The B&B
Guide 2009

Please use one of the Readers' Report Forms at the end of the guide or contact:
The Editor, AA B&B Guide, Fanum House Floor 13
Basing View, Basingstoke, Hampshire RG21 4EA
lifestyleguides@theAA.com

Advertisement Sales: advertisingsales@theaa.com

Cover photographs courtesy of: **Front cover (top)** The Stables Lodge, Tyne & Wear; **(bottom
left)** The Gainsborough, London; **(bottom right)** Burford House, Oxfordshire; **Back cover (left)**
Stockbyte Royalty Free; **(centre)** Rock House, Lynmouth; **(right)** AA/A Mockford & N Bonetti
Photographs in the gazetteer are provided by the establishments.

Typeset by Servis Filmsetting Ltd, Manchester
Printed by Printer Industria Grafica S.A., Barcelona

Published by AA Publishing, which is a trading name of Automobile
Association Developments Limited whose registered office is:
Fanum House, Basing View, Basingstoke, Hampshire RG21 4EA
Registered number 1878835

A CIP catalogue record for this book is available from the British Library.
ISBN-13: 978-0-7495-5786-7
A03685

Information on National Parks in England provided by The Countryside Agency (Natural England).
Information on National Parks in Scotland provided by Scottish Natural Heritage.
Information on National Parks in Wales provided by The Countryside Council for Wales.

Contents

How to Use the Guide

Sample entry

❶ CHEADLE   MAP 10 SK04

❷ ★★★★ 🛏 🥧 GUEST HOUSE
Elder Grange
Elder Rd ST10 4QR
☎ 01538 75633 📄 01538 72593
❸ **e-mail:** eldergrange@hotmail.com
❹ *dir: 1m E of Cheadle*

❺

This restored house stands in neat gardens and rolling countryside on the edge of the town. The stylish, well-equipped bedrooms offer flawless levels of comfort and the luxurious bathrooms have multi-jet walk-in ❻ power showers. Comprehensive breakfasts are served at an antique oak table, and fine Staffordshire pottery forms an attractive backdrop. ❽

❼ **Rooms** 3 en suite (smoking in 1 bedroom) S £45; D £80-£90 **Facilities** STV ❾
TVB tea/coffee **Parking** 10 **Notes** ⊗ No coaches ❿

❶ Each country is listed in alphabetical order by county then town/village. The Channel Islands and Isle of Man follow the England section and the Scottish islands follow the rest of Scotland. Establishments are listed alphabetically in descending order of Stars with any Yellow Stars first in each rating.

The map page number refers to the atlas at the back of the guide and is followed by the National Grid Reference. To find the town/village, read the first figure across and the second figure vertically within the lettered square. You can find routes at **theAA.com** or **AAbookings.ie**. **Farmhouse** entries also have a six-figure National Grid Reference, which can be used with Ordnance Survey maps or **www.ordnancesurvey.co.uk** We also show the name of the proprietors, as often farms are known locally by their name.

❷ **Establishment classification and designator**
See pages 6 and 7.

Five Star establishments are highlighted as Premier Collection, and they are listed on page 16.

If the establishment's name is shown in *italics*, then details have not been confirmed by the proprietor for this edition.

🏵 **Rosettes** The AA's food award, see page 11.

🛏 **Egg cups** and 🥧 **pies** These symbols indicate that, in the experience of the inspector, either breakfast or dinner are really special, and have an emphasis on freshly prepared local ingredients.

❸ **E-mail address and website** E-mail and website addresses are included where they have been specified by the establishment. Such websites are not under the control of The Automobile Association Developments Limited, who cannot accept any responsibility or liability in respect of any and all matters whatsoever relating to such websites.

❹ Distances in **directions** are given in miles (m) and yards (yds), or kilometres (km) and metres (mtrs) in the Republic of Ireland.

❺ Establishments may choose to include a **photograph**.

❻ **Description**. Written by the inspector at the time of his or her visit.

❼ **Rooms** The number of letting bedrooms (**rms**), or rooms with a bath or shower en suite are shown.

Bedrooms that have a private bathroom (**pri facs**) adjacent are indicated.

The number of bedrooms in an **annexe** of equivalent standard are also shown. Facilities may not be the same as in the main building.

Charges are per night:
S bed and breakfast per person
D bed and breakfast for two people sharing a room.

The **euro €** is the currency of the Republic of Ireland.

Prices are indications only, so check before booking. Some places may offer free accommodation to children provided they share their parents' room.

❽ **Facilities: TVB** stands for **tv in bedrooms.**
If it is shown **TV4B**, there is a tv in four rooms.
If **Dinner** is shown, you may have to order in advance. **Last d** is the last order time for dinner not the last time it is served.

For other abbreviations and symbols, see the table on the right.

9 The number of **parking** spaces available.

10 Notes Establishments that state **no dogs** ⊗ may accept assist/guide dogs. Some places that accept dogs may restrict the size and breed and the rooms into which they can be taken. Check the conditions when booking.

No children - children cannot be accommodated, or a minimum age may be specified, e.g. No children 4 yrs means no children under four years old.

Establishments with special facilities for children (**ch fac**) may include a babysitting service or baby-intercom system, playroom or playground, laundry facilities, drying and ironing facilities, cots, high chairs and special meals. If you have very young children, check before booking.

No coaches is published in good faith from details supplied by the establishment. Inns have well-defined legal obligations towards travellers; in the event of a query the customer should contact the proprietor or local licensing authority.

Additional facilities such as lifts or any leisure activities available are also listed.

LB indicates that Short or Leisure Breaks are available. Contact the establishment for details.

Establishments are open all year unless **Closed** dates/ months are shown. Some places are open all year but offer a restricted service (RS) in low season. If the text does not say what the restricted services are you should check before booking.

Civ Wed 50 The establishment is licensed for civil weddings and can accommodate 50 guests for the ceremony.

⊛ shows that **credit/debit cards are not accepted**, but check when booking. Where credit cards are accepted there may be an extra charge.

Smoking Since July 1st 2007 smoking is banned in all public places in the United Kingdom and Ireland. The proprietor can designate one or more bedrooms with ventilation systems where the occupants can smoke, but communal areas must be smoke-free. Communal areas include the interior bars and restaurants in pubs and inns. We indicate number of smoking rooms (if any).

Conference facilities **Conf** indicates that facilities are available. Total number of delegates that can be accommodated is shown, plus maximum numbers in various settings.

Key to Symbols and abbreviations

★☆	Classification (see page 6)
◉	AA Rosette award (see page 11)
A	Associate entry (see page 7)
U	Unclassified rating (see page 7)
☎	Phone number
▤	Fax number
⬢	A very special breakfast, with an emphasis on freshly prepared local ingredients
⬯	A very special dinner, with an emphasis on freshly prepared local ingredients
S	Single room
D	Double room (2 people sharing)
pri fac	Private facilities
fmly	Family bedrooms
GF	Ground floor bedroom
LB	Short/Leisure breaks
✳	2008 prices
Cen ht	Full central heating
ch fac	Special facilities for children
TVL	Lounge with television
TVB	Television in bedrooms
STV	Satellite television
FTV	Freeview television
Wi-fi	Wireless internet
⊛	Credit cards not accepted
tea/coffee	Tea and coffee facilities
Conf	Conference facilities
Last d	Last time dinner can be ordered
rms	Bedrooms in main building
Etr	Easter
fr	From
RS	Restricted service
⊗	No dogs
⊡	Indoor swimming pool
⊡	Heated indoor swimming pool
⌇	Outdoor swimming pool
⌇	Heated outdoor swimming pool
⌁	Croquet lawn
⌁	Tennis court
⌁	Golf course

5

AA Inspected Guest Accommodation

The AA inspects and classifies more than 3,400 guest houses, farmhouses and inns for its Guest Accommodation Scheme, under common quality standards agreed between the AA, VisitBritain, VisitScotland and VisitWales.

AA recognised establishments pay an annual fee according to the classification and the number of bedrooms. The classification is not transferable if an establishment changes hands.

The AA presents several awards within the Guest Accommodation scheme, including the **AA Friendliest Landlady of the Year**, which showcases the very finest hospitality in the country, **Guest Accommodation of the Year awards**, presented to establishments in Scotland, Ireland, Wales and England, **AA London B&B of the Year**, and **AA Funkiest B&B of the Year**. See pages 12 and 14 for this year's winners.

Stars

AA Stars classify guest accommodation at five levels of quality, from one at the simplest, to five offering the highest quality. In order to achieve a one Star rating an establishment must meet certain minimum entry requirements, including:

- A cooked breakfast, or substantial continental option is provided.
- The proprietor and/or staff are available for your arrival, departure and at all meal times.
- Once registered, you have access to the establishment at all times unless previously notified.
- All areas of operation meet minimum quality requirements for cleanliness, maintenance and hospitality as well as facilities and the delivery of services.
- A dining room or similar eating area is available unless meals are only served in bedrooms.

Our research shows that **quality** is very important to visitors. To obtain a higher Star rating, an establishment must provide increased quality standards across all areas, with particular emphasis in four key areas:

- Cleanliness and housekeeping
- Hospitality and service
- Quality and condition of bedrooms, bathrooms and public rooms
- Food quality

There are also particular requirements in order for an establishment to achieve three, four or five Stars, for example:

Three Stars and above
- access to both sides of all beds for double occupancy
- bathrooms/shower rooms cannot be used by the proprietor
- there is a washbasin in every guest bedroom (either in the bedrooms or the en suite/private facility)

Four Stars
- half of bedrooms must be en suite or have private facilities

Five Stars
- all bedrooms must be en suite or have private facilities

Establishments applying for AA recognition are visited by one of the AA's qualified accommodation inspectors as a **mystery guest**. Inspectors stay overnight to make a thorough test of the accommodation, food, and hospitality. After paying the bill the following morning they identify themselves and ask to be shown round the premises. The inspector completes a full report, resulting in a recommendation for the appropriate Star rating. After this first visit, the establishment will receive an annual visit to check that standards are maintained. If it changes hands, the new owners must re-apply for classification, as standards can change.

Guests can expect to find the following minimum standards at all levels:
- Pleasant and helpful welcome and service, and sound standards of housekeeping and maintenance
- Comfortable accommodation equipped to modern standards
- Bedding and towels changed for each new guest, and at least weekly if the room is taken for a long stay
- Adequate storage, heating, lighting and comfortable seating

- A sufficient hot water supply at reasonable times
- A full cooked breakfast. (If this is not provided, the fact must be advertised and a substantial continental breakfast must be offered)

When an AA inspector has visited a property, and evaluated all the aspects of the accommodation for comfort, facilities, attention to detail and presentation, you can be confident the Star rating will allow you to make the right choice for an enjoyable stay.

★ Highly Commended

Yellow Stars indicate that an accommodation is in the top ten percent of its Star rating. Yellow Stars only apply to 3, 4 or 5 Star establishments.

Accommodation Designators

Along with the Star ratings, six discriptive **designators** have been introduced. The proprietors, in discussion with our inspectors, choose which designator best describes their establishment:

B&B

A private house run by the owner with accommodation for no more than six paying guests.

GUEST HOUSE

Run on a more commercial basis than a B&B, the accommodation provides for more than six paying guests and there are usually more services; for example staff as well as the owner may provide dinner.

FARMHOUSE

The B&B or guest house accommodation is part of a working farm or smallholding.

INN

The accommodation is provided in a fully licensed establishment. The bar will be open to non-residents and can provide food in the evenings.

RESTAURANT WITH ROOMS

This is a destination restaurant offering overnight accommodation, with dining being the main business and open to non-residents. The restaurant should offer a high standard of food and restaurant service at least five nights a week. A liquor licence is necessary and there is a maximum of 12 bedrooms.

GUEST ACCOMMODATION

Any establishment that meets the minimum entry requirements is eligible for this general category.

U Unclassified entries

A small number of establishments in this guide have this symbol because their Star classification was not confirmed at the time of going to press. This may be due to a change of ownership or because the establishment has only recently joined the AA rating scheme. For up-to-date information on these and other new establishments check **theAA.com**.

A Associate entries

These establishments have been inspected and rated by VisitBritain, VisitScotland or VisitWales, and have joined the AA scheme on a marketing-only basis. A limited entry for these places appears in the guide, while descriptions for these establishments appear on **theAA.com**.

Useful Information

There may be restricted access to some establishments, particularly in the late morning and the afternoon, so do check when booking.

London prices tend to be higher than outside the capital, and normally only bed and breakfast is provided, although some establishments do provide a full meal service.

Farmhouses: Sometimes the land has been sold and only the house remains, but many are working farms and some farmers are happy to allow visitors to look around, or even to help feed the animals. However, you should always exercise care and never leave children unsupervised. Although the directory entry states the acreage and the type of farming, do check when booking to make sure that it matches your expectations. The farmhouses are listed under towns or villages, but do ask for directions when booking.

Inns: Traditional inns often have a cosy bar, convivial atmosphere, and good beer and pub food. Those listed in the guide will provide breakfast in a suitable room, and should also serve light meals during licensing hours. The character of the properties vary according to whether they are country inns or town establishments. Check before you book, including arrival times as these may be restricted to opening hours.

Useful Information *continued*

Booking

Book as early as possible, particularly for the peak holiday period (early June to the end of September) and for Easter and other public holidays. In some parts of Scotland the skiing season is also a peak holiday period.

Some establishments only accept weekly bookings from Saturday, and some require a deposit on booking.

Prices

Minimum and maximum prices are shown for one (S) and two people (D) per night and include a full breakfast. If dinner is also included this is indicated in brackets (including dinner). Where prices are for the room only, this is indicated.

Prices in the guide include VAT (and service where applicable), except the Channel Islands where VAT does not apply.

Where proprietors have been unable to provide us with their 2009 charges we publish the 2008 price as a rough guide (shown by an asterisk ✳). Where no prices are given, please make enquiries direct.

Cancellation

If you have to cancel a booking, let the proprietor know at once. If the room cannot be re-let you may be held legally responsible for partial payment; you could lose your deposit or be liable for compensation, so consider taking out cancellation insurance.

Food and drink

Some guest accommodation provides evening meals, ranging from a set meal to a full menu. Some even have their own restaurant. You may have to arrange dinner in advance, at breakfast, or on the previous day, so do ask when booking.

If you book on bed, breakfast and evening meal terms, you may find that the tariff includes only the set menu. If there is a carte you may be able to order from this and pay a supplement.

On Sundays, many establishments serve the main meal at midday, and provide only a cold supper in the evening. In some parts of Britain, particularly in Scotland, high tea (i.e. a savoury dish followed by bread and butter, scones and cakes) is sometimes served instead of, or as an alternative to, dinner. The last time at which high tea or dinner may be ordered on weekdays is shown, but this may vary at weekends.

Facilities for Disabled Guests

The **Disability Discrimination Act** (access to Goods and Services) means that service providers may have to consider making adjustments to their premises. For further information see **www.direct. gov.uk/en/DisabledPeople/RightsAndObligations/ DisabilityRights/DG_4001068.**

Ground-floor rooms are noted under **Facilities**. The establishments in this guide should all be aware of their responsibilities under the Act. Always phone in advance to ensure that the establishment you have chosen has appropriate facilities. See also www.**holidaycare.org.uk**.

AA Rosette awards

The AA awards Rosettes to some 2,000 restaurants as the best in the UK.

 Excellent local restaurants serving food prepared with care, understanding and skill, using good quality ingredients.

 The best local restaurants, which aim for and achieve higher standards and better consistency, and where a greater precision is apparent in the cooking. There will be obvious attention to the selection of quality ingredients.

Outstanding restaurants that demand recognition well beyond their local area.

Among the very best restaurants in the British Isles, where the cooking demands national recognition.

The finest restaurants in the British Isles, where the cooking compares with the best in the world.

AA Guest Accommodation of the Year

Every year we ask our inspectors to nominate those establishments they feel come closest to the ideal of what a B&B should be. They consider location, food standards and quality of furnishings and fittings, as well as charm and hospitality. From a shortlist of around 20, one is selected from each country in the guide.

England

The Stables Lodge
Gateshead, Tyne & Wear

Page 509

Janet MacPherson has been running The Stables Lodge for three years. In 1999 she had her own interior design business, when she bought some derelict farm buildings to convert into her new home. The concept of The Stables Lodge evolved during the conversion, when she realised the potential in these odd-shaped old buildings, and set herself the task of designing accommodation with a difference. Using her experience in interior design she created something slightly unconventional, and very different from home, but which would still be very homely. Wendy Turnbull, Gateshead Tourism manager said "The Stables oozes charm, comfort, quality and individuality, and such a warm welcome. Janet has a wonderful outgoing personality and is obviously willing to go the extra mile, and the Stables Lodge offers a unique and different experience for our visitors to the area."

This award sponsored by:

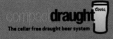

Scotland

Fauhope House
Melrose, Scottish Borders

Page 646

Born and bred in Aberdeenshire, Sheila Robson has plenty of experience in the hospitality industry. Along with husband Ian, she ran various restaurants for over 25 years. They retired from the restaurant business in 2006, and now Sheila concentrates on Fauhope House, which she launched in 1998. Designed by Sidney Mitchell, one of Scotland's leading 19th-century architects, the house has flourished in Sheila's hands. Her interests in interior decorating, gardening and flower arranging, have created an elegant, atmospheric and luxurious home for both her family and her guests. Here you will find close attention to detail in every area, a focus on providing a personalised and relaxing welcome to everyone who stays here and a dedication to providing the best of everything from the quality of the bed linen and the grand beds, to the smart toiletries and period furniture.

Wales

Tan-Y-Foel Country House
Betws-y-Coed, Conwy
Page 666

For six years Peter and Janet Pitman ran a B&B in the seaside town of Deal, Kent which included a formal restaurant. In 1991, having honed their skills they decided to establish a small luxury country house in North Wales. Tan-y-Foel Country House became a real family concern two years later when their daughter Kelly joined as a partner. Over the past 18 years the house has been refurbished to a very high standard, and for the past 10 years the restaurant there has achieved three AA Rosettes. The design ethic at Tan-y-Foel is stylishly contemporary, but also sympathetic to the environment. Most of the six en suite bedrooms, spectacular views over the Snowdonia Mountain range. The house has no staff, but is run in its entirety by Peter, Janet and Kelly. Although it's hard work at times, they feel that it allows them to maintain their consistently high standards.

Ireland

Killiane Castle
Wexford, Co Wexford
Page 754

The accommodation at this dramatic location is actually a 17th-century house attached to the castle itself, which is partly Norman, partly 15th century and now home to the very hospitable Mernagh family: Jack and Kathleen, and their sons David and Colin. In a recent visit report, one of our inspectors commented that: "Killiane Castle continues to impress. Not only is it a most interesting house, but also the hospitality of the Mernagh family is so genuine and welcoming." The breakfast is a real treat with a selection of stewed fruit from the garden, home bakery and a choice of hot dishes and yogurts which are made fresh daily. A new driving range has been opened on the farm and there are plans for an 18 hole pitch and put course. There are also a well-maintained tennis court and croquet lawn.

AA B&B Awards
2008-2009

SUPPORTED BY
LONDON
DEVELOPMENT
A G E N C Y
WORKING FOR THE MAYOR OF LONDON

Villeroy & Boch
1748

L to R: Giovanna Grossi, AA Hotel Services Group Area Manager; Margaret Frost, AA Friendliest Landlady of the Year 2008-2009; Simon Numphud, Manager Hotel Services; and Salvatore Scotti, AA Inspector

Each year the AA likes to celebrate those who are the cream of our Guest Accommodation Scheme crop. This year there is a new award to go alongside Friendliest Landlady and Funkiest B&B: London B&B of the Year, sponsored by the London Development Agency. This year's ceremony took place at the Mandarin Oriental, Hyde Park.

AA Friendliest Landlady of the Year

The winner of the AA Friendliest Landlady of the Year award, judged by the AA's expert panel of inspectors and selected from a shortlist including 19 other establishments, is Margaret Frost of Diggins Farm, Chipping Ongar in Essex.

Margaret has been welcoming guests at her home for eight years. The house is a 16th century, Grade II listed, oak-beamed farmhouse set in tranquil countryside and farmland overlooking the Roding Valley.

On a recent visit, one of our inspectors made this comment in his notes: "This establishment is clearly loved and cherished and continues to impress in all areas though the greatest asset of this property is the lady of the house. Mrs Frost greets her guests with a genuine welcome and provides high levels of guest care."

Real warmth and friendliness is the essence of this home from home, and Margaret always goes the extra mile for her guests. From welcoming visitors with tea and homemade cakes, or offering a complimentary taxi service to Stansted airport or local pubs, to gifting guests with a teddy bear if they stay for two nights or more, Margaret sets and maintains very high standards of customer care.

AA Funkiest B&B

The winner of the AA Funkiest B&B, selected by an independent judge, is the Enchanted Manor in Niton on the Isle of Wight.

This old manor house was originally known as Windcliffe Manor, and belonged to an Irish banking family. Ric and Maggie Hilton, the tireless current owners, have converted it into a magical boutique retreat.

Inspired by the work of fantasy artist Josephine Wall, Ric and Maggie have ensured that the

'enchanted' theme runs throughout the B&B, from ornately carved four-poster beds in each suite, to fantastical local artwork that adorns the house, and the garden and surrounding woodlands which have been landscaped to create enchanting individual areas adorned with local wooden sculptures and native wild flowers.

Artfully decorated rooms and suites successfully combine the fairytale theme with luxurious old world character. Enticingly named with promises such as Dreamtime, Serenity and Candlelight, each suite features a hand-carved four-poster bed and free-standing slipper bath.

Current plans include a fairytale hut for indoor BBQs, a refurbished swimming pool with its own mermaid, and a new castle-style garage for the "Spirit of Enchantment" carriage, which is being built to take guests on special tours and collect them from the ferry.

AA London B&B of the Year

Sponsored by the London Development Agency
The winner of our newest award for accommodation excellence is San Domenico House, Chelsea.

San Domenico House opened as a B&B more than ten years ago, and the owner, Mrs Melpignano, comments that she aims to give her guests "a comfortable and memorable stay with impeccable service."

Newly extended and redesigned, this B&B boasts 16 luxury bedrooms and suites, which offer privacy and comfort to guests wishing to relax. Each individually themed room has an en suite marble bathroom and is decorated with rich warm fabrics and dramatic furnishings.

The AA B&B Awards are a part of the AA's well established Hospitality Awards, covering the finest of all AA-inspected and rated hotels, restaurants, guesthouses and B&Bs. These accolades are presented in recognition of all round excellence, unfailing standards, outstanding service, as well as acknowledging the vital role played by those individuals who work to maintain the highest of standards within the industry. It is their eye for detail, dedication and good humour that make their guests' stays pleasant and memorable in every way.

For more information on the AA's awards go to:
www.AAHospitalityAwards.com

Above: The Enchanted Manor, Niton, Isle of Wight.

15

★★★★★ Premier Collection

These establishments have been awarded five Stars by the AA.

ENGLAND

BUCKINGHAMSHIRE
CHESHAM
Braziers Well

CAMBRIDGESHIRE
ELTON
The Crown Inn
HUNTINGDON
Cheriton House

CHESHIRE
CHESTER
Chester Stone Villa
Mitchell's of Chester Guest House
MALPAS
Tilston Lodge

CORNWALL & ISLES OF SCILLY
BOSCASTLE
Trerosewill Farm
DRYM
Drym Farm
FALMOUTH
Dolvean House
LAUNCESTON
Primrose Cottage
LOOE
The Beach House
PADSTOW
The Seafood Restaurant
Woodlands Country House
PENZANCE
Camilla House
Ennys
The Summer House
PERRANUTHNOE
Ednovean Farm
ST AUSTELL
Anchorage House
Highland Court Lodge
Lower Barn
Wisteria Lodge
ST BLAZEY
Nanscawen Manor House
Penarwyn House

ST IVES
Jamies
Porthglaze
Primrose Valley

CUMBRIA
AMBLESIDE
Drunken Duck Inn
BORROWDALE
Hazel Bank Country House
BOWNESS-ON-WINDERMERE
Oakbank House
BRAMPTON
The Hill On The Wall
CARTMEL
Hill Farm
L'Enclume
CATLOWDY
Bessiestown Country Guest House
CONISTON
Coniston Lodge
Wheelgate Country Guest House
CROSTHWAITE
The Punchbowl Inn at Crosthwaite
GRASMERE
Moss Grove Organic
HAWKSHEAD
West Vale Country House
KESWICK
The Grange Country Guest House
KIRKBY LONSDALE
Hipping Hall
The Sun Inn
LORTON
New House Farm
Winder Hall Country House
MILLOM
Underwood Country Guest House
NEAR SAWREY
Ees Wyke Country House
NEWBY BRIDGE
The Knoll Country House
PENRITH
Roundthorn Country House
TROUTBECK
Broadoaks Country House
WINDERMERE
Beaumont House
Low House

Newstead
The Howbeck
The Woodlands

DERBYSHIRE
ASHBOURNE
Turlow Bank
BELPER
Dannah Farm Country House Ltd.
BUXTON
Grendon Guest House
HOPE
Underleigh House
NEWHAVEN
The Smithy
WESTON UNDERWOOD
Park View Farm
WIRKSWORTH
The Old Lock Up
The Old Manor House

DEVON
AXMINSTER
Kerrington House
BARNSTAPLE
Halmpstone Manor
BUDLEIGH SALTERTON
Downderry House
CHAGFORD
Parford Well
CHILLATON
Tor Cottage
DARTMOUTH
Nonsuch House
HONITON
West Colwell Farm
HORNS CROSS
The Round House
LUSTLEIGH
Eastwrey Barton
Woodley House
LYDFORD
Moor View House
LYNMOUTH
Bonnicott House
Sea View Villa
The Heatherville
LYNTON
Highcliffe House

Victoria Lodge
SIDMOUTH
The Salty Monk
TEIGNMOUTH
Thomas Luny House
TORQUAY
The Marstan

DORSET
BEAMINSTER
Watermeadow House
BLANDFORD FORUM
Portman Lodge
BOURNEMOUTH
The Balincourt
BRIDPORT
The Roundham House
CHRISTCHURCH
Druid House
Seawards
The Lord Bute & Restaurant
DORCHESTER
Little Court
Poundbury B & B
The Casterbridge
FARNHAM
Farnham Farm House
WAREHAM
Kemps Country House
WIMBORNE MINSTER
Les Bouviers Restaurant with Rooms

CO DURHAM
BARNARD CASTLE
Greta House
Number 34

ESSEX
CHIPPING ONGAR
Diggins Farm
WIX
Dairy House Farm

GLOUCESTERSHIRE
BLOCKLEY
Lower Brook House
CHELTENHAM
Beaumont House
Cleeve Hill House
Georgian House
Lypiatt House
CHIPPING CAMPDEN
The Malt House
ST BRIAVELS
Prospect Cottage

TETBURY
Beaufort House

GREATER MANCHESTER
LITTLEBOROUGH
Hollingworth Lake Bed & Breakfast

HAMPSHIRE
ANDOVER
The Barn House B&B
BENTLEY
Bentley Green Farm
BROCKENHURST
The Cottage Lodge
LYMINGTON
The Olde Barn
MILFORD ON SEA
Ha'penny House
SOUTHAMPTON
Riverside Bed & Breakfast
WINCHESTER
Orchard House

HEREFORDSHIRE
HEREFORD
Somerville House
LEOMINSTER
Hills Farm
MOCCAS
Moccas Court
DATCHWORTH
Farmhouse B&B
HERTFORD HEATH
Rushen

KENT
AYLESFORD
Wickham Lodge
CANTERBURY
Great Weddington
Magnolia House
Yorke Lodge
DEAL
Sutherland House
DODDINGTON
The Old Vicarage
FARNINGHAM
Beesfield Farm
FOLKESTONE
The Relish
HAWKHURST
Southgate-Little Fowlers
IVYCHURCH
Olde Moat House

MARDEN
Merzie Meadows
ROYAL TUNBRIDGE WELLS
Danehurst House

LANCASHIRE
PRESTON
Whitestake Farm
WHITEWELL
The Inn at Whitewell
YEALAND CONYERS
The Bower

LEICESTERSHIRE
CROPSTON
Horseshoe Cottage Farm
KEGWORTH
Kegworth House
SHEPSHED
The Grange Courtyard

LINCOLNSHIRE
HEMSWELL
Hemswell Court
HOUGH-ON-THE-HILL
The Brownlow Arms
LINCOLN
Bailhouse & Mews
Charlotte House
MARKET RASEN
Blaven
NORMANTON
La Casita
STAMFORD
Rock Lodge
WINTERINGHAM
Winteringham Fields

LONDON POSTAL DISTRICTS
LONDON SW3
San Domenico House

NORFOLK
BLAKENEY
Blakeney House
CLEY NEXT THE SEA
Old Town Hall House
CROMER
Incleborough House
HINDRINGHAM
Field House
HOLT
Plantation House
Rose Cottage

NORTH WALSHAM
White House Farm
NORWICH
Catton Old Hall
SHERINGHAM
Fairlawns
The Eiders Bed & Breakfast
The Eight Acres
THURSFORD
Holly Lodge

NORTHAMPTONSHIRE
LAXTON
Spanhoe Lodge
STANWICK
The Courtyard Luxury Lodge

NORTHUMBERLAND
BELFORD
Market Cross Guest House
CORNHILL-ON-TWEED
Ivy Cottage
HEXHAM
Montcoffer Bed & Breakfast
ROTHBURY
The Orchard House
WOOLER
The Old Manse

NOTTINGHAMSHIRE
ELTON
The Grange
HOLBECK
Browns
NOTTINGHAM
Greenwood Lodge City Guest House

OXFORDSHIRE
ABINGDON
B&B Rafters
BURFORD
Burford House
HENLEY-ON-THAMES
Crowsley House
Lenwade
OXFORD
Burlington House
Gables Guest House
STADHAMPTON
The Crazy Bear

SHROPSHIRE
BRIDGNORTH
The Albynes
CHURCH STRETTON
Field House
Rectory Farm
The Orchards
Willowfield Guest House
CLUN
Birches Mill
IRONBRIDGE
The Library House
The Old Rectory at Broseley Ltd
LLANFAIR WATERDINE
The Waterdine
LUDLOW
De Greys of Ludlow
Line Farm
The Clive Bar & Restaurant with
Rooms
OSWESTRY
Greystones
TELFORD
Bridge House

SOMERSET
BATH
Apsley House
Athole House
Carfax
Cheriton House
Chestnut House
Dorian House
Haydon House
Meadowland
Paradise House
The Ayrlington
The County
The Villa Magdala
CHARD
Bellplot House & Thomas's Restaurant
CHEDDAR
Batts Farm
DULVERTON
Tarr Farm Inn
EAST HARPTREE
Harptree Court
FROME
Lullington House
NETHER STOWEY
Castle of Comfort Country House
TAUNTON
Elm Villa
WELLS
Beaconsfield Farm
Beryl
WESTON-SUPER-MARE
Church House
WITHYPOOL
Kings Farm
YEOVIL
Little Barwick House

STAFFORDSHIRE
CHEDDLETON
Choir Cottage and Choir House
RUGELEY
Colton House
TAMWORTH
Oak Tree Farm

SUFFOLK
BEYTON
Manorhouse
BURY ST EDMUNDS
Clarice House
HADLEIGH
Edge Hall
HOLTON
Valley Farm
LAVENHAM
Lavenham Great House 'Restaurant
With Rooms'
Lavenham Priory
SOUTHWOLD
Sutherland House
STOWMARKET
Bays Farm
Haughley House
YAXLEY
The Auberge

SURREY
CAMBERLEY
Maywood House
FARNHAM
Bentley Mill

EAST SUSSEX
EASTBOURNE
Ocklynge Manor
The Berkeley
The Gables
The Manse B & B
HALLAND
Tamberry Hall
HASTINGS & ST LEONARDS
Stream House
HERSTMONCEUX
Wartling Place

RYE
Jeake's House
Manor Farm Oast
Oaklands
White Vine House
Willow Tree House

WEST SUSSEX
CHICHESTER
Rooks Hill
The Royal Oak
West Stoke House
LINDFIELD
The Pilstyes
MIDHURST
Park House
Rivermead House
ROGATE
Mizzards Farm
SIDLESHAM
The Crab & Lobster

TYNE & WEAR
GATESHEAD
The Stables Lodge
SUNNISIDE
Hedley Hall Country House

WARWICKSHIRE
ATHERSTONE
Chapel House
ETTINGTON
Fulready Manor
GREAT WOLFORD
The Old Coach House
KENILWORTH
Loweridge Guest House
STRATFORD-UPON-AVON
Cherry Trees

WEST MIDLANDS
BIRMINGHAM
Westbourne Lodge

ISLE OF WIGHT
BONCHURCH
Winterbourne Country House
GODSHILL
Godshill Park Farm House
Koala Cottage
NITON
Enchanted Manor
SHANKLIN
Foxhills
VENTNOR
Hambrough

Horseshoe Bay House
The Leconfield

WILTSHIRE
BOX
Foggam Barn Bed and Breakfast
Spinney Cross
BRADFORD-ON-AVON
Bradford Old Windmill
DEVIZES
Blounts Court Farm
HIGHWORTH
Jesmonds of Highworth
PURTON
The Old Farmhouse

WORCESTERSHIRE
BEWDLEY
Number Thirty
BROADWAY
Mill Hay House
Russell's

EAST RIDING OF YORKSHIRE
BEVERLEY
Burton Mount Country House
BRIDLINGTON
Marton Grange

NORTH YORKSHIRE
AMPLEFORTH
Shallowdale House
APPLETREEWICK
Knowles Lodge
BEDALE
Mill Close Farm
GOLDSBOROUGH
Goldsborough Hall
GRASSINGTON
Ashfield House
HARROGATE
Cold Cotes
HELLIFIELD
Ribblecote Manor
KNARESBOROUGH
Gallon House
General Tarleton Inn
LEYBURN
Thorney Hall
PICKERING
17 Burgate
RIPON
Mallard Grange
The Old Coach House

SCARBOROUGH
Holly Croft
THIRSK
Spital Hill
THORNTON WATLASS
Thornton Watlass Hall
WHITBY
The Haven Guest House

ISLE OF MAN
PORT ST MARY
Aaron House

CHANNEL ISLANDS
JERSEY
ST AUBIN
The Panorama

SCOTLAND
ABERDEENSHIRE
FRASERBURGH
Lonmay Old Manse

ARGYLL & BUTE
APPIN
Bealach Country House
BOWMORE
The Harbour Inn and Restaurant
CARDROSS
Kirkton House
HELENSBURGH
Lethamhill
OBAN
Blarcreen House

DUMFRIES & GALLOWAY
MOFFAT
Well View
THORNHILL
Gillbank House

CITY OF EDINBURGH
EDINBURGH
Elmview
Kew House
The Witchery by the Castle

FIFE
PEAT INN
The Peat Inn
ST ANDREWS
The Paddock

HIGHLAND
AVIEMORE
The Old Minister's House
BRORA
Glenaveron
DAVIOT
Daviot Lodge
DORNOCH
2 Quail Restaurant and Rooms
FORT WILLIAM
Ashburn House
The Grange
GRANTOWN-ON-SPEY
An Cala Guest House
INVERNESS
Ballifeary Guest House
Trafford Bank
KINGUSSIE
The Cross at Kingussie
NEWTONMORE
Ard-Na-Coille
STRUAN
Ullinish Country Lodge

NORTH AYRSHIRE
SALTCOATS
Lochwood Farm Log Cabin

PERTH & KINROSS
ALYTH
Tigh Na Leigh Guesthouse
PITLOCHRY
Easter Dunfallandy House

SCOTTISH BORDERS
MELROSE
Fauhope House

SOUTH AYRSHIRE
AYR
The Crescent
MAYBOLE
Ladyburn

STIRLING
STRATHYRE
Creagan House

WEST LOTHIAN
EAST CALDER
Ashcroft Farmhouse
LINLITHGOW
Arden Country House

WALES

CARMARTHENSHIRE
ST CLEARS
Coedllys Country House

CEREDIGION
ABERAERON
The Harbourmaster
Ty Mawr Mansion
ABERYSTWYTH
Awel-Deg

CONWY
ABERGELE
The Kinmel Arms
BETWS-Y-COED
Penmachno Hall
Tan-y-Foel Country House
BYLCHAU
Hafod Elwy Hall
CONWY
Sychnant Pass Country House
The Old Rectory Country House
RHOS-ON-SEA
Plas Rhos

DENBIGHSHIRE
CORWEN
Bron-y-Graig
LLANDRILLO
Tyddyn Llan
LLANDYRNOG
Pentre Mawr Country House
ST ASAPH
Tan-Yr-Onnen Guest House

GWYNEDD
DOLGELLAU
Tyddynmawr Farmhouse
LLANDDEINIOLEN
Ty'n-Rhos Country House &
Restaurant

ISLE OF ANGLESEY
BEAUMARIS
Ye Olde Bulls Head Inn
MENAI BRIDGE
Wern Farm

MONMOUTHSHIRE
SKENFRITH
The Bell at Skenfrith
WHITEBROOK
The Crown at Whitebrook

NEWPORT
CAERLEON
Radford House
ST BRIDES WENTLOOGE
The Inn at the Elm Tree

PEMBROKESHIRE
SOLVA
Lochmeyler Farm Guest House

POWYS
BRECON
Canal Bank
The Coach House
BUILTH WELLS
The Drawing Room
CAERSWS
The Talkhouse
CRICKHOWELL
Glangrwyney Court
LLANDRINDOD WELLS
Guidfa House
WELSHPOOL
Moors Farm B&B

SWANSEA
MUMBLES
Little Langland
REYNOLDSTON
Fairyhill

NORTHERN IRELAND

ANTRIM
BUSHMILLS
Whitepark House

DOWN
BANGOR
Hebron House
HOLYWOOD
Rayanne House

LONDONDERRY
CASTLEDAWSON
The Inn at Castle Dawson
COLERAINE
Greenhill House

TYRONE
DUNGANNON
Grange Lodge

REPUBLIC OF IRELAND

CLARE

BALLYVAUGHAN
Rusheen Lodge

DOOLIN
Ballyvara House

LAHINCH
Moy House

SPANISH POINT
Admiralty Lodge

CORK

BLARNEY
Ashlee Lodge

CLONAKILTY
An Garran Coir

CORK
Lancaster Lodge

FERMOY
Ballyvolane House

KINSALE
Friar's Lodge
Perryville House
The Old Bank House

SHANAGARRY
Ballymaloe House

YOUGHAL
Ahernes

DONEGAL

LAGHEY
Coxtown Manor

DUBLIN

DUBLIN
Aberdeen Lodge
Blakes Townhouse
Butlers Town House
Glenogra Guest House
Harrington Hall
Merrion Hall
Pembroke Town House

GALWAY

CRAUGHWELL
St Clerans Manor House

KERRY

BALLYBUNION
Cashen Course House

CASTLEGREGORY
The Shores Country House

DINGLE
Castlewood House
Emlagh House
Gormans Clifftop House & Restaurant
Heatons Guest House
Milltown House

KILLARNEY
Earls Court House
Fairview Guest House
Foleys Town House
Kathleens Country House
Old Weir Lodge

KILLORGLIN
Carrig House Country House & Restaurant

KILDARE

ATHY
Coursetown Country House

LIMERICK

GLIN
Glin Castle

KILMALLOCK
Flemingstown House

LOUTH

CARLINGFORD
Beaufort House

SLIGO

ENNISCRONE
Seasons Lodge

TIPPERARY

THURLES
Inch House Country House & Restaurant
The Castle

WATERFORD

BALLYMACARBRY
Glasha Farmhouse
Hanoras Cottage

DUNGARVAN
Sliabh gCua Farmhouse
The Castle Country House

WATERFORD
Foxmount Country House
Sion Hill House & Gardens

WEXFORD

CAMPILE
Kilmokea Country Manor & Gardens

GOREY
Woodlands Country House

ROSSLARE HARBOUR
Churchtown House

WICKLOW

DUNLAVIN
Rathsallagh House

Blakeney, Norfolk

England

Brick Kiln Wood, /
North Mymms Country Park,
Hertfordshire

ENGLAND

BEDFORDSHIRE

ASTWICK
MAP 12 TL23

★★★ GUEST ACCOMMODATION
Tudor Oaks Lodge
Taylor's Rd SG5 4AZ
☎ 01462 834133 📠 01462 834133
e–mail: tudoroakslodge@aol.com
dir: *On A1 N, 1m past junct 10*

This 16th-century house has been renovated to create a cosy inn serving real ales and imaginative food. Bedrooms are smartly decorated and well equipped. Most have interesting bathrooms with a variety of modern jet showers and Italian marble detail. All bedrooms surround an attractive courtyard and there is ample private parking.

Rooms 13 en suite (13 GF) **Facilities** TVB tea/coffee Direct dial from bedrooms Cen ht Dinner Last d 10pm **Conf** Max 30 Thtr 30 Class 20 Board 12 **Parking** 200 **Notes** ⊗ No children 10yrs

See advert on this page

BEDFORD
MAP 12 TL04

★★★★ INN
Knife & Cleaver
The Grove, Houghton Conquest MK45 3LA
☎ 01234 740387 📠 01234 740900
e–mail: info@knifeandcleaver.com
web: www.knifeandcleaver.com

dir: *5m S of Bedford. Off A6, opp Houghton Conquest church*
In a pleasant village setting, this relaxing inn has a cosy bar and an elegant conservatory-restaurant. Interesting dishes are complemented by a good wine list. Bedrooms, located in a garden annexe, come in a variety of styles, all comfortably appointed and well equipped; the de luxe rooms are particularly good.

Rooms 9 annexe en suite (1 fmly) (9 GF) S £59–£69; D £59–£84✱ **Facilities** FTV TVB tea/coffee Direct dial from bedrooms Cen ht Dinner Last d 9.30pm Wi-fi available **Conf** Max 12 Thtr 16 Class 8 Board 12 **Parking** 35 **Notes** No coaches Closed 27–30 Dec

HARROLD
MAP 11 SP95

★★★ INN
The Muntjac
71 High St MK43 7BJ
☎ 01234 721500 📠 01234 721672
e–mail: russell@themuntjac.co.uk

dir: *In village centre opp butcher shop*
The Muntjac is a former 17th-century coaching inn situated in the picturesque village of Harrold. Bedrooms are modernised for the 21st century. The restaurant features an inglenook fireplace and a glass-covered well.

Rooms 4 en suite (4 GF) **Facilities** TVB tea/coffee Cen ht Dinner Last d 9.30pm **Parking** 7 **Notes** ⊗

MARSTON MORETAINE
MAP 11 SP94

★★★★ 🅐 BED & BREAKFAST
Twin Lodge
Lower Shelton Rd, Lower Shelton MK43 0LP
☎ 01234 767597
e–mail: pwillsmore@waitrose.com

dir: *Off A421 into Lower Shelton*
Rooms 4 en suite S £34–£37; D £60–£65✱ **Facilities** TVB tea/coffee Cen ht TVL **Parking** 5 **Notes** ⊗ 🍴

BERKSHIRE

BEENHAM   MAP 05 SU56

★★★★ INN
The Six Bells
The Green RG7 5NX
☎ 0118 971 3368
e–mail: info@thesixbells.net
web: www.thesixbells.net

dir: *Off A4 between Reading/Newbury, follow signs for Beenham Village*

Traditional village pub with a restaurant and bedrooms. Good access to Thatcham and Newbury, good atmosphere, friendly service and comfortable, well appointed accommodation.

Rooms 4 en suite S fr £59.95; D fr £79.95✳ **Facilities** FTV TVB tea/coffee Cen ht Dinner Last d 9pm **Conf** Max 40 Thtr 40 Class 40 Board 25 **Parking** 20 **Notes** ⊗ No coaches

---

BOXFORD   MAP 05 SU47

★★★★ FARM HOUSE
High Street Farm Barn *(SU424714)*
RG20 8DD
☎ 01488 608783 & 07768 324707 Mr & Mrs Boden
e–mail: nboden@uk2.net

dir: *0.5m W of village centre. Off B4000 to Boxford, farm 1st on left opposite pub*

A converted barn situated on a small holding in the Berkshire village of Boxford. Bedrooms are smartly furnished and a comfortable lounge is available for guests use. Breakfast, which is served at one table, includes free-range eggs from the farm and home made breads and marmalades.

Rooms 2 en suite (2 GF) S fr £50; D fr £65✳ **Facilities** TVB tea/coffee Cen ht **Parking** 4 **Notes** ⊗ 15 acres sheep ⊜

★★★ BED & BREAKFAST
White Hart Cottage
Westbrook RG20 8DN
☎ 01488 608410
e–mail: gillian@jones-parry.orangehome.co.uk

dir: *0.3m NW of Boxford. Off B4000 to Boxford, left for Westbrook, premises on right*

Guests are ensured of a friendly welcome at this pretty cottage, peacefully located in the delightful village of Boxford. Newbury and the M4 are both just a short drive away. Bedrooms are attractively appointed and guests have access to a small TV lounge. A hearty breakfast is served at the large kitchen table.

Rooms 3 rms (1 en suite) (2 pri facs) **Facilities** TV2B tea/coffee Cen ht TVL **Parking** 6 **Notes** ⊗ No children Closed 12 Dec–12 Jan ⊜

BRACKNELL   MAP 05 SU86

★★★★ BED & BREAKFAST
Angel Farm
Monks Alley RG42 5PA
☎ 01344 455539 📠 01344 484629
e–mail: sj@angelfarm.co.uk

dir: *Centre of Binfield, at rdbt turn onto Forest Rd signed Hurst. Turn right at 1st rdbt onto Wicks Green. Turn left onto Monks Alley, 3rd house on right*

This alluringly named farmhouse is the home of delightful Mrs Muir and her equally welcoming canine friends. The accommodation has been stylishly and thoughtfully converted. Breakfast is taken around a large imposing dining table and includes home produced free-range eggs. Although close to the motorway network, the farm enjoys a tranquil country setting.

Rooms 2 rms (2 pri facs) (2 GF) **Facilities** TVB tea/coffee Cen ht Wi-fi available 🐾 **Parking** 2 **Notes** ⊗ No children 10yrs RS Sat & Sun ⊜

CHIEVELEY   MAP 05 SU47

★★★★ 🅰 BED & BREAKFAST
The Old Farmhouse
Downend Ln RG20 8TN
☎ 01635 248361
e–mail: palletts@aol.com

dir: *0.5m N of Chieveley in Downend*

Rooms 1 en suite (1 fmly) (1 GF) S £45–£50; D £80–£85✳ **Facilities** STV TVB tea/coffee Cen ht TVL Wi-fi available Discounted day membership of local health club **Conf** Max 6 Thtr 6 Board 6 **Parking** 3 **Notes** ⊜

COOKHAM DEAN   MAP 05 SU88

★★★★ ⊛⊛ RESTAURANT WITH ROOMS
The Inn on the Green
The Old Cricket Common SL6 9NZ
☎ 01628 482638 📠 01628 487474
e–mail: reception@theinnonthegreen.com

dir: *In village centre*

A traditional English country inn set in rural Berkshire. Bedrooms are spacious and comfortable, with antique furnishings adding to the character. The building retains many traditional features including a wood panelled dining room and Old English bar with log fire. Food is imaginative and noteworthy and can be enjoyed outside in the garden or terrace in warmer months.

Rooms 9 en suite (4 GF) **Facilities** STV FTV TVB tea/coffee Direct dial from bedrooms Cen ht Dinner Last d 10pm Wi-fi available Hot tub, Outdoor games **Conf** BC Max 70 Thtr 70 Class 30 Board 20 **Parking** 50 **Notes** ⊗ RS Sun & Mon Civ Wed 100

HUNGERFORD MAP 05 SU36

★★★★ 🍴 INN
Crown & Garter
Great Common, Inkpen RG17 9QR
☎ 01488 668325
e–mail: gill.hern@btopenworld.com
web: www.crownandgarter.com

dir: *4m SE of Hungerford. Off A4 into Kintbury, opp corner stores onto Inkpen Rd, straight for 2m*

Peacefully located in the attractive village of Inkpen, this charming 17th-century inn has a bar with large inglenook log fire where interesting well-prepared dishes are offered. The bedrooms surround a pretty garden, and are comprehensively equipped and attractively decorated in a country cottage style.

Rooms 8 annexe en suite (8 GF) S £59.50; D £90✱ **Facilities** TVB tea/coffee Cen ht Dinner Last d 9.30pm Wi-fi available **Parking** 40 **Notes** LB ⊗ No children 10yrs No coaches RS No lunch Mon/Tue or evening meal Sun

★★★★ 🍴 INN
The Swan Inn
Craven Rd, Inkpen RG17 9DX
☎ 01488 668326 📠 01488 668306
e–mail: enquiries@theswaninn-organics.co.uk
web: www.theswaninn-organics.co.uk

dir: *3.5m SE of Hungerford. S on Hungerford High St past railway bridge, left to Hungerford Common, right signed Inkpen*

This delightful village inn dates back to the 17th century has open fires and beams in the bar, and the bonus of a smart restaurant. Bedrooms are generally spacious and well equipped. Organic produce is available
CONTINUED

from the on-site farm shop, so the bar, restaurant and breakfast menus all feature local organic produce too.

Rooms 10 en suite (2 fmly) S £60–£70; D £80–£95✱ **Facilities** TVB tea/coffee Direct dial from bedrooms Cen ht Dinner Last d 9.30pm Wi-fi available **Conf** Max 40 Thtr 40 Class 40 Board 12 **Parking** 50 **Notes** ⊗ Closed 25–26 Dec

★★★ BED & BREAKFAST
Beacon House
Bell Ln, Upper Green, Inkpen RG17 9QJ
☎ 01488 668640 📠 01488 668640
e–mail: l.g.cave@classicfm.net
web: www.beaconhouseinkpen.com

dir: *4m SE of Hungerford. Off A4 S into Kintbury, left onto Inkpen Rd, 1m over x-rds, right to common, 3rd left after Crown & Garter pub*

This large house is set in peaceful countryside. Bedrooms are comfortably furnished and overlook fields. As well as the lounge, there is usually an art exhibition and sale featuring watercolours, textiles, printmaking and pottery in the adjoining Gallery. Guests are always invited to view.

Rooms 3 rms S £34; D £68 **Facilities** TVB Cen ht TVL **Parking** 6 **Notes** LB ⊛

HURLEY MAP 05 SU88

★★★★ ◉◉ RESTAURANT WITH ROOMS
Black Boys Inn
Henley Rd SL6 5NQ
☎ 01628 824212
e–mail: info@blackboysinn.co.uk
web: www.blackboysinn.co.uk

dir: *1m W of Hurley on A4130*

Just a short drive from Henley, the traditional exterior of this friendly establishment is a contrast to the smart modernity within. Popular with locals, the restaurant is the stage for Simon Bonwick's imaginative cuisine, and offers a buzzing atmosphere. The well-appointed bedrooms are situated in converted barns close by.

Rooms 8 annexe en suite (5 GF) **Facilities** tea/coffee Cen ht Dinner Last d 9pm Wi-fi available **Conf** Max 10 Board 10 **Parking** 40 **Notes** ⊗ No children 12yrs Closed 24 Dec–9 Jan

NEWBURY MAP 05 SU46

★★★★ GUEST ACCOMMODATION
Pilgrims Guest House
Oxford Rd RG14 1XB
☎ 01635 40694 📠 01635 44873
e–mail: office@pilgrimsgh.co.uk
web: www.pilgrimsnewbury.co.uk

dir: *Off Waitrose A4 rdbt onto B4494 towards Wantage, 0.5m on left*

Located close to the town centre, this smartly presented house has stylish bedrooms with modern bathrooms, and some rooms are in a
CONTINUED

new annexe. Hearty breakfasts are served in the bright dining room. Large car park.

Rooms 13 rms (9 en suite) 4 annexe en suite (1 fmly) (3 GF) S £40–£55; D £52–£65✳ **Facilities** TVB tea/coffee Cen ht Wi-fi available **Parking** 17 **Notes** ⊗ Closed 24 Dec–2 Jan

★★★★ GUEST ACCOMMODATION
Rookwood Farm House

Stockcross RG20 8JX
☎ 01488 608676 📠 01488 657961
e–mail: charlotte@rookwoodfarmhouse.co.uk

dir: *2m W of Newbury, at junct A4 & A34 onto B4000, 0.75m to Stockcross, 1st right signed Woodspeen, bear left, 1st on right*

This farmhouse enjoys wonderful views and is very much a family home. Bedrooms are attractively presented and feature fine pieces of furniture. Breakfast is served on one large table in the kitchen. The coach house has a kitchen and sitting room. During the summer visitors can enjoy the beautiful gardens and outdoor pool.

Rooms 1 en suite 2 annexe en suite (1 fmly) **Facilities** TVB tea/coffee Cen ht TVL ⤳ ⤴ **Conf** Max 12 Board 12 **Parking** 3 **Notes** ⊗

★★★ GUEST ACCOMMODATION
Dolphin Inn

113 Bartholomew St RG14 5DT
☎ 01635 232425 📠 01635 230356
e–mail: room@dolphin-inns.com

dir: *In town centre. Off A339 Sainsbury's rdbt into town centre, signs for council offices, inn opp*

A warm welcome and attentive service are assured at this renovated 17th-century coaching inn, located within easy walking distance of the historic centre. Thoughtfully furnished bedrooms feature smart modern bathrooms, and spacious public areas include an attractive conservatory restaurant.

Rooms 4 en suite **Facilities** STV FTV TVB tea/coffee Direct dial from bedrooms Cen ht Dinner Last d 9pm **Conf** Max 50 Thtr 50 Class 50 Board 40 **Parking** 20 **Notes** ⊗ No children 16yrs

★★★ GUEST HOUSE
The Limes Guest House

368 London Rd RG14 2QH
☎ 01635 33082 📠 01635 580023
e–mail: s.j.sweeney@btinternet.com
web: www.limesguesthouse.co.uk

dir: *M4 junct 13, 3m S towards Newbury. Take A4 to towards Thatcham/Reading, 400yds past Newbury Business Park on left*

Built in 1910, the Edwardian house is convenient for Newbury and Thatcham, and Newbury Racecourse is only a mile away. The en suite bedrooms are individually decorated. Wi-fi internet access and ample parking are available. Dinner and breakfast is served in the light dining room overlooking the spacious gardens.

Rooms 17 en suite (2 fmly) (9 GF) S £58–£69; D £74–£87 **Facilities** FTV TVB tea/coffee Direct dial from bedrooms Cen ht TVL Dinner Last d 8pm Wi-fi available **Parking** 20 **Notes** ⊗ No coaches

---

PANGBOURNE   MAP 05 SU67

★★★★ GUEST ACCOMMODATION
Weir View House

9 Shooters Hill RG8 7DZ
☎ 0118 984 2120 📠 0118 984 3777
e–mail: info@weirview.co.uk
web: www.weirview.co.uk

dir: *A329 N from Pangbourne, after mini-rdbt under rail bridge, opp Swan pub*

A warm welcome is guaranteed at this delightful house, situated in the village of Pangbourne overlooking the River Thames. The spacious modern bedrooms have been finished to a very high standard and the thoughtful extras include a well-stocked minibar. A continental breakfast is served in the bright and airy dining room, and freshly cooked meals can be delivered to your room from the pub across the road.

Rooms 9 en suite (6 fmly) (3 GF) **Facilities** FTV TVB tea/coffee Direct dial from bedrooms Cen ht TVL Wi-fi available **Parking** 10 **Notes** ⊗ Closed 23 Dec–1 Jan

---

READING   MAP 05 SU77

★★★ BED & BREAKFAST
Chestnuts Bed & Breakfast

Basingstoke Rd, Spencers Wood RG7 1AA
☎ 0118 988 6171 & 07903 956397
e–mail: chestnuts4bb@hotmail.com

dir: *M4 junct 11, A33 for Basingstoke, next rdbt onto B3349 Three Mile Cross, over white-spot rdbt, Chestnuts 1m on left between chemist & bakery*

This detached Georgian house is convenient for the business parks of Reading, just 1.5m from the M4 and with easy access to the M3. The non-smoking house provides spacious bedrooms, warm hospitality, a good breakfast, and off-road parking.

Rooms 3 rms S £35–£40; D £50–£55✳ **Facilities** FTV TVB tea/coffee Cen ht Wi-fi available **Parking** 4 **Notes** ⊗ No children 16yrs ⊜

READING CONTINUED

Ⓤ
The New Inn
Chalkhouse Green Rd, Kidmore End RG4 9AU

☎ 0118 972 3115 📠 0118 972 4733

e–mail: thenewinn@live.co.uk

web: www.thenewinnrestaurant.co.uk

At the time of going to press the rating for this establishment had not been confirmed. Please check the AA website www.theAA.com for up-to-date information.

Rooms 6 en suite (3 GF) S £75–£110; D £75–£110✱ **Facilities** FTV TVB tea/coffee Direct dial from bedrooms Cen ht Dinner Last d 9.30pm Wi-fi available **Parking** 60 **Notes** LB

SLOUGH   MAP 06 SU97

★★★★ Ⓐ GUEST HOUSE
Furnival Lodge
53–55 Furnival Av SL2 1DH

☎ 01753 570333 📠 01753 670038

e–mail: info@furnival-lodge.co.uk

web: www.furnival-lodge.co.uk

dir: *Just off the A355 Farnham Rd adjacent to the BP garage*

Rooms 10 en suite (1 fmly) (3 GF) S £40–£55; D £50–£75✱ **Facilities** TVB Cen ht TVL Wi-fi available **Parking** 7 **Notes** ⊗

WINDSOR   MAP 06 SU97

★★★★ GUEST ACCOMMODATION
Park Farm
St Leonards Rd SL4 3EA

☎ 01753 866823

e–mail: stay@parkfarm.com

dir: *M4 junct 6, at end of dual-carriageway take 3rd exit. At junct, turn right, Park Farm on left*

Ideally situated between Windsor and Legoland, Park Farm offers a warm welcome and traditionally styled accommodation. Each bedroom has a lot of useful facilities. Some rooms also have romantic wrought-iron beds. The owners aim to offer guests a friendly and personal service including advice and information on where to eat or what to do in the area. Bunkbeds can be added for children.

Rooms 4 rms (3 en suite) (1 pri facs) (2 fmly) (2 GF) S £50–£85; D £79–£99✱ **Facilities** FTV TVB tea/coffee Cen ht Wi-fi available **Parking** 8 **Notes** ⊗ 🐾

★★★ GUEST HOUSE
Clarence Guest House
9 Clarence Rd SL4 5AE

☎ 01753 864436 📠 01753 857060

e–mail: clarence.hotel@btconnect.com

web: www.clarence-hotel.co.uk

dir: *M4 junct 6, dual-carriageway to Windsor, left at 1st rdbt onto Clarence Rd*

This Grade II listed Victorian house is in the heart of Windsor. Space in some rooms is limited, but all are well maintained and offer excellent value for money. Facilities include a lounge with a well-stocked bar, and a steam room. Breakfast is served in the dining room overlooking attractive gardens.

Rooms 20 en suite (6 fmly) (2 GF) (18 smoking) S £45–£72; D £55–£82 **Facilities** FTV TVB tea/coffee Licensed Cen ht TVL Wi-fi available Sauna Steam room **Parking** 4

WOKINGHAM   MAP 05 SU86

★★★★ GUEST ACCOMMODATION
Quarters
14 Milton Rd RG40 1DB

☎ 0118 979 7071 📠 0118 977 0057

e–mail: elaineizod@hotmail.com

dir: *From town centre on A321 towards Henley/Twyford. Left at 1st mini-rdbt onto Milton Rd*

Located just a short walk from the town centre, a guaranteed warm welcome is assured here. Stylishly decorated bedrooms are well equipped and spacious. A hearty breakfast is served around the communal dining table.

Rooms 3 en suite S £45–£50; D £55–£60✱ **Facilities** FTV TVB tea/coffee Cen ht Wi-fi available **Notes** ⊗ 🐾

BRISTOL

BRISTOL — MAP 04 ST57

★★★★ GUEST ACCOMMODATION
Westfield House
37 Stoke Hill, Stoke Bishop BS9 1LQ
☎ 0117 962 6119 📠 0117 962 6119
e-mail: admin@westfieldhouse.net
web: www.westfieldhouse.net
dir: *1.8m NW of city centre in Stoke Bishop*

A genuine welcome is assured at this friendly, family-run guest house in a quiet location on the edge of Durdham Downs. The very well-equipped bedrooms offer high levels of quality and comfort. Home-cooked dinners are available by arrangement and in summer they can be enjoyed on the patio overlooking the large rear garden.

Rooms 3 en suite S £69–£79; D £79–£108 **Facilities** FTV TVB tea/coffee Direct dial from bedrooms Cen ht TVL Dinner Last d 9.30pm Wi-fi available ⚓ **Conf** Max 10 Del from £150 ✳ **Parking** 5 **Notes LB** ⊗ No children 11yrs

★★★★ GUEST ACCOMMODATION
Downlands House
33 Henleaze Gardens, Henleaze BS9 4HH
☎ 0117 962 1639
e-mail: info@downlandshouse.co.uk
web: www.downlandshouse.com
dir: *2m NW of city centre off A4018. M5 junct 17, signs Westbury-on-Trym/City Centre, pass private girls schools, Henleaze Gdns on left*

This elegant Victorian property is convenient for Durdham Downs, Clifton village and Bristol Zoo. The attractive bedrooms have lots of

extra touches, there is a smart lounge, and breakfast is served in either the conservatory or the stylish dining room.

Rooms 10 rms (7 en suite) (3 pri facs) (1 fmly) (1 GF) S £40–£55; D £60–£75✳ **Facilities** FTV TVB tea/coffee Cen ht TVL Wi-fi available

★★★★ GUEST HOUSE
Downs Edge
Saville Rd, Stoke Bishop BS9 1JA
☎ 0117 968 3264 & 07885 866463 📠 0117 968 7063
e-mail: welcome@downsedge.com
dir: *M5 junct 17, A4018, 4th rdbt right onto B4054 Parrys Ln, 1st left onto Saville Rd, 3rd right onto Hollybush Ln, left after 2nd speed ramp*

This fetching country house has a quiet countryside setting in the heart of the city, on the edge of Bristol's famous Durdham Downs. It stands in glorious gardens and is furnished with period pieces and paintings. The pleasant, well-equipped bedrooms have facilities en suite and the added bonus of sweeping views across the Downs – a nice finishing touch to each room is a basket full with life's little necessities. Breakfast is an impressive variety of hot and cold dishes. There is a drawing room with an open fire, and a library containing many books on Bristol.

Rooms 4 en suite 3 annexe en suite S £55–£62; D £78–£82✳ **Facilities** TVB tea/coffee Cen ht Wi-fi available **Conf** Board 12 **Parking** 8 **Notes** ⊗ No children 6yrs No coaches Closed Xmas & New Year

★★★★ FARM HOUSE
Greenlands *(ST597636)*
BS39 4ES
☎ 01275 333487 📠 01275 331211 Mrs J Cleverley
(For full entry see Stanton Drew (Somerset))

★★★★ BED & BREAKFAST
Valley Farm
Sandy Ln BS39 4EL
☎ 01275 332723 & 07799 768161 📠 01275 332723
e-mail: valleyfarm2000@tiscali.co.uk
(For full entry see Stanton Drew (Somerset))

CONTINUED

BRISTOL CONTINUED

★★★★ GUEST HOUSE
Westbury Park Guest House
37 Westbury Rd, Westbury-on-Trym BS9 3AU

☎ 0117 962 0465 📠 0117 962 8607

e–mail: westburypark@btconnect.com

dir: *M5 junct 17, A4018, 3.5m opp gates of Badminton School*

On the edge of Durdham Downs, this detached guest house is ideally located for many of Bristol's attractions. Breakfast is served in the spacious dining room overlooking the front garden. Bedrooms and bathrooms offer a range of shapes and sizes including a room on the ground floor.

Rooms 8 en suite (3 fmly) (1 GF) **Facilities** TVB tea/coffee Licensed Cen ht **Parking** 4

★★★ GUEST HOUSE
Mayfair Lodge
5 Henleaze Rd, Westbury-on-Trym BS9 4EX

☎ 0117 962 2008 📠 0117 962 2008

e–mail: mayfairlodge@blueyonder.co.uk

dir: *M5 junct 17, A4018, after 3rd rdbt onto Henleaze Rd, Lodge 50yds on left*

This charming Victorian house is in a residential area close to Durdham Downs and Bristol Zoo. Mayfair Lodge has well-equipped bedrooms of varying sizes and a relaxed, friendly atmosphere. Breakfast is served at separate tables in the bright dining room. Off-road parking is available behind the property.

Rooms 9 rms (6 en suite) S £35–£55; D £70–£75 **Facilities** TVB tea/coffee Cen ht **Parking** 6 **Notes** ❷ No children 10yrs No coaches Closed Xmas & New Year

★★★ GUEST HOUSE
Washington
11–15 St Pauls Rd, Clifton BS8 1LX

☎ 0117 973 3980 📠 0117 973 4740

e–mail: washington@cliftonhotels.com

dir: *A4018 into city, right at lights opp BBC, house 200yds on left*

This large terrace house is within walking distance of the city centre and Clifton village. The bedrooms, many recently refurbished, are well equipped for business guests. Public areas include a modern reception lounge and a bright basement breakfast room. The property has secure parking and a rear patio garden.

Rooms 46 rms (40 en suite) (4 fmly) (10 GF) (7 smoking) S £35–£69; D £44–£87✳ **Facilities** STV TVB tea/coffee Direct dial from bedrooms Licensed Cen ht Wi-fi available Reduced rate pass for local health club **Parking** 16 **Notes** Closed 23 Dec–3 Jan

★★★ 🅰 GUEST HOUSE
Downs View
38 Upper Belgrave Rd, Clifton BS8 2XN

☎ 0117 973 7046 📠 0117 973 8169

e–mail: bookings@downsviewguesthouse.co.uk

dir: *1m NW of city centre. A4018 onto A4176, just before zoo*

Rooms 16 rms (9 en suite) (1 fmly) (2 GF) **Facilities** TVB tea/coffee Cen ht **Notes** ❷ Closed Xmas & New Year

★★ GUEST HOUSE
Shirehampton Lodge
62–64 High St, Shirehampton BS11 0DJ

☎ 0117 907 3480 📠 0117 907 3481

dir: *M5 junct 18, B4054 to Shirehampton for 1m, premises on left opp Texaco garage, entrance up ramp*

Situated above shops, this imaginatively converted warehouse offers easy access to the motorway and the city centre. The modern bedrooms are thoughtfully equipped for business and leisure, and there is a well-furnished lounge/dining room.

Rooms 11 en suite (3 fmly) S £40; D £55 **Facilities** STV TVB tea/coffee Cen ht **Parking** 10 **Notes** LB No children

---

EASTON-IN-GORDANO　　　　MAP 04 ST57

★★★ BED & BREAKFAST
The Tynings B & B
Martcombe Rd BS20 0QE

☎ 01275 372608

dir: *M5 junct 19, A369 towards Bristol (signed Clifton), 0.5m on right opp Rudgleigh Inn*

Located just a short drive from the M5, this popular house offers comfortable bedrooms and a relaxed atmosphere. There is a television lounge and a car park available to guests. A range of meals is available for dinner at the pleasant local pub opposite.

Rooms 7 rms (4 en suite) (4 fmly) (1 GF) S £35–£40; D £50–£55✳ **Facilities** TVB tea/coffee Cen ht TVL **Parking** 8 **Notes** ❷ Closed Xmas-New Year ⊛

BUCKINGHAMSHIRE

AMERSHAM
MAP 06 SU99

★★ BED & BREAKFAST

Morningside

Piggots Orchard HP7 0JG

☎ 01494 721134

dir: *250yds SE of Amersham Old Town. A413 onto A355, B&B 20yds on right*

A warm welcome is assured at this private home ideally located a few minutes walk from the old town. Smartly furnished bedrooms are equipped with lots of thoughtful extras and breakfast is taken at one table in an attractive pine furnished dining room or conservatory, during the warmer months.

Rooms 2 rms (2 pri facs) (1 fmly) S fr £30; D fr £60✷ **Facilities** TVB tea/coffee Cen ht **Parking** 2 **Notes** ⊗ ➡

BRILL
MAP 11 SP61

★★★★ FARM HOUSE

Poletrees Farm *(SP660160)*

Ludgershall Rd HP18 9TZ

☎ 01844 238276 📄 01844 238276 Mrs A Cooper

e–mail: poletrees.farm@virgin.net

dir: *S off A41 signed Ludgershall/Brill, after railway bridge 0.5m on left*

Located between the villages of Ludgershall and Brill, this 16th-century farmhouse retains many original features including a wealth of exposed beams. The bedrooms are in converted outbuildings. Breakfast is served in the cosy dining room, the setting for a wholesome breakfast.

Rooms 4 annexe en suite (4 GF) S £35–£40; D £60–£70✷ **Facilities** FTV TVB tea/coffee Cen ht TVL **Parking** 6 **Notes LB** ⊗ No children 10yrs 110 acres beef sheep

---

CHESHAM
MAP 06 SP90

Premier Collection

★★★★★ 🏠 BED & BREAKFAST

Braziers Well

Oak Ln, Braziers End HP5 2UL

☎ 01494 758956 & 07860 317762

e–mail: info@brazierswell.co.uk

web: www.brazierswell.co.uk

dir: *From Chesham N off A416 signed Bellingdon/Cholesbury, after 5m sharp left bend, Braziers Well 100yds on right*

Peacefully located within an unspoiled rural community, this impressive detached house provides a spacious, thoughtfully furnished bedroom with a wealth of homely extras and a smart modern shower room. Imaginative breakfasts, using quality produce, are served in an attractive conservatory-dining room and a warm welcome is assured.

Rooms 1 en suite (1 GF) S £50; D £65–£70✷ **Facilities** TVB tea/coffee Cen ht Table tennis **Parking** 4 **Notes** ⊗ No children 16yrs ➡

DENHAM
MAP 06 TQ08

★★★★ ➡ INN

The Falcon Inn

Village Rd UB9 5BE

☎ 01895 832125

e–mail: falcon.inn@btconnect.com

web: www.falconinn.biz

dir: *M40 junct 1 signed A40 Gerrards Cross. After approx 200yds, turn right into Old Mill Rd, follow road, pub opp village green.*

The 18th-century inn stands in the heart of the picturesque village, opposite the green. The bedrooms, with smart shower rooms en suite, are well equipped and display original features. Carefully prepared dishes and a good selection of wines are available for lunch and dinner in the cosy restaurant.

Rooms 3 en suite S £75–£95; D £95✷ **Facilities** TVB tea/coffee Cen ht Dinner Last d 9.30pm Wi-fi available **Notes LB** ⊗ No children 10yrs

ENGLAND

GAYHURST   MAP 11 SP84

★★★ FARM HOUSE
Mill Farm *(SP852454)*

MK16 8LT

☎ 01908 611489 & 07714 719640 🖷 01908 611489

Mrs K Adams

e–mail: adamsmillfarm@aol.com

web: www.millfarmgayhurst.co.uk

dir: *B526 from Newport Pagnell, 2.5m left onto Haversham Rd, Mill Farm 1st on left*

Within easy reach of Newport Pagnell and the M1, this historic farmhouse has a peaceful setting with wonderful views over farmland. Bedrooms are decorated in a homely style and have a host of thoughtful extras. The sumptuous lounge-dining room is enhanced with fine antiques, and the extensive grounds include a tennis court.

Rooms 3 rms (2 en suite) 1 annexe en suite (1 fmly) (1 GF) S £30–£35; D £50–£60 **Facilities** TVB tea/coffee Cen ht TVL 🏊 Fishing 🏌 **Parking** 13 **Notes** 550 acres mixed 🐾

HIGH WYCOMBE   MAP 05 SU89

★★★ GUEST HOUSE
Clifton Lodge

210 West Wycombe Rd HP12 3AR

☎ 01494 440095 & 529062 🖷 01494 536322

e–mail: sales@cliftonlodgehotel.com

web: www.cliftonlodgehotel.com

dir: *A40 from town centre towards Aylesbury, on right after BP station & opp phone box*

Located west of the town centre, this long-established, owner-managed establishment provides a range of bedrooms, popular with a regular commercial clientele. Public areas include an attractive conservatory-dining room and a cosy lounge. Ample parking behind the property.

Rooms 32 rms (20 en suite) (1 fmly) (7 GF) **Facilities** TVB tea/coffee Direct dial from bedrooms Licensed Cen ht TVL Dinner Last d 8.45pm **Conf** Max 30 Thtr 30 Class 20 Board 15 **Parking** 28 **Notes** 🐾

IVINGHOE   MAP 11 SP91

★★★★ GUEST ACCOMMODATION
The Brownlow B&B

LU7 9DY

☎ 01296 668787

e–mail: info@thebrownlow.com

dir: *A41 to Tring onto B488 to Ivinghoe/Dunstable. Follow Leighton Buzzard sign on B488*

The Brownlow at Ivinghoe was built in the early 1800s to serve the newly finished Grand Union Canal, it has remained in the same family ever since. The old stables have now been converted into well-appointed bedrooms, which offer plenty of modern amenities. Breakfast is served at the communal table overlooking the canal.

Rooms 5 en suite (5 GF) S £45–£55; D £75–£85✱ **Facilities** FTV TVB tea/coffee Cen ht TVL Wi-fi available **Parking** 6 **Notes** ⊗ No children 6yrs

CAMBRIDGESHIRE

BURWELL   MAP 12 TL56

★★★★ 🄰 GUEST ACCOMMODATION
The Meadow House

2A High St CB5 0HB

☎ 01638 741926 🖷 01638 741861

e–mail: hilary@themeadowhouse.co.uk

web: www.themeadowhouse.co.uk

dir: *A14 at Stow-cum-Quy onto B1102 to Burwell, Meadow House on left opposite phone box*

Rooms 7 rms (4 en suite) (4 fmly) (2 GF) S £30–£35; D £60–£70✱ **Facilities** TVB tea/coffee Cen ht **Parking** 16 **Notes** 🐾

CAMBRIDGE   MAP 12 TL45

★★★★ GUEST HOUSE
Aylesbray Lodge

5 Mowbray Rd CB1 7SR

☎ 01223 240089 🖷 01223 528678

e–mail: stay@aylesbray.com

web: www.aylesbray.com

dir: *1.5m SE of city centre on A1134*

A warm welcome is assured at this family-run guest house. The en suite bedrooms are well equipped, each with a modern shower room, and two rooms have attractive four-poster beds. Tasty English breakfasts are served in the elegant dining room and a lounge is available.

Rooms 6 en suite (1 fmly) (1 GF) **Facilities** STV TVB tea/coffee Direct dial from bedrooms Cen ht TVL Wi-fi available **Parking** 6 **Notes** ⊗

★★★★ BED & BREAKFAST
The Gate Lodge
2 Hinton Rd, Fulbourn CB1 5DZ

☎ 01223 881951 📄 08700 513050

e-mail: bandb@thegatelodge.co.uk

dir: *5m E of Cambridge. W side of Fulbourn village opp Bakers Arms pub*

This restful, lovingly restored house is in a sleepy village not far from Cambridge and the M11. The spacious bedrooms are well appointed with useful extras including internet connections, flat screen TV with Freeview and DVD facilities in all rooms. Breakfast is a feature, served round a large oak table in the attractive dining room.

Rooms 3 rms (1 en suite) (2 pri facs) (2 fmly) S £55–£75; D fr £80✳
Facilities FTV TVB tea/coffee Cen ht 🛳 **Parking** 5 **Notes** ⊗ No children 5yrs

★★★★ GUEST HOUSE
Lynwood House
217 Chesterton Rd CB4 1AN

☎ 01223 500776

e-mail: info@lynwood-house.co.uk

web: www.lynwood-house.co.uk

dir: *M11 N junct 13, A1303 towards city centre, left at mini-rdbt, house 1m on left*

Located close to the river and central attractions, this constantly improving guest house provides a range of thoughtfully equipped bedrooms, most of which have the benefit of modern en suite shower rooms. Organically sourced produce is a feature of the wholesome breakfasts which are taken in a stylish dining room and a warm welcome is assured.

Rooms 7 rms (5 en suite) (1 fmly) (2 GF) S £35–£75; D £65–£85✳
Facilities FTV TVB tea/coffee Cen ht Wi-fi available **Parking** 3 **Notes** ⊗ No children 12yrs No coaches

★★★★ BED & BREAKFAST
Rose Bungalow
68 High St, Great Wilbraham CB21 5JD

☎ 01223 882385 & 07876 426271

e-mail: rose.bungalow@btinternet.com

dir: *6m E of Cambridge in Great Wilbraham centre*

This attractive bungalow with pretty gardens stands in a quiet village very close to the Park and Ride for Cambridge and the Imperial War Museum. The comfortable bedrooms contain many thoughtful extras and the nutritious breakfast is a speciality. Off-road parking is an additional plus.

Rooms 2 en suite (2 GF) S £35–£40; D £55–£60✳ **Facilities** FTV TVB tea/coffee Cen ht Wi-fi available Golf 18 **Parking** 3 **Notes** ⊗ No children 12yrs 🍴

★★★★ BED & BREAKFAST
Rose Corner
42 Woodcock Close, Impington CB24 9LD

☎ 01223 563136 📄 01223 233886

e-mail: wsalmon.rosecorner@virgin.net

web: www.rose-corner.co.uk

dir: *4m N of Cambridge. A14 junct 32, B1049 N into Impington, off Milton Rd*

The detached property is in a quiet cul-de-sac in the popular village of Impington, north of the city. Its spacious bedrooms are carefully furnished and thoughtfully equipped, and breakfast is served in the comfortable lounge/dining room overlooking the rear gardens.

Rooms 5 rms (3 en suite) S £28–£30; D £55–£60 **Facilities** TVB tea/coffee Cen ht TVL Wi-fi available **Parking** 5 **Notes** ⊗ No children 11yrs

★★★ GUEST HOUSE
Alpha Milton
61–63 Milton Rd CB4 1XA

☎ 01223 311625 📄 01223 565100

e-mail: info@alphamilton.com

dir: *0.5m NE of city centre*

The Alpha Milton is in a residential area just a short walk from the city centre. The attractive lounge-dining room overlooks the rear garden, and the pleasant bedrooms are have a good range of facilities.

Rooms 8 rms (6 en suite) (1 pri facs) (2 fmly) (2 GF) S £30–£75; D £60–£120✳ **Facilities** TVB tea/coffee Cen ht TVL Wi-fi available **Parking** 8 **Notes** LB ⊗

★★★ GUEST HOUSE
Benson House
24 Huntingdon Rd CB3 0HH

☎ 01223 311594 📄 01223 311594

e-mail: bensonhouse@btconnect.com

dir: *0.5m NW of city centre on A604*

The popular guest house is well placed for the city centre and New Hall and Fitzwilliam colleges. Its pleasant bedrooms vary in size and style and are well equipped. Limited private parking behind the property.

Rooms 5 rms (4 en suite) (1 pri facs) (1 GF) **Facilities** TVB tea/coffee Cen ht **Parking** 5 **Notes** ⊗ No children 12yrs No coaches

CAMBRIDGE CONTINUED

★★★ GUEST HOUSE
Brooklands
95 Cherry Hinton Rd CB1 7BS
☎ 01223 242035 📠 01223 242035
e–mail: michelle@brooklandsguesthouse.co.uk

dir: *1m SE of city centre off A1307*

Located close to the ring road, this renovated Edwardian terrace house offers well-equipped homely bedrooms. Freshly cooked breakfasts are served in the cosy dining room and a sauna is available. Limited free parking is available nearby.

Rooms 5 en suite (1 fmly) **Facilities** STV TVB tea/coffee Direct dial from bedrooms Cen ht Snooker Sauna **Parking** 5 **Notes** No coaches

★★★ GUEST HOUSE
Fairways
143 Cherry Hinton Rd CB1 7BX
☎ 01223 246063 📠 01223 248306
e–mail: michaelslatter@btconnect.com
web: www.fairwaysguesthouse.com

dir: *M11 junct 11 onto A1309 to A1134. Left onto A1307, right onto Cherry Hinton Rd*

The large Victorian house provides well-equipped bedrooms convenient for the city centre and the ring road. Many of the rooms have attractive, handcrafted pine furniture, and the en suite rooms have modern showers. Breakfast is served in an attractive ground-floor dining room and ample car parking is available to the rear of property.

Rooms 16 rms (9 en suite) (3 fmly) (4 GF) S £32–£45; D £54–£70✳ **Facilities** TVB tea/coffee Cen ht Wi-fi available **Parking** 20 **Notes** ⊗ Closed 22 Dec–2 Jan

★★★ GUEST HOUSE
Hamden
89 High St, Cherry Hinton CB1 9LU
☎ 01223 413263 📠 01223 245960
e–mail: info@hamdenguesthouse.co.uk
web: www.hamdenguesthouse.co.uk

dir: *3m SE of city centre. Off A1134 to Cherry Hinton*

Expect a warm welcome at this small, family-run guest house, which is just a short drive from the city centre. The pleasant bedrooms are generally quite spacious and equipped with many thoughtful extras. Public rooms include a large kitchen-dining room where breakfast is served at individual tables.

Rooms 3 en suite (2 fmly) (1 GF) S £40; D £60✳ **Facilities** FTV TVB tea/coffee Direct dial from bedrooms Cen ht **Parking** 6 **Notes** LB ⊗ No children 5yrs No coaches

See advert on opposite page

★★★ GUEST HOUSE
Hamilton Lodge
156 Chesterton Rd CB4 1DA
☎ 01223 365664 📠 01223 314866
e–mail: hamiltonhotel@talk21.com

dir: *1m NE of city centre, off A1134 ring road*

Smartly maintained property situated just a short walk from the city centre. The pleasantly appointed bedrooms have coordinated fabrics and a good range of facilities to enhance guest comfort. The relaxing public areas include a large open plan restaurant/bar, where breakfast, evening meals and a range of snacks are available.

Rooms 25 rms (19 en suite) (4 fmly) (8 GF) S £30–£60; D £56–£85 **Facilities** TVB tea/coffee Direct dial from bedrooms Licensed Cen ht Dinner Last d 8pm Wi-fi available Pool Table ⤴ ⅃ **Parking** 20 **Notes** ⊗ Closed 25 & 26 Dec

★★★ GUEST HOUSE
Southampton Guest House
7 Elizabeth Way CB4 1DE
☎ 01223 357780 📄 01223 314297
e–mail: southamptonhouse@btinternet.com
web: www.southamptonguesthouse.com

dir: 0.5m E of city centre

The proprietors provide a friendly service at their terrace guest house, which is on the inner ring road, just a short walk from the Grafton Centre. The property has well-equipped bedrooms, and a comprehensive English breakfast is served.

Rooms 5 en suite (3 fmly) (1 GF) S £35–£45; D £48–£58✳
Facilities TVB tea/coffee Direct dial from bedrooms Cen ht **Parking** 8
Notes ⊗ ⊠

ENGLAND

CAMBRIDGE CONTINUED

★★ GUEST HOUSE
Ashtrees Guest House

128 Perne Rd CB1 3RR

☎ 01223 411233 📠 01223 411233

e–mail: ashtrees@cscuk.net

web: www.ashtreesguesthouse.co.uk

dir: *1.5m SE of city centre on A1134*

Service is informal, cheerful and helpful at Ashtrees, and the en suite bedrooms come in a variety of styles and sizes. A continental or full cooked breakfast is served at individual tables in the pleasant breakfast room. Some private parking is available to the rear of the property.

Rooms 5 en suite (1 fmly) (2 GF) **Facilities** TVB tea/coffee Cen ht
Parking 5

ELTON	MAP 12 TL09

Premier Collection

★★★★★ INN
The Crown Inn

8 Duck St PE8 6RQ

☎ 01832 280232

e–mail: inncrown@googlemail.com

web: www.thecrowninn.org

dir: *A1 junct 17 onto A605 W. After 3.5m turn right signed Elton, 0.9m turn left signed Nassington on village green*

Expect a warm welcome at this delightful village pub which is situated opposite the village green. The property dates back to the 16th century, and has recently undergone major refurbishment yet retains many of its original features, such as a large inglenook fireplace and oak-beamed ceilings. The smartly decorated bedrooms are tastefully appointed and thoughtfully equipped. Public rooms include a large open-plan lounge bar, a small relaxed dining area to the front, and a tastefully appointed circular restaurant.

Rooms 2 en suite 2 annexe en suite (2 GF) S £60–£120; D £80–£150✳
Facilities TVB tea/coffee Cen ht Last d 8.45pm Wi-fi available
Conf Max 40 Thtr 40 Class 40 **Parking** 15 **Notes** LB ⊗ No coaches
Closed 2wks Jan RS Sun eve & Mon (ex BH)

See advert on page 35

ELY	MAP 12 TL58

★★★★ ⊛ 🛡 RESTAURANT WITH ROOMS
The Anchor Inn

Sutton Gault CB6 2BD

☎ 01353 778537 📠 01353 776180

e–mail: anchorinn@popmail.bta.com

dir: *6m W of Ely. Sutton Gault signed off B1381 at S end of Sutton*

Located beside the New Bedford river with stunning country views, this 17th-century inn has a wealth of original features enhanced by period furniture. The spacious bedrooms are tastefully appointed and

CONTINUED

equipped with many thoughtful touches. The friendly team of staff offer helpful and attentive service.

Rooms 4 en suite (2 fmly) S £59.50–£155; D £79.50–£155✳
Facilities FTV TVB tea/coffee Direct dial from bedrooms Cen ht Dinner Last d 9pm Wi-fi available **Parking** 16 **Notes** LB ⊗

★★★ GUEST HOUSE
Castle Lodge

50 New Barns Rd CB7 4PW

☎ 01353 662276 📠 01353 666606

e–mail: castlelodgehotel@supanet.com

dir: *Off B1382 Prickwillow Rd NE from town centre*

Located within easy walking distance of the cathedral, this extended Victorian house offers well-equipped bedrooms in a variety of sizes. Public areas include a traditionally furnished dining room and a comfortable air-conditioned bar lounge. Service is friendly and helpful.

Rooms 11 rms (6 en suite) (3 fmly) S £32.50–£55; D fr £75✳
Facilities TVB tea/coffee Direct dial from bedrooms Licensed Cen ht TVL Dinner Last d 9pm **Conf** Max 40 Board 40 **Parking** 6 **Notes** No coaches

★★★ GUEST ACCOMMODATION
The Nyton

7 Barton Rd CB7 4HZ

☎ 01353 662459 📠 01353 666217

e–mail: nytonhotel@yahoo.co.uk

dir: *From S, A10 into Ely on Cambridge Rd, pass golf course, 1st right*

Set in 2 acres of mature gardens, this family-run establishment offers comfortable bedrooms in a range of sizes and styles. The pleasant public rooms include a wood-panelled restaurant, a smart bar, and a conservatory-lounge overlooking the gardens. Meals are available in the dining room and informal light meals are served in the lounge bar.

Rooms 10 en suite (3 fmly) (2 GF) **Facilities** FTV TVB tea/coffee Direct dial from bedrooms Cen ht TVL Dinner Last d 6.30pm Golf **Conf** Max 40 Board 40 **Parking** 25 **Notes** ⊗ Civ Wed 100

HILTON   MAP 12 TL26

★★★ INN
Prince of Wales

Potton Rd PE28 9NG
☎ 01480 830257 📠 01480 830257

dir: *A14 onto B1040 towards Biggleswade, 2m into village, Prince of Wales on left*

This popular village inn offers a choice of cosy traditional bars serving good food and real ales. The pleasantly decorated bedrooms are equipped with modern facilities. A hearty breakfast is served in the dining room at individual tables.

Rooms 4 en suite S £50; D £70✱ **Facilities** TVB tea/coffee Direct dial from bedrooms Cen ht Dinner Last d 8.45pm Pool Table **Parking** 12 **Notes** No children 5yrs

HUNTINGDON   MAP 12 TL27

★★★★★ Ⓐ GUEST ACCOMMODATION
Cheriton House

Mill St, Houghton PE28 2AZ
☎ 01480 464004 📠 01480 496960
e–mail: sales@cheritonhousecambs.co.uk

dir: *In village of Houghton, through village square, signed to river & mill*

Rooms 2 en suite 3 annexe en suite (3 GF) S £62–£68; D £70–£85✱ **Facilities** TVB tea/coffee Cen ht Wi-fi available ➷ **Conf** Max 15 Thtr 15 Class 6 Board 8 **Parking** 7 **Notes** LB ⊗ No children 14yrs

Ⓤ
The Three Horseshoes

Moat Ln, Abbots Ripton PE28 2PD
☎ 01487 773440 📠 01487 773440
e–mail: thethreehorseshoes.com@btconnect.com
web: www.thethreehorseshoes.com

dir: *3m N of Huntingdon. Off B1090 in Abbots Ripton*

At the time of going to press the rating for this establishment had not been confirmed. Please check the AA website www.theAA.com for up-to-date information.

Rooms 3 en suite 2 annexe en suite (1 fmly) (4 GF) **Facilities** TVB tea/coffee Cen ht Dinner Last d 9.30pm Wi-fi available **Parking** 80 **Notes** ⊗ RS Mon

See advert on this page

KIRTLING   MAP 12 TL65

★★★ BED & BREAKFAST
Hill Farm Guest House

CB8 9HQ
☎ 01638 730253 📠 01638 731957

dir: *0.5m NW of Kirtling*

Located on arable land south of Newmarket, in the heart of horse-breeding country, this 400-year-old property retains many original features. Public areas are furnished in keeping with the building's character, and hearty breakfasts are served at a family table in the elegant dining room.

Rooms 3 en suite S £35–£45; D £65✱ **Facilities** TVB tea/coffee Direct dial from bedrooms Cen ht TVL Wi-fi available ➷ **Parking** 15 **Notes** LB ⊛

PETERBOROUGH · MAP 12 TL19

★★★ GUEST ACCOMMODATION
Aaron Park

109 Park Rd PE1 2TR
☎ 01733 564849 📠 01733 564855
e–mail: aaronparkhotel@yahoo.co.uk

dir: *A1 onto A1139 to junct 5, to city centre on Boongate, over rdbt onto Crawthorne Rd, over lights, next left*

Family service is both friendly and helpful at this Victorian house, which is situated in a tree-lined avenue just a short walk from the city centre and cathedral. Bedrooms come in a variety of styles and sizes; each room is nicely presented and has a good range of modern facilities. Freshly cooked breakfasts are carefully presented and provide a good start to the day.

Rooms 10 en suite (3 fmly) (2 GF) **Facilities** STV TVB tea/coffee Cen ht **Parking** 8 **Notes** ⊗ Closed Xmas

ST NEOTS · MAP 12 TL16

★★★★ GUEST HOUSE
Agden Hill Farm

Agden Green, Great Staughton PE19 5EX
☎ 01480 869424 📠 01480 860996

dir: *4.5m NW of St Neots off B645*

Dating from the 18th century, this extended farmhouse stands amid 600 acres of arable farmland near Grafham Water, well known for its wildlife, fishing, sailing and cycling. The charming proprietors provide a very warm welcome, making every effort to put you at ease, while providing helpful service and good food. There are spacious lounges, a stylish dining room, and the bedrooms vary in style. The property is not suited to young children.

Rooms 2 rms 2 annexe en suite (2 GF) **Facilities** TV3B tea/coffee Cen ht TVL Dinner Last d 9.30pm **Conf** Max 10 Class 10 Board 8 **Parking** 20 **Notes** ⊗ No children 11yrs No coaches 🐾

STETCHWORTH · MAP 12 TL65

★★★★ BED & BREAKFAST
The Old Mill

Mill Ln CB8 9TR
☎ 01638 507839
e–mail: gbell839@aol.com

dir: *In village centre off Tea Kettle Ln*

Situated in a delightful village, the accommodation comprises a thoughtfully equipped self-contained flat sleeping four, with a small kitchen, quality pine furniture and a DVD player. Access is via a private staircase leading to a sun terrace overlooking mature gardens. Breakfast is served at a large communal table in the main house.

Rooms 1 annexe en suite **Facilities** TVB tea/coffee TVL Wi-fi available 🐾 **Parking** 2 **Notes** ⊗ 🐾

WILLINGHAM · MAP 12 TL47

★★★★ 🍴 GUEST ACCOMMODATION
Willingham House

50 Church St CB4 5HT
☎ 01954 260606 📠 01954 260603
e–mail: info@cimcol.com
web: www.cimcol.com

dir: *A14 junct 29 onto B1050 to Willingham*

A former rectory, this elegant Victorian house has been sympathetically renovated and extended to provide high standards of comfort and facilities. Bedrooms are thoughtfully furnished and imaginative dinners are served in an attractive dining room. Extensive conference facilities and pretty mature grounds are additional features.

Rooms 16 en suite 6 annexe en suite (7 GF) S £55–£79; D £60–£95 **Facilities** TVB tea/coffee Cen ht TVL Dinner Last d 10.30pm Wi-fi available Pool Table **Conf** Max 40 Thtr 40 Class 23 Board 24 Del from £100 **Parking** 25 **Notes** ⊗

CHESHIRE

AUDLEM · MAP 15 SJ64

★★★★ FARM HOUSE
Little Heath Farm *(SJ663455)*

CW3 0HE
☎ 01270 811324 Mrs H M Bennion
e–mail: hilaryandbob@ukonline.co.uk

dir: *Off A525 in village onto A529 towards Nantwich for 0.3m. Farm opposite village green*

The 200-year-old brick farmhouse retains much original character, including low beamed ceilings. The traditionally furnished public areas include a cosy sitting room and a dining room where you dine family style. The refurbished bedrooms are stylish, and the friendly proprietors create a relaxing atmosphere.

Rooms 3 en suite (1 fmly) S £30–£45; D £50–£65 **Facilities** TVB tea/coffee Cen ht TVL **Conf** Max 10 Board 10 **Parking** 6 **Notes** LB 50 acres mixed Closed Xmas & New Year 🐾

BURWARDSLEY	MAP 15 SJ55

★★★★ BED & BREAKFAST
Cheshire Cheese Cottage

Burwardsley Rd CH3 9NS
☎ 01829 770887 📄 01829 770887
e–mail: r.rosney@yahoo.co.uk

A very warm welcome awaits at this delightful little cottage, which is set in its own extensive grounds and colourful gardens on the outskirts of the village. The accommodation consists of one modern bedroom on ground floor level. This has its own conservatory which doubles as both lounge and breakfast room. Breakfasts are freshly cooked and hearty. Owner Rose Rosney is a qualified masseur and guests can book treatments if they wish.

Rooms 2 en suite (2 GF) D £75–£85✶ **Facilities** FTV TVB tea/coffee Direct dial from bedrooms Cen ht TVL Wi-fi available Golf 18 Riding **Parking** 4 **Notes** ⊗ No children ⊛

★★★★ BED & BREAKFAST
Sandhollow Farm B&B

Harthill Rd CH3 9NU
☎ 01829 770894
e–mail: paul.kickdrum@tiscali.co.uk

dir: From A41, turn off to Tattenhall, follow signs to Burwardsley. Continue past post office, 0.25m on right

Sandhollow Farm is a recently converted farmhouse commanding spectacular views of the Cheshire Plain and Welsh hills. Bedrooms have been carefully renovated and there is a comfortable lounge with a log fire. Substantial breakfasts using organic, homemade and local produce are served in the adjoining dining room with views across the garden and surrounding countryside.

Rooms 3 en suite (1 GF) S £60–£80; D £85–£120✶ **Facilities** TVB tea/coffee Cen ht Wi-fi available **Parking** 4 **Notes** LB ⊗ No children 12yrs Closed annual holiday ⊛

CHESTER	MAP 15 SJ46

See also Malpas

Premier Collection

★★★★★ 🏠 GUEST ACCOMMODATION
Chester Stone Villa

Stone Place, Hoole Rd CH2 3NR
☎ 01244 345014 📄 01244 345015
e–mail: enquiries@stonevillahotel.co.uk
web: www.stonevillahotel.co.uk

dir: 0.5m NE of city centre off A56 Hoole Rd

The attractive stone property offers stylish en suite bedrooms, all thoughtfully equipped with useful extras. Freshly cooked breakfasts are served in the elegant dining room, and there is a small lounge area and a private car park. Attentive friendly service is a highlight.

Rooms 10 en suite (4 fmly) (3 GF) S £50–£60; D £80–£90 **Facilities** STV FTV TVB tea/coffee Direct dial from bedrooms Cen ht Wi-fi available **Parking** 10 **Notes** LB ⊗

★★★★★ 🅰 GUEST HOUSE
Mitchell's of Chester

28 Hough Green CH4 8JQ
☎ 01244 679004 📄 01244 659567
e–mail: mitoches@dialstart.net
web: www.mitchellsofchester.com

dir: 1m SW of city centre. A483 onto A5104, 300yds on right in Hough Green

Rooms 7 en suite (2 fmly) (1 GF) S £40–£55; D £65–£75✶ **Facilities** FTV TVB tea/coffee Cen ht TVL Wi-fi available **Parking** 5 **Notes** LB ⊗ No coaches Closed 21–29 Dec

★★★★ GUEST ACCOMMODATION
Cheltenham Lodge

58 Hoole Rd, Hoole CH2 3NL
☎ 01244 346767
e–mail: cheltenhamlodge@btinternet.com
web: www.cheltenhamlodge.co.uk

dir: 1m NE of city centre on A56

The small, personally run guest house lies midway between the city centre and M53. Its attractive modern bedrooms, which include some on the ground floor and a family room, are well equipped, and a substantial breakfast is served in the smart dining room.

Rooms 5 en suite (2 fmly) **Facilities** TVB tea/coffee Cen ht **Parking** 5 **Notes** ⊗ Closed 23 Dec–7 Jan ⊛

ENGLAND

★★★★ GUEST ACCOMMODATION
Chester Brooklands

8 Newton Ln CH2 3RB
☎ 01244 348856 📄 01244 348856
e-mail: enquiries@chester-bandb.co.uk

dir: *M53 junct 12, A56 towards city, 1m right onto Newton Ln, on right*

Located in a mainly residential area close to Hoole village centre, this well-presented house has been carefully renovated to provide a range of thoughtfully furnished bedrooms with modern shower rooms en suite. Breakfast is served in the attractive dining room and a warm welcome is assured.

Rooms 5 en suite (1 fmly) **Facilities** FTV TVB tea/coffee Cen ht TVL Wi-fi available **Parking** 5 **Notes** ⊗ RS 2–3 wks in the year

★★★★ BED & BREAKFAST
Golborne Manor

Platts Ln, Hatton Heath CH3 9AN
☎ 01829 770310 & 07774 695268 📄 01829 770370
e-mail: info@golbornemanor.co.uk

dir: *5m S off A14 Whitchurch road. Right onto Platts Ln, 400yds on left*

The elegant Edwardian house stands in beautiful gardens with spectacular views across open countryside. Accommodation is in spacious bedrooms with either brass bedsteads or a richly carved antique Arabian bed. Breakfast is served around a large table in the dining room, and there is also a comfortable lounge.

Rooms 2 en suite (1 fmly) S £35–£45; D £60–£78✱ **Facilities** FTV TVB tea/coffee Cen ht 🏓 table tennis **Conf** Max 10 **Parking** 6 **Notes** LB ⊗ RS wknds 🐾

★★★★ GUEST HOUSE
Green Gables

11 Eversley Park CH2 2AJ
☎ 01244 372243 📄 01244 376352
e-mail: perruzza_d@hotmail.com

dir: *Off A5116 Liverpool Rd signed Countess of Chester Hospital, right at 3rd pedestrian lights to Eversley Park*

The attractive Victorian house, set in pretty gardens, is in a quiet residential area close to the city centre. The well-equipped bedrooms

CONTINUED

include a family room, and there is a choice of sitting rooms. The bright breakfast room is strikingly decorated.

Rooms 2 en suite (1 fmly) S £39–£45; D £56✱ **Facilities** FTV TVB tea/coffee Cen ht TVL Wi-fi available **Parking** 8 **Notes** ⊗ No coaches 🐾

★★★★ GUEST ACCOMMODATION
Hamilton Court

5–7 Hamilton St CH2 3JG
☎ 01244 345387 📄 01244 317404
e-mail: hamiltoncourth@aol.com

dir: *From town centre, All Saints church on left, 2nd turning on left*

Hamilton Court is a family run establishment, only 10 minutes walk from the city centre. All bedrooms are en suite and have useful facilities. Children are welcome and pets can be accommodated by arrangement.

Rooms 11 en suite (4 fmly) (1 GF) S £35–£45; D £65–£75✱ **Facilities** FTV TVB tea/coffee Cen ht Wi-fi available **Parking** 4 **Notes** Closed 24 Dec–3 Jan

★★★★ GUEST ACCOMMODATION
Lavender Lodge

46 Hoole Rd CH2 3NL
☎ 01244 323204 📄 01244 329821
e-mail: bookings@lavenderlodgechester.co.uk
web: www.lavenderlodgechester.co.uk

dir: *1m NE of city centre on A56, opp All Saints church*

A warm welcome is assured at this smart late Victorian house located within easy walking distance of central attractions. The bedrooms are equipped with thoughtful extras and have modern bathrooms. Quality breakfasts are served in the attractive dining room.

Rooms 5 en suite (2 fmly) S £35–£50; D £65–£80 **Facilities** FTV TVB tea/coffee Cen ht Wi-fi available **Parking** 7 **Notes** LB Closed 24 Dec–2 Jan

★★★★ BED & BREAKFAST
The Old Farmhouse B&B
9 Eggbridge Ln, Waverton CH3 7PE
☎ 01244 332124
e-mail: jmitchellgreenwalls@hotmail.com
dir: From A41 at Waverton turn left at Moor Ln, left onto Eggbridge Ln and over Canal Bridge, on the right
A warm welcome is assured at this 18th-century former farmhouse, located within a village community three miles south of the city centre. Cosy bedrooms are equipped with a wealth of thoughtful extras and hearty breakfasts feature local or home made produce.

Rooms 2 rms (1 en suite) (1 pri facs) S £35–£45; D £60–£65 **Facilities** TVB tea/coffee Cen ht TVL Wi-fi available **Parking** 5 **Notes LB** ⊗ No children 10yrs Closed 15 Feb–1 Mar RS 24–26 Dec

★★★★ GUEST HOUSE
Summerhill Guest House
4 Greenfield Ln, Hoole Village CH2 2PA
☎ 01244 400020 & 400334
e-mail: capricorn@taurusuk.net
dir: 1.5m NE of city centre. A56 onto A41, 1st right
Summerhill is a converted Edwardian house with comfortable, well-equipped accommodation. The helpful owners provide a friendly atmosphere and hearty breakfasts in the attractive dining room.

Rooms 4 en suite (1 fmly) S £30–£40; D £56–£70✱ **Facilities** FTV TVB tea/coffee Cen ht TVL **Parking** 4 **Notes LB** ⊗ No children 8yrs No coaches

★★★ GUEST HOUSE
The Glann
Stone Place CH2 3NR
☎ 01244 344800
e-mail: reception@theglannhotel.co.uk
web: www.theglannhotel.co.uk
dir: 0.5m NE of city centre off A56 Hoole Rd

Located in a quiet cul-de-sac in the fashionable Hoole district, this renovated Victorian house has a range of thoughtfully furnished bedrooms with modern shower rooms. Comprehensive breakfasts are served in the spacious dining room, which includes a lounge bar section. Large private car park.

Rooms 10 rms (9 en suite) (2 fmly) (1 GF) **Facilities** TVB tea/coffee Licensed Cen ht TVL **Parking** 10 **Notes** ⊗ No coaches

★★★ GUEST ACCOMMODATION
Glen Garth
59 Hoole Rd CH2 3NJ
☎ 01244 310260 📄 01244 310260
e-mail: glengarth@chester63.fsnet.co.uk
dir: Exit M53 onto A56, 0.5m E of city
Situated within easy walking distance of the city, family-run Glen Garth provides well-equipped bedrooms and hearty breakfasts served in the pleasant rear dining room. Friendly, attentive service is a strength here.

Rooms 5 rms (3 en suite) (2 pri facs) (3 fmly) S £35–£40; D £70–£80 **Facilities** TVB tea/coffee Cen ht **Parking** 5 **Notes LB** ⊗ 📷

★★★ 🅰 GUEST ACCOMMODATION
Bowman Lodge
52 Hoole Rd CH2 3NL
☎ 01244 342208
e-mail: jaynebowman@hotmail.com
dir: M56 junct 14 onto M53, follow signs to A56

Rooms 6 rms (5 en suite) (1 pri facs) (3 fmly) (2 GF) S £25–£35; D £50–£65✱ **Facilities** FTV TVB tea/coffee Cen ht **Parking** 4 **Notes** ⊗ 📷

CONGLETON   MAP 16 SJ86

★★★★ 🍽 INN
The Plough At Eaton
Macclesfield Rd, Eaton CW12 2NH
☎ 01260 280207 📄 01260 298458
e-mail: theploughinn@hotmail.co.uk
dir: On A536 Congleton Macclesfield road, 1.5m from Congleton town centre

A renovated traditional inn offering high quality meals and high class bedrooms in an adjacent building. Bedrooms and bathrooms are very new and offer modern facilities, and the gardens include discreet sitting areas. The restaurant is housed in a restored barn to the rear of the inn.

Rooms 17 annexe en suite (2 fmly) (8 GF) S £55; D £70✱ **Facilities** TVB tea/coffee Direct dial from bedrooms Cen ht Dinner Last d 9.30pm Wi-fi available **Parking** 78 **Notes LB** RS 25–26 Dec & 1 Jan Civ Wed 60

CONGLETON CONTINUED

KNUTSFORD   MAP 15 SJ77

★★★★ INN
Egerton Arms

Astbury Village CW12 4RQ

☎ 01260 273946 📄 01260 277273

e–mail: egertonastbury@totalise.co.uk

dir: 1.5m SW of Congleton off A34, by St Mary's Church

This traditional country inn stands opposite the church in the pretty village of Astbury. The creative, good-value menus in the bars and restaurant attract a strong local following, and the bedrooms have been refurbished to provide high standards of comfort and facilities.

Rooms 6 en suite S £50; D £70 **Facilities** TVB tea/coffee Cen ht Dinner Last d 9pm Wi-fi available **Conf** Max 40 Thtr 40 Class 30 Board 20 **Parking** 100 **Notes** LB ⊗ No coaches

★★★★ 🅰 GUEST ACCOMMODATION
Sandhole Farm

Hulme Walfield CW12 2JH

☎ 01260 224419 📄 01260 224766

e–mail: veronica@sandholefarm.co.uk

dir: 2m N of Congleton. Off A34 down driveway

Rooms 16 annexe en suite (3 fmly) (7 GF) S £58–£65; D £70–£75✳ **Facilities** TVB tea/coffee Direct dial from bedrooms Cen ht TVL Wi-fi available **Conf** Thtr 80 Class 80 Board 50 **Parking** 50 **Notes** RS Xmas wk Civ Wed 150

CREWE   MAP 15 SJ75

★★★★ BED & BREAKFAST
Valleybrook Guest House

29 Nevis Dr, Woolstanwood CW2 8UH

☎ 01270 588977 📄 01270 211119

e–mail: mail@valleybrookguesthouse.co.uk

web: www.valleybrookguesthouse.co.uk

dir: A530 onto A532 towards Crewe, 1st right, then 1st left, then 2nd right, 50yds on left

Located between Crewe and Nantwich, Valleybrook offers comfortable well equipped accommodation and a friendly welcome. Breakfast, using home-made and local produce, is served in the attractive dining room overlooking the garden.

Rooms 2 rms (1 en suite) (1 pri facs) S £32–£35; D £44–£50✳ **Facilities** FTV TVB tea/coffee Cen ht Wi-fi available **Parking** 2 **Notes** ⊗ ⊜

★★★★ GUEST HOUSE
The Hinton

Town Ln, Mobberley WA16 7HH

☎ 01565 873484

e–mail: the.hinton@virgin.net

dir: 1m NE on B5085 in Mobberley

This well-proportioned house offers a range of comfortable bedrooms with thoughtful extras. Comprehensive breakfasts, and dinners by arrangement, are served in the attractive dining room and a lounge is available.

Rooms 6 en suite (1 fmly) S £48; D £62✳ **Facilities** FTV TVB tea/coffee Licensed Cen ht Dinner Last d morning Wi-fi available **Parking** 8 **Notes** ⊗ No coaches

★★★★ INN
The Dog Inn

Well Bank Ln, Over Peover WA16 8UP

☎ 01625 861421 📄 01625 864800

e–mail: thedog-inn@paddockinnsfsnet.co.uk

web: www.doginn-overpeover.co.uk

dir: 4m SE of Knutsford. Off A50 at Whipping Stocks 2m to Peover Heath

Set in delightful Cheshire countryside, the front of this popular 18th-century inn is adorned with hanging baskets and tubs. The attractive bedrooms have many extras, while the lounge bar and restaurant offer a wide selection of ales and an extensive all-day menu using local produce.

Rooms 6 en suite S £60–£80; D £80–£100✳ **Facilities** FTV TVB tea/coffee Direct dial from bedrooms Cen ht Dinner Last d 9pm Wi-fi available Pool Table **Parking** 80

★★★★ GUEST HOUSE
Laburnum Cottage

Knutsford Rd, Mobberley WA16 7PU

☎ 01565 872464

e–mail: laburnum.cottage@hotmail.co.uk

dir: 1m NE of Knutsford on B5085 towards Mobberley

Set in attractive gardens, this cottage-style property is within easy reach of the M6, M56 and Manchester Airport. The attractive bedrooms are thoughtfully equipped, and imaginative and carefully prepared evening meals are available by arrangement. There is also a comfortable lounge.

Rooms 5 en suite S £46; D £64✳ **Facilities** TVB tea/coffee Cen ht TVL Dinner Last d 3pm **Parking** 6 **Notes** ⊗ No coaches

★★★★ BED & BREAKFAST
Rose Cottage Guest House
Newton Hall Ln, Mobberley WA16 7LL
☎ 01565 872430
e–mail: info@rose-cottage-guesthouse.com
web: www.rose-cottage-guesthouse.com

dir: *3m NE of Knutsford. B5085 E through Mobberley, before Bird in Hand pub left onto Newton Hall Ln, 0.5m on right*

Standing in extensive mature gardens on the outskirts of Mobberley, the Victorian house offers bedrooms with thoughtful extras in a extension. Comprehensive breakfasts are served in an attractive lounge-dining room overlooking a wildlife pond.

Rooms 3 en suite (2 GF) S £49; D £59✱ **Facilities** TVB tea/coffee Cen ht Wi-fi available **Parking** 10 **Notes** LB ⊗ No children 12yrs Closed 24 Dec–1 Jan

---

LOWER WITHINGTON   MAP 15 SJ86

★★★★ FARM HOUSE
Holly Tree Farm *(SJ802709)*
Holmes Chapel Rd SK11 9DT
☎ 01477 571257 🖺 01477 571257 Mrs Venables
web: www.hollytreefarm.org

dir: *On A535 Holmes Chapel Rd in front of Jodrell Bank*

Located close to Jodrell Bank, Holly Tree Farm offers a good base for the business person or for touring the local attractions. Rooms are located in the house adjacent to the farm and are attractive and well equipped. Hearty breakfasts are taken in the farmhouse, and the emphasis is on local produce from the farm's own shop.

Rooms 4 en suite (1 fmly) (1 GF) S £30–£35; D £55–£60✱ **Facilities** TV3B tea/coffee Cen ht TVL **Parking** 3 **Notes** LB ⊗ 100 acres Beef, sheep & poultry ⊜

MACCLESFIELD   MAP 16 SJ97

See also Rainow

★★ GUEST HOUSE
Penrose Guest House
56 Birtles Rd, Whirley SK10 3JQ
☎ 01625 615323 🖺 01625 432284
e–mail: info@penroseguesthouse.co.uk
web: www.penroseguesthouse.co.uk

dir: *A537 to rdbt and follow signs leisure centre, left at mini rdbt. 1st left into Birtles Rd*

Peacefully located in the suburb of Whirley, yet convenient for the hospital and the centre of town, this delightful home offers spacious comfortable bedrooms. Healthy breakfast is taken at one table looking over the lawned gardens, which are popular with an array of wild birds.

Rooms 3 rms S fr £25; D fr £50(room only) **Facilities** FTV TVB tea/coffee Cen ht Wi-fi available **Parking** 5 **Notes** LB ⊗ No children 7yrs No coaches

---

MALPAS   MAP 15 SJ44

Premier Collection

★★★★★ 🍴 GUEST ACCOMMODATION
Tilston Lodge
Tilston SY14 7DR
☎ 01829 250223 🖺 01829 250223

dir: *A41 S from Chester for 10m, turn right for Tilston. Left at T-junct. Lodge 200yds on right*

A former hunting lodge, this impressive Victorian house stands in 16 acres of rolling orchards and pasture, which are home to rare breeds of sheep and poultry. The spacious bedrooms are furnished with fine period pieces and a wealth of thoughtful extras. Ground-floor areas overlook immaculate gardens and a choice of lounges is available in addition to the elegant dining room, the setting for memorable breakfasts.

Rooms 3 en suite (1 fmly) S £48–£52; D £76–£84 **Facilities** FTV TVB tea/coffee Cen ht TVL 🍴 **Parking** 8 **Notes** LB ⊗ ⊜

★★★★ FARM HOUSE
Hampton House *(SJ505496)*
Stevensons Ln, Hampton SY14 8JS
☎ 01948 820588 🖺 01948 820588 Mrs E H Sarginson
e–mail: enquiries@hamptonhousefarm.co.uk

dir: *2m NE of Malpas. Off A41 onto Cholmondeley Rd, next left*

Parts of this house are reputed to date from 1600 and quality furnishing styles highlight the many retained period features including a wealth of exposed beams. It is located on a quiet dairy farm and offers thoughtfully appointed accommodation and a warm welcome.

Rooms 3 rms (2 en suite) (1 pri facs) S £30–£35; D £55–£60✱ **Facilities** tea/coffee Cen ht TVL Wi-fi available **Parking** 10 **Notes** ⊗ No children 12yrs 180 acres Mixed ⊜

MALPAS CONTINUED

★★★★ FARM HOUSE
Millmoor Farm (SJ518475)

Nomansheath SY14 8DY

☎ 01948 820304 Mrs S Chesters

e–mail: bookings@millmoorfarm.co.uk

dir: *2m E of Malpas. Off A41 into Nomansheath, left at mini rdbt in village, farm signed after 0.5m on right hand side (do not turn down back lane)*

Totally refurbished in 2008 and set in attractive gardens on a beef and dairy farm near Nomansheath, parts of this modernised farmhouse date from the late 17th century. Bedrooms, complimented by luxury modern bathrooms, are equipped with a wealth of thoughtful extras and day rooms include a spacious comfortable guest lounge and an attractive dining room, the setting for comprehensive breakfasts.

Rooms 2 en suite S £35; D £60✳ **Facilities** TVB tea/coffee Cen ht Dinner Last d noon Wi-fi available Fishing **Conf** Max 10 Board 10 Del from £40 ✳ **Parking** 11 **Notes LB** 270 acres dairy/beef/sheep

★★★ Ⓐ GUEST HOUSE
Mill House & Granary

Mill House, Higher Wych SY14 7JR

☎ 01948 780362 📠 01948 780566

e–mail: angela@videoactive.co.uk

web: www.millhouseandgranary.co.uk

dir: *3m S of Malpas. A41 onto B5395, next left by bus shelter, Mill House 1m on left*

Rooms 3 rms (2 en suite) S £25–£30; D £50 **Facilities** TVB tea/coffee Cen ht TVL Dinner Last d 6pm **Parking** 6 **Notes** ⊗ No coaches Closed Dec ⊜

See also Wybunbury

★★★★ FARM HOUSE
Henhull Hall (SJ641536)

Welshmans Ln CW5 6AD

☎ 01270 624158 📠 01270 624158 Mr & Mrs Percival

e–mail: philippercival@hotmail.com

dir: *M6 junct 16 onto A500 towards Nantwich, then A51 past Rease Heath, turn left onto Welshmans Ln, 0.25m on left*

Expect a warm welcome at Henhull Hall, which has been in the Percival family since 1924. The Hall stands on the site of the Battle of Nantwich fought in 1644. The farmhouse is amidst 250 acres of farmland with beautiful grounds and gardens surrounding the house. Bedrooms are spacious and individually decorated; breakfast is served in the attractive dining room and features fresh farm produce.

Rooms 2 rms (1 en suite) (1 pri facs) (1 fmly) S £35–£40; D £75–£80 **Facilities** TV1B tea/coffee Cen ht TVL ⚲ **Conf** Max 10 Thtr 10 Class 10 Board 10 **Parking** 4 **Notes** 345 acres Dairy, arable ⊜

★★★★ GUEST HOUSE
Oakland House

252 Newcastle Rd, Blakelow, Shavington CW5 7ET

☎ 01270 567134

e–mail: enquiries@oaklandhouseonline.co.uk

dir: *2m E of Nantwich. Off A500 into Shavington, house 0.5m W of village*

Oakland House offers a friendly and relaxed atmosphere. Bedrooms, some of which are in a separate chalet, are attractively furnished and well equipped. There is a spacious sitting room, and a modern conservatory overlooks the pretty garden and the Cheshire countryside beyond. Substantial breakfasts are served either around one large table or at separate tables.

Rooms 3 en suite 6 annexe en suite (1 fmly) (6 GF) S £34–£39; D £49–£54✳ **Facilities** TVB tea/coffee Cen ht TVL Wi-fi available **Parking** 13 **Notes LB** No coaches Closed 31 Dec

---

★★★ INN
The Red Lion

277 Chester Rd, Hartford CW8 1QL

☎ 01606 74597

e–mail: cathy.iglesias@tesco.net

web: www.redlionhartford.com

dir: *From A556 take Hartford turn off. Red Lion is 1st junct on left next to church*

Located within the community of Hartford opposite the parish church, this popular inn provides a range of real ales and traditional pub food within the cosy public areas and neat beer garden during the warmer months. Smart new bedrooms feature many thoughtful extras in addition to efficient en suite shower rooms.

Rooms 3 en suite (1 fmly) S £40–£44.95; D £50–£60✳ **Facilities** TVB tea/coffee Cen ht Dinner Last d 8pm Wi-fi available Pool Table **Parking** 6 **Notes** ⊗ No coaches

RAINOW
MAP 16 SJ97

★★★★ FARM HOUSE
Common Barn Farm B&B *(SJ965764)*
Smith Ln SK10 5XJ
☎ 01625 574878 & 07779 816098 Mrs R Cooper
e-mail: g_greengrass@hotmail.com
web: www.commonbarn.com

dir: *B5470 through Rainow towards Whaley Bridge, right onto Smith Ln, 0.5m on right down a drive*

Located high in the Pennines and straddling the border of Cheshire and the Peak District, this new barn conversion provides a popular destination for walkers. Bedrooms are spacious and stylish and all bathrooms offer modern power showers. A conservatory lounge is ideal for relaxation while enjoying stunning views. Hearty breakfasts are as memorable as the warmth of welcome. A coffee shop during the day provides light snacks and home-baked fayre.

Rooms 5 annexe en suite (1 fmly) (3 GF) S £35–£40; D £55–£60
Facilities TVB tea/coffee Cen ht TVL Wi-fi available Fishing **Conf** Max 25 **Parking** 40 **Notes** ⊗ 250 acres Sheep

TARPORLEY
MAP 15 SJ56

★★★★ ◓ INN
Alvanley Arms Inn
Forest Rd, Cotebrook CW6 9DS
☎ 01829 760200
web: www.alvanleyarms.co.uk

dir: *2m NE of Tarporley on A49 in Cotebrook*

Records show that there has been a pub on this site since the 16th century, and renovations have uncovered original beams in some of the stylish, well-equipped bedrooms. Wide-ranging menus are available in the cosy bars, and the adjoining Shire Horse Centre and Countryside Park is popular with families. Delamere Forest Park and Oulton Park race circuit are nearby.

Rooms 7 en suite **Facilities** TVB tea/coffee Cen ht Dinner Last d 9pm free entry for residents to Shire Horse Centre **Parking** 70 **Notes** No coaches

★★★★ FARM HOUSE
Hill House Farm *(SJ583626)*
Rushton CW6 9AU
☎ 01829 732238 📠 01829 733929 Mrs C Rayner
e-mail: aa@hillhousefarm-cheshire.co.uk
web: www.hillhousefarm-cheshire.co.uk

dir: *1.5m E of Tarporley. Off A51/A49 to Eaton, take Lower Ln, continue E for Rushton, right onto The Hall Ln, farm 0.5m*

This impressive brick farmhouse stands in very attractive gardens within 14 acres of rolling pastureland. The stylish bedrooms have en suite facilities, and there is a spacious lounge and a traditionally furnished breakfast room. Catherine Rayner was a finalist for the AA Friendliest Landlady of the Year 2008 Award.

Rooms 3 en suite 1 annexe en suite (1 fmly) S £45–£60; D £75–£95✱
Facilities TVB tea/coffee Cen ht TVL Wi-fi available **Parking** 6 **Notes LB** 14 acres non-working Closed Xmas & New Year

★★★ 🅰 INN
Foresters Arms
92 High St CW6 0AX
☎ 01829 733151 📠 01829 730020
e-mail: foresters-arms@btconnect.com

dir: *Off A49 into village centre*

Rooms 6 rms (5 en suite) (1 pri facs) **Facilities** TVB tea/coffee Cen ht Dinner Last d 8.30pm Pool Table **Parking** 20 **Notes** ⊗ No children 10yrs No coaches RS 25 & 31 Dec

WARRINGTON
MAP 15 SJ68

★★★ INN
Rams Head Inn
Church Ln, Grappen Hall WA4 3EP
☎ 01925 262814 📠 01925 860876
e-mail: mail@ramshead-inn.co.uk

dir: *A50 Warrington 1.5m, 1st left onto Bell House Ln 0.5m, Inn on left*

Located close to the church in this historic village and close to Warrington, the Rams Head Inn offers comfortable accommodation in a friendly atmosphere. Breakfast and a wide choice of meals are served in the character lounges and small functions are catered for.

Rooms 4 en suite (1 fmly) **Facilities** FTV TVB tea/coffee Direct dial from bedrooms Cen ht Dinner Last d 9pm Wi-fi available **Conf** Max 25 Thtr 25 Class 25 Board 25 **Parking** 80 **Notes** ⊗

WILMSLOW
MAP 16 SJ88

See Manchester Airport (Greater Manchester)

ENGLAND

WYBUNBURY
MAP 15 SJ64

★★★ FARM HOUSE
Lea Farm (SJ717489)
Wrinehill Rd CW5 7NS
☎ 01270 841429 Mrs J E Callwood
e–mail: leafarm@hotmail.co.uk

dir: *1m E of Wybunbury village church on unclassified road*

This working dairy farm is surrounded by delightful gardens and beautiful Cheshire countryside. The spacious bedrooms have modern facilities and there is a cosy lounge. Hearty breakfasts are served in the attractive dining room, which looks out over the garden, with its resident peacocks.

Rooms 3 rms (2 en suite) (1 fmly) S £29–£35; D £48–£56 **Facilities** TVB tea/coffee Cen ht TVL Fishing Pool Table **Parking** 24 **Notes** 150 acres Dairy & beef ☻

CORNWALL & ISLES OF SCILLY

BODMIN
MAP 02 SX06

★★★★ 🛏 BED & BREAKFAST
Roscrea
18 Saint Nicholas' St PL31 1AD
☎ 01208 74400 📠 01208 72361
e–mail: roscrea@btconnect.com

dir: *From Bodmin take B3268 to Lostwithiel. Roscrea is 0.25m on left*

Dating back to 1805, this fascinating house was once the home of a celebrated local schoolmaster. Now sympathetically restored to its former glory, this is an excellent location for anyone wishing to explore all that Cornwall has to offer. Comfort and quality are evident throughout all areas, matched by the warmth of the welcome. Breakfast is a treat here, featuring local produce and eggs from the resident hens. Dinner is also available by prior arrangement.

Rooms 3 rms (2 en suite) (1 pri facs) S £30–£40; D £60–£70✳ **Facilities** tea/coffee Cen ht TVL Dinner Last d 10am **Parking** 2 **Notes** LB ☻ ⊜

★★★★ 🛏 BED & BREAKFAST
The Stables at Welltown
Cardinham PL30 4EG
☎ 01208 821316 📠 01208 821673
e–mail: thestables@welltown.orangehome.co.uk

Enjoying a peaceful location away from hustle and bustle, this is a wonderful place to relax and enjoy the unspoilt delights of this rugged area. Guests are assured of a rewarding and pleasurable stay. Converted from stables, there is character and comfort in equal measure with an uncluttered contemporary feel. Breakfast from the Aga is a real treat with local produce in abundance. Additional facilities include a snug lounge and attractive garden.

Rooms 2 en suite S £30–£35; D £50–£55✳ **Facilities** FTV TVB tea/coffee Cen ht TVL Dinner Last d at breakfast **Parking** 2 **Notes** No children 12yrs ⊜

★★★ GUEST ACCOMMODATION
Tranack
26 Castle St PL31 2DU
☎ 01208 269095
e–mail: sandrambutler@onetel.com

dir: *A30 to St Petrocs church, 2nd exit at mini-rdbt, 1st right, 1st left, 150yds on left*

Situated in a quiet location within walking distance of the centre of town, this friendly and welcoming establishment combines comfort and character. Bedrooms are attractively furnished and equipped with useful extras. Breakfast is a real treat, served around the dining room table and featuring local produce and eggs fresh from the resident hens.

Rooms 2 en suite (2 fmly) **Facilities** TVB tea/coffee Cen ht **Notes** ⊛ Closed 23–27 Dec ⊜

★★★ GUEST ACCOMMODATION
Mount Pleasant Farm
Mount PL30 4EX
☎ 01208 821342
e–mail: info@mountpleasantcottages.co.uk

dir: *A30 from Bodmin towards Launceston for 4m, right signed Millpool, continue 3m*

Set in 10 acres, this is a wonderfully peaceful base from which to explore the delights of Cornwall. Originally a farmhouse dating back to the 17th-century, there is something here for all the family with extensive facilities including a games barn and heated swimming pool. Cosy bedrooms are well furnished, while public areas include a spacious sun lounge and extensive gardens. Breakfast, served in the well-appointed dining room, features local produce and is a highlight of a stay; home cooked evening meals are available by prior arrangement.

Rooms 6 en suite (3 fmly) D £54–£74✳ **Facilities** TVB tea/coffee Cen ht TVL Dinner Last d 10pm previous day ⊗ Pool Table Games barn **Parking** 8 **Notes** LB ⊜

BOSCASTLE   MAP 02 SX09

Premier Collection

★★★★★ FARM HOUSE
Trerosewill Farm *(SX095905)*
Paradise PL35 0DL
☎ 01840 250545 📄 01840 250727 Mr & Mrs Nicholls
e–mail: enquiries@trerosewill.co.uk
web: www.trerosewill.co.uk

dir: *Take B3266 at junct with B3263, towards Tintagel. After 0.2m, turn left by brown sign, 100yds along lane*

A genuine Cornish welcome, complete with tea and cake, is assured at the home of the Nicholls family. From this elevated position, the views over the village below to the sea beyond are truly spectacular. Bedrooms offer a host of thoughtful and generous extras from bath robes to Wi-fi access. Breakfast is a showcase of locally sourced and home made produce including eggs, sausages, breads and jams. Additional facilities include a hot-tub.

Rooms 6 en suite 2 annexe en suite (2 fmly) (2 GF) S £40–£81; D £67–£90✴ **Facilities** TVB tea/coffee Direct dial from bedrooms Licensed Cen ht TVL Wi-fi available Hot Tub **Parking** 10 **Notes LB** ⊗ No children 7yrs 50 acres beef lamb Closed mid Dec–mid Jan

★★★★ ◉◉ RESTAURANT WITH ROOMS
The Bottreaux, Restaurant, Bar & Rooms
PL35 0BG
☎ 01840 250231 📄 01840 250170
e–mail: info@boscastlecornwall.co.uk
web: www.boscastlecornwall.co.uk

dir: *A39 to Camelford – signs to Boscastle*

Built some 200 years ago, this property is within walking distance of the picturesque harbour. Refurbishment has resulted in a stylish establishment, where guests are genuinely welcomed. Bedrooms are light and airy, and some doubles have wonderful six-foot, teak framed beds. The bar is the ideal venue for a drink while perusing the imaginative menu that makes good use of local produce.

Rooms 7 en suite **Facilities** TVB tea/coffee Direct dial from bedrooms Dinner **Parking** 8 **Notes** ⊗ No children 10 yrs RS Mon & Sun

★★★★ GUEST ACCOMMODATION
Old Coach House
Tintagel Rd PL35 0AS
☎ 01840 250398 📄 01840 250346
e–mail: stay@old-coach.co.uk
web: www.old-coach.co.uk

dir: *In village at junct B3266 & B3263. 150yds from petrol station towards Tintagel*

Over 300 years old, the Old Coach House has lovely views over the village and the rolling countryside. The comfortable bedrooms are well equipped and include two rooms on the ground floor. A hearty breakfast is served in the conservatory, which overlooks the well-kept garden.

Rooms 8 en suite (3 fmly) (2 GF) S £32–£50; D £54–£64✴ **Facilities** TVB tea/coffee Cen ht TVL **Parking** 9 **Notes LB** Closed Xmas

★★★★ 🅰 GUEST HOUSE
Lower Meadows
Penally Hill PL35 0HF
☎ 01840 250570
e–mail: stay@lowermeadows.co.uk
web: www.lowermeadows.co.uk

dir: *A39 onto B3266 to Boscastle. Lower Meadows opp Coweb Inn*

Rooms 5 en suite D £60–£72 **Facilities** TVB tea/coffee Cen ht TVL Wi-fi available **Parking** 5 **Notes LB** ⊗ No children 12yrs No coaches Closed 22–28 Dec

★★★★ 🅰 GUEST ACCOMMODATION
Orchard Lodge
Gunpool Ln PL35 0AT
☎ 01840 250418
e–mail: orchardlodge@fsmail.net

dir: *From A39 follow signs for Boscastle, turn sharp right at petrol station*

Rooms 5 rms (4 en suite) (1 pri facs) D £54–£74✴ **Facilities** STV TVB tea/coffee Cen ht Wi-fi available **Parking** 6 **Notes LB** ⊗ No children 12yrs

★★★ BED & BREAKFAST
Pencarmol
5 Penally Ter, The Harbour PL35 0HA
☎ 01840 250435
e–mail: info@pencarmol.co.uk

dir: *Off B3263 to Boscastle harbour*

This lovely cottage has super views of the harbour and dramatic cliffs. The friendly proprietors are most welcoming and attentive hosts. There is a lovely garden and car parking is available. Bedrooms are compact and provide a good range of facilities. Breakfast features fresh mackerel, if any have been caught.

Rooms 3 en suite (1 fmly) D £50–£60✴ **Facilities** TVB tea/coffee Cen ht TVL **Parking** 3 **Notes LB** Closed 25 Dec–2 Jan ◉

BUDE　　　　　　MAP 02 SS20

★★★★ GUEST HOUSE
Bangors Organic
Poundstock EX23 0DP
☎ 01288 361297
e-mail: info@bangorsorganic.co.uk

dir: *4m S of Bude. On A39 in Poundstock*

Located a few miles south of Bude, this renovated Victorian establishment offers elegant accommodation with a good level of comfort. Bedrooms are furnished to a high standard and are located both in the main house and in an adjacent coach house, the latter being more contemporary in style. Bathrooms are a particular feature here, offering impressive levels of space and luxury. Breakfast and dinner, featuring organic, local and home-made produce, are served in the pleasant dining room. The establishment is Certified Organic by the Soil Association and was a runner-up for the AA Funkiest B&B of the Year 2008 Award.

Rooms 2 en suite 2 annexe en suite (1 GF) D £100–£130✱
Facilities FTV TVB tea/coffee Licensed Cen ht TVL Dinner Last d noon
Wi-fi available Badminton **Parking** 10 **Notes** ⊗ No children 12yrs
No coaches

★★★★ GUEST HOUSE
Dylan's Guest House
12 Downs View EX23 8RF
☎ 01288 354705
e-mail: dylansbude@tiscali.co.uk

dir: *From A39 onto A3073 at Stratton, at 2nd rdbt turn right to town centre, through town centre, signed to Downs View*

Recently refurbished to a high standard, this late Victorian house overlooks the golf course and is just a five minute walk from the beach. There is a refreshing and appealing style here, derived from a combination of original features and a crisp, contemporary décor. The well equipped bedrooms are light and airy with impressive levels of comfort. Breakfast and dinner (by prior arrangement) are carefully prepared from quality produce and served in the attractive dining room.

Rooms 4 rms (2 en suite) (2 pri facs) (2 fmly) S £30–£45; D £50–£65
Facilities FTV TVB tea/coffee Cen ht TVL Dinner Last d 1pm **Parking** 2
Notes LB ⊗ ⊜

★★★★ GUEST HOUSE
Fairway House
8 Downs View EX23 8RF
☎ 01288 355059
e-mail: enquiries@fairwayguesthouse.co.uk

dir: *N through town to Flexbury, brown tourist signs to Downs View from golf course*

Genuine hospitality and attentive service await you at this delightful Victorian terrace property, which overlooks the golf course and is close to the beach and town centre. The comfortable bedrooms are of a high standard and have many thoughtful extra facilities. A hearty breakfast, using local produce, is served at separate tables.

Rooms 7 rms (5 en suite) (1 fmly) S £24–£38.50; D £44–£59✱
Facilities FTV TVB tea/coffee Cen ht **Notes** LB ⊗ Closed Dec–Jan ⊜

★★★★ GUEST ACCOMMODATION
Bude Haven
Flexbury Av EX23 8NS
☎ 01288 352305 🖷 01288 352662
e-mail: enquiries@budehavenhotel.com
web: www.budehavenhotel.com

dir: *0.5m N of Bude in Flexbury village centre*

This charming, refurbished Edwardian property is in a quiet area within easy walking distance of Bude centre and Crooklets Beach. Bedrooms are bright and airy, and the restaurant offers an interesting menu at dinner. You can also relax in the lounge or the bar.

Rooms 10 en suite (1 fmly) S £30–£40; D £60–£80✱ **Facilities** FTV TVB
tea/coffee Cen ht TVL Dinner Last d 9pm Wi-fi available Hot tub
Parking 4 **Notes** LB ⊗

★★★★ GUEST HOUSE
The Cliff at Bude
Maer Down, Crooklets Beach EX23 8NG
☎ 01288 353110 & 356833 🖷 01288 353110
web: www.cliffhotel.co.uk

dir: *A39 through Bude, left at top of High St, pass Somerfields, 1st right between golf course, over x-rds, premises at end on left*

Overlooking the sea from a clifftop location, this friendly and efficient establishment provides spacious, well-equipped bedrooms. The various public areas include a bar and lounge and an impressive range of leisure facilities. Delicious dinners and tasty breakfasts are available in the attractive dining room.

Rooms 15 en suite (15 fmly) (8 GF) S £41.40–£47.40; D £69–£79✱
Facilities TVB tea/coffee Direct dial from bedrooms Licensed Cen ht TVL
Dinner Last d 7pm ⊙ ♨ Gymnasium Pool Table ♪ **Parking** 18
Notes LB No coaches Closed Nov–Mar

★★★★ GUEST HOUSE
Pencarrol
21 Downs View EX23 8RF
☎ 01288 352478
e-mail: pencarrolbude@aol.com

dir: *0.5m N of Bude. N from Bude into Flexbury village*

This cosy guest house is only a short walk from Bude centre and Crooklets Beach, and has glorious views over the golf course. Bedrooms are attractively furnished and there is a first-floor lounge. Breakfast is served at separate tables in the dining room.

Rooms 7 rms (3 en suite) (2 pri facs) (2 fmly) (2 GF) S £31–£37;
D £62–£74✱ **Facilities** TVB tea/coffee Cen ht TVL **Notes** LB ⊗
No coaches Closed Nov–Jan ⊜

★★★★ BED & BREAKFAST
Stonepark

Marine Dr, Widemouth Bay EX23 0DE
☎ 01288 361469 & 07974 940420
e–mail: info@stonepark-widemouth.co.uk

dir: *3m S of Bude. Off A39 at Coppathorne for Widemouth Bay, premises 0.5m*

A warm welcome awaits guests at this detached bungalow, with distant views of the rugged coastline and the sea. Just a 10 minute walk from the beach and Coastal Path, this is an ideal centre from which to explore the surrounding area. The two bedrooms are comfortable and equipped with numerous thoughtful extra facilities.

Rooms 2 en suite (2 fmly) (2 GF) D £50–£70✳ **Facilities** TVB tea/coffee Cen ht Wi-fi available ⤴ **Parking** 12 **Notes LB** ⊗ ⊛

★★★★ GUEST ACCOMMODATION
Stratton Gardens House

Cot Hill, Stratton EX23 9DN
☎ 01288 352500
e–mail: moira@stratton-gardens.co.uk
web: www.stratton-gardens.co.uk

dir: *A3072 in Stratton. Up hill left side of Kings Arms. Take 3rd right*

Tucked away in a quiet corner of this small town of Stratton, a mile from Bude, Stratton Gardens is a 16th-century house which was formerly owned by the church. Each of the bedrooms is distinctively furnished, and very comfortable. In the candlelit restaurant a varied menu is provided, offering innovative fare using the best of local produce. Specific diets can be catered for. Ample on-site parking is an added bonus.

Rooms 7 rms (6 en suite) (2 fmly) S £29–£36; D £62–£72✳ **Facilities** TVB tea/coffee Cen ht TVL Dinner Last d 8pm **Parking** 10 **Notes** ⊗

★★★★ 🅰 GUEST HOUSE
Surf Haven Guest House

31 Downs View EX23 8RG
☎ 01288 353923
e–mail: info@surfhaven.co.uk
web: www.surfhaven.co.uk

dir: *From A3072 follow signs to Bude town centre then follow sign for Crooklets Beach*

Rooms 8 rms (7 en suite) (1 pri facs) (4 fmly) (1 GF) S £30–£40; D £54–£60✳ **Facilities** TVB tea/coffee Cen ht TVL Dinner **Parking** 8 **Notes LB** No coaches

★★★ GUEST ACCOMMODATION
Sea Jade Guest House

15 Burn View EX23 8BZ
☎ 01288 353404
e–mail: seajadeguesthouse@yahoo.co.uk

dir: *A39 turn right follow signs for Bude & golf course*

A very well located bed and breakfast within a few minutes walk of both town and beaches. Very friendly hosts, comfortable bedrooms and hearty breakfast make this a very popular venue.

Rooms 8 rms (7 en suite) (1 pri facs) (4 fmly) (2 GF) S £28–£35; D £55–£60✳ **Facilities** FTV TVB tea/coffee Cen ht TVL **Notes LB** ⊗ ⊛

CALLINGTON   MAP 03 SX36

★★★★ GUEST HOUSE
Woodpeckers

Rilla Mill PL17 7NT
☎ 01579 363717
e–mail: alisonmerchant@virgin.net

dir: *5m NW of Callington. Off B3254 at Upton Cross x-rds for Rilla Mill*

Set in a conservation village, in a wooded valley, by a tumbling stream, this modern, detached house offers cosy, well equipped bedrooms with numerous thoughtful extras. Home-cooked dinners, using the best of local ingredients are available by arrangement. The hot tub in the garden is a welcome feature.

Rooms 3 en suite S £38; D £56–£60✳ **Facilities** STV FTV TVB tea/coffee Cen ht Dinner Last d Day before Gymnasium Spa/Hot Tub **Parking** 7 **Notes LB** ⊗ No coaches ⊛

ENGLAND

CALLINGTON CONTINUED

★★★★ 🅰 FARM HOUSE
Higher Manaton (SX336733)
Bray Shop PL17 8PX
☎ 01579 370460 📄 01579 370460 Mrs W Trewin
e–mail: dtrewin@manaton.fsnet.co.uk
dir: From A388 onto B3257, 300yds on left
Rooms 3 rms (2 en suite) (1 pri facs) (1 fmly) S £32–£37; D £58–£64
Facilities TVB tea/coffee TVL **Parking** 6 **Notes** LB ⊛ 100 acres Beef
Closed 20 Dec–3 Jan

★★★ BED & BREAKFAST
Green Pastures Bed & Breakfast
Longhill PL17 8AU
☎ 01579 382566
e–mail: greenpast@aol.com
dir: 0.5m E of Callington on A390 to Tavistock
Located on the southern side of Kit Hill, this friendly, homely
establishment has panoramic views across the Tamar Valley and distant
views of Dartmoor. The modern bungalow stands in five acres of land,
where Shetland ponies contentedly graze. Bedrooms are comfortably
furnished and there is a large lounge.
Rooms 3 rms (2 en suite) (1 pri facs) (3 GF) S £30–£35; D £50–£60✳
Facilities TVB tea/coffee Cen ht **Parking** 8 **Notes** ⊛ No children 18yrs
⊛

★★★ BED & BREAKFAST
The Olive Tree Bed & Breakfast
Maders PL17 7LL
☎ 01579 384392 📄 01579 384392
e–mail: kindredspirits@blueyonder.co.uk
dir: From M5 junct 31 A38 Plymouth A388 Callington through
town up hill on left
A warm welcome is assured at this single storey property, a mile north
of Callington. The attractive accommodation is spacious, and well
equipped with numerous extras. At breakfast an interesting choice is
offered, featuring home produced eggs from the hens in the garden.
Rooms 3 rms (2 en suite) (1 pri facs) (3 GF) S £30; D £55✳
Facilities TVB tea/coffee Cen ht Dinner Last d 24hrs Wi-fi available
Massage & reflexology available on site **Parking** 10 **Notes** LB ⊛

CAWSAND
MAP 03 SX45

★★★ GUEST ACCOMMODATION
Wringford Down
Hat Ln PL10 1LE
☎ 01752 822287
e–mail: a.molloy@virgin.net
web: www.cornwallholidays.co.uk
dir: A374 onto B3247, pass Millbrook, right towards Cawsand &
sharp right, 0.5m on right
This family-run establishment has a peaceful location near Rame Head
and the South West Coast Path, and is particularly welcoming to
families. There is a nursery, swimming pool, games room, and gardens
with play areas. A range of rooms, and some suites and self-catering
units are available. Breakfast and dinner are served in the dining room.
Rooms 7 en suite 4 annexe en suite (8 fmly) (4 GF) S £45–£55;
D £70–£100✳ **Facilities** TVB tea/coffee Cen ht TVL Dinner Last d 8pm
Wi-fi available ⊛ ⊛ Pool Table **Parking** 20 **Notes** LB ch fac Civ Wed
100

CONSTANTINE
MAP 02 SW72

★★★ ◉ INN
Trengilly Wartha Inn
Nancenoy TR11 5RP
☎ 01326 340332 📄 01326 340332
e–mail: reception@trengilly.co.uk
web: www.trengilly.co.uk
dir: Follow signs to Nancenoy, turn left towards Gweek until 1st
sign for inn, turn left & left again at next sign up to the Inn

Located in a very peaceful wooded valley, some one and a half miles
from the village of Constantine, this inn offers cosy, comfortable
accommodation with nicely appointed and well equipped bedrooms.
An interesting menu is offered in the restaurant together with a well
balanced wine list; there is also a wide selection of bar meals available
at lunch and dinner.
Rooms 6 en suite 2 annexe en suite (2 fmly) (2 GF) S £50; D £80–£96✳
Facilities TVB tea/coffee Direct dial from bedrooms Cen ht Dinner Last
d 9.30pm Boules **Conf** Max 30 Class 30 Board 30 **Parking** 60 **Notes** LB
RS 25 Dec

CRACKINGTON HAVEN   MAP 02 SX19

★★★★ FARM HOUSE
Lower Tresmorn Farm *(SX164975)*
EX23 0NU
☎ 01840 230667 📠 01840 230667 Rachel Crocker
e–mail: rachel.crocker@talk21.com
web: www.lowertresmorn.co.uk

dir: *Take Tresmorn turning off coast road 2m N of Crackington Haven*

Set in the North Cornwall Heritage Coast area, parts of this charming farmhouse date back to medieval times. The welcome is warm and genuine with a reviving cup of tea and piece of cake always on offer. Bedrooms are located in the main house and an adjacent converted barn, and all provide plenty of comfort. Breakfast and dinner (by prior arrangement) use local or farm produce.

Rooms 3 rms (2 en suite) 3 annexe en suite (2 fmly) (2 GF) S £30–£45; D £56–£74 **Facilities** TV4B tea/coffee TVL Dinner **Parking** 6 **Notes** ⊗ No children 8yrs 432 acres Beef/Sheep RS 20 Dec–5 Jan

★★★★ 🏠 🍴 GUEST HOUSE
Bears & Boxes Country Guest House
Penrose, Dizzard EX23 0NX
☎ 01840 230318
e–mail: rwfrh@btinternet.com
web: www.bearsandboxes.com

dir: *1.5m NE of St Gennys in Dizzard*

Dating in part from the mid 17th century, Bears and Boxes is a small, family-run guest house situated 500yds from the coastal path. You are welcomed with a tray of tea and home-made cake, and the caring owners are always around to help and advise about the locality. The cosy bedrooms have numerous thoughtful extras, and evening meals, using the very best of local ingredients and cooked with flair, are served by arrangement.

Rooms 3 en suite 1 annexe rms (1 annexe pri facs) (1 fmly) (1 GF) S fr £32; D fr £64✻ **Facilities** FTV TVB tea/coffee Cen ht TVL Dinner Last d noon Wi-fi available **Parking** 6 **Notes** No coaches

CRAFTHOLE   MAP 03 SX35

★★★★ GUEST ACCOMMODATION
The Liscawn
PL11 3BD
☎ 01503 230863
e–mail: enquiries@liscawn.co.uk
web: www.liscawn.co.uk

dir: *A374 onto B3247 to Crafthole, through village, left at rdbt, 0.3m on left*

A well established, friendly, family run inn with comfortable rooms. Serving food every night of the week, the Liscawn set in mature grounds and is a few minutes from the Coastal Path and Whitsand Bay.

Rooms 8 en suite 5 annexe en suite (3 fmly) (2 GF) S £45–£60; D £60–£90✻ **Facilities** TVB tea/coffee Cen ht Dinner Last d 8.30pm Children's play area **Conf** Max 60 Thtr 60 Class 40 Board 35 **Parking** 50 **Notes** Civ Wed 70

ENGLAND

CRANTOCK   MAP 02 SW76

★★★ GUEST ACCOMMODATION

Carrek Woth

West Pentire Rd TR8 5SA

☎ 01637 830530

web: www.carrekwoth.co.uk

dir: *W from Crantock village towards West Pentire*

Many guests return to this friendly, family-run house where hospitality and service are keynotes. Carrek Woth takes its name from the Cornish for Goose Rock, which can be seen in Crantock Bay. All the rooms are on the ground floor and the bedrooms are neatly furnished and some have good views. The lounge looks toward Newquay and the sea. Breakfast is served in the attractive dining room, where Sunday lunch is also available.

Rooms 6 en suite (1 fmly) (6 GF) S £44; D £66 **Facilities** TVB tea/coffee Cen ht TVL **Parking** 6 **Notes LB**

DEVORAN   MAP 02 SW73

★★★ BED & BREAKFAST

Pentrig

Greenbank Rd TR3 6PQ

☎ 01872 863597

dir: *A39 Truro to Falmouth, dual carriageway down hill to rdbt. Take exit signed Devoran*

Guests are assured of a warm welcome at this dormer bungalow, family home. Conveniently situated mid-way between Truro and Falmouth, Pentrig is an ideal centre from which to explore numerous attractions. A hearty breakfast is served, using free range eggs and local

produce where ever possible, at a communal table overlooking the well tended gardens. The comfortable bedrooms are well equipped.

Rooms 2 rms S £35–£45; D £45–£55✱ **Facilities** TVB tea/coffee Cen ht TVL **Parking** 10 **Notes** ⊗ No children 12yrs Closed 21 Dec–1 Jan

DRYM   MAP 02 SW63

Premier Collection

★★★★★ BED & BREAKFAST

Drym Farm

Drym, Nr Leedstown TR14 0NU

☎ 01209 831039

e-mail: drymfarm@hotmail.co.uk

web: www.drymfarm.co.uk

dir: *Off B3302 at Leedstown to Drym. Follow road until right turn to Drym. Farm drive on right after Drym House*

This delightful granite house stands in mature grounds and gardens within a lush, secluded valley. Guests are assured of a warm, friendly welcome. Bedrooms are stylishly simple and carefully furnished, with an emphasis on good linen and comfort. The comfortable lounge has a relaxing atmosphere; and breakfasts use local and organic produce.

Rooms 2 rms (2 pri facs) S £45–£60; D £80–£85✱ **Facilities** FTV TVB tea/coffee Cen ht Wi-fi available **Parking** 6 **Notes LB** ⊗

FALMOUTH   MAP 02 SW83

Premier Collection

★★★★★ GUEST ACCOMMODATION

Dolvean House

50 Melvill Rd TR11 4DQ

☎ 01326 313658 📠 01326 313995

e-mail: reservations@dolvean.co.uk

web: www.dolvean.co.uk

dir: *On A39 near town centre & Maritime Museum*

A Victorian house with high standards throughout. Rooms are comfortable and well equipped and there is a guest lounge. Well located for the beach and town alike with ample off-street parking.

CONTINUED

CONTINUED

Dolvean House

Rooms 10 en suite (2 GF) S £35–£41; D £70–£92✳ **Facilities** TVB tea/coffee Cen ht TVL Wi-fi available **Parking** 10 **Notes LB** ✹ Closed Xmas

★ ★ ★ ★ ☖ GUEST ACCOMMODATION

Prospect House

1 Church Rd, Penryn TR10 8DA
☎ 01326 373198 📄 01326 373198
e–mail: stay@prospecthouse.co.uk
web: www.prospecthouse.co.uk

dir: *Off A39 at Treluswell rdbt onto B3292, past Crosskeys pub & over lights, after 50yds right through white gates next to phone box*

Situated close to the waterside, Prospect House is an attractive building, which was built for a ship's captain around 1820. The original charm of the house has been carefully maintained. The attractive bedrooms are well equipped. A comfortable lounge is available, and freshly cooked breakfasts are served in the elegant dining room.

Rooms 3 en suite **Facilities** TVB tea/coffee Cen ht TVL Dinner Last d 9.30pm Wi-fi available **Conf** Max 6 **Parking** 4 **Notes** ✹

★ ★ ★ ★ GUEST ACCOMMODATION

The Rosemary

22 Gyllyngvase Ter TR11 4DL
☎ 01326 314669
e–mail: therosemary@tiscali.co.uk
web: www.therosemary.co.uk

dir: *A39 Melvill Rd signed to beaches & seafront, right onto Gyllyngvase Rd, 1st left*

Centrally located with splendid views over Falmouth Bay, this friendly establishment provides comfortable accommodation. The attractive bedrooms are thoughtfully equipped and some enjoy the benefit of the views. Guests can relax in the lounge with a drink from the well stocked bar. Also available is a sunny decking area at the rear in the pretty garden, facing the sea.

Rooms 10 en suite (4 fmly) S £37–£43; D £64–£76✳ **Facilities** FTV TVB tea/coffee Cen ht Wi-fi available **Parking** 3 **Notes** Closed Nov–Jan

See advert on this page

★ ★ ★ ★ GUEST ACCOMMODATION

Bosanneth Guest House

Gyllyngvase Hill TR11 4DW
☎ 01326 314649 📄 01326 314649
e–mail: bosanneth@fsbdial.co.uk

dir: *From Truro on A39 follow signs for beaches/docks, 3rd right mini-rdbt Melvin Rd, 3rd right onto Gyllyngvase Hill*

Well situated property with comfortable rooms and very friendly hosts. Some rooms have a sea view and dinner is served nightly. Undergoing gradual refurbishment. Clive and David were finalists for the AA Friendliest Landlady of the Year 2008 Award.

Rooms 8 en suite **Facilities** TVB tea/coffee Cen ht Dinner Last d 4pm Wi-fi available **Parking** 7 **Notes** ✹ No children 15yrs

FALMOUTH CONTINUED

★★★★ GUEST HOUSE
Cotswold House

49 Melvill Rd TR11 4DF

☎ 01326 312077

e-mail: info@cotswoldhousehotel.com

dir: *On A39 near town centre & docks*

This smart Victorian house has splendid sea views, and is just a short walk from the town. The atmosphere is relaxed, the bar is popular, and the lounge provides a good level of comfort. A hearty breakfast is served in the dining room and dinner, featuring home-cooked dishes, is available by prior arrangement.

Rooms 10 en suite (1 fmly) (1 GF) **Facilities** FTV TVB tea/coffee Licensed Cen ht TVL Dinner Last d noon **Parking** 10 **Notes** ⊗ Closed Xmas

★★★★ GUEST HOUSE
Esmond House

5 Emslie Rd TR11 4BG

☎ 01326 313214

e-mail: esmondhouse@btopenworld.com

web: www.esmondhouse.com

dir: *Off A39 Melvill Rd left onto Emslie Rd*

The friendly and comfortable Edwardian house is just a short easy walk from the beach. Bedrooms vary in size and some have sea views; the rooms are on the first and second floors. A hearty, freshly cooked breakfast is served in the spacious, traditionally furnished front room, whose large bay windows create a light and airy environment.

Rooms 5 en suite (1 fmly) S £26–£30; D £58–£65✱ **Facilities** TVB tea/coffee Cen ht **Notes LB** ⊗ No children 3yrs No coaches Closed Nov–Jan

★★★★ GUEST ACCOMMODATION
Gayhurst

10 Pennance Rd TR11 4EA

☎ 01326 315161

e-mail: jfjgriffin@yahoo.co.uk

web: www.falmouth-gayhurst.co.uk

dir: *A39 towards town centre, at end of Western Ter right at mini-rdbt onto Pennance Rd*

Many guests return to this friendly home, located in a quiet residential area close to the beaches. The spacious bedrooms are comfortably appointed, and some have sea views. Freshly cooked breakfasts are served in the bright dining room, which overlooks the attractive garden.

Rooms 5 en suite D £58–£64✱ **Facilities** TVB tea/coffee **Parking** 5 **Notes** ⊗ No children 5yrs Closed Nov–Etr

★★★★ GUEST HOUSE
Hawthorne Dene Guest House

12 Pennance Rd TR11 4EA

☎ 01326 311427 🖹 01326 311994

e-mail: enquiries@hawthornedenehotel.co.uk

web: www.hawthornedenehotel.com

dir: *A39 towards town centre, at end of Western Ter right at mini-rdbt onto Pennance Rd*

Picture windows in the lounge, dining room and many of the bedrooms of this late Victorian house look out over the sea. Cuisine is a feature, and dishes focus on the best of local and organic produce. A log fire burns in winter in the comfortable lounge. Sign language is understood.

Rooms 10 en suite (1 fmly) (1 GF) **Facilities** TVB tea/coffee Licensed Cen ht Dinner Last d 8.30pm **Parking** 7 **Notes** ⊗ No coaches

★★★★ GUEST HOUSE
Ivanhoe

7 Melvill Rd TR11 4AS

☎ 01326 319083

e-mail: info@ivanhoe-guesthouse.co.uk

web: www.ivanhoe-guesthouse.co.uk

dir: *Follow signs to town centre, through T-lights, over 2 rdbts, after 0.75m on right*

You are made to feel most welcome at this charming Edwardian guest house, where a relaxed atmosphere makes for an enjoyable stay. Bedrooms are thoughtfully equipped, and the cheerful breakfast room is an uplifting venue for an impressive range of choices, including vegetarian dishes and local produce.

Rooms 6 rms (4 en suite) (1 fmly) (1 GF) S £24–£26; D £52–£60 **Facilities** TVB tea/coffee Cen ht TVL **Notes LB** ⊗ No children 5yrs No coaches 🐾

★★★★ GUEST ACCOMMODATION
Lugo Rock

59 Melvill Rd TR11 4DF

☎ 01326 311344 📠 01326 311567

e–mail: info@lugorockhotel.co.uk

dir: On A39 near town centre & docks

The proprietor of this pleasant house provides comfortable and spacious accommodation and a friendly atmosphere. Bedrooms are attractively decorated and well equipped. There is a smart lounge and terrace overlooking the well-tended garden and ample car parking space is provided, there is also a small bar. Breakfast is served in the stylish dining room.

Rooms 11 en suite (3 fmly) (2 GF) **Facilities** TVB tea/coffee Cen ht TVL Wi-fi available **Parking** 12 **Notes** No children 12yrs

★★★★ GUEST ACCOMMODATION
Melvill House

52 Melvill Rd TR11 4DQ

☎ 01326 316645 📠 01326 211608

e–mail: melvillhouse@btconnect.com

dir: On A39 near town centre & docks

Well situated for the beach, the town centre and the National Maritime Museum on the harbour, Melvill House is a family-run establishment with a relaxed atmosphere. Some bedrooms have four-poster beds, and breakfast is served in the smart dining room. Ample parking.

Rooms 7 en suite (2 fmly) (1 GF) S £25–£30; D £54–£60 **Facilities** TVB tea/coffee Cen ht TVL **Parking** 8 **Notes LB** ⊗

★★★★ GUEST HOUSE
The Rathgowry

Gyllyngvase Hill TR11 4DN

☎ 01326 313482

e–mail: enquiries@rathgowry.co.uk

dir: Take A39 from Truro bypass Penryn follow signs for docks & beaches (avoid the town centre). A39 goes into Dracaena Avenue, Melvill Rd & right into Gyllyngvase Hill

A spacious Edwardian house, situated within easy walking distance of the town centre and beach. Bedrooms are bright, well maintained and comfortable, and four have sea views. A spacious lounge is available, and in the attractive dining room, evening meals are served by prior arrangement. The resident proprietors offer helpful and friendly service, and forecourt parking is provided.

Rooms 10 rms (8 en suite) (2 pri facs) (2 fmly) (1 GF) S £30–£40; D £60–£80✳ **Facilities** TVB tea/coffee Cen ht Dinner Last d 3pm **Parking** 10 **Notes LB** ⊗ No coaches Closed Oct–Apr 🐾

★★★★ GUEST ACCOMMODATION
Rosemullion

Gyllyngvase Hill TR11 4DF

☎ 01326 314690 📠 01326 210098

e–mail: gail@rosemullionhotel.demon.co.uk

Recognisable by its mock-Tudor exterior, this friendly establishment is well situated for both the town centre and the beach. Some of the comfortable bedrooms are on the ground floor, while a few rooms on the top floor have views to Falmouth Bay. Hospitality and service are strengths. Breakfast, served in the panelled dining room, is freshly cooked and there is a well appointed lounge.

Rooms 13 rms (11 en suite) (2 pri facs) (3 GF) S £35–£45; D £64–£74 **Facilities** FTV TVB tea/coffee Cen ht Wi-fi available **Parking** 18 **Notes LB** ⊗ No children Closed 23–29 Dec 🐾

★★★★ BED & BREAKFAST
Sienna Guest House

70 Trenoweth Rd TR11 5GH

☎ 01326 313756 📠 01326 313756

e–mail: susanashdown@yahoo.co.uk

dir: A39 to Maenporth, left at Treveglos Rd, 2nd left onto Penhale Rd

Sienna is a modern detached house close to Swanpool beach. The house enjoys rear sea views, and one of the double bedrooms has a luxury waterbed. Guests can relax in the Japanese gardens or lounge area. Complementary therapies also available by appointment.

Rooms 2 rms (1 en suite) (1 pri facs) **Facilities** TVB tea/coffee Cen ht TVL **Parking** 3 **Notes** ⊗ 🐾

★★★★ 🅐 GUEST HOUSE
Chellowdene

Gyllyngvase Hill TR11 4DN

☎ 01326 314950

e–mail: info@chellowdene.co.uk

Rooms 6 rms (4 en suite) (2 pri facs) (1 fmly) **Facilities** TVB tea/coffee Cen ht Dinner Last d 6pm **Parking** 6 **Notes** ⊗ No children 10yrs No coaches

ENGLAND

FALMOUTH CONTINUED

★★★ GUEST HOUSE
The Oasis Guest House
15 Dracaena Av TR11 2EG

☎ 01326 311457

e–mail: enquiries@theoasisguesthouse.com

dir: *From A30 take A390 through Truro into Falmouth, through lights, at Esso garage. House 200yds on left*

Guests are assured of a warm friendly welcome at this comfortable establishment. Conveniently situated for the town centre, the beaches and the numerous local attractions, the Oasis is an ideal location for both business and leisure guests. Some ground floor bedrooms are available, and a freshly cooked breakfast is served in the cosy dining room.

Rooms 7 rms (6 en suite) (1 pri facs) (2 fmly) (3 GF) S £28–£30; D £50–£60 **Facilities** FTV TVB tea/coffee Cen ht TVL Wi-fi available **Parking** 6 **Notes LB** ⊗ No coaches

★★★ GUEST HOUSE
The Observatory
27 Western Ter TR11 4QL

☎ 01326 314509

e–mail: theobservatory@talktalk.net

dir: *On A39, Dracaena Av onto Western Ter*

This interesting house is a pleasant place to stay, close to the town and harbour. The proprietors are very friendly hosts. Bedrooms come in a range of sizes, and freshly cooked breakfasts, with vegetarian options, are served in the dining room. On site parking is an added bonus.

Rooms 6 en suite (2 fmly) (3 GF) S £30–£50; D £50–£60 **Facilities** FTV TVB tea/coffee Cen ht **Parking** 6 **Notes LB** ⊗ ⊜

★★★ GUEST HOUSE
Penwarren
3 Avenue Rd TR11 4AZ

☎ 01326 314216

e–mail: penwarren@btconnect.com

Penwarren is in the heart of Falmouth, not far from Gyllyngvase beach. This friendly establishment is a winner of a Green Award for environmental awareness. Service is attentive and thoughtful and the fresh accommodation comes with considerate extras. A varied choice is offered at breakfast; a cosy lounge is also available.

Rooms 7 rms (6 en suite) (1 pri facs) (1 fmly) **Facilities** TVB tea/coffee Cen ht TVL **Parking** 7 **Notes** ⊗ No coaches Closed 20 Dec–6 Jan

★★★ GUEST HOUSE
The Tudor Court
55 Melvill Rd TR11 4DF

☎ 01326 312807

e–mail: enquiries@tudorcourthotel.com

dir: *A39 to Falmouth straight through Dracaena Ave, onto Melvill Road. Tudor Court 300yds on right*

This mock Tudor establishment offers bright, well-equipped bedrooms, some having the benefit of distant sea views. A comfortable bar/lounge is available for guests and in the dining room, which overlooks the attractive garden, a freshly cooked, full English breakfast is served.

Rooms 10 rms (9 en suite) (1 fmly) **Facilities** TVB tea/coffee Cen ht TVL **Parking** 10 **Notes** ⊗ No coaches

★★★ GUEST HOUSE
The Winnick
17 Castle Dr TR11 4NF

☎ 01326 313913

e–mail: sam@gourmetpicnics.co.uk

web: www.thewinnick.co.uk

dir: *Straight down Western Terrace onto Melvill Road turn right at Falmouth Hotel straight onto Castle Dr*

Within walking distance of the town centre, this personally run establishment has spectacular views across Falmouth Bay to the Helford River. Bedrooms vary in size and style, all having recently been upgraded. Guests enjoy a freshly cooked breakfast around a communal table in the dining room.

Rooms 4 rms (1 fmly) S £35–£65; D £55–£65✳ **Facilities** TVB tea/coffee Cen ht Wi-fi available **Parking** 4 **Notes LB** ⊗ No coaches Closed 25–26 Dec RS Xmas ⊜

★★ GUEST HOUSE
Trevoil
25 Avenue Rd TR11 4AY

☎ 01326 314145 & 07966 409782 🗎 01326 314145

e–mail: alan.jewel@btconnect.com

dir: *Off A39 Melvill Rd left onto Avenue Rd, B&B 150yds from Maritime Museum*

Located within walking distance of the town centre, the friendly Trevoil has a comfortable and relaxed environment. Breakfast is enjoyed in the light, pleasant dining room.

Rooms 8 rms (4 en suite) (3 fmly) (1 GF) **Facilities** TVB tea/coffee Cen ht **Parking** 6

| FLUSHING | MAP 02 SW83 |

★★★ FARM HOUSE
Trefusis Barton Farmhouse B & B
(SW815341)
TR11 5TD
☎ 01326 374257 & 07866 045646 ▤ 01326 374257
Mrs J Laity
e–mail: trefusisbarton@aol.com

dir: *Off A39 towards Carclew, follow signs to Mylor Bridge, left at mini-rdbt, after 0.5m straight across at x-rds*

This working farm is easily reached high above the village of Flushing. The friendly home is convenient for a relaxing break or for touring, and the comfortable bedrooms have many thoughtful extras. Breakfast is served at the farmhouse kitchen table, fresh from the Aga.

Rooms 3 en suite (1 GF) S fr £35; D fr £65✽ **Facilities** TVB tea/coffee Cen ht **Parking** 6 **Notes** ❸ 400 acres dairy arable ⬙

| FOWEY | MAP 02 SX15 |

★★★★ GUEST ACCOMMODATION
Trevanion
70 Lostwithiel St PL23 1BQ
☎ 01726 832602
e–mail: alisteve@trevanionguesthouse.co.uk
web: www.trevanionguesthouse.co.uk

dir: *A3082 into Fowey, down hill, left onto Lostwithiel St, Trevanion on left*

This 16th-century merchant's house provides friendly, comfortable accommodation within easy walking distance of the historic town of Fowey and is convenient for visiting the Eden Project. A hearty farmhouse-style cooked breakfast, using local produce, is served in the attractive dining room and other menu options are available.

Rooms 5 rms (4 en suite) (1 pri facs) (2 fmly) (1 GF) S £35–£40; D £55–£70 **Facilities** TVB tea/coffee Cen ht Wi-fi available **Parking** 5 **Notes** LB ⬙

| GOLDSITHNEY | MAP 02 SW53 |

★★★ GUEST ACCOMMODATION
Penleen
South Rd TR20 9LF
☎ 01736 710633
e–mail: jimblain@penleen.com
web: www.penleen.com

dir: *Off main street in village*

Penleen is a quiet home close to Penzance and Mount's Bay. The friendly proprietors ensure you have a comfortable stay. The lounge overlooks an attractive garden and freshly cooked breakfasts are served in the dining room. Bedrooms come with a good range of facilities.

Rooms 2 rms (1 en suite) (1 pri facs) D £55–£60✽ **Facilities** TVB tea/coffee Cen ht **Parking** 2 **Notes** ❸ No children 8yrs Closed 19 Dec–5 Jan ⬙

| GORRAN | MAP 02 SW94 |

★★★★ ⬙ FARM HOUSE
Tregerrick Farm B & B *(SW992436)*
PL26 6NF
☎ 01726 843418 ▤ 01726 843418 Mrs C Thomas
e–mail: fandc.thomas@btconnect.com
web: www.tregerrickfarm.co.uk

dir: *1m NW of Gorran. B3273 S from St Austell, right after Pentewan Sands campsite to The Lost Gardens of Heligan, continue 3m, farm on left*

Near many attractions, the family-run Victorian farmhouse offers a high standard of accommodation in peaceful countryside. Two of the attractive bedrooms are in the main house, the other is in a self-contained, two-bedroom suite. Delicious breakfasts, featuring home-made breads and preserves, are served around the large dining table.

Rooms 2 en suite 2 annexe rms (2 annexe pri facs) (1 fmly) (2 GF) D £60–£70✽ **Facilities** FTV TVB tea/coffee Cen ht TVL Wi-fi available **Parking** 4 **Notes** LB ❸ No children 4yrs 280 acres arable, beef Closed Nov–Jan

| GORRAN HAVEN | MAP 02 SX04 |

★★★★ BED & BREAKFAST
The Mead
PL26 6HU
☎ 01726 842981
e–mail: maureengoff@tiscali.co.uk
web: www.themeadcornwall.co.uk

dir: *A30 signed to St Austell continue towards Mevagissey. Signed for Gorran Haven, 1st right Wansford Meadows*

Guests are welcomed at this new, comfortable home, with a complimentary cream tea. Peacefully situated in Gorran Haven, within a ten minute walk of the sandy beach, Heligan and the Eden Project are a short drive away. The bedrooms feature larger than average beds and numerous extra facilities. Hearty breakfasts are served in the ground floor dining room, with free-range eggs from the owner's hens in the garden, when possible.

Rooms 2 en suite S £40; D £60 **Facilities** FTV TVB tea/coffee Cen ht Wi-fi available **Parking** 2 **Notes** ❸ No children Closed Xmas ⬙

| GRAMPOUND | MAP 02 SW94 |

★★★ GUEST ACCOMMODATION
Perran House
Fore St TR2 4RS
☎ 01726 882066 ▤ 01726 882936

dir: *On A390 in village centre*

Convenient for Truro or St Austell, Perran House dates from the 17th century and offers brightly decorated and coordinated bedrooms equipped with modern facilities. Breakfast is served in the airy dining room and there is ample off-road parking.

Rooms 5 rms (3 en suite) **Facilities** TVB tea/coffee Cen ht **Parking** 8 **Notes** ❸

ENGLAND

★★★ FARM HOUSE
Barton Farm *(SW692279)*

TR13 0QH

☎ 01326 572557 & 07814 942471 Mrs P Jenkin

e–mail: bartonfarm@talk21.com

dir: *1m NW of Gweek. Off A394 at Manhay x-rds towards Gweek, 1m left at T-junct, farm 150yds on left*

This dairy farm in a peaceful location near Gweek has been in the same family for four generations. The proprietors' warm hospitality brings guests back year after year. Scrumptious breakfasts are served in the traditionally furnished dining room.

Rooms 3 rms (1 pri facs) S £25–£35; D £50–£55✳ **Facilities** tea/coffee TVL **Parking** 5 **Notes** ⊗ 178 acres beef dairy Closed Nov–Feb 🅰

★★★★ GUEST ACCOMMODATION
Calize Country House

Prosper Hill, Gwithian TR27 5BW

☎ 01736 753268 📠 01736 753268

e–mail: jilly@calize.co.uk

dir: *2m NE of Hayle. B3301 in Gwithian at Red River Inn, house 350yds up hill on left*

The refurbished establishment has superb views of the sea and countryside, and is well located for the beaches and coves of West Penwith, walking, birdwatching, and the many gardens in the area. The attentive proprietors provide a most welcoming environment and invite you to share their comfortable lounge, which has a log-burning fire during colder months. Enjoyable breakfasts featuring delicious home-made fare are served around a communal table with sea views.

Rooms 4 en suite S £50–£55; D £80–£90 **Facilities** TVB tea/coffee Cen ht TVL **Parking** 6 **Notes** ⊗ No children 12yrs 🅰

★★★★ GUEST HOUSE
Treglisson Guest House

Wheal Alfred Rd TR27 5JT

☎ 01736 753141

e–mail: steve@treglisson.co.uk

dir: *A30 Hayle rdbt, 4th exit, 1st left at mini rdbt, guest house 1m on left*

This fine period house sits in the middle of some 130 acres of working arable farmland. The house has recently been sympathetically restored and the charming bedrooms are each individually furnished. Guests can relax and enjoy the warmth of the log burning stove during the colder months or make use of the swimming pool in the summer.

Rooms 4 en suite (2 fmly) D £55–£75 **Facilities** FTV TVB tea/coffee Cen ht Wi-fi available 🅾 Childrens play area **Parking** 6 **Notes** ⊗ No coaches Closed 23 Dec–2 Jan

---

See also St Keverne

Premier Collection

★★★★★ BED & BREAKFAST
Drym Farm

Drym, Nr Leedstown TR14 0NU

☎ 01209 831039

e–mail: drymfarm@hotmail.co.uk

web: www.drymfarm.co.uk

(For full entry see Drym)

★★★ INN
Copley Arms

PL11 3HJ

☎ 01503 240209 📠 01503 240766

e–mail: reservations@smallandfriendly.co.uk

dir: *On A387 in village*

The popular village inn is just a short drive from Plymouth, and is a good base for exploring east Cornwall. Its smart bedrooms have good levels of quality, and the extensive bar menu incorporates daily specials. Alfresco dining is popular on summer evenings. There is ample secure parking available.

Rooms 5 annexe rms (4 en suite) (1 annexe pri facs) (1 fmly) **Facilities** STV TVB tea/coffee Cen ht Dinner Last d 8.45pm **Parking** 40 **Notes** ⊗

LANLIVERY

MAP 02 SX05

★★★ INN
The Crown Inn

PL30 5BT

☎ 01208 872707 📠 01208 871208

e-mail: thecrown@wagtailinns.com

web: www.wagtailinns.com

dir: *Signed off A390, 2m W of Lostwithiel. Pub 0.5m down lane into village, opp church*

This characterful inn has a long history, reflected in its worn flagstone floors, aged beams, ancient well and open fireplaces. Dating in part from the 12th century, the Crown has recently undergone faithful restoration. Dining is a feature and menus offer a wide choice of fresh fish, local produce and interesting dishes. The bedrooms are more contemporary and are attractively and impressively appointed. The garden is a delight.

Rooms 2 en suite 7 annexe en suite (7 GF) S £39.95–£79.95; D £39.95–£79.95✶ **Facilities** FTV TVB tea/coffee Cen ht Dinner Last d 9pm Wi-fi available **Parking** 50

LAUNCESTON

MAP 03 SX38

Premier Collection

★★★★★ 🍴 GUEST ACCOMMODATION
Primrose Cottage

Lawhitton PL15 9PE

☎ 01566 773645

e-mail: enquiry@primrosecottagesuites.co.uk

web: www.primrosecottagesuites.co.uk

dir: *Exit A30 Tavistock, follow A388 through Launceston for Plymouth then B3362, Tavistock 2.5m*

Originally a cottage, this impressive property has been imaginatively developed to provide stylish accommodation. From its elevated position, views across the lush countryside are wonderful. Two of the spacious suites have external entrances, while the third is in the main house. All provide high levels of comfort with separate seating areas. Breakfast makes use of excellent local produce and a guest lounge is also available. Outside, guests can enjoy the garden, or perhaps take a stroll down to the river Tamar for a spot of fishing.

Rooms 2 en suite 1 annexe en suite (1 GF) S £70–£90; D £80–£130 **Facilities** FTV TVB tea/coffee Cen ht Dinner Last d 10am Fishing **Parking** 5 **Notes** ⊗ No children 12yrs

★★★★ 🏚 FARM HOUSE
Hurdon *(SX333828)*

PL15 9LS

☎ 01566 772955 Mrs M Smith

dir: *A30 onto A388 to Launceston, at rdbt exit for hospital, 2nd right signed Trebullett, premises 1st on right*

Genuine hospitality is assured at this delightful 18th-century granite farmhouse. The bedrooms are individually furnished and decorated, and equipped with numerous extras. The delicious dinners, by arrangement, use only the best local produce, and include home-made puddings and the farm's own clotted cream.

Rooms 6 en suite (1 fmly) (1 GF) S £30–£34; D £50–£66 **Facilities** FTV TVB tea/coffee Cen ht TVL Dinner Last d 4.30pm **Parking** 10 **Notes** ⊗ 400 acres mixed Closed Nov–Apr ⊛

★★★★ FARM HOUSE
Bradridge Farm *(SX328938)*

PL15 9RL

☎ 01409 271264 Mrs A Strout

e-mail: angela@bradridgefarm.co.uk

dir: *5.5m N of Launceston. Off B3254 at Ladycross sign for Boyton, Bradridge 2nd farm on right after Boyton school*

The late Victorian farmhouse stands in glorious countryside on the border of Devon and Cornwall. The well-presented bedrooms have numerous thoughtful extras, and the Aga-cooked breakfasts feature farm-fresh eggs.

Rooms 4 rms (3 en suite) (1 fmly) **Facilities** FTV TVB tea/coffee Cen ht TVL Fishing **Parking** 6 **Notes** 250 acres arable/beef/sheep/hens Closed Nov–Feb ⊛

ENGLAND

LAUNCESTON CONTINUED

★★★★ BED & BREAKFAST
Tyne Wells House
Pennygillam PL15 7EE

☎ 01566 775810

e-mail: btucker@talktalk.net

web: www.tynewells.co.uk

dir: *0.6m SW of town centre. Off A30 onto Pennygillam rdbt, house off rdbt*

Situated on the outskirts of the town, Tyne Wells House has panoramic views over the countryside. A relaxed and friendly atmosphere prevails and the cosy bedrooms are neatly furnished. A hearty breakfast is served in the dining room, which overlooks the garden. Evening meals are available by arrangement.

Rooms 3 rms (2 en suite) (1 pri facs) (1 fmly) S £30–£36; D £48–£60 **Facilities** TVB tea/coffee Cen ht Dinner Last d 11am Wi-fi available **Parking** 4 **Notes** LB ⊗ 🖾

★★★★ 🅐 BED & BREAKFAST
Oakside Farm Bungalow
Oakside, South Petherwin PL15 7JL

☎ 01566 86733

e-mail: janet.crossman@tesco.net

dir: *3m SW of Launceston. A30 W, 1st left after passing under Kennards House (A395) flyover*

Rooms 3 rms (2 en suite) (1 pri facs) (3 GF) S £25–£30; D £50–£60✳ **Facilities** TVB tea/coffee Cen ht TVL **Parking** 6 **Notes** ⊗ 🖾

★★★ BED & BREAKFAST
B&B @ Rose Cottage
Rose Cottage, 5 Lower Cleaverfield PL15 8ED

☎ 01566 779292

e-mail: info@rosecottagecornwall.co.uk

dir: *Exit A30 at Launceston Continue A388, Lower Cleaverfield 200yds left after 2nd mini rdbt*

A warm and genuine welcome is extended to all guests at this charming cottage, parts of which date back several hundred years. A homely atmosphere ensures a relaxing and enjoyable stay with every effort made to help with any local information required. Bedrooms offer good levels of comfort and breakfast is served in the attractive

CONTINUED

dining room with lovely views across the valley. Wi-fi access is also available.

Rooms 3 rms (2 en suite) (1 pri facs) S £26–£36; D £52–£80 **Facilities** TVB tea/coffee Cen ht TVL Wi-fi available **Parking** 4 **Notes** LB No children 9yrs

---

LISKEARD   MAP 02 SX26

See also Callington

★★★★ FARM HOUSE
Tregondale *(SX294643)*
Menheniot PL14 3RG

☎ 01579 342407 🖨 01579 342407 Mrs S Rowe

e-mail: tregondalefarm@btconnect.com

web: www.tregondalefarm.co.uk

dir: *3m E of Liskeard. Off A38 or A390 to Menheniot, 0.7m N of village, signed*

Located in a peaceful valley amid 210 acres of farmland, this working farm offers individually decorated bedrooms with thoughtful extras. Attention to detail is the hallmark here and every effort is made to ensure a comfortable stay. Delicious meals, using home-grown produce, are served in the airy dining room. Convenient for The Eden Project.

Rooms 3 en suite S fr £45; D £60–£76✳ **Facilities** FTV TVB tea/coffee Cen ht TVL Dinner Last d 9am 🍷 **Parking** 3 **Notes** LB ⊗ No children 5yrs 200 acres arable beef mixed sheep RS 24–25 Dec

★★★★ GUEST HOUSE
Pencubitt Country House
Lamellion Cross PL14 4EB

☎ 01579 342694

e-mail: hotel@pencubitt.com

dir: *From A38 head towards Liskeard and follow signs to railway station, signed on the right*

Located on the southern edge of the town, this well appointed property is peacefully set in two and a half acres of gardens; overlooking the rolling countryside of Looe Valley. The comfortable bedrooms feature numerous extra facilities. A spacious lounge and separate bar area are delightful areas for guests to relax in after a day exploring the many attractions in the area. Dinner is available by prior arrangement.

Rooms 8 en suite S £55–£65; D £90–£130✳ **Facilities** TVB tea/coffee Direct dial from bedrooms Licensed Cen ht TVL Dinner Last d 4pm Wi-fi available 🍷 **Parking** 15 **Notes** LB ⊗ No children 12yrs No coaches

★★★★ BED & BREAKFAST
Redgate Smithy

Redgate, St Cleer PL14 6RU
☎ 01579 321578
e–mail: enquiries@redgatesmithy.co.uk
web: www.redgatesmithy.co.uk

dir: *3m NW of Liskeard. Off A30 at Bolventor/Jamaica Inn onto St Cleer Rd for 7m, B&B just past x-rds*

This 200-year-old converted smithy is on the southern fringe of Bodmin Moor near Golitha Falls. The friendly accommodation offers smartly furnished, cottage style bedrooms with many extra facilities. There are several dining options nearby, and a wide choice of freshly cooked breakfasts are served in the conservatory.

Rooms 3 rms (2 en suite) (1 pri facs) S fr £40; D fr £60✳ **Facilities** FTV TVB tea/coffee Cen ht **Parking** 3 **Notes LB** No children 12yrs Closed Xmas & New Year 🐾

★★★★ GUEST ACCOMMODATION
Trecarne House

Penhale Grange, St Cleer PL14 5EB
☎ 01579 343543 📠 01579 343543
e–mail: trish@trecarnehouse.co.uk

dir: *B3254 N from Liskeard to St Cleer. Right at Post Office, 3rd left after church, 2nd right, house on right*

A warm welcome awaits you at this large family home, peacefully located on the edge of the village. The stylish and spacious bedrooms, which have magnificent country views, feature pine floors and have many thoughtful extras. The buffet-style breakfast offers a wide choice, which can be enjoyed in the dining room and sun-filled conservatory overlooking rolling countryside.

Rooms 3 en suite (2 fmly) S £45–£55; D £70–£90✳ **Facilities** TVB tea/coffee Cen ht TVL Table tennis Trampoline **Conf** Max 12 **Parking** 6 **Notes LB** 🐾

★★★ GUEST HOUSE
Elnor

1 Russell St PL14 4BP
☎ 01579 342472 📠 01579 345673
e–mail: infoelnorguesthouse@talktalk.net

dir: *Off A38 from Plymouth into town centre, house on right opp florist on road to railway station*

This well-established, friendly guest house is close to the town centre and railway station, and is just a short drive from Bodmin Moor and other places of interest. Bedrooms are neatly presented and well equipped, and some are on the ground floor. A cosy lounge and a small bar are available.

Rooms 6 rms (4 en suite) 3 annexe en suite (3 fmly) (4 GF) S £25–£30; D £48–£55✳ **Facilities** TVB tea/coffee Direct dial from bedrooms Licensed Cen ht TVL **Parking** 7 **Notes** 🐾 No coaches 🐾

★★★ BED & BREAKFAST
Moor Gate

Higher Rd, Pensilva PL14 5NJ
☎ 01579 362386
e–mail: sylviadoney@hotmail.co.uk

dir: *B3254 N from Liskeard for 4m, right to Pensilva, Moor Gate on right*

Having excellent country views, this friendly house stands in attractive grounds on the edge of the pleasant village of Pensilva, and the recently designated World Heritage Site of Caradon Hill. The two attractive bedrooms are well equipped, and freshly cooked breakfasts are served in the lounge overlooking the garden.

Rooms 2 rms (1 en suite) (1 pri facs) S £25–£27; D £50–£54✳ **Facilities** TVB tea/coffee Cen ht **Parking** 4 **Notes** 🐾 🐾

LIZARD   MAP 02 SW71

★★★ GUEST ACCOMMODATION
Penmenner House
Penmenner Rd TR12 7NR
☎ 01326 290370

dir: *A3083 into Lizard, right at green to sea, last house on right*

Interesting tales abound at this Victorian house, which has a splendid coastal setting. A friendly welcome is assured and the comfortable bedrooms, some having sea views, are equipped with modern facilities. Breakfast is a treat with local produce used whenever possible, thus ensuring a tasty and satisfying start to the day.

Rooms 6 rms (5 en suite) **Facilities** TVB tea/coffee Cen ht Dinner Last d 4pm **Parking** 10 **Notes** ⊗

LOOE   MAP 02 SX25

Premier Collection

★★★★★ 🏠 GUEST ACCOMMODATION
The Beach House
Marine Dr, Hannafore PL13 2DH
☎ 01503 262598 📠 01503 262298
e–mail: enquiries@thebeachhouselooe.co.uk
web: www.thebeachhouselooe.co.uk

dir: *From Looe W over bridge, left to Hannafore & Marine Dr, on right after Tom Sawyer Tavern*

This peaceful property has panoramic sea views and is just a short walk from the harbour, restaurants and town. Some rooms have been refurbished with stylish hand-made furniture, and the bedrooms are well equipped and have many extras. Hearty breakfasts are served in the first-floor dining room, a good start for the South West Coast Path that goes right by the house.

Rooms 5 en suite (4 GF) S £60–£70; D £80–£120 **Facilities** FTV TVB tea/coffee Cen ht Beauty treatment room **Parking** 6 **Notes LB** ⊗ No children 16yrs

★★★★ GUEST ACCOMMODATION
Barclay House
St Martin's Rd PL13 1LP
☎ 01503 262929 📠 01503 262632
e–mail: reception@barclayhouse.co.uk
web: www.barclayhouse.co.uk

dir: *1st house on left on entering Looe from A38*

Barclay House stands in six acres of grounds overlooking Looe harbour and is within walking distance of the town. The thoughtfully furnished bedrooms have modern facilities, and there is a sitting room, a spacious bar, a terrace where you can enjoy an aperitif during the summer. Enjoyable dinners are served (Wed–Sat and lunch on Sun) in the light and airy restaurant serving freshly prepared food; popular with locals and tourists alike. A heated swimming pool is also available.

Rooms 10 en suite 1 annexe en suite (1 fmly) (1 GF) S £70–£105; D £95–£140 **Facilities** STV TVB tea/coffee Direct dial from bedrooms Cen ht Dinner Last d 9pm Wi-fi available ⌁ Sauna Gymnasium **Conf** Max 40 Thtr 20 Class 10 Board 18 Del from £109 **Parking** 25 **Notes LB** ⊗

See advert on page 65

★★★★ 🍴 FARM HOUSE
Bay View Farm (SX282548)
St Martins PL13 1NZ
☎ 01503 265922 📠 01503 265922 Mrs E Elford
e–mail: mike@looebaycaravans.co.uk
web: www.looedirectory.co.uk/bay-view-farm.htm

dir: *2m NE of Looe. Off B3253 for Monkey Sanctuary, farm signed*

The renovated and extended bungalow has a truly spectacular location with ever-changing views across Looe Bay. The spacious bedrooms

CONTINUED

have many thoughtful extras. Add a genuine Cornish welcome, tranquillity and great food, and it's easy to see why guests are drawn back to this special place.

Bay View Farm

Rooms 3 en suite (3 GF) S £35–£38; D fr £65 **Facilities** TVB tea/coffee Cen ht TVL Dinner Last d 4pm **Parking** 3 **Notes LB** ⊗ No children 5yrs 56 acres Mixed, shire horses ☺

★ ★ ★ ★ GUEST ACCOMMODATION

Bucklawren Farm

St Martin-by-Looe PL13 1NZ

☎ 01503 240738 📄 01503 240481

e–mail: bucklawren@btopenworld.com

web: www.bucklawren.co.uk

dir: *2m NE of Looe. Off B3253 to Monkey Sanctuary, 0.5m right to Bucklawren, farmhouse 0.5m on left*

The spacious 19th-century farmhouse stands in 500 acres of farmland just a mile from the beach. The attractive bedrooms, including one on the ground floor, are well equipped, and the front-facing rooms have spectacular views across fields to the sea. Breakfast is served in the dining room, and tempting home-cooked evening meals are available at the nearby Granary Restaurant.

Rooms 6 en suite (3 fmly) (1 GF) S £35–£50; D £59–£70 **Facilities** TVB tea/coffee Cen ht TVL ⮶ **Parking** 6 **Notes LB** ⊗ No children 5yrs Closed Nov–Feb

★ ★ ★ ★ FARM HOUSE

Polgover Farm *(SX277586)*

Widegates PL13 1PY

☎ 01503 240248 Mrs L Wills

e–mail: enquiries@polgoverfarm.co.uk

dir: *4m NE of Looe. A38 S onto B3251 & B3252, B&B 0.5m on right*

This attractive house stands in farmland with fine views and is a peaceful place to stay. The welcoming proprietors ensure guests feel at home. Comfortable bedrooms are tastefully decorated with numerous thoughtful extras. Hearty breakfasts are served in the very pleasant lounge.

Rooms 3 rms (2 en suite) (1 pri facs) D £58–£62✳ **Facilities** FTV TVB tea/coffee Cen ht TVL **Parking** 9 **Notes LB** ⊗ No children 12yrs 93 acres arable sheep Closed Nov–Feb ☺

★ ★ ★ ★ ⇔ GUEST HOUSE

South Trelowia Barns

Widegates PL13 1QL

☎ 01503 240709

e–mail: madley.cornwall@virgin.net

dir: *A387 W from Hessenford, 1m left signed Trelowia, 0.75m down lane on right*

Set in a very peaceful rural location, this home offers a relaxing environment and is full of character. The proprietors provide a warm welcome and guests are made to feel at home. The comfortable bedrooms have lots of extra facilities. Cooking is accomplished and features home-grown and local produce.

Rooms 1 en suite 1 annexe en suite (2 fmly) S £30–£37; D £50–£54 **Facilities** TV1B tea/coffee Cen ht TVL Dinner Last d 10.30am **Parking** 6 **Notes LB** No coaches ☺

★ ★ ★ ★ 🛏 ⇔ GUEST ACCOMMODATION

Trehaven Manor

Station Rd PL13 1HN

☎ 01503 262028 📄 01503 265613

e–mail: enquiries@trehavenhotel.co.uk

web: www.trehavenhotel.co.uk

dir: *In East Looe between railway station & bridge. Trehaven drive adjacent to The Globe PH*

Run by a charming family, the former rectory has a stunning location with magnificent views of the estuary. Many of the attractive bedrooms have views, and all are particularly well equipped. There is also a cosy lounge bar. Dinner, by arrangement, specialises in Oriental cuisine, and breakfast features traditional fare; both meals are memorable.

Rooms 7 en suite (1 fmly) (1 GF) **Facilities** TVB tea/coffee Cen ht TVL Dinner Last d 11am **Parking** 8 **Notes** ⊗

ENGLAND

LOOE CONTINUED

★★★★ GUEST ACCOMMODATION
Coombe Farm

Widegates PL13 1QN
☎ 01503 240223
e–mail: coombe_farm@hotmail.com
web: www.coombefarmhotel.co.uk

dir: *3.5m E of Looe on B3253 just S of Widegates*

Set in ten acres of grounds and gardens, Coombe Farm has a friendly atmosphere. The bedrooms are in a converted stone barn, and are comfortable and spacious. Each has a dining area, with breakfast delivered to your room.

Rooms 3 annexe en suite (1 fmly) (3 GF) S £45–£55; D £70–£84 **Facilities** STV TVB tea/coffee Direct dial from bedrooms ↘ **Parking** 20 **Notes** Closed 15 Dec–5 Jan

★★★★ GUEST ACCOMMODATION
Down Ende Country House

Widegates PL13 1QN
☎ 01503 240213 📄 01503 240213
e–mail: teresa@downende.com
web: www.downende.com

dir: *A374 towards Looe, right A387 road becomes B3253 on left after Coombe Farm*

Set in its own grounds, guests are assured of a warm welcome here, at this young family's home. Bedrooms are comfortable and well equipped, the majority overlooking the gardens, to the front of the property. Home-cooked evening meals are a highlight and use the best of local produce, prepared with care and skill.

Rooms 7 en suite (1 fmly) (1 GF) S £40–£45; D £60–£80✳ **Facilities** TVB tea/coffee Cen ht Dinner Last d 12hr notice Wi-fi available **Conf** Max 20 **Parking** 9 **Notes** LB ⊗ Closed Dec

★★★★ ☐ ⊜ GUEST ACCOMMODATION
Polraen Country House

Sandplace PL13 1PJ
☎ 01503 263956
e–mail: enquiries@polraen.co.uk
web: www.polraen.co.uk

dir: *2m N of Looe at junct A387 & B3254*

This 18th-century stone house, formerly a coaching inn, nestles in the peaceful Looe valley. The charming hosts provide friendly service in a relaxed atmosphere, and bedrooms and public areas are stylishly coordinated and well equipped. The licensed bar, lounge and dining room overlook the garden, and there are facilities for children. Excellent evening meals feature local produce.

Rooms 5 en suite (2 fmly) D £60–£104✳ **Facilities** STV FTV TVB tea/coffee Cen ht TVL Dinner Last d 11am **Conf** Max 20 Thtr 16 Class 16 Board 16 **Parking** 20 **Notes LB** ⊗ Closed 25–27 Dec RS Nov–Feb (dinner by prior arrangement)

★★★★ GUEST ACCOMMODATION
Shutta House

Shutta PL13 1LS
☎ 01503 264233
e–mail: enquiries@shuttahouse.co.uk
web: www.shuttahouse.co.uk

dir: *From A58 Liskeard, follow A387 to Looe, opposite railway station*

This fine Victorian house was once the vicarage and has been sympathetically refurbished by the owners to create appealing and contemporary accommodation. Bedrooms all offer high standards of comfort with elegant styling and original character. Breakfast utilises

CONTINUED

locally sourced produce where possible, and is served in the light and airy dining room. Guests are also welcome to use the garden which overlooks the East Looe River.

Rooms 3 en suite **Facilities** TVB tea/coffee Cen ht Dinner Last d 24hrs notice **Parking** 1 **Notes** ⊗ No children 11yrs ☎

★★★★ BED & BREAKFAST
Southdown

Meadway PL13 1JT
☎ 01503 262222
e–mail: gjkmason@tiscali.co.uk
web: www.looebandb.com

dir: *A387 onto B3252, left onto Barbican Rd, left onto Hay Ln and right onto Meadway*

With spectacular views over the bay, Southdown is quietly situated on the East Cliff Downs, and is a ten minute walk along the coastal path from Looe beach and the town. The accommodation is ideally suited for a family or couple, with two bedrooms, one enjoying the superb view, the other overlooking the attractive rear garden. Guests are assured of a warm welcome and a hearty breakfast.

Rooms 2 en suite (1 fmly) D £50–£60✳ **Facilities** FTV TVB tea/coffee Cen ht TVL Wi-fi available **Notes LB** ⊗ ☎

★★★★ FARM HOUSE
Tremaine Farm *(SX194558)*

Pelynt PL13 2LT
☎ 01503 220417 📄 01503 220417 Mrs R Philp
e–mail: rosemary@tremainefarm.co.uk
web: www.tremainefarm.co.uk

dir: *5m NW of Looe. B3359 N from Pelynt, left at x-rds*

Convenient for Fowey, Looe and Polperro, this pleasant working farm offers a comfortable stay. The proprietors provide friendly hospitality and attentive service, and the spacious bedrooms are well equipped. A hearty breakfast is served in the dining room and there is a particularly pleasant lounge. This is a non-smoking house.

Rooms 2 rms (1 en suite) (1 pri facs) (1 fmly) S £35–£36; D £60–£64✳ **Facilities** TVB tea/coffee Cen ht TVL Wi-fi available **Parking** 6 **Notes LB** ⊗ No children 4yrs 300 acres Arable/sheep/potatoes ☎

★★★ GUEST HOUSE
Little Harbour

Church St PL13 2EX
☎ 01503 262474
e–mail: littleharbour@btinternet.com
web: www.looedirectory.co.uk

dir: *From harbourside West Looe, turn right into Princess Sq, on left*

Little Harbour is situated, almost on Looe's harbour-side, in the historic old town, car parking is available and this house has a pleasant and convenient location. The proprietors are friendly and attentive here. The bedrooms are well appointed and attractively decorated. Breakfast is served freshly cooked in the dining room.

Rooms 5 en suite (1 fmly) S £20–£30; D £40–£60✳ **Facilities** STV FTV TVB tea/coffee Cen ht **Parking** 3 **Notes LB** No children 12yrs

LOOE CONTINUED

★★★ BED & BREAKFAST
The Old Chapel
4 Summer Ln PL13 2LP
☎ 01503 220500
e–mail: mail@the-old-chapel.co.uk
web: www.the-old-chapel.co.uk
dir: *A390 onto B3359 7m. Reach Pelynt and Old Chapel, on right down hill*

Closed as a chapel since 1935, this attractive building was then used as a school canteen for the County Council. Sympathetically converted to a village house, the friendly owners welcome guests to their home. Bedrooms are comfortable, with the best use of the available space. A hearty breakfast is served at a communal table in the dining room. This is an ideal base for exploring the numerous attractions the area has to offer.

Rooms 2 rms (1 en suite) (1 pri facs) S £40; D £60✱ **Facilities** FTV TVB tea/coffee Cen ht Wi-fi available **Parking** 4 **Notes** ⊗ No children ⊜

★★★ BED & BREAKFAST
The Old Malt House
West Looe Hill PL13 2HE
☎ 01503 264976
e–mail: oldmalt@tiscali.co.uk
web: www.oldmalthouselooe.co.uk
dir: *A387 to Looe, 1st left after bridge, right behind fire station, 100yds on left*

A short, level stroll from the harbour front, the Old Malt House dates back to 1650 and is very conveniently situated for all of Looe's amenities. The cosy bedrooms are well equipped and are approached via an external stone staircase, while a hearty breakfast is served in the ground floor dining room.

Rooms 3 en suite (3 fmly) S £30–£50; D £40–£50✱ **Facilities** FTV TVB tea/coffee Cen ht **Parking** 3 **Notes** LB ⊗ No children

★★★ INN
The Ship Inn
Fore St PL13 1AD
☎ 01503 263124 📠 01503 263624
e–mail: reservations@smallandfriendly.co.uk
web: www.smallandfriendly.co.uk

This lively, family pub is located in the very heart of bustling East Looe and has a local following. The bedrooms are comfortable and equipped with all the expected facilities. A wide range of popular dishes is served at lunch times and during the evenings, with light refreshments available throughout the day.

Rooms 8 en suite (1 fmly) S £35; D £70✱ **Facilities** STV TVB tea/coffee Cen ht Dinner Last d 9pm Pool Table **Notes** LB ⊗

See advert on opposite page

LOSTWITHIEL MAP 02 SX15

★★★★ GUEST ACCOMMODATION
Penrose B&B
1 The Terrace PL22 0DT
☎ 01208 871417 📠 01208 871101
e–mail: enquiries@penrosebb.co.uk
web: www.penrosebb.co.uk
dir: *A390 Edgecombe Rd, Lostwithiel onto Scrations Ln, 1st right for parking*

Just a short walk from the town centre, this grand Victorian house offers comfortable accommodation and a genuine homely atmosphere. Many of the bedrooms have the original fireplaces and all are equipped with thoughtful extras. Breakfast is a generous offering and is served in the elegant dining room, with views over the garden. Wi-fi access is also available.

Rooms 7 rms (6 en suite) (1 pri facs) (3 fmly) (2 GF) S £30–£60; D £40–£80 **Facilities** TVB tea/coffee Cen ht Wi-fi available **Parking** 8 **Notes** LB ⊜

★★★ FARM HOUSE
Hartswell Farm *(SX119597)*
St Winnow PL22 0RB
☎ 01208 873419 📠 01208 873419 Mrs W Jordan
e–mail: hartswell@connexions.co.uk
web: www.connexions.co.uk/hartswell

dir: 1m E of Lostwithiel. S off A390 at Downend Garage, farm 0.25m up hill on left

The 17th-century farmhouse has a wonderfully peaceful setting, and offers generous hospitality and a homely atmosphere. The cosy bedrooms look across rolling countryside, and breakfast includes tasty eggs fresh from the farm. Two self-catering barn conversions are available, one with the 'Exceptional' Access award. Hartswell Farm boasts a small herd of Red Poll cows and calves.

Rooms 3 rms (2 en suite) (1 pri facs) S £30–£44; D £52–£68
Facilities TV1B tea/coffee Cen ht TVL Sailing days for 5 night stays
Parking 3 **Notes LB** ⊗ No children 6yrs 52 acres Rare breed cattle ◉

MANACCAN   MAP 02 SW72

★★★★ BED & BREAKFAST
The Hen House
Tregarne TR12 6EW
☎ 01326 280236
e–mail: henhouseuk@aol.com
web: www.thehenhouse-cornwall.co.uk

dir: A3083 onto B3293 left into Newtown, right at T-junct. After 2.3m, take left fork, then 1st right, last house

Cleverly converted from former farm buildings, this delightful little bed and breakfast is a haven of peace and tranquillity. It has many praiseworthy attributes, including its spacious and thoughtfully equipped modern bedrooms, both on ground floor level. However, by far the greatest strength here is the warm and friendly hospitality. Self-catering accommodation is also available.

Rooms 1 en suite 1 annexe en suite (2 GF) S £60; D £70–£80
Facilities TVB tea/coffee Cen ht Wi-fi available Tai-Chi workshops, Reflexology & Reiki therapies **Parking** 5 **Notes LB** No children 12yrs

---

MARAZION   MAP 02 SW53

★★★★ GUEST HOUSE
Glenleigh
Higher Fore St TR17 0BQ
☎ 01736 710308
e–mail: info@marazionhotels.com

dir: Off A394 to Penzance, opp the Fire Engine Inn

This proud granite house has an elevated position with wonderful views towards St Michael's Mount. The welcoming proprietors have owned this house for more than 30 years and many guests return. Dinners, by arrangement, are served in the comfortable dining room and feature fresh local produce where possible.

Rooms 9 en suite (1 fmly) (1 GF) S £32.50–£33.50; D £65–£67✳
Facilities TVB tea/coffee Licensed Cen ht TVL Dinner Last d noon
Parking 9 **Notes LB** ⊗ No children 3yrs No coaches Closed Nov–Mar ◉

MARAZION CONTINUED

★★★ GUEST ACCOMMODATION
Blue Horizon
Fore St TR17 0AW
☎ 01736 711199
e–mail: holidaybreaksmarazion@freeola.com

dir: *E end of village centre*
Located in the heart of this Market Town, the rear of this establishment is almost at the water's edge and offers superb views of the sea from its garden, some of the bedrooms and the breakfast room. The atmosphere is laid back and relaxed. There are a number of additional facilities available (charged), including a laundry room, sauna cabin and barbeque facilities. Ample parking is also available.

Rooms 6 rms (5 en suite) (1 pri facs) (2 GF) S £33; D £55–£65✳
Facilities TVB tea/coffee TVL Wi-fi available Sauna Hot tub & Bike hire **Parking** 7 **Notes LB** ✪ Closed Nov–mid Feb

---

MEVAGISSEY   MAP 02 SX04

★★★★ BED & BREAKFAST
Kerryanna Country House
Treleaven Farm, Valley Rd PL26 6SA
☎ 01726 843558 📇 01726 843558
e–mail: enquiries@kerryanna.co.uk

dir: *B3273 St Austell to Mevagissey road, right at bottom of hill, next to playground*
Located on the peaceful outskirts of this fishing village, Kerryanna stands in two acres of gardens and looks across the countryside to the sea. The attractive bedrooms are comfortably furnished, with one room on the ground floor. There are three cosy lounges, a swimming pool and a putting green.

Rooms 3 en suite D £70–£80✳ **Facilities** FTV TVB tea/coffee Cen ht ↖
Parking 6 **Notes LB** ✪ No children 12yrs Closed Nov–Apr 🐾

★★★ GUEST ACCOMMODATION
Headlands
Polkirt Hill PL26 6UX
☎ 01726 843453
e–mail: headlandshotel@talk21.com

dir: *One-way through village & ascend towards Port Mellon, Headlands on right*
Set on an elevated position with spectacular views over the bay, this family-run establishment offers friendly service and comfortable accommodation. The colourful bedrooms are well equipped, with many having sea views. Public rooms include a stylish lounge bar and dining room.

Rooms 14 rms (12 en suite) (1 fmly) (4 GF) S £40; D £80–£90✳
Facilities TVB tea/coffee Cen ht **Parking** 10 **Notes LB** ✪ Closed Dec–Jan

---

★★★ INN
The Ship
Fore St PL26 6UQ
☎ 01726 843324 📇 01726 844368
e–mail: reservations@smallandfriendly.co.uk

dir: *B3273 S from St Austell to Mevagissey, in central square*
The 400-year-old Ship Inn stands in the centre of this delightful fishing village. The popular bar, with low-beamed ceilings, flagstone floors and a strong nautical feel, offers a choice of menu or blackboard specials. The pine-furnished bedrooms are attractively decorated. Car park nearby.

Rooms 5 en suite (2 fmly) **Facilities** TVB tea/coffee Cen ht Dinner Last d 9pm

---

MORWENSTOW   MAP 02 SS21

★★★★ BED & BREAKFAST
West Point B&B
West Point, Crimp EX23 9PB
☎ 01288 331594
e–mail: bramhill@supanet.com

dir: *Take A361 to Barnstaple onto A39 towards Bude. 7m past Clovelly rdbt on right*
Ideally placed for exploring the beautiful countryside and coasts of North Cornwall and North Devon, this smartly appointed establishment is surrounded by colourful gardens with far reaching views to the rear. Guests are assured of a genuine welcome here with the freedom of all day access. Both bedrooms are comfortable, light and airy, with one having a four poster bed and patio doors leading to the garden. Additional facilities include a guest lounge, leading to the dining room, where local farm produce is utilised whenever possible.

Rooms 2 en suite (1 fmly) (2 GF) S £30–£35; D £50–£60 **Facilities** FTV TVB tea/coffee Cen ht TVL **Parking** 4 **Notes LB** ✪ Closed 22 Dec–2 Jan 🐾

MOUSEHOLE   MAP 02 SW42

★★★★ ◉◉ RESTAURANT WITH ROOMS
The Cornish Range Restaurant with Rooms
6 Chapel St TR19 6BD
☎ 01736 731488
e–mail: info@cornishrange.co.uk

dir: *Coast road through Newlyn into Mousehole, along harbour past Ship Inn, sharp right, then left, located on right*
This is a memorable place to eat and stay. Stylish rooms, with delightful Cornish home-made furnishings, and attentive, friendly service create a relaxing environment. Interesting and accurate cuisine relies heavily on freshly-landed, local fish and shellfish, as well as local meat and poultry, and the freshest fruit and vegetables.

CONTINUED

68

The Cornish Range Restaurant with Rooms

Rooms 3 en suite S £80–£100; D £80–£100✳ **Facilities** FTV TVB tea/coffee Cen ht Dinner Last d 9pm **Notes** ⊗

★★★★ INN
Ship Inn
TR19 6QX

☎ 01736 731234 📠 01736 732259

e–mail: reservations@smallandfriendly.co.uk

dir: *Off B3315 into village*

This smart harbourside inn is full of charm, and friendly locals and staff provide a relaxed atmosphere. Many bedrooms have views over the harbour and across Mount's Bay towards the Lizard peninsula. Fresh Newlyn fish and shellfish feature in the restaurant and in the bar.

Rooms 6 en suite **Facilities** TVB tea/coffee Cen ht Dinner Last d 9pm **Notes** No coaches

---

MULLION   MAP 02 SW61

★★★★ BED & BREAKFAST
Colvennor Farmhouse
Cury TR12 7BJ

☎ 01326 241208

e–mail: colvennor@aol.com

web: www.colvennorfarmhouse.com

dir: *A3083 Helston-Lizard, over rdbt at end of airfield, next right to Cury/Poldhu Cove, farm 1.4m on right at top of hill*

The friendly proprietors ensure guests have a comfortable stay at this Grade II listed building, which dates from the 17th century. Set in an acre of attractive and tranquil grounds, the house is a good base for

CONTINUED

touring the Lizard peninsula. Freshly cooked breakfasts are served in the dining room.

Rooms 3 en suite (1 GF) S £36–£40; D £56–£66 **Facilities** TVB tea/coffee Cen ht **Parking** 4 **Notes LB** ⊗ No children 10yrs Closed Dec & Jan

---

NEWQUAY   MAP 02 SW86

★★★★ FARM HOUSE
Degembris *(SW852568)*
St Newlyn East TR8 5HY

☎ 01872 510555 📠 01872 510230 Mrs K Woodley

e–mail: kathy@degembris.co.uk

dir: *3m SE of Newquay. A30 onto A3058 towards Newquay, 3rd left to St Newlyn East & 2nd left*

This delightful Grade II listed 16th-century farmhouse is convenient for The Eden Project and Newquay, and the warm hospitality and farmhouse breakfasts are highlights. The well-appointed bedrooms have lovely country views, as does the inviting sitting room.

Rooms 5 rms (3 en suite) (1 fmly) S £30; D £60–£70 **Facilities** FTV TVB tea/coffee Cen ht TVL Farm trail **Conf** Max 12 **Parking** 8 **Notes LB** ⊗ 30 acres Non Working Closed Xmas

★★★★ GUEST HOUSE
Dewolf Guest House
100 Henver Rd TR7 3BL

☎ 01637 874746

e–mail: holidays@dewolfguesthouse.com

dir: *A392 onto A3058 at Quintrell Downs Rdbt, Guesthouse on left just past mini rdbts*

Making you feel welcome and at home is the priority here. The bedrooms in the main house are bright and well equipped, and there are two more in a separate single storey building at the rear. The cosy lounge has pictures and items that reflect the host's interest in wildlife. The guesthouse is just a short walk from Porth Beach.

Rooms 4 en suite 2 annexe en suite (2 fmly) (3 GF) S £25–£40; D £50–£80 **Facilities** FTV TVB tea/coffee Licensed Cen ht **Parking** 6 **Notes LB** No coaches

ENGLAND

★★★★ GUEST HOUSE
Fairview House
2 Fairview Ter TR7 1RJ
☎ 01637 871179 & 07968 680957
e-mail: lindasheppsh@aol.com
web: www.fairviewhouse.org.uk

dir: *From A30 exit at Newquay onto A392. Turn right onto Trevemper Rd. At rdbt turn left. At the top of hill turn right at lights & left onto Fairview Terrace. Continue to the bottom, on left*

This very friendly guesthouse is conveniently located for access to the town centre, beaches and other amenities. It provides soundly maintained modern bedrooms and facilities include a lounge and bar.

Rooms 5 rms (3 en suite) (1 fmly) (1 GF) D £40–£60✶ **Facilities** TVB tea/coffee Licensed Cen ht **Notes LB** ⊗ No coaches ⊜

★★★★ GUEST ACCOMMODATION
Kallacliff
12 Lusty Glaze Rd TR7 3AD
☎ 01637 871704
e-mail: kallacliffhotel@btconnect.com

dir: *0.5m NE of town centre. A3058 to Newquay, right off Henver Rd onto Lusty Glaze Rd, 350yds on right*

This popular establishment is in a peaceful area close to the South West Coast Path. There are stunning views of the Atlantic from the bar and the breakfast dining room, and some of the attractive bedrooms also have sea views. Beaches and eateries are just a stroll away.

Rooms 8 en suite (3 fmly) (2 GF) D £66–£90 **Facilities** TVB tea/coffee Cen ht TVL **Parking** 10 **Notes LB** ⊗

★★★★ GUEST ACCOMMODATION
Windward
Alexandra Rd, Porth Bay TR7 3NB
☎ 01637 873185 📄 01637 851400
e-mail: enquiries@windwardhotel.co.uk

dir: *1.5m NE of town centre. A3508 towards Newquay, right onto B3276 Padstow road, 1m on right*

Windward is pleasantly located almost on Porth Beach and is convenient for the airport. It offers spectacular views, friendly hospitality, and a pleasant bar and terrace for relaxing. The spacious

CONTINUED

bedrooms, some with balcony, and many with sea views, are well equipped, and breakfast is served in the restaurant overlooking the beach.

Rooms 13 en suite (1 fmly) (3 GF) S £56–£66; D £76–£106✶ **Facilities** TVB tea/coffee Cen ht TVL Wi-fi available **Conf** Max 30 Thtr 30 Class 30 Board 30 **Parking** 15 **Notes LB** ⊗

★★★★ 🅰 GUEST HOUSE
Pine Lodge
91 Henver Rd TR7 3DJ
☎ 01637 850891 📄 01637 877804
e-mail: enquiries@pinelodgehotel.co.uk

dir: *1m E of town centre on A3058*

Rooms 12 en suite (4 fmly) (3 GF) **Facilities** TVB tea/coffee Licensed Cen ht TVL Dinner Last d 8pm Wi-fi available ⚲ Pool Table **Parking** 14 **Notes** ⊗ Closed 18 Dec–14 Feb

★★★ GUEST ACCOMMODATION
The Three Tees
21 Carminow Way TR7 3AY
☎ 01637 872055 📄 01637 872055
e-mail: greg@3tees.co.uk
web: www.3tees.co.uk

dir: *A30 onto A392 Newquay. Right at Quintrell Downs rdbt signed Porth, over double mini-rdbt & 3rd right*

Located in a quiet residential area just a short walk from the town and beach, this friendly family-run accommodation is comfortable and well equipped. There is a lounge, bar and a sun lounge for the use of guests. Breakfast is served in the dining room, where snacks are available throughout the day. Light snacks are available in the bar during the evenings.

Rooms 8 rms (7 en suite) (1 pri facs) 1 annexe en suite (4 fmly) (2 GF) D £60–£70✶ **Facilities** TVB tea/coffee Cen ht TVL Wi-fi available **Parking** 11 **Notes LB** Closed Nov–Feb

★★★ GUEST ACCOMMODATION
Tregarthen Guest House
1 Arundel Way TR7 3BB
☎ 01637 873554
e-mail: info@tregarthen.co.uk
web: www.tregarthen.co.uk

dir: *From A30 onto A392, at Quintrell onto A3058 Henver Rd, Arundel Way 4th turn on right*

Located in a quiet residential area just a short walk from the beaches and town centre of Newquay. The owners of this delightful detached property provide warm hospitality along with comfortable accommodation which is smartly furnished and well-equipped. Evening meals can be provided by arrangement, and the hearty breakfast is served at individual tables in the spacious ground floor dining room. There is also a cosy lounge facility where guests can sit and relax. Parking is ample to the front of the property.

Rooms 5 en suite 2 annexe en suite (2 fmly) (6 GF) S £35–£60; D £50–£70 **Facilities** FTV TVB tea/coffee Cen ht Dinner Last d 11am Wi-fi available **Parking** 7 **Notes LB** ⊗ Closed Xmas RS Oct–Jun

★★★ GUEST HOUSE
Wenden

11 Berry Rd TR7 1AU
☎ 01637 872604 📠 01637 872604
e–mail: wenden@newquay-holidays.co.uk
web: www.newquay-holidays.co.uk
dir: In town centre off seafront Cliff Rd, near station

The family-run guest house offers bright, modern accommodation near the beach and the town centre. Bedrooms have been carefully designed to make best use of space, and each is individually styled. Breakfast, served in the stylish dining room, is a filling start to the day.

Rooms 7 en suite D £45–£65✹ **Facilities** FTV TVB tea/coffee Cen ht **Parking** 7 **Notes LB** ⊗ No children 16yrs No coaches Closed 1wk Xmas

★★★ GUEST HOUSE
Copper Beech

70 Edgcumbe Av TR7 2NN
☎ 01637 873376
e–mail: info@copperbeechnewquay.co.uk
web: www.copperbeechnewquay.co.uk
dir: Exit A30 signed RAF St Mawgan, at rdbt take A3059 exit 6m. Turn right at T-junct, left at 1st mini rdbt and straight over 2nd. 3rd on right opposite tennis courts

Set amidst pleasant gardens, Copper Beech is located in a peaceful area of the town opposite Trenance Gardens. Bedrooms are light and airy, with ground floor rooms available. Comprehensive breakfasts are served in an attractive dining room and a warm welcome is assured.

Rooms 13 en suite (2 fmly) (3 GF) **Facilities** TVB tea/coffee Licensed Cen ht TVL Dinner Last d 7.30pm **Parking** 13 **Notes** ⊗

★★★ GUEST ACCOMMODATION
The Croft

37 Mount Wise TR7 2BL
☎ 01637 871520 📠 01637 871520
e–mail: info@the-crofthotel.co.uk
web: www.the-crofthotel.co.uk
dir: In town centre nr Towan Beach, junct Mount Wise & Mayfield Rd

Located just minutes away from the town centre and beach, this accommodation is comfortable and the friendly host creates a homely atmosphere. A full English breakfast is served in the informal bar-dining room.

Rooms 8 rms (6 en suite) (2 pri facs) (4 fmly) D £45–£75✹ **Facilities** TVB tea/coffee Cen ht Dinner Last d Breakfast **Parking** 7 **Notes LB** ⊗

★★★ GUEST HOUSE
Lazy Days Guest House

36 St Annes Rd TR7 2SA
☎ 01637 876074 📠 01637 876074
e–mail: susan.baker07@btinternet.com
dir: A30 onto A392 towards Quintrell Downs. A3088 towards Newquay, Henver Rd 3rd left, 1st right

Within walking distance of the town centre, this quietly situated, single storey property has recently been extended and extensively refurbished. In the stylishly decorated bedrooms, the best possible use has been made of the available space. Guests are assured a relaxed and friendly welcome, hearty breakfasts being served in the rear conservatory.

Rooms 4 en suite (3 GF) **Facilities** FTV TVB tea/coffee Cen ht TVL **Parking** 5 **Notes** ⊗ No children 18yrs No coaches Closed 21–29 Dec

★★★ GUEST ACCOMMODATION
Meadow View

135 Mount Wise TR7 1QR
☎ 01637 873132
e–mail: meadowview135@hotmail.com
web: www.meadowviewguesthouse.co.uk
dir: A392 into Newquay to Mountwise, Meadow View on left before rdbt to Pentire

Expect a warm welcome at this detached property which is ideally located just a short walk from the town of Newquay and the famous Fistral Beach, renowned for surfing. A short drive away are Waterworld, the Eden Project, and the Pentire Peninsular with its rolling green coastline. Accommodation is comfortable with some rooms having a countryside view. A hearty breakfast is served in the pleasant dining room and there is a cosy sun lounge to relax in.

Rooms 7 en suite (2 fmly) **Facilities** TVB tea/coffee Cen ht **Parking** 7 **Notes** ⊗ No children 5yrs Closed 7 Nov–mid Feb ⊛

NEWQUAY CONTINUED

★★★ GUEST HOUSE
Milber Guest House
11 Michell Av TR7 1BN
☎ 01637 872825
e-mail: suemilber@aol.com

dir: *A392 Newquay straight ahead at Quintrell rdbt to Henver Rd/
Berry Rd. Turn right onto Mount Wise, 2nd right to Michell Av*

This small and friendly guest house is situated in the centre of
Newquay. Bedrooms are comfortable and offer lots of useful facilities.
The bar is open most reasonable times, and guests get their own keys
so they can come and go as they please.

Rooms 6 rms (4 en suite) (6 fmly) (1 GF) S £25–£40; D £40–£60✳
Facilities TVB tea/coffee Licensed Cen ht **Notes LB** ⊗ No coaches ⊛

★★★ GUEST ACCOMMODATION
Pencrebar
4 Berry Rd TR7 1AT
☎ 01637 872037
e-mail: enquiries@pencrebar.com
web: www.pencrebar.com

dir: *A30 onto A392, then right at boating lake on entering
Newquay*

This friendly family-run house is a short walk from Newquay's popular
beaches and the town centre. Bedrooms are all spacious and well
planned. Delicious breakfasts are served in the attractive dining room.
Secure car parking is available for guests.

Rooms 7 en suite (2 fmly) S £25–£30; D £44–£56 **Facilities** TVB tea/
coffee Cen ht Parking charged all year **Parking** 5 **Notes LB** ⊗

★★★ GUEST ACCOMMODATION
The Pippin
2 Godolphin Way TR7 3BU
☎ 01637 873979
e-mail: thepippins@btinternet.com

dir: *A3058 to Newquay (Henver Rd), 1st right after double rdbt*

Well located bed and breakfast just a short walk from Newquay's north
beaches. The environment is friendly, the accommodation very clean
and the comfort is like home. Freshly cooked breakfasts are served in
the light and airy dining room which overlooks the well tended garden.
Good off road parking is a bonus.

Rooms 6 rms (3 en suite) (3 pri facs) (3 GF) D £45–£55✳ **Facilities** TVB
tea/coffee Cen ht **Parking** 6 **Notes** ⊗ No children 2yrs Closed Nov–Apr
⊛

★★★ GUEST HOUSE
Rolling Waves
Alexandra Rd, Porth TR7 3NB
☎ 01637 873236 📠 01637 873236
e-mail: enquiries@rollingwaves.co.uk

dir: *A30 onto A392, A3058 towards Newquay, then B3276 to
Porth, pass Mermaid public house*

A family owned and run guest house with great views across the bay.
Rooms are comfortable, the hosts friendly and welcoming, and dinner
is available on request.

Rooms 7 rms (6 en suite) (1 pri facs) (1 fmly) (3 GF) S £26–£34;
D £52–£68✳ **Facilities** TVB tea/coffee Licensed Cen ht TVL Dinner Last
d 10am **Parking** 7 **Notes** ⊗ No coaches

★★★ GUEST HOUSE
St Breca
22 Mount Wise TR7 2BG
☎ 01637 872745
e-mail: enquiries@stbreca.co.uk

dir: *A30 onto A392. Follow signs to Newquay, then to Mount
Wise*

This friendly guesthouse is conveniently located a few minutes walk
from the town centre, beaches and other amenities. It provides
soundly maintained, modern bedrooms and separate tables are
provided in the attractive breakfast room.

Rooms 10 rms (8 en suite) (2 pri facs) (3 fmly) (2 GF) **Facilities** TVB
tea/coffee Cen ht **Parking** 8 **Notes** ⊗

★★★ GUEST HOUSE
The Silver Jubilee
13 Berry Rd TR7 1AU
☎ 01637 874544
e-mail: andrew.hatton@tiscali.co.uk

dir: *Follow A3058 into Newquay. After railway station, left at
lights, 3rd house on left*

Silver Jubilee is a small establishment situated on the level in the heart
of Newquay. All amenities including shopping centre and beaches are
about three minutes walk away. Breakfast and dinner (Easter to
September) are served in the dining room. There is also a bar/lounge
for a pre-dinner drink or post-meal relaxation.

Rooms 7 en suite (3 fmly) S £30–£43; D £44–£70✳ **Facilities** TVB tea/
coffee Licensed Cen ht Dinner Last d 10am **Parking** 3 **Notes LB** ⊗
No coaches

★★★ GUEST HOUSE
Summer Breeze
20 Mount Wise TR7 2BG
☎ 01637 871518 📠 01637 879308
e–mail: karen.wilkins@tarsc.net
web: www.summer-breeze.info

dir: *A30 onto A392 signed to Newquay, turn right at Pentire rdbt, 0.5m on left*

Guests are assured of a warm welcome at this centrally located guest house; just a couple of minutes from the town centre and not that much further to the beaches. Bedrooms are neatly furnished and decorated, all equipped with modern facilities. Freshly cooked, hearty breakfasts are served each morning in the sunny breakfast room; prior notice is appreciated for the vegetarian option.

Rooms 6 en suite (3 fmly) (1 GF) D £50–£70 **Facilities** TVB tea/coffee Cen ht **Parking** 4 **Notes** LB ⊗ No coaches

★★★ GUEST ACCOMMODATION
Tir Chonaill
106 Mount Wise TR7 1QP
☎ 01637 876492
e–mail: tirchonailhotel@talk21.com
web: www.tirchonaill.co.uk

dir: *A392 into Newquay, last rdbt right onto Mount Wise*

Expect a warm welcome at the long-established and family-owned Tir Chonaill, situated close to the beaches and the town centre. Some of the neat bedrooms have wonderful views across town to the sea, and the hearty breakfasts are sure to satisfy.

Rooms 9 en suite (9 fmly) (1 GF) S £35–£45; D £55–£80✱ **Facilities** TVB tea/coffee Cen ht TVL **Parking** 10 **Notes** LB

PADSTOW   MAP 02 SW97

★★★★★ ◉◉◉ 🍴
RESTAURANT WITH ROOMS
The Seafood Restaurant
Riverside PL28 8BY
☎ 01841 532700 📠 01841 532942
e–mail: reservations@rickstein.com

dir: *Padstow town centre down hill, follow road round sharp bend, on left*

Food lovers continue to beat the well trodden path to this legendary establishment. This famous restaurant-with-rooms is situated on the edge of the harbour and just a stone's throw from the shops. The comfortable bedrooms are stylishly simple, equipped with numerous thoughtful extras, some have views of the estuary, while a couple have use of a stunning balcony. Service is relaxed and friendly, perfect for that break by the sea; booking is essential for both the accommodation and in the restaurant.

Rooms 14 en suite 6 annexe en suite (6 fmly) (3 GF) D £135–£265✱ **Facilities** STV TVB tea/coffee Direct dial from bedrooms Lift Cen ht Dinner Last d 10pm Cookery School **Parking** 12 **Notes** LB Closed 24–26 Dec RS 1 May

★★★★★ Ⓐ BED & BREAKFAST
Woodlands Country House
Treator PL28 8RU
☎ 01841 532426 📠 01841 533353
e–mail: info@woodlands-padstow.co.uk

dir: *1m W of Padstow on B3276*

Rooms 8 en suite (1 fmly) (2 GF) S £54–£76; D £92–£128✱ **Facilities** FTV TVB tea/coffee Direct dial from bedrooms Cen ht TVL Wi-fi available 🚶 Table tennis **Parking** 10 **Notes** LB Closed 16 Dec–1 Feb

ENGLAND

★★★★ GUEST HOUSE
The Old Mill House
PL27 7QT
☎ 01841 540388 📄 01841 540406
e-mail: enquiries@theoldmillhouse.com
web: www.theoldmillhouse.com
dir: *2m S of Padstow. In centre of Little Petherick on A389*

Situated in an Area of Outstanding Natural Beauty, the Old Mill House is a 16th-century corn mill with attractive secluded gardens beside a gentle stream. Guests enjoy an English breakfast in the mill room where the mill wheel still turns.

Rooms 7 en suite S £80–£120; D £80–£120✳ **Facilities** TVB tea/coffee
Direct dial from bedrooms Licensed Cen ht TVL **Parking** 20 **Notes** ⊗
No children 14yrs No coaches Closed Nov–Mar

★★★★ GUEST HOUSE
Penjoly Guest House
Padstow Rd PL28 8LB
☎ 01841 533535 📄 01841 532313
e-mail: penjoly.padstow@btopenworld.com
dir: *1m S of Padstow. Off A389 near Padstow Holiday Park*
Standing within 1 acre of grounds, this is a good base for exploring the beauty of North Cornwall. Bedrooms are carefully decorated and complemented with an impressive range of extras. Attention to detail is a hallmark throughout public areas. Breakfast is served in the attractive dining room or conservatory, and a lounge is also available.

Rooms 3 en suite (3 GF) **Facilities** STV TVB tea/coffee Cen ht TVL
Parking 10 **Notes** ⊗ No children 16yrs No coaches ⊜

★★★★ BED & BREAKFAST
Rick Stein's Cafe
10 Middle St PL28 8AP
☎ 01841 532700 📄 01841 532942
e-mail: reservations@rickstein.com
dir: *A389 into town, one way past church, 3rd right*
Another Rick Stein success story, this lively café by day, restaurant by night, offers good food, quality accommodation, and is just a short walk from the harbour. Three rooms are available, all quite different but sharing high standards of cosseting comfort. Friendly and personable staff complete the picture.

CONTINUED

Rooms 3 en suite (1 fmly) **Facilities** TVB tea/coffee Cen ht Dinner Last d 9.30pm **Notes** Closed 1 May BH RS 24–26 Dec

★★★★ BED & BREAKFAST
Roselyn
20 Grenville Rd PL28 8EX
☎ 01841 532756 📄 01841 532756
e-mail: padstowbbroselyn@bushinternet.com
web: www.padstowbbroselyn.co.uk
dir: *After blue Welcome to Padstow sign, Grenville Rd 1st left*

This charming small guest house is in a quiet residential area just a 10-minute walk from the centre of the delightful fishing port. Guests are assured of warm hospitality, and smartly furnished, well-equipped bedrooms. A good choice of breakfast options is available.

Rooms 3 en suite (1 fmly) S £35–£45; D £60–£65✳ **Facilities** TVB tea/coffee Cen ht **Parking** 4 **Notes LB** ⊗ RS Xmas ⊜

★★ BED & BREAKFAST
Little Pentyre
6 Moyle Rd PL28 8DG
☎ 01841 532246
e-mail: jujulloyd@aol.com
dir: *From A389, right onto Dennis Rd, bear right onto Moyle Rd*
Within easy, level walking distance of the town centre, Little Pentyre is situated in a quiet residential area, adjacent to the Camel Estuary and Trail. The comfortable bedrooms are well equipped and guests enjoy a freshly cooked breakfast, featuring eggs from the hens in the rear garden.

Rooms 2 en suite (2 GF) S fr £30; D fr £55✳ **Facilities** FTV TVB tea/coffee Cen ht **Parking** 2 **Notes** ⊜

Ⓤ
Treravel House
PL28 8LB
☎ 01841 532931
e-mail: mandytreravel@tiscali.co.uk
At the time of going to press the rating for this establishment had not been confirmed. Please check the AA website www.theAA.com for up-to-date information.

Rooms 3 en suite D £60–£79✳ **Facilities** FTV TVB tea/coffee Cen ht Wi-fi available **Parking** 6 **Notes LB** ⊗ ⊜

| PAR | MAP 02 SX05 | PENZANCE | MAP 02 SW43 |

★★★★ GUEST ACCOMMODATION
Elmswood House

73 Tehidy Rd, Tywardreath PL24 2QD
☎ 01726 814221 ▤ 01726 814399
e–mail: enquiries@elmswoodhousehotel.co.uk
web: www.elmswoodhousehotel.co.uk

dir: *Right from Par station, then 1st left to top of hill, opp village church*

Elmswood is a fine Victorian house set in the middle of the village opposite the church, where many guests return for the warm welcome. Bedrooms have quality furnishings and many extra facilities, and the attractive dining room, lounge and bar overlook a beautiful garden.

Rooms 7 rms (6 en suite) (1 pri facs) (1 fmly) (1 GF) S £35–£42; D £64–£84✳ **Facilities** TVB tea/coffee Cen ht TVL Wi-fi available **Parking** 7 **Notes** ⊗ No children 10yrs Closed Jan

★★★★ INN
The Royal Inn

66 Eastcliffe Rd, Tywardreath PL24 2AJ
☎ 01726 815601 ▤ 01726 816415
e–mail: info@royal-inn.co.uk

dir: *Adjacent to Par railway station*

Set opposite the local rail station, on the edge of the village of Tywardreath, this fully refurbished freehouse provides high standards of comfort and quality. Only 5 minutes from Par Sands and 4 miles from the Eden Project, this is an ideal base for exploring Cornwall. The open plan bar area has slate floors and a large open fire. The atmosphere is relaxed and diners can choose from the bar menu or more formal dining in the restaurant or conservatory. All rooms have en suite facilities, along with tv, clock radio, direct dial telephone, hairdryer and refreshment tray. All twin rooms have sofa beds (suitable for children under 14), and the family suite is suitable for families of 4 or 5.

Rooms 17 en suite (10 fmly) (4 GF) S £40–£57.50; D £55–£70✳ **Facilities** TVB tea/coffee Direct dial from bedrooms Cen ht Dinner Last d 9pm Wi-fi available Pool Table **Parking** 17 **Notes LB** Closed 23–26 Dec & 30 Dec–1 Jan

Premier Collection

★★★★★ GUEST HOUSE
Camilla House

12 Regent Ter TR18 4DW
☎ 01736 363771 ▤ 01736 363771
e–mail: enquiries@camillahouse.co.uk
web: www.camillahouse.co.uk

dir: *A30 to Penzance, at railway station follow road along harbour front onto Promenade Rd. Opp Jubilee Bathing Pool, Regent Ter 2nd right*

The friendly proprietors at this attractive Grade II listed terrace house do their utmost to ensure a comfortable stay. Wi-fi access is available throughout the house, and there is also access to computers in the lounge. Bedrooms and bathrooms are attractive providing many added extras. Some bedrooms and the dining room provide delightful sea views.

Rooms 8 rms (7 en suite) (1 pri facs) (1 GF) S £35–£39.50; D £70–£85✳ **Facilities** FTV TVB tea/coffee Licensed Cen ht TVL Dinner Last d 9pm Wi-fi available **Parking** 6 **Notes LB** ⊗ No coaches

Premier Collection

★★★★★ 🅶 GUEST ACCOMMODATION
Ennys

Trewhella Ln TR20 9BZ
☎ 01736 740262 ▤ 01736 740055
e–mail: ennys@ennys.co.uk
web: www.ennys.co.uk

(For full entry see St Hilary)

PENZANCE CONTINUED

Premier Collection

★★★★★ ◎◎ GUEST ACCOMMODATION

The Summer House

Cornwall Ter TR18 4HL

☎ 01736 363744 📄 01736 360959

e–mail: reception@summerhouse-cornwall.com

web: www.summerhouse-cornwall.com

dir: *A30 to Penzance, at railway station follow road along harbour front onto Promenade Rd, pass Jubilee Pool, right after Queens Hotel, Summer House 30yds on left*

This house, in a delightful residential location close to the seafront and harbour, is decorated in a Mediterranean style. The walled garden also reflects the theme, with sub-tropical plantings and attractive blue tables and chairs; dinner and drinks are served here on summer evenings. Expect warm hospitality and attentive service. Fresh local produce is simply prepared to provide memorable dishes on the daily changing menu.

Rooms 5 en suite S £85–£125; D £95–£125✱ **Facilities** FTV TVB tea/coffee Cen ht TVL Dinner Wi-fi available **Parking** 6 **Notes LB** ⊗ No children 13yrs Closed Nov–Feb

★★★★ 🏠 GUEST ACCOMMODATION

Blue Seas

13 Regent Ter TR18 4DW

☎ 01736 364744

e–mail: blueseas@ukonline.co.uk

dir: *A30 to Penzance, at railway station along harbour front onto Promenade Rd, opp Jubilee Bathing Pool, Regent Ter 2nd right*

Located within an elegant Regency terrace with stunning views across Mounts Bay, this is an ideal location for exploring the local area. There is an appealing contemporary style throughout with bedrooms providing a combination of comfort and quality, most with wonderful sea views. A guest lounge is also available, where you'll find lots of useful local information, books and magazines to peruse. Breakfast is a real treat here, featuring excellent local produce and a range of options from the generous continental buffet, vegetarian, fish options or the full English.

Blue Seas

Rooms 8 en suite (2 fmly) (2 GF) S £34–£38; D £70–£84 **Facilities** FTV TVB tea/coffee Cen ht Wi-fi available **Parking** 9 **Notes LB** Closed 15 Dec–Jan

★★★★ GUEST ACCOMMODATION

Chy-an-Mor

15 Regent Ter TR18 4DW

☎ 01736 363441

e–mail: reception@chyanmor.co.uk

dir: *From railway station, take left lane to promenade, 1st right in front of Stanley House*

This elegant Grade II listed Georgian house has been refurbished to provide high standards throughout. Bedrooms are individually designed and equipped with thoughtful extras; many have spectacular views of Mount's Bay. The spacious lounge has similar views, and tasty and satisfying breakfasts are served in the dining room. There is ample parking available.

Rooms 10 en suite (2 fmly) (4 GF) S £35–£40; D £70–£80✱ **Facilities** TVB tea/coffee Cen ht TVL **Parking** 12 **Notes LB** No children 10yrs Closed Xmas & New Year

★★★★ GUEST ACCOMMODATION

The Dunedin

Alexandra Rd TR18 4LZ

☎ 01736 362652 📄 01736 360497

e–mail: info@dunedinhotel.co.uk

web: www.dunedinhotel.co.uk

dir: *A30 to Penzance, at railway station along harbour front onto Promenade Rd, right onto Alexandra Rd, Dunedin on right*

The house is in a tree-lined avenue just a stroll from the promenade and town centre. The friendly proprietors provide a relaxed atmosphere. Bedrooms are well equipped and smartly decorated to a high standard. There is a cosy lounge and hearty breakfasts are served in the dining room.

Rooms 8 rms (8 pri facs) (2 fmly) (2 GF) S £27.50–£35; D £50–£65✱ **Facilities** FTV TVB tea/coffee Cen ht TVL Wi-fi available **Notes LB** ⊗ Closed 15 Dec–2 Jan 📧

CONTINUED

★★★★ BED & BREAKFAST
The Old Vicarage

Churchtown, St Hilary TR20 9DQ
☎ 01736 711508 & 07736 101230 🖹 01736 711508
e–mail: johnbd524@aol.com

dir: 5m E of Penzance. Off B3280 in St Hilary

Feel at home with a friendly welcome at this home. The spacious bedrooms are thoughtfully equipped, and there is a snooker room, a comfortable lounge and extensive gardens. Also available to guests, a trekking and riding school, run by the proprietors, who run a small stud farm as well.

Rooms 3 en suite (1 fmly) **Facilities** FTV TVB tea/coffee Cen ht TVL Riding Snooker **Parking** 8

★★★★ FARM HOUSE
Rose Farm *(SW446290)*

Chyanhal, Buryas Bridge TR19 6AN
☎ 01736 731808 🖹 01736 731808 Mrs P Lally
e–mail: penny@rosefarmcornwall.co.uk
web: www.rosefarmcornwall.co.uk

dir: 1.5m S of Penzance. Off A30 at Drift (behind phone box), 0.75m on left

Situated in peaceful countryside near Penzance, this working farm provides cosy accommodation with a genuine welcome and relaxed atmosphere. Bedrooms are attractively designed and well equipped, and some rooms have a private entrance. A hearty breakfast is served in the lounge-dining room at a refectory table.

Rooms 2 en suite 1 annexe en suite (1 fmly) (1 GF) D £60–£65✱ **Facilities** FTV TVB tea/coffee Cen ht **Parking** 8 **Notes LB** ⊗ 23 acres beef / Sheep Closed 24–27 Dec

★★★ GUEST HOUSE
The Carlton

Promenade TR18 4NW
☎ 01736 362081 🖹 01736 362081
e–mail: carltonhotelpenzance@talk21.com

dir: From A30 signs for harbour & Newlyn, on right after rdbt

Situated on the pleasant promenade and having sea views from some of its rooms, The Carlton is an easy stroll from the town centre and amenities. Bedrooms are traditionally styled. There is a guest lounge and spacious dining room, both sea facing.

Rooms 12 rms (9 en suite) (3 smoking) S £30–£35; D £65–£70 **Facilities** TVB tea/coffee TVL **Notes** ⊗ No coaches

★★★ GUEST ACCOMMODATION
Mount Royal

Chyandour Cliff TR18 3LQ
☎ 01736 362233 🖹 01736 362233
e–mail: mountroyal@btconnect.com

dir: Off A30 onto coast road into town

Part Georgian and part Victorian, the spacious Mount Royal has splendid views over Mount's Bay and is convenient for the town's attractions. The elegant dining room retains its original fireplace and ornate sideboard. Parking available to the rear of the property.

Rooms 7 en suite (3 fmly) (1 GF) D £70–£80✱ **Facilities** FTV TVB tea/coffee Cen ht **Parking** 10 **Notes LB** ⊗ Closed Nov–Mar 🐾

★★★ INN
Mount View

Longrock TR20 8JJ
☎ 01736 710416 🖹 01736 710416

dir: Off A30 at Marazion/Penzance rdbt, 3rd exit signed Longrock. On right after pelican crossing

The Victorian inn, just a short walk from the beach and half a mile from the Isles of Scilly heliport, is a good base for exploring West Cornwall. Bedrooms are well equipped, including a hospitality tray, and the bar is popular with locals. Breakfast is served in the dining room and a dinner menu is available.

Rooms 5 rms (3 en suite) (2 fmly) (2 smoking) S £20–£27.50; D £40–£55✱ **Facilities** TVB tea/coffee Dinner Last d 8.30pm Pool Table **Conf** Max 20 **Parking** 8 **Notes** RS Sun

ENGLAND

★★★ GUEST ACCOMMODATION
Penmorvah
61 Alexandra Rd TR18 4LZ
☎ 01736 363711

dir: *A30 to Penzance, at railway station follow road along harbour front pass Jubilee pool. At mini-rdbt, right onto Alexandra Rd*

A well situated bed and breakfast offering comfortable rooms, all of which are en suite. Penmorvah is just a few minutes walk from the sea front with convenient on-street parking nearby.

Rooms 10 en suite (2 fmly) (3 GF) S £24–£35; D £48–£70 **Facilities** FTV TVB tea/coffee Cen ht TVL **Notes LB** ⊛

★★★ GUEST HOUSE
Southern Comfort
Seafront, 8 Alexandra Ter TR18 4NX
☎ 01736 366333

dir: *0.5m SW of town centre. Follow seafront road, right after Lidl store, establishment signed*

This grand Victorian house is in a quiet location overlooking the bay and St Michael's Mount. A pleasant welcome awaits all guests, both tourist and business. Breakfast is served in the lower-ground dining room, and guests can enjoy a drink either outside in summer or in the bar or lounge.

Rooms 12 en suite (2 fmly) **Facilities** STV FTV TVB tea/coffee Licensed Cen ht TVL Dinner Last d noon **Parking** 6 **Notes** No coaches ⊛

★★★ INN
The Swordfish Inn
The Strand, Newlyn TR18 5HN
☎ 01736 362830
e–mail: info@swordfishinn.co.uk

dir: *1m SW of Penzance*

Situated in the very heart of the fishing village of Newlyn, The Swordfish was totally renovated a couple of years ago. The spacious, comfortable bedrooms are well appointed, as are the en suite shower rooms. This establishment is a popular venue for locals and tourists alike.

Rooms 4 en suite (1 smoking) S £30; D £50✻ **Facilities** FTV TVB tea/coffee Cen ht Wi-fi available **Notes LB** ⊛ No coaches

---

PERRANPORTH   MAP 02 SW75

★★★★ Ⓐ GUEST HOUSE
The Tides Reach
Ponsmere Rd TR6 0BW
☎ 01872 572188 ▤ 01872 572188
e–mail: jandf.boyle@virgin.net
web: www.tidesreachhotel.com

dir: *In village centre. Off St Piran's Rd onto Ponsmere Rd*

Rooms 9 rms (8 en suite) (1 pri facs) (1 fmly) (3 GF) S £30–£35; D £66–£76✻ **Facilities** TVB tea/coffee Licensed Cen ht TVL Dinner Last d noon Outdoor Hot Tub **Parking** 9 **Notes LB** ⊛ No children 8yrs No coaches RS Dec–Jan

---

PERRANUTHNOE   MAP 02 SW52

Premier Collection

★★★★★ FARM HOUSE
Ednovean Farm *(SW538295)*
TR20 9LZ
☎ 01736 711883 Mr & Mrs C Taylor
e–mail: info@ednoveanfarm.co.uk
web: www.ednoveanfarm.co.uk

dir: *Off A394 towards Perranuthnoe at Dynasty Restaurant, farm drive on left on bend by post box*

Tranquillity is guaranteed at this 17th-century farmhouse, which looks across the countryside towards Mount's Bay. The bedrooms are individually styled and are most comfortable. The impressive Mediterranean style gardens are ideal to relax in. In addition to the sitting room, there is also a garden room and several patios. Breakfast is served at a magnificent oak table.

Rooms 3 en suite (3 GF) S £77.50–£100; D £77.50–£100✻ **Facilities** TVB tea/coffee Cen ht **Parking** 4 **Notes** ⊛ No children 16yrs 22 acres grassland/horticultural Closed 24–28 Dec & New Year

★★★★ GUEST ACCOMMODATION
Ednovean House

TR20 9LZ

☎ 01736 711071

e–mail: clive@ednoveanhouse.co.uk

dir: *Off A394 at Perran x-rds between Penzance and Helston, 1st lane left, continue to end past farm*

Ednovean House is in a tranquil location with spectacular views of Mount's Bay and St Michael's Mount. It is ideal for a relaxing break or for touring the area. This establishment offers comfortable lounges and well-tended gardens and terraces. Bedrooms are comfortable and attractively decorated; ask for a room with a view.

Rooms 7 en suite S £32–£34; D £58–£88✳ **Facilities** TV1B tea/coffee Cen ht TVL **Parking** 12 **Notes** No children 7yrs Closed Xmas & New Year

★★★ ❀ INN
The Victoria Inn

TR20 9NP

☎ 01736 710309 📠 01736 719284

e–mail: enquiries@victoriainn-penzance.co.uk

dir: *Off A394 into village*

The attractive and friendly inn, popular with locals and visitors alike, reputedly originates from the Middle Ages. Daily specials in the cosy bar or the dining room include local fish, while the bedrooms are small but well equipped.

Rooms 2 en suite S £45–£65; D £65✳ **Facilities** TVB tea/coffee Dinner Last d 9pm **Parking** 10 **Notes** No children 18yrs

---

POLPERRO   MAP 02 SX25

★★★★ FARM HOUSE
Trenake Manor Farm *(SX190555)*

Pelynt PL13 2LT

☎ 01503 220835 📠 01503 220835 Mrs L Philp

e–mail: lorraine@cornishfarmhouse.co.uk

dir: *3.5m N of Polperro. A390 onto B3359 for Looe, 5m left at small x-rds*

The welcoming 15th-century farmhouse is surrounded by countryside and is a good base for touring Cornwall. Bedrooms have considerate finishing touches and there is a comfortable lounge. Breakfast, using local produce, is enjoyed in the cosy dining room (you may just spot the milking cows quietly passing the end of the garden).

Rooms 3 en suite (1 fmly) D £64–£70✳ **Facilities** TVB tea/coffee Cen ht TVL **Parking** 10 **Notes** LB 400 acres arable, dairy & beef ❀

★★★ GUEST ACCOMMODATION
Penryn House

The Coombes PL13 2RQ

☎ 01503 272157 📠 01503 273055

e–mail: chrispidcock@aol.com

web: www.penrynhouse.co.uk

dir: *A387 to Polperro, at mini-rdbt left down hill into village (ignore restricted access). 200yds on left*

Penryn House has a relaxed atmosphere and offers a warm welcome. Every effort is made to ensure a memorable stay. Bedrooms are neatly presented and reflect the character of the building. After a day exploring, enjoy a drink at the bar and relax in the comfortable lounge.

Rooms 12 rms (11 en suite) (1 pri facs) (3 fmly) S £35–£40; D £70–£90✳ **Facilities** TVB tea/coffee **Parking** 13 **Notes** LB

Ⓤ
Trenderway Farm

Pelynt PL13 2LY

☎ 01503 272214

e–mail: stay@trenderwayfarm.com

web: www.trenderwayfarm.co.uk

dir: *A387 from Looe to Polperro, farm signed, onto 2nd signed turning*

At the time of going to press the rating for this establishment had not been confirmed. Please check the AA website www.theAA.com for up-to-date information.

Rooms 2 en suite 4 annexe en suite (1 GF) D £75–£155 **Facilities** FTV TVB tea/coffee Cen ht Wi-fi available lakes **Conf** Max 15 Thtr 12 Class 12 Board 15 **Parking** 6 **Notes** LB ⊗ No children Closed Xmas & New Year

POLZEATH   MAP 02 SW97

★★★ GUEST HOUSE
Seaways

PL27 6SU

☎ 01208 862382

e–mail: pauline@seaways99.freeserve.co.uk

dir: *250yds E of village centre*

Seaways is just a short walk from the sandy beach popular with surfers and bathers. The house offers comfortable accommodation and a friendly environment, and an open fire burns in the cosy lounge on cooler evenings. Breakfast is served in a pleasant dining room.

Rooms 5 rms (3 en suite) (2 pri facs) (1 fmly) (1 GF) **Facilities** TVB tea/coffee Cen ht TVL **Parking** 5 **Notes** ⊗ No coaches Closed Xmas & New Year 🐾

PORTHLEVEN   MAP 02 SW62

★★★★ INN
Harbour Inn

Commercial Rd TR13 9JB

☎ 01326 573876 📄 01326 572124

e–mail: reservations@smallandfriendly.co.uk

dir: *In village by harbour*

This pleasant harbourside inn is decked with flowers in summer. The spacious bars offer local beers, and there is a good choice of freshly cooked dishes. The smart, contemporary bedrooms are very comfortable and well equipped, and many have harbour views.

Rooms 15 en suite (2 fmly) **Facilities** STV FTV TV10B tea/coffee Direct dial from bedrooms Cen ht TVL Dinner Last d 9pm Pool Table **Conf** Max 20 **Parking** 10 **Notes** ⊗ RS 24–25 Dec

★★★ ⊛ RESTAURANT WITH ROOMS
Kota Restaurant with Rooms

Harbour Head TR13 9JA

☎ 01326 562407 📄 01326 562407

e–mail: kota@btconnect.com

dir: *B3304 from Helston into Porthleven, Kota is on the harbour head opposite the slipway*

Overlooking the Harbour Head, this 300-year-old building is the home of Kota Restaurant (Kota being Maori for shellfish). The bedrooms are

approached from a granite stairway to the side of the building. The family room is spacious and has the benefit of harbour views, while the smaller, double room is at the rear of the property. The enthusiastic, young owners ensure guests enjoy their stay here and a meal in the restaurant is not to be missed. Breakfast features the best of local produce.

Rooms 2 annexe en suite (1 fmly) S £50–£70; D £65–£90✻ **Facilities** TVB tea/coffee Dinner Last d 9pm **Parking** 1 **Notes** ⊗ Closed Jan RS Nov–Mar

PORT ISAAC   MAP 02 SW98

★★★★ BED & BREAKFAST
The Corn Mill

Port Isaac Rd, Trelill PL30 3HZ

☎ 01208 851079

dir: *Off B3314, between Pendoggett and Trelill*

Dating from the 18th century, this mill has been lovingly restored to provide a home packed full of character. The bedrooms are individually styled and personal touches create a wonderfully relaxed and homely atmosphere. The farmhouse kitchen is the venue for a delicious breakfast.

Rooms 2 en suite (1 fmly) D £70–£75✻ **Facilities** TV1B tea/coffee Cen ht **Parking** 3 **Notes** Closed 24 Dec–5 Jan 🐾

PRAA SANDS   MAP 02 SW52

★★★★ GUEST ACCOMMODATION
Gwynoon

Chy-an-Dour Rd TR20 9SY

☎ 01736 763508

e–mail: enquiries@gwynoon.co.uk

web: www.gwynoon.co.uk

dir: *Off A394 at Germoe x-rds into village, 2nd left after Post Office, house on left*

Praa Sands is one of Cornwall's dazzling beaches. Gwynoon has excellent views from the front bedrooms, balcony and the well-tended gardens. Bedrooms are well furnished and have many extras. The hosts are very attentive and provide a peaceful atmosphere, and their enjoyable breakfasts feature fresh local produce.

CONTINUED

CONTINUED

Gwynoon

Rooms 3 en suite (2 fmly) (1 GF) S fr £32; D fr £64✳ **Facilities** TVB tea/coffee Cen ht Wi-fi available **Parking** 6 **Notes** ⊗ ☉

REDRUTH   MAP 02 SW64

★★★ GUEST HOUSE
Lansdowne Guest House

Lansdowne House, 42 Clinton Rd TR15 2QE
☎ 01209 216002 📠 01209 216002
e–mail: enquiries@lansdowne-guesthouse.co.uk
dir: *From train station turn down to lights, turn left, Guesthouse 200yds past library on right*

This detached Edwardian house, formerly owned by a tea merchant, is in a residential area within easy walking distance of the town centre and the railway station; a range of places to eat is available. The comfortable bedrooms are well equipped and a hearty breakfast is served in the cosy dining room.

Rooms 7 rms (3 en suite) (1 fmly) (1 GF) S £29–£45; D £58–£90✳ **Facilities** FTV TVB tea/coffee Cen ht Wi-fi available **Parking** 5 **Notes** ⊗

★★ INN
Lanner Inn

The Square, Lanner TR16 6EH
☎ 01209 215611 & 214065
web: www.lannerinn.co.uk
dir: *2m SE of Redruth. In Lanner on A393*

Conveniently situated for Redruth and the A30 this traditional inn is about to undergo refurbishment and is now under new ownership. Bedrooms are comfortable and staff very friendly.

Rooms 6 rms (4 en suite) 1 annexe en suite (2 fmly) (1 GF) S £30–£40; D £50–£70✳ **Facilities** TVB tea/coffee Cen ht Pool Table **Parking** 16

ROCHE   MAP 02 SW96

★★★ BED & BREAKFAST
Saffron Park

Belowda PL26 8NL
☎ 01726 890105 & 07930 572536
e–mail: saffron.park@btinternet.com
dir: *Exit new A30 at Victoria junct, after rdbt continue W along former A30. Pass Victoria Inn & Lodge 0.75m, right into narrow lane before Roche Cross junct, on left within 200yds*

Saffron Park is midway between the north and south coasts and very convenient for the Eden Project. Friendly hospitality and attentive service are provided, and there is a comfortable lounge and pleasant bedrooms. A hearty breakfast is served in the dining room.

Rooms 2 en suite (1 fmly) D £60✳ **Facilities** TVB tea/coffee Cen ht TVL Wi-fi available Sauna Spa bath **Parking** 5 **Notes** Closed 22 Dec–2 Jan ☉

RUAN MINOR   MAP 02 SW71

★★★★ GUEST ACCOMMODATION
The Coach House

Kuggar TR12 7LY
☎ 01326 291044
e–mail: mjanmakin@aol.com
dir: *1m N of Ruan Minor in Kuggar village*

This 17th-century house is close to Kennack Sands and Goonhilly Downs nature reserve. The friendly proprietors provide a warm welcome for their guests, who can relax in the spacious lounge-dining room where a fire burns in colder months. Bedrooms, two of which are in a converted stable block, are attractively decorated.

Rooms 3 en suite 2 annexe en suite (2 GF) S £35–£40; D £64–£70✳ **Facilities** STV TVB tea/coffee Cen ht TVL Wi-fi available **Parking** 10 **Notes LB** ⊗ Closed Xmas ☉

ST AGNES
MAP 02 SW75

★★★★ 👄 GUEST ACCOMMODATION
Driftwood Spars
Trevaunance Cove TR5 0RT
☎ 01872 552428 📠 01872 553701
e–mail: driftwoodspars@hotmail.com

dir: *A30 to Chiverton rdbt, right onto B3277 and follow road through village. Located 200yds before beach*

Partly built from ship-wreck timbers, this 18th-century inn attracts locals and visitors alike. The attractive bedrooms, some in an annexe, are decorated in bright, sea-side style and have many interesting features. Local produce served in the informal pub dining room or in the restaurant, ranges from hand-pulled beers to delicious, locally landed seafood.

Rooms 9 en suite 6 annexe en suite (4 fmly) (5 GF) S £45–£66; D £86–£101✱ **Facilities** TVB tea/coffee Direct dial from bedrooms Cen ht TVL Dinner Last d 9.30pm Wi-fi available Pool Table **Conf** Max 50 Thtr 50 Class 25 Board 20 **Parking** 40 **Notes** RS 25 Dec

★★★★ 🄰 GUEST ACCOMMODATION
Lambriggan Court
Penhallow TR4 9LU
☎ 01872 571636
e–mail: lynn_c_churchill@hotmail.com
web: www.lambriggancourt.com

Rooms 2 rms (1 en suite) (1 pri facs) (2 GF) **Facilities** FTV TVB tea/coffee Cen ht TVL Wi-fi available **Parking** 8 **Notes** ⊗ No children Closed 25 Dec 🐾

★★ GUEST HOUSE
Penkerris
Penwinnick Rd TR5 0PA
☎ 01872 552262 📠 01872 552262
e–mail: info@penkerris.co.uk
web: www.penkerris.co.uk

dir: *A30 onto B3277 to village, 1st house on right after village sign*

Set in gardens on the edge of the village, Penkerris is an Edwardian house with a relaxed atmosphere. The best possible use is made of space in the bedrooms, and home-cooked evening meals using local produce are served by arrangement. Ample parking available.

CONTINUED

Rooms 6 rms (3 en suite) (3 fmly) S £27.50–£42.50; D £45–£65✱ **Facilities** TVB tea/coffee Licensed TVL Dinner Last d 10.30pm **Parking** 9 **Notes LB** No coaches

ST AUSTELL
MAP 02 SX05

See also Gorran Haven, Roche & St Blazey

★★★★★ 🍴 👄 GUEST ACCOMMODATION
Anchorage House
Nettles Corner, Tregrehan Mills PL25 3RH
☎ 01726 814071 📠 01726 813462
e–mail: info@anchoragehouse.co.uk
web: www.anchoragehouse.co.uk

dir: *2 m E of town centre off A390, opposite St Austell Garden Centre*

This Georgian style house is set in an acre of carefully landscaped gardens at the end of a private lane. Guests are met upon arrival with afternoon tea, often served on the patio, and dinner is served in the evening by arrangement. The luxurious bedrooms are equipped to the highest standard and thoughtful extras include satellite television, fresh fruit, magazines, bottled water and chocolates. Guests also have use of the pool, hot tub, gym and sauna. The house is a short distance from the Eden Project, the Lost Gardens of Heligan, Carolyn Bay and Charlestown Harbour.

Rooms 4 en suite (1 GF) S £85–£120; D £110–£150 **Facilities** STV FTV TVB tea/coffee Cen ht Dinner Last d 24hrs Wi-fi available ⓢ Sauna Gymnasium Spa treatments, Hot tub **Parking** 6 **Notes** ⊗ No children 16yrs Closed Dec–Feb

★ ★ ★ ★ ★ ⚏ GUEST ACCOMMODATION

Penarwyn House

PL24 2DS

☎ 01726 814224 📠 01726 814224

e-mail: stay@penarwyn.co.uk

web: www.penarwyn.co.uk

(For full entry see St Blazey)

★ ★ ★ ★ ★ GUEST ACCOMMODATION

Highland Court Lodge

Biscovey Rd, Biscovey, Par PL24 2HW

☎ 01726 813320 📠 01726 813320

e-mail: enquiries@highlandcourt.co.uk

web: www.highlandcourt.co.uk

dir: *2m E of St Austell. A390 E to St Blazey Gate, right onto Biscovey Rd, 300yds on right*

Highland Court Lodge is extremely well presented and maintained, has stunning views over St Austell Bay and is just over one mile from the Eden Project. Its impressive en suite bedrooms have luxurious fabrics and each room opens onto a private patio. There is a lounge with deep sofas, and the terrace shares the fine views. The local Cornish catch features strongly in the freshly prepared dinners, which, like breakfast are not to be missed.

Rooms 5 en suite (2 fmly) (5 GF) S £85–£125; D £110–£190✳
Facilities FTV TVB tea/coffee Cen ht Dinner Last d 10am Wi-fi available
Conf Max 12 Class 12 Board 12 **Parking** 10 **Notes LB** ⊗

★ ★ ★ ★ ★ GUEST ACCOMMODATION

Lower Barn

Bosue, St Ewe PL26 6EU

☎ 01726 844881

e-mail: janie@bosue.co.uk

web: www.bosue.co.uk

dir: *3.5m SW of St Austell. Off B3273 at x-rds signed Lost Gardens of Heligan, Lower Barn signed 1m on right*

The converted barn, tucked away in countryside with easy access to local attractions, has huge appeal. Warm colours create a Mediterranean feel, complemented by informal and genuine hospitality. Bedrooms have a host of extras. Breakfast is served around a large table or on the patio deck overlooking the garden, which also has a hot tub.

Rooms 3 en suite (1 fmly) (1 GF) **Facilities** TVB tea/coffee Cen ht Dinner Last d Breakfast Sauna Gymnasium Hot tub Spa treatments **Parking** 7 **Notes** ⊗ Closed Jan

★ ★ ★ ★ ★ GUEST ACCOMMODATION

Nanscawen Manor House

Prideaux Rd, Luxulyan Valley PL24 2SR

☎ 01726 814488

e-mail: keith@nanscawen.com

web: www.nanscawen.com

(For full entry see St Blazey)

ENGLAND

ST AUSTELL CONTINUED

Premier Collection

★★★★★ GUEST HOUSE
Wisteria Lodge

Boscundle, Tregrehan PL25 3RJ
☎ 01726 810800 📠 0871 661 6213
e-mail: info@wisterialodgehotel.co.uk
web: www.wisterialodgehotel.co.uk

dir: *1m E of town centre off A390*

You are made to feel very welcome at this delightful guest house set in a quiet location on the outskirts of town. The very well-equipped accommodation includes rooms on the ground floor and there is a comfortable sitting room. Skilfully prepared meals are served in the conservatory-dining room, which overlooks the large garden.

Rooms 5 en suite (1 fmly) (2 GF) **Facilities** STV TVB tea/coffee Direct dial from bedrooms Licensed Cen ht Dinner Last d 1pm Hot Tub **Conf** Max 10 Board 10 **Parking** 5 **Notes** ⊗ No children 12yrs No coaches

★★★★ GUEST HOUSE
Hunter's Moon

Chapel Hill, Polgooth PL26 7BU
☎ 01726 66445 📠 01726 66445
e-mail: enquiries@huntersmooncornwall.co.uk

dir: *1.5m SW of town centre. Off B3273 into Polgooth, pass village shop on left, 1st right*

Hunter's Moon lies in a quiet village just a few miles from Heligan and within easy reach of the Eden Project. Service is friendly and attentive and the bedrooms are well equipped for business or leisure. There is a conservatory-lounge and a pretty garden to enjoy during warmer weather. Breakfast is served in the cosy dining room and the nearby village inn serves freshly prepared meals.

Rooms 4 en suite (2 fmly) S £44–£50; D £60–£70✳ **Facilities** FTV TVB tea/coffee Cen ht **Parking** 5 **Notes** ⊗ No children 14yrs No coaches ◉

★★★★ BED & BREAKFAST
Sunnyvale Bed & Breakfast

Hewas Water PL26 7JF
☎ 01726 882572
e-mail: jmuden@aol.com

dir: *4m SW of St Austell. Off A390 in Hewas Water*

This house has pleasant gardens in a peaceful location, and the very friendly proprietor makes you feel most welcome. The bedrooms are

both ground floor, one specifically designed for the disabled, and have an extensive range of facilities. Breakfast is either taken in the main house at separate tables, or for the less able in the bedroom, by prior arrangement.

Rooms 2 annexe en suite (2 GF) D £60–£65 **Facilities** FTV TVB tea/coffee Cen ht **Parking** 4 **Notes** ⊗ No children 16yrs ◉

★★★★ BED & BREAKFAST
Cooperage

37 Cooperage Rd, Trewoon PL25 5SJ
☎ 01726 70497 & 07854 960385
e-mail: lcooperage@tiscali.co.uk
web: www.cooperagebb.co.uk

dir: *1m W of St Austell. On A3058 in Trewoon*

Situated on the edge of the town, this late Victorian, semi-detached granite house has been renovated in a contemporary style. The comfortable bedrooms are well equipped and feature beautifully tiled en suites. Guests are assured of a friendly and relaxed welcome here and the property is conveniently positioned for the numerous amenities and attractions locally. Cooperage is suitable for both business and leisure guests. Pets welcome by arrangement.

Rooms 4 rms (3 en suite) (1 pri facs) S £35–£40; D £55–£60 **Facilities** TVB tea/coffee Cen ht Wi-fi available **Parking** 6 **Notes** LB

★★★★ BED & BREAKFAST
The Elms

14 Penwinnick Rd PL25 5DW
☎ 01726 74981 📠 01726 74981
e-mail: pete@edenbb.co.uk
web: www.edenbb.co.uk

dir: *0.5m SW of town centre. On A390 junct Pondhu Rd*

Well located for the Eden Project or for touring Cornwall, this accommodation offers a relaxed and friendly environment for leisure and business guests. Bedrooms, one with a four-poster bed, are well equipped and there is an inviting lounge. Breakfast is served in the conservatory dining room.

Rooms 3 annexe en suite **Facilities** TVB tea/coffee Cen ht TVL Wi-fi available Golf 18 **Parking** 3 **Notes** ⊗

★★★★ GUEST ACCOMMODATION
Elmswood House

73 Tehidy Rd, Tywardreath PL24 2QD
☎ 01726 814221 📠 01726 814399
e-mail: enquiries@elmswoodhousehotel.co.uk
web: www.elmswoodhousehotel.co.uk

(For full entry see Par)

CONTINUED

★★★★ GUEST ACCOMMODATION
Polgreen Farm
London Apprentice PL26 7AP
☎ 01726 75151
e–mail: polgreen.farm@btinternet.com
web: www.polgreenfarm.co.uk

dir: *1.5m S of St Austell. Off B3273, turn left entering London Apprentice & signed*

Guests return regularly for the friendly welcome at this peaceful accommodation located just south of St Austell. The spacious and well-equipped bedrooms are divided between the main house and an adjoining property, and each building has a comfortable lounge. Breakfast is served in a pleasant conservatory overlooking the garden.

Rooms 3 rms (2 en suite) (1 pri facs) 4 annexe en suite (1 fmly) (1 GF) S £30–£40; D £56–£64 **Facilities** FTV TVB tea/coffee Cen ht TVL **Parking** 8 **Notes** LB ⊗ ☺

★★★★ FARM HOUSE
Poltarrow *(SW998518)*
St Mewan PL26 7DR
☎ 01726 67111 📠 01726 67111 Mrs J Nancarrow
e–mail: enquire@poltarrow.co.uk

dir: *1.5m W of town centre. Off A390 to St Mewan, pass school, 2nd farm on left after 0.5m*

Set in 45 acres of gardens and pasture, this delightful traditional farmhouse retains many of original features, including open fires. The attractive bedrooms are comfortably furnished and decorated with style. Breakfast, cooked on an Aga, is served in the conservatory-dining room overlooking the gardens. An impressive indoor pool is available, together with a sports hall for badminton, bowls and short tennis.

Rooms 3 en suite 2 annexe en suite (1 fmly) S £50; D £75 **Facilities** FTV TVB tea/coffee Cen ht TVL Wi-fi available ⓒ Fishing Pool Table Indoor short tennis, badminton, bowls **Parking** 10 **Notes** LB ⊗ No children 5yrs 45 acres mixed Closed 16 Dec–5 Jan

★★★ GUEST ACCOMMODATION
Arches Bed & Breakfast
78 Bodmin Rd PL25 5AG
☎ 01726 64644
e–mail: nikki@archesbedandbreakfast.co.uk

A traditional bed and breakfast operation within minutes of the town centre with ample off-road parking. Rooms are well

CONTINUED

presented and maintained and hearty breakfast is served in the breakfast room.

Rooms 3 rms (2 en suite) (1 pri facs) **Facilities** FTV TVB tea/coffee Cen ht **Parking** 4 **Notes** ☺

★★★ GUEST HOUSE
T'Gallants
6 Charlestown Rd, Charlestown PL25 3NJ
☎ 01726 70203 📠 01726 70203

dir: *0.5m SE of town off A390 rdbt signed Charlestown*

The fine Georgian house partly dates from 1630. It overlooks the historic port of Charlestown, with its fleet of square-rigged sailing ships. Bedrooms are well presented and spacious, and one has a four-poster bed and views of the port. Breakfast is served in the attractive dining room with a choice of traditional or continental offered. A guest lounge is also available.

Rooms 7 en suite S £45–£50; D £70–£95 **Facilities** TVB tea/coffee Cen ht TVL Wi-fi available **Notes** ⊗ No coaches

---

ST BLAZEY   MAP 02 SX05

Premier Collection
★★★★★ 🏆 GUEST ACCOMMODATION
Penarwyn House
PL24 2DS
☎ 01726 814224 📠 01726 814224
e–mail: stay@penarwyn.co.uk
web: www.penarwyn.co.uk

dir: *A390 W through St Blazey, left at 2nd speed camera, house past school*

This impressive house stands in tranquil surroundings close to main routes, the Eden Project and many attractions. Painstakingly restored, the spacious house offers a host of facilities, and the bedrooms are particularly comfortable and delightfully appointed. Breakfast is another highlight here, and along with the proprietor's most welcoming hospitality, Penarwyn provides a memorable stay.

Rooms 4 en suite (1 fmly) S £68–£95; D £85–£150✱ **Facilities** FTV TVB tea/coffee Cen ht Wi-fi available 3/4 size snooker table **Parking** 6 **Notes** LB ⊗ No children 10yrs Closed 21 Dec–9 Jan

ST BLAZEY CONTINUED

Premier Collection

★★★★★ GUEST ACCOMMODATION
Nanscawen Manor House
Prideaux Rd, Luxulyan Valley PL24 2SR
☎ 01726 814488
e–mail: keith@nanscawen.com
web: www.nanscawen.com

dir: *A390 W to St Blazey, right after railway, Nanscawen 0.75m on right*

This renovated manor house originates from the 14th century and provides a high standard of accommodation, with elegant bedrooms and bathrooms with spa baths. There are extra touches throughout to pamper you, a spacious lounge with a well-stocked honesty bar, and five acres of pleasant gardens with splendid woodland views. Breakfast, served in the conservatory, features fresh local produce.

Rooms 3 en suite S £68–£98; D £78–£122✳ **Facilities** FTV TVB tea/coffee Direct dial from bedrooms Cen ht Wi-fi available ⤚ **Parking** 8 **Notes** ⊗ No children 12yrs

---

ST GENNYS   MAP 02 SX19

★★★★ GUEST ACCOMMODATION
Rosecare Villa Farm
EX23 0BG
☎ 01840 230474
e–mail: info@northcornwallholidays.com

dir: *9m S of Bude on A39, S of Wainhouse Corner*
This family-run establishment is close to the spectacular North Cornish coast, an area with a host of activities on offer. Dating back several hundred years, the house was once a slate captain's house and is now a smallholding complete with a small menagerie. Woodland walks are also available. Bedrooms are situated in the original stone barns surrounding the courtyard, and each has its own separate entrance. Breakfast features locally sourced produce with eggs from the resident hens. Dinner is also available by prior arrangement.

Rooms 5 annexe en suite (5 GF) S £33–£35; D £66–£70 **Facilities** FTV TVB tea/coffee Cen ht Dinner Last d at breakfast **Parking** 8 **Notes LB** Closed 22–28 Dec

---

ST HILARY   MAP 02 SW53

Premier Collection

★★★★★ 🛎 GUEST ACCOMMODATION
Ennys
Trewhella Ln TR20 9BZ
☎ 01736 740262 📠 01736 740055
e–mail: ennys@ennys.co.uk
web: www.ennys.co.uk

dir: *1m N of B3280 Leedstown-Goldsithney road at end of Trewhella Ln*

Set off the beaten track, this 17th-century manor house is a perfect place to unwind. A friendly welcome awaits you, and a complimentary afternoon tea is laid out in the kitchen. Ennys retains much original character and the rooms are impressively furnished. A delightful Cornish breakfast is served in the dining room, using a wealth of fresh local ingredients and home-produced fresh eggs. Three self-catering cottages available.

Rooms 3 en suite 2 annexe en suite (2 fmly) (1 GF) S £70–£115; D £85–£125✳ **Facilities** FTV TVB tea/coffee Cen ht Wi-fi available ⤚ 🦮 **Parking** 8 **Notes** ⊗ No children 5yrs Closed Nov–25 Mar

---

ST IVES   MAP 02 SW54

Premier Collection

★★★★★ GUEST ACCOMMODATION
Jamies
Wheal Whidden, Carbis Bay TR26 2QX
☎ 01736 794718
e–mail: info@jamiesstives.co.uk
web: www.jamiesstives.co.uk

dir: *A3074 to Carbis Bay, onto Pannier Ln, 2nd left*
Accomplished hosts, Felicity and Jamie, provide a most pleasant home for their guests at this attractive Cornish Villa, which has been thoughtfully renovated and stylishly appointed. Bedrooms are spacious and comfortable, all have sea views, and lots of thoughtful extras have been provided. Breakfast is a feature here and is taken in the elegant dining room at a large round table providing a memorable aspect to a stay at Jamies.

Rooms 3 en suite (1 GF) S £100; D £110✳ **Facilities** FTV TVB tea/coffee Cen ht **Parking** 4 **Notes** ⊗ No children 12yrs RS Dec–Feb 🦮

Premier Collection

★★★★★ 🏠 BED & BREAKFAST
Porthglaze

Steeple Ln TR26 2AY
☎ 01736 799409
e–mail: info@porthglaze.co.uk
web: www.porthglaze.co.uk

dir: *A3074 to St Ives, left at Cornish Arms, left onto Steeple Ln, Porthglaze 500yds on left*

Porthglaze is in a quiet residential area just a stroll from St Ives and Carbis Bay. You are made to feel relaxed and at home, and the impressive choice at breakfast is memorable. The spacious bedrooms are particularly well equipped, and there is also a pleasant garden. Parking available.

Rooms 2 en suite (2 GF) D £80–£92 **Facilities** STV TVB tea/coffee Cen ht TVL **Parking** 4 **Notes** ⊗ No children 14yrs

Premier Collection

★★★★★ 🏠 GUEST ACCOMMODATION
Primrose Valley

Porthminster Beach TR26 2ED
☎ 01736 794939 📠 01736 794939
e–mail: info@primroseonline.co.uk
web: www.primroseonline.co.uk

dir: *A3074 to St Ives, 25yds after town sign right onto Primrose Valley, left under bridge, along beach front, turn left back under bridge, property on left*

St Ives is just a short walk from this friendly, family-run establishment close to Porthminster Beach. The atmosphere is light and airy and modernisation provides a good level of comfort. Some bedrooms have balconies with stunning views. There is a lounge and bar area, and dinner is available. Breakfast features local produce and home-made items.

Rooms 9 en suite (2 fmly) D £100–£155✱ **Facilities** TVB tea/coffee Cen ht Dinner Last d 10.30pm Wi-fi available **Parking** 10 **Notes LB** ⊗ No children 8yrs Closed 23–27 Dec RS 2–29 Jan

★★★★ GUEST ACCOMMODATION
Borthalan

Off Boskerris Rd, Carbis Bay TR26 2NQ
☎ 01736 795946 📠 01736 795946
e–mail: borthalanhotel@btconnect.com

dir: *A3074 into Carbis Bay, right onto Boskerris Rd, 1st left onto cul-de-sac*

Quietly situated, this welcoming establishment is just a short walk from Carbis Bay station, from where you can take the 3-minute journey to St Ives without the hassle of car parking. The friendly proprietors provide a relaxing environment, with every effort made to ensure an enjoyable stay. Bedrooms are all well equipped and smartly presented, some with lovely sea views. There is a cosy lounge and an attractive garden, and breakfast is served in the bright dining room.

CONTINUED

Borthalan

Rooms 7 en suite **Facilities** TVB tea/coffee Cen ht TVL **Parking** 7 **Notes** ⊗ No children 12yrs Closed Xmas

★★★★ GUEST ACCOMMODATION
Glanmor

The Belyars TR26 2BX
☎ 01736 795613
e–mail: margaret@glanmor.net

dir: *A3074 to St Ives, left at Porthminster Hotel & up Talland Rd*

The relaxed and friendly atmosphere at the Glanmor draws guests back time after time. It is just a short walk from the town centre and beaches, and offers attractive, well equipped bedrooms. There is a comfortable lounge and conservatory, and the pretty landscaped gardens have seating on warm sunny days. Carefully prepared breakfasts are served in the light and airy dining room.

Rooms 6 en suite (3 fmly) (1 GF) D £52–£72✱ **Facilities** TVB tea/coffee Cen ht TVL Wi-fi available **Parking** 6 **Notes** ⊗ 🚭

★★★★ GUEST ACCOMMODATION
The Nook

Ayr TR26 1EQ
☎ 01736 795913
e–mail: info@nookstives.co.uk
web: www.nookstives.co.uk

dir: *A30 to St Ives left at Natwest, right at rdbt & left at top of hill*

Extensively refurbished in the last few years, the Nook is an ideal base for exploring Cornwall's spectacular coastline, gardens and countryside. The comfortable bedrooms are furnished in a modern, contemporary style and are equipped with numerous facilities. Guests enjoy the wide variety on offer at breakfast, from full English or continental, to scrambled eggs with smoked salmon and chunky sandwiches.

Rooms 10 en suite (2 fmly) S £36–£45; D £72–£95✱ **Facilities** FTV TVB tea/coffee Cen ht TVL Wi-fi available **Parking** 10 **Notes LB** ⊗

ST IVES CONTINUED

★★★★ 🏠 GUEST ACCOMMODATION

Pebble

4 Parc Av TR26 2DN

☎ 01736 794168

e–mail: info@pebble-hotel.co.uk

dir: *A3074 to St Ives, left at NatWest bank, left at mini-rdbt, pass car park, house 150yds on right*

The welcoming proprietors ensure you feel relaxed at this stylish, impeccably maintained house with spectacular views over St Ives Bay. Breakfast is an impressive choice, including vegetarian options, and local produce is used whenever possible. The stylish accommodation is well equipped and there is an inviting lounge.

Rooms 5 en suite D £80–£110✱ **Facilities** FTV TVB tea/coffee Cen ht TVL Wi-fi available **Parking** 6 **Notes** LB ⊗ No children 14yrs Closed Nov–Feb

★★★★ GUEST ACCOMMODATION

The Regent

Fernlea Ter TR26 2BH

☎ 01736 796195 📄 01736 794641

e–mail: keith@regenthotel.com

web: www.regenthotel.com

dir: *In town centre, near bus & railway station*

This popular and attractive property stands on an elevated position convenient for the town centre and seafront. The Regent has well-equipped bedrooms, some with spectacular sea vistas, and the comfortable lounge also has great views. The breakfast choices, including vegetarian, are excellent.

Rooms 9 rms (7 en suite) **Facilities** TVB tea/coffee Cen ht TVL Wi-fi available **Parking** 12 **Notes** ⊗ No children 16yrs

★★★★ GUEST ACCOMMODATION

Treliska

3 Bedford Rd TR26 1SP

☎ 01736 797678 📄 01736 797678

e–mail: info@treliska.com

web: www.treliska.com

dir: *A3074 to St Ives, fork at Porthminster Hotel into town, at T-junct facing Barclays Bank left onto Bedford Rd, house on right*

This stylish, friendly and relaxed home is close to the seafront, restaurants and galleries. There is a refreshing approach here with a contemporary feel throughout. Impressive bathrooms have invigorating showers, while the attractive bedrooms are configured to maximise comfort. Enjoyable, freshly cooked Cornish breakfasts are served in the lounge-dining room with a choice of coffee available at all times to guests. Additional facilities include internet and Wi-fi connections.

Rooms 5 en suite S £40–£60; D £70–£80 **Facilities** FTV TVB tea/coffee Cen ht Wi-fi available **Notes** ⊗ No children 10yrs ♿

★★★★ GUEST ACCOMMODATION

Bay View Guest House

5 Pednolver Ter TR26 2EL

☎ 01736 796765

e–mail: jamesvictorsimmons@hotmail.com

dir: *A30/A3704 to St Ives, follow signs for leisure centre, Pednolver Ter off Albert Rd*

Situated within 250 yards of Porthminster Beach, this small, friendly guesthouse provides comfortable accommodation and a warm welcome. Rear on-site car parking is a bonus.

Rooms 5 rms (3 en suite) (2 pri facs) (1 fmly) S £35✱ **Facilities** TVB tea/coffee TVL **Parking** 5 **Notes** ⊗ No children 5yrs Closed Oct–Etr ♿

★★★★ BED & BREAKFAST

Coombe Farmhouse

TR27 6NW

☎ 01736 740843

e–mail: coombefarmhouse@aol.com

web: www.coombefarmhouse.com

dir: *1.5m W of Lelant. Off A3074 to Lelant Downs*

Built of sturdy granite, this early 19th-century farmhouse is in a delightful location tucked away at the southern foot of Trencrom Hill, yet convenient for St Ives. The comfortable bedrooms are attractively decorated. There is a cosy lounge and substantial breakfasts, featuring farm-fresh eggs, are served in the dining room overlooking the garden.

Rooms 3 rms (2 en suite) (1 pri facs) S £40; D £70–£78✱ **Facilities** tea/coffee Cen ht TVL **Parking** 3 **Notes** ⊗ No children 12yrs Closed Dec ♿

★★★★ GUEST ACCOMMODATION

Edgar's

Chy-an-Creet, Higher Stennack TR26 2HA

☎ 01736 796559 📄 01736 796559

e–mail: stay@edgarshotel.co.uk

web: www.edgarshotel.co.uk

dir: *0.5m W of town centre on B3306, opp Leach Pottery*

High standards of comfort are provided at this friendly, family-run guest accommodation. Public areas are spacious and include a bar and a lounge, and bedrooms, some on the ground floor, are well equipped. Bar snacks are available and breakfast, served in the dining room, includes home-made preserves.

Rooms 8 en suite (2 fmly) (4 GF) S £39–£85; D £58.50–£100✱ **Facilities** TVB tea/coffee Cen ht TVL Wi-fi available **Parking** 8 **Notes** LB ⊗ Closed Nov–Feb

★★★★ BED & BREAKFAST
Halwell

Fore St, Lelant TR26 3EL

☎ 01736 752003

e-mail: RandSRook@aol.com

Situated in a historic village, a short drive from St Ives, Halwell is a detached property set within its own well maintained garden. Guests are assured of a warm friendly welcome at this family home. The bedrooms are particularly well equipped and very comfortable. A varied choice is offered at breakfast, served at separate tables in the dining room, overlooking the garden.

Rooms 3 en suite (2 GF) D £60–£70✷ **Facilities** TVB tea/coffee Cen ht **Parking** 5 **Notes LB** ⊗ No children 12yrs Closed 31Oct–Etr 🐾

★★★★ GUEST ACCOMMODATION
Headland House

Headland Rd, Carbis Bay TR26 2NS

☎ 01736 796647 📠 01736 796647

e-mail: headland.house@btconnect.com

dir: A30 onto A3074 towards St Ives, at Carbis Bay right to Porthepta Rd & 3rd on right

Newly renovated and furnished house with great views over Carbis Bay from many rooms. Headland House is a stylish and comfortable operation with very friendly hosts. Breakfast can be taken in the conservatory, and it benefits from off-road parking.

Rooms 6 en suite 1 annexe en suite (1 fmly) S £50–£75; D £75–£115✷ **Facilities** FTV TVB tea/coffee Cen ht TVL Wi-fi available **Parking** 7 **Notes LB** ⊗ No children 8yrs

★★★★ GUEST ACCOMMODATION
Lamorna Lodge

Boskerris Rd, Carbis Bay TR26 2NG

☎ 01736 795967

e-mail: lamorna@tr26.wanadoo.co.uk

dir: A30 onto A3074, right after playground in Carbis Bay, establishment 200yds on right

A truly genuine welcome is assured at this quietly situated establishment which is just a short walk from Carbis Bay beach. Wonderful views over St Ives Bay to Godrevy Lighthouse can be enjoyed from the spacious lounge, a view also shared by some of the stylish bedrooms. Breakfast and dinner are served in the elegant

CONTINUED

surroundings of the dining room where home-cooked food is prepared from local produce.

Rooms 9 en suite (4 fmly) (2 GF) D £76–£96✷ **Facilities** TVB tea/coffee Cen ht Dinner Last d 5pm **Conf** Max 18 Thtr 18 Class 18 Board 18 **Parking** 9 **Notes LB** ⊗ Closed 5 Nov–10 Mar

★★★★ GUEST HOUSE
The Mustard Tree

Sea View Meadows, St Ives Rd, Carbis Bay TR26 2JX

☎ 01736 795677

e-mail: enquiries@mustard-tree.co.uk

dir: A3074 to Carbis Bay, The Mustard Tree on right opp Methodist church

Set in delightful gardens and having sea views, the attractive house is just a short drive from the centre of St Ives. Alternatively, the coastal path leads from Carbis Bay to St Ives. The pleasant bedrooms are very comfortable and have many extra facilities. A splendid choice is offered at breakfast, with vegetarian or continental options; a range of 'lite bites' are available in the early evening.

Rooms 7 rms (6 en suite) (1 pri facs) (2 fmly) (4 GF) S £30–£38; D £60–£80✷ **Facilities** FTV TVB tea/coffee Cen ht TVL Dinner Last d 10am Wi-fi available **Conf** Max 16 **Parking** 7 **Notes** ⊗ No coaches

★★★★ BED & BREAKFAST
Nancherrow Cottage

7 Fish St TR26 1LT

☎ 01736 798496

e-mail: peterjean@nancherrowcottage.fsnet.co.uk

dir: A30 onto A3074, through Lelant to St Ives, along Harbour to Sloop Inn. Turn left onto Fish St

Situated a stone's throw from the harbour, in the centre of the town, Nancherrow Cottage is an attractive period property, with friendly, enthusiastic owners. The comfortable bedrooms are well equipped and boast numerous, thoughtful extras. Breakfast is served around a communal table, an interesting and varied choice is offered, including a full English cooked breakfast, scrambled eggs and smoked salmon on toasted muffin, and lots more.

Rooms 3 en suite D £75–£90✷ **Facilities** TVB tea/coffee Cen ht **Notes LB** ⊗ No children 12yrs Closed mid Nov–mid Feb 🐾

ST IVES CONTINUED

★★★★ GUEST HOUSE
The Old Count House
1 Trenwith Square TR26 1DQ
☎ 01736 795369 📄 01736 799109
e-mail: counthouse@btconnect.com
web: www.theoldcounthouse-stives.co.uk

dir: Follow signs to St Ives, located between leisure centre and school

Situated in a quiet residential area with on site parking, the Old Count House is a granite stone house, where mine workers collected their wages in Victorian times. Guests are assured of a warm welcome and an extensive choice at breakfast. Bedrooms vary in size, with all rooms being well equipped. The town centre and all its restaurant and 'eateries' is only a five minute walk away.

Rooms 10 rms (9 en suite) (1 pri facs) (2 GF) S £38–£42; D £72–£88✳
Facilities TVB tea/coffee Cen ht TVL Sauna **Parking** 9 **Notes** ✖
No children No coaches Closed 20–29 Dec

★★★★ GUEST HOUSE
Old Vicarage
Parc-an-Creet TR26 2ES
☎ 01736 796124
e-mail: stay@oldvicarage.com
web: www.oldvicarage.com

dir: Off A3074 in town centre onto B3306, 0.5m right into Parc-an-Creet

This former Victorian rectory stands in secluded gardens in a quiet part of St Ives and is convenient for the seaside, town and the Tate. The bedrooms are enhanced by modern facilities. A good choice of local produce is offered at breakfast, plus home-made yoghurt and preserves.

Rooms 5 en suite (4 fmly) S £60–£65; D £80–£90 **Facilities** TVB tea/coffee Licensed Cen ht TVL ♿ **Parking** 12 **Notes** No coaches Closed Dec–Jan

★★★★ GUEST ACCOMMODATION
Poppies
Headland Rd, Carbis Bay TR26 2NX
☎ 01736 796469 & 07756 078341 📄 01736 796469
e-mail: sandie@poppies.me.uk
web: www.poppies.me.uk

dir: A3074 into Carbis Bay, 1st right onto Porthrepta Rd, 3rd right onto Headland Rd

Located close to the beach and within easy reach of St Ives, this friendly home offers pleasant bedrooms with comfortable furnishings. The large lounge contains games and books and there is also a conservatory-lounge. The bar-dining room serves traditional home-cooked hearty breakfasts.

Rooms 8 en suite (1 fmly) (5 GF) S £37–£43; D £64–£76✳
Facilities TVB tea/coffee Cen ht TVL **Parking** 7 **Notes** LB ✖
No children 5yrs Closed 24–28 Dec

★★★★ GUEST HOUSE
Rivendell Guest House
7 Porthminster Ter TR26 2DQ
☎ 01736 794923 📄 01736 794923
e-mail: rivendellstives@aol.com
web: www.rivendell-stives.co.uk

dir: A3074 to St Ives, left at junct, left again & up hill, over road, 50yds on right

Just a short walk from the town centre and harbour, this friendly and welcoming establishment has much to offer those visiting this lovely area. Bedrooms are all well appointed with contemporary comforts; some also have the benefit of sea views. Breakfast and dinner (by prior arrangement) are served in the attractive dining room which leads through to the guest lounge.

Rooms 7 rms (6 en suite) (1 pri facs) (1 fmly) **Facilities** TVB tea/coffee Cen ht TVL Dinner Last d noon **Parking** 5 **Notes** ✖ No coaches Closed 23–25 Dec

★★★★ GUEST ACCOMMODATION
The Rookery
8 The Terrace TR26 2BL
☎ 01736 799401
e-mail: therookerystives@hotmail.com

dir: A3074 through Carbis Bay, right fork at Porthminster Hotel, The Rookery 500yds on left

This friendly establishment stands on an elevated position overlooking the town and sandy beach. The attractive bedrooms include one on the ground floor and a luxurious suite, all of which are well equipped and offer a good level of comfort. Breakfast is served in the first-floor dining room at separate tables.

Rooms 6 en suite (1 GF) **Facilities** STV TVB tea/coffee Cen ht **Parking** 6 **Notes** ✖ No children 7yrs

★★★★ ≜ BED & BREAKFAST
St Dennis

6 Albany Ter TR26 2BS
☎ 01736 795027
e-mail: stdennis007@btopenworld.com

dir: *A3074 to St Ives, pass St Ives Motor Co on right, continue down hill, Albany Ter 1st left, signed Edward Hain Hospital*

St Dennis is a friendly and comfortable place to stay within walking distance of the town and beaches. Breakfast is a real treat with an emphasis upon excellent local organic produce. The comprehensive menu includes plenty of variety for both meat eaters and vegetarians with lighter, healthier options also offered. Bedrooms are attractively decorated and have many thoughtful touches. Ample parking is available.

Rooms 3 en suite D £68–£90 **Facilities** FTV TVB tea/coffee Cen ht **Parking** 5 **Notes** ⊗ No children 12yrs Closed Nov–Feb

★★★★ GUEST ACCOMMODATION
Skidden House

Skidden Hill TR26 2DU
☎ 01736 796899
e-mail: skiddenhouse@tiscali.co.uk
web: www.skiddenhouse.co.uk

dir: *A3074 to St Ives, 1st right after bus/railway station*

Skidden House is in the heart of town and is reputed to have formerly been a jail, brothel and a pub, as well as St Ives' oldest hotel. The accommodation is now much more comfortable and welcoming, with pleasant, well-equipped rooms. Some parking is available.

Rooms 7 en suite (4 fmly) (2 GF) S £35–£42; D £70–£84 **Facilities** TVB tea/coffee Direct dial from bedrooms Cen ht TVL **Parking** 4 **Notes** LB ⊗

★★★★ GUEST ACCOMMODATION
Thurlestone Guest House

St Ives Rd, Carbis Bay TR26 2RT
☎ 01736 796369
e-mail: mandycartwright@btopenworld.com

dir: *A3074 to Carbis Bay, pass convenience store on left, 0.25m on left next to newsagent*

The granite chapel built in 1843 now offers stylish, comfortable accommodation. The welcoming proprietors provide a relaxed environment, and many guests return regularly. Recently totally upgraded, there is a cosy lounge bar, and some of the well-equipped bedrooms have sea views.

Rooms 7 en suite (1 fmly) (1 GF) **Facilities** TVB tea/coffee Cen ht TVL **Parking** 5 **Notes** ⊗

★★★★ GUEST ACCOMMODATION
The Tregorran

Headland Rd, Carbis Bay TR26 2NU
☎ 01736 795889
e-mail: book@carbisbay.com
web: www.carbisbay.com

dir: *Right at Carbis Bay to beach, along Porthrepta Rd, last right onto Headland Rd, Tregorran halfway along*

There are wonderful views of Carbis Bay and St Ives from the friendly, family-run Tregorran. Relax by the pool, in the garden or in the pleasant bar, and there is also a comfortable lounge, and a games room and a gym. Breakfast is served in an airy dining room, which has superb views.

Rooms 18 en suite (5 fmly) (4 GF) **Facilities** TVB tea/coffee Cen ht TVL ↘ Gymnasium Pool Table **Parking** 20 **Notes** Closed Nov–Etr

★★★★ GUEST ACCOMMODATION
Woodside

The Belyars TR26 2DA
☎ 01736 795681
e-mail: woodsidehotel@btconnect.com

dir: *A3074 to St Ives, left at Porthminster Hotel onto Talland Rd, 1st left onto Belyars Ln, Woodside 4th on right*

This attractive house is in a peaceful location overlooking St Ives Bay. The friendly proprietors provide a welcoming and relaxing environment, and the bedrooms, some with sea views, come in a range of sizes. Hearty breakfasts are served in the dining room, and there is a comfortable lounge and a well-stocked bar.

Rooms 10 en suite (3 fmly) S £40–£55; D £80–£120✳ **Facilities** TVB tea/coffee Cen ht TVL ↘ Pool Table **Parking** 12 **Notes** LB ⊗ No children 5yrs

★★★★ ◪ GUEST ACCOMMODATION
Beechwood House

St Ives Rd, Carbis Bay TR26 2SX
☎ 01736 795170 📠 01736 795170
e-mail: beechwood@carbisbay.wanadoo.co.uk

dir: *A3074 for St Ives, through Lelant to Carbis Bay, past Costcutter shop on left*

Rooms 8 en suite (2 fmly) (3 GF) **Facilities** TVB tea/coffee Cen ht TVL **Parking** 8 **Notes** ⊗

ST IVES CONTINUED

★★★ GUEST ACCOMMODATION
The Hollies
4 Talland Rd TR26 2DF
☎ 01736 796605 & 793495 📄 01736 796605
e–mail: theholliesstives@aol.com

dir: *A3074 to St Ives, left at Porthminster Hotel, 500yds bear left, bear left again, 3rd property on right*

The Hollies has an elevated position with fine views, and is within easy walking distance of the town and harbour. Some of the homely bedrooms have sea views, and families are particularly welcome. A hearty breakfast is served in the pleasant dining room.

Rooms 10 en suite (4 fmly) S £45–£60; D £60–£90✳ **Facilities** TVB tea/coffee Cen ht TVL Golf 9 **Parking** 10 **Notes LB** ⊗ No children 3yrs Closed Xmas

★★★ GUEST ACCOMMODATION
Atlantic
8 Atlantic Ter TR26 1JQ
☎ 01736 793957
e–mail: mail@atlantichouse.org.uk

dir: *In town centre via A3306 Fore St*

Situated on the hill above Tate St Ives, the Atlantic has sea views from all rooms. The property is beside a car park and within walking distance of the town's beaches. Bedrooms are well equipped, and a hearty breakfast featuring home-made bread is served in the pleasant front dining room around two large tables.

Rooms 3 en suite **Facilities** TVB tea/coffee Cen ht **Notes** ⊗ 🐾

★★★ GUEST ACCOMMODATION
Horizon
5 Carthew Ter TR26 1EB
☎ 01736 798069

With an elevated position, this family home affords pleasant sea views and is within walking distance of the town centre and beaches. The host welcomes guests as friends and creates a most homely atmosphere. Some of the attractive bedrooms have wonderful views, and there is a comfortable lounge. A traditional English cooked breakfast is served around a communal table. Dinner is available by prior arrangement and is house-party style.

Rooms 3 en suite **Facilities** Cen ht TVL Dinner Last d 10am **Parking** 2 **Notes** ⊗ No children Closed Nov–Apr 🐾

★★★ GUEST ACCOMMODATION
Portarlington
11 Parc Bean TR26 1EA
☎ 01736 797278 📄 01736 797278
e–mail: info@portarlington.co.uk
web: www.portarlington.co.uk

This pleasant home is convenient for the town, beaches and Tate St Ives. The friendly proprietors have long welcomed guests to their home and many return regularly. Bedrooms are well furnished and some have sea views. There is a comfortable lounge, and enjoyable breakfasts are served in the attractive dining room.

Rooms 4 en suite (3 fmly) **Facilities** TVB tea/coffee Cen ht TVL **Parking** 4 **Notes** ⊗ No children 3yrs Closed Nov–Jan 🐾

★★★ GUEST ACCOMMODATION
Porthminster View
13 Draycott Ter TR26 2EF
☎ 01736 795850 📄 01736 796811
e–mail: enquiry@porthminster.com
web: www.porthminster.com

dir: *A3074 entering town, 300yds past Ford station right onto Draycott Ter*

Built around 1896, this relaxed, family-friendly establishment was formerly home to the local stationmaster. It stands high above Porthminster Beach and has spectacular views. The bedrooms are thoughtfully equipped. Guests can use a well-appointed lounge, which has many books and videos. The portions at breakfast are generous.

Rooms 6 en suite (1 fmly) **Facilities** TVB tea/coffee Cen ht TVL **Parking** 1 **Notes** ⊗ No children 11yrs

★★★ GUEST HOUSE
St Margaret's Guest House
3 Parc Av TR26 2DN
☎ 01736 795785
e–mail: btrevena@aol.com
web: www.stmargaretsguesthouse.co.uk

dir: *A3074 to town centre, left onto Gabriel St & The Stennack, left onto Parc Av*

Guests feel comfortable at St Margaret's, with its panoramic views of the town and bay, and just a short walk from the sandy beaches. Breakfast is served in a pleasant dining room and dinner is available by arrangement.

Rooms 4 en suite (1 fmly) **Facilities** TVB tea/coffee Dinner Last d 8pm **Parking** 3 **Notes** No coaches

★★★ INN
Sloop
The Wharf TR26 1LP
☎ 01736 796584 📄 01736 793322
e–mail: sloopinn@btinternet.com
web: www.sloop-inn.co.uk

dir: *On St Ives harbour by middle slipway*

This attractive, historic inn has an imposing position on the harbour. Each of the guest rooms has a nautical name, many with pleasant views, and all have impressive modern facilities. A good choice of dishes is offered at lunch and dinner in the atmospheric restaurant-bar.

Rooms 18 rms (15 en suite) (6 fmly) (2 GF) (5 smoking) D £86–£90✱ **Facilities** FTV TVB tea/coffee Cen ht Dinner Last d 10pm Wi-fi available **Parking** 6 **Notes** LB No coaches

★★★ GUEST HOUSE
27 The Terrace
TR26 2BP
☎ 01736 797450 📄 01736 793623

dir: *On A3074 near town centre*

Well-located with splendid views across the harbour and St Ives Bay, this family-run property offers spacious bedrooms, many of which have sea views. Hearty breakfasts are served in the breakfast room overlooking the bay, and parking is available for all guests.

Rooms 7 en suite (2 fmly) (2 GF) **Facilities** TVB tea/coffee Licensed Cen ht TVL **Parking** 9 **Notes** No coaches Closed 24–26 Dec

★★★ BED & BREAKFAST
Wheal-e-Mine Bed & Breakfast
9 Belmont Ter TR26 1DZ
☎ 01736 795051 📄 01736 795051
e–mail: whealemine@btinternet.com
web: www.whealemine.co.uk

dir: *A3074 into town, left at x-rds onto B3306, right at rdbt, left at top of hill*

Guests are assured of a warm, friendly welcome at this Victorian, terraced property, which over the last few years has been fully upgraded with style and flair. Bedrooms are well appointed and each boasts distant sea views. A hearty breakfast is served each morning in the attractive dining room. On-site parking at the rear of the property is an added bonus.

Rooms 3 rms (2 en suite) (1 pri facs) (1 fmly) D £60–£76✱ **Facilities** TVB tea/coffee Cen ht **Parking** 3 **Notes** LB ⊗ No children 18yrs Closed Nov–Mar 🐾

ST JUST (NEAR LAND'S END) MAP 02 SW33

★★ INN
The Wellington
Market Square TR19 7HD
☎ 01736 787319 📄 01736 787906
e–mail: wellingtonhotel@msn.com

dir: *6m W of Penzance*

This friendly inn, situated in busy Market Square, offers comfortable accommodation and is popular with locals and visitors alike. Bedrooms are spacious and well equipped. Home-cooked food and local ales from the well-stocked bar make for a pleasant stay.

Rooms 5 en suite 6 annexe en suite (4 fmly) (3 GF) S £35–£40; D £60–£75✱ **Facilities** TVB tea/coffee Direct dial from bedrooms Cen ht Dinner Last d 9pm Pool Table **Conf** Max 20 **Notes** LB

ST KEVERNE MAP 02 SW72

★★★ GUEST HOUSE
Gallen-Treath Guest House
Porthallow TR12 6PL
☎ 01326 280400 📄 01326 280400
e–mail: gallentreath@btclick.com

dir: *1.5m S of St Keverne in Porthallow*

Gallen-Treath has super views over the countryside and sea from its elevated position above Porthallow. Bedrooms are individually decorated and feature many personal touches. Guests can relax in the large, comfortable lounge complete with balcony. Hearty breakfasts and dinners (by arrangement) are served in the bright dining room.

Rooms 5 rms (4 en suite) (1 pri facs) (1 fmly) (1 GF) S £25–£30; D £50–£60✱ **Facilities** FTV TVB tea/coffee Licensed Cen ht TVL Dinner Last d at breakfast **Parking** 6

ST MAWGAN   MAP 02 SW86

★★★★ INN
The Falcon
TR8 4EP
☎ 01637 860225 📄 01637 860884
e–mail: enquiries@thefalconinn-newquay.co.uk
web: www.thefalconinn-newquay.co.uk

dir: *In village centre*

The delightful early 19th-century inn stands opposite the village church in a quiet wooded valley. It is popular with locals and has a friendly atmosphere, with warming log fires. Bedrooms vary in size and are well equipped. There is a good choice for lunch and dinner, including local fish and cheeses.

Rooms 2 en suite D £84✳ **Facilities** TVB tea/coffee Direct dial from bedrooms Cen ht Dinner Last d 9.15pm Pool Table **Parking** 12 **Notes** RS Winter

---

SALTASH   MAP 03 SX45

★★★★ 🍴 🍷 FARM HOUSE
Smeaton Farm *(SX387634)*
PL12 6RZ
☎ 01579 351833 📄 01579 351833 Mr & Mrs Jones
e–mail: info@smeatonfarm.co.uk
web: www.smeatonfarm.co.uk

dir: *1m N of Hatt and 1m S of St Mellion just off A388*

This elegant Georgian farmhouse is surrounded by 450 acres of rolling Cornish farmland, providing a wonderfully peaceful place to stay. Home to the Jones family, the atmosphere is relaxed and hospitable, with every effort made to ensure a comfortable and rewarding break. Bedrooms are spacious, light and airy. Enjoyable dinners often feature home-reared meats and the sausages at breakfast come highly recommended.

Rooms 3 en suite (1 fmly) S £45–£55; D £60–£80 **Facilities** FTV TVB tea/coffee Licensed Cen ht TVL Dinner Last d 5pm Wi-fi available Riding **Parking** 8 **Notes** LB ⊗ ch fac 450 acres arable beef sheep organic

★★★★ INN
Weary Friar Inn
Pillaton PL12 6QS
☎ 01579 350238 📄 01579 350238
web: www.wearyfriar.co.uk

dir: *5m NW of Saltash. Off A388 into Pillaton*

Well located for touring east Cornwall and west Devon, this extended inn stands next to the medieval village church and is popular with locals and tourists. There are open fires, a wealth of beams, homely bedrooms, and a good choice of imaginative food.

Rooms 13 en suite **Facilities** TVB tea/coffee Cen ht TVL Dinner Last d 9pm **Conf** Max 45 **Parking** 30 **Notes** ⊗

★★★ GUEST ACCOMMODATION
Crooked Inn
Stoketon Cross, Trematon PL12 4RZ
☎ 01752 848177 📄 01752 843203
e–mail: info@crooked-inn.co.uk

dir: *1.5m NW of Saltash. A38 W from Saltash, 2nd left to Trematon, sharp right*

The friendly animals that freely roam the courtyard add to the relaxed country style of this delightful inn. The spacious bedrooms are well equipped, and freshly cooked dinners are available in the bar and conservatory. Breakfast is served in the cottage-style dining room.

Rooms 18 annexe rms (15 en suite) (5 fmly) (7 GF) S fr £52; D fr £80 **Facilities** TVB tea/coffee Cen ht Dinner ⊀ **Conf** Max 60 **Parking** 45 **Notes** Closed 25 Dec

See advert on opposite page

★★★ INN
The Holland Inn
Callington Rd, Hatt PL12 6PJ
☎ 01752 844044 📄 01752 849701
e–mail: hollandinn@myopal.net
web: www.hollandinn.co.uk

dir: *2m NW of Saltash on A388*

This popular country inn provides spacious and comfortable accommodation in countryside near the A38. The attractive bedrooms are in an annexe. The wide choice for lunch and dinner includes a carvery, and a good selection of ales and wines is available at the bar.

CONTINUED

Rooms 30 en suite (5 fmly) (30 GF) (11 smoking) S £45–£50; D £45–£50✱ (room only) **Facilities** FTV TVB tea/coffee Direct dial from bedrooms Cen ht Dinner Last d 9.30pm Pool Table **Conf** Max 20 **Parking** 30 **Notes** LB ⊗

SCILLY, ISLES OF (ST MARY'S) MAP 02 SV91

★★★★ GUEST HOUSE
Crebinick House

Church St TR21 0JT
☎ 01720 422968
e–mail: aa@crebinick.co.uk
web: www.crebinick.co.uk

dir: *Crebinick House 500yds from quay through Hugh Town. Airport bus to Crebinick House*

Many guests return to this friendly, family-run house close to the town centre and seafront. The granite Crebinick dates from 1760 and its smart bedrooms, with two on the ground floor, are well equipped. There is a quiet lounge for relaxing.

Rooms 6 en suite (2 GF) D £70–£84✱ **Facilities** TVB tea/coffee Cen ht TVL **Notes** ⊗ No children 10yrs No coaches Closed Nov–Mar ⊛

SENNEN   MAP 02 SW32

★★★★ BED & BREAKFAST
Mayon Farmhouse

TR19 7AD
☎ 01736 871757
e–mail: mayonfarmhouse@hotmail.co.uk
web: www.mayonfarmhouse.co.uk

dir: *A30 into Sennen, driveway opp Post Office*

Guests receive a genuine welcome and a cream tea at this 19th-century, granite former farmhouse. About one mile from Land's End, and conveniently situated for visiting the Minack Theatre, it has country and distant coastal views. The attractive bedrooms are comfortable and well equipped, and an imaginative choice is offered at breakfast.

Rooms 3 en suite (1 fmly) D £80 **Facilities** FTV TVB tea/coffee Cen ht TVL Wi-fi available **Parking** 30 **Notes** LB ⊗ No children 8yrs

---

TINTAGEL   MAP 02 SX08

★★★★ GUEST HOUSE
Pendrin House

Atlantic Rd PL34 0DE
☎ 01840 770560
e–mail: info@pendrintintagel.co.uk
web: www.pendrintintagel.co.uk

dir: *Through village, pass entrance to Tintagel Castle, last house on right before Headlands Caravan Park*

Located close to coastal walks, castle and the town centre, this Victorian house provides comfortable accommodation with most rooms having sea or country views. Delicious evening meals, using quality fresh ingredients, are available by arrangement. There is a cosy lounge.

CONTINUED

Rooms 9 rms (4 en suite) (3 pri facs) (2 fmly) S £25–£30; D £56–£70✱ **Facilities** TVB tea/coffee Cen ht TVL Dinner Last d 8.30pm **Parking** 6 **Notes** ⊗ No children 4yrs No coaches

★★★★ 🅰 GUEST HOUSE
The Bluff Centre

Treknow PL34 0EP
☎ 01840 770033 & 770920 📄 01840 770033
e–mail: book@bluffcentre.co.uk
web: www.bluffcentre.co.uk

dir: *A39 take B3314 over x-rds, right onto B3263 to Tintagel, left into Treknow*

Rooms 9 rms (6 pri facs) (1 fmly) (6 GF) S £30–£40; D £60–£70✱ **Facilities** FTV TVB tea/coffee Licensed Cen ht TVL Dinner Last d noon Wi-fi available Games room & library **Conf** Max 20 **Parking** 6 **Notes** LB ⊗ No coaches Closed 22 Dec–3 Jan

ENGLAND

TINTAGEL CONTINUED

★★★★ Ⓐ BED & BREAKFAST
The Cottage Teashop
Bossiney Rd PL34 0AH
☎ 01840 770639

dir: *Off A30, 2m past Launceston junct onto A395. Follow signs to Camelford then Tintagel*

Rooms 3 en suite 1 annexe en suite (1 GF) D £50–£60✳ **Facilities** TVB tea/coffee Cen ht **Parking** 4 **Notes LB** No children 12yrs Closed 25–26 Dec

★★★ INN
Port William Inn
Trebarwith Strand PL34 0HB
☎ 01840 770230 📄 01840 770936

The Port William has a superb location, perched on the cliff-side just south of Tintagel. The smartly appointed bedrooms all have wonderful sea views with the sound of the waves below ensuring a restful sleep. The spacious bar-restaurant has a conservatory and outside area, where the extensive menu can be enjoyed along with the spectacular scenery.

Rooms 8 en suite (1 fmly) S £69–£85; D £89–£105✳ **Facilities** TVB tea/coffee Cen ht Dinner Last d 8.45pm Wi-fi available Pool Table **Conf** Max 40 Thtr 40 Class 40 Board 40 **Parking** 45 **Notes LB** Civ Wed 150

★★★ BED & BREAKFAST
Tregosse House
Treknow PL34 0EP
☎ 01840 779230
e–mail: enquiries@tregossehouse.co.uk

dir: *A30 onto A395 to Tintagel, signed Treknow. At Atlantic View Hotel bear right, 0.5m on right*

Surrounded by open farmland, Tregosse House boasts probably one of the best views of the sea in North Cornwall. This family home, which has undergone extensive upgrading over the last few years, welcomes guests throughout the year, and offers a hearty, freshly cooked breakfast served at separate tables.

Rooms 3 en suite S £42–£51; D £50–£76✳ **Facilities** TVB tea/coffee Cen ht **Parking** 1 **Notes LB** ⊗ No children 12yrs

TRURO
MAP 02 SW84

★★★★ GUEST HOUSE
Bissick Old Mill
Ladock TR2 4PG
☎ 01726 882557
e–mail: enquiries@bissickoldmill.plus.com

dir: *6m NE of Truro. Off B3275 in Ladock village centre by Falmouth Arms pub*

This charming mill, family run, dates back some 300 years. Low ceilings, beams, stone walls and an impressive fireplace all contribute to its character. Equally inviting is the hospitality extended to guests, who are instantly made welcome. The breakfast menu offers a range of hot dishes, is freshly prepared and is a memorable aspect of any stay.

Rooms 3 en suite 1 annexe en suite (1 GF) S £50–£60; D £65–£90 **Facilities** TVB tea/coffee Direct dial from bedrooms Cen ht TVL Wi-fi available **Parking** 6 **Notes LB** ⊗ No coaches

★★★★ FARM HOUSE
Bodrean Manor Farm (SW851480)
Trispen TR4 9AG
☎ 01872 273227 & 07970 955857 Mrs M Marsh
e–mail: bodrean@hotmail.co.uk
web: www.bodreanmanorfarm.co.uk

dir: *3m NE of Truro. A30 onto A39 towards Truro, left after Trispen village signed Frogmore & Trehane, farm driveway 100yds*

This friendly farm house is located in peaceful countryside, convenient for Truro or as a touring base. It has all the charm of an historic house but is styled and fitted with modern facilities. Bedrooms are thoughtfully and extensively equipped, and the bathrooms are well

CONTINUED

provisioned with soft towels and a host of toiletries. The home-cooked breakfast served in the smartly appointed dining room, around a large communal table, is a feature. Storage for motorbikes and cycles is available.

Rooms 3 rms (2 en suite) (1 pri facs) (1 fmly) **Facilities** TVB tea/coffee Cen ht TVL **Parking** 6 **Notes** ⊗ 40 acres mixed ⊛

★★★★ GUEST ACCOMMODATION
Manor Cottage

Tresillian TR2 4BN
☎ 01872 520212
e–mail: manorcottage@live.co.uk

dir: *3m E of Truro on A390, on left opp river*

Located just a few minutes drive of Truro this well-run bed and breakfast is friendly and comfortable. Breakfast is served in the conservatory and dinner is available with prior notice.

Rooms 5 rms (2 en suite) (1 pri facs) (1 fmly) S £34–£45; D £60–£82 **Facilities** TVB tea/coffee Dinner Last d 7.30pm **Parking** 8 **Notes** LB ⊗

★★★★ BED & BREAKFAST
Oxturn House

Ladock TR2 4NQ
☎ 01726 884348
e–mail: oxturnhouse@hotmail.com
web: www.oxturnhouse.co.uk

dir: *6m NE of Truro. B3275 into Ladock, onto lane opp Falmouth Arms, up hill 200yds, 1st right after end 30mph sign, Oxturn on right*

A friendly welcome is assured at this large family house, set slightly above the village and close to a pub and several dining venues. Bedrooms are spacious and a pleasant lounge is available. In summer you can enjoy the country views from the patio. Hearty breakfasts are served in the dining room.

Rooms 2 rms (1 en suite) (1 pri facs) D £58–£68 **Facilities** TVB tea/coffee Cen ht TVL Wi-fi available **Parking** 4 **Notes** ⊗ No children 12yrs Closed Dec–Jan ⊛

★★★★ INN
The Whitehouse Inn & Luxury Lodge

Penhallow TR4 9LQ
☎ 01872 573306 📠 01872 572062
e–mail: whitehouseinn@btconnect.com
web: www.whitehousecornwall.co.uk

dir: *A3075 between Newquay and Redruth*

This popular inn now offers recently constructed, very well appointed bedrooms. Conveniently located mid-way between Truro and Newquay, the Whitehouse Inn has a busy bar and restaurant, appealing to all palates and pockets. In addition to the local and international artists performing at weekends, widescreen TVs, pool tables and both indoor and outdoor children's play areas are provided. A wide range of meals is available, including the carvery which offers great value for money.

Rooms 12 en suite (3 fmly) (6 GF) **Facilities** FTV TVB tea/coffee Direct dial from bedrooms Lift Cen ht Dinner Last d 9pm Wi-fi available Golf 9 Fishing Pool Table Go-Karts Crazy golf **Parking** 200 **Notes** ⊗

★★★ BED & BREAKFAST
Spires

45 Treyew Rd TR1 2BY
☎ 01872 277621

dir: *0.5m W of town centre on A39, opp Truro City Football Club*

This comfortable establishment enjoys a homely atmosphere and has a friendly host. The city centre is just a short drive away, or a walk for the more energetic (downhill there, uphill back). Bedrooms are light and airy; one room is spacious and has a splendid view of the city and cathedral. Breakfast is served in the cosy dining room. The nearby pub-restaurant offers an extensive choice of meals.

Rooms 2 rms (1 en suite) (1 pri facs) (1 fmly) S £35–£40; D £52–£58✱ **Facilities** TVB tea/coffee Cen ht **Parking** 2 **Notes** ⊗ ⊛

★★★ 🏠 GUEST ACCOMMODATION
Cliftons

46 Tregolls Rd TR1 1LA
☎ 01872 274116 📠 01872 274116
e–mail: cliftonsbandb@hotmail.com

dir: *0.5m NE of city centre on A390*

This lovely Victorian property has character, provides a relaxed atmosphere and is within walking distance of the city centre. Bedrooms, some on the ground floor, have considerate extras. There is a lounge for guest use, which exhibits a large tropical fish tank. The breakfast menu offers a good choice of dishes in the bright dining room.

Rooms 6 en suite (1 fmly) (1 GF) S £35–£45; D £56 **Facilities** TVB tea/coffee Cen ht TVL **Parking** 6 **Notes** ⊗

★★★ FARM HOUSE
Great Hewas Farm *(SW915531)*

Grampound Rd TR2 4EP
☎ 01726 882218 📠 01726 882218 Mrs A D Dymond
e–mail: greathewas@tiscali.co.uk.

dir: *From A30 follow Grampound Rd 2.25m, continue over x-rds, farm entrance is 500yds on right*

Rurally located at the end of its own long drive, guests are welcomed here with a cream tea, served in the conservatory overlooking the surrounding countryside. The bedrooms are comfortably furnished, one especially suitable for use as a family unit. A hearty breakfast is served each morning at separate tables.

Rooms 2 en suite D £55✱ **Facilities** TVB tea/coffee Cen ht **Parking** available **Notes** ⊗ No children 10yrs 140 acres arable beef Closed Nov–Mar RS Apr–Oct ⊛

TRURO CONTINUED

★★★ FARM HOUSE
Polsue Manor Farm (SW858462)

Tresillian TR2 4BP
☎ 01872 520234 📄 01872 520616 Mrs G Holliday
e–mail: geraldineholliday@hotmail.com

dir: *2m NE of Truro. Farm entrance on A390 at S end of Tresillian*
The 190-acre sheep farm is in peaceful countryside a short drive from Truro. The farmhouse provides a relaxing break from the city, with hearty breakfasts and warm hospitality. The spacious dining room has pleasant views and three large communal tables. Bedrooms do not offer televisions but there is a homely lounge equipped with a television and video recorder with a selection of videos for viewing.

Rooms 5 rms (2 en suite) (3 fmly) (1 GF) **Facilities** tea/coffee TVL **Parking** 5 **Notes** 190 acres mixed sheep horses working Closed 21 Dec–2 Jan

★★★ BED & BREAKFAST
The Terrace

2 Coronation Ter TR1 3HJ
☎ 01872 274514
e–mail: theterracecornwall@hotmail.co.uk

dir: *Opp railway station*
Located just a short distance from the city centre and close to the railway station, this Victorian accommodation is attentively cared for. Bedrooms, although not spacious, are clean and bright. A freshly prepared traditional English breakfast is taken in the pleasant dining room at the rear of the house.

Rooms 3 rms S fr £30; D fr £60✳ **Facilities** TVB tea/coffee Cen ht **Notes** No children 8yrs ●

★★★ FARM HOUSE
Trevispian Vean (SW850502)

St Erme TR4 9AT
☎ 01872 279514 Mr & Mrs E Dymond

dir: *3m N of Truro. A30 onto A39 for Truro, 2nd left in Trispin, 0.5m sharp left, farm 500yds on left*
This busy family-run farm is a good base for exploring the area. You are assured of a friendly welcome and many guests return regularly. Freshly cooked farmhouse breakfasts are served in the spacious dining room at separate tables.

Rooms 3 en suite (1 fmly) **Facilities** TVB tea/coffee TVL Fishing Snooker Pool Table **Parking** 20 **Notes** ⊗ 300 acres arable/pigs Closed Oct–Mar ●

VERYAN
MAP 02 SW93

★★★★ INN
The New Inn

TR2 5QA
☎ 01872 501362 📄 01872 501078
e–mail: jack@newinn-veryan.fsnet.co.uk

dir: *In village centre*
Popular with visitors and locals, the New Inn is a good base for touring the Roseland peninsula. Bedrooms are brightly decorated and have thoughtful extras. Dining is an enjoyable experience: fresh local produce graces much of the menu and the changing specials.

Rooms 3 rms (2 en suite) (1 pri facs) S £35; D £70✳ **Facilities** TVB tea/ coffee Cen ht Dinner Last d 9pm **Notes** ⊗ No children 14yrs No coaches

ZENNOR
MAP 02 SW43

★★★ ◉◉ INN
The Gurnard's Head

Treen TR26 3DE
☎ 01736 796928
e–mail: enquiries@gurnardshead.co.uk

dir: *5m from St Ives on B3306, 4.5m from Penzance via New Mill*
Ideally located for enjoying the beautiful coastline, this inn offers atmospheric public areas. The style is relaxed and very popular with walkers, keen to rest their weary legs. A log fire in the bar provides a warm welcome on colder days and on warmer days, outside seating is available. Lunch and dinner, featuring local home cooked food, is available either in the bar or the adjoining restaurant area. The dinner menu is not extensive but there are interesting choices and everything is home made, including the bread. Breakfast is served around a grand farm-house table.

Rooms 7 en suite S £60–£82.50; D £82.50–£140✳ **Facilities** tea/coffee Dinner Last d 9.30pm Wi-fi available **Parking** 40 **Notes** No coaches Closed 25 Dec

CUMBRIA

ALSTON   MAP 18 NY74

See also Cowshill (Co Durham)

★★★★ GUEST HOUSE
Lowbyer Manor Country House

Hexham Rd CA9 3JX

☎ 01434 381230 ▤ 01434 381425

e–mail: stay@lowbyer.com

web: www.lowbyer.com

dir: *250yds N of village centre on A686. Pass South Tynedale Railway on left, turn right*

Located on the edge of the village, this Grade II listed Georgian building retains many original features, which are highlighted by the furnishings and decor. Cosy bedrooms are filled with a wealth of thoughtful extras and day rooms include an elegant dining room, a comfortable lounge and bar equipped with lots of historical artefacts.

Rooms 9 en suite (1 fmly) S £33–£45; D £66–£80 **Facilities** TVB tea/coffee Licensed Cen ht **Parking** 9 **Notes LB** No coaches

★★★★ GUEST ACCOMMODATION
Nent Hall Country House

CA9 3LQ

☎ 01434 381584 ▤ 01434 382668

web: www.nenthall.com

dir: *From main cobbled street turn left at top onto A689. House 2m on right*

Enthusiastic new owners have considerably upgraded this delightful old house that stands in well-kept gardens. Warm and friendly hospitality is provided, with well-appointed and comfortable accommodation, some rooms being on the ground floor and others being suitable for families. There are two comfortable lounges and a pleasant bar serving bar meals and light snacks as well as a more formal dining room.

Rooms 18 en suite (3 fmly) (9 GF) **Facilities** TVB tea/coffee Direct dial from bedrooms TVL **Parking** 100 **Notes** ⊗ Civ Wed 200

AMBLESIDE   MAP 18 NY30

Premier Collection

★★★★★ ◉◉ INN
Drunken Duck

Barngates LA22 0NG

☎ 015394 36347 ▤ 015394 36781

e–mail: info@drunkenduckinn.demon.co.uk

web: www.drunkenduckinn.co.uk

dir: *B5285 S from Ambleside towards Hawkshead, 2.5m signed right, 0.5m up hill*

This 400-year-old, traditional coaching inn has been stylishly modernised to offer a high standard of accommodation. Superior

CONTINUED

rooms are in a courtyard house looking out over private gardens and a tarn. The bar retains its original character and is the hub of the inn. Fresh, local produce features on the imaginative menus served there and in the cosy restaurant. The on-site brewery ensures a fine selection of award-winning ales.

Rooms 8 en suite 8 annexe en suite (4 GF) S fr £90; D fr £120✳
Facilities TVB Direct dial from bedrooms Cen ht Dinner Last d 9pm Wi-fi available Fishing **Parking** 40 **Notes** ⊗ No coaches

★★★★ ⌂ GUEST ACCOMMODATION
The Fisherbeck

Lake Rd LA22 0DH

☎ 015394 33215 ▤ 015394 33600

e–mail: email@fisherbeckhotel.co.uk

web: www.fisherbeckhotel.co.uk

Set on the southern approach to the town, this well-presented and friendly establishment offers a high standard of accommodation. Many of the spacious, modern bedrooms have fine views. There is a choice of lounges, where refreshments are served, and the split-level breakfast room provides many interesting dishes.

Rooms 18 en suite (2 fmly) (4 GF) S £33–£65; D £60–£130✳
Facilities TVB tea/coffee Direct dial from bedrooms Cen ht TVL Wi-fi available Use of nearby leisure club, free fishing available **Conf** Max 18 **Parking** 20 **Notes LB** ⊗ Closed 24 Dec–24 Jan

★★★★ GUEST ACCOMMODATION
Lake House

Waterhead Bay LA22 0HD

☎ 015394 32360 ▤ 015394 31474

e–mail: info@lakehousehotel.co.uk

dir: *Exit M6 signed A591, Ambleside. Pass Ambleside sign, continue past lights, 1st right*

Set on a hillside with lake views, this delightful house has very stylish accommodation and a homely atmosphere. The bedrooms are all individual in style and include many homely extras. Dinner is available at the nearby sister property with complimentary transport, and leisure facilities are available there too. Breakfast is an interesting and substantial cold buffet.

Rooms 12 en suite (3 fmly) (2 GF) **Facilities** TVB tea/coffee Cen ht TVL Wi-fi available **Parking** 12 **Notes** ⊗

AMBLESIDE CONTINUED

★★★★ GUEST HOUSE
Riverside

Under Loughrigg LA22 9LJ

☎ 015394 32395 📄 015394 32440

e–mail: info@riverside-at-ambleside.co.uk

web: www.riverside-at-ambleside.co.uk

dir: *A593 from Ambleside to Coniston, over stone bridge, right onto Under Loughrigg Ln, Riverside 150yds left*

A friendly atmosphere prevails at this refurbished Victorian house, situated on a quiet lane by the River Rothay, below Loughrigg Fell. Bedrooms, all with lovely views, are very comfortable, stylishly furnished and feature homely extras; some have spa baths. A log-burning stove warms the lounge in winter. Guests can use the garden, which has seating for morning and evening sun.

Rooms 6 en suite (1 fmly) **Facilities** TVB tea/coffee Licensed Cen ht TVL Fishing Jacuzzi **Parking** 15 **Notes** ⊗ No children 5yrs No coaches Closed Xmas & New Year

★★★★ INN
Wateredge Inn

Waterhead Bay LA22 0EP

☎ 015394 32332 📄 015394 31878

e–mail: rec@wateredgeinn.co.uk

web: www.wateredgeinn.co.uk

dir: *On A59, at Waterhead, 1m S of Ambleside. Inn at end of promenade by lake*

This modern inn has an idyllic location on the shore of Windermere at Waterhead Bay. The pretty bedrooms are particularly smart and generally spacious, and all offer a high standard of quality and comfort.

CONTINUED

The airy bar-restaurant opens onto attractive gardens, which have magnificent lake views. There is also a comfortable lounge, bar and dining area.

Wateredge Inn

Rooms 15 en suite 7 annexe en suite (4 fmly) (3 GF) S £40–£65; D £80–£110✳ **Facilities** TVB tea/coffee Cen ht Dinner Last d 9pm Wi-fi available Complimentary membership of nearby leisure club **Parking** 40 **Notes LB** Closed 25–26 Dec

★★★★ GUEST HOUSE
Ambleside Lodge

Rothay Rd LA22 0EJ

☎ 015394 31681 📄 015394 34547

e–mail: enquiries@ambleside-lodge.com

web: www.ambleside-lodge.com

Located close to the centre of this historic market town, this Grade II listed 18th-century residence has a peaceful atmosphere. The stylishly decorated, elegant accommodation includes attractive bedrooms with antique and contemporary pieces, including four-poster beds. Attentive, personal service is provided.

Rooms 18 en suite (8 GF) **Facilities** FTV TVB tea/coffee Cen ht Wi-fi available **Parking** 20

★★★★ GUEST ACCOMMODATION
Brathay Lodge
Rothay Rd LA22 0EE
☎ 015394 32000
e–mail: brathay@globalnet.co.uk

dir: One-way system in town centre, Lodge on right opp church

This traditional property has been refurbished in a bright contemporary style. The pine-furnished bedrooms are mainly very spacious; some share a communal balcony and some of the ground-floor rooms have their own entrance. All rooms have spa baths. Breakfast is continental, self-service in the lounge or can be taken to your bedroom.

Rooms 14 en suite 7 annexe en suite (5 fmly) (6 GF) D £60–£129✳
Facilities TVB tea/coffee Cen ht Wi-fi available Use of Langdale Country Club **Parking** 24 **Notes** LB

★★★★ GUEST HOUSE
Broadview Guest House
Lake Rd LA22 0DN
☎ 015394 32431
e–mail: enquiries@broadviewguesthouse.co.uk
web: www.broadviewguesthouse.co.uk

dir: On A591 south side of Ambleside, opposite Garden Centre

Just a short walk from the centre of Ambleside this friendly, comfortable, non-smoking house offers thoughtfully equipped bedrooms and warm hospitality. Hearty breakfasts are served in the pleasant dining room.

Rooms 6 rms (3 en suite) (1 pri facs) D £50–£90✳ **Facilities** TVB tea/coffee Cen ht Wi-fi available **Notes** LB ⊗ No coaches

★★★★ GUEST HOUSE
Cherry Garth
Old Lake Rd LA22 0DH
☎ 015394 33128 ▤ 015394 33885
e–mail: reception@cherrygarth.com

dir: A591 N into Ambleside, over lights, 800yds on right

Set on the southern approach to the town, this detached house sits in well-landscaped gardens giving views of Loughrigg Fell and Wetherlam. Bedrooms offer a range of styles, are spacious and have modern fittings with all of the expected facilities. Traditional Lakeland breakfasts are served in the lounge-breakfast room overlooking the front garden.

Rooms 11 en suite (2 fmly) (3 GF) S £37.50–£60; D £75–£13
Facilities TVB tea/coffee Licensed Cen ht **Parking** 14 **Notes** LB

★★★★ GUEST HOUSE
Elterwater Park
Skelwith Bridge LA22 9NP
☎ 015394 32227
e–mail: enquiries@elterwater.com

dir: A593 from Ambleside to Coniston, 1m past Skelwith Bridge Hotel, layby on right fronts estate road to Elterwater Park, signed at gate

This 18th-century Lakeland house is set in 119 acres of parkland, and offers a unique setting and stunning views. The friendly proprietors are dedicated to becoming carbon neutral so the house has geothermal heating and its own water supply. Attractive, comfortable bedrooms include a ground floor annexe room. Evening meals are available by arrangement and there is a useful drying room too.

Rooms 5 en suite (1 GF) S £42–£48; D £64–£76✳ **Facilities** STV TVB tea/coffee Licensed Cen ht Dinner Last d Previous day Wi-fi available **Parking** 10 **Notes** **Notes** ⊗ No children 10yrs No coaches

ENGLAND

AMBLESIDE *CONTINUED*

★★★★ GUEST HOUSE
Kent House
Lake Rd LA22 0AD
☎ 015394 33279
e–mail: mail@kent-house.com
web: www.kent-house.com

dir: *From town centre, by Post Office on one-way system 300yds on left on terrace above main road*

From an elevated location overlooking the town, this traditional Lakeland house offers comfortable, well-equipped accommodation with attractive bedrooms. Traditional breakfasts featuring the best of local produce are served at individual tables in the elegant dining room.

Rooms 5 rms (4 en suite) (1 pri facs) (2 fmly) **Facilities** TVB tea/coffee Cen ht **Parking** 2 **Notes** No coaches

★★★★ GUEST ACCOMMODATION
Lakes Lodge
Lake Rd LA22 0DB
☎ 015394 33240 📠 015394 31474
e–mail: info@lakeslodge.co.uk

dir: *Enter Ambleside on A59, right around one-way system, on exiting town turn right onto Lake Rd*

Located in the centre of Ambleside, friendly service and simply furnished, contemporary bedrooms, in a range of sizes are offered. Wine, beer and champagne is available to be served to bedrooms during the day and evening, until 9pm. A continental breakfast buffet is served in the café-style breakfast room. Guests can arrange use of an indoor pool at a nearby hotel.

Rooms 12 en suite (4 fmly) (2 GF) S £59–£79; D £79–£110✳ **Facilities** TVB tea/coffee Cen ht Wi-fi available **Parking** 12 **Notes** LB ⊗

★★★★ ⊛ RESTAURANT WITH ROOMS
The Log House
Lake Rd LA22 0DN
☎ 015394 31077
e–mail: nicola@loghouse.co.uk
web: www.loghouse.co.uk

dir: *On left after Hayes Garden Centre on A591 (Lake Rd)*

This charming and historic Norwegian building is located midway between the town centre and the shore of Windermere, just five minutes walk to each. Guests can enjoy delicious meals in the attractive restaurant, which also has a bar area. There are three comfortable bedrooms available, each equipped with thoughtful accessories such as DVD/VCR players, Wi-fi and hairdryers.

Rooms 3 en suite S £60–£90; D £70–£90✳ **Facilities** TVB tea/coffee Cen ht Dinner Last d 9.30pm Wi-fi available **Parking** 3 **Notes** ⊗ Closed 7 Jan–7 Feb

★★★★ GUEST ACCOMMODATION
Rysdale Guesthouse
Rothay Rd LA22 0EE
☎ 015394 32140 📠 015394 33999
e–mail: info@rysdalehotel.co.uk

dir: *A591 into Ambleside, one-way system to A593, Rysdale on right facing church*

The comfortable Edwardian house is only a stroll from the village centre and overlooks the church and the park. The friendly proprietors offer attractive, well-equipped bedrooms and most have superb mountain views, as does the smart dining room. There is also a cosy lounge with an inglenook fire place.

Rooms 9 rms (7 en suite) (2 pri facs) (1 fmly) S £34–£45; D £68–£90 **Facilities** TVB tea/coffee Cen ht **Parking** 1 **Notes** ⊗ No children 4yrs Closed 23–27 Dec RS Jan ⊛

★★★★ GUEST HOUSE
Wanslea Guest House
Low Fold, Lake Rd LA22 0DN
☎ 015394 33884 📠 015394 33884
e–mail: information@wanslea.co.uk

dir: *On S side of town, opp garden centre*

Located between town centre and lakeside pier, this Victorian house provides a range of thoughtfully furnished bedrooms, some of which are individually themed and equipped with spa baths. Comprehensive breakfasts are served in the spacious dining room and a cosy lounge is available.

Rooms 8 en suite (2 fmly) S £30–£45; D £50–£90✳ **Facilities** FTV TVB tea/coffee Cen ht TVL Wi-fi available **Notes** LB ⊗ No children 6yrs No coaches Closed 23–26 Dec

★★★★ 🅰 GUEST ACCOMMODATION
The Old Vicarage

Vicarage Rd LA22 9DH
☎ 015394 33364 📠 015394 34734
e-mail: info@oldvicarageambleside.co.uk
web: www.oldvicarageambleside.co.uk

dir: *In town centre. Off Compston Rd onto Vicarage Rd*

Rooms 15 en suite (4 fmly) (2 GF) S £55–£140; D £90–£140✳
Facilities STV TVB tea/coffee Cen ht TVL Wi-fi available 🕐 🏊 Riding
Sauna Pool Table **Parking** 17 **Notes LB**

★★★★ 🅰 GUEST ACCOMMODATION
The Rothay Garth

Rothay Rd LA22 0EE
☎ 015394 32217 📠 015394 34400
e-mail: book@rothay-garth.co.uk

dir: *M6 junct 36, A591 to Ambleside. 1st lights straight over, then
left onto Wansfell Rd. At T-junct turn right, located on right*

Rooms 14 en suite 1 annexe en suite (3 fmly) (4 GF) D £74–£120✳
Facilities TVB tea/coffee Direct dial from bedrooms Cen ht TVL
Parking 18 **Notes LB**

★★★ GUEST HOUSE
Haven Cottage Guest House

Rydal Rd LA22 9AY
☎ 015394 33270
e-mail: enquiries@amblesidehavencottage.co.uk
web: www.amblesidehavencottage.co.uk

dir: *250yds N of town centre on A591*

A warm welcome awaits along with home baking and refreshments
served on arrival. Claire and Tim create a definite home away from
home making their guests feel very welcome. A well presented
property providing numerous extras and benefiting from off-road
parking, located on the edge of Ambleside. Very good breakfast; see
how many puzzles you can work out!

Rooms 7 rms (5 en suite) (2 fmly) S £30–£37; D £60–£76 **Facilities** TVB
tea/coffee Cen ht Wi-fi available **Parking** 6 **Notes LB** ⊗ No children
8yrs No coaches

★★★★ BED & BREAKFAST
Hall Croft

Dufton CA16 6DB
☎ 017683 52902
e-mail: r.walker@leaseholdpartnerships.co.uk

dir: *3m N of Appleby. In Dufton by village green*

Standing at the end of a lime-tree avenue, Hall Croft, built in 1882, has
been restored to its original glory. Bedrooms are comfortably
proportioned, traditionally furnished and well equipped. Breakfasts,
served in the lounge-dining room, are substantial and include a range
of home-made produce. Guests can enjoy the lovely garden, which has
views of the Pennines.

Rooms 3 rms (2 en suite) (1 pri facs) **Facilities** TVB tea/coffee Cen ht
Parking 3 **Notes** Closed 24–26 Dec ✇

★★★ GUEST HOUSE
Bongate House

Bongate CA16 6UE
☎ 017683 51245
e-mail: bongatehouse1@btconnect.com

dir: *0.5m from town centre on B6542 signed Brough*

This fine Georgian house dates from 1760 and offers comfortable,
thoughtfully equipped bedrooms. Guests are given a warm welcome
and are invited to enjoy the landscaped gardens or relax in the lounge.
Hearty breakfasts are served in the pleasant dining room.

Rooms 9 rms (6 en suite) (2 fmly) S fr £30; D £70✳ **Facilities** TVB tea/
coffee Cen ht TVL Wi-fi available **Parking** 10 **Notes** No coaches Closed
Dec–Jan

ARMATHWAITE
MAP 18 NY54

★★★ INN
The Dukes Head Inn

Front St CA4 9PB

☎ 016974 72226

e–mail: info@dukeshead-hotel.co.uk

web: www.dukeshead-hotel.co.uk

dir: *In village centre opp Post Office*

Located in the peaceful village of Armathwaite close to the River Eden, the Dukes Head offers comfortable accommodation in a warm friendly atmosphere. There is a relaxing lounge bar with open fires and a wide choice of meals are available either here or in the restaurant.

Rooms 5 rms (3 en suite) (2 pri facs) S fr £38.50; D fr £62.50✳
Facilities TV4B tea/coffee Cen ht Dinner Last d 9pm **Parking** 20
Notes LB Closed 25 Dec

BASSENTHWAITE
MAP 18 NY23

★★★★ GUEST HOUSE
Lakeside Country Guest House

CA13 9YD

☎ 017687 76358

e–mail: info@lakesidebassenthwaite.co.uk

web: www.lakesidebassenthwaite.co.uk

dir: *M6 junct 40, A66 towards Keswick/Cockermouth, right onto B5291, house on left*

Lakeside Country Guest House is an elegant Edwardian property offering comfortable accommodation. A warm welcome awaits all guests at this friendly and relaxing property where hosts Sharon and Arnold make you feel at home. Located on the shores of Bassenthwaite Lake, some rooms enjoy views over the lake and the Skiddaw mountain range. Lakeside is a great location for bird watchers, and there is an Osprey Bus that tours forests and bird viewing points. Walkers can enjoy the mountains or visit local towns such as Cockermouth, the birth place of William Wordsworth.

Rooms 8 rms (7 en suite) (1 pri facs) (1 fmly) (1 GF) S £35–£40;
D £65–£90✳ **Facilities** TVB tea/coffee Cen ht TVL Wi-fi available
Parking 8 **Notes LB** ⊗ No coaches Closed Xmas

BOOT
MAP 18 NY10

★★★★ INN
Brook House Inn

CA19 1TG

☎ 019467 23288 📄 019467 23160

e–mail: stay@brookhouseinn.co.uk

web: www.brookhouseinn.co.uk

dir: *In village centre. 0.5m NE of Dalegarth station*

Located in the heart of Eskdale, this impressive inn dates from the early 18th century and has been renovated to offer comfortable accommodation with smart, modern bathrooms for weary walkers and travellers. Wholesome meals using local produce are served in the

CONTINUED

traditionally furnished dining room or attractive bar, the latter featuring real ales and country memorabilia.

Rooms 7 en suite (2 fmly) **Facilities** FTV TVB tea/coffee Cen ht Dinner
Last d 8.30pm **Conf** Max 35 **Parking** 24 **Notes** Closed 25 Dec

★★★ INN
The Woolpack Inn

CA19 1TH

☎ 019467 23230

e–mail: enquiries@woolpack.co.uk

web: www.woolpack.co.uk

dir: *From Eskdale Green follow single track road towards Hardknott, 1m on left*

A traditional Lake District inn, at the head of Eskdale which dates back to the 16th century. A friendly welcome is guaranteed along with true peace, relaxation and tastefully modernised bedrooms. Enjoy the residents or walkers bar with beer from the Woolpack's own micro brewery. Restaurant offers imaginative homemade produce.

Rooms 8 rms (6 en suite) (2 fmly) S £45–£100; D £65–£120✳
Facilities STV TVB tea/coffee Cen ht Dinner Last d 8pm Wi-fi available
Parking 40 **Notes LB** No coaches

BORROWDALE
MAP 18 NY21

Premier Collection

★★★★★ ⊕ GUEST HOUSE
Hazel Bank Country House

Rosthwaite CA12 5XB

☎ 017687 77248 📄 017687 77373

e–mail: enquiries@hazelbankhotel.co.uk

web: www.hazelbankhotel.co.uk

dir: *A66 Keswick, follow B5289 signed Borrowdale, turn left before Rosthwaite over humped back bridge*

Set on an elevated position surrounded by four acres of well-tended lawns and woodland, this Victorian residence has magnificent views of Borrowdale. Bedrooms are well proportioned, thoughtfully equipped and carefully decorated. Set four-course dinners, cooked with imagination and skill, and excellent breakfasts are served in the delightful dining room. Service is attentive and the hospitality makes guests feel very much at home.

Rooms 8 en suite (2 GF) S £65–£95; D £130–£190✳ (incl. dinner)
Facilities TVB tea/coffee Licensed Cen ht Dinner Last d 3pm ⌣
Parking 12 **Notes** ⊗ No children 12yrs No coaches RS Xmas

BOWNESS-ON-WINDERMERE

See **Windermere**

BRAITHWAITE   MAP 18 NY22

★★★★ INN
The Royal Oak
CA12 5SY
☎ 017687 78533 📄 017687 78533
e–mail: theroyaloak@tp-inns.co.uk
web: www.tp-inns.co.uk

dir: In village centre

The Royal Oak, in the pretty village of Braithwaite, has delightful views of Skiddaw and Barrow, and is a good base for tourists and walkers. Some of the well-equipped bedrooms are furnished with four-poster beds. Hearty meals and traditional Cumbrian breakfasts are served in the restaurant, and there is an atmospheric, well-stocked bar.

Rooms 10 en suite (1 fmly) **Facilities** STV TVB tea/coffee Cen ht Dinner Last d 9pm Wi-fi available ☕ **Parking** 20

BRAMPTON   MAP 21 NY56

See also Castle Carrock & Gilsland (Northumberland)

Premier Collection

★★★★★ GUEST ACCOMMODATION
The Hill On The Wall
Gilsland CA8 7DA
☎ 016977 47214 📄 016977 47214
e–mail: info@hadrians-wallbedandbreakfast.com
web: http://hadrians-wallbedandbreakfast.com

dir: A69 into Gilsland & follow brown tourist signs for Birdoswald, The Hill on the Wall 0.5m on right

Overlooking Hadrian's Wall, this elegant house was originally built in the 16th century as a fortified farmhouse. The spacious, attractive bedrooms are well equipped. The lounge is comfortably furnished and stocked with books and games. Breakfast, using good local produce, is served in the smart dining room.

The Hill On the Wall

Rooms 3 rms (2 en suite) (1 pri facs) (1 GF) S £45–£50; D £60–£70✳ **Facilities** FTV TVB tea/coffee Cen ht TVL Wi-fi available Golf 18 **Parking** 8 **Notes LB** ⊛ No children 10yrs Closed Dec & Jan ⊛

★★★★ INN
The Blacksmiths Arms
Talkin Village CA8 1LE
☎ 016977 3452 & 42111 📄 016977 3396
e–mail: blacksmithsarmstalkin@yahoo.co.uk
web: www.blacksmithstalkin.co.uk

dir: B6413 from Brampton to Castle Carrock, after level crossing 2nd left signed Talkin

Dating from the early 19th century and used as a smithy until the 1950s, this friendly village inn offers good home-cooked fare and real ales, with two Cumbrian cask beers always available. Bedrooms are well equipped, and three are particularly smart. An extensive menu and daily specials are offered in the cosy bar lounges or the smart, panelled Old Forge Restaurant.

Rooms 5 en suite 3 annexe en suite (2 fmly) (3 GF) S £40–£50; D £60–£70 **Facilities** FTV TVB tea/coffee Direct dial from bedrooms Cen ht Dinner Last d 9pm **Parking** 20 **Notes** No coaches

CONTINUED

ENGLAND

BRAMPTON CONTINUED

★★★★ GUEST ACCOMMODATION
Hullerbank

Talkin CA8 1LB

☎ 016977 46668 🖥 016977 46668

e–mail: info@hullerbank.freeserve.co.uk

web: www.hullerbankbnb.co.uk

dir: *B6413 from Brampton for 2m, over railway & after golf club left to Talkin, onto Hallbankgate Rd & signs to Hullerbank*

Dating from 1635, Hullerbank is a delightful farmhouse set in well-tended gardens, convenient for Hadrian's Wall, the Lake District and the Borders. Bedrooms are comfortably proportioned, attractively decorated and well equipped. There is a cosy ground-floor lounge with an inglenook fireplace, and traditional hearty breakfasts are served in the dining room.

Rooms 3 rms (2 en suite) (1 pri facs) D £62–£64 **Facilities** TVB tea/coffee Cen ht TVL **Parking** 6 **Notes** ⊗ No children 12yrs Closed Dec–Mar

BRIGSTEER   MAP 18 SD48

★★★★ 🛎 ⇔ INN
The Wheatsheaf

LA8 8AN

☎ 015395 68254

e–mail: wheatsheaf@brigsteer.gb.com

web: www.brigsteer.gb.com

dir: *Off A591 signed Brigsteer, Wheatsheaf at bottom of hill*

Lying in the peaceful little hamlet of Brigsteer to the west of Kendal, just off the A591, the Wheatsheaf offers attractive, well-equipped en suite bedrooms, all of which have been refurbished to offer modern comforts. There is a cosy, well-stocked bar, and a spacious, charming dining room where delicious home-cooked fare is served at individual tables.

Rooms 3 en suite **Facilities** TVB tea/coffee Cen ht Dinner Last d 9pm **Parking** 25 **Notes** ⊗ No coaches

BROUGHTON-IN-FURNESS   MAP 18 SD28

See also Millom

★★★★ ⇔ INN
The Old Kings Head

Church St LA20 6HJ

☎ 01229 716293 🖥 01229 715165

e–mail: russelleclar7jw@wanadoo.co.uk

dir: *M6 junct 36, onto A591. After 2m onto A5900 signed Barrow, turn right at Greenodd (A5092) to Broughton*

This traditional family-run country inn offers a warm welcome, charming public areas and real ales. A wide choice of freshly cooked meals are served in the bar, restaurant or, during warmer months, the attractive beer garden. Bedrooms are varied in size but all are comfortable and tastefully presented.

Rooms 6 rms (5 en suite) (1 fmly) **Facilities** TVB tea/coffee Cen ht Dinner Last d 9pm **Parking** 6 **Notes** ⊗

★★★ 🛏 INN
The High Cross Inn
High Cross Brow LA20 6ES
☎ 01229 716272
e–mail: visiting@highcrossinn.com

dir: *Exit M6 junct 36 onto A590 towards Barrow. Right at junct with A595 at Greenodd and through Foxfield. Continue 2m, at top of hill*

Located on the brow of a hill overlooking Broughton-in-Furness and the Duddon Valley. A wide choice of delicious meals are served in the cosy oak beamed bar or pleasant conservatory restaurant. Bedrooms are comfortable and well equipped.

Rooms 4 en suite (1 fmly) S £30–£45; D £70–£90✱ **Facilities** TVB tea/coffee Cen ht Dinner Last d 9pm Wi-fi available **Conf** Max 12 Board 12 Del from £80 ✱ **Parking** 30 **Notes LB**

CALDBECK   MAP 18 NY34

★★★★ GUEST ACCOMMODATION
Swaledale Watch Farm
Whelpo CA7 8HQ
☎ 016974 78409 📠 016974 78409
e–mail: nan.savage@talk21.com
web: www.swaledale-watch.co.uk

dir: *1m SW of Caldbeck on B5299*

This attractive farmhouse, set within its own nature reserve, is in a peaceful location with a backdrop of picturesque fells. The en suite bedrooms are spacious and well equipped. Two rooms are in an adjacent converted farm building and share a comfortable sitting room. Traditional hearty breakfasts are served in the attractive dining room overlooking the garden, with views of the fells.

Rooms 2 en suite 2 annexe en suite (2 fmly) (4 GF) S £25–£31; D fr £50 **Facilities** TVB tea/coffee Cen ht TVL 100 acre Nature Reserve, badger watching evenings **Parking** 8 **Notes** Closed 24–26 Dec 🐾

CARLISLE   MAP 18 NY35
See also Brampton & Castle Carrock

★★★★★ 🛏 GUEST ACCOMMODATION
Bessiestown Country Guest House
CA6 5QP
☎ 01228 577219 & 577019 📠 01228 577219
e–mail: info@bessiestown.co.uk
web: www.bessiestown.co.uk

(For full entry see Catlowdy)

★★★★ GUEST HOUSE
Cambro House
173 Warwick Rd CA1 1LP
☎ 01228 543094
e–mail: davidcambro@aol.com

dir: *M6 junct 43, onto Warwick Rd, 1m on right before St Aidan's Church*

This smart Victorian house is close to the town centre and motorway. The beautifully refurbished and spacious bedrooms are brightly decorated, smartly appointed and thoughtfully equipped. A hearty Cumbrian breakfast is served in the cosy morning room.

Rooms 3 en suite (1 GF) S £30–£35; D £50–£60✱ **Facilities** FTV TVB tea/coffee Cen ht Wi-fi available **Parking** 2 **Notes LB** ⊗ No children 5yrs No coaches

★★★★ BED & BREAKFAST
No1 Guest House
1 Etterby St CA3 9JB
☎ 01228 547285 & 07899 948711
e–mail: sheila@carlislebandb.co.uk

dir: *M6 junct 44 onto A7, right at 7th lights onto Etterby St, house 1st on left*

This small friendly house is on the north side of the city within walking distance of the centre. The attractive, well-equipped en suite bedrooms consist of a double, a twin-bed and a single room. Hearty traditional breakfasts featuring the best of local produce are served in the ground-floor dining room.

Rooms 3 en suite S £27–£32; D £54–£64 **Facilities** FTV TVB tea/coffee Cen ht Dinner Last d 10am Wi-fi available **Parking** 1 **Notes LB** ⊗

CARLISLE CONTINUED

★★★ 🛏 GUEST ACCOMMODATION
Angus House & Almonds Restaurant
14–16 Scotland Rd CA3 9DG
☎ 01228 523546 📠 01228 531895
e–mail: hotel@angus-hotel.co.uk
web: www.angus-hotel.co.uk

dir: *0.5m N of city centre on A7*

Situated just north of the city, this family-run establishment is ideal for business and leisure. A warm welcome is assured and the accommodation is well equipped. Almonds Restaurant provides enjoyable food and home baking, and there is also a lounge and a large meeting room.

Rooms 10 en suite (2 fmly) S £52; D £76 **Facilities** FTV TVB tea/coffee Direct dial from bedrooms Cen ht Dinner Last d 8.45pm Wi-fi available **Conf** Max 25 Thtr 25 Class 16 Board 16 **Notes LB**

★★★ GUEST ACCOMMODATION
Marlborough House
2 Marlbourgh Gardens, Stanwix CA3 9NW
☎ 01228 512174
e–mail: ian_mc_brown@hotmail.com

dir: *M6 junct 44, 2m to Carlisle, left at Crown Inn*

A warm welcome awaits you at Marlborough House situated within easy walking distance of the city centre. This friendly guest house offers individually decorated, pleasantly furnished, and thoughtfully equipped bedrooms. There is a comfortable conservatory breakfast room where hearty breakfasts are served at individual tables. Parking is available.

Rooms 4 en suite (1 fmly) (1 GF) **Facilities** TVB tea/coffee Cen ht TVL Dinner Last d 8pm Wi-fi available Golf 18 **Parking** 8 **Notes** ⊗

CARTMEL   MAP 18 SD37

★★★★★ ◉◉◉◉
RESTAURANT WITH ROOMS
L'enclume
Cavendish St LA11 6PZ
☎ 015395 36362
e–mail: info@lenclume.co.uk

dir: *From A590 turn for Cartmel before Newby Bridge*

This 13th-century building offers 21st-century food in a destination restaurant that should not be missed. The accommodation varies in style depending on which house the room is in; all rooms are modern but some have a 'country house' feel. The menus often read like some kind of modern poetry, but the food will leave you satisfied. A truly unique experience.

Rooms 7 en suite 5 annexe en suite (3 fmly) (3 GF) S £68–£118; D £98–£198 (room only) **Facilities** STV TVB tea/coffee Cen ht Dinner Last d 9pm **Parking** 11 **Notes** Closed 1–8 Jan

★★★★★ 🛏 BED & BREAKFAST
Hill Farm
LA11 7SS
☎ 015395 36477 📠 015395 36636
e–mail: hillfarmbb@btinternet.com
web: www.hillfarmcartmel.co.uk

dir: *Exit village centre signed Cartmel Village Store, follow cul-de-sac signs then signs to Hill Farm*

Hill Farm, dating from 1539, stands on an elevated position on the edge of the village famous for its sticky toffee pudding. The farmhouse has been renovated to provide comfortable accommodation with original character, and the attractive bedrooms are thoughtfully equipped with many extra touches. The comfortable lounge has log fires, and delicious freshly cooked breakfasts are served at a large table in the dining room. Hill Farm is closed from November to January.

Rooms 3 en suite S £40–£45; D £80–£90✳ **Facilities** TVB tea/coffee Cen ht TVL Solarium **Parking** 3 **Notes LB** ⊗ No children 5yrs Closed Nov–Jan 🛏

CASTLE CARROCK　　　MAP 18 NY55

★★ FARM HOUSE
Gelt Hall Farm (NY542554)
CA8 9LT

☎ 01228 670260 📠 01228 670260 Mrs Annie Robinson

e–mail: robinson@gelthall.fsnet.co.uk

dir: *B6413 to Castle Carrock, farm in village centre*

This working farmhouse retains much of its original 17th-century character. The cheerful bedrooms are traditionally furnished and overlook the farmyard. Breakfast is served at a communal table in the cosy lounge, and warm hospitality is a particular feature.

Rooms 3 rms (1 en suite) (1 fmly) **Facilities** TV2B tea/coffee TVL **Parking** 7 **Notes** 400 acres beef dairy sheep mixed ⊛

CATLOWDY　　　MAP 21 NY47

Premier Collection

★★★★★ 🏠 GUEST ACCOMMODATION
Bessiestown Country Guest House
CA6 5QP

☎ 01228 577219 & 577019 📠 01228 577219

e–mail: info@bessiestown.co.uk

web: www.bessiestown.co.uk

dir: *From Longtown at Bush Hotel take road signed Penton-Catlowdy. At T-junct turn right onto B6318 1.5m, Catlowdy on left*

The owners have welcomed guests to this delightful farmhouse for the past 30 years. The stylish bedrooms, with refurbished bathrooms, include family rooms and the luxury Dovecote Suite, which has a king-size four-poster bed, separate dressing room and a spa bath. There is a choice of lounges and a heated indoor swimming pool. Freshly prepared dinners and hearty breakfasts with home-made bread and preserves are served in the smart dining room.

Rooms 5 en suite (1 fmly) (2 GF) **Facilities** TVB tea/coffee Cen ht TVL Dinner Last d 4pm 🕭 **Parking** 10 **Notes** ⊗

COCKERMOUTH　　　MAP 18 NY13

★★★★ 🏠 BED & BREAKFAST
Highside Farmhouse
Embleton CA13 9TN

☎ 01768 776893

e–mail: enquiries@highsidefarmhouse.co.uk

web: www.highsidefarmhouse.co.uk

dir: *A66 Keswick to Cockermouth, left at sign Lorton/Buttermere, left at T-junct. 300yds turn right opp church, farm at top of hill*

True to its name, this 17th-century farmhouse stands over 600 feet up Ling Fell with breathtaking views across to the Solway Firth and Scotland. Add warm hospitality, great breakfasts, an inviting lounge-dining room with open fire in winter, and pine-furnished bedrooms, and the trip up the narrow winding road is well worth it.

Rooms 2 en suite S £40–£42; D £60–£64✳ **Facilities** TVB tea/coffee Cen ht **Parking** 2 **Notes** No children 10yrs ⊛

★★★★ 🏠 GUEST HOUSE
Croft Guest House
6–8 Challoner St CA13 9QS

☎ 01900 827533

e–mail: info@croft-guesthouse.com

dir: *In town centre off Main St*

Croft Guest House, one of the town's oldest buildings, lies in the heart of Cockermouth. It has been carefully upgraded to offer generally spacious, stylish accommodation. Bedrooms are comfortable, well equipped and retain some original features. There is a cosy ground-floor lounge next to the spacious dining room, where delicious breakfasts from the extensive blackboard menu are served at individual tables.

Rooms 6 en suite (1 fmly) S fr £38; D fr £60✳ **Facilities** TVB tea/coffee Cen ht **Parking** 5 **Notes LB** No coaches

★★★★ GUEST HOUSE
Rose Cottage
Lorton Rd CA13 9DX

☎ 01900 822189 📠 01900 822189

e–mail: bookings@rosecottageguest.co.uk

dir: *A5292 from Cockermouth to Lorton/Buttermere, Rose Cottage on right*

This former inn is on the edge of town and has been refurbished to provide attractive, modern accommodation. The smart, well-equipped en suite bedrooms include a self-contained studio room with external access. There is a cosy lounge, and a smart dining room where delicious home-cooked dinners are a highlight.

Rooms 6 en suite 1 annexe en suite (2 fmly) (3 GF) S £42–£60; D £60–£85 **Facilities** TVB tea/coffee Licensed Cen ht Dinner Last d noon Wi-fi available **Parking** 12 **Notes LB** Closed 13–20 Feb RS 24–27 Dec

Premier Collection

★★★★★ 🏠 🍴 GUEST HOUSE

Coniston Lodge

Station Rd LA21 8HH
☎ 015394 41201 🖹 015394 41201
e-mail: info@coniston-lodge.com
web: www.coniston-lodge.com
dir: *Off A593 x-rds near fuel station up hill onto Station Rd*

Coniston Lodge stands in mature gardens and is adorned with artistic touches, collectables and beautiful fresh and dried flower arrangements. An open staircase leads to the lounge (with a balcony overlooking the gardens) and the dining room. The well-proportioned bedrooms are in an extension on columns above the car park. Breakfasts are memorable, as are dinners (by arrangement).

Rooms 6 en suite **Facilities** TVB tea/coffee Direct dial from bedrooms Licensed Cen ht Dinner Last d 10am **Parking** 9 **Notes** ⊗ No children 10yrs No coaches RS Sun–Tue

Premier Collection

★★★★★ 🏠 GUEST HOUSE

Wheelgate Country Guest House

Little Arrow LA21 8AU
☎ 015394 41418 🖹 015394 41114
e-mail: enquiry@wheelgate.co.uk
dir: *1.5m S of Coniston, on W side of road*

Dating from the 17th century, this charming farmhouse has original oak beams, panelling and low ceilings. An intimate bar, laundry facilities and a comfortable lounge with open fire are provided. There are impressive views over the well-tended gardens and the beautiful Lakeland countryside. A warm welcome can be expected.

Rooms 4 en suite 1 annexe en suite (1 GF) S £39–£42; D £74–£84✱ **Facilities** TVB tea/coffee Licensed Cen ht **Parking** 5 **Notes LB** ⊗ No children 8yrs No coaches Closed 3 Nov–Etr

Premier Collection

★★★★★ ◉ INN

The Punchbowl Inn at Crosthwaite

Lyth Valley LA8 8HR
☎ 015395 68237 🖹 015397 68875
e-mail: info@the-punchbowl.co.uk
dir: *M6 junct 36 signed Barrow, on A5074 towards Windermere, turn right for Crosthwaite. At E end of village beside church*

Located in the stunning Lyth Valley alongside the village church, this historic inn has been renovated to provide excellent standards of comfort and facilities. Its sumptuous bedrooms have a wealth of thoughtful extras, and imaginative food is available in the elegant restaurant or in the rustic-style bar with open fires. A warm welcome and professional service is assured.

Rooms 9 en suite S £93.75–£232.50; D £125–£310✱ **Facilities** TVB Direct dial from bedrooms Cen ht Dinner Last d 9.30pm Wi-fi available **Parking** 25 **Notes** No coaches Civ Wed 50

★★★★ GUEST HOUSE

Crosthwaite House

LA8 8BP
☎ 015395 68264 🖹 015395 68264
e-mail: bookings@crosthwaitehouse.co.uk
web: www.crosthwaitehouse.co.uk
dir: *A590 onto A5074, 4m right to Crosthwaite, 0.5m turn left*

Having stunning views across the Lyth Valley, this friendly Georgian house is a haven of tranquillity. Bedrooms are spacious and offer a host of thoughtful extras. The reception rooms include a comfortable lounge and a pleasant dining room with polished floorboards and individual tables.

Rooms 6 en suite S £26–£30; D £52–£60 **Facilities** FTV TVB tea/coffee Cen ht TVL **Parking** 10 **Notes** No coaches Closed mid Nov–Dec RS early Nov & Feb–Mar

ELTERWATER   MAP 18 NY30   GRASMERE   MAP 18 NY30

★★★ A INN
Britannia Inn
LA22 9HP
☎ 01539 437210
e–mail: info@britinn.co.uk

dir: *A593 from Ambleside, then B5343 to Elterwater*

Rooms 9 en suite **Facilities** Cen ht Last d 9.30pm **Parking** 10
Notes No coaches

FAUGH   MAP 18 NY55

U
The String of Horses Inn
CA8 9EG
☎ 01228 670297
e–mail: info@stringofhorses.com
web: www.stringofhorses.com

dir: *A69 turn towards Heads Nook at Corby Hill lights. 1m
through Heads Nook, turn left*

At the time of going to press the rating for this establishment had not
been confirmed. Please check the AA website www.theAA.com for
up-to-date information.

Rooms 11 en suite (1 fmly) S £40–55; D £50–£65✳ **Facilities** FTV TVB
tea/coffee Direct dial from bedrooms Cen ht TVL Dinner Last d 9pm
Wi-fi available **Conf** Max 60 Thtr 60 Class 30 Board 30 Del from £25 ✳
Parking 30 **Notes** LB ✖

GRANGE-OVER-SANDS   MAP 18 SD47

★★★★ 🛏 GUEST ACCOMMODATION
Corner Beech House
Methven Ter, Kents Bank Rd LA11 7DP
☎ 015395 33088
e–mail: info@cornerbeech.co.uk
web: www.cornerbeech.co.uk

dir: *M6 junct 36 onto A590, then off B5277 (Kents Bank Road)*

Overlooking Morecambe Bay this Edwardian house is well maintained
and offers a friendly atmosphere. Hearty breakfasts featuring
homemade and local produce are served in the attractive dining room.
All bedrooms are en suite and well equipped with sitting area,
widescreen digital televisions and DVD players.

Rooms 3 en suite S £49; D £70 **Facilities** FTV TVB tea/coffee Cen ht
Parking 5 **Notes** ✖ No children 14yrs

Premier Collection

★★★★★ 🛏 GUEST ACCOMMODATION
Moss Grove Organic
LA22 9SW
☎ 015394 35251 📠 015394 35306
e–mail: enquiries@mossgrove.com
web: www.mossgrove.com

dir: *From S, M6 junct 36 onto A591 signed Keswick, from N M6
junct 40 onto A591 signed Windermere*

Located in the centre of Grasmere, this impressive Victorian house has
been refurbished using as many natural products as possible with
ongoing dedication to causing minimal environmental impact. The
stylish bedrooms are decorated with beautiful wallpaper and natural
clay paints, featuring handmade beds and furnishings. Bose home
entertainment systems, flat screen TVs and luxury bathrooms add
further comfort. Extensive continental breakfasts are served in the
spacious kitchen, where guests can help themselves and dine at the
large wooden dining table in the guest lounge. Moss Grove Organic
was a runner-up for the AA Funkiest B&B of the Year 2008 Award.

Rooms 11 en suite (2 GF) S £125–£250; D £125–£250✳ **Facilities** STV
TVB tea/coffee Cen ht Wi-fi available **Parking** 11 **Notes** LB No children
14yrs Closed 24–25 Dec

★★★★ GUEST HOUSE
Silverlea Guest House
Easedale Rd LA22 9QE
☎ 015394 35657 📠 015394 35657
e–mail: info@silverlea.com

dir: *Easedale Rd opp village green, Silverlea 300yds on right*

A friendly welcome is assured at this ivy-clad Lakeland-stone house,
just a short walk from the village. Delicious home-cooked meals using
fresh produce are served in the cosy cottage dining room. Bedrooms,
some having their own sitting area, are fresh in appearance and very
comfortable. Silverlea is an ideal base for walking and exploring the
Lake District.

Rooms 4 en suite S £58–£66; D £76–£92✳ **Facilities** TVB tea/coffee
Cen ht **Parking** 5 **Notes** LB ✖ No children 11yrs No coaches 🐾

★★★★ 🛏 GUEST HOUSE
White Moss House
Rydal Water LA22 9SE
☎ 015394 35295 📠 015394 35516
e–mail: sue@whitemoss.com
web: www.whitemoss.com

dir: *On A591 1m S of Grasmere, 2m N of Ambleside*

This traditional Lakeland house was once bought by Wordsworth for
his son. It benefits from a central location and has a loyal following.
The individually styled bedrooms are comfortable and thoughtfully
equipped. There is also a two-room suite in a cottage on the hillside
above the house. Afternoon tea is served in the inviting lounge.

Rooms 5 en suite S £52–£62; D £84–£110✳ **Facilities** TVB tea/coffee Direct dial from bedrooms Licensed Cen ht Fishing Free use of local leisure club **Parking** 10 **Notes LB** ⊗ No coaches Closed Dec–Jan

---

GRIZEDALE   MAP 18 SD39

★★★★ GUEST ACCOMMODATION
Grizedale Lodge

LA22 0QL

☎ 015394 36532 📠 015394 36572

e–mail: enquiries@grizedale-lodge.com

web: www.grizedale-lodge.com

dir: *From Hawkshead signs S to Grizedale, Lodge 2m on right*

Set in the heart of the tranquil Grizedale Forest Park, this charming establishment provides particularly comfortable bedrooms, some with four-poster beds and splendid views. Hearty breakfasts are served in the attractive dining room, which leads to a balcony for relaxing on in summer.

Rooms 8 en suite (1 fmly) (2 GF) **Facilities** TVB tea/coffee Cen ht Dinner Last d 8.30pm **Conf** Max 10 **Parking** 20

HAWKSHEAD   MAP 18 SD39

See also Near Sawrey

Premier Collection

★★★★★ ⊚⊚ GUEST HOUSE
West Vale Country House

Far Sawrey LA22 0LQ

☎ 015394 42817 📠 015394 45302

e–mail: enquiries@westvalecountryhouse.co.uk

web: www.westvalecountryhouse.co.uk

dir: *Cross Windemere by car ferry at Bowness, B5285 for 1.25m to Far Sawrey, West Vale on left leaving village*

West Vale Country House is on the edge of the beautiful village of Far Sawrey, and has delightful views across the vale to Grizedale Forest. All the bedrooms have been furnished to a high standard, and there is a lounge and an elegant dining room, where traditional breakfasts and dinners are served at individual tables.

Rooms 7 en suite (1 fmly) **Facilities** TVB tea/coffee Licensed Cen ht Dinner Last d 5.30pm **Parking** 8 **Notes** ⊗ No children 12yrs

---

Premier Collection

★★★★★ ⊚ 🔔 GUEST HOUSE
Ees Wyke Country House

LA22 0JZ

☎ 015394 36393

e–mail: mail@eeswyke.co.uk

web: www.eeswyke.co.uk

(For full entry see Near Sawrey)

★★★★ 🔔 GUEST ACCOMMODATION
Sawrey Ground

Hawkshead Hill LA22 0PP

☎ 015394 36683

e–mail: mail@sawreyground.com

web: www.sawreyground.com

dir: *B5285 from Hawkshead, 1m to Hawkshead Hill, sharp right after Baptist chapel, signs to Tarn Hows for 0.25m. Sawrey Ground on right*

Set in the heart of the Lake District, this charming 17th-century farmhouse has a superb setting on the doorstep of Tarn Hows. The flagstone entrance hall leads to a sitting room with a beamed ceiling, where an open fire burns on winter nights. Hearty breakfasts featuring fresh fruit and home-baked bread are served in the dining room. The traditional bedrooms are furnished in pine and oak.

Rooms 3 en suite D £70–£82✳ **Facilities** TVB tea/coffee Cen ht **Parking** 6 **Notes** ⊗ No children 8yrs ⊜

★★★★ INN
The Sun Inn

Main St LA22 0NT

☎ 015394 36236 📠 015394 36747

e–mail: rooms@suninn.co.uk

web: www.suninn.co.uk

This 16th-century inn features a wood-panelled bar with low, oak-beamed ceilings and an open log fire. Substantial, carefully prepared meals are served in the bar and dining room. The bedrooms, three of which are in an adjacent cottage, are attractively furnished and include some four-poster rooms.

Rooms 8 en suite (1 fmly) D £85–£95✳ **Facilities** TVB tea/coffee Cen ht Dinner Last d 9.30pm Wi-fi available Fishing Pool Table **Conf** Max 20 Thtr 20 Class 20 Board 12 Del from £60 ✳ **Notes** ⊗

★★★ INN
Kings Arms
LA22 0NZ

☎ 015394 36372 📠 015394 36006

e–mail: info@kingsarmshawkshead.co.uk

web: www.kingsarmshawkshead.co.uk

dir: *In main square*

A traditional Lakeland inn in the heart of a conservation area. The cosy, thoughtfully equipped bedrooms retain much character and are traditionally furnished. A good choice of freshly prepared food is available in the lounge bar and the neatly presented dining room.

Rooms 9 rms (8 en suite) (3 fmly) **Facilities** TVB tea/coffee Direct dial from bedrooms Cen ht Dinner Last d 9.30pm Fishing **Parking** available **Notes** Closed 25 Dec

---

HELTON   MAP 18 NY52

★★★★ GUEST ACCOMMODATION
Beckfoot Country House
CA10 2QB

☎ 01931 713241 📠 01931 713391

e–mail: info@beckfoot.co.uk

dir: *M6 junct 39, A6 through Shap & left to Bampton. Through Bampton Grange and Bampton, house 2m on left*

This delightful Victorian country house stands in well-tended gardens surrounded by beautiful open countryside, yet is only a short drive from Penrith. Bedrooms are spacious and particularly well equipped. The four-poster room is particularly impressive. Public areas include an elegant drawing room, where guitar workshops are occasionally held, an oak-panelled dining room and a television lounge.

Rooms 7 en suite 1 annexe en suite (1 fmly) (1 GF) S £35–£39; D £78–£100✱ **Facilities** STV TVB tea/coffee Cen ht TVL Wi-fi available Childrens play area **Conf** Max 20 **Parking** 12 **Notes** LB Closed Dec–Feb

---

HOLMROOK   MAP 18 SD09

★★★ INN
The Lutwidge Arms
CA19 1UH

☎ 019467 24230 📠 019467 24100

e–mail: mail@lutwidge.co.uk

dir: *M6 junct 36 onto A590 towards Barrow. Follow A595 towards Whitehaven/Workington, in centre of Holmrook*

This Victorian roadside inn is family run and offers a welcoming atmosphere. The name comes from the Lutwidge family of Holmrook Hall, who included Charles Lutwidge Dodgson, better known as Lewis Caroll. The bar and restaurant offer a wide range of meals during the evening. Bedrooms are comfortably equipped.

Rooms 11 en suite 5 annexe en suite (5 fmly) (5 GF) S £40–£55; D £65–£75✱ **Facilities** FTV TVB tea/coffee Direct dial from bedrooms Cen ht TVL Dinner Last d 9pm Wi-fi available Pool Table **Parking** 30 **Notes** LB

KENDAL   MAP 18 SD59

See also Brigsteer

★★★★ BED & BREAKFAST
Burrow Hall Country Guest House
Plantation Bridge LA8 9JR

☎ 01539 821711 📠 01539 821711

e–mail: burrow.hall@virgin.net

web: www.burrowhall.co.uk

dir: *3m NW of Kendal on A591*

Dating from 1648, this charming country house has been restored to provide comfortable, modern accommodation. Some of the en suite bedrooms have lovely views of the fells, and all are neatly furnished and well equipped. Guests have a separate entrance to a comfortable lounge and the breakfast room.

Rooms 4 en suite S £35–£40; D £70–£80✱ **Facilities** TVB tea/coffee Cen ht TVL **Parking** 8 **Notes** ✖ No children 12yrs Closed 23–26 Dec

---

★★★★ 🅰 GUEST ACCOMMODATION
The Glen
Oxenholme LA9 7RF

☎ 01539 726386 📠 01539 724434

e–mail: greenintheglen@btinternet.com

web: www.glen-kendal.co.uk

dir: *2m S of Kendal. B6254 to Oxenholme, past railway station, driveway on right up hill*

Rooms 6 en suite (2 fmly) (1 GF) S £35–£47; D £60–£80✱ **Facilities** STV TVB tea/coffee Cen ht Wi-fi available Hot tub **Parking** 10 **Notes** Closed 31 Dec

ENGLAND

★★★ INN
Gilpin Bridge

Bridge End, Levens LA8 8EP
☎ 015395 52206 📠 015395 52444
e–mail: info@gilpinbridgeinn.co.uk
dir: M6 junct 36, 7m on A5074, 100yds from A590

Situated just outside Levens, this modern Tudor-style inn offers a creative and appealing bar and restaurant menu. The bedrooms offer comfortable accommodation, and there is a games room, a function suite, and an outside playground for children.

Rooms 9 en suite (1 fmly) S £50–£60; D £75–£90✱ **Facilities** FTV TVB tea/coffee Cen ht Dinner Last d 9pm Pool Table **Conf** Max 80 Thtr 80 Class 60 Board 40 Del from £45 ✱ **Parking** 50 **Notes LB**

★★★ BED & BREAKFAST
Millers Beck Country Guest House

Stainton LA8 0DU
☎ 015395 60877 📠 015395 60877
e–mail: millersbeck@aol.com
dir: M6 junct 36, A65, 1st left signed Crooklands/Endmoor, Millers Beck 3.5m on right

The delightful sound of cascading water can be heard from this converted 16th-century corn mill. Situated in the countryside, close to Kendal, this charming guest house offers cosy, modern bedrooms. Public areas include a choice of two comfortable gallery lounges, with hearty breakfasts served in the conservatory-dining room.

Rooms 3 en suite S £27–£35; D £49–£54✱ **Facilities** TVB tea/coffee Cen ht TVL **Parking** 4 **Notes LB** Closed Jan

KESWICK

MAP 18 NY22

See also Lorton

★★★★★ GUEST HOUSE
The Grange Country Guest House

Manor Brow, Ambleside Rd CA12 4BA
☎ 017687 72500 📠 0707 500 4885
e–mail: info@grangekeswick.com
dir: M6 junct 40, A66 15m. A591 for 1m, turn right onto Manor Brow

This stylish Victorian residence stands in beautiful gardens just a stroll from the town centre. It offers a relaxed atmosphere and professional service. The spacious bedrooms are well equipped, and some have beams and mountain views. Spacious lounges and ample parking are available. The proprietors are keen to give advice on walks and local activities.

Rooms 10 en suite S £71–£83; D £98–£106 **Facilities** FTV TVB tea/coffee Direct dial from bedrooms Licensed Cen ht Wi-fi available **Conf** Max 12 Board 12 **Parking** 10 **Notes LB** ⊗ No children 10yrs No coaches Closed Jan

★★★★ 🍴 GUEST ACCOMMODATION
Dalegarth House

Portinscale CA12 5RQ
☎ 017687 72817
e–mail: allerdalechef@aol.com
dir: Off A66 to Portinscale, pass Farmers Arms, 100yds on left

The friendly family-run establishment stands on an elevated position in the village of Portinscale, and has fine views from the well-tended

CONTINUED

garden. The attractive bedrooms are well equipped, and there is a peaceful lounge, a well-stocked bar, and a spacious dining room where the resident owner-chef produces hearty breakfasts and delicious evening meals.

Rooms 8 en suite 2 annexe en suite (2 GF) S £40–£45; D £80–£90✳
Facilities FTV TVB tea/coffee Cen ht Dinner Last d 6pm **Parking** 14
Notes LB ⊗ No children 12yrs Closed Dec–1 Mar

★★★★ GUEST HOUSE
Howe Keld

5/7 The Heads CA12 5ES
☎ 017687 72417 & 0800 783 0212 📄 017687 72417
e–mail: david@howekeld.co.uk
web: www.howekeld.co.uk

dir: *From town centre towards Borrowdale, right opp main car park, 1st on left*

Howe Keld has been completely refurbished to create spacious, contemporary natural style accommodation. Many rooms have solid wood floors and bespoke furniture made by local furniture maker Danny Frost along with local herdwick carpets. On the ground floor there is a bright new spacious dining room and lounge area where guests can relax. Breakfast is another highlight, with local and home-made produce a feature.

Rooms 15 en suite (3 fmly) (2 GF) S £45–£60; D £75–£110✳
Facilities TVB tea/coffee Licensed Cen ht Wi-fi available **Parking** 7
Notes LB No coaches Closed Xmas & Jan

★★★★ GUEST HOUSE
Amble House

23 Eskin St CA12 4DQ
☎ 017687 73288
e–mail: info@amblehouse.co.uk
web: www.amblehouse.co.uk

dir: *400yds SE of town centre. Off A5271 Penrith Rd onto Greta St & Eskin St*

An enthusiastic welcome awaits you at this Victorian mid-terrace house, close to the town centre. The thoughtfully equipped bedrooms have coordinated decor and are furnished in pine. Healthy breakfasts are served in the attractive dining room.

Rooms 5 en suite S £27–£45; D £56–£76✳ **Facilities** TVB tea/coffee
Cen ht **Notes LB** ⊗ No children 16yrs No coaches Closed 24–26 Dec

★★★★ GUEST ACCOMMODATION
Avondale

20 Southey St CA12 4EF
☎ 017687 72735
e–mail: enquiries@avondaleguesthouse.com
web: www.avondaleguesthouse.com

dir: *A591 towards town centre, left at war memorial onto Station St, sharp left onto Southey St, Avondale 100yds on right*

Expect efficient and friendly service at this pristine terrace house just a short walk from the town centre. Bright, modern, well-equipped bedrooms come in a variety of sizes. The cosy lounge has a collection of books and there is an airy dining room.

CONTINUED

Rooms 6 en suite S £30–£36; D £60–£72✳ **Facilities** TVB tea/coffee
Cen ht **Notes** ⊗ No children 12yrs

★★★★ GUEST HOUSE
Badgers Wood

30 Stanger St CA12 5JU
☎ 017687 72621 📄 017687 72621
e–mail: enquiries@badgers-wood.co.uk
web: www.badgers-wood.co.uk

dir: *In town centre off A5271 Main St*

A warm welcome awaits you at this delightful Victorian terrace house, located in a quiet area close to the town centre. The smart bedrooms are nicely furnished and well equipped, and the attractive breakfast room at the front of the house overlooks the fells. The house is non-smoking and vegetarians are gladly catered for.

Rooms 6 en suite S fr £33; D fr £62 **Facilities** TVB tea/coffee Cen ht
Parking 2 **Notes** ⊗ No children 12yrs No coaches Closed 3–31 Jan ⊛

★★★★ GUEST HOUSE
Charnwood

6 Eskin St CA12 4DH
☎ 017687 74111 & 07711 773925
e–mail: sue@excite.com

dir: *400yds SE of town centre. Off A5271 Penrith Rd onto Greta St & Eskin St*

This Grade II listed Victorian building is close to the town centre. Beautifully decorated and furnished in keeping with the period of the house, the individually styled bedrooms are well equipped. Delicious breakfasts and home-cooked dinners (by arrangement) are served in the spacious and stylish dining room. A comfortable lounge is available during summer.

Rooms 5 en suite (3 fmly) D £60–£75✳ **Facilities** TVB tea/coffee
Cen ht Dinner Last d 10am **Notes LB** ⊗ No children 5yrs No coaches
Closed 24–25 Dec

KESWICK CONTINUED

★★★★ GUEST ACCOMMODATION
Claremont House
Chestnut Hill CA12 4LT
☎ 017687 72089
e–mail: claremonthouse@btinternet.com
web: www.claremonthousekeswick.co.uk
dir: *A591 N onto Chestnut Hill, Keswick. Pass Manor Brow on left, Claremont House 100yds on right*

This attractive and well-maintained family home stands in mature grounds overlooking the town. Bedrooms are pine furnished and thoughtfully equipped, while the welcoming dining room has good views towards the fells.
Rooms 6 en suite D £60–£74 **Facilities** TVB tea/coffee Cen ht **Parking** 6 **Notes** LB ⊗ No children 12yrs Closed 23–26 Dec ⊛

★★★★ GUEST ACCOMMODATION
Craglands Guest House
Penrith Rd CA12 4LJ
☎ 017687 74406 & 07702 217017
e–mail: craglands@msn.com
dir: *0.5m E of Keswick centre on A5271 Penrith Rd at junct A591*
This Victorian house occupies an elevated position within walking distance of the town centre. The good value accommodation provides attractive, well equipped bedrooms. Pauline and Mark offer a warm welcome and serve delicious breakfasts with local produce and homemade breads.
Rooms 7 rms (5 en suite) S £27–£35; D £54–£80✱ **Facilities** TVB tea/coffee Cen ht Dinner Last d Previous Day Wi-fi available **Parking** 6 **Notes** LB ⊗ No children 8yrs

★★★★ GUEST ACCOMMODATION
Cragside
39 Blencathra St CA12 4HX
☎ 017687 73344 📠 017687 73344
e–mail: wayne-alison@cragside39blencathra.fsnet.co.uk
dir: *A591 Penrith Rd into Keswick, under railway bridge, 2nd left*
Expect warm hospitality at this guest house, located within easy walking distance of the town centre. The attractive bedrooms are well equipped, and many have fine views of the fells. Hearty Cumbrian

breakfasts are served in the breakfast room, which overlooks the small front garden. Visually or hearing impaired guests are catered for, with Braille information, televisions with teletext, and a loop system installed in the dining room.
Rooms 4 en suite (1 fmly) S £35–£40; D £50–£55 **Facilities** TVB tea/coffee Cen ht **Notes** No children 3yrs

★★★★ GUEST ACCOMMODATION
Dorchester House
17 Southey St CA12 4EG
☎ 017687 73256
e–mail: dennis@dorchesterhouse.co.uk
dir: *200yds E of town centre. Off A5271 Penrith Rd onto Southey St, 150yds on left*
A warm welcome awaits you at this guest house, just a stroll from the town centre and its amenities. The comfortably proportioned, well-maintained bedrooms offer pleasing coordinated decor. Hearty breakfasts are served in the attractive ground-floor dining room. This is a non-smoking establishment.
Rooms 8 rms (7 en suite) (2 fmly) S £27–£36; D £60–£70✱ **Facilities** TVB tea/coffee Cen ht **Notes** LB ⊗

★★★★ GUEST HOUSE
Eden Green
20 Blencathra St CA12 4HP
☎ 017687 72077 📠 017687 80870
e–mail: enquiries@edengreenguesthouse.com
web: www.edengreenguesthouse.com
dir: *A591 Penrith Rd into Keswick, under railway bridge, 2nd left, house 500yds on left*
This mid-terrace house, faced with local stone, offers well-decorated and furnished bedrooms, some suitable for families and some with fine views of Skiddaw. Traditional English and vegetarian breakfasts are served in the neat breakfast room, and packed lunches can be provided on request.
Rooms 6 en suite (1 fmly) (1 GF) S £30; D £54–£60✱ **Facilities** TVB tea/coffee Cen ht Wi-fi available **Notes** LB ⊗ No children 8yrs

★★★★ GUEST ACCOMMODATION
Hazelmere
Crosthwaite Rd CA12 5PG
☎ 017687 72445 📠 017687 74075
e–mail: info@hazelmerekeswick.co.uk
web: www.hazelmerekeswick.co.uk
dir: *Off A66 at Crosthwaite rdbt (A591 junct) for Keswick, Hazelmere 400yds on right*
This large Victorian house is only a short walk from Market Square and within walking distance of Derwentwater and the local fells. The attractive bedrooms are comfortably furnished and well equipped. Hearty Cumbrian breakfasts are served at individual tables in the ground-floor dining room, which has delightful views.
Rooms 6 en suite (1 fmly) S £34–£36; D £68–£72✱ **Facilities** TVB tea/coffee Cen ht Wi-fi available **Parking** 7 **Notes** No children 8yrs

CONTINUED

★★★★ GUEST HOUSE
Hazelwood Guesthouse
Chestnut Hill CA12 4LR
☎ 017687 73496
e-mail: info@hazelwoodkeswick.com
web: www.hazelwoodkeswick.com
dir: 0.5m E of town centre on A591
Hazelwood is ideally located on the edge of town and benefits from its own private car parking. Hospitality is warm and genuine, and the gardens enjoy superb views down into Keswick and on to the fells beyond.
Rooms 6 rms (5 en suite) (1 pri facs) S fr £35; D £65✱ **Facilities** TVB tea/coffee Cen ht Wi-fi available **Parking** 6 **Notes LB** ⊗ No coaches

★★★★ GUEST ACCOMMODATION
Heatherlea
26 Blencathra St CA12 4HP
☎ 017687 72430
e-mail: info@heatherlea-keswick.co.uk
dir: 300 yds E of town centre. Off A5271 Penrith Rd on Southey St & 2nd left
Just a stroll from the town centre, this end-of-terrace Victorian house provides well-equipped bedrooms. The proprietors give a friendly welcome, and substantial breakfasts are served in the dining room, which has lovely views of the surrounding fells.
Rooms 4 en suite (1 fmly) **Facilities** TVB tea/coffee Cen ht **Notes** ⊗ No children 5yrs Closed Jan ⊜

★★★★ GUEST HOUSE
Hedgehog Hill Guest House
18 Blencathra St CA12 4HP
☎ 017687 80654
e-mail: keith@hedgehoghill.co.uk
dir: M6 junct 40, take A66 to Keswick. Left onto Blencathra St
Expect warm hospitality at this Victorian terrace house. Hedgehog Hill is convenient for the town centre, the many walks and local attractions. Bedrooms are comfortably equipped and offer thoughtful extras. Hearty breakfasts are served in the light and airy dining room with vegetarians well catered for.
Rooms 6 rms (4 en suite) S £26–£35; D £56–£80✱ **Facilities** TVB tea/coffee Cen ht **Notes** ⊗ No children 12yrs No coaches

★★★★ GUEST ACCOMMODATION
The Hollies
Threlkeld CA12 4RX
☎ 017687 79216 📄 017687 79216
e-mail: info@theholliesinlakeland.co.uk
web: www.theholliesinlakeland.co.uk
dir: 3m E of Keswick. Off A66 into Threlkeld, The Hollies opp village hall
Built in 1900 using local stone, The Hollies is an impressive detached property in the heart of Threlkeld. Lying at the foot of Blencathra, it is on the coast-to-coast walk, and the sea-to-sea cycle route. The attractive bedrooms are well equipped, and hearty breakfasts served in the dining room feature the best of local produce and home-made bread.
Rooms 4 en suite **Facilities** STV TVB tea/coffee Cen ht **Parking** 6 **Notes** ⊜

★★★★ 🏠 BED & BREAKFAST
Honister House
1 Borrowdale Rd CA12 5DD
☎ 017687 73181
e-mail: honisterhouse@btconnect.com
web: www.honisterhouse.co.uk
dir: 100yds S of town centre, off Market Sq onto Borrowdale Rd

This charming family home is one of the oldest properties in Keswick, dating from the 18th century, and has attractive and well-equipped bedrooms. John and Susie Stakes are the friendly proprietors, who offer a warm welcome and serve hearty breakfasts utilising high quality local, organic and Fair Trade produce wherever possible.
Rooms 3 en suite **Facilities** TVB tea/coffee Cen ht **Notes** ⊗

ENGLAND

KESWICK CONTINUED

★★★★ GUEST ACCOMMODATION
Keswick Park

33 Station Rd CA12 4NA
☎ 017687 72072 🖥 017687 74816
e–mail: reservations@keswickparkhotel.com
web: www.keswickparkhotel.com

dir: *200yds NE of town centre. Off A5271 Penrith Rd onto Station Rd*

A friendly welcome awaits you at this comfortable Victorian house, situated within a short walking distance of the town centre. Bedrooms are mostly of a good size, and have homely extras. The breakfast room is in two sections, one with a good outlook, and there also is a cosy bar. Fine days can be enjoyed sitting on the front garden patio with a refreshment.

Rooms 16 en suite (2 fmly) S £35–£39; D £70–£100✷ **Facilities** TVB tea/coffee Direct dial from bedrooms Cen ht TVL Wi-fi available **Parking** 8 **Notes LB** ⊗

★★★★ GUEST HOUSE
Sunnyside Guest House

25 Southey St CA12 4EF
☎ 017687 72446
e–mail: enquiries@sunnysideguesthouse.com
web: www.sunnysideguesthouse.com

dir: *200yds E of town centre. Off A5271 Penrith Rd onto Southey St, Sunnyside on left*

This stylish guest house is in a quiet area close to the town centre. Bedrooms, which have been refurbished to a high standard, include a

family room, and are comfortably furnished and well equipped. There is a spacious and comfortable lounge with plenty of books and magazines. Breakfast is served at individual tables in the airy and attractive dining room, and private parking is available.

Rooms 7 en suite (1 fmly) S £40–£45; D £60–£74✷ **Facilities** TVB tea/coffee Cen ht **Parking** 8 **Notes LB** ⊗ No children 12yrs No coaches

★★★★ 🄰 BED & BREAKFAST
The Bungalows Country Guest House

The Bungalows, Sunnyside, Threlkeld CA12 4SD
☎ 01768 779679
e–mail: paulsunley@msn.com
web: www.thebungalows.co.uk

dir: *From A66 turn into Threlkeld follow the Bungalows signs*
Rooms 4 rms (3 en suite) (1 pri facs) (3 fmly) (4 GF) D £60–£70✷ **Facilities** STV FTV TVB tea/coffee Cen ht TVL **Parking** 14 **Notes LB**

★★★★ 🄰 GUEST HOUSE
Sandon Guesthouse

13 Southey St CA12 4EG
☎ 017687 73648
e–mail: enquiries@sandonguesthouse.com

dir: *200yds E of town centre. Off A5271 Penrith Rd onto Southey St*
Rooms 6 rms (5 en suite) (1 pri facs) S £28–£35; D £50–£70 **Facilities** TVB tea/coffee Cen ht **Notes** ⊗ No children 4yrs No coaches Closed 24 Dec (day), 25–26 Dec

★★★★ 🄰 GUEST HOUSE
Watendlath

15 Acorn St CA12 4EA
☎ 017687 74165 🖥 017687 74165
e–mail: info@watendlathguesthouse.co.uk

dir: *350yds SE of town centre. Off A5271 Penrith Rd onto Southey St, left onto Acorn St*
Rooms 4 en suite (2 fmly) D £50–£64✷ **Facilities** TVB tea/coffee Cen ht **Notes** ⊗ Closed Xmas ⊜

★★★ GUEST ACCOMMODATION
Brierholme

21 Bank St CA12 5JZ
☎ 017687 72938
e–mail: enquiries@brierholme.co.uk
web: www.brierholme.co.uk

dir: *On A591, 100yds from Post Office*
The house is just a short walk from the main square. Bedrooms are traditionally furnished and thoughtfully equipped, and the rear rooms have lovely views of Skiddaw. Hearty breakfasts are served in the neat breakfast room.

Rooms 6 en suite (2 fmly) D £60–£70✷ **Facilities** TVB tea/coffee Cen ht **Parking** 6 **Notes LB** No children 5yrs

CONTINUED

★★★ FARM HOUSE
Low Nest Farm B&B *(NY282224)*
Castlerigg CA12 4TF

☎ 017687 72378 Mrs A True

e-mail: info@lownestfarm.co.uk

dir: *2m S of Keswick, off A591 Windermere Rd*

Low Nest Farm is a small, family-run farm set in some typically breath-taking Cumbrian scenery. Bedrooms are comfortable, en suite and benefit from views of the aforementioned landscape. There are of course, any number of walks available in the area, and Keswick is just two miles away.

Rooms 3 en suite (3 GF) **Facilities** tea/coffee Cen ht TVL Wi-fi available **Parking** 10 **Notes** No children 16yrs 120 acres Mixed RS Nov–Mar ☻

KIRKBY LONSDALE   **MAP 18 SD67**

Premier Collection

★ ★ ★ ★ ★ ◉◉◉ RESTAURANT WITH ROOMS
Hipping Hall
Cowan Bridge LA6 2JJ

☎ 015242 71187 📄 015242 72452

e-mail: info@hippinghall.com

Close to the market town of Kirkby Lonsdale, Hipping Hall is surrounded by four Areas of Outstanding Natural Beauty – Eden Valley, Lake District, Yorkshire Dales and Trough of Bowland. The accommodation has spacious feature bedrooms, designed in tranquil colours. The dining room is a feature of the hall with fine culinary fare being served to a very high standard.

Rooms 6 en suite 3 annexe en suite (1 GF) S £152.50–£197.50; D £205–£295✳ (incl. dinner) **Facilities** TVB Direct dial from bedrooms Cen ht Dinner Last d 9.30pm **Parking** 30 **Notes** ☻ No children 12yrs Closed 1–29 Jan Civ Wed 40

Premier Collection

★★★★★ ◉ 🍴 INN
The Sun Inn
6 Market St LA6 2AU

☎ 015242 71965 📄 015242 72485

e-mail: email@sun-inn.info

web: www.sun-inn.info

dir: *From A65, follow signs to Kirkby town centre. Inn on main street*

A 17th-century inn situated in a historic market town, overlooking St Mary's Church. The atmospheric bar features stone walls, wooden beams and log fires with real ales available. Delicious meals are served in the bar and more formal, modern restaurant. Traditional and modern styles are blended together in the beautifully appointed rooms with excellent en suites.

Rooms 11 en suite (2 fmly) S £65–£110; D £90–£130✳ **Facilities** TVB tea/coffee Cen ht Dinner Last d 9–9.30pm Wi-fi available **Notes** No coaches

★★★★ ⬛ INN
The Snooty Fox Inn
33 Main St LA6 2AH

☎ 01524 271308 📄 01524 272642

e-mail: snootyfoxhotel@talktalk.net

dir: *M6 junct 36, A65 towards Skipton for 5.5m. At Kirkby Lonsdale follow signs for town centre, next to Market Sq*

Located on the Main Street, this charming Jacobean inn offers traditional yet fully equipped bedrooms. Public areas include a well furnished bar and restaurant, with log fires lit in the colder months. A variety of dishes are served utilising fresh local produce.

Rooms 9 en suite **Facilities** TVB tea/coffee Cen ht Dinner Last d 9pm Wi-fi available **Parking** 5 **Notes** No coaches

★★★ 🅰 GUEST ACCOMMODATION
The Copper Kettle
3–5 Market St LA6 2AU

☎ 015242 71714 📄 015242 71714

e-mail: gamble_p@btconnect.com

dir: *In town centre, down lane by Post Office*

Rooms 5 en suite (2 fmly) S £28; D £41–£48✳ **Facilities** TVB tea/coffee Dinner Last d 9pm **Parking** 3 **Notes** LB

KIRKBY STEPHEN   **MAP 18 NY70**

★★★★ GUEST HOUSE
Brownber Hall Country House
Newbiggin-on-Lune CA17 4NX

☎ 01539 623208

e-mail: enquiries@brownberhall.co.uk

web: www.brownberhall.co.uk

dir: *6m SW of Kirkby Stephen. Off A685 signed Great Asby, 60yds right through gatehouse, 0.25m sharp left onto driveway*

Having an elevated position with superb views of the surrounding countryside, Brownber Hall, built in 1860, has been restored to its original glory. The en suite bedrooms are comfortably proportioned, attractively decorated and well equipped. The ground floor has two lovely reception rooms, which retain many original features, and a charming dining room where traditional breakfasts, and by arrangement delicious dinners, are served. There is also a lift.

Rooms 6 en suite (1 GF) **Facilities** TVB tea/coffee Lift Cen ht Dinner Last d 24hrs in advance **Conf** Max 20 Board 20 **Parking** 12

KIRKBY STEPHEN CONTINUED

★★★ FARM HOUSE
Southview Farm (NY785105)

Winton CA17 4HS

☎ 01768 371120 & 07801 432184 Mrs J Marston

e–mail: southviewwinton@hotmail.com

dir: *1.5m N of Kirkby Stephen. Off A685 signed Winton*

A friendly family home, Southview lies in the centre of Winton village, part of a terrace with the working farm to the rear. Two well-proportioned bedrooms are available, and there is a cosy lounge-dining room where traditional breakfasts are served around one table.

Rooms 2 rms (2 fmly) S £30; D £42✱ **Facilities** TVB tea/coffee TVL Dinner Last d 8am **Parking** 2 **Notes** 280 acres beef, dairy ⊛

LONGTOWN   MAP 21 NY36

★★★★ GUEST HOUSE
Home from Home

6 English St CA6 5SD

☎ 01228 792474

e–mail: joy762bnb@yahoo.co.uk

dir: *M6 junct 44, follow signs for A7 Longtown, situated on main road next to chip shop*

A property that really lives up to its name, a warm and genuine welcome on arrival is assured and throughout your stay. Bedrooms are comfortable and well presented with good attention to detail. A hearty breakfast with ingredients locally sourced offers a great start to the day.

Rooms 5 en suite (2 fmly) (1 GF) S fr £30; D fr £56✱ **Facilities** TVB tea/coffee Cen ht **Parking** 5 **Notes** ⊗ No children 4yrs No coaches ⊛

LEGBURTHWAITE   MAP 18 NY31

★★★ FARM HOUSE
Stybeck Farm Experience (NY319188)

CA12 4TN

☎ 017687 73232 Mr & Mrs Hodgson

e–mail: stybeckfarm@farming.co.uk

web: http://members.farmline.com/stybeckfarm

dir: *On A591 near B5322 junct*

A traditional farmhouse set below Lakeland fells and crags. Three bedrooms, one on the ground floor, are in the main house, while another two are in a nearby barn conversion. Both properties have their own dining room where hearty breakfasts are served.

Rooms 3 en suite 2 annexe en suite (1 GF) S £32–£34; D £56–£68✱ **Facilities** TVB tea/coffee Cen ht TVL **Parking** 5 **Notes LB** ⊗ No children 5yrs 200 acres dairy mixed sheep working Closed 25 Dec ⊛

LITTLE LANGDALE   MAP 18 NY30

★★★★ INN
Three Shires Inn

LA22 9NZ

☎ 015394 37215 📄 015394 37127

e–mail: enquiry@threeshiresinn.co.uk

web: www.threeshiresinn.co.uk

Enjoying an outstanding rural location, this family-run inn was built in 1872. The brightly decorated bedrooms are individual in style and many offer panoramic views. The attractive lounge features a roaring fire in the cooler months and there is a traditional style bar with a great selection of local ales. Meals can be taken in either the bar or cosy restaurant.

LORTON   MAP 18 NY12

Premier Collection

★★★★★ 🏠 ⇔ FARM HOUSE
New House Farm (NY159227)

CA13 9UU

☎ 01900 85404 📄 01900 85478 Ms H Thompson

e–mail: enquiries@newhouse-farm.co.uk

web: www.newhouse-farm.com

dir: *6m S of Cockermouth on B5289 between Lorton & Loweswater*

A warm welcome awaits you at this restored Grade II listed, 17th-century farmhouse, situated in Lorton Vale. The inviting public areas and bedrooms have been stylishly decorated to complement the original features. Bedrooms are spacious and have thoughtful extras including home-baked biscuits, and many have period-style beds and romantic bathrooms. The daily changing, delicious five-course dinner menu and hearty breakfasts are highlights. Hazel Thompson was a finalist for the AA Friendliest Landlady of the Year 2008 Award.

Rooms 3 en suite 2 annexe en suite (2 GF) S £80–£100; D £160 **Facilities** tea/coffee Licensed Cen ht Dinner Last d 1pm Wi-fi available Hot spa in the garden **Conf** Max 12 **Parking** 30 **Notes LB** No children 6yrs 15 acres non-working

★★★★★ 🛏 🍽 GUEST ACCOMMODATION
Winder Hall Country House
CA13 9UP
☎ 01900 85107 📠 01900 85479
e–mail: stay@winderhall.co.uk
web: www.winderhall.co.uk

dir: *A66 W from Keswick, at Braithwaite onto B5292 to Lorton, left at T-junct signed Buttermere, Winder Hall 0.5m on right*

Impressive Winder Hall dates from the 14th century. The lounge is luxuriously furnished and the elegant, spacious dining room is the venue for skilfully prepared meals using local produce. The smart, individually styled bedrooms are thoughtfully equipped, and all are furnished with fine antiques or pine. Two rooms have beautiful four-poster beds.

Rooms 7 en suite (2 fmly) S £52–£104; D £82–£148✱ **Facilities** FTV TVB tea/coffee Direct dial from bedrooms Cen ht Dinner Last d 8pm Wi-fi available Fishing Sauna Hot tub **Conf** Max 25 Class 25 Board 25 Del from £97 ✱ **Parking** 10 **Notes LB** ⊗ Closed 2–31 Jan Civ Wed 65

★★★★ 🛏 🍽 GUEST HOUSE
The Old Vicarage
Church Ln CA13 9UN
☎ 01900 85656
e–mail: enquiries@oldvicarage.co.uk
web: www.oldvicarage.co.uk

dir: *B5292 onto B5289 N of Lorton. 1st left signed Church, house 1st on right*

This delightful Victorian house offers spacious accommodation in the peaceful Lorton Vale, at the heart of the Lake District National Park. A converted coach-house offers two rooms with exposed stone walls, and is ideal for families with older children. Bedrooms in the main house are well equipped and have excellent views of the distant mountains. Delicious home cooking is served in the bright dining room.

Rooms 6 rms (5 en suite) (1 pri facs) 2 annexe en suite (1 GF) S £75–£80; D £110–£120✱ **Facilities** TVB tea/coffee Licensed Cen ht Dinner Last d 10am Wi-fi available **Parking** 10 **Notes** ⊗ No children 8yrs No coaches

---

LOWESWATER   MAP 18 NY12

★★★★ 🍽 INN
Kirkstile Inn
CA13 0RU
☎ 01900 85219 📠 01900 85239
e–mail: info@kirkstile.com
web: www.kirkstile.com

dir: *A66 onto B5292 into Lorton, left signed Buttermere. Signs to Loweswater, left signed Kirkstile Inn*

This historic 16th-century inn lies in a valley surrounded by mountains. Serving great food and ale, its rustic bar and adjoining rooms are a mecca for walkers. There is also a cosy restaurant offering a quieter ambiance. Bedrooms retain their original character. A spacious family suite in an annexe, with two bedrooms, a lounge and a bathroom.

Rooms 7 en suite 1 annexe en suite (1 fmly) S £59.50–£87; D £87–£97✱ **Facilities** TV2B tea/coffee Cen ht TVL Dinner Last d 9pm **Parking** 30 **Notes LB** No coaches Closed 25 Dec

---

MILLOM   MAP 18 SD18

★★★★★ 🍽 GUEST HOUSE
Underwood Country Guest House
The Hill LA18 5EZ
☎ 01229 771116 📠 01229 719900
e–mail: enquiries@underwoodhouse.co.uk

dir: *A595 onto A5093 through village, The Green & The Hill, Underwood 0.5m after The Hill*

A warm welcome is assured at this Victorian vicarage standing in mature grounds overlooking the Duddon Estuary and Whicham Valley. Bedrooms are well appointed and have a wealth of thoughtful extras. Imaginative dinners, using local produce, are served in an attractive dining room and two lounges are also available. Additional features include a self-contained conference suite, an indoor swimming pool and a tennis court.

Rooms 5 en suite S £40–£60; D £80–£120✱ **Facilities** STV TVB tea/coffee Direct dial from bedrooms Licensed Cen ht TVL Dinner Last d 10.30am Wi-fi available ⊗ 🏊 Sauna 🎾 **Conf** Max 18 Thtr 18 Class 18 Board 18 Del from £97.50 ✱ **Parking** 20 **Notes LB** ⊗ No children 14yrs

NEAR SAWREY MAP 18 SD39

Premier Collection

★★★★★ ⊛ ⚏ GUEST HOUSE
Ees Wyke Country House
LA22 0JZ
☎ 015394 36393
e-mail: mail@eeswyke.co.uk
web: www.eeswyke.co.uk
dir: *On B5285 on W side of village*

A warm welcome awaits you at this elegant Georgian country house with views over Esthwaite Water and the surrounding countryside. The thoughtfully equipped bedrooms have been decorated and furnished with care. There is a charming lounge with an open fire, and a splendid dining room where a carefully prepared five-course dinner is served. Breakfasts have a fine reputation due to the skilful use of local produce.

Rooms 8 en suite (1 GF) S £49–£78; D £98–£126 **Facilities** TVB tea/coffee Licensed Cen ht Dinner Last d noon **Parking** 12 **Notes LB** ⊗ No children 12yrs No coaches

★★★★ GUEST HOUSE
Buckle Yeat
LA22 0LF
☎ 015394 36446 & 36538
e-mail: info@buckle-yeat.co.uk
dir: *In village centre*

Close to Beatrix Potter's former home, Buckle Yeat is mentioned in some of the author's well-known tales. This charming 200-year-old cottage retains many original features, including a beamed dining

CONTINUED

room where freshly cooked breakfasts and cream teas are served. Bedrooms are pretty and there is an elegant lounge.

Rooms 7 rms (6 en suite) (1 pri facs) (1 fmly) (1 GF) S £37.50–£40; D £75–£80 **Facilities** TVB tea/coffee Cen ht TVL **Parking** 9 **Notes** No coaches Closed Jan RS Nov–Dec

NEWBY BRIDGE MAP 18 SD38

Premier Collection

★★★★★ ⚏ ⊜ GUEST ACCOMMODATION
The Knoll Country House
Lakeside LA12 8AU
☎ 015395 31347 🖪 015395 30850
e-mail: info@theknoll-lakeside.co.uk
dir: *A590 W to Newby Bridge, over rdbt, signed right for Lake Steamers, house 0.5m on left*

This delightful Victorian house stands in a leafy dell on the western side of Windermere. Public areas have many original features, including an open fire in the cosy lounge. The attractive bedrooms vary in style and outlook, and are well maintained. Enthusiastic owners share the tasks – Tracey extends a very caring and natural welcome, and Jenny offers a good choice of excellent dishes at breakfast and dinner.

Rooms 8 en suite **Facilities** TVB tea/coffee Direct dial from bedrooms Cen ht TVL Dinner Last d 6pm Wi-fi available Use of nearby hotel leisure spa **Parking** 8 **Notes** ⊗ No children 16yrs Closed 24–26 Dec

★★★★ ⚏ BED & BREAKFAST
Hill Crest
Brow Edge LA12 8QP
☎ 015395 31766 🖪 015395 31986
e-mail: enquiries@hillcrest.gbr.cc
dir: *1m SW of Newby Bridge. Off A590 onto Brow Edge Rd, house 0.75m on right*

Set in picturesque surroundings with stunning views offering a high standard of en-suite accommodation at this well kept Lakeland home. All rooms are individual and well maintained. The lounge doubles as a breakfast room and opens out on to a large patio to the rear. The breakfast menu makes good use of fresh local produce. Warm and genuine hospitality is guaranteed.

Rooms 3 en suite (2 fmly) (1 GF) S £42–£50; D £56–£80 **Facilities** TVB tea/coffee Cen ht TVL Free use of local leisure club if staying 5 nights **Parking** 4 **Notes LB** ⊗ Closed 22–26 Dec

★★★★ 🏠 🍴 GUEST HOUSE
Lyndhurst Country House
LA12 8ND
☎ 015395 31245
e-mail: chris@lyndhurstcountryhouse.co.uk

dir: *On the junct of A590 and A592 at Newby Bridge rdbt*
This 1920s house is situated close to the southern tip of Lake Windermere. Accommodation consists of three comfortable, tastefully decorated bedrooms, each with en suite shower room. Evening meals and hearty breakfasts feature local produce and are served in the pleasant dining room, which also has a lounge area opening onto the garden.

Rooms 3 en suite S £40; D £60–£70✶ **Facilities** TVB tea/coffee Licensed Cen ht Dinner Last d noon **Parking** 3 **Notes** ⊗ No children 8yrs No coaches Closed 23–28 Dec

★★★★ BED & BREAKFAST
The Coach House
Hollow Oak LA12 8AD
☎ 015395 31622
e-mail: coachho@talk21.com
web: www.coachho.com

dir: *2.5m SW of Newby Bridge. Off A590 onto B5278 signed Cark & left into car park*
This converted coach house stands in delightful gardens south of Lake Windermere. The hosts offer a warm welcome and are a good source of local knowledge. The modern bedrooms are light and airy, and there is a cosy lounge. Breakfast is served in a converted stable.

Rooms 3 rms (2 en suite) (1 pri facs) S £35; D £55 **Facilities** tea/coffee Cen ht TVL **Parking** 3 **Notes LB** ⊗ No children 10yrs ◉

★★★★ GUEST HOUSE
Lakes End
LA12 8ND
☎ 015395 31260 📠 015395 31260
e-mail: info@lakes-end.co.uk
web: www.lakes-end.co.uk

dir: *On A590 in Newby Bridge, 100yds from rdbt*
In a sheltered, wooded setting away from the road, Lakes End is convenient for the coast and the lakes. The bedrooms have been thoughtfully furnished and equipped. Traditional English breakfasts are served, and delicious home-cooked evening meals can be provided by arrangement.

Rooms 4 en suite (1 fmly) (1 GF) S £35–£40; D £60–£70✶ **Facilities** STV FTV TVB tea/coffee Licensed Cen ht Dinner Last d 6pm **Parking** 4 **Notes LB** ⊗ No coaches

PENRITH   MAP 18 NY53

★★★★★ 🅰 GUEST ACCOMMODATION
Roundthorn Country House
Beacon Edge CA11 8SJ
☎ 01768 863952 📠 01768 864100
e-mail: enquiries@roundthorn.co.uk

dir: *1.2m NE of town centre. Off A686 signed Roundthorn*
Rooms 10 en suite (3 fmly) S £67–£74; D £95–£105✶ **Facilities** TVB tea/coffee Direct dial from bedrooms Cen ht Dinner Last d 9.30pm Wi-fi available **Conf** Max 200 Thtr 200 Class 200 Board 50 Del from £120 ✶ **Parking** 60 **Notes LB** ⊗ Civ Wed 100

★★★★ GUEST HOUSE
Brandelhow
1 Portland Place CA11 7QN
☎ 01768 864470
e-mail: enquiries@brandelhowguesthouse.co.uk
web: www.brandelhowguesthouse.co.uk

dir: *In town centre on one-way system, left at town hall*
Situated within easy walking distance of central amenities, this constantly improving and friendly guest house is also convenient for the Lakes and M6. The individually themed bedrooms are thoughtfully furnished and some are suitable for families. Breakfasts, utilising quality local produce, are served in a Cumbria-themed dining room overlooking the pretty patio garden.

Rooms 5 rms (4 en suite) (1 pri facs) (2 fmly) S £35; D £65–£75✶ **Facilities** FTV TVB tea/coffee Cen ht **Notes** ⊗ No coaches Closed 25–26, 31 Dec & 1 Jan

★★★★ GUEST HOUSE
Brooklands
2 Portland Place CA11 7QN
☎ 01768 863395 📠 01768 863395
e-mail: enquiries@brooklandsguesthouse.com
web: www.brooklandsguesthouse.com

dir: *From town hall onto Portland Place, 50yds on left*
A friendly welcome awaits at this delightful Victorian terrace house. Bedrooms are beautifully decorated, well equipped and have furniture made by local craftsmen. There is a family room and a four-poster suite. A hearty breakfast is served at individual tables in the stylish dining room. A courtesy collection service from the railway or bus station is available by arrangement. This is a non-smoking establishment.

Rooms 7 en suite (2 fmly) **Facilities** TVB tea/coffee Cen ht Wi-fi available **Parking** 2 **Notes** ⊗

PENRITH CONTINUED

★★★★ GUEST HOUSE
Acorn Guest House
Scotland Rd CA11 9HL
☎ 01768 868696
e–mail: acornguesthouse@fsmail.net
web: www.acorn-guesthouse.co.uk

The house, recently refurbished, is on the edge of the town and is
popular with walkers and cyclists. Bedrooms are generally spacious
and a substantial, freshly cooked breakfast is offered. Drying facilities
are available.
Rooms 8 en suite (1 fmly) **Facilities** TVB tea/coffee Licensed Cen ht
Parking 8 **Notes** ⊗

★★★★ GUEST ACCOMMODATION
Beckfoot Country House
CA10 2QB
☎ 01931 713241 📠 01931 713391
e–mail: info@beckfoot.co.uk
(For full entry see Helton)

★★★★ GUEST HOUSE
Glendale
4 Portland Place CA11 7QN
☎ 01768 210061
e–mail: glendaleguesthouse@yahoo.co.uk
web: www.glendaleguesthouse.com

dir: *M6 junct 40, town centre signs. Pass castle, turn left before
town hall*
This friendly family-run guest house is part of a Victorian terrace only a
stroll from the town centre and convenient for the lakes and Eden
Valley. Drying facilities are available. Bedrooms vary in size, but all are
attractive, and well equipped and presented. Hearty breakfasts are
served at individual tables in the charming ground-floor dining room.
Rooms 7 rms (6 en suite) (1 pri facs) (4 fmly) S £35; D £60✱
Facilities TVB tea/coffee Cen ht Wi-fi available

★★★★ 🅰 GUEST ACCOMMODATION
Tymparon Hall
Newbiggin, Stainton CA11 0HS
☎ 017684 83236
e–mail: margaret@tymparon.freeserve.co.uk
web: www.tymparon.freeserve.co.uk

dir: *M6 junct 40, A66 towards Keswick for 1.75m, right turn for
Newbiggin, Tymparon Hall on right*
Rooms 3 rms (2 en suite) (1 pri facs) (2 fmly) **Facilities** tea/coffee
Cen ht TVL **Parking** available **Notes** ⊗ No children 3 yrs RS Feb–Nov
🐾

★★★ GUEST HOUSE
Albany House
5 Portland Place CA11 7QN
☎ 01768 863072
e–mail: info@albany-house.org.uk

dir: *Turn left at town hall onto Portland Place. 30yds on the left*
A well maintained Victorian house located close to Penrith town centre.
Bedrooms are spacious, comfortable and thoughtfully equipped.
Wholesome breakfasts utilising local ingredients are served in the
attractive breakfast room.
Rooms 5 rms (2 en suite) (3 fmly) D £50–£70✱ **Facilities** TVB tea/
coffee Cen ht

★★★ GUEST HOUSE
Abbey House
7 Victoria Rd CA11 8HR
☎ 01768 863414 & 07949 771548 📠 01768 863414
e–mail: anneabbeyhouse@aol.com
web: www.abbeyhousebandb.co.uk

dir: *500yds SE of town centre on A6 Victoria Rd*
Located close to the centre of town, Abbey House offers a warm
atmosphere and comfortable accommodation. Breakfast is served in
the attractive downstairs dining room.
Rooms 4 en suite (1 fmly) (1 GF) **Facilities** TVB tea/coffee Cen ht
Parking 4 **Notes** ⊗ 🐾

🆄
The Black Swan Inn
Culgaith CA10 1QW
☎ 01768 88223
e–mail: info@blackswanculgaith.co.uk
At the time of going to press the rating for this establishment had not
been confirmed. Please check the AA website www.theAA.com for
up-to-date information.
Rooms 7 en suite S £39.50–£60; D £75–£80✱

See advert on opposite page

POOLEY BRIDGE — MAP 18 NY42

★★★★ GUEST HOUSE
Elm House
High St CA10 2NH
☎ 017684 86334
e-mail: enquiries@stayullswater.co.uk
web: www.stayullswater.co.uk

dir: *B5320 into village, next to church*

Mark and Anne offer a friendly welcome at this delightful stone built house at the edge of the village. The attractive bedrooms are thoughtfully equipped with ground floor and family rooms available. A good range is offered at breakfast in the conservatory style dining room looking over unspoilt gardens.

Rooms 8 rms (7 en suite) (1 pri facs) (1 fmly) (3 GF) S £50–£75; D £60–£90✳ **Facilities** TVB tea/coffee Cen ht Wi-fi available **Parking** 9 **Notes** ⊗ No coaches

RAVENSTONEDALE — MAP 18 NY70

★★★★ 🏠 🍽 INN
The Black Swan
CA17 4NG
☎ 015396 23204 📠 015396 23204
e-mail: enquiries@blackswanhotel.com

dir: *M6 junct 38. Situated on A685 W of Kirkby Stephen*

Set in the heart of this quiet village, the inn is popular with visitors and locals and offers a very friendly welcome. Bedrooms are individually styled and comfortably equipped. There is an informal atmosphere in the bar areas and homemade meals can be taken in the bar or the stylish dining room. Relax by the fire in the cooler months and enjoy the riverside garden in the summer.

Rooms 7 rms (6 en suite) (1 pri facs) 3 annexe en suite (3 fmly) (3 GF) **Facilities** TVB tea/coffee Cen ht Dinner Last d 9pm Wi-fi available Golf 9 🎣 Fishing Snooker **Conf** Max 14 Thtr 14 Class 14 Board 14 **Parking** 20

RAVENSTONEDALE CONTINUED

★★★ INN
The Kings Head
CA17 4NH
☎ 015396 23284
e-mail: enquiries@kings-head.net
web: www.kings-head.net
dir: *Off A685 into village centre*

This delightful village inn offers comfortably furnished bedrooms and public areas that display much character. The bar, warmed by roaring log fires in the cooler months, attracts a mix of locals and visitors, while the extensive menu, featuring local produce whenever possible, is served either here or in the candlelit restaurant.

Rooms 3 rms (2 en suite) (1 pri facs) (1 fmly) **Facilities** TVB tea/coffee Cen ht Dinner Last d 9pm Pool Table **Conf** Max 30 Thtr 30 Board 20 **Parking** 10

See advert on page 125

RYDAL   MAP 18 NY30

See Ambleside

SEASCALE   MAP 18 NY00

★★★★ ◉ RESTAURANT WITH ROOMS
Cumbrian Lodge
Gosforth Rd CA20 1JG
☎ 019467 27309 🖹 019467 27158
e-mail: cumbrianlodge@btconnect.com
web: www.cumbrianlodge.com

dir: *Off A595 at Gosforth onto B5344 signed Seascale, 2m on left*
A relaxed and friendly atmosphere prevails at this well-run restaurant with rooms, where well-prepared tasty dinners are a popular local attraction. Décor and fixtures are modern throughout, and the bedrooms are well-equipped for business and leisure guests. The new thatched garden buildings provide a delightful location for dining al fresco, an elegant setting for groups of up to eight.

Rooms 6 en suite (1 fmly) S £74.50; D £90✱ **Facilities** STV TVB tea/coffee Direct dial from bedrooms Cen ht Dinner Last d 9.30pm Wi-fi available ☁ **Parking** 15 **Notes** ⊗

SEDBERGH   MAP 18 SD69

★★★ INN
Cross Keys Temperance Inn
Cautley LA10 5NE
☎ 015396 20284 🖹 015396 21966
e-mail: clowes@freeuk.com

dir: *4m NE of Sedbergh on A683*
Built in the 1732, this charming inn retains many original features. No alcohol is sold at this temperance inn, though you can bring your own to go with the ambitious home-cooked dishes. Bedrooms are traditionally presented and thoughtfully equipped, and the conservatory has delightful views of the dales.

Rooms 2 en suite (1 fmly) **Facilities** tea/coffee Direct dial from bedrooms Cen ht Dinner Last d 9pm Riding **Parking** 9 **Notes** ⊗

SHAP   MAP 18 NY51

★★★★ GUEST HOUSE
Brookfield
CA10 3PZ
☎ 01931 716397 🖹 01931 716397
e-mail: info@brookfieldshap.co.uk

dir: *M6 junct 39, A6 towards Shap, 1st accommodation off motorway*
Having a quiet rural location within easy reach of the M6, this inviting house stands in well-tended gardens. Bedrooms are thoughtfully appointed and well maintained. There is a comfortable lounge, and a small bar area next to the traditional dining room where substantial, home-cooked breakfasts and dinners are served at individual tables.

Rooms 4 rms (3 en suite) **Facilities** TVB tea/coffee Licensed Cen ht TVL Dinner Last d 6pm **Conf** Max 20 **Parking** 20 **Notes** ⊗ No children 12yrs No coaches Closed Jan ⊜

TEBAY   MAP 18 NY60

★★★★ 🅰 GUEST ACCOMMODATION
Primrose Cottage
Orton Rd CA10 3TL
☎ 01539 624791 & 07778 520930
e-mail: primrosecottebay@aol.com

dir: *M6 junct 38, right at rdbt, 1st house on right*
Rooms 3 rms (1 en suite) (2 pri facs) (2 GF) S £30–£50; D £60–£70✱ **Facilities** TVB tea/coffee Direct dial from bedrooms Cen ht Wi-fi available **Parking** 8 **Notes** LB ⊜

TEMPLE SOWERBY   MAP 18 NY62

★★★ FARM HOUSE
Skygarth Farm (NY612261)
CA10 1SS

☎ 01768 361300 📠 01768 361300 Mrs Robinson
e–mail: enquire@skygarth.co.uk

dir: *Off A66 at Temple Sowerby for Morland, Skygarth 500yds on right, follow signs*

Skygarth is just south of the village, half a mile from the busy main road. The house stands in a cobbled courtyard surrounded by cowsheds and with gardens to the rear, where red squirrels feed. There are two well-proportioned bedrooms and an attractive lounge where tasty breakfasts are served.

Rooms 2 rms (2 fmly) S £25–£30; D £45–£50✳ **Facilities** FTV TVB tea/coffee Cen ht TVL **Parking** 4 **Notes** ⊗ 200 acres Mixed Closed Dec–Jan ⊜

THIRLMERE

See Legburthwaite

TROUBECK   MAP 18 NY32
(NEAR KESWICK)

★★★★ GUEST HOUSE
Lane Head Farm
CA11 0SY

☎ 017687 79220
e–mail: info@laneheadfarm.co.uk
web: www.laneheadfarm.co.uk

dir: *On A66 between Penrith & Keswick*

This delightful converted farmhouse dates from the 18th century and enjoys a peaceful location with magnificent views. Bedrooms are comfortable and well equipped, and two are furnished with four poster beds. One bedroom is on the ground floor. Public areas are well presented and include a comfortable lounge and spacious dining room with an open log fire. Meals are freshly prepared using local ingredients, and hosts Josette and Mark offer a warm welcome to all.

Rooms 7 en suite (1 GF) S £45–£80; D £68–£80✳ **Facilities** TVB tea/coffee Licensed Cen ht Dinner Last d 10am **Parking** 9 **Notes LB** ⊗ No children 12yrs No coaches

---

TROUBECK   MAP 18 NY40
(NEAR WINDERMERE)

★★★★★ ⊜ GUEST ACCOMMODATION
Broadoaks Country House
Bridge Ln LA23 1LA

☎ 015394 45566 📠 015394 88766

e–mail: enquiries@broadoakscountryhouse.co.uk
web: www.broadoakscountryhouse.co.uk

dir: *Exit A591 junct 36 pass Windermere. Filing station on left, 1st right 0.5m*

This impressive Lakeland stone house has been restored to its original Victorian grandeur and is set in seven acres of landscaped grounds with stunning views of the Troutbeck Valley. Individually furnished bedrooms are well appointed and en suite bathrooms feature either whirlpool or Victorian roll top baths. Spacious day rooms include the music room, featuring a Bechstein piano. Meals are served by friendly and attentive staff in the elegant dining room.

Rooms 11 en suite 3 annexe en suite (5 fmly) (4 GF) **Facilities** FTV TVB tea/coffee Direct dial from bedrooms Cen ht Dinner Last d 8pm Wi-fi available Fishing Snooker ⤙ ⚂ Arrangement with local leisure facility **Conf** Max 62 Thtr 40 Class 45 Board 45 **Parking** 40 **Notes** Civ Wed 62

★★★★ ⊜ INN
Queens Head
Town Head LA23 1PW

☎ 015394 32174 📠 015394 31938

e–mail: feast@queensheadhotel.com
web: www.queensheadhotel.com

dir: *A592 from Windermere for Penrith/Ullswater, Queens Head 2m on right*

This 17th-century coaching inn has stunning views of the Troutbeck valley. The delightful bedrooms, several with four-poster beds, are traditionally furnished and equipped with modern facilities. Beams, flagstone floors, and a bar that was once an Elizabethan four-poster, provide a wonderful setting in which to enjoy imaginative food, real ales and fine wines.

Rooms 10 en suite 5 annexe en suite (2 fmly) (2 GF) **Facilities** TVB tea/coffee Cen ht Dinner Last d 9pm **Parking** 100 **Notes** ⊗ No coaches Closed 25 Dec

ENGLAND

ULVERSTON
MAP 18 SD27

★★★★ BED & BREAKFAST
Church Walk House

Church Walk LA12 7EW
☎ 01229 582211
e–mail: martinchadd@btinternet.com

dir: *In town centre opp Stables furniture shop*

This Grade II listed 18th-century residence stands in the heart of the historic market town. Stylishly decorated, the accommodation includes attractive bedrooms with a mix of antiques and contemporary pieces. A peaceful atmosphere prevails with attentive service, and there is a small herbal garden and patio.

Rooms 3 rms (2 en suite) S £25–£40; D £55–£65✳ **Facilities** tea/coffee Cen ht TVL **Notes LB** ⊕

WATERMILLOCK
MAP 18 NY42

★★★★ 🛏 INN
Brackenrigg

CA11 0LP
☎ 017684 86206 🖷 017684 86945
e–mail: enquiries@brackenrigginn.co.uk
web: www.brackenrigginn.co.uk

dir: *6m from M6 onto A66 towards Keswick & A592 to Ullswater, right at lake & continue 2m*

An 18th-century coaching inn with superb views of Ullswater and the surrounding countryside. Freshly prepared dishes and daily specials are served by friendly staff in the traditional bar and restaurant. The bedrooms include six attractive rooms in the stable cottages.

Rooms 11 en suite 6 annexe en suite (8 fmly) (3 GF) **Facilities** TVB tea/coffee Cen ht Dinner Last d 9pm **Conf** Max 48 Thtr 36 Class 12 Board 16 **Parking** 40

WHITEHAVEN
MAP 18 NX91

★★★★ GUEST ACCOMMODATION
Corkickle Guest House

1 Corkickle CA28 8AA
☎ 01946 692073 🖷 01946 629073

dir: *500yds SE of town centre off A5094*

This delightful, beautifully maintained house has an elevated position at the end of a Georgian terrace fronted by a cobbled street. There is an inviting lounge and a smart dining room where breakfasts are served around one large table. The well-equipped bedrooms are individually styled and smartly decorated.

Rooms 6 rms (4 en suite) (1 pri facs) S £35; D £55✳ **Facilities** TVB tea/coffee Cen ht TVL **Parking** 2 **Notes LB** ⊗

★★★★ GUEST HOUSE
Glenfield Guest House

Back Corkickle CA28 7TS
☎ 01946 691911 & 07749 856784 🖷 01946 694060
e–mail: glenfieldgh@aol.com
web: www.glenfield-whitehaven.co.uk

dir: *0.5m SE of town centre on A5094*

The imposing, family-run Victorian house is in a conservation area close to the historic town centre and harbour. Margaret and Andrew provide a relaxed environment with friendly but unobtrusive service, and this is a good start point for the Sea to Sea (C2C) cycle ride.

Rooms 6 en suite (2 fmly) **Facilities** TVB tea/coffee Licensed Cen ht TVL Dinner Last d 7.30pm Wi-fi available **Notes** No coaches

WIGTON
MAP 18 NY24

★★★ INN
Wheyrigg Hall Inn

Nr Abbeytown CA7 0DH
☎ 016973 61242 🖷 016973 61020
e–mail: wheyrigg-hall@tiscali.co.uk
web: www.wheyrigg.co.uk

dir: *From S M6 junct 41 onto B5305 towards Wigton onto B5302. From N M6 junct 44 onto A595/A596 onto B5302 towards Abbeytown*

Wheyrigg Hall is popular with locals and offers a friendly welcome. Bedrooms are comfortably furnished and well equipped. There is an informal atmosphere in the bar areas and meals can be taken in the bar or restaurant. Two function rooms are available for conferences, weddings and other celebrations.

Rooms 14 en suite (2 fmly) (6 GF) S £40–£46; D £60–£66✳ **Facilities** FTV TVB tea/coffee Cen ht TVL Dinner Last d 8.55pm Pool Table **Conf** Max 50 Thtr 50 Class 40 Board 30 **Parking** 50 **Notes LB** ⊗ Closed 25 Dec

WINDERMERE   MAP 18 SD49

Premier Collection

★★★★★ GUEST HOUSE
Beaumont House
Holly Rd LA23 2AF
☎ 015394 47075 📠 015394 88311
e–mail: lakesbeaumont@btinternet.com
web: www.lakesbeaumont.co.uk

dir: *After one-way system left onto Ellerthwaite Rd & 1st left*

A warm welcome awaits you at this smart, traditional house, in a peaceful location just a stroll from the town centre. Bedrooms, some with four-poster beds, are individually furnished to a high standard, as are the modern bathrooms. The spacious lounge has an honesty bar, and hearty breakfasts are served in the smartly appointed dining room.

Rooms 10 en suite (4 GF) S £45–£60; D £80–£150✱ **Facilities** TVB tea/coffee Licensed Cen ht TVL Wi-fi available Membership of Country Club **Parking** 10 **Notes LB** ⊗ No children 12yrs

Premier Collection

★★★★★ GUEST HOUSE
The Howbeck
New Rd LA23 2LA
☎ 015394 44739
e–mail: relax@howbeck.co.uk

dir: *A591 through Windermere town centre, left towards Bowness*

Howbeck is a delightful Victorian villa, convenient for the village and the lake. Bedrooms are well appointed and feature lovely soft furnishings, some with new luxurious spa baths. There is a bright lounge with internet access and an attractive dining room where home-prepared dinners and hearty Cumbrian breakfasts are served at individual tables. This house is non-smoking.

Rooms 10 en suite 1 annexe en suite (3 GF) **Facilities** STV TVB tea/coffee Licensed Cen ht TVL Dinner Last d noon Wi-fi available **Parking** 12 **Notes** ⊗ No children 12yrs No coaches Closed 24–25 Dec

Premier Collection

★★★★★ BED & BREAKFAST
Low House
Cleabarrow LA23 3NA
☎ 015394 43156
e–mail: info@lowhouse.co.uk
web: www.lowhouse.co.uk

dir: *A591 N past Kendal, 1st left B5284 signed Crook. After 5m, past Windermere Golf Club, 1st right signed Heathwaite, Low House on right*

This delightful 17th-century house is in a quiet location just off the road that passes the golf club and a 25-minute country walk from Bowness. Restored to create a homely atmosphere, the bedrooms are well equipped and there are two lounges in addition to the breakfast room.

CONTINUED

An optional extra is the hire of the family's 1965 Bentley to visit local restaurants and attractions.

Rooms 3 rms (2 en suite) (1 pri facs) **Facilities** TVB tea/coffee Cen ht ⚓ **Parking** 5 **Notes** No children 12yrs

Premier Collection

★★★★★ GUEST HOUSE
Newstead
New Rd LA23 2EE
☎ 015394 44485 📠 015394 88904
e–mail: info@newstead-guesthouse.co.uk

dir: *0.5m from A591 between Windermere & Bowness*

A family home set in landscaped gardens, this spacious Victorian house offers very comfortable well-equipped accommodation. The attractive bedrooms are very individual and retain original features such as fireplaces and include many thoughtful extra touches. There is an elegant lounge and a smart dining room where freshly cooked breakfasts are served at individual tables.

Rooms 7 en suite (1 fmly) **Facilities** TVB tea/coffee Cen ht **Parking** 10 **Notes** ⊗ No children 7yrs ⚓

Premier Collection

★★★★★ GUEST HOUSE
Oakbank House
Helm Rd LA23 3BU
☎ 015394 43386 📠 015394 47965
e–mail: enquiries@oakbankhousehotel.co.uk
web: www.oakbankhousehotel.co.uk

dir: *Off A591 through town centre into Bowness, Helm Rd 100yds on left after cinema*

Oakbank House is just off the main street in Bowness village, overlooking Windermere and the fells beyond. Bedrooms are individually styled, attractive and very well equipped; most have stunning lake views. There is an elegant lounge with a perpetual coffee pot, and delicious breakfasts are served at individual tables in the dining room.

Rooms 12 en suite (3 GF) D £50–£110 **Facilities** TVB tea/coffee Licensed Cen ht Wi-fi available Free membership to local country club **Parking** 14 **Notes LB** ⊗ RS 20–26 Dec

WINDERMERE CONTINUED

Rooms 10 rms (9 en suite) (2 fmly) (3 GF) **Facilities** TVB tea/coffee Licensed Cen ht TVL Dinner Last d 24hrs ⬥ **Conf** Max 20 Thtr 20 Class 10 Board 12 **Parking** 10 **Notes** No children 6yrs

See advert on opposite page

Premier Collection

★★★★★ GUEST HOUSE
The Woodlands

New Rd LA23 2EE
☎ 015394 43915 🖷 015394 43915
e–mail: enquiries@woodlands-windermere.co.uk
web: www.woodlands-windermere.co.uk

dir: *One-way system through town down New Rd towards lake, premises by war memorial clock*

Just a short walk from Lake Windermere, guests can expect stylish accommodation and friendly, attentive service. Bedrooms (including two contemporary 4-poster rooms) have been individually decorated and feature quality furnishings and accessories, such as flat screen televisions. Guests are welcome to relax in the comfortable lounge where there is also a well stocked bar offering beers, wine, champagnes and rich Italian coffees. A wide choice is offered at breakfast which is served in the spacious dining room.

Rooms 14 en suite (2 fmly) (3 GF) **Facilities** TVB tea/coffee Licensed Cen ht Dinner Free facilities at local leisure/sports club **Parking** 17 **Notes** No coaches

★★★★ GUEST ACCOMMODATION
Dene House

Kendal Rd LA23 3EW
☎ 015394 48236 🖷 015394 48236
e–mail: denehouse@ignetics.co.uk

dir: *0.5m S of Bowness centre on A5074, next to Burnside Hotel*

A friendly welcome awaits you at this smart Victorian house, in a peaceful location just a short walk from the centre of Bowness. The elegant bedrooms are generally spacious, individually decorated and are particularly well equipped. Afternoon tea is served on the patio, which overlooks a well-tended garden. A car park is available.

Rooms 7 rms (5 en suite) (2 pri facs) (1 fmly) (1 GF) **Facilities** TVB tea/coffee Cen ht TVL Free use of adjacent leisure centre **Parking** 7 **Notes** ⊗ ☺

★★★★ 🏠 GUEST HOUSE
Fairfield House and Gardens

Brantfell Rd, Bowness-on-Windermere LA23 3AE
☎ 015394 46565 🖷 015394 46565
e–mail: tonyandliz@the-fairfield.co.uk
web: www.the-fairfield.co.uk

dir: *Into Bowness town centre, turn opp St Martin's Church & sharp left by Spinnery restaurant, house 200yds on right*

Situated just above Bowness and Lake Windermere this Lakeland country house is tucked away in a half acre of secluded, peaceful gardens. The house has been beautifully refurbished to combine Georgian and Victorian features with stylish, contemporary design. Guests are shown warm hospitality and can relax in the delightful lounge. Bedrooms are well furnished, varying in size and style with some featuring luxurious bathrooms. Delicious breakfasts are served in the attractive dining room or on the terrace in warmer weather.

CONTINUED

★★★★ ⊛ RESTAURANT WITH ROOMS
The Hideaway at Windermere

Phoenix Way LA23 1DB
☎ 015394 43070
e–mail: eatandstay@thehideawayatwindermere.co.uk
web: www.thehideawayatwindermere.co.uk

dir: *Exit A591 at B&B, The Hideaway is 100mtrs on right*

Tucked quietly away, as the name suggests, this beautiful Victorian Lakeland house is personally run by owners Richard and Lisa. Delicious food, individually designed bedrooms and warm hospitality ensure an enjoyable stay. There is a spacious lounge looking out to the garden, and the restaurant, split between two light and airy rooms, offers fresh, local ingredients and attentive, yet friendly service. Bedrooms vary in size and style; the largest feature luxury bathrooms.

Rooms 10 en suite 1 annexe en suite S £82.50–£97.50; D £90–£190✱ **Facilities** TVB tea/coffee Direct dial from bedrooms Cen ht Dinner Last d 9pm **Parking** 15 **Notes LB** ⊗ No children 12yrs Closed Jan–mid Feb RS Sun & Mon (low season)

★★★★ GUEST ACCOMMODATION
Blenheim Lodge

Brantfell Rd, Bowness-on-Windermere LA23 3AE
☎ 015394 43440
e–mail: enquiries@blenheim-lodge.com
web: www.blenheim-lodge.com

dir: *A591 Bowness village, left at mini-rdbt, 1st left & left again, house at top*

From a peaceful position above the town of Bowness, Blenheim Lodge has some stunning panoramic views of Lake Windermere. Bedrooms are well equipped featuring antique furnishings and pocket-sprung mattresses. Most beds are antiques these include two William IV four-posters and three Louis XV beds. There is a comfortable lounge and a beautifully decorated dining room.

Rooms 11 rms (10 en suite) (1 pri facs) (2 fmly) (2 GF) S £50–£55; D £77–£136 **Facilities** TVB tea/coffee TVL Free membership private nearby leisure facilities **Parking** 11 **Notes LB** ⊗ Closed 25 Dec RS 20–27 Dec

★★★★ GUEST ACCOMMODATION
The Coach House

Lake Rd LA23 2EQ
☎ 015394 44494
e–mail: enquiries@lakedistrictbandb.com
web: www.lakedistrictbandb.com

dir: *A591 to Windermere house 0.5m on right opp St Herbert's Church*

Expect a relaxed and welcoming atmosphere at this stylish house, which has a minimalist interior with bright decor and cosmopolitan furnishings. The attractive bedrooms are well equipped. There is a

CONTINUED

reception lounge, and a breakfast room where freshly prepared breakfasts feature the best of local produce.

Rooms 5 en suite (1 fmly) S £45–£75; D £52–£75✷ **Facilities** TVB tea/coffee Cen ht Wi-fi available **Parking** 5 **Notes** ⊗ No children 5yrs Closed 24–26 Dec

★★★★ 🏛 ➡ GUEST HOUSE
The Coppice
Brook Rd LA23 2ED
☎ 015394 88501 📄 015394 42148
e–mail: chris@thecoppice.co.uk
web: www.thecoppice.co.uk
dir: 0.25m S of village centre on A5074

This attractive detached house lies between Windermere and Bowness. There are colourful public rooms and bedrooms, and a restaurant serving freshly prepared local produce. The bedrooms vary in size and style and have good facilities.

Rooms 9 en suite (2 fmly) (1 GF) S £35–£45; D £56–£104✷ **Facilities** TVB tea/coffee Licensed Cen ht Dinner Last d 10am Wi-fi available Private leisure club membership **Parking** 10 **Notes** LB No coaches

★★★★ 🏛 GUEST ACCOMMODATION
The Cottage
Elleray Rd LA23 1AG
☎ 015394 44796
e–mail: enquiries@thecottageguesthouse.com
web: www.thecottageguesthouse.com
dir: A591, past Windermere Hotel, after 150yds turn left onto Elleray Rd, 150yds on left
Built in 1847, this attractive house has been extensively refurbished to offer a blend of modern and traditional styles. The tastefully furnished bedrooms are well equipped and comfortable. A wide choice of freshly cooked breakfasts are served in the spacious dining room at individual tables.

Rooms 8 en suite (2 GF) D £54–£98✷ **Facilities** FTV TVB tea/coffee Cen ht **Parking** 8 **Notes** ⊗ No children 11yrs Closed Nov–Jan

★★★★ GUEST HOUSE
The Cranleigh
Kendal Rd, Bowness LA23 3EW
☎ 015394 43293 & 44245 📄 015394 47283
e–mail: enquiries@thecranleigh.com
web: www.thecranleigh.com
dir: Lake Rd onto Kendal Rd, 150yds on right
Just a short walk from Lake Windermere this smartly appointed period property is being transformed to provide stylish accommodation. Bedrooms are divided between the main house and adjacent building. Luxury and superior rooms are impressive, featuring spa baths, illuminated showers and an excellent range of accessories. Guests have complimentary use of leisure facilities at a nearby hotel.

Rooms 11 en suite 6 annexe en suite (2 fmly) (1 GF) S £45–£100; D £60–£150✷ **Facilities** FTV TVB tea/coffee Direct dial from bedrooms Licensed Cen ht 🏊 Squash Sauna Solarium Gymnasium **Parking** 13 **Notes** LB ⊗

Fairfield House and Gardens

The Fairfield is a charming Georgian house set in quiet secluded grounds with its own car park. Located in a quiet cul-de-sac, yet just a few steps from the waterfront, shops, pubs, clubs and restaurants of Bowness.

A spacious terrace and a large lounge, where we are licensed for alcohol, and free Internet access and

Wi-fi are available. We have four-poster rooms, deluxe rooms with spa bath's and a rooftop penthouse.

Brantfell Road, Bowness Bay, Windermere, Cumbria LA23 3AE
Tel: 015394 46565   Fax: 015394 46564
Website: www.the-fairfield.co.uk

ENGLAND

★★★★ GUEST ACCOMMODATION
Fair Rigg
Ferry View LA23 3JB
☎ 015394 43941
e–mail: stay@fairrigg.co.uk
web: www.fairrigg.co.uk

dir: *0.5m S of village centre at junct A5074 & B5284*

This late Victorian house has been refurbished to provide spacious accommodation, while retaining many original features. The elegant dining room and many of the bedrooms have delightful views of the lake and to the mountains. Bedrooms are attractively decorated and well equipped.

Rooms 6 en suite (1 GF) S £40–£80; D £68–£90 **Facilities** TVB tea/coffee Cen ht **Parking** 6 **Notes** LB ⊗ No children 14yrs

★★★★ GUEST HOUSE
Fir Trees
Lake Rd LA23 2EQ
☎ 015394 42272 📄 015394 42512
e–mail: enquiries@fir-trees.com
web: www.fir-trees.co.uk

dir: *Off A591 through town, Lake Rd in 0.5m, Fir Trees on left after clock tower*

Located halfway between Windermere town and the lake, this spacious Victorian house offers attractive and well equipped accommodation. Bedrooms are generously proportioned and have many thoughtful extra touches. Breakfasts, featuring the best of local produce, are served at individual tables in the smart dining room.

Rooms 9 en suite (2 fmly) (3 GF) **Facilities** TVB tea/coffee Cen ht Dinner Last d 10am Free use of local country club (2 nights stay) **Parking** 9 **Notes** ⊗

★★★★ GUEST HOUSE
Glencree
Lake Rd LA23 2EQ
☎ 015394 45822 & 0797 469714
e–mail: h.butterworth@btinternet.com
web: www.glencreelakes.co.uk

dir: *From town centre signs for Bowness & The Lake, Glencree on right after large wooded area on right*

Colourful hanging baskets and floral displays adorn the car park and entrance to Glencree, which lies between Windermere and Bowness. Bedrooms are brightly decorated and individually furnished. The attractive lounge, with an honesty bar, is next to the dining room, where breakfasts are served at individual tables.

Glencree

Rooms 6 en suite (1 fmly) (1 GF) **Facilities** TVB tea/coffee Licensed Cen ht TVL Dinner Last d 2.30pm Wi-fi available **Parking** 6 **Notes** No coaches

★★★★ GUEST HOUSE
Glenville House
Lake Rd LA23 2EQ
☎ 015394 43371 📄 015394 48457
e–mail: mail@glenvillehouse.co.uk

dir: *Off A591 into Windermere, B5074 to Bowness, Glenville 0.5m on right next to St John's Church*

This traditional Lakeland stone house has a relaxing and friendly atmosphere, and is just a short walk from the town centre and Lake Windermere. Breakfast, including a wide choice of cooked dishes, is served in the pleasant dining room. Bedrooms are attractively decorated and furnished with good quality en suite bathrooms.

Rooms 6 en suite (1 GF) S £50–£80; D £59–£100✳ **Facilities** TVB tea/coffee Cen ht Wi-fi available **Parking** 6 **Notes** LB ⊗ No children No coaches Closed Xmas

★★★★ BED & BREAKFAST
The Haven
10 Birch St LA23 1EG
☎ 015394 44017
e–mail: thehaven.windermere@btopenworld.com

dir: *On A5074 enter one-way system, 3rd left onto Birch St*

Built from Lakeland slate and stone, this Victorian house is just a stroll from the town centre and shops. The bright, spacious bedrooms offer en suite or private facilities, and one has a Victorian brass bed. A hearty

CONTINUED

CONTINUED

Cumbrian breakfast is served in the well-appointed dining room that doubles as a lounge.

Rooms 3 rms (2 en suite) (1 pri facs) (2 fmly) D £50–£80✶
Facilities TVB tea/coffee Cen ht **Parking** 3 **Notes LB** ⊗ No children 7yrs

★★★★ GUEST ACCOMMODATION
Holly-Wood Guest House

Holly Rd LA23 2AF
☎ 015394 42219
e–mail: info@hollywoodguesthouse.co.uk
web: www.hollywoodguesthouse.co.uk

dir: A591 towards Windermere, left into town and left again onto Ellerthwaite Rd, next left Holly Rd

This attractive Victorian end terrace is located in a quiet residential area just a few minutes walk from the town centre. Guests are offered a friendly welcome, comfortable, well equipped bedrooms and a freshly prepared breakfast. Limited off street parking is also available.

Rooms 6 en suite (1 fmly) S £35–£47.50; D £70–£85 **Facilities** TVB tea/coffee Cen ht **Parking** 3 **Notes** ⊗ No children 7yrs Closed 3–25 Nov & 22–28 Dec

★★★★ GUEST HOUSE
Invergarry Guest House

3 Thornbarrow Rd LA23 2EW
☎ 015394 44561
e–mail: invergarryguesthouse@btinternet.com
web: www.invergarrywindermere.com

dir: Towards Bowness, turn left onto Thornbarrow Road

Just 10 minutes walk from the villages of Windermere and Bowness-on-Windermere, this 19th century traditional Lakeland house offers a warm welcome to all guests. Bedrooms and bathrooms are comfortable, well equipped and include a chalet room in the courtyard garden. Guests also have use of a cosy lounge. A wide choice is offered at breakfast and evening meals are available on request during winter months. Geoff and Muriel were finalists for the AA Friendliest Landlady of the Year 2008 Award.

Rooms 4 en suite 1 annexe en suite (1 GF) S £40–£50; D £60–£75✶
Facilities TVB tea/coffee Cen ht **Parking** 2 **Notes LB** ⊗ No children 16yrs No coaches ⊛

★★★★ GUEST HOUSE
The Old Court House

Lake Rd LA23 3AP
☎ 015394 45096
e–mail: alison@theoch.co.uk

dir: On Windermere-Bowness road at junct Longlands Rd

Guests are given a warm welcome at this attractive former Victorian police station and courthouse, located in the centre of Bowness. Comfortable, pine-furnished bedrooms offer a good range of extra facilities. Freshly prepared breakfasts are served in the bright ground-floor dining room.

Rooms 6 en suite (2 GF) S £30–£45; D £57–£75 **Facilities** TVB tea/coffee Cen ht **Parking** 6 **Notes LB** ⊗ No children 10yrs No coaches ⊛

★★★★ GUEST HOUSE
The Willowsmere

Ambleside Rd LA23 1ES
☎ 015394 43575 🖹 015394 44962
e–mail: info@thewillowsmere.com
web: www.thewillowsmere.com

dir: On A591, 500yds on left after Windermere station, towards Ambleside

Willowsmere is a friendly, family-run establishment within easy walking distance of the town centre. It stands in a colourful, well-tended garden, with a patio and water feature to the rear. The attractive bedrooms are spacious, and there is a choice of inviting lounges and a well-stocked bar. Delicious breakfasts are served at individual tables in the stylish dining room.

Rooms 12 en suite (1 GF) S £35–£50; D £64–£100✶ **Facilities** TVB tea/coffee Licensed Cen ht TVL Wi-fi available Free use of pool, sauna and gym at local hotel **Parking** 15 **Notes** ⊗ No children 12yrs

WINDERMERE CONTINUED

★★★★ Ⓐ GUEST HOUSE
Storrs Gate House
Longtail Hill LA23 3JD
☎ 015394 43272
e–mail: enquiries@storrsgatehouse.co.uk
dir: *At junct A592 & B5284, opposite Windermere Marina*

Rooms 7 en suite (2 GF) D £80–£150✱ **Facilities** STV TVB tea/coffee Licensed Cen ht Dinner Last d 9.30am Wi-fi available **Parking** 7 **Notes LB** ⊗ No children 10yrs No coaches Closed Xmas & New Year

See advert on this page

★★★ GUEST ACCOMMODATION
St Johns Lodge
Lake Rd LA23 2EQ
☎ 015394 43078 🖷 015394 88054
e–mail: mail@st-johns-lodge.co.uk
web: www.st-johns-lodge.co.uk
dir: *On A5074 between Windermere & lake*

Located between Windermere and Bowness, this large guest house offers a refreshingly friendly welcome. Bedrooms vary in size and style but all are neatly furnished and decorated. Freshly prepared traditional breakfasts, including vegetarian and vegan options, are served in the well-appointed basement dining room. Facilities include free internet access.

Rooms 12 en suite (1 fmly) S £40–£50; D £55–£110 **Facilities** TVB tea/coffee Cen ht Wi-fi available Free access to local leisure club **Parking** 3 **Notes LB** ⊗ No children 12yrs Closed Xmas

★★★ GUEST HOUSE
Adam Place Guest House
1 Park Av LA23 2AR
☎ 015394 44600 🖷 015394 44600
e–mail: adamplacewindermere@yahoo.co.uk
dir: *Off A591 into Windermere, through town centre, left onto Ellerthwaite Rd & Park Av*

Located in a mainly residential area within easy walking distance of lake and town centre, this stone Victorian house has been renovated to provide comfortable and homely bedrooms. Comprehensive breakfasts are served in the cosy dining room and there is a pretty patio garden.

Rooms 5 en suite (2 fmly) S £20–£36; D £40–£66✱ **Facilities** TVB tea/coffee Cen ht **Notes** ⊗ No children 6yrs

★★★ GUEST HOUSE
Broadlands
19 Broad St LA23 2AB
☎ 015394 46532
e–mail: enquiries@broadlandsbandb.co.uk
dir: *From A591 follow one-way system, left onto Broad St after pedestrian crossing*

A friendly welcome is offered at this attractive house opposite the park and library and convenient for central amenities. Bedrooms are pleasantly coordinated and comfortably furnished, and freshly prepared breakfasts are served in the ground-floor dining room.

Rooms 5 en suite (2 fmly) S £30–£35; D £54–£70✱ **Facilities** TVB tea/coffee Cen ht Wi-fi available **Notes LB** ⊗ No children 12yrs No coaches

★★★ INN
Eagle & Child Inn
Kendal Rd, Staveley LA8 9LP
☎ 01539 821320
e–mail: info@eaglechildinn.co.uk
web: www.eaglechildinn.co.uk
dir: *A591 from Kendal towards Windermere, sign for Staveley, pub 500yds on left*

Close to the beautiful Kentmere valley, this delightful village pub offers comfortable accommodation and good food. A choice of local cask ales can be enjoyed in either the tranquil riverside garden or the

CONTINUED

ENGLAND

spacious bar. Breakfast is served in the Redmond Suite, which is available for functions.

Rooms 5 en suite (1 fmly) **Facilities** TVB tea/coffee Cen ht Dinner Last d 8.45pm Local Leisure Club facilities can be arranged **Conf** Max 60 Board 40 **Parking** 16 **Notes** ⊗

★★★ GUEST ACCOMMODATION
Elim House

Biskey Howe Rd LA23 2JP

☎ 015394 42021 📇 015394 42021

e–mail: elimhouse@btopenworld.com

web: www.elimhouse.co.uk

dir: *Left off A5074, 150yds past police station, 1st house on left*

A short walk from the bustling village of Bowness and the lake, this attractive house has a colourful, well-kept garden. Bedrooms, some in an annexe, vary in size and style, but all offer sound levels of comfort. A hearty Cumbrian breakfast is served in the cheerful breakfast room.

Rooms 6 en suite 3 annexe en suite (1 fmly) S £35–£50; D £55–£100 **Facilities** TVB tea/coffee Wi-fi available **Parking** 7 **Notes** LB ⊗ No children 10yrs Closed 1–26 Dec RS Jan–Mar

★★★ GUEST HOUSE
Green Gables Guest House

37 Broad St LA23 2AB

☎ 015394 43886

e–mail: info@greengablesguesthouse.co.uk

dir: *Off A591 into Windermere, 1st left after pelican crossing, opp car park*

Aptly named, Green Gables is a friendly guest house looking onto Elleray Gardens. Just a short walk from the centre, the house is attractively furnished and offers bright, fresh and well appointed bedrooms. There is a comfortable bar-lounge, and substantial breakfasts are served in the spacious dining room.

Rooms 7 rms (4 en suite) (3 pri facs) (3 fmly) (1 GF) **Facilities** TVB tea/coffee Licensed Cen ht TVL **Notes** ⊗ No coaches Closed 23–27 Dec

DERBYSHIRE

ALFRETON   MAP 16 SK45

★★★ BED & BREAKFAST
Oaktree Farm

Matlock Rd, Oakerthorpe, Wessington DE55 7NA

☎ 01773 832957 & 07999 876969

e–mail: katherine770@btinternet.com

dir: *2m W of Alfreton. A615 W under railway bridge & past cottages, farmhouse on left*

Set in 22 acres, including a fishing lake, chicken run and kitchen garden, this mellow-stone house provides thoughtfully equipped bedrooms complemented by modern bathrooms. Breakfasts using the freshest ingredients are served in an attractive cottage-style dining room. The pretty floral patio is a bonus in summer.

Rooms 3 en suite S £27–£30; D £47–£50✳ **Facilities** STV TVB tea/coffee Cen ht TVL Fishing **Parking** 10 **Notes** ⊗ 🐾

ASHBOURNE MAP 10 SK14

Premier Collection

★★★★★ 🛎 BED & BREAKFAST

Turlow Bank

Hognaston DE6 1PW
☎ 01335 370299 📠 01335 370299
e-mail: turlowbank@w3z.co.uk
web: www.turlowbank.co.uk

dir: *Off B5035 to Hognaston (signed Hognaston only), through village towards Hulland Ward, Turlow Bank 0.5m, look for clock tower*

Set in delightful gardens on a superb elevated position close to Carsington Water, this extended 19th-century farmhouse provides high levels of comfort with excellent facilities. Bedrooms are equipped with many thoughtful extras and feature quality modern bathrooms. Comprehensive breakfasts, which include free-range chicken or duck eggs, are served at a family table in the cosy dining room. A spacious lounge is available. Hospitality is memorable.

Rooms 2 en suite S £45–£60; D £75–£85 **Facilities** tea/coffee Cen ht TVL 🐾 **Parking** 6 **Notes** ⊗ No children 12yrs Closed 25–27 Dec ⊜

★★★★ ⚛ RESTAURANT WITH ROOMS

Bramhall's of Ashbourne

6 Buxton Rd DE6 1EX
☎ 01335 346158 📠 01335 347453
e-mail: info@bramhalls.co.uk

dir: *From market square N onto Buxton Rd up hill, on left*

Located within the heart of the historic market town, this restaurant with rooms occupies a conversion of two cottages and an Edwardian

CONTINUED

house. It is increasingly popular for its imaginative food, attentive service and excellent value for money. Bedrooms are filled with thoughtful extras and a warm welcome is assured.

Rooms 10 rms (8 en suite) (2 pri facs) (2 fmly) (1 GF) S £55–£100; D £80–£100✳ **Facilities** FTV TVB tea/coffee Cen ht Dinner Last d 9pm Wi-fi available **Parking** 5 **Notes LB** ⊗

★★★★ GUEST ACCOMMODATION

Compton House

27–31 Compton DE6 1BX
☎ 01335 343100
e-mail: jane@comptonhouse.co.uk
web: www.comptonhouse.co.uk

dir: *A52 from Derby into Ashbourne, over lights at bottom of hill, house 100yds on left opp garage*

Within easy walking distance of the central attractions, this conversion of three cottages has resulted in a house with good standards of comfort and facilities. Bedrooms are filled with homely extras and comprehensive breakfasts are served in the cottage-style dining room.

Rooms 5 en suite (2 fmly) (1 GF) S £35–£45; D £55–£65 **Facilities** TVB tea/coffee Cen ht TVL **Parking** 6 **Notes LB**

★★★★ BED & BREAKFAST

Dove House B & B

Bridge Hill, Mayfield DE6 2HN
☎ 01335 343329
e-mail: dovehouse2000@yahoo.com

dir: *1m W of Ashbourne. A52 onto B5032, B&B 300yds on right*

Peacefully located in Mayfield, this well-proportioned Victorian house has many original features, highlighted by the furnishings and decor. The comfortable bedroom is equipped with thoughtful extras and has a spacious bathroom en suite. A lounge is also available.

Rooms 1 en suite D £55✳ **Facilities** tea/coffee Cen ht TVL **Parking** 1 **Notes** ⊗ No children ⊜

★★★★ FARM HOUSE

Mercaston Hall *(SK279419)*

Mercaston DE6 3BL
☎ 01335 360263 Mr & Mrs A Haddon
e-mail: mercastonhall@btinternet.com

dir: *Off A52 in Brailsford onto Luke Ln, 1m turn right at 1st x-rds, house 1m on right*

Located in a pretty hamlet, this medieval building retains many original features. Bedrooms are homely, and additional facilities include an all-weather tennis court and a livery service. This is a good base for visiting local stately homes, the Derwent Valley mills and Dovedale.

Rooms 3 en suite S £40–£45; D £60–£66✳ **Facilities** FTV TVB tea/coffee Cen ht 🐾 **Parking** 3 **Notes** No children 8yrs 60 acres mixed Closed Xmas ⊜

★★★★ BED & BREAKFAST
Mona Villas Bed & Breakfast

1 Mona Villas, Church Ln, Middle Mayfield DE6 2JS

☎ 01335 343773 📄 01335 343773

e–mail: info@mona-villas.fsnet.co.uk

web: www.mona-villas.fsnet.co.uk

dir: *2.5m SW of Ashbourne. B5032 to Middle Mayfield, onto Church Ln, 400yds on right*

This well-furnished house overlooks open fields close to the village. The bedrooms are very well equipped and have good facilities. Substantial breakfasts are served in the bright dining room and hospitality is a major strength.

Rooms 3 en suite (1 GF) S £30–£35; D £48–£52✱ **Facilities** FTV TVB tea/coffee Cen ht **Parking** 6 **Notes LB** ⊗ 🐾

★★★★ BED & BREAKFAST
The Wheel House

Belper Rd, Hulland Ward DE6 3EE

☎ 01335 372837 📄 01335 372837

e–mail: thewheelhouse@btinternet.com

dir: *Between Ashbourne and Belper on A517*

This comfortably furnished house is set in open countryside on the main road between Ashbourne and Belper. The bedrooms are well furnished and a cosy lounge is also available. Breakfasts are hearty, and guests can expect friendly and attentive service.

Rooms 3 en suite (1 fmly) S £40–£50; D £55–£65✱ **Facilities** TVB tea/coffee Cen ht TVL Wi-fi available **Parking** 5 **Notes LB** ⊗

★★★ BED & BREAKFAST
Homesclose House

DE6 2DA

☎ 01335 324475

e–mail: gilltom2@btinternet.com

dir: *Off A52 into village centre*

Stunning views of the surrounding countryside and manicured gardens are a feature of this beautifully maintained dormer bungalow. Bedrooms are filled with homely extras, and an attractive dining room with one family table is the setting for breakfast.

Rooms 3 rms (2 en suite) (1 fmly) (1 GF) **Facilities** TVB tea/coffee Cen ht TVL **Parking** 4 **Notes** Closed Dec–Jan 🐾

★★★ GUEST HOUSE
The Old Barn at Common End Farm

Common End Farm, Swinscoe DE6 2BW

☎ 01335 342342

e–mail: commonendbarn@hotmail.co.uk

web: www.commonendbarn.co.uk

dir: *4m W of Ashbourne. Off A52 at Swinscoe*

The converted barn provides a range of pine-furnished bedrooms with modern shower rooms en suite. Breakfast is served in the cosy dining room and a lounge is available.

Rooms 6 en suite (2 fmly) (4 GF) S £40–£42.50; D £60–£65 **Facilities** TVB tea/coffee Cen ht TVL **Parking** 10 **Notes LB** ⊗

★★★ BED & BREAKFAST
Stone Cottage

Green Ln, Clifton DE6 2BL

☎ 01335 343377

e–mail: info@stone-cottage.fsnet.co.uk

web: www.stone-cottage.fsnet.co.uk

dir: *1m from Ashbourne on A52 Leek-Uttoxeter. Left at sign for Clifton, 2nd house on right*

A good base for touring and only a short drive from the town centre, this well-maintained stone house stands in pretty gardens and provides homely bedrooms. Freshly cooked breakfasts are served in an attractive conservatory, and tourist information is available.

Rooms 3 en suite (1 fmly) S £28–£45; D £50–£64✱ **Facilities** STV TVB tea/coffee Cen ht TVL **Parking** 4 **Notes** ⊗ Closed 25 Dec

★★ FARM HOUSE
Air Cottage Farm *(SK142523)*

Ilam DE6 2BD

☎ 01335 350475 Mrs J Wain

dir: *A515 from Ashbourne, left signed Thorpe/Dovedale/Ilam, in Ilam right at memorial stone to Alstonfield, right at 1st cattle grid gate on right leaving village, 2nd farm on drive*

This 18th-century farmhouse has a magnificent elevated position with stunning views over the countryside and Dovedale. It provides traditional standards of accommodation and is very popular with serious walkers, climbers and artists visiting this beautiful part of the Peak District.

Rooms 3 rms (3 GF) S £25–£30; D £50–£55 **Facilities** tea/coffee Cen ht TVL **Parking** 4 **Notes** ⊗ 320 acres beef cattle sheep Closed Dec–Feb 🐾

BAKEWELL **MAP 16 SK26**

★★★★ GUEST ACCOMMODATION
Avenue House

The Avenue DE45 1EQ

☎ 01629 812467

dir: *Off A6 onto The Avenue, 1st house on right*

Located a short walk from the town centre, this impressive Victorian house has original features complemented by the décor and furnishings. Bedrooms have many thoughtful extras and the modern bathrooms contain power showers. Hearty English breakfasts are served in the traditionally furnished dining room.

Rooms 3 en suite S £39–£45; D £50–£60✱ **Facilities** TVB tea/coffee Cen ht **Parking** 3 **Notes** ⊗ 🐾

ENGLAND

BAKEWELL CONTINUED

★★★★ GUEST HOUSE
Bourne House
The Park, Haddon Rd DE45 1ET
☎ 01629 813274
web: www.bournehousebakewell.co.uk
dir: *300yds S of town centre on A6, on left before park*
This impressive former manse stands in mature gardens and is located overlooking the park a few minutes' walk from the town centre. Bedrooms are spacious and lots of thoughtful extras enhance guest comfort. Breakfast is taken in an attractive period-furnished dining room and a warm welcome is assured.
Rooms 3 en suite D fr £55✱ **Facilities** TVB tea/coffee Cen ht **Parking** 5 **Notes** ⊗ No children 7yrs No coaches Closed Dec–Feb ⊛

★★★★ GUEST HOUSE
Croft Cottages
Coombs Rd DE45 1AQ
☎ 01629 814101
e–mail: croftco@btopenworld.com
dir: *A619 E from town centre over bridge, right onto Station Rd & Coombs Rd*
A warm welcome is assured at this Grade II listed stone building close to the River Wye and town centre. Thoughtfully equipped bedrooms are available in the main house or in an adjoining converted barn suite. Breakfast is served in a spacious lounge dining room.
Rooms 3 rms (2 en suite) (1 pri facs) 1 annexe en suite (1 fmly) S £35–£45; D £58–£80 **Facilities** TVB tea/coffee Cen ht **Parking** 2 **Notes** LB No coaches ⊛

★★★★ BED & BREAKFAST
Holly Cottage
Pilsley DE45 1UH
☎ 01246 582245 🖷 01246 583177
e–mail: hollycottagebandb@btinternet.com
dir: *Follow brown tourist signs for Chatsworth and Pisley. Holly Cottage next to post office*
A warm welcome is assured at this mellow stone cottage, part of a combined Post Office and shop within the conservation area of Pilsley, which is owned by the adjacent Chatsworth Estate. The cosy bedrooms feature a wealth of thoughtful extras, and comprehensive breakfasts, utilising quality local produce, are taken in an attractive pine furnished dining room.
Rooms 3 en suite D £60–£70✱ **Facilities** TVB tea/coffee Cen ht Wi-fi available **Notes** LB ⊗ No children 10yrs

★★★★ BED & BREAKFAST
Wyedale
Wyedale House, 25 Holywell DE45 1BA
☎ 01629 812845
dir: *500yds SE of town centre, off A6 Haddon Rd*
Wyedale is close to the town centre and is ideal for relaxing or touring. Bedrooms, one of which is on the ground floor, are spacious and freshly decorated. Breakfast is served in the attractive dining room, which overlooks the rear patio.
Rooms 3 en suite (1 fmly) (1 GF) D £55–£65✱ **Facilities** TVB tea/coffee Cen ht **Parking** 4 **Notes** ⊗ Closed 31 Dec RS 24 Dec ⊛

★★★ INN
Castle Inn
Castle St DE45 1DU
☎ 01629 812103
web: www.oldenglish.co.uk
A traditional inn built in the 16th century and offering well furnished bedrooms and extensive bars. A wide range of well-prepared dishes is available and real ales are served.
Rooms 4 annexe en suite **Facilities** TVB Direct dial from bedrooms Last d all day **Notes** No coaches

★★★ GUEST HOUSE
Everton
Haddon Rd DE45 1AW
☎ 01629 815028
e–mail: trish@evertonbandb.co.uk
dir: *S of Bakewell on A6*
Ideally located opposite a public park and a few minutes walk from central attractions, this large semi-detached house provides comfortable homely bedrooms and an attractive pine-furnished dining room, the setting for comprehensive breakfasts.
Rooms 3 rms (2 en suite) (1 pri facs) (1 fmly) S £35–£45; D £50–£60✱ **Facilities** TVB tea/coffee Cen ht **Parking** 6 **Notes** LB Closed 24–26 Dec RS 30–31 Dec ⊛

★★★ INN
The George
Church St, Youlgreave DE45 1UW
☎ 01629 636292 🖷 01632 636292
dir: *3m S of Bakewell in Youlgreave, opp church*
The public bars of the 17th-century George are popular with locals and tourists. Bedroom styles vary, and all have shower rooms en suite. Breakfast is served in the lounge bar, and a range of bar meals and snacks is available.
Rooms 3 en suite (1 fmly) **Facilities** TVB tea/coffee Cen ht Dinner Last d 8.30pm Fishing **Parking** 12 **Notes** ⊛

★★★ BED & BREAKFAST
Wyeclose

5 Granby Croft DE45 1ET
☎ 01629 813702 📄 01629 813702
e-mail: h.wilson@talk21.com

dir: *Off A6 Matlock St onto Granby Rd & Granby Croft*

Located in a quiet cul-de-sac in the town centre, this Edwardian house provides thoughtfully furnished bedroom accommodation with smart modern bathrooms and an attractive dining room, the setting for comprehensive breakfasts. Original family art is a feature within the ground-floor areas.

Rooms 2 rms (1 en suite) (1 pri facs) D £52 **Facilities** STV TVB tea/coffee Cen ht **Parking** 3 **Notes** ⊗ No children 8yrs Closed Xmas & New Year ⊛

BAMFORD   MAP 16 SK28

★★★★ INN
Yorkshire Bridge Inn

Ashopton Rd S33 0AZ
☎ 01433 651361 📄 01433 651361
e-mail: info@yorkshire-bridge.co.uk
web: www.yorkshire-bridge.co.uk

A well-established country inn, ideally located beside Ladybower Dam and within reach of the Peak District's many beauty spots. The inn offers a wide range of excellent dishes in both the bar and dining area, along with a good selection of real ales. Bedrooms are attractively furnished, comfortable and well-equipped.

Rooms 14 en suite (3 fmly) (4 GF) S £55–£60; D £76–£110✶ **Facilities** STV TVB tea/coffee Direct dial from bedrooms Cen ht Dinner Last d 9pm **Conf** Max 20 **Parking** 50 **Notes** LB

See advert on page 135

★★★ GUEST ACCOMMODATION
Thornhill View

Hope Rd, Bamford, Hope Valley S33 0AL
☎ 01433 651823
e-mail: thornhill4bb@aol.com

dir: *0.5m SW of Bamford. On A6187 at Thornhill Ln junct*

Comfortable accommodation in a secluded location, set back from the main road running through the Hope Valley nearby to the Rising Sun Inn. Compact bedrooms are well equipped, and Jo Fairbairn is a caring hostess.

Rooms 3 rms (2 en suite) (1 pri facs) (2 GF) D £55–£60✶ **Facilities** TVB tea/coffee Cen ht **Parking** 3 **Notes** LB ⊛

★★★ BED & BREAKFAST
The White House

Shatton Ln S33 0BG
☎ 01433 651487 📄 01433 651487

dir: *A6187 Hathersage to Hope, left opp High Peak Garden Centre into Shatton, White House 250yds on left*

Set in a secluded lane among attractive gardens, this large detached family home offers spacious, nicely laid out bedrooms. Breakfast is served around a large communal table in the neat dining room, which overlooks the garden. The comfortable lounge has a television.

Rooms 5 rms **Facilities** TVB tea/coffee Cen ht TVL **Parking** 4 **Notes** ⊛

BEELEY   MAP 16 SK26

★★★★ INN
Devonshire Arms-Beeley

Devonshire Square DE4 2NR
☎ 01629 733259 📄 01629 734542
e-mail: enquiries@devonshirebeeley.co.uk

dir: *B6012 towards Matlock, pass Chatsworth House. After 1.5m turn left, 2nd entrance to Beeley village*

The Devonshire Arms is a picturesque country inn at the heart of village life. It offers all the charm and character of an historic inn with a warm and comfortable interior full of oak beams and stone crannies, but venture inside a little further and you will find the startlingly different décor of the brasserie with its contemporary bar, glass fronted wine store and colourful furnishings. For the ultimate escape, there are four stylish cottage bedrooms.

Rooms 4 en suite 4 annexe en suite (1 fmly) (2 GF) D fr £145✶ **Facilities** STV TVB tea/coffee Direct dial from bedrooms Cen ht Dinner Last d 9.30pm Wi-fi available **Parking** 40 **Notes** No coaches

BELPER   MAP 11 SK34

Premier Collection

★★★★★ 🏨 GUEST ACCOMMODATION

Dannah Farm Country House

Bowmans Ln, Shottle DE56 2DR
☎ 01773 550273 & 550630 📠 01773 550590
e–mail: reservations@dannah.co.uk
web: www.dannah.co.uk

dir: *A517 from Belper towards Ashbourne, 1.5m right into Shottle after Hanging Gate pub on right, over x-rds & right*

Located within the Chatsworth Estates at Shottle, on an elevated position with stunning views, this impressive Georgian house and outbuildings have been renovated to provide high standards of comfort and facilities. Many original features have been retained, and are enhanced by quality decor and furnishings. The bedrooms are filled with a wealth of thoughtful extras. One room has an outdoor hot tub. The Mixing Place restaurant is the setting for imaginative dinners and memorable breakfasts, which make use of the finest local produce.

Rooms 8 en suite (1 fmly) (2 GF) S £75–£110; D £110–£250
Facilities FTV TVB tea/coffee Direct dial from bedrooms Cen ht Dinner Last d noon Wi-fi available Sauna Leisure cabin, hot-tub **Conf** Max 10 Thtr 10 Class 10 Board 10 Del from £145 **Parking** 20 **Notes LB** ⊗ Closed 24–26 Dec Civ Wed 50

See advert on opposite page

★★★★ FARM HOUSE

Chevin Green Farm *(SK339471)*

Chevin Rd DE56 2UN
☎ 01773 822328 📠 01773 822328 Mr & Mrs Postles
e–mail: spostles@globalnet.co.uk
web: www.chevingreenfarm.org.uk

dir: *Off A6 opp Strutt Arms at Milford onto Chevin Rd, 1.5m on left*

You can be sure of a warm welcome at this 300-year-old farm overlooking the Derwent valley. Bedrooms are furnished with thoughtful extras and smart modern bathrooms. There is a comfortable lounge, and breakfast is served at separate tables in the cosy dining room. Self-catering units are also available.

Rooms 5 en suite (1 fmly) (1 GF) S £30–£38; D £50–£60✳
Facilities TVB tea/coffee Cen ht TVL **Parking** 5 **Notes** ⊗ 38 acres non-working Closed Xmas & New Year

★★★★ BED & BREAKFAST

The Hollins

45 Belper Ln DE56 2UQ
☎ 01773 823955
e–mail: emery.christine@googlemail.com

dir: *A6 onto A517 W, over bridge, right onto Belper Ln, 300yds up hill*

This immaculately maintained house is a 10-minute walk from the town centre. The bedroom is comfortable and equipped with many extras, and the dining room can be used for evening work or take-away food. The full English breakfast is a highlight.

Rooms 1 en suite (1 fmly) S £35; D £60✳ **Facilities** TVB tea/coffee Cen ht **Parking** 1 **Notes** ⊗ No children 4yrs 🏨

BIRCH VALE   MAP 16 SK08

★★★ INN

The Waltzing Weasel Inn

8 New Mills Rd SK22 1BT
☎ 01663 743402 📠 01663 744397
e–mail: w-weasel@zen.co.uk
web: www.w-weasel.co.uk

Located between Glossop and Chapel-en-le-Frith within the High Peak, this mellow stone inn enjoys a good local reputation for its range of real ales and imaginative food. Some of the spacious bedrooms offer fine rural views and a warm welcome is assured.

Rooms 8 en suite (1 fmly) (2 GF) **Facilities** TVB tea/coffee Cen ht Dinner Last d 9pm **Conf** Thtr 15 Class 12 Board 10 **Parking** 42

BONSALL   MAP 16 SK25

★★★★ GUEST HOUSE

Pig of Lead

Via Gellia Rd DE4 2AJ
☎ 01629 820040 📠 01629 820040
e–mail: pigoflead@aol.com

dir: *0.5m SE of Bonsall on A5012*

This delightful property dating back over two hundred years was once an inn named after a measurement of lead, which used to be mined locally. Only five minutes from Matlock Bath, this is a good base for exploring the area. Individually styled bedrooms are comfortable and well appointed. A warm welcome and hearty breakfasts featuring local produce can be assured here.

Rooms 3 en suite S £40; D £55–£65✳ **Facilities** TVB tea/coffee Cen ht Wi-fi available **Parking** 3 **Notes** No children 14yrs No coaches 🏨

BROUGH
MAP 16 SK18

★★★ INN
Travellers Rest
Brough Ln Head S33 9HG
☎ 01433 620363 📄 01433 623338
e–mail: elliottstephen@btconnect.com

dir: *On junct A6187 & B6049*

On the main road approaching the village of Hope, this stone inn has been totally refurbished to modern requirements. Open fires burn in the winter in the bar, which is popular with locals, and a wide range of bar food is also available. An excellent base for touring the Peak District.

Rooms 5 en suite **Facilities** TVB tea/coffee Cen ht Dinner Last d 9pm **Parking** 50 **Notes** No coaches Closed 25–26 Dec RS Nov–Mar

BUXTON
MAP 16 SK07

★★★★★ GUEST HOUSE
Grendon Guest House
Bishops Ln SK17 6UN
☎ 01298 78831
e–mail: grendonguesthouse@hotmail.com
web: www.grendonguesthouse.co.uk

dir: *0.75m from Buxton centre. Off A53 St Johns Rd, Bishops Ln 1st right after Otter Hole development*

A warm welcome is assured at this non-smoking Edwardian house, set in immaculate grounds just a short walk from the town centre. The spacious, carefully furnished bedrooms are filled with thoughtful extras and lots of local information. Stunning country views can be enjoyed from the elegant lounge-dining room, where imaginative dinners are served. The attractive breakfast room is the setting for comprehensive breakfasts using local produce.

Rooms 5 en suite S £38–£50; D £60–£90✱ **Facilities** TVB tea/coffee Cen ht TVL Dinner Last d 5pm Wi-fi available **Parking** 8 **Notes** LB No children 10yrs No coaches Closed 3 Jan–3 Feb

BUXTON CONTINUED

★★★★ ≜ GUEST ACCOMMODATION
The Grosvenor House
1 Broad Walk SK17 6JE
☎ 01298 72439
e–mail: grosvenor.buxton@btopenworld.com
dir: *In town centre*

This Victorian house is centrally located overlooking the Pavilion Gardens and Opera House. Bedrooms are carefully furnished and have many thoughtful extras. There is a comfortable period-style sitting room, and freshly prepared imaginative breakfasts are served in the cosy dining room.

Rooms 8 en suite (1 fmly) **Facilities** TVB tea/coffee Cen ht Wi-fi available **Conf** Max 8 **Parking** 2 **Notes** ⊗ Closed Xmas

★★★★ GUEST HOUSE
Oldfield
8 Macclesfield Rd SK17 9AH
☎ 01298 78264
e–mail: avril@oldfieldhousebuxton.co.uk
web: www.oldfieldhousebuxton.co.uk
dir: *On B5059 0.5m SW of town centre*

Located within easy walking distance of the centre, this impressive Victorian house provides spacious bedrooms with modern en suites. Comprehensive breakfasts are served in the bright dining room, and a cosy lounge is available.

Rooms 5 en suite (1 GF) D £64–£78✶ **Facilities** TVB tea/coffee Cen ht TVL **Parking** 7 **Notes LB** ⊗ No coaches Closed Xmas & New Year

★★★★ GUEST HOUSE
Roseleigh
19 Broad Walk SK17 6JR
☎ 01298 24904 ▤ 01298 24904
e–mail: enquiries@roseleighhotel.co.uk
web: www.roseleighhotel.co.uk

dir: *A6 to Safeway rdbt, onto Dale Rd, right at lights, 100yds left by Swan pub, down hill & right onto Hartington Rd*

This elegant property has a prime location overlooking Pavilion Gardens, and quality furnishings and décor highlight the many original features. Thoughtfully furnished bedrooms have smart modern shower rooms and a comfortable lounge is also available.

Rooms 14 rms (12 en suite) (2 pri facs) (1 GF) **Facilities** TVB tea/coffee Cen ht **Parking** 9 **Notes** ⊗ No children 6yrs No coaches Closed 16 Dec–16 Jan

★★★★ Ⓐ GUEST HOUSE
The Old Manse Guesthouse
6 Clifton Rd, Silverlands SK17 6QL
☎ 01298 25638
e–mail: info@oldmanse.co.uk
web: www.oldmanse.co.uk

dir: *From A6 approach Buxton via Morrisons rdbt onto B5059 Dale Rd, 200yds before bridge right onto Peveril Rd & Clifton Rd*

Rooms 7 rms (6 en suite) (1 pri facs) (2 fmly) S fr £27; D fr £56✶ **Facilities** TVB tea/coffee Cen ht **Parking** 4 **Notes LB** ⊗ No coaches

See advert on opposite page

★★★ BED & BREAKFAST
Wellhead Farm
Wormhill SK17 8SL
☎ 01298 871023 ▤ 0871 236 0267
e–mail: wellhead4bunkntrough@cbits.net

dir: *Between Bakewell and Buxton. Off A6 onto B6049 signed Millers Dale/Tideswell & left to Wormhill*

This 16th-century farmhouse is in a peaceful location, and has low beams and two comfortable lounges. The bedrooms, some with four poster beds, come with radios, beverage trays and many thoughtful extras. The proprietors provide friendly and attentive hospitality in their delightful home.

Rooms 4 en suite (1 fmly) S £40–£48; D £66–£70 **Facilities** tea/coffee Cen ht TVL Dinner Last d 9am **Parking** 4 **Notes LB** ⊗

CALVER MAP 16 SK27

★★★★ GUEST ACCOMMODATION
Valley View
Smithy Knoll Rd S32 3XW
☎ 01433 631407
e-mail: sue@a-place-2-stay.co.uk
web: www.a-place-2-stay.co.uk
dir: *A623 from Baslow into Calver, 3rd left onto Donkey Ln*

This detached stone house is in the heart of the village. It is very well-furnished throughout and delightfully friendly service is provided. A hearty breakfast is served in the cosy dining room, which is well-stocked with local guide books.

Rooms 3 en suite (1 fmly) D £52–£80 **Facilities** TVB tea/coffee Cen ht Wi-fi available **Parking** 6 **Notes LB** No children 5yrs

CARSINGTON MAP 16 SK25

★★★★ BED & BREAKFAST
Henmore Grange
Hopton DE4 4DF
☎ 01629 540420 📄 01629 540420
e-mail: henmoregrange@hotmail.com
dir: *B5035 into Hopton, Henmore Grange 2nd house on left*

Ideally located very close to Carsington Water, this stone built farmhouse has been tastefully restored and retains many original features. Bedrooms are comfortable and well appointed and a freshly cooked breakfast is served in the farmhouse style dining room. An ideal touring centre, offering secure cycle storage and ample parking.

Rooms 3 en suite (1 fmly) S £40–£50; D £70✳ **Facilities** TVB tea/coffee Cen ht **Parking** 10 **Notes LB** ⊗ 🐾

CASTLETON MAP 16 SK18

See also Hope

★★★★ GUEST ACCOMMODATION
The Rising Sun
Hope Rd S33 0AL
☎ 01433 651323 📄 01433 651601
e-mail: info@the-rising-sun.org
dir: *On A625 from Sheffield to Castleton*

Located at Thornhill Moor within the Hope Valley, this 18th-century inn has been renovated to provide high standards of comfort and facilities. Spacious luxury bedrooms offer quality furnishings and efficient modern bathrooms, and some have stunning views of the surrounding countryside. The staff are friendly and capable, and imaginative food is offered in the comfortable public areas.

Rooms 12 en suite (2 fmly) S £55.50–£69.50; D £60–£140✳
Facilities STV TVB tea/coffee Cen ht Dinner Last d 10pm Wi-fi available
Conf Max 200 Thtr 200 Class 200 Board 24 Del from £95 ✳
Parking 120 **Notes LB** Civ Wed 220

See advert on page 144

★★★ INN
Ye Olde Cheshire Cheese Inn
How Ln S33 8WJ
☎ 01433 620330 📄 01433 621847
e-mail: info@cheshirecheeseinn.co.uk
dir: *In the centre of Castleton on A6187*

A family-run, former 17th-century coaching inn offering a traditional friendly welcome with real ales and a popular bar where hearty meals are served. Bedrooms are comfortably equipped and are en suite. Ideal location for walking and an extensive car park makes this a good touring base in the Peak District.

Rooms 10 en suite (1 fmly) (2 GF) S £35–£40; D £65–£90✳ **Facilities** TVB tea/coffee Cen ht Dinner Last d 8.30pm Golf 18 Fishing Riding **Conf** Max 50 Class 30 Board 40 **Parking** 24 **Notes LB** ⊗ Closed 25 Dec

CHESTERFIELD MAP 16 SK37

★★★★ 🅰 INN
Batemans Mill
Mill Ln, Old Tupton S42 6AE
☎ 01246 862296 📄 01246 865672
e-mail: info@batemansmill.co.uk
dir: *6.5m S of Chesterfield. Off A61 at Clay Cross onto Holmgate Rd to Valley Rd & Mill Ln*

Rooms 8 en suite (1 fmly) (4 GF) **Facilities** FTV TVB tea/coffee Direct dial from bedrooms Cen ht Dinner Last d 9pm Wi-fi available **Conf** Max 50 Thtr 50 Class 30 Board 30 **Parking** 50 **Notes** Closed 1st wk Jan

See advert on page 145

The Old Manse
Guesthouse, Buxton

Our elegant Victorian stone property is ideally situated in a leafy residential area. The quiet location ensures our guests a delightfully warm and peaceful stay. It is just a short walk from the historic town centre of Buxton, its Opera House & Pavilion Gardens. Ideal for exploring the Peak District National Park.

6 Clifton Road, Silverlands, Buxton, SK17 6QL
Telephone: 01298 25638
Email: info@oldmanse.co.uk

The Rising Sun

'Winner of the East Midlands Small Hotel of Excellence Award 2005'

ETC

THIS IS NOT JUST ANOTHER INN, THIS IS AN EXPERIENCE!

The Rising Sun, an 18th Century Inn situated in the heart of the Peak District National Park, is privately owned and family run. The inn has been sympathetically restored with 12 individually designed de luxe bedrooms yet maintains its authentic country atmosphere. Fresh flowers in abundance and antiques together with friendly and efficient staff make this the place to stay. Quality fresh food, real ales and fine wines served daily in a relaxed and comfortable bar. Civil ceremonies & wedding receptions a speciality.

The Rising Sun, Thornhill Moor, Hope Road, Nr. Bamford, Hope Valley, Derbyshire S33 0AL
Telephone: 01433 651323 • Fax: 01433 651601
E-Mail: info@the-rising-sun.org • www.the-rising-sun.org

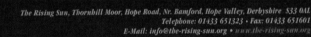

"Winner of the East Midlands Small Hotel of Excellence Award 2005."

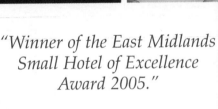

Weddings are our speciality. Hold your Civil Ceremony in our Oak Panelled Chatsworth Suite.

CROMFORD
MAP 16 SK25

★★★★ GUEST ACCOMMODATION
Alison House

Intake Ln DE4 3RH

☎ 01629 822211 📄 01629 822316

e–mail: alisonhouse@toch.org.uk

This very well furnished and spacious 18th-century house stands in seven acres of grounds just a short walk from the village. Public rooms are comfortable and bedrooms are mostly very spacious.

Rooms 16 en suite (1 fmly) (4 GF) S £49; D £79–£99✷ **Facilities** FTV TVB tea/coffee Direct dial from bedrooms Cen ht Dinner Last d 9pm Wi-fi available 🍴 **Conf** Max 40 Thtr 40 Class 40 Board 40 Del from £85 ✷ **Parking** 30 **Notes** Civ Wed 50

DARLEY DALE
MAP 16 SK26

★★★★ BED & BREAKFAST
Meadow House

Dale Rd North DE4 2HX

☎ 01629 734324

dir: 0.5m N of village centre on A6

Located within a short distance of Matlock, this friendly, non-smoking house stands in grounds and is well furnished throughout. Guests can enjoy substantial tasty breakfasts in the cosy lounge-dining room.

Rooms 3 rms (2 en suite) (1 pri facs) (1 fmly) S £30; D £50–£58✷ **Facilities** TVB tea/coffee Cen ht **Parking** 6 **Notes** ⊗ No children 8yrs 🚭

DERBY
MAP 11 SK33

See also Belper & Melbourne

★★★ GUEST ACCOMMODATION
Chambers House

110 Green Ln DE1 1RY

☎ 01332 746412

web: www.chambershouse.co.uk

dir: In city centre on Green Lane. Approach car park via Abbey St & Wilson St

Located a short walk from the centre, this impressive double-fronted Victorian house retains many original features. The attractive bedrooms

CONTINUED

are generally spacious, some are en-suite while others have shared facilities. A car park is available.

Rooms 12 rms (4 en suite) (2 fmly) (2 GF) **Facilities** TVB tea/coffee TVL **Parking** 6 **Notes** ⊗ 🚭

★★★ GUEST ACCOMMODATION
The Derby Conference Centre

London Rd DE24 8UX

☎ 01332 263137 📄 01322 264410

e–mail: enquiries@thederbyconferencecentre.com

web: www.thederbyconferencecentre.com

dir: A50/A52 onto A6, located at rdbt with Pride Park

Formerly a railway training centre, this Grade II-listed art deco building has undergone a major refurbishment to modernise the public areas, meeting rooms and accommodation, yet it still retains original features such as the wall paintings by Norman Wilkinson. Day rooms offer good flexibility and comforts, while updated conference facilities can cater for small to very large gatherings. The studio bedroom accommodation is soundly appointed and equipped.

Rooms 50 en suite (10 GF) S £35–£50; D £45–£60✷ **Facilities** STV TVB tea/coffee Cen ht TVL Dinner Last d 9pm Wi-fi available Pool Table **Conf** Max 1000 Thtr 400 Class 80 Board 50 Del from £89 ✷ **Parking** 200 **Notes** ⊗ No children 14yrs Civ Wed 400

ENGLAND

★★★ GUEST HOUSE
The Rose & Thistle Guest House
21 Charnwood St DE1 2GU
☎ 01332 344103 📠 01332 295944

dir: *Close to city centre and train station*

Just a short walk from the city centre, this Victorian terrace house is situated on the inner ring road. Rooms are pleasantly decorated and a warm welcome is provided. Breakfast is served in a light, modern dining room.

Rooms 8 rms (2 en suite) (5 fmly) (1 GF) S £25–£35; D £40–£50✳
Facilities TVB tea/coffee Cen ht **Notes** ⊗ No children 5yrs No coaches 🐾

★★★ INN
Bentley Brook Inn
DE6 1LF
☎ 01335 350278 📠 01335 350422
e–mail: all@bentleybrookinn.co.uk

dir: *2m N of Ashbourne at junct of A515 & B5056*

This popular inn is located within the Peak District National Park, just north of Ashbourne. It is a charming building with an attractive terrace, sweeping lawns, and nursery gardens. A well-appointed family restaurant dominates the ground floor, where a wide range of dishes is available all day. The character bar serves beer from its own micro-brewery. Bedrooms are well appointed and thoughtfully equipped.

Rooms 11 en suite (1 fmly) (2 GF) S £50–£60; D £60–£110✳
Facilities TVB tea/coffee Direct dial from bedrooms Cen ht TVL Dinner Last d 8.45pm Wi-fi available **Conf** Del from £120 ✳ **Parking** 60
Notes LB Civ Wed 40

★★★★ INN
The Bulls Head Inn
S32 5QR
☎ 01433 630873 📠 01433 631738
e–mail: wilbnd@aol.com

dir: *Off A623 into Foolow*

Located in the village centre, this popular inn retains many original features and offers comfortable, well-equipped bedrooms. Extensive and imaginative bar meals are served in the traditionally furnished dining room or in the cosy bar areas. The inn welcomes well-behaved dogs in the bar (and even muddy boots on the flagstone areas).

Rooms 3 en suite (1 fmly) S fr £50; D fr £70✳ **Facilities** TVB tea/coffee Cen ht Dinner Last d 8.45pm **Parking** 20

★★★★ ⊛ INN
The Chequers Inn
S32 3ZJ
☎ 01433 630231 📠 01433 631072
e–mail: info@chequers-froggatt.com

dir: *On A625 between Sheffield & Bakewell*

A very popular 16th-century inn offering an extensive range of well-cooked food. The bedrooms are comprehensively equipped with all modern comforts and the hospitality is professional and sincere. A good location for touring Derbyshire, the Peak Park, and visiting Chatsworth.

Rooms 5 en suite S £75–£100; D £75–£100✳ **Facilities** TVB tea/coffee Direct dial from bedrooms Cen ht Dinner Last d 9.15pm **Parking** 45
Notes LB ⊗ No coaches Closed 25 Dec

★★★★ 🛏 BED & BREAKFAST
Allmans Heath Cottage Bed & Breakfast
Woodhead Rd SK13 7QE
☎ 01457 857867
e–mail: julie@allmansheathcottage.co.uk

dir: *From Glossop town centre lights, proceed up Nolfolk St towards Woodhead for 1m. Continue through tunnel of trees, on left turning in at farm gate*

Just one mile from Glossop, this converted farm cottage has beamed ceilings, open fires and many original features. All the rooms command spectacular views over open countryside, and hospitality is warm and friendly.

Rooms 2 rms (1 en suite) (1 pri facs) S fr £40; D fr £60✳ **Facilities** TVB tea/coffee Cen ht TVL Wi-fi available **Parking** 6 **Notes** ⊗ 🐾

★★★★ BED & BREAKFAST
Woodlands

Woodseats Ln, Charlesworth SK13 5DP
☎ 01457 866568
e–mail: brian.mairs@sky.com
web: www.woodlandshighpeak.co.uk

dir: *3m SW of Glossop. Off A626, 0.5m from Charlesworth towards Marple*

This delightful Victorian house stands in well-tended grounds and offers very well-equipped and delightfully furnished bedrooms. There is a comfy lounge and a conservatory serving very good breakfasts, lunches and cream teas. Judy Mairs was a finalist for the AA Friendliest Landlady of the Year 2008 Award.

Rooms 3 rms (2 en suite) (1 pri facs) S £45; D £60–£70✳ **Facilities** FTV TVB tea/coffee Cen ht TVL **Parking** 6 **Notes** ⊗ No children 12yrs ⊜

★★★★ FARM HOUSE
Rock Farm *(SK027907)*

Monks Rd SK13 6JZ
☎ 01457 861086 & 07780 670568 📄 01457 861086
Mrs Dennett
e–mail: rockfarmbandb@btinternet.com

dir: *Off A624 onto Monks Rd, signed Charlesworth. After 1m, Rock Farm on left, follow farm track past Higher Plainsteads Farm*

Located down a winding track, with spectacular views over Kinder Scout and the surrounding hills from all rooms, Rock Farm is a restored family home. Walkers, horses, and riders, as well as young families, are offered a particularly warm welcome. Fresh eggs are used at breakfast.

Rooms 2 rms S £40; D £60✳ **Facilities** TVB tea/coffee Cen ht TVL Dinner **Parking** 4 **Notes** ⊗ 6 acres non-working ⊜

★★★★ ⬛ INN
Rock Tavern

Rock Tavern, Glossop Rd, Marple Bridge SK6 5RX
☎ 01457 899354
e–mail: info@rocktavern.co.uk

(For full entry see Marple, Greater Manchester)

★★★ BED & BREAKFAST
The Old House

Woodhead Rd, Torside SK13 1HU
☎ 01457 857527
e–mail: oldhouse@torside.co.uk

dir: *2m N of Glossop. On B6105 between sailing club & hairpin bend*

Set on the northwest-facing slopes above a reservoir, this smallholding commands superb views and offers all mod cons, including a drying room for people who are walking the nearby Pennine Way. Oak beams and rough plastered walls date from the 17th century, and hospitality is warm.

Rooms 3 en suite (1 fmly) (1 GF) **Facilities** tea/coffee Cen ht TVL **Parking** 5 **Notes** ⊜

★★★ GUEST ACCOMMODATION
Peakdale Lodge

49–53 High St East SK13 8PN
☎ 01457 854109 📄 01457 857080

dir: *On A57 in town centre near leisure centre*

This well-furnished guest house is in the centre of the town and offers friendly hospitality. Bedrooms have modern shower rooms and comprehensive breakfasts are served in the attractive dining room. A pretty rear patio garden is a feature during the summer.

Rooms 9 en suite (2 fmly) (1 GF) **Facilities** TVB tea/coffee Cen ht **Notes** ⊜

★★★ FARM HOUSE
White House Farm *(SK031963)*

Padfield SK13 1ET
☎ 01457 854695 📄 01457 854695 Mrs S Wynne

dir: *A628 from Sheffield to Tintwistle, signed to Padfield*

A 200-year-old farmhouse standing on the edge of Padfield village with fine views across the Longdendale Valley. The bedrooms are pleasantly furnished and comfortable. Breakfast is served around a large table in the dining room. There is a lounge and ample parking.

Rooms 1 rms 2 annexe rms (1 GF) **Facilities** FTV TVB tea/coffee Cen ht TVL **Parking** 10 **Notes** 40 acres mixed ⊜

GREAT HUCKLOW · · · · · · · · · · · · · · · MAP 16 SK17

★★★ ⬛ INN
The Queen Anne

SK17 8RF
☎ 01298 871246 📄 01298 873504
e–mail: angelaryan100@aol.com
web: www.queenanneinn.co.uk

dir: *Off A623 onto B6049 to Great Hucklow*

Set in the heart of this pretty village, the Queen Anne has been a licensed inn for over 300 years and the public areas retain many original features. The bedrooms are in a separate building with direct access, and have modern shower rooms en suite.

Rooms 2 annexe en suite (2 GF) S £40–£49; D £60–£69 **Facilities** TVB tea/coffee Cen ht TVL Dinner Last d 9pm **Parking** 20 **Notes LB** ⊗ No children 10yrs

HARTINGTON

MAP 16 SK16

★★★★ GUEST ACCOMMODATION

Bank House

Market Place SK17 0AL

☎ 01298 84465

dir: *B5054 into village centre*

Bank House is a very well-maintained Grade II listed Georgian building that stands in the main square of this delightful village. Bedrooms are neat and fresh in appearance, and there is a comfortable television lounge. A hearty breakfast is served in the ground-floor cottage-style dining room.

Rooms 5 rms (3 en suite) (3 fmly) S £25–£32; D £48–£54✻
Facilities TVB tea/coffee Cen ht TVL Dinner Last d noon **Parking** 2
Notes LB ⊗ Closed Xmas RS 22–28 Dec ⊚

HARTSHORNE

MAP 10 SK32

★★★★ ⊜ INN

The Mill Wheel

Ticknall Rd DE11 7AS

☎ 01283 550335 📄 01283 552833

e–mail: info@themillwheel.co.uk

web: www.themillwheel.co.uk

dir: *M42 junct 2 follow signs for A511 to Woodville, left onto A514 towards Derby until Hartshorne*

This popular inn and restaurant provides a wide range of well-prepared food and has a large mill wheel in the bar. Bedrooms are modern and well-equipped while friendly and attentive service is provided.

The Mill Wheel

Rooms 4 en suite (2 GF) **Facilities** TVB tea/coffee Cen ht Dinner Last d 9.15pm **Parking** 55 **Notes** ⊗

HATHERSAGE

MAP 16 SK28

★★★★ 🏠 BED & BREAKFAST

Cannon Croft

Cannonfields S32 1AG

☎ 01433 650005

e–mail: soates@cannoncroft.fsbusiness.co.uk

dir: *From George Hotel in village centre, 150yds W right onto single-track lane before bridge, Cannon Croft 130yds*

Set on the edge of the village with superb views of the surrounding countryside, this non-smoking home offers well-furnished and comprehensively equipped en suite bedrooms. An extensive choice of carefully prepared breakfasts is served in the conservatory-lounge. The enthusiastic hosts always offer a warm welcome.

Rooms 3 en suite (1 fmly) (3 GF) **Facilities** TVB tea/coffee Cen ht
Parking 5 **Notes** ⊗ No children 12yrs ⊚

★★★★ ◉ INN

Plough

Leadmill Bridge S32 1BA

☎ 01433 650319 📄 01433 651049

e–mail: sales@theploughinn-hathersage.co.uk

web: www.theploughinn-hathersage.co.uk

dir: *1m SE of Hathersage on B6001. Over bridge, 150yds beyond at Leadmill*

This delightful 16th-century inn with beer garden has an idyllic location by the River Derwent. A selection of real ales and imaginative food is served in the spacious public areas, and original open fires and exposed beams have been preserved. The thoughtfully equipped, well-appointed bedrooms include two impressive suites.

Rooms 3 en suite 2 annexe en suite (1 GF) S £60–£90; D £90–£120✻
Facilities TVB tea/coffee Direct dial from bedrooms Cen ht Dinner Last d 9.30pm **Parking** 50 **Notes LB** ⊗ No coaches Closed 25 Dec

CONTINUED

★★★★ GUEST ACCOMMODATION
Hillfoot Farm
Castleton Rd S32 1EG
☎ 01433 651673
e–mail: hillfootfarm@hotmail.com
web: www.hillfootfarm.com

dir: On A625 0.5m W from Hathersage on right

This 16th-century former inn and tollhouse is at the end of an old packhorse route, and you can expect a welcome from the friendly dog. The house has been extended to offer spacious, comfortable bedrooms and there is also a cosy lounge. Breakfast is served in the adjacent beamed dining room. This is a non-smoking establishment.

Rooms 4 en suite (1 fmly) (2 GF) S £30–£60; D £50–£60✳
Facilities TVB tea/coffee Cen ht **Parking** 12 **Notes LB** ⊗ No children 12yrs ⊛

★★★★ INN
Millstone
Sheffield Rd S32 1DA
☎ 01433 650258 📄 01433 651664
e–mail: jerry@millstoneinn.co.uk
web: www.millstoneinn.co.uk

dir: 0.5m SE of village on A6187

This timber and stone inn stands on an elevated position overlooking the Hope Valley. It offers modern, well-equipped bedrooms, and real ales and exciting food are served in the friendly bar. The smart Terrace fish restaurant offers fine dining with great views over the valley. Wi-fi and free use of the local gym are benefits.

Rooms 8 en suite (3 fmly) **Facilities** TVB tea/coffee Direct dial from bedrooms Cen ht Dinner Last d 9.30pm Wi-fi available Gym membership free to guests **Conf** Max 40 Thtr 40 Class 60 Board 40 **Parking** 80

★★★★ INN
The Scotsman's Pack Inn
School Ln S32 1BZ
☎ 01433 650253 📄 01433 650712
e–mail: scotsmans.pack@btinternet.com

dir: A625 into Hathersage, turn right onto School Ln towards the church, Scotsman's Pack 100yds on right

This comfortable inn on the edge of the village provides a wide range of well-prepared food. The bedrooms are compact, well-furnished and thoughtfully equipped, while the bar, which contains Little John's chair, is a great place to meet the locals. Hearty breakfasts are served in the separate dining room, and the staff are very friendly.

Rooms 5 en suite S £45; D £70–£75✳ **Facilities** TVB tea/coffee Cen ht Dinner Last d 9pm **Conf** Max 20 **Parking** 17 **Notes LB** ⊗ RS 25 Dec eve

★★★ BED & BREAKFAST
Moorgate
Castleton Rd S32 1EH
☎ 01433 650293

dir: On A6187 towards Hope, 100yds past George Hotel on right before railway bridge

This large Victorian house is set in attractive gardens and is just a short walk from the village centre. Traditionally furnished, spacious bedrooms come with interesting reading material and original artwork. Breakfast is served in the lounge-dining room that overlooks the delightful front garden.

Rooms 3 rms S £25; D £44 **Facilities** TVB tea/coffee Cen ht **Parking** 3 **Notes** ⊗ ⊛

HAYFIELD   MAP 16 SK08

★★★★ BED & BREAKFAST
Spinney Cottage B&B

Spinnerbottom SK22 1BL

☎ 01663 743230

dir: *A6 onto A6015 towards Hayfield, 2m turn left, 400yds on right*

Spinney Cottage lies a short distance from the picturesque village of Hayfield and is a good base for touring the area. Hospitality is warm, the attractive bedrooms are well equipped, and hearty breakfasts are served in the cottage-style dining room.

Rooms 3 rms (2 en suite) (1 pri facs) (1 fmly) S £27; D £54✳
Facilities TVB tea/coffee Cen ht TVL **Notes** ⊗ Closed Xmas & New Year
🐾

HOPE   MAP 16 SK18

Premier Collection

★★★★★ ≜ GUEST ACCOMMODATION
Underleigh House

Off Edale Rd S33 6RF

☎ 01433 621372 📠 01433 621324

e-mail: info@underleighhouse.co.uk
web: www.underleighhouse.co.uk

dir: *From village church on A6187 onto Edale Rd, 1m left onto lane*

Situated at the end of a private lane, surrounded by glorious scenery, Underleigh House was converted from a barn and cottage that dates from 1873, and now offers carefully furnished and attractively decorated bedrooms with modern facilities. One room has a private lounge and others have access to the gardens. There is a very spacious lounge with comfortable chairs and a welcoming log fire. Memorable breakfasts are served at one large table in the dining room.

Rooms 6 en suite (2 GF) S £55–£60; D £75–£95✳ **Facilities** TVB tea/coffee Direct dial from bedrooms Cen ht TVL **Parking** 6 **Notes LB** No children 12yrs Closed Xmas, New Year & 5 Jan–5 Feb

---

★★★★ ≜ GUEST ACCOMMODATION
Stoney Ridge

Granby Rd, Bradwell S33 9HU

☎ 01433 620538

e-mail: toneyridge@aol.com
web: www.stoneyridge.org.uk

dir: *From N end of Bradwell, Gore Ln uphill past Bowling Green Inn, turn left onto Granby Rd*

This large, split-level bungalow stands in attractive mature gardens at the highest part of the village and has extensive views. Hens roam freely in the landscaped garden, and their fresh eggs add to the hearty breakfasts. Bedrooms are attractively furnished and thoughtfully equipped, and there is a spacious comfortable lounge and a superb indoor swimming pool.

Rooms 4 rms (3 en suite) (1 pri facs) S £40–£42; D £54–£68✳
Facilities TVB tea/coffee Cen ht TVL Wi-fi available ☜ **Parking** 3
Notes LB No children 10yrs RS Winter

★★★ ≜ BED & BREAKFAST
Round Meadow Barn

Parsons Ln S33 6RB

☎ 01433 621347 & 07836 689422 📠 01433 621347

e-mail: rmbarn@bigfoot.com

dir: *Off A625 Hope Rd N onto Parsons Ln, over railway bridge, 200yds right into Hay barnyard, through gates, across 3 fields, house on left*

This converted barn, with original stone walls and exposed timbers, stands in open fields in the picturesque Hope Valley. The bedrooms are large enough for families and there are two modern bathrooms. Breakfast is served at one large table adjoining the family kitchen.

Rooms 4 rms (1 en suite) (1 fmly) S £30–£35; D £50–£60✳
Facilities TVB tea/coffee Cen ht Golf 18 Riding **Parking** 8 **Notes LB** 🐾

LONGFORD   MAP 10 SK23

★★★★ BED & BREAKFAST
Russets

Off Main St DE6 3DR

☎ 01335 330874 📠 01335 330874

e-mail: geoffreynolan@btinternet.com
web: www.russets.com

dir: *A516 in Hatton onto Sutton Ln, at T-junct right onto Long Ln, next right into Longford & right before phone box on Main St*

An indoor swimming pool is available at this beautifully maintained bungalow, which is in a peaceful location near Alton Towers. Bedrooms are well equipped and have smart modern bathrooms. Comprehensive breakfasts are served at a family table in a homely dining room, and a comfortable lounge is available.

Rooms 2 en suite (1 fmly) (2 GF) S £40; D £60–£63 **Facilities** STV TVB tea/coffee Cen ht TVL ☜ Gymnasium **Parking** 4 **Notes** Closed 3rd wk Dec–1st wk Jan 🐾

MARSTON MONTGOMERY   MAP 10 SK13

★★★★ ⊛ INN
The Crown Inn
Riggs Ln DE6 2FF
☎ 01889 590541 📠 01889 591576
e–mail: info@thecrowninn-derbyshire.co.uk

dir: From Ashbourne take A515 to Lichfield. After 5m turn right at Cubley x-rds, then follow signs to Marston Montgomery

This lovely inn stands at the heart of the peaceful village and provides modern bedrooms with informal dining in the bar and brasserie. Cooking shows much flair and imagination and the staff are friendly and caring.

Rooms 7 en suite (3 fmly) S £60–£65; D £65–£80✳ **Facilities** TVB tea/coffee Cen ht TVL Dinner Last d 9.30pm Wi-fi available **Conf** Max 10 Thtr 20 Class 10 Board 10 **Parking** 16 **Notes** ⊗ Closed 25 Dec & 1 Jan RS Sun

See advert on this page

MATLOCK   MAP 16 SK35

★★★★ ⇔ GUEST ACCOMMODATION
Holmefield
Dale Rd North, Darley Dale DE4 2HY
☎ 01629 735347
e–mail: holmefieldguesthouse@btinternet.com
web: www.holmefieldguesthouse.co.uk

dir: Between Bakewell & Matlock on A6. 1m from Rowsley & Chatsworth Estate, 0.5m from Peak Rail

Standing on mature grounds between Matlock and Bakewell, this elegant Victorian house has been furnished with flair to offer good levels of comfort and facilities. Imaginative dinners feature seasonal local produce, some from The Chatsworth Estate and warm hospitality and attentive services are assured.

Rooms 4 en suite (2 fmly) **Facilities** TVB tea/coffee Cen ht Dinner Last d 11am Pool Table Table tennis, badminton **Parking** 4 **Notes** ⊗ Closed 23 Dec–2 Jan

★★★★ 🏠 BED & BREAKFAST
Yew Tree Cottage
The Knoll, Tansley DE4 5FP
☎ 01629 583862 & 07799 541903
e–mail: enquiries@yewtreecottagebb.co.uk
web: www.yewtreecottagebb.co.uk

dir: 1.2m E of Matlock. Off A615 into Tansley centre

Located in a village, this 18th-century cottage has been renovated to provide high standards of comfort while retaining original character. Memorable breakfasts are served in the elegant dining room and a cosy lounge is available. A warm welcome and attentive service are assured.

Rooms 3 en suite D £70–£85✳ **Facilities** TVB tea/coffee Cen ht TVL Wi-fi available Sauna **Parking** 3 **Notes LB** ⊗ No children 12yrs

MATLOCK CONTINUED

★★★★ GUEST HOUSE
Glendon

Knowleston Place DE4 3BU
☎ 01629 584732
e–mail: sylvia.elliott@tesco.net

dir: *250yds SE of town centre. Off A615, car park before Glendon sign*

Glendon is set beside a park just a short walk from the town centre. The spacious bedrooms are pleasantly decorated and well equipped, and one is suitable for families. The comfortable third-floor lounge has lovely views over Bentley Brook and the local church.

Rooms 4 rms (2 en suite) (1 fmly) S £35–£40; D £58–£62 **Facilities** TVB tea/coffee Cen ht TVL **Parking** 4 **Notes** ⊗ No children 3yrs No coaches Closed Dec ⊛

★★★★ FARM HOUSE
Hearthstone Farm *(SK308583)*

Hearthstone Ln, Riber DE4 5JW
☎ 01629 534304 📄 01629 534372 Mrs Gilman
e–mail: enquiries@hearthstonefarm.co.uk
web: www.hearthstonefarm.co.uk

dir: *A615 at Tansley 2m E of Matlock, turn opp Royal Oak towards Riber, at gates to Riber Hall left onto Riber Rd and 1st left onto Hearthstone Ln, farmhouse on left*

Situated on a stunning elevated location, this traditional stone farmhouse retains many original features and is stylishly decorated throughout. Bedrooms are equipped with a wealth of homely extras and comprehensive breakfasts feature the farm's organic produce. There is a very comfortable lounge, and the farm animals in the grounds are an attraction.

Rooms 3 en suite S fr £50; D fr £70 **Facilities** TVB tea/coffee Cen ht TVL Wi-fi available **Parking** 6 **Notes** LB 150 acres organic beef lamb pigs Closed Xmas & New Year ⊛

★★★★ BED & BREAKFAST
Mount Tabor House

Bowns Hill, Crich DE4 5DG
☎ 01773 857008 & 07813 007478 📄 01773 857008
e–mail: mountabor@msn.com

dir: *6m SE of Matlock. On B5035 in Crich village centre*

This former Victorian Methodist chapel has fine surroundings. The first floor is a spacious living-dining area, where dinner and breakfast are served at one table – leaded Gothic windows and a superb wrought-iron balcony look across the Amber Valley. Interesting meals are created from quality local and organic produce, with dietary needs willingly catered for. The two bedrooms have a useful range of facilities, and the larger room has a king-size antique pine bed.

Rooms 2 en suite (3 fmly) (1 GF) **Facilities** TVB tea/coffee Cen ht Dinner jacuzzi **Parking** 3 **Notes** ⊗ No children Closed Xmas & New Year

★★★★ 🍴 BED & BREAKFAST
Old Sunday School

New St DE4 3FH
☎ 01629 583347 📄 01629 583347
e–mail: davhpatrick@hotmail.com

dir: *In town centre. Off A6 rdbt onto Bank Rd to Council Office car park, New St opp*

A warm welcome is assured at this converted Victorian chapel, built of mellow sandstone and just a short walk from central attractions. The homely bedroom is complemented by a modern shower room, and the spacious living area includes a period dining table, the setting for comprehensive breakfasts and (by arrangement) imaginative dinners.

Rooms 1 en suite (1 fmly) S £30; D £55 **Facilities** TVB tea/coffee Cen ht TVL Dinner Last d 5pm **Notes** LB ⊗ ⊛

★★★★ FARM HOUSE
Pear Tree Farm *(SK319572)*

Lea Main Rd, Lea Bridge DE4 5JN
☎ 01629 534215 & 07831 573688 📄 01629 534060
Mr & Mrs Barber
e–mail: sue@derbyshirearts.co.uk
web: www.derbyshirearts.co.uk

dir: *M1 junct 28, A38 S, A610 Ambergate, A6 Cromford. Turn right at lights, after 2m turn left at John Smedley Mills, 0.5m on left*

Set in 76 acres of woodland and pasture overlooking Lea Brook, this renovated farmhouse provides a range of thoughtfully furnished bedrooms, two of which have easier access. Comprehensive breakfasts are served in the oak-furnished dining room, and there is a spacious lounge with wood-burning stove and a separate art studio.

Rooms 8 en suite (1 fmly) (2 GF) **Facilities** TVB tea/coffee Cen ht TVL Dinner Studio (art based activities) **Conf** Max 15 **Parking** 10 **Notes** ⊗ 76 acres mixed, sheep

★★★★ INN
The Red Lion
Matlock Green DE4 3BT
☎ 01629 584888

dir: 500yds SE of town centre on A632

This comfortable inn is a good base for exploring Matlock and the surrounding Derbyshire countryside. Each bedroom is comfortable and furnished in quality pine. Public areas include a character bar with open fire and a restaurant where a wide selection of meals is on offer.

Rooms 6 en suite (1 fmly) **Facilities** TVB tea/coffee Cen ht Dinner Last d 9pm Pool Table **Parking** 20 **Notes** ⊗

★★★★ GUEST ACCOMMODATION
Sunnybank Guest House
37 Clifton Rd, Matlock Bath DE4 3PW
☎ 01629 584621
e–mail: sunnybank.matlock@btinternet.com

dir: Take A6 Matlock towards Cromford, on right between Temple and Newbath Hotels

A warm and friendly welcome awaits you in this attractive Victorian residence. Sunnybank is characterful, comfortable and charming. Situated in a quiet cul-de-sac amidst mature woodland surroundings. It has stunning views of the Derwent Valley and Wildcat Craggs, and is central to numerous walks, waterways and attractions.

Rooms 5 rms (4 en suite) (1 pri facs) (1 fmly) **Facilities** TVB tea/coffee Cen ht Last d Day before **Notes** ⊗ ⊛

★★★★ BED & BREAKFAST
Woodside
Stanton Lees DE4 2LQ
☎ 01629 734320 🗎 01629 734320
e–mail: kathpotter8378@woodsidestantonlees.co.uk
web: www.woodsidestantonlees.co.uk

dir: 4m NW of Matlock. A6 onto B5057 into Darley Bridge, opp pub right to Stanton Lees & right fork

Located on an elevated position with stunning views of the surrounding countryside, this mellow-stone house has been renovated to provide high standards of comfort and facilities. Carefully decorated bedrooms come with a wealth of thoughtful extras, and ground-floor areas include a comfortable lounge and conservatory overlooking the garden, which is home to a variety of wild birds.

Rooms 3 en suite D £50–£60✱ **Facilities** FTV TVB tea/coffee Cen ht TVL **Parking** 3 **Notes** ⊗ No children 3yrs ⊛

★★★ BED & BREAKFAST
Bradford Villa
26 Chesterfield Rd DE4 3DQ
☎ 01629 57147

dir: 500yds NE of town centre on A632, opp Lilybank hamlet

This non-smoking, semi-detached Victorian house is situated on an elevated position in neat gardens on the north edge of the town. Bedrooms are comfortably furnished and suitable for families. Small car park at rear.

Rooms 2 rms (1 en suite) (1 pri facs) (2 fmly) D £52 **Facilities** TVB tea/coffee Cen ht **Parking** 4 **Notes** ⊗ Closed 22 Dec–3 Jan ⊛

★★★ FARM HOUSE
Farley *(SK294622)*
Farley DE4 5LR
☎ 01629 582533 & 07801 756409 🗎 01629 584856
Mrs Brailsford
e–mail: eric.brailsford@btconnect.com

dir: 1m N of Matlock. From A6 rdbt towards Bakewell, 1st right, right at top of hill, left up Farley Hill, 2nd farm on left

You can expect a warm welcome at this traditional stone farmhouse. In addition to farming, the proprietors also breed dogs and horses. The bedrooms are pleasantly decorated and equipped with many useful extras. Breakfast is served round one large table (dinner is available by arrangement).

Rooms 2 en suite (3 fmly) S £35; D £50–£55 **Facilities** TVB tea/coffee Cen ht TVL Dinner Last d 5pm Riding **Parking** 8 **Notes** LB 165 acres arable beef dairy ⊛

★★★ GUEST ACCOMMODATION
Red House Carriage Museum
Old Rd, Darley Dale DE4 2ER
☎ 01629 733583 🗎 01629 733583
e–mail: redhousestables@hotmail.co.uk

dir: 2m N of Matlock, left off A6, 200yds on left

Located within a famous working carriage-driving school and museum, this detached house provides homely and thoughtfully equipped bedrooms, one on the ground floor and one in a former stable. Comprehensive breakfasts are served at a family table in an attractive dining room, and the comfortable lounge area overlooks the spacious gardens.

Rooms 2 rms (1 en suite) 2 annexe en suite (1 fmly) (1 GF) S £30–£40; D £70–£75✱ **Facilities** TVB tea/coffee Cen ht **Parking** 5 **Notes** ⊗ ⊛

MELBOURNE   MAP 11 SK32

★★★★ GUEST HOUSE

The Coach House

69 Derby Rd DE73 8FE

☎ 01332 862338 📄 01332 695281

e-mail: enquiries@coachhouse-hotel.co.uk

web: www.coachhouse-hotel.co.uk

dir: *Off B587 in village centre*

Located within the heart of a conservation area and close to Donington Park and East Midlands Airport, this traditional cottage has been restored to provide good standards of comfort and facilities. Bedrooms are thoughtfully furnished, and two are in converted stables. A lounge and secure parking are available.

Rooms 6 en suite (1 fmly) (3 GF) S £39–£40; D £60✳ **Facilities** TVB tea/coffee Cen ht TVL Wi-fi available **Parking** 6 **Notes LB** ⊗ No coaches

★★★ INN

The Melbourne Arms

92 Ashby Rd DE73 8ES

☎ 01332 864949 📄 01332 865525

e-mail: info@melbournearms.co.uk

web: www.melbournearms.co.uk

dir: *3m from East Midlands Airport*

Well located for the airport and Donington Park, this Grade II listed inn provides modern, thoughtfully equipped bedrooms, one of which is in a converted outbuilding. Ground-floor areas include two bars, a coffee shop and an elegant Indian restaurant.

Rooms 7 en suite (1 fmly) **Facilities** TVB tea/coffee Cen ht TVL Dinner Last d 11pm Bouncy Castle for children (weather permitting) **Conf** Max 25 Thtr 15 Class 15 Board 15 **Parking** 52 **Notes** ⊗

See advert on opposite page

NEWHAVEN   MAP 16 SK16

Premier Collection

★★★★★ 🏠 GUEST ACCOMMODATION

The Smithy

SK17 0DT

☎ 01298 84548 📄 01298 84548

e-mail: thesmithy@newhavenderbyshire.freeserve.co.uk

web: www.thesmithybedandbreakfast.co.uk

dir: *0.5m S of Newhaven on A515. Next to Biggin Ln, private driveway opp Ivy House*

Set in a peaceful location close to the Tissington and High Peak trails, the 17th-century drovers' inn and blacksmith's workshop have been carefully renovated. Bedrooms, which are in a former barn, are well equipped. Enjoyable breakfasts, which include free-range eggs and home-made preserves, are served in the forge, which features the original bellows on the vast open hearth.

CONTINUED

The Smithy

Rooms 4 en suite (2 GF) S £40–£60; D £70–£90 **Facilities** TVB tea/coffee Cen ht TVL **Conf** Max 20 Thtr 15 Board 10 **Parking** 8 **Notes LB** ⊗ ⊜

NEW MILLS   MAP 16 SK08

★★★★ 🅰 INN

Pack Horse Inn

Mellor Rd SK22 4QQ

☎ 01663 742365 📄 01663 741674

e-mail: info@packhorseinn.co.uk

dir: *A6 onto A6015, left at lights. Right at rdbt, after 0.5m left, onto Mellor Rd*

Rooms 7 en suite 5 annexe en suite (1 fmly) (2 GF) S £45–£75; D £60–£95✳ **Facilities** TVB tea/coffee Cen ht Dinner Last d 9pm Wi-fi available **Parking** 50 **Notes** ⊗ No coaches

REPTON   MAP 10 SK32

★★★ INN

The Boot Inn

12 Boot Hill DE65 6FT

☎ 01283 703327

e-mail: susie_goulden@yahoo.co.uk

web: www.thebootinn.co.uk

dir: *Off A38 or A50, follow signs for Willington and then Repton. Turn left at 'cross' rdbt*

Situated in the centre of the village, this traditional old inn offers pleasingly furnished bedrooms and busy bars. A wide choice of food is available and the service is friendly and attentive.

Rooms 5 en suite (1 fmly) S £35–£45; D £65–£75✳ **Facilities** TVB tea/coffee Cen ht Dinner Last d 8.30pm Wi-fi available **Parking** 8

RISLEY   MAP 11 SK43

[U]

Braeside Guest House
113 Derby Rd DE72 3SS
☎ 0115 939 5885
e–mail: bookings@braesideguesthouse.co.uk
web: www.braesideguesthouse.co.uk
dir: *W end of village on B5010*

At the time of going to press the rating for this establishment had not been confirmed. Please check the AA website www.theAA.com for up-to-date information.

Rooms 6 annexe en suite (6 GF) S £45; D £60✳ **Facilities** TVB tea/coffee Cen ht **Parking** 10 **Notes** ⊗ Closed 25–26 Dec

ROWSLEY   MAP 16 SK26

★★★ INN
The Grouse and Claret
Station Rd DE4 2EB
☎ 01629 733233 📄 01629 735194
e–mail: grouseandclaret.matlock@marstons.co.uk
dir: *M1 junct 28, A6 5m from Matlock, 3m from Bakewell*
A busy inn with a wide range of dishes available in the spacious bars. Bedrooms are pleasantly furnished and staff are friendly and attentive.
Rooms 8 en suite (2 fmly) S £69.95; D £69.95 **Facilities** STV FTV TVB tea/coffee Cen ht Dinner Last d 9pm Wi-fi available **Parking** 78 **Notes** ⊗ No coaches

SWADLINCOTE   MAP 10 SK21

★★★★ BED & BREAKFAST
Manor Farm
Coton in the Elms DE12 8EP
☎ 01283 760340 📄 01283 760340
dir: *Off A38 for Walton-on-Trent & sign for Coton in the Elms, Manor Farm on right*
This splendid traditional farmhouse retains its original staircase and many other interesting features. The spacious bedrooms are furnished with antiques. Located in a pleasant village, but not far from major roads for touring.
Rooms 3 en suite (1 fmly) **Facilities** TVB tea/coffee Cen ht **Parking** 8 **Notes** ⊗ ⊛

★★★ BED & BREAKFAST
Overseale House
Acresford Rd, Overseal DE12 6HX
☎ 01283 763741 📄 01283 760015
e–mail: oversealehouse@hotmail.com
web: www.oversealehouse.co.uk
dir: *On A444 between Burton upon Trent & M42 junct 11*
Located in the village, this well-proportioned Georgian mansion, built for a renowned industrialist, retains many original features including a magnificent dining room decorated with ornate mouldings. The period-furnished ground-floor areas include a cosy sitting room, and bedrooms contain many thoughtful extras.
Rooms 4 en suite 1 annexe rms (3 fmly) (2 GF) S £30–£45; D £60–£70✳ (room only) **Facilities** TVB tea/coffee Cen ht **Conf** Max 14 Board 14 **Parking** 6 **Notes** ⊛

TIDESWELL   MAP 16 SK17

★★★ GUEST ACCOMMODATION
Poppies
Bank Square SK17 8LA
☎ 01298 871083
e–mail: poptidza@dialstart.net
dir: *On B6049 in village centre opp NatWest bank*
A friendly welcome is assured at this non-smoking house, located in the heart of a former lead-mining and textile community, a short walk from the 14th-century parish church. Bedrooms are homely and practical.
Rooms 3 rms (1 en suite) (1 fmly) S £22–£25; D £44–£53✳ **Facilities** TVB tea/coffee Cen ht Dinner Last d previous day **Notes** ⊛

WESTON UNDERWOOD — MAP 10 SK24

Premier Collection

★★★★★ 🏠 🍽 FARM HOUSE
Park View Farm (SK293425)

DE6 4PA
☎ 01335 360352 & 07771 573057 📠 01335 360352
Mrs Adams
e–mail: enquiries@parkviewfarm.co.uk
web: www.parkviewfarm.co.uk

dir: *From A52/A38 rdbt W of Derby, take A38 N, 1st left to Kedleston Hall. Continue for 1.5m past x-rds*

An impressive Victorian farmhouse surrounded by beautiful gardens and 370 acres of arable land. Each bedroom has an antique four-poster bed, attractive decor, period furniture and a wealth of homely extras. Quality ornaments and art enhance the many original features and ground-floor rooms include a spacious comfortable lounge and an elegant dining room.

Rooms 3 en suite S £50–£60; D £80–£85 **Facilities** TVB tea/coffee Cen ht TVL Wi-fi available **Parking** 10 **Notes LB** ✖ No children 5yrs 370 acres Organic arable/sheep Closed Xmas 🐾

WINSTER — MAP 16 SK26

★★★★ 🅐 GUEST ACCOMMODATION
Brae Cottage

East Bank DE4 2DT
☎ 01629 650375

dir: *A6 onto B5057, driveway on right past pub*

Rooms 2 annexe en suite (1 fmly) (2 GF) S £37–£48; D £48✳ **Facilities** TVB tea/coffee Cen ht **Parking** 2 **Notes** ✖ No children 11yrs 🐾

WIRKSWORTH — MAP 16 SK25

Premier Collection

★★★★★ GUEST HOUSE
The Old Lock-Up

North End DE4 4FG
☎ 01629 826272 📠 01629 826272
e–mail: wheeler@theoldlockup.co.uk

dir: *Off A6, in village centre off Coldwell St*

A really unique guest house which is a conversion of a police station with cells and also an adjacent chapel. The house is delightfully furnished throughout, while service and hospitality is quite special.

Rooms 2 en suite 2 annexe en suite S £45–£90; D £80–£150✳ **Facilities** TVB tea/coffee Cen ht TVL Dinner Last d 6pm Air bath with aromatherapy oils **Parking** 5 **Notes LB** ✖ No children No coaches 🐾

Premier Collection

★★★★★ BED & BREAKFAST
The Old Manor House

Coldwell St DE4 4FB
☎ 01629 822502
e–mail: ivan@spurrier-smith.fsnet.co.uk

dir: *On B5035 Coldwell St off village centre*

Located on the village edge, this impressive period house has been lovingly renovated to provide high standards of comfort and facilities. Quality furnishing and décor highlight the many original features and the spacious bedroom has a wealth of thoughtful extras. Comprehensive breakfasts are served in the elegant dining room and a spacious drawing room is available.

Rooms 1 rms (1 pri facs) S £50–£55; D £80–£85✳ **Facilities** TVB tea/coffee Cen ht Pool Table 🏓 **Parking** 1 **Notes** ✖ No children 12yrs Closed Xmas & New Year 🐾

YOULGREAVE — MAP 16 SK26

★★★ BED & BREAKFAST
The Old Bakery

Church St DE45 1UR
☎ 01629 636887
e–mail: corcot@tiscali.co.uk

dir: *Off A515/A6, in village centre*

Located in the heart of this unspoiled village, the former bakery has been renovated to provide a range of thoughtfully furnished bedrooms, one of which is in a converted barn. Breakfast is served in the original baker's shop and furnishings enhance the retained features.

Rooms 2 rms 1 annexe en suite S £28–£40; D £42–£64✳ **Facilities** TV2B Cen ht TVL **Parking** 2 **Notes** Closed Xmas 🐾

DEVON

ASHBURTON
MAP 03 SX77

★★★★ GUEST ACCOMMODATION

Greencott

Landscove TQ13 7LZ

☎ 01803 762649

dir: *3m SE of Ashburton. Off A38 at Peartree junct, Landscove signed on slip road, village green 2m on right, opp village hall*

Greencott has a peaceful village location and superb country views. Your hosts extend a very warm welcome and there is a relaxed home-from-home atmosphere. Service is attentive and caring and many guests return time and again. Bedrooms are attractive, comfortable and very well equipped. Delicious country cooking is served around an oak dining table.

Rooms 2 en suite S £24–£25; D £48–£50 **Facilities** tea/coffee Cen ht TVL Dinner Last d by arrangement **Parking** 3 **Notes** LB ⊗ Closed 25–26 Dec ☜

★★★★ FARM HOUSE

Sladesdown Farm *(SX765684)*

Landscove TQ13 7ND

☎ 01364 653973 🖹 01364 653973 Mr & Mrs Mason

e–mail: sue@sladesdown.co.uk

dir: *2m S of Ashburton. Off A38 at Peartree junct, Landscove signed on slip road, left at 2nd x-rds, farm 100yds right*

Set in 50 acres of tranquil pasture and well-tended gardens, and convenient for the A38, this modern farmhouse offers very spacious, attractive accommodation. There's a friendly atmosphere, with relaxation assured either in the lounge or on the terrace in finer weather. Guests are welcome to wander across the land where a series of ponds have been created attracting abundant wildlife. A hearty breakfast featuring delicious local and home-made produce is the perfect start to the day.

Rooms 4 rms (2 en suite) (2 pri facs) (1 fmly) **Facilities** TVB tea/coffee Cen ht **Parking** available **Notes** ⊗ 14 acres beef goats turkeys ☜

★★★★ GUEST ACCOMMODATION

Gages Mill Country Guest House

Buckfastleigh Rd TQ13 7JW

☎ 01364 652391 🖹 01364 652641

e–mail: richards@gagesmill.co.uk

dir: *Off A38 at Peartree junct, turn right then left at fuel station, Gages Mill 500yds on left*

Set in delightful grounds and well-tended gardens, Gages Mill lies on the edge of Dartmoor National Park and is an attractive former wool mill dating back to the 14th century. This family-run house offers a warm welcome and a home-from-home atmosphere. Breakfast is served in the dining room at individual tables, and there is a lounge where you can play games or watch television.

Rooms 7 en suite (1 fmly) (1 GF) S £45; D £62–£74✻ **Facilities** tea/coffee Cen ht TVL Wi-fi available **Parking** 7 **Notes** ⊗ No children 8yrs Closed 23 Oct–1 Mar ☜

★★★★ ⌂ INN

The Rising Sun

Woodland TQ13 7JT

☎ 01364 652544

e–mail: admin@therisingsunwoodland.co.uk

dir: *A38, exit signed Woodland/Denbury, continue straight on for 1.5m Rising Sun on left*

Peacefully situated in scenic south Devon countryside, this inn is just a short drive from the A38. A friendly welcome is extended to all guests, business, leisure and families alike. Bedrooms are comfortable and well equipped. Dinner and breakfast feature much local and organic produce. A good selection of homemade puddings, West Country cheeses, local wines and quality real ales are available.

Rooms 5 en suite (2 fmly) (2 GF) D £75✻ **Facilities** FTV TVB tea/coffee Cen ht Dinner Last d 9.15pm **Parking** 30 **Notes** No coaches

ATHERINGTON
MAP 03 SS52

★★★★ ⌂ FARM HOUSE

West Down *(SS582228)*

Little Eastacombe EX37 9HP

☎ 01769 560551 🖹 01769 560551 Mr & Mrs Savery

e–mail: info@westdown.co.uk

web: www.westdown.co.uk

dir: *0.5m from Atherington on B3227 to Torrington, turn right, 100yds on left*

Set within 25 acres of lush Devon countryside, this establishment makes a good base for exploring the area. Peace and caring hospitality are assured. Bedrooms are equipped with a host of thoughtful extras, and every effort is made to ensure an enjoyable stay. A choice of homely lounges is available, and breakfast and scrumptious dinners are served in the sun lounge.

Rooms 2 en suite 2 annexe en suite (2 GF) S £36–£40; D £68–£70✻ **Facilities** TVB tea/coffee Cen ht TVL Dinner Last d 1pm Wi-fi available **Parking** 8 **Notes** LB ⊗ 25 acres Sheep chicken ☜

AXMINSTER MAP 04 SY29

Premier Collection

★★★★★ 🛏 🍽 GUEST ACCOMMODATION

Kerrington House

Musbury Rd EX13 5JR

☎ 01297 35333 📠 01297 35345

e-mail: jreaney@kerringtonhouse.com

web: www.kerringtonhouse.com

dir: *0.5m from Axminster on A358 towards Seaton, house on left*

Set in landscaped gardens, this delightful house has been lovingly restored. The carefully decorated bedrooms are equipped with many thoughtful touches, and personal treasures adorn the light and airy drawing room. Breakfast offers a good selection of dishes prepared with flair and imagination. The house is available with exclusive use for small house parties.

Rooms 5 en suite **Facilities** TVB tea/coffee Direct dial from bedrooms Cen ht Dinner Last d 7pm **Conf** Max 12 Board 12 **Parking** 6 **Notes** ⊗

BAMPTON MAP 03 SS92

★★★★ 🍽 GUEST ACCOMMODATION

The Bark House

Oakford Bridge EX16 9HZ

☎ 01398 351236

dir: *A361 to rdbt at Tiverton onto A396 for Dulverton and onto Oakfordbridge, on right*

Located in the stunning Exe Valley, this is a perfect place to relax and unwind, surrounded by wonderful unspoilt countryside. Hospitality is a hallmark here and a cup of tea by the fireside is always on offer. Both breakfast and dinner make use of the excellent local produce, and are served in the attractive dining room, overlooking fields and the river. Bedrooms all have a homely, cottage-style feel with comfy beds to ensure a peaceful night's sleep.

Rooms 6 rms (5 en suite) (1 pri facs) S £48.50–£64; D £77–£128✳ **Facilities** TVB tea/coffee Cen ht Dinner Last d 7.30pm **Parking** 6 **Notes LB**

★★★★ 🍽 FARM HOUSE

Newhouse Farm *(SS892228)*

EX16 9JE

☎ 01398 351347 Mrs A Boldry

e-mail: anne.boldry@btconnect.com

web: www.newhouse-farm-holidays.co.uk

dir: *5m W of Bampton on B3227*

Set in 42 acres of rolling farmland, this delightful farmhouse provides a friendly and informal atmosphere. The smart, rustic-style bedrooms are well equipped with modern facilities, and imaginative and delicious home-cooked dinners, using the best local produce, are available by arrangement. Home-made bread and preserves feature at breakfast.

Rooms 3 en suite (1 GF) S £40; D £65–£70 **Facilities** FTV TVB tea/coffee Cen ht Dinner Last d 4pm Fishing **Parking** 3 **Notes LB** ⊗ No children 10yrs 42 acres Beef, sheep Closed Xmas & New Year

BARNSTAPLE MAP 03 SS53

Premier Collection

★★★★★ 🛏 🍽 GUEST ACCOMMODATION

Halmpstone Manor

Bishop's Tawton EX32 0EA

☎ 01271 830321 & 831003 📠 01271 830826

e-mail: jane@halmpstonemanor.co.uk

web: www.halmpstonemanor.co.uk

dir: *3m SE of Barnstaple. Off A377 E of river & rail bridges*

Halmpstone Manor was mentioned in the Domesday Book and parts of the later medieval manor house survive. The Manor now provides quality accommodation, personal service and fine cuisine. Delightful day rooms include a spacious lounge complete with deep sofas and a roaring fire, and a creative, daily changing menu is offered in the elegant restaurant. Superb hospitality and excellent value make this a great choice for a restful break.

Rooms 4 en suite **Facilities** TVB tea/coffee Dinner Last d 7.30pm **Parking** 12 **Notes** Closed Xmas & New Year

★★★ GUEST HOUSE

Cresta Guest House

26 Sticklepath Hill EX31 2BU

☎ 01271 374022

e-mail: peter.davis170@virgin.net

dir: *On A3215 0.6m W of town centre, top of hill on right*

A warm welcome is assured at this family-run establishment, situated on the western outskirts of Barnstaple. The well-equipped, individually styled bedrooms, are comfortably appointed and include ground floor rooms. A hearty breakfast is served in the modern and comfortable dining room.

CONTINUED

Cresta Guest House

Rooms 6 rms (4 en suite) (2 pri facs) 2 annexe en suite (2 fmly) (2 GF)
S £25; D £49✱ **Facilities** TVB tea/coffee Cen ht Wi-fi available
Parking 6 **Notes** No coaches Closed 2 wks Xmas

★★★ FARM HOUSE
Rowden Barton *(SS538306)*
Roundswell EX31 3NP
☎ 01271 344365 Mrs VJ Dallyn

dir: *2m SW of Barnstaple on B3232*
Rowden Barton offers a friendly and homely environment where
guests can feel they are part of the family. The two comfortable
bedrooms share an adjoining bathroom, and both rooms have views
of the surrounding countryside. Delicious breakfasts, featuring
home-made bread and preserves, provide a fine start to the day.

Rooms 2 rms S £25–£27; D £45–£47✱ **Facilities** Cen ht TVL **Parking** 4
Notes ✗ No children 12yrs 90 acres beef & sheep ☺

BERRYNARBOR   MAP 03 SS54
★★★★ GUEST ACCOMMODATION
Berry Mill House
Mill Ln EX34 9SH
☎ 01271 882990
e–mail: enquiries@berrymillhouse.co.uk
web: www.berrymillhouse.co.uk

dir: *500yds NW of village centre. A399 W through Combe Martin,
2nd left at bottom of the hill, house on left*
In a wooded valley on the edge of the village, this former grain mill is a
5-minute walk on the coastal path. Guests are assured of a warm
reception from the owners, who enjoy welcoming guests to their
home. The freshly-cooked breakfast provides a substantial start to the
day while home-cooked evening meals are available by arrangement.

Rooms 3 en suite S £42.50; D £60–£65✱ **Facilities** TVB tea/coffee
Cen ht TVL Dinner Last d 5pm ☘ **Parking** 6 **Notes** LB ✗ No children
12yrs Closed Nov & Xmas ☺

BIDEFORD   MAP 03 SS42
See also Westward Ho!

★★★★ GUEST HOUSE
The Mount
Northdown Rd EX39 3LP
☎ 01237 473748 ▤ 01271 373813
e–mail: andrew@themountbideford.co.uk
web: www.themountbideford.co.uk

dir: *Bideford turning off A39, right after Rydon garage, premises
on right after 600yds at mini-rdbt*
A genuine warm welcome is assured at this delightful, centrally located
Georgian property. Bedrooms are comfortably furnished and well
equipped, and a ground-floor room is available for easier access. A
hearty breakfast is served in the elegant dining room and there is a
cosy sitting room.

Rooms 8 en suite (3 fmly) (1 GF) S £33–£37.50; D £66–£75
Facilities TVB tea/coffee Licensed Cen ht Wi-fi available **Parking** 5
Notes LB ✗ No coaches Closed Xmas

★★★★ GUEST ACCOMMODATION
Pines at Eastleigh
The Pines, Eastleigh EX39 4PA
☎ 01271 860561 ▤ 01271 861689
e–mail: pirrie@thepinesateastleigh.co.uk

dir: *A39 onto A386 signed East-The-Water. 1st left signed
Eastleigh, 500yds next left, 1.5m to village, house on right*
Friendly hospitality is assured at this Georgian farmhouse, set in
seven acres of gardens. Two of the comfortable bedrooms are located
in the main house, the remainder in converted barns around a
charming courtyard, with a pretty pond and well. A delicious breakfast
featuring local and home-made produce is served in the dining room
and a lounge and honesty bar are also available.

Rooms 6 en suite (1 fmly) (4 GF) S £45; D £75–£100 **Facilities** TVB
tea/coffee Direct dial from bedrooms Cen ht Wi-fi available ☘ Table
Tennis, Archery, Table Football **Conf** Max 25 Thtr 20 Board 20 **Parking** 20
Notes LB No children 9yrs

BOVEY TRACEY   MAP 03 SX87
★★★ INN
The Cromwell Arms
Fore St TQ13 9AE
☎ 01626 833473 ▤ 01626 836873
e–mail: thecromwellarms@fsmail.net
web: www.thecromwellarms.co.uk

dir: *In town centre*
This inn at the heart of the town dates from the 17th century. Rooms
are stylish with quality furnishings, and two are suitable for families.
There is a choice of dining in either the bar or restaurant.

Rooms 12 en suite (2 fmly) S £52.50–£60; D £65–£70✱ **Facilities** FTV
TVB tea/coffee Direct dial from bedrooms Cen ht Dinner Last d 9pm
Conf Max 40 Thtr 40 Class 25 Board 25 **Parking** 25

BRAUNTON
MAP 03 SS43

★★★★ Ⓐ BED & BREAKFAST
Denham House

North Buckland EX33 1HY

☎ 01271 890297 📄 01271 890106

e–mail: info@denhamhouse.co.uk

web: www.denhamhouse.co.uk

dir: *From Barnstaple A361, 2nd left after Knowle, follow lane into North Buckland, house on right*

Rooms 6 en suite (2 fmly) S £35–£40; D £50–£70✱ **Facilities** TVB tea/coffee Cen ht TVL Snooker Pool Table Table tennis Skittle Alley **Parking** 7 **Notes LB** ⊗

BRIXHAM
MAP 03 SX95

★★★★ GUEST HOUSE
Anchorage Guest House

170 New Rd TQ5 8DA

☎ 01803 852960

e–mail: enquiries@brixham-anchorage.co.uk

web: http://brixham-anchorage.co.uk

dir: *A3022, enter Brixham, left at lights, 1st on right*

This smartly appointed establishment is conveniently located within walking distance of the town centre and harbour. The Anchorage stands in its own grounds and guests have use of the garden; there is also ample safe parking. The dining room and bedrooms all share a light, bright contemporary style with many extra facilities provided in rooms to ensure a comfortable stay.

Rooms 7 rms (6 en suite) (1 pri facs) (1 fmly) (4 GF) S £24–£33; D £52–£66✱ **Facilities** TVB Cen ht TVL Wi-fi available **Parking** 7 **Notes LB** ⊗ No coaches

★★★ GUEST ACCOMMODATION
Harbour View Brixham

65 King St TQ5 9TH

☎ 01803 853052 📄 01803 853052

dir: *A3022 to town centre/harbour, left at lights, right at T-junct, premises on right of inner harbour*

This comfortable house looks across the harbour towards Torbay. The friendly proprietors provide attractive, well-equipped accommodation, and there is a pleasant lounge area in the dining room. Breakfasts are traditional, well-cooked and appetising.

Rooms 8 rms (7 en suite) (1 pri facs) (1 fmly) S £31–£40; D £50–£62✱ **Facilities** TVB tea/coffee Cen ht **Parking** 7 **Notes LB** ⊗

BUCKFAST
MAP 03 SX76

★★★ GUEST ACCOMMODATION
Furzeleigh Mill

Old Ashburton Rd TQ11 0JP

☎ 01364 643476

e–mail: enquiries@furzeleigh.co.uk

web: www.furzeleigh.co.uk

dir: *Off A38 at Dartbridge junct, right at end slip road, right opp Little Chef signed Ashburton/Prince Town (do not cross River Dart bridge), 200yds right*

This Grade II listed 16th-century converted corn mill stands in grounds and is a good base for touring Dartmoor. Spacious family rooms are available as well as a lounge and a bar. All meals are served in the dining room and use local produce.

Rooms 14 en suite (2 fmly) **Facilities** TVB tea/coffee Cen ht TVL Dinner Last d 8.10pm Wi-fi available **Conf** Max 20 Thtr 20 **Parking** 32 **Notes** No children 8yrs Closed 23 Dec–2 Jan

BUCKFASTLEIGH   MAP 03 SX76

★★★★ ≜ ⊜ GUEST ACCOMMODATION

Kilbury Manor

Colston Rd TQ11 0LN
☎ 01364 644079
e-mail: visit@kilburymanor.co.uk
web: www.kilburymanor.co.uk

dir: Off A38 onto B3380 to Buckfastleigh, left onto Old Totnes Rd, at bottom turn right, Kilbury Manor on left

Dating back to the 17th century, this charming Devon longhouse is situated in the tranquil surroundings of the Dart Valley with access to the river across the meadow. Bedrooms have lots of character and are located in the main house or in adjacent converted barns, all of which provide high levels of comfort with period furnishings. Breakfast is served in the elegant dining room with local produce very much in evidence.

Rooms 4 rms (3 en suite) (1 pri facs) (1 fmly) (1 GF) S £40–£50; D £65–£80✱ **Facilities** FTV TVB tea/coffee Cen ht Dinner Last d noon **Parking** 5 **Notes** No children 8yrs ⊛

★★★ INN

Kings Arms

15 Fore St TQ11 0BT
☎ 01364 642341

dir: In town centre opp tourist office & The Valiant Soldier
This long-established, friendly and popular inn provides a well-appointed base from which to explore this picturesque area. Bedrooms are comfortably furnished, while public areas include a choice of bars, dining area and an attractive patio and garden.

Rooms 4 rms (1 en suite) S £35–£45; D £50–£75 **Facilities** TVB tea/coffee Dinner Last d 9pm **Conf** Max 20 Thtr 20 Class 14 Board 14 Del from £70 ✱ **Parking** 1 **Notes** No coaches

★★★ 🅰 INN

Dartbridge Inn

Totnes Rd TQ11 0JR
☎ 01364 642214 📠 01364 643839
e-mail: dartbridgeinn@oldenglishinns.co.uk
web: www.oldenglishinns.co.uk

dir: 0.5m NE of town centre. A38 onto A384, 250yds on left

Rooms 10 en suite (1 fmly) **Facilities** tea/coffee Direct dial from bedrooms Last d 9.30pm **Conf** Max 150 Thtr 150 Class 75 Board 40 **Parking** 100

BUDLEIGH SALTERTON   MAP 03 SY08

Premier Collection

★★★★★ ≜ GUEST ACCOMMODATION

Downderry House

10 Exmouth Rd EX9 6AQ
☎ 01395 442663 📠 01395 442663
e-mail: info@downderryhouse.co.uk
web: www.downderryhouse.co.uk

dir: From M5 signed for Budleigh Salterton. From A303 exit at Daisy Mount and follow B3180

Just a short stroll from the town and seafront, this lovely house stands in an acre of gardens with views across meadows. Quality is the hallmark here with spacious and stylish bedrooms offering impressive levels of comfort. In addition, the luxurious bathrooms come complete with robes and fluffy towels. Breakfast provides a wonderful taste of the local area, served in the attractive dining room overlooking the gardens. An elegant guest lounge is also available, complete with honesty bar.

Rooms 5 en suite (1 GF) S £65–£89; D £79–£99✱ **Facilities** FTV TVB tea/coffee Cen ht Wi-fi available ♨ **Conf** Max 10 Thtr 10 Class 10 Board 10 **Parking** 9 **Notes** LB No children 10yrs

BUDLEIGH SALTERTON CONTINUED

★★★★ GUEST ACCOMMODATION
Hansard House

3 Northview Rd EX9 6BY
☎ 01395 442773 📄 01395 442475
e–mail: enquiries@hansardhotel.co.uk
web: www.hansardhousehotel.co.uk

dir: 500yds W of town centre

Hansard House is quietly situated a short walk from the town centre. Many of the well-presented bedrooms have commanding views across the town to the countryside and estuary beyond. Several are located on the ground floor and have easier access. Guests enjoy a varied selection at breakfast including a range of healthy options. The dining room and lounge are both comfortably furnished and dinners are sometimes available with prior notification.

Rooms 12 en suite (1 fmly) (3 GF) S £39–£47; D £79–£93✳
Facilities STV TVB tea/coffee Direct dial from bedrooms Lift Cen ht TVL Dinner Last d noon **Parking** 11 **Notes LB**

CHAGFORD   MAP 03 SX78

Premier Collection

★★★★★ GUEST ACCOMMODATION
Parford Well

Sandy Park TQ13 8JW
☎ 01647 433353
e–mail: tim@parfordwell.co.uk
web: www.parfordwell.co.uk

dir: A30 onto A382, after 3m left at Sandy Park towards Drewsteignton, house 50yds on left

Set in delightful grounds on the edge of Dartmoor, this attractive house is a restful and friendly home. Quality and style are combined in the comfortable bedrooms, the lounge overlooks the well-tended gardens, and breakfast is served at tables dressed with silver and crisp linen in one of two dining rooms. Carefully cooked, top local ingredients are hallmarks of a breakfast that's a perfect start for exploring the moors.

Parford Well

Rooms 3 rms (2 en suite) (1 pri facs) S £45–£85; D £70–£85
Facilities Cen ht TVL Wi-fi available **Parking** 4 **Notes** ⊗ No children 8yrs ⌨

★★★★ GUEST ACCOMMODATION
Easton Court

Easton Cross TQ13 8JL
☎ 01647 433469
e–mail: stay@easton.co.uk
web: www.easton.co.uk

dir: 1m NE of Chagford at junct A382 & B3206

Set in Dartmoor National Park, the age of this picturesque house is reflected in the oak beams and deep granite walls. Guests can come and go via a separate entrance. Relaxation is obligatory, either in the lovely garden or in the snug surroundings of the lounge. The delightful bedrooms all have country views.

Rooms 5 en suite (2 GF) S £50–£65; D £60–£80✳ **Facilities** TVB tea/coffee Cen ht Wi-fi available **Parking** 5 **Notes** No children 10yrs

★★★ INN
The Sandy Park Inn

TQ13 8JW
☎ 01647 433267
e–mail: sandyparkinn@aol.com

dir: 1m NE of Chagford off A382

This popular, thatched country inn is conveniently located a short drive from the A30. The busy bar is full of character and is well stocked. There is a separate restaurant and smaller cosy rooms. Bedrooms are contemporary in style and well appointed with comfortable furnishings. A good choice of hearty dishes is also available.

CONTINUED

CONTINUED

Rooms 5 rms (2 en suite) (3 pri facs) S fr £55; D fr £92 Facilities TVB tea/coffee Cen ht Dinner Last d 9pm Wi-fi available Fishing Gofl Course nearby Parking 4 Notes No coaches

---

CHERITON BISHOP   MAP 03 SX79

★ ★ ★ ★ ⇔ INN

The Mulberry

EX6 6JH

☎ 01647 24227

e–mail: the.mulberry@btconnect.com

dir: 0.25m off A30 Exeter to Okehampton road

Handy for the A30, this popular inn has been totally refurbished with impressive results. Bedrooms all provide high levels of quality and comfort, allied with contemporary bathrooms complete with robes and fluffy towels. A choice of bars is available with well-kept local ales, while the exciting menu is served in the stylish restaurant.

Rooms 6 en suite (2 fmly) S fr £79; D £79–£89✳ Facilities FTV TVB tea/coffee Cen ht Dinner Last d 9pm Parking 30

CHERITON FITZPAINE   MAP 03 SS80

★ ★ ★ FARM HOUSE

Lower Burrow Coombe Farm (SS883054)

EX17 4JS

☎ 01363 866220 Mrs Kekwick

dir: M5 junct 27 to Tiverton, follow signs to Exeter. At Bickleigh take A3072 towards Crediton, 3m on right, sign for farm

Situated in one of Devon's most beautiful valleys, Lower Burrow Coombe Farm is an unspoilt smallholding, conveniently located midway between Exmoor and Dartmoor. Guests receive a warm and friendly welcome here and will enjoy the tranquillity of this home. While two of the bedrooms are in the original Elizabethan part of the property, the other room benefits from its own private sitting room.

Rooms 3 rms (1 pri facs) (1 fmly) S £30–£35; D £60–£80✳ Facilities TVB tea/coffee Cen ht TVL Parking available Notes ⊗ 48 acres Sheep, poultry Closed Oct–Mar ⊜

CHILLATON   MAP 03 SX48

★ ★ ★ ★ ★ ⊜ GUEST ACCOMMODATION

Tor Cottage

PL16 0JE

☎ 01822 860248 ▤ 01822 860126

e–mail: info@torcottage.co.uk

web: www.torcottage.co.uk

dir: A30 Lewdown exit through Chillaton towards Tavistock, 300yds after Post Office right signed 'Bridlepath No Public Vehicular Access' to end

Tor Cottage, located in its own valley with 18 acres of grounds, is a welcome antidote to the fast pace of everyday life. Rooms are spacious and elegant; the cottage-wing bedroom has a separate sitting room, and the garden rooms have their own wood burners. The gardens are delightful, with a stream and heated outdoor pool. An exceptional range of dishes is offered at breakfast, which can be enjoyed either in the conservatory dining room or on the terrace.

Rooms 1 en suite 3 annexe en suite (3 GF) S £94; D £140 Facilities FTV TVB tea/coffee Cen ht TVL Dinner Last d 24hrs Wi-fi available ⌁ Parking 8 Notes LB ⊗ No children 14yrs Closed 17 Dec–7 Jan

---

CHULMLEIGH   MAP 03 SS61

★ ★ ★ ★ ⊜ GUEST HOUSE

Old Bakehouse

South Molton St EX18 7BW

☎ 01769 580074 & 580137 ▤ 01769 580074

e–mail: oldbakehouse@colinandholly.co.uk

web: www.colinandholly.co.uk

dir: A377 onto B3096 into village, left into South Molton St, 100yds on left

This 16th-century thatched house is situated in the centre of the medieval town. The cosy licensed restaurant offers fixed-price menus which feature local produce; dishes are imaginative and made with care. Some of the charming bedrooms are located across a courtyard in the former village bakery.

Rooms 3 en suite 1 annexe en suite (1 fmly) (1 GF) S £40–£45; D £57–£65 Facilities TVB tea/coffee Licensed Cen ht Dinner Last d 10am Notes LB ⊗ No children 5yrs No coaches

ENGLAND

CLOVELLY   MAP 03 SS32

★★★★ ≜ FARM HOUSE
East Dyke Farmhouse *(SS312235)*
East Dyke Farm, Higher Clovelly EX39 5RU
☎ 01237 431216 Mrs H Goaman
e–mail: steve.goaman@virgin.net
dir: A39 onto B3237 at Clovelly Cross rdbt, farm 500yds on left

Adjoining Clovelly's Iron Age hill fort, the working farm has glorious
views across Bideford Bay in the distance. The farmhouse has a friendly
atmosphere and offers attractively co-ordinated bedrooms. A major
attraction is the breakfast, where local produce and delicious
home-made preserves are served around one large table.

Rooms 3 rms (2 en suite) (1 pri facs) (1 fmly) S fr £30; D £50–£60
Facilities FTV TVB tea/coffee Cen ht TVL Wi-fi available **Parking** 6
Notes ⊗ 350 acres Beef/Arable Closed 24–26 Dec ⊛

COLEFORD   MAP 03 SS70

Ⓤ
The New Inn
EX17 5BZ
☎ 01363 84242 🖹 01363 85044
e–mail: enquiries@thenewinncoleford.co.uk
web: www.thenewinncoleford.co.uk
dir: Off A377 into Coleford, inn after 1.5m
At the time of going to press the rating for this establishment had not
been confirmed. Please check the AA website www.theAA.com for
up-to-date information.

Rooms 7 en suite (1 fmly) (1 GF) S £65; D £85–£110 **Facilities** TVB
tea/coffee Direct dial from bedrooms Cen ht Dinner Last d 9.30pm
Parking 50 **Notes LB** Closed 25–26 Dec

COLYFORD   MAP 04 SY29

★★★★ BED & BREAKFAST
Lower Orchard
Swan Hill Rd EX24 6QQ
☎ 01297 553615
e–mail: robin@barnardl.demon.co.uk
dir: On A3052 in Colyford, between Lyme Regis & Sidmouth
This modern ranch-style family home looks over the Axe Valley. The
spacious ground-floor bedrooms are very well equipped. Breakfast is
served in the lounge-dining room with patio doors leading to a private
sun terrace, well-tended gardens and splash pool. The owners have
also created a motoring memories museum and a classic car
showroom nearby.

Rooms 2 rms (1 en suite) (1 pri facs) (2 GF) D £55–£65 **Facilities** TVB
tea/coffee Cen ht TVL ⭦ **Parking** 3 **Notes** ⊛

CROYDE   MAP 03 SS43

★★★★ ≜ ⊜ GUEST HOUSE
The Whiteleaf
Croyde Rd EX33 1PN
☎ 01271 890266
dir: On B3231 entering Croyde, on left at 'Road Narrows' sign
A warm, family welcome awaits guests at this attractive house within
easy walking distance of the pretty village and the sandy surfing beach.
Each of the well-equipped bedrooms has its own charm, and three
rooms have decked balconies. Ambitious and imaginative dinners,
using fresh seasonal produce, are served every evening in the
restaurant.

Rooms 5 en suite (2 fmly) S £54–£62; D £72–£88✳ **Facilities** TVB tea/
coffee Direct dial from bedrooms Licensed Cen ht Dinner Last d 9pm
Parking 10 **Notes LB** No coaches Closed 24–26 Dec

CULLOMPTON   MAP 03 ST00

★★★★ FARM HOUSE
Weir Mill Farm *(ST040108)*
Jaycroft, Willand EX15 2RE
☎ 01884 820803 Mrs R Parish
e–mail: rita@weirmill-devon.co.uk
web: www.weirmill-devon.co.uk
*dir: 2m N of Cullompton. M5 junct 27, B3181 to Willand, left at
rdbt onto B3340 signed Uffculme, 50yds right onto Willand Moor
Rd, after Lupin Way left onto lane*
Set in extensive farmland, this charming 19th-century farmhouse offers
comfortable accommodation with a relaxed and homely atmosphere.
The spacious bedrooms are attractively decorated and equipped with
an impressive range of thoughtful extras. A good choice is offered at
breakfast in the well-appointed dining room. The farmhouse is
non-smoking.

Rooms 3 en suite (1 fmly) S £35; D £55✳ **Facilities** TVB tea/coffee
Cen ht TVL **Parking** 5 **Notes** ⊗ 100 acres arable & beef

★★★ FARM HOUSE
Wishay Farm *(SS994056)*

Trinity EX15 1PE

☎ 01884 33223 📠 01884 33223 Mrs Baker

e–mail: wishayfarm@btopenworld.com

web: www.wishayfarm-bandb-devon.co.uk

dir: *2m SW of Cullompton. From town centre onto Colbrook Ln, 1.5m to junct, continue over, farm 200yds on left*

Wishay Farm is a 280 acre, working arable and beef farm with a modernised Grade II listed farmhouse offering some interesting features. The peaceful location offers some pleasant views over the surrounding countryside. The two bedrooms are spacious and comfortably furnished. A traditional farmhouse breakfast is served in the dining room and a separate guest lounge is also available.

Rooms 2 rms (1 en suite) (1 pri facs) (2 fmly) S £30; D £46–£50✳
Facilities TVB tea/coffee Cen ht TVL **Parking** 3 **Notes LB** ⊗ 280 acres Arable, beef

---

DARTMEET   MAP 03 SX67

★★★★ 🏨 🍴 GUEST ACCOMMODATION
Hunter's Lodge B & B

PL20 6SG

☎ 01364 631173 & 07840 905624

e–mail: huntlodge@pobox.com

dir: *A38 at Ashburton onto B3357 to Dartmeet, Hunter's Lodge 1st right after 3rd bridge over Dart River*

Situated between the East and West Dart rivers, Hunter's Lodge is located at the very heart of Dartmoor. The house offers splendid views and the bedrooms are attractively and comfortably presented. Dinner, available by arrangement, features a wide range of fresh foods and local farm produce. German, French and Spanish are spoken here.

Rooms 3 rms (2 en suite) 1 annexe en suite (1 fmly) S £30–£45; D £45–£80✳ **Facilities** FTV TV1B tea/coffee Cen ht Dinner Last d 2 days prior Spa bath **Parking** 6 **Notes LB** Closed 24–26 Dec RS Mon & Tue

★★★ GUEST ACCOMMODATION
Brimpts Farm

PL20 6SG

☎ 01364 631450 📠 01364 631179

e–mail: info@brimptsfarm.co.uk

web: www.brimptsfarm.co.uk

dir: *Dartmeet at E end of B3357, establishment signed on right at top of hill*

A popular venue for walkers and lovers of the great outdoors, Brimpts is peacefully situated in the heart of Dartmoor and has been a Duchy of Cornwall farm since 1307. Bedrooms are simply furnished and many have wonderful views across Dartmoor. Dinner is served by arrangement. Additional facilities include a children's play area and sauna and spa. Brimpts is also home to the Dartmoor Pony Heritage Trust.

CONTINUED

Brimpts Farm

Rooms 10 en suite (2 fmly) (7 GF) S fr £30; D £50–£60 **Facilities** TV1B tea/coffee Cen ht TVL Dinner Last d 24hrs notice Wi-fi available Sauna Pool Table Farm walks & trails **Conf** Max 60 Thtr 60 Class 40 Board 25 Del from £73.50 ✳ **Parking** 50 **Notes LB**

DARTMOUTH   MAP 03 SX85

Premier Collection

★★★★★ 🏨 🍴 GUEST ACCOMMODATION
Nonsuch House

Church Hill, Kingswear TQ6 0BX

☎ 01803 752829 📠 01803 752357

e–mail: enquiries@nonsuch-house.co.uk

web: www.nonsuch-house.co.uk

dir: *A3022 onto A379 2m before Brixham. Fork left onto B3205. Left up Higher Contour Rd, down Ridley Hill, house on bend on left at top of Church Hill*

This delightful Edwardian property has fabulous views across the Dart estuary. The marvellous hosts combine friendliness with unobtrusive service. Bedrooms are spacious and superbly appointed, each with a spectacular panorama of the harbour. Fresh, local ingredients are served at dinner, including top-quality meat and fish, along with farmhouse cheeses. Breakfast, on the patio in good weather, features freshly squeezed juice, local sausages and home-baked bread.

Rooms 4 en suite (2 GF) S £80–£105; D £100–£135✳ **Facilities** FTV TVB tea/coffee Cen ht Dinner Last d 8pm Wi-fi available **Parking** 3 **Notes LB** ⊗ No children 10yrs RS Sat & Tue–Wed

★★★★ 🏨 BED & BREAKFAST
Woodside Cottage

TQ9 7BL

☎ 01803 898164

e–mail: theaa@woodsidedartmouth.co.uk

web: www.woodsidedartmouth.co.uk

dir: *Off A3122 to Dartmouth. After golf club brown sign right to house, sharp right, 0.5m on right*

This delightful and comfortable house lies in a scenic valley within easy reach of Dartmouth, and is ideal for walkers and for touring. The charming proprietors are very welcoming, and the bedrooms are attractive. Local and organic produce, cooked on an Aga, and home-made marmalade and fresh eggs feature at breakfast.

Rooms 3 en suite D £75–£90✳ **Facilities** FTV TVB tea/coffee Wi-fi available Concessions at Dartmouth Golf Club **Parking** 4 **Notes** ⊗ No children 18yrs Closed 25–26 Dec

DARTMOUTH CONTINUED

★★★★ GUEST ACCOMMODATION
Captain's House

18 Clarence St TQ6 9NW

☎ 01803 832133

e–mail: thecaptainshouse@aol.com

web: www.captainshouse.co.uk

dir: *B3122 into Dartmouth, Clarence St is parallel with the river*

Dating from 1730, this charming house retains many original features and is only a short walk from the quayside and town centre. The attractive bedrooms are comfortable and well-equipped. Enjoyable breakfasts are served in the dining room and include local produce and a large selection of quality preserves.

Rooms 5 en suite **Facilities** TVB tea/coffee Cen ht **Notes** ⊗ No children 5yrs

★★★★ GUEST ACCOMMODATION
Cherub's Nest

15 Higher St TQ6 9RB

☎ 01803 832482

e–mail: cherubsnest4bb@aol.com

web: www.cherubsnest.co.uk

dir: *From Lower Dartmouth ferry along Lower St, left onto Smith St, left onto Higher St, Cherub's Nest 50yds on left*

Dating from 1710, this former merchant's house, bedecked with flowers during the summer, is located in the very heart of historic Dartmouth. Full of character, the individually decorated bedrooms vary in size, but all are attractive and well equipped. A choice of breakfasts is served in the cosy dining room.

Rooms 3 en suite S £45–£70; D £65–£90 **Facilities** TVB tea/coffee Cen ht Wi-fi available **Notes** LB ⊗ No children 10yrs

★★★★ ⊜ GUEST ACCOMMODATION
New Angel Rooms

51 Victoria Rd TQ6 9RT

☎ 01803 839425 📠 01803 839567

e–mail: reservations@thenewangel.co.uk

dir: *A38 onto A384 for Totnes, turn right onto A381 and left onto A3122 for Dartmouth. After 2nd rdbt turn 2nd right into Victoria Rd*

Just a level stroll from the acclaimed New Angel restaurant, this terrace property offers very comfortable, contemporary accommodation,

CONTINUED

equipped with numerous extra facilities including a complimentary half bottle of Champagne. Breakfast is a feature, with freshly squeezed orange juice: specials such as eggs Benedict and scrambled eggs with smoked salmon are not to be missed.

New Angel Rooms

Rooms 6 en suite (3 fmly) S fr £110; D fr £130✳ **Facilities** TVB tea/coffee Cen ht Dinner Last d 10pm ⅏ **Notes** ⊗ Closed Jan

★★★★ ⊜ BED & BREAKFAST
Triatic

13a Ridge Hill TQ6 9PE

☎ 01803 835954

web: www.triatic.co.uk

dir: *From Riverside via A3122/A379, 1st right then 2nd left onto Ridge Hill*

Just a five minute walk from the historic town centre of Dartmouth, Triatic enjoys a prominent position overlooking the town and the harbour. Accommodation is of a high standard and the sole bedroom is equipped with a host of thoughtful extras. A warm welcome is assured from the conscientious owners of this lovely house.

Rooms 1 en suite S £55; D £65–£75✳ **Facilities** TVB tea/coffee Cen ht **Parking** 1 **Notes** LB ⊗ No children Closed 2 Jan–mid Mar

---

EXETER   MAP 03 SX99

See also Cheriton Bishop, Rockbeare & Whimple

★★★★ ⬛ RESTAURANT WITH ROOMS
Chi Restaurant & Bar with Accommodation

Fore St, Kenton EX6 8LD

☎ 01626 890213 📠 01626 891678

e–mail: enquiries@chi-restaurant.co.uk

web: www.chi-restaurant.co.uk

dir: *5m S of Exeter. M5 junct 30, A379 towards Dawlish, in Kenton village centre*

This former pub has been spectacularly transformed into a chic and contemporary bar that is allied with a stylish Chinese restaurant. Dishes are beautifully presented with an emphasis upon quality produce and authenticity, resulting in a memorable dining experience. Bedrooms are well equipped and all provide good levels of space and comfort, along with modern bathrooms.

CONTINUED

Rooms 5 en suite (2 fmly) S £37; D £63–£69(room only) **Facilities** FTV TVB tea/coffee Direct dial from bedrooms Cen ht TVL Dinner Last d 10pm Wi-fi available **Parking** 26 **Notes** ⊗

★★★★ GUEST HOUSE
The Edwardian
30–32 Heavitree Rd EX1 2LQ
☎ 01392 276102
e–mail: michael@edwardianexeter.co.uk
web: www.edwardianexeter.co.uk

dir: M5 junct 29, right at lights signed city centre, on left after Exeter University School of Education

Friendly proprietors offer a warm welcome at this attractive Edwardian terrace property, which is situated within easy walking distance of the city centre. The bedrooms vary in size but are well presented and comfortable, and offer a range of extra accessories. Breakfast is served in the spacious dining room, while the separate inviting lounge offers comfort and relaxation.

Rooms 13 en suite (3 fmly) (4 GF) **Facilities** FTV TVB tea/coffee Direct dial from bedrooms Cen ht Wi-fi available **Parking** 5 **Notes** No coaches

★★★★ GUEST ACCOMMODATION
Holbrook Farm
Clyst Honiton EX5 2HR
☎ 01392 367000 📠 01392 367000
e–mail: heatherglanvill@holbrookfarm.co.uk
web: www.holbrookfarm.co.uk

dir: M5, A3052 for Sidmouth, pass Westpoint (county showground) & Cat and Fiddle pub, 500yds left at Hill Pond caravans, signed for 1m

This friendly, modern farmhouse stands in lush rolling countryside and has spectacular views. All bedrooms are located on the ground floor, have their own entrance and offer bright, attractive and spacious accommodation. Breakfast features the best fresh local produce. Holbrook Farm is convenient for Exeter, the coast and moor, and there are several popular inns and restaurants nearby.

Rooms 3 en suite (1 fmly) (3 GF) S £35–£50; D £50–£60✳ **Facilities** TVB tea/coffee Cen ht Wi-fi available **Parking** 4 **Notes** LB ⊗

★★★★ FARM HOUSE
Mill Farm (SX959839)
Kenton EX6 8JR
☎ 01392 832471 Mrs D Lambert
e–mail: info@millfarmstay.co.uk

dir: A379 from Exeter towards Dawlish, over mini-rdbt by Swans Nest, farm 1.75m on right

Located just a short drive from the Powderham Estate, this imposing working farmhouse is surrounded by pastureland. Each of the spacious bedrooms is comfortably furnished and has co-ordinated décor; many rooms have views across the countryside. Breakfast is served in the sunny dining room and a lounge is also provided.

Rooms 5 en suite (3 fmly) S £37–£40; D £55–£60 **Facilities** TVB tea/coffee Cen ht Wi-fi available **Parking** 12 **Notes** LB ⊗ No children 6yrs 30 acres Horses Closed Xmas ☺

★★★★ FARM HOUSE
Rydon Farm (SX999871)
Woodbury EX5 1LB
☎ 01395 232341 📠 01395 232341 Mrs S Glanvill
e–mail: sallyglanvill@aol.com
web: www.rydonfarmwoodbury.co.uk

dir: A376 & B3179 from Exeter into Woodbury, right before 30mph sign

Dating from the 16th century, this Devon longhouse has been run by the same family for eight generations. The farmhouse provides spacious bedrooms, which are equipped with many useful extra facilities and one has a four-poster bed. There is a television lounge and a delightful garden in which to relax. Breakfast is served in front of an inglenook fireplace.

Rooms 3 rms (2 en suite) (1 pri facs) (1 fmly) S £40–£55; D £62–£74✳ **Facilities** FTV TVB tea/coffee Cen ht TVL **Parking** 3 **Notes** LB 450 acres dairy

★★★★ Ⓐ GUEST HOUSE
Raffles
11 Blackall Rd EX4 4HD
☎ 01392 270200 📠 01392 270200
e–mail: raffleshtl@btinternet.com

dir: M5, exit at Exeter services, follow signs for Middlemore & City Centre

Rooms 6 en suite (2 fmly) S £38–£45; D £68✳ **Facilities** STV TVB tea/coffee Cen ht TVL Wi-fi available **Parking** 6 **Notes** LB No coaches

EXETER CONTINUED

★★★ GUEST HOUSE
Chimneys

The Strand, Starcross EX6 8PA
☎ 01626 890813
e–mail: tuckmrgrt@aol.com
web: www.chimneys-bandb.co.uk

dir: *M5 junct 30, follow signs for A379 (Dawlish). On entering Starcross, 3rd house on right*

This grand house dates back to the 1880s and looks out across the Exe Estuary. All bedrooms offer good levels of comfort, and some also have the bonus of lovely views across the river. Elegant public rooms have plenty of character with a very welcoming and homely feel. Breakfast provides a satisfying start to the day, and dinner is also available by prior arrangement.

Rooms 5 en suite (2 fmly) S £40–£45; D £50–£70✱ **Facilities** TVB tea/coffee Licensed Cen ht Dinner Last d 10am **Parking** 5 **Notes LB** ⊗ No coaches Closed Dec–Feb

★★★ BED & BREAKFAST
Culm Vale Country House

Culm Vale, Stoke Canon EX5 4EG
☎ 01392 841615 ▤ 01392 841615
e–mail: culmvale@hotmail.com

dir: *A396 from Exeter towards Tiverton, after Stoke Canon sign Culm Vale 5th property on right*

A warm welcome is extended at this impressive house situated on the edge of pretty Stoke Canon. Culm Vale is family run, full of character and offers very spacious, comfortable accommodation. Breakfast, featuring eggs laid by the family's own hens, can be enjoyed in the grand dining room.

Rooms 4 rms (1 en suite) S £30–£50; D £40–£60✱ **Facilities** FTV TVB tea/coffee Cen ht **Parking** 4 **Notes** ⊗

★★★ GUEST HOUSE
Dunmore Guest House

22 Blackall Rd EX4 4HE
☎ 01392 431643 ▤ 01392 431643
e–mail: dunmorehtl@aol.com
web: www.dunmorehotel.co.uk

dir: *M5 junct 29, through city centre, right at mini-rdbt, house on left*

Convenient for the city centre, Exeter College and the railway station, Dunmore Guest House provides comfortable accommodation. The bedrooms are attractive and well presented, and many have been redecorated to provide very good standards. Traditional English breakfasts are served in the dining room.

Rooms 9 rms (6 en suite) (3 fmly) (1 GF) S £38–£40; D £50–£60✱ **Facilities** FTV TVB tea/coffee Cen ht **Parking** 1 **Notes LB** ⊗

★★★ GUEST HOUSE
The Sunnymede Guest House

24 New North Rd EX4 4HF
☎ 01392 273844 ▤ 01392 273844
e–mail: seldonsnnymds@aol.com

dir: *600yds N of cathedral. On one-way system pass Central station in Queen St, at clocktower rdbt turn right, Sunnymede on left*

The Sunnymede has a central location in this historic city and is convenient for the college, shopping centre and attractions. A compact guest house, it offers well-presented, comfortable bedrooms, well suited for business or leisure guests. A good choice is available at breakfast.

Rooms 9 rms (5 en suite) (1 fmly) **Facilities** TVB tea/coffee Cen ht TVL **Notes** ⊗ No coaches Closed 20 Dec–15 Jan

EXMOUTH   MAP 03 SY08

★★★★ ⌂ GUEST ACCOMMODATION
Barn

Foxholes Hill, Marine Dr EX8 2DF
☎ 01395 224411 ▤ 01395 225445
e–mail: info@barnhotel.co.uk
web: www.barnhotel.co.uk

dir: *M5 junct 30- take A376 to Exmouth, then signs to seafront. At rdbt last exit into Foxholes Hill. Located on right*

This Grade II-listed establishment has a prime location, close to miles of sandy beaches. Equally pleasurable is the impeccable rear garden, which is sea-facing and features a terrace and swimming pool for use during the summer. Service is attentive and friendly, and spectacular sea views are enjoyed from most of the considerably equipped bedrooms and public rooms. Breakfast, featuring freshly squeezed juices and local produce, is served in the pleasant dining room.

Rooms 11 en suite (4 fmly) S £35–£52; D £70–£104✱ **Facilities** TVB tea/coffee Direct dial from bedrooms Cen ht ⌖ **Parking** 30 **Notes LB** ⊗ Closed 23 Dec–10 Jan

★★★★ GUEST ACCOMMODATION
The Devoncourt
16 Douglas Av EX8 2EX
☎ 01395 272277 📠 01395 269315
e–mail: enquiries@devoncourt.com
web: www.devoncourthotel.com

dir: M5/A376 to Exmouth, follow seafront to Maer Rd, right at T-junct

The Devoncourt stands in four acres of mature, subtropical gardens, sloping gently towards the sea and overlooking two miles of sandy beaches. It offers extensive leisure facilities, and the smartly furnished bedrooms are exceptionally well equipped. Public areas are spacious and shared with timeshare owners. For meals guests can choose between the informal bar and dining in the restaurant.

Rooms 10 en suite (1 fmly) **Facilities** FTV TVB tea/coffee Direct dial from bedrooms Lift Cen ht TVL Dinner Last d 9pm (Sun 8pm) Wi-fi available ⊗ ↖ ♨ Snooker Sauna Solarium Gymnasium ♨ ♨ Sun shower, Jacuzzi **Parking** 50 **Notes** ⊗ Civ Wed

---

HARTLAND   MAP 02 SS22
★★★ GUEST HOUSE
Fosfelle
EX39 6EF
☎ 01237 441273 📠 01237 441273
dir: 500yds SE of village on B3248

Dating from the 17th century, this delightful manor house offers comfortable accommodation close to the village of Hartland. It is set in 6 acres of gardens with two fishing lakes. Guests can enjoy pool or darts in the welcoming bar, and the restaurant offers a range of freshly prepared dishes.

Rooms 7 rms (4 en suite) (2 fmly) S £35–£40; D £65–£80 **Facilities** TV6B tea/coffee Licensed Cen ht TVL Dinner Last d 9pm Fishing Pool Table **Parking** 20 **Notes** LB

HOLSWORTHY   MAP 03 SS30
★★★★ GUEST ACCOMMODATION
Leworthy Farm House
Lower Leworthy, Nr Pyworthy EX22 6SJ
☎ 01409 259469 📠 01409 259469
e–mail: leworthyfarmhouse@yahoo.co.uk
web: www.leworthyfarmhouse.co.uk

dir: From Holsworthy onto Bodmin St towards North Tamerton, 4th left signed Leworthy/Southdown

Located in an unspoiled area of north Devon with three acres of gardens, meadows, a copse and a fishing lake, this delightful farmhouse provides bright, comfortable accommodation with numerous extra facilities. Breakfast is served in the large lounge-dining room.

Rooms 7 en suite (1 fmly) S £45–£65; D £65–£70✱ **Facilities** TVB tea/coffee TVL Fishing **Parking** 8 **Notes** LB ⊗ ☺

★★★★ ⇔ INN
Bickford Arms
Brandis Corner EX22 7XY
☎ 01409 221318 📠 01409 220085
e–mail: info@bickfordarms.com
dir: 4m E of Holsworthy on A3072

This roadside inn has been providing rest and sustenance for weary travellers for many years, and the tradition continues today with a genuine welcome and relaxed atmosphere. The spacious bar is warmed by a crackling fire in cooler months and guests can choose to eat either here or in the restaurant, with a choice of bar menu and specials board. The attractive bedrooms provide high levels of comfort, likewise the impressive and well-appointed bathrooms.

Rooms 5 en suite (1 fmly) **Facilities** TVB tea/coffee Cen ht Dinner Last d 9pm Wi-fi available **Conf** Max 30 Thtr 40 Board 20 **Parking** 50 **Notes** ⊗ No coaches

ENGLAND

ENGLAND

★★★★ GUEST HOUSE
Clawford Vineyard

Clawton EX22 6PN
☎ 01409 254177 📠 01409 254177
e-mail: john.ray@clawford.co.uk

dir: *A388 (Holsworth to Launceston road), left at Clawton x-rds, 1.5m to T-junct, left, 0.5m left again*

Situated in the peaceful Claw Valley and having splendid views over fishing lakes and woods, this working cider orchard and vineyard offers spacious and comfortable bedrooms. There is a large lounge, a well-stocked bar, a conservatory and a restaurant. Freshly cooked dishes are well prepared and attractively presented at dinner and breakfast. Self-catering apartments are also available, overlooking the lakes.

Rooms 11 en suite (7 fmly) **Facilities** TVB tea/coffee Licensed Cen ht TVL Dinner Last d 9pm Fishing Pool Table Coarse & game fishing **Parking** 60 **Notes** ❽ No children 6yrs

★★★ FARM HOUSE
The Hollies Farm Guest House
(SS371001)

Clawton EX22 6PN
☎ 01409 253770 & 07929 318033 Mr & Mrs G Colwill
e-mail: theholliesfarm@hotmail.com
web: www.theholliesfarm.co.uk

dir: *Off A388 at Clawton village signed vineyard, Hollies 2m in lane on left after T-junct, signed*

This sheep and beef farm offers comfortable, modern accommodation in a family atmosphere. There are pleasant views across the countryside from most bedrooms, and all of them are well appointed. Breakfast is served in the conservatory and dinner is available by arrangement. There is also a barbecue area with a gazebo.

Rooms 3 en suite (3 fmly) S £25–£35; D £45–£60✻ **Facilities** TVB tea/coffee Cen ht TVL Dinner Last d early morning ⤳ **Parking** 6 **Notes** LB ❽ 25 acres Beef, sheep Closed 24–25 Dec ☻

HONITON   MAP 04 ST10

Premier Collection

★★★★★ 🏠 BED & BREAKFAST
West Colwell Farm

Offwell EX14 9SL
☎ 01404 831130 📠 01404 831769
e-mail: stay@westcolwell.co.uk

dir: *Off A35 to village, at church downhill, farm 0.5m on right*

Peacefully situated down a country lane, in an Area of Outstanding Natural Beauty, West Colwell Farm offers stylish bedrooms in a converted dairy. The two rooms on the ground floor have direct access to their own terraces. Breakfast is served overlooking the wooded valley and fields in the split-level dining room, with a roaring log-burning stove in cooler months.

Rooms 3 en suite (2 GF) D £70–£80✻ **Facilities** FTV TVB tea/coffee Cen ht **Parking** 3 **Notes** LB ❽ No children 12yrs Closed Xmas

★★★★ FARM HOUSE
Courtmoor Farm (ST207068)

Upottery EX14 9QA
☎ 01404 861565 Mr & Mrs Buxton
e-mail: courtmoor.farm@btinternet.com
web: www.courtmoor.farm.btinternet.co.uk

dir: *4m NE of Honiton off A30*

This farmhouse is set in attractive grounds, with stunning views over the Otter Valley. All of the bedrooms share the views, and are spacious, comfortable and well equipped. Breakfast provides a tasty and substantial start to the day with local produce used whenever possible. Guests have access to the leisure room, gym and sauna. Self-catering cottages are also available.

Rooms 3 en suite (1 fmly) S £37; D £60✻ **Facilities** FTV TVB tea/coffee Cen ht Fishing Sauna Gymnasium **Parking** 20 **Notes** ❽ 17 acres non-working Closed 20 Dec–1 Jan

★★★★ GUEST ACCOMMODATION
Ridgeway Farm

Awliscombe EX14 3PY
☎ 01404 841331 📠 01404 841119
e-mail: jessica@ridgewayfarm.co.uk

dir: *3m NW of Honiton. A30 onto A373, through Awliscombe to near end of 40mph area, right opp Godford Farm, farm 500mtrs up narrow lane*

This 18th-century farmhouse has a peaceful location on the slopes of Hembury Hill, and is a good base for exploring nearby Honiton and the east Devon coast. Renovations have brought the cosy accommodation to a high standard and the atmosphere is relaxed and homely. The proprietors and their family pets assure a warm welcome.

Rooms 2 en suite S £30–£34; D £52–£58✻ **Facilities** TVB tea/coffee Cen ht TVL Dinner Last d morning **Parking** 4 **Notes** LB ☻

★★★ BED & BREAKFAST
Threshays

Awliscombe EX14 3QB
☎ 01404 43551 & 07811 675800 📠 01404 43551
e-mail: threshays@btinternet.com

dir: *2.5m NW of Honiton on A373*

A converted threshing barn, situated on a non-working farm, Threshays has wonderful views over open countryside. With tea and cake offered on arrival, this family-run establishment provides comfortable accommodation in a friendly atmosphere. The lounge-dining room is a light and airy setting for the enjoyment of good breakfasts. Ample parking is a bonus.

Rooms 2 rms (1 fmly) S £28; D £48 **Facilities** tea/coffee Cen ht TVL Wi-fi available **Parking** 6 **Notes** ❽ RS Sun–Tue ☻

HOPE COVE	MAP 03 SX64

★★★ GUEST ACCOMMODATION

Cottage

TQ7 3HJ

☎ 01548 561555 📠 01548 561455

e–mail: info@hopecove.com

web: www.hopecove.com

dir: *From Kingsbridge on A381 to Salcombe. 2nd right at Marlborough, left for Inner Hope*

Glorious sunsets can be seen over the attractive bay from this popular accommodation. Friendly and attentive service from the staff and management mean many guests return here. Bedrooms, many with sea views and some with balconies, are well equipped. The restaurant offers an enjoyable dining experience.

Rooms 35 rms (26 en suite) (5 fmly) (7 GF) Facilities FTV TV29B tea/coffee Direct dial from bedrooms TVL Dinner Last d 8.30pm Wi-fi available Conf Max 70 Thtr 60 Class 60 Board 30 Parking 50 Notes Closed early Jan–early Feb

HORNS CROSS	MAP 03 SS32

Premier Collection

★★★★★ GUEST HOUSE

The Round House

EX39 5DN

☎ 01237 451687

e–mail: michael.m.clifford@btinternet.com

web: www.the-round-house.co.uk

dir: *1m W of Horns Cross on A39, 0.5m past Hoops Inn towards Bude*

This charming converted barn stands in landscaped gardens within easy reach of Clovelly. Guests receive a warm welcome and a complimentary cream tea on arrival, which may be served in the lounge with its exposed beams and inglenook fireplace. Bedrooms are comfortable with numerous thoughtful extra facilities. A varied choice is offered at breakfast.

Rooms 3 en suite (1 fmly) (1 GF) S £40; D £60–£65✳ Facilities FTV TVB tea/coffee Cen ht TVL Parking 8 Notes ⊗ No children 12yrs No coaches

ILFRACOMBE	MAP 03 SS54

★★★★ GUEST ACCOMMODATION

Strathmore

57 St Brannock's Rd EX34 8EQ

☎ 01271 862248 📠 01271 862248

e–mail: peter@small6374.fsnet.co.uk

web: www.the-strathmore.co.uk

dir: *A361 from Barnstaple to Ilfracombe, Strathmore 1.5m from Mullacot Cross entering Ilfracombe*

Situated within walking distance of the town centre and beach, this charming Victorian property offers a very warm welcome. The attractive bedrooms are comfortably furnished, while public areas include a well-stocked bar, an attractive terraced garden, and an elegant breakfast room.

Rooms 8 en suite (3 fmly) S £32–£35; D £65–£76✳ Facilities TVB tea/coffee Cen ht Wi-fi available Parking 7 Notes LB

★★★★ GUEST HOUSE

Collingdale Guest House

13 Larkstone Ter EX34 9NU

☎ 01271 863770 📠 01271 863867

e–mail: stay@thecollingdale.co.uk

web: www.thecollingdale.co.uk

dir: *Take A399 E through Ilfracombe, on left past B3230 turning*

Built in 1869, this friendly establishment is within easy walking distance of the town centre and seafront. The well presented bedrooms, many with sweeping sea views, are equipped with modern facilities, and the comfortable lounge also has magnificent views over the sea. Dinner is available by arrangement and there is a cosy bar.

Rooms 9 rms (8 en suite) (1 pri facs) (3 fmly) D £60–£80 Facilities TVB tea/coffee Licensed TVL Dinner Last d 2pm Wi-fi available Notes LB ⊗ No children 8yrs No coaches Closed Nov–Feb

★★★★ GUEST HOUSE
Marine Court
Hillsborough Rd EX34 9QQ
☎ 01271 862920
e-mail: marinecourthotel@btconnect.com

dir: *M5 junct 27, A361 to Barnstaple, continue to Ilfracombe*
This friendly and welcoming establishment offers comfortable and homely accommodation opposite the Old Thatched Inn. The well-presented bedrooms all provide good levels of comfort with thoughtful extras. Freshly prepared evening meals and breakfast are served in the spacious dining room which is next to the bar. On-site and adjacent parking is a bonus.

Rooms 8 en suite (2 fmly) S £36.50–£42; D £58–£68 **Facilities** TVB tea/coffee Licensed Cen ht Dinner Last d noon **Parking** 3 **Notes LB** No coaches

★★★★ GUEST HOUSE
Norbury House
Torrs Park EX34 8AZ
☎ 01271 863888
e-mail: info@norburyhouse.co.uk

dir: *From A399 continue to end of High St/Church St. At mini-rdbt after lights take 1st exit onto Church Rd. Bear left onto Osbourne Rd. At T-junct turn left onto Torrs Park, at top of hill on right*
This detached Victorian residence has a refreshingly different, contemporary style. The welcome is warm and genuine, allied with a helpful and attentive approach. A variety of bedrooms types are offered, all of which provide impressive levels of comfort and quality. An elegant lounge leads through to a conservatory, which has an honesty bar. Outside, the terraced gardens offer a quiet spot to enjoy the lovely views. Cuisine is taken seriously here, with breakfast and dinner (by prior arrangement) featuring quality, local produce.

Rooms 6 en suite (2 fmly) **Facilities** TVB tea/coffee Licensed Cen ht Dinner Last d 10.30am Wi-fi available **Conf** Max 18 Thtr 14 Class 14 Board 12 **Parking** 6 **Notes** No coaches

★★★★ A GUEST HOUSE
The Dorchester Guest House
59 St Brannocks Rd EX34 8EQ
☎ 01271 865472
e-mail: edwardsna@btinternet.com

dir: *A361 from Barnstaple to Ilfracombe, Dorchester 1.5m from Millacot entering Ilfracombe*
Rooms 6 en suite (2 fmly) S £35–£40; D £55–£65 **Facilities** TVB tea/coffee Licensed Cen ht TVL Dinner Last d 2pm Wi-fi available **Parking** 5 **Notes LB** No children 5yrs

★★★ GUEST HOUSE
Avalon
6 Capstone Crescent EX34 9BT
☎ 01271 863325 📄 01271 866543
e-mail: avalon_ilfracombe@yahoo.co.uk
web: www.avalon-hotel.co.uk

dir: *A361 to Ilfracombe, left at 1st lights, straight on 2nd lights, left at end of one-way system & left again*
Conveniently located near the centre of Ilfracombe, this well established guest house has magnificent sea views from the bedrooms and dining room. This friendly establishment offers well-equipped bedrooms, one of which is located on the ground floor. Breakfast is served at separate tables in the well-appointed dining room and parking is available free of charge not far from Avalon.

Rooms 9 en suite (3 fmly) (1 GF) S £30–£32; D £50–£60✳ **Facilities** TVB tea/coffee Dinner Last d 2.30pm **Notes LB** ⊗ No coaches Closed Xmas & New Year

★★★ INN
The Wayfarer Inn
Ln End EX39 4LB
☎ 01271 860342
web: www.thewayfarerinstow.co.uk

Tucked away in a coastal village, this family-run pub offers a real West Country welcome. Most of the bedrooms benefit from sea views. The inn serves real ales from the barrel and a wide range of meals to suit all palates and pockets. Food is locally sourced and includes fresh fish from their own boat. A sun trap beer garden is also available for alfresco eating, all within 20 yards of Instow's sandy beach and the Atlantic Ocean.

Rooms 6 en suite (2 fmly) S £45; D £70✳ **Facilities** TVB tea/coffee Cen ht Dinner Last d 8.45pm Fishing **Notes** ⊗ No coaches

★★★★ 🏠 GUEST ACCOMMODATION
Stowford House
EX20 4BZ
☎ 01566 783415
e-mail: alison@stowfordhouse.com
web: www.stowfordhouse.com

dir: *1m W of Lewdown in Stowford village near church*
This delightful Georgian country house within secluded gardens provides a tranquil base for exploring the area. Guests can enjoy a varied choice at breakfast in the smart dining room, and an elegant drawing room is available. The bedrooms have high standards of comfort and numerous extras.

CONTINUED

Stowford House

Rooms 4 en suite S £47–£57; D £67–£77✱ **Facilities** TVB tea/coffee Cen ht TVL **Parking** 5 **Notes LB** ⊗ No children 14yrs Closed Xmas RS 23–29 Dec

---

LIFTON   MAP 03 SX38

★★★★ BED & BREAKFAST
The Old Coach House

The Thatched Cottage, Sprytown PL16 0AY
☎ 01566 784224 📄 01566 784334
e–mail: tochsprytown@aol.com
web: www.theoldcoach-house.co.uk

dir: *Off A30 through Lifton, 0.75m E to Sprytown x-rds, right to Thatched Cottage in 100yds*

Set in a colourful cottage garden near the Cornwall border, the Old Coach House provides a warm welcome. The comfortable bedrooms have numerous extras, including a welcome basket. Hearty breakfasts, served in the beamed dining room of the adjacent Thatched Cottage, feature good local produce including vegetarian options.

Rooms 4 annexe en suite (3 fmly) (2 GF) **Facilities** TVB tea/coffee Direct dial from bedrooms **Parking** 6 **Notes** ⊗

★★★★ ◉ RESTAURANT WITH ROOMS
Tinhay Mill Guest House and Restaurant

Tinhay PL16 0AJ
☎ 01566 784201 📄 01566 784201
e–mail: tinhay.mill@talk21.com
web: www.tinhaymillrestaurant.co.uk

dir: *A30/A388 approach Lifton, establishment at bottom of village on right*

The former mill cottages are now a delightful restaurant with rooms of much charm. Beams and open fireplaces set the scene, with everything geared to ensure a relaxed and comfortable stay. Bedrooms are spacious and well equipped, with many thoughtful extras. Cuisine is taken seriously here, using the best of local produce.

Rooms 5 en suite (1 GF) S £59.50; D £80–£85✱ **Facilities** FTV TVB Cen ht TVL Dinner Last d 9.30pm Wi-fi available **Parking** 19 **Notes LB** ⊗ No children 12yrs

LUSTLEIGH   MAP 03 SX78

★★★★★ ⇔ GUEST ACCOMMODATION
Eastwrey Barton

Moretonhampstead Rd TQ13 9SN
☎ 01647 277338 📄 01647 277133
e–mail: info@eastwreybarton.co.uk
web: www.eastwreybarton.co.uk

dir: *On A382 between Bovey Tracey and Moretonhampstead, 6m from A38 (Drumbridges junct)*

Warm hospitality and a genuine welcome are hallmarks at this family-run establishment, situated inside the Dartmoor National Park. Built in the 18th century, the house retains many original features and has views across the Wray Valley. Bedrooms are spacious and well equipped, while public areas include a snug lounge warmed by a crackling log fire. Breakfast and dinner are showcases for local produce with an impressive wine list to accompany the latter.

Rooms 5 en suite (1 fmly) S £60–£68; D £80–£96✱ **Facilities** FTV TVB tea/coffee Cen ht Dinner Last d noon **Parking** 18 **Notes** ⊗ No children 10yrs

★★★★★ GUEST ACCOMMODATION
Woodley House

Caseley Hill TQ13 9TN
☎ 01647 277214 📄 01647 277126

dir: *Off A382 into village, at T-junct right to Caseley, house 2nd on left*

Set just a stroll from the village pub, church and tea room, Woodley House is a peaceful and tranquil retreat, with super views over the rolling countryside. A hearty breakfast, featuring as many as 12 home-made preserves, home-baked bread and a vast range of cooked breakfast options, can be enjoyed in the charming dining room. A good base for walkers, and dogs are welcome too.

Rooms 2 en suite S £50; D £68–£70✱ **Facilities** TVB tea/coffee Cen ht TVL **Parking** 3 **Notes** No children 10yrs ◉

ENGLAND

LYDFORD   MAP 03 SX58

Premier Collection

★★★★★ ⊜ GUEST ACCOMMODATION

Moor View House

Vale Down EX20 4BB

☎ 01822 820220 📄 01822 820220

dir: *1m NE of Lydford on A386*

Built around 1870, this charming house once changed hands over a game of cards. The elegant bedrooms are furnished with interesting pieces and retain many original features. Breakfast, and dinner by arrangement, is served house-party style at a large oak table. The two acres of moorland gardens give access to Dartmoor.

Rooms 4 en suite S fr £50; D fr £70✱ **Facilities** TVB tea/coffee Cen ht TVL Dinner Last d 24hrs prior ⤴ **Parking** 15 **Notes** LB ⊗ No children 12yrs ⊜

LYNMOUTH   MAP 03 SS74

See also Brendon

Premier Collection

★★★★★ 🏠 ⊜ GUEST ACCOMMODATION

Sea View Villa

6 Summer House Path EX35 6ES

☎ 01598 753460 📄 01598 753496

e–mail: seaviewenquiries@aol.com

web: www.seaviewvilla.co.uk

dir: *A39 from Porlock, 1st left after bridge, Sea View Villa on right 20yds along path opp church*

This charming Georgian villa, built in 1721, has been appointed to a high standard by owners Steve Williams and Chris Bissex. Tucked away from the bustle of the main streets, the house provides elegant and peaceful accommodation. All bedrooms are equipped with thoughtful extras and have impressive views of the harbour and sea. The proprietors' genuine hospitality assures a relaxed and comfortable stay. Dinner and breakfast are not to be missed. Beauty therapies are available by prior arrangement.

Rooms 5 rms (3 en suite) (1 fmly) S £40–£45; D £100–£110✱ **Facilities** TVB tea/coffee Cen ht TVL Dinner Last d 5pm Wi-fi available **Notes** LB ⊗ No children 14yrs Closed Jan

Premier Collection

★★★★★ 🏠 ⊜ GUEST HOUSE

Bonnicott House

10 Watersmeet Rd EX35 6EP

☎ 01598 753346

e–mail: stay@bonnicott.com

web: www.bonnicott.com

dir: *A39 from Minehead over East Lyn River Bridge, left onto Watersmeet Rd, 50yds on right opp church*

Bonnicott House is set in attractive gardens with spectacular views over the harbour towards the sea and cliffs. Bedrooms, most with sea views, are very well equipped, with comfortable furnishings and thoughtful extra facilities. Dinner offers fresh local produce, imaginatively presented, and at breakfast hearty portions are served fresh from being cooked on the Aga.

Rooms 8 rms (7 en suite) (1 pri facs) S £37–£86; D £45–£96 **Facilities** TVB tea/coffee Licensed Cen ht Dinner Last d noon Wi-fi available **Conf** Max 16 Board 16 Del from £93 **Notes** LB ⊗ No children 14yrs No coaches

Premier Collection

★★★★★ 🏠 ⊜ GUEST ACCOMMODATION

The Heatherville

Tors Park EX35 6NB

☎ 01598 752327 📄 01598 752634

web: www.heatherville.co.uk

dir: *Off A39 onto Tors Rd, 1st left fork into Tors Park*

With its secluded and elevated south-facing position, the Heatherville has splendid views over Lynmouth and surrounding woodland.

CONTINUED

Lovingly restored over the last few years to a very high standard, both the bedrooms and the lounge give a feeling of luxury, with the charm of a large country house. By arrangement, enjoyable evening meals feature organic and free-range produce whenever possible. There is also an intimate bar.

The Heatherville

Rooms 6 en suite D £60–£90✳ **Facilities** TVB tea/coffee Cen ht Dinner Last d breakfast **Parking** 7 **Notes LB** No children 16yrs Closed Nov–Feb

★★★★ 🍴 GUEST HOUSE
Bay View House

Clooneavin Path EX35 6EE
☎ 01598 752270 📠 01598 752270
e–mail: enquiries@bayviewhouselynmouth.co.uk

dir: *Enter Lynmouth, cross a bridge over Lyn River (do not take left turn by Shelly's Hotel) continue up hill towards Lynton, Clooneavin Path 2nd right. (NB very sharp turning)*

Nestling in a peaceful, wooded location, yet within a couple of minutes walk of Lynmouth and the water-powered cliff railway to Lynton, this late Victorian house boasts stunning views over the harbour, the sea and the surrounding coastline. The refurbished bedrooms are very well equipped and all take full advantage of the views. Using the best of fresh, local ingredients, dinner is available by prior arrangement; not licensed though guests may bring their own wine if they wish.

Rooms 3 en suite D £62–£78 **Facilities** FTV TVB tea/coffee Cen ht Dinner Last d 11am **Parking** 3 **Notes LB** No children 8yrs No coaches Closed Nov–Feb

★★★★ GUEST ACCOMMODATION
Glenville House

2 Tors Rd EX35 6ET
☎ 01598 752202
e–mail: tricia@glenvillelynmouth.co.uk
web: www.glenvillelynmouth.co.uk

dir: *Off A39 at bottom of Countisbury Hill, 200yds along Tors Rd*

A friendly welcome awaits at this delightful Victorian house overlooking the East Lyn River. The attractive bedrooms feature co-ordinated soft furnishings, and traditional breakfasts are served at separate tables in the dining room. A comfortable first-floor lounge is also available, with river views and an attractive garden, where cream teas can be enjoyed in summer.

Rooms 5 rms (3 en suite) (2 pri facs) (1 GF) D £56–£64✳
Facilities TV4B tea/coffee Cen ht TVL **Notes LB** ⊗ No children 14yrs Closed mid Nov–early Mar 🐾

CONTINUED

★★★★ GUEST ACCOMMODATION
Rock House

Manor Grounds EX35 6EN
☎ 01598 753508 📠 01598 753796
e–mail: enquiries@rock-house.co.uk

dir: *On A39, at foot of Countisbury Hill right onto drive, pass Manor green/play area to Rock House*

Located next to the river with wonderful views of the harbour and out to sea, this enchanting establishment dates back to the 18th century and has much to offer. Bedrooms are all well appointed, and many have the benefit of wonderful views of the rolling waves. A choice of menus is offered, either in the spacious lounge/bar or in the smart dining room. The garden is a popular venue for cream teas in the summer.

Rooms 8 en suite (1 GF) **Facilities** TVB tea/coffee Cen ht TVL Dinner Last d 9pm 🛁 ♨ **Parking** 8 **Notes** Closed 24–25 Dec

★★★ GUEST ACCOMMODATION
River Lyn View

26 Watersmeet Rd EX35 6EP
☎ 01598 753501
e–mail: riverlynview@aol.com

dir: *On A39, 200yds past St John's church on right*

A warm welcome awaits you at the River Lyn View, just a stroll away from the picturesque harbour at Lynmouth. Exmoor National Park is a short drive away or you can enjoy a walk along the East Lyn's tranquil tree lined banks. Much of the accommodation overlooks the river, but all is comfortable and includes a good range of extras. There is a choice of lounges, and a hearty breakfast is served at individual tables in the open-plan dining area.

Rooms 4 en suite (2 fmly) S £30–£40; D £52–£60 **Facilities** FTV TVB tea/coffee Cen ht TVL Wi-fi available

LYNMOUTH CONTINUED

★★★ GUEST ACCOMMODATION
Countisbury Lodge

6 Tors Park, Countisbury Hill EX35 6NB

☎ 01598 752388

e–mail: paulpat@countisburylodge.co.uk

dir: *Off A39 Countisbury Hill just before Lynmouth centre, signed Countisbury Lodge*

From its peaceful elevated position high above the town, this former Victorian vicarage has spectacular views of the harbour and countryside. The atmosphere is friendly and informal with attentive service. The comfortable bedrooms are attractively decorated, and breakfast is served in the pleasant dining room.

Rooms 4 en suite (1 fmly) **Facilities** FTV TVB tea/coffee Cen ht TVL Dinner Last d breakfast **Parking** 6

LYNTON   MAP 03 SS74

Premier Collection

★★★★★ 🛎 🍽 GUEST ACCOMMODATION
Victoria Lodge

30–31 Lee Rd EX35 6BS

☎ 01598 753203

e–mail: info@victorialodge.co.uk

web: www.victorialodge.co.uk

dir: *Off A39 in village centre opp Post Office*

A warm welcome awaits you at this elegant villa, built in the 1880s and located in the heart of Lynton. Named after Queen Victoria's children and grandchildren, and reflecting the style of the period, bedrooms are decorated in rich colours and feature coronets, half-testers and a four-poster bed.

Rooms 8 en suite S £59.50–£119; D £70–£140✳ **Facilities** TVB tea/coffee Cen ht Wi-fi available **Parking** 6 **Notes** ⊗ No children 11yrs Closed Nov–23 Mar

Premier Collection

★★★★★ 🛎 🍽 GUEST ACCOMMODATION
Highcliffe House

Sinai Hill EX35 6AR

☎ 01598 752235

e–mail: info@highcliffehouse.co.uk

web: www.highcliffehouse.co.uk

dir: *Off A39 into Lynton, signs for Old Village, at Crown pub up steep hill, house 150yds on left*

Highcliffe House has stunning views of Exmoor and the coast, and across to South Wales. Built in the 1880s as a summer residence, this wonderful house is a good base for exploring the area. Bedrooms are spacious and elegant, likewise the lounges and candlelit conservatory restaurant with its spectacular outlook. Dinner, served Friday to Sunday, is an imaginative choice of home-made dishes.

Rooms 7 en suite **Facilities** TVB tea/coffee Cen ht TVL Dinner Last d 11am (wknds only) Wi-fi available **Parking** 7 **Notes** ⊗ No children 16yrs Closed Dec–mid Feb RS Dinner served wknds only

★★★★ 🛎 🍽 GUEST ACCOMMODATION
North Walk House

North Walk EX35 6HJ

☎ 01598 753372

e–mail: northwalkhouse@btinternet.com

web: www.northwalkhouse.co.uk

dir: *In town centre. Off Castle Hill by church down North Walk Hill, on left*

With fabulous views over the Bristol Channel to the Welsh coastline, North Walk House has recently been completely refurbished. Guests receive a friendly welcome from the owners, who are happy to advise on local walks. The contemporary bedrooms are comfortable and well equipped, with rooms featuring DVDs and ironing equipment. Evening meals, by arrangement, utilise organic produce whenever possible.

Rooms 6 en suite (1 GF) S fr £42; D fr £80✳ **Facilities** FTV TVB tea/coffee Cen ht Dinner Last d 5pm Wi-fi available **Conf** Board 12 **Parking** 6 **Notes LB** ⊗ No children 14yrs

★★★★ GUEST ACCOMMODATION
Alford House
3 Alford Ter EX35 6AT
☎ 01598 752359
e–mail: enquiries@alfordhouse.co.uk
web: www.alfordhouse.co.uk

dir: *B3234 into Lynton onto Station Rd & 2nd right (Normans Cleave), onto Alford Terrace, on right*

Having splendid views over Lynton, the coastline and Wales in the distance, Alford House is a charming Georgian property. Most of the well-appointed bedrooms have delightful views and all are equipped with considerate extras. Guests are assured of a warm and friendly atmosphere. Additional features include a cosy bar/lounge.

Rooms 6 en suite S £32–£35; D £64–£70✱ **Facilities** TVB tea/coffee Cen ht TVL **Notes LB** ⊗ No children 10yrs Closed Xmas

★★★★ GUEST HOUSE
Pine Lodge
Lynway EX35 6AX
☎ 01598 753230
e–mail: info@pinelodgelynton.co.uk
web: www.pinelodgelynton.co.uk

dir: *500yds S of town centre off Lynbridge Rd opp Bridge Inn*

Built in the 19th century, this charming house is set in an acre of landscaped gardens and overlooks the beautiful West Lyn Valley. Understandably, this a popular area for walkers with many spectacular walks right on the doorstep. The quaint village of Lynton is close by, and visitors can take the Cliff Railway 500 feet down to Lynmouth. Bedrooms all offer impressive levels of comfort with lovely views and a relaxing atmosphere. Breakfast is served in the attractive dining room with an adjacent conservatory lounge for guests.

Rooms 4 en suite D £60–£72 **Facilities** TVB tea/coffee Cen ht **Parking** 6 **Notes** ⊗ No children 12yrs No coaches

★★★★ 🍴 GUEST ACCOMMODATION
St Vincent House & Restaurant
Castle Hill EX35 6JA
☎ 01598 752244 🖨 01598 752244
e–mail: welcome@st-vincent-hotel.co.uk
web: www.st-vincent-hotel.co.uk

dir: *Off Lynmouth Hill onto Castle Hill, take left fork after NCP car park. 50mtrs on right, next to Exmoor museum*

Expect a warm welcome at this attractive Grade II listed house. The individually furnished bedrooms are well equipped, and an open fire burns in the charming drawing room during cooler months, the venue for a pre-dinner drink. Exmoor produce is used in the restaurant alongside signature dishes such as Provençal Bouillabaisse and Noir de Noir Marquise along with classic Belgian beers.

Rooms 6 en suite S £65; D £70–£75✱ (room only) **Facilities** TVB tea/coffee Cen ht Dinner Last d 8.30pm Wi-fi available **Parking** 2 **Notes LB** ⊗ No children 14yrs Closed Nov–Etr RS Mon eve (ex BH)

★★★★ GUEST ACCOMMODATION
Sinai House
Lynway EX35 6AY
☎ 01598 753227 🖨 01598 752663
e–mail: enquiries@sinaihouse.co.uk

dir: *A39 onto B3234 through town, pass church, house on right overlooking main car park*

This Victorian residence has spectacular views over Lynton, Lynmouth and across the Bristol Channel. Guests are assured of a friendly welcome from the owners. Bedrooms are well furnished and the comfortable public rooms include a spacious, well-appointed lounge, a cosy bar and smartly presented dining room.

Rooms 8 rms (6 en suite) (2 pri facs) **Facilities** TVB tea/coffee Cen ht TVL **Parking** 8 **Notes** ⊗ No children 12yrs Closed 15 Nov–28 Dec & 3 Jan–15 Feb

---
MARSH   **MAP 04 ST21**

★★★★ GUEST ACCOMMODATION
Cottage B & B
EX14 9AJ
☎ 01460 234240
e–mail: buttonstephens@btopenworld.com

dir: *A303 (Ilminster to Honiton), left off dual-carrigeway, 1st right under bridge, 1st house on right*

Set in the beautiful Blackdown Hills on the border of Devon and Somerset, this accommodation has been refurbished to a high quality standard. Bedrooms are all at ground level, with walk-in shower rooms. Each room has its own entrance from the small courtyard where visitors, resident and non-resident, can sit in warmer weather and enjoy afternoon tea from the on-site tea shop (seasonal afternoon opening times). Breakfast features eggs from the host's own chickens and local produce.

Rooms 4 en suite (4 GF) **Facilities** TVB tea/coffee Cen ht **Parking** 4 **Notes** ⊛

MORETONHAMPSTEAD MAP 03 SX78

★★★★ 🛏 BED & BREAKFAST

Hazlecott Bed & Breakfast

Manaton TQ13 9UY

☎ 01647 221521 & 07800 994928 📠 01647 221405

e-mail: hazelcott@dartmoordays.com

web: www.dartmoordays.com

dir: *A38 onto A382 through Bovey Tracey to Manaton. Pass Kestor Inn, right at x-rds, 0.5m past church*

A home-from-home is provided at this delightful house secluded on the edge of Dartmoor. Rooms vary in size but all have superb views of the locality. Breakfasts are a feature, when local produce is used confidently. This is an ideal venue for ramblers. A Wi-fi connection is also now available here.

Rooms 3 en suite (1 fmly) (1 GF) S £40–£50; D £60–£80 **Facilities** TVB tea/coffee Cen ht TVL Dinner Last d previous day Wi-fi available Hot Spa **Parking** 6 **Notes LB**

★★★★ GUEST HOUSE

Moorcote Country Guest House

Chagford Cross TQ13 8LS

☎ 01647 440966

e-mail: moorcote@smartone.co.uk

dir: *500yds NW of village centre on A382, past hospital on right*

Perched on a hill overlooking the town and surrounded by attractive mature country gardens, this Victorian house is a good base for exploring Dartmoor and only a short walk from the town centre. Friendly owners Pat and Paul Lambert extend a warm welcome to their guests, many of whom return on a regular basis.

Rooms 4 en suite (2 fmly) **Facilities** TVB tea/coffee Cen ht **Parking** 6 **Notes** ⊗ No children 5yrs No coaches Closed Dec 🔄

★★★★ 🅰 FARM HOUSE

Great Sloncombe (SX737864)

TQ13 8QF

☎ 01647 440595 📠 01647 440595 Mrs T Merchant

e-mail: hmerchant@sloncombe.freeserve.co.uk

dir: *A382 from Moretonhampstead towards Chagford, 1.5m left at sharp double bend & farm 0.5m up lane*

Rooms 3 en suite S fr £40; D £70–£76 **Facilities** TVB tea/coffee Cen ht **Parking** 3 **Notes** No children 8yrs 170 acres beef/horses

★★★★ 🅰 FARM HOUSE

Great Wooston Farm (SX764890)

TQ13 8QA

☎ 01647 440367 📠 01647 440367 Mrs M Cuming

e-mail: info@greatwoostonfarm.com

web: www.greatwoostonfarm.com

dir: *Onto Lime St (opp library) for 1.5m over cattle grid, fork left over 2nd cattle grid, 2nd house on right*

Rooms 3 en suite S £35–£40; D £62–£66 **Facilities** TVB tea/coffee Cen ht TVL **Parking** 3 **Notes LB** ⊗ No children 8yrs 320 acres mixed

★★★ GUEST HOUSE

Cookshayes Country Guest House

33 Court St TQ13 8LG

☎ 01647 440374 📠 01647 440453

e-mail: cookshayes@aol.co.uk

web: www.cookshayes.co.uk

dir: *A38 onto A382 to Moretonhampstead. Take B3212 towards Princetown. Cookshayes 400yds on left*

A genuine welcome awaits at this secluded Victorian house, a perfect base for exploring the delights of Dartmoor. Bedrooms are comfortably furnished and well appointed, and one has a four-poster bed. The smart dining room is the venue for scrumptious breakfasts and excellent dinners, where local produce is cooked with skill and enthusiasm. Additional facilities include a cosy lounge, which overlooks the attractive garden.

Rooms 7 rms (5 en suite) (1 fmly) (1 GF) S £25–£27.50; D £45–£60 **Facilities** TVB tea/coffee Licensed Cen ht TVL Dinner Last d 9am **Conf** Max 16 Class 10 Board 10 **Parking** 10 **Notes LB** No children 5yrs No coaches

NEWTON ABBOT MAP 03 SX87

See also Widecombe in the Moor

★★★★ 🛏 FARM HOUSE

Bulleigh Park (SX860660)

Ipplepen TQ12 5UA

☎ 01803 872254 📠 01803 872254 Mrs A Dallyn

e-mail: bulleigh@lineone.net

web: www.southdevonaccommodation.co.uk

dir: *3.5m S of Newton Abbot. Off A381 at Parkhill Cross by Power station for Compton, continue 1m, signed*

Bulleigh Park is a working farm, producing award-winning Aberdeen Angus beef. The owners have also won an award for green tourism by reducing the impact of the business on the environment. Expect a friendly welcome at this family home set in glorious countryside, where breakfasts are notable for the wealth of fresh, local and home-made produce, and the porridge is cooked from a secret recipe.

Rooms 2 en suite 1 annexe en suite S £38–£40; D £70–£76 **Facilities** FTV TVB tea/coffee Cen ht TVL Wi-fi available **Parking** 6 **Notes LB** ⊗ 60 acres beef, sheep, hens Closed Dec–1 Feb

★★★★ BED & BREAKFAST
Lyndale Bed and Breakfast
Lyndale Leygreen, Teigngrace TQ12 6QW
☎ 01626 332491
e–mail: sue.haddy@btinternet.com

dir: *Going S from Exeter on A38, pass Chudleigh exit, after 1.5m exit for Teigngrace. 1m on right*

Peacefully located in the quiet village of Teigngrace, Lyndale is a modern detached bungalow surrounded by pleasant countryside views. The two well decorated and comfortably furnished bedrooms and bathrooms provide guests with plenty of space and comfort. Breakfast is taken in the bright conservatory overlooking the gardens and outdoor seating is available for sunnier days.

Rooms 2 en suite (2 GF) S £30–£35; D £56–£60✱ **Facilities** TVB tea/coffee Cen ht **Parking** 4 **Notes** ⊗ No children ⊛

★★★★ ⊛ GUEST ACCOMMODATION
Sampsons Farm & Restaurant
Preston TQ12 3PP
☎ 01626 354913 📄 01626 354913
e–mail: nigel@sampsonsfarm.com
web: www.sampsonsfarm.com

dir: *A380 onto B3195 signed Kingsteignton. Pass Ten Tors Inn on left & 2nd right B3193 to Chudleigh. At rdbt 3rd exit, left after 1m*

This attractive thatched 16th-century farmhouse stands in a quiet location. Accommodation is provided in the main house and in adjacent converted stables; all rooms are well-equipped and pleasantly appointed. Cuisine is a notable feature and menus at dinner and breakfast feature fresh local produce and accomplished cooking.

Rooms 5 rms (2 en suite) 6 annexe en suite (2 fmly) S £59.50–£115; D £65–£140✱ **Facilities** TVB tea/coffee Direct dial from bedrooms Cen ht Dinner Last d 9.15pm Wi-fi available **Conf** Max 16 Class 20 Board 12 **Parking** 20 **Notes LB** ⊗ No children 14yrs

---

NEWTON POPPLEFORD MAP 03 SY08

★★★ ⊛⊛ RESTAURANT WITH ROOMS
Moores Restaurant & Rooms
6 Greenbank, High St EX10 0EB
☎ 01395 568100
e–mail: mooresrestaurant@aol.com

dir: *On A3052 in village centre*

Centrally located in the village, this small restaurant offers very comfortable, practically furnished bedrooms. Guests are assured of a friendly welcome and relaxed, efficient service. Lunches and dinners are provided; good quality, locally sourced ingredients are used to produce imaginative dishes full of honest, natural flavour.

Rooms 3 rms (1 en suite) (2 fmly) S £40–£60; D £50–£60 **Facilities** TVB tea/coffee Cen ht Dinner Last d 9.30pm **Conf** Max 12 Board 12 **Notes LB** ⊗ Closed 1st 2wks Jan

---

OKEHAMPTON

See also Holsworthy & Lewdown

★★★★ 🏠 🍴 GUEST HOUSE
Pressland Country House
Hatherleigh EX20 3LW
☎ 01837 810871
e–mail: giles@presslandhouse.co.uk
web: www.presslandhouse.co.uk

dir: *6m N of Okehampton on A386 towards Hatherleigh*

A friendly welcome is assured at Pressland Country House, a delightful Victorian house surrounded by landscaped gardens. The elegant bedrooms have views over the countryside and are provided with excellent extras and accessories. It is worth booking in advance for one of the delicious dinners.

Rooms 4 rms (3 en suite) (1 pri facs) 2 annexe en suite (2 GF) **Facilities** TVB tea/coffee Licensed Cen ht TVL Dinner Last d 6pm 🍴 **Conf** Max 12 Thtr 12 Class 12 Board 12 **Parking** 10 **Notes** ⊗ No children 8 yrs No coaches Closed mid Dec–mid Mar

★★★★ FARM HOUSE
Week Farm *(SX519913)*
Bridestowe EX20 4HZ
☎ 01837 861221 📄 01837 861221 Mrs Margaret Hockridge
e–mail: margaret@weekfarmonline.com
web: www.weekfarmonline.com

dir: *1m NE of Bridestowe. Off junct A30 & A386 towards Bridestowe, fork right, left at x-rds to Week Farm*

A delicious complimentary cream tea awaits at this 17th-century farmhouse. Surrounded by undulating countryside, the farm also has three coarse fishing lakes, set in a conservation area. Traditional farmhouse breakfasts can be enjoyed in the dining room. The comfortable bedrooms are furnished in traditional style, and one ground-floor room has easier access.

Rooms 5 en suite (2 fmly) (1 GF) S £30–£35; D £56–£60✱ **Facilities** FTV TVB tea/coffee Cen ht TVL ⌇ Fishing 3 Coarse fishing lakes **Conf** Max 12 **Parking** 10 **Notes LB** 180 acres sheep/cattle Closed 25 Dec

---

OTTERY ST MARY MAP 03 SY19

★★ BED & BREAKFAST
Fluxton Farm *ANN FORTH.* ✗
Fluxton EX11 1RJ
☎ 01404 812818 📄 01404 814843
web: www.fluxtonfarm.co.uk

dir: *2m SW of Ottery St Mary. B3174 W from Ottery over river, left, next left to Fluxton*

A haven for cat lovers, Fluxton Farm offers comfortable accommodation with a choice of lounges and a large garden, complete with pond and ducks. Set in peaceful farmland four miles from the coast, this 16th-century longhouse has a wealth of beams and open fireplaces.

Rooms 7 en suite S £27.50; D £55✱ **Facilities** TVB tea/coffee Cen ht TVL **Parking** 15 **Notes LB** No children 8yrs RS Nov–Apr ⊛

★★★★ GUEST HOUSE
The Clydesdale
5 Polsham Park TQ3 2AD
☎ 01803 558402
e–mail: theclydesdale@hotmail.co.uk

dir: *Off A3022 Torquay Rd onto Lower Polsham Rd, 2nd right into Polsham Park*

The friendly proprietors warmly welcome guests to their home with a splendid garden, just a short walk from the town centre and seafront. Two bedrooms are on the ground floor, and home-cooked evening meals are available by arrangement; the home-made cakes are a speciality.

Rooms 7 en suite (1 fmly) (2 GF) S £24–£27; D £48–£54✱ **Facilities** FTV TVB tea/coffee Cen ht TVL Dinner Last d noon **Parking** 6 **Notes LB** No coaches Closed Xmas & New Year

See advert on opposite page

★★★★ GUEST ACCOMMODATION
The Commodore
14 Esplanade Rd TQ4 6EB
☎ 01803 553107 📠 01803 557040
e–mail: info@commodorepaignton.com
web: www.commodorepaignton.com

dir: *A379 to Paignton, A3022 to seafront. Pass multiplex cinema, property on right*

With an excellent seafront location, all the popular attractions of the town including shopping, the harbour, cinema and restaurants, are all just a short stroll from this family-run accommodation. Bedrooms are generally spacious and well furnished and some enjoy sea views. Guests are welcome to use the lounge and a small downstairs bar is also available.

Rooms 11 en suite (5 fmly) (3 GF) S £36–£70; D £52–£80 **Facilities** FTV TVB tea/coffee Cen ht TVL Dinner Last d 8.45am Wi-fi available **Parking** 10 **Notes LB**

See advert on opposite page

★★★★ GUEST HOUSE
The Wentworth Guest House
18 Youngs Park Rd, Goodrington TQ4 6BU
☎ 01803 557843
e–mail: enquiries@wentworthguesthouse.co.uk

dir: *Through Paignton on A378, 1m left at rdbt, sharp right onto Roundham Rd, right & right again onto Youngs Park Rd*

Within 200 yards of the beach, this Victorian house overlooks Goodrington Park and is convenient for many attractions and the town centre. The bedrooms are attractively decorated, well equipped, and feature many thoughtful extras. The traditional English breakfast is a tasty start to the day, and additional facilities include a comfortable bar and a spacious lounge.

Rooms 10 en suite (2 fmly) (1 GF) S £20–£27; D £40–£54✱ **Facilities** TVB tea/coffee Licensed Cen ht TVL **Parking** 4

★★★★ ᴀ GUEST HOUSE
Earlston House
31 St Andrews Rd TQ4 6HA
☎ 01803 558355
e–mail: stay@earlstonhouse.co.uk
web: www.earlstonhouse.co.uk

dir: *From Paignton seafront at mini-rdbt onto Sands Rd, 2nd left onto St Andrews Rd, establishment at brow of hill on left*

Rooms 8 en suite (4 fmly) S £24–£32; D £48–£60✱ **Facilities** FTV TVB tea/coffee Licensed Cen ht TVL Dinner Last d noon Wi-fi available **Parking** 8 **Notes LB** ⊗ No coaches Closed Xmas & New Year

★★★ GUEST HOUSE
Aquamarine Guesthouse
8 St Andrews Rd TQ4 6HA
☎ 01803 551193
e–mail: enquiries@aquamarine-hotel.co.uk

dir: *Along Esplanade with sea on left, at mini-rdbt right onto Sands Rd, St Andrews Rd 2nd left*

Located in a quiet road, just a short stroll from the town centre and the seafront, this smartly appointed establishment is well placed to explore Torbay. Bedrooms all provide good levels of comfort with spacious en suite facilities. Additional facilities include a choice of lounges, small bar and a lovely garden with decking and hot-tub.

Rooms 7 en suite (2 fmly) S £24–£27; D £48–£54✱ **Facilities** FTV TVB tea/coffee Licensed Cen ht TVL Dinner Last d 8pm Wi-fi available **Parking** 5 **Notes LB** ⊗ No coaches

★★★ GUEST ACCOMMODATION
Bay Cottage
4 Beach Rd TQ4 6AY
☎ 01803 525729

dir: *Along B3201 Esplanade Rd past Paignton Pier, Beach Rd 2nd right*

Quietly located in a level terrace, the seafront, park, harbour and shops are all just a short stroll away. Run in a friendly and relaxed manner, Bay Cottage offers a range of bedrooms of various shapes and sizes, with a guest lounge also made available. Dinner is offered by prior arrangement and includes enjoyable home cooking in hearty portions.

Rooms 8 en suite (3 fmly) S £20–£25; D £40–£50 **Facilities** TVB tea/coffee Cen ht TVL Dinner Last d 10am **Notes LB** ⊗

★★★ GUEST ACCOMMODATION
The Park
Esplanade Rd TQ4 6BQ
☎ 01803 557856 📠 01803 555626
e–mail: stay@parkhotel.me.uk

dir: *On Paignton seafront, nearly opp pier*

This large establishment has a prominent position on the seafront with excellent views of Torbay. The pleasant bedrooms are all spacious and available in a number of options, and several have sea views. Entertainment is provided on some evenings in the lounge. Dinner and

CONTINUED

breakfast are served in the spacious dining room, which overlooks the attractive front garden.

Rooms 47 en suite (5 fmly) (3 GF) S £26–£43; D £54–£90✱
Facilities TVB tea/coffee Lift Cen ht Dinner Last d 6pm Wi-fi available Pool Table Games room with 3/4 snooker table & table tennis
Conf Max 120 Board 12 **Parking** 38 **Notes** LB

★★★ GUEST HOUSE
Redcliffe Lodge

1 Marine Dr TQ3 2NJ
☎ 01803 551394 📄 01803 551394
e-mail: davies.valleyview@tiscali.co.uk

dir: Follow A3022 to Paignton seafront. At the end of Marine Drive on the right adjacent to Paignton Green

Handily placed across the road from the seafront, this is an ideal base for those visiting the Torbay area. Bedrooms are furnished in traditional style with some having the benefit of sea views. The dining room has lovely views over the garden to the sea beyond and guests also have a choice of lounges and bar.

Rooms 17 en suite (2 fmly) (3 GF) **Facilities** TVB tea/coffee Licensed Cen ht TVL Dinner Last d 5.30pm **Conf** Max 40 Class 40 **Parking** 16 **Notes** ⊗

See advert on page 183

★★★ GUEST HOUSE
The Sealawn

Sea Front, 20 Esplanade Rd TQ4 6BE
☎ 01803 559031 📄 01803 666113

dir: On seafront between pier & cinema

With an ideal location right on the seafront, this traditional guest house is understandably popular. Bedrooms are comfortably decorated and furnished, and guests are also welcome to use the lounge and bar area. The large forecourt to the front of the accommodation includes some outdoor seating and much useful parking space.

Rooms 10 en suite (2 fmly) (2 GF) **Facilities** TVB tea/coffee Cen ht TVL Dinner Last d 9.30am **Parking** 12 **Notes** LB ⊗ No coaches

PLYMOUTH   MAP 03 SX45

★★★★ GUEST ACCOMMODATION
Berkeley's of St James

4 St James Place East, The Hoe PL1 3AS

☎ 01752 221654 📄 01752 221654

e–mail: enquiry@onthehoe.co.uk

dir: *Off A38 towards city centre, left at sign The Hoe, over 7 sets of lights, left onto Athenaeum St, right to Crescent Av, 1st left*

Located in a quiet square close to The Hoe and just a short walk from the city centre, this is a good choice for business and leisure. Bedrooms are comfortable, attractive and equipped with a number of thoughtful extras. An enjoyable breakfast using organic and local produce, whenever possible, is served in the dining room.

Rooms 5 en suite (1 fmly) (1 GF) S £40–£45; D £60–£65 **Facilities** TVB tea/coffee Cen ht **Parking** 3 **Notes LB** ⊗ Closed 23 Dec–1 Jan

★★★★ GUEST ACCOMMODATION
Brittany Guest House

28 Athenaeum St, The Hoe PL1 2RQ

☎ 01752 262247 📄 01752 268843

e–mail: enquiries@brittanyguesthouse.co.uk

web: www.brittanyguesthouse.co.uk

dir: *A38/City Centre follow signs for Pavillions, bear left at mini-rdbt, turn left at lights onto Athenaeum St*

Situated in a pleasant street, within walking distance of Plymouth's many attractions, this well presented house offers comfortable and well-equipped accommodation. The proprietors provide friendly hospitality, along with a freshly cooked breakfast served in the attractive dining room. Parking available.

Rooms 10 en suite (3 fmly) (1 GF) S £30–£45; D £45–£55 **Facilities** TVB tea/coffee Cen ht Wi-fi available **Parking** 6 **Notes** ⊗ No children 3yrs Closed 20 Dec–2 Jan

★★★★ GUEST ACCOMMODATION
Grosvenor

9 Elliot St, The Hoe PL1 2PP

☎ 01752 260411 📄 01752 668878

e–mail: grosvenorhotel@btinternet.com

dir: *Off A38 for city centre & Barbican, left to Walrus, over junct on left*

The Grosvenor is convenient for The Hoe, ferry port and the city's attractions. Bedrooms are well equipped with some family rooms, and you can relax in the smart bar-lounge. A light meal/snack menu is available during the evening in the pleasant dining room, where breakfast is also served. Limited parking is available at the rear of the property.

Rooms 28 en suite (3 fmly) (1 GF) **Facilities** TVB tea/coffee Cen ht TVL Dinner Last d 8pm **Parking** 6 **Notes** ⊗ Closed 22 Dec–2 Jan

★★★★ GUEST ACCOMMODATION
Jewell's

220 Citadel Rd, The Hoe PL1 3BB

☎ 01752 254760 📄 01752 254760

dir: *A38 towards city centre, follow sign for Barbican, then The Hoe. Left at lights, right at top of road onto Citadel Rd. Jewell's 0.25m*

This smart, comfortable, family-run guest house is only a short walk from The Hoe and is convenient for the city centre and the Barbican. Bedrooms come with a wide range of extra facilities, and breakfast is served in the pleasant dining room. Some secure parking is available.

Rooms 10 rms (7 en suite) (5 fmly) (2 smoking) S £25–£30; D £45–£55✳ **Facilities** FTV TVB tea/coffee Cen ht Wi-fi available **Parking** 3 **Notes LB** ⊗

★★★★ 🅰 GUEST HOUSE
Four Seasons

207 Citadel Rd East, The Hoe PL1 2JF

☎ 01752 223591

e–mail: f.seasons@btconnect.com

dir: *Off A38 for city centre & The Hoe*

Rooms 7 rms (5 en suite) (2 pri facs) (1 GF) S £31–£46; D £47–£62✳ **Facilities** TVB tea/coffee Cen ht Wi-fi available **Notes** No coaches

★★★ GUEST ACCOMMODATION
The Cranbourne

278–282 Citadel Rd, The Hoe PL1 2PZ
☎ 01752 263858 & 224646 & 661400 📠 01752 263858
e–mail: cran.hotel@virgin.net
web: www.cranbournehotel.co.uk

dir: *Behind the Promenade, Plymouth Hoe*

This attractive Georgian terrace house has been extensively renovated, and is located just a short walk from The Hoe, The Barbican and the city centre. Bedrooms are practically furnished and well equipped. Hearty breakfasts are served in the elegant dining room and there is also a cosy bar.

Rooms 40 rms (28 en suite) (5 fmly) (1 GF) S £25–£40; D £44–£60✳
Facilities TVB tea/coffee Cen ht TVL **Parking** 14

★★★ GUEST ACCOMMODATION
Ashgrove House

218 Citadel Rd, The Hoe PL1 3BB
☎ 01752 664046 📠 01752 252112
e–mail: ashgroveho@aol.com

dir: *Follow signs for The Hoe*

Conveniently situated within walking distance of all the city's attractions, this personally-run establishment offers well-presented accommodation; ideal for commercial visitors and also welcoming to children. Freshly-cooked breakfasts are provided and a comfortable lounge is available for guests.

Ashgrove House

Rooms 10 en suite (10 fmly) **Facilities** TVB tea/coffee Cen ht TVL
Notes ⊗ Closed mid Jan–mid Dec

★★★ GUEST ACCOMMODATION
Devonshire

22 Lockyer Rd, Mannamead PL3 4RL
☎ 01752 220726 📠 01752 220766
e–mail: devonshiregh@blueyonder.co.uk

dir: *At Hyde Park pub on traffic island turn left onto Wilderness Rd. After 60yds turn left onto Lockyer Rd*

This comfortable Victorian house is located in a residential area close to Mutley Plain high street, from where there is a regular bus service to the city centre. The well-proportioned bedrooms are bright and attractive, and a comfy lounge is available. Parking is available.

Rooms 10 rms (5 en suite) (4 fmly) (3 GF) **Facilities** TVB tea/coffee
Cen ht TVL Wi-fi available **Parking** 6 **Notes** ⊗

CONTINUED

★★★ GUEST ACCOMMODATION
The Lamplighter

103 Citadel Rd, The Hoe PL1 2RN

☎ 01752 663855 & 07793 360815 📠 01752 228139

e–mail: stay@lamplighterplymouth.co.uk

web: www.lamplighterplymouth.co.uk

dir: *Near war memorial*

With easy access to The Hoe, The Barbican and the city centre, this comfortable guest house provides a good base for leisure or business. Bedrooms, including family rooms, are light and airy and furnished to a consistent standard. Breakfast is served in the dining room, which has an adjoining lounge area.

Rooms 9 rms (7 en suite) (2 pri facs) (2 fmly) S £30; D £50✳
Facilities TVB tea/coffee Cen ht TVL Wi-fi available **Parking** 4

★★★ GUEST HOUSE
Rainbow Lodge Guest House

29 Athenaeum St, The Hoe PL1 2RQ

☎ 01752 229699 📠 01752 229357

e–mail: info@rainbowlodgeplymouth.co.uk

web: www.rainbowlodgeplymouth.co.uk

dir: *A38 onto A374. Follow City centre signs for 3m. Move into left lane and follow signs to Pavillions mini rdbt. Turn left and go through 6 sets of lights, turn left*

Just a short stroll from the Hoe, this small and friendly establishment is well placed for exploring the city. Bedrooms are varied in size and style, some of which are suitable for family use. Substantial breakfasts are served in the homely dining room.

Rooms 11 rms (7 en suite) (1 pri facs) (2 fmly) (1 GF) S £30–£50;
D £45–£65✳ **Facilities** TVB tea/coffee Cen ht **Parking** 6 **Notes** ⊗
No children 6yrs No coaches Closed 22 Dec–5 Jan

★★★ GUEST HOUSE
Riviera

8 Elliott St, The Hoe PL1 2PP

☎ 01752 667379 📠 01752 667379

e–mail: riviera-hoe@btconnect.com

dir: *Follow signs to city centre, then The Hoe, located off Citadel Road*

This late Victorian building retains many of the features typical of the period, and is only a short walk from Plymouth Hoe where Sir Francis Drake finished playing his game of bowls prior to defeating the approaching Spanish armada in 1588. Linda and Lester Wrench are committed to providing a highly personalised guest experience. Guests have use of a lounge and bar, and breakfast is served in the breakfast room.

Rooms 11 rms (8 en suite) S £30–£35; D £53–£57✳ **Facilities** TVB tea/
coffee Direct dial from bedrooms Licensed Cen ht TVL Wi-fi available
Notes No children 16yrs No coaches Closed mid Dec–early Jan

★★ GUEST ACCOMMODATION
The Firs Guest House

13 Pier St, West Hoe PL1 3BS

☎ 01752 262870 & 300010

e–mail: thefirsguesthouse@hotmail.co.uk

A well-located and-well established house on the West Hoe with convenient on-street parking. Friendly owners and comfortable rooms make it a popular destination.

Rooms 7 rms (2 en suite) (2 fmly) S £20–£30; D £40–£50✳
Facilities FTV TVB tea/coffee Cen ht Dinner Last d Breakfast time
Notes LB

ROCKBEARE MAP 03 SY09

★★★ BED & BREAKFAST
3 Cherry Tree Close

EX5 2HF

☎ 01404 822047

dir: *In village centre between bridge & church. 3.5m from M5 off old A30*

Guests are assured of a warm welcome and a homely atmosphere at this spacious bungalow set in its own garden in the village of Rockbeare. 3 Cherry Tree Close is convenient for the M5, Exeter International Airport and Westpoint Arena, and its only a short drive from Dartmoor. One of the two bedrooms overlooks fields, and both come complete with tea- and coffee-making facilities. A TV lounge is available for guests, and breakfast is served in the dining room.

Rooms 2 rms (2 GF) S £20; D £40✳ **Facilities** tea/coffee Cen ht TVL
Parking 3 **Notes** LB ⊗ No children Closed 23 Dec–4 Jan ⊜

SEATON MAP 04 SY29

★★★★ ▤ ⊜ GUEST ACCOMMODATION
Mariners

East Walk Esplanade EX12 2NP

☎ 01297 20560

dir: *Off A3052 signed Seaton, Mariners on seafront*

Located just yards from the beach and cliff paths, this comfortable accommodation has a friendly and relaxed atmosphere. Bedrooms, some having sea views, are well equipped, and public rooms are light and airy. The dining room is the venue for enjoyable breakfasts utilising quality local produce, and afternoon teas are also available on the seafront terrace.

Rooms 10 en suite (1 fmly) (2 GF) S £37–£45; D £66–£72✳
Facilities TVB tea/coffee Cen ht Dinner **Parking** 10 **Notes** LB ⊗
No children 5yrs RS Nov–Jan

SHALDON MAP 03 SX97

See Teignmouth

SIDMOUTH

MAP 03 SY18

See also Ottery St Mary

Premier Collection

★★★★★ ⚫⚫ RESTAURANT WITH ROOMS

The Salty Monk

Church St, Sidford EX10 9QP

☎ 01395 513174

e–mail: saltymonk@btconnect.com

web: www.saltymonk.biz

dir: *On A3052 opposite church*

Set in the village of Sidford, this attractive property dates from the 16th century. Some of the well-presented bedrooms feature spa baths or special showers, and a ground-floor courtyard room has a king-size water bed. Meals are served in the restaurant, where the two owners both cook. They use fresh local produce to ensure that the food is of a high standard and thoroughly enjoyable.

Rooms 5 en suite (3 GF) S £70–£90; D £110–£180✳ **Facilities** FTV TVB tea/coffee Cen ht Dinner Last d 9pm Wi-fi available **Conf** Max 14 Board 14 Del from £110 ✳ **Parking** 20 **Notes LB** Closed 2wks Nov & 3wks Jan

★★★★ INN

Blue Ball Inn

Stevens Cross, Sidford EX10 9QL

☎ 01395 514062 & 516564 📠 01395 519584

e–mail: rogernewton@blueballinn.net

dir: *On A3052, at Sidford straight over lights, inn 600yds*

Ideally placed for exploring the many delights of East Devon, this long established inn has been overseen by five generations of the Newton family since 1912 and can trace its history back to 1385. After a devastating fire in 2006, the inn has been lovingly re-built and now provides impressive levels of comfort and quality. The bedrooms and stylish bathrooms provide an appealing blend of old and new with individuality and flair. Extensive bars offer cosy nooks to enjoy the food and drink offerings with an attractive garden also available.

Rooms 9 en suite (2 fmly) (1 GF) S £60; D £95 **Facilities** FTV TVB tea/coffee Cen ht Dinner Last d 9pm Wi-fi available **Conf** Max 65 Del from £80 **Parking** 80 **Notes** ⊗

★★★★ GUEST ACCOMMODATION

The Old Farmhouse

Hillside Rd EX10 8JG

☎ 01395 512284

dir: *A3052 from Exeter to Sidmouth, right at Bowd x-rds, 2m left at rdbt, left at mini-rdbt, next right, over hump-back bridge, bear right on the corner*

This beautiful 16th-century thatched farmhouse, in a quiet residential area just a stroll from the Esplanade and shops, has been lovingly restored. Bedrooms are attractively decorated and the charming public rooms feature beams and an inglenook fireplace. The welcoming

proprietors provide memorable dinners using traditional recipes and fresh local ingredients.

The Old Farmhouse

Rooms 3 en suite 3 annexe en suite (1 fmly) (1 GF) D £56–£70✳ **Facilities** TV3B tea/coffee Cen ht TVL Dinner Last d am **Parking** 4 **Notes LB** No children 12yrs Closed Nov–Feb ⊛

★★★★ GUEST HOUSE

Avalon – A Haven for Non Smokers

Vicarage Rd EX10 8UQ

☎ 01395 513443

e–mail: owneravalon@aol.com

web: www.avalonsidmouth.co.uk

dir: *0.5m N of seafront on A375*

With an award-winning front garden and naturally friendly and welcoming hospitality, this well appointed, small establishment is a short, level walk from the town centre and seafront beyond. Bedrooms are attractively co-ordinated and there is a comfortable lounge area where guests can relax.

Rooms 4 en suite D £56–£70✳ **Facilities** FTV TVB tea/coffee Cen ht TVL **Parking** 4 **Notes LB** ⊗ No children 18yrs No coaches Closed 10 Dec–15 Jan ⊛

★★★★ ⊜ INN

Dukes

The Esplanade EX10 8AR

☎ 01395 513320 📠 01395 519318

e–mail: dukes@hotels-sidmouth.co.uk

web: www.hotels-sidmouth.co.uk

dir: *A3052, take 1st exit to Sidmouth on right, left onto Esplanade*

Situated in the heart of Sidmouth, this stylish inn offers a relaxed and convivial atmosphere with a great team of attentive staff. Bedrooms provide good levels of comfort with a number having the benefit of sea views. The menu employs the seasonable best from the area, with a choice of dining areas available, including the patio garden, perfect for soaking up the sun.

Rooms 13 en suite (5 fmly) S £34–£45; D £68–£116✳ **Facilities** FTV TVB tea/coffee Cen ht Dinner Last d 9pm Wi-fi available **Notes LB** RS 25 Dec

CONTINUED

SIDMOUTH CONTINUED

★★★★ GUEST HOUSE
The Glendevon

Cotmaton Rd EX10 8QX

☎ 01395 514028

e–mail: enquiries@glendevon-hotel.co.uk

web: www.glendevon-hotel.co.uk

dir: *A3052 onto B3176 to mini-rdbt. Right, house 100yds on right*

Located in a quiet residential area just a short walk from the town centre and beaches, this stylish Victorian house offers neat, comfortable bedrooms. Guests are assured of a warm welcome from the resident owners, who provide attentive service and wholesome home-cooked evening meals by arrangement. A lounge is also available.

Rooms 8 en suite **Facilities** TVB tea/coffee Licensed Cen ht Dinner Last d 9am **Notes** ⊗ No children No coaches ⊚

★★★★ GUEST HOUSE
The Groveside

Vicarage Rd EX10 8UQ

☎ 01395 513406

web: www.thegroveside.co.uk

dir: *0.5m N of seafront on A375*

Conveniently situated a short level walking distance from the town centre, the Groveside offers comfortable, well-equipped accommodation. Guests are assured of attentive service and a relaxed and friendly atmosphere with every effort made to facilitate an enjoyable stay. Home-cooked evening meals are served by prior arrangement and on-site parking is an added bonus.

Rooms 9 rms (7 en suite) (2 pri facs) **Facilities** TVB tea/coffee Licensed Cen ht Dinner **Parking** 9 **Notes** ⊗ No coaches ⊚

★★★ GUEST HOUSE
Bramley Lodge Guest House

Vicarage Rd EX10 8UQ

☎ 01395 515710

e–mail: haslam@bramleylodge.fsnet.co.uk

dir: *0.5m N of seafront on A375*

Guests are assured of a warm and friendly welcome at this family-run, small guesthouse, located about a half mile from the seafront. The neatly furnished bedrooms vary in size, and all are equipped to a good standard. Home-cooked evening meals are available, by prior arrangement, with special diets on request.

Rooms 6 rms (5 en suite) (1 fmly) S £29–£31; D £58–£62 **Facilities** FTV TVB tea/coffee Cen ht TVL Dinner Last d 1pm **Parking** 6 **Notes** No coaches Closed Dec–Jan ⊚

See advert on opposite page

★★ GUEST HOUSE
Enstone

Lennox Av EX10 8TX

☎ 01395 514444

e–mail: enstone1@hotmail.co.uk

dir: *A375 Vicarage Rd into Sidmouth, left onto Lennox Av*

Situated in colourful gardens at the end of a quiet cul de sac, this family-run guest house is just 200 yards from the town centre, and a short walk from the seafront. Bedrooms are neatly furnished with the best use made of the available space.

Rooms 4 rms (2 en suite) (1 fmly) (1 GF) S £23–£24; D £40–£54✱ **Facilities** TVB tea/coffee Cen ht TVL Dinner Last d 11am **Parking** 5 **Notes LB** ⊗ No children 2yrs No coaches Closed Oct–Mar ⊚

SOURTON
MAP 03 SX59

★★★★ 🍴 INN
Bearslake Inn
Lake EX20 4HQ
☎ 01837 861334 🖷 01837 861108
e-mail: enquiries@bearslakeinn.com

dir: *A30 from Exeter onto A386 signed Sourton/Tavistock, 2m on left from junct*

Situated on the edge of the Dartmoor National Park, this thatched inn is believed to date back to the 13th century and was originally a working farm. There is character in abundance here with beams, flagstone floors and low ceilings, all of which contribute to an engaging atmosphere. Bedrooms have great individuality and all provide period features combined with contemporary comforts. Local produce is very much in evidence on the menu with dinner served in the attractive Stable Restaurant. The beer garden is bordered by a moorland stream with wonderful views across open countryside.

Rooms 6 en suite (3 fmly) (1 GF) S fr £55; D fr £80✳ **Facilities** TVB tea/coffee Cen ht Dinner Last d 8:45pm **Parking** 35 **Notes** No coaches RS Sun eve

SOUTH MOLTON
MAP 03 SS72

★★★ INN
Old Coaching Inn
Queen St EX36 3BJ
☎ 01769 572526

dir: *In town centre*

There is a warm welcome at this popular inn in a bustling market town. Bedrooms are soundly appointed, and the extensive menu in the bar or restaurant provides a range of good value dishes. Additional facilities include a large function room.

Rooms 10 en suite (2 fmly) **Facilities** TVB tea/coffee Cen ht Dinner Last d 9.30pm Pool Table **Conf** Max 100 Thtr 100 Class 100 Board 50 **Parking** 26 **Notes** ⊗

★★★ 🍴 RESTAURANT WITH ROOMS
Stumbles
134 East St EX36 3BU
☎ 01769 574145 🖷 01769 572558
e-mail: info@stumbles.co.uk

dir: *M5 junct 27 to South Molton on A361. Establishment in town centre*

Located in the centre of this bustling town, Stumbles is a charming place with a friendly and welcoming atmosphere. Bedrooms are individual in style and all have lots of character and good levels of comfort. A small conservatory area is also available for guests. The restaurant is a popular venue for locals and visitors alike, with a varied menu on offer both at lunchtime and in the evenings.

Rooms 6 en suite 4 annexe en suite (1 fmly) (2 GF) **Facilities** FTV TVB tea/coffee Direct dial from bedrooms Cen ht Dinner Last d 9pm **Conf** Max 50 Thtr 30 Class 50 Board 50 **Parking** 25

ENGLAND

STRETE   MAP 03 SX84

★★★★ GUEST HOUSE
Strete Barton House
Totnes Rd TQ6 0RU
☎ 01803 770364 📄 01803 771182
e–mail: info@stretebarton.co.uk
web: www.stretebarton.co.uk
dir: *Off A379 into village centre, just below church*

This delightful 16th-century farmhouse has been refurbished to blend stylish accommodation with its original character. Bedrooms are very comfortably furnished and well equipped with useful extras. Breakfast utilises quality local produce and is served in the spacious dining room. Guests are also welcome to use the very comfortable lounge complete with real log burner for the cooler months. The village lies between Dartmouth and Kingsbridge and has easy access to the natural beauty of the South Hams as well as local pubs and restaurants.

Rooms 5 rms (4 en suite) (1 pri facs) 1 annexe en suite (2 fmly) (1 GF) S £65–£90; D £75–£100✱ **Facilities** FTV TVB tea/coffee Cen ht Wi-fi available **Parking** 4 **Notes LB** No children 3yrs No coaches

See advert on page 187

TAVISTOCK   MAP 03 SX47

Premier Collection

★★★★★ 🏠 GUEST ACCOMMODATION
Tor Cottage
PL16 0JE
☎ 01822 860248 📄 01822 860126
e–mail: info@torcottage.co.uk
web: www.torcottage.co.uk
(For full entry see Chillaton)

★★★ GUEST ACCOMMODATION
The Coach House
PL19 8NS
☎ 01822 617515 📄 01822 617515
e–mail: estevens255@aol.com
web: www.thecoachousehotel.co.uk
dir: *2.5m NW of Tavistock. A390 from Tavistock to Gulworthy Cross, at rdbt take 3rd exit towards Chipshop Inn turn right to Ottery, 1st building in village*

Dating from 1857, this building was constructed for the Duke of Bedford and converted by the current owners. Some bedrooms are on the ground floor and in an adjacent barn conversion. Dinner is available in the cosy dining room or the restaurant, which leads onto the south-facing garden.

Rooms 6 en suite 3 annexe en suite (4 GF) S £47; D £65✱ **Facilities** TVB tea/coffee Direct dial from bedrooms Cen ht Dinner Last d 9pm **Parking** 24 **Notes LB** No children 5yrs

★★★ BED & BREAKFAST
Sampford Manor
Sampford Spiney PL20 6LH
☎ 01822 853442 📄 01822 855691
e–mail: manor@sampford-spiney.fsnet.co.uk
web: www.sampford-spiney.fsnet.co.uk
dir: *B3357 towards Princetown, right at 1st x-rds. Next x-rds Warren Cross left for Sampford Spiney. 2nd right, house below church*

Once owned by Sir Francis Drake, this manor house is tucked away in a tranquil corner of Dartmoor National Park. The family home is full of character, with exposed beams and slate floors, while outside, a herd of award winning alpacas graze in the fields. Genuine hospitality is assured together with scrumptious breakfasts featuring home-produced eggs. Children, horses (stabling available) and dogs are all equally welcome.

Rooms 3 rms (2 pri facs) (1 fmly) S £27–£35; D £50–£70✱ **Facilities** TVB tea/coffee Cen ht Golf 19 **Parking** 3 **Notes** Closed Xmas
🐾

TEIGNMOUTH
MAP 03 SX97

Premier Collection

★★★★★ 🏠 GUEST ACCOMMODATION

Thomas Luny House

Teign St TQ14 8EG

☎ 01626 772976

e–mail: alisonandjohn@thomas-luny-house.co.uk

dir: *A381 to Teignmouth, at 3rd lights turn right to quay, 50yds turn left onto Teign St, after 60yds turn right through white archway*

Built in the late 18th century by marine artist Thomas Luny, this charming house offers unique and comfortable accommodation in the old quarter of Teignmouth. Bedrooms are individually decorated and furnished, and all are well equipped with a good range of extras. An elegant drawing room with French windows leads into a walled garden with a terraced sitting area. A superb breakfast, featuring local produce, is served in the attractive dining room.

Rooms 4 en suite **Facilities** TVB tea/coffee Direct dial from bedrooms Cen ht Wi-fi available **Parking** 8 **Notes** ⊗ No children 12yrs

★★★★ GUEST ACCOMMODATION

Potters Mooring

30 The Green, Shaldon TQ14 0DN

☎ 01626 873225 📄 01626 872909

e–mail: mail@pottersmooring.co.uk

web: www.pottersmooring.co.uk

dir: *A38 onto A380 signed Torquay, B3192 to Teignmouth & Shaldon, over river signs to Potters Mooring*

A former sea captain's residence dating from 1625, Potters Mooring has been refurbished to provide charming accommodation of a very high standard, including a four-poster room. The friendly proprietors make every effort to ensure an enjoyable stay and the Captain Potter's breakfast features tasty local produce.

Rooms 6 rms (5 en suite) (1 pri facs) (2 fmly) **Facilities** TVB tea/coffee Cen ht **Parking** 8

★★★ BED & BREAKFAST

The Minadab Cottage

60 Teignmouth Rd TQ14 8UT

☎ 01626 772044

e–mail: enquiries@minadab.co.uk

dir: *M5 onto A380, 2nd left onto B3192, left at T-lights onto A379, cottage approx 1m*

This unusual thatched building offers plenty of character and interest throughout. The friendly owners will be pleased to discuss the history of the property, including its unusual name. Bedrooms provide a range of shapes and sizes and include one on the ground floor. Enjoyable home-cooked dinners are usually available by prior arrangement.

Rooms 3 rms (1 en suite) (2 pri facs) (1 GF) S £40–£45; D £60–£70✳ **Facilities** TVB tea/coffee Cen ht Dinner Last d 24hrs notice DVD's & games available for use **Parking** 4 **Notes** ⊗ No children 16yrs

THORVERTON
MAP 03 SS90

★★★ INN

Thorverton Arms

EX5 5NS

☎ 01392 860205

e–mail: info@thethorvertonarms.co.uk

web: www.thethorvertonarms.co.uk

dir: *Turn off A396 at Ruffwell. Continue for 1m to centre of Thorverton. The Thorverton Arms on left*

Mid-way between Exeter and Tiverton, this 16th-century, former coaching inn is situated at the heart of a picturesque village. The open-plan bar is the hub of village life, offering a range of real ales, wines and spirits and a varied selection of locally sourced and freshly prepared meals. At the rear of the property, there's a patio and south-facing beer garden, featuring one of the oldest wisteria in Devon.

Rooms 6 en suite (1 fmly) S £50–£52.50; D £68.50–£85✳ **Facilities** FTV TVB tea/coffee Cen ht Dinner Last d 9pm Pool Table **Parking** 15 **Notes LB** RS Mon–Fri

TIVERTON
MAP 03 SS91

★★★★ 🖺 FARM HOUSE
Hornhill Farmhouse *(SS965117)*

Exeter Hill EX16 4PL
☎ 01884 253352 Mrs B Pugsley
e-mail: hornhill@tinyworld.co.uk
web: www.hornhill-farmhouse.co.uk

dir: *Signs to Grand Western Canal, right fork up Exeter Hill.
Farmhouse on left at top of hill*

Hornhill has a peaceful hilltop setting with panoramic views of the
town and the Exe Valley. Elegant décor and furnishings enhance the
character of the farmhouse, which in part dates from the 18th century.
Bedrooms are beautifully equipped with modern facilities and there is
a lovely sitting room with a log fire. Breakfast is served at one large
table in the spacious dining room.

Rooms 3 rms (1 en suite) (2 pri facs) (1 GF) S £35–£40; D £60–£65✱
Facilities TVB tea/coffee 🍴 **Parking** 5 **Notes** ⊗ No children 12yrs
75 acres beef sheep ☺

★★★★ FARM HOUSE
Rhode Farm House *(SS967102)*

Exeter Hill EX16 4PL
☎ 01884 242853 📠 01884 242853 Mr & Mrs D Boulton
e-mail: david@rhodefarmhouse.com
web: www.rhodefarmhouse.com

dir: *Signs to Grand Western Canal, right fork signed Exeter Hill,
farmhouse 3m on left*

Guests receive a very warm welcome at Rhode Farm House. It stands
in 5 acres with stables in the yard, a 30-minute drive from Exeter city

CONTINUED

centre. Bedrooms are finished with many considerate extras and there
is an inviting lounge with a log fire for colder nights. A delicious
breakfast, featuring local produce, is served around a communal table
in the dining room. Carefully prepared and presented dinners are
available by arrangement.

Rooms 2 en suite (2 fmly) S £35–£40; D £65–£70 **Facilities** TVB tea/
coffee Cen ht TVL Dinner Last d noon Riding **Parking** 5 **Notes** ⊗
4 acres

★★★ FARM HOUSE
Quoit-At-Cross *(ST923188)*

Stoodleigh EX16 9PJ
☎ 01398 351280 📠 01398 351351 Mrs L Hill

dir: *M5 junct 27 3.5m N of Tiverton. A396 N for Bampton, 3.5m
left over bridge for Stoodleigh, farmhouse on junct*

A friendly welcome is assured at this delightful stone-built working
farmhouse with views over rolling Devonshire countryside. The
comfortable, attractive bedrooms are well furnished, and have many
extra facilities. A lounge and pretty garden are available.

Rooms 3 en suite S fr £30; D fr £60✱ **Facilities** TVB tea/coffee Cen ht
TVL Wi-fi available **Parking** 3 **Notes** ⊗ 160 acres organic mixed Closed
Dec–Apr ☺

TORBAY
MAP 03 SX86

*See **Brixham, Paignton** and **Torquay***

TORQUAY
MAP 03 SX96

★★★★★ GUEST HOUSE
The Marstan

Meadfoot Sea Rd TQ1 2LQ
☎ 01803 292837 📠 01803 299202
e-mail: enquiries@marstanhotel.co.uk

dir: *A3022 to seafront, left onto A379 Torbay Rd & Babbacombe
Rd, right onto Meadfoot Rd, Marstan on right*

This elegant mid–19th-century villa provides high levels of comfort and
quality throughout. The hospitality and service are excellent, and every
effort is made to create a relaxed and enjoyable atmosphere. Public
areas include an impressive dining room, a bar and a comfortable
lounge. Outdoors guests can enjoy a heated swimming pool and hot
tub in the pleasant garden.

CONTINUED

Rooms 9 en suite (1 fmly) (2 GF) S £55–£65; D £80–£138✱
Facilities FTV TVB tea/coffee Direct dial from bedrooms Licensed Cen ht
Wi-fi available ⚲ **Conf** Max 12 Thtr 12 Class 12 Board 12 **Parking** 8
Notes LB ⊗ No coaches

★★★★ 🏠 GUEST ACCOMMODATION

The Colindale

20 Rathmore Rd, Chelston TQ2 6NY
☎ 01803 293947
e–mail: rathmore@blueyonder.co.uk
web: www.colindalehotel.co.uk

dir: *From Torquay station 200yds on left in Rathmore Rd*

Having attractive, well-tended gardens, the Colindale is located in a
quiet area close to the seafront. It is an elegant establishment and
service is exemplary. Rooms, some with views over Torbay, are
comfortable and attractively co-ordinated. Memorable breakfasts are
enjoyed in the relaxing dining room.

Rooms 8 rms (6 en suite) (2 pri facs) **Facilities** TVB tea/coffee Cen ht
TVL Dinner Last d 10.30am Wi-fi available **Parking** 6 **Notes** ⊗
No children 12yrs Closed Dec

★★★★ GUEST ACCOMMODATION

Linden House

31 Bampfylde Rd TQ2 5AY
☎ 01803 212281
e–mail: lindenhouse.torquay@virgin.net
web: www.lindenhousetorquay.co.uk

dir: *Onto A3022, 1st left opposite playing fields*

This elegant Victorian building has been refurbished in a classic style
with soft neutral colours providing charm and elegance. An especially

warm welcome is provided by the enthusiastic proprietors. Bedrooms
and bathrooms provide a range of welcome extras and include a
garden room with its own patio. Delicious home-cooked dinners utilise
fresh local produce and are available by prior arrangement.

Linden House

Rooms 7 en suite (1 GF) S £50–£55; D £65–£80
Facilities FTV TVB tea/coffee Cen ht TVL Dinner Last d 3pm **Parking** 7
Notes LB ⊗ No children

★★★★ GUEST ACCOMMODATION

Meadfoot Bay Guest House

Meadfoot Sea Rd TQ1 2LQ
☎ 01803 294722 📄 01803 214473
e–mail: stay@meadfoot.com

dir: *A3022 to seafront, onto A379 & right onto Meadfoot Rd, 0.5m
on right*

This detached Victorian Villa dates from 1850 and was originally a
gentleman's residence. It's just a short stroll from Meadfoot Beach, the
town and the harbour. A number of the smart bedrooms have private
balconies or patios and ground floor rooms are also available. Public
areas offer high levels of comfort and quality with a choice of lounges,
and the elegant dining room where fresh local produce is utilised.
Outside, there are four lovely decked areas for relaxing with a drink.
Additional planned facilities include a fully equipped golfing studio.

Rooms 19 en suite (3 GF) S £32–£44; D £64–£148✱ **Facilities** FTV TVB
tea/coffee Cen ht TVL Wi-fi available **Parking** 14 **Notes** LB ⊗
No children 14yrs

★★★★ GUEST ACCOMMODATION

Millbrook House

1 Old Mill Rd, Chelston TQ2 6AP
☎ 01803 297394

The delightful, personally run Millbrook House is within easy walking
distance of Torquay's attractions and has a friendly and relaxed
atmosphere. The well-maintained bedrooms provide many useful
facilities; a king-size bed and a four-poster are available. There is a bar
on the lower ground floor with pool and darts and the garden has a
summer house for guests to relax in on hotter days.

Rooms 10 en suite (1 fmly) (2 GF) **Facilities** FTV TVB tea/coffee Cen ht
TVL Pool Table **Parking** 8 **Notes** ⊗ Closed Nov–Feb

CONTINUED

TORQUAY CONTINUED

★★★★ GUEST ACCOMMODATION
Ashfield Guest House

9 Scarborough Rd TQ2 5UJ

☎ 01803 293537

e–mail: enquiries@ashfieldguesthouse.co.uk

web: www.ashfieldguesthouse.co.uk

dir: *Torquay Seafront onto Belgrave Rd, 300mtrs turn right onto Scarborough Rd, 100mtrs on left*

On a quiet side street yet just a short walk from the bustling town centre, Ashfield Guest House offers comfortable bedrooms in a fine old mid terrace property. The house has been sympathetically restored in recent years and guests have the sole use of the large lounge and breakfasts are served at individual tables in the bright airy dining room.

Rooms 6 en suite (2 fmly) (2 GF) S £30–£35; D £55–£60 **Facilities** FTV TVB tea/coffee Cen ht TVL **Parking** 3 **Notes LB** ⊗ Closed Dec–Mar

★★★★ GUEST ACCOMMODATION
Aveland House

Aveland Rd, Babbacombe TQ1 3PT

☎ 01803 326622 🖷 01803 328940

e–mail: avelandhouse@aol.com

web: www.avelandhouse.co.uk

dir: *A379 into Babbacombe, off Babbacombe Rd onto Reddenhill Rd & right onto Cary Av, 2nd left*

Set in well-tended gardens in a peaceful area of Babbacombe, close to Cary Park, beaches, shops and attractions, Aveland House is within easy walking distance of Torquay harbour and town. This family-run house offers warm and attentive service. The attractive bedrooms are well equipped, and free Wi-fi is a feature. A pleasant bar and two comfortable lounges are available. Hearing-impaired visitors are especially welcome, as both the proprietors are OCSL signers. Evening meals and bar snacks are available by arrangement.

Rooms 10 en suite (3 fmly) S £30–£35; D £60–£70 **Facilities** tea/coffee Cen ht TVL Dinner Last d noon Wi-fi available **Parking** 10 **Notes LB** ⊗ RS Sun

★★★★ GUEST ACCOMMODATION
Babbacombe Hall

17 Manor Rd, Babbacombe TQ1 3JX

☎ 01803 325668 🖷 01803 325668

e–mail: glyn.aida.rees@lineone.net

dir: *A379 to Babbacombe, onto Manor Rd*

This family-run establishment offers friendly and attentive service. The bedrooms are very well equipped and decorated in colourful styles, and there are many useful facilities. Dinner is a varied menu of traditional and Oriental dishes freshly prepared by the resident proprietors.

Rooms 7 en suite D £52–£70✶ **Facilities** TVB tea/coffee Cen ht TVL Dinner Last d 4pm ⌁ **Parking** 7 **Notes LB** ⊗ No children 10yrs RS Mon

★★★★ GUEST HOUSE
Berkeley House

39 Babbacombe Downs Rd, Babbacombe TQ1 3LN

☎ 01803 322429

e–mail: reception@berkeleyhousetorquay.co.uk

dir: *A380 to Babbacombe, off Babbacombe Rd onto Princes St to seafront*

Warm and friendly hospitality awaits you at this very pleasant guest house, which is situated on the Babbacombe seafront. The bedrooms vary in size and style, but all are thoughtfully equipped. Three rooms including one on ground floor level, have sea views. Separate tables are provided in the dining room, where hearty breakfasts are served.

Rooms 5 en suite (1 fmly) (1 GF) S £40–£55; D £50–£65✶ **Facilities** TVB tea/coffee Cen ht Wi-fi available **Parking** 4 **Notes** ⊗ No children 5yrs No coaches

★★★★ GUEST ACCOMMODATION
Blue Conifer

Higher Downs Rd, The Seafront, Babbacombe TQ1 3LD

☎ 01803 327637

dir: *Signs for Babbacombe & seafront, premises 500yds from model village*

Surrounded by neat gardens and having splendid views across beaches to the bay, this attractive property provides a relaxed and friendly atmosphere. Bedrooms, many with sea views, are well-equipped and one is on the ground floor. A relaxing lounge and spacious car park are welcome additions.

Rooms 7 en suite (3 fmly) (1 GF) S £35–£41; D £54–£70✶ **Facilities** TVB tea/coffee Cen ht **Parking** 9 **Notes LB** Closed Nov–Feb ⊛

★★★★ GUEST HOUSE
Court Prior

St Lukes Rd South TQ2 5NZ

☎ 01803 292766

e–mail: courtprior@btconnect.com

dir: *A380 to Torquay, at Halfords right at lights onto Avenue Rd to seafront, left at next lights up Sheddon Hill, 2nd lights onto St Lukes Rd*

Located in a quiet residential area within walking distance of the seafront and town centre, this charming house, built in 1860, offers comfortable accommodation. Rooms are spacious, well decorated and pleasantly furnished throughout. Traditional home-made dishes are served at dinner. There is also a large comfortable lounge.

Rooms 10 en suite (3 fmly) (2 GF) S £27–£29; D £34–£58 **Facilities** FTV TVB tea/coffee Cen ht TVL Dinner Last d 4pm **Parking** 10 **Notes LB** ⊗ No children 12yrs No coaches

★★★★ GUEST ACCOMMODATION
Crown Lodge

83 Avenue Rd TQ2 5LH
☎ 01803 298772 📄 01803 291155
e–mail: john@www.crownlodgehotel.co.uk

dir: *A380 through Kingskerswell, over rbt & 3 lights, right at Torre station, 200yds on left*

Located within walking distance of the harbour and seafront and close to the town centre, Crown Lodge offers stylish and comfortable accommodation. Bedrooms have been appointed to a high standard, each individually furnished with flair. The ground floor rooms are suitable for disabled guests. Well-cooked breakfasts are a delight.

Rooms 6 en suite (1 fmly) (2 GF) S £30–£59; D £49–£79✷
Facilities FTV TVB tea/coffee Cen ht Dinner Last d at breakfast Wi-fi available **Parking** 7 **Notes LB** ⊗ No children 9yrs

★★★★ GUEST ACCOMMODATION
Glenorleigh

26 Cleveland Rd TQ2 5BE
☎ 01803 292135 📄 01803 213717
e–mail: glenorleighhotel@btinternet.com
web: www.glenorleigh.co.uk

dir: *A380 from Newton Abbot onto A3022, at Torre station lights right onto Avenue Rd & 1st left, across 1st junct, 200yds on right*

Located in a residential area, the Glenorleigh provides a range of smart bedrooms, some on the ground floor. With facilities such as a solarium, an outdoor pool and terrace, and a convivial bar, this family-run establishment is ideal for leisure or business.

Rooms 15 rms (14 en suite) (6 fmly) (7 GF) S £30–£40; D £60–£80✷
Facilities TVB tea/coffee Cen ht TVL Dinner Last d 2pm ⌇ Solarium Pool Table **Parking** 10 **Notes LB** ⊗

★★★★ 🏠 GUEST HOUSE
Headland View

37 Babbacombe Seafront, Babbacombe TQ1 3LN
☎ 01803 312612
e–mail: reception@headlandview.com
web: www.headlandview.com

dir: *A379 S to Babbacombe, off Babbacombe Rd left onto Portland Rd & Babbacombe Downs Rd & seafront*

There are spectacular views of the bay and the Downs from the lounge and many of the bedrooms of Headland View. The attentive proprietors offer a friendly welcome, and several of the attractive bedrooms have balconies. Breakfast is memorable for the well-cooked quality ingredients.

Rooms 6 rms (4 en suite) (2 pri facs) S £40–£50; D £64–£68✷
Facilities TVB tea/coffee Cen ht TVL Wi-fi available **Parking** 4
Notes LB ⊗ No children 5yrs No coaches Closed Nov -Feb ◉

★★★★ 🍽 GUEST HOUSE
Kingsholm

539 Babbacombe Rd TQ1 1HQ
☎ 01803 297794
e–mail: enquiries@kingsholmhotel.co.uk

dir: *A3022 left onto Torquay seafront, left at clock tower rdbt, Kingsholm 400mtrs on left*

Guests will no doubt enjoy the friendly and welcoming atmosphere created here by the resident proprietors. A range of well furnished and decorated bedrooms and bathrooms provide guests with plenty of comfort and quality. A relaxing guest lounge, small bar area and car park to the rear are all welcome features. Dinner featuring seasonal, home cooking is available by prior arrangement and should not be missed.

Rooms 9 en suite S £27–£35; D £54–£70✷ **Facilities** FTV TVB tea/coffee Licensed Cen ht Dinner Last d 12 noon **Parking** 4 **Notes LB** No coaches No children 10yrs

ENGLAND

★★★★ GUEST ACCOMMODATION
Riviera Lodge

26 Croft Rd TQ2 5UE

☎ 01803 209309 📠 0560 1136425

e–mail: stay@rivieralodgehotel.co.uk

This establishment offers a relaxed atmosphere within walking distance of the promenade, shopping centre and the many attractions. Bedrooms vary in size, with the best use being made of available space; all rooms are well equipped. There is a spacious bar and lounge area and dinner, by arrangement, offers a choice of dishes.

Rooms 21 en suite (1 GF) S £35–£45; D £66–£79✳ **Facilities** TVB tea/coffee Cen ht TVL Dinner Last d 7.30pm Wi-fi available ⤢ **Parking** 20 **Notes LB** ⊗ No children 14yrs

★★★★ GUEST ACCOMMODATION
Summerlands

19 Belgrave Rd TQ2 5HU

☎ 01803 299844

e–mail: summerlands@blueyonder.co.uk

web: www.summerlandsguesthousetorquay.co.uk

dir: *A3022 onto Newton Rd, towards seafront and town centre, onto Belgrave Rd, Summerlands on left, just past T-lights*

Friendliness is the key word in this stylish guest house, which is situated within walking distance of the town centre and the seafront. Well-appointed bedrooms are individually designed and equipped with a range of thoughtful guest accessories. Freshly prepared breakfasts are served in the attractively decorated dining room and there is also a comfortable lounge.

Rooms 7 en suite (2 fmly) (1 GF) S £25–£35; D £45–£55✳ **Facilities** TVB tea/coffee Cen ht TVL Dinner Last d noon **Parking** 4 **Notes** ⊗

★★★★ 🅰 GUEST HOUSE
Grosvenor House

Falkland Rd TQ2 5JP

☎ 01803 294110

e–mail: aa@grosvenorhousehotel.co.uk

dir: *From Newton Abbot to Torquay, at Torre station right by Halfords, left at 2nd lights onto Falkland Rd*

Rooms 10 en suite (4 fmly) (3 GF) S fr £35; D fr £55✳ **Facilities** FTV TVB tea/coffee Licensed Cen ht TVL Dinner Last d 4.30pm Wi-fi available **Parking** 7 **Notes LB** ⊗ Closed Oct–Etr

★★★★ 🅰 GUEST ACCOMMODATION
The Westgate

Falkland Rd TQ2 5JP

☎ 01803 295350 📠 01803 213710

e–mail: stay@westgatehotel.co.uk

dir: *A380 to Torquay, at A3022 junct sharp left onto Falkland Rd, 300yds on left*

Rooms 10 en suite (2 fmly) (1 GF) S £29.50–£49.50; D £59–£89✳ **Facilities** FTV TVB tea/coffee Cen ht TVL Dinner Last d 2pm Wi-fi available **Parking** 10 **Notes LB** ⊗ No children 5yrs

★★★ GUEST ACCOMMODATION
Stover Lodge

29 Newton Rd TQ2 5DB

☎ 01803 297287 📠 01803 297287

e–mail: enquiries@stoverlodge.co.uk

web: www.stoverlodge.co.uk

dir: *Signs to Torquay town centre, at station/Halfords left lane, Lodge on left after lights*

Located close to the town centre, the family-run Stover Lodge is relaxed and friendly. Children and babies are welcome, and a cot and high chair can be provided on request. Hearty breakfasts, with a vegetarian option, are served in the dining room. There is a garden to enjoy in summer.

Rooms 9 rms (8 en suite) (1 pri facs) (3 fmly) (2 GF) S £25–£40; D £48–£56✳ **Facilities** FTV TVB tea/coffee Cen ht Wi-fi available **Parking** 10 **Notes LB** ⊗ `

★★★ GUEST ACCOMMODATION
Abberley House

100 Windsor Rd, Babbacombe TQ1 1SU

☎ 01803 392787

e–mail: stay@abberleyguesthouse.co.uk

web: www.abberleyguesthouse.co.uk

dir: *A38, A380, B3199 to Plainmoor, turn onto Warbro Rd, right onto Hingston Rd, left onto Windsor Rd*

Quietly located in a residential area, Abberley House is just a ten to fifteen minute walk from either the town centre or Babbacombe Downs. The friendly proprietors offer a warm welcome, alongside comfortable bedrooms in a variety of sizes with some ground floor rooms available. Carefully prepared, home-cooked dinners are offered by prior arrangement.

Rooms 7 en suite (1 fmly) (2 GF) **Facilities** TVB tea/coffee Cen ht TVL Dinner Last d 10am Wi-fi available

★★★ GUEST HOUSE
Ashleigh House

61 Meadfoot Ln TQ1 2BP
☎ 01803 294660
e–mail: dawnsmale@btinternet.com
web: www.ashleighhousetorquay.co.uk

Quietly located in a residential area of Torquay, and only a five minute downhill walk from the town or harbour, this pleasant accommodation includes roadside permit parking. Relaxed and friendly hospitality is provided and guests are welcome to use the large, well furnished lounge. Bedrooms offer a range of shapes and sizes and include some useful extras. A carefully prepared breakfast is served in the bright, comfortable dining room.

Rooms 4 rms (3 en suite) (1 pri facs) (3 fmly) **Facilities** TVB tea/coffee Cen ht TVL Dinner Last d 11am **Notes** ⊛

★★★ GUEST ACCOMMODATION
Atlantis

68 Belgrave Rd TQ2 5HY
☎ 01803 292917 🖹 01803 292917
e–mail: info@atlantishotel.freeserve.co.uk

dir: *Signs to Torquay seafront, turn left, left at lights onto Belgrave Rd, over next lights, premises on left*

Convenient for the beach, theatre and conference centre, the Atlantis offers a thoughtfully equipped home-from-home. There is a well-stocked bar and a comfortable lounge, and the hearty breakfasts in the dining room are a tasty start to the day.

Rooms 11 rms (9 en suite) (7 fmly) **Facilities** TVB tea/coffee Cen ht TVL **Parking** 3 **Notes** ⊛

★★★ GUEST ACCOMMODATION
Briarfields

84–86 Avenue Rd TQ2 5LF
☎ 01803 297844
e–mail: briarfields@aol.com

dir: *Exeter to Torquay on A380 on to A3022. Past Torre Station 400yds on right.*

Briarfields is conveniently located and is a short walk from the seafront and all the main tourist attractions. Bedrooms are comfortable, well equipped and thoughtfully furnished. Guests can also make use of the sun terrace at the rear of the property and soak up the early evening sun. Breakfasts are served at individual tables in the main dining room and a warm welcome is guaranteed.

Rooms 9 en suite (5 fmly) **Facilities** FTV TVB tea/coffee Cen ht **Parking** 9

★★★ GUEST ACCOMMODATION
Doogals

74 Belgrave Rd TQ2 5HY
☎ 01803 295966 🖹 01803 295966
e–mail: skey@sky.com

dir: *Town centre signs, pass police station on right, through small shopping area, premises on right*

This privately owned and personally run guest house is convenient for the town centre and attractions. It provides friendly hospitality and well-equipped accommodation, which includes family rooms and bedrooms on the ground floor.

Rooms 7 en suite (2 fmly) (3 GF) S £25–£35; D £50–£70✳
Facilities FTV TVB tea/coffee Cen ht TVL Dinner Last d noon **Parking** 4 **Notes** LB ⊛

★★★ GUEST ACCOMMODATION
Mariners Guest House

35 Belgrave Rd TQ2 5HX
☎ 01803 291604
e–mail: marinersguesthouse@btinternet.com
web: www.marinerstorquay.co.uk

dir: *A380 onto A3022 to seafront, left onto Belgrave Rd, left at lights onto Lucius St, then 1st left*

This personally run guest house provides friendly hospitality and willing service. It is within easy reach of the town centre, and the modern bedrooms are being refurbished to a good standard. Separate tables are provided in the attractive breakfast room.

Rooms 7 en suite (2 fmly) (2 GF) S £25–£35; D £45–£65✳
Facilities TVB tea/coffee Cen ht **Parking** 4 **Notes** LB ⊛

TORQUAY CONTINUED

★★★ GUEST ACCOMMODATION
Newton House

31 Newton Rd, Torre TQ2 5DB
☎ 01803 297520 📠 01803 297520
e-mail: newtonhouse_torquay@yahoo.com
web: www.newtonhouse-tq.co.uk

dir: *From Torre station bear left at lights, Newton House 40yds on left*

You are assured of a warm welcome at Newton House, which is close to the town centre and attractions. The comfortable bedrooms, some at ground level, have thoughtful extras, and a lounge is available. Breakfast is enjoyed in the pleasant dining room.

Rooms 9 en suite (3 fmly) (5 GF) S £29–£52; D £48–£64 **Facilities** TVB tea/coffee Cen ht Wi-fi available **Parking** 15 **Notes** LB ⊗

★★★ GUEST ACCOMMODATION
Silverlands B & B

27 Newton Rd TQ2 5DB
☎ 01803 292013
e-mail: enquiries@silverlandsguesthouse.co.uk
web: www.silverlandsguesthouse.co.uk

dir: *A380 onto A3022 for Torquay, premises on left after Torre station lights*

Convenient for the town centre and the beaches, this friendly establishment has a homely atmosphere. Some of the well-presented bedrooms are on the ground floor, and a hearty, freshly cooked breakfast is served in the dining room.

Rooms 9 rms (7 en suite) (2 pri facs) (3 fmly) (4 GF) (9 smoking) S £20–£28; D £50–£56✱ **Facilities** TVB tea/coffee Cen ht **Parking** 10 **Notes** LB ⊗

★★★ GUEST ACCOMMODATION
Tyndale

68 Avenue Rd TQ2 5LF
☎ 01803 380888

dir: *A380 onto A3022, pass Torre station onto Avenue Rd, 1st lights right onto Old Mill Rd & right into car park*

Close to the seaside attractions and the town centre, this neatly presented house is only a short level walk from the railway station. Bedrooms are brightly decorated in a range of sizes. A comfortable CONTINUED

lounge is provided and a freshly cooked, traditional British breakfast is served in the dining room.

Rooms 3 en suite (1 GF) D £36 **Facilities** FTV TVB tea/coffee Cen ht TVL **Parking** 5 **Notes** LB ⊗ ⊜

Ⓤ
Burleigh House

25 Newton Rd TQ2 5DB
☎ 01803 291557
e-mail: enquiry@burleigh-house.co.uk

dir: *A380, at Torre station, bear left at lights, 4th guest house on left*

At the time of going to press the rating for this establishment had not been confirmed. Please check the AA website www.theAA.com for up-to-date information.

Rooms 8 rms (6 en suite) (4 GF) S £25–£27; D £50–£54✱ **Facilities** TVB tea/coffee Cen ht Wi-fi available **Parking** 8 **Notes** ⊗ No children

---

TOTNES   MAP 03 SX86

★★★★ ⊜ INN
Durant Arms

Ashprington TQ9 7UP
☎ 01803 732240
e-mail: info@thedurantarms.com
web: www.thedurantarms.com

dir: *A381 from Totnes for Kingsbridge, 1m left for Ashprington*

This delightful inn, the focal point of the picturesque village of Ashprington, offers comfortable bedrooms in the main building or annexe, which are very well appointed and attractively decorated. A range of carefully prepared dishes from blackboard menus can be enjoyed in the character bar or dining room and local ales, juices and wines also feature.

Rooms 3 en suite 5 annexe en suite (2 GF) S £50; D £80✱ **Facilities** TV4B tea/coffee Cen ht TVL Dinner Last d 9.15pm **Conf** Max 20 Board 15 **Parking** 8 **Notes** LB ⊗ No children Closed 25–26 Dec evenings

★★★★ GUEST HOUSE
The Old Forge at Totnes

Seymour Place TQ9 5AY
☎ 01803 862174
e–mail: enq@oldforgetotnes.com

dir: *From Totnes town centre cross river bridge & 2nd right*

Over 600 years old, this delightful property is close to the town centre and Steamer Quay. A range of bedroom styles is offered from spacious suites to cosy cottage-style. All are thoughtfully equipped with numerous extras. Public areas include a conservatory complete with hot tub, which overlooks the garden. Breakfast is a leisurely and enjoyable affair, served in the pleasantly appointed dining room.

Rooms 10 rms (9 en suite) (1 pri facs) (2 fmly) (2 GF) S £47–£72; D £64–£88✱ **Facilities** TVB tea/coffee Licensed Cen ht Wi-fi available **Parking** 7 **Notes** LB ⊗ No coaches

★★★★ ⊜ INN
Steam Packet Inn

St Peter's Quay TQ9 5EW
☎ 01803 863880 ▤ 01803 862754
e–mail: steampacket@buccaneer.co.uk
web: www.steampacketinn.co.uk

dir: *Off A38 at Totnes to Dartington & Totnes. Over 1st lights, pass railway station, signs for town centre at next rdbt. Over mini-rdbt, River Dart on left, inn 100yds on left*

This friendly and popular riverside inn offers a warm welcome to visitors and locals alike. Complete with its own quay, the inn has a long history. Public areas offer a choice of dining options, including the extensive waterside patio. Bedrooms are well equipped and comfortable and some have river views. Choices at lunch and dinner offer interesting and well-cooked dishes, while breakfast provides a satisfying start to the day.

Rooms 4 en suite (1 fmly) S £59.50; D £79.50✱ **Facilities** TVB tea/coffee Cen ht Dinner Last d 9pm **Parking** 15 **Notes** LB ⊗ No coaches

WESTWARD HO! MAP 03 SS42

★★★ GUEST HOUSE
Culloden House

Fosketh Hill EX39 1UL
☎ 01237 479421
e–mail: enquiry@culloden-house.co.uk
web: www.culloden-house.co.uk

dir: *S of town centre. Off B3236 Stanwell Hill onto Fosketh Hill*

A warm welcome is assured in this family-friendly Victorian property stands on a wooded hillside with sweeping views over the beach and coast. Guests can relax in the spacious lounge with its log-burning fire and enjoy the wonderful sea views.

Rooms 5 en suite (3 fmly) (1 GF) **Facilities** TVB tea/coffee Cen ht TVL **Parking** available **Notes** No coaches Closed Xmas

WHIMPLE MAP 03 SY09

★★★★ Ⓐ BED & BREAKFAST
Strete Ralegh Farm

EX5 2PP
☎ 01404 822464 ▤ 01404 822464
e–mail: info@streteraleghfarm.co.uk

dir: *A30 onto B3180 towards Exmouth. 1st right, 1st right again, farmhouse 0.25m*

Rooms 3 rms (2 en suite) (1 pri facs) S £40–£50; D £60–£70✱ **Facilities** tea/coffee Cen ht TVL Dinner Last d 24hrs **Parking** 3 **Notes** LB ⊛

WIDECOMBE IN THE MOOR   MAP 03 SX77

★★★ BED & BREAKFAST
Manor Cottage

TQ13 7TB

☎ 01364 621218

dir: *A382 to Bovey Tracey, left onto B3387 to Widecombe, cottage with Post Office*

Located in the centre of the historic village, this attractive cottage stands in a large and pleasant garden and has a lot of character. It offers friendly hospitality and spacious and comfortable bedrooms. Breakfast is served in the cosy dining room and features good home cooking using fresh local produce.

Rooms 3 rms (1 en suite) D £50–£60✳ **Facilities** TV2B tea/coffee Cen ht **Parking** 3 **Notes** ⊗ No children 15yrs Closed Xmas ⊛

WOOLACOMBE   MAP 03 SS44

★★★★ GUEST ACCOMMODATION
The Castle

The Esplanade EX34 7DJ

☎ 01271 870788 📠 01271 870812

e–mail: the.castlehotel@amserve.net

dir: *A361 from Barnstaple to Ilfracombe, turn right at Woolacombe sign*

Built in 1898 in the style of a castle, this Victorian stone folly has stunning views over the bay. The attractively decorated bedrooms are comfortable and well equipped. The lounge has a carved-wood ceiling and interesting panelling. There is also a lounge-bar, and breakfast is served in the elegant dining room.

Rooms 8 en suite (2 fmly) S £34–£37; D £68–£74✳ **Facilities** TVB tea/coffee Cen ht TVL **Parking** 8 **Notes** ⊗ No children 5yrs Closed Oct–Mar

---

YELVERTON   MAP 03 SX56

★★★★ ☕ GUEST ACCOMMODATION
Harrabeer Country House

Harrowbeer Ln PL20 6EA

☎ 01822 853302

e–mail: reception@harrabeer.co.uk

web: www.harrabeer.co.uk

dir: *In village. Off A386 Tavistock Rd onto Grange Rd, right onto Harrowbeer Ln*

A warm welcome awaits you at this historic Devon longhouse situated on the edge of Dartmoor. Providing an excellent base for exploring this beautiful area, the accommodation has all the expected modern comforts with a lounge, bar and dining room overlooking the garden. There are also two self-catering units. Dinners are available by arrangement with special diets catered for.

Rooms 6 rms (5 en suite) (1 pri facs) (2 fmly) (1 GF) S £55–£80; D £65–£95 **Facilities** TVB tea/coffee Direct dial from bedrooms Cen ht TVL Dinner Last d 9am Wi-fi available **Conf** Max 20 Board 20 **Parking** 10 **Notes** Closed 3rd wk Dec, 2nd wk Jan

---

★★★★ 🅰 GUEST HOUSE
Overcombe House

Old Station Rd, Horrabridge PL20 7RA

☎ 01822 853501 📠 01822 853602

e–mail: enquiries@overcombehotel.co.uk

web: www.overcombehotel.co.uk

dir: *Signed 100yds off A386 at Horrabridge*

Rooms 8 en suite (2 GF) S £39.50–£45; D £70–£80 **Facilities** TVB tea/coffee Licensed Cen ht TVL Wi-fi available **Parking** 7 **Notes** ⊗ No children 5yrs No coaches Closed 25 Dec

---

DORSET

ABBOTSBURY   MAP 04 SY58

★★★ FARM HOUSE
East Farm House *(SY578853)*

2 Rosemary Ln DT3 4JN

☎ 01305 871363 📠 01305 871363 Mrs W M Wood

e–mail: wendy@eastfarmhouse.co.uk

web: www.eastfarmhouse.co.uk

dir: *B3157 W into Abbotsbury, Swan Inn on left, farmhouse 1st right onto Rosemary Ln*

This unspoiled and charming farmhouse is in the centre of the pretty village and has been in the owner's family since 1729. The house has a homely atmosphere, traditionally furnished with much character, and filled with memorabilia. Hearty breakfasts are served in the lounge-dining room, where a log fire burns in winter.

Rooms 3 en suite **Facilities** TVB tea/coffee Cen ht Dinner Last d breakfast **Parking** 3 **Notes** No children 14yrs 20 acres Horse stud, rare breed pigs

---

ASKERSWELL   MAP 04 SY59

★★★★ INN
The Spyway Inn

DT2 9EP

☎ 01308 485250 📠 01308 485250

e–mail: tim.wilkes@btconnect.com

dir: *A35, turn signed Askerswell, follow Spyway Inn sign*

Peacefully located in the rolling Dorset countryside, this family-run inn offers a warm and genuine welcome to all. Bedrooms are spacious and well appointed with a number of extras provided, including bath robes. Real ales are on tap in the bar, where locals congregate to put the world to rights. Menus feature home cooked food with many dishes utilising local produce both at dinner and breakfast. The extensive beer garden is popular in summer with wonderful views a bonus.

Rooms 3 en suite (1 fmly) D £50–£80✳ **Facilities** TVB tea/coffee Cen ht Dinner Last d 9pm **Parking** 40 **Notes** LB ⊗

BEAMINSTER

MAP 04 ST40

★★★★★ Ⓐ FARM HOUSE
Watermeadow House *(ST535001)*

Bridge Farm, Hooke DT8 3PD

☎ 01308 862619 📄 01308 862619 Mrs P M Wallbridge

e–mail: enquiries@watermeadowhouse.co.uk

web: www.watermeadowhouse.co.uk

dir: *3m E of Beaminster. In Hooke village*

Rooms 2 rms (1 en suite) (1 pri facs) (1 fmly) S £30–£40; D £60–£65✳ **Facilities** TVB tea/coffee Cen ht **Parking** 6 **Notes** LB ⊗ 280 acres dairy beef Closed Nov–Mar

---

BLANDFORD FORUM

MAP 04 ST80

Premier Collection

★★★★★ BED & BREAKFAST
Portman Lodge

Whitecliff Mill St DT11 7BP

☎ 01258 453727 📄 01258 453727

e–mail: enquiries@portmanlodge.co.uk

dir: *On NW end of Blandford's one-way system, to access follow signs from town centre to Shaftesbury & hospital*

Built in the Victorian period and once used as a music school, this house now provides elegant accommodation and a genuinely warm welcome. Carefully decorated and adorned with artefacts and pictures from the proprietors' extensive travels, the public rooms are spacious and inviting. A delicious breakfast is prepared with skill and served at a communal table. Dinner is available by prior arrangement.

Rooms 3 en suite **Facilities** TVB tea/coffee Cen ht Dinner Last d noon Wi-fi available **Parking** 6 **Notes** ⊗ No children 10yrs

★★★★ INN
The Anvil Inn

Salisbury Rd, Pimperne DT11 8UQ

☎ 01258 453431 📄 01258 480182

e–mail: theanvil.inn@btconnect.com

dir: *2m NE of Blandford on A354 in Pimperne*

Located in a village near Blandford, this 16th-century thatched inn provides a traditional country welcome with plenty of character.

CONTINUED

Bedrooms have been refurbished to high standards. Dinner is a varied selection of home-made dishes with a tempting variety of hand-pulled ales and wines by the glass.

Rooms 12 en suite S £75–£80; D £100–£130✳ **Facilities** STV TVB tea/coffee Direct dial from bedrooms Cen ht Dinner Last d 9.30pm **Parking** 18 **Notes** LB No coaches

See advert on this page

★★★★ BED & BREAKFAST
St Martin's House

Whitecliff Mill St DT11 7BP

☎ 01258 451245 & 07748 887719

e–mail: info@stmartinshouse.co.uk

dir: *Off Market Pl onto Salisbury St & left onto White Cliff Mill St, on right before traffic island*

Dating from 1866, this restored property was once part of the chorister's house for a local church. The bedrooms are comfortable and well equipped. The hosts offer warm hospitality and attentive service. Breakfast, which features local and home-made items, is enjoyed around a communal table. Carefully prepared dinners are available by arrangement.

Rooms 2 rms (2 pri facs) (1 fmly) S £45–£50; D £65–£70✳ **Facilities** TVB tea/coffee Cen ht Dinner Last d 24hrs before Wi-fi available **Parking** 3 **Notes** Closed 22 Dec–6 Jan ⊛

ENGLAND

★★★ BED & BREAKFAST
The Old Bakery
Church Rd, Pimperne DT11 8UB
☎ 01258 455173 & 07799 853784
e–mail: jjtanners@hotmail.com
web: www.theoldbakerydorset.co.uk
dir: *2m NE of Blandford. Off A354 into Pimperne village*
Dating from 1890 and once, as the name suggests, the village bakery, this family home offers comfortable accommodation in a convenient location. Popular with business travellers, families can also be accommodated, with cots available. Substantial breakfasts featuring home-made bread and marmalade are served in the dining room.

Rooms 3 en suite (1 GF) **Facilities** TVB tea/coffee Cen ht TVL Dinner Last d 9am **Parking** 2 **Notes** ✉

★★★ FARM HOUSE
Pennhills Farmhouse *(ST819101)*
Sandy Ln, Shillingstone DT11 0TF
☎ 01258 860491 Mrs Watts
dir: *6.5m NW of Blandford. Off A357 at Shillingstone Post Office onto Gunn Ln, bear right to T-junct, left onto Lanchard Ln, signed*
Located in a quiet setting with far views over the surrounding countryside, this delightful, family-run farmhouse provides spacious rooms. The substantial English breakfast consists of home-produced items, served house-party style around one large table in the lounge-dining room, where an open fire burns during the winter.

Rooms 2 en suite (1 fmly) (1 GF) **Facilities** TVB tea/coffee Cen ht TVL **Notes** ⊗ 120 acres mixed Closed 22 Dec–3 Jan ✉

BOURNEMOUTH
MAP 05 SZ09

Premier Collection

★★★★★ GUEST ACCOMMODATION
The Balincourt
58 Christchurch Rd BH1 3PF
☎ 01202 552962 🖹 01202 552962
e–mail: rooms@balincourt.co.uk
web: www.balincourt.co.uk
dir: *On A35 between Lansdowne & Boscombe Gardens, opp Lynton Court pub*
The friendly Balincourt offers high standards of accommodation within easy reach of the town centre and beaches. Bedrooms are individually decorated and equipped with a host of thoughtful extras. There is a lounge and bar, and freshly prepared evening meals are available in the attractive dining room.

Rooms 12 en suite S £50–£90; D £80–£100✱ **Facilities** TVB tea/coffee Cen ht TVL Dinner Last d 4pm **Conf** Max 20 **Parking** 11 **Notes** LB ⊗ No children 16yrs Closed Xmas

★★★★ GUEST ACCOMMODATION
Fenn Lodge
11 Rosemount Rd, Alum Chine BH4 8HB
☎ 01202 761273 🖹 01202 761273
e–mail: fennlodge@btconnect.com
web: www.fennlodge.co.uk
dir: *A338 into Poole, at rdbt onto B3065 signed Alum Chime & Sandbanks. Left at lights, right at rdbt onto Alumhurst Rd, 3rd left onto Rosemount Rd*

Located within walking distance of Alum Chine and the beach, this stylish accommodation is friendly and relaxed. The hosts ensure their guests are well cared for and provide many thoughtful extras. Bournemouth and Poole are just a short drive away. Guests have use of an elegant comfortable lounge.

Rooms 11 rms (10 en suite) (1 pri facs) (1 fmly) (1 GF) S £24–£30; D £48–£60✱ **Facilities** TVB tea/coffee Cen ht TVL Wi-fi available **Parking** 6 **Notes** LB ⊗ Closed Nov–mid Mar

★★★★ GUEST HOUSE
Fielden Court
20 Southern Rd, Southbourne BH6 3SR
☎ 01202 427459 🖹 01202 427459
e–mail: enquiries@fieldencourthotel.co.uk
dir: *A338 onto A3060, at 2nd rdbt onto Christchurch Rd, left at lights, right onto Chestnut Av & Southern Rd*
This delightful guest house is close to the lift to the beach and provides comfortable, well-equipped bedrooms. There is a cosy guest lounge, breakfast is served in the airy dining room, and home-cooked evening meals are available by arrangement.

Rooms 7 en suite (1 fmly) **Facilities** TVB tea/coffee Cen ht TVL Dinner Last d 10am **Parking** 5 **Notes** ⊗

★★★★ BED & BREAKFAST
The Maples
1 Library Rd, Winton BH9 2QH
☎ 01202 529820
e–mail: jeffreyhurrell@yahoo.co.uk
dir: *1.5m N of town centre. Off A3060 Castle Ln West onto Wimborne Rd, The Maples 1m on right after police station*
A warm welcome awaits you at the Maples, which is just off Winton High Street. The atmosphere is friendly and bedrooms are quiet,

CONTINUED

comfortable and equipped with considerate extras. Breakfast is enjoyed in the pleasant dining room around a communal table.

Rooms 2 en suite (1 fmly) S £25–£30; D £50–£60 **Facilities** FTV TVB tea/coffee Cen ht **Parking** 2 **Notes** ⊛ No children 7yrs ⊜

★★★★ GUEST ACCOMMODATION
Newlands

14 Rosemount Rd, Alum Chine BH4 8HB
☎ 01202 761922 📠 01202 769872
e–mail: newlandshotel@totalise.co.uk
web: www.newlandshotel.com

dir: *A338/A35 to Liverpool Victoria rdb, exit for Alum Chine, left at lights, right at small rdbt onto Alumhurst Rd, 3rd left*

A warm welcome is guaranteed at this attractive Edwardian house which is in a quiet area near Alum Chine beach and within easy driving distance of Bournemouth and Poole centres. Offering comfortable accommodation with Wi-fi and a guest lounge.

Rooms 8 en suite (3 fmly) S £26–£35; D £52–£70 **Facilities** TVB tea/coffee Cen ht Wi-fi available **Parking** 8 **Notes** LB ⊛ Closed Dec & Jan

★★★★ GUEST ACCOMMODATION
The Thanet

2 Drury Rd, Alum Chine BH4 8HA
☎ 01202 761135
e–mail: thanethotel@hotmail.com

dir: *Signs for Alum Chine Beach. On corner of Alumhurst Rd & Drury Rd*

A warm welcome is assured at this delightful Edwardian house, located within easy walking distance of fashionable Westbourne and Alum Chine Beach. The bedrooms are filled with many homely extras. A lounge is also available. Imaginative dinners and comprehensive breakfasts are served in the attractive dining room.

Rooms 8 rms (5 en suite) (1 fmly) **Facilities** FTV TVB tea/coffee Cen ht Dinner Last d 4pm **Parking** 6 **Notes** ⊛ No children 7yrs Closed Nov–Mar

★★★★ GUEST HOUSE
Westcotes House

9 Southbourne Overcliff Dr, Southbourne BH6 3TE
☎ 01202 428512 📠 01202 428512
web: www.westcoteshousehotel.co.uk

dir: *2m E of town centre. A35 onto B3059, turn down Grand Av continue to end and turn right, house on right*

The refurbished Westcotes House has spectacular views across Poole Bay. Situated on the quiet side of the town, it has well-equipped bedrooms, with one on the ground floor. There is a conservatory lounge, and enjoyable home-cooked dinners are available by arrangement.

Rooms 6 en suite (1 GF) S £44–£48; D £64–£74✳ **Facilities** TVB tea/coffee Cen ht TVL Dinner Last d 5pm **Parking** 6 **Notes** ⊛ No children 10yrs No coaches ⊜

★★★★ GUEST ACCOMMODATION
Wood Lodge

10 Manor Rd, East Cliff BH1 3EY
☎ 01202 290891 📠 01202 290892
e–mail: enquiries@woodlodgehotel.co.uk
web: www.woodlodgehotel.co.uk

dir: *A338 to St Pauls rdbt, 1st exit left. Straight over next 2 rdbts, immediate left*

Expect a warm welcome from this family-run guest house. Set in beautiful gardens minutes from the seafront and a 10 minute walk from the town centre. Bedrooms, which vary in size, are well presented. Home-cooked evening meals and hearty breakfasts are served in the smart dining room.

Rooms 15 rms (14 en suite) (1 pri facs) (1 fmly) (4 GF) S £34–£55; D £68–£110 **Facilities** TVB tea/coffee Cen ht TVL Dinner Last d 1pm Wi-fi available ⏃ ⏂ Use of pools, jacuzzi and sauna at nearby hotel **Conf** Max 30 **Parking** 12 **Notes** LB

ENGLAND

★★★★ GUEST HOUSE
The Woodside
29 Southern Rd BH6 3SR
☎ 01202 427213 📠 01202 427213
e-mail: enquiries@woodsidehotel.co.uk

dir: *Follow A35 from Bournemouth. Take B3059 at Pokesdown Station. Right at Boots. Straight on to Southern Rd*

Well located with some off street parking The Woodside offers comfortable rooms and is run by friendly hosts. Dinner is available by prior arrangement and is served in a light, airy dining room.

Rooms 7 rms (6 en suite) (1 pri facs) S £30–£40; D £56–£70 **Facilities** FTV TVB tea/coffee Licensed Cen ht Dinner Last d 1pm Wi-fi available **Parking** 5 **Notes LB** ⊗ No children 16yrs

★★★★ 🅰 BED & BREAKFAST
Blue Palms
26 Tregonwell Rd, West Cliff BH2 5NS
☎ 01202 554968 📠 01202 294197
e-mail: bluepalmshotel@btopenworld.com
web: www.bluepalmshotel.com

dir: *Off A338 at Bournemouth West rdbt signed town centre, Triangle, next rdbt onto Durley Chine Rd, at rdbt onto West Hill Rd, Tregonwell Rd 3rd left*

Rooms 10 en suite (2 fmly) (2 GF) S £35–£42; D £60–£74 **Facilities** FTV TVB tea/coffee Cen ht TVL Wi-fi available **Parking** 8 **Notes LB**

★★★★ 🅰 GUEST ACCOMMODATION
Cransley
11 Knyveton Rd, East Cliff BH1 3QG
☎ 01202 290067 📠 07092 381721
e-mail: info@cransley.com
web: www.cransley.com

dir: *Off A338 at St Pauls rdbt by ASDA store, over next rdbt, Knyveton Rd 1st left*

Rooms 11 rms (10 en suite) (1 pri facs) (2 GF) S £35–£40; D £70–£80✳ **Facilities** FTV TVB tea/coffee Cen ht TVL Wi-fi available **Parking** 8 **Notes** ⊗ No children 14yrs Closed Xmas & New Year

★★★ GUEST ACCOMMODATION
Denewood
1 Percy Rd, Boscombe BH5 1JE
☎ 01202 394493 & 309913 📠 01202 391155
e-mail: info@denewood.co.uk

dir: *500yds NE of Boscombe Pier, signed*

Located within walking distance of the beach and Boscombe shopping centre, and close to Bournemouth centre, the Denewood offers individually decorated bedrooms. A full English breakfast is served at individual tables in the delightful dining room. The beauty salon is perfect for a little indulgence.

Rooms 10 en suite (3 fmly) S £25–£38; D £50–£74✳ **Facilities** STV TVB tea/coffee Cen ht TVL Solarium health & beauty salon **Parking** 14 **Notes LB**

★★★ GUEST ACCOMMODATION
Pinedale
40 Tregonwell Rd, West Cliff BH2 5NT
☎ 01202 553733 & 292702 📠 01202 553733
e-mail: thepinedalehotel@btconnect.com

dir: *A338 at Bournemouth West rdbt, signs to West Cliff, Tregonwell Rd is 3rd left after passing Wessex Hotel*

This friendly guest accommodation is enthusiastically run by two generations of the same family, and offers comfortable accommodation within a short walk of the seafront and local attractions. The fresh-looking bedrooms are equipped with useful extras. There is also an attractive licensed bar and an airy dining room where you can enjoy wholesome home-cooked meals.

Rooms 15 rms (9 en suite) (1 fmly) S £19–£37; D £38–£78✳ **Facilities** TVB tea/coffee Direct dial from bedrooms TVL Dinner Last d 3pm Wi-fi available **Parking** 15 **Notes** ⊗

★★★ 🅰 INN
Commodore
Overcliff Dr, Southbourne BH6 3TD
☎ 01202 423150 📠 01202 423519
e-mail: 7688@greeneking.co.uk
web: www.thecommodore.co.uk

dir: *1m E of town centre on seafront*

Rooms 9 en suite (1 fmly) S £55; D £85✳ **Facilities** TVB tea/coffee Lift Cen ht Dinner Last d 9pm **Conf** Max 30 Thtr 30 Class 12 Board 20 **Parking** 12 **Notes LB** ⊗ No coaches

★★ GUEST ACCOMMODATION
The Alum Grange
1 Burnaby Rd, Alum Chine BH4 8JF
☎ 01202 761195 & 760973 📠 01202 760973
e-mail: alumgrange@aol.com

dir: *B3065 The Avenue towards Canford Cliffs, left onto Tower Rd & Mountbatten Rd, over x-rds, 1st right*

Located between the town centres of Bournemouth and Poole, this spacious accommodation is only a short stroll from the beautiful, sandy

CONTINUED

Alum Chine Beach. All bedrooms are brightly decorated and one room has a four-poster bed. Guests can choose from the daily-changing menu, served in the open-plan dining room/lounge bar.

Rooms 13 rms (11 en suite) (2 pri facs) (6 fmly) (2 GF) S fr £45; d fr £70✳ **Facilities** TVB tea/coffee Cen ht TVL Dinner Last d mid afternoon **Conf** Max 40 **Parking** 11 **Notes LB**

BRIDPORT
MAP 04 SY49

See also Chideock

Premier Collection

★★★★★ GUEST ACCOMMODATION

The Roundham House

Roundham Gardens, West Bay Rd DT6 4BD
☎ 01308 422753 📄 01308 421500
e–mail: cyprencom@compuserve.com

dir: *A35 into Bridport, at the Crown Inn rdbt take exit signed West Bay. House 400yds on left*

The hosts here are invariably on hand to extend a warm welcome to their lovely home, which is complete with well-tended gardens and views to the nearby coast. Bedrooms come in a variety of sizes and are all filled with useful extras. Public areas include a comfortable lounge and well-appointed dining room.

Rooms 8 rms (7 en suite) (1 fmly) S £49–£57; D £85–£118✳
Facilities TVB tea/coffee Cen ht **Parking** 10 **Notes** No children 6yrs
Closed Jan–Feb

★★★★ INN

The Shave Cross Inn

Marshwood Vale DT6 6HW
☎ 01308 868358 📄 01308 867064
e–mail: roy.warburton@virgin.net
web: www.theshavecrossinn.co.uk

dir: *From B3165 turn at Birdsmoorgate and follow brown signs.*

A newly-built property in the grounds of an historic inn. Rooms are extremely well appointed and equipped, staff are very friendly, and dinner with a Trinidadian theme is available in the restaurant.

Rooms 7 en suite (1 fmly) (3 GF) **Facilities** STV FTV TVB tea/coffee Direct dial from bedrooms Cen ht Dinner Last d 9pm Wi-fi available Pool Table **Parking** 29 **Notes** No children No coaches RS Mon (ex BH)

★★★★ GUEST ACCOMMODATION

Britmead House

West Bay Rd DT6 4EG
☎ 01308 422941 & 07973 725243
e–mail: britmead@talk21.com
web: www.britmeadhouse.co.uk

dir: *1m S of town centre, off A35 onto West Bay Rd*

Britmead House is located south of Bridport, within easy reach of the town centre and West Bay harbour. Family-run, the atmosphere is friendly and the accommodation well-appointed and comfortable.

CONTINUED

Suitable for business and leisure, many guests return regularly. A choice of breakfast is served in the light and airy dining room.

Britmead House

Rooms 8 en suite (2 fmly) (2 GF) **Facilities** TVB tea/coffee Cen ht TVL **Parking** 12 **Notes** Closed 24–27 Dec

★★★★ FARM HOUSE

Oxbridge Farm (SY475977)

DT6 3UA
☎ 01308 488368 & 07766 086543 Mrs C Marshall
e–mail: jojokillin@hotmail.com
web: www.oxbridgefarm.co.uk

dir: *From A3066 Bridport to Beaminster. Take 1st right signed Oxbridge 1m*

Oxbridge Farm is nestled in the rolling hills of West Dorset in an Area of Outstanding Natural Beauty. The bedrooms are well equipped and offer a very good degree of comfort. A hearty breakfast is served in the attractive dining room overlooking the wonderful views.

Rooms 3 rms (2 en suite) (1 pri facs) **Facilities** TV1B tea/coffee Cen ht TVL Dinner Last d noon **Parking** 6 **Notes** ⊗ 40 acres Sheep ⊛

CHIDEOCK
MAP 04 SY49

★★★★ BED & BREAKFAST

Rose Cottage

Main St DT6 6JQ
☎ 01297 489994 & 07980 400904
e–mail: enquiries@rosecottage-chideock.co.uk

dir: *On A35 in village centre*

Located in the centre of the charming village, this 300-year-old cottage provides very well-appointed, attractive accommodation. A friendly welcome is assured. A delicious breakfast can be enjoyed in the renovated dining room which has many interesting features, and in finer weather you can relax in the pretty garden.

Rooms 2 en suite S £40–£60; D £60✳ **Facilities** FTV TVB tea/coffee Cen ht **Parking** 2 **Notes LB** ⊗

★★★★ GUEST ACCOMMODATION
Betchworth House

DT6 6JW
☎ 01297 489478 📄 01297 489932
e–mail: info@betchworthhouse.co.uk
web: www.betchworthhouse.co.uk

dir: *On A35 in village*

There is a warm welcome and thoughtful and attentive service at this Grade II listed 19th-century house. Bedrooms, including one on the ground floor, are attractive and all feature numerous extra touches. Breakfast is served in the comfortable dining room, where a good choice of hot and cold options is provided. Guests can unwind in the garden and off-road parking is available.

Rooms 5 rms (3 en suite) (2 pri facs) (1 fmly) (1 GF) S £35; D £50–£55✱ **Facilities** TVB tea/coffee Cen ht **Parking** 5 **Notes** LB ⊗ No children 8yrs Closed Xmas

★★★ GUEST ACCOMMODATION
Warren House

DT6 6JW
☎ 01297 489996
e–mail: kathy@warren-house.com

dir: *Off A35 in village centre signed North Chideock, parking signed 60yds*

Expect a friendly welcome upon arrival at this thatched long house built in the early 17th century, situated in the picturesque Dorset village of Chideock. Bedrooms, which are all named after local hills are spacious and comfortable. Enjoy afternoon tea in the secluded garden. Private car park to the rear.

Rooms 4 en suite (2 fmly) S £35; D £55✱ **Facilities** TVB tea/coffee Cen ht Wi-fi available **Parking** 5 **Notes** LB Closed Xmas ➌

Premier Collection

★★★★★★ ◉◉ GUEST ACCOMMODATION
The Lord Bute & Restaurant

179–181 Lymington Rd, Highcliffe on Sea BH23 4JS
☎ 01425 278884 📄 01425 279258
e–mail: mail@lordbute.co.uk
web: www.lordbute.co.uk

dir: *A337 towards Highcliffe*

The elegant Lord Bute stands directly behind the original entrance lodges of Highcliffe Castle close to the beach and historic town of Christchurch. Bedrooms have been finished to a very high standard with many thoughtful extras including spa baths and satellite television. Excellent food is available in the smart restaurant, and conferences and weddings are catered for.

Rooms 9 en suite 4 annexe en suite (3 fmly) (6 GF) D £98–£225✱ **Facilities** FTV TVB tea/coffee Direct dial from bedrooms Cen ht Dinner Last d 9.45pm **Conf** Max 25 Thtr 25 Class 15 Board 18 **Parking** 40 **Notes** LB RS Mon

Premier Collection

★★★★★ 🛏 GUEST ACCOMMODATION
Druid House

26 Sopers Ln BH23 1JE
☎ 01202 485615 📄 01202 473484
e–mail: reservations@druid-house.co.uk
web: www.druid-house.co.uk

dir: *A35 exit Christchurch main rdbt onto Sopers Ln, establishment on left*

Overlooking the park, this delightful family-run establishment is just a stroll from High Street, the Priory and the Quay. Bedrooms, some with balconies, are very comfortably furnished, and the many welcome extras include CD players. There is a pleasant rear garden, patio and relaxing lounge and bar areas.

CONTINUED

Druid House

Rooms 8 en suite (3 fmly) (4 GF) **Facilities** STV TVB tea/coffee Direct dial from bedrooms Cen ht **Parking** 8 **Notes** ⊗

Premier Collection

★★★★★ 🏠 BED & BREAKFAST
Seawards

13 Avon Run Close, Friars Cliff BH23 4DT

☎ 01425 273188 & 07811 934059

e–mail: seawards13@hotmail.com

web: www.seawards13.plus.com

dir: *A35 onto A337 towards Highcliffe, right towards Mudeford, down the Runway, onto Bure Ln, 2nd left onto Island Av, then 1st right, then right again*

Set in a peaceful cul-de-sac just a stroll from the beach, Seawards offers home-from-home comfort in thoughtfully equipped bedrooms. For those not wanting to go to the beach there is a pretty, well-tended garden and one of the rooms has a conservatory. Breakfast offers plenty of choice and quality ingredients.

Rooms 2 en suite (2 GF) D £60–£90✳ **Facilities** STV FTV TVB tea/ coffee Cen ht TVL **Parking** 7 **Notes LB** ⊗ No children 12yrs Closed 21 Dec–14 Jan 🐾

★★★★ BED & BREAKFAST
Windy Willums

38 Island View Av BH23 4DS

☎ 01425 277046 & 07950 481433

e–mail: enquiries@windywillums.co.uk

dir: *A35 Somerford rdbt take A337 for Highcliffe, mini-rdbt last exit 2nd left after Sandpiper pub*

Just a two minute walk from Mudeford beach, this establishment is an ideal base for windsurfing, sailing or for exploring the New Forest. The proprietor is passionate about gardening and has created a truly beautiful and peaceful outdoor place for guests to relax in.

Rooms 3 rms (2 en suite) (1 pri facs) (3 fmly) S £30–£50; D £50–£75✳ **Facilities** TVB tea/coffee Cen ht Wi-fi available **Parking** 3 **Notes LB** ⊗ No children 🐾

★★★★ GUEST ACCOMMODATION
Ashbourne

47 Stour Rd BH23 1LN

☎ 01202 475574 📠 01202 482905

e–mail: ashcroft.b@hotmail.com

dir: *A35 Christchurch to Bournemouth, left at lights onto Stour Rd, over lights, 4th house on right*

Convenient for the historic market town of Christchurch, the scenic River Stour, the New Forest and nearby beaches, this delightful guest house provides a relaxed and friendly environment. Bedrooms and bathrooms are all neatly furnished and equipped with many extra facilities. Large cooked breakfasts are served in the bright dining room.

Rooms 7 rms (5 en suite) (1 fmly) **Facilities** STV TVB tea/coffee Cen ht **Parking** 6 **Notes** ⊗ Closed Xmas & New Year 🐾

★★★★ BED & BREAKFAST
Beautiful South

87 Barrack Rd BH23 2AJ

☎ 01202 568183 & 07958 597686

e–mail: kevin.lovett1@ntlworld.com

web: www.christchurchbandb.co.uk

dir: *0.25m from Christchurch town centre on A35, opp Pizza Hut at Bailey Bridge*

A convenient location near to the main road on the outskirts of Christchurch makes this friendly guest house a good choice for leisure and business. Totally refurbished throughout by the proprietor, public areas and bedrooms are bright and inviting, and hearty dinners, by arrangement, can be enjoyed in the pleasantly appointed dining room.

Rooms 3 en suite (1 fmly) S £45–£55; D £60–£75 **Facilities** FTV TVB tea/coffee Cen ht Dinner Last d 10am **Parking** 4 **Notes LB** ⊗ 🐾

ENGLAND

ENGLAND

CHRISTCHURCH CONTINUED

★★★★ GUEST ACCOMMODATION
The Beech Tree

2 Stuart Rd, Highcliffe BH23 5JS
☎ 01425 272038 📠 01425 272038
e–mail: hkowalski@beechtree.info
web: www.beechtree.info

The Beech Tree is a superb family-run guest house in Highcliffe, with a very high standard of accommodation, cleanliness and facilities, offering an excellent full English breakfast and buffet. Situated on the edge of the New Forest, it is five minutes walk away from an award-winning village and beach, shop and restaurants. Activities close by include golf, walking, riding and sailing.

Rooms 7 en suite (2 GF) S £30–£40; D £55–£60✳ **Facilities** TVB tea/coffee Cen ht TVL **Parking** 14 **Notes LB** ⊗

★★★★ GUEST HOUSE
Grosvenor Lodge

53 Stour Rd BH23 1LN
☎ 01202 499008 📠 01202 486041
e–mail: bookings@grosvenorlodge.co.uk

dir: *A35 from Christchurch to Bournemouth, at 1st lights left onto Stour Rd, Lodge on right*

A friendly and popular guest house near the centre of this historic town. The bedrooms are brightly and individually decorated and have lots of useful extras. Hearty breakfasts are served in the cheerful dining room. There is an extensive selection of local restaurants for lunch and dinner.

Rooms 7 en suite (4 fmly) (1 GF) **Facilities** FTV TVB tea/coffee Cen ht **Parking** 10 **Notes** ⊗

★★★★ GUEST ACCOMMODATION
Riversmead

61 Stour Rd BH23 1LN
☎ 01202 487195
e–mail: riversmead.dorset@googlemail.com

dir: *A338 to Christchurch. Left turn to town centre, turn right over railway bridge*

Ideally located close to the town centre, beaches and the New Forest with excellent access to all local transport, Riversmead is the perfect base for a short break or longer stay. This comfortable house offers a range of facilities including enclosed off road parking, fridges in rooms and an excellent breakfast.

Rooms 3 en suite (1 fmly) **Facilities** FTV TVB tea/coffee Cen ht Wi-fi available **Parking** 9 **Notes** ⊗ No children 5yrs ⊛

★★★★ GUEST ACCOMMODATION
The Rothesay

175, Lymington Rd, Highcliffe BH23 4JS
☎ 01425 274172
e–mail: reservations@therothesayhotel.com
web: www.rothesay.net

dir: *A337 to Highcliffe towards The Castle, 1m on left*

Set on the edge of Highcliffe village, the Rothesay is a great base for exploring the Dorset-Hampshire coast. Highcliffe Castle is just a 5 minute walk, and there are clifftop walks and views to the Isle of Wight. The indoor pool is a real benefit, as are the pretty gardens and large car park.

Rooms 12 en suite 3 annexe en suite (1 fmly) (7 GF) **Facilities** TVB tea/coffee Cen ht TVL Wi-fi available ⊛ Sauna **Conf** Max 30 Thtr 20 Class 20 Board 20 **Parking** 21 **Notes** ⊗ No children 12yrs

★★★★ BED & BREAKFAST
Three Gables

11 Wickfield Av BH23 1JB
☎ 01202 481166 & 486171
e–mail: rfgill@threegables.plus.com
web: www.3gables-christchurch.co.uk

dir: *Off rdbt top of High St onto Sopers Ln, 1st left*

A short walk from the town and the Quay, Three Gables is a relaxed, family-run guest house with a home from home style. Guests are encouraged to join in the banter with the proprietors, especially at breakfast. Bedrooms include one on the ground floor with its own small patio.

Rooms 3 en suite (1 fmly) (1 GF) S £25–£30; D £50–£60✳ **Facilities** STV TVB tea/coffee Cen ht TVL **Parking** 5 **Notes LB** ⊗ No children 5yrs Closed Xmas & New Year ⊛

★★★★ GUEST ACCOMMODATION
The White House

428 Lymington Rd, Highcliffe on Sea BH23 5HF

☎ 01425 271279 📄 01425 276900

e–mail: enquiries@thewhitehouse-christchurch.co.uk

web: www.thewhitehouse-christchurch.co.uk

dir: *Off A35, signs to Highcliffe. After rdbt The White House 200yds on right*

This charming Victorian house is just a short drive from Highcliffe beach, the New Forest and the historic town of Christchurch. Comfortable, well-appointed accommodation is provided, and a generous, freshly-cooked breakfast is served in the cosy dining room. Private car park.

Rooms 6 rms (5 en suite) (1 pri facs) **Facilities** TVB tea/coffee Cen ht Wi-fi available **Parking** 6 **Notes** ⊗

★★★★ 🅰 BED & BREAKFAST
Four Seasons B&B

2 Nea Rd, Highcliffe on Sea BH23 4NA

☎ 01425 273408

e–mail: melbar1940@aol.com

dir: *A35 from Lyndhurst, left into Hinton Wood Ave, right at T-junct onto Lymington Rd, 2nd right onto Nea Rd, 1st left*

Rooms 2 en suite **Facilities** TVB tea/coffee Cen ht **Parking** 3 **Notes** ⊗ No children ⊜

★★★ GUEST ACCOMMODATION
Brantwood Guest House

55 Stour Rd BH23 1LN

☎ 01202 473446 📄 01202 473446

e–mail: pam.brantwood@ntlworld.com

dir: *A338 Bournemouth, 1st exit Christchurch right after railway bridge cross lights, 200yds on right*

Relaxed and friendly guest house where the proprietors create a home-from-home atmosphere. Bedrooms and bathrooms are all well decorated and comfortably furnished. The town centre is just a stroll away and off-road parking is available.

Rooms 5 en suite (2 fmly) **Facilities** TVB tea/coffee Cen ht **Parking** 5 **Notes** ⊗ ⊜

★★★ BED & BREAKFAST
Bure Farmhouse

107 Bure Ln, Friars Cliff BH23 4DN

☎ 01425 275498

e–mail: info@burefarmhouse.co.uk

dir: *A35 & A337 E from Christchurch towards Highcliffe, 1st rdbt right onto The Runway. Bure Lane 3rd turn sharp right onto service road, farmhouse on left*

A friendly welcome is assured at this family home. Individually decorated bedrooms offer comfort and provide useful extras. Hearty breakfasts are served farmhouse style in the dining room overlooking the attractive gardens.

Rooms 3 rms (2 en suite) (1 pri facs) S £30–£40; D £50–£72 **Facilities** TVB tea/coffee Cen ht **Parking** 3 **Notes** LB ⊗ No children 4yrs ⊜

★★★ GUEST ACCOMMODATION
Seapoint

121 Mudeford BH23 4AF

☎ 01425 279541 📄 01425 279541

web: www.seapointb-b.com

Expect a friendly welcome at Seapoint, a pleasant white-painted house in a prime location at the entrance to Mudeford Quay, just a few minutes walk from Christchurch Harbour. Enjoy the sea views while having your full English or Continental breakfast in the first floor breakfast room. The comfortable ground floor bedrooms include one with a four poster. Guests are welcome to make use of the colourful garden.

Rooms 4 rms (2 en suite) (2 pri facs) (2 fmly) (4 GF) S fr £25; D £50–£85 **Facilities** TVB tea/coffee Cen ht TVL **Parking** 4 **Notes** LB ⊗ ⊜

★★★ GUEST ACCOMMODATION
Southern Comfort Guest House

51 Stour Rd BH23 1LN

☎ 01202 471373

e–mail: scomfortgh@aol.com

dir: *A338 onto B3073 towards Christchurch, 2m onto B3059 (Stour Rd)*

Convenient for Bournemouth, Christchurch and Southbourne, this practical and friendly guest house offers spacious bedrooms. Breakfast, served in the bright lounge-dining room, is a relaxed affair with a good choice of hot items.

Rooms 3 en suite (3 fmly) S £22.50–£30; D £45–£60✶ **Facilities** FTV TVB tea/coffee Cen ht TVL **Parking** 4 **Notes** LB ⊗ ⊜

★★★ GUEST ACCOMMODATION
Stour Villa

67 Stour Rd BH23 1LN

☎ 01202 483379 📄 01202 483379

e–mail: stourvilla@hotmail.com

web: www.stourvilla.co.uk

dir: *A35 Christchurch to Bournemouth, left at lights onto Stour Rd, Villa 150yds right*

Stour Villa is well located for visiting the New Forest and local beaches, being just a 5-minute walk from the town centre. Bright and comfortable with a relaxed and friendly atmosphere, the bedrooms and bathrooms are neatly furnished and decorated. A substantial cooked breakfast is served in the cosy dining room.

Rooms 6 en suite (2 fmly) **Facilities** TVB tea/coffee Cen ht **Parking** 7 **Notes** No children 3yrs ⊜

CONTINUED

CORFE MULLEN

MAP 04 SY99

★★★ BED & BREAKFAST
Kenways
90a Wareham Rd BH21 3LQ
☎ 01202 694655
e-mail: eileen@kenways.com
web: www.kenways.com

dir: *2m SW of Wimborne. Off A31 to Corfe Mullen. Over B3074 rdbt, B&B 0.3m on right*

Expect to be welcomed as one of the family at this homely guest house between Wimborne Minster and Poole. The spacious bedrooms are well provisioned with thoughtful extras, and breakfast is served in the pleasant conservatory overlooking the attractive gardens.

Rooms 3 rms (3 pri facs) (2 GF) S £30; D £60✱ **Facilities** TVB tea/coffee Cen ht TVL Wi-fi available Table tennis Snooker table **Parking** 4 **Notes** ❀

CRANBORNE

MAP 05 SU01

★★★★ ❀ RESTAURANT WITH ROOMS
La Fosse at Cranborne
London House, The Square BH21 5PR
☎ 01725 517604
e-mail: mac@la-fosse.com
web: www.la-fosse.com

dir: *M27(W) onto A31 to Ringwood, left onto B3081 to Verwood & Cranborne*

Mac and Sue La Fosse have been welcoming guests to their charming home for over 20 years, where the emphasis is on fine food and relaxation. A stay revolves around Mac's accomplished cooking in the attractive restaurant, and the bedrooms offer comfort and many thoughtful extras.

Rooms 3 en suite **Facilities** TVB tea/coffee Direct dial from bedrooms Cen ht Dinner Last d 9.30pm **Notes** ❀

DORCHESTER

MAP 04 SY69

See also Sydling St Nicholas

Premier Collection

★★★★★ 🏨 GUEST ACCOMMODATION
The Casterbridge
49 High East St DT1 1HU
☎ 01305 264043 📠 01305 260884
e-mail: reception@casterbridgehotel.co.uk
web: www.casterbridgehotel.co.uk

dir: *In town centre, 75yds from town clock*
Within a short walk of the town centre, this Georgian property provides well-maintained and comfortable bedrooms, some of which are situated off a concealed courtyard annexe at the rear of the property; a few ground floor rooms are available. Public areas consist of a bar-library, a drawing room, and a dining room and conservatory where a particularly good breakfast is provided.

Rooms 9 en suite 5 annexe en suite (1 fmly) (2 GF) S £65–£70; D £99–£130 **Facilities** STV FTV TVB tea/coffee Direct dial from bedrooms Cen ht TVL Wi-fi available **Conf** Max 12 Thtr 12 Class 12 Board 12 **Parking** 4 **Notes** LB ❀ Closed 24–26 Dec

Premier Collection

★★★★★ GUEST ACCOMMODATION
Little Court
5 Westleaze, Charminster DT2 9PZ
☎ 01305 261576 📠 01305 261359
e-mail: info@littlecourt.net
web: www.littlecourt.net

dir: *A37 from Dorchester, 0.25m right at Loders Garage, Little Court 0.5m on right*

Built in 1909 in the style of Lutyens, Little Court nestles in over 4 acres of attractive grounds and gardens. The property has been refurbished to a very high standard and the friendly proprietors are on hand to ensure a pleasant stay. A delicious breakfast, including home-grown produce, can be enjoyed in the stylish dining room.

Rooms 8 en suite (1 fmly) S £79; D £89✱ **Facilities** FTV TVB tea/coffee Cen ht Wi-fi available 🏊 ⛳ **Conf** Max 30 Thtr 30 Class 20 Board 20 **Parking** 10 **Notes** LB ❀

Premier Collection

★★★★★ BED & BREAKFAST
Poundbury B & B

37 Peverell Av East, Poundbury DT1 3RH

☎ 01305 250838 & 07759 667771

e–mail: info@poundburybandb.co.uk

web: www.poundburybandb.co.uk

dir: *Off junct A35 & A37 onto B3150 for Dorchester town centre, left at 2nd rdbt & straight across*

Built in a traditional style, this large detached house is situated on the development overseen by HRH The Prince of Wales. Expect a warm and friendly welcome at this modern home. The exceptionally well-equipped bedrooms are comfortable, and the hospitality is relaxed and welcoming. A variety of options is offered at breakfast, including eggs Benedict and the full cooked breakfast, along with home-made bread.

Rooms 2 rms (1 en suite) (1 pri facs) S £52–£60; D £65–£75✱
Facilities TVB tea/coffee Cen ht **Parking** 3 **Notes LB** ⊗ No children 16 yrs Closed 12 Dec–12 Jan RS Dec & Jan 🐾

★★★★ BED & BREAKFAST
Baytree House Dorchester

4 Athelstan Rd DT1 1NR

☎ 01305 263696

e–mail: info@baytreedorchester.com

dir: *0.5m SE of town centre*

Friendly, family-run bed and breakfast situated in the heart of Dorchester – the birth place of Thomas Hardy. Three newly refurbished contemporary and spacious bedrooms offer high levels of comfort. Breakfast is farmhouse style in open plan kitchen/dining area. Parking available.

Rooms 3 en suite **Facilities** FTV TVB tea/coffee Cen ht TVL **Parking** 3 **Notes** ⊗ 🐾

★★★★ GUEST ACCOMMODATION
Beggars Knap

2 Weymouth Av DT1 1QS

☎ 01305 268191

e–mail: beggarsknap@hotmail.co.uk

Conveniently situated in the heart of the town, this renovated, detached Victorian property has connections with the local brewery and Thomas Hardy. Guest arrivals are handled with efficiency and warmth. Bedrooms are spacious, and furnished with a variety of styles of furnishings. The freshly-cooked breakfast features the best of locally sourced ingredients, with guests sitting around one large table. Off-street parking available.

Rooms 3 en suite S £45–£60; D £60–£85✱ **Facilities** TVB tea/coffee Cen ht TVL **Parking** 3 **Notes** 🐾

★★★★ GUEST ACCOMMODATION
Westwood House

29 High West St DT1 1UP

☎ 01305 268018

e–mail: reservations@westwoodhouse.co.uk

web: www.westwoodhouse.co.uk

dir: *On B2150 in town centre*

Originally built in 1815, Westwood House is centrally located in the historic town of Dorchester and is ideal for leisure visitors to the area as well as the business traveller. This attractive property, run by husband and wife team, offers well-appointed rooms with modern facilities in an informal yet stylish non-smoking environment.

Rooms 7 rms (5 en suite) (2 pri facs) (2 fmly) S £45–£60; D £70–£90
Facilities FTV TVB tea/coffee Cen ht Wi-fi available **Notes** ⊗

Chapel House

Ford Down Lane, Henley, Dorchester, Dorset DT2 7BN

Tel: 01300 345822 **Mobile:** 07814 705225
Website: www.chapelhousebandb.com
Email: enquiries@malcolmscholes.com

Old furniture and battered leather sofas, stuffed birds, paintings, roaring log fires and candles, combine to create an eccentric atmosphere in this unusual and intriguing house with rooms more reminiscent of a scottish hunting lodge.

Breakfasts in the large aga kitchen. Bedrooms mainly large and comfortable, one has an 1820 Georgian four poster another an 1805 Napoleon bed. Bathrooms are neat and modern. No televisions anywhere, 1960s Roberts radios everywhere. Shoes off to go upstairs. Casual yet comfortable in a very quiet location.

★★★★ Bed and Breakfast

DORCHESTER CONTINUED

★★★★ GUEST ACCOMMODATION
Yellowham Farmhouse

Yellowham Wood DT2 8RW

☎ 01305 262892 🖹 01305 848155

e-mail: mail@yellowham.freeserve.co.uk

web: www.yellowham.co.uk

dir: *1.5m NE of Dorchester, 500yds off A35*

Located north-east of Dorchester in the heart of Hardy Country, the farm stands amid fields and the tranquil 130 acres of Yellowham Wood. There are spectacular views, and the comfortable bedrooms are all on the ground floor. Thomas Hardy's Cottage and Puddletown Heath are only half a mile to the south.

Rooms 4 en suite (1 fmly) (4 GF) S £45–£60; D £65–£80 **Facilities** TVB tea/coffee Cen ht **Parking** 8 **Notes LB** No children 4yrs

★★★ BED & BREAKFAST
Bramlies

107 Briport Rd DT1 2NH

☎ 01305 265778

e-mail: bramlies@btinternet.com

web: www.bramlies.co.uk

dir: *On B3150 on W side of Dorchester*

A traditional bed and breakfast operation on the outskirts of the town within easy walking distance of the centre and close to the hospital. The hospitality is excellent and the proprietors do all they can to make guests feel at home.

Rooms 1 en suite 2 annexe en suite (1 fmly) (2 GF) S £35–£45; D £60–£75✳ **Facilities** FTV TVB tea/coffee Cen ht **Parking** 5 **Notes LB** ⊗ No children 12yrs ◉

★★★ GUEST ACCOMMODATION
Higher Came Farmhouse

Higher Came DT2 8NR

☎ 01305 268908 🖹 01305 268908

e-mail: enquiries@highercame.co.uk

Higher Came Farmhouse is nestled in beautiful countryside yet only five minutes drive from Dorchester and less than half an hour from the coastal town of Weymouth. Spacious bedrooms are attractively presented and a hearty breakfast is served family style in the bright dining room. Parking and the provision of a lounge with comfortable seating are bonuses.

Rooms 3 rms (1 en suite) (2 pri facs) S £35–£45; D £75–£85✳ **Facilities** TVB tea/coffee Cen ht **Parking** 6 **Notes** No children 5yrs

 🔘

Yalbury Cottage & Restaurant

Lower Bockhampton DT2 8PZ

☎ 01305 262382

e-mail: yalburyemails@aol.com

dir: *Off A35 past Thomas Hardys cottage, over x-rds, 400yds on left, past telephone box, opp village pump*

At the time of going to press the rating for this establishment had not been confirmed. Please check the AA website www.theAA.com for up-to-date information.

Rooms 8 en suite (1 fmly) (6 GF) **Facilities** TVB tea/coffee Direct dial from bedrooms Cen ht Dinner Last d 9pm **Parking** 16

EVERSHOT	MAP 04 ST50

★★★★ ◉ INN
The Acorn Inn

DT2 0JW

☎ 01935 83228 🖹 01935 83707

e-mail: stay@acorn-inn.co.uk

web: www.acorn-inn.co.uk

dir: *0.5m off A37 between Yeovil and Dorchester, signed Evershot, Holywell*

This delightful 16th-century coaching inn is located at the heart of the village. Several of the bedrooms feature interesting four-poster beds, and all have been individually decorated and furnished. Public rooms retain many original features including oak panelling, open fires and stone-flagged floors. Fresh local produce is included on the varied menu.

Rooms 10 en suite (2 fmly) **Facilities** STV TVB tea/coffee Direct dial from bedrooms Cen ht TVL Dinner Last d 9pm Pool Table **Conf** Max 30 Thtr 30 Class 60 Board 30 **Parking** 40

FARNHAM MAP 04 ST91

Premier Collection
★★★★★ GUEST ACCOMMODATION
Farnham Farm House
DT11 8DG

☎ 01725 516254 📠 01725 516306

e–mail: info@farnhamfarmhouse.co.uk

dir: *Off A354 Thickthorn x-rds into Farnham, continue NW from village centre T-junct, 1m bear right at sign*

Farnham Farm House is a country house in 350 acres of arable farmland, offering a high level of quality, comfort and service. The atmosphere is friendly and the accommodation charming and spacious. In the winter, a log fire burns in the attractive dining room, where a delicious breakfast featuring local produce is served, and views across the rolling countryside can be enjoyed. Added features include the outdoor pool and the Sarpenela Treatment room in the converted stable.

Rooms 3 en suite (1 fmly) S £50–£60; D £80✳ **Facilities** TVB tea/coffee ↖ 🌙 Holistic Therapies Centre **Parking** 7 **Notes** ✪ Closed 25–26 Dec

HENLEY MAP 04 ST60

★★★★ BED & BREAKFAST
Chapel House
DT2 7BN

☎ 01300 345822 & 07814 705225

e–mail: enquiries@malcolmscholes.com

web: www.chapelhousebandb.com

dir: *B3143 N of Dorchester. 1st left after Henley Hillbillies, at x-rds turn left and continue 50yds*

This sympathetically converted chapel offers easy access to Dorchester and has high quality bedrooms, bathrooms and public areas. The host, Malcolm Scholes has a relaxed, informal style.

Rooms 3 rms (2 en suite) (1 pri facs) D £70✳ **Facilities** Cen ht Dinner Last d 24hrs **Parking** 3 **Notes LB** ✪ No children Closed Xmas

See advertisement under DORCHESTER on page 209

HIGHCLIFFE MAP 05 SZ29

*For accommodation details see **Christchurch***

LOWER ANSTY MAP 04 ST70

★★★★ INN
The Fox Inn
DT2 7PN

☎ 01258 880328 📠 01258 881440

e–mail: fox@anstyfoxinn.co.uk

web: www.anstyfoxinn.co.uk

dir: *Off A354 at Millbourne St Andrew, follow brown signs to Ansty*

This popular inn has a long and interesting history including strong links to the Hall and Woodhouse brewery. Surrounded by beautiful lush Dorset countryside, this is a great base for exploring the area. Bedrooms are smartly appointed and offer generous levels of comfort. The interesting menu focuses upon excellent local produce, with a choice of dining options including the oak-panelled dining room. An extensive garden and patio area is also available.

Rooms 11 en suite (7 fmly) S £40–£70; D £60–£100✳ **Facilities** TVB tea/coffee Cen ht TVL Dinner Last d 9pm ↩ **Conf** Max 60 Thtr 60 Class 40 Board 45 Del from £62 ✳ **Parking** 30 **Notes LB**

LYME REGIS MAP 04 SY39

See also Axminster (Devon)

★★★★ GUEST ACCOMMODATION
Old Lyme Guest House
29 Coombe St DT7 3PP

☎ 01297 442929

e–mail: oldlyme.guesthouse@virgin.net

web: www.oldlymeguesthouse.co.uk

dir: *In town centre. Off A3052 Church St onto Coombe St*

Comfort is a high priority at this delightful 18th-century former post office, which is just a short walk from the seafront. Bedrooms, which vary in size, are all well equipped and include many thoughtful extras. A wide choice is offered at breakfast, served in the cheerful dining room.

Rooms 5 rms (4 en suite) (1 pri facs) (1 fmly) D £68–£75✳ **Facilities** TVB tea/coffee Cen ht TVL **Notes LB** ✪ No children 5yrs 🖾

★★★★ GUEST ACCOMMODATION
Albany
Charmouth Rd DT7 3DP

☎ 01297 443066

e–mail: albany@lymeregis.com

dir: *300yds NE of town centre on A3052*

Situated on the fringe of this popular town within easy walking distance of the seafront, this attractive house provides comfortable accommodation and a home-from-home atmosphere. Bedrooms are comfortably furnished, public rooms inviting, and guests are welcome to use the garden. Breakfast, featuring local ingredients, is served in the homely dining room.

Rooms 6 en suite (1 fmly) (1 GF) S fr £37; D fr £64✳ **Facilities** TVB tea/coffee Cen ht TVL **Parking** 6 **Notes** ✪ No children 5yrs 🖾

★★★★ GUEST HOUSE
The Orchard Country House

Rousdon DT7 3XW
☎ 01297 442972 📠 01297 443670
e–mail: reception@orchardcountryhotel.com
web: www.orchardcountryhotel.com

dir: *Take B3052 from Lyme Regis towards Sidmouth, on right after garage*

Located in the peaceful village of Rousdon and set in attractive orchard gardens, this friendly and comfortable establishment is a good base for exploring the area. The hop-on hop-off bus stop just outside provides relaxed means to visit many of the local attractions. There is a spacious lounge, and breakfast and dinner are served in the pleasant dining room.

Rooms 11 en suite (1 fmly) (1 GF) S £50; D £88–£100✱ **Facilities** FTV TVB tea/coffee Licensed Cen ht Dinner Last d 6pm **Parking** 25

★★★★ GUEST HOUSE
The White House

47 Silver St DT7 3HR
☎ 01297 443420
e–mail: whitehouselyme@btopenworld.com

dir: *On B3165 (Axminster-Lyme Regis road) 50yds from A3052 junct*

This charming guest house dates from 1770 and is located at the top of town, within walking distance of the beach and the harbour. The well-equipped bedrooms are cheerful and bright. Guests have use of a spacious lounge and an attractive dining room where hearty breakfasts are served.

Rooms 6 en suite D fr £60✱ **Facilities** TVB tea/coffee Cen ht TVL **Parking** 7 **Notes LB** No children 10yrs No coaches Closed Xmas 🐾

★★★ BED & BREAKFAST
Berrydown

Highcliff Rd DT7 3EW
☎ 01297 444448

dir: *0.5m W of town centre on A3052*

Located at the top of Lyme Regis with pleasant views towards the sea, this welcoming establishment offers two comfortable bedrooms including one on the ground floor. Guests are encouraged to use the pleasant rear garden with terrace seating. A carefully prepared breakfast is served in the relaxing conservatory.

Rooms 2 rms (2 pri facs) (1 GF) S £35–£45; D £55–£65✱ **Facilities** TVB tea/coffee Cen ht **Parking** 4 **Notes** 🚫 🐾

MILTON ABBAS   MAP 04 ST80

★★★ FARM HOUSE
Fishmore Hill Farm *(ST799013)*

DT11 0DL
☎ 01258 881122 📠 01258 881122 Mr & Mrs N Clarke
e–mail: neal.clarke@btinternet.com

dir: *Off A354 signed Milton Abbas, 3m left on sharp bend, up steep hill, 1st left*

This working sheep farm and family home is surrounded by beautiful countryside and is close to historic Milton Abbey and a short drive from the coast. Bedrooms, which vary in size, are comfortable and finished with considerate extras. The atmosphere is friendly and relaxed. Breakfast is served in the smart dining room around a communal table.

Rooms 3 en suite **Facilities** TVB tea/coffee Cen ht **Parking** 4 **Notes** 50 acres Sheep and horses Closed Xmas & New Year 🐾

MOTCOMBE   MAP 04 ST82

★★★ 🅰 INN
The Coppleridge Inn

SP7 9HW
☎ 01747 851980 📠 01747 851858
e–mail: thecoppleridgeinn@btinternet.com
web: www.coppleridge.com

dir: *Off A350 to Motcombe, under railway bridge, 400yds right to Mere, inn 300yds on left*

Rooms 10 en suite (2 fmly) (10 GF) S £45–£50; D £80–£85✱ **Facilities** TVB tea/coffee Direct dial from bedrooms Cen ht TVL Dinner Last d 9pm Wi-fi available 🎱 **Conf** Max 60 Thtr 60 Class 60 Board 30 Del from £70 ✱ **Parking** 100 **Notes LB** Civ Wed 80

PIDDLEHINTON   MAP 04 SY79

★★★★ BED & BREAKFAST
Longpuddle

4 High St DT2 7TD
☎ 01300 348532
e–mail: ann@longpuddle.co.uk

dir: *From Dorchester (A35) take B3143, after entering village 1st thatched house on left*

Now refurbished, this purpose-built annexed accommodation is perfectly located for exploring the delightful Dorset countryside and coast. Bedrooms are spacious, very well furnished and equipped with thoughtful extras such as mini fridges. Breakfast is served in the dining room of the main house.

Rooms 2 annexe en suite (2 fmly) D £80–£100 **Facilities** TVB tea/coffee Cen ht TVL Wi-fi available **Parking** 3 **Notes** RS Dec–Jan 🐾

ENGLAND

★★★★ INN
The Piddle Inn
DT2 7QF
☎ 01300 348468 🖹 01300 348102
e–mail: piddleinn@aol.com
web: www.piddleinn.co.uk
dir: *7m N of Dorchester on B3143 in middle of Piddletrenthide*
The Piddle Inn is situated deep in the heart of the Dorset countryside
in the Piddle Valley. Fresh flowers are put in each bedroom, and most
have lovely views. Dinner is served in the friendly bar downstairs and
the menu includes the fresh fish of the day. The gardens are perfect for
alfresco dining.
Rooms 3 en suite (1 fmly) S £45–£50; D £70–£80✳ **Facilities** TVB tea/
coffee Direct dial from bedrooms Cen ht Dinner Last d 9pm Wi-fi
available Pool Table **Parking** 15 **Notes** No coaches

★★★★ INN
The Poachers
DT2 7QX
☎ 01300 348358 🖹 01300 348153
e–mail: info@thepoachersinn.co.uk
web: www.thepoachersinn.co.uk
dir: *N of Dorchester on B3143, inn on left*

This friendly, owner-run inn combines original 16th-century character
with contemporary style in the bar and dining areas. Home-cooked
meals are a feature, and the smart, en suite bedrooms open onto a
courtyard. In fine weather guests can lounge round the swimming pool
or relax in the garden.
Rooms 21 en suite (3 fmly) (12 GF) S fr £54; D fr £74✳ **Facilities** TVB
tea/coffee Direct dial from bedrooms Cen ht Dinner Last d 9.30pm Wi-fi
available ↖ **Conf** Class 20 **Parking** 42 **Notes** LB

★★★★ GUEST HOUSE
Bees Knees Guest House
28 Davies Rd, Branksome BH12 2BB
☎ 01202 734509
e–mail: bees.knees1@ntlworld.com
web: www.beesknees-guesthouse.com
Situated just a short distance from the Sand Banks peninsular, close to
the Jurassic Coast, between Bournemouth and Poole. Your hosts,
Graham and Michelle, offer attentive service and warm, friendly
hospitality. Rooms are well appointed, offer above average facilities and
are equipped with a good range of amenities. Both breakfast and
dinner are served in the attractive conservatory, overlooking the
garden.
Rooms 3 en suite D £69–£80✳ **Facilities** FTV TVB tea/coffee Licensed
Cen ht TVL Dinner Last d 7pm Wi-fi available **Conf** Max 8 Thtr 8 Class 6
Board 8 **Parking** 3 **Notes** ⊗ No children 18yrs No coaches

★★★★ GUEST ACCOMMODATION
Acorns
264 Wimborne Rd, Oakdale BH15 3EF
☎ 01202 672901 🖹 01202 672901
e–mail: enquiries@acornsguesthouse.co.uk
web: www.acornsguesthouse.co.uk
dir: *On A35, approx 1m from town centre, opp Texaco station*
A warm welcome is assured at Acorns, located with easy access to the
town, ferry terminal, business parks and attractions. The bedrooms are
furnished to a high standard, and an English breakfast is served in the
charming dining room. There is also a quiet cosy lounge.
Rooms 4 en suite (1 GF) D £56–£60 **Facilities** FTV TVB tea/coffee
Cen ht TVL Wi-fi available **Parking** 6 **Notes** LB ⊗ No children 14yrs
Closed 23 Dec–1 Jan ☺

★★★★ GUEST ACCOMMODATION
Blue Shutters
109 North Rd, Parkstone BH14 0LU
☎ 01202 748129
e–mail: stay@blueshutters.co.uk
web: www.blueshutters.co.uk
dir: *0.5m from Poole Park and Civic Centre buildings*
The friendly, family-run Blue Shutters is close to the civic centre and
offers brightly decorated, well-equipped bedrooms. Sound,
home-cooked meals are served in the well-presented dining room
overlooking the attractive garden. The guest lounge provides comfort
and quiet.
Rooms 7 en suite (2 fmly) (1 GF) S £35–£45; D £60–£70✳
Facilities TVB tea/coffee Cen ht TVL **Parking** 7 **Notes** ⊗ No children
5yrs Closed 24 Dec–2 Jan

ENGLAND

POOLE CONTINUED

★★★ GUEST HOUSE
Towngate
58 Wimborne Rd BH15 2BY
☎ 01202 668552
e–mail: ayoun19@ntlworld.com

dir: *B3093 from town centre, guest house on right*

Guests are assured of a warm welcome at this centrally located house, within walking distance of the town centre and harbour, and just a short drive from the ferry terminal. The well-equipped bedrooms are comfortable and nicely furnished.

Rooms 3 en suite S £45–£50; D £55–£60✱ **Facilities** TVB tea/coffee Cen ht **Parking** 4 **Notes** ⊗ No children 10yrs No coaches Closed mid Dec–mid Jan ⊕

★★★ GUEST ACCOMMODATION
The Burleigh
76 Wimborne Rd BH15 2BZ
☎ 01202 673889 📄 01202 685283

dir: *Off A35 onto A349*

Suited to business and leisure, this well-kept guest house is close to the town centre and ferry terminal. The individually furnished and decorated bedrooms are of a good standard. Breakfast is served on separate tables and there is a small, attractive lounge.

Rooms 8 rms (4 en suite) (1 fmly) S £27–£35; D £50–£55✱ **Facilities** TVB tea/coffee Cen ht TVL Wi-fi available **Parking** 5

★★★ GUEST HOUSE
Centraltown
101 Wimborne Rd BH15 2BP
☎ 01202 674080 📄 01202 674080

dir: *From town centre onto A3093, Barclays International building on left, guest house 500yds*

This friendly and well-maintained guest house is within easy access of the town centre, ferry terminals, speedway and many other attractions. Bedrooms are attractive and equipped with many useful extra facilities. A full English breakfast is served in the bright, cosy dining room.

Rooms 3 en suite S £40; D £55✱ **Facilities** TVB tea/coffee Cen ht **Parking** 6 **Notes** ⊗ No children No coaches ⊕

★★★ GUEST ACCOMMODATION
Seacourt
249 Blandford Rd, Hamworthy BH15 4AZ
☎ 01202 674995

dir: *Off A3049/A35 signed to Hamworthy*

Within a short distance of the ferry port and town centre, this friendly establishment is well maintained and efficiently run. The comfortable bedrooms, some located on the ground floor, are all nicely decorated and equipped with useful extra facilities. Breakfast is served in the pleasant dining room at separate tables.

Rooms 5 en suite (1 fmly) (3 GF) (5 smoking) S £40–£54; D £54 **Facilities** TVB tea/coffee Cen ht **Parking** 5 **Notes** ⊗ No children 5yrs ⊕

★★★ INN
Shah of Persia
173 Longfleet Rd BH15 2HS
☎ 01202 676587 📄 01202 679327
e–mail: shahofpersia.poole@marstons.co.uk

dir: *On A35, 0.5m from Poole General Hospital*

The Shah of Persia is located just a short distance from the town centre of Poole and is popular with visitors and locals alike. The accommodation consists of well equipped en suite rooms, some located in an adjacent annexe. The carvery restaurant has a friendly atmosphere and offers a wide range of freshly prepared dishes, and a large drinks selection including beers and wines which is available all day.

Rooms 11 en suite 4 annexe en suite (3 fmly) (4 GF) S £49.95–£59.95; D £59.95–£69.95✱ **Facilities** TVB tea/coffee Direct dial from bedrooms Cen ht Dinner Last d 9.30pm Wi-fi available **Parking** 40 **Notes** No coaches

★★ GUEST ACCOMMODATION
Holly House
97 Longfleet Rd BH15 2HP
☎ 01202 677839 📄 01202 461722
e–mail: maxine.curr@ntlworld.com

dir: *Just off A35*

Holly House is across the road from Poole Hospital and is well situated for the town centre and the ferry terminal. It has a friendly and relaxed atmosphere. The comfortable bedrooms are simply furnished and are ideal for business or leisure.

Rooms 4 en suite (3 fmly) **Facilities** TVB tea/coffee Cen ht TVL **Parking** 7 **Notes** ⊗ Closed 20 Dec–5 Jan RS 6 Jan ⊕

PORTLAND   MAP 04 SY67

★★★★ GUEST ACCOMMODATION
Queen Anne House
2/4 Fortuneswell DT5 1LP
☎ 01305 820028
e–mail: margaretdunlop@tiscali.co.uk

dir: *A354 to Portland then Fortuneswell. House on left 200yds past Royal Portland Arms*

This delightful Grade II listed building is a charming and comfortable place to stay. A particular pleasure is the Italianate gardens to the rear. Ideal for business and for leisure, Queen Anne House is close to the famous Chesil Beach, Portland Bill and Weymouth. Bedrooms are particularly attractive and pleasantly furnished. At breakfast, where guests are seated at one large table, there is a wide choice of options.

Rooms 3 en suite **Facilities** FTV TVB tea/coffee Cen ht TVL Wi-fi available **Parking** 4 **Notes** ⊗ ⊕

ENGLAND

★★★ GUEST HOUSE
Beach House
51 Chiswell DT5 1AW
☎ 01305 821155
e–mail: roy@beach-house-bandb.co.uk

dir: *A354, after causeway take right hand lane to Victoria Square & into Chiswell. 150mtrs on right*

Dating back to the early 19th century, this grand building was formerly a public house, but more recently has been providing relaxed and welcoming accommodation. Situated at the side of the stunning sweep of Chesil Beach, the establishment is also handy for the sailing academy. Bedrooms all provide good levels of comfort and quality, many having stripped wooden floors and a simple, stylish feel. A lounge and bar are also available, together with a light and airy breakfast room.

Rooms 6 rms (5 en suite) (1 pri facs) (2 fmly) S £30–£42; D £65–£70✱
Facilities TVB tea/coffee Licensed Cen ht Wi-fi available **Parking** 8
Notes LB ⊗ No coaches

★★★ GUEST ACCOMMODATION
Portland Lodge
Easton Ln DT5 1BW
☎ 01305 820265 📄 01305 860359
e–mail: info@portlandlodge.com

dir: *Signs to Easton/Portland Bill, rdbt at Portland Heights Hotel 1st right. Portland Lodge 200yds*

Situated on the fascinating Island of Portland, this modern, lodge style establishment provides comfortable accommodation including a number of ground floor bedrooms. Breakfast is served in the spacious dining room with a friendly team of staff on hand. This is an ideal location for those wishing to explore the World Heritage coastline with many stunning views.

Rooms 24 annexe en suite (9 fmly) (7 GF) S £38–£44; D £48–£54✱ (room only) **Facilities** TVB tea/coffee Cen ht **Parking** 50 **Notes LB** ⊗

★★★★ GUEST ACCOMMODATION
Offley Bed & Breakfast
Looke Ln DT2 9BD
☎ 01308 897044 & 07792 624977

dir: *Off B3157 into village centre*

With magnificent views over the Bride Valley, this village house provides comfortable, quality accommodation. Guests are assured of a warm, friendly welcome; an ideal venue to enjoy the numerous local attractions. There are several local inns, one in the village, just a gentle stroll away.

Rooms 3 rms (2 en suite) S £40; D £65 **Facilities** TV2B tea/coffee Cen ht TVL **Parking** 3 **Notes LB** ☺

★★★★ ⊛⊛ RESTAURANT WITH ROOMS
La Fleur de Lys Restaurant with Rooms
Bleke St SP7 8AW
☎ 01747 853717 📄 01747 853130
e–mail: info@lafleurdelys.co.uk
web: www.lafleurdelys.co.uk

dir: *0.25m off junct of A30 with A350 at Shaftesbury towards town centre*

Located just a few minutes walk from the famous Gold Hill, this light and airy restaurant with rooms combines efficient service in a relaxed and friendly atmosphere. Bedrooms, are suitable for both business and leisure guests, vary in size but all are well equipped, comfortable and tastefully furnished. A relaxing guest lounge and courtyard are available for afternoon tea or pre-dinner drinks.

Rooms 7 en suite (2 fmly) (1 GF) **Facilities** FTV TVB tea/coffee Direct dial from bedrooms Cen ht TVL Dinner Last d 10pm **Conf** Max 12 Board 10 **Parking** 10 **Notes** ⊗

★★★★ BED & BREAKFAST
Avalon Townhouse
South St DT9 3LZ
☎ 01935 814748
e–mail: enquiries@avalontownhouse.co.uk
web: www.avalontownhouse.co.uk

dir: *A30 from Shaftesbury, towards Sherborne town centre, left onto South St*

"Avalon" is a spacious and comfortable Edwardian townhouse in the heart of historic Sherborne. The building was recently refurbished to a high standard, and the husband and wife team provide a warm welcome and fine, freshly prepared food using local produce.

Rooms 3 en suite S £70–£80; D £80–£90✱ **Facilities** FTV TVB tea/coffee Cen ht TVL Wi-fi available **Notes** ⊗ No children 18yrs

ENGLAND

★★★★ BED & BREAKFAST
Thorn Bank
Long St DT9 3BS
☎ 01935 813795
e–mail: savileplatt@hotmail.com

dir: *A30 onto North Rd, then St Swithin's Rd. Right onto Long St, 75yds on right*

Located just a short walk from the centre of town and the Abbey, this elegantly appointed Grade II listed Georgian townhouse is a perfect base from which to explore this delightful area. Attentive service is a hallmark here with every effort made to ensure an enjoyable and relaxing stay. The spacious bedroom provides impressive quality and comfort with lovely views over the garden. Breakfast makes use of local Dorset produce and in summer months guests are welcome to eat al fresco on the lovely patio.

Rooms 1 en suite D £75–£80✹ **Facilities** FTV TVB tea/coffee Cen ht 🐾 **Parking** 2 **Notes** ⊗ No children 18yrs ⬚

★★★★ BED & BREAKFAST
The Alders
Sandford Orcas DT9 4SB
☎ 01963 220666 🖹 01963 220666
e–mail: jonsue@btinternet.com
web: www.thealdersbb.com

dir: *3m N of Sherborne. Off B3148 signed Sandford Orcas, near Manor House in village*

Located in the charming conservation area of Sandford Orcas and set in a lovely walled garden, this delightful property offers attractive, well-equipped bedrooms. There is a huge inglenook with a wood-burning fire in the comfortable sitting room, which features the owner's watercolours.

Rooms 3 en suite (1 fmly) S £45–£58; D £55–£68✹ **Facilities** TVB tea/coffee Cen ht TVL Wi-fi available **Parking** 4 **Notes** ⊗ ⬚

★★★★ FARM HOUSE
Stowell Farm *(ST686223)*
Stowell DT9 4PE
☎ 01963 370200 Mrs E Kingman
e–mail: stowellfarm@btconnect.com

dir: *5m NE of Sherborne. Off A357 to Stowell, farm next to church*

This 15th-century working dairy farm is situated in rolling countryside 5 miles from Sherborne and handy for the main roads. Guests receive a friendly welcome and can look forward to a peaceful stay. Bedrooms are attractively decorated, furnished with comfortable beds, and have good views. The spacious bathrooms are equipped with showers and baths.

Rooms 2 rms (1 en suite) (1 pri facs) S £40–£45; D £60 **Facilities** TVB tea/coffee TVL Riding **Parking** 6 **Notes** LB ⊗ No children 12yrs 240 acres dairy beef sheep Closed 30 Nov–Jan ⬚

★★★ BED & BREAKFAST
Cross House
North St, Milborne Port DT9 5ET
☎ 01963 250032 & 07881 580130
e–mail: cellwood@sherborne.org

dir: *3m E of Sherborne. Off A30 High St in Milborne Port*

This delightful family home stands in the centre of Milborne Port. You are welcomed into the kitchen to join the owners for breakfast straight from the Aga. Bedrooms are comfortable and compact, and there is a large comfortable lounge with a seasonal wood-burning fire.

Rooms 2 rms (2 pri facs) (2 fmly) S fr £30; D fr £60✹ **Facilities** tea/coffee Cen ht TVL **Notes** LB ⬚

★★★ FARM HOUSE
Venn *(ST684183)*
Milborne Port DT9 5RA
☎ 01963 250598 🖹 01963 250598 Mrs Pauline Tizzard

dir: *3m E of Sherborne on A30 on edge of Milborne Port*

Expect a friendly welcome at this farmhouse, which is set in a good location for exploring west Dorset, and specialises in training National Hunt racehorses. The individually furnished bedrooms are comfortable and bathrooms are fitted with power showers. Downstairs a farmhouse breakfast is served in the lounge-dining room.

Rooms 3 en suite S fr £30; D fr £52✹ **Facilities** TVB tea/coffee Cen ht TVL Fishing **Parking** 6 **Notes** 375 acres dairy/mixed/race horses Closed Xmas ⬚

STURMINSTER NEWTON   MAP 04 ST71

★★★★ BED & BREAKFAST
Skylands
Lower Rd, Stalbridge DT10 2SW
☎ 01963 362392
e–mail: alison@skylands.co.uk

dir: *A357 in village, onto Lower Rd signed Marnhill/village hall. After 0.75m Skylands sign, drive on left before x-rds*

Located on the edge of the Blackmore Vale, this 17th-century farmhouse provides well-presented accommodation. The two bedrooms have private facilities. Guests can bring their own horses, and there is a British Horse Society instructor on site.

Rooms 2 rms (2 pri facs) S fr £35; D fr £70✹ **Facilities** TVB tea/coffee Cen ht TVL Wi-fi available Fishing Stables for guests horses **Parking** 20 **Notes** ⊗ No children 12yrs ⬚

★★★★ GUEST HOUSE
Stourcastle Lodge
Goughs Close DT10 1BU
☎ 01258 472320 📠 01258 473381
e–mail: enquiries@stourcastle-lodge.co.uk
dir: *Off town square opp cross*

Tucked away off the market square, this charming 18th-century house is set in delightful gardens and offers warm hospitality. Bedrooms are spacious, well presented and comfortably appointed. A lounge, complete with crackling log fire, is also available. Satisfying, Aga-cooked meals are served at dinner and breakfast in the attractive dining room.

Rooms 5 en suite S £51–£58; D £84–£98✳ Facilities TVB tea/coffee Direct dial from bedrooms Cen ht Dinner Last d 7pm Wi-fi available Parking 8 Notes LB ⊗ No children 18yrs No coaches

★★★★ 🅰 BED & BREAKFAST
Northwood Cottages
2 Northwood Cottages, Manston DT10 1HD
☎ 01258 472666 📠 01258 473950
e–mail: info@northwoodcottages.co.uk
dir: *M3 to A303 then A350 to Shaftesbury. B3091 to Sturminster Newton. At Manston Village sign take next right to Gillingham, 3rd building on right*

Rooms 4 en suite 2 annexe rms (1 en suite) (1 annexe pri facs) (1 fmly) (2 GF) S £43–£49; D £84–£99 Facilities FTV TVB tea/coffee Cen ht TVL Dinner Last d am Wi-fi available Parking 10 Notes LB ⊗

★★★ 🍽 FARM HOUSE
Honeysuckle House (ST772102)
1995 Fifehead St Quintin DT10 2AP
☎ 01258 817896 & 07980 085107 Mrs J Miller
dir: *Off A357 up Glue Hill signed Hazelbury Bryan. Left after sharp bend, continue 2.5m*

The young proprietors of this 400-acre dairy farm offer a particularly friendly welcome and ensure all guests are very well looked after. The lovely rural setting is a delight, with contented cows grazing in the fields awaiting milking time. Bedrooms are comfortable and include some welcome extras. Breakfasts are enormous, and be sure to book for dinner which is a real highlight.

Rooms 3 en suite (1 fmly) Facilities TVB tea/coffee Cen ht TVL Dinner Last d Previous day ⌇ Fishing Riding 🐎 Pony rides, farm tours, children's tractor rides Parking 6 Notes 400 acres Dairy Closed 22 Dec–2 Jan ⊛

★★★ GUEST HOUSE
The Sandringham
20 Durlston Rd BH19 2HX
☎ 01929 423076 📠 01929 423076
e–mail: silk@sandhot.fsnet.co.uk
dir: *From centre follow signs for Durlston Country Park*

This delightful property stands high above the town, close to the beach, and just half a mile from the beautiful Durlston Country Park. It offers attractive, well-equipped bedrooms and comfortable public rooms, which include a conservatory-bar.

Rooms 11 rms (9 en suite) (5 fmly) (1 GF) S £30–£40; D £60–£80 Facilities TVB tea/coffee Licensed Cen ht TVL Parking 6 Notes LB ⊗ No coaches Closed Xmas & New Year

🅄
Railway Cottage
26 Victoria Cottage BH19 1AP
☎ 01929 425542
e–mail: enquiries@railway-cottage.co.uk
At the time of going to press the rating for this establishment had not been confirmed. Please check the AA website www.theAA.com for up-to-date information.

Rooms 6 en suite (1 fmly) (1 GF) S £25–£55; D £50–£80 Facilities TVB tea/coffee Cen ht Dinner Last d 24 hrs prior Parking 5 Notes LB ⊛

★★★★ 🍽 INN
Greyhound Inn
26 High St DT2 9PD
☎ 01300 341303
e–mail: info@thegreyhounddorset.co.uk
dir: *Off A37 into village centre*

Situated in this traditional English village complete with stream, the Greyhound Inn is well located for exploring Hardy Country. Stylish, well-equipped rooms, three at ground floor level, are available. Flagstone floors and attractive, relaxed surroundings make this inn a popular place for dining. An interesting and wide range of meals are offered in either the restaurant, bar or conservatory.

Rooms 6 en suite (3 fmly) (3 GF) D £70–£90✳ Facilities TVB tea/coffee Cen ht Dinner Last d 9pm Wi-fi available Parking 30 Notes RS Sun eve

TARRANT MONKTON   MAP 04 ST90

★★★★ ◉ INN
The Langton Arms

DT11 8RX

☎ 01258 830225 📠 01258 830053

e-mail: info@thelangtonarms.co.uk

dir: *Off A354 in Tarrant Hinton to Tarrant Monkton, through ford, Langton Arms opp*

Tucked away in this sleepy Dorset village, the Langton Arms offers light and airy, stylish accommodation and is a good base for touring this attractive area. Bedrooms, all situated at ground level in the modern annexe, are very well equipped and comfortable. There is a choice of dining options, the relaxed bar-restaurant or the more formal Stables restaurant (open Wednesday to Saturday evenings and Sunday lunch time), which offers innovative and appetising dishes. Breakfast is served in the conservatory dining room, just a few steps through the pretty courtyard.

Rooms 6 annexe en suite (6 fmly) (6 GF) S £70; D £90✶ **Facilities** TVB tea/coffee Direct dial from bedrooms Cen ht Dinner Last d 9.30pm **Conf** Max 70 Thtr 70 Class 70 Board 70 Del from £40 ✶ **Parking** 100 **Notes LB** Civ Wed 50

VERWOOD   MAP 05 SU00

★★★★ BED & BREAKFAST
Farleigh

38 Dewlands Rd BH31 6PN

☎ 01202 826424 📠 01202 826424

e-mail: jeanettehamp@waitrose.com

dir: *A31 onto B3081, 3m from A31 into Verwood, pass fire station, over rdbt, 1st left*

There is a warm welcome at this dormer bungalow in the peaceful village; the New Forest, Bournemouth and the coast are all within easy reach. The attractive bedrooms are thoughtfully equipped and have stylish modern en suites, and a hearty breakfast is served in the smart dining room.

Rooms 2 en suite S £25–£40; D £40–£63✶ **Facilities** TVB tea/coffee Cen ht **Parking** 3 **Notes LB** ⊗ 🖾

WAREHAM   MAP 04 SY98

Premier Collection

★★★★★ ◉ GUEST ACCOMMODATION
Kemps Country House

East Stoke BH20 6AL

☎ 0845 8620315 📠 0845 8620316

e-mail: info@kempscountryhouse.co.uk

web: www.kempshotel.com

dir: *Follow A352 W from Wareham, 3m on right in village of East Stoke*

Located within easy reach of the Dorset coastline, this former rectory provides a calming, friendly atmosphere and is the perfect base for touring the area. The refurbished bedrooms are spacious and well appointed, and benefit from plenty of modern extras; super king-size beds, flat screen TV and power showers. Breakfast and dinner are served in the elegant dining room and offer an imaginative choice of modern British cuisine.

Rooms 12 annexe en suite (2 fmly) (6 GF) **Facilities** FTV TVB tea/coffee Direct dial from bedrooms Cen ht Dinner Wi-fi available **Parking** 24

★★★★ ♟ 🍽 GUEST ACCOMMODATION
Purbeck Vineyard

Valley Rd, Harmans Cross BH20 5HU

☎ 01929 481525 & 07780 614050

e-mail: theresa@vineyard.uk.com

dir: *On A351 in Harmans Cross, on right*

This unique establishment situated on a working vineyard benefits from several bedrooms which overlook the stunning countryside and is only a few minutes drive from the equally scenic south coast. Accommodation is comfortable and furnished to a very high standard; bathrooms have powerful showers with generously sized fluffy towels. Enjoy a freshly prepared dinner made using a number of locally sourced ingredients and try a glass of the delicious house wine from the vineyard. Breakfast is heartily substantial, creating a fabulous start to the day.

Rooms 6 en suite (1 fmly) (1 GF) S £60–£65; D £95✶ **Facilities** FTV TVB tea/coffee Direct dial from bedrooms Cen ht Dinner Wi-fi available **Conf** Max 24 Thtr 12 Class 12 Board 12 **Parking** 8 **Notes LB** ⊗

★★★★ BED & BREAKFAST
Hyde Cottage Bed & Breakfast

Furzebrook Rd, Stoborough BH20 5AX

☎ 01929 553344

e-mail: hydecottbb@yahoo.co.uk

dir: *2m S of Wareham. Off A351 rdbt for Furzebrook/Blue Pool, premises on right*

Easy to find, on the Corfe Castle side of Wareham, this friendly guest house has a great location. Bedrooms are all large with lounge seating and are suitable for families. All are well equipped with extras such as fridges. Meals are served en famille in the dining area downstairs.

Rooms 3 en suite (2 fmly) (1 GF) S £30–£35; D £50–£64✶ **Facilities** FTV TVB tea/coffee Cen ht Dinner Last d Breakfast same day **Parking** 4 **Notes LB** ⊗ Closed 24–27 Dec 🖾

★★★★ FARM HOUSE
The Old Granary *(SY886858)*
West Holme Farm BH20 6AQ
☎ 01929 552972 Mrs Venn Goldsack
e–mail: venngoldsack@lineone.net
web: www.theoldgranarybandb.co.uk
dir: *A352 from Wareham onto B3090, turn into Holme Nurseries, house on right*

A friendly, well run bed and breakfast with an experienced host, this is a former granary to the working farm, architect-designed with high ceilings and lots of light. Rooms are comfortable and well maintained and the hearty breakfast is a great start to the day.

Rooms 2 en suite (1 GF) D £60–£70 **Facilities** TVB tea/coffee Cen ht **Parking** 2 **Notes** ⊗ No children 16yrs 50 acres Horticultural Closed 19 Dec–3 Jan

★★★ GUEST ACCOMMODATION
Luckford Wood House
East Stoke BH20 6AW
☎ 01929 463098 & 07888 719002
e–mail: johnbarnes@ukipemail.co.uk
web: www.luckfordleisure.co.uk
dir: *3m W of Wareham. Off A352, take B3070 to Lulworth, turn right onto Holme Ln. 1m right on Church Ln*
Rurally situated about 3 miles west of Wareham, this family home offers comfortable accommodation. Situated on the edge of woodland, wildlife is in abundance. Guests can be assured of a friendly welcome and an extensive choice at breakfast.

Rooms 6 rms (3 en suite) (1 pri facs) (3 fmly) (1 GF) S £25–£55; D £50–£80 **Facilities** TVB tea/coffee Cen ht TVL Wi-fi available **Parking** 6 **Notes** LB

WEST LULWORTH   MAP 04 SY88

★★★ GUEST ACCOMMODATION
The Lulworth Beach
Main Rd BH20 5RQ
☎ 01929 400404 📠 01929 400159
e–mail: info@lulworthbeachhotel.com
Set into the hill above Lulworth Cove with great views from a number of rooms, the Lulworth Beach is under new ownership and
CONTINUED

refurbishment is well underway. The young team of staff are very friendly and helpful and food is freshly prepared and served in the attractive restaurant.

Rooms 11 en suite S £60–£70; D £90–£110✳ **Facilities** STV TVB Direct dial from bedrooms Cen ht TVL Dinner Last d 9.30pm Wi-fi available **Notes** LB ⊗ No children 12yrs RS Xmas

WEYMOUTH   MAP 04 SY67
See also Portland

★★★★ GUEST HOUSE
Channel View
10 Brunswick Ter, The Esplanade DT4 7RW
☎ 01305 782527
e–mail: leggchannelview@aol.com
dir: *Off A353 The Esplanade onto Dorchester Rd, right onto Westerall Rd, 1st left at lights to Brunswick Ter*
Just off The Esplanade, this guest house is in a superb spot close to the beach and within walking distance of the attractions. Bedrooms are on three floors and vary in size. Some have lovely views over the bay and all offer good levels of comfort and decor. Guests receive a warm welcome and breakfast is served in the well-appointed dining room.

Rooms 7 rms (6 en suite) (1 fmly) S £29–£36; D £60–£70 **Facilities** TVB tea/coffee Cen ht TVL **Notes** ⊗ No coaches

WEYMOUTH *CONTINUED*

★★★★ GUEST ACCOMMODATION
The Esplanade

141 The Esplanade DT4 7NJ
☎ 01305 783129 📄 01305 783129
e–mail: theesplanade@o2email.co.uk
web: www.theesplanadehotel.co.uk

dir: *On seafront, between Jubilee Clock and pier bandstand*

Dating from 1835, this attractive Georgian property has public rooms, including a first floor lounge, that all enjoy the splendid sea views. A warm welcome is assured from the friendly owners. Bedrooms are well furnished and nicely decorated, including many thoughtful extras. Some bedrooms also have sea views.

Rooms 11 en suite (2 fmly) (2 GF) S £35–£50; D £60–£100✶ **Facilities** TVB tea/coffee Cen ht TVL **Parking** 9 **Notes LB** ⊗

See advert on page 219

★★★★ GUEST ACCOMMODATION
The Heritage

8 East St, Chickerell DT3 4DS
☎ 01305 783093 📄 01305 786668
e–mail: mail@turksheadhotel.co.uk

dir: *In village centre*

A stone building dating back over 250 years, in the village of Chickerell just outside Weymouth. Family run, this is a popular restaurant with six individually decorated, spacious bedrooms that come with plentiful accessories.

Rooms 6 en suite (2 fmly) **Facilities** TVB tea/coffee Cen ht Dinner Last d 9pm **Conf** Max 14 Board 14 **Parking** 10

★★★★ GUEST HOUSE
Letchworth Guest House

5 Waterloo Place, The Esplanade DT4 7NY
☎ 01305 786663 📄 01305 759203
e–mail: letchworth.hotel@virginnet.co.uk
web: www.letchworthweymouth.co.uk

dir: *Off A31 at Bere Regis to Weymouth, signs to seafront & The Esplanade*

Expect a warm welcome at this well-maintained, licensed guest house on the seafront. The bedrooms are brightly decorated and thoughtfully equipped with many useful extras, and there is also a cosy lounge.

Rooms 6 rms (4 en suite) (2 fmly) S £30–£45; D £60–£64 **Facilities** TVB tea/coffee Licensed TVL **Parking** 6 **Notes LB** ⊗ No children 5yrs No coaches

★★★★ GUEST ACCOMMODATION
The Pebbles

18 Kirtleton Av DT4 7PT
☎ 01305 784331 📄 01305 784331
e–mail: info@thepebbles.co.uk
web: www.thepebbles.co.uk

dir: *On A354, take 2nd exit at Manor rdbt onto Dorchester Rd South. After 1m, turn right at brown sign onto Carlton Rd North, then 1st left*

Situated in a quiet residential avenue and just a short walk from the seafront, this Victorian establishment is an excellent base for all the local attractions. A warm welcome is assured, and every effort is made to ensure an enjoyable and relaxing stay. Bedrooms are neatly presented with thoughtful extras provided – a ground floor room is also available. The refurbished dining room is the venue for satisfying breakfasts.

Rooms 8 rms (6 en suite) (1 fmly) (1 GF) **Facilities** TVB tea/coffee Cen ht Wi-fi available **Parking** 8 **Notes** ⊗

★★★★ GUEST ACCOMMODATION
St John's Guest House

7 Dorchester Rd DT4 7JR
☎ 01305 775523
e–mail: stjohnsguesthouse@googlemail.com

Located just 70 yards from the beach, this elegant Victorian property was built around 1880. Hospitality here is warm and genuine and recent refurbishment means that standards are high throughout with an appealing simple, uncluttered style. Bedrooms are all well equipped with such extras as DVD players, Wi-fi access and comfy beds. Breakfast is served in the light and airy dining room with a lounge area also available for guests.

Rooms 7 en suite (2 fmly) (3 GF) S £27–£34; D £54–£68✶ **Facilities** TVB tea/coffee Cen ht Wi-fi available **Parking** 10 **Notes LB** ⊗ No children 4yrs

CONTINUED

★★★★ GUEST HOUSE
The Seaham
3 Waterloo Place DT4 7NU
☎ 01305 782010
e–mail: seanhourigan2001@yahoo.co.uk

dir: *500yds N of town centre off A353 The Esplanade*

This well-presented establishment, stands on the seafront close to the town centre. It's a good base for exploring the area, and offers attractive bedrooms with many useful extras. Generous breakfasts are served in the well-appointed dining room, which has an adjoining lounge.

Rooms 5 en suite D £64–£80✶ **Facilities** TVB tea/coffee TVL **Notes LB** ⊗ No children Closed Jan ☺

★★★★ BED & BREAKFAST
Squires Lodge
71 Preston Rd DT3 6PY
☎ 01305 835912
e–mail: paulandbeverley@hotmail.co.uk
web: www.squireslodge.co.uk

dir: *On right of A353 between Chalbury Corner and Overcombe Beach*

Newly converted bungalow with comfortable rooms, friendly service and hearty breakfasts. Off-street parking is available and its within minutes of the beach and town centre.

Rooms 2 en suite (2 GF) **Facilities** TVB tea/coffee Cen ht Wi-fi available **Parking** 2 **Notes** No children Closed Nov–Feb ☺

★★★★ GUEST ACCOMMODATION
Wenlock House
107 The Esplanade DT4 7EE
☎ 01305 786674

dir: *On A353 (the Esplanade) King St junct*

The Wenlock offers a good standard of accommodation and a friendly atmosphere on the seafront, just a short walk from the station and town centre. The hosts are very attentive and always happy to help. The attractive bedrooms are well equipped and many have excellent views.

Rooms 11 rms (8 en suite) (2 fmly) S £35–£40; D £60–£70✶ **Facilities** TVB tea/coffee Cen ht **Parking** available **Notes LB** ⊗ No children 5yrs Closed 30 Nov -Dec

★★★ GUEST HOUSE
Kimberley Guest House
16 Kirtleton Av DT4 7PT
☎ 01305 783333 📄 01305 839603
e–mail: kenneth.jones@btconnect.com

dir: *Off A384 Weymouth road right onto Carlton Rd North, opp Rembrandt Hotel, Kirtleton Av on left*

This friendly guest house is in a quiet residential area near the seafront. Bedrooms are well presented, and in addition to a hearty breakfast, traditional home-cooked meals using fresh local and seasonal produce are served by arrangement.

Rooms 11 rms (7 en suite) (2 fmly) (1 GF) S £20–£22; D £44–£48✶ **Facilities** TVB tea/coffee Cen ht Dinner Last d morning **Parking** 8 **Notes LB** ⊗ No coaches Closed 1–29 Dec ☺

★★★ GUEST HOUSE
The Alendale Guest House
4 Waterloo Place DT4 7NX
☎ 01305 788817
e–mail: bowie538@aol.com

dir: *Turn left at clock tower, through 2nd set of lights, Alendale 20mtrs on left*

This friendly property is located just 50 yards from the beach, and provides a warm, homely environment with easy access to the town centre and ferry terminals. Bedrooms are light and airy with an uncluttered contemporary style and come equipped with useful extras. The attractive dining room is the venue for excellent local Dorset produce which is utilised in the imaginative and extensive breakfast menu, including both full English and Scottish options. Ample off-road parking is also a bonus here.

Rooms 5 en suite (3 fmly) S £33–£42; D £58–£66✶ **Facilities** TVB tea/coffee Cen ht TVL **Parking** 6 **Notes LB** ⊗ No coaches

★★★ GUEST HOUSE
Beachcomber
6 Waterloo Place DT4 7PD
☎ 01305 783078 📄 01305 768254
e–mail: raycousins@beachcomberat6.co.uk

dir: *On seafront 250yds from Jubilee Clock*

A warm welcome is assured at this friendly family-run guest house located close to the beach and within easy walking distance of the town centre and places of interest. Bedrooms are cosy and well furnished. There is a lounge and tasty home-cooked evening meals are available by arrangement.

Rooms 8 rms (6 en suite) (2 fmly) S £23–£32; D £46–£64✶ **Facilities** TVB tea/coffee Licensed Cen ht TVL Dinner Last d 10am Wi-fi available **Parking** 8 **Notes LB** ⊗ No coaches

ENGLAND

★★★ GUEST ACCOMMODATION
Bedford House
17 The Esplanade DT4 8DT

☎ 01305 786995 📄 01305 786995

dir: *Along The Esplanade W towards harbour, turn right around amusement gardens (one-way), Bedford House on left*

Known locally as the Bear House, because of the ever-growing collection of bears of every shape and description, Bedford House offers comfortable accommodation. Guests are assured of a friendly welcome and a relaxed atmosphere. Bedrooms are stylishly decorated. The front-facing rooms are popular for their views over the bay, while rear-facing rooms look to the harbour.

Rooms 9 en suite (3 fmly) S £30–£36; D £52–£60✱ **Facilities** TVB tea/coffee Cen ht TVL **Notes LB** ⊗ Closed mid Nov–mid Feb ⊛

★★★ GUEST HOUSE
Molyneux Guest House
9 Waterloo Place, The Esplanade DT4 7PD

☎ 01305 774623 & 07947 883235

e–mail: stay@molyneuxguesthouse.co.uk
web: www.molyneuxguesthouse.co.uk

dir: *A354 to Weymouth seafront, onto The Esplanade, The Molyneux on right*

Located close to the seafront and beautiful beaches of Weymouth, this guest house offers a genuine warm welcome. Bedrooms are brightly decorated and comfortable and there is a lounge. Breakfast is enjoyed in the smart dining room. Off-road parking to the rear is a bonus.

Rooms 6 rms (5 en suite) (1 pri facs) (1 fmly) (1 GF) S £25–£35; D £45–£64✱ **Facilities** TVB tea/coffee Licensed Cen ht TVL **Parking** 6 **Notes LB** ⊗

★★★ GUEST HOUSE
Tara
10 Market St DT4 8DD

☎ 01305 766235

dir: *From Alexandra Gardens on The Esplanade right onto Belle Vue, right & left onto Market St*

Neatly presented, this welcoming establishment is set just back from the seafront at the harbour end of town. Strictly non-smoking, the guest house provides a relaxed and friendly atmosphere. Bedrooms offer good levels of comfort. Home-cooked evening meals are served every day except Sundays.

Rooms 6 en suite (1 fmly) S £22–£26; D £44–£52 **Facilities** TVB tea/coffee Cen ht Dinner Last d breakfast **Notes LB** ⊗ No children 4yrs No coaches ⊛

★★★ GUEST ACCOMMODATION
Wadham Guesthouse
22 East St DT4 8BN

☎ 01305 779640

dir: *Off S end of A353 The Esplanade*

The pleasant guest house offers a range of rooms in the town centre, and is a good base for touring or for a short stay. The comfortable bedrooms are attractively decorated, and home-cooked breakfasts are served in the ground-floor dining room. Parking permits available.

Rooms 9 en suite (3 fmly) (1 GF) S £25–£30; D £50–£60 **Facilities** TVB tea/coffee Cen ht TVL **Notes LB** ⊗ No children 4yrs Closed Xmas ⊛

★★★ 🅰 GUEST ACCOMMODATION
The Channel
93 The Esplanade DT4 7AY

☎ 01305 785405 📄 01305 785405

e–mail: stay@channelhotel.co.uk

dir: *From A354 continue to seafront and Jubilee Clock. Turn right, 100yds on right*

Rooms 11 en suite (4 fmly) (3 GF) S £30–£38; D £60–£76✱ **Facilities** TVB tea/coffee Cen ht TVL Wi-fi available **Notes LB** ⊗ Closed 15–30 Dec

★★ GUEST HOUSE
Charlotte Guest House
5 Commercial Rd DT4 7DW

☎ 01305 772942 & 07719 576744

e–mail: charlottegh1@aol.com

dir: *On A353 Esplanade, at clock turn right onto Kings St. At rdbt take 1st left and then left again onto Commercial Rd*

A warm welcome is offered at this small renovated guest house within easy walking distance of the town's amenities. The breakfast room is light and airy and bedrooms vary in size.

Rooms 12 rms (7 en suite) (3 fmly) (1 GF) S £25–£30; D £45–£60✱ **Facilities** TVB tea/coffee Cen ht **Parking** 3 **Notes LB** ⊛

★★ GUEST ACCOMMODATION
Ferndown Guest House

47 Walpole St DT4 7HQ

☎ 01305 775228

e–mail: odpjean@yahoo.co.uk

dir: *Off A353 The Esplanade before Queen Victoria statue onto William St & Walpole St*

Just a short walk from the seafront and the town centre, this neat, mid-terrace guest house provides comfortable accommodation. Rooms are simply furnished and pleasantly decorated, and downstairs there is a lounge-dining room where guests can enjoy breakfast.

Rooms 6 rms (2 en suite) S £20–£25; D £35–£45✱ **Facilities** TVB tea/coffee TVL **Notes LB** ⊗ No children 5yrs Closed Oct–Apr ☻

★★ GUEST ACCOMMODATION
Field Barn House

44 Fieldbarn Dr, Southill DT4 0EE

☎ 01305 779140 & 07955 180934

dir: *1m NW of town centre. Off A354 Weymouth Way rdbt onto Fieldbarn Dr (Southill), 300yds on right*

Located on a residential estate on the outskirts of the town, yet only a short drive from the sandy beaches and town centre, this modern home is family run and provides guests with comfortable accommodation. A full English breakfast is taken at a communal table overlooking the well-tended rear garden.

Rooms 3 rms (1 fmly) **Facilities** TVB Cen ht **Parking** 2 **Notes** ⊗ No children 3yrs Closed 15–31 Dec ☻

WIMBORNE MINSTER   MAP 05 SZ09

Premier Collection

★★★★★ ◉◉ RESTAURANT WITH ROOMS
Les Bouviers Restaurant with Rooms

Arrowsmith Rd, Canford Magna BH21 3BD

☎ 01202 889555 📄 01202 639428

e–mail: info@lesbouviers.co.uk

web: www.lesbouviers.co.uk

dir: *A31 on to A349. In 0.6m turn left. In approx 1m turn right onto Arrowsmith Rd. Establishment approx 100yds on right*

A very well patronised restaurant with rooms in a great location, set in six acres of grounds. Food is a highlight of any stay here as is the friendly, attentive service. Bedrooms are extremely well equipped and beds are supremely comfortable.

Rooms 6 en suite (4 fmly) S £102–£170; D £120–£200✱ (room only) **Facilities** FTV TVB tea/coffee Direct dial from bedrooms Cen ht Dinner Last d 9.30pm Wi-fi available All bathrooms have steam showers or air baths **Conf** Max 100 Thtr 100 Class 100 Board 100 **Parking** 50 **Notes LB** RS Sun eve Civ Wed

★★★★ GUEST ACCOMMODATION
Ashton Lodge

10 Oakley Hill BH21 1QH

☎ 01202 883423 📄 01202 883423

e–mail: ashtonlodge@ukgateway.net

web: www.ashton-lodge.co.uk

dir: *Off A31 S of Wimborne onto A349 for Poole, left next rdbt signed Wimborne/Canford Magna, house 200yds on right*

A warm welcome is assured at this delightful modern home, which provides comfortable bedrooms, stylishly furnished with attractively coordinated decor and fabrics. All rooms are well equipped, with many extra facilities provided. Hearty breakfasts are served in the spacious dining room, which overlooks the well-maintained garden.

Rooms 5 rms (2 en suite) (1 pri facs) (2 fmly) S £36; D £62–£66✱ **Facilities** TVB tea/coffee Cen ht TVL Wi-fi available **Parking** 4 **Notes LB** ⊗ ☻

★★ Ⓐ INN
The Albion Inn

19 High St BH21 1HR

☎ 01202 882492 📄 01202 639333

e–mail: albioninn-wimborne@tiscali.co.uk

dir: *Off town square opp Wimborne Minster*

Rooms 4 rms (1 en suite) (1 fmly) **Facilities** TVB tea/coffee Cen ht **Parking** 14

WINFRITH NEWBURGH   MAP 04 SY88

★★★ INN
The Red Lion

DT2 8LE

☎ 01305 852814 📄 01305 851768

dir: *On A352, N of village*

Situated between Dorchester and Wareham, this traditional longhouse is surrounded by rolling countryside and is a good centre for touring the numerous attractions in the area. The Red Lion's characterful public areas offer an extensive range of dishes, and booking is essential at weekends. The comfortable bedrooms are well equipped.

Rooms 3 en suite S £50–£70; D £70–£80✱ **Facilities** TVB tea/coffee Cen ht Dinner Last d 9.15pm **Parking** 70 **Notes LB** ⊗ No children 12yrs No coaches

ENGLAND

WINTERBORNE WHITECHURCH

MAP 04 ST80

★★★★ BED & BREAKFAST

Shalom

Blandford Hill DT11 0AA

☎ 01258 881299

e-mail: tranquillity@shalom2414.freeserve.co.uk

dir: On A354 5m SW from Blandford

A warm welcome awaits guests to Shalom, situated in a village within an Area of Outstanding Natural Beauty. The comfortable modern house has attractive bedrooms enhanced with thoughtful extras. A delicious breakfast featuring organic and local produce is enjoyed in the dining room. Walkers and cyclists are welcome (garage for bicycles).

Rooms 2 en suite D £62–£64✱ **Facilities** TVB tea/coffee Cen ht **Parking** 3 **Notes** ⊗ No children Closed Xmas & New Year 🅿

CO DURHAM

BARNARD CASTLE

MAP 19 NZ01

Premier Collection

★★★★★ 🏠 BED & BREAKFAST

Greta House

89 Galgate DL12 8ES

☎ 01833 631193 📠 01833 631193

e-mail: kathchesman@btinternet.com

dir: 400yds NE of town centre on A67

Expect very warm hospitality at this spacious Victorian villa built in 1870. Greta House is convenient for the Bowes Museum, local antiques shops, High Force and Raby Castle, and is a truly comfortable home from home. Bedrooms come with a wealth of thoughtful extras, and memorable breakfasts are served in the elegant dining room.

Rooms 3 en suite D £65–£68✱ **Facilities** FTV TVB tea/coffee Cen ht **Notes** ⊗ No children 5yrs 🅿

Premier Collection

★★★★★ GUEST ACCOMMODATION

Number 34

34 The Bank DL12 8PN

☎ 01833 631304

e-mail: evasreid@aol.com

web: www.number34.com

dir: 3m from A66, on left after Butter Market rdbt

This delightful house has its share of history: the regal dining room dates back to Elizabethan times. A warm welcome is always guaranteed, and bedrooms are generally spacious, well equipped and very stylishly furnished. One room is en suite and two have private facilities. Guests can relax in the lounge or use the garden in the warmer weather. Breakfasts are a treat with homemade and local produce a feature.

Rooms 3 rms (1 en suite) (2 pri facs) S £40–£50; D £55–£80✱ **Facilities** TVB tea/coffee Cen ht **Notes LB** ⊗ No children 12yrs 🅿

★★★★ 🏠 GUEST ACCOMMODATION

Homelands

85 Galgate DL12 8ES

☎ 01833 638757

e-mail: enquiries@homelandsguesthouse.co.uk

web: www.homelandsguesthouse.co.uk

dir: 400yds NE of town centre on A67

A warm welcome awaits you at this central guest house. The Victorian property has been renovated to provide attractive and well-equipped bedrooms, and a hearty breakfast using local and home-made produce is served in the elegant dining room overlooking the garden. Light snacks are available in the stylish lounge.

Rooms 4 rms (3 en suite) (1 pri facs) 1 annexe en suite (1 GF) S £35–£47; D £60–£70✱ **Facilities** TVB tea/coffee Cen ht **Notes** ⊗ No children 5yrs Closed 23 Dec–2 Jan

---

★★★★ 🏠 FARM HOUSE

Wilson House (NZ081124)

Barningham DL11 7EB

☎ 01833 621218 Mrs H Lowes

e-mail: helowes@tiscali.co.uk

dir: 5m SE of Barnard Castle. S off A66 at Greta Bridge to Barningham, 2nd farm on right

The attractive farmhouse, set in 475 acres among superb Pennine scenery, is an ideal retreat for a relaxing break. You can expect good home cooking, flexible bedrooms, and guests can wander around the farm and enjoy the spectacular views.

Rooms 4 rms (2 en suite) (2 GF) S fr £30; D £56–£70 **Facilities** TVB tea/coffee Cen ht Dinner Last d 2pm **Parking** 5 **Notes LB** ⊗ No children 5yrs 475 acres mixed livestock Closed 30 Nov–1 Mar 🅿

COWSHILL

MAP 18 NY84

★★★★ 🏠 ☕ FARM HOUSE

Low Cornriggs Farm (NY845413)

Cowshill-in-Weardale DL13 1AQ

☎ 01388 537600 & 07818 843159 Mrs J Elliott

e-mail: cornriggsfarm@btconnect.com

web: www.britnett.net/lowcornriggsfarm

dir: 0.6m NW of Cowshill on A689

Situated in the heart of Weardale yet also close to Cumbria, this delightful farmhouse has stunning views. Original stone and stripped

CONTINUED

ENGLAND

pine are combined to provide a house with real character. Excellent home-cooked dinners are offered along with charming hospitality. Bedrooms are attractive and thoughtfully equipped with many homely extras. There is a riding stable available on the farm.

Rooms 3 en suite 2 annexe en suite (1 fmly) (2 GF) S £36–£40; D £54–£58 **Facilities** TVB tea/coffee Cen ht TVL Dinner Last d noon **Parking** 6 **Notes LB** ⊗ No children 14yrs 42 acres beef

---

DARLINGTON   MAP 19 NZ21

*See **Aldbrough St John** (Yorkshire, North)*

DURHAM   MAP 19 NZ24

★★★★ GUEST ACCOMMODATION
Farnley Tower
The Avenue DH1 4DX
☎ 0191 375 0011 & 384 6655 🖳 0191 383 9694
e–mail: enquiries@farnley-tower.co.uk
web: www.farnley-tower.co.uk

dir: *Exit A1(M) junct 62 ,onto A690, continue straight over 4 rdbts. After 4th rdbt take 4th turning on right*

Built in 1875, this former manse stands in gardens on the edge of the city, enjoying a quiet location, yet minutes walk away from the City centre. The house is popular with both business and leisure guests. Bedrooms are thoughtfully equipped and vary in size. Food is fast becoming a real feature here with skilfully prepared meals served each evening in the stylish basement Gourmet Spot restaurant.

Rooms 15 rms (13 en suite) (2 fmly) (5 GF) S £60–£65; D £85–£95✳ **Facilities** STV FTV TVB tea/coffee Direct dial from bedrooms Cen ht Dinner Last d 9.30pm Wi-fi available **Conf** Max 30 Thtr 30 Class 30 Board 15 Del from £45 ✳ **Parking** 20 **Notes LB** RS Sun

★★★★ INN
The Old Mill
Thinford Rd, Metal Bridge DH6 5NX
☎ 01740 652928 🖳 01740 657230
e–mail: office@theoldmill.uk.com
web: www.theoldmill.uk.com

dir: *5m S of Durham. A1(M) junct 61, onto A688 S for 1.5m, left at rdbt & sharp right*

This traditional-style, family-owned inn offers a friendly welcome. The stylish bedrooms are very well equipped, and the bar offers a comprehensive list of wines and beer, and a very good selection of meals.

Rooms 8 en suite **Facilities** STV TVB tea/coffee Direct dial from bedrooms Cen ht Dinner Last d 9pm Jacuzzi/Spa **Conf** Max 40 Thtr 40 Class 40 Board 25 **Parking** 40 **Notes** ⊗ RS 25 Dec

★★★★ 🅐 GUEST ACCOMMODATION
Cathedral View Town House
212 Lower Gilesgate DH1 1QN
☎ 0191 386 9566
e–mail: cathedralview@hotmail.com

dir: *In town centre off A690 Gilesgate rdbt*

Rooms 6 en suite (2 GF) S £60–£80; D £80–£90✳ **Facilities** FTV TVB tea/coffee Cen ht TVL Wi-fi available **Notes** ⊗ No children 11yrs

---

HASWELL PLOUGH   MAP 19 NZ34

★★★ 🅐 GUEST ACCOMMODATION
The Gables
Front St DH6 2EW
☎ 0191 526 2982 🖳 0191 526 2982
e–mail: jmgables@aol.com
web: www.thegables.co.uk

dir: *On B1283 in village centre*

Rooms 5 en suite (1 fmly) S £48–£54; D £62–£70✳ **Facilities** STV FTV TVB tea/coffee Cen ht TVL Dinner Last d 7.30pm Wi-fi available **Parking** 30

MIDDLETON-IN-TEESDALE   MAP 18 NY92

★★★★ 🅐 GUEST HOUSE
Brunswick House
55 Market Place DL12 0QH
☎ 01833 640393
e–mail: enquiries@brunswickhouse.net

dir: *In town centre on B6277 opp St Mary's Church*

Rooms 5 en suite S £40; D £60–£65 **Facilities** TVB tea/coffee Licensed Cen ht Dinner Last d 7pm **Parking** 5 **Notes LB** ⊗ No coaches

---

PETERLEE   MAP 19 NZ44

★★★ 🅐 GUEST HOUSE
The Bell Guest House
Sunderland Rd, Horden SR8 4PF
☎ 0191 586 3863 🖳 0191 586 3863
e–mail: bar-is.thebell@unicombox.co.uk

Rooms 5 en suite (1 fmly) S £35; D £50✳ (room only) **Facilities** FTV TVB tea/coffee Licensed Cen ht TVL Wi-fi available Pool Table **Parking** 2 **Notes** ⊗ No coaches

STANLEY　　　　　　　　　　MAP 19 NZ15

★★★ FARM HOUSE
Bush Blades Farm *(NZ168533)*

Harperley DH9 9UA

☎ 01207 232722 Mrs P Gibson

e–mail: bushbladesfarm@hotmail.com

dir: *2m W of Stanley. A693 W from Stanley for Consett, 0.5m right to Harperley, farm 0.5m on right*

The farmhouse stands on a peaceful plateau of farming land with very good views. Well located for visiting Beamish and Durham, Bush Blades has a friendly and relaxed atmosphere, and spacious, traditionally furnished bedrooms.

Rooms 2 en suite (1 GF) S £35–£40; D £60–£65 **Facilities** TVB tea/coffee Cen ht TVL **Parking** 4 **Notes** ⊗ No children 12yrs 50 acres sheep Closed 20 Dec–2 Jan ⊚

STOCKTON-ON-TEES　　　MAP 19 NZ41

★★★ INN
The Parkwood Inn

64–66 Darlington Rd, Hartburn TS18 5ER

☎ 01642 587933

e–mail: theparkwoodhotel@aol.com

web: www.theparkwoodhotel.com

dir: *1.5m SW of town centre. A66 onto A137 signed Yarm & Stockton West, left at lights onto A1027, left onto Darlington Rd*

A very friendly welcome awaits you at this family-run establishment. The well-equipped en suite bedrooms come with many homely extras

CONTINUED

and a range of professionally prepared meals are served in the cosy bar lounge, conservatory, or the attractive dining room.

Rooms 6 en suite **Facilities** TVB tea/coffee Cen ht Dinner Last d 9.15pm **Parking** 36 **Notes** ⊗ No coaches

★★★ Ⓐ GUEST ACCOMMODATION
The Grange Guest House

33 Grange Rd, Norton TS20 2NS

☎ 01642 552541

e–mail: grangeguesthouse@tiscali.co.uk

dir: *A19 onto A139 sliproad to Norton, over 1st rdbt with Red Lion pub on right, 2nd left onto Grange Rd*

Rooms 8 rms (4 en suite) S £28–£35; D £44–£54✱ **Facilities** STV TVB tea/coffee Cen ht **Notes** ⊗ No children 2yrs Closed Xmas & New Year ⊚

ESSEX

CHELMSFORD　　　　　　MAP 06 TL70

★★★ GUEST ACCOMMODATION
Beechcroft

211 New London Rd CM2 0AJ

☎ 01245 352462 & 250861　▤ 01245 347833

e–mail: enquiries@beechcrofthotel.com

dir: *0.5m SW of town centre. A12 onto A414, over 3 rdbts, left at 4th rdbt, on right after lights*

The Beechcroft is just a short walk from the town centre. Bedrooms vary in size and style but all are pleasantly decorated and equipped with modern facilities. Breakfast is served at separate tables in the smart dining room and there is a cosy lounge.

Rooms 20 rms (13 en suite) (2 fmly) (6 GF) **Facilities** TVB tea/coffee Cen ht TVL **Parking** 14 **Notes** ⊗

CHIPPING ONGAR　　　　MAP 06 TL50

AA FRIENDLIEST LANDLADY OF THE YEAR 2008
Premier Collection

★★★★★ FARM HOUSE
Diggins Farm *(TL582082)*

Fyfield CM5 0PP

☎ 01277 899303　▤ 01277 899015 Mrs M Frost

dir: *B184 N from Fyfield, right after Black Bull pub, farm 0.75m on left*

This delightful Grade II listed 16th-century farmhouse is set amid open farmland in the Roding Valley, and is only a short drive from Stansted Airport. The spacious bedrooms are attractively decorated, carefully furnished and well equipped.

Rooms 2 rms (1 en suite) (1 pri facs) **Facilities** TVB tea/coffee Cen ht **Parking** 20 **Notes** ⊗ No children 12yrs 440 acres Arable Closed 15 Dec–3 Jan ⊚

CLACTON-ON-SEA   MAP 07 TM11

★★★★ GUEST ACCOMMODATION
Chudleigh
13 Agate Rd, Marine Pde West CO15 1RA
☎ 01255 425407 📠 01255 470280
e-mail: reception@chudleighhotel.com

dir: *With sea on left, cross lights at pier, turn onto Agate Rd*
Conveniently situated for the seafront and shops, this immaculate property has been run by the friendly owners Peter and Carol Oleggini for the last 30 years. Bedrooms are most attractive with co-ordinating décor and well chosen fabrics. Breakfast is served in the smart dining room and there is a cosy lounge with plush sofas.

Rooms 10 en suite (2 fmly) (2 GF) S £45–£47; D £70–£72 **Facilities** TVB tea/coffee Direct dial from bedrooms Cen ht TVL **Parking** 7 **Notes** No children 2yrs RS Oct–Mar

★★★★ GUEST ACCOMMODATION
The Sandrock
1 Penfold Rd, Marine Pde West CO15 1JN
☎ 01255 428215 📠 01255 428215
e-mail: thesandrock@btinternet.com
web: www.thesandrock.co.uk

dir: *A133 to seafront, turn right, pass lights at pier, then take 2nd right*
A warm welcome is offered at this Victorian property, just off the seafront and within easy walking distance of the town centre. The attractive bedrooms vary in size and style, are thoughtfully equipped, and some have sea views. Breakfast is served in the smart bar-restaurant and there is also a cosy lounge.

Rooms 9 en suite (1 fmly) (1 GF) S £40–£42; D £58–£60✶ **Facilities** TVB tea/coffee Cen ht TVL Wi-fi available **Parking** 5 **Notes** LB

★★★ GUEST ACCOMMODATION
The Beeches Guest Accommodation
12/14 Ellis Rd CO15 1ER
☎ 01255 421713 & 07947 259048 📠 01255 421713
e-mail: info@thebeechesclacton.co.uk
web: www.thebeechesclacton.co.uk

The Beeches is ideally located for an easy reach of the beach Pier and shopping area. The husband and wife team, welcome you to their home, where the service is attentive, hospitality genuine and rooms nicely decorative and comfortable. The attractive dining room provides the perfect venue for a hearty breakfast.

Rooms 13 rms (10 en suite) (4 fmly) (4 GF) S £25–£28; D £50–£56✶ **Facilities** TVB tea/coffee **Parking** 7

COLCHESTER   MAP 13 TL92

See also Nayland (Suffolk)

★★★★ FARM HOUSE
Fridaywood Farm *(TL985213)*
Bounstead Rd CO2 0DF
☎ 01206 573595 📠 01206 547011 Mrs J Lochore
e-mail: lochorem8@aol.com

dir: *3m S of Colchester, follow signs from A12 for zoo to Mersea, cross B1026 at Maypole pub, right for Bounstead Rd*

A traditional farmhouse surrounded by wooded countryside. Bedrooms are generally quite spacious, and each one is carefully decorated, furnished with well-chosen pieces, and equipped with many thoughtful touches. Public rooms include an elegant dining room where breakfast is served at a large communal table, and a cosy sitting room.

Rooms 2 en suite S £40–£50; D £60–£70✶ **Facilities** TVB tea/coffee Cen ht Wi-fi available 🐾 🍴 **Parking** 6 **Notes** ⊗ No children 12yrs 500 acres sheep/arable 🐾

★★★★ GUEST ACCOMMODATION
Old Manse
15 Roman Rd CO1 1UR
☎ 01206 545154 📠 01206 545153
e-mail: wendyanderson15@hotmail.com
web: www.theoldmanse.uk.com

dir: *In town centre, 250yds E of castle. Off High St-East Hill onto Roman Rd*

Expect a warm welcome from the caring host at this Victorian house, situated just a short walk from the castle and High Street. Bedrooms are carefully decorated with coordinated soft furnishings and equipped with many thoughtful touches. Breakfast is served seated at a large communal table in the attractive dining room and there is a comfortable lounge.

Rooms 3 rms (2 en suite) (1 pri facs) S £45–£60; D £68–£72 **Facilities** TVB tea/coffee Cen ht **Parking** 1 **Notes** ⊗ No children 8yrs Closed 23–31 Dec 🐾

COLCHESTER CONTINUED

★★★ GUEST HOUSE
Globe

71 North Station Rd CO1 1RQ

☎ 01206 576496 & 07734 442799 📠 01206 562543

e–mail: info@the_globehotel.com

Expect a warm welcome at this former inn which is situated close to the town centre. The property has undergone a refurbishment programme and offers a range of comfortable, well-equipped bedrooms. In addition there is a smart restaurant on the ground floor serving Indian cuisine.

Rooms 11 en suite (2 fmly) **Facilities** TVB tea/coffee Wi-fi available **Conf** Board 25 **Parking** 15

DEDHAM   MAP 13 TM03

★★★★ ⇔ INN
The Sun Inn

High St CO7 6DF

☎ 01206 323351 📠 01206 323964

e–mail: office@thesuninndedham.com

dir: *In village centre opp church*

A charming 15th-century coaching inn situated in the centre of Dedham opposite the church. The carefully decorated bedrooms have many features that include four-poster and half tester beds, along with many thoughtful touches. The open-plan public rooms have a wealth of character with inglenook fires, oak beams and fine oak panelling.

Rooms 5 en suite S fr £65; D £85–£130✳ **Facilities** TVB tea/coffee Cen ht Dinner Last d 10pm **Parking** 15 **Notes** LB Closed 25–28 Dec Civ Wed 100

FELSTED   MAP 06 TL62

★★★ FARM HOUSE
Potash Farmhouse *(TL686196)*

Cobblers Green, Causeway End Rd CM6 3LX

☎ 01371 820510 Mr & Mrs R Smith

e–mail: jill@potashfarm.co.uk

web: www.potashfarm.co.uk

dir: *B1417 S from Felsted, 0.5m left signed Cobbler's Green, farm signed 400yds on left*

A Grade II listed, 15th-century house situated on the outskirts of Felsted amid extensive, half-moated mature gardens. There are original exposed beams and open fireplaces, and the bedrooms are carefully decorated and thoughtfully equipped. Public rooms include an attractive dining room, a comfortable lounge and a conservatory.

Rooms 3 rms (1 pri facs) S £40–£45; D £55–£60 **Facilities** TVB tea/coffee Cen ht TVL ⤸ **Parking** 6 **Notes** ⊗ No children 12yrs 40 acres arable ⊜

FRINTON-ON-SEA   MAP 07 TM22

★★★ GUEST ACCOMMODATION
Uplands

41 Hadleigh Rd CO13 9HQ

☎ 01255 674889 📠 01255 674889

e–mail: info@uplandsguesthouse.co.uk

web: www.uplandsguesthouse.com

dir: *B1033 into Frinton, over level crossing, Hadleigh Rd 3rd left, Uplands 250yds on left*

This large Edwardian house stands in a peaceful side road just a short walk from the shops and seafront. Bedrooms are pleasantly decorated and thoughtfully equipped with a good range of useful extras. Public rooms include a large lounge-dining room where breakfast is served at individual tables.

Rooms 4 rms (2 en suite) S £25–£29; D £54–£58✳ **Facilities** TVB tea/coffee Cen ht TVL Dinner Last d 10am Wi-fi available **Parking** 4 **Notes** LB ⊗

★★★★ GUEST ACCOMMODATION

Homelye Farm

Homelye Chase, Braintree Rd CM6 3AW
☎ 01371 872127 📠 01371 876428
e–mail: homelyebandb@btconnect.com
web: www.homelyfarm.com

dir: *1.5m E of Great Dunmow. Off B1256 at water tower*

Expect a warm welcome at this working farm situated in a peaceful rural location just a short drive from the town centre. The spacious bedrooms are in converted outbuildings; each one features exposed beams, co-ordinated fabrics and attractive pine furnishings. Breakfast is taken at individual tables in the original farmhouse.

Rooms 13 annexe en suite (1 fmly) (13 GF) S £45–£55; D £55–£75
Facilities TVB tea/coffee Cen ht **Parking** 16 **Notes** ⊗ Closed 24–27 Dec

★★★★ 🅰 GUEST HOUSE

Harwood Guest House

52 Stortford Rd CM6 1DN
☎ 01371 874627
e–mail: info@harwoodguesthouse.com

dir: *M11 junct 8 onto A120, follow signs to Great Dunmow town centre (B1256)*

Rooms 6 en suite (1 fmly) (3 GF) S £55; D £65✳ **Facilities** FTV TVB tea/coffee Licensed Cen ht Wi-fi available **Conf** Max 12 Board 12 Del £90 ✳ **Parking** 18 **Notes** ⊗

★★★ FARM HOUSE

Lancasters Farm *(TL544149)*

Chelmsford Rd CM22 7BB
☎ 01279 730220 📠 01279 730220 Mrs M Hunt

dir: *A1060 from Hatfield Heath for Chelmsford, 1m left on sharp right bend, through white gates*

Guests are made to feel at home at this delightfully spacious house, which is the heart of this large working arable farm close to Stansted Airport. Bedrooms vary in size and style but all are smartly decorated and thoughtfully equipped. Garaging arrangements can be made, as can transport to and from the airport.

Rooms 4 rms (1 en suite) S fr £30; D fr £70✳ **Facilities** TVB tea/coffee Cen ht **Parking** 6 **Notes** ⊗ No children 12yrs 260 acres arable Closed 14 Dec–4 Jan ⊜

★★★ GUEST ACCOMMODATION

Crouch Valley Lodge & Blue Toad Restaurant

Burnham Rd CM3 6EX
☎ 01621 740770 📠 01621 743355
e–mail: info@crouchvalley.com
web: www.crouchvalley.com

dir: *B1018 through village, at mini rdbt turn right, lodge 300yds on right*

Situated in rural Essex, this modern establishment offers comfortable, well-equipped chalet-style accommodation, with two rooms having easier access. Breakfast is served in the adjoining restaurant, and an interesting choice of dishes is available for dinner.

Rooms 10 en suite (8 fmly) (10 GF) S £40–£60; D £50–£80(room only) **Facilities** STV FTV TVB tea/coffee Cen ht Dinner Last d 9.30pm Wi-fi available **Parking** 50 **Notes** LB

★★★ GUEST HOUSE

Homesdale

Lower Rd CM22 7QY
☎ 01279 600647 📠 01279 600647
e–mail: info@homesdale.net
web: www.homesdale.net

dir: *A1060 through village, 200yds past sign to Wrights Green*

Conveniently situated near Stansted Airport, this charming B&B provides ideal accommodation for a short stopover or a weekend break in the Bishop's Stortford area. The atmosphere is homely, dinner can be arranged and breakfast is served in the dining room overlooking the garden. The pool is a refreshing bonus for the warmer summer months.

Rooms 4 en suite (1 fmly) (1 GF) (1 smoking) S £35–£40; D £45–£55✳ **Facilities** STV FTV TVB tea/coffee Cen ht Dinner Last d breakfast Wi-fi available ⤾ **Parking** 5 **Notes** No coaches

MANNINGTREE — MAP 13 TM13

Premier Collection

★★★★★ FARM HOUSE

Dairy House *(TM148293)*

Bradfield Rd CO11 2SR

☎ 01255 870322 🖹 01255 870186 Mrs B Whitworth

e–mail: bridgetwhitworth@btinternet.com

web: www.dairyhousefarm.info

(For full entry see Wix)

SAFFRON WALDEN — MAP 12 TL53

★★★★ ◉ INN

The Cricketers Arms

Rickling Green CB11 3YG

☎ 01799 543210 🖹 01799 543512

e–mail: reservations@cricketers.demon.co.uk

web: www.thecricketersarms.com

dir: *Off B1383 at Quendon, premises 300yds, opp cricket green*

Parts of this fully refurbished inn, which overlooks Rickling village green, date from the 16th century. A selection of real ales and imaginative food is available within the character bar and smart modern restaurant. In warm weather you can enjoy a drink on the landscaped decking area. Bedrooms, furnished in an understated colonial style, are comfortable and well equipped.

Rooms 9 en suite (3 fmly) (2 GF) S £65–£85; D £95–£120 **Facilities** FTV TVB tea/coffee Direct dial from bedrooms Cen ht Dinner Last d 9.30pm Wi-fi available **Conf** Max 12 Board 12 **Parking** 40 **Notes** LB

★★★★ BED & BREAKFAST

Warner's Farm

Top Rd, Wimbish Green CB10 2XJ

☎ 01799 599525 & 07989 562316

e–mail: nettymawson@aol.com

web: www.warnersfarm.co.uk

dir: *4m SE of Saffron Walden. Off B184 to Wimbish Green*

Expect a warm welcome at this delightful property set in five acres of grounds and surrounded by open countryside. The comfortable bedrooms have a wealth of character; each one has coordinated fabrics and many thoughtful touches. Breakfast is taken in the smart dining room and guests have the use of a lounge with an open fireplace.

Rooms 4 rms (2 en suite) (2 pri facs) **Facilities** TVB tea/coffee Cen ht TVL Dinner Last d 8hrs notice ⚡ Sauna Gymnasium **Parking** 13 **Notes** No children 10yrs Closed Nov–Feb ⊛

SOUTHEND-ON-SEA — MAP 07 TQ88

★★★★ GUEST ACCOMMODATION

Ilfracombe House

9–13 Wilson Rd SS1 1HG

☎ 01702 351000 🖹 01702 393989

e–mail: info@ilfracombehotel.co.uk

web: www.ilfracombehotel.co.uk

dir: *500yds W of town centre. Off A13 at Cricketers pub onto Milton Rd, 3rd left onto Cambridge Rd, 4th right, car park in Alexandra Rd*

Ilfracombe House lies in Southend's conservation area, just a short walk from the cliffs, gardens and the beach. The public rooms include

CONTINUED

a dining room, lounge and a cosy bar, and the well-equipped bedrooms include deluxe options and two four-poster rooms.

Rooms 20 en suite (3 fmly) (2 GF) **Facilities** STV FTV TVB tea/coffee Direct dial from bedrooms Cen ht TVL Dinner Last d 7pm **Parking** 9

★★★ GUEST ACCOMMODATION
Terrace Guest House

8 Royal Ter SS1 1DY

☎ 01702 348143 📄 01702 348143

e–mail: info@terraceguesthouse.co.uk

dir: *From pier up Pier Hill onto Royal Terrace*

Set on a terrace above the Western Esplanade, this comfortable guest house has an informal atmosphere. There is a cosy bar, and an elegant sitting room and breakfast room. The spacious, well-planned bedrooms consist of en suite front and rear-facing rooms, and several front-facing rooms that share two bathrooms.

Rooms 9 rms (6 en suite) (2 fmly) (1 smoking) S £35–£45; D £45–£65✳ **Facilities** TVB tea/coffee Cen ht TVL **Notes** LB Closed 21 Dec–4 Jan

---

STANSTED AIRPORT — MAP 06 TL52

See also Bishops Stortford (Hertfordshire)

★★★★ GUEST ACCOMMODATION
The White House

Smiths Green CM22 6NR

☎ 01279 870257 📄 01279 870423

e–mail: enquiries@whitehousestansted.co.uk

web: www.whitehousestansted.co.uk

dir: *Leave M11 junct 8 take B1256 towards Takeley through lights at Four Ashes x-rds 400yds corner of B1256 & Smiths Green*

The White House is a delightful 16th-century property situated close to Stansted Airport (but not on the flight path). The stylish bedrooms feature superb beds, luxurious bathrooms and many thoughtful touches. Traditional breakfasts are served in the farmhouse-style kitchen, using local ingredients. Evening meals are available at the Lion and Lamb, a nearby pub/restaurant owned by the proprietors, who can usually provide transport.

Rooms 3 rms (2 en suite) (1 pri facs) (3 fmly) S £60; D £65✳ **Facilities** TVB tea/coffee Cen ht Dinner Last d 10pm Wi-fi available **Parking** 6 **Notes** ❂ Closed 24–25, 31 Dec & 1 Jan

★★★★ GUEST ACCOMMODATION
Little Bullocks Farm

Hope End CM22 6TA

☎ 01279 870464 📄 01279 871430

e–mail: julie@waterman-farm.demon.co.uk

web: www.littlebullocksfarm.co.uk

dir: *M11 junct 8, B1256 to Takeley, over lights, 1st right to Hope End, left at triangle island, on left at bottom of lane*

Expect a friendly welcome at this pleasant, family-run guest house, which is situated in a peaceful rural location just a short drive from the M11 and Stansted Airport. The bedrooms are cheerfully decorated, with coordinated soft furnishings and many thoughtful touches. Breakfast is served at individual tables in the smart dining room.

Rooms 4 en suite (2 fmly) (4 GF) **Facilities** TVB tea/coffee Cen ht TVL **Parking** 15 **Notes** ❂ 🐾

THAXTED — MAP 12 TL63

★★★★ GUEST ACCOMMODATION
Thaxted Bed & Breakfast

Totmans Farm, Dunmow Rd CM6 2LU

☎ 01371 830233 📄 01371 831545

e–mail: stay@thaxtedandstanstedbandb.co.uk

web: www.thaxtedandstanstedbandb.co.uk

dir: *On brow of B184 at S end of Thaxted*

There is a warm welcome at this charming property situated just a short drive from Stansted airport and close to major roads. The spacious, thoughtfully equipped bedrooms are in a converted outbuilding. Each room has a separate lounge-dining area and a door to the communal west-facing conservatory.

Rooms 5 en suite (1 fmly) (1 GF) **Facilities** TVB tea/coffee Cen ht TVL **Parking** 5 **Notes** ❂

★★★ INN
The Farmhouse Inn

Monk Street CM6 2NR

☎ 01371 830864 📄 01371 831196

e–mail: info@farmhouseinn.org

web: www.farmhouseinn.org

dir: *M11 to A120 to B184 1m from Thaxted, between Thaxted and Great Dunmow*

This 16th-century inn overlooks the Chelmer Valley, and is surrounded by open countryside. The property is ideally situated in the quiet hamlet of Monk Street about two miles from the historic town of Thaxted. Bedrooms are pleasantly decorated and equipped with modern facilities. Public rooms include a cosy lounge bar and a large smartly appointed restaurant.

Rooms 11 annexe en suite **Facilities** FTV TVB tea/coffee Cen ht Dinner Last d 9pm Wi-fi available **Conf** Max 80 Thtr 80 Class 60 Board 50 **Parking** 35

ENGLAND

THORPE BAY — MAP 07 TQ98

See Southend-on-Sea

TOPPESFIELD — MAP 12 TL73

★★★ BED & BREAKFAST
Ollivers Farm

CO9 4LS

☎ 01787 237642 📄 01787 237602

e–mail: bandbolliversfarm@tesco.net

web: www.essex-bed-breakfast.co.uk

dir: *500yds SE of village centre. Off A1017 in Great Yeldham to Toppesfield, farm 1m on left before T-junct to village*

Impressive 16th-century farmhouse full of charm and character set amid pretty landscaped gardens in a peaceful rural location. Bedrooms are pleasantly decorated and thoughtfully equipped. Public rooms have a wealth of original features including exposed beams and a huge open fireplace in the reception hall.

Rooms 3 rms (1 en suite) (1 pri facs) S £30; D £60–£80✹
Facilities TV2B tea/coffee Shed for bikes **Parking** 4 **Notes** ⊗ No children 10yrs Closed 23 Dec–1 Jan ⊜

WESTCLIFF-ON-SEA — MAP 07 TQ88

See also Southend-on-Sea

★★★ GUEST ACCOMMODATION
Chilton House

3 Trinity Av SS0 7PU

☎ 01702 342282 & 07994 705902

e–mail: manager@thechilton.fsbusiness.co.uk

dir: *A13 to Milton Rd, at lights turn right towards Cliffs pavilion, left onto Cambridge Rd and right onto Trinity Avenue*

A two minute walk from the Cliff Pavilion and Westcliff Pier, this charming Victorian property provides a cheerful welcome. The well-presented bedrooms and bathrooms vary in size but all ensure a comfortable stay. A hearty breakfast is served in the cosy dining room/ lounge

Rooms 7 rms (4 en suite) (3 pri facs) (2 fmly) (1 GF) S £30–£35; D £52–£59.50✹ **Facilities** FTV TVB tea/coffee Cen ht TVL **Notes LB** ⊗ No children 3yrs

★★★ 🅰 GUEST HOUSE
The Rose House

21/23 Manor Rd SS0 7SR

☎ 01702 341959 📄 01702 390918

e–mail: joe@joegibson8.wanadoo.co.uk

dir: *Manor Rd opposite Westcliff-on-Sea railway station*

Rooms 19 en suite (2 fmly) (2 GF) S £25–£30; D £50–£60✹
Facilities STV FTV TVB tea/coffee Licensed Cen ht TVL Dinner Last d 8.30pm **Parking** 6 **Notes** ⊗ No coaches

---

WIX — MAP 13 TM12

★★★★★ FARM HOUSE
Dairy House *(TM148293)*

Bradfield Rd CO11 2SR

☎ 01255 870322 📄 01255 870186 Mrs B Whitworth

e–mail: bridgetwhitworth@btinternet.com

web: www.dairyhousefarm.info

dir: *Off A120 into Wix, turn at x-rds to Bradfield, farm 1m on left*

This Georgian house stands amid 700 acres of arable land, with stunning views of the surrounding countryside. Extensively renovated in the Victorian style, it still retains original decorative tiled floors, moulded cornices and marble fireplaces. The spacious bedrooms are carefully furnished and equipped with many thoughtful touches. Breakfast is served in the elegant antique-furnished dining room and there is a cosy lounge.

Rooms 2 en suite S £38–£42; D £57–£65 **Facilities** TVB tea/coffee Cen ht TVL 🐾 **Parking** 8 **Notes** ⊗ No children 12yrs 700 acres arable, fruit ⊜

GLOUCESTERSHIRE

ALDERTON — MAP 10 SP03

★★★★ BED & BREAKFAST
Tally Ho Bed & Breakfast

20 Beckford Rd GL20 8NL

☎ 01242 621482

e–mail: tallyhobb@aol.com

dir: *3m NW of Winchcombe. Off B4077 into Alderton village*

Convenient for the M5, this friendly establishment stands in a delightful quiet village. Bedrooms, including two on the ground floor, offer modern comforts and attractive coordinated furnishings. Breakfast is served in the stylish dining room with the village pub just a stroll away for dinner.

Rooms 3 en suite (1 fmly) (2 GF) S £40–£45; D £60–£70 **Facilities** TVB tea/coffee Cen ht **Parking** 3 **Notes LB** ⊜

See advert on opposite page

ARLINGHAM
MAP 04 SO71

★★★★ ◉◉ ♨ RESTAURANT WITH ROOMS
The Old Passage Inn
Passage Rd GL2 7JR
☎ 01452 740547 📄 01452 741871
e–mail: oldpassage@ukonline.co.uk
dir: *A38 onto B4071 through Arlingham, located by river*
Delightfully located on the very edge of the River Severn, this relaxing restaurant with rooms combines high quality food with an air of tranquillity. Outdoor terrace seating is available in warmer months. The menu offers a wide range of seafood and shellfish dishes including crab, oysters and lobsters from Cornwall kept live in seawater tanks. Bedrooms and bathrooms are decorated in a modern style and include a range of welcome extras such as air conditioning and a well stocked mini bar.
Rooms 3 en suite S £75–£130; D £95–£130✱ **Facilities** STV TVB tea/coffee Cen ht Dinner Last d 9.30pm Wi-fi available **Parking** 30 **Notes** ❌ Closed 24–27 Dec

BERKELEY
MAP 04 ST69

★★★ INN
The Malt House
22 Marybrook St GL13 9BA
☎ 01453 511177 📄 01453 810257
e–mail: the-malthouse@btconnect.com
web: www.themalthouse.uk.com
dir: *A38 into Berkeley, at town hall follow road to right, premises on right past hospital & opposite school*

Well located for business and leisure, this family-run inn has a convivial atmosphere. Bedrooms are soundly appointed while public areas include a choice of bars, a skittle alley and an attractive restaurant area. Local attractions include Berkeley Castle and the Slimbridge Wildfowl and Wetlands Trust.
Rooms 10 rms (9 en suite) (2 fmly) S £50–£58; D £70–£85✱ **Facilities** FTV TVB tea/coffee Cen ht Dinner Last d 9pm Pool Table Skittle Alley **Parking** 30 **Notes** LB ❌

BIBURY
MAP 05 SP10

★★★★ BED & BREAKFAST
Cotteswold House
Arlington GL7 5ND
☎ 01285 740609 📄 01285 740609
e–mail: enquiries@cotteswoldhouse.org.uk
web: www.cotteswoldhouse.org.uk
dir: *On B4425, 500yds W of village centre*
Convenient for exploring the Cotswolds, Cotteswold House offers a warm welcome and high levels of comfort and quality. Spacious bedrooms are equipped with thoughtful extras, and there is a cosy lounge with useful local information.
Rooms 3 en suite S fr £48; D fr £68 **Facilities** TVB tea/coffee Cen ht **Parking** 3 **Notes** LB ❌

233

BIRDWOOD   MAP 10 SO71

★★★ INN
Kings Head
GL19 3EF

☎ 01452 750348 📄 01452 750348

dir: *On A40 in village of Birdwood*

Located between Gloucester and Ross-on-Wye, this attractive roadside inn offers attractive, bright bedrooms, two of which have patios. The spacious public areas are themed with military memorabilia, and the cosy dining room is the setting for breakfast and popular bar meals.

Rooms 8 en suite (1 fmly) (2 GF) (2 smoking) S fr £38; D fr £48✳ **Facilities** TVB tea/coffee Cen ht TVL Dinner Last d 9pm Golf 9 Pool Table **Conf** Max 70 **Parking** 100 **Notes** ✪ Closed 24–26 Dec

BLOCKLEY   MAP 10 SP13

Premier Collection

★★★★★ 🏠 🍴 GUEST ACCOMMODATION
Lower Brook House
Lower St GL56 9DS

☎ 01386 700286 📄 01386 701400

e–mail: info@lowerbrookhouse.com
web: www.lowerbrookhouse.com

dir: *In village centre*

Dating from the 17th century, this enchanting house is the perfect place to relax. Genuine hospitality and attentive service are hallmarks here, and bedrooms come in all shapes and sizes. There's a lot of character in the public areas, with beams, flagstone floors, huge fireplace and deep stone walls. Enjoy a delicious breakfast and an aperitif in the garden, but leave room for the skilfully prepared dinner.

Rooms 6 en suite S £80–£175; D £95–£175✳ **Facilities** TVB tea/coffee Cen ht Dinner Last d 9pm Wi-fi available **Parking** 8 **Notes** No children 10yrs

BOURTON-ON-THE-WATER   MAP 10 SP12

★★★★ GUEST HOUSE
Coombe House
Rissington Rd GL54 2DT

☎ 01451 821966 📄 01451 810477

e–mail: info@coombehouse.net

dir: *Off A429 through village, past Birdland on right, 300yds on left*

A warm welcome is assured at this immaculately presented house, set in a mature garden. Bedrooms are equipped with a wealth of homely extras and ground-floor rooms are available. Facilities include a comfortable lounge and sun terrace, and breakfast is served in the attractive breakfast room overlooking the flower-filled garden.

Rooms 6 en suite (2 GF) S £50–£65; D £65–£85✳ **Facilities** TVB tea/coffee Cen ht TVL **Parking** 6 **Notes** ✪ No children 12yrs No coaches RS Nov -Feb

★★★★ BED & BREAKFAST
Larks Rise
Old Gloucester Rd GL54 3BH

☎ 01451 822613 & 07884 438498

e–mail: larks.rise@virgin.net
web: www.larksrisehouse.co.uk

dir: *0.5m W of village. A249 onto A436, 1st driveway on left*

A relaxed and welcoming home, sitting in its own acre of gardens on the edge of the village of Bourton-on-the-Water. Comfort and style are of paramount importance at this delightful property where the proprietors offer a very warm welcome. Accommodation is most comfortable using cotton sheets on pocket sprung beds, with high standards of en suite facilities and toiletries. Breakfasts feature locally sourced produce and there is ample parking to the front of the property.

Rooms 3 rms (2 en suite) (1 pri facs) (1 GF) **Facilities** TVB tea/coffee Cen ht **Parking** 6 **Notes** ✪ No children 12yrs

★★★★ BED & BREAKFAST
The Lawns
Station Rd GL54 2ER

☎ 01451 821195

e–mail: the.lawns@virgin.net
web: www.cotswoldbedandbreakfast.net

dir: *A429, at lights continue into village, 1st house on right*

A warm welcome awaits all guests at the Lawns B&B, a traditional Cotswold stone property set on the edge of the village of Bourton-on-the-Water. Accommodation is situated in a separate building and consists of very spacious and comfortable rooms which are tastefully furnished and en suite. Breakfast is served in the main house dining room at separate tables.

Rooms 3 annexe en suite (1 GF) S £50–£65; D £60–£75✳ **Facilities** TVB tea/coffee Cen ht **Parking** 6 **Notes** ✪ 🐾

★★★ BED & BREAKFAST
The Cotswold House
Lansdowne GL54 2AR

☎ 01451 822373

e–mail: meadowscotswoldhouse@btinternet.com

dir: *Off A429 into Landsdowne & continue 0.5m to Cotswold House on right opp Paragon Garage*

A warm welcome is assured at this well maintained, mellow-stone house. Just a short walk from the church and the many attractions of this popular village, this is a great base for touring the Cotswolds. Bedrooms are comfortably furnished, and one is a self-contained conversion of the former village telephone exchange, set within immaculate gardens.

Rooms 3 en suite 1 annexe en suite (1 fmly) S £30–£60; D £55–£65 **Facilities** TVB tea/coffee Cen ht TVL **Parking** 5 **Notes** LB ✪ 🐾

★★★ BED & BREAKFAST
Strathspey

Lansdowne GL54 2AR
☎ 01451 810321 & 07889 491993
e–mail: information@strathspey.org.uk
web: www.strathspey.org.uk

dir: *Off A429 into Lansdowne, 200yds on right*

This friendly Edwardian-style cottage is just a short riverside walk from the charming village centre, perfume factory and the famous model village. Bedrooms, one at ground floor level having its own front door, are well presented with many useful extras, and substantial breakfasts are part of the caring hospitality.

Rooms 2 en suite 1 annexe en suite (1 fmly) (1 GF) S fr £40; D fr £55✳
Facilities TVB tea/coffee Cen ht TVL **Parking** 4 **Notes LB** ☻

CHELTENHAM   **MAP 10 SO92**

★★★★★ GUEST ACCOMMODATION
Beaumont House

56 Shurdington Rd GL53 0JE
☎ 01242 223311 🖹 01242 520044
e–mail: reservations@bhhotel.co.uk
web: www.bhhotel.co.uk

dir: *S side of town on A46 to Stroud*

Built as a private residence, this popular establishment exudes genteel charm. Public areas include a large lounge and an elegant dining room which overlooks the garden. Many improvements have taken place recently and include new studio bedrooms on the top floor, which complement the already completed 'Out of Asia' and 'Out of Africa' bedrooms which are luxuriously furnished and very well equipped. Bedrooms situated to the rear of the building have views over Leckhampton Hill and there are also bedrooms on the lower ground floor.

Rooms 16 en suite (3 fmly) S £63–£74; D £86–£201✳ **Facilities** STV FTV TVB tea/coffee Direct dial from bedrooms Cen ht Dinner Last d 8.30pm **Parking** 16 **Notes LB** ☻ No children 5yrs

★★★★★ GUEST ACCOMMODATION
Cleeve Hill House

Cleeve Hill GL52 3PR
☎ 01242 672052 🖹 01242 679969
e–mail: info@cleevehill-hotel.co.uk

dir: *3m N of Cheltenham on B4632*

This large detached property was built in Edwardian times and both the lounge and many of the bedrooms have spectacular views across to the Malvern Hills. Rooms vary for shapes and sizes but all are comfortably furnished with many welcome extras and include some with four poster beds. In addition to the relaxing guest lounge, an honesty bar is in place. Breakfast, served in the pleasant conservatory, offers a good selection of carefully presented hot and cold items.

Rooms 10 rms (9 en suite) (1 pri facs) (1 GF) S £45–£65; D £75–£95✳
Facilities STV FTV TVB tea/coffee Direct dial from bedrooms Cen ht Wi-fi available **Parking** 11 **Notes** ☻ No children 8yrs

★★★★★ BED & BREAKFAST
Georgian House

77 Montpellier Ter GL50 1XA
☎ 01242 515577 🖹 01242 545929
e–mail: penny@georgianhouse.net
web: www.georgianhouse.net

dir: *M5 junct 11, A40 into town centre & onto Montpellier Ter, Georgian House on right after park*

Dating from 1807, this elegant Georgian house is located in the fashionable area of Montpellier. Renovation has resulted in delightful accommodation with quality and comfort throughout. Bedrooms are individually styled, with contemporary comforts cleverly interwoven with period furnishings to great effect. Warm hospitality and attentive service ensure a memorable stay.

Rooms 3 en suite S £60–£70; D £80–£105 **Facilities** FTV TVB tea/coffee Cen ht Wi-fi available **Parking** 2 **Notes** ☻ No children 16yrs Closed Xmas & New Year

★★★★★ 🅰 GUEST HOUSE
Lypiatt House

Lypiatt Rd GL50 2QW
☎ 01242 224994 🖹 01242 224996
e–mail: stay@lypiatt.co.uk

dir: *M5 junct 11 to town centre. At Texaco petrol station mini-rdbt take exit signed Stroud. Fork right, pass shops, turn sharp left onto Lypiatt Rd*

Rooms 10 en suite (2 GF) S £70–£90; D £80–£170✳ **Facilities** FTV TVB tea/coffee Direct dial from bedrooms Licensed Cen ht **Conf** Max 10 Board 10 **Parking** available **Notes LB** ☻ No children 10yrs No coaches

CHELTENHAM CONTINUED

★★★★ GUEST ACCOMMODATION
Butlers
Western Rd GL50 3RN
☎ 01242 570771 📠 01242 528724
e–mail: info@butlers-hotel.co.uk

dir: *M5 junct 11, over 2 rdbts & 2 lights onto Landsdown Rd, left at next lights to end of Christchurch Rd, left at mini-rdbt onto Malvern Rd, Western Rd 2nd on right*

This elegant late Regency house has a quiet location yet is only a stroll from the Promenade, Montpellier and the town centre. Decor and furnishings are stylish, and the spacious, elegant bedrooms (named after butlers from literature and history) are extremely well equipped, and all have PCs. Public rooms include an inviting sitting room and a charming breakfast room that overlooks the delightful rear garden.

Rooms 7 en suite (2 fmly) (1 GF) **Facilities** TVB tea/coffee Direct dial from bedrooms Cen ht TVL Wi-fi available **Parking** 8 **Notes** No children 5yrs

★★★★ GUEST ACCOMMODATION
Badger Towers
133 Hales Rd GL52 6ST
☎ 01242 522583 📠 01242 574800
e–mail: mrbadger@badgertowers.co.uk
web: www.badgertowers.co.uk

dir: *Off A40 London Rd onto Hales Rd, 0.5m on right towards Prestbury Village and racecourse*

Located in the residential area of Battledown, close to the racecourse, town centre and GCHQ, this elegant Victorian house offers thoughtfully furnished bedrooms, a light and airy breakfast room, and a spacious lounge complete with piano. The well-cooked breakfasts, with an emphasis on local produce, are a satisfying start to the day.

Rooms 7 en suite (2 GF) S £50–£70; D £70–£105✴ **Facilities** FTV TVB tea/coffee Cen ht Wi-fi available **Parking** 7 **Notes LB** Closed Xmas & New Year

★★★★ GUEST HOUSE
The Battledown
125 Hales Rd GL52 6ST
☎ 01242 233881
e–mail: battledown125@hotmail.com

dir: *0.5m E of town centre. A40 onto B4075, 0.5m on right*

This elegant and well-proportioned Grade II listed house offers comfortable accommodation close to the town centre and racecourse. The refurbished bedrooms and bathrooms provide plenty of quality and comfort with some welcome extras, while the smart dining room is an attractive setting for breakfast.

Rooms 7 en suite (2 fmly) S £48; D £68✴ **Facilities** TVB tea/coffee Cen ht Wi-fi available **Parking** 7 **Notes LB** ⊗ No coaches Closed Xmas

★★★★ GUEST ACCOMMODATION
Clarence Court
Clarence Square GL50 4JR
☎ 01242 580411 📠 01242 224609
e–mail: enquiries@clarencecourthotel.co.uk
web: www.clarencecourthotel.com

Situated in an attractive, tree-lined Georgian square, this property was once owned by the Duke of Wellington. Sensitive refurbishment is returning the building to its former glory with elegant public rooms reflecting the grace of a bygone age. Spacious bedrooms offer ample comfort and quality with many original features retained. The convenience of the peaceful location is a great asset, only a 5-minute stroll from the town centre.

Rooms 21 rms (19 en suite) (3 fmly) (7 GF) **Facilities** TVB tea/coffee Direct dial from bedrooms Cen ht **Parking** 21

★★★★ GUEST ACCOMMODATION
The Prestbury House
The Burgage, Prestbury GL52 3DN
☎ 01242 529533 📠 01242 227076
e–mail: enquiries@prestburyhouse.co.uk
web: www.prestburyhouse.co.uk

dir: *1m NE of Cheltenham. Follow all signs for racecourse, Evesham (A435) and Prestbury (B4632) From racecourse follow Prestbury signs. 2nd left signed Prestbury House, 500yds from racecourse entrance*

Standing its own grounds, this impressive house offers a wealth of history along with spacious and comfortable accommodation.

CONTINUED

Bedrooms are divided between the larger rooms of the main house and an adjacent former coach house. The public areas are full of character and include a comfy bar, traditional breakfast room and delightful surrounding gardens.

Rooms 7 en suite 8 annexe en suite (3 GF) S £65–£89; D £70–£128 **Facilities** STV TVB tea/coffee Direct dial from bedrooms Cen ht TVL Wi-fi available Gymnasium ⚐ Archery, Bike hire, Trim trail, Hill walking **Conf** Max 40 Thtr 40 Class 25 Board 20 Del from £115 **Parking** 40 **Notes** ⊗ Civ Wed 60

★★★★ GUEST ACCOMMODATION
33 Montpellier

33 Montpellier Ter GL50 1UX

☎ 01242 526009 🖹 01242 579793

e-mail: montpellierhotel@btopenworld.com

dir: M5 junct 11, A40 to rdbt at Montpellier, over rdbt & 100yds on right

The friendly and welcoming Montpellier forms part of an elegant Georgian terrace overlooking the municipal gardens in a fashionable area of town convenient for shops, restaurants and amenities. Bedrooms are light, airy and well equipped with a range of practical extras and thoughtful touches. Breakfast is served in the lower ground dining room.

Rooms 7 en suite (5 fmly) S £45–£65; D £65–£85✳ **Facilities** FTV TVB tea/coffee Direct dial from bedrooms Cen ht TVL **Notes LB** ⊗ 🐾

★★★★ GUEST ACCOMMODATION
White Lodge

Hatherley Ln GL51 6SH

☎ 01242 242347 🖹 01242 242347

e-mail: pamela@whitelodgebandb.wanadoo.co.uk

dir: M5 junct 11, A40 to Cheltenham, 1st rdbt 4th exit Hatherley Ln, White Lodge 1st on right

Built around 1900, this well cared for, smart and friendly establishment is convenient for access to the M5. Bedrooms, of varied size, offer quality and many extra facilities, including fridges and Wi-fi. The very comfortable dining room, where breakfast is served around a grand table, looks out across the pleasant backdrop of White Lodge's extensive gardens.

Rooms 4 en suite (1 GF) S £39–£42; D £55–£60✳ **Facilities** FTV TVB tea/coffee Cen ht Wi-fi available **Parking** 6 **Notes** 🐾

★★★★ GUEST ACCOMMODATION
Wishmoor House

147 Hales Rd GL52 6TD

☎ 01242 238504 🖹 01242 226090

e-mail: wishmoor@hotmail.co.uk

dir: A40 onto B4075 Hales Rd signed Prestbury, racecourse, crematorium, 0.5m on right

Wishmoor House is an elegantly modernised spacious Victorian residence, situated between the town centre and racecourse with easy access from all major roads and ample parking. Inside you can expect charming period features, wonderful views and a warm welcome. Free Wi-fi is available.

Rooms 10 rms (9 en suite) (1 pri facs) (2 fmly) S £39–£49; D £65–£72✳ **Facilities** TVB tea/coffee Cen ht Wi-fi available **Conf** Max 10 Thtr 10 Class 10 Board 10 **Parking** 9 **Notes** ⊗

★★★★ 🅰
The Cheltenham Townhouse

12–14 Pittville Lawn GL52 2BD

☎ 01242 221922 🖹 01242 244687

e-mail: info@cheltenhamtownhouse.com

web: www.cheltenhamtownhouse.com

dir: A435 to Evesham, turn right into Wellington Rd, at lights turn into Pittville Lawn

Rooms 22 rms (21 en suite) (1 pri facs) (8 fmly) (11 GF) **Facilities** FTV TVB tea/coffee Lift Cen ht TVL Wi-fi available **Parking** 14 **Notes** ⊗ RS 23–27 Dec

★★★ GUEST ACCOMMODATION
Hope Orchard

Gloucester Rd, Staverton GL51 0TF

☎ 01452 855556 🖹 01452 530037

e-mail: info@hopeorchard.com

web: www.hopeorchard.com

dir: A40 onto B4063 at Arlecourt rdbt, Hope Orchard 1.25m on right

Situated midway between Gloucester and Cheltenham, this is a good base for exploring the area. The comfortable bedrooms are next to the main house, and all are on the ground floor and have their own separate entrances. There is a large garden, and ample off-road parking is available.

Rooms 8 en suite (8 GF) **Facilities** FTV TVB tea/coffee Direct dial from bedrooms Cen ht Wi-fi available **Parking** 10

★★★ INN
The Beaufort Arms

184 London Rd GL52 6HJ

☎ 01242 526038 🖹 01242 526038

e-mail: beaufort.arms@blueyonder.co.uk

dir: On A40

Located on the main road, just outside of the town centre, this traditional inn offers a friendly welcome and a relaxed style of service and hospitality. Bedrooms, some with en suite and some sharing bathrooms, have been recently refurbished to provide sound standards throughout. A range of home cooked meals and a selection of real ales are available.

Rooms 5 rms (2 en suite) (1 fmly) D £50–£56✳ **Facilities** FTV TVB tea/coffee Cen ht TVL Dinner Last d 8pm Pool Table **Parking** 5 **Notes** ⊗

CONTINUED

CHELTENHAM CONTINUED

★★★ GUEST ACCOMMODATION
Lonsdale House

Montpellier Dr GL50 1TX
☎ 01242 232379 📄 01242 232379
e–mail: lonsdalehouse@hotmail.com

dir: *Off A46 towards Stroud, 0.25m from town centre by Eagle Tower tall building*

A warm welcome awaits you at this centrally located guest house with private parking. This Regency house has been renovated and provides comfortable accommodation. Bedrooms range in size, with all featuring homely extras. Breakfast is served in the smart dining room, and a small lounge is available.

Rooms 9 rms (3 en suite) (1 pri facs) (3 fmly) S £35–£49; D £60–£75 **Facilities** TVB tea/coffee Cen ht **Parking** 6 **Notes** ⊗

★★★ Ⓐ BED & BREAKFAST
Cheltenham Guest House

145 Hewlett Rd GL52 6TS
☎ 01242 521726 📄 0871 661 4405
e–mail: info@cheltenhamguesthouse.biz

dir: *A40 London Rd into town, follow GH signs to hospital, Hewlett Rd on right after A&E*

Rooms 9 rms (7 en suite) (1 fmly) **Facilities** FTV TVB tea/coffee Cen ht Wi-fi available **Parking** 6

CHIPPING CAMPDEN   MAP 10 SP13

See also Blockley

Premier Collection

★★★★★ GUEST HOUSE
The Malt House

Broad Campden GL55 6UU
☎ 01386 840295 📄 01386 841334
e–mail: info@malt-house.co.uk
web: www.malt-house.co.uk

dir: *0.8m SE of Chipping Campden in Broad Campden, by church*

Formed from the village malt house and adjacent cottages, this beguiling house dates from the 16th century. Original features are mixed with contemporary comforts, and bedrooms have quality soft fabrics and period furniture. There is a choice of lounges, an elegant breakfast room, and a wonderful garden with croquet lawn and relaxing seating.

The Malt House

Rooms 4 en suite 3 annexe en suite (3 fmly) (1 GF) S £85; D £143✱ **Facilities** FTV TVB tea/coffee Licensed Cen ht TVL Wi-fi available 🍴 **Conf** Max 8 Board 8 **Parking** 10 **Notes** ⊗ No coaches Closed 22–28 Dec

★★★★ BED & BREAKFAST
Bramley House

6 Aston Rd GL55 6HR
☎ 01386 840066 & 07855 760113
e–mail: povey@bramleyhouse.co.uk

dir: *Off High St onto B4081 towards Mickleton, house 0.5m opp cul-de-sac Grevel Ln & post box*

A warm welcome and refreshment on arrival await you to Bramley House. With ample off-road parking and just a stroll from the centre of this popular market town, this friendly family home offers attractively coordinated accommodation, with many thoughtful extras. The rear room offers superb tranquil field views. A delicious breakfast, featuring organic produce whenever possible, is served in the smart dining room around a large communal table.

Rooms 2 en suite **Facilities** TVB tea/coffee Cen ht **Parking** 3 **Notes** ⊗ No children 12yrs Closed 16 Dec–Jan 🐾

★★★★ ◉ RESTAURANT WITH ROOMS
The Kings

The Square GL55 6AW
☎ 01386 840256 & 841056 📄 01386 841598
e–mail: info@kingscampden.co.uk

dir: *In centre of town square*

Located in the centre of historic Chipping Campden, this Grade II listed late Georgian property is popular with visitors and locals alike, and the friendly and good-humoured staff all contribute to the convivial buzz. Bedrooms offer ample comfort with period features and mod cons combined to stylish effect. The menus show a range of flavour-packed dishes, complemented by a particularly good selection of wines by the glass.

Rooms 14 en suite (2 fmly) **Facilities** FTV TVB tea/coffee Direct dial from bedrooms Cen ht Dinner Last d 9.30pm Wi-fi available **Conf** Thtr 30 Class 20 Board 20 **Parking** 8

CONTINUED

★ ★ ★ ★ BED & BREAKFAST
Poppy Bank
4 Aston Rd GL55 6HR
☎ 01386 840424
e–mail: junebritton@dsl.pipex.com

dir: *A44 onto B4081 through Chipping Campden towards Mickleton House, 0.25m from village centre on right*
Just a few minutes easy walk away from the village centre, this recently developed accommodation is well equipped, light and airy. Bedrooms are spacious with comfortable seating, and one room has French doors overlooking the pretty rear garden and open farm land. Breakfast is taken in the cosy dining room/lounge at separate tables.

Rooms 2 en suite (1 fmly) D £65–£80✱ **Facilities** TVB tea/coffee Cen ht Wi-fi available **Parking** 6 **Notes LB** ⊗ RS Xmas wk ➌

★ ★ ★ ★ BED & BREAKFAST
Staddlestones
7 Aston Rd GL55 6HR
☎ 01386 849288
e–mail: info@staddle-stones.com
web: www.staddle-stones.com

dir: *B4081 signed to Mickleton, out of Chipping Campden 200mtrs. House on right opp gravel lane*
A warm welcome can be expected from the host Pauline Kirton at this delightful property, situated just a short walk from the Cotswold village of Chipping Campden and an ideal base for walking, cycling, golf or just relaxing. The accommodation consists of three comfortable bedrooms offering some thoughtful extras for guests use. A hearty breakfast is taken in the dining room around the communal table, and offers a good choice using mostly organic produce from local farms. Dinner can be provided by arrangement.

Rooms 2 en suite 1 annexe en suite (1 fmly) D £65–£85✱ **Facilities** FTV TVB tea/coffee Cen ht Dinner Last d previous day **Parking** 6 **Notes** No children 12yrs ➌

★ ★ ★ ★ BED & BREAKFAST
Catbrook House
Catbrook GL55 6DE
☎ 01386 841499 & 07731 953365
e–mail: m.klein@virgin.net

dir: *B4081 into Chipping Campden, signs for Broad Campden until Catbrook House on right*
Having stunning rural views and just a short walk from the town centre, this mellow-stone house provides comfortable, homely bedrooms. The attentive hosts extend a friendly welcome. A traditional English breakfast is served in the comfortably furnished dining room.

Rooms 3 rms (1 en suite) (2 pri facs) S fr £42; D fr £52✱ **Facilities** TV2B tea/coffee Cen ht **Parking** 3 **Notes** ⊗ No children 9yrs Closed Xmas ➌

★ ★ ★ ★ BED & BREAKFAST
Holly House
Ebrington GL55 6NL
☎ 01386 593213
e–mail: hutsbybandb@aol.com
web: www.hollyhousebandb.co.uk

dir: *B4035 from Chipping Campden towards Shipston on Stour, 0.5m left to Ebrington & signed*
Set in the heart of the pretty Cotswold village of Ebrington, this late Victorian house offers thoughtfully equipped accommodation. Bedrooms are housed in buildings that were formerly used by the local wheelwright, and offer level access, seclusion and privacy. Quality English breakfasts are served in the light and airy dining room. For other meals, the village pub is just a short walk away.

Rooms 2 en suite 1 annexe en suite (1 fmly) (3 GF) S £45–£60; D £65–£70 **Facilities** TVB tea/coffee Cen ht Last d am **Parking** 5 **Notes** ⊗ Closed Xmas ➌

★ ★ ★ ★ FARM HOUSE
Manor Farm *(SP124412)*
Weston Subedge GL55 6QH
☎ 01386 840390 & 07889 108812 📄 0870 1640638
Mrs L King
e–mail: lucy@manorfarmbnb.demon.co.uk
web: www.manorfarmbnb.demon.co.uk

dir: *2m NW of Chipping Campden. On B4632 in Weston Subedge*
A genuine welcome is extended at this 17th-century mellow Cotswold-stone farmhouse. The welcome also extends to pets, and stabling is available by arrangement. Bedrooms are comfortable and homely with thoughtful extras. Facilities include a lounge with a wood-burning stove, and an elegant dining room where mouth-watering breakfasts are served.

Rooms 3 en suite S £50–£70; D £65–£70 **Facilities** FTV TVB tea/coffee Cen ht TVL **Parking** 8 **Notes LB** ⊗ 800 acres arable, cattle, horses, sheep

★ ★ ★ GUEST ACCOMMODATION
Stonecroft Bed & Breakfast
Stonecroft, George Ln GL55 6DA
☎ 01386 840486
e–mail: info@stonecroft-chippingcampden.co.uk
Quietly located in a residential area just a stroll from the High Street, this well-maintained property offers relaxing accommodation. Guests have the key to their own entrance and can come and go as they please. Breakfast is served around one large table in the compact but well-furnished dining room.

Rooms 3 en suite D £60–£65✱ **Facilities** TVB tea/coffee Cen ht **Parking** 2 **Notes** ⊗ No children 12yrs ➌

ENGLAND

U

Myrtle House

High St, Mickleton GL55 6SA

☎ 01386 430032

e–mail: louanne@myrtlehouse.co.uk

dir: *A46 onto B4632 towards Broadway. In Mickleton, on left opp Three Ways House*

At the time of going to press the rating for this establishment had not been confirmed. Please check the AA website www.theAA.com for up-to-date information.

Rooms 5 en suite (2 fmly) S £45–£55; D £65–£85✳ **Facilities** TVB tea/coffee Cen ht Dinner Last d 24hrs before arrival Wi-fi available **Parking** 2 **Notes** LB

CHIPPING SODBURY   MAP 04 ST78

★★★★ GUEST ACCOMMODATION

The Moda House

1 High St BS37 6BA

☎ 01454 312135 📄 01454 850090

e–mail: enquiries@modahotel.com

web: www.modahotel.com

dir: *In town centre*

This popular Grade II listed Georgian house has an imposing position at the top of the High Street. It has been refurbished to provide modern bedrooms of varying shapes and sizes and comfortable public areas, while retaining many original features. Room facilities include satellite TV and phones.

Rooms 7 en suite 3 annexe en suite (1 fmly) (3 GF) **Facilities** STV TVB tea/coffee Direct dial from bedrooms Cen ht TVL Wi-fi available **Conf** Max 20 Thtr 10 Board 10

CIRENCESTER   MAP 05 SP00

★★★★ ◉ INN

Hare & Hounds

Fosse-Cross, Chedworth GL54 4NN

☎ 01285 720288

e–mail: stay@hareandhoundsinn.com

web: www.hareandhoundsinn.com

dir: *4.5m NE of Cirencester. On A429 by speed camera*

This traditional country inn built of Cotswold stone offers delicious home-cooked food in the garden, orangerie or one of the elegant dining rooms. The smart and comfortable en suite bedrooms surround a peaceful courtyard. Ample car parking to the rear of the inn.

Rooms 10 en suite (2 fmly) (8 GF) **Facilities** TVB tea/coffee Direct dial from bedrooms Cen ht Dinner Last d 9.30pm Wi-fi available **Parking** 40 **Notes** ⊗

COLEFORD   MAP 04 SO51

★★★★ GUEST ACCOMMODATION

Chapel Cottage

3 Chapel Rd, Berry Hill GL16 7QY

☎ 01594 836547

e–mail: chapelcottagefod@btinternet.com

dir: *Off A4136 at Five Acres onto Park Rd. 1st left, 200yds on left*

This lovely 19th-century cottage is well situated for exploring the Forest of Dean. The welcome here is genuine and every effort is made to ensure a relaxing and comfortable stay. Bedrooms are attractively styled to a high standard with a host of thoughtful extras, and the contemporary bathrooms are of a high quality. Breakfast is a tasty and satisfying feast, served in the light and airy dining room.

Rooms 3 en suite S £40–£45; D £60–£65✳ **Facilities** TVB tea/coffee Cen ht Dinner Last d prior notice needed **Parking** 3 **Notes** ⊗ ⊜

★ ★ ★ ★ FARM HOUSE
Dryslade Farm *(SO581147)*
English Bicknor GL16 7PA
☎ 01594 860259 📠 01594 860259 Mrs D Gwilliam
e–mail: daphne@drysladefarm.co.uk
web: www.drysladefarm.co.uk

dir: *3m N of Coleford. Off A4136 onto B4432, right towards English Bicknor, farm 1m*

You are warmly welcomed at this 184-acre working farm, which dates from 1780 and has been in the same family for almost 100 years. The en suite bedrooms are attractively furnished in natural pine and are well equipped. The lounge leads onto a conservatory where hearty breakfasts are served.

Rooms 3 en suite (1 GF) S £45–£50; D £60–£70 **Facilities** TVB tea/coffee Cen ht TVL **Parking** 6 **Notes LB** 184 acres Beef 🐾

★ ★ ★ BED & BREAKFAST
Cor Unum
Monmouth Rd, Edge-End GL16 7HB
☎ 01594 837960
e–mail: antony@jones3649.freeserve.co.uk

dir: *On A4136 in village of Edge End*

A genuine welcome is assured at this comfortably appointed bungalow which is located in the heart of the Forest of Dean. Bedrooms are neatly furnished, and the lounge has wonderful views across the garden of the Welsh mountains. Breakfast, served in the cosy dining room, is a tasty and fulfilling start to the day.

Rooms 3 rms (2 en suite) (3 GF) S £25–£35; D £50–£80✳
Facilities TVB tea/coffee Cen ht TVL **Parking** 1 **Notes LB** No children 🐾

COWLEY   MAP 10 SO91
★ ★ ★ ★ 🍴 INN
The Green Dragon
Cockleford GL53 9NW
☎ 01242 870271
e–mail: green-dragon@buccaneer.co.uk

The Green Dragon offers all the charm and character of an English country pub combined with a light and airy relaxed atmosphere and carefully prepared food made from local produce. Bedrooms, some at ground floor level, are located in an annexe beside and behind the main building and vary in size. There is a terrace to the front where guests may enjoy a cool drink on warm sunny days.

Rooms 9 en suite (4 GF) **Facilities** tea/coffee Direct dial from bedrooms Cen ht Dinner Last d 10pm **Conf** Max 65 Thtr 65 Class 65 Board 65 **Parking** 11

DIDMARTON   MAP 04 ST88
★ ★ ★ ★ 🍴 INN
The Kings Arms
The Street GL9 1DT
☎ 01454 238245 📠 01454 238249
e–mail: bookings@kingsarmsdidmarton.co.uk

dir: *In village centre*

Located on the fringes of the Beaufort Estate close to Westonbirt Arboretum, this 17th-century coaching inn has considerable charm, with original features cleverly interwoven with contemporary comforts. Local produce features on the menu, which can be enjoyed in either of the bars or the attractive restaurant. The comfortable bedrooms are light and neatly presented.

Rooms 4 en suite (1 fmly) **Facilities** TVB tea/coffee Cen ht Dinner bowls pitch **Conf** Max 22 **Parking** 22 **Notes** ⊗ RS 25–26 Dec & 1 Jan

EBRINGTON	MAP 10 SP14

★★★★ ⊛ INN
The Ebrington Arms
GL55 6NH
☎ 01386 593223
e–mail: info@theebringtonarms.co.uk
web: www.theebringtonarms.co.uk
dir: *From Chipping Campden take B4035 towards Shipston-on-Stour, left to Ebrington*

Located in the quiet, unspoilt village of Ebington, just a couple of miles from Chipping Campden, this 17th-century inn provides an excellent selection of real ales, fine wines and really enjoyable homemade dishes utilising the finest of produce. Food can be enjoyed in the traditional ambience of the bar or the cosy dining room with roaring open fire. Bedrooms are full of character and include some welcome extras. A large beer garden and car park are also available.

Rooms 3 en suite D £90–£100 **Facilities** FTV TVB tea/coffee Cen ht Dinner Last d 9pm **Conf** Max 32 Thtr 32 Class 32 Board 25 **Parking** 10 **Notes** LB

FORD	MAP 10 SP02

★★★★ ⇔ INN
The Plough Inn
GL54 5RU
☎ 01386 584215 📄 01386 584042
e–mail: info@theploughinnatford.co.uk
web: www.theploughinnatford.co.uk
dir: *On B4077 in village*

Popular with locals and the racing fraternity, this charming 16th-century inn retains many original features such as Cotswold stone walls, open fires and beamed ceilings. Cheltenham, Tewkesbury and many popular Cotswold towns and villages are within close proximity. Home-cooked food featuring local produce is a highlight. Bedrooms are situated in a restored stable block across a courtyard, adjacent to the delightful beer garden.

Rooms 3 annexe en suite (2 fmly) **Facilities** FTV TVB tea/coffee Cen ht Dinner Last d 9pm **Conf** Max 30 **Parking** 50 **Notes** ⊗

FOSSEBRIDGE	MAP 05 SP01

★★★★ INN
The Inn at Fossebridge
GL54 3JS
☎ 01285 720721 📄 01285 720793
e–mail: info@fossebridgeinn.co.uk
dir: *Situated on A429, 3m S of A40 & 6m N of Cirencester*
The Inn at Fossebridge is around 300 years old, and used to be a coaching inn on the Fossway. Today, it is a beautiful Cotswold retreat, with wonderful accommodation and grounds, located not too far from Stratford-upon-Avon, Cheltenham and Cirencester. Fine food is served in the character bar and dining areas, and a warm welcome awaits all travellers resting at this delightful inn.

Rooms 8 en suite (1 fmly) S £90–£130; D £100–£140✳ **Facilities** STV TVB tea/coffee Cen ht TVL Dinner Last d 9.30pm Fishing **Conf** Max 40 Thtr 40 Class 40 Board 12 **Parking** 30 **Notes** LB No coaches Civ Wed 70

FRAMPTON MANSELL   MAP 04 SO90

★★★★ INN
The Crown Inn
GL6 8JG
☎ 01285 760601
e-mail: enquiries@thecrowninn-cotswolds.co.uk
web: www.thecrowninn-cotswolds.co.uk
dir: *Off A419 signed Frampton Mansell, 0.75m at centre of village*

The Crown Inn is a 17th-century, former cider house, complete with roaring log fires, locally brewed ales and traditional, home-cooked food. There are some splendid views across the golden valley. The bedrooms are in an annexe, and ample parking is available.

Rooms 12 en suite (1 fmly) (4 GF) S fr £50; D fr £80✱ **Facilities** TVB tea/coffee Cen ht Dinner Last d 9.30pm Wi-fi available **Conf** Max 40 **Parking** 25 **Notes** LB

GLOUCESTER   MAP 10 SO81

★★★ A GUEST HOUSE
Brookthorpe Lodge
Stroud Rd, Brookthorpe GL4 0UQ
☎ 01452 812645 📄 01452 812645
e-mail: enq@brookthorpelodge.demon.co.uk
dir: *3m S of Gloucester on A4173*

Rooms 10 rms (6 en suite) (1 fmly) (3 GF) S £30–£45; D £60–£70✱ **Facilities** TVB tea/coffee Licensed Cen ht Wi-fi available **Parking** 15 **Notes** LB ⊗ No coaches Closed Xmas & New Year

GUITING POWER   MAP 10 SP02

★★★★ GUEST HOUSE
Guiting Guest House
Post Office Ln GL54 5TZ
☎ 01451 850470
e-mail: info@guitingguesthouse.com
web: www.guitingguesthouse.com
dir: *In village centre*

In keeping with all the surrounding houses, this engaging family home is built of mellow Cotswold stone. Charming and comfortable bedrooms offer both individuality and character, as do the public rooms, which include the stylish dining room and snug lounge. Breakfast (and dinner by arrangement) uses excellent local produce whenever possible.

Rooms 3 rms (2 en suite) (1 pri facs) 4 annexe rms (3 en suite) (1 annexe pri facs) (1 fmly) (2 GF) **Facilities** TVB tea/coffee Cen ht Dinner Last d 48hrs prior **Parking** 3 **Notes** No coaches

LAVERTON   MAP 10 SP03

★★★★ GUEST ACCOMMODATION
Leasow House
Laverton Meadows WR12 7NA
☎ 01386 584526 📄 01386 584596
e-mail: leasow@hotmail.com
web: www.leasow.co.uk
dir: *2m SW of Broadway. Off B4632 towards Wormington, 500yds on right*

Located in countryside to the south-west of Broadway, this 16th-century former farmhouse has been restored to provide high standards of comfort. Bedrooms have a wealth of extras and the attractive dining room is the setting for comprehensive breakfasts. There is also an elegant library lounge and a warm welcome is assured.

Rooms 5 en suite 2 annexe en suite (2 fmly) (1 GF) **Facilities** TVB tea/coffee Direct dial from bedrooms Cen ht **Parking** 10 **Notes** No children 8yrs Closed Xmas & New Year

ENGLAND

LECHLADE ON THAMES   MAP 05 SU29

★★★★ GUEST ACCOMMODATION
Cambrai Lodge

Oak St GL7 3AY
☎ 01367 253173 & 07860 150467
e–mail: info@cambrailodgeguesthouse.co.uk
web: www.cambrailodgeguesthouse.co.uk
dir: *In town centre, off High St onto A361 Oak St*

This delightful non-smoking house is just a stroll from the centre of the historic market town. Individually styled bedrooms, some in a pretty cottage across the garden, include a four-poster room and two ground-floor bedrooms. Breakfast is served in the conservatory overlooking the gardens.

Rooms 2 en suite 3 annexe en suite (1 fmly) (2 GF) S £45–£65;
D £55–£75✳ **Facilities** TVB tea/coffee Cen ht **Parking** 12 **Notes** ☺

LONGHOPE   MAP 10 SO61

★★★★ FARM HOUSE
New House Farm B&B *(SO685229)*

Barrel Ln, Aston Ingham GL17 0LS
☎ 01452 830484 & 07768 354922 📠 01452 830484
Ms R Smith
e–mail: scaldbrain@btinternet.com

dir: *A40 onto B4222, Barrel Ln on right before Aston Ingham*
Located in tranquil wooded countryside, this working farm is a good touring base on the Gloucestershire-Herefordshire border. Set in 65 acres, the welcoming farmhouse will certainly appeal to nature lovers, and there is a comfortable lounge and bar. Breakfast consists of a good selection of carefully prepared local produce.

Rooms 3 en suite (1 fmly) S £38–£50; D £60–£80✳ **Facilities** TVB tea/
coffee Cen ht TVL Wi-fi available 🍴 **Conf** Max 15 **Parking** 10 **Notes** LB
☺ No children 10yrs 65 acres Sheep woodland RS Xmas & New Year

MARSHFIELD   MAP 04 ST77

★★★ INN
Lord Nelson Inn

SN14 8LP
☎ 01225 891820
e–mail: thelordnelsoninn@btinternet.com
web: www.thelordnelsoninn.info

dir: *M4 junct 18 onto A46 towards Bath. Left at Cold Ashton rdbt towards Marshfield*
Located at one end of the pleasant village of Marshfield, the Lord Nelson is a traditional coaching inn with a pleasant ambience. The spacious bar provides a good opportunity to mix with the locals, while the candlelit restaurant offers a quieter environment in which to enjoy the excellent selection of carefully prepared homemade dishes. Bedrooms and bathrooms are all well decorated and furnished.

Rooms 3 en suite S £42.50; D £75✳ **Facilities** TVB tea/coffee Cen ht
Dinner Last d 9pm **Conf** Max 30 **Notes** ☺

MINCHINHAMPTON   MAP 04 SO80

★★★★ BED & BREAKFAST
Hyde Wood House

Cirencester Rd GL6 8PE
☎ 01453 885504
e–mail: info@hydewoodhouse.co.uk
web: www.hydewoodhouse.co.uk

dir: *From Stroud A419 to Cirencester, after village of Chalford, turn right at top of hill signed Minchinhampton & Aston Down. House 1m on right*

Located within extensive mature grounds, this well-proportioned mellow-stone house provides bedrooms filled with a range of homely extras. Comprehensive breakfasts are taken in an elegant dining room and a spacious comfortable lounge is also available. A warm welcome is assured and afternoon tea includes delicious home-made cake.

Rooms 3 en suite D fr £65✳ **Facilities** TVB Cen ht TVL **Parking** 6
Notes LB ☺ No children 14yrs ☺

NAILSWORTH   MAP 04 ST89

★★★★ BED & BREAKFAST
Hazelwood
Church St GL6 0BP
☎ 01453 839304
e–mail: karen@hazelwood.me.uk
web: www.hazelwood.me.uk
dir: *Off A46 in town centre onto A4014 Avening Rd, 1st right*
Quietly located just a stroll from the centre of this interesting town, Hazelwood offers a comfortable and relaxing base for exploring the Cotswolds. The spacious bedrooms have many thoughtful extras, and the pleasant garden and off-road parking are welcome benefits.

Rooms 3 rms (2 en suite) (1 pri facs) S £35–£40; D £50–£60✱
Facilities TVB tea/coffee Cen ht **Parking** 3 **Notes** ⊗ No children 12yrs ⊜

★★★★ ⊛⊛ RESTAURANT WITH ROOMS
Heavens Above
3 Cossack Square GL6 0DB
☎ 01453 832615
e–mail: info@wild-garlic.co.uk
dir: *In town centre. Off A46 onto Spring Hill, left onto Old Market*
Situated in a quiet corner of this charming Cotswold town, this restaurant with rooms offers a delightful combination of welcoming and relaxed hospitality with high quality cuisine. Bedrooms are located above the restaurant and are spacious and well equipped. A small and friendly team of staff ensure guests are very well looked after throughout their stay.

Rooms 3 rms (1 en suite) S £70–£80; D £70–£80✱ **Facilities** tea/coffee Cen ht Dinner Last d 9pm Wi-fi available **Notes** ⊗

★★★★ BED & BREAKFAST
Highlands
Shortwood GL6 0SJ
☎ 01453 832591 ▤ 01453 833590
dir: *Off A46 rdbt in Nailsworth onto Nympsfield road, turn left, pass bus station, fork left at Britannia Inn, follow signs for Wallow Green, Highlands opp church*

This friendly guest house occupies a quiet elevated position on the outskirts of Nailsworth. The homely bedrooms are filled with stylish furniture and accessories, and there is a comfortable conservatory-lounge and an attractive breakfast dining room.

Rooms 3 en suite S £30–£35; D £50–£60✱ **Facilities** TVB tea/coffee Cen ht TVL Wi-fi available **Parking** 3 **Notes** LB ⊗ No children 8yrs

NAUNTON   MAP 10 SP12

★★★★ GUEST HOUSE
Mill View
2 Mill View GL54 3AF
☎ 01451 850586 ▤ 01451 850970
e–mail: ralph.boult@care4free.net
web: www.millviewguesthousecotswolds.com
dir: *Off B4068 to E end of village*
Lying opposite a historic watermill, this former family home has been extended and modernised to provide every comfort. A warm welcome and attentive care is assured in this non-smoking house, which has one bedroom equipped for easier access. A good base for walkers or for touring Gloucestershire.

Rooms 3 en suite (1 GF) S £40–£50; D £55–£75 **Facilities** TVB tea/coffee Cen ht TVL Dinner Last d 2pm **Parking** 4 **Notes** LB ⊗ No coaches ⊜

NETHER WESTCOTE   MAP 10 SP22

★★★★ 🅰 INN
Westcote Inn
OX7 6SD
☎ 01993 830888 ▤ 01993 831657
e–mail: julia.reed@virgin.net
dir: *From Burford high street, over small bridge, at mini-rdbt take 1st exit A424 towards Stow. Turn right after 6m, follow signs*

Rooms 4 en suite (1 fmly) S £85–£110; D £95–£110✱ **Facilities** STV TVB tea/coffee Direct dial from bedrooms Cen ht TVL Dinner Last d 9.30pm Wi-fi available Riding Gymnasium 🎣 **Conf** Max 40 Thtr 40 Class 40 Board 30 **Parking** 50 **Notes** LB Civ Wed 50

NEWENT   MAP 10 SO72

★★★★ ⊛⊛ RESTAURANT WITH ROOMS
Three Choirs Vineyards
GL18 1LS
☎ 01531 890223 ▤ 01531 890877
e–mail: info@threechoirs.com
web: www.threechoirs.com
dir: *On B4215 N of Newent, follow brown tourist signs*
This thriving vineyard continues to go from strength to strength and provides a wonderfully different place to stay. The restaurant, which overlooks the 100-acre estate, enjoys a popular following thanks to well-executed dishes making good use of local produce. Spacious, high quality bedrooms are equipped with many extras and each opens on to a private patio area, from where wonderful views can be enjoyed.

Rooms 11 annexe en suite (1 fmly) (11 GF) S £85–£145; D £95–£165✱ **Facilities** FTV TVB tea/coffee Direct dial from bedrooms Cen ht Dinner Last d 9pm Wine tasting Vineyard Tours **Conf** Max 20 Thtr 20 Class 15 Board 20 Del from £135 ✱ **Parking** 11 **Notes** LB Closed 24 Dec–5 Jan

NEWENT CONTINUED

★★★ BED & BREAKFAST
Malswick Mill B+B

Malswick Mill, Malswick GL18 1HF

☎ 01452 790680

web: www.malswickmill.co.uk

dir: *N from Mailswick Mill on A40, on right 1m after petrol station*

Malswick Mill is a family run B&B with a small, high quality fishery, located on the outskirts of The Forest of Dean. Bedrooms are located in a newly refurbished annexe building while a separate converted barn provides an ideal area in which to enjoy breakfast or a drink from the bar in the evening. In addition to fishing, guests can enjoy the delightful surrounding grounds or simply sit by the lake and relax.

Rooms 3 en suite (1 fmly) (3 GF) **Facilities** TVB tea/coffee Cen ht TVL Fishing **Parking** 20 **Notes** ⊗ Closed 22 Dec–3 Jan ⊜

NORTHLEACH   MAP 10 SP11

★★★★ GUEST ACCOMMODATION
Northfield Guest House

Cirencester Rd GL54 3JL

☎ 01451 860427 📠 01451 860427

e–mail: p.loving@sky.com

dir: *Signed off A429 Northleach-Cirencester road, 1m from Northleach lights*

Located south of the historic town, this Cotswold stone house offers homely bedrooms, two of which have direct access to the immaculate gardens. Tasty eggs from the contented resident hens feature at breakfast, served in the elegant dining room. A comfortable lounge is also provided.

Rooms 2 en suite 1 annexe en suite (1 fmly) (3 GF) D £65–£75 **Facilities** TVB tea/coffee Cen ht TVL **Parking** 10 **Notes** ⊗ Closed Dec–Feb

---

★★★★ ⊛⊛ INN
The Puesdown Inn

Compton Abdale GL54 4DN

☎ 01451 860262 📠 01451 861262

e–mail: inn4food@btopenworld.com

web: www.puesdown.cotswoldinns.com

dir: *3m W from Northleach on A40*

A friendly welcome awaits you at this long-established inn, a popular stop-off between Cheltenham and Oxford. The stylish modern restaurant provides an enjoyable and informal environment for sampling accomplished cuisine. Individually designed bedrooms, which are accessed externally, have great appeal and offer high standards of contemporary quality.

Rooms 3 en suite (1 fmly) (3 GF) S £50–£60; D £85–£130✳ **Facilities** TVB tea/coffee Cen ht Dinner Last d 10.30pm **Conf** Max 60 Thtr 60 Class 20 Board 20 Del from £85.50 ✳ **Parking** 80 **Notes LB** Closed 1 wk Jan RS Sun eve

OLD SODBURY
MAP 04 ST78

★★★ GUEST HOUSE
The Sodbury House
Badminton Rd BS37 6LU
☎ 01454 312847 📄 01454 273105
e–mail: sodburyhouse.hotel@virgin.net
web: www.sodburyhouse.co.uk

dir: *M4 junct 18, A46 N, 2m left onto A432 to Chipping Sodbury, house 1m on left*

This comfortably furnished 19th-century farmhouse stands in 6 acres of grounds. The bedrooms, many located on the ground floor and in buildings adjacent to the main house, have many extra facilities. Breakfast is a varied choice served in the spacious breakfast room.

Rooms 6 en suite 9 annexe en suite (2 fmly) (7 GF) **Facilities** TVB tea/coffee Direct dial from bedrooms Cen ht TVL Wi-fi available
Conf Thtr 40 Class 25 Board 20 **Parking** 30 **Notes** ⊗ Closed 24 Dec–3 Jan

ST BRIAVELS
MAP 04 SO50

Premier Collection

★★★★★ 🍽 BED & BREAKFAST
Prospect Cottage
Lower Wye Valley Rd, Bigsweir GL15 6RR
☎ 01594 530566 📄 01594 530566
e–mail: enquiries@prospectcottage.com
web: www.prospectcottage.com

dir: *1m W of St Briavels. Off A466 onto track adjoining Bigsweir Bridge lights, continue 1m*

With a peaceful riverside location, this relaxing accommodation will have special appeal to guests with an interest in wildlife. A variety of birds can be observed from the comfortable balcony and guests also have use of a well-furnished lounge. Friendly and attentive service is a highlight of any stay here as are the carefully prepared, delicious home-cooked dinners.

Rooms 2 rms (2 pri facs) **Facilities** STV TVB tea/coffee Cen ht TVL Dinner Last d 48hrs prior Fishing **Parking** 8 **Notes** ⊗ No children 11yrs

★★★★ GUEST ACCOMMODATION
The Florence
Bigsweir GL15 6QQ
☎ 01594 530830 📄 01594 530830
e–mail: enquiries@florencehotel.co.uk

dir: *On A466 between Monmouth & Chepstow*

Located on the Wye Valley road, the Florence has delightful views across the river and stands in over five acres of gardens and woodland walks. Bedrooms come in a range of sizes and styles, with some in the main house and the others in an adjacent cottage. You can enjoy a cream tea in the garden, a drink in the snug, and choose from a wide selection of carefully prepared dishes at lunch and dinner.

Rooms 4 en suite 4 annexe en suite (1 fmly) (2 GF) S £35–£46; D £70–£92✳ **Facilities** TVB tea/coffee Cen ht Dinner Last d 9pm Fishing **Conf** Max 12 Thtr 12 Class 12 Board 12 **Parking** 30 **Notes** LB ⊗

STOW-ON-THE-WOLD
MAP 10 SP12

★★★★ BED & BREAKFAST
Aston House
Broadwell GL56 0TJ
☎ 01451 830475
e–mail: fja@netcomuk.co.uk

dir: *A429 from Stow-on-the-Wold towards Moreton-in-Marsh, 1m right at x-rds to Broadwell, Aston House 0.5m on left*

Peacefully located on the edge of the village of Broadwell, this is an ideal base from which to explore the charming delights of the Cotswolds. A warm and genuine welcome is assured and every effort is made to ensure a relaxed and enjoyable stay. Great care and attention are hallmarks here, and bedrooms come equipped with many thoughtful extras such as electric blankets.

Rooms 3 rms (2 en suite) (1 pri facs) (1 GF) D £64–£68 **Facilities** TVB tea/coffee Cen ht stairlift **Parking** 3 **Notes** ⊗ No children 10yrs Closed Nov–Feb

STOW-ON-THE-WOLD CONTINUED

★★★★ ⊚ INN
Kings Head Inn & Restaurant
The Green, Bledington OX7 6XQ
☎ 01608 658365 📄 01608 658902
e–mail: kingshead@orr-ewing.com
web: www.kingsheadinn.net
dir: *4m SE off B4450*

Located on the delightful village green near the river, this 16th-century inn has spacious public areas with open fires, wobbly floors, beams and wood furnishings. The comfortable restaurant offers excellent dining and the bedrooms have been creatively decorated and well furnished; some rooms are in a converted annexe.

Rooms 6 en suite 6 annexe en suite (3 GF) **Facilities** FTV TVB tea/coffee Direct dial from bedrooms Cen ht TVL Dinner Last d 9pm Sun–Thu Wi-fi available **Parking** 24 **Notes** ⊗ No coaches Closed 25–26 Dec

★★★★ GUEST ACCOMMODATION
Woodlands Guest House
Upper Swell GL54 1EW
☎ 01451 832346
e–mail: amandak247@talktalk.net
dir: *Upper Swell 1m from Stow-on-the-Wold, take B4077 (Tewkesbury Road)*
Situated in the small hamlet of Upper Swell, Woodlands provides an ideal base for exploring many charming nearby villages. This establishment enjoys delightful rural views and has comfortably appointed bedrooms with a good range of extra accessories. Breakfast is served in the welcoming dining room around the communal dining table. Off-road parking is available.

Rooms 4 en suite (2 GF) S £35–£45; D £60–£70✳ **Facilities** FTV TVB tea/coffee Cen ht **Parking** 8 **Notes** LB ⊗ ⊜

★★★ FARM HOUSE
Corsham Field Farmhouse *(SP217249)*
Bledington Rd GL54 1JH
☎ 01451 831750 📄 01451 832247 Mr R Smith
e–mail: farmhouse@corshamfield.co.uk
dir: *2m SE of Stow on B4450*
This establishment, which has views of the surrounding countryside from its elevated position, is a popular choice with walking groups and

families. The modern bedrooms are practically equipped and located in two separate houses. Enjoyable breakfasts are taken in the spacious dining room, which also provides a lounge. The local pub is just a short walk away and has a reputation for good food.

Rooms 7 rms (5 en suite) (3 fmly) (2 GF) S £35–£45; D £48–£60✳ **Facilities** TVB tea/coffee Cen ht Wi-fi available **Parking** 10 **Notes** LB ⊗ 100 acres arable ⊜

★★★ GUEST ACCOMMODATION
Limes
Evesham Rd GL54 1EJ
☎ 01451 830034 📄 01451 830034
e–mail: thelimes@zoom.co.uk
dir: *500yds from village centre on A424*
Just a short walk from the village centre, this Victorian house provides a comfortable base from which to explore this beautiful area. Bedroom styles vary, with four-poster and ground-floor rooms offered. A warm and genuine welcome is extended, and many guests return on a regular basis. A spacious lounge is available and breakfast is served in the light and airy dining room.

Rooms 5 en suite 1 annexe en suite (2 fmly) (2 GF) S £35–£52; D £50–£60✳ **Facilities** STV TVB tea/coffee Cen ht TVL **Parking** 4 **Notes** Closed Xmas ⊜

Ⓤ
Crestow House
GL54 1JX
☎ 01451 830969 📄 01451 832129
e–mail: fsimonetti@btinternet.com
web: www.crestow.co.uk
dir: *At W end of village at junct A429 & B4068*
At the time of going to press the rating for this establishment had not been confirmed. Please check the AA website www.theAA.com for up-to-date information.

Rooms 4 en suite **Facilities** TVB tea/coffee Cen ht ⤳ Sauna Gymnasium **Parking** 4 **Notes** ⊗ No children 15yrs Closed Feb

STROUD	MAP 04 SO80

★★★★ ⌂ BED & BREAKFAST
1 Woodchester Lodge
Southfield Rd, North Woodchester GL5 5PA
☎ 01453 872586
e–mail: anne@woodchesterlodge.co.uk
dir: *A46 onto Selsley Rd, take 2nd left, 200yds on the left*
Close to the newly re-routed Cotswold Way, this late Victorian former timber merchant's house is set in the peaceful village of North Woodchester and is just a short drive from Stroud. Set in landscaped gardens this large house has spacious, sympathetically restored bedrooms and a comfortable lounge. Evening meals and freshly prepared breakfasts are not to be missed.

CONTINUED

CONTINUED

Bedrooms offer countryside views; public areas are spacious with a choice of seating areas, and there is a selection of real ales to choose from. Bar snacks or full meals are available and there is a fine-dining restaurant which opens Friday evening to Sunday lunch. Outside furniture enables guests to relax and enjoy a drink amidst the lovely Cotswold countryside.

Rooms 6 en suite **Facilities** STV TVB tea/coffee Direct dial from bedrooms Cen ht Dinner Last d 10pm Golf 18 ⅃ **Conf** Max 150 Class 100 **Parking** 100

1 Woodchester Lodge

Rooms 2 rms (1 en suite) (1 pri facs) (1 fmly) S £35–£40; D £55–£65✲ **Facilities** TVB tea/coffee Cen ht TVL Dinner Last d 10am Wi-fi available Golf 18 ⌘ Squash Riding **Parking** 4 **Notes** ❸ Closed Xmas & Etr

★★★★ BED & BREAKFAST
Hyde Crest

Cirencester Rd GL6 8PE
☎ 01453 731631
e–mail: anthea@hydecrest.demon.co.uk
web: www.hydecrest.co.uk

dir: *Off A419, 5m E of Stroud, signed Minchinhampton & Aston Down, house 3rd right opp Ragged Cot pub*

Hyde Crest lies on the edge of the picturesque Cotswold village of Minchinhampton. Bedrooms are located at ground floor level, each with a private patio where welcome refreshments are enjoyed upon arrival (weather permitting). Guests are attentively cared for and scrumptious breakfasts are served in the small lounge-dining room around a communal table.

Rooms 3 en suite (3 GF) S fr £40; D fr £65✲ **Facilities** TVB tea/coffee Cen ht TVL Wi-fi available **Parking** 6 **Notes** No children 10yrs RS Xmas & New Year ⊜

★★★★ INN
The Old Lodge

Minchinhampton Common GL6 9AQ
☎ 01453 832047 ⬛ 01453 834033
e–mail: info@thelodgeminchinhampton.com
web: www.thelodgeminchinhampton.com

dir: *From A419 Cirencester – Stroud, left onto Cirencester Rd. After 4m turn left to Nailsworth. Inn is 2nd on right*

Located right on Minchinhampton Common, beside the golf course, this inn has been fully refurbished to offer stylish accommodation.

TETBURY MAP 04 ST89

Premier Collection

★★★★★ BED & BREAKFAST
Beaufort House

Willesley GL8 8QU
☎ 01666 880444

dir: *4m SW of Tetbury. A433 to Willesley, House set back from road*

Within easy reach of Bath and Bristol, this former staging post and inn built of beautiful local stone, dates back to the 17th century. Bedrooms, all with spacious en suites, are thoughtfully equipped and elegantly furnished. There is also a deeply comfortable guest lounge. Breakfast, featuring organic items (when available), is served in the dining room around one grand table. A delightful walled garden may be enjoyed in warmer weather.

Rooms 4 en suite **Facilities** TVB tea/coffee Cen ht TVL **Parking** 8 **Notes** ❸ No children 10yrs ⊜

CONTINUED

249

TETBURY CONTINUED

★★★ GUEST ACCOMMODATION
Folly Farm B&B & Cottages
Folly Farm, Long Newton GL8 8XA
☎ 01666 502475 📄 01666 502358
e–mail: info@gtb.co.uk
web: www.gtb.co.uk

dir: *M4 junct 17, B4014 signed Tetbury, on right after Welcome to Tetbury sign*

Folly Farm is located among rolling countryside just a 10-minute walk from Tetbury. The well-equipped bedrooms are next to a huge tithe barn with pleasant surrounding grounds, making this a popular venue for weddings. Breakfast is continental only, to be taken at guests' leisure in the bedroom where a refrigerator and dining table is provided.

Rooms 16 en suite (2 fmly) (6 GF) **Facilities** TVB tea/coffee Cen ht ⬥ **Conf** Max 180 Thtr 100 Class 64 Board 65 **Parking** 100 **Notes** ⊗ Civ Wed 180

TEWKESBURY   MAP 10 SO83

★★★ GUEST ACCOMMODATION
Willow Cottages
Shuthonger Common GL20 6ED
☎ 01684 298599 📄 01684 298599
e–mail: RobBrd1@aol.com

dir: *1m N of Tewkesbury, on A38, right hand side, or 1m S of M50 junct 1, on A38, left hand side*

Located north of Tewkesbury in pretty rural surroundings, this welcoming house offers comfortable homely bedrooms with efficient modern bathrooms and a cosy, pine furnished breakfast room. An excellent base for those visiting this picturesque area for work or pleasure.

Rooms 3 en suite (1 fmly) S £32; D £54✳ **Facilities** TVB tea/coffee Cen ht Dinner Last d noon **Parking** 6 **Notes LB** ⊛

WILLERSEY   MAP 10 SP13

★★★★ 🄰 FARM HOUSE
Lowerfield Farm *(SP098406)*
WR11 7HF
☎ 01386 858273 📄 01386 854608 Mr & Mrs Atkinson
e–mail: info@lowerfieldfarm.com

dir: *At mini rdbt in Willersey, take Badsey Ln. On right after 0.75m*

Rooms 6 en suite (2 fmly) (2 GF) S £54–£58; D £60–£78 **Facilities** FTV TVB tea/coffee Licensed Cen ht TVL Dinner Last d 9am Wi-fi available **Parking** 10 **Notes** 6 acres Mixed

---

WINCHCOMBE   MAP 10 SP02

★★★★ 🏠 FARM HOUSE
Sudeley Hill Farm *(SP038276)*
GL54 5JB
☎ 01242 602344 📄 01242 602344 Mrs B Scudamore
e–mail: scudamore4@aol.com

dir: *Off B4632 in Winchcombe onto Castle St, White Hart Inn on corner, farm 0.75m on left*

Located on an 800-acre mixed arable and sheep farm, this 15th-century mellow-stone farmhouse is full of original features including fires and exposed beams. Genuine hospitality is always on offer here with a relaxed and welcoming atmosphere. The comfortable bedrooms are filled with thoughtful extras, and memorable breakfasts are served in the elegant dining room overlooking immaculate gardens.

Rooms 3 en suite (1 fmly) S £35–£45; D £70–£75✳ **Facilities** TVB tea/coffee Cen ht TVL **Parking** 10 **Notes** ⊗ 800 acres sheep arable Closed Xmas ⊛

★★★★ ⊛⊛ RESTAURANT WITH ROOMS
Wesley House
High St GL54 5LJ
☎ 01242 602366 📄 01242 609046
e–mail: enquiries@wesleyhouse.co.uk
web: www.wesleyhouse.co.uk

dir: *In town centre*

A 15th-century, half-timbered property named after John Wesley, founder of the Methodist Church, who stayed here while preaching in the town. Bedrooms are comfortably appointed. A unique lighting system changes colour to suit the mood required and to highlight floral

CONTINUED

creations by a world-renowned flower arranger. A glass atrium now covers the outside terrace.

Rooms 5 en suite S £65; D £80–£95 **Facilities** TVB tea/coffee Direct dial from bedrooms Cen ht Dinner Last d 2pm Wi-fi available **Conf** Thtr 30 Class 40 **Notes** LB ⊗ RS Sun eve Civ Wed 60

GREATER LONDON

BARNET   MAP 06 TQ29

★★★ ⊚ GUEST ACCOMMODATION
206

206 High St EN5 5SZ
☎ 020 8449 9888 📄 020 8449 7444
e–mail: hotelx206@yahoo.co.uk
web: www.savoro.co.uk

dir: M25 junct 23 on A1000 in crescent behind Hadley Green Jaguar Garage

Set back from the main High Street the traditional frontage of this establishment belies the stylishly modern bedrooms and well designed bathrooms within. The award-winning restaurant is an additional bonus.

Rooms 11 rms (9 en suite) (2 pri facs) (2 fmly) (3 GF) S £40–£75; D £70–£110✱ (room only) **Facilities** FTV TVB tea/coffee Cen ht Dinner Last d 10.30pm Wi-fi available **Parking** 9 **Notes** ⊗

BRENTFORD

See London Plan 1 C3

★★★★ BED & BREAKFAST
Primrose House

56 Boston Gardens TW8 9LP
☎ 020 8568 5573
e–mail: information@primrosehouse.com
web: www.primrosehouse.com

dir: Off A3002 Boston Manor Rd near Boston Manor tube station

A warm welcome is assured at this delightful guest house, set in a quiet residential area convenient for central London and Heathrow by tube or road. The individually styled bedrooms are carefully appointed and feature numerous thoughtful extras. A continental breakfast is served in the dining room overlooking the garden.

Rooms 4 rms (2 en suite) S £45–£55; D £58–£68 **Facilities** FTV TVB tea/coffee Cen ht TVL Wi-fi available **Parking** 2 **Notes** ⊗

BROMLEY

See London Plan 1 H1

★★★ GUEST ACCOMMODATION
Glendevon House

80 Southborough Rd, Bickley BR1 2EN
☎ 020 8467 2183 📄 020 8295 0701
e–mail: glendevonhousehotel@hotmail.co.uk

dir: At turning with Park Hill, 400yds from Bickley tube station

This large Victorian property is ideally situated close to London-bound Bickley Station and within easy reach of Bromley. Comfortable bedrooms provide a wealth of amenities including internet access and Freeview. A plentiful breakfast is served in the bright dining room.

Rooms 12 en suite (3 fmly) (2 GF) **Facilities** FTV TVB tea/coffee Direct dial from bedrooms Cen ht **Parking** 7 **Notes** No children 2yrs Closed 23 Dec–7 Jan

CRANFORD

See London Plan 1 A3

For accommodation details see **Heathrow Airport**

CROYDON

See London plan 1 F1

★★★ GUEST ACCOMMODATION
Kirkdale

22 St Peters Rd CR0 1HD
☎ 020 8688 5898 📄 020 8680 6001
e–mail: reservations@kirkdalehotel.co.uk

dir: A23 onto A232 W & A212 Lower Coombe St, 500yds right

Close to the town centre, this Victorian property retains many original features. Public areas include a small lounge bar and an attractive breakfast room, and the bedrooms have good facilities. There is a sheltered patio for the summer.

Rooms 19 en suite (6 GF) S £50–£65; D £60–£75✱ **Facilities** TVB tea/coffee Direct dial from bedrooms Cen ht TVL Wi-fi available **Parking** 12 **Notes** ⊗ Closed Xmas & New Year

FELTHAM

See **London Plan 1 A2**

For accommodation details see **Heathrow Airport**

HARROW

See **London Plan 1 B5**

★★★ GUEST ACCOMMODATION
Brent X

165 Preston Hill HA3 9UY

☎ 020 8904 9394 📠 020 8904 1155

e–mail: info@brentxhotel.com

dir: *1m from Wembley stadium and arena*

This renovated guest house provides comfortable accommodation within easy reach of many attractions, including The New Wembley Stadium, which is visible from some rooms. Bedrooms feature modern decor and amenities. Public areas include a pleasant dining area where breakfast only is served. Some off-road parking is available.

Rooms 19 rms (17 en suite) (1 fmly) (6 GF) **Facilities** TVB tea/coffee Direct dial from bedrooms Cen ht Wi-fi available **Parking** 5 **Notes** ⊗

HARROW ON THE HILL

See **London Plan 1 B5**

★★★ GUEST ACCOMMODATION
Old Etonian

36–38 High St HA1 3LL

☎ 020 8423 3854 & 8422 8482 📠 020 8423 1225

e–mail: info@oldetonian.com

web: www.oldetonian.com

dir: *In town centre. On B458 opp Harrow School*

In the heart of this historic part of London and opposite the prestigious school, this friendly guest house is a delight. Recently redecorated bedrooms are attractive, well appointed and comfortable. A continental breakfast is served in the dining room, which in the evening is home to a lively restaurant. On-road parking available.

Rooms 9 en suite (1 GF) S £60–£75; D £70–£75✱ **Facilities** FTV TVB tea/coffee Direct dial from bedrooms Cen ht TVL Dinner Last d 10.30pm **Conf** Max 30 Thtr 20 Class 20 Board 20 Del from £28 ✱ **Parking** 3 **Notes** ⊗

HAYES

See **London Plan 1 A3**

For accommodation details see **Heathrow Airport**

HEATHROW AIRPORT

See **London Plan 1 A3**

★★★★ GUEST ACCOMMODATION
The Cottage

150–152 High St TW5 9WB

☎ 020 8897 1815

e–mail: info@the-cottage.eu

dir: *M4 junct 3, A312 towards Feltham, left at lights, left after 1st pub on left*

This beautiful property is a peacefully situated oasis, family run within five minutes of Heathrow Airport. It offers comfortable and spacious accommodation, tastefully decorated in the main house and six new bedrooms located at the rear of the garden, connected to the main building by a covered walkway overlooking the stunning courtyard.

Rooms 14 en suite 6 annexe en suite (4 fmly) (12 GF) S £55–£65; D £74.50–£84.50 **Facilities** TVB tea/coffee Cen ht **Parking** 20 **Notes** ⊗ Closed 24–26 Dec & 31 Dec–1 Jan

★★★ GUEST ACCOMMODATION
Harmondsworth Hall

Summerhouse Ln, Harmondsworth Village UB7 0BG
☎ 020 8759 1824 & 07713 104229 📠 020 8897 6385
e–mail: elaine@harmondsworthhall.com
web: www.harmondsworthhall.com

dir: M4 junct 4, A3044 Holloway Ln onto Harmondsworth High St, left after Crown pub

Hidden away in the old part of the village, this delightful property has been restored and converted into a spacious guest house. It is well located for the airport and motorways. Breakfast is served in an attractive wood-panelled dining room overlooking the gardens and there is a spacious lounge. The well-equipped bedrooms are all individually furnished.

Rooms 10 en suite (4 fmly) (2 GF) S £65–£70; D £75–£80✳
Facilities STV FTV TVB tea/coffee Direct dial from bedrooms Cen ht TVL Dinner Last d by arrangement Wi-fi available **Conf** Max 25 Thtr 25 Class 25 Board 15 **Parking** 10 **Notes LB**

★★★ GUEST ACCOMMODATION
Shepiston Lodge

31 Shepiston Ln UB3 1LJ
☎ 020 8573 0266 📠 020 8569 2536
e–mail: shepistonlodge@aol.com
web: www.shepistonlodge.co.uk

dir: M4 junct 4, 1st A408 rdbt onto Shepiston Ln, opp Great Western pub

Located close to Heathrow Airport, the Shepiston Lodge offers smart, well-equipped bedrooms. Public rooms include an informal bar, and a spacious dining room where freshly cooked breakfasts (and dinners by request) are served. Ample secure parking is available.

Rooms 22 en suite (2 fmly) (9 GF) **Facilities** FTV TVB tea/coffee Cen ht TVL Dinner Last d 6pm **Parking** 20 **Notes** ⊗

Ⓤ
Crompton Guest House

49 Lampton Rd TW3 1JG
☎ 020 8570 7090 📠 020 8577 2975
e–mail: cromptonguesthouse@btinternet.com

At the time of going to press the rating for this establishment had not been confirmed. Please check the AA website www.theAA.com for up-to-date information.

Rooms 11 en suite S £69–£120; D £79–£120

HOUNSLOW

*See London **Plan 1 B2***

*For accommodation details see under **Heathrow Airport***

ILFORD

★★ Ⓐ GUEST ACCOMMODATION
Cranbrook

22–24 Coventry Rd IG1 4QR
☎ 020 8554 6544 📠 020 8518 1463
e–mail: manager@expresslodging.co.uk

dir: From M25 to A406 east, exit at junct A123 past Ilford station, on right

Rooms 45 rms (25 en suite) (4 fmly) (17 GF) **Facilities** STV FTV TVB tea/coffee **Conf** Max 30 Thtr 30 Class 30 Board 30 **Parking** 35 **Notes** ⊗

★★ Ⓐ GUEST ACCOMMODATION
The Park

327 Cranbrook Rd IG1 4UE
☎ 020 8554 9616 📠 020 8518 2700
e–mail: manager@expresslodging.co.uk
web: www.parkhotelilford.com

dir: Exit A406 onto A123, pass Ilford station, Macdonalds and Pizza Hut, located on left

Rooms 30 rms (25 en suite) (2 fmly) (11 GF) **Facilities** STV FTV TVB tea/coffee **Conf** Max 50 Thtr 50 Class 50 Board 50 **Parking** 30 **Notes** ⊗

ENGLAND

RICHMOND (UPON THAMES)

See London Plan 1 C2

★★★ GUEST ACCOMMODATION
Hobart Hall

43–47 Petersham Rd TW10 6UL
☎ 020 8940 0435 📄 020 8332 2996
e–mail: hobarthall@aol.com
dir: *200yds S of Richmond Bridge on A307*

Built around 1690, the friendly establishment stands beside the River Thames close to Richmond Bridge. Many of the spacious bedrooms have river views and a good range of modern facilities. There is an impressive reception, a comfortable lounge, an attractive breakfast room, and a meeting room that overlooks the river.

Rooms 33 rms (18 en suite) (5 fmly) (3 GF) S £55–£70; D £75–£95 **Facilities** TVB tea/coffee Direct dial from bedrooms Cen ht TVL Wi-fi available **Parking** 14 **Notes** ⊗ RS 25–26 Dec & 1 Jan

SUTTON   MAP 06 TQ26

★★★ BED & BREAKFAST
Ashling Tara

50 Rosehill SM1 3EU
☎ 020 8641 6142 & 8296 9866 📄 020 8644 7872
e–mail: info@ashlingtarahotel.com
web: www.ashlingtarahotel.com
Situated only a few minutes away from Sutton station, and a short walk from the town centre, this is a handy location for business travellers requiring access to the City. Bedrooms are generally spacious with comfortable easy chairs and the landing has a communal seating area for people travelling together.

Rooms 9 en suite (2 fmly) (4 GF) **Facilities** TVB tea/coffee Cen ht **Parking** 10 **Notes** ⊗

WEST DRAYTON

For accommodation details see Heathrow Airport

GREATER MANCHESTER

BOLTON   MAP 15 SD70

★★★ GUEST HOUSE
Broomfield House

33–35 Wigan Rd, Deane BL3 5PX
☎ 01204 61570 📄 01204 650932
e–mail: chris@broomfield.force9.net
dir: *M61 junct 5, A58 to 1st lights, straight onto A676, premises on right*

A friendly relaxed atmosphere prevails at Broomfield House, close to the motorway and west of the town centre. There is a comfy lounge and separate bar area. Hearty breakfasts are served in the separate dining room.

Rooms 20 en suite (2 fmly) (2 GF) (9 smoking) S £40–£44; D fr £54✱ **Facilities** TVB tea/coffee Licensed Cen ht TVL Wi-fi available **Parking** 12

DELPH   MAP 16 SD90

★★★★ GUEST ACCOMMODATION
Wellcroft House

Bleak Hey Nook OL3 5LY
☎ 01457 875017
e–mail: wellcrofthouse@hotmail.co.uk
dir: *Off A62 on Standedge Foot Rd near A670 junct*

Commanding superb views down the valley below this former weaver's cottage offers warm traditional hospitality to walkers on the Pennine Way and those simply touring the Pennine towns and villages. Modern comforts in all bedrooms and transport from local railway or walks is routinely provided by the friendly proprietors.

Rooms 3 rms (2 en suite) (1 GF) S £30–£35; D £50–£60✱ **Facilities** TVB tea/coffee Cen ht TVL Dinner Last d 6pm Pool Table **Parking** 1 **Notes** LB ⊛

DIGGLE   MAP 16 SE00

★★★★ INN
The Hanging Gate

217 Huddersfield Rd OL3 5PQ
☎ 01457 871164
e–mail: info@thehanginggate.co.uk
dir: *A627 to Oldham, then A62 to Saddleworth, follow signs for Diggle, in centre of village*

Located within the village of Diggle in the heart of Saddleworth, this 200-year-old inn, with its award-winning frontage, has been sympathetically renovated to provide high standards of comfort with a warm welcome. Bedrooms combine modern facilities with creature comforts and imaginative food is available in the attractive public areas.

Rooms 4 en suite (1 fmly) **Facilities** TVB tea/coffee Cen ht Dinner Last d 8.30pm Pool Table **Parking** 20

★★ GUEST ACCOMMODATION
Sunfield Accommodation

Diglea OL3 5LA

☎ 01457 874030

e–mail: sunfield.accom@lineone.net

dir: *Off A670 to Diggle village, off Huddersfield Rd onto Sam Rd to Diggle Hotel & signs for Diggle Ranges*

This friendly, family-run operation is located within easy reach of Manchester and the M62, and affords wonderful views over the Pennines; bedrooms are on the ground floor and pets are made welcome. Breakfast is served at one large table and a couple of good pubs serving food are located at the bottom of the lane.

Rooms 4 en suite (1 fmly) (4 GF) S £35–£40; D £50–£60✳
Facilities FTV TVB tea/coffee Cen ht TVL **Parking** 11 **Notes** ⊕

LITTLEBOROUGH   MAP 16 SD91

★★★★★ 🅰 GUEST ACCOMMODATION
Hollingworth Lake Bed & Breakfast

164 Smithy Bridge Rd OL15 0DB

☎ 01706 376583 📄 01706 374054

dir: *M62 junct 21, brown signs to Hollingworth Lake Country Park, at T-junct onto small rdbt, right onto Smithy Bridge Rd, 50yds on right*

Rooms 3 en suite 2 annexe en suite (1 fmly) (2 GF) S £35; D £50
Facilities FTV TVB tea/coffee Cen ht Wi-fi available **Conf** Max 10
Parking 8 **Notes** RS 25–26 Dec & 1 Jan

MANCHESTER   MAP 15 SJ89

★★★★ GUEST ACCOMMODATION
The Ascott

6 Half Edge Ln, Ellesmere Park, Eccles M30 9GJ

☎ 0161 950 2453 📄 0161 661 7063

e–mail: ascottmanchester@talk21.com

web: www.ascotthotel.co.uk

dir: *M602 junct 2, left onto Wellington Rd, 0.25m right onto Abbey Grove & left onto Half Edge Ln*

Set in a mainly residential area close to major routes, this early Victorian house, once the home of the mayor of Eccles, has been renovated to provide thoughtfully furnished bedrooms with smart modern bathrooms. A choice of breakfast rooms is available and there is an elegant lounge.

Rooms 14 rms (13 en suite) (1 pri facs) (1 fmly) (4 GF) S £45–£75; D £55–£95✳ **Facilities** TVB tea/coffee Direct dial from bedrooms Cen ht TVL Wi-fi available **Parking** 12 **Notes** ⊗ Closed 22 Dec–2 Jan RS Sun

★★★ GUEST ACCOMMODATION
New Central Guest House

144–146 Heywood St, Off Cheetham Hill Rd M8 0DF

☎ 0161 205 2169 📄 0161 211 9299

e–mail: info@newcentralhotel.com

dir: *1.5m N of city centre. Off A665 Cheetham Hill Rd opp Esso station onto Heywood St*

Located within easy reach of the city, this refurbished property offers very good hospitality and modern bedrooms. There is a cosy lounge and secure parking, and ample breakfasts are served in the spacious dining room.

Rooms 9 rms (5 en suite) (3 fmly) **Facilities** TVB tea/coffee Cen ht TVL
Parking 2 **Notes** ⊗ No children 5yrs

★★★ GUEST HOUSE
Thistlewood

203 Urmston Ln, Stretford M32 9EF

☎ 0161 865 3611 📄 0161 866 8133

e–mail: iain.campbell30@ntlworld.com

dir: *M60 junct 7, A56 towards Stretford, left onto A5181 & Sandy Ln, left onto A5213*

This grand Victorian house is set in attractive grounds in a residential area close to the M60. Within easy reach are Old Trafford football and cricket grounds, and the airport. The bedrooms are well equipped, and the public rooms, including a lounge, are spacious and comfortable.

Rooms 9 en suite S £40; D £52 **Facilities** TVB tea/coffee Licensed Cen ht TVL **Parking** 12 **Notes** ⊗ No coaches

★★★ 🅰 GUEST ACCOMMODATION
Luther King House

Brighton Grove, Off Wilmslow Rd M14 5JP

☎ 0161 224 6404 📄 0161 248 9201

e–mail: reception@lkh.co.uk

web: www.lkh.co.uk

dir: *S of city centre opp Platt Fields park*

Rooms 46 en suite (7 fmly) (6 GF) **Facilities** STV TVB tea/coffee Direct dial from bedrooms Cen ht Dinner Last d 8.30pm Pool Table
Conf Max 125 Thtr 70 Class 70 Board 54 **Parking** 45 **Notes** Closed 24 Dec–2 Jan Civ Wed 125

MANCHESTER AIRPORT MAP 15 SJ88

★★★ GUEST ACCOMMODATION
Rylands Farm Guest House
Altrincham Rd SK9 4LT
☎ 01625 535646 & 548041 📠 01625 255256
e–mail: info@rylandsfarm.com
web: www.rylandsfarm.com
dir: *M56 junct 6, A538 towards Wilmslow, house 1.5m on left after Wilmslow Moat House*

Situated in pretty gardens and convenient for Manchester Airport, this property provides a range of bedrooms, some of which are well furnished and located in a separate building. Breakfast is taken in an attractive conservatory dining room, which also contains a comfortable lounge area with honesty bar.

Rooms 3 en suite 6 annexe en suite (3 fmly) (3 GF) **Facilities** TVB tea/coffee Cen ht TVL Dinner Last d 6pm **Conf** Max 30 Class 30 **Parking** 15 **Notes** Closed 24–25 Dec & 31 Dec–1 Jan

MARPLE MAP 16 SJ98

★★★★ 🍴 INN
Rock Tavern
Rock Tavern, Glossop Rd, Marple Bridge SK6 5RX
☎ 01457 899354
e–mail: info@rocktavern.co.uk
dir: *Situated midway between Glossop and Marple on A626*

Situated in an elevated position amidst rolling countryside this comfortable inn has a popular reputation locally thanks to its extensive menu with local produce and carefully prepared dishes. The bedrooms are modern and although compact, offer modern facilities. The Rock Tavern also provides a hearty breakfast and extensive car parking.

Rooms 5 en suite **Facilities** TVB tea/coffee Cen ht Dinner Last d 9pm **Parking** 80 **Notes** ⊗

MELLOR MAP 16 SJ98

★★★★ INN
The Moorfield Arms
Shiloh Rd SK6 5NE
☎ 0161 427 1580 📠 0161 427 1582
e–mail: info@moorfieldarms.co.uk
dir: *1m NE of Mellor. Off A6015 towards Mellor, right onto Shiloh Rd, 0.3m on left*

Located in an elevated position with stunning views of the surrounding countryside including Kinder Scout, this 400-year-old property has been renovated and extended to provide spacious, comfortable public areas and tastefully furnished modern bedrooms within a sympathetic barn conversion.

Rooms 4 annexe en suite (1 fmly) (3 GF) **Facilities** TVB tea/coffee Cen ht Dinner Last d 9.30pm **Conf** Max 90 Class 40 Board 25 **Parking** 100 **Notes** ⊗

SALE MAP 15 SJ79

★★★★ GUEST HOUSE
Brooklands Lodge
208 Marsland Rd M33 3NE
☎ 0161 973 3283
e–mail: enquiries@brooklandslodge.co.uk
web: www.brooklandslodge.co.uk
dir: *M60 junct 6, 1m on A6144 Marsland Rd*

This long established, privately run guest house is well located for Manchester Airport, the city centre, Old Trafford and the Trafford Centre. The comfortably furnished accommodation includes thoughtful extras to provide a home from home. Breakfast can be taken either in your room or in the attractive dining room.

Rooms 8 en suite (3 fmly) (5 GF) S £35–£45; D £45–£55✴ **Facilities** FTV TVB tea/coffee Cen ht TVL Dinner Last d 6pm Wi-fi available **Conf** Max 16 Thtr 16 Class 16 Board 16 **Parking** 9 **Notes** LB No children 5yrs No coaches

WIGAN MAP 15 SD50

★★★ RESTAURANT WITH ROOMS
The Beeches
School Ln, Standish WN6 0TD
☎ 01257 426432 & 421316 📠 01257 427503
e–mail: mail@beecheshotel.co.uk
dir: *M6 junct 27, A5209 into Standish on School Ln*

Located a short drive from M6, this elegant Victorian house has been renovated to provide high standards of comfort. Bedrooms are equipped with practical and homely extras, and public areas include spacious lounges, a popular brasserie, and a self-contained function suite.

Rooms 10 en suite (4 fmly) **Facilities** FTV TVB tea/coffee Cen ht Dinner Last d 9.45pm **Conf** Max 120 Thtr 100 Board 40 **Parking** 120 **Notes** ⊗ Civ Wed 60

★★★ GUEST HOUSE
Bel Air
236 Wigan Ln WN1 2NU
☎ 01942 241410
e-mail: sales@belairhotel

Located between major road links and the town centre, this popular guest house is equipped for both business and leisure customers, especially visitors to the nearby sporting stadia. A range of bedrooms includes family accommodation, and the public areas are decorated with interesting art and ornaments from around the world. Bar meals are available at weekends and a warm welcome is assured.

Rooms 11 en suite (11 smoking) S fr £39.50; D fr £49.50✶
Facilities TVB tea/coffee Direct dial from bedrooms Licensed Cen ht TVL
Parking 8

HAMPSHIRE

ALRESFORD   MAP 05 SU53

See New Alresford

ALTON   MAP 05 SU73

★★★★ GUEST ACCOMMODATION
Beech Barns Guest House
61 Wellhouse Rd, Beech GU34 4AQ
☎ 01420 85575 & 07759 723112 📠 01420 85575
e-mail: timsiggs@yahoo.com

dir: *1.5m W of Alton. Off A339 towards Beech, 2nd right onto Wellhouse Rd, 0.5m on left*

This well-appointed property has easy access to the motorway system. Set on the outskirts of Alton in its own grounds at the end of a quiet lane, there is no shortage of walking and cycling around this picturesque village location. The proprietors are welcoming and friendly, and bedrooms are smartly appointed in contemporary style to provide a good range of facilities. A separate lounge is available for guest use, and dinner can be offered on request.

Rooms 9 en suite (2 fmly) (6 GF) **Facilities** TVB tea/coffee Cen ht TVL
Dinner ⌣ **Conf** Max 18 Class 18 **Parking** 12

ANDOVER   MAP 05 SU34

★★★★★ 🅰 BED & BREAKFAST
The Barn House B&B
Forton SP11 6NU
☎ 01264 720544
e-mail: hello@thebarnhousebandb.co.uk
web: www.thebarnhousebandb.co.uk

dir: *M3 junct 8 onto A303, onto B3048 to Longparish. Right to Forton, 2nd drive on left*

Rooms 2 en suite S £60–£75; D £80–£105 **Facilities** FTV TVB tea/coffee
Cen ht **Parking** 4 **Notes** ⊗

See advert on this page

★★★★ BED & BREAKFAST
Forest Edge
Andover Down SP11 6LJ
☎ 01264 364526
e-mail: david@forest-edge.co.uk
web: www.forest-edge.co.uk

dir: *1.5m E of Andover. A303 onto A3093 & B3400, 1m on right*

Forest Edge is situated in the beautiful Hampshire countryside, a few miles from Andover and within easy reach of the A303, M3, Basingstoke, Winchester and Salisbury. The property is set in over an acre of landscaped and eco-friendly gardens where guests can relax or walk at their leisure.

Rooms 4 en suite (4 GF) S £45; D £65✶ **Facilities** TVB tea/coffee
Cen ht Dinner Last d 24hrs Wi-fi available ⌣ **Conf** Max 8 **Parking** 4
Notes ⊗

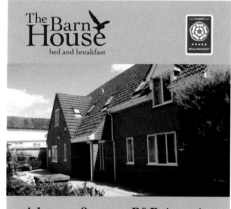

ANDOVER CONTINUED

★★★★ GUEST ACCOMMODATION
May Cottage
SP11 8LZ
☎ 01264 771241 & 07768 242166 🖷 01264 771770
e-mail: info@maycottage-thruxton.co.uk
web: www.maycottage-thruxton.co.uk

dir: 3.5m W of Andover. Off A303 signed Thruxton (Village Only), opp George Inn

Excellent customer care is assured at this 18th-century, part-thatched house, which stands in pretty gardens within the heart of the village. Fine art and furnishings enhance the original features, and bedrooms are filled with a wealth of thoughtful extras. Comprehensive breakfasts are served in the attractive dining room.

Rooms 3 en suite S £45–£55; D £65–£85✳ **Facilities** STV TVB tea/coffee Cen ht TVL **Parking** 5 **Notes LB** ⊗ 🖷

ASHURST   MAP 05 SU31

★★★★ 🅰 GUEST HOUSE
Forest Gate Lodge
161 Lyndhurst Rd SO40 7AW
☎ 023 8029 3026 🖷 023 8029 3026

dir: On A35 in village

Rooms 4 en suite (1 fmly) S £15–£30✳ **Facilities** TVB tea/coffee Cen ht **Parking** 6 **Notes LB** ⊗ No children 5yrs No coaches 🖷

BENTLEY   MAP 05 SU74

Premier Collection

★★★★★ BED & BREAKFAST
Bentley Green Farm
The Drift GU10 5JX
☎ 01420 23246
e-mail: enquiries@bentleygreenfarm.co.uk
web: www.bentleygreenfarm.co.uk

dir: 500yds S of village. Off A31 Farnham-Alton signed Bentley, left at T-junct & 1st right

Off the A31 a short drive from the village centre this Grade II listed farm offers outstanding luxury. The first floor smaller double in the
CONTINUED

main house boasts a private bathroom and wet room shower. A separate ground floor private lounge with fireplace is the ideal place to sample owners Glenda and Chris Powell's excellent hospitality. The annexe suite of rooms includes lounge, dining and kitchen area overlooking the gardens and swimming pool. A total of 39 acres surrounds the house boasting a tennis court, spa pool and its own private fishing. Breakfast is served in the dining room around a big oak table.

Rooms 1 rms (1 pri facs) 1 annexe en suite (1 fmly) (1 GF) S £85; D £95 **Facilities** STV FTV TVB tea/coffee Cen ht TVL ⚲ ♨ Fishing Trampolines, tree house **Parking** 13 **Notes** ⊗ 🖷

BRANSGORE   MAP 05 SZ19

★★★★ 🏠 BED & BREAKFAST
Tothill House
Black Ln, off Forest Rd BH23 8EA
☎ 01425 674414 🖷 01425 672235

dir: M27 onto A31 or A35, house is 0.75m NE of Bransgore centre
Built for an admiral in 1908, Tothill House is located in the southern part of the New Forest. The garden backs on to the forest, where deer, ponies and other wildlife are frequent visitors. The spacious bedrooms are furnished to a high standard, reflecting the character of the house. There is an elegant library, and a generous breakfast is served in the dining room.

Rooms 3 rms (2 en suite) (1 pri facs) **Facilities** TVB tea/coffee Cen ht **Parking** 6 **Notes** ⊗ No children 16yrs Closed Nov–Feb 🖷

BROCKENHURST   MAP 05 SU30

Premier Collection

★★★★★ GUEST ACCOMMODATION
The Cottage Lodge
Sway Rd SO42 7SH
☎ 01590 622296 🖷 01590 623014
e-mail: enquiries@cottagelodge.co.uk
web: www.cottagelodge.co.uk

dir: Off A337 opp Careys Manor Hotel onto Grigg Ln, 0.25m over x-rds, cottage next to war memorial

This 17th-century forester's cottage in the town centre is a good base for exploring the New Forest. The comfortable bedrooms are individually furnished and thoughtfully equipped. There is a cosy bar lounge with a fire, where tea can be served and a small selection of drinks is available.
CONTINUED

Rooms 9 en suite 3 annexe en suite (6 GF) S £50–£120; D £50–£170 **Facilities** TVB tea/coffee Cen ht **Parking** 14 **Notes LB** No children 10yrs Closed Xmas & New Year

★★★★ GUEST ACCOMMODATION
Little Heathers Guest House
13 Whitemoor Rd SO42 7QG
☎ 01590 623512
e–mail: littleheathers@msn.com
Set in a quiet cul-de-sac on the outskirts of the village, this modern guesthouse offers well-appointed and comfortable ground floor accommodation. A well-prepared and hearty breakfast can be enjoyed overlooking the gardens, and is a perfect start to a day spent in exploring the New Forest and other attractions.

Rooms 3 rms (2 en suite) (1 pri facs) (1 fmly) (3 GF) **Facilities** TVB tea/coffee Cen ht **Parking** 4 **Notes** ⊛ ⊜

★★★ BED & BREAKFAST
Crossings Cottage
Lyndhurst Rd SO42 7RL
☎ 01590 622478
e–mail: lisa@crossings-brockenhurst.co.uk
dir: In centre just before rail crossing & opp cycle hire shop
Situated close to the town, Crossings is named due to its proximity to the station and level crossing. The friendly proprietor provides a warm welcome, and the rooms are comfortably furnished and equipped. Full English breakfasts are served at individual tables.

Rooms 3 rms S £35–£40; D £48–£55 **Facilities** FTV TVB tea/coffee Cen ht Wi-fi available **Parking** 2 **Notes LB** ⊛ Closed 24–26 Dec ⊜

★★★ BED & BREAKFAST
Seraya
8 Grigg Ln SO42 7RE
☎ 01590 622426
e–mail: edwin.ward@btinternet.com
web: www.serayanewforest.co.uk
dir: Off A337 opp Careys Manor Hotel onto Grigg Ln, 500yds on corner Horlock Rd
Well placed for visiting the New Forest, and close to the centre of town with its good eating options, this delightful guest house offers attractive rooms with a broad selection of extra facilities. A hearty breakfast is served around the communal dining table.

Rooms 3 rms (1 en suite) **Facilities** TVB tea/coffee Cen ht **Parking** 3 **Notes** ⊜

★★★★ BED & BREAKFAST
Walnut Cottage
Old Romsey Rd SO40 2NP
☎ 023 8081 2275 📄 023 8081 2275
dir: M27 junct 1, Cadnam rdbt onto A3090, Old Romsey Rd 1st left
This charming, mid–19th-century cottage is convenient for the New Forest or nearby business areas. The comfortable bedrooms are brightly decorated. An inviting lounge is available, and hearty English breakfasts are enjoyed around a large table in the cosy dining room.

Rooms 3 rms (2 en suite) (1 pri facs) (1 GF) S fr £40; D fr £55 **Facilities** TVB tea/coffee Cen ht TVL **Parking** 3 **Notes** ⊛ No children 14yrs Closed 24–26 Dec ⊜

★★★ BED & BREAKFAST
Tower Hill House
Tower Hill, Winchester Rd RG25 2AL
☎ 01256 398340 📄 01256 398340
e–mail: martin.hyndman@virgin.net
web: www.towerhill-guesthouse.co.uk
dir: In village. M3 junct 7, onto A30 towards Winchester, 2nd left, opp sign for North Waltham
Ideally situated for access to the M3 and A30, while overlooking fields and countryside, this family-run bed and breakfast is in the pretty village of Dummer, just 10 minutes away from the centre of Basingstoke. Bedrooms are simply, but comfortably furnished and a well-made breakfast is served in the cheerful dining room.

Rooms 4 rms S £25–£30; D £50–£55✳ **Facilities** TVB tea/coffee Cen ht Wi-fi available **Parking** 6 **Notes** ⊜

★★★★ ⊛⊛ INN
The Star Inn
SO51 0LW
☎ 01794 340225
e–mail: info@starinn.co.uk
dir: 1m S of East Tytherley
This charming coaching inn offers bedrooms in a purpose-built annexe, separate from the main pub. The spacious rooms have high levels of quality and comfort, and an outdoor children's play area is available. The inn has a loyal following of locals and visitors, drawn especially by the excellent food.

Rooms 3 annexe en suite (3 GF) S £50–£75; D £80✳ **Facilities** FTV TVB tea/coffee Cen ht Dinner Last d 9pm Wi-fi available **Conf** Max 30 Thtr 24 Class 24 Board 30 **Parking** 50 **Notes LB** RS Sun eve & Mon

EMSWORTH
MAP 05 SU70

★★★★ ◉◉◉ RESTAURANT WITH ROOMS
36 on the Quay
47 South St PO10 7EG
☎ 01243 375592 & 372257

Occupying a prime position with far reaching views over the estuary, this 16th-century house is the scene for some accomplished and exciting cuisine. The elegant restaurant occupies centre stage with peaceful pastel shades, local art and crisp napery together with glimpses of the bustling harbour outside. The contemporary bedrooms offer style, comfort and thoughtful extras.

Rooms 5 en suite S £70–£100; D £95–£200✳ **Facilities** TVB tea/coffee Cen ht Dinner Last d 10pm **Parking** 6 **Notes LB** Closed 3wks Jan, 1wk late May & 1 wk late Oct

★★★★ BED & BREAKFAST
Hollybank House
Hollybank Ln PO10 7UN
☎ 01243 375502 📠 01243 378118
e–mail: anna@hollybankhouse.com
web: www.hollybankhouse.com

dir: *1m N of town centre. A259 onto B2148, 1m right onto Southleigh Rd, 3rd left onto Hollybank Ln, house at top*

The Georgian country house stands in a 10-acre woodland garden with a tennis court on the outskirts of Emsworth, and looks out to Chichester Harbour. Emsworth has a variety of restaurants, pubs and harbour walks.

Rooms 4 rms (3 en suite) (1 pri facs) (1 fmly) S £45–£50; D £70–£75✳ **Facilities** TVB tea/coffee Cen ht Wi-fi available 🐾 ⚓ **Parking** 85

★★★★ GUEST ACCOMMODATION
Jingles
77 Horndean Rd PO10 7PU
☎ 01243 373755
e–mail: info@thejingles.co.uk

dir: *A3(M) junct 2, follow signs for Emsworth, continue for 4m and Jingles is the 1st building in Emsworth*

Jingles is a family-run business, located in the charming maritime village of Emsworth. Set adjacent to open farmland, it's a great location for discovering both Portsmouth and Chichester. All bedrooms are en suite and decorated to a high standard. The dining room is the setting for a cooked English breakfast, and a drawing room is available for relaxing in. Wi-fi is available if required, and guests have complimentary use of the health and fitness club which is only one and a half miles away.

Rooms 20 en suite 7 annexe en suite (2 fmly) (7 GF) **Facilities** FTV TVB tea/coffee Cen ht Wi-fi available **Parking** 24 **Notes** ⊗

FAREHAM
MAP 05 SU50

★★★★ BED & BREAKFAST
Wisteria House
14 Mays House, Stubbington PO14 2EP
☎ 01329 511940
e–mail: info@wisteria-house.co.uk

dir: *Exit M27 junct 9, take A27 to Fareham. Turn right onto B3334, at rdbt turn left onto Mays Ln*

Wisteria House is located on the edge of the village of Stubbington, just a short walk from local amenities, and only one mile from the beach at Lee-on-the-Solent. The charming and comfortable bedrooms have en suite bathrooms, are all located on the ground floor, and also now have Wi-fi. Off-road parking is available.

Rooms 2 en suite (2 GF) S £47; D £62✳ **Facilities** FTV TVB tea/coffee Cen ht Wi-fi available **Parking** 2 **Notes** ⊗ No children 8yrs

★★★ GUEST ACCOMMODATION
Travelrest – Solent Gateway
22 The Avenue PO14 1NS
☎ 01329 232175 📠 01329 232196
e–mail: solentreservations@travelrest.co.uk
web: www.travelrest.co.uk

dir: *0.5m from town centre on A27. 500yds from railway station*

Situated just west of the town centre, this well-presented accommodation is convenient for the ferry terminals and naval heritage sites. The comfortable bedrooms are spacious and well equipped, and one has a four-poster bed. Breakfast is served in the cosy conservatory-dining room and conference rooms are available.

Rooms 19 en suite (3 fmly) (6 GF) S £45–£65; D £49.50–£80✳ (room only) **Facilities** FTV TVB tea/coffee Direct dial from bedrooms Cen ht Dinner Last d 10pm Wi-fi available **Parking** 27

★★ 🅰 BED & BREAKFAST
Catisfield Cottage
1 Catisfield Ln PO15 5NW
☎ 01329 843301

dir: *Off A27 at Highlands Rd lights, Catisfield Ln 2nd left*

Rooms 6 rms (3 en suite) (1 fmly) S £26.75–£40; D £53–£70✳ **Facilities** TVB tea/coffee Cen ht TVL **Parking** 6 **Notes** Closed 24 Dec–5 Jan

FARNBOROUGH   MAP 05 SU85

★★★★ GUEST HOUSE
Tudorwood Guest House
164 Farnborough Rd GU14 7JJ
☎ 01252 541123
e–mail: pshutak@btinternet.com

dir: *Off A325 Farnborough Rd onto Sycamore Rd, next 3 left turns onto Cedar Rd, right onto Old Farnborough Rd*

A delightful Tudor-style house located within minutes of the town centre. Individually decorated bedrooms are well appointed with a range of useful facilities. Public areas include a pleasant conservatory lounge and intimate dining room where home-cooked dinners are available. Ample parking is provided to the front of the property.

Rooms 2 en suite 4 annexe en suite (1 fmly) (4 GF) S £50–£60; D £60–£75✱ Facilities TVB tea/coffee Cen ht TVL Dinner Last d 6pm Wi-fi available DVD library Conf Max 10 Board 10 Del from £120 Parking 7 Notes ✖ No coaches Closed 24–29 Dec

★★ GUEST HOUSE
The Silverdale
68 Alexandra Rd GU14 6DD
☎ 01252 541891 ▤ 01252 370461
e–mail: thesilverdalehotel@hotmail.co.uk

This bay-fronted Victorian House is located alongside the A325 at the North Camp end of the town. Guest rooms are varied and all benefit from free Wi-Fi connection. There's a small licensed resident lounge that adjoins the dining room where breakfast is served.

Rooms 9 rms (7 en suite) (2 pri facs) (1 fmly) (2 GF) Facilities TVB tea/coffee Licensed Cen ht TVL Parking 12 Notes ✖ No coaches

FORDINGBRIDGE   MAP 05 SU11

★★★★ GUEST ACCOMMODATION
Alderholt Mill
Sandleheath Rd SP6 1PU
☎ 01425 653130 ▤ 01425 652868
e–mail: alderholt-mill@zetnet.co.uk
web: www.alderholtmill.co.uk

dir: *1m W from Fordingbridge, left at x-rds in Sandleheath, 0.5m over bridge on right*

Fresh bread made from home-ground flour can be relished around the communal breakfast table at this delightful working mill. Guests can also enjoy milling demonstrations, cream teas, barbecues by the river, and private fishing. The bedrooms, lounge and dining room are all well appointed.

Rooms 5 rms (4 en suite) S £28–£32; D £30–£37.50✱ Facilities TVB tea/coffee Cen ht TVL Fishing Parking 10 Notes LB No children 8yrs Closed 24–26 Dec

★★★ BED & BREAKFAST
Witts Cottage
65 Church St SP6 1BB
☎ 01425 655065 & 650905
e–mail: pamelaclarke1@btinternet.com

dir: *On A338 between Salisbury and Ringwood. Close to St. Mary's church and High St*

Situated in the riverside town of Fordingbridge close to the New Forest and within reach of Salisbury, Winchester, Bournemouth and Poole. Two smartly presented double bedrooms, one en suite and one with private bathroom. Breakfast is at a communal table in the dining room.

Rooms 2 rms (1 en suite) (1 pri facs) S £40; D £60✱ Facilities TVB tea/coffee Cen ht Parking 2 Notes LB ✖ No children 12yrs Closed 20 Dec–3 Jan ⊛

★★★ BED & BREAKFAST
Merrimead
12 Station Rd, Alderholt SP6 3RB
☎ 01425 657544
e–mail: merrimead@ic24.net
web: www.explorethenewforest.co.uk/merrimead.htm

dir: *B3078 from Fordingbridge, 3m on left*

With easy access to the New Forest, Merrimead offers a peaceful and relaxing environment. The attractive bedrooms are light and airy and breakfast, which includes home-made preserves and bread, can be enjoyed around the communal dining table. For those guests who wish to indulge in a more creative breakfast, a variety of alternatives to the traditional English are offered. There is a small conservatory lounge, which overlooks the pleasant garden.

Rooms 2 rms (1 en suite) (1 pri facs) S £27–£33; D £48–£60✱ Facilities TVB tea/coffee Lift Cen ht Wi-fi available Parking 3 Notes LB ✖ No children 10yrs Closed 21 Dec–2 Jan ⊛

GOSPORT   MAP 05 SZ69

★★★★ BED & BREAKFAST
Thirty Three A
33a Anglesey Rd, Alverstoke PO12 2EG
☎ 023 9251 0119 & 07866 400700 ▤ 023 9251 0119
e–mail: rob.turnerchina@ntlworld.com

dir: *1m W of town centre. Off B3333 onto Anglesey Rd*

Close to Alverstoke church, the house is tucked away in its secluded garden. The friendly proprietors have made the two bedrooms stylish and comfortable, both have flat screen TVs. Breakfast is a gourmet treat that is served in the open-plan kitchen/lounge that overlooks the garden.

Rooms 2 en suite (1 fmly) (2 GF) S £65–£69; D £75–£79✱ Facilities FTV TVB tea/coffee Cen ht Wi-fi available Parking 2 Notes ✖

HAWKLEY   MAP 05 SU72

★★★ INN
The Hawkley Inn
Pococks Ln GU33 6NE
☎ 01730 827205 📠 01730 827954
e–mail: info@hawkleyinn.co.uk

dir: *A3 Liss rdbt towards Liss B3006. Right at Spread Eagle 2.5m turn left at Pococks Ln*

The Hawkley Inn is conveniently situated just off the A3. The inn is perfect for ramblers, locals and business guests alike. The rustic bar areas contrast hugely in style to the contemporary and modern, thoughtfully equipped bedrooms and bathrooms with powerful showers. Delicious home-made comfort food is on offer during lunch times and evenings and breakfast provides a great start to the day.

Rooms 5 en suite (1 fmly) (1 GF) **Facilities** FTV TVB tea/coffee Cen ht Dinner Last d 9.15pm **Parking** 2 **Notes** ⊗ No coaches

HAYLING ISLAND   MAP 05 SU70

★★★★ BED & BREAKFAST
Ravensdale
19 St Catherines Rd PO11 0HF
☎ 023 9246 3203 & 07802 188259 📠 023 9246 3203
e–mail: phil.taylor@tayloredprint.co.uk
web: www.ravensdale-hayling.co.uk

dir: *A3023 at Langstone, cross Hayling Bridge & continue 3m until mini rdbt, right onto Manor Rd 1m. Right by Barley Mow onto Station Rd, 3rd left onto St Catherines Rd*

A warm welcome awaits you to this comfortable home, quietly situated near the beach and golf course. Bedrooms are attractive, very

CONTINUED

comfortable and enhanced with numerous thoughtful extras. Home cooking can be enjoyed at breakfast (and dinner by arrangement) in the dining room, and there is also a lounge area.

Rooms 3 rms (2 en suite) S fr £38; D fr £66 **Facilities** TVB tea/coffee Cen ht TVL Dinner Last d Breakfast **Parking** 4 **Notes LB** ⊗ No children 8yrs Closed last 2 wks Dec ☻

★★ BED & BREAKFAST
Redwalls
66 Staunton Av PO11 0EW
☎ 023 9246 6109
e–mail: daphne@redwalls66.freeserve.co.uk

dir: *A3023 to South Hayling seafront, right along seafront & 4th right*

Built around the turn of the 20th century, the characterful home of Daphne and Noel Grover offers a peaceful retreat close to the seafront and local attractions. The bedrooms and public areas enjoy a homely ambience and there is a garden and conservatory lounge for guests to use.

Rooms 3 en suite D £50✶ **Facilities** TVB tea/coffee Cen ht TVL **Parking** 4 **Notes** ⊗ No children Closed Xmas & New Year ☻

HIGHCLERE   MAP 05 SU45

★★★ INN
The Furze Bush Inn
Hatt Common, East Woodhay RG20 0NQ
☎ 01635 253228 📠 01635 254883
e–mail: info@furzebushinn.co.uk
web: www.furzebushinn.co.uk

dir: *Highclere exit from A34, turn left, then 1st left to Ball Hill*

A traditional inn nestled in the countryside on the Hampshire/Berkshire border. Rooms are air conditioned, spacious and well-equipped. The smart restaurant offers a good range of dishes, but bar food is available, too. There is one air-conditioned conference room accommodating up to 16 people. Large front beer garden and ample parking.

Rooms 10 en suite (4 GF) **Facilities** FTV TVB tea/coffee Direct dial from bedrooms Cen ht Dinner Last d 10pm Wi-fi available Snooker Pool Table **Conf** Max 16 Board 16 **Parking** 60 **Notes** ⊗

HOOK   MAP 05 SU75

★★★★ GUEST HOUSE
Oaklea Guest House
London Rd RG27 9LA
☎ 01256 762673 📠 01256 762150
e–mail: reception@oakleaguesthouse.co.uk

dir: *From village centre, 500yds on right on A30 towards Basingstoke*

You can be sure of a warm welcome at this Victorian house located just a short drive from the M3. Bedrooms are well appointed with modern facilities. There is a comfortable lounge, and the large dining room has a bar.

CONTINUED

Rooms 15 en suite (2 fmly) (1 GF) S £45–£52; D £60–£65✳
Facilities TVB tea/coffee Licensed Cen ht TVL Wi-fi available
Parking 15 **Notes** No coaches Closed Xmas & New Year

★★★ GUEST ACCOMMODATION
Cherry Lodge Guest House
Reading Rd RG27 9DB
☎ 01256 762532 📠 01256 766068
e–mail: cherrylodge@btinternet.com
dir: *On B3349 Reading Rd, next to Hook garden centre*
This pleasant bungalow is peacefully set back from the Reading road,
and is convenient for the M3. Cherry Lodge provides extremely friendly
hospitality and is popular with business guests. Breakfast is served from
6.30 am. A spacious lounge is provided and bedrooms are well
equipped.
Rooms 10 en suite (1 fmly) (10 GF) S fr £45; D fr £60 **Facilities** STV
TVB tea/coffee Direct dial from bedrooms Cen ht TVL Wi-fi available
Parking 20 **Notes** Closed Xmas-New Year

HYTHE   MAP 05 SU40

★★★★ BED & BREAKFAST
Four Seasons B&B
Hamilton Rd SO45 3PD
☎ 023 8084 5151 📠 023 8084 6285
e–mail: fourseasonshythe@btconnect.com
web: www.the-four-seasons.co.uk
dir: *M27 junct 2 onto A326. Exit at Holbury/Hardley, 1st left then
next left*
Set in a quiet residential area close to good transport links across the
south. Bedrooms are well presented, very comfortable and are
enhanced by many thoughtful extras. There is a comfortable lounge,
and a traditional English breakfast is served in the attractive dining
room. Ample car parking is available.
Rooms 12 rms (7 en suite) (4 fmly) (2 GF) S £30–£35; D £60–£71✳
Facilities FTV TVB tea/coffee Cen ht TVL Wi-fi available **Parking** 11
Notes LB ⊗

ISLE OF WIGHT

See **Wight, Isle of**

LEE-ON-THE-SOLENT   MAP 05 SU50

★★★★ GUEST ACCOMMODATION
West Wind Guest House
197 Portsmouth Rd PO13 9AA
☎ 023 9255 2550
e–mail: maggie@west-wind.co.uk
dir: *M27 junct 11, onto A32, then onto B3385 for Lee-on-the-
Solent, left at beach, 800mtrs on left*
This well cared for white-painted house is situated just a short walk
from the seafront and imposing views across the Solent, and offers
good comfortable standards in bedrooms and bathrooms. The
freshly-cooked breakfasts include locally-made sausages. *CONTINUED*

Rooms 6 en suite (1 GF) S £45–£55; D £60✳ **Facilities** FTV TVB tea/
coffee Cen ht Wi-fi available **Parking** 6 **Notes** ⊗ No children 10yrs
Closed Xmas & New Year

★★★ BED & BREAKFAST
Apple Tree Cottage B&B
159 Portsmouth Rd PO13 9AD
☎ 023 9255 1176 📠 023 9235 2492
e–mail: appletreecottage@ntlworld.com
web: www.leeonthesolentbedandbreakfast.com
dir: *From Marine Pde, pass Old Ship public house, onto
Portsmouth Rd. Pass Inn by the Sea on right, 4th house along*
Apple Tree Cottage is a small, family-run B&B that offers a warm
welcome, individual attention, and high standards of comfort, just
50 yards from the seafront and Sailing Club. The area has easy access
to Southampton and Portsmouth. Both rooms have a maritime theme
and enjoy a wide range of useful facilities including DVD players and
Wi-fi. Rooms are decorated and furnished to a high standard, with high
quality linen and towels. The Lighthouse Room has a 4-poster with
drapes, and the Solent can be seen from both rooms. Breakfast is
served in the pretty dining room.
Rooms 2 en suite (1 fmly) D £48–£55✳ **Facilities** FTV TVB tea/coffee
Cen ht Wi-fi available **Parking** 3 **Notes** ⊗ No children 6yrs ⊛

LYMINGTON   MAP 05 SZ39

See also Milford-on-Sea

Premier Collection

★★★★★ BED & BREAKFAST
The Olde Barn
Christchurch Rd, Downton SO41 0LA
☎ 01590 644939 & 07813 679757 📠 01590 644939
e–mail: julie@theoldebarn.co.uk
dir: *On A337 3m W of Lymington, in Downton*
A 17th-century barn and associated buildings have been restored to
provide stylish accommodation. Bedrooms are smartly decorated and
furnished, and the spacious bathrooms have power showers. There is a
comfortable lounge, and a traditional English breakfast is served
around a farmhouse table in the attractive dining room.
Rooms 3 en suite (1 fmly) (3 GF) S £45–£70; D £60–£70✳
Facilities STV TVB tea/coffee Cen ht TVL **Parking** 6 **Notes** No children
10yrs

ENGLAND

LYMINGTON CONTINUED

★★★★ BED & BREAKFAST
1 Honeysuckle Gardens
Everton SO41 0EH
☎ 01590 641282
e-mail: mway286978@aol.com
web: www.newforest-uk.com/honeysucklebandb

dir: *Off A337 Lymington to Christchurch onto Everton Rd, Honeysuckle Gardens 3rd left*

Located in a new residential development in the village of Everton, this charming house is a good base for visiting Lymington, New Milton and the New Forest. Bedrooms are well furnished and decorated, and a range of useful extra facilities is provided. Full English breakfasts are served around one large table. The owner has won an award for green tourism by reducing the impact on the environment.

Rooms 3 rms (2 en suite) (1 pri facs) (2 fmly) S £35–£40; D £62 **Facilities** TVB tea/coffee Cen ht Wi-fi available **Parking** 3 **Notes LB** No children 3yrs ☺

★★★★ BED & BREAKFAST
Auplands
22 Southampton Rd SO41 9GG
☎ 01590 675944
e-mail: sue@auplands.com
web: www.auplands.com

dir: *On A337 before town centre, opp supermarket*

Located just a short walk from High Street, this friendly family-run establishment provides comfortable, neatly decorated and well-equipped bedrooms. Hearty English breakfasts are served at individual tables in the attractive dining room. Off-road parking.

Rooms 3 en suite **Facilities** TVB tea/coffee Cen ht **Parking** 8 **Notes** ⊗ No children 5yrs ☺

★★★★ BED & BREAKFAST
Elsburn
Pennington SO41 8HF
☎ 01590 676309 & 07817 762455
e-mail: shirley.measures@tesco.net

dir: *1m W of town centre. Off A337 Milford Rd rdbt onto North St & Ramley Rd, Elsburn 50yds past Pennington Garage*

Set in a village close to the yachting haven of Lymington and the beautiful New Forest, this guest house has been extensively refurbished to provide a relaxing and comfortable base. The smart bedrooms are filled with thoughtful extras, and a continental breakfast is served in the modern, café-style dining room.

Rooms 3 en suite **Facilities** TVB tea/coffee Cen ht **Parking** 3 **Notes** ⊗ No children 15yrs ☺

★★★★ BED & BREAKFAST
Harts Lodge
242 Everton Rd, Everton SO41 0HE
☎ 01590 645902

dir: *From Lymington 2.5m W to Everton, off A337 onto Everton Rd, 0.5m on left*

This attractive bungalow is situated in 3 acres of peaceful gardens and paddocks. The bedrooms are furnished to a high standard and feature many thoughtful touches; one room has outside access. Public areas include a lounge and a pleasant breakfast room, with views of the garden and a small pond.

Rooms 3 en suite (1 fmly) (3 GF) S £35–£60; D £55–£65✶ **Facilities** TVB tea/coffee Cen ht **Parking** 6 **Notes LB** ⊗ No children 8yrs ☺

★★★★ BED & BREAKFAST
Jevington
47 Waterford Ln SO41 3PT
☎ 01590 672148 ▤ 01590 672148
e-mail: jevingtonbb@lineone.net

dir: *From High St at St Thomas's Church onto Church Ln, left fork onto Waterford Ln*

Situated within walking distance of the town centre and marinas, Jevington offers attractive bedrooms furnished to a high standard with coordinated soft furnishings. An appetising breakfast is served at two tables in the dining room, and the friendly proprietors can suggest local places for dinner.

Rooms 3 en suite (1 fmly) S £30–£45; D £58✶ **Facilities** FTV TVB tea/coffee Cen ht **Parking** 3 **Notes** No children 5yrs ☺

★★★★ 🅰 BED & BREAKFAST
Glenhurst
86 Wainsford Rd, Everton SO41 0UD
☎ 01590 644256 & 07763 322519 ▤ 01590 644256
e-mail: a.rose@virgin.net
web: www.newforest-bedbreakfast.co.uk

dir: *2m W of Lymington. Off A337 into Everton village, off Old Christchurch Rd onto Wainsford Rd, Glenhurst 0.25m*

Rooms 2 en suite 1 annexe rms (1 annexe pri facs) (3 GF) D £55–£75✶ **Facilities** STV FTV TVB tea/coffee Cen ht Dinner Last d 24hrs Wi-fi available **Parking** 4 **Notes LB**

★★★ GUEST HOUSE
Gorse Meadow Country House

Sway Rd SO41 8LR

☎ 01590 673354 📄 01590 673336

e–mail: gorse.meadow.guesthouse@wildmushrooms.co.uk

web: www.gorsemeadowguesthouse.co.uk

dir: *Off A337 from Brockenhurst, right onto Sway Rd before Toll House pub, Gorse Meadow 1.5m on right*

This imposing Edwardian house is situated within 14 acres of grounds and most bedrooms enjoy views across the gardens and paddocks. Situated just one mile from Lymington, this is an excellent base to enjoy the many leisure pursuits that the New Forest has to offer. Meals are also available here, and Mrs Tee often uses the local wild mushrooms in her dishes.

Rooms 5 en suite (2 fmly) (2 GF) **Facilities** TVB tea/coffee Cen ht Dinner Last d 6pm Wi-fi available **Conf** Max 12 Board 12 **Parking** 20 **Notes** No coaches

★★★ BED & BREAKFAST
Passford Farm

Southampton Rd SO41 8ND

☎ 01590 674103 📄 01590 677074

dir: *Opp Welcome to Lymington sign*

Set in 5 acres with delightful gardens and a pond, parts of this charming thatched cottage date back 700 years. With its wealth of beams and fireplaces, Passford Farm is full of character. The proprietors adopt a relaxed and friendly approach, and ensure you enjoy the comfortable facilities.

Rooms 3 en suite (1 fmly) S £35–£50; D £70✳ **Facilities** STV TVB tea/coffee Cen ht TVL **Parking** 20 **Notes LB** ⊗ No children 12yrs ⊛

★★★ BED & BREAKFAST
Rosewood B&B

45 Ramley Rd SO41 8GZ

☎ 01590 677970

dir: *M27 to Lyndhurst then A337 to Lymington, continue towards Christchurch, turn right before shops at Pennington into South St, past church into Ramley Rd, Rosewood 0.5m on right*

Expect a warm welcome with an African theme at this family-run establishment. Located opposite Pennington Common on the edge of Lymington, this is an ideal area for exploring the area around the New

Forest. Breakfast is served in the dining room which leads into a large conservatory.

Rooms 3 rms (1 en suite) (1 pri facs) S £30–£35; D £50–£60✳ **Facilities** TVB tea/coffee Cen ht **Parking** 2 **Notes LB** Closed Xmas ⊛

LYNDHURST   MAP 05 SU30

★★★★ GUEST ACCOMMODATION
Temple Lodge

2 Queens Rd SO43 7BR

☎ 023 8028 2392 📄 023 8028 4910

e–mail: templelodge@btinternet.com

web: www.templelodge-guesthouse.com

dir: *M27 junct 2/3 onto A35 to Ashurst/Lyndhurst, Temple Lodge on 2nd corner on right, opposite forest*

Temple Lodge is a well appointed Victorian house with very friendly hosts. Guests will enjoy easy access to the New Forest and Lyndhurst town centre, with good off-road parking. The bedrooms feature lots of thoughtful extras including mini bars. Breakfast is not to be missed.

Rooms 6 en suite (2 fmly) D £80–£120✳ **Facilities** TVB tea/coffee Cen ht TVL Wi-fi available **Parking** 6 **Notes LB** ⊗ No children 12yrs

★★★★ BED & BREAKFAST
Clayhill House

SO43 7DE

☎ 023 8028 2304 📄 023 8028 2093

e–mail: clayhillhouse@tinyworld.co.uk

web: www.clayhillhouse.co.uk

dir: *Exit M27 junct 2. A35 to Lyndhurst then A332 marked Brockenhurst 0.75m from village*

Set at the edge of this attractive town, and convenient for visiting the New Forest and coastal attractions nearby, Clayhill House is a well-appointed house, which offers friendly service and comfortable accommodation. The bedrooms are particularly well equipped with thoughtful extras. Freshly-cooked breakfasts are served in the dining room.

Rooms 3 en suite (1 fmly) S £40–£50; D £60–£65✳ **Facilities** FTV TVB tea/coffee Cen ht **Parking** 6 **Notes LB** No children 7yrs Closed 22 Dec–4 Jan

CONTINUED

ENGLAND

LYNDHURST CONTINUED

★★★★ GUEST ACCOMMODATION
Rufus House

Southampton Rd SO43 7BQ
☎ 023 8028 2930
e–mail: rufushouse@aol.com
web: www.rufushouse.com

dir: *From Lyndhurst centre onto A35 Southampton Rd, 300yds on left*

Located on the edge of town, this delightful family-run Victorian property is well situated for exploring the New Forest. The brightly decorated bedrooms are appointed to a high standard, while the turret lounge and the garden terrace are great spots for relaxing.

Rooms 11 en suite (1 fmly) (2 GF) **Facilities** TVB tea/coffee Cen ht TVL **Parking** 15 **Notes** ⊗ No children 6yrs

★★★★ ⌂ GUEST ACCOMMODATION
Whitemoor House

Southampton Rd SO43 7BU
☎ 023 8028 3043
e–mail: whitemoor@tiscali.co.uk
web: www.whitemoorhouse.co.uk

dir: *0.5m NE of town centre on A35*

A warm welcome is assured at this well-run establishment in the New Forest. The comfortable bedrooms are brightly decorated and well equipped. A full English breakfast is served with homemade preserves in the tastefully appointed breakfast room.

Rooms 6 en suite (1 fmly) S £35–£50; D £60–£85 **Facilities** FTV TVB tea/coffee Cen ht TVL Wi-fi available **Parking** 6 **Notes** ⊗ No children 12yrs Closed 27 Dec–15 Jan ◉

★★★★ 🅰 GUEST ACCOMMODATION
Burwood Lodge

27 Romsey Rd SO43 7AA
☎ 023 8028 2445 📄 023 8028 4722
e–mail: burwoodlodge@yahoo.co.uk
Rooms 7 en suite (2 fmly) (1 GF) **Facilities** TVB tea/coffee Cen ht TVL **Parking** 10 **Notes** No children 6yrs ◉

★★★ GUEST ACCOMMODATION
Heather House

Southampton Rd SO43 7BQ
☎ 023 8028 4409 📄 023 8028 4431
e–mail: enquiries@heatherhouse.co.uk
web: www.heatherhouse.co.uk

dir: *M27 junct 1, A337 to Lyndhurst. At lights in centre turn left, establishment 800yds on left*

This impressive double-fronted Edwardian house stands in attractive gardens on the edge of town with views of the New Forest. Bedrooms are comfortably appointed with some suitable for families. Breakfast is served in the pleasant dining room.

Rooms 10 en suite (1 fmly) (1 GF) **Facilities** TVB tea/coffee Cen ht TVL **Parking** 12 **Notes** ⊗ Closed 23 Dec–2 Jan

★★★ BED & BREAKFAST
Little Hayes

43 Romsey Rd SO43 7AR
☎ 023 8028 3816
e–mail: info@littlehayes.co.uk

dir: *M27 junct 1 onto A337. On entering Lyndhurst, 200yds on right*

A friendly, well run bed and breakfast located within a few moments walk of the town centre, pubs and restaurants. Breakfast featuring local produce is served in the cosy dining room. Little Hayes provides an ideal base for touring the New Forest National Park, and benefits from off-road parking.

Rooms 3 en suite **Facilities** FTV TVB tea/coffee Cen ht Wi-fi available **Parking** 6 **Notes** ⊗

★★★ BED & BREAKFAST
The Willows

72 Lyndhurst Rd, Ashurst SO40 7BE
☎ 023 8029 2745 📄 023 8029 2745
e–mail: the_willows_ashurst@hotmail.com

dir: *3m NE of Lyndhurst on A35 in Ashurst*

Located north-east of Lyndhurst, this delightful property has good access to Southampton, the New Forest and numerous places of interest. Rooms are comfortable and well equipped. A full English breakfast or alternative choices are served at individual tables in the cosy and light dining room.

Rooms 3 rms (2 en suite) (1 fmly) S £28–£35; D £60–£70✳ **Facilities** TVB tea/coffee Cen ht TVL **Parking** 4 **Notes** LB ⊗ No children 10yrs

ENGLAND

MILFORD ON SEA MAP 05 SZ29

Premier Collection

★★★★★ 🏠 GUEST ACCOMMODATION
Ha'penny House
16 Whitby Rd SO41 0ND
☎ 01590 641210
e–mail: info@hapennyhouse.co.uk
web: www.hapennyhouse.co.uk

dir: *A337 at Everton onto B3058, through village onto Cliff Rd, right onto Cornwallis Rd, right at T-junct onto Whitby Rd, house 50yds on left*

This delightful house is in a peaceful residential area close to the clifftop with its stunning views towards the Isle of Wight. Individually styled bedrooms are beautifully appointed and equipped with a host of thoughtful extras. There is a stylish lounge, and an elegant dining room where superb breakfasts are served.

Rooms 4 en suite **Facilities** TVB tea/coffee Cen ht TVL Wi-fi available **Parking** 7 **Notes** ⊗ No children 12yrs

★★★★ BED & BREAKFAST
Alma Mater
4 Knowland Dr SO41 0RH
☎ 01590 642811
e–mail: bandbalmamater@aol.com
web: www.newforestalmamater.co.uk

dir: *A337 at Everton onto B3058 to Milford on Sea. Pass South Lawn Hotel, right onto Manor Rd, 1st left onto Knowland Dr, 3rd bungalow on right*

Alma Mater is in a quiet residential area within walking distance of the village centre and beaches. The comfortable bedrooms are all well appointed with many thoughtful touches including digital TV and toiletries. One room is on the ground floor and has twin beds, and the elegant dining room also has a conservatory where a wide choice of breakfasts can be enjoyed.

Rooms 3 en suite (1 GF) S £50; D £64–£70✳ **Facilities** TVB tea/coffee Cen ht TVL **Parking** 4 **Notes LB** ⊗ No children 15yrs ⊕

★★★★ GUEST ACCOMMODATION
Pilgrims Rest
Westover Rd SO41 0PW
☎ 01590 641167
e–mail: pilgrimsrestbandb@yahoo.co.uk

dir: *From Lymington follow signs New Milton, continue 2m left onto B3058 through village 2nd left*

A traditional bed and breakfast with friendly hosts, very well appointed rooms and a breakfast that is a great start to the day. Pilgrims Rest lies within walking distance of the beach and the town of Milford on Sea. All rooms are en suite or have private facilities.

Rooms 4 en suite S £40–£50; D £60–£70✳ **Facilities** FTV TVB tea/coffee Cen ht **Parking** 6 **Notes LB** ⊗ No children 10yrs ⊕

NEW ALRESFORD MAP 05 SU53

★★★ 🅰 BED & BREAKFAST
Haygarth
82 Jack Lyns Ln SO24 9LJ
☎ 01962 732715 & 07986 372895
e–mail: valramshaw@aol.com

dir: *B3046 from New Alresford centre for Cheriton, Haygarth 0.5m on right*

Rooms 3 rms (2 en suite) (1 pri facs) (3 GF) **Facilities** TVB tea/coffee Cen ht TVL **Parking** 7 **Notes** ⊗ ⊕

PETERSFIELD   MAP 05 SU72

See also Rogate (West Sussex)

★★★★ 🛏 BED & BREAKFAST
Quinhay Farmhouse
Alton Rd, Froxfield GU32 1BZ
☎ 01730 827183 📄 01730 827184
e–mail: janerothery@hotmail.com
web: www.quinhaybandb.co.uk

dir: *4m NW of Petersfield. Off A3 at A272 junct towards Petersfield, at rdbt exit signed Froxfield/Steep, 3.5m on right*

Jane Rothery takes great delight in welcoming you to her delightful modern home set in rolling countryside outside Petersfield. The spacious bedrooms are designed with comfort in mind and have a wealth of thoughtful extras, and the large lounge comes with comfy sofas and a wood-burning stove for colder months.

Rooms 3 rms (1 en suite) (2 pri facs) S £30–£40; D £60–£70 **Facilities** TVB tea/coffee Cen ht TVL Wi-fi available **Parking** 12 **Notes** ⊗ No children 12yrs Closed 15 Dec–15 Jan

★★★★ INN
The Good Intent
40–46 College St GU31 4AF
☎ 01730 263838 📄 01730 302239
e–mail: paul@stuartinns.com

dir: *In town centre on one-way system*

Named after the ship whose timbers are incorporated into the building, this cosy inn is full of character. Two en suite bedrooms are, comfortable and equipped with thoughtful extras. A popular carte menu is offered in the restaurant and simple snacks and real ales are also available.

Rooms 3 rms (2 en suite) (1 pri facs) (1 fmly) **Facilities** FTV TVB tea/coffee Cen ht Dinner Last d 9.30pm **Parking** 10 **Notes** No coaches

PLAITFORD   MAP 05 SU21

★★★★ 🅰 INN
The Shoe Inn
Salisbury Rd SO51 6EE
☎ 01794 322397 📄 01794 322405
e–mail: theshoeinn@btinternet.com
web: www.shoeinn.co.uk

dir: *On A36 at Plaitford*

Rooms 5 en suite **Facilities** TVB tea/coffee Cen ht Dinner Last d 9.15pm Pool Table **Parking** 40 **Notes** No coaches

PORTSMOUTH & SOUTHSEA MAP 05 SU60

★★★★ GUEST ACCOMMODATION
Hamilton House
95 Victoria Rd North, Southsea PO5 1PS
☎ 023 9282 3502 📄 023 9282 3502
e–mail: sandra@hamiltonhouse.co.uk
web: www.hamiltonhouse.co.uk

dir: *M275 Portsmouth, at Charles Dickens rdbt take 1st exit, across 3 rdbts onto Victoria Rd North*

This spacious Victorian property, carefully renovated by Graham and Sandra Tubb, provides bright, comfortable accommodation with many thoughtful facilities. The property is convenient for exploring historic Portsmouth and is close to the university. Breakfast is available from 6am for guests catching the cross-channel ferry. On-road parking available.

Rooms 9 rms (5 en suite) (3 fmly) S £50–£60; D £60–£70 **Facilities** TVB tea/coffee Cen ht TVL **Notes** ⊗

★★★★ GUEST HOUSE
St Margaret's Lodge
3 Craneswater Gate PO4 0NZ
☎ 023 9282 0097 📄 023 9282 0097
e–mail: enquiries@stmargarets-southsea.co.uk
web: www.stmargarets-southsea.co.uk

dir: *From South Parade Pier E along A288 St Helens Parade, 2nd left*

This establishment is in a quiet residential area close to the seafront and town centre. The attractive bedrooms have coordinated soft furnishings and many thoughtful extras. Breakfast is served in the smart dining room and there are two lounges and a cosy bar.

Rooms 14 en suite (1 fmly) S £30–£36; D £52–£70✳ **Facilities** TVB tea/coffee Cen ht TVL Wi-fi available **Parking** 5 **Notes** ⊗ No coaches Closed 21 Dec–2 Jan

ENGLAND

★★★★ GUEST ACCOMMODATION
Upper Mount House
The Vale, Off Clarendon Rd, Southsea PO5 2EQ
☎ 023 9282 0456 📄 023 9282 0456
e–mail: uppermountportsmouth@btconnect.com

dir: Off M275 for D-Day Museum onto road opposite Museum, over x-rds, right at T-junct, right again

Upper Mount House is peacefully located in a residential cul-de-sac. This impressive Victorian villa retains many original features. Public areas include a comfortable lounge and an attractive dining room where a fine collection of Venetian glassware is displayed. The bedrooms are spacious and well equipped and come in a variety of styles.

Rooms 16 en suite (3 fmly) (7 GF) S £40–£65; D £65–£70✳
Facilities FTV TVB tea/coffee Direct dial from bedrooms Cen ht TVL Wi-fi available **Parking** 17 **Notes** ⊗ Closed 2 wks Xmas

★★★★ Ⓐ GUEST ACCOMMODATION
Victoria Court
29 Victoria Rd North, Southsea PO5 1PL
☎ 023 9282 0305
e–mail: stay@victoriacourt.co.uk
web: www.victoriacourt.co.uk

dir: M275 junct 12, A3 into Portsmouth, onto A2030, 2nd rdbt right onto A2151 Victoria Rd North

Rooms 6 en suite (2 fmly) (1 GF) S £40–£60; D £50–£75✳
Facilities FTV TVB tea/coffee Cen ht Wi-fi available **Notes** ⊗

★★★ GUEST ACCOMMODATION
The Festing Grove
8 Festing Grove, Southsea PO4 9QA
☎ 023 9273 5239
e–mail: thefestinggrove@ntlworld.com

dir: E along seafront to South Parade Pier, after pier sharp left, around lake 3rd left & 2nd right

A well-presented property situated within easy walking distance of the seafront and pier. A continual programme of upgrading has ensured that the rooms enjoy a high standard of decor and comfort. Breakfast is served in the homely dining room, and there is a well-appointed lounge.

Rooms 6 rms (1 en suite) (2 fmly) **Facilities** TVB tea/coffee Cen ht TVL **Notes** ⊗

★★★ GUEST HOUSE
Abbey Lodge
30 Waverley Rd, Southsea PO5 2PW
☎ 023 9282 8285 📄 023 9287 2943
e–mail: linda@abbeylodge.co.uk

dir: Off A288 South Parade near pier onto B2155 Clarendon Rd & Waverley Rd

A warm welcome awaits you at this attractive property close to the seafront and within walking distance of the shops. It offers well-equipped bedrooms, and breakfast is served in a cosy dining room at individual tables.

Rooms 9 rms (3 en suite) (2 fmly) S £45; D £55✳ **Facilities** TVB tea/coffee Cen ht Wi-fi available **Notes** ⊗ No children 5yrs No coaches Closed Xmas & New Year

★★★ GUEST ACCOMMODATION
Amberley Court
97 Waverley Rd, Southsea PO5 2PL
☎ 023 9273 7473 📄 023 9275 2343
e–mail: mail@amberleycourt.co.uk

dir: Off A288 South Parade near pier onto B2155 Clarendon Rd & Waverley Rd

Amberley Court has a convenient location just 0.4m from the seafront and attractions. The comfortable bedrooms have bright modern coordinated fabrics, and come with good facilities. Some rooms and a smart conservatory-dining room are in a second house nearby.

Rooms 9 en suite (4 fmly) **Facilities** TVB tea/coffee Cen ht TVL **Parking** 4 **Notes** ⊗

★★★ GUEST ACCOMMODATION
Norfolk House
25 Granada Rd, Southsea PO4 0RD
☎ 023 9282 4162
e–mail: jbpnorfolk@ntlworld.com
web: www.thenorfolksouthsea.com

dir: From South Parade Pier E along A288 St Helens Parade, 1st left

Situated within walking distance of Southsea's attractions, Norfolk House is suited for business and leisure. The attractive rooms come with a range of useful extras, and some include a workspace. A lounge is also available.

Rooms 8 en suite (2 fmly) S £30–£35; D £46–£58 **Facilities** FTV TVB tea/coffee Cen ht **Parking** 5 **Notes** ⊗ Closed Xmas

PORTSMOUTH & SOUTHSEA CONTINUED

U

Collingham

89 St Ronans Rd, Southsea PO4 0PR

☎ 023 9282 1549

dir: From South Parade Pier E along A288 St Helens Parade, left onto Festing Rd, left at T-junct, left onto St Ronans Rd

At the time of going to press the rating for this establishment had not been confirmed. Please check the AA website www.theAA.com for up-to-date information.

Rooms 6 rms (3 fmly) S £23–£25; D £46–£50✱ **Facilities** TVB tea/coffee Cen ht TVL **Notes** No children 4yrs Closed 25 Dec 🐾

RINGWOOD   MAP 05 SU10

★★★★ GUEST ACCOMMODATION

Moortown Lodge

244 Christchurch Rd BH24 3AS

☎ 01425 471404 📄 01425 476527

e–mail: enquiries@moortownlodge.co.uk

web: www.moortownlodge.co.uk

dir: 1m S of Ringwood. Off A31 at Ringwood onto B3347, signs to Sopley, Lodge next to David Lloyds Leisure Club

The light and airy accommodation is finished to a very high standard, with digital television and broadband available in each room. Two of the well-equipped bedrooms are on ground level and another features a four-poster bed. Breakfast is served in the smart lounge-dining room at separate tables.

Rooms 7 en suite (3 fmly) (2 GF) S £67.50; D £84–£94✱ **Facilities** FTV TVB tea/coffee Direct dial from bedrooms Cen ht Wi-fi available Access to facilities of adjoining leisure club **Parking** 9 **Notes** LB

★★★★ GUEST ACCOMMODATION

Amberwood

3/5 Top Ln BH24 1LF

☎ 01425 476615 📄 01425 476615

e–mail: maynsing@aol.com

web: www.amberwoodbandb.co.uk

dir: A31 onto B3347, over rdbt, left onto School Ln, left onto Top Ln

This delightful Victorian home is situated in a quiet residential area within easy walking distance of the town centre. Bedrooms are attractively furnished and decorated, with many thoughtful extras. A substantial breakfast is served around one large table in the conservatory, which overlooks the well-tended garden. A lounge is also available.

Rooms 2 en suite **Facilities** TVB tea/coffee Direct dial from bedrooms Cen ht TVL **Parking** 2 **Notes** No children 12yrs Closed Xmas & New Year 🐾

★★★★ GUEST HOUSE

Little Forest Lodge

Poulner Hill BH24 3HS

☎ 01425 478848 📄 01425 473564

dir: 1.5m E of Ringwood on A31

A warm welcome is given to you and your pets, at this charming Edwardian house set in two acres of woodland. Bedrooms are pleasantly decorated and equipped with thoughtful extras. Both the attractive wood-panelled dining room and the delightful lounge, with bar and wood-burning fire, overlook the gardens. Home-cooked evening meals by arrangement.

Rooms 6 en suite (3 fmly) (1 GF) S £45–£50; D £80✱ **Facilities** TVB tea/coffee Licensed Cen ht Dinner Last d 7.30pm 🏸 badminton **Parking** 10 **Notes** No coaches

★★★★ GUEST ACCOMMODATION

Old Stacks

154 Hightown Rd BH24 1NP

☎ 01425 473840

e–mail: oldstacksbandb@aol.com

dir: Off A31 1m E of Ringwood signed Hightown, left onto Eastfield Ln, 0.5m right

This delightful bungalow is set in charming gardens. Of the two bedrooms, the twin bedroom has an en suite and its own garden entrance, while the double room has an adjoining bathroom. There is

CONTINUED

a comfortable lounge for guests' use and a hearty breakfast is served around a large table in the dining room.

Rooms 2 rms (1 en suite) (1 pri facs) (2 GF) D £58–£65 **Facilities** TVB tea/coffee Cen ht TVL **Parking** 4 **Notes LB** ⊗ No children 12yrs Closed Xmas & New Year ⊜

★★★★ BED & BREAKFAST
Picket Hill House
Picket Hill BH24 3HH
☎ 01425 476173 🖹 01425 470022
e–mail: b+b@pickethill.freeserve.co.uk

dir: *From Burley junct/services 2m E of Ringwood, off A31 to Ringwood, 250yds left to Hightown & Crow*

This is a good choice as a base for exploring the beautiful New Forest, where guests will be assured of a warm welcome. The comfortable bedrooms are well furnished and equipped with many extra facilities, and there is a spacious and comfortable first-floor lounge overlooking the delightful gardens. Delicious breakfasts are enjoyed at one large table in the dining room.

Rooms 3 en suite **Facilities** tea/coffee Cen ht TVL Golf **Parking** 6 **Notes** ⊗ No children 12yrs Closed 23 Dec–2 Jan

★★★★ BED & BREAKFAST
Valley View
Cowpits Ln, North Poulner BH24 3JX
☎ 01425 475855 & 07930 463134 🖹 01425 472542
e–mail: es-brown@tiscali.co.uk

dir: *A31 E 0.75m, E of Ringwood. Left to Hangelsley, 1st right 0.5m to x-rds, 75yds on right*

This establishment is set in a peaceful location with easy access to the New Forest, the Dorset coast and Salisbury. The bedroom has many considerate extras, and breakfast, featuring home-made preserves, is served in the family dining room. A home-cooked dinner is available by arrangement.

Rooms 2 rms (2 pri facs) S £30–£32; D £56–£60✱ **Facilities** TVB tea/coffee Cen ht Dinner Last d 4pm **Parking** 5 **Notes LB** ⊗ ⊜

★★★★ BED & BREAKFAST
Zarabanda
Horton Rd, Ashley Heath BH24 2EB
☎ 01425 475566
e–mail: stantonborley@waitrose.com

dir: *2m SW of Ringwood. Off A31 onto Horton Rd, 100yds right onto cul de sac*

A warm welcome is guaranteed at Zarabanda, set in a residential area close to routes for the Dorset coast and the New Forest. The new self-contained annexe is excellently equipped with a kitchen, television lounge and dining room, and overlooks the pretty family garden.

Rooms 1 annexe en suite (1 GF) **Facilities** TVB tea/coffee Cen ht TVL **Parking** 1 **Notes** ⊗ ⊜

★★★★ 🄰 BED & BREAKFAST
Fraser House
Salisbury Rd, Blashford BH24 3PB
☎ 01425 473958 🖹 01425 473958
e–mail: mail@fraserhouse.net

dir: *Off A31 at Ringwood onto A338 Salisbury Rd, house 1m on right*

Rooms 6 en suite S £45–£50; D £65–£75✱ **Facilities** TVB tea/coffee Cen ht TVL **Parking** 6 **Notes** No children 12yrs

★★★ GUEST HOUSE
Candlesticks Inn
136 Christchurch Rd BH24 3AP
☎ 01425 472587 🖹 01425 471600
e–mail: info@hotelnewforest.co.uk
web: www.hotelnewforest.co.uk

dir: *0.5m SE of town centre on B3347*

The 15th-century thatched property offers accommodation with a restaurant on the edge of town, and is convenient for Bournemouth and the New Forest National Park. Ample parking.

Rooms 8 annexe en suite (1 fmly) (4 GF) S £50–£70; D £55–£85 **Facilities** TVB tea/coffee Direct dial from bedrooms Licensed Cen ht Dinner Last d 9pm Sauna Sauna available for wheelchair users **Parking** 30 **Notes LB** ⊗ No coaches Closed 23 Dec–10 Jan

★★★ BED & BREAKFAST
Lochend
Hurst Corner, Salisbury Rd BH24 1AX
☎ 01425 473836
e–mail: kenburnsbrown@btinternet.com

dir: *A31 onto A338 towards Fordingbridge, 0.25m right onto Hurst Rd*

Located on the north side of town with easy access to the shops, the New Forest and various places of interest, this delightful property has both of its spacious, comfortable bedrooms on the ground floor. A charming garden is also available to guests, and English breakfasts are served at one large table.

Rooms 2 rms (1 en suite) (1 fmly) (2 GF) S £35; D £50 **Facilities** TVB tea/coffee Cen ht **Parking** 4 **Notes LB** Closed 20 Dec–3 Jan ⊜

ENGLAND

ROMSEY MAP 05 SU32

See also East Tytherley

★★★★ BED & BREAKFAST
Greenvale Farm
Melchet Park, Sherfield English SO51 6FS
☎ 01794 884858
e–mail: suebrown@greenvalefarm.com
web: www.greenvalefarm.com

dir: *5m W of Romsey. On S side of A27 through red-brick archway for Melchet Court, Greenvale Farm 150yds on left, left at slatted barn*

Located 4 miles from the New Forest and within easy reach of Winchester and Salisbury, this self-contained accommodation has plentiful facilities. With a working farm next door, don't be surprised if you are woken by a cockerel crow in the morning or hear guinea fowl chattering at night. The hearty breakfast, with freshly laid eggs if you're lucky, will set you up for the day.

Rooms 1 annexe en suite (1 GF) D £60–£65 **Facilities** STV TVB tea/coffee Cen ht Wi-fi available **Parking** 10 **Notes LB** ⊗ No children 14yrs ⊛

★★★★ BED & BREAKFAST
Country Accommodation Guest House
The Old Post Office, New Rd, Michelmersh SO51 0NL
☎ 01794 368739
e–mail: oldpodingo@aol.com

dir: *3m N of Romsey, off A3057 onto New Rd into Michelmersh*

This attractive guest house is decorated with country memorabilia that reflect the history of this delightful property. The comfortable bedrooms have excellent facilities and many useful extras. This is a good location for business or for touring the beautiful Hampshire countryside.

Rooms 3 annexe en suite (1 fmly) (3 GF) S £35; D £60 **Facilities** TVB tea/coffee Cen ht **Parking** 5 **Notes** ⊗ No children 12yrs

★★★ BED & BREAKFAST
The Courtyard
49 The Hundred SO51 8GE
☎ 01794 516434 & 07879 000000
e–mail: babidge@btinternet.com

dir: *From A27 follow signs to town centre. Follow one way system, past the bus station, follow road round to rdbt and turn right*

Centrally located in the village of Romsey, this recently refurbished property offers en suite bedrooms located above a traditional and charming tea room. The rooms are fresh with a contemporary outlook. Staff are friendly and attentive, and a hearty breakfast utilises top notch ingredients.

Rooms 3 en suite S £45–£50; D £70✳ **Facilities** TVB tea/coffee Cen ht **Conf** Max 20 Thtr 20 Board 20 **Parking** 3 **Notes** Closed 20 Dec–5 Jan ⊛

SOUTHAMPTON MAP 05 SU41

Premier Collection

★★★★★ BED & BREAKFAST
Riverside Bed & Breakfast
4 Tides Reach, 53 Whitworth Rd SO18 1GE
☎ 023 8063 0315 ▤ 023 8063 0315
e–mail: gordon-funnelle@supanet.com

dir: *2m NE of city centre. M27 junct 5, A335 onto Thomas Lewis Way, left onto A3035 over river, sharp right onto Whitworth Crescent & Whitworth Rd*

Located in a quieter part of Southampton, just five minutes walk away from public transport links and a ten-minute drive from the airport, this small and homely house has wonderful river views. Bedrooms have many thoughtful touches and guests have their own comfortable lounge. A wonderful continental breakfast is served in the dining room or on the balcony in warmer weather.

Rooms 2 rms (2 pri facs) D £60–£80✳ **Facilities** FTV TVB tea/coffee Cen ht **Parking** 1 **Notes** ⊗ No children 14yrs ⊛

★★★★ ◉ INN
White Star Tavern, Dining and Rooms
28 Oxford St SO14 3DJ
☎ 023 8082 1990 ▤ 023 8090 4982
e–mail: reservations@whitestartavern.co.uk
web: www.whitestartavern.co.uk

dir: *M3 junct 14 onto A33, towards Ocean Village*

This stylish tavern is conveniently located within the popular Oxford Street area, a moment's walk to the city centre. Bedrooms take their name from the ships of the White Star line, and are smartly appointed and well equipped with many thoughtful extras. The main bar and restaurant areas provide comfortable seating in well styled surroundings. Award winning cuisine is served in the White Star restaurant whilst in the morning an à la carte breakfast is served in the bar area. Private meeting space is also available.

CONTINUED

Rooms 13 en suite D £79–£179✱ (room only) **Facilities** FTV TVB tea/coffee Direct dial from bedrooms Cen ht TVL Dinner Last d 10pm Wi-fi available **Conf** Max 12 Board 12 Del from £145 ✱ **Notes** LB

See advert on this page

★★★★ GUEST ACCOMMODATION
Alcantara Guest House

20 Howard Rd, Shirley SO15 5BN
☎ 023 8033 2966 📄 023 8049 6163
e–mail: alcantara@btconnect.com

dir: *0.5m NW of city centre. Off A3057 onto Howard Rd*

A warm welcome is assured at this Victorian property, named after the ocean liner to reflect the establishment's shipping connections and location close to the city centre. Bedrooms are comfortable and well decorated and have many thoughtful extras. An appetising breakfast can be served in the bright and airy dining room. Secure off-road parking is available.

Rooms 9 rms (6 en suite) (3 fmly) (2 GF) S £30–£45; D £70–£80✱
Facilities FTV TVB tea/coffee Cen ht Wi-fi available **Parking** 7 **Notes** ⊗
No children 12yrs RS 2 wks Xmas

★★★★ GUEST ACCOMMODATION
Hunters Lodge

25 Landguard Rd, Shirley SO15 5DL
☎ 023 8022 7919
e–mail: hunterslodge.hotel@virgin.net
web: www.hunterslodgehotel.net

dir: *500yds NW of Southampton Central station. Off A3057 Shirley Rd onto Languard Rd*

Located in a leafy residential area close to the city centre and convenient for the docks, ferry terminal, university and hospital, this double-fronted Victorian house provides business and leisure guests with comfortable, well-equipped bedrooms. Full English breakfast is served at shared tables in the elegant dining room. There is also a television lounge and a well-stocked bar.

Rooms 14 en suite (1 fmly) (1 GF) S £44–£57; D £72–£75✱
Facilities TVB tea/coffee Direct dial from bedrooms Cen ht TVL Wi-fi available **Parking** 16 **Notes** ⊗

★★★ GUEST HOUSE
Landguard Lodge

21 Landguard Rd SO15 5DL
☎ 023 8063 6904 📄 023 8063 2258
e–mail: landguard.lodge@mail.com
web: www.landguardlodge.co.uk

dir: *500yds NW of Southampton Central station. Off A3057 Shirley Rd onto Landguard Rd*

This Victorian house is in a quiet residential area a short walk from the railway station. The bedrooms are bright, comfortable and well equipped with many thoughtful extras.

Rooms 10 en suite (1 fmly) (1 GF) **Facilities** TVB tea/coffee Cen ht
Parking 3 **Notes** ⊗ No children 5yrs No coaches

★★★ 🅰 GUEST HOUSE
Mayview

30 The Polygon SO15 2BN
☎ 023 8022 0907 & 07973 874194 📄 07977 017921
e–mail: info@mayview.co.uk

Rooms 9 rms (1 en suite) (1 fmly) (1 GF) **Facilities** TVB tea/coffee Cen ht **Notes** ⊗ Closed 25 Dec

★★ GUEST ACCOMMODATION
The Brimar

10–14 High St, Totton SO40 9HN
☎ 023 8086 2950 📄 023 8086 1301
e–mail: info@brimar-guesthouse.co.uk

dir: *3m W of city centre, off A35 in Totton High St*

This guest house offers practical, comfortable accommodation at reasonable prices. Not all rooms are en suite but bathrooms are well situated. Breakfast is served in the dining room or as a take-away option. The Brimar is well placed for the M27 and Southampton docks, and off-road parking is available.

Rooms 21 rms (8 en suite) (2 fmly) (8 GF) (3 smoking) S £30–£35;
D £50–£70✱ **Facilities** TVB Cen ht **Parking** 20 **Notes** ⊗

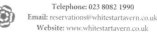

ENGLAND

SOUTHSEA   MAP 05 SZ69

See Portsmouth & Southsea

STOCKBRIDGE   MAP 05 SU33

★★★★ BED & BREAKFAST
Old Drapery Guesthouse
Middle Wallop SO20 8HN
☎ 01264 781301 📠 01264 781301
e–mail: amanda@olddraperyguesthouse.co.uk
web: www.olddraperyguesthouse.co.uk

dir: *A303 onto A343, turn right at x-rds by George Inn, 2nd on left*
A Georgian family home in the Wallops, close to Stockbridge and set just off the main road in mature gardens. A warm welcome and attentive service awaits guests and accommodation provides good levels of comfort throughout. Off-street parking is available.

Rooms 4 en suite S £40; D £80–£90✻ **Facilities** TVB tea/coffee Cen ht Dinner Last d 6.30pm **Parking** 5 **Notes** ✪ No children 12yrs Closed 24–26 & 31 Dec–1 Jan 🐾

★★★★ BED & BREAKFAST
York Lodge
Five Bells Ln, Nether Wallop SO20 8HE
☎ 01264 781313
e–mail: bradley@york-lodge.co.uk
web: www.york-lodge.co.uk

dir: *Turn off A30 or A343 onto B3084, turn onto Hosketts Ln, fork left, 1st house on right*
Located in the picturesque village famous for Agatha Christie's Miss Marple series, this charming house has comfortable accommodation in a self-contained wing. Bedrooms are stylishly presented with many thoughtful extra facilities. The dining room overlooks peaceful gardens, and delicious dinners are available by arrangement.

Rooms 2 en suite (2 GF) S £35–£55; D £70–£75✻ **Facilities** TVB tea/coffee Cen ht Wi-fi available **Parking** 4 **Notes** No children 8yrs 🐾

★★★ INN
The Three Cups Inn
High St SO20 6HB
☎ 01264 810527 📠 08708 913158
e–mail: manager@the3cups.co.uk

A former coaching inn on the high street in a popular town, with its own parking. Rooms are comfortable and well equipped, and food is available every evening.

Rooms 8 en suite (3 fmly) S fr £62; D fr £72✻ **Facilities** TVB tea/coffee Cen ht Dinner Last d 9.25pm Wi-fi available **Parking** 15

SWAY   MAP 05 SZ29

★★★★ 🍴 ☕ GUEST ACCOMMODATION
The Nurse's Cottage Restaurant with Rooms
Station Rd SO41 6BA
☎ 01590 683402
e–mail: nurses.cottage@lineone.net
web: www.nursescottage.co.uk

dir: *Off B3055 in village centre, close to shops*
Smart and appealing accommodation, excellent hospitality and service, and carefully prepared food contribute to an enjoyable stay at this former district-nurse's cottage. Sight, sound and accessibility facilities further enhance the experience for guests at this delightful establishment. The bedrooms offer comfort with numerous thoughtful extras, and lovely toiletries and fluffy towels are provided in the bathrooms. The conservatory-restaurant is popular with locals and guests.

Rooms 5 en suite (5 GF) S £90; D £170–£190(incl. dinner) **Facilities** FTV TVB tea/coffee Direct dial from bedrooms Cen ht Dinner Last d 8pm Wi-fi available **Parking** 5 **Notes LB** No children 10yrs Closed Feb–Mar & Nov (3 wks)

★★★★ BED & BREAKFAST
Acorn Shetland Pony Stud

Meadows Cottage, Arnewood Bridge Rd SO41 6DA
☎ 01590 682000
e–mail: meadows.cottage@virgin.net

dir: *M27 junct 1, A337 to Brockenhurst, B3055 to Sway, pass Birchy Hill Nursing Home, over x-rds, 2nd entrance left*
Located on the outskirts of Sway, this comfortable establishment is set in over 6 acres of pony paddocks and a water garden. The ground-floor bedrooms are well furnished and have direct access onto patios. The enjoyable, freshly cooked breakfasts use a range of fine produce including delicious home-made bread.

Rooms 3 en suite (1 fmly) (3 GF) S fr £27; D fr £56✱ **Facilities** TVB tea/coffee Cen ht Carriage driving with Shetland ponies **Parking** 3 **Notes** LB ⊜

★★★ INN
The Forest Heath

Station Rd SO41 6BA
☎ 01590 682287 ▤ 01590 682626
e–mail: forestheathhotel@hotmail.co.uk

dir: *M27 junct 1, A337 to Brockenhurst, B3055 to Sway, onto Church Ln & Station Rd*
Located in a New Forest village, this late Victorian inn is a popular meeting place for the local community. Bedrooms are well equipped and comfortable, and a range of real ales and imaginative meals is offered in the bars and the conservatory dining room.

Rooms 4 en suite (2 fmly) **Facilities** TVB tea/coffee Cen ht Dinner Last d 8.45pm Wi-fi available Pool Table boules, petanque **Parking** 20 **Notes** ⊗

WINCHESTER   MAP 05 SU42

Premier Collection

★★★★★ BED & BREAKFAST
Orchard House

3 Christchurch Gardens, St Cross SO23 9TH
☎ 01962 861544 ▤ 01962 861988
e–mail: hopefamily@hotmail.co.uk

dir: *B3335 to Winchester & St Cross, after 2nd lights turn left onto Barnes Close and right onto Christchurch Rd, right again onto Christchurch Gardens, last house on the right*
This friendly, family-run B&B is in a peaceful cul-de-sac, close to Winchester and the famous college, yet within easy access of the M3. It offers a relaxed atmosphere, professional service and warm hospitality. The bedroom is spacious, comfortable and very well equipped for either the business or leisure guest alike. Gardens are well tended, and the balcony overlooking the rear garden can be used for breakfast on warmer summer mornings, and there is also ample parking available.

Rooms 1 en suite S £50–£60; D £80–£100 **Facilities** STV TVB tea/coffee Cen ht TVL **Parking** 2 **Notes** ⊗ No children 6yrs ⊜

★★★★ GUEST ACCOMMODATION
The Grange

Sleeper Hill SO22 4NA
☎ 01962 851419 & 07771 927012 ▤ 01962 851419
e–mail: jeannesaywell@aol.com

dir: *From Romsey Rd turn onto Sleepers Hill, 1st lane on left to the Grange*
A large family house within minutes of the city centre, its cathedral, and shopping centre. The hosts are friendly and welcoming, rooms are very comfortable and well equipped, and the freshly cooked breakfast is a great start to the day.

Rooms 3 en suite (3 fmly) **Facilities** FTV TVB tea/coffee Cen ht TVL Gymnasium Outdoor Jacuzzi **Parking** 8 **Notes** ⊗ No children 12yrs Closed Xmas & New Year

★★★★ BED & BREAKFAST
Heybridge

Clifton Rd SO22 5BP
☎ 01962 865007 & 07779 436305
e–mail: jacquiekennedy@yahoo.co.uk

dir: *500yds W of city centre. Off A3040 Romsey Rd onto Clifton Rd*
Close to the town centre in a quiet suburb, overlooking the park, Heybridge offers a quiet location with very comfortable accommodation. The two bedrooms are both en suite, comfortable and very smartly appointed. A substantial breakfast is served in the spacious dining room.

Rooms 2 en suite S £50–£55; D £70✱ **Facilities** TVB tea/coffee Cen ht **Parking** 1 **Notes** ⊗ ⊜

★★★★ INN
The Old Vine

8 Great Minster St SO23 9HA
☎ 01962 854616
e–mail: reservations@oldvinewinchester.com
web: www.oldvinewinchester.com

dir: *M3 junct 11 towards St Cross, turn right at Green Man Pub, left onto Symonds St*
Overlooking the cathedral this historic inn has been extensively and sympathetically restored and updated. Rooms are named and themed after various designers, there is permit parking, and food is served in the restaurant and bar downstairs.

Rooms 5 en suite (1 fmly) S £90–£150; D £100–£160✱ **Facilities** FTV TVB tea/coffee Cen ht Dinner Last d 9.30pm **Notes** ⊗ No coaches

WINCHESTER CONTINUED

★★★★ ֎֎ INN
The Running Horse

88 Main Rd, Littleton SO22 6QS

☎ 01962 880218 📠 01962 886596

e–mail: runninghorseinn@btconnect.com

dir: B3049 out of Winchester 1.5m, turn right into Littleton after 1m, Running Horse on right

Situated in a pretty rural location, yet with easy access to the M3, this is a great location for business and leisure travellers visiting Hampshire. Offering quality accommodation, the Running Horse is minimalist in its design, and provides comfortable beds and a small workstation area. Highlights of a stay here are a meal in the smart restaurant or a drink in the bar.

Rooms 9 annexe en suite (1 fmly) (9 GF) S £65; D £75✳ **Facilities** TVB tea/coffee Cen ht Dinner Last d 9.30pm **Parking** 70 **Notes** ֎ No coaches Closed 25 Dec

★★★ BED & BREAKFAST
31 St Anne's Close

Badgers Farm SO22 4LQ

☎ 01962 622553

e–mail: reelhall@yahoo.co.uk

dir: M3 junct 11, onto A3090 Badger Farm Rd, right onto Ridgeway, right onto St Anne's Close

This friendly, family-run home is in the quiet residential area of Badgers Farm. It offers a cosy bedroom with a sitting room that bursts coordinated furnishings, a television and a hospitality tray. A full English breakfast is provided.

Rooms 1 rms (1 pri facs) S £30; D £45 **Facilities** TVB tea/coffee Cen ht TVL **Parking** 1 **Notes** ֎ No children Closed 16 Dec–4 Jan ֎

★★★ BED & BREAKFAST
24 Clifton Road

SO22 5BU

☎ 01962 851620

e–mail: a.williams1997@btinternet.com

dir: 500yds NW of city centre. B3040 Romsey Rd W from city centre, Clifton Rd 2nd right

This delightful house is in a quiet residential area close to the railway station and High Street. It combines town-house elegance with a

CONTINUED

homely cottage charm, and is handy for local walks. The bedroom is comfortably furnished and the bathroom has a deep claw-foot bath. There is a lounge and a dining room.

Rooms 1 rms (1 pri facs) S £35; D £50 **Facilities** tea/coffee Cen ht TVL **Parking** 2 **Notes** ֎ No children 6yrs ֎

★★★ INN
The Westgate Inn

2 Romsey Rd SO23 8TP

☎ 01962 820222 📠 01962 820222

e–mail: wghguy@yahoo.co.uk

dir: From junct Upper High St & High St onto Romsey Rd, premises beyond Westgate arch

The Westgate Inn is well placed at the west end of the city near the castle. A popular restaurant serves good, home-prepared Indian meals and snacks. The traditional bar remains busy. The attractive and good-sized bedrooms on two floors are well-equipped.

Rooms 8 rms (6 en suite) (8 smoking) D £70–£85 **Facilities** TVB tea/coffee Direct dial from bedrooms Cen ht Dinner Last d 9.30pm **Conf** Max 12 **Notes** No children No coaches Closed 25–26 Dec

★★ BED & BREAKFAST
Casadele

61 Stanmore Ln SO22 4AH

☎ 01962 813412

e–mail: adeleradichetti@yahoo.com

dir: 1m SE of city centre. M3 junct 11 onto B3335 for Winchester, 1m left at lights onto Lower Stanmore Ln & Stanmore Ln

This small bed and breakfast is situated in a residential area just outside of the centre of the town and is easily reached by car or public transport. Both rooms are compact in size yet comfortable, and there is ample parking.

Rooms 2 rms **Facilities** TVB tea/coffee Cen ht TVL **Parking** 2 **Notes** ֎ No children 15yrs ֎

HEREFORDSHIRE

ADFORTON
MAP 09 SO47

★★★★ 🏠 BED & BREAKFAST
Brick House Farm

SY7 0NF

☎ 01568 770870

e–mail: info@adforton.com

web: www.adforton.com

dir: On A4110 in Adforton village. Opposite St Andrews Church

Located at the heart of the village community, this 16th-century longhouse has been sympathetically renovated to provide high standards of comfort and facilities. Superb beds are only one feature of the thoughtfully furnished accommodation, and smart modern bathrooms are an additional benefit. Comprehensive breakfasts feature locally-sourced produce, served in a cosy combined sitting/dining room and a warm welcome is assured.

Rooms 2 rms (2 pri facs) D £75✳ **Facilities** STV FTV TVB tea/coffee Cen ht TVL Dinner Last d 48hrs notice Wi-fi available Riding **Parking** 4 **Notes** No children 12yrs

BROCKHAMPTON

MAP 10 SO53

★★★★ ⇔ GUEST HOUSE
Ladyridge Farm
HR1 4SE

☎ 01989 740220 ▤ 01989 740220

e–mail: carolgrant@ladyridgefarm.fsworld.co.uk

dir: Off B4224 signed Brockhampton Church between How Caple & Fownhope. 400yds on right after thatched church

This working farm, set in delightful countryside, provides a peaceful haven and is also home to rare breed ducks, poultry and sheep. Bedrooms are spacious, traditional and thoughtfully equipped. Meals are served family-style in the attractive dining room, using local fresh ingredients and home-produced free-range eggs.

Rooms 3 rms (2 pri facs) (1 fmly) S £28; D £52–£56✱ **Facilities** TVB tea/coffee Cen ht Dinner Last d 24hrs prior Riding **Parking** 6 **Notes LB** No coaches ⊛

BROMYARD

MAP 10 SO65

★★★★ BED & BREAKFAST
Little Hegdon Farm House
Hegdon Hill, Pencombe HR7 4SL

☎ 01885 400263 & 07779 595445

e–mail: howardcolegrave@hotmail.com

web: www.littlehegdonfarmhouse.co.uk

dir: 4m SW of Bromyard. From Bromyard to Pencombe, 1.5m towards Risbury, at top of Hegdon Hill down farm lane for 500yds

Located in a pretty hamlet, this traditional house has been renovated to provide high standards of comfort. Original features include exposed beams and open fires, and the bedrooms are equipped with lots of thoughtful extras. They also enjoy stunning views of the surrounding countryside.

Rooms 2 en suite S £35; D £60 **Facilities** TVB tea/coffee Cen ht TVL Riding Pool Table ⚒ **Parking** 4 **Notes** ⊛

★★★★ FARM HOUSE
Linton Brook Farm *(SO676538)*
Malvern Rd, Bringsty WR6 5TR

☎ 01885 488875 ▤ 01885 488875 Mrs S Steeds

dir: Off A44 1.5m E of Bromyard onto B4220 signed Malvern. Farm 0.5m on left

Dating back some 400 years, this large house has a wealth of character and has been renovated to provide modern comforts. Accommodation is spacious and there is a comfortable sitting room with a welcoming wood-burning stove. The breakfast room has exposed beams, antique furniture and an inglenook fireplace.

Rooms 3 rms (2 en suite) (1 pri facs) S £30–£40; D £60–£70 **Facilities** TVB tea/coffee Cen ht TVL Dinner **Parking** 12 **Notes** LB ⊗ 68 acres grassland Closed Xmas & New Year RS end Oct -end Apr ⊛

FOWNHOPE

MAP 10 SO53

★★★★ ⇔ GUEST ACCOMMODATION
Bowens Country House
HR1 4PS

☎ 01432 860430 ▤ 01432 860430

e–mail: thebowenshotel@aol.com

web: www.thebowenshotel.co.uk

dir: 6m SE of Hereford on B4224. In Fownhope, opp church

This 17th-century former farmhouse, set in well-tended grounds, is peaceful and relaxing. The house provides modern and comfortable facilities. Bedrooms are attractively decorated and have many extra touches; family rooms are available, including a two-bedroom suite. An honesty bar is provided in the lounge, and at dinner delicious home-cooked dishes are served at individual tables.

Rooms 6 en suite 4 annexe en suite (3 fmly) (4 GF) S fr £40; D fr £80✱ **Facilities** TVB tea/coffee Direct dial from bedrooms Cen ht Dinner Last d 8pm ⚑ ⚒ ♪ **Parking** 15 **Notes LB**

GOODRICH   MAP 10 SO51

★★★★ BED & BREAKFAST
Granton House B&B

HR9 6JE

☎ 01600 890277

e-mail: info@grantonhouse.co.uk

web: www.grantonhouse.co.uk

dir: *A40 S from Ross-on-Wye, 2nd Goodrich exit into village, pass Cross Keys continue straight for approx 0.5m*

A genuinely warm and friendly welcome awaits at Granton House, parts of which date back to the late 18th century. It is situated in extensive grounds and gardens, in a picturesque rural area on the edge of Goodrich village. The house, which was once the home of Victorian artist Joshua Cristall, has been extensively and tastefully renovated to provide high quality, thoughtfully equipped accommodation.

Rooms 3 en suite (1 fmly) S £55–£65; D £75–£85 **Facilities** TVB tea/coffee Cen ht Wi-fi available **Parking** 4 **Notes LB** ⊗ No children 6yrs Closed 18 Dec–2 Jan ⊜

HEREFORD   MAP 10 SO53

See also Little Dewchurch & Moccas

Premier Collection

★★★★★ GUEST ACCOMMODATION
Somerville House

12 Bodenham Rd HR1 2TS

☎ 01432 273991   📠 01432 268719

e-mail: enquiries@somervillehouse.net

web: www.somervillehouse.net

dir: *A465, at Aylestone Hill rdbt continue towards city centre, left at Southbank Rd, leading to Bodenham Rd*

Somerville House is a detached late-Victorian villa situated in a quiet tree-lined residential road, offering a boutique style bed and breakfast. Expect a warm and friendly welcome from Rosie and Bill, the new partners who offer quality accommodation with high standards of luxury and comfort. All bedrooms are spacious, and provide a good range of quality extras. Breakfast is served in the light and contemporary dining room at individual tables. There is a terraced garden to the rear where guests can sit and relax, or indoors, make use

of the comfortable lounge. There is ample car parking to the front of the property.

Rooms 12 en suite (3 fmly) (1 GF) S £50; D £65–£99✳ **Facilities** FTV TVB tea/coffee Cen ht Wi-fi available **Conf** Max 10 Thtr 10 Class 10 Board 10 **Parking** 10 **Notes** ⊗

★★★★ 🍴 INN
Bay Horse Inn

236 Kings Acre Rd HR4 0SD

☎ 01432 273351

e-mail: info@thebayhorsehereford.co.uk

dir: *On A438, pass Wyevale, 1000yds on left*

This delightful inn is set on the outskirts of Hereford, and is personally run by Mr and Mrs Morgan. Bedrooms are purpose built and recently completed to a high standard, situated adjoining the main building. Four are on the ground floor, and one has wheelchair access along with a wet room shower facility. All bedrooms are tastefully decorated, spacious with comfortable beds, and a good range of extras. Public areas have comfortable seating around a log fireplace as well as casual dining tables. Both dinner and breakfast offer extensive choice and quality and are served in the dining room at separate tables.

Rooms 8 annexe en suite (1 fmly) (4 GF) S £55–£65; D £65–£75✳ **Facilities** FTV TVB tea/coffee Direct dial from bedrooms Cen ht TVL Dinner Last d 9pm Wi-fi available **Conf** Max 40 Thtr 40 Class 40 Board 32 Del from £100 ✳ **Parking** 30 **Notes LB** ⊗ No children 12yrs

★★★★ FARM HOUSE
Holly House Farm *(SO456367)*

Allensmore HR2 9BH

☎ 01432 277294 & 07889 830223 📠 01432 261285

Mrs D Sinclair

e-mail: hollyhousefarm@aol.com

web: www.hollyhousefarm.org.uk

dir: *A465 S to Allensmore, right signed Cobhall Common, at small x-rds right into lane, house on right*

Surrounded by open countryside, this spacious farmhouse is a relaxing base for those visiting this beautiful area. The homely and comfortable bedrooms offer lovely views over the fields. Breakfast makes use of local produce together with home-made jams and marmalade. Pets are very welcome here and the proprietor is happy to look after them during the day if required.

Rooms 2 rms (1 en suite) (1 pri facs) D £56–£76 **Facilities** TVB tea/coffee Cen ht **Parking** 32 **Notes** 11 acres Horses Closed 25–26, 31 Dec & 1 Jan ⊜

★★★★ GUEST ACCOMMODATION
Norfolk House

23 Saint Martin St HR2 7RD

☎ 01432 340900

e-mail: info@norfolkhousehereford.co.uk

web: www.norfolkhousehereford.co.uk

Norfolk House is a large mid-terraced Georgian property situated south of the River Wye in Hereford, only 100 metres from the city's old bridge and the Left Bank Village. An ideal location for exploring the

CONTINUED

CONTINUED

nearby towns of Leominster, Ludlow, Ledbury, Kington, Ross-on-Wye and Worcester. The accommodation provides five comfortable en suite bedrooms and offer both doubles (with king-sized beds) and twin rooms. In the welcoming dining room a hearty breakfast made from fresh local produce is provided to start the day. Wi-fi is available.

Rooms 5 en suite (1 fmly) S £40–£50; D £60–£70✱ **Facilities** FTV TVB tea/coffee Cen ht Wi-fi available **Parking** 3 **Notes** ⊛ No children 5yrs

★★★★ 🚍 GUEST ACCOMMODATION
Priors Mead
Ruckhall Ln HR2 9SB
☎ 01432 277209
e–mail: priorsmead@accessbb.co.uk

dir: *From Belmont Abbey on the A465 Abergavenny Rd, turn onto Ruckhall Ln. Priors Mead is located 1.5m on left*

Priors Mead was built in the 1930s, and has been completely refurbished throughout by the present owners over the last seven years. It is located approximately four miles from the centre of Hereford in some very peaceful surroundings with views to the Black Mountains. Bedrooms are spacious with quality fittings and thoughtful extras, and the bathrooms have been designed to a high standard. Dinner is available on request with all dishes freshly prepared from locally sourced and home-grown produce.

Rooms 3 rms (1 en suite) (1 pri facs) S £40–£45; D £60–£76✱ **Facilities** tea/coffee Cen ht TVL Dinner Last d 10am Wi-fi available Golf 18 ⛳ **Parking** 8 **Notes** No children 12yrs 🐾

★★★★ FARM HOUSE
Sink Green *(SO542377)*
Rotherwas HR2 6LE
☎ 01432 870223 📠 01432 870223 Mr D E Jones
e–mail: enquiries@sinkgreenfarm.co.uk
web: www.sinkgreenfarm.co.uk

dir: *3m SE of city centre. Off A49 onto B4399 for 2m*

This charming 16th-century farmhouse stands in attractive countryside and has many original features, including flagstone floors, exposed beams and open fireplaces. Bedrooms are traditionally furnished and one has a four-poster bed. The pleasant garden has a comfortable summer house, hot tub and barbecue.

Rooms 3 en suite S £28–£33; D £54–£67✱ **Facilities** TVB tea/coffee Cen ht TVL Wi-fi available Fishing Hot Tub **Parking** 10 **Notes** LB 180 acres beef 🐾

★★★★ 🅰 GUEST ACCOMMODATION
Hedley Lodge
Belmont Abbey, Abergavenny Rd HR2 9RZ
☎ 01432 374747 📠 01432 374754
e–mail: hedley@belmontabbey.org.uk
web: www.hedleylodge.com

dir: *2m SW of city centre. Off A465 signed Belmont Abbey*

Rooms 17 en suite (1 fmly) S £45–£55; D £65–£75✱ **Facilities** TVB tea/coffee Direct dial from bedrooms Cen ht Dinner Last d 8pm Wi-fi available **Conf** Max 200 Thtr 200 Class 50 Board 40 Del from £65 ✱ **Parking** 200 **Notes** ⊛

★★★ 🅰 GUEST HOUSE
Charades Guest House
34 Southbank Rd HR1 2TJ
☎ 01432 269444 📠 01432 269444
e–mail: stay@charadeshereford.co.uk

dir: *Off A4103 Ayelstone Hill, right onto Southbank Rd, 500yds on right*

Rooms 14 en suite (5 fmly) (3 GF) S £40–£45; D £65–£75✱ **Facilities** TVB tea/coffee Cen ht TVL Wi-fi available **Parking** 16 **Notes** LB No coaches

★★★ 🅰
Graiseley House
180 Whitecross Rd HR4 0DJ
☎ 01432 358289 & 07870 499542
e–mail: janespearpoint@yahoo.co.uk

dir: *A438, 0.75m from Hereford city centre, just past Holy Trinity Church*

Rooms 4 rms (2 en suite) S £28–£35; D £55–£65 **Facilities** TVB tea/coffee Cen ht TVL Wi-fi available **Parking** 3 **Notes** ⊛

★★★ 🅰 BED & BREAKFAST
Heron House
Canon Pyon Rd, Portway HR4 8NG
☎ 01432 761111 📠 01432 760603
e–mail: info@theheronhouse.com
web: www.theheronhouse.com

dir: *A4103 onto A4110 until Portway x-rds, Heron House 200yds on left*

Rooms 2 rms (1 en suite) S £25; D £56✱ **Facilities** TVB tea/coffee Cen ht **Parking** 5 **Notes** ⊛ No children 10yrs 🐾

LEDBURY   MAP 10 SO73

★★★★ 🏛 FARM HOUSE
Bodenham Farm *(SO653318)*
Much Marcle HR8 2NJ
☎ 01531 660222 & 07754 415604 Mrs L Morgan
e–mail: bodenhamfarm@lineone.net
web: www.bodenhamfarm.co.uk
dir: *5m SW of Ledbury. 0.5m S of Much Marcle on A449*

Set in well-tended gardens, this impressive and attractive Grade II listed house dates from the 18th century. Full of character, the comfortable accommodation retains many original features including exposed beams and four-poster beds, along with modern facilities. The welcoming proprietors make you feel very much at home.

Rooms 3 en suite S £40; D £65 **Facilities** TVB tea/coffee Cen ht TVL **Parking** 8 **Notes** ⊗ No children 12yrs 5 acres highland cattle chickens 🐾

★★★★ FARM HOUSE
Church Farm *(SO718426)*
Coddington HR8 1JJ
☎ 01531 640271 Mrs West
web: www.dexta.co.uk
A warm welcome awaits you at Church Farm which provides comfortable accommodation in a Grade II-listed farm house. Aga-cooked breakfasts are served around the shared kitchen table or in the dining room. The farm house is in a peaceful and tranquil location in the depths of rural Herefordshire. There is much to explore in the area, with numerous activities including golf, canoeing, cycling and various walks, with the Malvern Hills only five miles away.

Rooms 3 rms (2 en suite) (1 pri facs) S fr £40; D fr £72✳ **Facilities** TV1B tea/coffee Cen ht TVL **Conf** Max 12 **Parking** 6 **Notes** 100 acres sheep/arable Closed 16 Dec–15 Jan 🐾

★★★★ FARM HOUSE
Moor Court Farm *(SO639447)*
Stretton, Grandison HR8 2TP
☎ 01531 670408 📠 01531 670408 Mrs E Godsall
dir: *1.5m E of A417 at Upper Eggleton*

This 15th-century house is situated on a mixed farm with working oast houses where hops are dried. Bedrooms are thoughtfully equipped and furnished, and one has a four-poster. Public areas include a comfortable lounge with an impressive stone fireplace and a dining room, where breakfast includes local produce and eggs from the farm.

Rooms 3 en suite **Facilities** TVB tea/coffee Licensed Cen ht Dinner Last d 6.30pm Fishing **Parking** 5 **Notes** ⊗ No children 8yrs 200 acres Mixed livestock hops 🐾

★★★★ GUEST ACCOMMODATION
Wall Hills House
Hereford Rd HR8 2PR
☎ 01531 632833 📠 01531 632833
e–mail: wallhills@btinternet.com
dir: *Leave Ledbury on A438, entrance to drive within 200yds on left after rdbt*
Expect a friendly welcome at Wall Hills House, which is set amongst the fields and woodland half a mile from the main road and close to the old market town of Ledbury. The area is ideal for walkers, with the wonderful scenery of the Malvern Hills nearby. Bedrooms are spacious, reflecting the Georgian era in which the house was built, and front-facing rooms command views over rural Herefordshire. Dinner is freshly prepared using fresh, local ingredients with vegetables usually

CONTINUED

picked from the owner's garden and served in the cosy dining room at individually set tables.

Rooms 3 rms (2 en suite) (1 pri facs) S £60–£78; D £78–£85✱
Facilities tea/coffee Cen ht Dinner Last d 8.15pm Wi-fi available
Parking 6 **Notes** LB ⊗ Closed Xmas & New Year

★★★ GUEST ACCOMMODATION
Hillstow

21 Bank Crescent HR8 1AD
☎ 01531 632196 📠 0800 902 0176
e–mail: sales@hillstow.co.uk
web: www.stayinledbury.com

dir: Off main Ledbury High St

This property is situated two minutes walk from historic Ledbury town centre, one mile from Eastnor Castle, and five miles from Malvern. The luxury bedroom is very comfortable and there are many thoughtful extras provided for guest comfort. Continental breakfast is served to the bedroom and uses a very good selection of fresh ingredients. There is a set of stairs from the hallway to the bedroom with a toilet and washbasin at the bottom of the stairs all within the accommodation area, and parking is available for one car.

Rooms 1 en suite D £65✱ **Facilities** FTV TVB tea/coffee Cen ht Wi-fi available **Parking** 1 **Notes** ⊜

LEOMINSTER   MAP 10 SO45

Premier Collection
★★★★★ FARM HOUSE
Hills Farm (SO564638)

Leysters HR6 0HP
☎ 01568 750205 Mrs J Conolly
e–mail: j.conolly@btconnect.com
web: www.thehillsfarm.co.uk

dir: Off A4112 Leominster to Tenbury Wells, on edge of Leysters

Set in a peaceful location with views of the surrounding countryside, this property dates in part from the 16th century. The friendly, attentive proprietors provide a relaxing and homely atmosphere. The attractive bedrooms, in the converted barns, are spacious and comfortable. Breakfasts, served in the dining room and conservatory, feature fresh local produce.

Rooms 3 annexe en suite (1 GF) S £35–£42; D £70–£84 **Facilities** FTV TVB tea/coffee Cen ht **Parking** 8 **Notes** ⊗ No children 12yrs 120 acres arable Closed Dec & Jan

★★★★ FARM HOUSE
Heath House (SO535552)

Stoke Prior HR6 0NF
☎ 01568 760385 & 07720 887393 Mr & Mrs Cholerton
e–mail: heathhouse@onetel.com

dir: A44 turn right at x-rds, signed Risbury & brown tourist sign for Broadfield vineyard, house located on left after 1m

A warm and friendly welcome awaits all guests at this pleasant property, which is situated in a peaceful rural location. This former 17th-century farmhouse has an attractive garden and retains many original features including exposed beams and open fireplace. The bedrooms are spacious and comfortable, and provide some thoughtful guest extras. A carefully prepared breakfast, including eggs from the owners' own hens, can be taken at the communal table in the kitchen. Horses and dogs are welcome by arrangement.

Rooms 1 en suite 1 annexe en suite (1 fmly) S £40; D £65✱
Facilities TVB tea/coffee Cen ht **Parking** 3 **Notes** LB No children 5yrs 5 acres Non-Working/Horses Closed Dec–1 Feb ⊜

★★★ FARM HOUSE
Woonton Court Farm (SO548613)

Leysters HR6 0HL
☎ 01568 750232 📠 01568 750232 Mrs E M Thomas
e–mail: thomas@woontoncourtfarm.co.uk
web: www.woontoncourt.co.uk

dir: 3m NE of Leominster. Off A4112 for Woonton (SE of Leysters), farm 0.5m

This attractive 15th-century farmhouse is set in tranquil countryside, has many original features, and displays family mementoes. Bedrooms are well equipped, with comfortable furnishings and many extra facilities. Freshly cooked breakfasts include farm-produced eggs, local sausages and home-made marmalade, served in the comfortable dining room.

Rooms 2 en suite 1 annexe en suite S £30–£40; D £60–£70✱
Facilities STV FTV TVB tea/coffee Cen ht TVL **Parking** 4 **Notes** LB ⊗ 250 acres mixed Closed 22–27 Dec ⊜

LITTLE DEWCHURCH   MAP 10 SO53

★★★★ FARM HOUSE
Cwm Craig (SO535322)

HR2 6PS
☎ 01432 840250 📠 01432 840250 Mrs G Lee

dir: Off A49 into Little Dewchurch, turn right in village, Cwm Craig 1st farm on left

This Georgian farmhouse is situated on the outskirts of the village in glorious countryside and offers spacious accommodation. Bedrooms are carefully furnished and public areas consist of a comfortable lounge, games room and dining rooms, one of which is offered for the use of families. A hearty breakfast is supplemented by eggs from the farm's hens.

Rooms 3 en suite (1 fmly) S £28–£34; D £52–£64 **Facilities** TVB tea/coffee Cen ht TVL Pool Table **Parking** 6 **Notes** ⊗ 190 acres Organic arable ⊜

MOCCAS	MAP 09 SO34

ROSS-ON-WYE — MAP 10 SO52

See also Goodrich

Premier Collection

★★★★★ 🛏 ⛵ GUEST ACCOMMODATION

Moccas Court

HR2 9LH

☎ 01981 500019 📄 01981 500095

e–mail: bencmaster@btconnect.com

dir: *A438, 10m turn right to Bredwardine then right at T junct approx 2.5m turn left to Moccas Court.*

This memorable Grade I listed Georgian family home is of such historic interest that it is open to the public as a stately home. You can dwell in the lap of luxury, attended to by the most charming and genial hosts. A delicious dinner, served around a large circular table in the splendid dining room, should not be missed.

Rooms 5 rms (4 en suite) (1 pri facs) S £126–£203; D £140–£225✳
Facilities FTV TVB tea/coffee Cen ht TVL Dinner Last d noon Wi-fi available Fishing ⚓ **Parking** 35 **Notes LB** ⊗ No children 16yrs Closed Feb–1 Apr Civ Wed 60

PETERCHURCH	MAP 09 SO33

★★★ BED & BREAKFAST

Hinton Green Country House B&B

Hinton Green HR2 0SH

☎ 01981 550135

e–mail: info@hintongreen.com

web: www.hintongreen.com

dir: *B4348 to Peterchurch, turn left at Nags Head 3rd house on right*

A warm and friendly welcome awaits guests at this fine 16th-century property which has been lovingly restored by the present proprietors, Pat and Sandy, who have created three guest bedrooms with quality fittings. Bedrooms are comfortable and offer a good range of extras. Peterchurch is in the centre of the Golden Valley with many local walks and an historic village and church. Hinton Green is within easy walking distance of the village centre with shops, restaurants and pubs.

Rooms 3 en suite 1 annexe en suite (1 fmly) S £25–£35; D £50–£70✳
Facilities TVB tea/coffee Cen ht TVL **Conf** Max 8 **Parking** 4 **Notes LB** ⊗ 📠

★★★★ GUEST ACCOMMODATION

Brookfield House

Over Ross St HR9 7AT

☎ 01989 562188

e–mail: info@brookfield-house.co.uk

web: www.brookfield-house.co.uk

dir: *500yds N of town centre. Off B4234 Over Ross St onto Brookmead & up driveway*

Dating from the 18th century, this large detached house lies just north of the town centre. Refurbished to a high standard throughout, the bedrooms are spacious, comfortably appointed and well equipped. Breakfast is served in the light and airy dining room. A relaxing lounge is also available for guest use, as are the attractive gardens.

Rooms 3 en suite (1 fmly) D £64–£72✳ **Facilities** TVB tea/coffee Cen ht Wi-fi available **Parking** 12 **Notes** ⊗ No children 12yrs

★★★★ ⊛⊛ RESTAURANT WITH ROOMS

Bridge House

Wilton HR9 6AA

☎ 01989 562655 📄 01989 567652

e–mail: info@bridge-house-hotel.com

web: www.bridge-house-hotel.com

dir: *Off junct A40 & A49 into Ross-on-Wye, 300yds on left*

Built about 1740, this elegant house is just a stroll across the bridge from delightful Ross-on-Wye. Standards here are impressive and bedrooms offer ample space, comfort and genuine quality. Period features in the public areas add to the stylish ambience, and the gardens run down to the river. The restaurant serves accomplished cuisine.

Rooms 9 en suite **Facilities** TVB tea/coffee Direct dial from bedrooms Cen ht Dinner Last d 9pm Fishing **Conf** Max 12 **Parking** 20 **Notes** ⊗ No children 14yrs

★★★★ GUEST ACCOMMODATION
Lea House
Lea HR9 7JZ
☎ 01989 750652 🖹 01989 750652
e–mail: enquiries@leahouse.co.uk
web: www.leahouse.co.uk

dir: *4m SE of Ross on A40 towards Gloucester, in Lea village*

This former coaching inn near Ross is a good base for exploring the Forest of Dean and the Wye Valley. The individually furnished bedrooms are thoughtfully equipped with many extras and toiletries, and the atmosphere is relaxed and homely. Breakfast in the oak-beamed dining room is a tasty choice including freshly squeezed fruit juices, fish and local sausages.

Rooms 3 rms (2 en suite) (1 pri facs) (1 fmly) S £35–£45; D £60–£70✳
Facilities TVB tea/coffee Cen ht TVL Dinner Last d by prior arrangement Wi-fi available **Parking** 4 **Notes LB**

★★★★ BED & BREAKFAST
Lumleys
Kern Bridge, Bishopswood HR9 5QT
☎ 01600 890040 🖹 0870 706 2378
e–mail: helen@lumleys.force9.co.uk
web: www.thelumleys.co.uk

dir: *Off A40 onto B4229 at Goodrich, over Kern Bridge, right at Inn On The Wye, 400yds opp picnic ground*

This pleasant and friendly guest house overlooks the River Wye, and has been a hostelry since Victorian times. It offers the character of a bygone era combined with modern comforts and facilities. Bedrooms are individually and carefully furnished and one has a four-poster bed and its own patio. Comfortable public areas include a choice of sitting rooms.

Rooms 3 en suite D £65–£75 **Facilities** STV FTV TVB tea/coffee Direct dial from bedrooms Cen ht TVL Dinner Last d 7pm Wi-fi available **Parking** 15 **Notes** 🐾

★★★★ GUEST ACCOMMODATION
Sunnymount
Ryefield Rd HR9 5LS
☎ 01989 563880 🖹 01989 566251
e–mail: sunnymount@tinyworld.co.uk

dir: *M50 junct 4, A449 for Ross, next rdbt onto A40 Gloucester, B4260 for Ross town centre, 2nd right*

Built in the 1920s, this large house is in a quiet suburb close to the M50 and the A40. Immaculately maintained throughout, the bedrooms are comfortable and well equipped, and the public areas are spacious. A hearty breakfast is provided and served in the pleasant, airy dining room.

Rooms 6 en suite S £35–£40; D £55–£65✳ **Facilities** TVB tea/coffee Cen ht Dinner Last d 4pm **Parking** 7 **Notes LB** RS 21–31 Dec

★★★★ GUEST ACCOMMODATION
Thatch Close
Llangrove HR9 6EL
☎ 01989 770300
e–mail: info@thatchclose.co.uk
web: www.thatchclose.com

dir: *Off A40 at Symonds Yat West/Whitchurch junct to Llangrove, right at x-rds after Post Office, Thatch Close 0.6m on left*

Standing in 13 acres, this sturdy farmhouse dating from 1760 is full of character. There is a wonderfully warm atmosphere here with a genuine welcome from your hosts. The homely bedrooms are equipped for comfort with many thoughtful extras. Breakfast and dinner are served in the elegant dining room, and a lounge is available. The extensive patios and gardens are popular in summer, providing plenty of space to find a quiet corner and relax with a good book.

Rooms 3 en suite **Facilities** TVB tea/coffee Cen ht TVL Dinner Last d 9am **Parking** 8 **Notes** 🐾 🐕

ENGLAND

SHOBDON   MAP 09 SO46

★★★★ INN
The Bateman Arms
HR6 9LX
☎ 01568 708374 📠 08701 236418
e–mail: diana@batemanarms.co.uk
web: www.batemanarms.co.uk
dir: *On B4362 in Shobdon village*

Located in the village, parts of this refurbished inn date back over four hundred years. Now under the new ownership of Bill and Diana Mahood who offer a warm welcome to all their guests as well as accommodation which comprises six modern style bedrooms located in the separate refurbished building and three bedrooms in the main building. All are comfortable and well appointed. Much of the character has been retained with plenty of oak beams and a large log fire adding to the ambience in the public areas. In addition to the friendly welcome, the food here is a key feature with carefully prepared local produce.

Rooms 3 en suite 6 annexe en suite (2 fmly) (3 GF) S £55–£65; D £85–£95✱ **Facilities** FTV TVB tea/coffee Cen ht Dinner Last d 8.45pm Wi-fi available Pool Table Games room **Parking** 40

SYMONDS YAT (EAST)   MAP 10 SO51

★★★★ GUEST ACCOMMODATION
Garth Cottage
HR9 6JL
☎ 01600 890364
e–mail: val.eden@virgin.net
web: www.garthcottage-symondsyat.com
dir: *Off A40 onto B4229, signs for Symonds Yat East*

The Eden family's warm hospitality and attention to guest comfort is evident in this attractive and impeccably maintained 18th-century house. The bedrooms are well equipped, and breakfast and dinner are served in the conservatory-dining room overlooking the River Wye. There is also a cosy bar and a choice of lounges, including a sun lounge that also looks over the river.

Rooms 4 en suite D £72✱ **Facilities** tea/coffee Cen ht TVL Dinner Last d noon Fishing **Parking** 9 **Notes** ⊛ No children 12yrs Closed Nov–Mar ⌂

★★★★ INN
Saracens Head Inn
HR9 6JL
☎ 01600 890435 📠 01600 890034
e–mail: contact@saracensheadinn.co.uk
web: www.saracensheadinn.co.uk
dir: *Off A40 at Little Chef, signed Symonds Yat East*

Dating from the 16th century, the friendly, family-run Saracens Head faces the River Wye and has wonderful views. The well-equipped bedrooms are decorated in a cottage style, and there is a cosy lounge, an attractive dining room, and a popular public bar with a riverside patio. All meals are offered from a comprehensive menu changed regularly, and include locally-sourced produce.

Rooms 8 en suite 2 annexe en suite (1 fmly) (1 GF) S £50–£70; D £78–£130 **Facilities** FTV TVB tea/coffee Direct dial from bedrooms Cen ht TVL Dinner Last d 9pm Wi-fi available Fishing Pool Table **Conf** Max 25 Thtr 25 Class 25 Board 25 **Parking** 35 **Notes LB** No children 7yrs No coaches

---

★★★ GUEST ACCOMMODATION
The Royal Lodge
HR9 6JL
☎ 01600 890238 📠 01600 891425
e–mail: info@royalhotel-symondsyat.com
web: www.royallodgesymondsyat.co.uk
dir: *Midway between Ross and Monmouth. Turn off at signs for Goodich B4229 to Symonds Yat East*

The Royal Lodge is under new ownership and stands at the top end of the village overlooking the River Wye. Bedrooms are spacious and comfortable and there is a cosy lounge with an open fireplace, along with a television. The bedrooms do not have TVs, as the Lodge operates a quiet policy. Meals are offered in the welcoming restaurant which provides carefully prepared fresh and local ingredients. Staff are pleasant and friendly and there are many outside seating areas where you can enjoy a drink from the bar or take lunch on warmer days.

Rooms 20 en suite (5 fmly) S £30–£50; D £50–£130✱ **Facilities** tea/coffee Direct dial from bedrooms Cen ht TVL Dinner Last d 9pm Wi-fi available **Conf** Max 70 Thtr 70 Class 20 Board 30 **Parking** 150 **Notes LB**

SYMONDS YAT (WEST) MAP 10 SO51

★★★★ 🏠 ➰ GUEST ACCOMMODATION
Norton House

Whitchurch HR9 6DJ
☎ 01600 890046 📄 01600 890045
e-mail: su@norton.wyenet.co.uk
web: www.norton-house.com

dir: *0.5m N of Symonds Yat West. Off A40 into Whitchurch village and left onto Old Monmouth Rd*

Built as a farmhouse, Norton House dates back 300 years and retains a lot of character, with features such as flagstone floors and beamed ceilings. The bedrooms, including a four-poster room, are individually styled and furnished for maximum comfort. Excellent local produce is used to create an imaginative range of breakfast and dinner options. The charming public areas include a snug lounge, with a wood-burning stove. Self-catering cottages are also available.

Rooms 3 en suite S £45–£50; D £60–£90 **Facilities** TVB tea/coffee Cen ht TVL Dinner Last d 9am **Parking** 5 **Notes** No children 12yrs Closed 25–26 Dec ⊛

VOWCHURCH MAP 09 SO33

★★★★ 🅰 BED & BREAKFAST
Yew Tree House

Bacho Hill HR2 9PF
☎ 01981 251195 📄 01981 251195
e-mail: enquiries@yewtreehouse-hereford.co.uk
web: www.yewtreehouse-hereford.co.uk

dir: *On B4348 between Kingstone & Vowchurch*

Rooms 3 en suite (2 fmly) S £40–£50; D £60–£75✻ **Facilities** TVB tea/coffee Cen ht TVL Dinner Last d 8.30pm Wi-fi available **Parking** 4 **Notes LB** ⊛

WHITCHURCH MAP 10 SO51

★★★★ GUEST ACCOMMODATION
Portland House Guest House

HR9 6DB
☎ 01600 890757
e-mail: info@portlandguesthouse.co.uk
web: www.portlandguesthouse.co.uk

dir: *Off A40 between Monmouth and Ross on Wye. Take turn for Whitchurch/Symonds Yat West*

Portland House is an impressive dwelling, dating in part back to the 17th century, and situated in the picturesque Wye Valley. The accommodation consists of comfortable bedrooms which include a large family room, an accessible bedroom on the ground floor, and a four-poster suite. All have a thoughtful range of extras provided. Walkers can use the Boot Room and guests have use of the laundry, the terrace garden area, and the attractive lounge. Breakfast with ingredients from local suppliers, home-made bread and up to eight kinds of home-made preserve, is served around the shared dining table, or at a separate table in the cosy elegant dining room. With prior arrangement, evening meals can be provided.

Rooms 6 en suite (2 fmly) (1 GF) S £40–£50; D £60–£86✻ **Facilities** TVB tea/coffee Cen ht TVL Dinner Last d noon Wi-fi available **Parking** 6 **Notes LB** ⊗ Closed 25–26 Dec & Jan

WHITNEY-ON-WYE
MAP 09 SO24

★★★★ INN
The Rhydspence Inn
HR3 6EU

☎ 01497 831262 📠 01497 831751

e–mail: info@rhydspence-inn.co.uk

dir: *N side of A438 1m W of Whitney*

Dating back to the 14th century this large, privately owned and personally run hostelry is three miles north of Hay-on-Wye. Surrounded by attractive gardens and with a stream that forms part of the boundary between England and Wales, the inn provides modern accommodation, and public rooms that include a very attractive restaurant and two quaint bars with low beamed ceilings and log fires.

Rooms 7 en suite S fr £42.50; D fr £85✱ **Facilities** TVB tea/coffee Cen ht Dinner Last d 9pm **Parking** 60 **Notes** LB ⊗ No coaches

---

YARKHILL
MAP 10 SO64

★★★★ FARM HOUSE
Garford Farm *(SO600435)*
HR1 3ST

☎ 01432 890226 📠 01432 890707 Mrs H Parker

e–mail: garfordfarm@btconnect.com

dir: *Off A417 at Newtown x-rds onto A4103 for Hereford, farm 1.5m on left*

This black and white timber-framed farmhouse, set on a large arable holding, dates from the 17th century. Its character is enhanced by period furnishings, and fires burn in the comfortable lounge during colder weather. The traditionally furnished bedrooms, including a family room, have modern facilities.

Rooms 2 en suite (1 fmly) S fr £40; D fr £60✱ **Facilities** TVB tea/coffee Cen ht Fishing ⌣ **Parking** 6 **Notes** No children 2yrs 700 acres arable Closed 25–26 Dec ⊜

BISHOP'S STORTFORD
MAP 06 TL42

★★★ BED & BREAKFAST
Broadleaf Guest House
38 Broadleaf Av CM23 4JY

☎ 01279 835467

e–mail: b-tcannon@tiscali.co.uk

dir: *1m SW of town centre. Off B1383 onto Whittinton Way & Friedburge Av, Broadleaf Av 6th left*

A delightful detached house situated in a peaceful residential area close to the town centre, and within easy striking distance of the M11 and Stansted Airport. The pleasantly decorated bedrooms are carefully furnished and equipped with many thoughtful touches. Breakfast is served in the smart dining room, which overlooks the pretty garden.

Rooms 2 rms (1 fmly) S £30–£35; D £55–£60✱ **Facilities** TVB tea/coffee Cen ht **Parking** 2 **Notes** ⊜

★★★ GUEST ACCOMMODATION
Pearse House
Parsonage Ln CM23 5BQ

☎ 01279 757400 📠 01279 506591

e–mail: pearsehouse@btconnect.com

dir: *M11 junct 8, A120, A1250 into Bishops Stortford. Right at rdbt onto Parsonage Ln, house 1st on left*

An imposing, half-timbered Victorian house situated on the edge of town and just a short drive from Stansted Airport. Bedrooms are smartly appointed and equipped with modern facilities. The spacious public areas include a bar, lounge, dining room and conference facilities.

Rooms 13 en suite 24 annexe en suite (2 fmly) (1 GF) **Facilities** TVB tea/coffee Direct dial from bedrooms Cen ht TVL Dinner Last d 8pm Wi-fi available Small fitness room **Conf** Max 300 Thtr 150 Class 60 Board 30 **Parking** 100 **Notes** ⊗ Closed Xmas & New Year Civ Wed 60

BUNTINGFORD
MAP 12 TL32

★★★★ INN
Sword Inn Hand
Westmill SG9 9LQ

☎ 01763 271356

e–mail: welcome@theswordinnhand.co.uk

web: www.theswordinnhand.co.uk

dir: *In village of Westmill, off A10 S of Buntingford*

Set within the peaceful village of Westmill amid rolling countryside, this charming 14th-century inn offers excellent accommodation and a friendly and relaxed atmosphere. Purpose-built ground-floor bedrooms are located just off the rear gardens; these very well-equipped and carefully appointed rooms have their own access. Character public rooms within the inn, include a choice of restaurant and bar dining options, along with a choice of draught ales.

Rooms 4 en suite (4 GF) **Facilities** STV FTV TVB tea/coffee Cen ht TVL Dinner Last d 9.30pm Wi-fi available **Parking** 25 **Notes** ⊗

DATCHWORTH   MAP 06 TL21

★★★★★ BED & BREAKFAST
Farmhouse B&B

Hawkins Grange Farm, Hawkins Hall Ln SG3 6TF

☎ 01438 813369 📄 01438 813369

e–mail: mail@hawkinsgrangefarm.com

web: www.hawkinsgrangefarm.com

dir: *A1(M) junct 7 onto A602 (Hertford). From Bragbury End onto Bragbury Ln, 2m on left after phone box*

This detached property is set in several acres of grassland on the edge of the pretty village of Datchworth. A warm and professional welcome is provided by your host Jane. Bedrooms are comfortably furnished with an abundance of accessories. Full English or continental breakfast is served, including organic, local produce and home-made items.

Rooms 3 rms (2 en suite) (1 pri facs) S £37.50–£47.50; D £65–£75✳
Facilities FTV TVB tea/coffee Cen ht Wi-fi available **Parking** 8 **Notes** ⊗

HARPENDEN   MAP 06 TL11

★★★★ ◉ INN
The Silver Cup

5 St Albans Rd AL5 2JF

☎ 01582 713095 📄 01582 469713

e–mail: info@silvercup.co.uk

web: www.silvercup.co.uk

dir: *200yds SW of Harpenden station on A1081 St Albans Rd*

Located south of Harpenden high street opposite the common, this small family-owned inn offers comfortable, well equipped rooms with many additional extras such as an honesty bar and home-made biscuits. Public areas are stylish and well presented and the attractive restaurant serves a superior quality menu complemented by real ales and a good wine list. Service is friendly and helpful.

Rooms 6 en suite (1 fmly) S £75; D £95✳ **Facilities** TVB tea/coffee
Cen ht TVL Dinner Last d 9.30pm Wi-fi available **Parking** 7 **Notes** ⊗
No coaches

See advert on this page

HEMEL HEMPSTEAD   MAP 06 TL00

★★ GUEST HOUSE
AA Recommended Guest House

27A High St HP1 3AA

☎ 01442 392828

e–mail: info@casamigos.co.uk

dir: *On Old High St, opp St Mary's Church*

Located in the old town with its high street setting. Good value accommodation is provided in thoughtfully equipped rooms. Breakfast is served in a pub just a moments walk away.

Rooms 4 rms (1 en suite) (2 pri facs) (4 fmly) S £25–£35; D £50–£60✳
Facilities FTV TVB tea/coffee Cen ht **Parking** 4 **Notes** LB ⊗

★★ GUEST ACCOMMODATION
Alexandra

40/42 Alexandra Rd HP2 5BP

☎ 01442 242897 📄 01442 211829

e–mail: alexhous@aol.com

dir: *Off B487 Queensway in town centre*

This well-managed guest house has a regular business clientele and provides well-equipped bedrooms with practical extras. Breakfast is served in the ground-floor dining room, which also contains a lounge area. There is a good selection of tourist information.

Rooms 16 rms (3 fmly) (3 GF) **Facilities** STV TVB tea/coffee Lift Cen ht
TVL Wi-fi available **Parking** 6 **Notes** ⊗ No children 2yrs Closed
23 Dec–2 Jan

HERTFORD   MAP 06 TL31

★★★★ GUEST ACCOMMODATION
Mulberry Lodge

Newgate St SG13 8NQ

☎ 01707 879652 📄 01707 879653

e–mail: bookings@mulberrylodge.org.uk

web: www.mulberrylodge.org.uk

dir: *M25 junct 25, signs for Paradise Wildlife Park, left at T-junct, Lodge on left*

Mulberry Lodge offers carefully furnished accommodation in a smart barn conversion in peaceful rural surroundings at Epping Green. The spacious bedrooms have king-size doubles (or twins) and are very well equipped for business travellers, providing safes, direct dial telephones with modem points, and modern bathrooms. Freshly cooked breakfasts are served in the open-plan diner, which has an adjacent small lounge area and a 24-hour manned reception desk. Secure parking is a bonus.

Rooms 12 en suite (12 GF) S £62.50–£69; D £62.50–£75✳
Facilities TVB tea/coffee Direct dial from bedrooms Cen ht TVL
Parking 15 **Notes** Closed 24–26, 31 Dec & 1 Jan

★★★★ GUEST ACCOMMODATION
Orchard Cottage

East End Green SG14 2PD

☎ 01992 583494 & 07885 747000

e–mail: looadams@sky-mail.net

dir: *2m SW of Hertford. Off A414 at East End Green sign, 5th drive left on gravel road*

A friendly welcome awaits at Orchard Cottage, set in a peaceful rural location yet only 5 minutes from Hertford. This large cottage sits in lovely gardens and has views of the countryside. Bedrooms offer comfortable accommodation with beamed ceilings.

Rooms 4 rms (2 en suite) (2 pri facs) (1 fmly) S £35–£45; D £60–£75✳
Facilities FTV TVB tea/coffee Cen ht TVL Wi-fi available **Parking** 6
Notes ⊗ Closed Xmas & New Year 🐾

HERTFORD HEATH   MAP 06 TL31

Premier Collection

★★★★★ BED & BREAKFAST
Rushen

Mount Pleasant SG13 7QY

☎ 01992 581254 📄 01992 534737

e–mail: wilsonamwell@btinternet.com

dir: *From A10 exit at Hertford slip road, 1st left onto B1502. 1st right at top of lane, bear left at village green. Rushen on left at end of green*

You will find a warm welcome at Rushen, which is situated at the end of the village green in Hertford Heath. Rooms are comfortable and well appointed. Breakfast offers a good range of choice using local and organic produce when possible.

Rooms 2 rms (1 en suite) S £35–£40; D £60–£70 **Facilities** FTV TVB
tea/coffee Cen ht Wi-fi available **Parking** 3 **Notes** ⊗ Closed
22 Dec–3 Jan

Ⓤ
Brides Farm

The Roundings SG13 7PY

☎ 01992 466687 & 463315 📄 01992 478776

dir: *Take B1197 to Hertford Heath. Right at College Arms into the Roundings. Take left fork to Brides Farm*

At the time of going to press the rating for this establishment had not been confirmed. Please check the AA website www.theAA.com for up-to-date information.

Rooms 3 en suite S £40; D £60✳ **Facilities** TVB tea/coffee Cen ht
Parking 10 **Notes** LB 🐾

HITCHIN
MAP 12 TL12

★★★ INN
The Greyhound

London Rd, St Ippollitts SG4 7NL

☎ 01462 440989

e-mail: greyhound@freenet.co.uk

dir: *On B656, 1m S of Hitchin*

A popular inn situated on the outskirts of town amid open farmland. Service is friendly and helpful, and a range of interesting meals is readily available in the bar and dining area. Bedrooms are well equipped and have cheerful colour schemes.

Rooms 5 en suite (1 fmly) S £40–£45; D £42.50–£50✼ (room only) **Facilities** TVB tea/coffee Cen ht Dinner Last d 9pm **Conf** Max 30 **Parking** 25 **Notes LB**

See advert on this page

MUCH HADHAM
MAP 06 TL41

★★★★ BED & BREAKFAST
High Hedges Bed & Breakfast

High Hedges, Green Tye SG10 6JP

☎ 01279 842505

e-mail: info@high-hedges.co.uk

dir: *From B1004 turn off to Green Tye at Prince of Wales pub, turn into private road, 1st on right*

Expect a warm welcome at High Hedges. Bedrooms are well presented and comfortable, and come with many thoughtful extra touches. A substantial breakfast is served in the comfortable dining room. Half Moon Holistic Therapies is part of the B&B, and offers a range of massages and other treatments.

Rooms 3 rms (2 en suite) (1 pri facs) (1 GF) S fr £35; D £55–£60✼ **Facilities** FTV TVB tea/coffee Cen ht Wi-fi available Holistic therapies **Parking** 3 **Notes** ⊗ Closed 25–26 Dec & 31 Dec–1 Jan ⊛

NUTHAMPSTEAD
MAP 12 TL43

★★★ INN
The Woodman Inn

SG8 8NB

☎ 01763 848328 📠 01763 848328

e-mail: woodman.inn@virgin.net

dir: *A505 to Royston, take right onto B1368 to Barkway village, 1st left past Tally Ho, 2m turn right, situated on left*

This 17th-century inn has many fine features, and is close to the Duxford Imperial War Museum. The practical bedrooms are decorated in a traditional style. The kitchen offers a good range of British meals, plus a generous breakfast.

Rooms 4 en suite (2 GF) **Facilities** TV2B tea/coffee Cen ht TVL Dinner Last d 9pm Pool Table **Parking** 30 **Notes** ⊗ Closed 25 Dec RS Sun eve

---

289

ST ALBANS   MAP 06 TL10

★★★★ Ⓐ BED & BREAKFAST
Fern Cottage
116 Old London Rd AL1 1PU
☎ 01727 834200
e–mail: bookinginfo@ferncottage.uk.net

dir: *M25 junct 22, A1081 to St Albans, 3rd exit off London Coney rdbt for 1m, under railway bridge, over mini-rdbt & 2nd left onto Old London Rd. Fern Cottage 400yds on left*

Rooms 3 en suite (1 GF) **Facilities** TVB tea/coffee Cen ht Wi-fi available **Parking** 3 **Notes** ⊛

★★★ Ⓐ BED & BREAKFAST
Tresco
76 Clarence Rd AL1 4NG
☎ 01727 864880
e–mail: pat_leggatt@hotmail.com

dir: *Off A1057 Hatfield Rd onto Clarence Rd at Crown pub, B&B 300yds on right*

Rooms 2 rms S £30–£36; D £50–£58 **Facilities** FTV TVB tea/coffee Cen ht **Parking** 1 **Notes** ⊛ No children 10yrs ⊜

STAPLEFORD   MAP 06 TL31

★★★ INN
Papillon Woodhall Arms
17 High Rd SG14 3NW
☎ 01992 535123 🖷 01992 582772
e–mail: papillonwoodhall@aol.com
web: www.papillon-woodhallarms.co.uk

dir: *2.5m from Hertford town (A414)*

Located in the village centre, this former Victorian house has been sympathetically renovated and extended to provide good standards of comfort and facilities. Bedrooms are equipped with both practical and thoughtful extras and public areas include a spacious restaurant offering a wide range of international dishes.

Rooms 10 en suite **Facilities** TVB tea/coffee Cen ht TVL Dinner Last d 10pm **Conf** Max 50 Thtr 60 Class 30 Board 20 **Parking** 33 **Notes** ⊛

WATFORD   MAP 06 TQ19

★★★ GUEST ACCOMMODATION
Travel Stop Inn
26–28 Upton Rd WD18 0JF
☎ 01923 224298 🖷 01923 253553
e–mail: info@travelstopinn.com
web: www.travelstopinn.com

dir: *M1 junct 5, A4008 to Watford centre*

Located within easy walking distance of the town centre, this renovation of two Edwardian houses provides a range of bedrooms equipped with lots of homely extras. There is a cocktail bar and

CONTINUED

restaurant in the White House Hotel opposite, which is under the same ownership and is where registration takes place as well as being the venue for breakfast.

Rooms 26 annexe en suite (1 fmly) (7 GF) S £54.95–£59.95; D £59.95–£65✱ (room only) **Facilities** STV TVB tea/coffee Direct dial from bedrooms Cen ht TVL Dinner Last d 9.45pm **Conf** Max 200 Thtr 200 Class 80 Board 60 Del from £140 ✱ **Parking** 35 **Notes** ⊛ RS Xmas/New Year Civ Wed 120

WELWYN GARDEN CITY   MAP 06 TL21

★★★ GUEST ACCOMMODATION
The Fairway Tavern
Old Herns Ln AL7 2ED
☎ 01707 336007 & 339349 🖷 01707 376154
e–mail: info@fairwaytavern.co.uk
web: www.fairwaytavern.co.uk

dir: *Exit A1 junct 6 take B1000 through Digswell for 2m and follow signs for Golf complex*

Enjoying a picturesque location, this property is located on Panshanger Golf Complex, with lodge style bedrooms opening out onto views of the golf course and rolling countryside. Bedrooms are smartly presented and are well equipped for business and leisure guests. Breakfast and meals up to 5pm are served by the friendly staff in the adjacent pub. A large peaceful garden and a function room for private hire are available.

Rooms 7 en suite (2 fmly) (7 GF) D £50–£70✱ (room only) **Facilities** TVB tea/coffee Direct dial from bedrooms Lift Cen ht Dinner Last d 9pm Golf 18 Squash ♨ **Conf** Thtr 120 Class 80 Board 25 **Parking** 200 **Notes** ⊛

★★ INN
The Brocket Arms
Ayot St Lawrence AL6 9BT
☎ 01438 820250 🖷 01438 820068
e–mail: bookings@brocketarms.com
web: www.brocketarms.com

dir: *A1(M) junct 4 signed B653 Welwyn Garden City to Luton road, in village of Ayot St Lawrence*

This delightful 14th-century hostelry retains most of the traditional features of a country pub, offers accommodation with en suite or private bathroom, which are comfortable and full of character. The bars and restaurant with their low ceilings and oak beams, offer an array of real ales and a seasonal menu.

Rooms 3 rms (3 pri facs) 3 annexe en suite (3 GF) S £70; D £85✱ **Facilities** TVB tea/coffee Dinner Last d 9.30pm Fishing **Parking** 6

★★ BED & BREAKFAST
23 Wheatley Close
AL7 3LJ
☎ 01707 884218 & 07836 571578 🖷 01707 884218

Tucked away in a quiet residential part of Welwyn Garden City, 23 Wheatley Close is an ideal base for visiting the local area. The rooms are well-equipped, and Alan and Barbara will ensure a good welcome. Breakfast is served in the downstairs dining room at a communal table.

Rooms 2 rms **Facilities** TVB tea/coffee Cen ht **Notes** ⊛ ⊜

KENT

ASHFORD
MAP 07 TR04

★★★ GUEST ACCOMMODATION
Croft
Canterbury Rd, Kennington TN25 4DU
☎ 01233 622140 📠 01233 635271
e–mail: info@crofthotel.com

dir: *M20 junct 10, 2m on A28 signed Canterbury*

An attractive red-brick house situated in 2 acres of landscaped grounds just a short drive from Ashford railway station. The generously proportioned bedrooms are in the main house and in pretty cottages; all are pleasantly decorated and thoughtfully equipped. Public rooms include a smart Italian restaurant, a bar, and a cosy lounge.

Rooms 27 en suite (6 fmly) (8 GF) **Facilities** TVB tea/coffee Direct dial from bedrooms Cen ht TVL Dinner Last d 9.30pm **Conf** Max 40 Thtr 40 Class 20 Board 22 **Parking** 30 **Notes** Civ Wed 40

★★ BED & BREAKFAST
Cornerstone B&B
25a High St TN24 8TH
☎ 01233 630520 📠 01233 638529
e–mail: info@cornerstonebandb.co.uk

This charming listed property is situated in the heart of the historic town centre, walking distance from Ashford International Station. Bedrooms vary in size but all are bright, airy and stylishly decorated; some with en suite. Shared bathrooms are well equipped and spacious. There is a choice of English or Continental breakfast. Limited parking available.

Rooms 10 rms (3 en suite) (2 fmly) (1 GF) S £40–£50; D £60–£70✳
Facilities TVB tea/coffee Cen ht Dinner Last d 5.15pm **Parking** 1
Notes LB ⊗ Closed 24–25 & 31 Dec

AYLESFORD
MAP 06 TQ75

★★★★★ 🅰 GUEST ACCOMMODATION
Wickham Lodge
The Quay, 73 High St ME20 7AY
☎ 01622 717267 📠 01622 792855
e–mail: wickhamlodge@aol.com
web: www.wickhamlodge.co.uk

dir: *M20 junct 5, signs to Aylesford village, The Quay is on a small road beside Chequers pub*

Rooms 3 rms (2 en suite) (1 pri facs) (1 fmly) (1 GF) S £45; D £90✳
Facilities FTV TVB tea/coffee Cen ht Wi-fi available **Parking** 4

BIDDENDEN
MAP 07 TQ83

★★★★ GUEST ACCOMMODATION
Heron Cottage
TN27 8HH
☎ 01580 291358 📠 01580 291358
e–mail: susantwort@hotmail.com
web: www.heroncottage.info

dir: *1m NW of Biddenden. A262 W from Biddenden, 1st right, 0.25m across sharp left bend through stone pillars, left onto unmade road*

Expect a warm welcome at this picturesque extended cottage, set in immaculate mature gardens in peaceful Kent countryside. The bedrooms are thoughtfully equipped and have coordinated soft furnishings. Breakfast is served in the smart dining room, and the cosy sitting room has an open fireplace.

Rooms 7 rms (6 en suite) (2 fmly) (1 GF) S £45–£55; D £65–£70
Facilities TVB tea/coffee Cen ht TVL Dinner Last d 9am Fishing 🎣
Conf Max 20 Board 20 **Parking** 8 **Notes** Closed Dec–Feb ⊛

BROADSTAIRS
MAP 07 TR36

★★★★ GUEST ACCOMMODATION
West View House B&B
26 Callis Court Rd CT10 3AF
☎ 01843 862039
e–mail: westviewhouse@aol.com

dir: *From A299 onto A253 signed Broadstairs onto A256. At Broadstairs turn left onto St Peter's Park Rd and left again onto Bairds Hill, West View House on left*

This attractively remodelled house is an easy distance from Broadstairs town centre and the coast. Bathrooms are luxurious and spacious, and bedrooms are stylish and comfortably furnished with plenty of amenities for business and leisure guests. Hospitality from cheerful owners Lynn and Guy ensures guests are well catered for. A hearty breakfast of local produce is served in the spacious dining room. Lynne Philp was a finalist for the Friendliest Landlady of the Year 2008 Award.

Rooms 2 en suite S £40–£45; D £70–£80✳ **Facilities** TVB tea/coffee Cen ht Wi-fi available **Parking** 2 **Notes** ⊗ No children ⊛

BROADSTAIRS CONTINUED

★★★★ GUEST ACCOMMODATION
Bay Tree House

12 Eastern Esplanade CT10 1DR

☎ 01843 862502 📄 01843 860589

dir: *A255 onto Rectory Rd & Eastern Esplanade*

Expect a warm welcome at this family-run establishment, situated on an elevated position overlooking East Cliff. The attractive bedrooms are well equipped and some have a balcony with a sea view. There is a comfortable lounge bar, and a good breakfast and dinner menu is offered in the dining room.

Rooms 10 en suite (1 GF) S £41–£71; D £82–£92 **Facilities** TVB tea/coffee Cen ht TVL Dinner Last d breakfast **Parking** 11 **Notes** LB ⊗ No children 10yrs Closed Xmas & New Year

---

CANTERBURY   **MAP 07 TR15**

Premier Collection

★★★★★ GUEST ACCOMMODATION
Magnolia House

36 St Dunstan's Ter CT2 8AX

☎ 01227 765121 & 07776 236459 📄 01227 765121

e–mail: info@magnoliahousecanterbury.co.uk

web: www.magnoliahousecanterbury.co.uk

dir: *A2 E onto A2050 for city centre, 1st rdbt left signed University of Kent. St Dunstan's Ter 3rd right*

A charming property, combining a warm welcome with superbly appointed bedrooms, full of extra amenities including internet access. Evening meals (by arrangement from November to February) are delightful, served in the dining room overlooking the attractive walled garden. Breakfast is also of merit, with a wide choice on offer.

Rooms 7 en suite (1 GF) S £55–£65; D £95–£150✳ **Facilities** FTV TVB tea/coffee Cen ht Dinner Last d 9am Wi-fi available **Parking** 5 **Notes** ⊗ No children 12yrs

Premier Collection

★★★★★ GUEST ACCOMMODATION
Yorke Lodge

50 London Rd CT2 8LF

☎ 01227 451243 📄 01227 462006

e–mail: info@yorkelodge.com

web: www.yorkelodge.com

dir: *From London M2/A2, 1st exit signed Canterbury. At 1st rdbt left onto London Rd*

The charming Victorian property stands in a tree-lined road just ten minutes walk from the town centre and railway station. The spacious bedrooms are thoughtfully equipped and carefully decorated; some rooms have four-poster beds. The stylish dining room leads to a conservatory-lounge, which opens onto a superb terrace.

Rooms 8 en suite (1 fmly) S £52–£58; D £85–£98 **Facilities** FTV TVB tea/coffee Cen ht Wi-fi available **Parking** 5 **Notes** LB

★★★★★ 🅰 BED & BREAKFAST
Great Weddington

CT3 2AR

☎ 01304 813407 📄 01304 812531

e–mail: traveltale@aol.com

web: www.greatweddington.co.uk

Rooms 3 en suite (1 GF) S £70–£82; D £106–£112✳ **Facilities** FTV TVB tea/coffee Cen ht Dinner Last d 3 days Wi-fi available **Parking** 6 **Notes** Closed Xmas & New Year

★★★★ GUEST ACCOMMODATION
Castle House

28 Castle St CT1 2PT
☎ 01227 761897
e–mail: enquiries@castlehousehotel.co.uk
dir: *Opposite Canterbury Castle ruins, off A28 ring road*

Built in the 1730s, this magnificent house takes its name from the Norman ruins standing opposite, and is close to the city centre. The bright and spacious bedrooms are well equipped and the décor enhances the character of the property. A hearty breakfast is served in the grand dining room. Ample parking is available.

Rooms 7 en suite (2 fmly) **Facilities** TVB tea/coffee Cen ht TVL Wi-fi available **Parking** 12 **Notes** ⊗ ➂

★★★★ FARM HOUSE
Chislet Court Farm *(TR224644)*

Chislet CT3 4DU
☎ 01227 860309 📠 01227 860444 Mr & Mrs M Wilkinson
e–mail: kathy@chisletcourtfarm.com
web: www.chisletcourtfarm.com
dir: *Off A28 in Upstreet, farm on right 100yds past church*

This delightful 18th-century house is situated in a pretty village six miles from Canterbury. The house is smartly maintained and set in delightful grounds. The en suite bedrooms are extremely spacious, well appointed, and have smart modern bathrooms. A hearty Aga-cooked breakfast is served in the charming conservatory overlooking the garden. Kathy Wilkinson was a finalist for the Friendliest Landlady of the Year 2008 Award.

Rooms 2 en suite S £50; D £75✳ **Facilities** FTV TVB tea/coffee Cen ht Wi-fi available **Parking** 4 **Notes** ⊗ No children 12yrs 800 acres arable Closed Xmas ➂

★★★★ GUEST ACCOMMODATION
The White House

6 St Peters Ln CT1 2BP
☎ 01227 761836
e–mail: info@whitehousecanterbury.co.uk
dir: *A290 into city, through Westgate, sharp left onto Pound Ln, 1st right into St Peters Lane*

This attractive Regency house is in a quiet road close to the High Street and next to the Marlowe Theatre. Both contemporary and traditionally-styled bedrooms are comfortably furnished and provide an abundance of thoughtful extras. Fresh quality produce is offered at breakfast which is served in the smart dining room. This is a non-smoking establishment.

Rooms 7 en suite (1 fmly) S £55–£65; D £80–£100✳ **Facilities** TVB tea/coffee Cen ht **Notes** ⊗ No children 16yrs

★★★★ GUEST ACCOMMODATION
Beech Bank

Duckpit Ln, Waltham CT4 5QA
☎ 01227 700302 📠 01227 700302
e–mail: grandbeech@hotmail.com
dir: *5.5m S of Canterbury. Off B2068 through Petham, left by telephone onto Duckpit Ln, 2m on left*

A 15th-century coach house set in landscaped grounds with magnificent views of the surrounding countryside. Original features include a minstrels' gallery, oak beams and exposed brickwork. Bedrooms are carefully decorated and thoughtfully equipped, and one room has a four-poster bed. Breakfast is served in the elegant Victorian conservatory.

Rooms 3 rms (2 en suite) (1 pri facs) (1 fmly) (2 GF) **Facilities** TVB tea/coffee Cen ht ♨ ⅋ **Parking** 10 **Notes** ⊗ No children 4yrs Closed 20 Dec–5 Jan ➂

★★★ GUEST ACCOMMODATION
Ersham Lodge

12 New Dover Rd CT1 3AP
☎ 01227 463174
e–mail: info@ersham-lodge.co.uk
dir: *From Canterbury ring road signs for Dover, premises on right just after lights by Blockbuster Video*

This attractive twin-gabled Victorian house is just a short walk from the college, cathedral and the city's attractions. Bedrooms are smartly decorated and comfortable, and there is a cosy lounge and a spacious breakfast room which looks out onto the well-kept patio and garden. Free guest parking is available.

Rooms 10 en suite (1 fmly) (5 GF) S £45; D £80✳ **Facilities** TVB tea/coffee Cen ht Wi-fi available **Conf** Max 30 Class 30 Board 20 **Parking** 10 **Notes** LB ⊗

CANTERBURY CONTINUED

★★★ INN
Canterbury Pilgrims
18 The Friars CT1 2AS
☎ 01227 464531 📠 01227 762514
e–mail: pilgrimshotel@aol.com

dir: *Signs for Marlowe Theatre, establishment opp*

Situated in the centre of historic Canterbury opposite the Marlowe Theatre, parts of the Pilgrims date back some 350 years. Bedrooms are comfortably appointed and well equipped. The newly refurbished public rooms include a spacious bar, a smart meeting room and a contemporary style restaurant, where a good selection of dishes is available.

Rooms 15 en suite (1 fmly) **Facilities** TVB tea/coffee Direct dial from bedrooms Cen ht Dinner Last d 9.30pm **Conf** Max 30 Thtr 25 Class 25 Board 20 **Parking** 10 **Notes** ⊗

★★★ GUEST ACCOMMODATION
St Stephens Guest House
100 St Stephens Rd CT2 7JL
☎ 01227 767644 📠 01227 767644

dir: *A290 from city Westgate & sharp right onto North Ln, 2nd rdbt left onto St Stephens Rd, right onto Market Way, car park on right*

A large, privately-owned guest house situated close to the university and within easy walking distance of the city centre. The pleasant bedrooms are equipped with a good range of useful extras, and there is a cosy lounge. Breakfast is served at individual tables in the smart dining room.

Rooms 12 rms (11 en suite) (2 fmly) (3 GF) S £39–£45; D £59–£68✶ **Facilities** TVB tea/coffee Cen ht TVL **Parking** 11 **Notes** No children 5yrs Closed 18 Dec–mid Jan ⊜

★★★ GUEST ACCOMMODATION
Cathedral Gate
36 Burgate CT1 2HA
☎ 01227 464381 📠 01227 462800
e–mail: cgate@cgate.demon.co.uk

dir: *In city centre. Next to main gateway into cathedral precincts*

Dating from 1438, this house has an enviable central location next to the Cathedral. Old beams and winding corridors are part of the character of the property. Bedrooms are traditionally furnished, equipped to modern standards and many have cathedral views. Luggage can be unloaded at reception before parking in a local car park.

Rooms 13 rms (2 en suite) 12 annexe rms (10 en suite) (5 fmly) S £31.75–£103.50; D £61.50–£103.50 **Facilities** TVB tea/coffee Direct dial from bedrooms Cen ht Dinner Last d 8pm **Notes LB**

CRANBROOK   MAP 07 TQ73

★★★★ BED & BREAKFAST
Apple Trees B&B
Goddards Green, Benenden TN17 4AR
☎ 01580 240622
e–mail: garryblanch@aol.com
web: www.appletreesbandb.co.uk

dir: *3m E of Cranbrook. Off A262 at Sissinghurst S onto Chaple Ln, over x-rds, 2m left to Goddards Green, 1m on right*

This spacious rural cottage is situated in the heart of the Kentish countryside close to the famous Chapeldown and Biddenden Vineyards. Bedrooms are attractively presented and include plenty of thoughtful extras. TV can be watched in the comfortable lounge, and breakfast is served in the rustic dining room with picturesque views of the garden.

Rooms 3 rms (1 en suite) (2 pri facs) (3 GF) S £50–£65; D £60–£70 **Facilities** tea/coffee Cen ht TVL Wi-fi available **Parking** 6 **Notes** ⊗ ⊜

DARTFORD   MAP 06 TQ57

★★★ INN
Rising Sun
Fawkham Green DA3 8NL
☎ 01474 872291 📠 01474 872779

dir: *M25 junct 3, A20 Brands Hatch. Turn onto Scratchers Ln until sign for Fawkham. Left onto Brandshatch Rd, inn on left*

This popular inn overlooks the village green just a short drive from Brands Hatch. All the en suite bedrooms are spacious, pleasantly decorated and comfortable. There is a busy character bar, restaurant, and a patio for alfresco dining in warmer weather.

Rooms 5 en suite (1 fmly) (2 GF) S £50–£55; D £65–£75✳
Facilities TVB tea/coffee Cen ht Dinner Last d 9.30pm **Parking** 20
Notes ⊗ No coaches

See advert on this page

DEAL   MAP 07 TR35

Premier Collection

★★★★★ 🍴 GUEST ACCOMMODATION
Sutherland House
186 London Rd CT14 9PT
☎ 01304 362853 📠 01304 381146
e–mail: info@sutherlandhouse.fsnet.co.uk

dir: *0.5m W of town centre/seafront on A258*

This stylish accommodation demonstrates impeccable taste with its charming, well-equipped bedrooms and a comfortable lounge. Fully stocked bar, books, free Wi-fi, Freeview TV and radio are some of the many amenities offered. The elegant dining room is the venue for a hearty breakfast and dinner is available by prior arrangement.

Rooms 4 en suite (1 GF) S £55–£60; D £65–£70✳ **Facilities** FTV TVB tea/coffee Direct dial from bedrooms Cen ht Dinner Last d 6.30pm Wi-fi available **Conf** Max 12 Thtr 12 Class 12 Board 12 Del £105 ✳ **Parking** 7 **Notes LB** No children 5yrs

★★★★ INN
The Plough Inn
Church Ln, Ripple CT14 8JH
☎ 01304 360209
e–mail: plough@sutton-vale.co.uk

This charming country inn in the rural village of Ripple is ideally located for easy access to Dover and Deal. Bedrooms are attractively decorated, bright and spacious with plenty of thoughtful extras for guest comfort. Home-cooked food and real ale are served at lunch and dinner, as well as a hearty breakfast to start the day.

Rooms 3 en suite (1 fmly) D fr £55✳ **Facilities** FTV TVB tea/coffee Cen ht TVL Dinner Last d 8pm Wi-fi available Golf 18 ⚲ Fishing Squash Riding Pool Table **Parking** 31 **Notes LB**

★★★ GUEST ACCOMMODATION
Sondes Lodge
14 Sondes Rd CT14 7BW
☎ 01304 368741 📠 01304 368050
e–mail: sondes.lodge@tiscali.co.uk
web: www.sondeslodge.co.uk

dir: *From Dover take A25 to Deal, pass Deal Castle and continue towards town centre, take 4th right onto Sondes Rd*

Expect a warm welcome at this smart guest house situated in a side road just off the seafront and a short walk from the town centre. The pleasant bedrooms have co-ordinated fabrics and many thoughtful touches. Breakfast is served at individual tables in the lower ground-floor dining room.

Rooms 3 en suite (1 fmly) (1 GF) S £40; D £56✳ **Facilities** TVB tea/coffee Cen ht

---

DODDINGTON
MAP 07 TQ95

Premier Collection

★★★★★ GUEST ACCOMMODATION

The Old Vicarage

Church Hill ME9 0BD

☎ 01795 886136 🖹 01795 886136

e–mail: claire@oldvicaragedoddington.co.uk

dir: From A2 take Faversham Rd signed Doddington for 4.4m. Turn right towards church.

Stunning Grade II listed property situated at the edge of the village beside the old church. Spacious rooms with flat screen TVs, and special touches like binoculars and bird reference books. Guests can relax in the elegant lounge and a bountiful breakfast is served in the stylish dining room overlooking endless green fields and trees.

Rooms 3 en suite (1 fmly) S £48; D £69✱ **Facilities** FTV TVB tea/coffee Cen ht Wi-fi available Pool Table ♨ **Parking** 6 **Notes** ⊗ No children 3yrs Closed 25 Dec–2 Jan 🐾

DOVER
MAP 07 TR34

★★★★ GUEST ACCOMMODATION

Beulah House

94 Crabble Hill, London Rd CT17 0SA

☎ 01304 824615 🖹 01304 828850

e–mail: owen@beulahhouse94.freeserve.co.uk

web: www.beulahguesthouse.co.uk

dir: On A256

An impressive Victorian house located just a stroll from the town centre and close to the ferry port. The spacious bedrooms are pleasantly decorated and thoughtfully equipped. Public rooms include two conservatories and a comfortable lounge. The impressive garden has an interesting display of topiary and a small menagerie.

Rooms 9 rms (7 en suite) D £60–£68✱ **Facilities** TVB tea/coffee Cen ht TVL **Parking** 11 **Notes** LB ⊗ Closed Dec–Feb

★★★★ GUEST ACCOMMODATION

Hubert House

9 Castle Hill Rd CT16 1QW

☎ 01304 202253 🖹 01304 210142

e–mail: huberthouse@btinternet.com

web: www.huberthouse.co.uk

dir: On A258 by Dover Castle

This charming Georgian house is within walking distance of the ferry port and the town centre. Bedrooms are pleasantly decorated and furnished in a modern style. Breakfast, including full English and healthy options, is served in the smart coffee house, which is open all day. Families are especially welcome.

Rooms 7 en suite (4 fmly) S £40–£50; D £50–£75✱ (room only) **Facilities** FTV TVB tea/coffee Cen ht Dinner Last d 2pm Wi-fi available **Parking** 6 **Notes** LB Closed Jan–Feb

★★★★ INN

The Swingate Inn

Deal Rd CT15 5DP

☎ 01304 204043 🖹 01304 204043

e–mail: info@swingate.com

dir: Dover Easton Docks. Turn right at rdbt up Jubille Way for 1m, at rdbt turn right onto the A258 to Deal

Pleasantly located on the edge of Dover and very convenient for the ferry, this friendly inn has spacious modern accommodation. The bar offers informal dining while the restaurant carte provides greater choice. The Wednesday jazz evenings are particularly popular and family entertainment is provided on Sunday evenings.

Rooms 10 en suite (2 fmly) **Facilities** TVB tea/coffee Cen ht Dinner Last d 9pm Wi-fi available **Conf** Max 30 Thtr 30 Class 30 Board 20 **Parking** 60 **Notes** ⊗ Civ Wed 120

★★★ GUEST ACCOMMODATION

Bleriot's

Belper House, 47 Park Av CT16 1HE

☎ 01304 211394

e–mail: info@bleriots.net

dir: A20 to Dover, left onto York St, right at lights into Ladywell. Bear left at next lights onto Park Av

This large, family-run Victorian property is convenient for the ferry port and town centre. Guests receive a warm welcome and can enjoy a

CONTINUED

range of comfortable, spacious en suite bedrooms. The attractive dining room is the venue for a wholesome breakfast to start the day. Martin Casey was a finalist for the Friendliest Landlady of the Year 2008 Award.

Rooms 8 en suite (2 fmly) S £25–£40; D £54–£58 **Facilities** TVB tea/coffee Cen ht **Parking** 8 **Notes LB** ⊗

★★★ GUEST ACCOMMODATION
Ardmore Guest House
18 Castle Hill Rd CT16 1QW
☎ 01304 205895 📠 01304 208229
e–mail: res@ardmoreph.co.uk
web: www.ardmoreph.co.uk

dir: *On A258 by Dover Castle*

Dating from 1796, this delightful house is adjacent to Dover Castle. Convenient for the town centre and ferry port, the Ardmore offers comfortable accommodation and friendly hospitality. The non-smoking bedrooms are spacious and airy. Public rooms include a comfortable lounge and a well-appointed breakfast room.

Rooms 4 en suite (1 fmly) D £48–£65✶ **Facilities** TVB tea/coffee Cen ht **Notes** ⊗ Closed Xmas

★★★ GUEST ACCOMMODATION
Kernow
189 Folkestone Rd CT17 9SJ
☎ 01304 207797

dir: *B2011 W from town centre onto Folkestone Rd*

This welcoming guest house is convenient for the ferries and railway station. The neat accommodation is well maintained, and two bathrooms are available. There is adequate parking at the front of the property, and breakfast can be arranged to suit your travel arrangements.

Rooms 3 rms **Facilities** TVB tea/coffee Cen ht TVL **Parking** 4 **Notes** ⊛

★★★ GUEST ACCOMMODATION
St Martins
17 Castle Hill Rd CT16 1QW
☎ 01304 205938 📠 01304 208229
e–mail: res@stmartinsgh.co.uk
web: www.stmartinsgh.co.uk

dir: *On A258 by Dover Castle*

Located close to the castle, ferry port and town centre, this smart guest house offers a friendly welcome. The thoughtfully equipped en suite bedrooms are attractively decorated, and most rooms enjoy a sunny aspect. Breakfast is served in the pine-furnished dining room, and there is also a comfortable lounge.

➤ **Rooms** 6 en suite (3 fmly) D £48–£55✶ **Facilities** TVB tea/coffee Cen ht **Notes** ⊗ Closed Xmas

★★★★ GUEST ACCOMMODATION
Waterside
15 Hythe Rd TN29 0LN
☎ 01303 872253 📠 01303 872253
e–mail: info@watersideguesthouse.co.uk

dir: *M20 junct 11 onto A259 follow signs for Hythe then Dymchurch, 0.5m past village sign*

Waterside is located overlooking a picturesque stream, and sandy beaches are a few minutes away. Bedrooms are comfortably appointed and have sparkling en suite bathrooms. Breakfast is served in the cosy dining room and a small bar and lounge is provided for added guest comfort. Parking is available.

Rooms 5 en suite (1 fmly) S £36–£65; D £60–£65 **Facilities** TVB tea/coffee Cen ht TVL Dinner Last d 4pm Wi-fi available **Parking** 6 **Notes** ⊗

Premier Collection

★★★★★ FARM HOUSE
Beesfield Farm *(TQ554660)*
Beesfield Ln DA4 0LA
☎ 01322 863900 📠 01322 863900 Mr & Mrs D Vingoe
e–mail: kim.vingoe@btinternet.com

dir: *From village centre S onto Beesfield Ln, farm 0.5m on left*

Set amid mature gardens and surrounded by open farmland, this attractive house is close to major roads, Brands Hatch and Bluewater Shopping Centre. Individually decorated bedrooms and bathrooms are beautifully appointed and have many thoughtful touches. Breakfast is served at a large polished table in the elegant dining room, and there is a stylish lounge with plush furnishings.

Rooms 3 en suite S £65–£70; D £80–£90 **Facilities** FTV TVB tea/coffee Cen ht TVL Wi-fi available **Parking** 10 **Notes LB** ⊗ No children 12yrs 400 acres arable dairy mixed Closed 8 Dec–Jan ⊜

FAVERSHAM MAP 07 TR06

★★★★ GUEST ACCOMMODATION
Court Lodge B&B

Court Lodge, Church Rd, Oare ME13 0QB
☎ 01795 591543 📄 01795 591543
e-mail: d.wheeldon@btconnect.com

dir: A2 onto B2045, left onto The Street, right onto Church Road, 0.25m on left

Nestled amongst fields of flowers, and commanding fabulous views, this charming farmhouse has been restored to a very high standard. Inside is a mini museum of antique furniture and Victorian fittings include caringly restored bathtubs, sinks and kitchen appliances. Modern additions such as free Wi-fi enhance guest comfort. Home-made cakes and jams and the warm hospitality of owners Dennise and John guarantee a memorable stay.

Rooms 2 rms (1 en suite) (1 pri facs) S £40; D £60✱ **Facilities** TVB tea/coffee Cen ht Wi-fi available **Parking** 10 **Notes** ⊗ Closed Dec–Jan 🐾

FOLKESTONE MAP 07 TR23

Premier Collection

★★★★★ GUEST ACCOMMODATION
The Relish

4 Augusta Gardens CT20 2RR
☎ 01303 850952 📄 01303 850958
e-mail: reservations@hotelrelish.co.uk
web: www.hotelrelish.co.uk

dir: Off A2033 Sandgate Rd

Expect a warm welcome at this impressive Victorian terrace property, which overlooks Augusta Gardens in the fashionable West End of town. The bedrooms feature beautiful contemporary natural-wood furniture, lovely co-ordinated fabrics and many thoughtful extras like DVD players and free Broadband access. Public rooms include a modern lounge-dining room, and a sun terrace where breakfast is served in the summer.

Rooms 10 en suite (2 fmly) **Facilities** TVB Direct dial from bedrooms Cen ht Wi-fi available **Conf** Max 20 Thtr 20 Class 10 Board 20 **Notes** ⊗ Closed 22 Dec–2 Jan

★★★ GUEST ACCOMMODATION
Chandos Guest House

77 Cheriton Rd CT20 1DG
☎ 01303 851202 & 07799 886297
e-mail: froggydon@aol.com
web: www.chandosguesthouse.co.uk

dir: M20 junct 13. Right towards Folkstone. At 2nd set of lights, middle lane. Continue for 1m, straight over rdbt, premises located 0.25m on right

Close to the town centre and only a five minute drive from the Eurotunnel, this pleasant guest house is ideal for continental travellers. Bedrooms and bathrooms are well equipped, bright and comfortable. Free Wi-fi is a recent addition. A hearty breakfast is served in the spacious ground-floor dining room. Early morning departures are catered for.

Rooms 9 rms (6 en suite) (4 fmly) S £25–£30; D £50–£55 **Facilities** FTV TVB tea/coffee Cen ht Wi-fi available **Notes LB** ⊗

★★★ GUEST ACCOMMODATION
Langhorne Garden

10–12 Langhorne Gardens CT20 2EA
☎ 01303 257233 📄 01303 242760
e-mail: info@langhorne.co.uk
web: www.langhorne.co.uk

dir: Exit M20 junct 13 and follow signs for The Leas 2m

Once a Victorian seaside villa, Langhorne Garden is close to the seafront, shops and restaurants. Bright spacious bedrooms are traditionally decorated with plenty of original charm. Public rooms include a choice of comfortable lounges and a bar, a spacious dining

CONTINUED

room and a popular local bar in the basement with billiards, darts and a fussbol table.

Rooms 29 en suite (8 fmly) S £35–£49; D £59–£65✱ **Facilities** STV FTV TVB tea/coffee Direct dial from bedrooms Lift Cen ht Dinner Last d 7pm Wi-fi available Pool Table **Conf** Thtr 40 Class 20 Board 20 **Notes LB** Closed Xmas RS Jan–Etr

★★★ INN
The Lighthouse Inn & Restaurant
111 Old Dover Rd, Capel-le-Ferne CT18 7HT
☎ 01303 223300 📠 01303 842270
e–mail: sales@thelighthouseinn.co.uk

Situated on the cliff top with stunning panoramic sea views, this newly refurbished inn is handy for the EuroTunnel, Folkstone and Dover ferry terminals. Spacious bedrooms are tastefully decorated and thoughtfully equipped; including free Wi-fi. Some rooms boast lovely sea views, while the public rooms include a popular restaurant and bar. The newly decked terrace is ideal for warmer months.

Rooms 8 en suite S fr £45; D fr £55✱ **Parking** available

★★★ 🅰 GUEST HOUSE
Kentmere Guest House
76 Cheriton Rd CT20 1DG
☎ 01303 259661 📠 01303 220208
e–mail: enquiries@kentmere-guesthouse.co.uk

Rooms 7 en suite (4 fmly) (1 GF) S £25–£28; D £50–£52 **Facilities** TVB tea/coffee Cen ht Wi-fi available **Parking** 3

GOUDHURST   MAP 06 TQ73

★★★★ 🍴 INN
The Star & Eagle
High St TN17 1AL
☎ 01580 211512 📠 01580 212444
e–mail: starandeagle@btconnect.com
web: www.starandeagle.co.uk

dir: *Off A21 to Hastings rd, take A262, inn is at the top of the village next to the church*

A hearty welcome is assured at this 15th-century inn located in the heart of this delightful village. Within easy reach of Royal Tunbridge Wells and The Weald this is a great base for walkers. Both bedrooms and public areas boast original features and character. A wide range of delicious home-made dishes is available in the restaurant and bar.

Rooms 10 rms (8 en suite) S £50–£130; D £70–£130 **Facilities** FTV TVB Direct dial from bedrooms Cen ht Dinner Last d 9.30pm Wi-fi available **Conf** Max 30 Thtr 30 Class 15 Board 12 **Parking** 20 **Notes** ⊗ RS 24–26 Dec Civ Wed 50

HAWKHURST   MAP 07 TQ73

Premier Collection

★★★★★ 🏠 GUEST ACCOMMODATION
Southgate-Little Fowlers
Rye Rd TN18 5DA
☎ 01580 752526 📠 01580 752526
e–mail: susan.woodard@southgate.uk.net
web: www.southgate.uk.net

dir: *0.25m E of Hawkhurst on A268*

A warm welcome is assured at this wonderful 300-year-old former dower house. Set in immaculate mature gardens, the renovated property provides attractive accommodation throughout. Spacious bedrooms are carefully decorated and equipped with many thoughtful extras. A hearty breakfast is served at individual tables in the delightful Victorian conservatory.

Rooms 2 en suite (1 fmly) S £55–£60; D £70–£85 **Facilities** TVB tea/coffee Cen ht TVL Wi-fi available **Parking** 5 **Notes** ⊗ No children 8yrs Closed Nov–Feb 🐾

HYTHE   MAP 07 TR13

★★★★ GUEST ACCOMMODATION
Seabrook House
81 Seabrook Rd CT21 5QW
☎ 01303 269282 📠 01303 237822
e–mail: seabrookhouse@hotmail.co.uk
web: www.seabrook-house.co.uk

dir: *0.9m E of Hythe on A259*

A stunning Victorian house situated just a few miles from the M20 and Eurotunnel. The property is set in pretty gardens and within easy walking distance of the beach. The attractive bedrooms are carefully furnished and thoughtfully equipped. Public rooms include an elegant lounge, where tea and coffee are served in the evening, a sunny conservatory and large dining room.

Rooms 13 en suite (4 fmly) (4 GF) S £35–£45; D £65–£75✱ **Facilities** TVB tea/coffee Cen ht TVL **Parking** 13 **Notes** ⊗

IVYCHURCH   MAP 07 TR02

Premier Collection

★★★★★ GUEST ACCOMMODATION
Olde Moat House

TN29 0AZ
☎ 01797 344700 📠 01797 343919
e-mail: oldemoathouse@hotmail.com
web: www.oldemoathouse.co.uk

dir: Off junct A2070 & A259 into Ivychurch, left & 0.75m on left

Situated eight miles north-east of Rye this charming character property sits peacefully amongst carefully tended gardens. Spacious bedrooms are elegantly furnished and an abundance of accessories are provided for guest comfort. The elegant dining room overlooks the gardens, and a cosy lounge with oak beams and open fireplace is furnished with comfortable sofas.

Rooms 3 en suite **Facilities** TVB tea/coffee Cen ht TVL Dinner Last d 24 hours notice **Parking** 10 **Notes** ⊗ No children 16yrs

---

MAIDSTONE   MAP 07 TQ75

See also Marden

★★★★ INN
The Black Horse Inn

Pilgrims Way, Thurnham ME14 3LD
☎ 01622 737185 & 630830 📠 01622 739170
e-mail: info@wellieboot.net
web: www.wellieboot.net/home_blackhorse.htm

dir: M20 junct 7, N onto A249. Right into Detling, opp pub onto Pilgrims Way for 1m

This charming inn dates from the 17th century, and the public areas have a wealth of oak beams, exposed brickwork and open fireplaces. The stylish bedrooms are in a series of cosy cabins behind the premises; each one is attractively furnished and thoughtfully equipped.

Rooms 16 annexe en suite (4 fmly) (11 GF) S £65–£90; D £80–£90✶ **Facilities** FTV TVB tea/coffee Cen ht Dinner Last d 10pm Wi-fi available **Parking** 40 **Notes LB** No coaches

---

★★★★ GUEST ACCOMMODATION
Langley Oast

Langley Park, Langley ME17 3NQ
☎ 01622 863523 📠 01622 863523
e-mail: margaret@langleyoast.freeserve.co.uk

dir: 2.5m SE of Maidstone off A274. After Parkwood Business Estate lane signed Maidstone Golf Centre

This traditional Kent oast house is a short drive from the town centre and has views of the surrounding countryside. Bedrooms are spacious and well appointed. Two are in the 24-foot diameter towers and one has a Jacuzzi bath. Breakfast is served in an elegant dining room around one large table and an attractive garden is an additional feature.

Rooms 3 rms (2 en suite) (1 fmly) S £35–£55; D £55–£95 **Facilities** TVB tea/coffee Cen ht Jacuzzi in 1 bedroom **Parking** 5 **Notes** ⊗ Closed Xmas ◉

★★★★ GUEST ACCOMMODATION
Ringlestone House

Ringlestone Hamlet, Harrietsham ME17 1NX
☎ 01622 859911 📠 01622 859740
e-mail: bookings@ringlestonehouse.co.uk
web: www.ringlestonehouse.co.uk

dir: M20 junct 8, A20, at rdbt opp Ramada Hotel left to Hollingbourne, through village, right at x-rds at top of hill

This picturesque converted farmhouse sits prettily amongst beautiful landscaped grounds. Bedrooms are carefully decorated and furnished to an excellent level. An abundance of thoughtful extras are provided in each room including a substantial Continental breakfast, and by prior arrangement a hearty English breakfast can be served in the rustic dining room overlooking the garden

Rooms 3 en suite (1 fmly) **Facilities** TVB tea/coffee Direct dial from bedrooms Cen ht TVL Wi-fi available Day membership to local Health Club **Conf** Max 50 Thtr 50 Class 30 Board 24 **Parking** 40 **Notes** ⊗ Closed 25 Dec–3 Jan

---

★★★★ GUEST ACCOMMODATION
Aylesbury House

56–58 London Rd ME16 8QL
☎ 01622 762100 📠 01622 664673
e-mail: mail@aylesburyhouse.co.uk

dir: 5mins from M20 junct 5 on A20 to Maidstone. Aylesbury House on left before town centre

Located just a short walk from the town centre, this smartly maintained establishment offers a genuine welcome. The carefully decorated bedrooms have co-ordinated soft fabrics and many thoughtful touches. Breakfast is served in the smart dining room overlooking a walled garden.

Rooms 8 en suite S £50–£55; D £60–£75 **Facilities** TVB tea/coffee Cen ht Wi-fi available **Parking** 8

★★★★ GUEST ACCOMMODATION
Conway House

12 Conway Rd ME16 0HD
☎ 01622 688287 📠 01622 726323
e−mail: t.griffiths295@btinternet.com

dir: *Exit M20 junct 5 onto A20 to Maidstone 0.5m, turn right at BP garage*

This large, modern, family house is a short drive from the M20 and Maidstone town centre. Bedrooms are beautifully furnished and have spacious en suite bathrooms. Plentiful amenities and warm hospitality make this a perfect choice for business and leisure guests.

Rooms 2 en suite **Facilities** FTV TVB tea/coffee Cen ht **Parking** 2 **Notes** ⊗

★★★★ GUEST HOUSE
Roslin Villa

11 St Michaels Rd ME16 8BS
☎ 01622 758301 📠 01622 761459
e−mail: info@roslinvillaguesthouse.com
web: www.roslinvillaguesthouse.com

dir: *0.6m W of town centre. Off A26 Tonbridge Rd, brown tourist signs to Roslin Villa*

Expect a warm welcome from the caring hosts at this delightful detached Victorian house, which is within easy walking distance of the town centre and only a short drive from the M20. The smart bedrooms are carefully furnished and equipped with many thoughtful touches. Public rooms include a cosy lounge and an elegant dining room.

Rooms 5 en suite (1 fmly) S £48−£50; D £65−£75✱ **Facilities** TVB tea/coffee Cen ht TVL Wi-fi available **Conf** Max 15 Class 15 Board 15 **Parking** 10 **Notes** No children 12yrs No coaches

★★★★ ◉ GUEST ACCOMMODATION
Stone Court

28 Lower St ME15 6LX
☎ 01622 769769 📠 01622 769888
e−mail: stonecourt@ohiml.com
web: www.oxfordhotelsandinns.com

dir: *M20 junct 6, 2nd exit at next 2 rdbts onto A229 towards Hastings. Stay in right lane at lights, just past police station*

This former judiciary chambers is a listed building and contrary to its contemporary façade has many interesting internal features. The popular fine-dining restaurant boasts an impressive menu selection and wine list. Bedrooms are spacious and comfortably appointed.

Rooms 16 en suite (2 fmly) **Facilities** TVB tea/coffee Direct dial from bedrooms Wi-fi available **Parking** 12 **Notes** Civ Wed 60

See advert on this page

★★★ GUEST ACCOMMODATION
Rock House Bed & Breakfast

102 Tonbridge Rd ME16 8SL
☎ 01622 751616 📠 01622 756119
e−mail: rock.house@btconnect.com

dir: *On A26, 0.5m from town centre*

This friendly, family-run guest house is just a short walk from the town centre. Breakfast is served in the conservatory-dining room that overlooks the attractive walled garden. Bedrooms are brightly decorated and equipped with modern facilities.

Rooms 14 rms (8 en suite) (4 fmly) **Facilities** TVB tea/coffee Cen ht TVL Wi-fi available **Parking** 7

MAIDSTONE CONTINUED

★★★ 🅰 GUEST ACCOMMODATION
Maidstone Lodge
22/24 London Rd ME16 8QL
☎ 01622 758778 📄 01622 609984
e–mail: maidstonelodge@btinternet.com

dir: *400yds W of town centre on A20*

Rooms 14 rms (1 GF) (7 smoking) S £35–£45; D £60✲ **Facilities** TVB tea/coffee Cen ht TVL **Parking** 15 **Notes** ⊗ Closed 24 Dec–1 Jan

---

MARDEN
MAP 06 TQ74

Premier Collection

★★★★★ BED & BREAKFAST
Merzie Meadows
Hunton Rd TN12 9SL
☎ 01622 820500 📄 01622 820500
e–mail: pamela@merziemeadows.co.uk

dir: *A229 onto B2079 for Marden, 1st right onto Underlyn Ln, 2.5m large Chainhurst sign, right onto drive*

A detached property set in 20 acres of mature gardens in the Kent countryside. The generously proportioned bedrooms are housed in two wings, which overlook a terrace; each room is carefully decorated, thoughtfully equipped and furnished with well-chosen pieces. The attractive breakfast room has an Italian tiled floor and superb views of the garden.

Rooms 2 en suite (1 fmly) (2 GF) D £80–£95✲ **Facilities** STV FTV TVB tea/coffee Cen ht TVL Wi-fi available **Parking** 4 **Notes** ⊗ No children 15yrs Closed mid Dec–mid Feb ⊜

NEW ROMNEY
MAP 07 TR02

★★★★ FARM HOUSE
Honeychild Manor Farmhouse
(TR062276)
St Mary In The Marsh TN29 0DB
☎ 01797 366180 & 07951 237821 📄 01797 366925
Mrs V Furnival
e–mail: honeychild@farming.co.uk

dir: *2m N of New Romney off A259. S of village centre*

This imposing Georgian farmhouse is part of a working dairy farm on Romney Marsh. Walkers and dreamers alike will enjoy the stunning views and can relax in the beautifully landscaped gardens or play tennis on the full-sized court. A hearty breakfast is served in the elegant dining room and features quality local produce. Bedrooms are pleasantly decorated, well furnished and thoughtfully equipped. This establishment is pet friendly.

Honeychild Manor Farmhouse

Rooms 3 rms (1 en suite) (1 fmly) **Facilities** TVB tea/coffee Cen ht Dinner Last d 4pm ♨ **Parking** 10 **Notes** 1500 acres Arable & Dairy ⊜

ROLVENDEN
MAP 07 TQ83

★★★ GUEST ACCOMMODATION
The Vicarage B&B
Maytham Rd TN17 4ND
☎ 01580 241235 📄 01580 241235
e–mail: vicarage1965@btinternet.com

dir: *A28 through Rolvenden. Left turn at the church into Matham Rd. 1st driveway on right after 150mtrs*

White-painted vicarage nestled next to the handsome village church. Bedrooms are fresh and bright with lush garden views. A hearty breakfast provides the perfect start to the day. The village of Tenterden and celebrated English vineyards are located nearby.

Rooms 3 rms S £25–£35; D £50–£60✲ **Facilities** TV2B tea/coffee Cen ht **Parking** 3 **Notes** LB ⊗ Closed Xmas & Etr ⊜

SANDHURST
MAP 07 TQ82

★★ FARM HOUSE
Hoads Farm *(TQ805282)*
Crouch Ln TN18 5PA
☎ 01580 850296 📄 01580 850296 Mrs A Nicholas
e–mail: ca.nicholas@btinternet.com

dir: *Off A268 0.5m E from Sandhurst onto Crouch Ln*

Situated in peaceful countryside, this 16th-century farmhouse still forms part of a working farm. Public rooms include a spacious beamed lounge with a welcoming open fire in winter. Breakfast is served at a large table in the dining room, which overlooks the garden. Hoads Farm produces its own beer and award-winning wines.

Rooms 3 rms (1 fmly) **Facilities** tea/coffee Cen ht TVL Dinner Last d by arrangement **Parking** 6 **Notes** ⊗ 350 acres Apple Hops Vines Plums

CONTINUED

ENGLAND

SANDWICH

MAP 07 TR35

★★★ 🍴 INN

The Blue Pigeons Inn

The Street, Worth CT14 0DE

☎ 01304 613245 📄 01304 621177

e-mail: info@bluepigeons.co.uk

web: www.bluepigeons.co.uk

dir: *From A258 (Deal to Sandwich road), turn right onto The Street, 600mtrs on left*

This popular local inn is close to historic Canterbury and the village of Sandwich. Bedrooms vary in size and all are en suite and comfortably presented. A hearty English breakfast is served in the restaurant and evening dining offers plentiful fresh, local produce. Bar meals are also available. Child-friendly environment.

Rooms 4 en suite 2 annexe en suite (2 fmly) (2 GF) S £39.95–£65; D £49.95–£75 **Facilities** FTV TVB tea/coffee Cen ht TVL Dinner Last d 9.30pm Pool Table **Conf** Max 250 Thtr 150 Class 150 Board 100 **Parking** 10 **Notes** LB Civ Wed 250

★★★ INN

The New Inn

2 Harnet St CT13 9ES

☎ 01304 612335 📄 01304 619133

e-mail: new.inn@thorleytaverns.com

dir: *Off A256, one-way system into town centre, inn on right*

A popular inn situated in the heart of this busy historic town. The large open-plan lounge bar offers an extensive range of beers and an interesting choice of home-made dishes. Bedrooms are furnished in pine and have many useful extras.

Rooms 5 en suite (3 fmly) (2 smoking) **Facilities** STV TVB tea/coffee Direct dial from bedrooms Cen ht Dinner Last d 8pm **Parking** 17 **Notes** ⊗ No coaches

SEVENOAKS

MAP 06 TQ55

See also Farningham

★★★★ GUEST ACCOMMODATION

The Studio at Double Dance

Tonbridge Rd, Ightham TN15 9AT

☎ 01732 884198 📄 01732 780363

e-mail: pennycracknell@doubledance.co.uk

dir: *A227 S from Ightham towards Tonbridge, 1st left onto Mill Ln, driveway 1st right*

Close to Sevenoaks this delightful contemporary annexe sits within peaceful gardens and boasts impressive views of the North Downs. Comfortable accommodation is self-contained with private access and a wide range of facilities. An ample continental breakfast is provided and home-made cakes and pastries are a speciality.

Rooms 1 annexe en suite S £50–£60; D £50–£60 **Facilities** TVB tea/coffee Cen ht Wi-fi available 🍴 **Parking** 2 **Notes** ⊗ 🐾

★★★★ GUEST ACCOMMODATION

Yew Tree Barn

Long Mill Ln, Crouch, Borough Green TN15 8QB

☎ 01732 780461

e-mail: bartonje@hotmail.com

dir: *A25 Maidstone Road turn left after Esso garage. Crouch Lane 1m, right to Crouch, on left*

Situated in the quiet picturesque village of Crouch this attractively converted barn is in an ideal position from which to explore the beautiful Kent countryside. Brands Hatch racing circuit is just a short drive away as well as Leeds and Lullingstone Castles. Welcoming hosts Tricia and James offer spaciously comfortable bedrooms as well as an attractive guest lounge and dining room overlooking the beautiful gardens.

Rooms 2 en suite (2 fmly) (1 GF) S £50; D £65–£75 **Facilities** TVB tea/coffee Cen ht TVL Wi-fi available **Parking** 5 **Notes** ⊗ Closed 21 Dec–7 Jan 🐾

SITTINGBOURNE

MAP 07 TQ96

★★★★ GUEST ACCOMMODATION

The Beaumont

74 London Rd ME10 1NS

☎ 01795 472536 📄 01795 425921

e-mail: info@thebeaumont.co.uk

web: www.thebeaumont.co.uk

dir: *From M2 or M20 take A249 N. Exit at A2, 1m on left towards Sittingbourne*

Originally a Georgian farmhouse, this charming family-run property offers the best of hospitality and service. Comfortable bedrooms and bathrooms are well equipped for business and leisure guests. Breakfast in the bright, spacious conservatory makes good use of local produce and homemade preserves. Off-road parking is available.

Rooms 9 rms (6 en suite) (3 pri facs) (3 GF) S £45–£75; D £75–£85 **Facilities** STV TVB tea/coffee Direct dial from bedrooms Cen ht TVL Wi-fi available **Conf** Max 12 Thtr 12 Class 12 Board 12 **Parking** 9 **Notes** Closed 24 Dec–1 Jan

SITTINGBOURNE CONTINUED

★★★ GUEST ACCOMMODATION
Sandhurst Farm Forge

Seed Rd, Newnham ME9 0NE
☎ 01795 886854
e–mail: rooms.forge@btinternet.com

dir: *Off A2 into Newnham, onto Seed Rd by church,
establishment 1m on right*

A warm welcome is assured at this peaceful location, which also
features a working forge. The spacious bedrooms are in a converted
stable block and provide smartly furnished accommodation. Breakfast
is served in the dining room adjoining the bedrooms. The owner has
won an award for green tourism by reducing the impact of the
business on the environment.

Rooms 2 en suite (2 GF) S £30; D £58✳ **Facilities** TVB tea/coffee
Cen ht Wi-fi available **Parking** 6 **Notes** No children 12yrs Closed
23 Dec–1 Jan ⊜

SUTTON   MAP 07 TR34

★★★ GUEST ACCOMMODATION
Sutton Vale Country Club

Vale Rd CT15 5DH
☎ 01304 366233 & 374155 🖹 01304 381132
e–mail: office@sutton-vale.co.uk

dir: *In village centre*

Surrounded by countryside yet only a short distance from the historical
town of Dover, Sutton Vale provides a wealth of activities including
indoor pool. Comfortable bedrooms in the main house are stylishly
decorated and annexe rooms have private terraces. Breakfast is served
in the dining room and evening entertainment is available in high
season.

Rooms 4 en suite **Facilities** TVB tea/coffee Cen ht TVL Dinner Last
d 8pm ⊗ Pool Table **Conf** Max 100 Thtr 100 Class 60 Board 50
Parking 50 **Notes** ⊗

TENTERDEN   MAP 07 TQ83

★★★★ GUEST ACCOMMODATION
Collina House

5 East Hill TN30 6RL
☎ 01580 764852 & 764004 🖹 01580 762224
e–mail: enquiries@collinahousehotel.co.uk
web: www.collinahousehotel.co.uk

dir: *Off High St E onto B2067 Oaks Rd, property on left opp
orchard*

This attractive, restored half-timbered Edwardian house has a peaceful
location just a short walk from the town centre. The smart en suite
bedrooms are spacious and thoughtfully equipped. Public areas
include a formal bar and an elegant restaurant offering imaginative
home-made dishes.

Rooms 12 en suite 3 annexe en suite (8 fmly) S £50–£60; D £75–£100
Facilities TV14B tea/coffee Direct dial from bedrooms Cen ht Dinner
Last d 8.30pm **Parking** 15 **Notes** LB ⊗ Closed 21 Dec–11 Jan

---

TUNBRIDGE WELLS (ROYAL) MAP 06 TQ53

Premier Collection

★★★★★ GUEST ACCOMMODATION
Danehurst House

41 Lower Green Rd, Rusthall TN4 8TW
☎ 01892 527739 🖹 01892 514804
e–mail: info@danehurst.net
web: www.danehurst.net

dir: *1.5m W of Tunbridge Wells in Rusthall. Off A264 onto Coach
Rd & Lower Green Rd*

Situated in pretty gardens in a quiet residential area, this Victorian
gabled house is located to the west of the historic spa town. The house
retains many original features and is attractively decorated throughout.
Public areas include a comfortable lounge with a small bar. The
homely bedrooms come with a wealth of thoughtful extras, and
excellent breakfasts are served in the conservatory.

Rooms 4 en suite S £59.50–£69.50; D £69.50–£99.50✳ **Facilities** TVB
tea/coffee Cen ht **Parking** 6 **Notes** ⊗ No children 8yrs Closed Xmas &
1st 2wks Feb

★★★★ ⊜ INN
The Beacon

Tea Garden Ln, Rusthall TN3 9JH
☎ 01892 524252 🖹 01892 534288
e–mail: beaconhotel@btopenworld.com
web: www.the-beacon.co.uk

dir: *1.5m W of Tunbridge Wells. Signed off A264 onto Tea
Garden Ln*

This charming 18th-century inn is situated on an elevated position
amid sixteen acres of land and surrounded by open countryside. The
open-plan public areas are full of character and include ornate
fireplaces and stained glass windows. The spacious bedrooms are
attractively decorated, comfortably furnished and have many
thoughtful touches.

Rooms 3 en suite S fr £68.50; D fr £97✳ **Facilities** TV2B tea/coffee
Direct dial from bedrooms Cen ht Dinner Last d 9.30pm Wi-fi available
Fishing **Conf** Thtr 50 Class 40 Board 30 **Parking** 42 **Notes** Civ Wed 100

ENGLAND

★★★★ GUEST ACCOMMODATION
Bentham Hill Stables
Stockland Green Rd TN3 0TJ
☎ 01892 516602
e–mail: d-waddell@sky.com

dir: *2m NW of Tunbridge Wells. Off A26 signed Salomons/ Speldhurst, 1m right onto Bentham Hill/Stockland Green Rd, sharp right again*

This converted stable block is located in peaceful woodlands only a short drive from the town. Bedrooms are light and airy with tiled floors and shuttered windows, and some rooms have small private terraces. A freshly cooked breakfast is served in the delightful dining room.

Rooms 3 en suite (3 GF) S £45–£55; D £65–£75 **Facilities** tea/coffee Cen ht **Parking** 3 **Notes** ⊗ No children 8yrs Closed 23–27 Dec ☺

WESTERHAM   MAP 06 TQ45

★★★★ GUEST ACCOMMODATION
Corner Cottage
Toys Hill TN16 1PY
☎ 01732 750362 📠 01732 750754
e–mail: szeman@jshmanco.com

dir: *A25 to Brasted, onto Chart Ln signed Fox & Hounds. Turn right onto Puddledock Ln, 1st house on left*

Settled in a charming village this spacious, well equipped annexe is comfortably furnished and includes many thoughtful touches. In the main cottage a hearty Aga-cooked breakfast is served in the rustic dining room with stunning views of the countryside.

Rooms 1 annexe en suite (1 fmly) S fr £50; D fr £70✱ **Facilities** TVB tea/coffee Cen ht Dinner Last d noon Wi-fi available **Parking** 2 **Notes** ☺

WHITSTABLE   MAP 07 TR16

★★★★ GUEST ACCOMMODATION
Cherries
25 Cherry Orchard, Chestfield CT5 3NH
☎ 01227 792600 📠 01227 792600
e–mail: info@lets4you.com
web: www.thecherries.net

dir: *A229 onto A2290, straight over 1st two rdbts, turn right at 3rd rdbt onto Chestfield Rd, Cherry Orchard on the right*

This modern child-friendly house is set in a quiet street an easy distance from Whitstable and ideally located for Sandwich and the coast. Spacious bedrooms are stylishly furnished with plenty of amenities for business and leisure guests. Hospitality is a keynote here. A hearty breakfast includes home-made jams and dinner is available on request.

Rooms 2 en suite (1 fmly) **Facilities** STV TVB tea/coffee Cen ht TVL Dinner Last d 10am Hot tub **Parking** 4 **Notes** ⊗ ☺

WROTHAM HEATH   MAP 06 TQ65

★★★★ GUEST ACCOMMODATION
Pretty Maid House B&B
London Rd TN15 7RU
☎ 01732 886445 📠 01732 886439
e–mail: stay@prettymaid.co.uk

dir: *M26 junct 2A towards Maidstone on A20, through lights, 300mtrs on left*

Situated close to Brands Hatch Circuit, and within easy reach of Bluewater and Lullingstone Castle, this family home has been carefully designed to offer spacious, comfortable accommodation. Well appointed bedrooms vary in size and provide many thoughtful extras including free Wi-fi. Breakfast is served in the large, bright dining room or can be offered as room service

Rooms 7 rms (6 en suite) (1 pri facs) (2 fmly) (2 GF) S £47–£52; D £62–£72✱ **Facilities** FTV TVB tea/coffee Cen ht Wi-fi available **Parking** 7

LANCASHIRE

ACCRINGTON   MAP 18 SD72

★★★★ GUEST ACCOMMODATION
The Maple Lodge
70 Blackburn Rd, Clayton-le-Moors BB5 5JH
☎ 01254 301284 📠 0560 112 5380
e–mail: info@stayatmaplelodge.co.uk

dir: *M65 junct 7, signs for Clayton-le-Moors, right at T-junct onto Blackburn Rd*

This welcoming house is convenient for the M65, and provides comfortable, well-equipped bedrooms. There is an inviting lounge with well-stocked bar, and freshly cooked dinners (by arrangement) and hearty breakfasts are served in the attractive dining room.

Rooms 4 en suite 4 annexe en suite (1 fmly) (4 GF) S £44; D £62✱ **Facilities** FTV TVB tea/coffee Direct dial from bedrooms Cen ht TVL Dinner Last d 8pm Wi-fi available **Parking** 6 **Notes** LB

★★★ GUEST HOUSE
Pilkington's Guest House
135 Blackburn Rd BB5 0AA
☎ 01254 237032 📠 01254 237032
e–mail: pilkybuses@hotmail.com

Located close to the railway station, this family-run property has two comfortable bedrooms in the main house and four further bedrooms in the carefully refurbished terrace a short way along the street. Home cooked breakfasts are served in the main house.

Rooms 2 rms (2 pri facs) 4 annexe rms (2 fmly) (2 GF) **Facilities** TVB tea/coffee Cen ht Snooker Pool Table **Conf** Max 100 Thtr 100 Class 100 Board 100 **Parking** 6 **Notes** ⊗ No coaches ☺

BLACKBURN   MAP 18 SD62

★★★ BED & BREAKFAST
Old Dad's Barn

Mellor Ln, Mellor BB2 7EN

☎ 01254 812434

dir: *3m NW of town centre, off A677 into Mellor*

Located between Preston and Blackburn and part of a riding centre and garden nursery, bedrooms here are thoughtfully furnished and have smart modern shower rooms. Some rooms have country views. Comprehensive breakfasts, using quality local produce, are served in the traditionally furnished dining room, which also has a lounge area.

Rooms 4 en suite S £35; D £60✱ **Facilities** TVB tea/coffee Cen ht TVL Riding **Parking** 6 **Notes LB** ⊗ No children 11yrs ⊜

BLACKPOOL   MAP 18 SD33

★★★★ GUEST ACCOMMODATION
Bona Vista

104–106 Queens Promenade FY2 9NX

☎ 01253 351396 ▤ 01253 594985

e–mail: enquires@bonavistahotel.com

dir: *0.25m N of Uncle Toms Cabin & Castle Casino*

The Bona Vista has a peaceful seafront location on North Shore within reach of the town's attractions. Its attractive bedrooms are well equipped and some have sea views. There is a spacious dining room and a comfortable bar and lounges. Sixteen parking spaces are available, a boon in busy Blackpool.

Rooms 19 rms (17 en suite) (4 fmly) **Facilities** TVB tea/coffee Cen ht TVL Dinner Last d 4pm Pool Table **Conf** Max 50 Thtr 50 Class 50 Board 50 **Parking** 16

★★★★ GUEST HOUSE
The Craigmore

8 Willshaw Rd, Gynn Square FY2 9SH

☎ 01253 355098

e–mail: enquiries@thecraigmore.com

web: www.thecraigmore.com

dir: *1m N of Tower. A584 N over Gynn rdbt, 1st right onto Willshaw Rd. The Craigmore 3rd on left*

This well-maintained property is in an attractive location overlooking Gynn Square gardens, with the Promenade and tram stops just yards

CONTINUED

away. Several of the smart modern bedrooms are suitable for families. There is a comfortable lounge, a sun lounge and patio, and the pretty dining room has a small bar.

Rooms 8 en suite (4 fmly) S £30–£40; D £48–£68✱ **Facilities** TVB tea/coffee Licensed Cen ht TVL Dinner Last d 1pm **Notes LB** ⊗ Closed Dec–Jan RS Feb–Mar

★★★★ GUEST ACCOMMODATION
The Ramsay

90–92 Queen Promenade FY2 9NS

☎ 01253 352777 ▤ 01253 351207

e–mail: enquiries@theramsayhotel.co.uk

On Blackpool's North Shore and within easy reach of the town centre this friendly hotel offers comfortable, well equipped bedrooms, many with sea views. Meals are served in the attractive dining room and lighter snacks are also available in the bar.

Rooms 20 en suite (2 fmly) **Facilities** Lift Cen ht TVL Dinner Last d 10am **Parking** 10 **Notes** ⊗ Closed Nov–Mar

★★★★ GUEST HOUSE
Sunny Cliff

98 Queens Promenade, Northshore FY2 9NS

☎ 01253 351155

dir: *On A584 1.5m N of Blackpool Tower, just past Uncle Toms Cabin*

Under the same ownership for four decades, this friendly guest house overlooking the seafront offers a genuine home-from-home atmosphere. The pretty bedrooms, some with sea views, are neatly furnished. There is a cosy bar, a sun lounge, a comfortable lounge, and a smart dining room where good home cooking features.

Rooms 9 en suite (3 fmly) (2 smoking) S £25.50–£29; D £51–£58✱ **Facilities** TVB tea/coffee Licensed Cen ht TVL Dinner Last d 5pm **Parking** 6 **Notes LB** ⊗ No coaches Closed 9 Nov–Etr ⊜

★★★★ 🅰 GUEST ACCOMMODATION
Windsor Carlton Guest Accommodation

6 Warley Rd, North Shore FY1 2JU

☎ 01253 354924 ▤ 0870 7536305

e–mail: info@windsorcarlton.com

web: www.windsorcarlton.com

dir: *From M55 follow signs for Promenade & North Shore. Warley Rd adjacent Hilton Hotel off seafront. Windsor Carlton on left*

Rooms 11 en suite (4 fmly) S £28–£34; D £56–£66 **Facilities** FTV TVB tea/coffee Cen ht TVL Dinner Last d 7pm Wi-fi available **Notes** Closed Xmas

★★★ GUEST ACCOMMODATION
Hartshead

17 King Edward Av, North Shore FY2 9TA
☎ 01253 353133 & 357111
e-mail: info@hartshead-hotel.co.uk

dir: *M55 junct 4, A583 & A584 to North Shore, off Queens Promenade onto King Edward Av*

Popular for its location near the seafront, this enthusiastically run establishment has modern bedrooms of various sizes, equipped with a good range of practical extras. A veranda-sitting room is available, in addition to a comfortable lounge bar, and breakfast and pre-theatre dinners are served in the attractive dining room.

Rooms 10 en suite (3 fmly) S £20–£33; D £40–£60✳ **Facilities** FTV TVB tea/coffee Cen ht TVL Dinner Last d 2pm **Parking** 6 **Notes LB** ⊗

★★★ GUEST HOUSE
Burlees

40 Knowle Av FY2 9TQ
☎ 01253 354535 📄 01253 354535
e-mail: marrasimpson@aol.com
web: www.burlees-hotel.co.uk

dir: *Off seafront Queen's Promenade at Uncle Tom's Cabin onto Knowle Av*

A genuine welcome awaits you at this well-maintained house, just a stroll from the promenade. Smartly decorated bedrooms are thoughtfully equipped, and there is a comfortable lounge and a cosy bar. Hearty breakfasts and evening meals by arrangement are served in the pine-furnished dining room.

Rooms 9 en suite (2 fmly) (1 GF) S £20–£28; D £40–£56 **Facilities** TVB tea/coffee Licensed Cen ht TVL Dinner Last d prev evening **Parking** 4 **Notes LB** No coaches Closed 16 Dec–7 Jan

★★★ GUEST HOUSE
Denely

15 King Edward Av FY2 9TA
☎ 01253 352757
e-mail: denely@tesco.net

dir: *1m N of Blackpool Tower*

Just a stroll from this Promenade and Gynn Square gardens, the welcoming guest house offers a spacious lounge and a bright dining room along with simply furnished bedrooms. The friendly resident

owners provide attentive service, and evening meals are available by arrangement.

Rooms 9 en suite (3 fmly) S fr £18; D fr £36✳ **Facilities** FTV TVB tea/coffee Cen ht TVL Dinner Last d 1pm **Parking** 6 **Notes LB** ⊗ Closed Dec–Jan

★★★ GUEST ACCOMMODATION
Derby Lodge

8 Derby Rd FY1 2JF
☎ 01253 753444 📄 01253 753444
e-mail: derbylodgehotel@btconnect.com

dir: *From M55 follow signs for Promenade, north (with sea on left), right onto Derby Rd, located on right*

Located close to the seafront and close to the town centre Derby Lodge offers spacious well equipped accommodation in a friendly atmosphere. Dinner is available in the attractive restaurant and there is a small bar.

Rooms 7 en suite (3 fmly) S £30–£50; D £50–£60 **Facilities** FTV TVB tea/coffee Dinner Last d 9.30pm Wi-fi available **Conf** Max 24 Thtr 24 Class 24 Board 20 Del from £29 ✳ **Parking** 4 **Notes LB** ⊗ ⊛

★★★ GUEST ACCOMMODATION
Funky Towers

297 The Promenade FY1 6AL
☎ 01253 400123
e-mail: stay@funkytowers.com
web: www.funkytowers.com

dir: *On A584 Promenade between Central Pier & South Pier*

The friendly, family-run guest house has a prime location facing the sea, between the Pleasure Beach and Central Pier. There is a spacious bar and a modern café with direct access to seafront. The bedrooms are equipped with lots of extras; some feature four posters and others have great sea views.

Rooms 14 en suite (5 fmly) (1 GF) S fr £38✳ **Facilities** TVB tea/coffee Cen ht TVL Wi-fi available Pool Table **Notes** ⊗ Closed Jan

★★★ GUEST HOUSE
The Sandalwood

3 Gynn Av FY1 2LD
☎ 01253 351795 📄 01253 351795
e-mail: peter.gerald@btconnect.com
web: www.sandalwoodhotel.co.uk

dir: *North of tower, proceed along prom. Take 1st right, then 1st left after Hilton Hotel.*

Situated on Blackpool's North Shore Sandalwood offers a friendly atmosphere and attractive, well-equipped accommodation. There is a comfortable lounge, and dinner or lighter snacks are available by arrangement.

Rooms 9 rms (7 en suite) (2 fmly) **Facilities** TVB tea/coffee Licensed Cen ht TVL Dinner Last d 11.30am **Parking** 2 **Notes** ⊗ No coaches Closed 20–30 Dec

CONTINUED

ENGLAND

BLACKPOOL CONTINUED

★★★ GUEST HOUSE
Wilmar
42 Osborne Rd FY4 1HQ
☎ 01253 346229 🖻 01253 200343
e–mail: info@thehotelwilmar.co.uk

dir: *From M55 follow Main Parking Area, right at Waterloo Rd exit, left at lights, left at 2nd lights, bear right at Grand Hotel & right again*

This friendly, family-run guest house has a convenient location close to the Pleasure Beach, Sandcastles and all the resort's major South Promenade attractions. Bedrooms are brightly appointed, smartly maintained and include a family suite. A cosy lounge and bar are available and dinner is served by arrangement.

Rooms 7 rms (6 en suite) (1 pri facs) (1 fmly) S £20–£28; D £40–£50 **Facilities** FTV TVB tea/coffee Licensed Cen ht TVL Dinner Last d 10am **Notes LB** ⊗ No coaches

★★★ GUEST HOUSE
Windsor Park
96 Queens Promenade FY2 9NS
☎ 01253 357025
e–mail: info@windsorparkhotel.net

dir: *Queens Promenade, North Shore*

Having stunning views, this family-run guest house on the peaceful North Shore is just a tram ride from the attractions. Home-cooked meals and substantial breakfasts are served in the elegant dining room, and there is a pleasant bar area and a sun lounge. The bedrooms have modern amenities.

Rooms 9 en suite (1 fmly) **Facilities** TVB tea/coffee Licensed Cen ht TVL Dinner Last d 4pm Stair lift **Parking** 6 **Notes** ⊗ No coaches Closed 8 Nov–Etr (ex Xmas/New Year)

★★★ Ⓐ GUEST ACCOMMODATION
The Vidella
80–82 Dickson Rd FY1 2BU
☎ 01253 621201 🖻 01253 620319
e–mail: info@videllahotel.com
web: www.videllahotel.com

dir: *N from North Pier on A584, right onto Cocker St, left at x-rds*

Rooms 29 en suite (6 fmly) (3 GF) (9 smoking) S £22.50–£42.50; D £45–£85 **Facilities** FTV TVB tea/coffee Cen ht Dinner Last d noon Wi-fi available Pool Table **Parking** 5 **Notes LB**

★★ Ⓐ GUEST ACCOMMODATION
Briny View
2 Woodfield Rd FY1 6AX
☎ 01253 346584
e–mail: brinyviewhotel@aol.com

dir: *Off A584 Promenade between Central Pier & South Pier, opposite St Chads headland*

Rooms 11 rms (7 en suite) (1 pri facs) (4 fmly) S £20–£26; D £40–£56✳ **Facilities** TVB tea/coffee Cen ht TVL **Notes LB** ⊗ Closed Dec

Ⓤ
Lancaster House
170 – 274 Central Dr FY1 5JB
☎ 01253 341928 🖻 01253 402878
e–mail: maria@lancasterhousehotel.co.uk

At the time of going to press the rating for this establishment had not been confirmed. Please check the AA website www.theAA.com for up-to-date information.

CONTINUED

Rooms 11 en suite (2 fmly) S £28–£38; D £56–£76✱ **Facilities** FTV TVB Cen ht TVL Dinner Last d 9.30pm Wi-fi available **Parking** 11 **Notes** ⊗ Closed Jan

BOLTON-BY-BOWLAND   MAP 18 SD74

★★★★ GUEST HOUSE
Middle Flass Lodge
Settle Rd BB7 4NY
☎ 01200 447259 🖹 01200 447300
e–mail: middleflasslodge@btconnect.com
web: www.middleflasslodge.co.uk

dir: *2m N of Bolton by Bowland. Off A59 for Sawley, N to Forest Becks, over bridge, 1m on right*

Set in peaceful countryside within the Forest of Bowland, this smart house provides a warm welcome. Stylishly converted from farm outbuildings, exposed timbers feature throughout, including the attractive restaurant and cosy lounge. The modern bedrooms include a family room. Thanks to the accomplished chef, the restaurant is also popular with non-residents.

Rooms 5 en suite 2 annexe en suite (1 fmly) S £40–£50; D £60–£75 **Facilities** TVB tea/coffee Licensed Cen ht TVL Dinner Last d 6.30pm **Parking** 14 **Notes** LB ⊗ No coaches

BURNLEY   MAP 18 SD83

★★★ GUEST ACCOMMODATION
Ormerod House
121/123 Ormerod Rd BB11 3QW
☎ 01282 423255

dir: *Burnley centre onto A682, 200yds N after rdbt right onto Ormerod Rd, pass Burnley College, 300yds on right*

The welcoming guest house is a short walk from the town centre and is handy for Queens Park, Thompson's Park and Burnley FC. The bright modern bedrooms are well equipped and there is a comfortable lounge. Separate tables are provided in the smart breakfast room.

Ormerod House

Rooms 9 en suite (2 fmly) **Facilities** TVB tea/coffee Cen ht TVL **Parking** 8 **Notes** ⊜

CHORLEY   MAP 15 SD51

See Eccleston

CLITHEROE   MAP 18 SD74

★★★★ GUEST HOUSE
Brooklyn
32 Pimlico Rd BB7 2AH
☎ 01200 428268 & 07971 917664

dir: *500yds N of town centre. A671 rdbt onto B6478 Well Terrace, right at next rdbt*

This elegant and welcoming Victorian house is in a peaceful residential area just a stroll from the centre of town. The bedrooms are equipped with lots of thoughtful extras and the attractive dining room has a comfortable lounge area.

Rooms 4 en suite S £32–£35; D £60✱ **Facilities** TVB tea/coffee Cen ht **Notes** ⊗ No coaches ⊜

ECCLESTON   MAP 15 SD51

★★★★ GUEST ACCOMMODATION
Parr Hall Farm
8 Parr Ln PR7 5SL
☎ 01257 451917 🖹 01257 453749
e–mail: enquiries@parrhallfarm.com

dir: *Off B5250 at the Green/Towngate junct turn into Parr Ln, 1st property on left*

This attractive well-maintained farmhouse, located in a quiet corner of the village, yet close to the M6, dates back to the 18th century. The majority of bedrooms are located in a sympathetic barn conversion and include luxury en suite bathrooms and lots of thoughtful extras. A comprehensive continental breakfast is included in the room price.

Rooms 4 en suite 9 annexe en suite (1 fmly) (5 GF) S £40–£50; D £70–£90 **Facilities** TVB tea/coffee Cen ht Wi-fi available 🚶 Guided Walks **Conf** Class 15 Board 10 Del from £80 **Parking** 20 **Notes** ⊗

CONTINUED

FLEETWOOD

MAP 18 SD34

★★★ GUEST HOUSE
Normandy

100 Promenade Rd FY7 6RF
☎ 01253 872961 📄 01253 872961
e–mail: normandy-house@btconnect.com

dir: *From A585, Marine Hall on right, left onto Mount Rd & Promenade Rd*

This friendly family-run guest house is close to the town centre and the beach and its attractions. Bedrooms are comfortable and carefully decorated and well equipped, There is also a small lounge and dinner is served by arrangement in the dining room which has a small bar.

Rooms 3 en suite (1 fmly) S £25; D £50✱ **Facilities** FTV TVB tea/coffee Licensed Cen ht TVL Dinner Last d 10am **Notes LB** ✖ Closed 24 Dec–5 Jan 🌐

LANCASTER

MAP 18 SD46

★★★ 🅰 GUEST ACCOMMODATION
Lancaster Town House

11/12 Newton Ter, Caton Rd LA1 3PB
☎ 01524 65527 📄 01524 383148
e–mail: hedge-holmes@talk21.com

dir: *M6 junct 34, 1m towards Lancaster, house on right*

Rooms 7 en suite (1 fmly) S £32; D £55–£60✱ **Facilities** TVB tea/coffee Cen ht TVL Wi-fi available **Notes** ✖

LYTHAM ST ANNES

MAP 18 SD32

★★★ GUEST ACCOMMODATION
Strathmore

305 Clifton Dr South FY8 1HN
☎ 01253 725478

dir: *In centre of St Annes opp Post Office*

This friendly, family-run property has a central location close to the promenade. The long-established Strathmore offers smartly furnished and well-equipped bedrooms. There is an elegant lounge where you can enjoy a relaxing drink, and a smart dining room.

Rooms 8 rms (5 en suite) S £28–£30; D £56–£60 **Facilities** TVB tea/coffee Cen ht **Parking** 10 **Notes LB** ✖ No children 9yrs 🌐

MORECAMBE

MAP 18 SD46

★★★★ GUEST HOUSE
Morecambe Bay Guest House

35 Marine Rd West LA3 1BZ
☎ 01524 426593
e–mail: info@morecambebayguesthouse.co.uk

This friendly family-run house has a stunning outlook over Morecambe Bay. The contemporary bedrooms, including a ground floor room, are spacious and well furnished with good quality en suites. Breakfast is

CONTINUED

served in the pleasant downstairs dining room, and there is also a lounge area.

Rooms 4 en suite (1 GF) **Facilities** FTV TVB tea/coffee Cen ht Wi-fi available **Notes** ✖ No children No coaches

★★★ GUEST ACCOMMODATION
Beach Mount

395 Marine Rd East LA4 5AN
☎ 01524 420753
e–mail: beachmounthotel@aol.com

dir: *M6 junct 34/35, follow signs to Morecambe, Beach Mount 0.5m from town centre on the E Promenade*

This spacious property overlooks the bay and features a range of room styles that includes a family room and a junior suite. Guests have ue of a comfortable lounge with fully licensed bar, and breakfasts are served in a pleasant separate dining room

Rooms 10 en suite (1 GF) (10 smoking) S £27–£43; D £50–£58✱ **Facilities** FTV TVB tea/coffee Cen ht **Notes LB** Closed Nov–Mar

★★★ GUEST ACCOMMODATION
Belle Vue

330 Marine Rd LA4 5AA
☎ 01524 411375 📄 01524 411375

dir: *On seafront between lifeboat house & bingo hall*

Having fine views over the promenade and Morecambe Bay, the Belle Vue provides a range of bedrooms styles on three floors, with most accessible by lift. There are comfortable lounges, and a spacious lounge bar where entertainment is provided when busy. A choice of dishes is available in the large dining room.

Rooms 41 rms (34 en suite) (3 fmly) S £35–£38; D £70–£76 **Facilities** TVB tea/coffee Lift Cen ht TVL Dinner Last d 5pm **Parking** 3 **Notes LB** ✖ No children 14yrs Closed Jan–Mar

★★★ GUEST HOUSE
The Craigwell

372 Marine Rd East LA4 5AH
☎ 01524 410095
e–mail: craigwellhotel@tiscali.co.uk
web: www.craigwellhotel.co.uk

dir: *A589 to seafront, left, Craigwell 400yds*

This house is part of a Victorian terrace and looks out over Morecambe

CONTINUED

Bay to the distant Cumbrian hills. There is also a stylish lounge with fine views and a spacious breakfast room to the rear. Bedrooms are pleasantly decorated, with all expected facilities; six enjoy views of the Bay. There is a private car park at the rear.

Rooms 12 en suite (1 fmly) S £26–£30; D £54–£60 **Facilities** TVB tea/coffee Cen ht TVL Dinner Last d noon Wi-fi available **Conf** Thtr 30 Class 15 Board 20 **Parking** 4 **Notes** LB No coaches

★★★ GUEST ACCOMMODATION
The Sea Lynn Guest House
29 West End Rd LA4 4DJ
☎ 01524 411340
e–mail: thesealynn@hotmail.com

dir: *Signs for West End seafront, turn right, then 3rd right, 50yds on right*

Set just back from the promenade and Morecambe's tourist attractions, this terrace house with a tidy front patio area, offers accommodation on four floors. Guests have use of a cosy lounge on the ground floor and a comfortable breakfast room on the first floor. Bedrooms are fresh in design, with all the expected facilities; all guests are given a warm welcome.

Rooms 12 rms (3 en suite) (1 fmly) (3 GF) S £22–£24; D £44–£48✱ **Facilities** FTV TVB tea/coffee Cen ht TVL Wi-fi available **Notes** ⊗

★★★ GUEST ACCOMMODATION
The Trevelyan
27 West End Rd LA4 4DJ
☎ 01524 412013
e–mail: contact@thetrevelyanhotel.co.uk

dir: *M6 junct 34, signed Morecambe then West End. At seafront right & 3rd right onto West End Rd, 50yds on right*

You are assured of a warm welcome at The Trevelyan, a family-run guest house some 50 yards from the seafront and well located for Morecambe's attractions. Bedrooms are comfortably proportioned and well equipped, and there is an inviting lounge, a cosy bar, and a bright airy dining room where delicious freshly cooked evening meals (by arrangement), and traditional English breakfasts, are served at individual tables.

Rooms 10 rms (2 en suite) (1 fmly) (2 GF) S £22–£25; D £44–£50✱ **Facilities** FTV TVB tea/coffee Cen ht TVL Dinner Last d 4pm Wi-fi available **Notes** ⊗

★★★ GUEST HOUSE
Yacht Bay View
359 Marine Rd East LA4 5AQ
☎ 01524 414481
e–mail: yachtbayview@hotmail.com

dir: *0.5m NE of town centre on seafront promenade*

Overlooking Morecambe Bay, this family-run property offers comfortable bedrooms, some with impressive views, and all with en suite shower rooms. Guests are given a warm welcome and breakfast is served in the dining room, which also has a lounge area.

Rooms 7 en suite (1 fmly) **Facilities** TVB tea/coffee TVL Dinner Last d at time of booking **Notes** ⊗ No coaches

---

PRESTON
MAP 18 SD52

See also Blackburn

Premier Collection

★★★★★ BED & BREAKFAST
Whitestake Farm
Pope Ln, Whitestake PR4 4JR
☎ 01772 619392 📠 01772 611146
e–mail: enquiries@gardenofedenspa.co.uk
web: www.gardenofedenspa.co.uk

dir: *M6 junct 29, A582 Lytham St Annes Penwortham Way, left onto Chain House Lane, right onto Pope Lane, on right*

A warm welcome awaits at this attractive white farmhouse, peacefully located just minutes from Preston and the M6, within easy reach of Southport and Lytham. Beautifully appointed bedrooms and bathrooms are spacious and thoughtfully equipped. Carefully prepared, substantial breakfasts are taken around a huge table in the elegant dining room. Guests can also make use of the indoor swimming pool and two treatment rooms.

Rooms 2 en suite S £60; D £120 **Facilities** STV TVB tea/coffee Cen ht TVL Dinner Last d 8pm Wi-fi available ⊗ **Parking** 6 **Notes** ⊗

★★★ BED & BREAKFAST
Birch Croft Bed & Breakfast
Gill Ln, Longton PR4 4SS
☎ 01772 613174 📠 01772 613174
e–mail: johnsuts@btinternet.com
web: www.birchcroftbandb.co.uk

dir: *From A59 right at rdbt to Midge Hall. Premises 4th on left*

Located only 10 minutes away from major motorway links (M6, M65, M61) this establishment is on the doorstep of many local attractions and close to Southport, Preston and Blackpool. This is a friendly, family run business which offers comfortable accommodation and a very peaceful location.

Rooms 3 en suite (1 fmly) S £25–£35; D £48–£50✱ **Facilities** TVB tea/coffee Cen ht TVL Wi-fi available **Parking** 11 **Notes** LB ⊗ ⊜

PRESTON CONTINUED

★★★ GUEST ACCOMMODATION
Claremont

516 Blackpool Rd, Ashton on Ribble PR2 1HY
☎ 01772 729738 📄 01772 726274
e-mail: claremonthotel@hotmail.co.uk

dir: *M6 junct onto A59 towards Preston. Right at hilltop onto A583. Claremont on right past pub & over bridge*

This family-run accommodation offers a relaxed and informal atmosphere for its mainly business clientele. Bedrooms are comfortable and well equipped, and public areas include a cosy bar lounge and adjacent dining room offering a modest choice of good value, home-cooked dishes during the week.

Rooms 12 en suite (1 fmly) (1 GF) S £40; D £60✴ **Facilities** TVB tea/coffee Direct dial from bedrooms Cen ht TVL Dinner Last d 7pm Wi-fi available **Conf** Max 60 Thtr 60 Class 40 Board 30 **Parking** 27

★ GUEST ACCOMMODATION
Ashton Lodge Guest House

37 Victoria Pde, Ashton PR2 1DT
☎ 01772 728414 📄 01772 720580
e-mail: greathospitality@btconnect.com

dir: *M6 junct 31, A59 onto A5085, 3.3m onto A5072 Tulketh Rd, 0.3m onto Victoria Pde*

This detached Victorian Guest House offers good value accommodation. Bedrooms vary in size, with some bedrooms located on the ground floor. The dining room on the ground floor is the setting for hearty traditional breakfasts served at individual tables.

Rooms 8 rms (6 en suite) (5 fmly) (3 GF) S £28–£38; D £40–£50✴ **Facilities** FTV TVB tea/coffee Cen ht TVL Wi-fi available **Notes** ⊗

WHITEWELL   MAP 18 SD64

Premier Collection

★★★★★ 🏵 INN
The Inn at Whitewell

Forest of Bowland, Clitheroe BB7 3AT
☎ 01200 448222 📄 01200 448298
e-mail: reception@innatwhitewell.com

dir: *M6 junct 31a, B6243 to Longridge. Bear left at mini-rdbt. After 3 rdbts leave Longridge. Approx 3m, sharp left bend with white railings, then right. Approx 1m then left, right at T junct. Next left, then 3m to Whitewell.*

This long-established culinary destination is hidden away in quintessential Lancashire countryside just 20 minutes from the M6. The fine dining restaurant is complemented by two historic and cosy bars with roaring fires, real ales and polished service. Bedrooms are richly furnished with antiques and eye-catching bijouterie, while many of the bathrooms have Victorian brass showers.

Rooms 19 en suite 4 annexe en suite (1 fmly) (1 GF) S £70–£135; D £96–£172✴ **Facilities** STV TVB tea/coffee Direct dial from bedrooms Cen ht Dinner Last d 9.30pm Fishing **Conf** BC Max 45 Thtr 45 Board 35 **Parking** 60 **Notes** No coaches Civ Wed 80

YEALAND CONYERS   MAP 18 SD57

Premier Collection

★★★★★ BED & BREAKFAST
The Bower

LA5 9SF
☎ 01524 734585 📄 01524 734585
e-mail: info@thebower.co.uk
web: www.thebower.co.uk

dir: *M6 junct 35, A6 towards Milnthorpe for 0.75m, under narrow bridge, take next left onto Snape Ln & bear left an end*

This Georgian house stands in grounds in a charming village. The spacious bedrooms are comfortably furnished. There is a welcoming and homely drawing room, warmed by open fires during colder months. Breakfast is served at a communal table in the kitchen.

Rooms 2 rms (1 en suite) (1 pri facs) (1 fmly) **Facilities** TVB tea/coffee Cen ht TVL Wi-fi available ⚓ Bridge games/lessons **Parking** 6 **Notes** ⊗ No children 12yrs

LEICESTERSHIRE

ASHBY-DE-LA-ZOUCH   MAP 11 SK31

See Coalville

BARROW UPON SOAR   MAP 11 SK51

★★★★ INN
The Hunting Lodge

38 South St LE12 8LZ
☎ 01509 412337 📄 01509 410838
web: www.thehuntinglodgebarrowonsoar.co.uk

The themed bedrooms at this modern inn include a Fagin room, a Chopin room and a Dali room; all are well equipped and have good facilities. There is a popular bar and a good range of interesting food is served in the brasserie.

Rooms 6 en suite (2 fmly) S £80–£120; D £80–£120✴ **Facilities** TVB tea/coffee Direct dial from bedrooms Cen ht Dinner Last d 9.30pm Wi-fi available **Conf** Max 50 Thtr 50 Class 50 Board 30 **Parking** 60 **Notes** ⊗

BELTON
MAP 11 SK42

★★★★ ◉◉ RESTAURANT WITH ROOMS
The Queen's Head
2 Long St LE12 9TP
☎ 01530 222359 🖥 01530 224680
e–mail: enquiries@thequeenshead.org
web: www.thequeenshead.org

dir: *From Loughborough turn left onto B5324, 3m into Belton*
This well furnished establishment is found in the village centre and has
public rooms with a modern feel. Bedrooms are also along modern
lines while quality cooking is provided in the delightful dining room.

Rooms 6 en suite **Facilities** TVB tea/coffee Cen ht Dinner Last d 9.30pm
Wi-fi available **Conf** Max 40 Thtr 40 Class 18 Board 30 **Parking** 20
Notes Civ Wed 50

BELVOIR
MAP 11 SK83

★★★★ BED & BREAKFAST
Woodside Farm
Long Ln, Barkestone-le-Vale NG13 0HQ
☎ 01476 870336 & 07703 299291
e–mail: hickling-woodside@supanet.com

dir: *1m SE of Barkestone. Off A52 at Bottesford for Harby &
Belvoir Castle, after Redmile x-rds, left onto lane, farm 0.5m*
A warm welcome awaits at this friendly farm, located on the Belvoir
Castle estate in the peaceful Vale of Belvoir within easy reach of
Nottingham and Grantham. The smart bedrooms have beautiful views
over open countryside, and hearty breakfasts are served in the
lounge-dining room. Packed lunches are available on request.

Rooms 2 en suite (1 fmly) (1 GF) **Facilities** tea/coffee Cen ht Golf
Fishing Riding **Parking** 5 **Notes** ⊗ RS mid Sep–mid May ⊛

BUCKMINSTER
MAP 11 SK82

★★★★ ◉◉ GUEST ACCOMMODATION
The Tollemache Arms
48 Main St NG33 5SA
☎ 01476 860007
e–mail: enquiries@thetollemachearms.com

dir: *Off A1 Colsterworth rdbt onto B676 to Buckminster*
This revamped village property has a minimalist decor of neutral
colours, and strong shades in the pictures, brown leather chairs and
crisp white table linen. Its busy restaurant serves high quality food.

Rooms 4 en suite (3 fmly) S £50; D £75✶ **Facilities** TVB tea/coffee
Cen ht Dinner Last d 9.30pm **Conf** Max 20 Class 20 Board 20
Parking 21 **Notes LB** RS Sun–Mon

CASTLE DONINGTON
MAP 11 SK42

See East Midlands Airport

COALVILLE
MAP 11 SK41

★★★★ 🖥 GUEST HOUSE
Ravenstone Guesthouse
Church Lane, Ravenstone LE67 2AE
☎ 01530 810536
e–mail: annthorne@ravenstone-guesthouse.co.uk
web: www.ravenstone-guesthouse.co.uk

dir: *1.5m W of Coalville. Off A447 onto Church Ln for
Ravenstone, 2nd house on left*
Situated in the heart of Ravenstone village, this early 18th-century
house is full of character. The bedrooms are individually decorated and
feature period furniture, and local produce is used for dinner and in
the extensive breakfast menu. The beamed dining room has an
honesty bar and there is also a cosy lounge.

Rooms 3 en suite **Facilities** tea/coffee Licensed Cen ht TVL Dinner Last
d noon Painting tuition **Parking** 6 **Notes** No children 18yrs No coaches
Closed 23–30 Dec & 1 Jan

CROPSTON
MAP 11 SK51

★★★★★ 🅰 BED & BREAKFAST
Horseshoe Cottage Farm
Hallgates LE7 7HQ
☎ 0116 235 0038
e–mail: Lindajee@ljee.freeserve.co.uk
web: www.horseshoecottagefarm.com

Rooms 3 en suite (1 GF) S £55; D £90 **Facilities** TVB tea/coffee Cen ht
TVL Dinner Last d at breakfast **Conf** Max 8 Board 8 **Parking** 6 **Notes** ⊗

EAST MIDLANDS AIRPORT
MAP 11 SK42

Premier Collection

★★★★★ GUEST HOUSE
Kegworth House
42 High St DE74 2DA
☎ 01509 672575 🖥 01509 670645
e–mail: info@kegworthhouse.co.uk
web: www.kegworthhouse.co.uk

dir: *M1 junct 24, A6 to Loughborough. 0.5m 1st right onto
Packington Hill. Left at junct, Kegworth House 50yds on left*
Convenient for major roads and East Midlands Airport, this impressive
Georgian house with an immaculate walled garden has been lovingly
restored. The individually styled bedrooms are luxuriously appointed
and equipped with a wealth of thoughtful extras. The elegant dining
room is the setting for memorable dinners by arrangement, and
wholesome breakfasts featuring local produce are served in the
attractive kitchen.

Rooms 11 en suite (2 fmly) (2 GF) S £55–£139; D £65–£250✶
Facilities TVB tea/coffee Direct dial from bedrooms Licensed Cen ht TVL
Dinner Last d 24hrs before Wi-fi available **Conf** Max 12 Board 12
Parking 25 **Notes** ⊗ No coaches

★★★★ GUEST ACCOMMODATION
Donington Park Farmhouse

Melbourne Rd, Isley Walton DE74 2RN
☎ 01332 862409 📠 01332 862364
e–mail: info@parkfarmhouse.co.uk
web: www.parkfarmhouse.co.uk

dir: *Off A453 at Isley Walton to Melbourne, premises 0.5m on right*

Located adjacent to Donington Park and convenient for East Midlands Airport, this 17th-century former farmhouse has been renovated to a high standard. The thoughtfully furnished bedrooms, some of which are in converted outbuildings, are equipped with a range of homely extras. Imaginative dinners, served in the attractive kitchen-dining room, make use of home-grown produce.

Rooms 9 en suite 10 annexe en suite (3 fmly) (5 GF) S £65–£85; D £100–£140✶ **Facilities** TVB tea/coffee Direct dial from bedrooms Cen ht Dinner Last d 9.30pm Wi-fi available Caravan site with play area, Deer stalking courses **Conf** Max 150 Thtr 100 Class 20 Board 30 Del from £110 ✶ **Parking** 60 **Notes** LB Closed Xmas Civ Wed 160

HALLATON   MAP 11 SP79

★★★★ INN
The Bewicke Arms

1 Eastgate LE16 8UB
☎ 01858 555784
e–mail: bewickearms@aol.com

dir: *2m S of A47, in village centre*

This 400-year-old thatched country inn offers interesting food in the restaurant and tea room, the main inn provides a traditional bar featuring open fires and cask ales. Smartly appointed accommodation is provided in the nicely converted stable block, across the pub courtyard; the freshly cooked breakfasts are served within the adjacent tea room.

Rooms 3 annexe en suite (2 GF) S £35–£40; D £45–£55✶ **Facilities** TVB tea/coffee Cen ht Dinner Last d 9pm **Parking** 20 **Notes** ⊗ No coaches

---

HUSBANDS BOSWORTH   MAP 11 SP68

★★★★ FARM HOUSE
Croft Farm B&B (SP634860)

Leicester Rd LE17 6NW
☎ 01858 880679 Mrs Smith
e–mail: janesmith06@aol.com
web: www.croftfarm.org.uk

dir: *Take A5199 from Husbands Bosworth towards Leicester, Croft Farm 0.25m on left*

This very spacious and delightfully furnished house stands on the edge of the village in very well cared for grounds. Bedrooms are thoughtfully equipped and there is a very comfortable guests' lounge. Expect a substantial breakfast together with friendly and attentive service.

Rooms 3 en suite (2 fmly) **Facilities** TVB tea/coffee Cen ht TVL Wi-fi available **Parking** 15 **Notes** ⊗ 350 acres Sheep arable beef mixed ⊜

KEGWORTH   MAP 11 SK42

See East Midlands Airport

KNIPTON   MAP 11 SK83

★★★★ ⊛ GUEST ACCOMMODATION
The Manners Arms

Croxton Rd NG32 1RH
☎ 01476 879222 📠 01476 879228
e–mail: info@mannersarms.com
web: www.mannersarms.com

dir: *Off A607 into Knipton*

Part of the Rutland Estate and built as a hunting lodge for the 6th Duke, the Manners Arms has been renovated to provide thoughtfully furnished bedrooms designed by the present Duchess. Public areas include the intimate themed Beater's Bar and attractive Red Coats Restaurant, popular for imaginative dining.

Rooms 10 en suite (1 fmly) S £55–£65; D £80–£120✶ **Facilities** TVB tea/coffee Direct dial from bedrooms Cen ht TVL Dinner Last d 8.45pm, 7.45pm Sun Wi-fi available **Conf** Max 50 Thtr 50 Class 25 Board 20 Del from £110 ✶ **Parking** 60 **Notes** Civ Wed 50

See advertisement under Preliminary Section

LEICESTER — MAP 11 SK50

★★★ GUEST ACCOMMODATION
Stoney Croft

5–7 Elmfield Av, Off London Rd LE2 1RB
☎ 0116 270 7605 📧 0116 270 6067
e–mail: reception@stoneycrofthotel.co.uk
web: www.stoneycrofthotel.co.uk

dir: *Near city centre on A6 to Market Harborough*

Stoney Croft provides comfortable accommodation and helpful service. Public rooms include a foyer-lounge area, breakfast room and conference facilities. There is also a large restaurant-bar where a good selection of freshly cooked dishes is available. The modern bedrooms come with desks.

Rooms 41 en suite (4 fmly) (6 GF) **Facilities** TVB tea/coffee Direct dial from bedrooms Cen ht TVL Dinner Last d 9.30pm Pool Table **Conf** Max 150 Thtr 150 Class 20 Board 30 **Parking** 30

★★★ 🅰 GUEST HOUSE
Abinger Guest House

175 Hinckley Rd LE3 0TF
☎ 0116 255 4674 📧 0116 271 9833
e–mail: abinger@btinternet.com
web: www.leicesterguest.co.uk

dir: *0.5m W of city centre, off A47 or A5460*

Rooms 8 rms (2 fmly) (2 GF) S £33–£38; D £44–£50✳ **Facilities** FTV TVB tea/coffee Cen ht Wi-fi available **Notes** ⊗ No coaches Closed Xmas

LONG CLAWSON — MAP 11 SK72

★★★★ INN
The Crown & Plough

East End LE14 4NG
☎ 01664 822322
e–mail: crownandplough@btconnect.com

dir: *3m off A606 from Melton Mowbray-Nottingham*

This country pub sits in the heart of the village of Long Clawson, within the Vale of Belvoir. The rustic inn offers enjoyable food and drink, in a relaxed atmosphere. The annexe accommodation consists of individually appointed bedrooms, mostly of a generous size, that are complemented by stylish bathrooms. Breakfast is self-service and dinner is available in the restaurant.

Rooms 5 en suite (5 fmly) (3 GF) **Facilities** tea/coffee Cen ht Dinner Last d 9pm Golf 18 **Conf** Max 20 Class 20 Board 20 **Parking** 6

LOUGHBOROUGH — MAP 11 SK51

★★★ INN
The Falcon Inn

64 Main St, Long Whatton LE12 5DG
☎ 01509 842416 📧 01509 646802
e–mail: enquiries@thefalconinnlongwhatton.com

This late 18th century traditional country pub sits within the quiet village of Long Whatton. Within the pub the relaxed and friendly atmosphere is complemented by a good choice of freshly made meals, real ales and efficient service. Smartly appointed bedrooms are housed in a converted former school house and stable block at the rear of the main inn. Ample private parking is provided.

Rooms 11 annexe en suite (5 GF) **Facilities** FTV TVB tea/coffee Cen ht Dinner Last d 8.45pm Wi-fi available petanque pitch **Conf** Max 30 Thtr 20 Class 20 Board 20 **Parking** 46 **Notes** ⊗

MARKET BOSWORTH — MAP 11 SK40

★★★ GUEST ACCOMMODATION
Softleys

2 Market Place CV13 0LE
☎ 01455 290464
e–mail: softleysrestaurant@tiscali.co.uk

dir: *On B585 in Market Place*

Softleys is a Grade II listed building dating back to 1794. The bedrooms are en suite set on the third floor offering picturesque views over Market Bosworth. Quality food is served using locally sourced ingredients.

Rooms 3 en suite S £65; D £75✳ **Facilities** TVB tea/coffee Direct dial from bedrooms Cen ht Dinner Last d 9.30pm Wi-fi available **Conf** Max 24 Thtr 24 Class 24 Board 24 **Notes** RS Sun eve & Mon

MARKET HARBOROUGH — MAP 11 SP78

See also Medbourne

★★★★ 🅰 BED & BREAKFAST
Hunters Lodge

By Foxton Locks, Gumley LE16 7RT
☎ 0116 279 3744 📧 0116 279 3855
e–mail: info@hunterslodgefoxton.co.uk

dir: *M1 junct 20, A4304 for Market Harborough, after 8m in Lubenham 2nd left signed Foxton. Next left signed Laughton, pass village hall, 1.5m over hump backed bridge. Next right Gumley in 200yds right, signed Foxton*

Rooms 2 en suite (1 fmly) (2 GF) S £38–£40; D £60✳ **Facilities** STV TVB tea/coffee Cen ht TVL Wi-fi available **Parking** 5

MEDBOURNE   MAP 11 SP89

★★★★ ◉◉ RESTAURANT WITH ROOMS
The Horse & Trumpet
Old Green LE16 8DX
☎ 01858 565000 📄 01858 565551
e–mail: info@horseandtrumpet.com

dir: *In village centre, opposite church*

Tucked away behind the village bowling green, this carefully restored and re-thatched former farmhouse and pub now offers fine dining and quality accommodation. The golden stone three-storey building hosts three dining rooms, in which chef Gary Maganani and his team provides imaginative food from high quality produce; service is both professional and friendly. The smartly appointed bedrooms are located to the rear of the building in a barn conversion; attractively furnished and thoughtfully equipped for modern travellers.

Rooms 4 annexe en suite (2 GF) S £75; D £75✱ **Facilities** TVB tea/coffee Direct dial from bedrooms Cen ht Dinner Last d 9.30pm **Conf** Max 25 **Notes** ⊗ No children 5yrs RS Sun eve & Mon

★★★★ FARM HOUSE
Medbourne Grange (SP815945)
LE16 8EF
☎ 01858 565249 & 07730 956116 📄 01858 565257
Mrs S Beaty

dir: *2m NE of Medbourne. Between Market Harborough & Uppingham off B664*

This 150-year-old working farm has unrivalled views of the Welland Valley and is well situated for Rutland Water, Uppingham or Market Harborough. Mrs Beaty is a natural host, ensuring that guests receive a warm welcome and friendly service. Individually furnished bedrooms are complemented by comfortable day rooms, and freshly prepared breakfasts are served in the smart dining room.

Rooms 3 en suite **Facilities** TVB tea/coffee Cen ht TVL ⤳ **Parking** 6 **Notes** ⊗ 500 acres arable 🐾

Ⓤ
The Nevill Arms
12 Waterfall Way LE16 8EE
☎ 01858 565288 📄 01858 565509
e–mail: info@thenevillarms.net
web: www.thenevillarms.net

dir: *From Uppingham follow B664 SW for 7m. From Market Harborough follow B664 NE for 5m.*

At the time of going to press the rating for this establishment had not been confirmed. Please check the AA website www.theAA.com for up-to-date information.

Rooms 11 en suite (1 fmly) S £69; D £89✱ **Facilities** FTV TVB tea/coffee Cen ht Dinner Last d 9.30pm Wi-fi available **Conf** Max 30 Thtr 18 Class 30 **Parking** 25 **Notes** ⊗

MELTON MOWBRAY   MAP 11 SK71

★★★★ GUEST ACCOMMODATION
Bryn Barn
38 High St, Waltham-on-the-Wolds LE14 4AH
☎ 01664 464783 & 07791 215614
e–mail: glenarowlands@onetel.com
web: www.brynbarn.co.uk

dir: *4.5m NE of Melton. Off A607 in Waltham village centre*

A warm welcome awaits at this attractive, peacefully located cottage within easy reach of Melton Mowbray, Grantham, Rutland Water and Belvoir Castle. Bedrooms are smartly appointed and comfortably furnished, while public rooms include an inviting lounge overlooking a wonderful courtyard garden. Meals are available at one of the nearby village pubs.

Rooms 4 rms (3 en suite) (1 pri facs) (2 fmly) (1 GF) S £30–£40; D £50–£60 **Facilities** FTV TVB tea/coffee Cen ht TVL Wi-fi available **Parking** 4 **Notes** LB Closed 21 Dec–4 Jan RS wknds

★★★ Ⓐ FARM HOUSE
Dairy Farm (SK744141)
8 Burrough End, Great Dalby LE14 2EW
☎ 01664 562783 Mrs L Parker
e–mail: dairyfarm@tesco.net

dir: *3m S of Melton Mowbray on B6407. 1st left after Chapel, Dairy Farm on right*

Rooms 3 rms (2 en suite) (1 pri facs) **Facilities** TVB tea/coffee Cen ht TVL **Parking** 5 **Notes** 300 acres beef dairy sheep 🐾

★★ INN
Noels Arms

31 Burton St LE13 1AE

☎ 01664 562363

dir: *On A606 S of town centre at junct Mill St*

The traditional inn lies close to the town centre. The bar is the focal point of the inn, where breakfast is served and staff and locals generate a relaxed and friendly atmosphere. Bedrooms come in a variety of co-ordinated styles and sizes, each furnished in pine.

Rooms 6 rms (4 en suite) (2 fmly) S fr £26; D fr £50✱ **Facilities** TVB tea/coffee Cen ht Pool Table **Notes** ⊛

MOUNTSORREL   MAP 11 SK51

★★★★ INN
The Swan Inn

10 Loughborough Rd LE12 7AT

☎ 0116 230 2340 📠 0116 237 6115

e-mail: office@swaninn.eu

web: www.the-swan-inn.eu

dir: *In village centre*

This traditional 17th-century inn is in the centre of the village and offers well produced meals in the bar, together with a wide range of real ales. The accommodation consists of a luxury suite which includes a double bedroom, a lounge, a large bathroom and an office. Continental breakfast is available in the suite.

Rooms 1 en suite S £70–£98; D £70–£98✱ **Facilities** FTV TVB tea/coffee Direct dial from bedrooms Cen ht TVL Dinner Last d 9pm Wi-fi available **Parking** 12 **Notes** No coaches

---

NARBOROUGH   MAP 11 SP59

★★★★ GUEST HOUSE
Fossebrook

Coventry Rd, Croft LE9 3GP

☎ 01455 283517 📠 01455 283517

dir: *0.6m SE of village centre on B4114*

This friendly guest house stands in a quiet rural location with good access to major roads. Bedrooms are spacious, very comfortable and offer an excellent range of facilities including videos in all rooms. Breakfast is served in the bright dining room, which overlooks pleasant gardens and grounds.

Rooms 4 en suite (4 GF) S fr £40; D fr £40✱ **Facilities** TVB tea/coffee Cen ht **Parking** 16 **Notes** ⊛ No coaches Closed 24 Dec–2 Jan

---

ORTON-ON-THE-HILL   MAP 10 SK30

★★★ FARM HOUSE
Hall Farm Accommodation *(SK304038)*

Hall Farm CV9 3NG

☎ 01827 881041 & 07967 636718 Mrs Elaine Smith

e-mail: epenhaulsmith@aol.com

dir: *M42 junct 11, A444 S to Nuneaton. Right at 1st sign to Orton-on-the-Hill, left at road end, right immediately past church*

Hall Farm dates back to the 15th century and is set in beautiful countryside on the Leicestershire/Warwickshire border. Luxury serviced accommodation with modern accessories provide extra special home-from-home comfort.

Rooms 1 annexe en suite S fr £70; D fr £90 **Facilities** tea/coffee Cen ht Wi-fi available **Parking** 10 **Notes** ⊗ 10 acres non-working ⊛

REDMILE   MAP 11 SK73

⊛ [U]
The Peacock Inn

Main St NG13 0GA

☎ 01949 842554

e-mail: reservations@thepeacockinnredmile.co.uk

dir: *Off A52 between Bingham & Bottesford, follow signs for Belvoir Castle, then Redmile*

At the time of going to press the rating for this establishment had not been confirmed. Please check the AA website www.theAA.com for up-to-date information.

Rooms 10 en suite (1 fmly) S £55–£65; D £74.95–£99.95✱ **Facilities** TVB tea/coffee Direct dial from bedrooms Cen ht Dinner Last d 9pm **Conf** Max 50 Thtr 40 Class 50 Board 40 Del from £124.95 ✱ **Parking** 40 **Notes** LB

ENGLAND

SHEPSHED   MAP 11 SK41

Premier Collection

★★★★★ GUEST ACCOMMODATION
The Grange Courtyard
Forest St LE12 9DA
☎ 01509 600189 📄 01509 603834
e–mail: linda.lawrence@thegrangecourtyard.co.uk
web: www.thegrangecourtyard.co.uk

dir: *M1 junct 23, right at lights onto Leicester road, over mini-rdbt onto Forest St*

Dating from 18th century, this Grade II listed building, set in attractive mature gardens and grounds, with the added bonus of secure private parking. The accommodation is housed in individually appointed cottage bedrooms, each immaculately presented and extensively equipped. Guests also have access to fully equipped kitchens. Attentive personal service from the charming proprietor and her helpful team makes a stay here a home-from-home experience.

Rooms 20 en suite (1 fmly) (12 GF) **Facilities** TVB tea/coffee Direct dial from bedrooms Cen ht **Conf** Max 12 Class 12 Board 12 **Parking** 15 **Notes** No children 8yrs RS Xmas & Etr

---

WIGSTON   MAP 11 SP69

[U]
Plough Inn
44 Bushloe Rd LE18 2BA
☎ 0116 281 0078 📄 0116 210 0674
e–mail: theploughwigston@ntlworld.com

dir: *Just off A599 (old A50), next to All Saints church*

At the time of going to press the rating for this establishment had not been confirmed. Please check the AA website www.theAA.com for up-to-date information.

Rooms 7 annexe en suite (1 fmly) (7 GF) **Facilities** TVB tea/coffee Cen ht Dinner Last d 9pm **Parking** 32 **Notes** ⊗

WOODHOUSE EAVES   MAP 11 SK51

★★★ ⇔ INN
The Wheatsheaf Inn
90 Brand Hill LE12 8SS
☎ 01509 890320
e–mail: richard@wheatsheafinn.net
web: www.wheatsheafinn.net

Originally built around 1800 by the local miners of Swithland slate mines, this charming inn offers a friendly service, good food and modern accommodation in the adjacent self-contained cottage. The first floor restaurant proves very popular with locals, offering Specials and Bistro menus that include traditional English fayre and fresh fish features on the blackboard specials.

Rooms 3 annexe en suite (1 GF) S £60; D £80✳ **Facilities** FTV TVB tea/coffee Cen ht TVL Dinner Last d 9.30pm Wi-fi available **Conf** Thtr 18 Class 12 Board 14 **Parking** 70 **Notes** No coaches

LINCOLNSHIRE

BOSTON   MAP 12 TF34

★★★★ GUEST ACCOMMODATION
Palethorpe House
138 Spilsby Rd PE21 9PE
☎ 01205 359000 & 07888 758608 📄 01205 359000

dir: *0.5m from town centre on left, 200yds from Pilgrim Hospital*

Friendly and welcoming, this Grade II listed Victorian villa, built by John Palethorpe in 1853, stands in a conservation area within easy walking distance of the town centre. The house is appointed to a very good standard, offering carefully furnished day rooms that include a lounge with satellite television and a pleasant breakfast room. A continental breakfast only is available during the week, with cooked options at the weekend. Bedrooms are thoughtfully equipped, have quality beds and well-appointed bathrooms.

Rooms 2 en suite (2 fmly) **Facilities** STV TVB tea/coffee Cen ht TVL **Parking** 3 **Notes** ⊗ ⊜

★★★★ INN
The Red Lion
Revesby PE22 7NU
☎ 01507 568665
e–mail: richardsandy@btconnect.com

dir: *At junct of B1183 and A155 between Boston and Horncastle*
Built in the 1840s as a coaching inn, this country pub sits on the edge of the Lincolnshire Wolds, which offers many fine walks and historical sites. A warm and welcoming environment, alongside hearty home cooked fare, ensures that The Red Lion is equally popular with guests and locals alike. Modern bedrooms are of good comfortable proportions and well appointed; broadband internet is also available. Please note that 'live music' is played on Saturday evenings.

Rooms 4 en suite S fr £40; D fr £60✳ **Facilities** TVB tea/coffee Cen ht Dinner Last d 8.30pm Pool Table **Parking** 50 **Notes** ⊗ No children 10yrs

---

BRIGG   MAP 17 TA00

★★★ INN
The Queens Head
Station Rd, North Kelsey Moor LN7 6HD
☎ 01652 678055 ▤ 01652 678954
e–mail: info@queens-head.biz
web: www.queens-head.biz

dir: *6m SE of Brigg. Off B1434 to North Kelsey Moor*

A small and friendly family-run inn with purpose-built en suite bedrooms. The rear car park overlooks a small garden. A wide range of ales and wines is available in the locals' bar, and an extensive menu can be enjoyed either in the bar or popular restaurant.

Rooms 5 en suite (5 GF) **Facilities** TVB tea/coffee Cen ht Dinner Last d 9pm **Conf** Max 50 Thtr 50 Class 50 Board 50 **Parking** 50 **Notes** ⊗

CLEETHORPES   MAP 17 TA30

★★★★ GUEST ACCOMMODATION
Adelaide
41 Isaac's Hill DN35 8JT
☎ 01472 693594 ▤ 01472 329717
e–mail: adelaide.hotel@ntlworld.com

dir: *500yds W of seafront. Junct A180 & A46 onto A1098 Isaac's Hill, on right at bottom of hill*

This beautifully presented house offers well-equipped bedrooms and comfortable public rooms, and hospitality is a major strength. Good home cooking is provided and there is a small lounge with a bar. Secure parking is available.

Rooms 5 rms (3 en suite) (1 fmly) **Facilities** STV TVB tea/coffee Cen ht TVL Dinner Last d noon **Notes** ⊗ No children 4yrs

★★★★ GUEST ACCOMMODATION
The Comat
26 Yarra Rd DN35 8LS
☎ 01472 694791 & 591861 ▤ 01472 694791
e–mail: comat-hotel@ntlworld.com
web: www.comat-hotel.co.uk

dir: *Off A1098 Alexandra Rd, on left of the library*

A short walk from the shops and seafront, the welcoming Comat offers cosy, well-equipped bedrooms, one with a four-poster bed. Tasty English breakfasts are served in the bright dining room, and a quiet sitting room and bar overlook the colourful flower terrace.

Rooms 6 en suite (1 fmly) (2 GF) S £40–£50; D £60–£73✳ **Facilities** TVB tea/coffee Cen ht TVL Wi-fi available **Notes LB** ⊗ No children 3yrs

★★★★ GUEST ACCOMMODATION
Sherwood Guest House
15 Kingsway DN35 8QU
☎ 01472 692020 ▤ 01472 239177
e–mail: sherwood.guesthouse@ntlworld.com

dir: *On A1098 seafront road*

This non-smoking Victorian house stands on the seafront overlooking the promenade and the beach, and is a short walk the town centre. Bedrooms are immaculate and the hearty breakfast comes with attentive service. There is a lounge, and limited off-road parking is available.

Rooms 6 rms (3 en suite) **Facilities** TVB tea/coffee Cen ht Wi-fi available **Parking** 2 **Notes** ⊗ No children

CLEETHORPES CONTINUED

★★★★ GUEST HOUSE
Tudor Terrace
11 Bradford Av DN35 0BB
☎ 01472 600800 📠 01472 501395
e–mail: tudor.terrace@ntlworld.com
dir: *Off seafront onto Bradford Av*
This guest house offers attractive bedrooms that are thoughtfully designed and furnished to a high standard. Guests can relax in the lounge, or outside on the patio in the well-maintained garden. Very caring and friendly service is provided, and the house is non-smoking except in the garden. Mobility scooter rental is available.
Rooms 6 en suite (1 GF) **Facilities** TVB tea/coffee Cen ht TVL Dinner Last d 2pm **Parking** 3 **Notes** No children No coaches

★★★ GUEST ACCOMMODATION
Alpine House
55 Clee Rd DN35 8AD
☎ 01472 690804
e–mail: nw.sanderson@ntlworld.com
dir: *On A46 before junct A180 & A1098 Isaac's Hill rdbt*
Carefully run by the resident owners, and convenient for the town centre and attractions, this friendly guest house offers compact, well-equipped bedrooms and a comfortable lounge.
Rooms 5 rms (2 fmly) **Facilities** TVB tea/coffee Cen ht TVL **Parking** 3 **Notes** ⊗ No children 2yrs 🐾

★★★ GUEST ACCOMMODATION
Brier Park Guest House
27 Clee Rd DN35 8AD
☎ 01472 605591
e–mail: graham.sherwood2@ntlworld.com
dir: *Left at bottom of Isaac's Hill, 150yds on left*
A private house personally managed by the owner offering a friendly atmosphere and comfortable compact bedrooms that are brightly decorated. Breakfast is freshly cooked to order and convenient parking in front is a bonus.
Rooms 6 rms (3 en suite) (1 fmly) (2 GF) **Facilities** TVB tea/coffee Cen ht TVL Wi-fi available **Parking** 2 **Notes** ⊗ No children 5yrs 🐾

★★★ GUEST ACCOMMODATION
Holmhirst
3 Alexandra Rd DN35 8LQ
☎ 01472 692656 📠 01472 692656
Overlooking the sea and the pier, this Victorian terrace house offers comfortable well-equipped bedrooms, many with showers en suite. Tasty English breakfasts and a range of lunchtime and evening meals are available. There is a well-stocked bar, and the resident owners are fluent in several languages.
Rooms 8 rms (5 en suite) **Facilities** TV7B tea/coffee Cen ht TVL Dinner Last d 8pm **Notes** ⊗ No children 4yrs

★★★ 🅰 GUEST ACCOMMODATION
Ginnies
27 Queens Pde DN35 0DF
☎ 01472 694997 📠 01472 593153
e–mail: enquiries@ginnies.co.uk
dir: *On A1098 Queens Parade, off seafront Kingsway*
Rooms 7 rms (5 en suite) (2 pri facs) (3 fmly) (1 GF) S £25–£35; D £40–£60✱ **Facilities** FTV TVB tea/coffee Cen ht TVL Wi-fi available **Parking** 4 **Notes** LB ⊗ RS 24 Dec–2 Jan

★★ GUEST HOUSE
Mallow View
9–11 Albert Rd DN35 8LX
☎ 01472 691297
e–mail: info@mallowviewhotel.co.uk
dir: *Off seafront A1098 Alexandra Rd onto Albert Rd*
Located within a short walk from the seafront, this large terrace house offers comfortable modern bedrooms. A small number of the rooms benefit from en suites, while others share well equipped bath/shower rooms. Breakfast is served in the pleasant dining room and guests also have use of a comfortable lounge and bar area.
Rooms 13 rms (3 en suite) (2 fmly) **Facilities** TVB tea/coffee Cen ht TVL Video library **Notes** ⊗

COLSTERWORTH   MAP 11 SK92

★★★★ BED & BREAKFAST
Stone Cottage
24 Bourne Rd NG33 5JE
☎ 01476 860620 📠 01476 860620
e–mail: jan003@hotmail.co.uk
dir: *From A1 into Colsterworth, 0.25m onto Bourne Rd, Stone Cottage on left*
Located on the edge of this vibrant rural community and close to major road links, this new property provides two modern bedrooms, furnished in minimalist style and equipped with a range of both practical and thoughtful extras. Smart efficient en-suite bathrooms are an additional benefit and comprehensive breakfasts, utilising local produce are taken in an attractive dining room.
Rooms 2 en suite (1 fmly) S £35–£40; D £60–£70✱ **Facilities** TVB tea/coffee Cen ht **Parking** 6 **Notes** ⊗ 🐾

★★★★ GUEST ACCOMMODATION
White Lion Lodge
12 High St NG33 5NF
☎ 01476 860120 📠 01476 860120
e–mail: info@whitelionlodge.co.uk
dir: *A1 Colsterworth Island turn in Colsterworth village. White Lion Lodge is opposite Pub in centre of village*
The White Lion Lodge is on the high street, almost opposite its sister property, the White Lion pub, where guests can take refreshments and

CONTINUED

evening meals in a comfortable environment. Parking is available on pub forecourt. The Lodge's lounge is stylish and comfortable and the breakfast room is the setting for continental breakfasts served at one large shared table. Bedrooms are similarly contemporary in style with en suite shower rooms.

Rooms 6 rms (3 en suite) (1 fmly) (1 GF) **Facilities** STV FTV TV5B tea/coffee Cen ht TVL Dinner Last d 8.30pm Wi-fi available Pool Table **Conf** Max 60 Class 60 **Parking** 30 **Notes** ⊗

CORBY GLEN   MAP 11 TF02

★★★★ ⊜ INN
The Coachman Inn
2 Bourne Rd NG33 4NS
☎ 01476 550316
e–mail: suzi.pearson@virgin.net

dir: *On A151 in village*

An impressive village inn offering smart en suite bedrooms, some with direct external access. There is a popular restaurant and a wide selection of real ales and wines is available in the friendly bar.

Rooms 2 en suite 3 annexe en suite (2 fmly) (3 GF) **Facilities** TVB tea/coffee Cen ht Dinner Last d 9pm **Parking** 40

DONINGTON ON BAIN   MAP 17 TF28

★★★ INN
The Black Horse Inn
Main Rd LN11 9TJ
☎ 01507 343640 📠 01507 343640
e–mail: barrett@blackhorse1125.freeserve.co.uk

dir: *In village centre*

An ideal touring base for the Viking Way, nearby Cadwell Park, Market Rasen or the market town of Louth. A wide range of food and beers is available in this popular inn, and the spacious bedrooms are comfortable and all en suite.

Rooms 8 en suite (4 GF) **Facilities** TVB tea/coffee Cen ht Dinner Last d 9pm Pool Table **Parking** 60

EPWORTH   MAP 17 SE70

★★★★ GUEST ACCOMMODATION
Wesley Guest House
16 Queen St DN9 1HG
☎ 01427 874512 📠 01427 874592
e–mail: enquiries@wesleyguesthouse.com
web: www.wesleyguesthouse.com

dir: *In town centre, 200yds off Market Place*

Situated near the Market Cross and close to The Old Rectory, this detached guest house offers a friendly welcome, modern, non-smoking en suite rooms, and secure off-road parking. Finningley airport is close by.

Rooms 4 en suite 2 annexe en suite (1 fmly) (1 GF) S £50–£60; D £80–£90 **Facilities** FTV TVB tea/coffee Cen ht Wi-fi available **Parking** 5 **Notes** LB ⊗

FILLINGHAM   MAP 17 SK98

★★★★ BED & BREAKFAST
Church Farm B & B
High St DN21 5BS
☎ 01427 668279
e–mail: enquiries@churchfarm-fillingham.co.uk
web: www.churchfarm-fillingham.co.uk

dir: *Off B1398 into village, 1st house on right*

A traditional stone farmhouse, close to antiques centres and the base of the Red Arrows. Warm hospitality and very comfortable bedrooms with modern décor provide a good touring base.

Rooms 3 rms (1 en suite) S £38; D £55✳ **Facilities** tea/coffee Cen ht TVL **Parking** 6 **Notes** ⊗ No children 5yrs Closed 24 Dec–1 Jan ◉

GAINSBOROUGH   MAP 17 SK88

See also Marton

★★★★ GUEST HOUSE
Eastbourne House
81 Trinity St DN21 1JF
☎ 01427 679511 📠 01427 679511
e–mail: info@eastbournehouse.co.uk

dir: *In town centre. Off A631 onto A159 Trinity St*

Located in a residential area west of the town centre, this impressive Victorian house has been restored to provide high standards of comfort and facilities. Bedrooms are thoughtfully furnished and the comprehensive breakfast uses quality local produce.

Rooms 5 rms (3 en suite) (2 pri facs) (1 fmly) S £35; D £50–£70✳ **Facilities** FTV TVB tea/coffee Cen ht Wi-fi available **Parking** 1 **Notes** ⊗ No coaches

---

GRANTHAM   MAP 11 SK93

Premier Collection

★★★★★ ⊜ BED & BREAKFAST
La Casita
Frith House, Main St NG32 3BH
☎ 01400 250302 & 07836 695282 📠 01400 250302
e–mail: jackiegonzalez@btinternet.com
web: www.lacasitabandb.co.uk

(For full entry see Normanton)

★★★★ GUEST HOUSE
Beechleigh Guest House
55 North Pde NG31 8AT
☎ 01476 572213 📠 01476 566058
e–mail: info@beechleigh.co.uk
web: www.beechleigh.co.uk
dir: *0.5m N of town centre. A52 onto B1174 by Asda, 200yds on left*

This Edwardian house sits just a short walk from the town centre on the northern approach. Offering comfortably appointed bedrooms that are equipped with many thoughtful extras (Wi-fi access provided). Freshly cooked breakfasts are taken in the pleasant dining room, and off-road parking is available.
Rooms 3 rms (1 fmly) **Facilities** STV TVB tea/coffee Cen ht Dinner Last d noon **Parking** 5 **Notes** No children 5yrs No coaches

★★★★ GUEST ACCOMMODATION
Belvoir Vale Cottage
Stenwith, Woolsthorpe-By-Belvoir NG32 2HE
☎ 01949 842434
e–mail: reservations@belvoirvale-cottage.co.uk
web: www.belvoirvale-cottage.co.uk

dir: *A1/A52 junct towards Nottingham, at Sedgebrook S to Stenwith & Woolsthorpe for 1.5m, immediately past T-junct*
This pair of early Victorian cottages is located on the edge of the beautiful Vale of Belvoir with views of the castle. Fully modernised and extended, the cottages retain their character and offer well-appointed accommodation, with crisp cotton sheets, powerful showers and freshly cooked and tasty breakfasts.
Rooms 3 en suite (1 GF) S £45–£55; D £65–£80✱ **Facilities** TVB tea/coffee Cen ht TVL Dinner Wi-fi available **Parking** 6 **Notes** LB ⊛ No children 12yrs ⊜

★★★★ INN
The Welby Arms
The Green, Allington NG32 2EA
☎ 01400 281361 📠 01400 281361

dir: *4m NW of Grantham. Off A52 into Allington village*
Three purpose built en suites in a former byre behind a popular village inn that serves a wide range of real ales and an extensive menu that is

CONTINUED

---

very popular with the locals. Just off the busy A1, handy for Grantham, but deep in the countryside.
Rooms 3 annexe en suite (3 GF) **Facilities** TVB tea/coffee Cen ht Dinner Last d 9.30pm **Parking** 35 **Notes** ⊛ No coaches

---

GRASBY   MAP 17 TA00

★★★★ 🅐 BED & BREAKFAST
Little Hen Bed & Breakfast
Brigg Rd DN38 6AQ
☎ 01652 629005
e–mail: polly@littlehen.co.uk
web: www.littlehen.co.uk

dir: *Exit M180 junct 5. A1084 to Grasby, on right next to Pub*
Rooms 2 en suite (1 GF) S £39.99; D £59.50 **Facilities** TVB tea/coffee Cen ht TVL Dinner Last d 7pm **Parking** 4 **Notes** No children ⊛

HEMSWELL   MAP 17 SK99

Premier Collection

★★★★★ 🍴 GUEST ACCOMMODATION
Hemswell Court
Lancaster Green, Hemswell Cliff DN21 5TQ
☎ 01427 668508 📠 01427 667335
e–mail: function@hemswellcourt.com

dir: *1.5m SE of Hemswell on A631 in Hemswell Cliff*
Originally an officers' mess, Hemswell Court is now a venue for conferences, weddings or private gatherings. The modern bedrooms and many suites are ideal for families or groups of friends, and all rooms are well equipped. The lounges and dining rooms are enhanced by many antique pieces.
Rooms 23 en suite (2 fmly) (4 GF) **Facilities** TV4B tea/coffee Cen ht TVL Dinner Last d 48hrs before Wi-fi available ⊜ ⍩ **Conf** Max 200 Thtr 200 Class 150 Board 150 **Parking** 150 **Notes** ⊛ Closed Xmas & New Year Civ Wed 200

HOLBEACH   MAP 12 TF32

★★★★ GUEST ACCOMMODATION
Elloe Lodge
37 Barrington Gate PE12 7LB
☎ 01406 423207 📠 01406 423207
e–mail: norman.vasey@btinternet.com
web: www.elloelodge.co.uk

dir: *From town centre onto Church St, 2nd left, 1st house on right*
This delightful house is peacefully situated in extensive well-tended grounds and gardens, just a short walk from the town centre. Bedrooms are well appointed and comfortably furnished. Spacious public areas include an inviting lounge and an attractive dining room, where hearty breakfasts are served at individual tables.
Rooms 4 en suite (2 fmly) S £35; D £59✱ **Facilities** tea/coffee Cen ht TVL **Parking** 10 **Notes** LB ⊛

★★★★ GUEST HOUSE
The Mansion House
45 High St PE12 7DY
☎ 01406 426919 & 425270 📠 01406 426848
e–mail: rickerby3@aol.com
web: www.holbeachhotels.com

dir: *A17 into Holbeach, at rdbt turn left along High St, on left past church opposite health food shop*

Expect a warm welcome at this delightful period property which dates back to the 16th century. This historic building has been sympathetically restored and retains much of its original character; public rooms include a choice of dining rooms, a cosy lounge and a smart bar. The bedrooms have co-ordinated soft furnishings, stripped pine furniture and modern facilities.

Rooms 8 en suite 1 annexe en suite (3 fmly) (1 GF) S £65–£77.50; D £75–£90✶ **Facilities** FTV TVB tea/coffee Licensed Cen ht TVL Dinner Last d 9pm Wi-fi available **Conf** Max 20 Thtr 20 Class 16 Board 16 **Parking** 5 **Notes LB** No coaches RS Xmas-New Year

---

HORNCASTLE   MAP 17 TF26

★★★★ FARM HOUSE
Greenfield Farm *(TF175745)*
Mill Ln/Cow Ln, Minting LN9 5PJ
☎ 01507 578457 & 07768 368829 📠 01507 578457
Mrs J Bankes Price
e–mail: greenfieldfarm@farming.co.uk

dir: *A158 NW from Horncastle. 5m left at The New Midge pub, farm 1m on right*

Located on the outskirts of Minting village, this impressive red-brick farmhouse has fine views over its gardens across the Lincolnshire countryside. The spacious house offers comfortable en suite bedrooms and a cosy lounge.

Rooms 3 en suite D £54–£60✶ **Facilities** TVB tea/coffee Cen ht TVL Wi-fi available **Parking** 12 **Notes LB** ⊗ No children 10yrs 387 acres arable Closed Xmas & New Year 🐾

HOUGH-ON-THE-HILL   MAP 11 SK94

Premier Collection

★★★★★ ⊛ INN
The Brownlow Arms
High Rd NG32 2AZ
☎ 01400 250234 📠 01400 271193
e–mail: paulandlorraine@thebrownlowarms.com
web: www.thebrownlowarms.com

This beautiful 16th-century property enjoys a peaceful location in the picturesque village, located between Newark and Grantham. Tastefully appointed and spacious public areas have many original features and include a choice of luxurious lounges and an elegant restaurant offering imaginative cuisine. The bedrooms are stylish, comfortable and particularly well equipped.

Rooms 4 en suite S £65–£70; D £96–£110 **Facilities** TVB tea/coffee Direct dial from bedrooms Dinner Last d 9.30pm **Parking** 20 **Notes** ⊗ No children 14yrs No coaches Closed 25–27 Dec & 31 Dec–20 Jan

---

LINCOLN   MAP 17 SK97

See also Horncastle, Marton & Swinderby

Premier Collection

★★★★★ GUEST ACCOMMODATION
Bailhouse & Mews
34 Bailgate LN1 3AP
☎ 01522 520883 & 07976 112233 📠 01522 521829
e–mail: info@bailhouse.co.uk

dir: *100yds N of cathedral*

This renovated 18th-century building in the cathedral quarter offers high levels of modern comfort. One room has an exposed cruck beam of a surviving 14th-century hall. A private car park surrounds an old chapel, and customer care is of the highest standard.

Rooms 10 en suite (1 fmly) (2 GF) **Facilities** TVB tea/coffee Direct dial from bedrooms Cen ht TVL Dinner Last d 9pm Wi-fi available ⌁ In Room Spa and Beauty Treatments **Conf** Max 20 Board 20 **Parking** 16 **Notes** ⊗

Premier Collection

★★★★★ GUEST ACCOMMODATION
Charlotte House
The Lawn, Union Rd LN1 3BJ
☎ 01522 541000 📠 08718 724396
e–mail: info@charlottehouselincoln.com

Expect a warm welcome at this 1930s Art Deco building which is situated in the cathedral quarter opposite Lincoln Castle. The property has been completely refurbished to a very high standard by the current owner, and the individually decorated bedrooms are tastefully appointed and thoughtfully equipped. Public areas include an impressive south facing lounge with plush sofas, a large period bar and a brasserie style dining room.

Rooms 14 en suite D £145–£245✶ (room only) **Facilities** FTV TVB Direct dial from bedrooms cen ht TVL Dinner Last d 10pm Wi-fi available **Conf** Max 100 Thtr 100 Class 60 Board 50 **Parking** 10

★★★★ GUEST ACCOMMODATION
6 Lee Road
LN2 4BH
☎ 01522 522577
e–mail: carolemann@gmail.com

dir: *0.5m NE of the cathedral. Off A15 onto Lee Rd*

A private house in a residential suburb within the cathedral quarter of the city that offers a high level of comfort and careful hospitality. There is off-road parking, and the landscaped gardens offer an oasis of tranquillity, but all the delights of the city are close by.

Rooms 1 en suite D £55–£65 **Facilities** TVB tea/coffee Cen ht **Parking** 2 **Notes** ⊗ No children 🐾

ENGLAND

LINCOLN CONTINUED

★★★★ GUEST HOUSE
Carholme Guest House
175 Carholme Rd LN1 1RU
☎ 01522 531059
e–mail: root@carholmeguesthouse.com
dir: *From A1 take A57. From A46 take A57, 0.5m on left after racecourse*

Situated a short walk from the Marina and Lincoln University, this small family-run guest house provides well appointed accommodation that is attractively decorated and well maintained, equipped with many useful extras; a ground floor bedroom is available. A freshly cooked breakfast is served in a pleasant dining area and guests have use of a comfortable ground floor lounge.

Rooms 5 rms (4 en suite) (1 pri facs) (1 fmly) (1 GF) S £30–£40; D £50–£60✻ **Facilities** TVB tea/coffee Cen ht TVL **Parking** 3 **Notes** ⊗ No coaches Closed 23 Dec–2 Jan

★★★★ GUEST HOUSE
Carline
1–3 Carline Rd LN1 1HL
☎ 01522 530422 📄 01522 530422
e–mail: sales@carlineguesthouse.co.uk
dir: *Left off A1102, A15 N. Premises 1m from A46 bypass & A57 into city*

This smart double-fronted Edwardian house is within easy walking distance of the castle and the cathedral. Bedrooms are particularly smartly appointed and have a host of useful extras. Breakfast is served at individual tables in the spacious dining room.

Rooms 9 en suite (1 fmly) (3 GF) S £38–£50; D £58–£60 **Facilities** TVB tea/coffee Cen ht Wi-fi available **Parking** 6 **Notes LB** ⊗ No children 3yrs No coaches Closed Xmas & New Year ⊛

★★★★ GUEST ACCOMMODATION
Eagles Guest House
552A Newark Rd, North Hykeham LN6 9NG
☎ 01522 686346
e–mail: eaglesguesthouse@yahoo.co.uk
dir: *A46 onto A1434, signed Lincoln south, North Hykeham, South Hykeham, 0.5m on right*

This large detached house is very convenient for the bypass and is well furnished and thoughtfully equipped. The bedrooms are bright and fresh, and there is a conservatory. Substantial breakfasts are served in the pleasant dining room.

Rooms 5 en suite (1 fmly) (1 GF) S £35–£40; D £50–£60✻ **Facilities** TVB tea/coffee Cen ht **Parking** 6 **Notes** ⊗ No children 9yrs

★★★★ GUEST ACCOMMODATION
Fairview Bed & Breakfast
35 Long Leys Rd LN1 1DP
☎ 01522 829879
e–mail: info@fairviewlincoln.co.uk
dir: *N on A46 turn left on A57 for 0.2m. Right onto Long Leys Rd for 1.4m*

Within easy walking distance of the city centre and Lincoln Cathedral, Fairview offers outstanding views of the West Common, Lincoln Grandstand and the Trent Valley. The guest bedroom is a large modern contemporary styled room with a superb bathroom and quality furnishings. Renata and Paul guarantee that guests will remember their stay as an enjoyable experience.

Rooms 1 en suite S £50–£75; D £65–£90✻ **Facilities** FTV TVB tea/coffee Cen ht Wi-fi available Golf 18 **Parking** 2 **Notes LB** ⊗ No children 10yrs ⊛

★★★★ GUEST ACCOMMODATION
The Loudor
37 Newark Rd, North Hykeham LN6 8RB
☎ 01522 680333 📄 01522 680403
e–mail: info@loudorhotel.co.uk
dir: *3m from city centre. A46 onto A1434 for 2m, on left opp shopping centre*

Originally a private residence, now refurbished, The Loudor offers high quality en suite accommodation in a friendly relaxing atmosphere. With ample parking, it is located three miles from Lincoln centre and within walking distance of shops, pubs and restaurants

Rooms 9 en suite (1 fmly) S fr £37; D fr £50✻ **Facilities** TVB tea/coffee Cen ht **Parking** 9 **Notes** ⊗ Closed 2wks Xmas & New Year

★★★★ ⊛⊛ RESTAURANT WITH ROOMS
The Old Bakery
26/28 Burton Rd LN1 3LB
☎ 01522 576057
e–mail: enquiries@theold-bakery.co.uk
web: www.theold-bakery.co.uk
dir: *Exit A46 at Lincoln North follow signs for cathedral. 3rd exit at 1st rdbt, 1st exit at next rdbt*

Situated close to the castle at the top of the town, this converted bakery offers well-equipped bedrooms and a delightful dining

CONTINUED

operation. The cooking is international and uses much local produce. Expect good friendly service from a dedicated staff.

Rooms 4 rms (2 en suite) (2 pri facs) (1 fmly) **Facilities** FTV TVB tea/coffee Cen ht Dinner Last d 9.30pm Wi-fi available **Notes** ⊗

★★★★ GUEST ACCOMMODATION
Orchard House

119 Yarborough Rd LN1 1HR

☎ 01522 528795

e–mail: enquiries@guesthouselincoln.com

dir: *Take A1 onto A57 into Lincoln – just off A46 bypass*

Close to the shopping centre and cathedral, this detached Edwardian house is situated in immaculate gardens complete with an apple orchard. Bedrooms are well equipped and homely, and the bright, attractive dining room has views out over the valley.

Rooms 5 rms (3 en suite) (2 pri facs) (1 fmly) S £25–£30; D £55–£65✻ **Facilities** FTV TVB tea/coffee Cen ht **Parking** 6 **Notes** ⊗ ☻

★★★★ BED & BREAKFAST
Stables B&B

32 Saxon St LN1 3HQ

☎ 01522 851750

e–mail: info@stablesbandb.com

dir: *A46/A15 to Cathedral, right onto Rasen Ln, 2nd right on Saxon St, then Saint Nicholas St*

This Victorian stable was converted to B&B accommodation in 2007. The quiet location with courtyard parking, and proximity to the Cathedral Quarter and uphill restaurants, make it ideal for relaxing breaks and business visits to Lincoln. Stables offers modern comfortable rooms with Wi-fi. Breakfasts are freshly prepared to order using local produce.

Rooms 3 en suite (1 GF) S £40–£75; D £55–£80✻ **Facilities** TVB tea/coffee Cen ht Wi-fi available **Parking** 3 **Notes** ⊗ No children 10yrs

★★★★ GUEST HOUSE
The Tennyson

7 South Park LN5 8EN

☎ 01522 521624 📄 01522 521355

e–mail: tennyson.hotel@virgin.net

web: www.tennysonhotel.com

dir: *S of city centre on A15, near South Park Common*

This smart house is just one mile from the city centre, situated on the ring road overlooking South Park. Bedrooms are attractively appointed and have a host of thoughtful extras. There is a modern lounge and a smart dining room where impressive breakfasts are served.

Rooms 8 en suite S £45; D £55✻ **Facilities** TVB tea/coffee Cen ht Wi-fi available **Parking** 8 **Notes** LB ⊗ No coaches Closed 24–31 Dec

★★★ GUEST HOUSE
Archers Lodge Guest House

133 Yarborough Rd LN1 1HR

☎ 01522 520201

e–mail: sue.scorer@tiscali.co.uk

dir: *A46 onto A57, at Horse & Groom pub, bear left onto B1273. 0.5m on the right*

Located a few minutes walk from central attractions, this elegant Victorian house has been sympathetically renovated to provide good standards of comfort and facilities. Bedrooms are equipped with lots of thoughtful extras and a warm welcome is assured.

Rooms 4 en suite (1 fmly) S £40; D £60 **Facilities** TVB tea/coffee Cen ht **Parking** 4 **Notes** No coaches

★★★ GUEST ACCOMMODATION
Elma

14 Albion Crescent, Off Long Leys Rd LN1 1EB

☎ 01522 529792 📄 01522 529792

e–mail: ellen.guymer@ntlworld.com

web: www.elma-guesthouse.co.uk

dir: *Off A57 onto Long Leys Rd signed St Georges Hospital. 1m left onto Albion Crescent*

This friendly family-run guest house lies in a quiet residential area within walking distance of the city centre. Attractive bedrooms are comfortably furnished and thoughtfully equipped. Breakfast is served around a large table in the dining room and there is a shared lounge.

Rooms 4 rms (1 en suite) S £28; D £45–£54✻ **Facilities** TVB tea/coffee Cen ht TVL **Parking** 5 **Notes** LB ⊗ No children 8yrs ☻

★★★ GUEST HOUSE
Newport

26–28 Newport Rd LN1 3DF

☎ 01522 528590 📄 01522 542868

e–mail: info@newportguesthouse.co.uk

web: www.newportguesthouse.co.uk

dir: *On Roman Rd, 600mtrs N of cathedral*

Situated in the quieter upper part of the city and just a few minutes' walk from the cathedral, this double-fronted terrace house offers well-equipped and comfortable bedrooms with broadband access. The pleasing public areas include a very comfortable sitting room and a bright and attractive breakfast room.

Rooms 9 en suite (2 GF) S £37–£60; D £55–£60✻ **Facilities** FTV TVB tea/coffee Cen ht TVL Wi-fi available **Parking** 4 **Notes** No coaches

ENGLAND

LINCOLN CONTINUED

★★★ GUEST HOUSE
South Park Guest House
11 South Park LN5 8EN
☎ 01522 528243 📠 01522 524603
e–mail: sparky824937@ntlworld.com

dir: *1m S of city centre on A15*

A Victorian house situated on the inner ring road facing South Park. The staff are friendly and attentive, and bedrooms, though compact, are well equipped. Breakfast is served in a modern dining room overlooking the park.

Rooms 6 en suite 1 annexe en suite (2 fmly) (1 GF) S £30–£40; D £48–£50✳ **Facilities** FTV TVB tea/coffee Cen ht **Parking** 7 **Notes LB** ⊗ No coaches

★★ GUEST ACCOMMODATION
Jaymar
31 Newland St West LN1 1QQ
☎ 01522 532934 📠 01522 820182
e–mail: ward.jaymar4@ntlworld.com

dir: *A46 onto A57 to city, 1st lights left onto Gresham St, then 2nd right, 500yds on left*

Situated within easy walking distance of the city, this small, friendly guest house has two well-equipped bedrooms. A full English breakfast, with vegetarian options, is served in the cosy dining room, and an early breakfast, from 5am onwards, is available on request. Children and pets are welcome, and guests can be collected from the bus or railway stations if required.

Rooms 2 rms (1 fmly) S £20; D £40✳ **Facilities** TVB tea/coffee
Notes ⊜

Ⓤ
Minster Lodge
3 Church Ln LN2 1QJ
☎ 01522 513220 📠 01522 513220
e–mail: info@minsterlodge.co.uk

dir: *400yds N of cathedral*

At the time of going to press the rating for this establishment had not been confirmed. Please check the AA website www.theAA.com for up-to-date information.

Rooms 6 en suite (3 fmly) S £65–£120; D £75–£120 **Facilities** TVB tea/coffee Direct dial from bedrooms Cen ht TVL Wi-fi available **Parking** 11
Notes LB

See advert on opposite page

Ⓤ
St Clements Lodge
21 Langworth Gate LN2 4AD
☎ 01522 521532 📠 01522 521532
e–mail: enquiries@stclementslodge.co.uk

dir: *350yds E of cathedral, down Eastgate onto Langworth Gate*

At the time of going to press the rating for this establishment had not been confirmed. Please check the AA website www.theAA.com for up-to-date information.

Rooms 3 rms (2 en suite) (1 pri facs) (1 fmly) S fr £45; D fr £60✳
Facilities TVB tea/coffee Cen ht Wi-fi available **Parking** 3 **Notes** ⊗ ⊜

LITTLE BYTHAM　　　　　　　　MAP 11 TF01

★★★★ Ⓐ INN
The Willoughby Arms
Station Rd NG33 4RA
☎ 01780 410276
e–mail: lkhulme@tiscali.co.uk
web: www.willoughbyarms.co.uk

dir: *A1 Stretton junct 5m, turn right in village centre B1176*
Rooms 3 rms (2 en suite) (1 pri facs) (1 fmly) **Facilities** TVB tea/coffee Cen ht Dinner Last d 8.55pm Pool Table **Parking** 30 **Notes** ⊗

LONG BENNINGTON　　　　　　MAP 11 SK84

★★★ BED & BREAKFAST
Shepherds Bush Farm
Main Rd NG23 5EB
☎ 01400 282163
e–mail: culverhay@hotmail.com

dir: *A1 S, 4m S of Newark, house driveway opp Fen Ln*

Dating from the 19th century, the converted farmhouse and barn lie in arable farmland set back from, but with direct access to the A1. The atmosphere is relaxed and informal, and the proprietors offer a friendly welcome. Bedrooms are individually appointed and have nearby private bathrooms.

Rooms 3 rms (3 pri facs) (2 fmly) (1 GF) S £30; D £50 **Facilities** TVB tea/coffee Cen ht **Parking** 4 **Notes** ⊗ ⊜

LOUTH   MAP 17 TF38

★★★ BED & BREAKFAST
The Manse B&B
Middlesykes Ln, Grimoldby LN11 8TE
☎ 01507 327495
e-mail: knowles578@btinternet.com

dir: *Grimoldby 4m from Louth on B1200 onto Tinkle St, turn right onto Middlesykes Ln*

Located in a quiet country lane, this pleasantly appointed house offers comfortable accommodation and a warm welcome. Proprietors are enthusiastic and helpful, making every effort to make guests feel welcomed to their home; freshly cooked evening meals are available by prior arrangement. An ideal location for exploring the delights of the Wolds.

Rooms 4 rms (3 en suite) (1 pri facs) (1 fmly) (1 GF) S £40–£45; D £55–£70✱ **Facilities** TVB tea/coffee Cen ht TVL Dinner Last d 5pm Wi-fi available **Parking** 5 **Notes** LB ⊗ No children 5yrs Closed 25 Dec ⊜

MABLETHORPE   MAP 17 TF58

★★★ GUEST HOUSE
Park View Guest House
48 Gibraltar Rd LN12 2AT
☎ 01507 477267   🖹 01507 477267
e-mail: malcolm@pvgh.freeserve.co.uk

dir: *Take A1104, at beach turn right onto Gibraltar Rd*

This well-established guest house is ideally situated just beside Mablethorpe's golden beach and the Queens Park, and also within easy walking distance of the main town centre amenities. Service is both helpful and friendly, provided by the resident proprietors, Debbie and Malcolm. The accommodation is soundly presented and of varying sizes, the ground-floor bedrooms proving particularly popular.

Rooms 5 rms (2 en suite) (1 fmly) (3 GF) S £22.50–£25; D £45–£50 **Facilities** TVB tea/coffee Licensed Cen ht TVL Dinner Last d Breakfast **Parking** 6 **Notes** LB No coaches ⊜

MARKET RASEN   MAP 17 TF18

Premier Collection

★★★★★ BED & BREAKFAST
Blaven
Walesby Hill, Walesby LN8 3UW
☎ 01673 838352
e-mail: blavenhouse@hotmail.com

dir: *A46 Market Rasen to Grimsby, right at junct with A1103, left at T-junct, Blaven 100yds on right*

On the edge of the village of Walesby, this smart house offers warm hospitality and comfortable en suite bedrooms. Freshly prepared breakfasts are served around one table in the dining room, while a large conservatory-lounge overlooks immaculate gardens.

Rooms 3 rms (2 en suite) (1 pri facs) S £45; D £55✱ **Facilities** TVB tea/coffee Cen ht TVL **Parking** 4 **Notes** ⊗ No children 10yrs Closed Xmas & New Year ⊜

★★★★ BED & BREAKFAST
Chuck Hatch
Kingerby Rd, West Rasen LN8 3NB
☎ 01673 842947 & 07745 288463   🖹 01673 842947
e-mail: info@chuckhatch.co.uk

dir: *A631 West Rasen follow signs Osgodby and North Owersby, house 0.5m on left*

Built in 1780, Chuck Hatch stands in grounds in peaceful open countryside. The en suite bedrooms are individually styled and well equipped. Public rooms include a lounge and a delightful breakfast room, which looks out over the lake and grounds beyond. Smoking is not permitted in the house.

Rooms 4 en suite S £40–£60; D £60–£70✱ **Facilities** TVB tea/coffee Cen ht TVL Fishing **Parking** 6 **Notes** LB ⊗ No children 16yrs ⊜

ENGLAND

MARKET RASEN *CONTINUED*

★★★ BED & BREAKFAST
Wold View House B&B
Bully Hill Top, Tealby LN8 6JA
☎ 01673 838226 📄 01673 838226
e–mail: irene@woldviewhouse.co.uk

dir: *A46 onto B1225 towards Horncastle, after 7m Wold View House at x-rds*

Situated at the top of Bully Hill with expansive views across The Wold, this smart teashop with guest house offers modern bedrooms and warm hospitality. Ideal for walking, riding, or touring the charming nearby villages and coastline, the house is also only a short drive from Lincoln.

Rooms 3 rms (1 en suite) **Facilities** TVB tea/coffee Cen ht TVL Dinner Last d 8pm Riding **Parking** 15 **Notes** ⊗ ⊜

MARTON (VILLAGE) MAP 17 SK88

★★★★ GUEST ACCOMMODATION
Black Swan Guest House
21 High St DN21 5AH
☎ 01427 718878
e–mail: info@blackswanguesthouse.co.uk
web: www.blackswanguesthouse.co.uk

dir: *On A156 in village centre at junct A1500*

Centrally located in the village, this 18th-century former coaching inn retains many original features, and offers good hospitality and homely bedrooms with modern facilities. Tasty breakfasts are served in the cosy dining room and a comfortable lounge with Wi-fi access is available. Transport to nearby pubs and restaurants can be provided.

Rooms 6 en suite 4 annexe en suite (3 fmly) (4 GF) S £45–£55; D £68–£75✻ **Facilities** FTV TVB tea/coffee Cen ht TVL Wi-fi available **Parking** 10 **Notes LB**

NORMANTON MAP 11 SK94

★★★★★ 🛏 BED & BREAKFAST
La Casita
Frith House, Main St NG32 3BH
☎ 01400 250302 & 07836 695282 📄 01400 250302
e–mail: jackiegonzalez@btinternet.com
web: www.lacasitabandb.co.uk

dir: *In village centre on A607*

A self-contained one bedroom family suite (can sleep four) built in the gated gardens of the owner's house. Furnished to a high standard and with many extras offering both comfort and luxury, the owners give careful service.

Rooms 1 annexe en suite (1 fmly) (1 GF) S £95; D £125 **Facilities** STV FTV TVB tea/coffee Direct dial from bedrooms Cen ht TVL Wi-fi available **Parking** 3 **Notes LB** ⊗

SKEGNESS MAP 17 TF56

★★★ 🅰 GUEST HOUSE
Amber
19 Scarbrough Av PE25 2SZ
☎ 01754 766503
e–mail: info@theamberhotel.co.uk

Rooms 8 en suite (2 fmly) S £25; D £50✻ **Facilities** TVB tea/coffee Licensed Cen ht TVL Dinner Last d 10am **Parking** 2 **Notes LB**

★★ GUEST HOUSE
Manderlay Guest House
49 Grosvenor Rd PE25 2DD
☎ 01754 899029 & 07795 124055 📄 01754 899029
e–mail: mikecaroline@fsmail.net

A warm welcome is assured here, as Caroline and Mike Austin make every effort to ensure their guests' needs are met. Bedrooms are well equipped, and come in a variety of sizes, some of cosy dimensions. Breakfast is served at individual tables in the dining room, and dinner is available by arrangement.

Rooms 3 en suite (1 fmly) D £40–£50✻ **Facilities** TVB tea/coffee Cen ht Dinner Last d 3pm **Parking** 2 **Notes LB** No coaches

ENGLAND

SKILLINGTON   MAP 11 SK82   STAMFORD   MAP 11 TF00

★★★ INN
The Cross Swords Inn
The Sqaure NG33 5HB

☎ 01476 861132

e–mail: harold@thecross-swordsinn.co.uk

dir: *Between Grantham and Stamford, W off A1 at Colsterworth rdbt*

Located at the crossroads at the centre of the award-winning village of Skillington, and very popular with the local community, this traditional inn offers three modern, well-equipped bedrooms that are housed in an attractive cottage at the top of the courtyard, and named in keeping with the history of the village. All are very comfortable and are coupled with smart modern bathrooms. The inn provides imaginative food and a range of real ales within a rustic period atmosphere.

Rooms 3 annexe en suite (3 GF) S fr £45; D fr £58✱ **Facilities** FTV TVB tea/coffee Cen ht Dinner Last d 9.30pm **Parking** 12 **Notes** ⊗ No children 10yrs RS Mon

Premier Collection

★★★★★ GUEST ACCOMMODATION
Rock Lodge
1 Empingham Rd PE9 2RH

☎ 01780 481758 📄 01780 481757

e–mail: rocklodge@innpro.co.uk

dir: *Off A1 at A606 signed Oakham, into Stamford, Rock Lodge 1.25m on left*

Philip and Jane Sagar have considerable experience in managing luxury hotels and offer a warm welcome to their imposing 1900 house near the town centre. The attractive bedrooms are individually furnished and have a good range of facilities. Character public rooms include the oak-panelled drawing room with mullion windows. Breakfast is served in a sunny room overlooking the gardens.

Rooms 6 en suite (1 fmly) (2 GF) S £65–£70; D £80–£110✱ **Facilities** STV FTV TVB tea/coffee Cen ht TVL Wi-fi available **Parking** 7 **Notes** ⊗

Ⓤ
Candlesticks
1 Church Ln PE9 2JU

☎ 01780 764033 📄 01780 756071

e–mail: info@candlestickshotel.co.uk

dir: *On B1081 High Street St Martins. Church Ln opposite St Martin Church*

At the time of going to press the rating for this establishment was not confirmed. This may be due to a change of ownership or because it has only recently joined the AA rating scheme. For further details please see the AA website. www.theAA.com

Rooms 8 en suite S £50–£75; D £65–£75✱ **Facilities** STV FTV TVB tea/coffee Direct dial from bedrooms Cen ht Dinner Last d 9.30pm **Parking** 8 **Notes** LB ⊗ RS No restaurant or bar service Mon

ENGLAND

SUTTON-ON-SEA   MAP 17 TF58

★★★ GUEST ACCOMMODATION
Athelstone Lodge

25 Trusthorpe Rd LN12 2LR

☎ 01507 441521

dir: *On A52 N of vilage*

Situated between Mablethorpe and Skegness and close to the
promenade, Athelstone Lodge has pleasant, soundly maintained
bedrooms equipped with many useful extras. Breakfast is served in the
dining room and a bar and a lounge are also available. A variety of
enjoyable home-cooked dinners is served.

Rooms 6 rms (5 en suite) (1 fmly) S £28–£30; D £56–£60✳
Facilities TVB tea/coffee Cen ht TVL Dinner Last d 4.30pm **Parking** 6
Notes LB Closed Nov–Feb

SWINDERBY   MAP 17 SK86

★★★ GUEST ACCOMMODATION
Halfway Farm Motel

Newark Rd (A46) LN6 9HN

☎ 01522 868749 📄 01522 868082

e–mail: halfwayfarmmotel@hotmail.com

web: www.halfway-farm-motel.co.uk

dir: *On A46 opp Swinderby rbt*

This 300-year-old farmhouse is set back from the A46, midway
between Lincoln and Newark. Spacious bedrooms are traditional in the
main house, while motel-style rooms are located around a courtyard to
the rear. There is a bright, airy dining room and comfortable lounge. A
good base for touring or antique hunting.

Rooms 6 rms (5 en suite) 10 annexe en suite (1 fmly) (13 GF)
Facilities TVB tea/coffee Direct dial from bedrooms Cen ht **Conf** Max 30
Parking 25 **Notes** ⊗ RS Dec–Jan

TIMBERLAND   MAP 17 TF15

★★★★ INN
The Penny Farthing

Station Rd LN4 3SA

☎ 01522 523230

e–mail: pennyfarthing@talktalkbusiness.net

dir: *Junct of B1191 & B1189, signed 1m to Timberland*

A warm welcome awaits at this charming inn situated in the heart of a
delightful Lincolnshire village. Public areas include a large open plan
lounge/bar/dining area as well as an additional restaurant to the front
of the property. The bedrooms are tastefully decorated and
thoughtfully equipped with a good range of useful facilities.

The Penny Farthing

Rooms 7 en suite (1 fmly) D £50–£60✳ **Facilities** FTV TVB tea/coffee
Cen ht Dinner Wi-fi available **Parking** 12 **Notes** ⊗

TORKSEY   MAP 17 SK87

★★★ ⊜ INN
The Hume Arms

Main St LN1 2EE

☎ 01427 718613 📄 01522 703841

e–mail: charles.allen@thehumearms.co.uk

web: www.thehumearms.co.uk

dir: *On A156 between Gainsborough and Saxilby*

This refurbished village inn (totally non-smoking throughout) offers a
good base for touring, just a mile north of Torksey Lock on the
Chesterfield Canal. An extensive range of imaginative meals and snacks
are available through the smart lounge bar areas or the restaurant.
Bedrooms are comfortably appointed and spacious, and all are
en suite. There is a children's play area, and extensive parking.

Rooms 4 en suite (1 fmly) S fr £55; D fr £65✳ **Facilities** TVB tea/coffee
Cen ht Dinner Last d 9pm Wi-fi available **Conf** Max 100 **Parking** 120

WHAPLODE   MAP 12 TF32

★★★★ BED & BREAKFAST
Westgate House & Barn

Little Ln PE12 6RU

☎ 01406 370546

e–mail: bandb@westgatehouse.f9.co.uk

web: www.westgatehouse.f9.co.uk

dir: *Follow brown signs in village of Whaplode (on A151)*

Located in a peaceful rural location, in well-established cottage gardens
and grounds, Westgate House offers comfortably appointed
accommodation in a delightful barn conversion. Breakfast is taken in
the main house, in a charming room with wood-burning stove and
garden views. The freshly cooked breakfast includes good locally
sourced ingredients and homemade preserves.

Rooms 2 annexe en suite **Facilities** TVB tea/coffee Cen ht **Parking** 2
Notes ⊗ ⊜

CONTINUED

WINTERINGHAM   MAP 17 SE92

Premier Collection

★ ★ ★ ★ ★ ★ ◉◉ RESTAURANT WITH ROOMS

Winteringham Fields

DN15 9PF

☎ 01724 733096 📄 01724 733898

e–mail: wintfields@aol.com

dir: *In centre of village at x-rds*

This highly regarded restaurant with rooms, located deep in the countryside in Winteringham village, is six miles west of the Humber Bridge. Public rooms and bedrooms, some of which are housed in renovated barns and cottages, are delightfully cosseting. Award-winning food is available in the restaurant.

Rooms 4 en suite 6 annexe en suite (3 GF) S £105–£145; D £145–£215✳
Facilities TVB tea/coffee Direct dial from bedrooms Cen ht Dinner Last d 9pm **Conf** Max 50 Thtr 50 Class 50 Board 50 **Parking** 14 **Notes LB** Closed 25 Dec for 2 wks, last wk Oct, 2 wks Aug

---

WOODHALL SPA   MAP 17 TF16

★ ★ GUEST ACCOMMODATION

Claremont Guest House

9/11 Witham Rd LN10 6RW

☎ 01526 352000

web: www.woodhall-spa-guesthouse-bedandbreakfast.co.uk

dir: *In town centre on B1191 near mini-rdbt*

This large guest house is located close to the town centre, and has been owned and run by Mrs Brennan for many number of years. The bedrooms are homely, generally quite spacious, traditionally furnished, and well equipped. The public areas contain original features, while breakfast includes home made jams.

Rooms 11 rms (5 en suite) (5 fmly) (2 GF) **Facilities** TVB tea/coffee
Parking 5 **Notes** ✪

WOOLSTHORPE   MAP 11 SK83

★ ★ ★ ★ ◉ INN

The Chequers Inn

Main St NG32 1LU

☎ 01476 870701 📄 01476 870085

e–mail: justinnabar@yahoo.co.uk

dir: *In village opp Post Office*

A 17th-century coaching inn set in the lee of Belvoir Castle next to the village cricket pitch and having its own pétanque pitch. Exposed beams, open fireplaces and original stone and brickwork, with 24 wines by the glass, a gastro menu, and real ales. Comfortable bedrooms are in the former stable block.

Rooms 4 annexe en suite (1 fmly) (3 GF) S £49; D £59 **Facilities** TVB
tea/coffee Cen ht TVL Dinner Last d 9.30pm **Conf** Max 80 Thtr 80
Class 50 Board 25 **Parking** 40

LONDON

N1

★ ★ ★ Ⓐ BED & BREAKFAST

Kandara   PLAN 1-F4

68 Ockendon Rd N1 3NW

☎ 020 7226 5721 📄 020 7226 3379

e–mail: admin@kandara.co.uk

web: www.kandara.co.uk

dir: *At Highbury corner rdbt on A1 onto St Pauls Rd for 0.5m, right at junct onto Essex Rd, Ockendon Rd 5th left*

Rooms 10 rms 2 annexe rms (4 fmly) (2 GF) S £47–£59; D £67–£79✳
Facilities TVB tea/coffee Cen ht **Notes** ⊗ Closed 20–25 Dec

---

N4

★ ★ ★ ★ GUEST HOUSE

Mount View   PLAN 1-F5

31 Mount View Rd N4 4SS

☎ 020 8340 9222

e–mail: info@mountviewguesthouse.com

web: www.mountviewguesthouse.com

dir: *Off A1201 Crouch Hill in Crouch End*

This delightful Victorian house is in a quiet, tree-lined residential area with good transport links to the City and the West End. The bedrooms and public areas are carefully furnished and facilities include a washing machine and access to the internet. Well-prepared breakfasts are served at a large communal table and the resident owners provide very friendly hospitality.

Rooms 3 rms (2 en suite) S fr £55; D £70–£90✳ **Facilities** TVB tea/coffee Cen ht Wi-fi available **Notes** ⊗ No coaches

See advert on page 333

N4 CONTINUED

★★★ BED & BREAKFAST
Ossian House
PLAN 1-F5

20 Ossian Rd N4 4EA

☎ 020 8340 4331 📄 020 8340 4331

e–mail: ann@ossianguesthouse.co.uk

web: www.ossianguesthouse.co.uk

dir: *Off A1201 Crouch Hill onto Mount View Rd, 1st right down hill, 1st left*

This pleasant guest house is in a quiet location north of the city. Bedrooms are stylishly furnished, with a very good range of facilities and accessories. Breakfast is served round one large table in the attractive dining room.

Rooms 3 en suite **Facilities** TVB tea/coffee Cen ht TVL **Notes** ⊗ ⊜

★★ GUEST ACCOMMODATION
Majestic
PLAN 1-F5

392/394 Seven Sisters Rd, Finsbury Park N4 2PQ

☎ 020 8800 2022 📄 020 8802 4131

e–mail: Hotelmaj@aol.com

web: www.majestic-hotel.sageweb.co.uk

dir: *On A503 near Manor House tube station*

The nearby tube station provides good access to the City and the West End. Bedrooms vary in size and style and include a number of family rooms. Public areas include an attractive lounge and breakfast room. Free parking is a bonus.

Rooms 36 rms (20 en suite) (13 fmly) (7 GF) **Facilities** TVB tea/coffee Cen ht TVL Use of local leisure club **Conf** Max 25 **Parking** 25 **Notes** ⊗ RS Xmas/New Year

N6

★★★ GUEST ACCOMMODATION
Winchester Pub
PLAN 1-E5

206 Archway Rd, Highgate N6 5BA

☎ 020 8374 1690 & 0777 037 8818 📄 020 8374 1690

e–mail: valatwinch@aol.com

web: www.winchester-hotel.com

dir: *A1 S to City, pass Highgate tube station on left, premises on left*

This delightful traditional Victorian property is close to Highgate tube station and within easy reach of the M1. The smart spacious bedrooms are well equipped and there is a well-stocked and popular bar-lounge. Hearty breakfasts and a good choice of home-cooked meals are served in the dining area.

Rooms 6 en suite (3 fmly) **Facilities** STV TVB tea/coffee Cen ht Dinner Last d 9.30pm **Notes** ⊗ RS 25 Dec

N8

★★★ GUEST ACCOMMODATION
White Lodge
PLAN 1-F5

1 Church Ln, Hornsey N8 7BU

☎ 020 8348 9765 📄 020 8340 7851

e–mail: info@whitelodgehornsey.co.uk

web: www.whitelodgehornsey.co.uk

dir: *A406 to Bounds Green, Hornsey High Rd & Church Ln*

This well-maintained, friendly guest house is in a convenient location close to shops and restaurants. Bedrooms are traditionally appointed and airy public areas include an attractive lounge and spacious dining room where continental breakfast is served.

Rooms 16 rms (8 en suite) (5 fmly) (1 GF) S £34–£36; D £42–£54✳ **Facilities** TVB tea/coffee Cen ht Wi-fi available **Notes** ⊗

NW1

★★★★ 🛏 GUEST ACCOMMODATION

MIC Conferences and Accommodation
PLAN 2-D5

81–103 Euston St NW1 2EZ

☎ 020 7380 0001 📄 020 7387 5300

e–mail: sales@micentre.com

web: www.micentre.com

dir: *Euston Rd left at lights onto Melton St, 1st left onto Euston St, MIC 100yds on left*

Located within walking distance of Euston station, this smart property is convenient for central London. Stylish air-conditioned bedrooms are thoughtfully equipped for business and leisure. The airy Atrium Bar and Restaurant offers drinks, light snacks and an evening menu. Extensive conference and meeting facilities are available.

Rooms 28 en suite (2 fmly) **Facilities** STV TVB tea/coffee Direct dial from bedrooms Lift Cen ht TVL Dinner Last d 8.45pm Wi-fi available **Conf** Max 150 Thtr 150 Class 50 Board 45 **Notes** ⊗

★★★ GUEST ACCOMMODATION

Euston Square
PLAN 2-C5

152–156 North Gower St NW1 2LU

☎ 020 7388 0099 📄 020 7383 7165

e–mail: reservations@euston-square-hotel.com

web: www.euston-square-hotel.com

dir: *On junct Euston Rd, next to Euston Sq tube station*

Over the tube station, this property has undergone a total transformation and is ideal for the business and leisure markets. The smart compact bedrooms and en suite bathrooms are well designed. Small conference facilities and a modern reception area are available. Breakfast and light meals are served in FAB, the bar lounge area.

Rooms 75 en suite (4 GF) **Facilities** STV TVB tea/coffee Direct dial from bedrooms Lift Cen ht TVL Dinner Last d 9.45pm Wi-fi available **Conf** Thtr 120 Class 50 Board 50 **Notes** ⊗

NW3

★★★★ GUEST ACCOMMODATION

The Langorf
PLAN 2-E5

20 Frognal, Hampstead NW3 6AG

☎ 020 7794 4483 📄 020 7435 9055

e–mail: info@langorfhotel.com

web: www.langorfhotel.com

dir: *Off A41 Finchley Rd, near Finchley Rd tube station*

Located on a leafy and mainly residential avenue within easy walking distance of shops and restaurants, this elegant Edwardian property has been renovated to provide high standards of comfort and facilities. Bedrooms are furnished with flair and a warm welcome is assured.

Rooms 31 en suite (4 fmly) (3 GF) S £55–£82; D £65–£110✳ **Facilities** STV TVB tea/coffee Direct dial from bedrooms Lift Cen ht TVL Wi-fi available **Conf** Max 30 Thtr 30 Class 20 Board 15 **Parking** available **Notes** LB ⊗

ENGLAND

★★★ GUEST ACCOMMODATION
La Gaffe
PLAN 2-E5

107–111 Heath St NW3 6SS

☎ 020 7435 4941 & 7435 8965 📠 020 7794 7592

e–mail: info@lagaffe.co.uk

dir: *On A502, 250yds N of Hampstead tube station*

This family owned and run guest house, just north of Hampstead High Street, offers charm and warm hospitality. The Italian restaurant, which is open most lunchtimes and for dinner, is popular with locals. Bedrooms are compact, but all are en suite.

Rooms 11 en suite 7 annexe en suite (2 fmly) (2 GF) **Facilities** TVB tea/coffee Direct dial from bedrooms Cen ht Dinner Last d 11pm Wi-fi available **Conf** Max 10 **Notes** ⊗

NW6

★★★ GUEST ACCOMMODATION
Dawson House
PLAN 1-E4

72 Canfield Gardens NW6 3EG

☎ 020 7624 0079 & 7328 4857 📠 020 7624 6525

e–mail: booking@dawsonhousehotel.com

web: www.dawsonhouse.com

dir: *From Finchley Rd tube station right onto Canfield Gardens*

A friendly welcome awaits guests at Dawson House, situated in a residential area of South Hampstead. Bedrooms are brightly appointed and well equipped for business and leisure, and there are attractive front and rear gardens.

Rooms 15 en suite (2 fmly) (1 GF) **Facilities** TVB tea/coffee Direct dial from bedrooms Cen ht **Notes** ⊗ No children 3yrs

---

NW8

★★★ INN
The New Inn
PLAN 1-E4

2 Allitsen Rd, St Johns Wood NW8 6LA

☎ 020 7722 0726 📠 020 7722 0653

e–mail: thenewinn@gmail.com

web: www.newinnlondon.co.uk

dir: *Off A41 by St Johns Wood tube station onto Acacia Rd, last right, to end on corner*

Built in 1810, this popular inn is in a leafy suburb only a stroll from Regents Park. Bedrooms are appointed to a high standard, while Thai cuisine and traditional fare are offered in the atmospheric bar lounge.

Rooms 5 en suite S £75; D £75(room only) **Facilities** FTV TVB tea/coffee Cen ht Dinner Last d 9.30pm Wi-fi available **Notes** ⊗ No coaches

---

NW9

★★★ GUEST ACCOMMODATION
Kingsland
PLAN 1-C5

Kingsbury Circle, Kingsbury NW9 9RR

☎ 020 8206 0666 📠 020 8206 0555

e–mail: stay@kingslandhotel.co.uk

web: www.kingslandhotel.co.uk

dir: *Kingsbury Circle junct A4006 & A4140*

Located at the roundabout near Kingsbury Station, shops, restaurants and Wembley complex, the Kingsland provides modern bedrooms with smart bathrooms en suite. A continental breakfast is supplied, and a passenger lift and car park are available.

Rooms 28 en suite (5 fmly) (6 GF) **Facilities** STV TVB tea/coffee Direct dial from bedrooms Lift Cen ht Wi-fi available **Parking** 30 **Notes** ⊗

SW1

★★★★ GUEST ACCOMMODATION
Best Western Corona
PLAN 2-D1

87–89 Belgrave Rd SW1V 2BQ

☎ 020 7828 9279 📠 020 7931 8576

e–mail: info@coronahotel.co.uk

Centrally located, this elegant Victorian property is of a high standard. Smartly appointed and well-equipped bedrooms offer comfortable,

CONTINUED

ENGLAND

modern accommodation. A continental breakfast is served in the basement dining room and room service is also available.

Rooms 51 en suite (8 fmly) (7 GF) **Facilities** TVB tea/coffee Direct dial from bedrooms Lift **Notes** ⊗

coach stations. The bedrooms have en suite shower rooms. A buffet-style breakfast is served in the basement dining room.

Rooms 50 en suite (4 fmly) (4 GF) **Facilities** STV TVB tea/coffee Direct dial from bedrooms Lift Cen ht TVL **Notes** ⊗

★★★★ GUEST ACCOMMODATION
Best Western Victoria Palace   PLAN 2-C1

60–64 Warwick Way SW1V 1SA
☎ 020 7821 7113 📄 020 7630 0806
e-mail: info@bestwesternvictoriapalace.co.uk
web: www.bestwesternvictoriapalace.co.uk

An elegant, 19th-century building located in the heart of London, near to Belgravia and a five minute walk from Victoria rail, underground and

CONTINUED

★★★★ GUEST ACCOMMODATION
Sidney London-Victoria   PLAN 2-C1

68–76 Belgrave Rd SW1V 2BP
☎ 020 7834 2738 📄 020 7630 0973
e-mail: reservations@sidneyhotel.com
web: www.sidneyhotel.com

dir: *A202 Vauxhall Bridge Rd onto Charlwood St & junct with Belgrave Rd*

This smart property near Pimlico offers brightly decorated bedrooms that are well equipped for business use, while several rooms are suitable for families. Public areas include a bar lounge and an airy breakfast room.

Rooms 82 en suite (13 fmly) (9 GF) **Facilities** STV TVB tea/coffee Direct dial from bedrooms Lift Cen ht TVL Wi-fi available **Conf** Thtr 30 Class 25 Board 14 **Notes** ⊗

See advert on this page

ENGLAND

SW1 *continued*

★★★★ GUEST ACCOMMODATION

The Windermere
PLAN 2-C1

142/144 Warwick Way, Victoria SW1V 4JE

☎ 020 7834 5163 🖺 020 7630 8831

e–mail: reservations@windermere-hotel.co.uk

web: www.windermere-hotel.co.uk

dir: *On B324 off Buckingham Palace Rd, at junct Alderney St*

The Windermere is a relaxed, informal and family-run establishment within easy reach of Victoria Station and many of the capital's attractions. Bedrooms, although varying in size, are stylish, comfortable and well equipped. The Pimlico restaurant serves delicious evening meals and hearty cooked breakfasts.

Rooms 20 en suite (3 fmly) (3 GF) S fr £89; D £119–£139✷
Facilities FTV TVB tea/coffee Direct dial from bedrooms Cen ht TVL Dinner Last d 10.30pm Wi-fi available **Conf** Max 20 **Notes** ⊗

★★★ GUEST ACCOMMODATION

Elizabeth
PLAN 2-C1

37 Eccleston Square SW1V 1PB

☎ 020 7828 6812 🖺 020 7828 6814

e–mail: info@elizabethhotel.com

web: www.elizabethhotel.com

dir: *500yds S of Victoria station. Off A3213 Belgrave Rd onto Eccleston Sq*

This friendly, well-run property is just a short walk from Victoria Station and within easy reach of central London attractions. The well-equipped bedrooms include some spacious apartments ideal for families.

Rooms 42 rms (39 en suite) (10 fmly) (4 GF) S £75–£85; D £105–£115✷
Facilities TVB tea/coffee Direct dial from bedrooms Lift Cen ht TVL Wi-fi available **Notes** ⊗

★★★ GUEST ACCOMMODATION

Comfort Inn
PLAN 2-C1

8–12 St Georges Dr SW1V 4BJ

☎ 020 7834 2988 🖺 020 7821 5814

e–mail: info@comfortinnbuckinghampalacerd.co.uk

dir: *Off Buckingham Palace Rd onto Elizabeth Bridge & St George's Dr*

Located just a short walk south from Victoria station, this establishment is a good base for visiting the capital's attractions. All bedrooms and public areas are smartly appointed and offer very good levels of comfort. An extensive continental breakfast is served.

Rooms 51 en suite (4 fmly) (7 GF) **Facilities** STV TVB tea/coffee Direct dial from bedrooms Lift Cen ht TVL **Conf** Max 20 Thtr 20 Class 20 Board 20 **Notes** ⊗

★★★ GUEST ACCOMMODATION

Comfort Inn Victoria
PLAN 2-C1

18–24 Belgrave Rd, Victoria SW1V 1QF

☎ 020 7233 6636 🖺 020 7932 0538

e–mail: stay@comfortinnvictoria.co.uk

Having a prime location close to Victoria station, this property offers brightly appointed en suite accommodation that is thoughtfully equipped for business and leisure guests. A continental breakfast is offered in the basement dining room.

Rooms 48 en suite (16 fmly) (9 GF) S £49–£119; D £59–£139✷
Facilities STV TVB tea/coffee Direct dial from bedrooms Lift Cen ht TVL Wi-fi available **Notes** ⊗

★★★ GUEST HOUSE

Victoria Inn
PLAN 2-C1

65–67 Belgrave Rd, Victoria SW1V 2BG

☎ 020 7834 6721 & 7834 0182 🖺 020 7931 0201

e–mail: welcome@victoriainn.co.uk

web: www.victoriainn.co.uk

dir: *On A3213 0.4m SE of Victoria station, near Pimlico tube station*

A short walk from Victoria station, this Victorian property offers modern, well-equipped accommodation for business and leisure guests. There is a comfortable reception lounge, and a limited self-service buffet breakfast is available in the basement breakfast room.

Rooms 43 en suite (7 fmly) **Facilities** STV TVB tea/coffee Direct dial from bedrooms Lift Cen ht **Notes** ⊗ No coaches

★★★ GUEST ACCOMMODATION
Winchester
PLAN 2-C1

17 Belgrave Rd SW1V 1RB
☎ 020 7828 2972 📄 020 7828 5191
e-mail: info@winchester-hotel.net
web: www.winchester-hotel.net

dir: *On A3213 300yds SE of Victoria station*

Conveniently located close to Victoria this welcoming, well maintained house provides an ideal base for tourists. Bedrooms vary in size and style but all are well equipped, decorated in bright colours and boast comfortable modern beds. Freshly cooked breakfasts are served in the traditionally styled dining room. Staff are friendly and keen to please.

Rooms 19 en suite (2 fmly) (2 GF) **Facilities** STV TVB tea/coffee Direct dial from bedrooms Cen ht **Notes** ⊗ No children 5yrs

★★ 🅰 GUEST ACCOMMODATION
The Dover – Victoria
PLAN 2-C1

42–44 Belgrave Rd, Victoria SW1V 1RG
☎ 020 7821 9085 📄 020 7834 6425
e-mail: reception@dover-hotel.co.uk
web: www.dover-hotel.co.uk

dir: *300yds SE of Victoria station on A3213*

Rooms 33 rms (29 en suite) (8 fmly) (5 GF) S £50–£85; D £55–£85 **Facilities** STV TVB tea/coffee Direct dial from bedrooms Cen ht Wi-fi available **Notes** LB ⊗

★★ 🅰 BED & BREAKFAST
Stanley House
PLAN 2-C1

19–21 Belgrave Rd, Victoria SW1V 1RB
☎ 020 7834 5042 & 7834 7292 📄 020 7834 8439
e-mail: cmahotel@aol.com
web: www.londonbudgethotels.co.uk

dir: *Near Victoria station*

Rooms 44 rms (32 en suite) (7 fmly) (8 GF) S £45–£50; D £60–£65✱ **Facilities** FTV TVB Direct dial from bedrooms Cen ht TVL Wi-fi available **Notes** LB ⊗ No children 5yrs

SW3

AA LONDON B&B OF THE YEAR
Premier Collection

★ ★ ★ ★ ★ GUEST ACCOMMODATION
San Domenico House
PLAN 2-B1

29–31 Draycott Place SW3 2SH
☎ 020 7581 5757 📄 020 7584 1348
e-mail: info@sandomenicohouse.com

This stunning property in the heart of Chelsea offers beautifully individually styled bedrooms, all with antique and period pieces, and well appointed en suites complete with Italian Spa toiletries. A sumptuous drawing room with wonderful works of art is available for guests to relax in or maybe to enjoy afternoon tea. Breakfast is served either to guests' bedrooms or in the lower ground floor elegant dining room. Staff are friendly and attentive.

Rooms 15 en suite (9 smoking) S £246.75–£334.88; D £276.13–£423✱ (room only) **Facilities** STV Direct dial from bedrooms Lift Cen ht **Notes** ⊗

★★★ 🍴 GUEST ACCOMMODATION
Claverley
PLAN 2-B3

13–14 Beaufort Gardens, Knightsbridge SW3 1PS
☎ 020 7589 8541 📄 020 7584 3410
e-mail: reservations@claverleyhotel.co.uk
web: www.claverleyhotel.co.uk

dir: *Off A4 Brompton Rd, 350yds SW of Knightsbridge tube station*

This pleasant establishment has a peaceful location set in a leafy close. The frontage and lounge provide a smart and welcoming arrival. The staff here offer a friendly service and there is a complimentary tea and coffee service in the lounge. Breakfast is not to be missed and offers an impressive range of choice as well as quality, service here is also attentive.

Rooms 29 rms (26 en suite) (3 pri facs) (7 fmly) (2 GF) **Facilities** STV TVB Direct dial from bedrooms Lift Cen ht Wi-fi available **Conf** Max 40 Thtr 30 Class 14 **Notes** ⊗

SW5

★★★★ GUEST ACCOMMODATION
Best Western Shaftesbury Kensington
PLAN 1-D3

33–37 Hogarth Rd, Kensington SW5 0QQ
☎ 020 7370 6831 📄 0207 373 6179

Well appointed to a high standard, this property has a smart modern feel and is conveniently located for the exhibition centre, the West End and local transport links. Bedrooms are furnished and decorated to a very high standard, offering guests a comprehensive range of modern facilities and amenities.

Rooms 133 en suite (7 GF) **Facilities** STV TVB tea/coffee Direct dial from bedrooms Lift Cen ht Gymnasium **Conf** Max 15 Board 15 **Notes** ⊗

SW5 CONTINUED

★★★★ GUEST ACCOMMODATION
The Mayflower
PLAN 1-D3

26–28 Trebovir Rd SW5 9NJ

☎ 020 7370 0991 📄 020 7370 0994

e-mail: info@mayflower-group.co.uk

web: www.mayflowerhotel.co.uk

dir: *Left from Earls Court tube station & 1st left into Trebovir Rd, premises on left*

This smart guest house is a short walk from Earls Court, and close to Olympia and West London's museums and attractions. Stylish, individually designed bedrooms vary in size but all are extremely well equipped and have smart, modern en suites. There is a comfortable, stylish lounge and an airy dining room where breakfast is served.

Rooms 47 en suite (4 fmly) (5 GF) S £69–£89; D £92–£175✳
Facilities STV FTV TVB tea/coffee Direct dial from bedrooms Lift Cen ht Wi-fi available **Conf** Max 25 Class 25 Board 25 **Parking** 4 **Notes LB** ⊗

See advert on this page

★★★★ GUEST ACCOMMODATION
Quality Crown Kensington
PLAN 1-D3

162 Cromwell Rd, Kensington SW5 0TT

☎ 020 7244 2400 📄 020 7244 2500

e-mail: stay@qualitycrown.com

This delightful property enjoys a prime location adjacent to the famous Cromwell Road hospital, within easy reach of the V&A Museum and the chic shops of Knightsbridge and South Kensington. Bedrooms are extremely well equipped and along with the comfortable public areas have a stylish, contemporary feel. The popular smart bar is a feature.

Rooms 82 en suite **Facilities** STV TVB tea/coffee Direct dial from bedrooms Lift Cen ht TVL Dinner Last d 10pm **Parking** 8 **Notes** ⊗

★★★ GUEST ACCOMMODATION
Henley House
PLAN 1-D3

30 Barkston Gardens, Earls Court SW5 0EN

☎ 020 7370 4111 📄 020 7370 0026

e-mail: reservations@henleyhousehotel.com

web: www.henleyhousehotel.com

dir: *A4 Cromwell Rd S onto A3220 Earls Court Rd, left onto Barkston Gardens after tube station*

Situated close to Earls Court in the relative peace of Barkston Gardens, this Victorian house has been sympathetically renovated to provide modern comforts. There is a pleasant foyer-lounge and breakfast is served in a conservatory-style dining room. Bedrooms are well equipped and some boast small balconies.

Rooms 21 en suite (1 fmly) (1 GF) **Facilities** STV TVB tea/coffee Direct dial from bedrooms Lift Cen ht Wi-fi available **Notes** ⊗

★★★ GUEST ACCOMMODATION
My Place
PLAN 1-D3

1–3 Trebvoir Rd SW5 9LS

☎ 020 7373 0833 📄 020 7373 9998

e-mail: info@myplacehotel.co.uk

web: www.myplacehotel.co.uk

dir: *A4 West Cromwell Rd onto Earls Court Rd, 3rd right*

This Victorian house is in a quiet residential street close to Earls Court station with easy access to the West End. The smart bedrooms vary in

CONTINUED

size and have an extremely good range of modern facilities. Breakfast is served in the dining room overlooking a spacious garden. Free entry to the on-site nightclub is included.

Rooms 50 en suite (6 fmly) S £55–£65; D £75–£85 **Facilities** STV TVB Direct dial from bedrooms Lift Cen ht TVL Wi-fi available Night Club **Conf** Max 100 Thtr 100 Class 100 Board 20 Del from £145 ✳ **Notes** LB ⊗

SW7

★★★★ GUEST ACCOMMODATION
Ashburn
PLAN 2-A1

111 Cromwell Rd SW7 4DP
☎ 020 7244 1999 ≜ 020 7244 1998
e–mail: reservations@ashburn-hotel.co.uk

dir: *On Cromwell Rd, close to crossing with Gloucester Rd*

This stunning establishment benefits from a great location in a peaceful Kensington side street which is less than a five minute walk from Gloucester Road Underground. All areas including the guest lounge, bar, dining room and accommodation have been stylishly renovated to a very high standard with guest's comfort a priority. Light hot and cold snacks are available during the day and evening. A Continental or full English breakfast is served in the attractive dining room located on the lower ground floor.

Rooms 38 en suite (3 GF) **Facilities** STV FTV TVB tea/coffee Direct dial from bedrooms Lift Cen ht TVL Dinner Last d 10.30pm Wi-fi available **Notes** ⊗

★★★★ GUEST ACCOMMODATION
The Gallery
PLAN 2-A1

8–10 Queensberry Place, South Kensington SW7 2EA
☎ 020 7915 0000 ≜ 020 7970 1805
e–mail: reservations@eeh.co.uk
web: www.eeh.co.uk

dir: *Off A4 Cromwell Rd opp Natural History Museum, near South Kensington tube station*

This stylish property, close to Kensington and Knightsbridge, offers friendly hospitality, attentive service and sumptuously furnished bedrooms, some with a private terrace. Public areas include a choice of lounges (one with internet access) and an elegant bar. There is an option of English or continental breakfast, and 24-hour room service is available.

CONTINUED

The Gallery

Rooms 36 en suite **Facilities** STV TVB tea/coffee Direct dial from bedrooms Lift Cen ht Dinner Wi-fi available **Conf** Max 40 Thtr 40 Board 30 **Notes** ⊗

★★★★ GUEST ACCOMMODATION
The Gainsborough
PLAN 2-A1

7–11 Queensberry Place, South Kensington SW7 2DL
☎ 020 7957 0000 ≜ 020 7970 1805
e–mail: reservations@eeh.co.uk
web: www.eeh.co.uk

dir: *Off A4 Cromwell Rd opp Natural History Museum, near South Kensington tube station*

This smart Georgian house is in a quiet street near South Kensington's museums. Bedrooms are individually designed with fine fabrics, quality furnishings and co-ordinated colours. A choice of breakfasts is offered in the attractive dining room. There is also a delightful lobby lounge and 24-hour room service is available.

Rooms 48 en suite (5 fmly) **Facilities** STV TVB tea/coffee Direct dial from bedrooms Lift Cen ht Dinner Wi-fi available **Conf** Max 40 Class 40 Board 30 **Notes** ⊗

W1

★★★★ GUEST ACCOMMODATION

Best Western Premier Shaftesbury

PLAN 2-D3

65–73 Shaftesbury Av W1D 6EX

☎ 020 7871 6000

e–mail: reservations@shaftesburyhotel.co.uk

dir: *From Piccadilly Circus 300yds up Shaftesbury Ave, at junct with Dean Street*

In the centre of the West End, this boutique accommodation offers plenty of warm, traditional hospitality. The Shaftesbury is next to two major underground stations, with comfortably sized public areas, a refreshment lounge, the Premier Bar, restaurants, conference facilities, and a fitness room.

Rooms 67 en suite (2 fmly) **Facilities** STV TVB tea/coffee Direct dial from bedrooms Lift Gymnasium **Conf** Max 12 Board 12 **Notes** ⊗

★★★★ GUEST ACCOMMODATION

Hart House

PLAN 2-B4

51 Gloucester Place, Portman Sq W1U 8JF

☎ 020 7935 2288 📠 020 7935 8516

e–mail: reservations@harthouse.co.uk

web: www.harthouse.co.uk

dir: *Off Oxford St behind Selfridges, near Baker St or Marble Arch tube stations*

This elegant Georgian house is only a short walk from Oxford Street, Selfridges and Madame Tussaud's. Bedrooms and public areas are smartly furnished, stylishly decorated and have been carefully restored to retain much of the house's original character. English breakfast is served in the stylish dining room.

Rooms 15 en suite (4 fmly) (4 GF) S £80–£90; D £110–£125 **Facilities** FTV TVB tea/coffee Direct dial from bedrooms Cen ht Wi-fi available **Notes** ⊗

See advert on opposite page

★★★★ GUEST ACCOMMODATION

The St George

PLAN 2-B4

49 Gloucester Place W1U 8JE

☎ 020 7486 8586 & 7486 6567 📠 020 7486 6567

e–mail: reservations@stgeorge-hotel.net

dir: *Off Marylebone Rd, between Marble Arch & Baker St tube stations*

This attractive, Grade II listed house is in the heart of the West End near Oxford St. Bedrooms are furnished to a high standard and offer many facilities such as modem points, safes, hairdryers and mini-fridges. There is a smart breakfast room and the friendly staff offer a very warm welcome. The St George was a runner-up for the AA London B&B of the Year 2008 Award.

Rooms 19 en suite (3 fmly) (3 GF) S £75–£95; D £100–£125✳ **Facilities** STV FTV TVB tea/coffee Direct dial from bedrooms Cen ht TVL Wi-fi available **Conf** Max 20 Thtr 15 Class 20 Board 20 **Notes** ⊗

★★★ GUEST ACCOMMODATION

Mermaid Suite

PLAN 2-C4

3–4 Blenheim St W1S 1LA

☎ 020 7629 1875 📠 020 7499 9475

e–mail: info@mermaidsuite.com

dir: *Off New Bond St near Bond St tube station*

Located just off Oxford St, the Mermaid Suite provides excellent accommodation in one of London's best-known shopping areas. Bedrooms, on several floors and different buildings, are all smartly presented and well equipped. There is also a popular Italian restaurant, which is open all day.

Rooms 30 rms (29 en suite) (4 fmly) (2 smoking) **Facilities** STV TVB tea/coffee Direct dial from bedrooms Cen ht Dinner Last d 10pm **Notes** ⊗ Closed 23 Dec RS 28 Dec

★★★ GUEST ACCOMMODATION

The Regency

PLAN 2-C4

19 Nottingham Place W1U 5LQ

☎ 020 7486 5347 📠 020 7224 6057

e–mail: enquiries@regencyhotelwestend.co.uk

web: www.regencyhotelwestend.co.uk

dir: *A501 Marylebone Rd S onto Baker St, left onto Paddington St, left onto Nottingham Place*

The Regency, a converted mansion, is close to Baker Street tube station, Madame Tussaud's, West End shops and Harley Street. Bedrooms are well equipped and some rooms are suitable for families. Breakfast is served in the brightly appointed basement breakfast room. Free Wi-fi available.

Rooms 20 en suite (2 fmly) (5 smoking) S £65–£72; D £89–£94✳ **Facilities** STV TVB tea/coffee Direct dial from bedrooms Lift Cen ht TVL Dinner Last d 6pm Wi-fi available **Notes LB** ⊗

★★ GUEST ACCOMMODATION

Lincoln House
PLAN 2-B4

33 Gloucester Place W1U 8HY

☎ 020 7486 7630 🖹 020 7486 0166

e–mail: reservations@lincoln-house-hotel.co.uk

web: www.lincoln-house-hotel.co.uk

dir: *Walking from Marble Arch Station, turn left onto Oxford St, then left onto Portman St which continues onto Gloucester Place*

This impressive Georgian property, located close to Oxford Street, is a friendly, family-run establishment. Comfortable bedrooms vary in size and many benefit from air-conditioning. Public areas are decorated to a high standard with a cottage-style breakfast room on the lower ground floor.

Rooms 24 en suite (5 fmly) (6 GF) **Facilities** STV TVB tea/coffee Direct dial from bedrooms Wi-fi available **Parking** 10 **Notes** ⊗

★★ 🅰 BED & BREAKFAST

Marble Arch Inn
PLAN 2-B3

49–50 Upper Berkeley St, Marble Arch W1H 5QR

☎ 020 7723 7888 🖹 020 7723 6060

e–mail: sales@marblearch-inn.co.uk

web: www.marblearch-inn.co.uk

dir: *Near Marble Arch rdbt. A5 N on Edgware Rd, 3rd right*

Rooms 29 rms (23 en suite) (9 fmly) (7 GF) S £40–£80; D £40–£80 **Facilities** STV TVB tea/coffee Direct dial from bedrooms Cen ht Wi-fi available **Notes** ⊗

W2

★★★★ GUEST ACCOMMODATION

Best Western Mornington
PLAN 2-A3

12 Lancaster Gate W2 3LG

☎ 020 7262 7361 🖹 020 7706 1028

e–mail: london@mornington.co.uk

dir: *N of Hyde Park, off A402 Bayswater Rd*

This fine Victorian building is located in a quiet road close to Lancaster Gate station for easy access to the West End. The bedrooms have been appointed to provide comfortable, stylish accommodation. There is a lounge/bar and an attractive dining room where an extensive Scandinavian-style breakfast is served.

Rooms 66 en suite (9 fmly) (2 GF) (20 smoking) S £75–£99; D £89–£135 **Facilities** STV TVB tea/coffee Direct dial from bedrooms Lift Cen ht Wi-fi available **Conf** Max 14 Thtr 20 Class 14 Board 14

★★★★ GUEST ACCOMMODATION

Best Western Shaftesbury Paddington Court London
PLAN 2-A3

27 Devonshire Ter W2 3DP

☎ 020 7745 1200 🖹 020 7745 1221

e–mail: info@paddingtoncourt.com

web: www.paddingtoncourt.com

dir: *From A40 take exit before Paddington flyover, follow Paddington Station signs. Devonshire Terr is off Craven Rd*

This establishment benefits from its convenient location close to Paddington mainline train station including links to the underground stations and the Heathrow Express terminal. Situated next to Hyde Park and Kensington Palace Gardens this establishment offers smart and comfortable guest accommodation and a guaranteed substantial breakfast. Club Rooms are also available with additional extras provided including exclusive use of the Club Lounge. A room is available for small meetings by prior arrangement.

Rooms 165 en suite 35 annexe en suite (43 fmly) **Facilities** STV TVB tea/coffee Direct dial from bedrooms Lift TVL **Notes** ⊗

W2 *CONTINUED*

★★★★ GUEST ACCOMMODATION
Byron
PLAN 2-A3

36–38 Queensborough Ter W2 3SH
☎ 020 7243 0987 📠 020 7792 1957
e–mail: byron@capricornhotels.co.uk
web: www.byronhotel.co.uk

dir: *Off Bayswater Rd near Queensway tube station*

This charming terrace house has been thoughtfully restored to retain many original features. Bedrooms are carefully decorated, and thoughtfully equipped with air conditioning, trouser presses and safes. Breakfast is served in the attractive dining room and there is an elegant lounge and a smart conservatory.

Rooms 45 en suite (5 fmly) **Facilities** STV TVB tea/coffee Direct dial from bedrooms Lift Cen ht TVL Wi-fi available **Notes** ⊗

★★★★ GUEST ACCOMMODATION
Hyde Park Radnor
PLAN 2-A5

7–9 Sussex Place, Hyde Park W2 2SX
☎ 020 7723 5969 📠 020 7262 8955
e–mail: hydeparkradnor@btconnect.com
web: www.hydeparkradnor.com

dir: *Off A402 Bayswater Rd onto Lancaster Ter & Sussex Gardens, right onto Sussex Place*

This smart property is within walking distance of Paddington station and close to all London's central attractions. The smart bedrooms are brightly appointed, well equipped and have modern en suites. English breakfast is served in the lower ground-floor dining room.

Rooms 36 en suite (10 fmly) (5 GF) **Facilities** STV TVB tea/coffee Direct dial from bedrooms Lift Cen ht TVL **Parking** 2 **Notes** ⊗

★★★★ GUEST HOUSE
The New Linden
PLAN 1-D4

59 Leinster Square, Notting Hill W2 4PS
☎ 020 7221 4321 📠 020 7727 3156
e–mail: newlindenhotel@mayflower-group.co.uk

dir: *Off A402, Bayswater Rd*

The friendly New Linden has a good location north of Kensington Gardens. Its stylish en suite bedrooms are richly furnished and thoughtfully equipped with CD players and safes. A good continental breakfast is served in the basement dining room. The New Linden was a runner-up for the AA London B&B of the Year 2008 Award.

Rooms 52 en suite S £79–£89; D £99–£155✱ **Facilities** STV TVB tea/coffee Direct dial from bedrooms Lift Cen ht Wi-fi available **Notes** ⊗

See advert on opposite page

★★★★ GUEST ACCOMMODATION
Quality Crown Hyde Park
PLAN 2-A3

8–14 Talbot Square W2 1TS
☎ 020 7262 6699 📠 020 7723 3233
e–mail: quality-p@lth-hotels.com

dir: *SE of Paddington station off Sussex Gardens*

This well-presented property is convenient for Hyde Park, Paddington and Marble Arch. The modern bedrooms are furnished to a good standard and the executive rooms are particularly impressive. Public areas include a compact but stylish bar and lounge, and a basement restaurant where hearty breakfasts are served.

Rooms 75 en suite (8 fmly) (8 GF) **Facilities** STV TVB tea/coffee Direct dial from bedrooms Lift Cen ht TVL **Notes** ⊗

★★★★ GUEST ACCOMMODATION
Quality Crown Paddington
PLAN 2-A4

144 Praed St, Paddington W2 1HU
☎ 020 7706 8888 📠 020 7706 8800
e–mail: seay@qualitycrown.com

This contemporary, stylish property enjoys a central location, adjacent to Paddington Station. Bedrooms and en suites vary in size but all are extremely smartly appointed and boast a host of extra facilities including CD players, flat screen TVs, room safes and internet access. A small gym, stylish lounge and meeting rooms are also available.

Rooms 83 en suite **Facilities** STV TVB tea/coffee Direct dial from bedrooms Lift Cen ht TVL Dinner Last d noon **Conf** Max 22 Board 22 **Notes** ⊗

★★★★ GUEST ACCOMMODATION
Shaftesbury Hyde Park
Paddington
PLAN 2-A4

78–82 Westbourne Ter, Paddington W2 6QA

☎ 020 7262 4521 📄 020 7262 7610

e–mail: reservations@londonpremierhotels.co.uk

dir: *Off A40 onto Lancaster Ter, at crossing left onto slip road*

This attractive property enjoys a central location within easy reach of central London shops and attractions. The en suite bedrooms and public areas have a smart contemporary feel. Although rooms vary in size, all boast many useful facilities such as free internet access, mini-fridges and irons.

Rooms 119 en suite (2 GF) **Facilities** STV TVB tea/coffee Direct dial from bedrooms Lift Wi-fi available **Parking** 12 **Notes** ⊗

★★★ GUEST ACCOMMODATION
Admiral
PLAN 2-A3

143 Sussex Gardens, Hyde Park W2 2RY

☎ 020 7723 7309 📄 020 7723 8731

The Admiral is a short walk from Paddington station and is convenient for Hyde Park and the West End. The smart bedrooms are enhanced with attractive artworks, and a full English breakfast is provided.

Rooms 21 en suite (12 fmly) (2 GF) S £50–£70; D £68–£88✳
Facilities STV FTV TVB tea/coffee Direct dial from bedrooms Cen ht TVL Dinner Last d 7pm Wi-fi available **Conf** Max 30 Class 20 **Parking** available **Notes** LB ⊗

★★★ GUEST ACCOMMODATION
Kingsway Park
Guest Accommodation
PLAN 2-A4

139 Sussex Gardens W2 2RX

☎ 020 7723 5677 & 7724 9346 📄 020 7402 4352

e–mail: info@kingswaypark-hotel.com

web: www.kingswaypark-hotel.com

This Victorian property has a central location within walking distance of Marble Arch, Hyde Park and Paddington. Bedrooms offer well-equipped value accommodation. Public areas include a reception lounge and a basement breakfast room adorned with interesting artwork. A limited number of parking spaces is available.

CONTINUED

Kingsway Park Guest Accommodation

Rooms 22 en suite (5 fmly) (2 GF) S £50–£70; D £68–£88✳ (room only)
Facilities STV FTV TVB tea/coffee Direct dial from bedrooms Cen ht TVL Dinner Last d 7pm **Conf** Max 30 **Parking** 3 **Notes** LB ⊗

★★★ GUEST ACCOMMODATION
Park Lodge
PLAN 2-A3

73 Queensborough Ter, Bayswater W2 3SU

☎ 020 7229 6424 📄 020 7221 4772

e–mail: info@hotelparklodge.com

dir: *Off Bayswater Rd near Queensway tube station*

A short walk from Kensington Gardens and fashionable Queensway, this former house has been converted to provide good, practically equipped bedrooms. Bathrooms are bright and well appointed. Breakfast is served in the basement dining room.

Rooms 29 en suite (1 fmly) (3 GF) **Facilities** STV TVB tea/coffee Direct dial from bedrooms Lift Cen ht **Notes** ⊗

W2 CONTINUED

★★★ GUEST ACCOMMODATION
Parkwood at Marble Arch   PLAN 2-B3
4 Stanhope Place, Marble Arch W2 2HB
☎ 020 7402 2241 🖷 020 7402 1574
e–mail: reception@parkwoodhotel.com
web: www.parkwoodhotel.com
dir: *Near Marble Arch tube station*

Located in a quiet residential street next to Marble Arch and Oxford Street, the friendly Parkwood provides a central base for budget-conscious shoppers and tourists. Family rooms are available, and a freshly cooked breakfast is served in the attractive basement dining room.

Rooms 16 rms (12 en suite) (1 fmly) (2 GF) **Facilities** STV TVB tea/coffee Direct dial from bedrooms Cen ht TVL **Notes** ⊗

★★★ GUEST ACCOMMODATION
Princes Square   PLAN 2-A3
23–25 Princes Square, off Ilchester Gardens, Bayswater W2 4NJ
☎ 020 7229 9876 🖷 020 7229 4664
e–mail: info@princessquarehotel.co.uk
dir: *From Bayswater take 1st left onto Moscow Rd, then 3rd turning on right into Ilchester Gardens*
This fine building is in a quiet road close to tube stations for easy access to the West End. The comfortable bedrooms provide stylish accommodation, and there is a small bar and an attractive dining room where a continental breakfast is served.

Rooms 50 en suite (3 fmly) (6 GF) **Facilities** STV TVB tea/coffee Direct dial from bedrooms Lift Cen ht Wi-fi available **Notes** ⊗

★★★ 🅰 BED & BREAKFAST
Barry House   PLAN 2-A4
12 Sussex Place, Hyde Park W2 2TP
☎ 020 7723 7340 🖷 020 7723 9775
e–mail: hotel@barryhouse.co.uk
web: www.barryhouse.co.uk
dir: *300yds SE of Paddington station*

Rooms 18 rms (15 en suite) (5 fmly) (2 GF) S £42–£59; D £75–£89✳ **Facilities** FTV TVB tea/coffee Direct dial from bedrooms Cen ht Wi-fi available **Notes** ⊗

W6

★★ GUEST ACCOMMODATION
Orlando   PLAN 1-D3
83 Shepherds Bush Rd W6 7LR
☎ 020 7603 4890 🖷 020 7603 4890
e–mail: hotelorlando@btconnect.com
web: www.hotelorlando.co.uk
dir: *On A219 between Hammersmith & Shepherd's Bush tube stations*
The Orlando is part of a Victorian terrace within easy walking distance of tube stations. Bedrooms, varying in size and style, are soundly furnished and well maintained. Breakfast is served at individual tables in the smart basement dining room.

Rooms 14 en suite (3 fmly) **Facilities** TVB tea/coffee Direct dial from bedrooms Cen ht **Notes** ⊗

W7

★★ BED & BREAKFAST
Hanwell Bed and Breakfast   PLAN 1-B4
110A Grove Av, Hanwell W7 3ES
☎ 020 8567 5015
e–mail: tassanimation@aol.com
web: www.ealing-hanwell-bed-and-breakfast.co.uk/new/about.html
dir: *1.5m from Greenford Rd*

Hanwell Bed and Breakfast occupies a convenient and peaceful location close to regular bus routes and within walking distance of Ealing Hospital and near to Ealing golf course. An array of restaurants offering menus to suit all palates is available within minutes. Accommodation is comfortable and the top floor en suite bedroom is available for longer term stays (minimum seven nights). Breakfast provides an excellent start to the day.

CONTINUED

Hanwell Bed and Breakfast

Rooms 2 rms (1 en suite) (1 pri facs) (2 fmly) **Facilities** TVB tea/coffee Cen ht Dinner Last d 3pm Wi-fi available **Parking** 2 **Notes** ⊗ Closed 25 Dec ☻

W11

Ⓤ
Portobello Gold
PLAN 1-D4

95/97 Portobello Rd W11 2QB

☎ 020 7460 4910

e–mail: reservations@portobellogold.com

web: www.portobellogold.com

At the time of going to press the rating for this establishment had not been confirmed. Please check the AA website www.theAA.com for up-to-date information.

Rooms 8 en suite (1 fmly) (1 smoking) D £80–£170✳ **Facilities** STV TVB tea/coffee Direct dial from bedrooms Cen ht Dinner Last d 11.15pm Wi-fi available **Conf** Max 20 Thtr 20 Board 10

W14

Ⓤ
Avonmore
PLAN 1-D3

66 Avonmore Rd W14 8RS

☎ 020 7603 4296 & 7603 3121 ▤ 056 0153 5230

e–mail: reservations@avonmorehotel.co.uk

web: www.avonmorehotel.co.uk

dir: *Off Hammersmith Rd opp Olympia Exhibition Centre*

At the time of going to press the rating for this establishment had not been confirmed. Please check the AA website www.theAA.com for up-to-date information.

Rooms 9 rms (7 en suite) (3 fmly) (2 GF) S £75–£85; D £95–£105✳ **Facilities** TVB tea/coffee Direct dial from bedrooms Cen ht TVL Wi-fi available **Notes LB** ⊗

WC1

★★★ GUEST ACCOMMODATION
Euro
PLAN 2-D5

51–53 Cartwright Gardens, Russell Square WC1H 9EL

☎ 020 7387 4321 ▤ 020 7383 5044

e–mail: reception@eurohotel.co.uk

dir: *Off Euston Rd onto Judd St, right onto Leigh St & Cartwright Gardens. Near Euston tube station*

This friendly guest house is in a leafy Georgian crescent only a short walk from Russell Square tube station with its direct link to Heathrow. Bedrooms are well equipped and many have en suite bathrooms. Breakfast is served at individual tables in the attractive dining room.

Rooms 31 rms (23 en suite) (6 pri facs) (9 fmly) (4 GF) **Facilities** STV TVB tea/coffee Direct dial from bedrooms Cen ht Wi-fi available ☕ **Notes** ⊗

★★★ GUEST ACCOMMODATION
The George
PLAN 2-D5

58–60 Cartwright Gardens WC1H 9EL

☎ 020 7387 8777 ▤ 020 7387 8666

e–mail: ghotel@aol.com

web: www.georgehotel.com

dir: *From St Pancras 2nd left onto Marchmont St & 1st left onto Cartwright Gardens*

The George is within walking distance of Russell Square and the tube, and convenient for London's central attractions. The brightly appointed bedrooms vary in size, many have en suites, and some rooms are suitable for families. A substantial breakfast is served in the attractive ground-floor dining room.

Rooms 40 rms (14 en suite) (14 fmly) (4 GF) **Facilities** STV TVB tea/coffee Direct dial from bedrooms Cen ht TVL ☕ Free Internet access **Notes** ⊗

★★★ GUEST ACCOMMODATION
The Jesmond Dene
PLAN 2-D5

27 Argyle St, Kings Cross WC1H 8EP

☎ 020 7837 4654 ▤ 020 7833 1633

e–mail: info@jesmonddenehotel.co.uk

web: www.jesmonddenehotel.co.uk

Less than five minutes walk from the mainline and underground station of Kings Cross is The Jesmond Dene. Accommodation comprises comfortable bedrooms most of which benefit from their own en suite facilities; (some bathroom facilities are shared). Warm service and hospitality is provided along with a well cooked breakfast served in the bright dining room.

Rooms 22 rms (11 en suite) (4 fmly) (5 GF) S £50–£95; D £60–£110✳ **Facilities** STV FTV TVB tea/coffee Cen ht Wi-fi available **Parking** 6 **Notes** ⊗

WC1 CONTINUED

★★ GUEST ACCOMMODATION

Mentone
PLAN 2-D5

54–56 Cartwright Gardens, Bloomsbury WC1H 9EL

☎ 020 7387 3927 & 7388 4671 📠 020 7388 4671

e–mail: bookings@mentonehotel.com

web: www.mentonehotel.com

dir: *Between Euston Rd & Russell Sq*

Overlooking pleasant gardens and tennis courts, this Georgian terrace is within easy reach of many central London attractions. Good value accommodation is provided in thoughtfully equipped rooms. Free internet access is provided in the reception area. Traditional breakfasts are served in the smart dining room.

Rooms 43 en suite (14 fmly) **Facilities** TVB tea/coffee Direct dial from bedrooms Lift Wi-fi available ♨ **Notes** ⊗

MERSEYSIDE

BIRKENHEAD
MAP 15 SJ38

★★★ A GUEST ACCOMMODATION

Shrewsbury Lodge

31 Shrewsbury Rd, Oxton CH43 2JB

☎ 0151 652 4029 📠 0151 653 3593

e–mail: info@shrewsbury-hotel.com

web: www.shrewsbury-hotel.com

Rooms 16 en suite S £30–£48; D £65–£75✱ (room only)

LIVERPOOL
MAP 15 SJ39

★★★ GUEST ACCOMMODATION

Aachen

91 Mount Pleasant L3 5TB

☎ 0151 709 3477 & 709 3633 📠 0151 709 1126

e–mail: enquiries@aachenhotel.co.uk

web: www.aachenhotel.co.uk

dir: *Signs for city centre & Mount Pleasant car park*

The friendly Aachen is within easy walking distance of the cathedrals, university and the city centre. Its attractive bedrooms are extremely well equipped for business and leisure, and there is a cosy lounge bar.

Rooms 17 rms (11 en suite) (6 fmly) (3 GF) **Facilities** STV TVB tea/coffee Direct dial from bedrooms Cen ht TVL Wi-fi available **Conf** Max 30 **Parking** 2 **Notes** ⊗ Closed 22 Dec–2 Jan

MAGHULL
MAP 15 SD30

★★★★ 🗑 FARM HOUSE

Goose Meadow B&B *(SD357044)*

Gore House Farm, Acres Ln L31 4EX

☎ 0151 526 0519 Ms L Edwards

e–mail: edwards@goosemeadow.co.uk

dir: *2m NW of town centre. A5147 onto B5195 for Formby, 1m left onto Acres Ln, 1m on right*

Goose Meadow is a historic, ivy-covered farmhouse dating from 1685. The accommodation is spacious and well equipped and there is a comfortable lounge and dining room where traditional farmhouse breakfasts are served. One room is en suite and another has private facilities in a wing of the farmhouse.

Rooms 2 rms (1 en suite) (1 pri facs) (1 GF) S £50; D £66–£80✱ **Facilities** FTV TVB tea/coffee Cen ht TVL Fishing **Parking** 4 **Notes** LB ⊗ No children 5yrs 675 acres Arable, Pigs

SOUTHPORT
MAP 15 SD31

★★★★ GUEST ACCOMMODATION

Bay Tree House B & B

No1 Irving St, Marine Gate PR9 0HD

☎ 01704 510555 📠 0870 753 6318

e–mail: baytreehouseuk@aol.com

web: www.baytreehousesouthport.co.uk

dir: *Off Leicester St*

A warm welcome is assured at this immaculately maintained house, located a short walk from promenade and central attractions. Bedrooms are equipped with a wealth of thoughtful extras, and delicious imaginative breakfasts are served in an attractive dining room overlooking the pretty front patio garden.

Rooms 6 en suite **Facilities** FTV TVB tea/coffee Direct dial from bedrooms Cen ht Dinner Last d 10am Wi-fi available **Parking** 2 **Notes** Closed 14 Dec–1 Feb

★★★★ GUEST ACCOMMODATION

The Baytrees

4 Queens Rd PR9 9HN

☎ 01704 536513 📠 01704 536513

e–mail: stay@baytreeshotel.freeserve.co.uk

web: www.baytreeshotel.co.uk

dir: *From B565 Lord St towards fire station, right at rdbt onto Manchester Rd, left at lights, 200yds on right*

Located a short walk from Lord Street, this elegant late Victorian house has been appointed to provide thoughtfully furnished bedrooms with smart modern en suite bathrooms. Breakfast is served in the attractive dining room overlooking the pretty rear garden, and a lounge is also available.

Rooms 12 en suite (5 fmly) (2 GF) S £29.50–£32.50; D £53–£59✱ **Facilities** TVB tea/coffee Cen ht TVL **Parking** 11 **Notes** ⊗ Closed Xmas

ENGLAND

★★★★ GUEST ACCOMMODATION
Bowden Lodge

18 Albert Rd PR9 0LE
☎ 01704 543531 📄 01704 539112
e–mail: stay@bowdenlodge.co.uk
web: www.bowdenlodge.co.uk

dir: *A565 N from town centre, over rdbt, 150yds on right*

This stylish house is in a quiet residential area just a stroll from Lord Street and the town's attractions. Bedrooms, many suitable for families, are smartly furnished and well equipped. Day rooms include a lounge with deep sofas, and a bright dining room where hearty cooked breakfasts are served. Value for money and a friendly welcome are assured.

Rooms 10 en suite (3 fmly) S £30–£40; D £60–£100✳ **Facilities** TVB tea/coffee Cen ht TVL Dinner Last d 10am Wi-fi available **Parking** 10 **Notes** LB ⊗

★★★★ GUEST ACCOMMODATION
Rosedale

11 Talbot St PR8 1HP
☎ 01704 530604 📄 01704 530604
e–mail: info@rosedale-hotel.co.uk

dir: *A570 into Southport, left onto Talbot St*

The smart and friendly Rosedale stands in a quiet street only a short walk from the town's attractions. The bright bedrooms are thoughtfully equipped, and there is a comfortable lounge, a cosy bar and a lovely garden.

Rooms 9 rms (8 en suite) (1 pri facs) (2 fmly) **Facilities** TVB tea/coffee Cen ht TVL Dinner **Parking** 6 **Notes** ⊗ Closed 21 Dec–3 Jan

★★★★ GUEST ACCOMMODATION
The White Lodge

12 Talbot St PR8 1HP
☎ 01704 536320 📄 01704 536320
dir: *In town centre. Off A570 Eastbank St onto Talbot St, 100yds on right*

Expect a genuine welcome at this family-run, non-smoking guest house, just a stroll from the town centre. Bedrooms, including one on the ground floor, are thoughtfully equipped, and the public areas feature a comfy lounge and a cosy cellar bar. Evening meals are available by arrangement.

Rooms 8 rms (6 en suite) (2 fmly) (1 GF) S £35–£50; D £70–£85 **Facilities** TVB tea/coffee Cen ht Dinner Last d 6pm **Parking** 6 **Notes** LB ⊗ 📶

★★★★ GUEST ACCOMMODATION
Whitworth Falls

16 Lathom Rd PR9 0JH
☎ 01704 530074
e–mail: whitworthfalls@rapid.co.uk

dir: *A565 N from town centre, over rdbt, 2nd left onto Alexandra Rd, 4th right*

Located on a mainly residential avenue within easy walking distance of seafront and Lord Street shops, this Victorian house has been renovated to provide a range of practical but homely bedrooms. Breakfasts and pre-theatre dinners are served in the attractive dining room, and a comfortable sitting room and lounge bar are also available.

Rooms 12 en suite (2 fmly) (1 GF) **Facilities** TVB tea/coffee Direct dial from bedrooms Cen ht TVL Dinner Last d noon **Parking** 8

★★ GUEST HOUSE
Lyndhurst

101 King St PR8 1LQ
☎ 01704 537520 & 07759 526864 📄 01704 537520

dir: *Off A570 Eastbank St at McDonalds onto King St*

This well maintained friendly guest house is situated just a short walk from Lord Street and the town's main attractions. It offers brightly decorated, comfortable accommodation. Public areas include a cosy lounge that leads onto the breakfast room.

Rooms 6 rms **Facilities** TVB tea/coffee Cen ht TVL **Parking** 2 **Notes** No children 12yrs No coaches Closed Xmas & New Year 📶

NORFOLK

ALBURGH   MAP 13 TM28

★★★★ ⊛⊛ RESTAURANT WITH ROOMS
The Dove Restaurant with Rooms

Holbrook Hill IP20 0EP
☎ 01986 788315 📄 01986 788315
e–mail: thedovenorfolk@freeula.com

dir: *Between Harleston & Bungay at junct A143 & B1062*

A warm welcome awaits at this restaurant with rooms, situated just off the A143 between Harleston and Bungay. Bedrooms are pleasantly decorated, furnished with pine pieces and have modern facilities. Public rooms include a lounge area with a small bar, and a smart restaurant with well-spaced tables.

Rooms 2 rms (1 en suite) (1 pri facs) (1 fmly) S £37; D £57✳ **Facilities** TVB tea/coffee Cen ht Dinner Last d 9pm **Parking** 20 **Notes** ⊗

CONTINUED

ATTLEBOROUGH MAP 13 TM09

★★★★ BED & BREAKFAST
Rylstone B&B
Bell Rd, Rockland St Peter NR17 1UL
☎ 01953 488199 📠 0870 1320816
e–mail: margaret@hneale.f9.co.uk

dir: *4m W of Attleborough. B1077 to Rockland St Peter, at x-rds onto Chapel St & Bell Rd*

A delightful detached property situated in a peaceful rural location on the edge of the village. The pleasantly decorated bedrooms have co-ordinated fabrics and many thoughtful touches. Public rooms include a large lounge with a log burner and a conservatory, which has views of the surrounding countryside.

Rooms 3 rms (2 en suite) (1 pri facs) D fr £60✱ **Facilities** TVB tea/coffee Cen ht **Parking** 3 **Notes** LB ⊗ 🐾

⊛ [U]
Sherbourne House
8 Norwich Rd NR17 2JX
☎ 01953 454363
e–mail: stay@sherbourne-house.co.uk
web: www.sherbourne-house.co.uk

dir: *Off B1077*

At the time of going to press the rating for this establishment had not been confirmed. Please check the AA website www.theAA.com for up-to-date information.

Rooms 8 en suite (1 fmly) (1 GF) S £40–£70; D £70–£80✱ **Facilities** FTV TVB tea/coffee Cen ht Dinner Last d 8.30pm Wi-fi available **Conf** Max 30 Thtr 30 Class 16 Board 20 Del from £100 ✱ **Parking** 30 **Notes** Civ Wed 40

BACTON MAP 13 TG33

★★ BED & BREAKFAST
Grange Cottage B&B
1 Grange Cottage, Pollard St NR12 0LH
☎ 01692 652219
e–mail: grangecottage1@yahoo.co.uk

dir: *North Walsham to Edingthorpe on B1150. Continue to Pollard St, B&B sign on right*

Expect a warm welcome from the caring hosts at this delightful cottage situated in a peaceful rural location surrounded by open countryside. Bedrooms are smartly decorated and equipped with a good range of thoughtful touches. Breakfast is served at a large communal table in the cheerful dining room which overlooks the garden.

Rooms 3 rms (1 en suite) S £30; D £50–£58✱ **Facilities** TVB tea/coffee Cen ht **Parking** 3 **Notes** ⊗ Closed 24–26 Dec 🐾

BARNEY MAP 13 TF93

★★★★ BED & BREAKFAST
The Old Brick Kilns
Little Barney Ln NR21 0NL
☎ 01328 878305 📠 01328 878948
e–mail: enquiries@old-brick-kilns.co.uk
web: www.old-brick-kilns.co.uk

dir: *Off B1354 to Barney, 0.3m left onto Little Barney Ln, B&B 0.75m at end*

This delightful country house, originally three separate cottages, provides attractive accommodation in peaceful grounds. Breakfasts are served at a communal table in the lounge-dining room. Due to the narrow access road, no arrivals can be accepted until after 1pm.

Rooms 3 en suite S £30–£35; D £59–£65✱ **Facilities** TVB tea/coffee Cen ht TVL Wi-fi available Fishing Pool Table **Parking** 20 **Notes** ⊗ No children 16yrs

---

BLAKENEY MAP 13 TG04

Premier Collection

★★★★★ GUEST HOUSE
Blakeney House
High St NR25 7NX
☎ 01263 740561 📠 01263 741750
e–mail: admin@blakeneyhouse.com
web: www.blakeneyhouse.com

dir: *In village centre*

A stunning Victorian manor house set amid two acres of attractive landscaped grounds just a short walk from the quay and town centre. The stylish, individually decorated bedrooms have co-ordinated fabrics and many thoughtful touches. Breakfast is served at individual tables in the smart dining room, which overlooks the well-stocked front garden.

Rooms 8 rms (7 en suite) (1 pri facs) (1 fmly) **Facilities** TVB tea/coffee Cen ht Wi-fi available **Parking** 8 **Notes** ⊗ No children 12yrs No coaches

BRISLEY MAP 13 TF92

★★★ INN

The Brisley Bell Inn & Restaurant

The Green NR20 5DW

☎ 01362 668686

e-mail: info@brisleybell-inn.co.uk

web: www.brisleybell-inn.co.uk

dir: *Between Fakenham and East Dereham on B1145*

Delightful village inn situated in a peaceful location just a short drive from the town centre. The bedrooms are generally quite spacious, each one is smartly appointed with modern furniture and co-ordinated soft furnishings. Public rooms include a beamed bar and a cosy restaurant serving an interesting choice of dishes.

Rooms 3 rms (1 en suite) (1 fmly) (3 GF) **Facilities** FTV TVB tea/coffee Cen ht Dinner Last d 6pm **Parking** 30 **Notes** ⊗

BROOKE MAP 13 TM29

★★★★ 🍴 BED & BREAKFAST

Old Vicarage

48 The Street NR15 1JU

☎ 01508 558329

dir: *Off B1332 in village centre near church*

Set in mature gardens in a peaceful village, this charming house is within easy driving distance of Norwich. The individually decorated bedrooms are thoughtfully furnished and equipped, and one room has a lovely four-poster bed. There is an elegant dining room and a cosy lounge, and dinner is available by arrangement. Service is genuinely helpful, provided in a relaxed and friendly manner.

Rooms 2 en suite S £40; D £60 **Facilities** tea/coffee Cen ht TVL Dinner Last d day before **Parking** 4 **Notes LB** ⊗ No children 15yrs 🐾

BURNHAM MARKET MAP 13 TF84

See also Wells-next-the-Sea

★★★★ FARM HOUSE

Whitehall Farm *(TF856412)*

Burnham Thorpe PE31 8HN

☎ 01328 738416 & 07050 247390 📠 01328 730937

Mrs V Southerland

e-mail: barrysoutherland@aol.com

web: www.whitehallfarm-accommodation.com

dir: *From Lord Nelson pub in Burnham towards Holkam/Wells, last building on right leaving village*

The large farmhouse forms part of a working arable farm. The property stands in large landscaped gardens with a menagerie of animals and offers a relaxing and informal atmosphere. Bedrooms are spacious, comfortable and equipped with DVDs, televisions and many extras. Communal hearty breakfasts are served in the cosy dining room.

Rooms 3 en suite (1 fmly) S £36–£72; D £72–£80✻ **Facilities** FTV TVB tea/coffee Cen ht Wi-fi available **Parking** 7 **Notes LB** 560 acres arable

---

CLEY NEXT THE SEA MAP 13 TG04

Premier Collection

★★★★★ 🍴 BED & BREAKFAST

Old Town Hall House

Coast Rd NR25 7RB

☎ 01263 740284

web: www.oldtownhallhouse.co.uk

dir: *On A149 in centre of Cley. Opposite old red phone box*

Expect a warm welcome from the caring hosts at this delightful detached property situated in the heart of a bustling North Norfolk village, which has been designated as an Area of Outstanding Natural Beauty, and has a superb bird watching reserve on its outskirts. The tastefully appointed bedrooms have lovely co-ordinated soft fabrics and many thoughtful touches. Breakfast, using locally sourced produce, is served at individual tables in the stylish dining room.

Rooms 3 en suite D £75–£95✻ **Facilities** tea/coffee Cen ht **Notes** ⊗ No children Closed Xmas & Jan

---

COLTISHALL MAP 13 TG21

★★★★ GUEST ACCOMMODATION

The Hedges

Tunstead Rd NR12 7AL

☎ 01603 738361 📠 01603 738983

e-mail: info@hedgesbandb.co.uk

web: www.hedgesbandb.co.uk

dir: *Off B1354 onto White Lion Rd & right fork*

A delightful family-run guest house situated close to the Norfolk Broads. The spacious bedrooms have co-ordinated fabrics and many thoughtful touches; most rooms have lovely views of the surrounding countryside. Breakfast is served in the dining room and guests have the use of a smart conservatory which overlooks the garden.

Rooms 5 en suite (2 fmly) (2 GF) **Facilities** TVB tea/coffee Cen ht TVL **Parking** 5 **Notes** ⊗ Closed 23–28 Dec

---

COLTON MAP 13 TG10

Ⓤ

The Ugly Bug Inn

High House Farm Ln NR9 5DG

☎ 01603 880794

e-mail: john_lainchbury@hotmail.com

dir: *A47 Ringland rdbt, take Colton exit, follow signs approx 2m*

At the time of going to press the rating for this establishment had not been confirmed. Please check the AA website www.theAA.com for up-to-date information.

Rooms 4 en suite (1 GF) D £60–£80✻ **Facilities** TVB tea/coffee Cen ht Dinner Last d 9pm Fishing **Parking** 40 **Notes LB**

ENGLAND

CROMER

MAP 13 TG24

See also Sheringham

★★★★★ BED & BREAKFAST

Incleborough House

Lower Common, East Runton NR27 9PG

☎ 01263 515939 ▤ 01263 510022

e–mail: enquiries@incleboroughhouse.co.uk

web: www.incleboroughhouse.co.uk

dir: *On A149 turn left onto Felbrigg road, 150mtrs on left*

Guests can look forward to tea and home-made cake on arrival at this large, award-winning, 16th-century property which has been lovingly restored by the current owners. The attractively decorated bedrooms are carefully furnished throughout with lovely co-ordinated fabrics, and have a wealth of useful extras. The spacious public areas include a luxurious drawing room with plush leather sofas and an open fireplace. Breakfast is served at individual tables in the large open-plan conservatory which has a lush indoor tropical garden.

Rooms 3 en suite (1 GF) S £112.50–£123.75; D £150–£165✱
Facilities STV FTV TVB tea/coffee Cen ht Dinner Last d 7.30pm Wi-fi available Pool Table **Parking** 7 **Notes LB** No children 14yrs

See advert on opposite page

★★★★ FARM HOUSE

Shrublands Farm *(TG246393)*

Church St, Northrepps NR27 0AA

☎ 01263 579297 ▤ 01263 579297 Mrs A Youngman

e–mail: youngman@farming.co.uk

web: www.broadland.com/shrublands

dir: *Off A149 to Northrepps, through village, past Foundry Arms, cream house 50yds on left*

Expect a warm welcome from the caring host at this delightful 18th-century farmhouse, set in landscaped grounds and surrounded by 300 acres of arable farmland. Public areas include a cosy lounge with a wood-burning stove, and breakfast is served at a communal table in the elegant dining room.

Shrublands Farm

Rooms 3 rms (1 en suite) (2 pri facs) S £42–£45; D £64–£70✱
Facilities FTV TVB tea/coffee Cen ht TVL **Parking** 5 **Notes LB** ⊛
No children 12yrs 300 acres arable

★★★★ GUEST HOUSE

Beachcomber Guest House

17 Macdonald Rd NR27 9AP

☎ 01263 513398

e–mail: info@beachcomber-guesthouse.co.uk

dir: *Off A149 Runton Rd, 500yds W of pier*

A smartly maintained Edwardian house situated in a peaceful side road close to the seafront and town centre. The pleasant bedrooms are carefully furnished and equipped with many thoughtful touches. Breakfast is served in the smart dining room and there is a comfortable lounge with plush sofas.

Rooms 5 rms (4 en suite) (1 pri facs) (1 fmly) S £35–£45; D £56–£60✱
Facilities TVB tea/coffee Cen ht TVL **Notes LB** ⊛ No children 8yrs
No coaches Closed Xmas ☺

★★★★ GUEST HOUSE

Bon Vista

12 Alfred Rd NR27 9AN

☎ 01263 511818

e–mail: jim@bonvista-cromer.co.uk

web: www.bonvista-cromer.co.uk

dir: *From pier onto A148 (Coast road), 400yds left onto Alfred Rd*

This delightful Victorian terrace house, situated in a peaceful side road adjacent to the seafront and just a short walk from the town centre,

CONTINUED
CONTINUED

extends a warm welcome. The individually decorated bedrooms have co-ordinated soft fabrics and many thoughtful touches. Public rooms include an attractive dining room and a spacious first floor lounge.

Rooms 5 en suite (2 fmly) **Facilities** TVB tea/coffee Cen ht TVL
Parking 2 **Notes** ⊛ No coaches ☺

★★★★ GUEST ACCOMMODATION
Westgate Lodge B&B
10 MacDonald Rd NR27 9AP
☎ 01263 512840

dir: *Along seafront & left after the Cliftonville Hotel, Westgate Lodge 50yds on right*

Situated in a peaceful side road next to the seafront and just a short walk from the centre of town. Bedrooms vary in size and style; each one is pleasantly decorated and has many thoughtful touches. Breakfast is served in the smart dining room and there is a cosy lounge.

Rooms 3 en suite D £52–£64✳ **Facilities** TVB tea/coffee Cen ht
Parking 5 **Notes LB** ⊛ No children Closed Xmas & New Year ☺

★★★★ BED & BREAKFAST
White Cottage
9 Cliff Dr NR27 0AW
☎ 01263 512728
e–mail: jboocock@whitecottagecromer.freeserve.co.uk

dir: *Off A149 Norwich Rd onto Overstrand Rd, 2nd right*

A delightful detached house situated on an elevated position above the beach with panoramic views of the sea. The immaculate property offers a high degree of comfort. The spacious bedrooms are pleasantly decorated and equipped with many useful extras, and breakfast is served in an elegant lounge-dining room.

Rooms 3 en suite **Facilities** TVB tea/coffee Cen ht **Parking** 3 **Notes** ⊛
No children 18yrs Closed Xmas ☺

★★★ GUEST HOUSE
Glendale
33 Macdonald Rd NR27 9AP
☎ 01263 513278
e–mail: glendalecromer@aol.com

dir: *A149 coast road from Cromer centre, 4th left*

Victorian property situated in a peaceful side road adjacent to the seafront and just a short walk from the town centre. Bedrooms are pleasantly decorated, well maintained and equipped with a good range of useful extras. Breakfast is served at individual tables in the smart dining room.

Rooms 5 rms (1 en suite) S £23–£32; D £46–£64 **Facilities** TVB tea/coffee **Parking** 2 **Notes LB** No coaches Closed 20 Oct–3 Apr

CROMER CONTINUED

★★★ GUEST HOUSE
The Sandcliff

Runton Rd NR27 9AS
☎ 01263 512888 🖹 01263 512888
e–mail: bookings@sandcliffcromer.co.uk

dir: *500yds W of town centre on A149*

Ideally situated on the seafront overlooking the beach and sea beyond, just a short walk from the town centre. Public rooms include a large lounge bar with comfortable seating and a spacious dining room where breakfast and dinner are served. The bedrooms are pleasantly decorated and thoughtfully equipped, and some have superb sea views.

Rooms 22 rms (16 en suite) (10 fmly) (3 GF) S £47–£55; D £64–£80✶
Facilities TVB tea/coffee Licensed TVL Dinner Last d 8pm **Conf** Max 50 Thtr 50 Class 50 Board 50 Del from £80 ✶ **Parking** 10 **Notes LB**

See advert on page 351

Ⓤ
White Horse

34 High St, Overstrand NR27 0AB
☎ 01263 579237
e–mail: reservations@whitehorseoverstrand.co.uk

dir: *From A140, before Cromer, turn right onto Mill Rd. At bottom turn right onto Overstrand Rd. After 2m, bear left onto High St, White Horse on left*

At the time of going to press the rating for this establishment had not been confirmed. Please check the AA website www.theAA.com for up-to-date information.

Rooms 7 en suite (1 fmly) S £55–£75; D £75–£95✶ **Facilities** TVB tea/coffee Cen ht TVL Dinner Wi-fi available Pool Table **Parking** 6 **Notes LB**

DEREHAM   MAP 13 TF91

★★★★ INN
The Yaxham Mill

Norwich Rd, Yaxham NR19 1RP
☎ 01362 851182 🖹 01362 691482
e–mail: yaxhammill@hotmail.co.uk
web: www.yaxhammill.co.uk

dir: *1.5m S of Dereham. B1135 into Yaxham, at E end of village*

This popular inn is situated in a peaceful rural location just a short drive from the market town of Dereham. The comfortable lounge bar and smart restaurant offer a good choice of dishes. The bedrooms are housed in two wings adjacent to the main building; each one has attractive pine furnishings and many thoughtful touches.

Rooms 6 en suite 6 annexe en suite (5 fmly) (7 GF) **Facilities** TVB tea/coffee Cen ht Dinner Last d 9pm **Parking** 45 **Notes** ⊗ No coaches

DOCKING   MAP 13 TF73

★★★★ GUEST ACCOMMODATION
Jubilee Lodge

Station Rd PE31 8LS
☎ 01485 518473 🖹 01485 518473
e–mail: eghoward62@hotmail.com
web: www.jubilee-lodge.com

dir: *400yds N of village centre on B1153*

Ideally placed for touring the North Norfolk coast, with Sandringham, Hunstanton, Burnham Market and Fakenham within easy striking distance. Bedrooms are pleasantly decorated, thoughtfully equipped and come with en suite facilities. Public rooms include a cosy guest lounge and breakfast is served at individual tables in the smart dining room.

Rooms 3 en suite S £30; D £50 **Facilities** TVB tea/coffee Cen ht TVL Fishing **Parking** 3 **Notes LB** ⊗ No children 16yrs ◉

DOWNHAM MARKET   MAP 12 TF60

★★★ BED & BREAKFAST
Crosskeys Riverside House

Bridge St, Hilgay PE38 0LD
☎ 01366 387777 🖹 01366 387777
e–mail: crosskeyshouse@aol.com
web: www.crosskeys.info

dir: *2m S of Downham Market. Off A10 into Hilgay, Crosskeys on bridge*

Situated in the small village of Hilgay on the banks of the River Wissey, this former coaching inn offers comfortable accommodation that includes a number of four-poster bedrooms; many rooms have river views. Public rooms include a dining room with oak beams and inglenook fireplace, plus a small, rustic residents' bar.

Rooms 4 en suite (1 fmly) (2 GF) S £30–£50; D £50–£60✶ **Facilities** TVB tea/coffee Cen ht Fishing Rowing boat for guests use **Parking** 10

★★★ GUEST ACCOMMODATION
The Old Shop

24 London Rd PE38 9AW
☎ 01366 382051
e–mail: kcorrall@aol.com

dir: *Off A10 at Downham Market exit. Left at lights, house on right after next mini-rdbt*

The Old Shop was once three separate cottages and has been refurbished to keep much original character. Breakfast is served at individual tables in the cosy cottage-style lounge-dining room. The smartly decorated bedrooms are furnished with pine pieces, have co-ordinated soft fabrics and many thoughtful touches.

Rooms 3 en suite S £30–£35; D £40–£50✶ **Facilities** TVB tea/coffee Cen ht **Notes LB** ⊗ ◉

EAST HARLING
MAP 13 TL98

★★★ INN
The Nags Head
Market St NR16 2AD
☎ 01953 718140 📠 01953 718140
e-mail: wgallant.nagshead@tiscali.co.uk

dir: On B1111 in centre of East Harling, 2m off A11 and 3m off A1066

A popular inn situated in the heart of the village. Public areas include a choice of lounge bars, a large restaurant and a further open-plan bar with lounge seating. Bedrooms are pleasantly decorated with co-ordinated fabrics and have a good range of useful facilities.

Rooms 4 en suite **Facilities** TVB tea/coffee Cen ht TVL Dinner Last d 9pm Wi-fi available Pool Table **Parking** 30 **Notes** ⊗ No coaches

FAKENHAM
MAP 13 TF92

See also Barney

★★★★ BED & BREAKFAST
Holly Tree
40 Sandy Ln NR21 9EZ
☎ 01328 851955 📠 01328 851955
e-mail: gartcarving@aol.com
web: www.hollytreebandb.co.uk

dir: Off junct A1065 & A148 onto Wells Rd into town centre, 1st right

Expect a warm welcome from the caring hosts at this small family-run B&B, which is situated in a quiet road on the west edge of town. The smart bedrooms have co-ordinated soft furnishings and many thoughtful touches. Breakfast is served in an attractive dining room that overlooks the neat gardens.

Rooms 2 en suite (2 GF) S £30–£50; D £50✶ **Facilities** TVB tea/coffee Cen ht **Parking** 2 **Notes** ⊗ No children 10yrs 🐾

★★★★ INN
White Horse
Fakenham Rd, East Barsham NR21 0LH
☎ 01328 820645 📠 01328 820645

dir: A148 onto B1105 towards Walsingham, inn 2m on left just before Barsham Manor

Delightful inn situated in a peaceful, rural location just to the north of Fakenham town centre, in the small village of East Barsham. The smart bedrooms are carefully furnished and well equipped. An interesting choice of dishes is served in the public areas, which include a small dining room and a cosy, well-stocked lounge bar.

White Horse

Rooms 3 en suite (1 fmly) **Facilities** TVB tea/coffee Cen ht Dinner Last d 9.30pm Organised bird watching tours **Parking** 50 **Notes** ⊗

★★★ FARM HOUSE
Abbott Farm *(TF975390)*
Walsingham Rd, Binham NR21 0AW
☎ 01328 830519 📠 01328 830519 Mrs E Brown
e-mail: abbot.farm@btinternet.com
web: www.abbottfarm.co.uk

dir: NE of Fakenham. From Binham SW onto Walsingham Rd, farm 0.6m on left

A detached red-brick farmhouse set amidst 190 acres of arable farmland and surrounded by open countryside. The spacious bedrooms are pleasantly decorated and thoughtfully equipped; they include a ground-floor room with a large en suite shower. Breakfast is served in the attractive conservatory, which has superb views of the countryside.

Rooms 3 en suite (2 GF) S £26–£30; D £52–£60 **Facilities** TVB tea/coffee Cen ht TVL **Parking** 20 **Notes** 190 acres arable Closed 24–26 Dec 🐾

★★★ GUEST HOUSE
Fieldview Guest House
West Barsham Rd, East Barsham NR21 0AR
☎ 01328 820083
e-mail: info@fieldview.net

dir: From A148 at Fakenham take B1105 to E Barsham, 1st left after village sign

Delightful detached Norfolk flint property ideally situated for touring the North Norfolk coast. Breakfast is served at individual pine tables in the dining room which has superb views of the surrounding countryside. Bedrooms are pleasantly decorated and equipped with a good range of useful extras.

Rooms 5 rms (2 en suite) (1 fmly) (1 GF) **Facilities** TVB tea/coffee Cen ht TVL **Parking** 5 **Notes** ⊗ No children 7yrs No coaches 🐾

CONTINUED

ENGLAND

GORLESTON ON SEA   MAP 13 TG50

★★★★ GUEST ACCOMMODATION
Avalon
54 Clarence Rd NR31 6DR
☎ 01493 662114 ▤ 01493 668528
e–mail: info@avalon-gorleston.co.uk
web: www.avalon-gorleston.co.uk

dir: *A12 past James Paget Hospital. Take 2nd exit at rdbt towards Gorleston. Next rdbt 2nd exit, 1st right*
This Edwardian terrace house is just a short walk from the promenade and beach. Breakfast and evening meals are served in the smart dining room and there is a cosy lounge bar; service is both helpful and friendly. Bedrooms are pleasantly appointed, each thoughtfully equipped and well furnished.

Rooms 10 en suite (6 fmly) (1 GF) S £25–£35; D £50–£60✴
Facilities TVB tea/coffee Cen ht TVL Dinner Last d 7.15pm Wi-fi available **Notes** ⊗

★★★ GUEST HOUSE
Jennis Lodge
63 Avondale Rd NR31 6DJ
☎ 01493 662840 ▤ 01493 662840
e–mail: mandy@jennislodge.co.uk
web: www.jennis-lodge.co.uk

dir: *A12 past James Paget Hosp, rdbt 2nd exit, next rdbt 2nd exit, left and 2nd right*

A genuine welcome awaits at this small, family-run guest house, situated just off the seafront and close to the town centre. Bedrooms are attractively decorated and thoughtfully equipped. Public rooms include a smart dining room and an elegant lounge. Dinner is available by arrangement.

Rooms 7 rms (6 en suite) (1 pri facs) (2 fmly) S £20–£30; D £44–£54
Facilities TVB tea/coffee Cen ht TVL Dinner Last d before 10am
Notes LB ⊗

GREAT ELLINGHAM   MAP 13 TM09

★★★★ GUEST ACCOMMODATION
Aldercarr Hall
Attleborough Rd NR17 1LQ
☎ 01953 455766 & 07710 752213 ▤ 01953 457993
e–mail: bedandbreakfast@aldercarr-limited.com

dir: *On B1077 500yds SE of village*
Situated amidst extensive grounds and surrounded by open countryside on the edge of Great Ellingham. Public rooms include a comfortably appointed conservatory and a delightful dining room where breakfast is served around a large table. The excellent facilities include a health, beauty and hairdressing studio, an indoor swimming pool, a Jacuzzi and a large function suite.

Rooms 3 annexe en suite (1 fmly) (3 GF) **Facilities** TVB tea/coffee Cen ht TVL ⊙ Golf Fishing Riding Snooker Sauna Pool Table **Conf** Max 125 Board 9 **Parking** 200 **Notes** ⊗

GREAT YARMOUTH   MAP 13 TG50

☆☆☆☆ BED & BREAKFAST
Barnard House
2 Barnard Crescent NR30 4DR
☎ 01493 855139 ▤ 01493 843143
e–mail: enquiries@barnardhouse.com

dir: *0.5m N of town centre. Off A149 onto Barnard Crescent*
A friendly, family-run guest house, set in mature landscaped gardens in a residential area. The smartly decorated bedrooms have co-ordinated fabrics and many thoughtful touches. Breakfast is served in the stylish dining room and there is an elegant lounge with plush sofas. A warm welcome is assured.

Rooms 3 rms (2 en suite) (1 pri facs) S £40–£42; D £60–£65
Facilities FTV TVB tea/coffee Cen ht TVL Wi-fi available **Parking** 3
Notes LB Closed Xmas & New Year

★★★★ GUEST HOUSE
All Seasons Guest House
10 Nelson Rd South NR30 3JL
☎ 01493 852713
e–mail: m.kenmore@sky.com

dir: *From sea front (sea on left) turn onto Kings Rd, Nelson Rd S, 150yds on right*
Expect a warm welcome at this well maintained terrace property situated just a short walk from the beach and town centre. Bedrooms are pleasantly decorated with co-ordinated fabrics and have a good range of useful facilities. Breakfast is served at individual tables in the dining room and guests have the use of a cosy lounge with plush sofas.

CONTINUED

All Seasons Guest House

Rooms 8 en suite (2 fmly) (1 GF) S £20–£33; D £40–£66✱
Facilities STV TVB tea/coffee Cen ht TVL Dinner Last d 11am Wi-fi
available **Conf** Max 16 Thtr 16 Class 16 Board 16 Del from £50 ✱
Notes LB ⊗ No coaches

★★★★ GUEST HOUSE

Bonheur

3 Norfolk Square NR30 1EE
☎ 01493 843042 📄 01493 745235
e–mail: enq@bonheur-hotel.co.uk

dir: *From North Dr on seafront, turn onto Albemarle Rd opposite
bowling greens. 100mtrs on left*

Delightful property situated in a peaceful side road just a short walk
from the seafront and town centre. Bedrooms are pleasantly decorated
and have a good range of useful facilities. Breakfast is served in the
lower ground floor dining room/bar, and guests also have the use of a
large lounge with plush sofas.

Rooms 8 en suite (3 fmly) (2 GF) S £35–£60; D £45–£60✱
Facilities TVB tea/coffee Licensed Cen ht TVL **Notes LB** ⊗ No coaches

★★★★ GUEST HOUSE

The Chequers

27 Nelson Rd South NR30 3JA
☎ 01493 853091
e–mail: mitchellsatchequers@hotmail.co.uk

dir: *Off A47 signed Seafront, right onto Marine Parade & Kings
Rd, 1st right*

Guests will receive a warm welcome from the caring hosts at this
privately run establishment situated just a short walk from Wellington
pier and the beach. Public rooms include a cosy bar, residents' lounge
and a smart dining room. Bedrooms are cheerfully decorated and have
many thoughtful touches.

Rooms 8 rms (7 en suite) (1 pri facs) (2 fmly) S £22–£30; D £44–£60✱
Facilities FTV TVB tea/coffee Licensed Cen ht TVL Dinner Last d
4.30pm Wi-fi available **Notes LB** ⊗ No coaches

★★★★ BED & BREAKFAST

The Classic Lodge

13 Euston Rd NR30 1DY
☎ 01493 852851 📄 01493 852851
web: www.classiclodge.com

dir: *A12 to A47, follow signs for seafront. Turn left Sainsbury's,
ahead at lights 200mtrs on right*

An impressive Victorian villa (situated just a short stroll from the
seafront and town centre) where guests are greeted warmly. Breakfast
is served at individual tables in the large lounge-dining room, and the
spacious bedrooms are carefully furnished and equipped with a very
good range of facilities.

Rooms 3 en suite S £30–£50; D £50–£60 **Facilities** FTV TVB tea/coffee
Cen ht TVL Wi-fi available **Parking** 3 **Notes LB** ⊗ No children 18yrs
Closed Nov–Apr ⊛

★★★★ GUEST HOUSE

The Corner House

Albert Square NR30 3JH
☎ 01493 842773
e–mail: t90len@aol.com
web: www.thecornerhousehotel.info

dir: *From A47/a12 follow signs to Seafront. Opposite Wellington
Pier, left onto Albert Sq*

The proprietors at this immaculate bay-fronted Victorian house situated
in a side road adjacent to the seafront offer a warm welcome. Public
rooms are on the lower ground floor; they include a smart lounge bar
and a spacious dining room. The generous bedrooms are pleasantly
decorated with co-ordinated fabrics and have many thoughtful
touches. Please note, this is a totally non-smoking establishment, and
children are not accepted.

Rooms 8 en suite (1 fmly) (2 GF) S £30–£60; D £60–£100✱
Facilities FTV TVB tea/coffee Licensed Cen ht TVL Dinner Wi-fi
available **Parking** 8 **Notes LB** ⊗ No children 16yrs No coaches ⊛

★★★★ GUEST ACCOMMODATION

The Hamilton

23–24 North Dr NR30 4EW
☎ 01493 844662
e–mail: enquiries@hamilton-hotel.co.uk
web: www.hamilton-hotel.co.uk

dir: *Off A47 to seafront, left at Britannia Pier, 0.5m N on seafront*

A friendly, family-run establishment, which is situated at the quieter
end of town overlooking the Venetian Waterways and beach. Breakfast
and dinner are served in the smart dining room, and there is a cosy
bar and a lounge. The pleasant bedrooms are thoughtfully equipped.

Rooms 23 en suite 1 annexe en suite (1 GF) S £36.50–£42; D £50–£70✱
Facilities STV TVB tea/coffee Cen ht Dinner Last d 8.30pm Wi-fi
available **Conf** Max 26 **Parking** 24 **Notes LB** ⊗ No children 16yrs

ENGLAND

★★★★ GUEST ACCOMMODATION
Knights Court

22 North Dr NR30 4EW
☎ 01493 843089 📄 01493 850780
e-mail: enquiries@knights-court.co.uk

dir: *600yds N of Britannia Pier, opp Waterways and Gardens*
Knights Court stands on the seafront overlooking the Venetian Waterways and the beach. The spacious bedrooms are carefully decorated and equipped with many thoughtful touches, and most rooms have lovely sea views. Breakfast and dinner are served in the smart dining room and there is a cosy lounge bar.

Rooms 14 en suite 6 annexe en suite (5 fmly) (6 GF) S £30–£42; D £56–£70✳ **Facilities** FTV TVB tea/coffee Direct dial from bedrooms Cen ht Dinner Last d 11am Wi-fi available **Parking** 21 **Notes LB** ⊗ Closed 28 Oct–16 Mar

★★★★ GUEST ACCOMMODATION
Marine Lodge

19–20 Euston Rd NR30 1DY
☎ 01493 331120
e-mail: res@marinelodge.co.uk

This establishment's enviable seafront position has panoramic views of the bowling greens and beach, and is within easy walking distance of Britannia Pier. Bright modern bedrooms are complemented by smart public areas that include a bar area where light snacks are available during the evening. Guests also have complimentary use of the indoor swimming pool at the sister Palm Court Hotel.

Rooms 40 en suite (5 fmly) (5 GF) **Facilities** FTV TVB tea/coffee Lift Cen ht TVL Wi-fi available **Conf** Thtr 50 Class 35 Board 25 **Parking** 38 **Notes** ⊗

★★★★ GUEST HOUSE
Taunton House

9 Nelson Rd South NR30 3JL
☎ 01493 850043
A friendly welcome awaits at this modern refurbished terrace property situated just a short walk from the beach and town centre. Bedrooms are decorated in a contemporary style with coordinated fabrics, and have a range of useful facilities. Breakfast is served at individual tables in the open-plan lounge/dining room.

Rooms 8 en suite D £50–£60✳ **Facilities** TVB Licensed Cen ht TVL **Notes LB**

★★★★ GUEST ACCOMMODATION
The Winchester

12 Euston Rd NR30 1DY
☎ 01493 843950
e-mail: enquiries@winchesterprivatehotel.com

dir: *A12 onto A47, signs for seafront, left at Sainsbury over lights, premises 400yds on right*
The friendly hosts at The Winchester give a warm welcome at this guest house just off the seafront. The pleasant bedrooms vary in size and style and are thoughtfully equipped. Public rooms include a large lower ground-floor dining room, a small conservatory and a foyer with plush sofas.

Rooms 14 en suite (2 fmly) (5 GF) S £25–£30; D £50–£60✳ **Facilities** TVB tea/coffee Cen ht TVL Dinner Last d 10am Wi-fi available **Parking** 10 **Notes LB** ⊗ No children 12yrs Closed Dec–Jan RS Oct–Etr ⊜

★★★★ 🅰 GUEST ACCOMMODATION
Kensington

29 North Dr NR30 4EW
☎ 01493 844145 📄 01493 852364
e-mail: enquiries@kensington-hotel.co.uk
web: www.kensington-hotel.co.uk

dir: *On seafront opp Venetian Waterways*
Rooms 26 en suite (7 fmly) (3 GF) S £30–£35; D £60–£70✳ **Facilities** FTV TVB tea/coffee Lift Cen ht Dinner Last d noon **Conf** Thtr 50 Class 50 Board 30 **Parking** 25 **Notes LB**

★★★ GUEST ACCOMMODATION
Amber Lodge

21 Princes Rd NR30 2DG
☎ 01493 843371
e-mail: paul@amberlodgehotel.co.uk

dir: *From A47 follow signs to seafront, turn right onto Wellesley Rd, 2nd left onto Princes Rd*
Smartly maintained Victorian bay-fronted property situated in a side road close to the seafront and Britannia Pier. Public rooms include a lounge bar, dining room and further residents' lounge on the first floor. Bedrooms are cheerfully decorated, have co-ordinated fabrics and a range of useful extras.

Rooms 10 rms (8 en suite) (2 fmly) **Facilities** TVB tea/coffee Cen ht TVL Dinner Last d noon **Notes** ⊗ ⊜

★★★ GUEST HOUSE
Andover House
28–30 Camperdown NR30 3JB
☎ 01493 843490 📄 01493 852546
e–mail: info@andoverhouse.co.uk
web: www.andoverhouse.co.uk

dir: *Opp Wellington Pier, turn right onto Shadingfield Cl, right again onto Kimberley Terrace, follow road round*

Guests receive a warm welcome at this well-maintained property situated in a peaceful side road, just a short walk from the seafront and town centre. Breakfast and dinner are served in the basement dining room, and there is a cosy lounge and a smart bar. Bedrooms are pleasantly decorated and equipped with a good range of facilities.

Rooms 20 en suite S £79; D £98–£118✳ **Facilities** STV FTV TVB tea/coffee Direct dial from bedrooms Licensed Cen ht TVL Dinner Last d 9.30pm Wi-fi available Golf **Conf** Max 100 Thtr 40 Class 60 Board 14 **Notes** ⊗ No children No coaches

★★★ GUEST HOUSE
The Elmfield
38 Wellesley Rd NR30 1EU
☎ 01493 859827
e–mail: stay@theelmfield.co.uk
web: www.theelmfield.co.uk

Expect a warm welcome at this family-run guest house situated just a short walk from the beach and shops. Bedrooms are pleasantly decorated with matching soft furnishings and have a range of useful extras; some rooms have sea views. Public rooms include a cosy lounge bar with a large-screen TV and breakfast is served in the smart dining room.

Rooms 9 en suite (3 fmly) S £22.50–£32.50; D £45–£50✳ **Facilities** TVB tea/coffee Licensed Cen ht TVL Wi-fi available **Parking** 5 **Notes LB** ⊗ No coaches

★★★ GUEST ACCOMMODATION
Harbour
20 Pavilion Rd, Gorleston on Sea NR31 6BY
☎ 01493 661031 📄 01493 661031
e–mail: jeffchambers@harbourhotel.freeserve.co.uk

dir: *A12 into Gorleston on Sea centre & signs to beach, premises near lighthouse*

A friendly guest house near the harbour. The pleasant, well-equipped bedrooms vary in size and style, and some rooms have lovely sea views. Breakfast is served in the spacious dining room, and evening snacks are available in the lounge bar.

Rooms 8 rms (4 en suite) (6 fmly) S £35–£54; D £54–£68✳ **Facilities** tea/coffee Cen ht TVL **Parking** 3 **Notes LB** ⊗ ⊜

★★★ GUEST HOUSE
The Haydee
27 Princes Rd NR30 2DG
☎ 01493 844580 📄 01493 844580
e–mail: info@haydee.co.uk
web: www.haydee.co.uk

dir: *Off A47 to seafront, Princes Rd opp Britannia Pier*

The Haydee is in a side road just a stroll from the seafront, pier and town centre. The pleasant bedrooms vary in size and style, but all are well equipped. Breakfast is served in the smart dining room and there is a cosy lounge bar.

Rooms 8 en suite (2 fmly) (2 smoking) S £20–£24; D £40–£48✳ **Facilities** TVB tea/coffee Licensed Cen ht TVL **Notes LB** ⊗ No coaches

★★★ GUEST ACCOMMODATION
Kingsley House
68 King St NR30 2PP
☎ 01493 850948 📄 01493 850948
e–mail: serina@kingsleyhousehotel.com

dir: *Along Hall Quay, left at Nottingham Way, right onto King St, 100yds on left*

A friendly welcome is to be expected at this well maintained terrace property situated just a short walk from the town centre and seafront. Public rooms feature a superb bar with an original brick and flint wall that dates back to the 15th century. Bedrooms are smartly decorated and have many useful extras.

Rooms 7 en suite (2 fmly) **Facilities** TVB tea/coffee Cen ht Dinner Last d 5pm **Notes** ⊗

★★★ GUEST ACCOMMODATION
Senglea Lodge
7 Euston Rd NR30 1DX
☎ 01493 859632
e–mail: senglealodge@fsmail.net

dir: *From A47 straight over 1st 2 rdbts. At lights turn left towards seafront. Through next lights, lodge on right*

Delightful terrace property situated just off the sea front and very close to the town centre. Bedrooms are pleasantly decorated, have co-ordinated soft furnishing and a good range of useful extras. Breakfast is served at individual tables in the smart open-plan lounge/dining room.

Rooms 6 rms (4 en suite) (2 fmly) (2 smoking) S £20–£25; D £40–£45✳ **Facilities** FTV TVB tea/coffee Cen ht TVL **Notes LB** ⊗ Closed 23 Dec–2 Jan

GREAT YARMOUTH CONTINUED

★★★ GUEST HOUSE
Shemara Guest House

11 Wellesley Rd NR30 2AR

☎ 01493 844054

e–mail: info@shemaraguesthouse.co.uk

dir: *A47 to Great Yarmouth, follow signs for seafront, take 4th right, Shemara on right*

Shemara is ideally situated in the heart of this busy resort, as it is just a short walk from the town centre and seafront. Bedrooms come in a variety of sizes and styles, each one is pleasantly decorated and well equipped. Breakfast is served at individual tables in the open-plan lounge/dining room.

Rooms 7 en suite (2 fmly) S £18–£25; D £36–£50 **Facilities** TVB tea/coffee Cen ht TVL Dinner Last d Breakfast **Notes LB** ⊗ ⊜

★★★ GUEST ACCOMMODATION
Swiss Cottage B&B Just for Non Smokers

31 North Dr NR30 4EW

☎ 01493 855742 & 08450 943949 📠 0870 2846294

e–mail: info@swiss-cottage.info

web: www.swisscottagebedandbreakfast.co.uk

dir: *0.5m N of town centre. Off A47 or A12 to to seafront, 750yds N of pier. Turn left at Britannia Pier. Swiss Cottage on left opposite Water Gardens*

A charming property situated at the quieter end of town overlooking the Venetian waterways and the sea beyond. The comfortable bedrooms are pleasantly decorated with co-ordinated fabrics and have many useful extras. Breakfast is served in the smart dining room and guests have use of an open-plan lounge area.

Rooms 9 en suite (1 fmly) (2 GF) S £27–£38; D £48–£71✻ **Facilities** FTV TVB tea/coffee Cen ht Wi-fi available **Parking** 9 **Notes LB** No children 8yrs Closed Nov–Feb

★★★ GUEST HOUSE
Victoria

2 Kings Rd NR30 3JW

☎ 01493 843872 & 842132 📠 01493 843872

e–mail: jhemsley@ukonline.co.uk

web: www.hotelvictoria.org.uk

dir: *Off seafront, opposite model village*

Large detached property situated just off the seafront close to Wellington Pier and the town centre. Bedrooms come in a variety of sizes and styles; each one is pleasantly decorated and thoughtfully equipped. Dinner and breakfast are served in the open plan lounge/dining room. The Victoria also has a smart outdoor swimming pool.

Rooms 35 rms (30 en suite) (3 pri facs) (12 fmly) (2 GF) S £25–£30; D £40–£60✻ **Facilities** FTV TVB tea/coffee Licensed Lift Cen ht TVL Dinner Last d 10.30pm Wi-fi available ⚓ Pool Table **Conf** Max 50 Thtr 50 Class 50 Board 30 **Parking** 20 **Notes LB** ⊗

★★ GUEST HOUSE
Rhonadean

110–111 Wellesley Rd NR30 2AR

☎ 01493 842004

e–mail: barbara@6wheeler0.wanadoo.co.uk

dir: *500yds N of town centre. Off A47 onto B1141 Fuller's Hill towards seafront, onto St Nicholas Rd & 3rd right*

Rhonadean is situated in a side road adjacent to the seafront and just a short walk from the town centre. Public rooms include a small lounge bar and a dining room where breakfast and dinner are served at individual tables. Bedrooms vary in size and style; each one is pleasantly decorated and well equipped.

Rooms 18 rms (17 en suite) (1 pri facs) (7 fmly) (8 GF) **Facilities** TVB tea/coffee Licensed Cen ht TVL Dinner Last d 11am Pool Table **Notes** ⊗ Closed 24–26 Dec

HEVINGHAM
MAP 13 TG12

★★★★ **A** INN
Marsham Arms Inn
Holt Rd NR10 5NP
☎ 01603 754268
e–mail: nigelbradley@marshamarms.co.uk
web: www.marshamarms.co.uk

dir: *N of Norwich. Off A140 near Norwich Airport onto B1149, through Horsford, establishment 2m on right*

Rooms 11 annexe en suite (8 fmly) (11 GF) S £54.50–£59.50; D £95–£100 **Facilities** TVB tea/coffee Direct dial from bedrooms Cen ht Dinner Last d 9.30pm Wi-fi available **Conf** Max 50 Thtr 50 Class 30 Board 30 **Parking** 100 **Notes LB**

HINDRINGHAM
MAP 13 TF93

Premier Collection

★★★★★ BED & BREAKFAST
Field House
Moorgate Rd NR21 0PT
☎ 01328 878726
e–mail: stay@fieldhousehindringham.co.uk
web: www.fieldhousehindringham.co.uk

dir: *Off A148 to Hindringham, onto Moorgate Rd at Lower Green, Field House on left*

A warm friendly welcome and genuine hospitality are to be expected from the caring hosts at this delightful property. Field House is situated in a peaceful rural location amid pretty landscaped gardens. The individually decorated bedrooms are tastefully furnished and have coordinated soft fabrics as well as many thoughtful touches. Breakfast is served in the lounge-dining room and features quality, locally sourced produce.

Rooms 2 en suite 1 annexe en suite S £70–£75; D £90–£110 **Facilities** FTV TVB tea/coffee Cen ht Wi-fi available **Parking** 3 **Notes LB** ⊗ No children 10yrs Closed 25–26 Dec ⊛

HOLT
MAP 13 TG03

Premier Collection

★★★★★ GUEST HOUSE
Plantation House
Ashburn, Old Cromer Rd, High Kelling NR25 6AJ
☎ 01263 710121
e–mail: info@plantation-house.net
web: www.plantation-house.net

dir: *Signs for Kelling Hospital on A148, 1st left & sharp right, 1st house*

A charming property situated on the outskirts of Holt in the wooded village of High Kelling. The property has been lovingly restored by the current owners and provides stylish accommodation throughout. Public rooms feature a colonial-style lounge-dining room with darkwood tables and a leather Chesterfield. The elegant bedrooms have a bright and airy feel; each one has attractive solid wood furniture, co-ordinated fabrics and many thoughtful touches.

Rooms 4 en suite S £60–£70; D£80–£95✱ **Facilities** TVB tea/coffee Cen ht Wi-fi available **Parking** 5 **Notes** ⊗ No children 12yrs

Premier Collection

★★★★★ BED & BREAKFAST
Rose Cottage
Cley Rd NR25 7DX
☎ 01263 714013
e–mail: rosecottageholt@hotmail.com

dir: *Turn into Holt high street from A148. Take the road opposite Kings Head pub which leads onto Cley Rd. Rose cottage 0.5m on left*

A delightful detached Norfolk flint cottage situated just a short walk from the town centre. The spacious bedrooms are in an adjacent barn conversion; each one is tastefully appointed with co-ordinated fabrics and has many thoughtful touches. Breakfast, which includes locally-sourced produce, is served in the main house dining room which overlooks the extensive grounds.

Rooms 2 annexe en suite (2 GF) S £85; D £95✱ **Facilities** FTV TVB tea/coffee Cen ht **Parking** 2 **Notes** ⊗ No children 14yrs RS Xmas & New Year ⊛

ENGLAND

HOLT CONTINUED

★★★★ ⑥ RESTAURANT WITH ROOMS
The Lawns
26 Station Rd NR25 6BS
☎ 01263 713390
e–mail: mail@lawnsatholt.co.uk

dir: *A148 (Cromer Rd). 0.25m from Holt rdbt, turn left, 400yds along Station Rd*

Superb Georgian house situated in the centre of this delightful North Norfolk market town. The open-plan public areas include a large wine bar with plush sofas, a conservatory and a smart restaurant. The spacious bedrooms are tastefully appointed with co-ordinated soft furnishings and have many thoughtful touches.

Rooms 8 en suite D £85–£110✳ **Facilities** FTV TVB tea/coffee Cen ht Dinner Last d 9pm Wi-fi available **Parking** 14 **Notes LB**

★★★★ BED & BREAKFAST
The Old Telephone Exchange Bed & Breakfast
37 New St NR25 6JH
☎ 01263 712992
e–mail: christopher.manders@btinternet.com

dir: *Off High St onto New St, establishment 200yds on left*

Expect a warm welcome at this small, family-run bed and breakfast situated in a quiet side road close to the town centre. The immaculate bedrooms are tastefully appointed and equipped with many thoughtful touches. Public rooms feature a comfortable lounge-dining area with a wide-screen television, plush sofas, books and games.

Rooms 3 en suite (3 GF) S £50–£65; D £60–£75 **Facilities** TVB tea/coffee Cen ht TVL **Parking** 2 **Notes LB** ⊗ No children 10yrs ⊜

★★★★ GUEST ACCOMMODATION
White Cottage B&B
Norwich Rd NR25 6SW
☎ 01263 713353
e–mail: enquiries@whitecottageholt.co.uk

dir: *From A148 from Holt take B1149, 0.5m on left after police station*

A delightful detached cottage situated just a short walk from this busy town centre. Breakfast is served at individual tables in the smart dining room and guests have the use of a cosy lounge with plush sofas. The bedrooms are pleasantly decorated and equipped with a good range of useful extras.

Rooms 2 en suite D £60–£70✳ **Facilities** TVB tea/coffee Cen ht **Notes LB** ⊗ No children 10yrs Closed 21 Dec–Jan ⊜

★★★★ GUEST HOUSE
Claremont
35 Greevegate PE36 6AF
☎ 01485 533171
e–mail: claremontgh@tiscali.co.uk

dir: *Off A149 onto Greevegate, house before St Edmund's Church*

This Victorian guest house, close to the shops, beach and gardens, has individually decorated bedrooms with a good range of useful extras. There is also a ground-floor room as well as two feature rooms, one with a four poster, and another with a canopied bed.

Rooms 7 en suite (1 fmly) (1 GF) S £26–£35; D £57–£70 **Facilities** TVB tea/coffee Cen ht TVL **Parking** 4 **Notes LB** No children 5yrs No coaches Closed 15 Nov–15 Mar ⊜

★★★★ ⑥⑥⑥ RESTAURANT WITH ROOMS
The Neptune Inn & Restaurant
85 Old Hunstanton Rd, Old Hunstanton PE36 6HZ
☎ 01485 532122
e–mail: reservations@theneptune.co.uk
web: www.theneptune.co.uk

dir: *On A149, past Hunstanton, 200mtrs on left after post office*

This charming 18th-century coaching inn, now a restaurant with rooms, is ideally situated for touring the Norfolk coastline. The smartly appointed bedrooms are brightly finished with co-ordinated fabrics and handmade New England furniture. Public rooms feature white clapboard walls, polished dark wood floors, fresh flowers and Lloyd Loom furniture. The food is very much a draw here with the carefully prepared, award-winning cuisine utilising excellent local produce, from oysters and mussels from Thornham to quinces grown on a neighbouring farm.

Rooms 7 en suite S £55–£110; D £90–£110✳ **Facilities** FTV TVB tea/coffee Direct dial from bedrooms Cen ht Dinner Last d 9.15pm **Parking** 6 **Notes** ⊗ No children 10yrs Closed last 2 wks in Jan RS Oct–Apr

★★★★ Ⓐ INN
The King William IV
Heacham Rd, Sedgeford PE36 5LU
☎ 01485 571765 📠 01485 571743
e–mail: info@thekingwilliamsedgeford.co.uk
web: www.thekingwilliamsedgeford.co.uk

dir: *A149 to Hunstanton, right at Norfolk Lavender in Heacham onto B1454, signed Docking. 2m to Sedgeford*

Rooms 4 en suite (2 fmly) S £50–£60; D £75–£90✳ **Facilities** TVB tea/coffee Cen ht Dinner Last d 8.50pm Golf Leisure/Tennis centre 0.5m **Parking** 50 **Notes LB** No coaches RS 24–25 Dec

★★★★ 🅰 GUEST ACCOMMODATION
Rosamaly

14 Glebe Av PE36 6BS

☎ 01485 534187 & 07775 724484

e–mail: vacancies@rosamaly.co.uk

dir: *A149 to Hunstanton. At rdbt take 3rd exit staying on A149 towards Cromer. In 1m church on left, Glebe Av is 2nd left, Rosamaly is 50yds on left*

Rooms 6 en suite (2 fmly) (1 GF) S £35–£60; D £54–£62✳
Facilities TVB tea/coffee Cen ht TVL Dinner Last d 1pm **Notes LB** Closed 24 Dec–1 Jan 🐾

★★★ GUEST HOUSE
Richmond House Bed & Breakfast

6–8 Westgate PE36 5AL

☎ 01485 532601

dir: *Off A149 onto Westgate*

This well-maintained house is well situated for the seafront and town centre. Its pleasant bedrooms vary in size and style, but all are well equipped and some rooms have superb sea views. Public rooms feature a smart restaurant and a cosy lounge bar.

Rooms 14 rms (10 en suite) (5 GF) S £30–£35; D £50–£55✳
Facilities TVB tea/coffee Licensed Lift Cen ht Dinner Last d 9pm **Notes** ⊗ No children 18yrs No coaches Closed Nov–Etr 🐾

★★★ GUEST ACCOMMODATION
The White Cottage

19 Wodehouse Rd PE36 6JW

☎ 01485 532380

A charming cottage situated in a quiet side road in Old Hunstanton. The property has been owned and run by Mrs Burton for over 25 years. The spacious bedrooms are attractively decorated, and some have lovely sea views. Dinner is served in the smart dining room and there is a cosy sitting room with a television.

Rooms 3 rms (1 en suite) **Facilities** TV1B Cen ht TVL Dinner Last d 6.30pm **Parking** 11 **Notes** No children 3yrs 🐾

KELLING MAP 13 TG04

★★★★ BED & BREAKFAST
Sandpipers Bed & Breakfast

The Street NR25 7EL

☎ 01263 588604

e–mail: ina@sandpipersbandb.co.uk

web: www.sandpipersbandb.co.uk

dir: *From A149 into Kelling, 200mtrs on right next to phone box*

A delightful property situated just a short walk from the beach in the picturesque village of Kelling. The tastefully appointed, well-equipped bedroom has its own separate lounge with a kitchenette. Breakfast, which includes locally sourced produce, is served in the smart dining room. A warm welcome is offered.

Rooms 1 annexe en suite (1 GF) D £65 **Facilities** STV TVB tea/coffee Cen ht TVL **Parking** 1 **Notes** ⊗ No children 🐾

★★★★ 🏠 GUEST ACCOMMODATION
Fairlight Lodge

79 Goodwins Rd PE30 5PE

☎ 01553 762234 📠 01553 770280

e–mail: enquiries@fairlightlodge.co.uk

dir: *Off A17/A47 onto A148 into town, over rdbt onto B1144 Vancouver Av, left onto Goodwins Rd*

This well-maintained Victorian house stands in attractive gardens on the outskirts of town. The friendly proprietors ensure that good standards are maintained, and the bedrooms and bathrooms are smartly appointed and attractively co-ordinated. Some delightful ground-floor annexe rooms are available and open onto the garden. A hearty breakfast is served in the bright, cosy dining room.

Rooms 5 rms (4 en suite) (1 pri facs) 2 annexe en suite (1 fmly) (4 GF) S £33–£35; D £50–£52✳ **Facilities** TVB tea/coffee Cen ht **Parking** 6 **Notes** ⊗ Closed 24 Dec–2 Jan

★★★ GUEST ACCOMMODATION
Guanock

10–11 Guanock Place PE30 5QJ

☎ 01553 772959 📠 01553 772959

dir: *Signs to town centre, premises on right of South Gates*

Located within easy walking distance of the town centre, this friendly, family-run guest house offers comfortable, practical accommodation. Public areas include a lounge bar, pool room, and a bright dining room where breakfast is served at individual tables. There is also a delightful little roof garden.

Rooms 17 rms (5 fmly) (1 GF) S £29–£31; D fr £50✳ **Facilities** STV TVB tea/coffee Cen ht Dinner Last d day before Pool Table **Parking** 8 **Notes** ⊗ Closed 24 Dec–3 Jan

---

★★★★ BED & BREAKFAST
Bramley

Weasenham Rd PE32 2QT

☎ 01328 701592 📠 01328 701592

e–mail: bramleybandb@hotmail.co.uk

web: www.bramley-litcham.co.uk

dir: *A1065 onto B1145. Left at x-rds, left at school, 4th house on left*

A warm welcome awaits at this delightful detached house, set in a peaceful location on the village fringe, with ample safe parking in generous grounds. The mostly spacious bedrooms are thoughtfully furnished to ensure guest comfort and have smartly appointed en suite shower rooms. A hearty, freshly-cooked breakfast is served at individual tables in the separate elegant dining room.

Rooms 3 en suite (1 fmly) S £30; D £60✳ **Facilities** TVB tea/coffee Cen ht **Parking** 3 **Notes LB** ⊗ 🐾

ENGLAND

LITTLE WALSINGHAM

MAP 13 TF93

★★★★ GUEST HOUSE
The Old Bakehouse Tea Room & Guest House

33 High St NR22 6BZ
☎ 01328 820454 📄 01328 820454
e-mail: theoldbakehouseguesthouse@yahoo.co.uk

dir: *Exit A148 (Fakenham Bypass) to Wells & Walsingham (B1105). Do not turn left at x-rds, continue straight ahead into Walsingham. Next to post office*

Ideally situated in the heart of the historical shrine village of Little Walsingham, The Old Bakehouse offers spacious bedrooms with pine furniture, co-ordinated soft furnishings and many thoughtful touches. Breakfast is served in the large dining room, which is now a traditional tea room during the day.

Rooms 3 en suite S £40; D £70✱ **Facilities** TVB tea/coffee Cen ht Dinner Last d 5pm **Notes** ⊗ No coaches

LUDHAM

MAP 13 TG31

★★★★ 🅰 BED & BREAKFAST
Broadland Bed & Breakfast

West End Lodge, Norwich Rd NR29 5PB
☎ 01692 678420
e-mail: info@bedbreakfast-norfolkbroads.co.uk

Rooms 3 rms (2 en suite) (1 pri facs) **Facilities** TVB tea/coffee Cen ht **Parking** 10 **Notes** ⊗ No children 12yrs

NARBOROUGH

MAP 12 TF71

★★★★ 🅰 BED & BREAKFAST
Mill View Rooms

Main Rd PE32 1TE
☎ 01760 338005
e-mail: narfish@supanet.com

dir: *0.5m from A47 (King's Lynn to Swaffham road), turn off at Narborough/Trout Lakes and follow to gates*

Rooms 3 annexe en suite (3 GF) S £30.75–£35; D £55–£60✱ **Facilities** TVB tea/coffee Cen ht Fishing **Conf** Max 14 **Parking** 3 **Notes** LB ⊗ No children 12yrs

NEATISHEAD

MAP 13 TG32

★★★★ GUEST ACCOMMODATION
Regency

The Street NR12 8AD
☎ 01692 630233 📄 01692 630233
e-mail: regencywrigley@btinternet.com

dir: *3m from Wroxham. Village 1m from A1151*

A charming 17th-century property, situated in a picturesque village close to the Norfolk Broads. The attractive bedrooms have co-ordinated soft furnishings and many thoughtful touches. Breakfast is served in the smart dining room and there are two comfortable lounges with plush sofas.

Rooms 3 en suite (1 fmly) D £62–£68✱ **Facilities** TVB tea/coffee Dinner **Parking** 6 **Notes** LB ⊛

NORTH WALSHAM

MAP 13 TG23

Premier Collection

★★★★★ GUEST ACCOMMODATION
White House Farm

Knapton NR28 0RX
☎ 01263 721344 & 07879 475220
e-mail: info@whitehousefarmnorfolk.co.uk

The caring host at this delightful Grade II listed 18th-century flint cottage is particularly welcoming. The property is surrounded by open farmland and has been restored to retain many of its original features. Bedrooms are attractively decorated, tastefully furnished and equipped with many thoughtful touches. Breakfast is served in the smart dining room and guests have the use of a cosy lounge with plush sofas.

Rooms 3 en suite (1 fmly) **Facilities** FTV TVB tea/coffee Cen ht TVL Wi-fi available **Parking** 8 **Notes** ⊗ No children 12yrs

★★★★ 🛏 BED & BREAKFAST
Chimneys
51 Cromer Rd NR28 0HB
☎ 01692 406172 & 07952 117701
e–mail: jenny.harmer@8virgin.net
dir: *0.5m NW of town centre on A149*

A delightful Edwardian-style town house set amidst mature secluded grounds close to the town centre. Bedrooms are tastefully furnished and thoughtfully equipped, the superior room has a Jacuzzi bath. Breakfast is served in the smart dining room and guests are welcome to sit on the balcony, which overlooks the garden. Dinner is available by prior arrangement.

Rooms 3 en suite (1 fmly) **Facilities** TVB tea/coffee Cen ht Dinner Last d 4.30pm Pool Table **Parking** 5 **Notes** ⊛

★★★★ BED & BREAKFAST
Green Ridges
104 Cromer Rd NR28 0HE
☎ 01692 402448 📄 01692 402448
e–mail: admin@greenridges.com
web: www.greenridges.com
dir: *On A149 from North Walsham to Cromer, at junct of B1145 to Aylsham*

Expect a warm welcome at this attractive detached property, situated on the edge of this busy market town. The smartly appointed, thoughtfully equipped bedrooms include two new rooms situated in an annexe with wheelchair access and superb wet rooms. Breakfast is served in the smart dining room, which overlooks the mature gardens.

Rooms 3 en suite (1 fmly) (3 GF) **Facilities** TVB tea/coffee Cen ht Dinner Last d Previous day **Parking** 6 **Notes** ⊛

★★★ INN
Kings Arms
Kings Arms St NR28 9JX
☎ 01692 403054 📄 01692 500095
dir: *In town centre*

A former coaching inn situated in the heart of this bustling market town. The spacious public areas include a public bar, lounge bar and a popular restaurant. The bedrooms are pleasantly decorated and equipped with a good range of useful extras.

Rooms 7 en suite **Facilities** TVB tea/coffee Cen ht Dinner Last d 8.45pm Pool Table **Conf** Max 100 **Parking** 15 **Notes** ⊛

NORWICH   MAP 13 TG20

Premier Collection

★★★★★ 🛏 GUEST HOUSE
Catton Old Hall
Lodge Ln, Old Catton NR6 7HG
☎ 01603 419379 📄 01603 400339
e–mail: enquiries@catton-hall.co.uk
web: www.catton-hall.co.uk
dir: *2m N of city centre in Old Catton. A1042 N onto B1150, left onto White Woman Ln, straight over at lights onto Lodge Ln*

This is a superb Jacobean house which dates back to 1632. The property is situated just a short drive from the city centre and airport. Original features include brick and flint walls, oak timbers and reused Caen stone. The stylish bedrooms offer a high degree of comfort; each one is individually decorated and tastefully furnished. The elegant public areas include a dining room and a cosy lounge with plush furnishings.

Rooms 7 en suite S fr £75; D £75–£130✳ **Facilities** TVB tea/coffee Direct dial from bedrooms Licensed Cen ht TVL Dinner Last d noon Wi-fi available **Parking** 11 **Notes** LB No children 12yrs No coaches

★★★★ GUEST ACCOMMODATION
Gothic House Bed & Breakfast
King's Head Yard, Magdalen St NR3 1JE
☎ 01603 631879
e–mail: charvey649@aol.com
dir: *Follow signs for A147, turn off at rdbt past flyover into Whitefriars. Right again onto Fishergate, at end, right onto Magdalen St*

This bed and breakfast establishment is an elegant Grade II listed Regency townhouse set in a quiet courtyard in the heart of Norwich. The property has been lovingly restored and retains much of its original character. The spacious bedrooms are individually decorated and have many thoughtful touches. Breakfast, which includes locally sourced produce, is served in the elegant dining room.

Rooms 2 rms (2 pri facs) D £90✳ **Facilities** STV FTV TVB tea/coffee Cen ht Wi-fi available **Parking** 2 **Notes** ⊛ No children 18yrs Closed Feb ⊛

NORWICH CONTINUED

★★★★ GUEST ACCOMMODATION

Old Thorn Barn

Corporation Farm, Wymondham Rd, Hethel NR14 8EU

☎ 01953 607785 & 07726 961530 📠 01953 601909

e–mail: enquires@oldthornbarn.co.uk

dir: *6m SW of Norwich. Follow signs for Lotus Cars from A11 or B1113, on Wymondham Rd*

A delightful Grade II listed barn situated in a peaceful rural location just a short drive from the city centre. The property has stylish, thoughtfully equipped bedrooms with polished wood floors and antique pine furniture. Breakfast is served in the open-plan barn, which also has a wood-burning stove and a cosy lounge area.

Rooms 5 en suite 2 annexe en suite (7 GF) S £33–£39; D £56–£60 **Facilities** FTV TVB tea/coffee Cen ht TVL Wi-fi available **Parking** 14 **Notes** ⊗

★★★★ GUEST HOUSE

Arrandale Lodge Guest House

431 Earlham Rd NR4 7HL

☎ 01603 250150 📠 01603 250150

e–mail: info@arrandalelodge.co.uk

The caring hosts extend a friendly welcome at this well maintained detached property, situated within easy striking distance of both Norwich City centre and the University of East Anglia. The individually decorated bedrooms are thoughtfully equipped and have many useful extras. A hearty breakfast is served in the smart dining room.

Rooms 6 en suite (1 GF) S £38–£40; D £60–£65 **Facilities** FTV TVB tea/coffee Cen ht TVL Wi-fi available **Parking** 7 **Notes** ⊗ Closed Xmas

★★★★ BED & BREAKFAST

Beaufort Lodge

60/62 Earlham Rd NR2 3DF

☎ 01603 667402

e–mail: beaufortlodge@aol.com

dir: *Off A140 onto B1108 Earlham Rd for 0.5m towards city centre*

This large Victorian property is conveniently located just a short walk from the city centre. Bedrooms, generally spacious, are comfortably and attractively furnished. Breakfast is served at individual tables in the light and airy dining room, overlooking the garden.

Rooms 10 rms (9 en suite) (1 pri facs) **Facilities** TV4B tea/coffee Cen ht **Parking** 10 **Notes** ⊗ No children 10yrs Closed 28 Dec–2 Jan RS Xmas ▣

★★★★ GUEST ACCOMMODATION

Church Farm

Church St, Horsford NR10 3DB

☎ 01603 898020 📠 01603 891649

e–mail: churchfarmguesthouse@btopenworld.co.uk

dir: *5m NW of city centre. A140 onto B1149, right at x-rds*

Set in a peaceful rural location just a short drive from Norwich airport and the city centre. The spacious bedrooms are smartly decorated, pleasantly furnished and have many thoughtful touches. Breakfast is served at individual tables in the conservatory-style lounge-dining room, which overlooks the garden and sun terrace.

Rooms 10 en suite (1 fmly) (3 GF) S £35–£45; D £55–£65✳ **Facilities** TVB tea/coffee Cen ht TVL **Parking** 20 **Notes** ⊗

★★★★ GUEST HOUSE

Cringleford Guest House

1 Gurney Ln, Cringleford NR4 7SB

☎ 01603 451349 & 07775 725933

e–mail: robandkate@cringlefordguesthouse.co.uk

web: www.cringlefordguesthouse.co.uk

dir: *From A11/A47 Thickthorn rdbt signs to Norwich, 0.25m slip road to Cringleford, left at junct onto Colney Ln, Gurney Ln 5th on right*

A delightful property situated just a short drive from the hospital, University of East Anglia and major roads. The pleasant, well-equipped bedrooms have co-ordinated fabrics and pine furniture. Breakfast is served at individual tables in the smart dining room. CONTINUED

Rooms 5 en suite (3 fmly) (1 GF) **Facilities** TVB tea/coffee Cen ht Wi-fi available **Parking** 5 **Notes** ⊗ No coaches Closed 2wks Xmas

★★★ GUEST ACCOMMODATION
Edmar Lodge
64 Earlham Rd NR2 3DF
☎ 01603 615599 📄 01603 495599
e-mail: mail@edmarlodge.co.uk
web: www.edmarlodge.co.uk

dir: Off A47 S bypass onto B1108 Earlham Rd, follow university and hospital signs

Located just a ten minute walk from the city centre, this friendly family-run guest house offers a convenient location and ample private parking. Individually decorated bedrooms are smartly appointed and well equipped. Freshly prepared breakfasts are served within the cosy dining room; a microwave and a refrigerator are also available.

Rooms 5 en suite (1 fmly) S £38–£43; D £43–£48✳ **Facilities** FTV TVB tea/coffee Cen ht Wi-fi available **Parking** 6

★★★ GUEST ACCOMMODATION
The Larches
345 Aylsham Rd NR3 2RU
☎ 01603 415420 📄 01603 465340
e-mail: lynda@thelarches.com
web: www.thelarches.com

dir: On A140 500yds past ring road, on left adjacent to Lloyds Bank

A modern, detached property situated only a short drive from the city centre and airport. The spacious, well-equipped bedrooms are brightly decorated, pleasantly furnished and have co-ordinated soft fabrics. Breakfast is served at individual tables in the smart lounge-dining room.

Rooms 7 en suite (2 fmly) (1 GF) S fr £30; D fr £50✳ **Facilities** STV FTV TVB tea/coffee Cen ht TVL Wi-fi available **Parking** 10

★★★ GUEST HOUSE
Marlborough House
22 Stracey Rd, Thorpe Rd NR1 1EZ
☎ 01603 628005 📄 01603 628005
e-mail: marlbhouse@btconnect.com

dir: Off A1242 0.5m E of city centre

A friendly family-run property situated close to the railway station, football ground and just a short walk from the city centre. Its pleasant bedrooms have modern facilities, and the public rooms include a cosy lounge bar and a traditionally furnished breakfast room with separate tables.

Rooms 12 rms (7 en suite) (2 fmly) (1 GF) S £30–£44; D £54–£60 **Facilities** TVB tea/coffee Licensed Cen ht TVL **Parking** 5 **Notes** LB ⊗ Closed 25–30 Dec 🐾

[U]
Wensum Guest House
225 Dereham Rd NR2 3TF
☎ 01603 621069 📄 01603 618445
e-mail: info@wensumguesthouse.co.uk
web: www.wensumguesthouse.co.uk

dir: From A47 1st exit into Norwich A1074 Dereham Rd

At the time of going to press the rating for this establishment had not been confirmed. Please check the AA website www.theAA.com for up-to-date information.

Rooms 9 rms (5 en suite) (4 pri facs) 9 annexe rms (7 en suite) (2 annexe pri facs) (4 fmly) (8 GF) S £27–£45; D £55–£80✳ **Facilities** FTV TVB tea/coffee Cen ht Wi-fi available **Parking** 16 **Notes** LB ⊗ Closed 24 Dec–3 Jan

RINGSTEAD   MAP 12 TF74

★★★★ ⊛ INN
The Gin Trap Inn
6 High St PE36 5JU
☎ 01485 525264
e-mail: thegintrap@hotmail.co.uk

dir: A149 from Kings Lynn towards Hunstanton. In 15m turn right at Heacham for Ringstead into village centre

This delightful 17th-century inn is in a quiet village just a short drive from the coast. The public rooms include a large open-plan bar and a cosy restaurant. The accommodation is luxurious. Each individually appointed bedroom has been carefully decorated and thoughtfully equipped.

Rooms 3 en suite S £49–£80; D £78–£140✳ **Facilities** TVB tea/coffee Cen ht Dinner Last d 9.30pm Fri/Sat Wi-fi available **Parking** 20 **Notes** No children No coaches

SHERINGHAM
MAP 13 TG14

Premier Collection

★★★★★ BED & BREAKFAST

The Eight Acres

Glebe Farm, Holt Rd, Aylmerton NR11 8QA

☎ 01263 838094 📄 01263 838094

dir: *On A148 3m from Cromer 6m from Holt*

A warm welcome is assured at this modern detached farmhouse, which is set amid open countryside just off the A148. Bedrooms are smartly decorated with co-ordinated soft furnishings and lovely pine furniture. Public rooms feature a large open-plan lounge dining room with plush sofas.

Rooms 2 en suite S £50; D £60–£65 **Facilities** FTV TVB tea/coffee Cen ht DVD players available in rooms **Parking** 2 **Notes** ⊗ No children Closed Oct–Mar ⊜

Premier Collection

★★★★★ GUEST HOUSE

Fairlawns

26 Hooks Hill Rd NR26 8NL

☎ 01263 824717

e–mail: info@fairlawns-sheringham.co.uk

web: www.fairlawns-sheringham.com

dir: *A148 (Kings Lynn to Cromer), exit A1082. Turn left at 1st rdbt, next left into Holt Rd, left into Vicarage Rd, then right into Hooks Hill Rd*

A lovely Victorian property which is situated just a few minutes' walk from the town centre and beach. The attractively decorated bedrooms are tastefully furnished and equipped with many thoughtful touches. The stylish public areas include a comfortable lounge with a small corner bar, a conservatory dining room and a lovely garden with croquet pitch.

Rooms 5 en suite (1 fmly) S £60; D £80–£90 **Facilities** TVB tea/coffee Direct dial from bedrooms Licensed Cen ht TVL ⚑ ♨ **Notes** ⊗ No coaches ⊜

Premier Collection

★★★★★ BED & BREAKFAST

The Eiders Bed & Breakfast

Holt Rd, Aylmerton NR11 8QA

☎ 01263 837280

e–mail: eidersnorfolk@aol.com

web: www.eiders.co.uk

dir: *From Cromer on A148, past Roman Camp Hotel in Aylmerton, 300mtrs on right*

A delightful detached property set amidst landscaped grounds in the beautiful North Norfolk countryside. Public areas include a smart lounge with plush sofas and a conservatory dining room. Guests also have the use of an outdoor swimming pool. The spacious bedrooms are tastefully appointed and three rooms open out onto a decked terrace.

CONTINUED

Rooms 6 en suite (2 fmly) (6 GF) S £50; D £70–£100✱ **Facilities** TVB tea/coffee Cen ht TVL Wi-fi available �‑ **Parking** 12 **Notes** LB ⊗ No children 2yrs Closed Jan–Feb ⊜

★★★★ BED & BREAKFAST

At Knollside

43 Cliff Rd NR26 8BJ

☎ 01263 823320 & 07771 631 980 📄 01263 823320

e–mail: millar@knollside.free-online.co.uk

web: www.broadland.com/knollsidelodge.html

dir: *250yds E of town centre. A1082 to High St, onto Wyndham St & Cliff Rd*

Expect a warm welcome from the caring hosts at this delightful Victorian house overlooking the beach and sea. Bedrooms are tastefully furnished, have co-ordinated fabrics and enjoy many thoughtful touches. Breakfast is served in the elegant dining room and features local produce. Guests also have the use of a comfortable lounge.

Rooms 3 en suite (1 fmly) **Facilities** TVB tea/coffee Cen ht ♨ **Parking** 3 **Notes** ⊗ No children 3yrs ⊜

★★★★ GUEST HOUSE

Amberleigh House

19 Cromer Rd NR26 8AB

☎ 01263 823081

dir: *From A148 Holt to Cromer road, turn left to Sheringham. At rdbt turn right, 0.5m on left*

A large detached property situated on the outskirts of the town centre on the coast road. The smartly furnished bedrooms are pleasantly decorated, have co-ordinated fabrics and many thoughtful touches. Breakfast is served in the stylish dining room, which has striped wood flooring and individual light oak tables.

Rooms 3 en suite **Facilities** TVB tea/coffee Cen ht Dinner Last d noon **Parking** 7 **Notes** No coaches Closed Oct–Mar ⊜

★★★★ GUEST HOUSE

Bay Leaf Guest House

10 St Peters Rd NR26 8QY

☎ 01263 823779 📄 01263 820041

e–mail: bayleafgh@aol.com

dir: *A149 Weybourne Rd onto Church St, 2nd right*

A lovely Victorian property situated just a short walk from the golf course, steam railway and town centre. There is a smart lounge bar, and breakfast is served in the conservatory-dining room which overlooks the patio.

Rooms 7 en suite (2 fmly) (2 GF) S £38–£50; D £54–£72 **Facilities** TVB tea/coffee Licensed Cen ht **Parking** 5 **Notes** LB ⊗ No children 8yrs No coaches ⊜

★★★★ GUEST ACCOMMODATION
Brambles Bed & Breakfast

5 Nelson Rd NR26 8BT

☎ 01263 825567 🗎 01263 825567

e-mail: enquiries@stayatbrambles.co.uk

web: www.stayatbrambles.co.uk

dir: *Leave A148 into Sheringham across rdbt, right at Lobster pub. Left onto Cliff Rd, right onto Nelson Rd*

A warm welcome is offered by the caring hosts at this delightful detached property situated just a short walk from the seafront and town centre. The bedrooms are pleasantly decorated with co-ordinated fabrics and have many thoughtful touches. Breakfast is served in the smart dining room.

Rooms 3 en suite (1 fmly) (1 GF) S £45–£55; D £55–£65 **Facilities** TVB tea/coffee Cen ht **Parking** 6 **Notes** LB ⊗ ☺

★★★★ GUEST HOUSE
Highfield

5 Montague Rd NR26 8LN

☎ 01263 825524 & 07769 628817

e-mail: gmcaldwell@aol.com

dir: *Off A148, left at mini rdbt, 1st right. Left at church, left onto South St & Montague Rd*

This delightful guest house is situated in a peaceful side road within easy walking distance of the shops and beach. It offers smart, thoughtfully equipped bedrooms, and breakfast is served at individual tables in the attractive dining room.

Rooms 6 rms (5 en suite) (1 pri facs) (2 fmly) S £45–£50; D £50–£75 **Facilities** TVB tea/coffee Cen ht TVL **Conf** Max 20 Board 20 **Parking** 2 **Notes** LB ⊗ No children 8yrs Closed 22 Dec–1 Feb ☺

★★★★ GUEST HOUSE
Homefield Guest House

48 Cromer Rd, West Runton NR27 9AD

☎ 01263 837337

web: www.homefieldguesthouse.co.uk

dir: *A149 towards Sheringham, B&B on left in West Runton*

This imposing detached property, dating from 1890, is on the A149 in the village of West Runton. Bedrooms are cheerfully decorated in pastel shades, with attractive co-ordinated fabrics and well-chosen furniture; some rooms have superb sea views. Breakfast is served at individual tables in the smart dining room.

Rooms 6 en suite S £40–£70; D £60–£70✳ **Facilities** TVB tea/coffee Cen ht **Parking** 6 **Notes** LB ⊗ No children 12yrs No coaches Closed Dec–Jan

★★★★ BED & BREAKFAST
Magnolia Cottage

8 Holt Rd NR26 8NA

☎ 01263 824635

e-mail: abolderstone@btinternet.com

dir: *A148 onto A1082, at rdbt left onto A149. 1st left onto Holt Rd, 200yds on right*

Delightful detached cottage set in pretty landscaped grounds in a peaceful residential area just a short walk from the centre of town. The bedrooms are tastefully decorated, have co-ordinated fabrics and many thoughtful touches. Breakfast is served at individual tables in the smart conservatory which overlooks the neat gardens.

Rooms 2 rms (1 en suite) (1 pri facs) D £44–£60 **Facilities** TVB tea/coffee Cen ht TVL Golf 18 **Parking** 2 **Notes** ⊗ No children ☺

★★★★ 🅰 GUEST ACCOMMODATION
The Old Barn

Cromer Rd, West Runton NR27 9QT

☎ 01263 838285

dir: *A149 from Cromer to West Runton, 2m opp church*

Rooms 3 rms (2 en suite) (1 pri facs) (1 GF) **Facilities** TVB tea/coffee Cen ht TVL **Parking** 6 **Notes** ⊗ No children 18yrs ☺

ENGLAND

SWAFFHAM
MAP 13 TF80

★★★★ GUEST ACCOMMODATION
Corfield House

Sporle PE32 2EA
☎ 01760 723636
e–mail: info@corfieldhouse.co.uk
web: www.corfieldhouse.co.uk

dir: *3m E of Swaffham on S edge of village, 0.5m from A47*

A delightful 19th-century property set in attractive landscaped gardens on the outskirts of Swaffham. Bedrooms (one of which is on the ground floor) are carefully furnished with co-ordinated fabrics, and have many thoughtful touches. Public rooms include a quiet lounge and a comprehensive breakfast menu is served in the elegant dining room.

Rooms 4 en suite (1 GF) S £35; D £56 **Facilities** TVB tea/coffee Cen ht **Parking** 5 **Notes** Closed mid Dec–early Jan

★★ INN
Red Lion Motel

87 Market Place PE37 7AQ
☎ 01760 721022 🖹 01760 720664
e–mail: gwhoare@aol.com

dir: *In town centre next to Woolworths*

Located in the central Market Place, this popular inn offers a range of real ales, meals and snacks in the lounge bar. Accommodation is in a motel-style block across the rear courtyard and includes bedrooms with modern facilities and some rooms suitable for families.

Rooms 9 annexe en suite (9 GF) **Facilities** TVB tea/coffee Cen ht Dinner Last d 9.30pm **Parking** 8 **Notes** ⊗

THOMPSON
MAP 13 TL99

★★★★ 🅰 INN
The Chequers Inn

Griston Rd IP24 1PX
☎ 01953 483360 🖹 01953 488092
e–mail: richard@chequers-inn.wanadoo.co.uk

dir: *NE of Thetford. Off A1075 to Thompson village x-rds*

Rooms 3 annexe en suite (1 fmly) (3 GF) **Facilities** TVB tea/coffee Direct dial from bedrooms Cen ht Dinner Last d 9.15pm Fishing **Parking** 35

THORNHAM
MAP 12 TF74

★★★★ ◉◉ RESTAURANT WITH ROOMS
The Orange Tree

High St PE36 6LY
☎ 01485 512213 🖹 01485 512424
e–mail: email@theorangetreethornham.co.uk
web: www.theorangetreethornham.co.uk

dir: *On A149 in centre of village.*

The Orange Tree is a smart restaurant with rooms on the north Norfolk coast. Bedrooms are located in an annexe adjacent to the main building; each one is pleasantly decorated and thoughtfully equipped. Public areas feature a contemporary open-plan bar/restaurant where an interesting choice of freshly prepared dishes is on offer.

Rooms 6 en suite (1 fmly) (6 GF) S £45; D £80 **Facilities** FTV TVB tea/coffee Cen ht Dinner Last d 9pm Wi-fi available **Parking** 24

THURNING
MAP 13 TG02

★★ FARM HOUSE
Rookery Farm *(TG078307)*

NR24 2JP
☎ 01263 860357 Mrs A M Fisher

dir: *Off B1354 S through Briston, left at x-rds signed Saxthorpe, farm 0.6m on left*

A delightful 300-year-old red-brick farmhouse, set amid landscaped grounds in peaceful countryside. The spacious bedrooms are pleasantly decorated and well equipped. Breakfast is served at a large table in the dining room, which doubles as a sitting room.

Rooms 2 rms (1 en suite) (1 fmly) S £25; D £50✳ **Facilities** tea/coffee TVL Dinner Last d By arrangement **Notes** ⊗ 400 acres arable Closed Dec–Jan

THURSFORD
MAP 13 TF93

Premier Collection

★★★★★ 🛏 BED & BREAKFAST
Holly Lodge

The Street NR21 0AS
☎ 01328 878465 🖷 01328 878465
e–mail: info@hollylodgeguesthouse.co.uk
dir: *Off A148 into Thursford village*

An award-winning 18th-century property situated in a picturesque location surrounded by open farmland. The stylish cottage bedrooms are in a converted stable block, each room individually decorated, beautifully furnished and equipped with many useful extras. The attractive public rooms have a wealth of character, with flagstone floors, oak beams and open fireplaces. There are also superb landscaped grounds to enjoy.

Rooms 3 en suite (3 GF) S £70–£100; D 90–£120 **Facilities** TVB tea/coffee Cen ht TVL Dinner Last d before arrival Wi-fi available **Parking** 6 **Notes** LB ⊗ No children 14yrs Closed Jan

★★★ ⊚ RESTAURANT WITH ROOMS
The Old Forge Seafood Restaurant

Seafood Restaurant, Fakenham Rd NR21 0BD
☎ 01328 878345
e–mail: sarah.goldspink@btconnect.com
dir: *On A148 (Fakenham to Holt road), next to garage at Thursford*

Expect a warm welcome at this delightful relaxed restaurant with rooms. The open-plan public areas include a lounge bar area with comfy sofas, and a intimate restaurant with pine tables. Bedrooms are pleasantly decorated and equipped with a good range of useful facilities.

Rooms 2 rms (1 en suite) (1 pri facs) S £25–£35; D £55–£65 **Facilities** FTV TVB tea/coffee Dinner Last d 9pm **Conf** Max 28 Class 28 **Parking** 10 **Notes** No children 6yrs

WELLS-NEXT-THE-SEA
MAP 13 TF94

★★★ FARM HOUSE
Branthill Farm (TF900407)

NR23 1SB
☎ 01328 710246 🖷 01328 711524 Mrs Maufe
e–mail: branthill.farms@macunlimited.net
web: www.therealaleshop.co.uk
dir: *1.5m SW of Wells off B1105*

Branthill is a friendly family-run farmhouse situated in peaceful countryside just a short drive from the north Norfolk coast. A hearty breakfast is served at the large communal table in the attractive dining

room. The one bedroom is equipped with many useful extras and offers a good degree of comfort. A real ale shop is a successful addition to the farm.

Rooms 1 en suite **Facilities** TVB tea/coffee Cen ht ↖ ♨ **Parking** 2 **Notes** ⊗ No children 12yrs 1000 acres arable ⊚

★★★ BED & BREAKFAST
Kilcoroon

Chancery Ln NR23 1ER
☎ 01328 710270
e–mail: terry@kilcoroon.co.uk
dir: *Turn off B1105 onto Mill Rd. Take 3rd right onto Buttlands. Left of Crown Hotel*

Delightful detached period property situated by the green, just off the Buttlands and a short walk from the town centre. The spacious bedrooms are pleasantly decorated with co-ordinated fabrics and equipped with modern facilities. Breakfast is served at a large communal table in the elegant dining room.

Rooms 3 rms (1 en suite) S £40–£45; D £60–£75✱ **Facilities** TVB tea/coffee Cen ht **Notes** ⊗ No children 10yrs Closed 23–31 Dec ⊚

The Ollands Guest House

The house is well situated in approximately ¾ acre of garden overlooking farmland. It is reached via a short loke (Norfolk word for walk) from the centre of the village of Worstead and is within easy walking distance of the Post Office, New Inn Public House and the C14th Church.

The Lounge with open fire is always open for guests to use.

Breakfast is served in the Dining Room and we provide a full English breakfast using our own freshly laid eggs, home-made bread and preserves, locally produced bacon and sausages. A two course table d'hôte evening meal is available on request. The kitchen has received an AA dinner award.

Swanns Loke, Worstead, Nr. North Walsham, Norfolk NR28 9RP
Tel: 01692 535150   **Fax:** 01692 535150
Email: theollands@btinternet.com
Website: www.ollandsfarm.com

CONTINUED

369

ENGLAND

WEST RUNTON   MAP 13 TG14

★★★★ BED & BREAKFAST
Corner House

2 Station Rd NR27 9QD

☎ 01263 838540 & 07769 800831 📠 01263 838540

e–mail: linjimhoward@btinternet.com

web: www.cornerhousenorfolk.com

dir: *Station Rd N off A149, in centre of village, B&B first on right*

A warm welcome is to be expected from the caring hosts at this delightful property situated just off the main coast road on the outskirts of Sheringham. Bedrooms are cheerfully decorated, have co-ordinated fabrics, and benefit from many thoughtful touches. Public areas include a large breakfast room and a cosy TV lounge.

Rooms 3 rms (1 en suite) (2 pri facs) S £35–£40; D £60–£66
Facilities tea/coffee Cen ht TVL **Notes** ⊗ No children 8yrs ⊛

WORSTEAD   MAP 13 TG32

★★★★ 🛏 GUEST HOUSE
The Ollands

Swanns Yard NR28 9RP

☎ 01692 535150 📠 01692 535150

e–mail: theollands@btinternet.com

dir: *Off A149 to village x-rds, off Back St*

This charming detached property is set in the heart of the picturesque village of Worstead. The well-equipped bedrooms are pleasantly decorated and carefully furnished, and breakfast served in the elegant dining room features local produce.

Rooms 3 en suite (1 GF) S £35.50–£37.50; D £56–£60* **Facilities** TVB tea/coffee Cen ht TVL Dinner Last d 9am **Parking** 8 **Notes LB** No coaches

See advert on page 369

WROXHAM   MAP 13 TG31

★★★★ 🅰 BED & BREAKFAST
Wroxham Park Lodge Guest House

142 Norwich Rd NR12 8SA

☎ 01603 782991

e–mail: parklodge@computer-assist.net

dir: *On A1151 in village centre*

Rooms 3 en suite S £36–£42; D £56–£60 **Facilities** TVB tea/coffee Cen ht Golf **Parking** 4 **Notes LB** ⊗ No children ⊛

★★★ BED & BREAKFAST
Beech Tree House

Wroxham Rd, Rackheath NR13 6NQ

☎ 01603 781419 & 07889 152063 📠 01603 781419

e–mail: beechtree@talk21.com

dir: *1.5m SW of Wroxham on A1151 opp Green Man pub*

This detached property, set amid pretty landscaped grounds and surrounded by farmland, is just a short drive from Norwich and Wroxham Broads. The spacious bedrooms are pleasantly decorated with co-ordinated soft furnishings and have many useful extras. Breakfast is served in the conservatory-lounge that overlooks the garden.

Rooms 3 rms (1 en suite) (3 fmly) **Facilities** TVB tea/coffee Cen ht TVL Golf ⛳ **Parking** 5 **Notes** Closed 23 Dec–1 Jan ⊛

WYMONDHAM   MAP 13 TG10

★★★★ 🅰 BED & BREAKFAST
Witch Hazel

55 Church Ln, Wicklewood NR18 9QH

☎ 01953 602247 📠 01953 602247

e–mail: witchhazel@tiscali.co.uk

web: www.witchhazel-norfolk.co.uk

dir: *2m W of Wymondham. Off B1135 to Wicklewood village x-rds, onto Church Ln, 200yds on right*

Rooms 3 en suite S £35–£37; D £52–£56 **Facilities** TVB tea/coffee Cen ht TVL Dinner Last d 10.30am **Parking** 3 **Notes** ⊗ No children 15yrs

---

NORTHAMPTONSHIRE

BRAUNSTON   MAP 11 SP56

★★★★ GUEST ACCOMMODATION
Braunston Manor

NN11 7HS

☎ 01788 890267 📠 01788 891515

e–mail: info@braunstonmanor.com

dir: *From A45 join High St at T-junct, right into parking area*

Braunston Manor has been family owned for almost a century. A beautiful, nostalgic, Tudor residence built of Northamptonshire stone, set in over ten acres of land. The Manor offers uninterrupted views over open countryside and is close to one of the countries oldest canal network systems. The bedrooms and bathrooms provide good comfort, space and ease of use. This establishment also offers easy access to main motorway networks.

Rooms 6 rms (5 en suite) (1 pri facs) 4 annexe en suite (2 GF) S £60–£85; D £85–£140(room only) **Facilities** FTV TVB tea/coffee TVL Wi-fi available **Conf** Max 40 Thtr 40 Class 40 Board 40 Del from £120 ✳ **Parking** 50 **Notes** ⊗ No children Civ Wed 85

COLLYWESTON — MAP 11 SK90

★★★★ ⑳ INN
The Collyweston Slater
87 Main Rd PE9 3PQ
☎ 01780 444288
e–mail: info@thecollywestonslater.co.uk

dir: *4m SW of Stamford on A43*

A major refurbishment at this pleasing village inn has seen all public areas and bedrooms brought up to a smart modern standard. Individually appointed bedrooms are stylish and well equipped, while the ground floor public areas are given over to a smart brasserie concept. The food is worthy of note, offering monthly changing menus that are supplemented by daily specials, in a modern British style.

Rooms 5 en suite (1 fmly) S £45–£60; D £60–£120✳ **Facilities** TVB tea/coffee Cen ht Dinner Last d 9pm Wi-fi available Petanque Piste **Conf** Max 12 Thtr 12 Class 6 Board 10 **Parking** 30 **Notes LB** ⊗

CORBY — MAP 11 SP88

★★★★★ Ⓐ GUEST ACCOMMODATION
Spanhoe Lodge
Harringworth Rd NN17 3AT
☎ 01780 450328
e–mail: jennie.spanhoe@virgin.net

(For full entry see Laxton)

KILSBY — MAP 11 SP57

★★★★ GUEST ACCOMMODATION
Hunt House Quarters
Main Rd CV23 8XR
☎ 01788 823282
e–mail: luluharris@hunthouse.fsbusiness.co.uk
web: www.hunthousekilsby.com

dir: *On B3048 in village*

This thatched 17th-century hunting lodge has been renovated to provide quality bedrooms with smart modern bathrooms in a converted stable block. Comprehensive breakfasts are served in the adjacent courtyard building.

Rooms 4 en suite (1 fmly) (4 GF) S £59.95–£75; D £75–£85✳ **Facilities** TVB tea/coffee Cen ht Wi-fi available **Parking** 8 **Notes LB** ⊗

LAXTON — MAP 11 SP99

★★★★★ Ⓐ GUEST ACCOMMODATION
Spanhoe Lodge
Harringworth Rd NN17 3AT
☎ 01780 450328
e–mail: jennie.spanhoe@virgin.net

dir: *Off A43 to Laxton, through village, Spanhoe Lodge 0.5m on right*

Rooms 4 en suite 8 annexe en suite (2 fmly) (11 GF) S £60–£85; D £80–£90✳ **Facilities** FTV TVB tea/coffee Cen ht TVL Dinner Last d 8.30pm Wi-fi available Snooker Hot Tub **Conf** Max 70 Thtr 70 Class 34 Board 36 **Parking** 50 **Notes LB**

OLD STRATFORD — MAP 11 SP74

★★★ BED & BREAKFAST
The Lodge
Furtho Manor Farm MK19 6NR
☎ 01908 543765 📠 01908 542139
e–mail: dsansome@talktalk.net

dir: *Just off A5, on A508 towards Northampton*

Situated on a dairy farm, bedrooms in this family bungalow overlook the countryside. There are three bedrooms, one of which has self-catering facilities. Breakfast is served farmhouse style in the open-plan kitchen/dining room.

Rooms 3 rms (2 en suite) (1 pri facs) (3 GF) S £25–£35; D £50–£65✳ **Facilities** FTV TVB tea/coffee Cen ht Wi-fi available Fishing ⛵ **Parking** 6 **Notes** ⊗ RS 24 Dec–1 Jan ⊛

ENGLAND

OUNDLE
MAP 11 TL08

★★★★ BED & BREAKFAST
Bridge Cottage Bed & Breakfast
Oundle Rd, Woodnewton PE8 5EG
☎ 01780 470779 & 07979 644864 📠 01780 470860
e-mail: judycolebrook@btinternet.com

dir: *A1 onto A605, right at 1st rdbt, through Fortheringham towards Woodnewtown. 1st house on left entering village*

A delightful and peaceful location on the periphery of the village of Woodnewton (next to the bridge) and bordered by open countryside, this lovely B&B offers real home-from-home comforts with tastefully appointed accommodation. A warm welcome and a tasty, freshly cooked breakfast ensure that guests return time and again. Breakfast is taken in the open-plan kitchen, which overlooks (as will the new conservatory) lovely gardens that have a summer house, bubbling brook and an abundance of birdlife (spot the Kingfisher).

Rooms 3 rms (2 en suite) (1 pri facs) S £37.50–£50; D £70–£85 **Facilities** STV TVB tea/coffee Cen ht **Parking** 3 **Notes** RS 24–26 Dec ⌨

STANWICK
MAP 11 SP97

Premier Collection

★★★★★ GUEST ACCOMMODATION
The Courtyard Luxury Lodge
Rutland Lodge, West St NN9 6QY
☎ 01933 622233 📠 01933 622276
e-mail: bookings@thecourtyard.me.uk
web: www.thecourtyard.me.uk

dir: *A45 rdbt to Stanwick, entrance immediately on right*

Standing in extensive and delightful gardens and on the edge of the village, this very well-furnished detached house offers guests every possible comfort, and the lounge is especially relaxing. Quality breakfasts are served around a large oak table and hospitality is really special.

Rooms 12 en suite (10 GF) S £60; D £75 **Facilities** FTV TVB tea/coffee Cen ht TVL Dinner Last d 9pm Wi-fi available **Conf** Max 30 Thtr 30 Class 20 Board 20 Del from £100 ✳ **Parking** 50 **Notes** LB Civ Wed 100

NORTHUMBERLAND

ALNWICK
MAP 21 NU11

★★★★ GUEST HOUSE
Bondgate House
20 Bondgate Without NE66 1PN
☎ 01665 602025
e-mail: enquiries@bondgatehouse.co.uk
web: www.bondgatehouse.co.uk

dir: *A1 onto B6346 into town centre, 200yds past war memorial on right*

Originally a doctor's house, this Georgian building stands close to the historic gateway into the town centre. Friendly service complements an attractive breakfast room and cosy lounge. Bedrooms are all well equipped and thoughtfully furnished and include three rooms in converted stables set in a secluded garden behind the house.

Rooms 3 en suite 3 annexe en suite (1 fmly) (1 GF) D £75–£85✳ **Facilities** TVB tea/coffee Cen ht TVL Aromatherapy massage **Parking** 8 **Notes** ⊗ No coaches Closed Xmas ⌨

★★★★ GUEST ACCOMMODATION
Rock Farm House B & B
Rock NE66 3SE
☎ 01665 579367
e-mail: stay@rockfarmhouse.co.uk

dir: *Off A1 into village centre*

Do not be misled by the surroundings of this old farmhouse. Inside, a loving restoration has transformed it into a delightful home. The spacious and comfortable bedrooms upstairs look out onto walled gardens, and downstairs there is a cosy lounge with a wood-burning stove and a charming dining room where breakfast (with healthy options) is served at a large pine table.

Rooms 3 en suite (1 fmly) **Facilities** FTV TVB tea/coffee Cen ht **Parking** 10

BARDON MILL MAP 21 NY76

★★★★ Ⓐ FARM HOUSE
Gibbs Hill Farm B&B (NY749693)
NE47 7AP
☎ 01434 344030 📄 01434 344030 Mrs V Gibson
e–mail: val@gibbshillfarm.co.uk

dir: *Off A69 at Bardon Mill, signs to Oncebrewed, over B6318, up hill, 1m right at sign to Gibbs Hill*

Rooms 3 en suite (1 fmly) **Facilities** TVB tea/coffee Cen ht TVL Fishing Riding **Parking** 10 **Notes** ⊗ No children 10yrs 750 acres Mixed Closed Oct–Apr

---

BELFORD MAP 21 NU13

Premier Collection

★★★★★ 🍴 GUEST ACCOMMODATION
Market Cross
1 Church St NE70 7LS
☎ 01668 213013
e–mail: info@marketcross.net
web: www.marketcross.net

dir: *Off A1 into village, opp church*

Lying in the heart of the village, this Grade II listed building offers delightful, individually styled and thoughtfully equipped bedrooms. Breakfast is a real treat, an extensive and impressive range of delicious cooked dishes using local produce. Jill and John Hodge were finalists for the Friendliest Landlady of the Year 2008 Award.

Rooms 3 en suite S £40–£80; D £70–£110 **Facilities** FTV TVB tea/coffee Cen ht TVL Wi-fi available **Parking** 3 **Notes LB**

BERWICK-UPON-TWEED MAP 21 NT95

★★★ INN
Lindisfarne Inn
Beal TD15 2PD
☎ 01289 381223 📄 01289 381223
e–mail: enquiries@lindisfarneinn.co.uk

dir: *On A1, turn off for Holy Island*

The Lindisfarne Inn stands on the site of the old "Plough Hotel" at Beal, on the road leading to Holy Island. Now totally refurbished and re-opened with a traditional bar, rustic style restaurant and comfortably equipped courtyard bedrooms in the adjacent wing. Food is available all day.

Rooms 21 annexe en suite (20 fmly) (10 GF) S £55; D £75✶ **Facilities** FTV TVB tea/coffee Cen ht TVL Dinner Last d 9pm **Parking** 25

CORNHILL-ON-TWEED MAP 21 NT83

Premier Collection

★★★★★ 🍴 GUEST ACCOMMODATION
Ivy Cottage
1 Croft Gardens, Crookham TD12 4ST
☎ 01890 820667 📄 01890 820667
e–mail: ajoh540455@aol.com
web: www.ivycottagecrookham.co.uk

dir: *4m E of Cornhill. Off A697 onto B6353 into Crookham village*

Hospitality is second to none at this pristine modern house set in delightful gardens in a quiet village. One bedroom is furnished in bright modern style while the upstairs room has antique pine; each room has a super private bathroom and host of thoughtful touches. Delicious Aga-cooked breakfasts are served either in the farmhouse-style kitchen or the cosy dining room. Guests can enjoy tea in the summerhouse.

Rooms 2 rms (2 pri facs) (1 GF) S £45; D £68–£78✶ **Facilities** TVB tea/coffee Cen ht Dinner Last d am same day **Parking** 2 **Notes LB** No children 5yrs ⊛

ENGLAND

FALSTONE
MAP 21 NY78

★★★★ INN
Pheasant

Stannersburn NE48 1DD
☎ 01434 240382 📠 01434 240382
e–mail: enquiries@thepheasantinn.com
web: www.thepheasantinn.com

dir: *1m S of Falstone. Off B6320 to Kielder Water, via Bellingham or via Hexham A69 onto B6320 via Wall-Wark-Bellingham*

This charming establishment epitomises the traditional country inn; it has character, good food and warm hospitality. Bright modern bedrooms, some with their own entrances, are all contained in stone buildings adjoining the inn. Delicious home-cooked meals are served in the bar with its low-beamed ceilings and exposed stone walls, or in the attractive dining room.

Rooms 8 annexe en suite (1 fmly) (5 GF) S £50–£55; D £85–£90
Facilities TVB tea/coffee Cen ht Dinner Last d 8.50pm **Parking** 40
Notes LB No coaches Closed Xmas RS Nov–Feb (closed Mon/Tue)

★★★ INN
The Blackcock Inn

NE48 1AA
☎ 01434 240200 📠 01434 240200
e–mail: thebcinn@yahoo.co.uk

dir: *In village centre, towards to Kielder Water*

This traditional family-run village inn lies close to Kielder Water. A cosy pub, it has a very homely atmosphere, with a welcoming fire in the bar in the colder weather. Evening meals are served here in the cosy restaurant, which is reminiscent of a Victorian parlour. The inn is closed during the day on Tuesdays throughout winter.

Rooms 6 rms (4 en suite) (1 fmly) S fr £40; D fr £70✱ **Facilities** TVB tea/coffee Cen ht Dinner Last d 8.30pm Fishing Pool Table **Parking** 15
Notes LB RS Tue

FELTON
MAP 21 NU10

★★★ GUEST ACCOMMODATION
Birchwood House

Kitswell Dene NE65 9NZ
☎ 01670 787828 📠 01670 787828
e–mail: gbblewitt@btinternet.com
web: www.gbblewitt.co.uk

dir: *Situated just off A1. Take Swarland exit, bear left, left again*

Conveniently situated close to the A1, this smart house offers warm hospitality and spacious, well-equipped en suite bedrooms. Freshly prepared, hearty breakfasts are served in the dining room and guests can also enjoy the separate lounge. Bedrooms are all on the ground floor.

Rooms 4 en suite (1 fmly) (4 GF) S £30–£35; D £60–£70✱
Facilities FTV TVB tea/coffee Cen ht TVL Wi-fi available **Parking** 10
Notes Closed 24 Dec–1 Mar RS Nov–24 Dec & 2 Mar–Apr ⊛

GILSLAND
MAP 21 NY66

★★★★ ≜ BED & BREAKFAST
Brookside Villa

CA8 7DA
☎ 016977 47300
e–mail: brooksidevilla@hotmail.co.uk

dir: *A69, take Spadeadam/Gisland/Denton exit, continue for 2m, left onto B6318, Brookside Villa 100yds on left*

This Victorian stone built villa is ideally located for the Hadrian's Wall trail. Walkers and cyclists are well catered for with great consideration given to their needs. The stylish bedrooms offer fresh, minimalist décor with contemporary en suites. Sky TV is available in the cosy lounge where guests can relax in front of the fire, or enjoy breakfast and a great view at the dining table.

Rooms 2 en suite (1 fmly) **Facilities** FTV TV1B tea/coffee Cen ht Dinner Last d 7pm Wi-fi available **Parking** 2 **Notes** ⊛

★ ★ ★ ★ GUEST HOUSE
Bush Nook
Upper Denton CA8 7AF
☎ 016977 47194 📄 016977 47194
e–mail: info@bushnook.co.uk
web: www.bushnook.co.uk

dir: *Halfway between Brampton and Haltwhistle, off A69 signed Spadeadam, Birdoswald, Bush Nook*

Located in open countryside, this converted farmhouse offers comfortable bedrooms, split between the main house and the barn, with many original features. Other guest areas include the spacious breakfast room, cosy lounge and impressive conservatory leading out to a large, well maintained garden. Particularly popular with walkers and cyclists, although a warm welcome is given to all.

Rooms 6 en suite **Facilities** TVB tea/coffee Licensed Cen ht Dinner Last d noon Wi-fi available **Parking** 6 **Notes** ⊗ No coaches Closed Xmas & New Year

---

HALTWHISTLE   MAP 21 NY76

See also Brampton (Cumbria)

★ ★ ★ ★ GUEST HOUSE
Vallum Lodge
Military Rd, Twice Brewed NE47 7AN
☎ 01434 344248 📄 01434 344488
e–mail: stay@vallum-lodge.co.uk
web: www.vallum-lodge.co.uk

dir: *On B6318, 400yds W of Once Brewed National Park visitors centre*

Set in the Northumberland National Park, a real home from home atmosphere is found at this well-equipped roadside guest house, which provides easy access to Hadrian's Wall. The en suite bedrooms have been refurbished and feature homely extras. Breakfast is served in the smart dining room and there is a cosy lounge. The Lodge is licensed and all accommodation is on the ground floor.

Rooms 6 en suite (1 fmly) (6 GF) S £50–£60; D £70✳ **Facilities** TVB tea/coffee Licensed Cen ht TVL **Parking** 15 **Notes** ⊗ No coaches Closed Nov–Feb

---

★ ★ ★ ★ 🅰 FARM HOUSE
Wydon Farm B&B *(NY682634)*
Wydon Farm NE49 0LG
☎ 01434 321702 📄 01434 321702 Mrs Linda Ogle
e–mail: stay@wydon-haltwhistle.co.uk
web: www.wydon-haltwhistle.co.uk

dir: *A69 to Haltwhistle, take Alston rd S, after 5yds turn right over cattle grid into Wydon Farm*

Rooms 3 en suite (2 fmly) (3 GF) S £45–£50; D £60–£80✳ **Facilities** STV TVB tea/coffee Cen ht Wi-fi available Fishing **Parking** 10 **Notes** 366 acres Beef, Sheep

---

HEXHAM   MAP 21 NY96

Premier Collection

★ ★ ★ ★ ★ 📖 BED & BREAKFAST
Montcoffer
Bardon Mill NE47 7HZ
☎ 01434 344138
e–mail: john-dehlia@talk21.com

dir: *Off A69 4m W of Haydon Bridge signed Bardon Mill, 0.25m into village on left*

John's passion for period pieces and collectables and Dehlia's design skills have transformed the former stables into a stylish guest house. Dehlia's adjacent studio specialises in fabrics and decorative wall hangings and many of her works adorn the house. The bedrooms have headboards made with reclaimed timber from the chapel at Bagshot House, home of the Earl and Countess of Wessex.

Rooms 2 en suite (1 fmly) (2 GF) **Facilities** TVB tea/coffee Cen ht Fishing **Parking** 12 **Notes** ⊗ 🐾

HEXHAM CONTINUED

★★★★ BED & BREAKFAST
Peth Head Cottage

Juniper NE47 0LA
☎ 01434 673286 📠 01434 673038
e–mail: peth_head@btopenworld.com
web: www.peth-head-cottage.co.uk

dir: *B6306 S from Hexham, 200yds fork right, next left. Continue 3.5m, house 400yds on right after Juniper sign*

Warm and caring hospitality is assured at this lovely sandstone cottage located within the peaceful hamlet of Juniper. Guests can enjoy home-made biscuits on arrival and home-baked bread and preserves at breakfast. The attractive bedrooms are equipped with lots of thoughtful extras and day rooms feature a cosy lounge-breakfast room. Self-catering is also available.

Rooms 2 en suite S £29; D £58 **Facilities** TVB tea/coffee Cen ht TVL **Parking** 2 **Notes** LB ⊗

★★★★ Ⓐ GUEST ACCOMMODATION
Rye Hill

Slaley NE47 0AH
☎ 01434 673259 📠 01434 673259
e–mail: info@ryehillfarm.co.uk

dir: *5m S of Hexham off B6306, 1st right after Travellers Rest pub then 1st farm road right*

Rooms 4 en suite (1 fmly) S £40; D £60 **Facilities** TVB tea/coffee Cen ht Dinner Last d 24hrs Wi-fi available Pool Table Games barn, Skittle alley, Table tennis **Parking** 4 **Notes** LB

KIRKWHELPINGTON   MAP 21 NY98

★★★ FARM HOUSE
Horncastle Farm *(NY985846)*

NE19 2RA
☎ 01830 540247 Mrs S Pittendrigh
e–mail: jspitt@horncastle.wanadoo.co.uk

dir: *On A696 opp village of Kirkwhelpington*

A relaxed atmosphere and friendly welcome are assured at this upland farmhouse that is set in sheltered gardens and reached by a long farm track leading across pastureland. It is a family home and offers a

CONTINUED

ground floor and an upstairs bedroom, plus a lounge and a dining room where hearty breakfasts are served.

Rooms 2 rms (1 en suite) (1 pri facs) (1 GF) **Facilities** tea/coffee Cen ht TVL **Parking** 5 **Notes** ⊗ 370 acres beef mixed sheep Closed Apr ⬛

NEWTON-ON-THE-MOOR   MAP 21 NU10

★★★★ ⬭ INN
The Cook and Barker Inn

NE65 9JY
☎ 01665 575234 📠 01665 575234

dir: *North on A1, pass Morpeth. A1 becomes single carriageway for 8m, then dual carriageway, travel up slight incline 3m, look for signs on left to Newton-on-the-Moor*

Set in the heart of this quiet village yet close to the A1, the inn is popular with visitors and locals. The emphasis is on food here with interesting home-made dishes offered in the restaurant and bar areas. Bedrooms are smartly furnished and well equipped and are split between the main house and the adjacent annexe.

Rooms 4 en suite 14 annexe en suite (2 fmly) (7 GF) S £57–£67; D £75–£85✳ **Facilities** TVB tea/coffee Cen ht Dinner Last d 9pm **Conf** Max 50 Thtr 50 Class 50 Board 25 Del from £100 ✳ **Parking** 64 **Notes** LB ⊗

ROTHBURY   MAP 21 NU00

Premier Collection

★★★★★ 🍴 GUEST ACCOMMODATION
The Orchard House

High St NE65 7TL
☎ 01669 620684
e–mail: graham@orchardhouserothbury.com
web: www.orchardhouserothbury.com

dir: *In village centre*

This delightful accommodation is located in an attractive Georgian period house within easy walking distance of the village amenities. Full of character the restful atmosphere is enhanced by genuinely friendly service and hospitality. Individually styled bedrooms are all finished to a high standard and are very well equipped. The elegant lounge is richly styled and very comfortable, the elegant dining room has an honesty bar and interesting breakfasts featuring the best of local and

CONTINUED

organic produce are served here. Orchard House was the AA Guest Accommodation of the Year for England 2007–2008.

Rooms 5 en suite (1 fmly) **Facilities** TVB tea/coffee Cen ht Golf 18 **Notes** ⊛ Closed Xmas & New Year

See advert on this page

WOOLER
MAP 21 NT92

Premier Collection

★★★★★ 🏠 GUEST ACCOMMODATION
The Old Manse
New Rd, Chatton NE66 5PU
☎ 01668 215343
e–mail: chattonbb@aol.com
web: www.oldmansechatton.co.uk

dir: *4m E of Wooler. On B6348 in Chatton*

Built in 1875, this elegant former manse is located on the edge of the village convenient for St Cuthbert's Way. There is a four poster and double rooms upstairs, and a ground-floor room with its own entrance, sitting room and patio; all are thoughtfully equipped with a wealth of thoughtful extras including fridge with fruit, CD player, juices and biscuits. Sumptuous day rooms include wood burning stoves, impressive breakfasts are served in a conservatory overlooking the pretty gardens and a warm welcome is assured.

Rooms 3 en suite (1 GF) S £40–£60; D £80–£95✳ **Facilities** TVB tea/coffee Cen ht TVL **Parking** 4 **Notes** ⊛ No children 13yrs Closed Nov – Feb ☻

The Orchard House
High Street, Rothbury, NE65 7TL
Tel: 01669 620684
www.orchardhouserothbury.com

Egyptian cotton linen, luxury-bathoils, antiques, fresh-flowers and delicious-organic breakfasts in the setting of a delightful Georgian House.

★★★ BED & BREAKFAST
Winton House
39 Glendale Rd NE71 6DL
☎ 01668 281362
e–mail: enquiries@wintonhousebandb.co.uk
dir: *Off A697 into Wooler, Glendale Rd off High St, 150mtrs on left*

Located on a quiet residential avenue close to town centre, this elegant Edwardian house is popular with cyclists and walkers for St Cuthbert's Way, providing comfortable bedrooms equipped with thoughtful extras. Breakfast, featuring the best of local produce is taken in an attractive dining room and a warm welcome is assured.

Rooms 3 rms (2 en suite) D £54–£76 **Facilities** TVB tea/coffee Cen ht **Notes** ⊛ No children 4yrs Closed Nov–Feb

NOTTINGHAMSHIRE

BINGHAM
MAP 11 SK73

★★★ GUEST ACCOMMODATION
Yeung Sing
15 Market St NG13 8AB
☎ 01949 831831 & 831222 📠 01949 838833
e–mail: manager@yeung-sing.co.uk
dir: *Off junct A52 & A46*

This family-run guest house is in the centre of the market town. The smart ground-floor public rooms include a bar and the highly successful Yeung Sing restaurant, which serves a fine selection of Cantonese and regional Chinese dishes. The bedrooms are well equipped and have modern suites.

Rooms 15 en suite (2 fmly) S £48; D £68✳ **Facilities** TVB tea/coffee Direct dial from bedrooms Lift Cen ht TVL Dinner Last d 9.30pm **Conf** Max 100 Thtr 100 Class 30 Board 30 **Parking** 30 **Notes** LB ⊛ Closed 25–26 Dec

COTGRAVE
MAP 11 SK63

★★★★ FARM HOUSE
Jerico Farm *(SK654307)*
Fosse Way NG12 3HG
☎ 01949 81733 Mrs S Herrick
e–mail: info@jericofarm.co.uk
web: www.jericofarm.co.uk

dir: *Farm driveway off A46, 1m N of junct A46 & A606*

A friendly relaxed atmosphere is offered at this attractive farmhouse, which stands in peaceful extensive grounds just off the A46, close to Nottingham, Melton Mowbray and the Vale of Belvoir. Day rooms include a comfortable lounge and a separate dining room overlooking the gardens, in which substantial tasty breakfasts are served. Spacious bedrooms are beautifully appointed and thoughtfully equipped.

Rooms 3 en suite S £45–£50; D £65–£70 **Facilities** TVB tea/coffee Cen ht TVL Wi-fi available Fishing **Conf** Max 6 **Parking** 4 **Notes** ⊛ No children 10yrs 150 acres mixed Closed 24 Dec–2 Jan

ENGLAND

EDWINSTOWE
MAP 16 SK66

Ⓤ

The Forest Lodge

Church St NG21 9QA
☎ 01623 824443 🖹 01623 824686
e-mail: audrey@forestlodgehotel.co.uk

dir: *A614 into Edwinstowe. On B6034, opp St Mary's church*
At the time of going to press the rating for this establishment had not been confirmed. Please check the AA website www.theAA.com for up-to-date information.

Rooms 8 en suite 5 annexe en suite (2 fmly) (5 GF) S £55; D £70–£80✳
Facilities TVB tea/coffee Cen ht Dinner Last d 9pm Wi-fi available
Conf Max 75 Thtr 75 Class 45 Board 50 **Parking** 35 **Notes** ⊗

ELTON
MAP 11 SK73

Premier Collection

★★★★★ BED & BREAKFAST

The Grange

Sutton Ln NG13 9LA
☎ 07887 952181
e-mail: d.bmasson@btinternet.com
web: www.thegrangebedandbreakfastnotts.co.uk

dir: *From Grantham A1 onto A52 to Elton x-rds, left 200yds, B&B on right*
Parts of this lovely house date back to the early 17th century and the rooms command fine views across the gardens and rolling open countryside. Bedrooms contain many thoughtful extras and fine hospitality is assured from the proprietors.

Rooms 3 en suite **Facilities** FTV TVB tea/coffee Cen ht TVL **Parking** 8
Notes ⊗ ⊛

FARNSFIELD
MAP 16 SK65

★★★ GUEST ACCOMMODATION

Grange Cottage

Main St NG22 8EA
☎ 01623 882259
e-mail: bedandbreakfast@grange-cottage.co.uk
web: www.grange-cottage.co.uk

dir: *In village opp Plough Inn car park*
Grange Cottage is a charming 18th-century Georgian building set in two acres of delightful gardens and grounds behind security gates. The bedrooms are comfortable and homely, each individually furnished with lots of family touches. A freshly-cooked breakfast is served at one large table in the elegant dining room.

Rooms 4 rms (1 en suite) (1 pri facs) 1 annexe en suite (1 GF)
S £25–£30; D £50–£60✳ **Facilities** TVB tea/coffee Cen ht **Parking** 6
Notes LB ⊛

HOLBECK
MAP 16 SK57

Premier Collection

★★★★★ BED & BREAKFAST

Browns

The Old Orchard Cottage, Holbeck Ln S80 3NF
☎ 01909 720659 🖹 01909 720659
e-mail: browns@holbeck.fsnet.co.uk

dir: *0.5m off A616 Sheffield-Newark road, turn for Holbeck at x-rds*
Set amid beautifully tended gardens with lily-ponds and extensive lawns, this mid 18th-century cottage is a tranquil rural hideaway. Breakfasts are served in the Regency-style dining room, and the elegant bedrooms have four-poster beds and many extras. The friendly owners provide attentive service, including courtesy transport to nearby restaurants if required.

Rooms 3 annexe en suite (3 GF) S £55–£62; D £72–£82✳ **Facilities** TVB tea/coffee Cen ht **Parking** 3 **Notes** ⊗ No children 15yrs Closed Xmas wk ⊛

HOLME PIERREPONT
MAP 11 SK63

★★★ GUEST ACCOMMODATION

Holme Grange Cottage

Adbolton Ln NG12 2LU
☎ 0115 981 0413
e-mail: jean.colinwightman@talk21.com

dir: *Off A52 SE of Nottingham, opp National Water Sports Centre*
A stone's throw from the National Water Sports Centre, this establishment with its own all-weather tennis court is ideal for the active guest. Indeed, when not providing warm hospitality and freshly cooked breakfasts, the proprietor is usually on the golf course.

Rooms 3 rms (1 en suite) (1 fmly) S £28–£34; D £48–£54✳
Facilities TVB tea/coffee Cen ht TVL 🏌 **Parking** 6 **Notes** LB Closed Xmas ⊛

MANSFIELD
MAP 16 SK56

★★★ GUEST HOUSE

Bridleways Holiday Homes & Guest House

Newlands Rd, Forest Town NG19 0HU
☎ 01623 635725 🖹 01623 635725
e-mail: bridleways@webnet2000.net
web: www.stayatbridleways.co.uk

dir: *Off B6030*
Beside a quiet bridleway that leads to Vicar Water Country Park and Sherwood Pines Forest Park this friendly guest house is a good touring base for walkers, cyclists or sightseeing. The new double, twin and family bedrooms are particularly spacious and all bedrooms are en suite. Lovely breakfasts are served in a cottage style dining room.

Bridleways Holiday Homes & Guest House

Rooms 9 en suite (1 fmly) (2 GF) S £35; D £66✷ **Facilities** TVB tea/coffee Wi-fi available **Parking** 14 **Notes** ⊗

★★★ GUEST ACCOMMODATION
Parkhurst

28 Woodhouse Rd NG18 2AF

☎ 01623 627324 🖷 01623 452442

e–mail: phil.fletcher@mansfieldhotel.co.uk

web: www.parkhurstguesthouse.co.uk

dir: *0.25m N of town centre. Off A60 Woodhouse Rd onto Park Av*

This well-furnished Victorian property is only a 10-minute walk from the centre of town. A cosy bar with television is available, and good breakfasts are served in the traditional style dining room. Bedrooms are comfortably appointed.

Rooms 11 rms (6 en suite) (4 fmly) (3 GF) **Facilities** TVB tea/coffee Cen ht TVL **Conf** Max 12 Thtr 25 Class 16 Board 20 **Parking** 9 **Notes** ⊗

NEWARK-ON-TRENT   MAP 17 SK75

★★★★ GUEST HOUSE
Compton House

117 Baldertongate NG24 1RY

☎ 01636 708670

e–mail: info@comptonhousenewark.com

web: www.comptonhousenewark.com

dir: *500yds SE of town centre. Off B6326 onto Sherwood Av, 1st right onto Baldertongate*

Located a short walk from the central attractions, this elegant period house has been renovated to provide high standards of comfort. Individually themed bedrooms come with a wealth of thoughtful extras and smart modern bathrooms. Comprehensive breakfasts, and wholesome dinners by arrangement, are served in the attractive dining room and a lounge is available.

Rooms 7 rms (6 en suite) (1 pri facs) (1 fmly) (1 GF) S £45–£65.50; D £79.50–£110✷ **Facilities** FTV TVB tea/coffee Cen ht Dinner Last d 2pm Wi-fi available **Conf** Max 10 Thtr 10 Class 10 Board 10 Del from £85✷ **Parking** 2 **Notes** ⊗ No coaches

★★★★ BED & BREAKFAST
Greystones Guest Accommodation

Main St, South Scarle NG23 7JH

☎ 01636 893969 🖷 01636 893969

e–mail: sheenafowkes@greystonesguests.co.uk

web: www.greystonesguests.co.uk

dir: *A1 onto A46. A1133 to Collingham, signed to South Scarle*

Service is both friendly and helpful at the Greystones, a tranquil 400-year-old Grade II-listed former farmhouse, which sits in the conservation village of South Scarle. The building has been sympathetically renovated to retain much of the original character (this includes the quirky uneven floors and walls). Bedrooms are individually appointed, comfortable and well equipped.

Rooms 2 rms (1 en suite) (1 pri facs) S £45–£60; D £60✷ **Facilities** FTV TVB tea/coffee Cen ht Dinner Last d at breakfast **Parking** 3 **Notes** LB ⊗ No children ☺

★★★ GUEST HOUSE
Willow Tree Cottages

Long Ln, Barnby-in-the-Willows NG24 2SG

☎ 01636 626613 🖷 01636 626060

e–mail: howard@willowinn.f9.co.uk

web: www.willowtreecottages.co.uk

dir: *Off A1/A17 3.5m to Newark Golf Course, 300yds to Barnby sign, turn right & 1m to guest house*

The Willow Tree offers purpose-built modern accommodation in a rustic style that fits in well with the surrounding area. Bedrooms are of varying styles and each room is well equipped. There is secure off-street parking and a separate breakfast room which can also be used for meetings.

Rooms 8 annexe en suite (2 fmly) (8 GF) S fr £45; D fr £55 **Facilities** TVB tea/coffee Direct dial from bedrooms Cen ht **Parking** 8 **Notes** No children 5yrs No coaches RS 25–26 Dec

ENGLAND

NOTTINGHAM
MAP 11 SK53

See also Cotgrave

Premier Collection

★★★★★ GUEST HOUSE
Greenwood Lodge City Guest House
5 Third Av, Sherwood Rise NG7 6JH
☎ 0115 962 1206 📠 0115 962 1206
e–mail: pdouglas71@aol.com
web: www.greenwoodlodgecityguesthouse.co.uk

dir: *A60 Mansfield Rd from city, 1st rdbt onto 1st exit to small rdbt, 2nd exit onto A692 Sherwood Rise, 3rd left*

A warm welcome is assured at this fine house, built in 1834, located in a quiet residential area one mile from the city centre. Day rooms include an elegant drawing room and a conservatory-dining room overlooking the secluded garden. Individually furnished bedrooms, equipped with many thoughtful extras, are decorated in a traditional style, complementing the antique furniture. Off-road parking is a bonus.

Rooms 6 en suite S £47.50; D £95 **Facilities** TVB tea/coffee Licensed Cen ht Wi-fi available **Parking** 6 **Notes** ⊗ No children 10yrs No coaches Closed 24–28 Dec

★★★★ GUEST ACCOMMODATION
Beech Lodge
222 Porchester Rd NG3 6HG
☎ 0115 952 3314
web: www.beechlodgeguesthouse.com

dir: *Off A684 onto Porchester Rd, 8th left, Punchbowl pub on right corner, Beech Lodge on left corner*

A friendly welcome is assured at Beech Lodge and the modern accommodation is well presented and suitably equipped. The ground-floor lounge is particularly comfortable, and there is a small conservatory. Breakfast is a good choice of freshly cooked and carefully presented fare served in the dining area next to the lounge.

Rooms 4 en suite (1 fmly) S fr £35; D fr £60✶ **Facilities** FTV TVB tea/coffee Cen ht TVL Wi-fi available **Parking** 4 **Notes** LB ⊗ No children 8yrs

★★★★ GUEST ACCOMMODATION
The Yellow House
7 Littlegreen Rd, Woodthorpe NG5 4LE
☎ 0115 926 2280
e–mail: suzanne.prewsmith1@btinternet.com
web: www.theyellowhousenottingham.co.uk

dir: *Off A60 Mansfield Rd N from city centre onto A6211, over rdbt, 1st right to x-rds, left, house on left*

A semi-detached private house in a quiet residential suburb to the north-east of the city, with easy access. A warm welcome is assured; the one purpose-built bedroom contains many thoughtful extras, and the family pet dog is also very friendly.

Rooms 1 en suite **Facilities** TVB tea/coffee Cen ht TVL **Parking** 1 **Notes** ⊗ No children ⊛

★★★ GUEST HOUSE
The Acorn
4 Radcliffe Rd, West Bridgford NG2 5FW
☎ 0115 981 1297 📠 0115 981 7654
e–mail: reservations@acorn-hotel.co.uk

dir: *A6011 onto A6520, next to Trent Bridge Cricket Ground*

Located a short walking distance from county cricket ground and football stadia, this property provides a range of bedrooms with en suite facilities. Breakfast is taken in a pine-furnished dining room. Car parking and a guest lounge are additional benefits.

Rooms 12 en suite (2 fmly) (1 GF) **Facilities** TVB tea/coffee Cen ht TVL Wi-fi available **Parking** 12 **Notes** ⊗ No coaches

★★★ GUEST ACCOMMODATION
Andrews
310 Queens Rd, Beeston NG9 1AJ
☎ 0115 925 4902
e–mail: andrews.hotel@ntlworld.com

dir: *A52 onto B6006 to Beeston, right at 4th lights onto Queens Rd, 200yds on right*

This pleasant establishment is close to the shops and park in Beeston, and is popular with business people and tourists alike. Guests have the use of a comfortable lounge and a separate dining room. Bedrooms, which vary in size, are well presented and suitably equipped.

Rooms 10 rms (3 en suite) (1 fmly) (1 GF) S £25–£35; D £50–£55✶ **Facilities** TVB tea/coffee Cen ht TVL **Parking** 6 **Notes** ⊛

★★★ GUEST ACCOMMODATION
Hall Farm House
Gonalston NG14 7JA
☎ 0115 966 3112
web: www.hallfarmhousebandb.com

dir: *NE of Nottingham. Off A612 x-rds into Gonalston, 1st right after post box*

The charming 17th-century former farmhouse is tucked away behind trees in the pretty village of Gonalston. Bedrooms are comfortable, and the beamed living rooms are full of character. The extensive grounds include a heated outdoor swimming pool and a tennis court, and there is a good choice of pubs for evening meals nearby.

Rooms 4 rms (2 en suite) (1 fmly) S £40; D £60✶ **Facilities** TV3B tea/coffee Cen ht TVL ⚐ ⚒ **Parking** 5 **Notes** LB ⊗ Closed 20 Dec–2 Jan ⊛

★★★ 🍴 BED & BREAKFAST
Old Rectory Farm B&B
Main St, Strelley Village NG8 6PE
☎ 0115 929 8838
e–mail: enq@oldrectoryfarm.com
web: www.oldrectoryfarm.com

dir: *M1 junct 26 onto A6002, after 1m turn right to Strelley village, 0.5m opp church*

Located within the pretty hamlet of Strelley opposite the notable All Saints parish church, this period property has been sympathetically

CONTINUED

restored to provide modern comfort in a home from home atmosphere. Bedrooms are equipped with lots of thoughtful extras and memorable breakfasts feature eggs from the farm's own chickens and home made preserves.

Rooms 4 rms (2 en suite) (1 fmly) (1 GF) S £35–£44; D £50–£60✳
Facilities TVB tea/coffee Cen ht TVL Wi-fi available **Parking** 6
Notes LB ⊛

★★ GUEST ACCOMMODATION
Fairhaven
19 Meadow Rd, Beeston NG9 1JP
☎ 0115 922 7509 📄 0870 130 4866
e–mail: info@fairhaven-hotel.com

dir: *A52 onto B6005 for Beeston station, 200yds after bridge*
This well-established guest house is in the quiet residential suburb of Beeston on the outskirts of Nottingham. The public rooms offer a stylish reception lounge, and breakfast is served in the cosy dining room. The bedrooms vary in style and size.

Rooms 14 rms (10 en suite) (1 fmly) (1 GF) S £29–£40; D £49✳
Facilities TVB tea/coffee Cen ht Wi-fi available **Parking** 13

SOUTHWELL   MAP 17 SK65

★★★ GUEST HOUSE
The Old Forge
Burgage Ln NG25 0ER
☎ 01636 812809 📄 01636 816302
e–mail: theoldforgesouthwell@yahoo.co.uk

dir: *Off A612 past Minster, Church St, left onto Newark Rd, 2nd left onto Burgage Ln*
An interesting house packed with pictures and antique furniture, the Old Forge is central and handy for the Minster, while its own parking also makes this a good touring base. Bedrooms are comfortable and a secluded conservatory-lounge and spacious breakfast room are available.

Rooms 3 en suite 1 annexe en suite (1 GF) S £48–£60; D £78✳
Facilities TVB tea/coffee Direct dial from bedrooms Cen ht **Parking** 4
Notes No coaches

WELLOW   MAP 17 SK66

★★★ BED & BREAKFAST
Scotts Farm B & B
Wellow Park Stables, Rufford Ln NG22 0EQ
☎ 01623 861040 & 07860 869378 📄 01623 835292
e–mail: judithcadman1973@aol.com
web: www.wellowpark.co.uk

dir: *A616 SE from New Ollerton, 1m right onto Rufford Ln*
Scotts Farm is a part of Wellow Park Stables, a family equestrian centre located on the quiet outskirts of Wellow in Sherwood Forest. The resident proprietors provide helpful service, and well-proportioned bedrooms that share a bathroom. Breakfast is served in the kitchen. Stabling, dressage instruction, show jumping and cross-country rides are available by arrangement.

Rooms 3 rms (1 en suite) (3 fmly) **Facilities** TVB tea/coffee Cen ht
Riding **Parking** 6 **Notes** ⊗

WORKSOP   MAP 16 SK57

★★★★ GUEST ACCOMMODATION
Acorn Lodge
85 Potter St S80 2HL
☎ 01909 478383 📄 01909 478383
e–mail: les.wheatcroft@btinternet.com

dir: *A1 onto A57. Take B6040 (town centre) through Manton, Lodge on right, 100mtrs past Priory*

Originally part of the community house of the Priory Church, this property has been modernised to offer comfortable, well-appointed accommodation. Good breakfasts are served in the pleasant breakfast room and ample private parking is available at the rear.

Rooms 7 en suite (2 fmly) S £35–£40; D £45–£55✳ **Facilities** FTV TVB tea/coffee Cen ht Wi-fi available **Parking** 15 **Notes** ⊗

OXFORDSHIRE

ABINGDON   MAP 05 SU49

Premier Collection

★★★★★ 🏠 BED & BREAKFAST
B&B Rafters
Abingdon Rd OX13 6NU
☎ 01865 391298 📄 01865 391173
e–mail: enquiries@bnb-rafters.co.uk
web: www.bnb-rafters.co.uk

dir: *A34 onto A415 towards Witney, Rafters on A415 in Marcham by 1st street light on right*
Set amid immaculate gardens, this modern house is built in a half-timbered style and offers spacious accommodation together with a warm welcome. Bedrooms are stylishly furnished and equipped with a range of homely extras. Comprehensive breakfasts feature local and organic produce when possible.

Rooms 4 rms (2 en suite) (2 pri facs) S £45–£75; D £60–£110
Facilities TVB tea/coffee Cen ht Wi-fi available **Parking** 9 **Notes** ⊗
Closed Xmas & New Year

ENGLAND

ABINGDON CONTINUED

★★★★ 🅰 BED & BREAKFAST
Kingfisher Barn

Rye Farm OX14 3NN

☎ 01235 537538 & 527590 📄 01235 537538

e–mail: info@kingfisherbarn.com

web: www.kingfisherbarn.com

dir: *0.5m SE of town centre. A415 S from town centre over River Thames, left into pay & display car park & onto single-track road*

Rooms 10 en suite (4 fmly) (10 GF) S £64; D £81✱ **Facilities** FTV TVB tea/coffee Cen ht Wi-fi available ⏱ **Parking** 20 **Notes** LB

ARDINGTON
MAP 05 SU48

★★★★ ◉◉ INN
The Boar's Head

Church St OX12 8QA

☎ 01235 833254 📄 01235 833254

e–mail: info@boarsheadardington.co.uk

dir: *In village next to church*

This characterful inn has been serving the local community for over 150 years and is set in a beautiful and seemingly timeless village. Great care has gone into creating a stylish and welcoming ambience in the comfortable bedrooms and the welcoming bar and restaurant where Bruce Buchan's accomplished cuisine can be enjoyed.

Rooms 3 en suite (1 fmly) S £75–£85; D £85–£130✱ **Facilities** TVB tea/coffee Direct dial from bedrooms Cen ht Dinner Last d 9.30pm Wi-fi available **Parking** 20 **Notes** No coaches

---

BAMPTON
MAP 05 SP30

★★★★ BED & BREAKFAST
Upham House Bed & Breakfast

The Lanes OX18 2JG

☎ 01993 852703 & 07946 625563 📄 01993 852703

e–mail: encompass5@aol.com

dir: *A4095 between Faringdon and Brize Norton*

Set in the Cotswold village of Bampton, a few minutes drive from Witney, a warm welcome awaits you from the owner and resident cats when you arrive at this family home. All stylishly furnished, this is very much a home from home. Breakfast is served farmhouse style in the dining room and choices differ from day to day.

Rooms 2 rms (1 en suite) (1 pri facs) D £55–£70 **Facilities** TVB tea/coffee Cen ht TVL Wi-fi available **Parking** 2 **Notes** ⊗ No children 6yrs Closed 23 Dec–2 Jan ◉

BANBURY
MAP 11 SP44

★★★★ GUEST ACCOMMODATION
The Mill House Country Guest House

North Newington Rd OX15 6AA

☎ 01295 730212 📄 01295 730363

e–mail: lamadonett@aol.com

web: www.themillhousebanbury.com

dir: *M40 junct 11, signs to Banbury Cross, onto B4035 (Shipston-on-Stour), 2m right for Newington*

This 17th-century miller's house belongs to the paper mill first mentioned in Shakespeare's Henry VI. It stands in peaceful gardens not far from the Banbury Cross. There are individually styled bedrooms in the main house or refurbished cottages across the courtyard with

CONTINUED

lounge-kitchens and en suite bedrooms. There is also a pleasant lounge-bar and meeting facilities within the main house.

Rooms 3 en suite 4 annexe en suite (2 fmly) S £69–£85; D £85–£125 **Facilities** TVB tea/coffee Direct dial from bedrooms Cen ht TVL **Conf** Max 12 Board 12 **Parking** 20 **Notes** LB ⊗ Closed 2wks Xmas

★★★ INN
The Blinking Owl

Main St, North Newington OX15 6AE

☎ 01295 730650

dir: *B4035 from Banbury, 2m sharp bend, right to North Newington, inn opp the green*

An important part of the community in the pretty village of North Newington, this former 17th-century inn retains many original features including impressive open fires. Straight forward food and a range of real ales are served in the beamed bar-lounges. The converted barn houses the three bedrooms and the restaurant, which is open at weekends.

Rooms 3 en suite S £50–£60; D £65–£75 **Facilities** TVB tea/coffee Cen ht Dinner Last d 9pm **Parking** 14 **Notes** ⊗ ⊜

★★★ GUEST ACCOMMODATION
Fairlawns

60 Oxford Rd OX16 9AN

☎ 01295 262461 & 07831 330220 📠 01295 261296

e-mail: fairlawnsgh@aol.com

dir: *0.5m S of town centre on A4260 near hospital*

This extended Edwardian house retains many original features and has a convenient location. Bedrooms are mixed in size, and all are neatly furnished, some with direct access to the car park. A comprehensive breakfast is served in the traditional dining room and a selection of soft drinks and snacks is also available.

Rooms 12 rms (11 en suite) 6 annexe en suite (5 fmly) (9 GF) S £48; D £58✳ **Facilities** TVB tea/coffee Direct dial from bedrooms Cen ht Wi-fi available **Parking** 18

★★★ GUEST ACCOMMODATION
Lampet Arms

Main St, Tadmarton OX15 5TB

☎ 01295 780070 📠 01295 788066

dir: *4m W of Banbury on B4035 in Tadmarton, opp church*

Located between Banbury and Shipston on Stour, this well-proportioned Victorian property provides warm and inviting open-plan public areas, the setting for home-cooked food and fine wines. The spacious, thoughtfully equipped bedrooms are in a converted coach house.

Rooms 4 annexe en suite (3 fmly) (2 GF) S fr £45; D £65–£68✳ **Facilities** TVB tea/coffee Direct dial from bedrooms Cen ht Dinner Last d 8.45pm Pool Table **Conf** Board 20 **Parking** 15

BICESTER
MAP 11 SP52

★★★★ BED & BREAKFAST
Manor Farm B&B

Hethe OX27 8ES

☎ 01869 277602

e-mail: chrmanor@aol.com

web: www.freewebs.com/manorfarm

dir: *Off B4100 signed Hardwick, after 2m village of Hethe, 1st house after church*

Guests are warmly welcomed at this delightful stone farmhouse in the peaceful village of Hethe, a short drive from the M40, Bicester Village and within easy access of Oxford. The property retains many original features such as Georgian beams and open fireplaces, and offers comfortable spacious accommodation with beautiful stylish bathrooms. A hearty breakfast with home made preserves is included.

Rooms 2 rms (1 en suite) (1 pri facs) **Facilities** TVB tea/coffee Cen ht **Parking** 2 **Notes** ⊜

BURFORD
MAP 05 SP21

Premier Collection

★★★★★ ⌂ GUEST ACCOMMODATION
Burford House

99 High St OX18 4QA

☎ 01993 823151 📠 01993 823240

e-mail: stay@burfordhouse.co.uk

web: www.burfordhouse.co.uk

dir: *Off A40 into town centre*

Set in the heart of this famous Cotswold market town, Burford House, marked by a half-timbered and stone exterior, is a haven for travellers. The charming bedrooms come with thoughtful homely extras, and there are two comfortable lounges with roaring log fires. Superb breakfasts and light meals are served in the dining room. The caring hosts ensure that a visit to their home is a memorable one.

Rooms 8 en suite (1 fmly) (1 GF) **Facilities** STV TVB Direct dial from bedrooms Cen ht Wi-fi available **Notes** ⊗

The **Highway Inn** dating 1480 is set in the middle of the bustling village of Burford, where the beautiful River Windrush passes through. We are 30 minutes from the Historic cities of Oxford and Cheltenham, as well as being centrally located to visits all of the Cotswold's.

A true Cotswold Inn, where locals and visitors come to mix. Plenty of character, creaky floorboards and beams throughout, however modern touches subtly fit in. Beautiful antiques and clutter from the past adorn all rooms. Bedrooms are individual in style but all are very cosy.

Come to escape, do business, relax with friends or unwind. Feet up or eyes down, you set the pace.

So, enjoy a glass of vino, Local ale, or simply chill with a cappuccino and your favourite newspaper. This is your home from home, do what you want!

We have a number of dining areas, the main bar and snug or outside seating, where you can watch the world go by or sit and listen to birds song in our sunny, restored medieval courtyard. We also have a cellar dining room for private dining that seats 20 banquet style, comfortably, very atmospheric.

The Highway offers guests a choice of 9 bedrooms.

The design, look and furnishings in each bedroom is unique, designed to make the whole experience more like staying in a friends country house, than in a hotel or pub.

All the rooms have spotless bathrooms, ensuite or Private, with efficient plumbing and LCD TV's with Freeview for a range of television channels. Several of the larger rooms specifically accommodate cots provided. And as we are in the country, certain rooms can accommodate dogs. (Please see dog policy)

Overall, the emphasis is on comfort, cleanliness, functionality and a healthy pinch of individuality or maybe eccentricity? We'll let you make your own minds up on that one!

The Highway Inn, 117 High St, Burford, Oxfordshire, OX18 4RGT
Tel: 01993 823661   **Fax:** 01993 824740
Website: www.thehighwayinn.co.uk
Email: info@thehighwayhotel.co.uk

ENGLAND

BURFORD CONTINUED

★ ★ ★ ★ ◉◉ RESTAURANT WITH ROOMS
The Angel at Burford
14 Witney St OX18 4SN
☎ 01993 822714 📄 01993 822069
e–mail: paul@theangelatburford.co.uk
web: www.theangelatburford.co.uk

dir: *Off A40 at Burford rdbt, down hill, 1st right onto Swan Ln, 1st left to Pytts Ln, left at end onto Witney St*

Once a coaching inn in the 16th century, this establishment is situated in the centre of Burford, the Gateway to The Cotswolds. Three attractively decorated en suite bedrooms offer plentiful accessories and share a cosy resident's lounge. The award-winning restaurant is open for lunch and dinner. The peaceful courtyard and walled garden are perfect for relaxing in the summer.

Rooms 3 en suite S £70–£85; D £93–£110✶ **Facilities** TVB tea/coffee Direct dial from bedrooms Cen ht Dinner Last d 9pm Wi-fi available **Notes** No children 9yrs RS Mon & Sun eve

★ ★ ★ ★ ◉ INN
The Highway Inn
117 High St OX18 4RG
☎ 01993 823661
e–mail: enquiries@thehighwayhotel.co.uk
This traditional inn is located at the top of this popular Costwold high street. Bedrooms are individual in size and style and incorporate many unique features. The traditional courtyard is the place to enjoy a long cool drink during the summer months. The restaurant serves interesting dishes using local produce, along with attentive friendly service.

Rooms 9 rms (8 en suite) (1 pri facs) (1 fmly) S £65–£95; D £75–£130✶ **Facilities** STV FTV TVB tea/coffee Direct dial from bedrooms Cen ht Dinner Last d 9pm Wi-fi available **Conf** Max 20 Thtr 20 Class 20 Board 20 Del from £150 ✶ **Notes** LB No coaches Closed 25–26 Dec & 1st wks Jan RS Sun eve & Tue (winter)

See advert on opposite page

★ ★ ★ ★ FARM HOUSE
Potters Hill Farm *(SP300148)*
Leafield OX29 9QB
☎ 01993 878018 📄 01993 878018 Mrs K Stanley
e–mail: potterabout@freenet.co.uk

dir: *4.5m NE of Burford. A361 onto B4437, 1st right, 1st left, 1.5m on left*

Located on a working farm in peaceful parkland with diverse wildlife, this converted coach house stands next to the farmhouse. It has been refurbished to offer comfortable bedrooms with many original features. Breakfast served in the main farmhouse features local produce.

Rooms 3 annexe en suite (1 fmly) (2 GF) S £40–£50; D £60–£65✶ **Facilities** TVB tea/coffee Cen ht **Parking** 5 **Notes** ⊗ 770 acres mixed/sheep ◉

CHARLBURY   MAP 11 SP31

★ ★ ★ BED & BREAKFAST
Tulip Tree House
Chruch St OX7 3PP
☎ 01608 810609 📄 01608 810609

dir: *A44 onto B4437 into Charlbury, turn onto Church St, behind Bell Hotel*

Tucked away in the market town of Charlbury, this charming property offers nicely appointed rooms, with good standards of comfort. Breakfast is served in the bright conservatory overlooking the well-tended gardens, which help to create a peaceful and charming atmosphere.

Rooms 3 rms (2 en suite) (1 pri facs) (1 fmly) **Facilities** TVB tea/coffee Cen ht TVL **Parking** 4 **Notes** ◉

CHIPPING NORTON   MAP 10 SP32

See also Long Compton (Warwickshire)

★ ★ ★ GUEST HOUSE
Nortens
10 New St OX7 5LJ
☎ 01608 645060 📄 01608 645060
e–mail: enquiries@nortens.co.uk

dir: *On A44 in town centre*

A warm welcome is assured at this sympathetically renovated period house, at the heart of the village. Bedrooms are thoughtfully furnished and some feature original features such as oak beams that blend seamlessly with contemporary décor. Comprehensive breakfasts are served in a cosy ground floor café, which leads to a craft shop. Free parking is available within easy walking distance.

Rooms 5 en suite S £40–£50; D £60–£70✶ **Facilities** TVB tea/coffee Licensed Cen ht Dinner Last d 9pm Wi-fi available **Notes** ⊗ No coaches

CHISLEHAMPTON   MAP 05 SU59

★★★ ⇔ INN

Coach & Horses

Watlington Rd OX44 7UX

☎ 01865 890255 📄 01865 891995

e–mail: enquiries@coachhorsesinn.co.uk

dir: *On B480*

Located six miles south-east of Oxford, this 16th-century inn retains original exposed beams and open fires, while furniture styles enhance the character of the building. A wide range of imaginative food is served, and the practically equipped chalet-style bedrooms have lovely rural views.

Rooms 9 annexe en suite **Facilities** TVB tea/coffee Direct dial from bedrooms Cen ht Dinner Last d 9.45pm **Conf** Max 12 **Parking** 30

FARINGDON   MAP 05 SU29

★★★★ FARM HOUSE

Chowle Farmhouse Bed & Breakfast

(SU272925)

Great Coxwell SN7 7SR

☎ 01367 241688 📄 07775 669102 Mr & Mrs Muir

e–mail: info@chowlefarmhouse.co.uk

web: www.chowlefarmhouse.co.uk

dir: *From Faringdon rdbt on A420, 2m W on right. From Watchfield rdbt 1.5m E on left*

Chowle is a delightful, friendly and quiet modern farmhouse just off the A420. Bedrooms are very well equipped with a charming and airy downstairs breakfast room. There is ample parking, and the location is ideal for visiting Oxford and Swindon. Great breakfasts, and dinner is available; pre-booking preferred.

Rooms 4 en suite (1 GF) S fr £55; D fr £75✱ **Facilities** FTV TVB tea/coffee Cen ht Dinner Last d 4pm Wi-fi available Fishing ⌇ Clay pigeon shooting **Parking** 10 **Notes LB** 10 acres Pedigree Beef Cattle ⊜

HENLEY-ON-THAMES   MAP 05 SU78

Premier Collection

★★★★★ BED & BREAKFAST

Crowsley House

Crowsley Rd, Lower Shiplake RG9 3JT

☎ 0118 940 6708

e–mail: info@crowsleyhouse.co.uk

dir: *A4155 onto Station Rd in Shiplake. Right onto Crowsley Rd, 2nd house on right*

Situated close to the popular village of Henley-on-Thames and a moments walk from Shiplake railway station. Bedrooms are smartly appointed and very well equipped with many thoughtful extras. A comfortable lounge area and beautifully landscaped gardens provide areas in which to relax. Breakfast is served around the dining table in the well styled dual aspect dining room. A two or three course dinner option is available on request.

CONTINUED

Rooms 3 rms (2 en suite) (1 pri facs) S £75–£95; D £95–£125✱ **Facilities** FTV TVB Cen ht Dinner Wi-fi available **Parking** 6 **Notes** ⊗ No children 14yrs

Premier Collection

★★★★★ BED & BREAKFAST

Lenwade

3 Western Rd RG9 1JL

☎ 01491 573468 & 0777 4941629 📄 01491 411664

e–mail: jacquie@lenwade.com

web: www.lenwade.com

dir: *From Henley town centre take Reading Rd (A4155), right onto St Andrew's Rd, 2nd left onto Western Rd*

The friendly and relaxed Victorian home is within easy walking distance of the town centre and the Thames Path. The hallway has a feature stained-glass window, while the attractive, well-equipped bedrooms come with free Wi-fi. Breakfast is a treat of fresh juices and fruit, yogurts, home-made bread and the best of local produce. There is a lounge with satellite television and parking is also available.

Rooms 3 rms (2 en suite) (1 pri facs) S £50–£55; D £70–£75✱ **Facilities** FTV TVB tea/coffee Cen ht TVL Wi-fi available **Parking** 2 **Notes** ⊗ Closed 24–26 Dec ⊜

★★★★★ ⊛ INN

The Cherry Tree Inn

Stoke Row RG9 5QA

☎ 01491 680430

e–mail: info@thecherrytreeinn.com

web: www.thecherrytreeinn.com

dir: *W of Henley. Off B841 into Stoke Row*

This stylish inn is situated in a peaceful rural setting, just 20 minutes away from Reading and motorway connections. Bedrooms are of a modern design, and have spacious bathrooms with luxurious toiletries. The cosy, contemporary dining room is the setting for imaginative and hearty food.

Rooms 4 annexe en suite (4 GF) D £95 **Facilities** TVB tea/coffee Cen ht Dinner Last d 10pm Wi-fi available **Parking** 30 **Notes** No coaches Closed 25–26 Dec

ENGLAND

★★★★ 🍽 INN
The Baskerville

Station Rd, Lower Shiplake RG9 3NY
☎ 0118 940 3332 📠 0118 940 4735
e–mail: enquiries@thebaskerville.com

dir: *2m S of Henley in Lower Shiplake. Off A4155 onto Station Rd, signed*

Located close to Shiplake station and just a short drive from Henley, this smart accommodation is perfect for a business or leisure break. It is a good base for exploring the Oxfordshire countryside, and the enjoyable hearty meals served in the cosy restaurant use good local produce.

Rooms 5 rms (4 en suite) (1 fmly) S £75; D £85✱ **Facilities** TVB tea/coffee Cen ht Dinner Last d 9.30pm Wi-fi available **Conf** Max 15 Thtr 15 Class 15 Board 15 **Parking** 15 **Notes** No coaches RS 23 Dec–2 Jan

★★★★ 🅰 BED & BREAKFAST
Apple Ash

Woodlands Rd, Harpsden Woods RG9 4AB
☎ 01491 574198 📠 01491 578183
e–mail: appleash@fsmail.net

dir: *From Henley exit A4155 towards Caversham, turn right onto Woodlands Rd, house is 0.5m on right*

Rooms 4 rms (3 en suite) (1 pri facs) **Facilities** TVB tea/coffee Cen ht **Parking** 6 **Notes** ⊗ No children 10yrs ⊜

★★★ 🅰 BED & BREAKFAST
Slater's Farm

Peppard Common RG9 5JL
☎ 01491 628675 📠 01491 628675
e–mail: stay@slatersfarm.co.uk

dir: *3m W of Henley. A4130 onto B481 to Rotherfield Peppard, pass The Dog pub & fork left to primary school, farm 200yds on right*

Rooms 3 rms (1 pri facs) S £38–£40; D £58–£60 **Facilities** TVB tea/coffee Cen ht Dinner Last d at breakfast ⟶ **Parking** 5 **Notes** ⊗ Closed Xmas ⊜

★★★★ 🍽 INN
The Gate Hangs High

OX15 5DF
☎ 01608 737387 📠 01608 737870
e–mail: gatehangshigh@aol.com

dir: *0.6m N of village on x-rds*

This delightful inn located between Banbury and Chipping Norton is convenient for Oxford and the Cotswolds. Stylish spacious bedrooms are situated around a courtyard in a carefully converted barn. They are comfortably furnished and extremely well-equipped. Carefully prepared food is served in the bar or the attractive restaurant.

Rooms 4 en suite (1 fmly) (4 GF) **Facilities** FTV TVB tea/coffee Direct dial from bedrooms Cen ht Dinner Last d 10pm Golf Riding **Parking** 40

★★★★ FARM HOUSE
Bould Farm *(SP244209)*

OX7 6RT
☎ 01608 658850 📠 01608 658850 Mrs L Meyrick
e–mail: meyrick@bouldfarm.co.uk
web: www.bouldfarm.co.uk

dir: *Off A424 signed Idbury, through village, down hill, round two bends, on right*

This delightful 17th-century farmhouse stands amid pretty gardens between Stow-on-the-Wold and Burford. The spacious bedrooms are carefully furnished and thoughtfully equipped, and some have stunning views of the surrounding countryside. Breakfast is served in the cosy dining room which features a cast-iron stove and stone-flagged floors.

Rooms 3 rms (2 en suite) (1 pri facs) (1 fmly) S £45–£65; D £65–£70✱ **Facilities** TVB tea/coffee Cen ht TVL **Parking** 6 **Notes** ⊗ 400 acres arable/sheep ⊜

★★★★ ◉ INN
The Kingham Plough

The Green OX7 6YD
☎ 01608 658327 📠 01608 658327
e–mail: book@thekinghamplough.co.uk

dir: *On village green*

Situated on the village green, in 'Englands favourite village', Kingham, this quintessential Cotswold inn has seven boutique en suite bedrooms that have been beautifully created for maximum comfort. The restaurant is housed in the historic tithe barn leading on from the bar area. A great countryside retreat for good food in a welcoming, relaxed environment

Rooms 4 en suite 3 annexe en suite S £70–£80; D £85–£110 **Facilities** TVB tea/coffee Cen ht Dinner Last d 8.45pm **Parking** 25 **Notes** No coaches Closed 25 Dec RS Mon & Sun eve

387

KINGHAM *CONTINUED*

★★★★ 🏠 GUEST ACCOMMODATION

Moat End

The Moat OX7 6XZ

☎ 01608 658090 & 07765 278399

e–mail: info@moatend.com

web: www.moatend.co.uk

dir: *Off B4450/A436 into village centre*

The converted barn lies in a peaceful Cotswold village and has splendid country views. Its well-appointed bedrooms either have a Jacuzzi or large shower cubicles, one with hydro-massage jets. The attractive dining room leads to a comfortable beamed sitting room with a stone fireplace. Quality local ingredients are used in the wholesome breakfasts. The owner has won an award for green tourism by reducing the impact of the business on the environment.

Rooms 3 en suite (1 fmly) S £40–£50; D £60–£70✻ **Facilities** TVB tea/coffee Cen ht TVL **Parking** 4 **Notes LB** Closed Xmas & New Year

★★★★ 🍽 INN

The Tollgate Inn & Restaurant

Church St OX7 6YA

☎ 01608 658389

e–mail: info@thetollgate.com

Situated in the idyllic Cotswold village of Kingham, this Grade II-listed Georgian building has been lovingly restored to provide a complete home-from-home among some of the most beautiful and historic countryside in Britain. The Tollgate provides comfortable, well-equipped accommodation in pleasant surroundings. A good choice of menu for lunch and dinner is available with fine use made of fresh and local produce. You can also be sure of a hearty breakfast provided in the modern, well-equipped dining room.

Rooms 5 en suite 4 annexe en suite (1 fmly) (4 GF) **Facilities** TVB tea/coffee Cen ht Dinner Last d 9/9.30pm Fri/Sat **Conf** Max 15 **Parking** 12

MILTON COMMON MAP 05 SP60

★★★★ 🏠 BED & BREAKFAST

Byways

Old London Rd OX9 2JR

☎ 01844 279386 📄 01844 279386

e–mail: byways.molt@tiscali.co.uk

web: www.bywaysbedandbreakfast.co.uk

dir: *Between M40 junct 7 & 8A*

A friendly welcome awaits you at Byways, situated a few minutes from the M40. Bedrooms are comfortable and tastefully decorated, and the emphasis is on a peaceful and relaxing stay away from it all. Breakfast is home produced, organic and obtained locally where possible. There is a large garden for guests to enjoy. Please note that Byways is a TV-free establishment.

Rooms 3 rms (2 en suite) (1 pri facs) (3 GF) S £35–£40; D £60–£70✻ **Facilities** tea/coffee Cen ht **Parking** 3 **Notes** ⊗ No children 7yrs

---

OXFORD MAP 05 SP50

Premier Collection

★★★★★ 🏠 GUEST ACCOMMODATION

Burlington House

374 Banbury Rd, Summertown OX2 7PP

☎ 01865 513513 📄 01865 311785

e–mail: stay@burlington-house.co.uk

dir: *Opposite Oxford Conference Centre on A4165 on corner of Hernes Rd & Banbury Rd*

Guests are assured of a warm welcome and attentive service at this smart, beautifully maintained Victorian house, within walking distance of Summertown's fashionable restaurants. Elegant, contemporary bedrooms are filled with a wealth of thoughtful extras, and some open onto a pretty patio garden. Memorable breakfasts, served in the delightful dining room, include home-made preserves, fruit breads, granola and excellent coffee.

Rooms 10 en suite 2 annexe en suite S £65–£75; D £85–£95✻ **Facilities** FTV TVB tea/coffee Direct dial from bedrooms Cen ht **Parking** 5 **Notes** ⊗ No children 12yrs Closed 24 Dec–2 Jan

★★★★★ 🅰 GUEST ACCOMMODATION

Gables Guest House

6 Cumnor Hill OX2 9HA

☎ 01865 862153 📄 01865 864054

e–mail: stay@gables-oxford.co.uk

web: www.gables-guesthouse.co.uk

dir: *A34 onto A420. At rdbt take Oxford/Botley exit, right at lights, 500yds on right*

Rooms 5 en suite (1 GF) S £48–£55; D £68–£80✻ **Facilities** STV TVB tea/coffee Direct dial from bedrooms Cen ht TVL Wi-fi available Pool Table **Parking** 6 **Notes LB** ⊗ No children 10yrs Closed 24 Dec–2 Jan

★★★★ GUEST ACCOMMODATION
Cotswold House
363 Banbury Rd OX2 7PL
☎ 01865 310558 📄 01865 310558
e–mail: d.r.walker@talk21.com
web: www.cotswoldhouse.co.uk

dir: *A40 onto A423 into Oxford city centre, following signs to Summertown, 0.5m on right*

Situated in a leafy avenue close to the northern ring road and Summertown, this well-maintained house offers comfortable, well-equipped bedrooms and a relaxed atmosphere. Enjoy a traditional, hearty breakfast with vegetarian choice, including home-made muesli and fresh fruit, served in the bright attractive dining room.

Rooms 8 en suite (2 fmly) (2 GF) S £55–£65; D £80–£100 **Facilities** FTV TVB tea/coffee Cen ht Wi-fi available **Parking** 6 **Notes** ⊗ No children 5yrs

★★★★ GUEST ACCOMMODATION
Conifers Guest House
116 The Slade, Headington OX3 7DX
☎ 01865 763055 📄 01865 742232
e–mail: stay@conifersguesthouse.co.uk
web: www.conifersguesthouse.co.uk

dir: *Off ring road onto A420 towards city centre. Left onto B4495, house on left past hospital*

Located in a residential area close to the hospitals, this impressive Edwardian house has been renovated to provide attractive, pine-furnished bedrooms. Breakfast is served in a smart, front-facing dining room. Private car park.

Rooms 8 en suite (1 fmly) S £45–£65; D £65–£75✱ **Facilities** TVB tea/coffee Cen ht **Parking** 8 **Notes** ⊗

★★★★ GUEST ACCOMMODATION
Galaxie
180 Banbury Rd OX2 7BT
☎ 01865 515688 📄 01865 556824
e–mail: info@galaxie.co.uk
web: www.galaxie.co.uk

dir: *1m N of Oxford centre, on right before shops in Summertown*

Situated in the popular Summertown area of the city, the Galaxie has a welcoming atmosphere and very good quality accommodation. The well-equipped bedrooms are all very comfortable and have a good range of extra facilities. The attractive conservatory-dining room looks over the Oriental garden.

Rooms 32 rms (28 en suite) (3 fmly) **Facilities** TV31B tea/coffee Direct dial from bedrooms Lift Cen ht TVL **Parking** 30 **Notes** ⊗

★★★★ GUEST ACCOMMODATION
Highfield
91 Rose Hill OX4 4HT
☎ 01865 774083
e–mail: highfield.house@tesco.net

dir: *Off A4142 Eastern Bypass Rd onto A4158, continue 250yds*

This attractive detached house stands in immaculate gardens close to Cowley and provides homely bedrooms equipped with quality pine furniture. The attractive front dining room is the setting for comprehensive breakfasts and there is also a spacious lounge.

Rooms 7 rms (5 en suite) **Facilities** FTV TVB tea/coffee Cen ht TVL **Parking** 6 **Notes** ⊗ Closed Xmas

ENGLAND

OXFORD *CONTINUED*

★★★★ GUEST ACCOMMODATION
Marlborough House

321 Woodstock Rd OX2 7NY
☎ 01865 311321 📠 01865 515329
e-mail: enquiries@marlbhouse.co.uk
web: www.marlbhouse.co.uk

dir: *1.5m N of city. Centre. Off junct A34 & A44 for city centre, onto A4144 Woodstock Rd, premises on right by lights*

Marlborough House is just 1.5 miles north of Oxford's historic City Centre, and is within easy reach of the M40 and the A34 ring road. Custom built in 1990 to a traditional design, the house sits comfortably alongside its Victorian neighbours in a predominantly residential area. All 17 bedrooms have en suite facilities, kitchenettes and mini-bars so guests aren't tied to any routine. Wi-fi covers the lounge and many of the rooms.

Rooms 13 en suite 4 annexe en suite (2 fmly) (4 GF) S £73–£82; D £85–£95 **Facilities** STV TVB tea/coffee Direct dial from bedrooms Cen ht Wi-fi available **Parking** 6 **Notes** ⊗

★★★★ GUEST HOUSE
Pickwicks

15–17 London Rd, Headington OX3 7SP
☎ 01865 750487 📠 01865 742208
e-mail: pickwicks@tiscali.co.uk
web: www.pickwicksguesthouse.co.uk

dir: *Off ring road onto A420 towards city centre, Pickwicks 0.9m on right at junct with Sandfield Rd*

Just a short walk from the bustling community of Headington, this double-fronted Edwardian house has been renovated to provide good standards of overall comfort. Bedrooms offer a useful range of facilities, and an attractive breakfast room overlooks the pretty gardens.

Rooms 15 rms (13 en suite) (2 pri facs) (4 fmly) (4 GF) S £30–£50; D £70–£90✶ **Facilities** FTV TVB tea/coffee Direct dial from bedrooms Licensed Cen ht TVL Wi-fi available **Parking** 12 **Notes** Closed 23 Dec–2 Jan

★★★★ GUEST HOUSE
Red Mullions Guest House

23 London Rd, Headington OX3 7RE
☎ 01865 742741 📠 01865 769944
e-mail: stay@redmullions.co.uk

dir: *M40 junct 8 onto A40. At Headington rdbt, 2nd exit signed Headington onto London Rd*

Red Mullions takes its name from the brick columns between the windows of the building. Modern bedrooms provide comfortable accommodation set within easy reach of motorway networks and Oxford city centre. Hearty breakfasts provide a good start to any day.

Rooms 12 rms (11 en suite) (1 pri facs) (3 fmly) (3 GF) S £50–£75; D £70–£90✶ **Facilities** FTV TVB tea/coffee Cen ht Wi-fi available **Parking** 9 **Notes** ⊗ No coaches

★★★ GUEST ACCOMMODATION
Sports View Guest House

106–110 Abingdon Rd OX1 4PX
☎ 01865 244268 📠 01865 249270
e-mail: stay@sportsviewguesthouse.co.uk
web: www.sportsviewguesthouse.co.uk

dir: *Exit Oxford S at Kennington rdbt towards city centre, 1.25m on left*

This family-run Victorian property, overlooks the Queens College sports ground. Situated south of the city it is within walking distance of the

CONTINUED

centre. Rooms are comfortable, and the property benefits from off-road parking.

Rooms 20 rms (19 en suite) (1 pri facs) (4 fmly) (5 GF) S £38–£52; D £64–£76✱ **Facilities** TVB tea/coffee Direct dial from bedrooms Cen ht Wi-fi available **Parking** 10 **Notes** ⊗ No children 3yrs

★★★ GUEST ACCOMMODATION
Acorn Guest House

260–262 Iffley Rd OX4 1SE

☎ 01865 247998

e–mail: acorn@kpattullo.wanadoo.co.uk

dir: *Off ring road onto A4158 towards city centre, 1m on left after VW garage*

This double-fronted Victorian house is located between the ring road and the city centre, and offers good-value accommodation. The lounge leads out to a quiet enclosed rear garden.

Rooms 15 rms (6 en suite) (1 pri facs) (1 fmly) **Facilities** TVB tea/coffee Lift Cen ht **Parking** 6

★★★ GUEST ACCOMMODATION
All Seasons

63 Windmill Rd, Headington OX3 7BP

☎ 01865 742215 🖨 01865 429667

e–mail: info@allseasonshouse.com

web: www.allseasonshouse.com

dir: *Off ring road onto A420 towards city centre. 1m left at lights onto Windmill Rd, house 300yds on left*

Within easy walking distance of the suburb of Headington, this double-fronted Victorian house provides comfortable homely bedrooms equipped with practical and thoughtful extras. The elegant dining room features an original fireplace, and secure parking is available behind the property.

Rooms 6 rms (4 en suite) S £35–£70✱ **Facilities** TVB tea/coffee Cen ht TVL Wi-fi available **Parking** 6 **Notes** ⊗ No children 4yrs

★★★ GUEST ACCOMMODATION
Athena Guest House

255 Cowley Rd, Cowley OX4 1XQ

☎ 01865 425700 & 07748 837144 🖨 01865 240566

e–mail: info@athenaguesthouse.com

web: www.athenaguesthouse.com

dir: *1.5m SE of city centre on B480*

Located close to the shops and amenities in Cowley, this Victorian brick house offers smart modern bedrooms on three floors with many useful extras. Breakfast is served in the bright and relaxing dining room, and limited parking is available.

Rooms 6 en suite (2 fmly) (2 GF) S £48–£53; D £60–£68 **Facilities** STV TVB tea/coffee Cen ht TVL Wi-fi available **Conf** Max 15 **Parking** 4 **Notes** LB ⊗

★★★ GUEST ACCOMMODATION
Green Gables

326 Abingdon Rd OX1 4TE

☎ 01865 725870 🖨 01865 723115

e–mail: green.gables@virgin.net

web: www.greengables.uk.com

dir: *Off ring road onto B4144 towards city centre, Green Gables 0.5m on left*

A warm welcome is assured at this Edwardian house, located within easy walking distance of the city centre. Bedrooms are equipped with a range of practical and homely extras, and a comprehensive breakfast is served in the cosy dining room. Guests have free access to the internet in the smart conservatory-lounge and private parking is available.

Rooms 11 en suite (2 fmly) (4 GF) S £48–£52; D £68–£75 **Facilities** TVB tea/coffee Direct dial from bedrooms Cen ht TVL Wi-fi available **Parking** 9 **Notes** ⊗ Closed 23–31 Dec

★★★ GUEST ACCOMMODATION
Heather House

192 Iffley Rd OX4 1SD

☎ 01865 249757 🖨 01865 249757

e–mail: stay@heatherhouseoxford.com

web: www.heatherhouseoxford.com

dir: *Off A40 at Headington rdbt S onto A4142 to Littlemore rdbt, onto A4158 Iffley Rd, house 1.25m. On left after pelican crossing, near Chester St*

A short walk from the colleges and city centre, this detached Edwardian house stands in a residential area and has its own parking. The en suite bedrooms, lounge and dining room are bright and comfortable, and one bedroom is on the ground floor. Room facilities include CD and DVD players. There is a choice of breakfasts, Wi-fi, a computer station (with Skype) and lots of tourist information available.

Rooms 6 rms (5 en suite) (1 pri facs) (2 fmly) (1 GF) S £36–£46; D £66–£80✱ **Facilities** FTV TVB tea/coffee Direct dial from bedrooms Cen ht TVL Wi-fi available **Parking** 4 **Notes** ⊗

OXFORD CONTINUED

★★★ GUEST ACCOMMODATION
Kings Guest House
363 Iffley Rd OX4 4DP
☎ 01865 205333 📄 01865 711544
e–mail: KingsGuestHouse@email.com

dir: *M40 junct 9, ring road towards A34 turn right on 2nd rdbt*
Enthusiastically run by friendly owners, this property is situated on a residential avenue leading to the city centre. Bedrooms are practically equipped, some with shower rooms en suite. Guests take breakfast at separate tables in dining room.

Rooms 7 rms (4 en suite) (2 fmly) **Facilities** TVB tea/coffee Cen ht TVL **Parking** 10

★★★ 🅰 BED & BREAKFAST
Beaumont
234 Abingdon Rd OX1 4SP
☎ 01865 241767 📄 01865 241767
e–mail: info@beaumont.sagehost.co.uk

dir: *Off ring road onto A4144 towards city centre, Beaumont 1m on left*

Rooms 4 rms (3 en suite) (1 fmly) (1 GF) **Facilities** TVB tea/coffee Cen ht **Notes** ⊗

★★★ 🅰 BED & BREAKFAST
Newton House
82–84 Abingdon Rd OX1 4PL
☎ 01865 240561 📄 01865 244647
e–mail: newton.house@btinternet.com

dir: *On A4144 Abingdon Rd*

Rooms 13 rms (2 en suite) (11 pri facs) (4 fmly) (4 GF) **Facilities** TVB tea/coffee Direct dial from bedrooms Cen ht Wi-fi available **Parking** 8 **Notes** ⊗

STADHAMPTON   MAP 05 SU69

Premier Collection

★★★★★ ❀❀ GUEST ACCOMMODATION
The Crazy Bear
Bear Ln OX44 7UR
☎ 01865 890714 📄 01865 400481
e–mail: enquiries@crazybear-oxford.co.uk
web: www.crazybearhotel.co.uk

dir: *M40 junct 7, into Stadhampton, over mini-rdbt at fuel station, 2nd left*

This popular and attractive restaurant with rooms successfully combines modern chic with old world character. Cuisine is extensive and varied, with award-winning Thai and English restaurants under the same roof (both with AA rosette status). Those choosing to make a night of it can enjoy the concept bedrooms, all presented to a very high standard and styled in exciting themes; the 'infinity suites' have state-of-the-art facilities.

Rooms 5 en suite 12 annexe en suite (3 fmly) (4 GF) **Facilities** STV TVB Direct dial from bedrooms Cen ht Dinner Last d 10pm Wi-fi available **Conf** Max 40 Thtr 30 Class 30 Board 30 **Parking** 100 **Notes** ⊗ Civ Wed 100

WALLINGFORD   MAP 05 SU68

★★★★ 🅰 BED & BREAKFAST
Bed & Breakfast at Little Gables
166 Crowmarsh Hill OX10 8BG
☎ 01491 837834 & 07860 148882 📄 01491 834426
e–mail: jill@stayingaway.com
web: www.stayingaway.com

dir: *1m E of Wallingford. Off A4130 at Crowmarsh Gifford rdbt onto Crowmarsh Hill & right*

Rooms 3 rms (2 en suite) (1 pri facs) (3 fmly) (1 GF) S £50–£65; D £60–£75 **Facilities** FTV TVB tea/coffee Cen ht Wi-fi available **Parking** 7 **Notes** LB ⊛

WANTAGE   MAP 05 SU38

★★★ BED & BREAKFAST
Bramley House
Mill Orchard, East Hanney OX12 0JH
☎ 01235 868314

dir: *Off A338 East Hanney W towards West Hanney, Bramley House 3rd on right on Mill Orchard*

This friendly guest house has a village location within easy driving distance of Oxford and the historic town of Wantage. The bedrooms are filled with thoughtful extras, while the hearty breakfasts are freshly prepared.

Rooms 2 rms (1 en suite) (1 pri facs) (1 fmly) S £25–£30; D £45–£50✳ **Facilities** TVB tea/coffee Cen ht **Parking** 2 **Notes** ⊗ No children 10yrs ⊛

★★★ GUEST HOUSE
Greensands Guest House
Reading Rd OX12 8JE
☎ 01235 833338 📠 01235 821632
e-mail: janemccourt@aol.com
web: www.greensandsguesthouse.co.uk
dir: *A4185 to Rowstock rdbt, take A417, 1m on right*

This guest house in a peaceful rural setting has good access to local towns, attractions and transport networks. Bedrooms vary in size and are comfortably appointed. Hearty breakfasts are served overlooking the attractive gardens. Ample parking available.

Rooms 7 rms (6 en suite) (1 pri facs) (2 fmly) (3 GF) S £35–£55; D £60–£80✱ **Facilities** TVB tea/coffee Cen ht Wi-fi available **Parking** 9

★★ FARM HOUSE
Down Barn Farm *(SU332852)*
Sparsholt Down OX12 9XD
☎ 01367 820272 Mrs P A Reid
e-mail: pendomeffect@aol.com
dir: *4m SW of Wantage. Off B4507 S onto Kingston Lisle-Seven Barrows road*

Popular with walkers and horse riders (stabling is available), this working farm has glorious views over the Downs and is near to the famous Ridgeway. Bedrooms and public areas have a homely and comfortable aspect while home-produced veal, beef and pork can be anticipated for dinner.

Rooms 3 rms (1 en suite) (3 GF) S £25–£35; D fr £70✱ **Facilities** Cen ht TVL Dinner Last d 1pm Riding **Parking** 4 **Notes LB** 100 acres Organic beef & pig Closed Xmas 🐾

★★★★ GUEST ACCOMMODATION
Corn Croft Guest House
69–71 Corn St OX28 6AS
☎ 01993 773298 📠 01993 773298
e-mail: richardturner4@btconnect.com
web: www.corncroft.co.uk
dir: *A40 to town centre, from Market Square onto Corn Street, 400mtrs on left*

Located in the quieter end of town, yet close to the centre, Corn Croft offers comfortable well equipped accommodation in a friendly atmosphere. Substantial breakfasts featuring local produce are served in the attractive dining room.

Rooms 9 en suite (1 fmly) (2 GF) **Facilities** FTV TVB tea/coffee Cen ht Wi-fi available **Notes** Closed 24–26 Dec

★★★★ 🏠 BED & BREAKFAST
The Laurels
40 Hensington Rd OX20 1JL
☎ 01993 812583 📠 01993 810041
e-mail: stay@laurelsguesthouse.co.uk
dir: *Off A44 onto Hensington Rd by pedestrian lights, 500yds on right opp Catholic church*

Located in a peaceful area just a short walk from the historic centre, the Victorian house has been renovated to provide high standards of comfort. Bedrooms come with thoughtful extras, and the elegant period-furnished dining room is the setting for imaginative breakfasts, which feature organic produce whenever possible.

Rooms 2 en suite S £65–£70; D £70–£80✱ **Facilities** TVB tea/coffee Cen ht **Notes** ⊗ No children 10yrs Closed Xmas & New Year

WOODSTOCK *CONTINUED*

★★★★ INN
Duke of Marlborough Country Inn
A44, Woodleys OX20 1HT
☎ 01993 811460 📄 01993 810165
e–mail: sales@dukeofmarlborough.co.uk

dir: *1m N of Woodstock on A44 x-rds*

The Duke of Marlborough is just outside the popular town of Woodstock, convenient for local attractions including Blenheim Palace. Bedrooms and bathrooms are in an adjacent lodge-style building and offer high standards of quality and comfort. Dinner includes many tempting home-cooked dishes complemented by a good selection of ales and wines.

Rooms 13 annexe en suite (2 fmly) (7 GF) S £65–£95; D £80–£120✳ **Facilities** TVB tea/coffee Direct dial from bedrooms Cen ht Dinner Last d 9.30pm Wi-fi available **Conf** Max 20 Thtr 20 Class 16 Board 12 Del from £125 ✳ **Parking** 42 **Notes LB** ⊗

See advert on opposite page

★★★★ GUEST ACCOMMODATION
Kings Head House
Chapel Hill, Wootton OX20 1DX
☎ 01993 811340
e–mail: t.fay@kings-head.co.uk
web: www.kings-head.co.uk

dir: *2m N of Woodstock. Off A44 to Wootton, close to village church*

Set in the pretty village of Wootton, this mellow-stone house retains many original features, including exposed beams and open fireplaces,

and is decorated in keeping with the style of the building. The homely bedrooms, including one in a barn conversion, are equipped with good practical extras, and imaginative food is served in the spacious, open-plan public areas. Currently undergoing re-building work until Autumn 2008.

Rooms 2 en suite 1 annexe en suite (1 fmly) (1 GF) S £60–£65; D £70–£85✳ **Facilities** TVB tea/coffee Cen ht Dinner Last d 24hrs notice Wi-fi available **Parking** 2 **Notes LB** ⊗ No children 12yrs Closed Xmas

★★★★ 🅰 GUEST ACCOMMODATION
The Blenheim Guest House & Tea Rooms
17 Park St OX20 1SJ
☎ 01993 813814 📄 01993 813810
e–mail: theblenheim@aol.com
web: www.theblenheim.com

dir: *Off A44 in Woodstock to County Museum, B&B after museum on left*

Rooms 6 rms (5 en suite) (1 pri facs) (2 fmly) S £50; D £60–£70✳ **Facilities** TVB tea/coffee Cen ht Wi-fi available

★★★ BED & BREAKFAST
Woodstock's Own
59 Oxford St OX20 1TJ
☎ 01993 810040
e–mail: enquiries@woodstocksown.co.uk

dir: *A44 N, take 1st slip rd on left after Kings Arms Hotel*

Situated in the Oxfordshire town of Woodstock, between Oxford and Chipping Norton, Woodstock's Own was recently renovated with wooden floors and stone walls. A tapas bar is open all day and there are en suite double bedrooms. There's a plentiful choice at breakfast.

Rooms 4 en suite S £45–£55; D £75–£90✳ **Facilities** TVB tea/coffee Cen ht TVL Wi-fi available **Notes** ⊗

★★★ INN
Sturdys Castle
Banbury Rd, Tackley OX5 3EP
☎ 01869 331328 📄 01869 331686
e–mail: enquiries@sturdyscastle.com

dir: *On A4260 Oxford to Banbury Rd*

Within easy reach of the historic Woodstock and Blenheim Palace this well-presented inn is a good touring base. Purpose-built accommodation is located to the rear of the attractive pub where a wide range of traditional fare is on offer. Bedrooms are comfortable and well appointed.

Rooms 20 en suite (4 fmly) (10 GF) **Facilities** TVB tea/coffee Direct dial from bedrooms Lift Cen ht Dinner Last d 10pm **Conf** Max 50 **Parking** 40 **Notes** ⊗

CONTINUED

WOOLSTONE

MAP 05 SU28

★★★ INN
The White Horse Inn

SN7 7QL

☎ 01367 820726 📄 01367 820566

e–mail: angusdtucker@aol.com

dir: *Just off B4507 nestling at the foot of Uffington White Horse Hill*

Located in the delightful village of Woolstone, The White Horse is a traditional country inn complete with friendly staff, a resident dog in the bar and an excellent selection of real ales and carefully prepared, quality home cooking. Bedrooms are located in an annexe adjacent to the inn and are generally spacious and comfortable. In addition to the relaxing bar and dining room, guests are welcome to enjoy the outdoor seating in the warmer months.

Rooms 5 annexe en suite (5 GF) S £75–£85; D £80–£90✶ **Facilities** TVB tea/coffee Cen ht Dinner Last d 9pm Wi-fi available **Parking** 40

The Duke of Marlborough *AA* ★★★★

A44 WOODSTOCK, OXFORD, OX20 1HT
Tel: 01993-811460

Quiet and friendly, this inn is situated on the edge of historic Woodstock, one mile from Blenheim Palace & 9 miles from Oxford.

Ample parking. All rooms are new, fitted to a high standard, en-suite & with all facilities associated with 4-stars.

e-mail: sales@dukeofmarlborough.co.uk
Web site: www.dukeofmarlborough.co.uk

RUTLAND

CLIPSHAM

MAP 11 SK91

★★★★ ◉◉ INN
Beech House

Main St LE15 7SH

☎ 01780 410355 📄 01780 410000

e–mail: rooms@theolivebranchpub.com

dir: *From A1 take B668 junct signed to Stretton and Clipsham*

This well furnished house stands over the road from the Olive Branch restaurant. It offers very well furnished bedrooms which include DVD players. Breakfasts are served in the Olive Branch. Excellent lunches and dinners are also available.

Rooms 5 en suite 1 annexe en suite (2 fmly) (3 GF) S £85–£150; D £100–£170✶ **Facilities** TVB tea/coffee Direct dial from bedrooms Cen ht Dinner Last d 9.30pm **Parking** 10 **Notes** No coaches Closed 24–26 Dec & 1 Jan

---

EMPINGHAM

MAP 11 SK90

★★★ INN
The White Horse Inn

Main St LE15 8PS

☎ 01780 460221 📄 01780 460521

e–mail: info@whitehorserutland.co.uk

web: www.whitehorserutland.co.uk

dir: *On A606 (Oakham to Stamford road)*

This attractive stone-built inn, offering bright, comfortable accommodation, is conveniently located just minutes from the A1. Bedrooms in the main building are spacious and include a number of family rooms. Public areas include a well-stocked bar, a bistro and restaurant where a wide range of meals is served.

Rooms 4 en suite 9 annexe en suite (3 fmly) (5 GF) **Facilities** TVB tea/coffee Direct dial from bedrooms **Parking** 60 **Notes** Closed 25 Dec

---

OAKHAM

MAP 11 SK80

★★★★ BED & BREAKFAST
Kirkee House

35 Welland Way LE15 6SL

☎ 01572 757401

e–mail: carolbeech@kirkeehouse.demon.co.uk

dir: *S of town centre. Off A606 High St onto Mill St, over level crossing, 400yds on left*

Located on a leafy avenue a short walk from the town centre, this immaculately maintained modern house provides comfortable bedrooms filled with homely extras. Comprehensive breakfasts, including local sausages and home-made jams, are served in the elegant conservatory-dining room, which overlooks the pretty garden.

Rooms 2 en suite D £55–£65 **Facilities** FTV TVB tea/coffee Cen ht **Parking** 2 **Notes** ⊗ No children 7yrs ▣

395

OAKHAM CONTINUED

★★★★ ◉◉ RESTAURANT WITH ROOMS
Nick's Restaurant at Lord Nelson's House

11 Market Place LE15 6HR

☎ 01572 723199

e–mail: simon@nicksrestaurant.co.uk

web: www.nicksrestaurant.co.uk

dir: *A1(M) onto A606, after 2nd rdbt, Market Place on right*

Tucked away in the corner of Oakham's market square, this restaurant with rooms offers fine dining and four individually appointed bedrooms with a range of antiques and knick-knacks. Service is attentive and helpful, and the food a delight, offering a selection of carefully crafted dishes using the best of quality seasonal produce.

Rooms 4 en suite S £55–£85; D £65–£115✶ **Facilities** TVB tea/coffee Direct dial from bedrooms Cen ht Dinner Last d 10pm Wi-fi available **Parking** 3 **Notes LB** ⊗

STRETTON   MAP 11 SK91

★★★ INN
Ram Jam Inn

Great North Rd LE15 7QX

☎ 01780 410776 📄 01780 410361

e–mail: ramjam@ohiml.com

web: www.oxfordhotelsandinns.com

dir: *A1 Nbound 200yds past B668 junct to Oakham*

The Ram Jam Inn is a popular destination situated just off the A1 in the village of Stretton. The open-plan public rooms include a large restaurant area, a bar and a comfortable lounge at the rear. Bedrooms are pleasantly decorated and equipped with modern facilities.

Rooms 7 en suite (1 fmly) S fr £45; D fr £55✶ **Facilities** TVB tea/coffee Cen ht Dinner Last d 7pm Wi-fi available **Conf** Max 40 Thtr 40 Class 30 Board 18 **Parking** 68 **Notes** ⊗ Closed 25 Dec & 1 Jan RS 24 & 26 Dec

---

UPPINGHAM   MAP 11 SP89

★★★★ ◉◉ RESTAURANT WITH ROOMS
The Lake Isle

16 High St East LE15 9PZ

☎ 01572 822951 📄 01572 824400

e–mail: info@lakeisle.co.uk

web: www.lakeisle.co.uk

dir: *From A47, turn left at 2nd set of lights, 100yds on right*

This attractive, townhouse hotel centres round a delightful restaurant and small elegant bar. There is also an inviting first-floor guest lounge. Bedrooms are extremely well appointed and thoughtfully equipped and include spacious split-level cottage suites situated in a quiet courtyard. Imaginative cooking and an extremely impressive wine list are highlights.

Rooms 9 en suite 2 annexe rms (2 annexe pri facs) (1 fmly) S £55–£65; D £75–£100✶ **Facilities** FTV TVB tea/coffee Direct dial from bedrooms Cen ht Dinner Last d 9.30pm Wi-fi available **Conf** Max 16 **Parking** 7

WING   MAP 11 SK80

★★★★ ◉ INN
Kings Arms Inn & Restaurant

13 Top St LE15 8SE

☎ 01572 737634 📄 01572 737255

e–mail: info@thekingsarms-wing.co.uk

web: www.thekingsarms-wing.co.uk

dir: *1.5m off A6003 in village centre*

This traditional village inn, with its open fires, flagstone floors and low beams, dates from the 17th century. The refurbished restaurant is more contemporary and offers a wide range of interesting freshly produced dishes. Service is attentive and friendly. The spacious, well-equipped bedrooms are in The Old Bake House and Granny's Cottage, in the nearby courtyard.

Rooms 8 en suite (4 fmly) (4 GF) **Facilities** TVB tea/coffee Direct dial from bedrooms Cen ht Dinner Last d 8.30pm **Conf** Max 20 Thtr 16 Class 16 Board 16 **Parking** 30 **Notes** ⊗ RS Nov–Mar

---

SHROPSHIRE

BISHOP'S CASTLE   MAP 15 SO38

★★★★ 🍽🛏 INN
The Sun at Norbury

Norbury SY9 5DX

☎ 01588 650680

web: www.sunatnorbury.co.uk

dir: *3m NE of Bishop's Castle. Off A488/A489 into Norbury village*

The delightful stone inn stands in the quiet village of Norbury. Exposed beams and log-burning stoves are enhanced by period furnishings, and the attractive, traditionally furnished bedrooms have modern facilities. Wholesome home-cooked food is available in the elegant dining room or in the popular bar.

Rooms 3 rms (2 en suite) (1 pri facs) 3 annexe en suite (1 GF) D £90–£120✶ **Facilities** TVB tea/coffee Cen ht Dinner Last d 9pm **Parking** 20 **Notes LB** ⊗ No children 14yrs No coaches

---

★★★★ BED & BREAKFAST
Shuttocks Wood

Norbury SY9 5EA

☎ 01588 650433 📄 01588 650433

e–mail: info@shuttocks.co.uk

dir: *From A489, turn left signed Norbury 3m, on the left past Norbury school*

Peacefully located in the rural hamlet of Norbury, this modern detached house, stands on pretty mature gardens and provides good standards of comfort and facilities. Bedrooms are equipped with thoughtful extras and breakfasts feature local fresh produce.

Rooms 3 en suite (1 fmly) (1 GF) S £35–£40; D £60–£70✶ **Facilities** TVB tea/coffee Cen ht Dinner Last d 24hrs notice **Parking** 10 **Notes LB** No children 10yrs

BRIDGNORTH

MAP 10 SO79

Premier Collection

★★★★★ BED & BREAKFAST

The Albynes

Nordley WV16 4SX

☎ 01746 762261

e-mail: thealbynes@hotmail.com

dir: *In Nordley on B4373, 500yds past Nordley village sign*

This imposing farmhouse features grand staircases, high ceilings and idyllic views. Melissa Woolley is a charming hostess, while husband Hayden looks after the crops and sheep. Bedrooms are comfortable, spacious and offer many thoughtful extras. Day rooms retain many original features and guests can enjoy traditional breakfasts, home-cooked on the Aga.

Rooms 3 en suite S £40–£45; D £60–£70 **Facilities** TVB tea/coffee Cen ht TVL **Parking** 6 **Notes** ⊗ No children 12yrs Closed Xmas-New Year ⊜

★★★★ GUEST ACCOMMODATION

Bearwood Lodge Guest House

10 Kidderminster Rd WV15 6BW

☎ 01746 762159

dir: *On A442, 50yds S of Bridgnorth bypass island*

This friendly guest house is situated on the outskirts of Bridgnorth. It provides soundly maintained modern accommodation, including one bedroom on the ground floor. The bright and pleasant breakfast room has an adjacent conservatory, which opens onto the attractive and colourful garden. There is also a comfortable lounge.

Rooms 5 en suite (1 GF) S £45; D £60 **Facilities** TVB tea/coffee Cen ht TVL **Parking** 8 **Notes** LB ⊜

The Crown Inn

Hopton Wafers, Cleobury Mortimer DY14 0NB

Surrounded by farmland, wooded valleys and tumbling streams, this 16th-century coaching inn offers fine hospitality. The bedrooms vary: you can choose between the original oak-beamed rooms of the inn, self-contained cottage-style rooms, and luxurious new rooms. Each is decorated in cottage style, with quality fabrics. Cosy sofas in the public areas are inviting, and there is a choice of dining rooms. The menus feature modern cuisine, which is imaginatively prepared using fresh local produce.

Tel: 01299 270372   Fax: 01299 271127
Website: www.crownathopton.co.uk
Email: desk@crownathopton.co.uk

Red Gables Country B&B

Longford, Newport, Shropshire TF10 8LN

Red Gables is a beautiful country house, set in five acres of private land situated in Longford near Newport, Shropshire. There is a newly converted three bedroomed (all ensuite) Coach House situated at the rear of the property. Accommodation is separate to the main house, guests have their own lounge, patio area and full use of modern kitchen once breakfasts have been served. Guests can enjoy the formal gardens which have open views of the grounds and neighbouring farmland.

Tel/Fax: 01952 811118
Website: www.red-gables.com
Email: sandracorbett@red-gables.com

BRIDGNORTH CONTINUED

★★★★ GUEST HOUSE
The Laurels

Broadoak, Six Ashes WV15 6EQ

☎ 01384 221546

e-mail: george.broadoak75@btinternet.com

web: www.thelaurelsbandb.co.uk

dir: *On right 5m from Bridgnorth travelling towards Stourbridge on A458*

Located on pretty gardens in a hamlet between Bridgnorth and Stourbridge, this immaculately maintained property provides a range of homely bedrooms, some of which are within conversion stables. Breakfast is served in an attractive conservatory-dining room, and a lounge and indoor swimming pool are additional attractions.

Rooms 2 en suite 5 annexe en suite (1 fmly) (5 GF) S £25–£30; D £50–£55✻ **Facilities** TV6B tea/coffee Cen ht TVL Wi-fi available ☒ **Parking** 9 **Notes** ☒ No coaches Closed Xmas & New Year ☒

★★★ INN
The Halfway House Inn

Cleobury Mortimer Rd WV16 5LS

☎ 01746 762670 📄 01746 768063

e-mail: info@halfwayhouseinn.co.uk

web: www.halfwayhouseinn.co.uk

dir: *1m from town centre on A4363 to Cleobury Mortimer*

Located in a rural area, this 16th-century inn has been renovated to provide good standards of comfort, while retaining original character. The bedrooms, most of which are in converted stables and cottages, are especially suitable for families and groups.

Rooms 10 en suite (10 fmly) (6 GF) **Facilities** TVB tea/coffee Cen ht TVL Dinner Last d 9pm Fishing Pool Table **Conf** Max 30 Thtr 30 Class 24 Board 20 **Parking** 30 **Notes** ☒ RS Sun eve (ex BHs)

★★★ BED & BREAKFAST
Little Brug

Oldbury Wells WV16 5JB

☎ 01746 761042

e-mail: helen@littlebrug.co.uk

dir: *A442 onto B4363, left at Oldbury Wells, left onto Captains Rd*

Located close to the historic Severn Valley Railway, this 300-year-old former farmhouse has been sympathetically renovated and extended to provide modern comfort while retaining original character. Thoughtfully furnished bedrooms share a smart modern bathroom and day rooms include a comfortable lounge with open fire.

Rooms 2 rms (1 pri facs) (1 fmly) S £15–£20; D £45–£65✻ **Facilities** TVB tea/coffee Cen ht TVL **Parking** 4 **Notes** LB ☒ ☒

★★★ BED & BREAKFAST
Severn View Accommodation

8 Sabrina Rd WV15 6DQ

☎ 01746 769337

e-mail: krystiana12558@hotmail.co.uk

dir: *Off A442 turn into Wellmeadow, 3rd right to Sabrina Rd*

Located on a peaceful residential estate a few minutes walk from Lower Town, this modern detached house provides two comfortable bedrooms, furnished in minimalist styles, with the benefit of smart en suite shower rooms. Comprehensive breakfasts are taken in an attractive dining room overlooking the pretty rear garden and a hot tub is also available at a small extra charge.

Rooms 2 en suite (1 GF) **Facilities** TVB tea/coffee Cen ht TVL Outdoor hot tub **Parking** 4 **Notes** ☒ ☒

★★ GUEST ACCOMMODATION
Sandward House

47 Cartway WV16 4BG

☎ 01746 765913 & 07703 649569 📄 01746 765913

Located beside the River Severn near original stone bridge, this 400-year-old property, which once included a butcher's shop, retains many original features and provides a range of bedrooms, some with modern en suite facilities. Hearty breakfasts are taken in an attractive pine furnished dining room and a warm welcome is assured.

Rooms 8 rms (3 en suite) (3 fmly) (1 GF) **Facilities** FTV TV7B tea/coffee Cen ht **Notes** ☒ RS Xmas

★★ BED & BREAKFAST
Wyndene

57 Innage Ln WV16 4HS

☎ 01746 764369 & 07977 943074

e-mail: wyndene@bridgnorth2000.freeserve.co.uk

dir: *500yds NW of town centre. Off B4373 onto Innage Ln*

Situated within walking distance of the centre of Bridgnorth, this small guest house is a home from home. Bedrooms are carefully decorated and one has a four-poster bed. Home-cooked breakfasts are served in an attractive dining room and parking space is available.

Rooms 3 rms (1 en suite) S £30; D £50–£54✻ **Facilities** TVB tea/coffee Cen ht TVL **Parking** 3 **Notes** ☒ ☒

CHURCH STRETTON　　　　　　　MAP 15 SO49

Premier Collection

★★★★★ BED & BREAKFAST
The Orchards

Eaton Rd, Ticklerton SY6 7DQ

☎ 01694 722268

e-mail: lnutting@btinternet.com

web: www.theorchardsticklerton.com

dir: *2m SE of Church Stretton. Off B4371 to Ticklerton village*

This large new house stands in the quiet hamlet of Ticklerton, two miles south-east of Church Stretton. Surrounded by four and a

CONTINUED

half acres of grounds, garden and orchard, it overlooks picturesque rural views. The comfortable accommodation is thoughtfully equipped and warm hospitality is a major strength here.

Rooms 3 rms (2 en suite) (1 pri facs) (1 fmly) S £28–£35; D £56–£70 **Facilities** TVB tea/coffee Cen ht **Parking** 6 **Notes** ⊗ No children 3yrs 🐾

Premier Collection

★★★★★ GUEST HOUSE
Field House
Cardington Moor, Cardington SY6 7LL
☎ 01694 771485
e–mail: pjsecrett@talktalk.net

This delightful old cottage is surrounded by 9 acres of grounds and gardens and is quietly located in a picturesque valley. It has been considerably renovated and extended to provide tastefully appointed, modern accommodation including a bedroom on ground floor level. Evening meals are available and separate tables are provided in the pleasant dining room. There is also a conservatory lounge.

Rooms 3 en suite (1 GF) **Facilities** TVB tea/coffee Direct dial from bedrooms Licensed Cen ht Dinner Last d 10.30am **Parking** 3 **Notes** ⊗ No coaches Closed Nov–Feb 🐾

Premier Collection

★★★★★ FARM HOUSE
Rectory Farm *(SO452985)*
Woolstaston SY6 6NN
☎ 01694 751306 📠 01694 751306 Mrs A Rodenhurst
e–mail: d.rodenhurst@btconnect.com

dir: *1.5m from A49 Shrewsbury to Ludlow road, turn by Copper Kettle*

Located in immaculate grounds within the pretty hamlet of Woolstaston, this early 17th-century half-timbered longhouse retains many original features including a wealth of exposed beams. The spacious bedrooms feature many thoughtful extras and ground-floor areas include two sitting rooms and an elegant dining room.

Rooms 2 en suite S £40✳ **Facilities** TVB tea/coffee Cen ht TVL **Parking** 6 **Notes** ⊗ No children 12yrs 10 acres non-working 🐾

Premier Collection

★★★★★ GUEST HOUSE
Willowfield Guest House
Lower Wood SY6 6LF
☎ 01694 751471
e–mail: willowfieldlowerwood@tiscali.co.uk

dir: *A5 onto A49 to Leebotwood, follow sign for Lower Wood, 0.5m on left*

Set in spacious and immaculate gardens, this Edwardian house, parts of which are much older, provides high standards of comfort. The bedrooms are well equipped and have many thoughtful extras as well as stunning views, while stylish décor and period furnishings add to the charm. A comfortable lounge is available, plus two elegant dining rooms where wholesome home-cooked dinners and hearty breakfasts are served.

Rooms 6 en suite (1 GF) S £40–£45; D £60–£70✳ **Facilities** TVB tea/coffee Cen ht Dinner Last d 6.30pm **Parking** 6 **Notes LB** ⊗ No coaches 🐾

★★★★ GUEST HOUSE
Belvedere
Burway Rd SY6 6DP
☎ 01694 722232 📠 01694 722232
e–mail: info@belvedereguesthouse.co.uk

dir: *Off A49 into town centre, over x-rds onto Burway Rd*

Located on the lower slopes of the Long Mynd, this impressive, well-proportioned Edwardian house has a range of homely bedrooms, equipped with practical extras and complemented by modern bathrooms. Ground-floor areas include a cottage-style dining room overlooking the pretty garden and a choice of lounges.

Rooms 7 rms (6 en suite) (2 fmly) **Facilities** tea/coffee Cen ht TVL Wi-fi available **Parking** 9 **Notes** No coaches

★★★★ FARM HOUSE
Brereton's Farm *(SO424871)*
Woolston SY6 6QD
☎ 01694 781201 📠 01694 781201 Mrs J Brereton
e–mail: info@breretonsfarm.co.uk
web: www.breretonsfarm.co.uk

dir: *A49 N from Craven Arms, at Jewsons turn left A489. Under bridge turn right Wistonstow, top of the village signed left 1.75m to Woolston. Farm on right*

Located among undulating hills within the pretty hamlet of Woolston, this impressive early-Victorian red-brick house provides thoughtfully equipped bedrooms with stunning country views. Comprehensive breakfasts are served in an elegant dining room, and the lounge has a wood-burning fireplace.

Rooms 2 en suite S £32; D £60 **Facilities** tea/coffee Cen ht TVL **Parking** 6 **Notes** 350 acres Mixed Closed 30 Nov–Mar 🐾

CHURCH STRETTON CONTINUED

★★★★ FARM HOUSE
Court Farm (SO514951)

Gretton SY6 7HU

☎ 01694 771219 📠 01694 771219

dir: *Turn off B4371at Longville, left at x-rds, 1st on left*

Located in the pretty village of Gretton, this 17th-century impressive stone-built Tudor house has been sympathetically renovated to provide high standards of comfort and facilities. Bedrooms overlook the pretty gardens and are equipped with a wealth of thoughtful extras. Comprehensive breakfasts are taken in an elegant dining room and a comfortable guest lounge is also available.

Rooms 2 en suite S £35–£40; D £60–£65✶ **Facilities** TVB tea/coffee Cen ht TVL **Parking** 4 **Notes** ⊗ No children 12yrs 330 acres Mixed ⊛

★★★★ FARM HOUSE
Gilberries Hall Farm (SO514938)

Gilberries Ln SY6 7HZ

☎ 01694 771723 Mrs Katherine Hotchkiss

dir: *B4371 E 4m, after Plough Inn left signed Gretton, house 1st on left*

With stunning views of the surrounding countryside, this well-proportioned house stands in pretty, mature gardens and has a large indoor swimming pool. Bedrooms are filled with homely extras and have modern bathrooms. Public areas include an elegant dining room and a lounge.

Rooms 3 en suite (1 fmly) (1 GF) **Facilities** TVB tea/coffee Cen ht TVL Dinner Last d by 10am on day ⊗ **Parking** 6 **Notes** ⊗ No children 10yrs 320 acres dairy arable Closed Dec–Jan ⊛

★★★★ BED & BREAKFAST
North Hill Farm

Cardington SY6 7LL

☎ 01694 771532

e–mail: cbrandon@btinternet.com

dir: *From Cardington village S onto Church Stretton road, right signed Cardington Moor, farm at top of hill on left*

This delightful house has been modernised to provide comfortable accommodation. It is located on a fairly remote 20-acre sheep-rearing holding amid the scenery of the Shropshire hills. The lounge, with exposed beams, has log fires in cold weather. Guests share one large table in the breakfast room.

Rooms 2 rms (2 pri facs) 1 annexe en suite (1 GF) S £30; D £50–£60✶ **Facilities** TVB tea/coffee Cen ht **Parking** 6 **Notes** LB No children 10yrs Closed Xmas ⊛

★★★ FARM HOUSE
Malt House Farm (SO459979)

Lower Wood SY6 6LF

☎ 01694 751379 📠 01694 751379 Mr & Mrs D Bloor

dir: *A49 N 3m, left signed Lower Wood, 0.5m to farm*

Located on an elevated position north of the town, this house was refashioned in 1772 and retains many original features. Modern

CONTINUED

bathrooms complement the homely bedrooms. Comprehensive breakfasts, which include free-range eggs, are served in the cosy dining room and a lounge is also available.

Rooms 3 en suite **Facilities** TVB tea/coffee Cen ht Dinner Last d 9am **Parking** 3 **Notes** ⊗ No children 100 acres beef sheep Closed Nov–Mar ⊛

Ⓤ
The Bucks Head

42 High St SY6 6BX

☎ 01694 722898

e–mail: lloyd.nutting@btconnect.com

web: www.the-bucks-head.co.uk

dir: *A49 N or S, turn into Church Stretton. At top of town turn left, Bucks Head on right*

At the time of going to press the rating for this establishment had not been confirmed. Please check the AA website www.theAA.com for up-to-date information.

Rooms 4 en suite S £30–£35; D £60–£70✶ **Facilities** TVB tea/coffee Cen ht Dinner Last d 9pm **Notes** ⊗ No children 5yrs

---

CLEOBURY MORTIMER   MAP 10 SO67

★★★★ INN
The Crown Inn

Hopton Wafers DY14 0NB

☎ 01299 270372 📠 01299 271127

e–mail: desk@crownathopton.co.uk

web: www.crownathopton.co.uk

dir: *In village on A4117 2m W of Cleobury Mortimer*

Set in extensive gardens with a duck pond, this 16th-century inn retains original exposed beams and has roaring log fires. Bedrooms are individually furnished and have modern facilities. Public areas include an elegant restaurant and spacious bars, where real ales and imaginative food are served.

Rooms 18 rms (2 GF) **Facilities** TV11B tea/coffee Direct dial from bedrooms Cen ht TVL Dinner Last d 9.45pm **Conf** Max 50 Thtr 50 Class 50 Board 50 **Parking** 50

See advertisement on page 397

★★★★ INN
The New Country Inn

10 Lower St DY14 8AA

☎ 01299 270395

e–mail: celia@countrybreak.co.uk

web: www.countrybreak.co.uk

dir: *On A4117 in village centre*

The New Country Inn has an excellent location with easy access to Birmingham, the West Midlands, and Shropshire. The accommodation is located in a nearby annexe and rooms are spacious and well equipped. Good honest farmhouse style food features in the attractive pine-furnished dining room.

CONTINUED

Rooms 6 annexe en suite (3 GF) **Facilities** TVB tea/coffee Cen ht Dinner Last d 11pm Wi-fi available **Conf** Max 30 Thtr 30 Class 16 Board 30 **Parking** 10 **Notes** ⊗ No children 12yrs

★★★ 🛏 BED & BREAKFAST
Old Bake House

46–47 High St DY14 8DQ
☎ 01299 270193

dir: *On A4117 in village 100yds from church*

A conversion of two 18th-century houses, a village inn and a bakery has resulted in a homely and carefully furnished guest house providing bedrooms filled with a wealth of thoughtful extras. Spacious ground-floor areas include comfortable sitting rooms and a dining section, the setting for memorable breakfasts.

Rooms 3 rms (2 en suite) (1 pri facs) S fr £30; D fr £60 **Facilities** tea/coffee Cen ht TVL Dinner Last d 7pm **Parking** 2 **Notes** ⊛

CLUN   MAP 09 SO38

Premier Collection

★★★★★ 🛏 BED & BREAKFAST
Birches Mill

SY7 8NL
☎ 01588 640409 📠 01588 640224
e–mail: gill@birchesmill.fsnet.co.uk
web: www.birchesmill.co.uk

dir: *A488 N from Clun for Bishop's Castle, 1st left to Bicton, in Bicton 2nd left for Mainstone, pass farm & 1st right*

Located in mature, pretty gardens beside a river in an Area of Outstanding Natural Beauty, this 17th-century former mill retains many original features, enhanced by the décor and furnishing schemes throughout. Bedrooms are filled with lots of thoughtful extras and a comfortable lounge is available.

Rooms 3 rms (2 en suite) (1 pri facs) D £76–£84✳ **Facilities** tea/coffee Cen ht TVL **Parking** 3 **Notes** ⊗ No children 12yrs Closed Nov–Mar

---

CRAVEN ARMS   MAP 09 SO48

★★★★ BED & BREAKFAST
The Firs

Norton SY7 9LS
☎ 01588 672511 📠 01588 672511
e–mail: thefirs@wrb.me.uk

dir: *Off A49 at Craven Arms onto B4368 towards Bridgnorth. 2m right at x-rds & B&B sign to Norton. Pass farm on left to next left, house 100yds on left*

Located in immaculate grounds on an elevated position within the hamlet of Norton, this impressive Victorian house retains many original features, highlighted by period furnishings and quality decor. Bedrooms are filled with thoughtful extras and have stunning views. Breakfast makes use of local produce and is served in an elegant dining room.

Rooms 3 rms (2 en suite) (1 pri facs) S £35–£50; D £60–£80✳ **Facilities** TVB tea/coffee Cen ht **Parking** 5 **Notes** ⊗ ⊛

★★★★ BED & BREAKFAST
Castle View

Stokesay SY7 9AL
☎ 01588 673712
e–mail: castleviewb_b@btinternet.com

dir: *On A49 S of Craven Arms opp turning to Stokesay Castle*

The Victorian cottage, extended about 20 years ago, stands in delightful gardens on the southern outskirts of Craven Arms, close to Stokesay Castle. Bedrooms are thoughtfully furnished, and breakfasts, featuring local produce, are served in the cosy, traditionally-furnished dining room.

Rooms 3 rms (1 en suite) (2 pri facs) S £35–£40; D £55–£60✳ **Facilities** TVB tea/coffee Cen ht **Parking** 4 **Notes** LB No children 3yrs ⊛

★★★★ FARM HOUSE
Strefford Hall Farm *(SO444856)*

Strefford SY7 8DE
☎ 01588 672383 📠 0870 132 3818 Mrs C Morgan
e–mail: strefford@btconnect.com

dir: *A49 from Church Stretton, South for 5.5m to Strefford, 0.25m past Travellers Rest Inn signed left. Strefford Hall 0.25m on right.*

This well-proportioned Victorian house stands at the foot of Wenlock Edge. The spacious bedrooms, filled with homely extras, have stunning views of the surrounding countryside. Breakfast is served in the elegant dining room and a comfortable lounge is also available.

Rooms 3 en suite (3 smoking) S fr £35; D £60–£70✳ **Facilities** TVB tea/coffee Cen ht TVL **Parking** 3 **Notes** LB ⊗ 350 acres arable, beef, sheep, pigs RS end Feb–end Oct ⊛

CRESSAGE   MAP 10 SJ50

★★★★ BED & BREAKFAST
The Old House B&B

4 Shrewsbury Rd SY5 6AA
☎ 01952 510198
e–mail: theoldhouse.bedandbreakfast@virgin.net

dir: *0.3m W of Cressage war memorial on A458*

A warm welcome awaits you at this delightful 17th-century cottage, which has been carefully renovated and extended to provide modern furnished accommodation, including a bedroom on the ground floor. A welcoming wood-burning stove is a feature of the comfortable lounge-breakfast room.

Rooms 2 en suite **Facilities** TVB tea/coffee Cen ht **Parking** 4 **Notes** ⊗ No children 12yrs

DORRINGTON   MAP 15 SJ40

★★★★ BED & BREAKFAST
Ashton Lees
Ashton Lees SY5 7JW
☎ 01743 718378
dir: *On N edge of village on A49. From Shrewsbury, Ashton Lees on right on entering village*

Located in immaculate mature gardens, this well-proportioned mid–20th-century house has been renovated to provide high standards of comfort and facilities. Bedrooms are filled with thoughtful extras, and public areas include a cosy lounge-dining room and a separate sitting room, both featuring open fires.

Rooms 3 rms (2 en suite) S £27.50–£30; D £55–£60✳ **Facilities** TVB tea/coffee Cen ht TVL **Parking** 6 **Notes** ⊗ Closed Dec–Jan ☺

★★★ BED & BREAKFAST
Caro's Bed & Breakfast
1 Higher Netley SY5 7JY
☎ 01743 718790 & 07739 285263
e-mail: info@carosbandb.co.uk
dir: *1m SW of Dorrington. Off A49 in Dorrington signed Picklescott, 1m left onto driveway by stone bridge, signed Higher Netley*

Self-contained guest accommodation is provided in this converted barn, south-west of Dorrington. Bedrooms, with smart modern bathrooms, are equipped with thoughtful extras and the open-plan ground-floor area contains a dining area and a comfortable lounge with a wood-burning stove.

Rooms 2 en suite S £40–£55; D £55✳ **Facilities** TVB tea/coffee Cen ht Wi-fi available **Parking** 4 **Notes** ⊗ Closed 21–28 Dec ☺

ELLESMERE   MAP 15 SJ33

★★★★ BED & BREAKFAST
Hordley Hall
Hordley SY12 9BB
☎ 01691 622772 📄 01691 622772
e-mail: hordleyhall@hotmail.co.uk
dir: *Leave A5 at Queens Head junct signed Hordley 4m. Take 1st left after village sign, 1st large cream house on right*

This large former farmhouse has a wealth of charm and character. Surrounded by large and attractive gardens, it is quietly located at Hordley, some three miles south-west of Ellesmere. It provides traditionally furnished, modern-equipped accommodation, which is equally suitable for both tourists and business visitors. Facilities include a comfortable lounge.

Rooms 4 rms (2 en suite) (2 pri facs) S £30; D £60✳ **Facilities** TVB tea/coffee Cen ht TVL **Parking** 4 **Notes LB** ⊗ ☺

HADNALL   MAP 15 SJ52

★★★★ BED & BREAKFAST
Hall Farm House
Shrewsbury Rd SY4 4AG
☎ 01939 210269
e-mail: hallfarmhouse@tiscali.co.uk
web: www.hallfarmhouse.co.uk
dir: *On A49 in centre of Hadnall*

Parts of this elegant former farmhouse, situated within pretty, mature gardens in the village, date from the 16th century. Accommodation is offered in two twin-rooms, and there is a traditionally furnished and spacious breakfast room.

Rooms 2 en suite S £30–£35; D £50–£60✳ **Facilities** TVB tea/coffee Cen ht **Parking** 6 **Notes LB** ⊗ No children 1yr ☺

★★★★ ◉ RESTAURANT WITH ROOMS
Saracens at Hadnall
Shrewsbury Rd SY4 4AG
☎ 01939 210877 📄 01939 210877
e–mail: reception@saracensathadnall.co.uk
web: www.saracensathadnall.co.uk

dir: *M54 onto A5, at junct of A5/A49 take A49 towards Whitchurch. Follow A49 until Hadnall, diagonal from church*

This Georgian Grade II listed former farmhouse and village pub has been tastefully converted into a very smart restaurant-with-rooms, without any loss of its original charm and character. The bedrooms are thoughtfully equipped and include a family room. Skilfully prepared meals are served in either the elegant dining room or the adjacent conservatory where the glass-topped well is a feature.

Rooms 5 en suite (1 fmly) **Facilities** TVB tea/coffee Cen ht Dinner Last d 9.30pm **Parking** 20 **Notes** ⊗ RS Sun eve-Mon

IRONBRIDGE   MAP 10 SJ60

★★★★★ 🏠 GUEST ACCOMMODATION
The Library House
11 Severn Bank TF8 7AN
☎ 01952 432299
e–mail: info@libraryhouse.com
web: www.libraryhouse.com

dir: *50yds from Iron Bridge*

A warm welcome is assured at this renovated Georgian house, once the local library. Bedrooms, named after writers of note, have a wealth of thoughtful extras and the immaculate gardens and hanging baskets are stunning during spring and summer. Memorable breakfasts are served in the pine- and copper-furnished dining room and a comfortable guest lounge is also available.

Rooms 4 en suite S £60–£75; D £70–£90✳ **Facilities** TVB tea/coffee Cen ht TVL Wi-fi available **Notes** LB ⊗ No children

★★★★★ GUEST ACCOMMODATION
The Old Rectory at Broseley Ltd
46 Ironbridge Rd TF12 5AF
☎ 01952 883399 📄 01952 882857
e–mail: info@theoldrectoryatbroseley.co.uk
web: www.theoldrectoryatbroseley.co.uk

The Old Rectory was built in 1893 and stands in a secluded and private position, the house is only minutes away from the centre of Ironbridge. Each bedroom has been tastefully furnished with the accent on luxury and comfort. There are four poster beds, Jacuzzi tubs and each room decorated in rich colour schemes using quality fabric. Breakfast is a real highlight to the day.

Rooms 10 en suite (3 fmly) (3 GF) S £49.95–£79.95; D £69.95–£129.95✳
Facilities FTV TVB tea/coffee Cen ht Wi-fi available **Parking** 30
Notes LB ⊗ Closed 24 Dec–2 Jan

See advert on this page

ENGLAND

IRONBRIDGE CONTINUED

★★★★★ A GUEST ACCOMMODATION
Bridge House
Buildwas Rd TF8 7BN
☎ 01952 432105 📄 01952 432105
e–mail: the-bridgehouse@btconnect.com

dir: *At bottom of Buildwas Bank (A4169) left & next left into car park*

Rooms 4 en suite (1 fmly) S £50–£55; D £70–£75 **Facilities** TVB tea/coffee Cen ht TVL Fishing **Parking** 6 **Notes** ⊗ Closed Xmas-New Year RS Dec–Jan

★★★★ GUEST HOUSE
Broseley House
1 The Square, Broseley TF12 5EW
☎ 01952 882043 📄 01952 882043
e–mail: info@broseleyhouse.co.uk
web: www.broseleyhouse.co.uk

dir: *1m S of Ironbridge in Broseley town centre*

A warm welcome is assured at this impressive Georgian house in the centre of Broseley. Quality individual décor and soft furnishings highlight the many retained original features, and thoughtfully furnished bedrooms are equipped with a wealth of homely extras. Comprehensive breakfasts are taken in an elegant dining room and a stylish apartment is also available.

Rooms 4 en suite (1 fmly) (1 GF) **Facilities** TVB tea/coffee Cen ht **Notes** No children 5yrs

★★★★ BED & BREAKFAST
Woodlands Farm Guest House
Beech Rd TF8 7PA
☎ 01952 432741 📄 01952 432741
e–mail: woodlandsfarm@ironbridge68.fsnet.co.uk
web: www.woodlandsfarmguesthouse.co.uk

dir: *Off B4373 rdbt in Ironbridge onto Church Hill & Beech Rd, house on private lane 0.5m on right*

Originally a brick works and then a working farm before conversion to spacious comfortable en suite bedrooms. Stylish furnishing and comfortable beds feature alongside warm hospitality. Wholesome breakfast is taken overlooking the pretty garden.

Rooms 5 en suite (1 fmly) (3 GF) S £35–£70; D £60–£80 **Facilities** STV FTV TVB tea/coffee Cen ht **Parking** 8 **Notes** LB No children 5yrs Closed 24 Dec–1 Jan

KNOCKIN   MAP 15 SJ32

★★★★ GUEST HOUSE
Top Farm House
SY10 8HN
☎ 01691 682582 📄 01691 682070
e–mail: p.a.m@knockin.freeserve.co.uk
web: www.topfarmknockin.co.uk

dir: *Off B4396 in village centre*

This impressive half-timbered Tudor house, set amid pretty gardens, retains many original features including a wealth of exposed beams and open fires. Bedrooms are equipped with many thoughtful extras, and the open-plan ground-floor area includes a comfortable sitting room and elegant dining section, where imaginative comprehensive breakfasts are served. Pam Morrissey was a finalist for the Friendliest Landlady of the Year 2008 Award.

Rooms 3 en suite (1 fmly) S £35–£45; D £65–£75✳ **Facilities** TVB tea/coffee Cen ht TVL **Parking** 6 **Notes** LB No coaches

LLANFAIR WATERDINE   MAP 09 SO27

Premier Collection

★★★★★ ◉◉ RESTAURANT WITH ROOMS
The Waterdine
LD7 1TU
☎ 01547 528214
e–mail: info@waterdine.com

dir: *Off B4355 into village, last property on left before church*

Standing in pretty, mature gardens within an Area of Outstanding Natural Beauty, which includes part of Offa's Dyke, this former 16th-century drovers' inn retains much of its original character. Bedrooms are filled with a wealth of thoughtful extras and have modern bathrooms. Public areas include a cosy lounge bar and an elegant restaurant, the setting for imaginative dinners that use quality, seasonal local produce.

Rooms 3 en suite S £95–£125; D £170✳ (incl. dinner) **Facilities** TVB tea/coffee Cen ht Dinner Last d 9pm **Parking** 12 **Notes** LB ⊗ No children 12yrs Closed 1wk Autumn & 1wk Spring RS Sun & Mon (ex BHs)

LUDLOW   MAP 10 SO57

Premier Collection

★★★★★ ◉◉ RESTAURANT WITH ROOMS

The Clive Bar & Restaurant with Rooms

Bromfield SY8 2JR

☎ 01584 856565 & 856665 📄 01584 856661

e-mail: info@theclive.co.uk

web: www.theclive.co.uk

dir: 2m N of Ludlow on A49 in village of Bromfield

The Clive is just two miles from the busy town of Ludlow and is a convenient base for visiting the local attractions or for business. The bedrooms are spacious and very well equipped, and some are suitable for families. Meals are available in the well-known Clive Restaurant or the Cookhouse café bar. A small meeting room is also available.

Rooms 15 annexe en suite (9 fmly) (11 GF) S £60–£85; D £85–£110✳ **Facilities** TVB tea/coffee Direct dial from bedrooms Cen ht Dinner Last d 9.30pm Wi-fi available **Conf** Max 40 Thtr 40 Class 40 Board 24 Del from £93.95 ✳ **Parking** 100 **Notes LB** ⊗ Closed 25–26 Dec

Premier Collection

★★★★★ GUEST HOUSE

De Greys of Ludlow

5–6 Broad St SY8 1NG

☎ 01584 872764 📄 01584 879764

e-mail: degreys@btopenworld.com

web: www.degreys.co.uk

dir: Off A49, in town centre, 50yds beyond the clock tower

This 16th-century timber-framed property is situated in the town centre. It has recently been extensively refurbished to provide high

quality accommodation with modern facilities, including two suites and one bedroom on ground floor level, all with the added confidence of an electronic security system. Careful renovation of the original beams combined with lush fabrics and beautiful wooden furniture has created a real fusion of the past and present. Breakfast is taken in the adjacent tearoom/restaurant and bakery shop.

De Greys of Ludlow

Rooms 9 en suite (1 GF) S £60–£120; D £80–£180✳ **Facilities** TVB tea/coffee Licensed Cen ht **Notes LB** ⊗ Closed 26 Dec & 1 Jan

Premier Collection

★★★★★ BED & BREAKFAST

Line Farm

Tunnel Ln, Orleton SY8 4HY

☎ 01568 780400

dir: Signed from A49 in Ashton. B&B signs in Tunnel Ln to Line Farm

A warm welcome is assured at this well-maintained non-smoking farmhouse, which is set in immaculate gardens to the south of Ludlow. Bedrooms, one of which is located in a superb Scandinavian style chalet, and can also be used for self-catering, are filled with a wealth of thoughtful extras and have modern efficient bathrooms. Comprehensive breakfasts are served in an elegant dining room, and a spacious lounge is available.

Rooms 3 en suite **Facilities** TVB tea/coffee Direct dial from bedrooms Cen ht TVL **Parking** 6 **Notes** ⊗ No children Closed Nov–Feb ◉

★★★★ 🍴 BED & BREAKFAST

Number Twenty Eight

28 Lower Broad St SY8 1PQ

☎ 01584 875466 📄 01584 875466

e-mail: enquiries@no28ludlow.co.uk

web: www.no28ludlow.co.uk

dir: In town centre. Over Ludford Bridge onto Lower Broad St, 3rd house on right

This 200-year-old property is just a stroll from the centre and has a wealth of character. It provides two double bedrooms, each well-equipped and containing thoughtful extra welcoming touches. There is a cosy lounge-breakfast room and a pleasant small garden.

Rooms 2 en suite S £65–£75; D £80–£90 **Facilities** TVB tea/coffee Cen ht **Notes** ⊗ No children 16yrs Closed Nov–May

CONTINUED

LUDLOW CONTINUED

★★★★ BED & BREAKFAST
Angel House

Bitterley SY8 3HT

☎ 01584 891377

e–mail: lockett1956@yahoo.co.uk

dir: *On A4117 towards Kidderminster*

Formerly "The Angel Inn", this sympathetically renovated 17th-century establishment, located four miles east of the town centre, provides comfortable bedrooms, with stunning views of the surrounding countryside. Breakfast is taken in an attractive dining room and a comfortable lounge and valley facing conservatory sitting area is also available.

Rooms 2 en suite (1 fmly) **Facilities** TVB tea/coffee Cen ht Dinner
Parking 30 **Notes** No children 5yrs ⊛

★★★★ BED & BREAKFAST
Bromley Court B & B

58 Bridgewood Rise SY8 2ND

☎ 01584 876996

e–mail: phil@ludlowhotels.com

dir: *Off B4361 at bridge into town centre*

Located close to the river and attractions of this historic town, this award-winning renovation of Georgian cottages provides split-level suites. All have comfortable sitting areas and kitchenettes; the carefully furnished bedrooms are filled with thoughtful extras and a peaceful patio garden is also available. Comprehensive continental breakfasts are available in each suite and cooked English breakfasts are available at the town centre Bull Hotel (under the same ownership).

Rooms 3 en suite S £75–£115; D £75–£115 **Facilities** TVB tea/coffee
Cen ht TVL **Notes** LB

★★★★ INN
Church Inn

The Buttercross SY8 1AW

☎ 01584 872174 📠 01584 877146

web: www.thechurchinn.com

dir: *In town centre at top of Broad St*

Set right in the heart of the historic town, this Grade II listed inn has been renovated to provide quality accommodation with smart modern bathrooms, some with spa baths. Other areas include a small lounge, a

CONTINUED

well-equipped meeting room, and cosy bar areas where imaginative food and real ales are served.

Rooms 8 en suite (3 fmly) S £40–£90; D £70–£90✳ **Facilities** TVB tea/
coffee Direct dial from bedrooms Cen ht TVL Dinner Last d 9pm
Conf Max 38 **Notes** No coaches

★★★★ BED & BREAKFAST
The Long House

The Sheet SY8 4JT

☎ 01584 874939

e–mail: mark.hudson@care4free.net

dir: *Off A49 towards Ludlow park & ride. Continue towards Caynham, 400yds on right*

Located one and a half miles from historic centre and only 400 yards from A49 by-pass, this 400-year-old former farmhouse has been sympathetically renovated to provide good standards of comfort and facilities. The spacious bedroom is equipped with lots of thoughtful extras and breakfast features local produce, homemade preserves and home grown fruit when in season.

Rooms 1 en suite (1 fmly) S £35–£40; D £60–£70 **Facilities** FTV TVB
tea/coffee Cen ht **Parking** 2 **Notes** LB ⊗ ⊛

★★★★ BED & BREAKFAST
Marcle House

Brimfield SY8 4NE

☎ 01584 711459 📠 01584 711459

e–mail: bill.pig@hotmail.co.uk

dir: *4m S of Ludlow, off A49 into village, almost opposite Roebuck Pub*

Located on pretty landscaped gardens, south of Ludlow within the village of Brimfield, this sympathetically renovated period property retains many original features including exposed beams and the interior is highlighted by quality décor and furnishings. Bedrooms are equipped with many thoughtful extras and a warm welcome is assured.

Rooms 3 en suite S £40; D £70 **Facilities** TVB tea/coffee Cen ht ⬥
Parking 3 **Notes** LB ⊗ No children 14yrs ⊛

★★★★ GUEST HOUSE
Moor Hall

Cleedownton SY8 3EG

☎ 01584 823209 📠 08715 041324

e–mail: enquiries@moorhall.co.uk

dir: *A4117 Ludlow to Kidderminster, left to Brignorth. B4364, follow for 3.5m, Moor Hall on right*

This impressive Georgian house, once the home of Lord Boyne, is surrounded by extensive gardens and farmland. Bedrooms are richly decorated, well equipped, and one room has a sitting area. Public areas are spacious and comfortably furnished. There is a choice of sitting rooms and a library bar. Guests dine family-style in an elegant dining room.

Rooms 3 en suite (1 fmly) S £40–£45; D £60–£70✳ **Facilities** TVB tea/
coffee Licensed Cen ht Dinner Last d day before Fishing **Conf** Max 14
Thtr 14 Class 14 Board 14 **Parking** 7 **Notes** LB No coaches Closed
25–26 Dec ⊛

★★★★ ◉◉ INN
Roebuck Inn
Brimfield SY8 4NE
☎ 01584 711230
e-mail: info@theroebuckludlow.co.uk
web: www.theroebuckinnludlow.co.uk
dir: *On A49, turn off at Brimfield*

Located in the rural village of Brimfield, this former 15th-century inn has been sympathetically renovated to provide good standards of comfort and facilities. Bedrooms offer a good range of homely extras and public areas include a lounge bar, which retains original period features and an elegant restaurant, in minimalist style, the setting for imaginative cooking.

Rooms 3 en suite D £75–£85✱ (room only) Facilities TVB tea/coffee Cen ht Dinner Last d 9pm Parking 20 Notes ⊗

★★★★ GUEST HOUSE
Southcot
Livesey Rd SY8 1EZ
☎ 01584 879655 & 07787 533718 📄 01584 878372
e-mail: gillandjohn@southcotbandb.co.uk
dir: *From lights at Tesco up Station Dr, past station to next lights, left & 1st right, Southcot on left*
Located in select residential area just five minutes walk from the historic centre. The bedrooms are comfortable, spacious and very well equipped with thoughtful extra touches and smart modern bathrooms. One ground floor room has been adapted for disabled guests. Facilities include a cosy lounge and breakfast room.
Rooms 5 en suite (1 GF) S £50–£75; D £60–£75✱ Facilities TVB tea/coffee Cen ht TVL Parking 6 Notes ⊗ No coaches

★★★★ BED & BREAKFAST
Tean House
8 Ledwyche Close, Middleton SY8 3EP
☎ 01584 875891
dir: *A4117 onto B4364, 0.7m on right*
Located in a small rural hamlet a few minutes drive from the town centre, this impressive modern detached house offers comfortable bedrooms equipped with a range of homely extras. Comprehensive breakfasts provide a good start to the day and a warm welcome is assured.
Rooms 3 rms (1 en suite) (1 pri facs) S £38; D £60✱ Facilities TVB tea/coffee Cen ht TVL Wi-fi available Parking 2 Notes ⊗ No children 5yrs ✉

★★★★ BED & BREAKFAST
37 Gravel Hill
SY8 1QR
☎ 01584 877524
e-mail: derekstraker@gravelhill.plus.com
dir: *Close to town centre*
This charming old house is within walking distance of the town centre. It provides good quality, thoughtfully equipped accommodation, and there is also a comfortable sitting room. Guests share one large table in the elegant breakfast room.
Rooms 2 rms (1 en suite) (1 pri facs) Facilities TVB tea/coffee Cen ht TVL Notes ✉

★★★ FARM HOUSE
Haynall Villa *(SO543674)*
Little Hereford SY8 4BG
☎ 01584 711589 📄 01584 711589 Mrs R Edwards
e-mail: rachelmedwards@hotmail.com
web: www.haynallvilla.co.uk
dir: *A49 onto A456, at Little Hereford turn right signed Leysters and Middleton on the Hill, 1m on right*

Located in immaculate gardens in the pretty hamlet of Little Hereford, this Victorian house retains many original features, which are enhanced by the furnishings and décor. Bedrooms are filled with lots of homely extras and the lounge has an open fire.
Rooms 3 rms (2 en suite) (1 fmly) S fr £30; D fr £56✱ Facilities TVB tea/coffee Cen ht TVL Dinner Last d 3pm Fishing Parking 3
Notes No children 6yrs 72 acres arable Closed mid Dec–mid Jan ✉

ENGLAND

LUDLOW CONTINUED

U

The Charlton Arms

Ludford Bridge SY8 1PJ

☎ 01584 872813

dir: From town centre onto Broad St, over Ludford Bridge, Charlton Arms located on right

At the time of going to press the rating for this establishment had not been confirmed. Please check the AA website www.theAA.com for up-to-date information.

Rooms 9 en suite (1 fmly) S £40–£90; D £80–£200✱ **Facilities** TVB tea/coffee Cen ht TVL Dinner Last d 9pm Fishing **Conf** Max 100 Thtr 100 Class 80 Board 70 **Parking** 25

MARKET DRAYTON   MAP 15 SJ63

★ ★ ★ ★ ⊛ RESTAURANT WITH ROOMS

Ternhill Farm House & The Cottage Restaurant

Ternhill TF9 3PX

☎ 01630 638984 🗎 01630 638752

e-mail: info@ternhillfarm.co.uk

web: www.ternhillfarm.co.uk

dir: On junct A53 & A41, archway off A53 to back of property

The elegant Grade II listed Georgian farmhouse stands in a large pleasant garden and has been modernised to provide quality accommodation. There is a choice of comfortable lounges, and the Cottage Restaurant features imaginative dishes using local produce. Secure parking is an additional benefit.

Rooms 5 en suite (2 fmly) S £35–£55; D £60–£80✱ **Facilities** TVB tea/coffee Cen ht Dinner Last d 9pm Wi-fi available **Parking** 15 **Notes LB** ⊗

★ ★ ★ INN

The Four Alls Inn

Woodseaves TF9 2AG

☎ 01630 652995 🗎 01630 653930

e-mail: inn@thefouralls.com

web: www.thefouralls.com

dir: On A529 1m S of Market Drayton

This country inn provides spacious open-plan public areas and has a strong local following for its imaginative food and real ales. Bedrooms, which are in a purpose-built chalet block, offer a good balance between practicality and homeliness. Superb beer gardens adorned with attractive floral displays are a feature during the summer.

The Four Alls Inn

Rooms 9 annexe en suite (4 fmly) (9 GF) **Facilities** TVB tea/coffee Direct dial from bedrooms Cen ht Dinner Last d 2pm **Conf** Max 100 Thtr 100 Class 100 **Parking** 60 **Notes** ⊗ Closed 24–26 Dec

---

MINSTERLEY   MAP 15 SJ30

★ ★ ★ ★ BED & BREAKFAST

Pool Cottage

Gravels SY5 0JD

☎ 01743 891621

e-mail: reservations@poolcottage.com

dir: Off A488, signed Pool Cottage

This small, pleasant and friendly guest house is quietly located amid open countryside 5 miles south of Minsterley and is set well back from the A488. It provides well-maintained, modern accommodation, as well as a cosy breakfast room where guests are seated around one table.

Rooms 3 en suite (1 fmly) (1 GF) S £35; D £60✱ **Facilities** TVB tea/coffee Cen ht TVL **Parking** 51 **Notes** ⊗ Closed Xmas ⊛

MUCH WENLOCK   MAP 10 SO69

★ ★ ★ ★ FARM HOUSE

Yew Tree *(SO543958)*

Longville In The Dale TF13 6EB

☎ 01694 771866 Mr & Mrs A Hilbery

e-mail: hilbery@tiscali.co.uk

dir: 5m SW of Much Wenlock. N off B4371 at Longville, left at pub, right at x-rds, farm 1.2m on right

Peacefully located between Much Wenlock and Church Stretton in ten acres of unspoiled countryside, where pigs, sheep and chickens are reared, and own produce is a feature on the comprehensive breakfast menu. Bedrooms are equipped with thoughtful extras and a warm welcome is assured.

Rooms 2 rms (1 en suite) (1 pri facs) S £30–£35; D £50–£60✱ **Facilities** TVB tea/coffee Cen ht TVL **Parking** 4 **Notes LB** 10 acres small holding, sheep, pigs ⊛

CONTINUED

★★★★ Ⓐ BED & BREAKFAST
Old Quarry Cottage

TF13 6JR

☎ 01746 785596 📄 01746 785596

e–mail: triciawebb.oldquarrycottage@virgin.net

web: www.oldquarrycottage.co.uk

dir: B4378 Much Wenlock to Ludlow, right at x-rds in Brockton towards Easthope. After 200yds, on right

Rooms 2 en suite 1 annexe en suite (1 GF) S £42–£47; D £60–£72 **Facilities** TVB tea/coffee Cen ht **Parking** 5 **Notes** ⊗ No children 12yrs ☞

★★★ INN
The Fox

46 High St TF13 6AD

☎ 01952 727292

e–mail: welcome@the-fox-inn.co.uk

Dating from the 17th century this inn offers a warm welcome and hospitality, creative cooking, and spacious comfortable en suite bedrooms equipped with many thoughtful extras. Private parking facilities.

Rooms 5 en suite 2 annexe en suite (2 fmly) S £60–£65; D £80–£85✳ **Facilities** TVB tea/coffee Cen ht Dinner Last d 9.30pm **Conf** Thtr 25 **Parking** 5 **Notes LB** No coaches

See advert on this page

★★★ Ⓐ INN
Talbot Inn

High St TF13 6AA

☎ 01952 727077 📄 01952 728436

e–mail: the_talbot_inn@hotmail.com

web: www.the-talbot-inn.com

dir: In village centre on A458

Rooms 6 annexe en suite (1 GF) **Facilities** TVB tea/coffee Direct dial from bedrooms Cen ht TVL Dinner Last d 8.45pm **Parking** 6 **Notes** ⊗ Closed 25 Dec

MUNSLOW   MAP 10 SO58

★★★★ ◉◉ 🍴 INN
Crown Country Inn

SY7 9ET

☎ 01584 841205

e–mail: info@crowncountryinn.co.uk

dir: Off B4368 into village

Located between Much Wenlock and Craven Arms, this impressive pastel-coloured and half-timbered Tudor inn is full of character and charm with stone floors, exposed beams and blazing log fires during winter. Smart pine-furnished bedrooms are in a converted stable block and spacious public areas include two dining rooms.

Rooms 3 en suite (1 fmly) (1 GF) S £50–£70; D £70–£75✳ **Facilities** TVB tea/coffee Cen ht Dinner Last d 8.45pm Wi-fi available **Conf** Max 30 Thtr 30 Class 30 Board 20 **Parking** 20 **Notes LB** ⊗ Closed 25 Dec RS Closed Sun eve

NEWPORT   MAP 15 SJ71 | OSWESTRY   MAP 15 SJ22

★★★★ FARM HOUSE
Moreton Hall Farm *(SJ789174)*
Moreton TF10 9DY
☎ 01952 691544 ▤ 01952 691544 Mrs S Bloor
e–mail: sarabloor@moretonhallfarm.com

dir: *Exit M54 junct 3, A41 Chester. Turn right Stockton, Moreton, Church Eaton 1.5m, turn left to farm*

Peacefully located close to major road links, a warm welcome is assured at this 18th-century farmhouse, which stands in pretty mature gardens and benefits from a swimming pool. Bedrooms are equipped with lots of homely extras and locally-sourced produce is featured on the breakfast selection.

Rooms 3 rms (2 en suite) (1 pri facs) (1 fmly) S £24–£35; D £48–£60 **Facilities** TVB tea/coffee Cen ht ⏱ **Parking** 6 **Notes** 200 acres Dairy ⊜

★★★★ 🅰 BED & BREAKFAST
Red Gables Country B&B
Longford TF10 8LN
☎ 01952 811118 ▤ 01952 811118
e–mail: sandracorbett@red-gables.com

dir: *From Newport onto Salters Ln/Longford Rd, left at T-junct, 100yds on left*

Rooms 3 annexe en suite S fr £50; D £60–£70 **Facilities** FTV TVB tea/coffee Cen ht TVL Wi-fi available **Parking** 10 **Notes** LB ⊗ ⊜

See advertisement under BRIDGNORTH

Premier Collection

★★★★★ ⊜ BED & BREAKFAST
Greystones
Crickheath SY10 8BW
☎ 07976 740141
e–mail: cbeard@netcomuk.co.uk
web: www.stayatgreystones.co.uk

dir: *From A483 follow B4396, turn right through village take No Through road, Greystones on right*

A warm welcome is assured at this impressive detached house, located on pretty mature gardens within the hamlet of Crickheath. Bedrooms are equipped with a wealth of thoughtful extras and smart modern bathrooms. Hearty breakfasts and imaginative dinners are available in an elegant dining room and a comfortable guest lounge is also available.

Rooms 3 en suite (2 fmly) **Facilities** FTV TVB tea/coffee Cen ht TVL Dinner Last d 24hrs before arrival **Parking** available **Notes** ⊗ No children 14yrs

★★★★ INN
The Bradford Arms
Llanymynech SY22 6EJ
☎ 01691 830582 ▤ 01691 839009
e–mail: cateloo@tesco.net

dir: *5.5m S of Oswestry on A483 in Llanymynech*

Once a coaching inn on the Earl of Bradford's estate, the Bradford Arms provides a range of carefully furnished bedrooms with a wealth of thoughtful extras. The elegant ground-floor areas include lounges, bars, and a choice of formal or conservatory restaurants, the settings for imaginative food and fine wines.

Rooms 5 en suite (2 fmly) (2 GF) S £35–£40; D £60–£70✳ **Facilities** TVB tea/coffee Direct dial from bedrooms Cen ht Dinner Last d 9pm Golf 18 Fishing Riding Pool Table **Parking** 20 **Notes** RS Mon

★★★★ BED & BREAKFAST
Pear Tree Cottage
Crickheath SY10 8BJ
☎ 01691 830766
e-mail: mike.bossen@virgin.net
web: www.stayatpeartree.co.uk

dir: *A5 onto B4396 through Knockin village, left after Lloyd Animal Feed Mill onto Crickheath Ln, house on right*
This 200-year-old property, reputedly once a pub, is set in quiet gardens alongside a disused section of the Montgomery Canal, which is currently being restored. The well-maintained accommodation consists of two thoughtfully equipped bedrooms. Warm hospitality is assured and hearty breakfasts take full advantage of local produce.
Rooms 2 en suite S £38; D £55✱ **Facilities** TVB tea/coffee Cen ht TVL **Parking** 3 **Notes** ⊗ No children 12yrs ⊜

 GUEST HOUSE
The Pentre
Trefonen SY10 9EE
☎ 01691 653952
e-mail: helen@thepentre.com
web: www.thepentre.com

dir: *4m SW of Oswestry. Off Oswestry-Treflach road onto New Well Ln & signed The Pentre*
This 500-year-old stone farmhouse retains many original features, including a wealth of exposed beams and a superb inglenook fireplace with blazing wood burner during colder months. Bedrooms are equipped with a range of thoughtful extras, and breakfast and dinner are memorable, with quality produce cooked with flair on an Aga.
Rooms 3 en suite (1 fmly) (1 GF) S £40–£50; D £64–£70✱ **Facilities** TVB tea/coffee Cen ht TVL Dinner Last d 9pm **Parking** 10 **Notes** LB ⊗ No coaches ⊜

★★★★ GUEST HOUSE
Top Farm House
SY10 8HN
☎ 01691 682582 📄 01691 682070
e-mail: p.a.m@knockin.freeserve.co.uk
web: www.topfarmknockin.co.uk

(For full entry see Knockin)

★★★★ GUEST ACCOMMODATION
Ashfield Farmhouse
Maesbury SY10 8JH
☎ 01691 653589 & 07989 477414
e-mail: marg@ashfieldfarmhouse.co.uk

dir: *1m S of Oswestry near Maesbury village school & white church*
The farmhouse is located in the hamlet of Maesbury and dates in part from the 16th century. It has been carefully preserved and original features include open fireplaces and a superb polished staircase.

CONTINUED

Bedrooms, one in a renovated coach house that can also be used for self-catering, are equipped with modern facilities and homely extras. There is a comfortable lounge and a traditionally furnished breakfast room.
Rooms 3 en suite (2 fmly) S £35–£50; D £58–£80✱ **Facilities** TVB tea/coffee Cen ht TVL **Parking** 5 **Notes** LB

★★★ BED & BREAKFAST
Carreg-Y-big Farm
Carreg-y-big, Selattyn SY10 7HX
☎ 01691 654754
e-mail: info@carreg-y-bigfarm.co.uk

dir: *Off B4580 at Old Racecourse, signed Selattyn. 1m on right on Offa's Dyke*
Incorporated within The Oswestry Equestrian Centre on the edge of Selattyn, this former farmhouse provides a range of simply appointed bedrooms, ideal for walkers of nearby Offas's Dyke. Comprehensive breakfasts and dinners, by arrangement, are served at one pine table in an attractive beamed dining room, and a small guest lounge is also available.
Rooms 4 rms (1 pri facs) (1 GF) **Facilities** Cen ht TVL Dinner Last d 6pm Riding **Parking** 10 **Notes** ⊜

★★★ INN
The Red Lion
Bailey Head SY11 1PZ
☎ 01691 656077 📄 01691 655932

dir: *In town centre. Off Castle St onto Powis Place, 1st left into car park signed Red Lion Complex*
Located in the historic town square, this well-maintained inn provides spacious, well-furnished open-plan public areas, the setting for a wide range of real ales and bar meals. Bedrooms are well equipped and have modern en suite shower rooms.
Rooms 5 en suite (1 fmly) (2 smoking) S £30–£40; D £40✱ **Facilities** TVB tea/coffee Cen ht Dinner Last d 8.30pm Pool Table **Parking** 4 **Notes** LB ⊗

RUYTON-XI-TOWNS MAP 15 SJ32

★★★ BED & BREAKFAST
Brownhill House
SY4 1LR
☎ 01939 261121 📄 01939 260626
e-mail: brownhill@eleventowns.co.uk
web: www.eleventowns.co.uk

dir: *Leave A5 onto B4397, 2m to Ruyton-XI-Towns. Through village, Brownhill House on left of a right-hand bend*
A warm welcome is assured at this charming guest house, parts of which date from the 18th century. The large terraced garden has been painstakingly created on the side of a steep hill above the River Perry, and guests are welcome to explore. All bedrooms have modern facilities and guests share one large table in a cosy kitchen-dining room.
Rooms 3 en suite (1 GF) S £23–£27; D £41–£52✱ **Facilities** tea/coffee Cen ht TVL Fishing ⛵ **Parking** 5 **Notes** LB ⊗ RS Xmas

SHIFNAL

MAP 10 SJ70

★★★ INN
The Hare and Hounds Inn
Crackley Bank TF11 8QT
☎ 01952 460597 📠 01952 462254
e–mail: hareandhoundsinn@btconnect.com
web: www.hareandhoundsinn.co.uk

dir: *On A5 between Red Hill and Weston-under-Lizard*

Located between Weston and Telford, this country inn, formerly part of the Weston Estate, provides cosy bars and an attractive modern restaurant, overlooking a pretty garden. Bedrooms converted from barns are very well equipped and comfortable, with two designed for use by disabled guests.

Rooms 6 en suite (3 GF) D £70✷ **Facilities** TVB tea/coffee Direct dial from bedrooms Cen ht TVL Dinner Last d 9pm **Conf** Max 60 Class 40 Board 30 Del £100 ✷ **Parking** 100 **Notes** ⊗

SHREWSBURY

MAP 15 SJ41

See also Criggion (Powys), Ruyton-XI-Towns, Wem & Westbury

★★★★ GUEST HOUSE
Fieldside
38 London Rd SY2 6NX
☎ 01743 353143 📠 01743 354687
e–mail: robrookes@btinternet.com

dir: *A5 onto A5064, premises 1m on left*

Located on manicured grounds within easy walking distance of town centre, this well maintained, early Victorian house provides a range of tastefully furnished bedrooms equipped with a wealth of thoughtful extras. Breakfast is taken in an elegant spacious dining room and a warm welcome is assured.

Rooms 4 en suite S £40; D £60–£65✷ **Facilities** TVB tea/coffee Cen ht **Parking** 8 **Notes** ⊗ No children 10yrs No coaches ☻

★★★★ BED & BREAKFAST
Old Park House
37 Abbey Foregate SY2 6BL
☎ 01743 289750
e–mail: oldparkhouse@yahoo.co.uk

dir: *From Shrewsbury town centre down Wyle Cop, over English Bridge. Left, behind The Abbi continue for 400yds Old Park House on left.*

Located behind the ancient Shrewsbury Abbey and reputed to have been the home of the Abbot, this 16th-century house has been sympathetically renovated to provide high standards of comfort and facilities for the 21st-century traveller, while retaining original intrinsic charm. Spacious bedrooms are equipped with lots of thoughtful extras and a spacious guest lounge is also available. Comprehensive breakfasts, featuring local produce, are taken at one large family table and a warm welcome is assured.

Rooms 3 en suite **Facilities** FTV TVB tea/coffee Cen ht TVL Wi-fi available **Conf** Max 15 Board 15 **Parking** 3 **Notes** ⊗ No children 9yrs ☻

★★★★ GUEST HOUSE
Abbey Court
134 Abbey Foregate SY2 6AU
☎ 01743 364416 📠 01743 358559
e–mail: info@abbeycourt.biz
web: www.abbeycourt.biz

dir: *N of river off A5112*

Located within easy reach of the town centre, this Grade II listed house offers a range of homely bedrooms, some of which are in an attractive extension. Comprehensive breakfasts are served in a cosy dining room and a warm welcome is assured.

Rooms 6 en suite 4 annexe en suite (1 fmly) (4 GF) **Facilities** TVB tea/coffee Direct dial from bedrooms Cen ht **Parking** 10 **Notes** ⊗ RS 23–27 Dec

★★★★ GUEST ACCOMMODATION
Abbots Mead
9 St Julian's Friars SY1 1XL
☎ 01743 235281 📠 01743 369133
e–mail: res@abbotsmeadhotel.co.uk
web: www.abbotsmeadhotel.co.uk

dir: *Entering town from S over English Bridge, 1st left*
This nicely maintained Georgian town house is located in a quiet
cul-de-sac, near the English Bridge and close to both the River Severn
and town centre. Bedrooms are compact, neatly decorated and well
equipped. The Abbots Mead also has a bright dining room, overlooking
the garden, and a bar featuring horse racing pictures.

Rooms 16 en suite (2 fmly) S £50–£55; D £65–£75✳ **Facilities** TVB tea/
coffee Direct dial from bedrooms Cen ht TVL Wi-fi available **Conf** Thtr 20
Parking 10 **Notes** Closed 24–26 Dec

★★★★ INN
The Bull Inn
7 Butcher Row SY1 1UW
☎ 01743 344728
e–mail: markglenister@btconnect.com
web: www.bull-inn.co.uk

dir: *Off High St onto Butcher Row, next to Prince Rupert Hotel*

Originally a slaughter house and situated in the heart of the town's
pedestrianised area, this timber-framed hostelry has a wealth of charm
and character. Now renovated, it provides modern equipped
accommodation and spacious bar and restaurant areas, where a wide
range of food is available. A pleasant beer garden is also available.

Rooms 6 rms (4 en suite) (2 pri facs) (1 fmly) **Facilities** TVB tea/coffee
Cen ht Dinner Last d 9pm **Notes** ⊗

★★★★ 🍴 GUEST HOUSE
Tudor House
2 Fish St SY1 1UR
☎ 01743 351735 & 07870 653040
e–mail: enquiry@tudorhouseshrewsbury.co.uk
web: www.tudorhouseshrewsbury.co.uk

dir: *Enter town over English Bridge, ascend Wyle Cop, in 50yds
take 1st right*
Located in the beautiful medieval town centre, this fine 15th-century
house has original beams and fireplaces, enhanced by the décor and
furnishings. Bedrooms are filled with thoughtful extras and breakfast
features local organic produce.

Rooms 3 rms (2 en suite) (1 pri facs) **Facilities** TVB tea/coffee Cen ht
Notes ⊗ No children 11yrs No coaches ⊛

★★★ GUEST HOUSE
Shenandoah Guest House
Sparrow Ln, Off Abbey Ln SY2 5EP
☎ 01743 363015 📠 01743 244918
web: www.shenandoah.org.uk

dir: *A5 onto A5064, turn onto Abbey Foregate after 100yds right
onto Sparrow Ln*
Located between The Lord Hill Monument and Abbey, and within easy
walking distance of town centre, this peacefully located modern house
provides a range of thoughtfully furnished bedrooms with en suite
shower rooms. Hearty breakfasts are taken in an attractive dining room
and a warm welcome is assured.

Rooms 4 en suite (3 fmly) S £35; D £50–£55 **Facilities** TVB tea/coffee
Cen ht **Parking** 6 **Notes LB** No coaches

TELFORD   MAP 10 SJ60

★★★★ BED & BREAKFAST
Avenue Farm
Uppington TF6 5HW
☎ 01952 740253 & 07711 219453 📠 01952 740401
e–mail: jones@avenuefarm.fsnet.co.uk
web: www.virtual-shropshire.co.uk/avenuefarm

dir: *M54 junct 7, B5061 for Atcham, 2nd left signed Uppington.
Right after sawmill, farm 400yds on right*
This impressive, well-proportioned house stands within immaculate
mature gardens in the hamlet of Uppington. Quality furnishings and
décor highlight the many original features, and the bedrooms are
homely. A comfortable sitting room is also available.

Rooms 3 en suite (1 fmly) S £35–£40; D £55–£60✳ **Facilities** TV2B
tea/coffee TVL Riding **Parking** 4 **Notes** Closed Xmas ⊛

TELFORD CONTINUED

★★★ BED & BREAKFAST
Potford House
Little Bolas, Wellington TF6 6PS
☎ 01952 541362
e-mail: dsadler@potford.fsnet.co.uk
web: www.shropshirebedandbreakfast.com

dir: *7m N of Wellington on A442, turn right signed Little Bolas, 1m from pub. Potford House on left*

Located in a peaceful hamlet north of Wellington, this spacious detached house provides a warm welcome and homely bedrooms with thoughtful extras. Wholesome breakfasts using local produce are served in an attractive dining room overlooking the pretty gardens.

Rooms 4 rms (1 en suite) (2 fmly) **Facilities** TV3B tea/coffee Cen ht TVL **Conf** Board 10 **Parking** 3 **Notes** ⊗ ⊛

WEM   MAP 15 SJ52

★★★★ ⇔ GUEST ACCOMMODATION
Soulton Hall
Soulton SY4 5RS
☎ 01939 232786 ▤ 01939 234097
e-mail: enquiries@soultonhall.co.uk
web: www.soultonhall.co.uk

dir: *A49 between Shrewsbury & Whitchurch turn onto B5065 towards Wem. Soulton Hall 2m NE of Wem on B5065*

Located two miles from historic Wem, this late 17th-century former manor house incorporates part of an even older building. The house stands in 560 acres and provides high levels of comfort. Bedrooms are equipped with homely extras and the ground-floor areas include a spacious hall sitting room, lounge-bar and an attractive dining room, the setting for imaginative dinners.

Rooms 4 en suite 3 annexe en suite (2 fmly) (3 GF) S £56.50–£74.75; D £83–£119.50✱ **Facilities** FTV TVB tea/coffee Direct dial from bedrooms Cen ht Dinner Last d 8.30pm Wi-fi available Fishing ⤳ Birdwatching in 50 acre private woodland **Conf** Max 100 Thtr 100 Class 60 Board 50 Del from £56 ✱ **Parking** 52 **Notes** **LB** Civ Wed 100

WESTBURY   MAP 15 SJ30

★★★★ BED & BREAKFAST
Barley Mow House
Aston Rogers SY5 9HQ
☎ 01743 891234 ▤ 01743 891234
e-mail: colinrigby@astonrogers.fsnet.co.uk
web: www.stmem.com/barleymowhouse

dir: *2m S of Westbury. Off B4386 into Aston Rogers, house 400yds opp Aston Hall*

Dating in part from the 17th century and extended in the 18th century, this charming property has been restored to provide comfortable accommodation with modern facilities. The house stands in a peaceful village and is surrounded by beautifully maintained gardens.

Rooms 3 en suite (1 fmly) **Facilities** TV2B tea/coffee Cen ht TVL **Parking** 4 **Notes** ⊗ ⊛

WESTON-UNDER-REDCASTLE MAP 15 SJ52

★★★★ ▤ BED & BREAKFAST
Greensboro
SY4 5UX
☎ 01939 200215
e-mail: bookings@greensboro.co.uk
web: www.greensboro.co.uk

dir: *Off A49 into village towards Hawkestone Park Hotel, Greensboro on left*

A warm welcome is assured at this immaculately maintained house set among pretty gardens near Hawkstone Park. The comfortable bedroom has a wealth of thoughtful extras, and memorable breakfasts are served in an elegant dining room overlooking the adjacent golf course practice area.

Rooms 1 en suite D £70–£80 **Facilities** TVB tea/coffee Cen ht **Parking** 1 **Notes** **LB** ⊗ No children ⊛

SOMERSET

BATH   MAP 04 ST76

For other locations surrounding Bath

*See also **Farmborough** and **Frome** (Somerset), **Box** (Wiltshire), **Bradford-on-Avon** (Wiltshire), **Trowbridge** (Wiltshire)*

Premier Collection

★★★★★ GUEST ACCOMMODATION

Ayrlington

24/25 Pulteney Rd BA2 4EZ

☎ 01225 425495 📄 01225 469029

e-mail: mail@ayrlington.com

web: www.ayrlington.com

dir: *A4 onto A36, pass Holburne Museum, premises 200yds on right*

The charm of this impressive Victorian house is evident in the attractive exterior and throughout the rooms, many of which feature Oriental artefacts and pictures. The bedrooms, some with spa baths, four-poster beds and views over Bath cricket ground, are very comfortable. Breakfast is served in the elegant dining room, which shares the enjoyable view.

Rooms 14 en suite (3 fmly) (3 GF) **Facilities** TVB tea/coffee Direct dial from bedrooms Cen ht Unlimited free golf at local golf club **Conf** Max 15 **Parking** 14 **Notes** ⊗ No children 14 yrs Closed 22 Dec–5 Jan

Premier Collection

★★★★★ 🛏 BED & BREAKFAST

Bradford Old Windmill

4 Masons Ln BA15 1QN

☎ 01225 866842 📄 01225 866648

e-mail: aa@bradfordoldwindmill.co.uk

(For full entry see Bradford-on-Avon)

Premier Collection

★★★★★ 🛏 GUEST HOUSE

Haydon House

9 Bloomfield Park BA2 2BY

☎ 01225 444919 & 424042

e-mail: stay@haydonhouse.co.uk

web: www.haydonhouse.co.uk

dir: *A36 onto A367 Wells Rd, right onto Bloomfield Rd, 2nd right*

This charming house offers excellent standards of comfort and hospitality. The delightful rooms include four-poster and canopied beds, are decorated with Laura Ashley fabrics, and are provided with many thoughtful extras. Special rates are available November to March. Breakfast is excellent – one option is the Scotch whisky or rum porridge.

Rooms 5 en suite (1 fmly) S £60–£95; D £70–£145✲ **Facilities** TVB tea/coffee Cen ht Wi-fi available **Parking** 1 **Notes** ⊗ No coaches

Premier Collection

★★★★★ 🛏 BED & BREAKFAST

Apsley House

Newbridge Hill BA1 3PT

☎ 01225 336966 📄 01225 425462

e-mail: info@apsley-house.co.uk

web: www.apsley-house.co.uk

dir: *1.2m W of city centre on A431*

Built in 1830 for the Duke of Wellington, Apsley House is within walking distance of the city centre. The house is extremely elegant, and the spacious bedrooms have pleasant views. There are family rooms and rooms with four-poster beds, while two rooms have direct access to the charming garden. A smart dining room and a delightful lounge are also available.

Rooms 11 en suite (2 fmly) (2 GF) **Facilities** STV FTV TVB tea/coffee Direct dial from bedrooms Cen ht Wi-fi available **Parking** 12 **Notes** ⊗ Closed 1wk Xmas

ENGLAND

BATH CONTINUED

Premier Collection

★★★★★ 🏠 GUEST ACCOMMODATION

Athole House

33 Upper Oldfield Park BA2 3JX

☎ 01225 320000 📠 01225 320009

e–mail: info@atholehouse.co.uk

web: www.atholehouse.co.uk

dir: *A36 onto A367 Wells Rd, 1st right*

Appointed to offer very high standards of comfort, this detached house stands in a quiet location just a 15-minute walk from the city centre. It has modern, well-equipped bedrooms and bathrooms, and the varied breakfast menu includes fresh fruit salad and home-made bread. There is a lovely garden to enjoy in summer, and secure parking with electronic gates.

Rooms 4 en suite (1 fmly) S £55–£65; D £75–£88 **Facilities** STV FTV TVB tea/coffee Direct dial from bedrooms Cen ht Wi-fi available **Parking** 7 **Notes LB** ⊗

Premier Collection

★★★★★ GUEST ACCOMMODATION

Cheriton House

9 Upper Oldfield Park BA2 3JX

☎ 01225 429862 📠 01225 428403

e–mail: info@cheritonhouse.co.uk

web: www.cheritonhouse.co.uk

dir: *A36 onto A367 Wells Rd, 1st right*

Expect a friendly welcome and a relaxed atmosphere at this well-presented Victorian house with panoramic views over Bath. The carefully decorated bedrooms are well equipped and include a two-bedroom suite in a converted coach house. A substantial breakfast is served in the conservatory-breakfast room overlooking the rear garden. There is also a comfortable lounge.

Rooms 11 en suite (2 fmly) (2 GF) **Facilities** TVB tea/coffee Direct dial from bedrooms Cen ht **Parking** 11 **Notes** ⊗ No children 12yrs

See advert on opposite page

Premier Collection

★★★★★ 🏠 GUEST ACCOMMODATION

Chestnuts House

16 Henrietta Rd BA2 6LY

☎ 01225 334279 📠 01225 312236

e–mail: reservations@chestnutshouse.co.uk

web: www.chestnutshouse.co.uk

Located just a few minutes walk from the city centre and totally renovated using light shades and oak, the accommodation is fresh and airy. Bedrooms are attractively co-ordinated, well equipped and comfortable. Added enhancements, such as Wi-fi, make the rooms suitable for both business and leisure. Breakfast, which features quite an extensive buffet and daily specials, is served in the dining room that opens onto the pretty rear garden. There is a cosy lounge, and the small car park is a bonus.

Rooms 5 en suite (1 fmly) (2 GF) S £65–£85; D £75–£105✳ **Facilities** STV FTV TVB tea/coffee Cen ht TVL Wi-fi available Riding **Parking** 5 **Notes** ⊗

Premier Collection

★★★★★ 🏠 GUEST ACCOMMODATION

The County

18/19 Pulteney Rd BA2 4EZ

☎ 01225 425003 📠 01225 466493

e–mail: reservations@county-hotel.co.uk

web: www.county-hotel.co.uk

Built at the turn of the century, The County was originally two separate houses. It became a hotel in the 1940s, and was taken over in 2000 as a family business. Overlooking the county cricket ground, it remains part of a green belt in the heart of Bath. Bedrooms are decorated very

CONTINUED

elegantly, and one has a four-poster. Breakfast is served in the dining room, and although evening meals are not served, Bath has no shortage of excellent restaurants.

Rooms 22 en suite S £90–£95; D £115–£190✳ **Facilities** FTV TVB tea/coffee Direct dial from bedrooms Cen ht Wi-fi available **Parking** 35
Notes ⊗ No children 12yrs Closed 20 Dec–10 Jan

Premier Collection

★★★★★ GUEST ACCOMMODATION
Dorian House

1 Upper Oldfield Park BA2 3JX
☎ 01225 426336 📠 01225 444699
e-mail: info@dorianhouse.co.uk
web: www.dorianhouse.co.uk

dir: *A36 onto A367 Wells Rd, right onto Upper Oldfield Park, 3rd building on left*

This elegant Victorian property has stunning views over the city. The atmosphere is welcoming and the accommodation of high quality. Several of the rooms have fine period four-poster beds and all offer a range of extra facilities. The attractive lounge has an honesty bar and views of the terraced gardens.

Rooms 11 en suite (1 fmly) (2 GF) S £65–£95; D £89–£165✳
Facilities FTV TVB tea/coffee Direct dial from bedrooms Cen ht Wi-fi available **Parking** 11 **Notes** LB ⊗

Premier Collection

★★★★★ GUEST ACCOMMODATION
Meadowland

36 Bloomfield Park BA2 2BX
☎ 01225 311079 📠 01225 311079
e-mail: stay@meadowlandbath.co.uk

dir: *A367 signed Exeter/Wells, past the Bear pub, take right fork onto Bloomfield Rd. 2nd right into Bloomfield Park*

Peacefully located in a residential area, yet just a twenty minute stroll from Bath, Meadowland offers a relaxing retreat with plenty of quality and comfort throughout. The three bedrooms are all spacious and equipped with welcome extras. Guests are also welcome to use the very comfortable lounge. Breakfast is a highlight, with a range of carefully prepared, good quality produce.

Rooms 3 en suite S £60–£65; D £80–£115 **Facilities** TVB tea/coffee
Cen ht **Parking** 4 **Notes** LB ⊗ No children 4yrs

BATH CONTINUED

Premier Collection

★★★★★ GUEST ACCOMMODATION
Paradise House

Holloway BA2 4PX

☎ 01225 317723 📠 01225 482005

e-mail: info@paradise-house.co.uk

web: www.paradise-house.co.uk

dir: *A36 onto A367 Wells Rd, 3rd left, down hill onto cul-de-sac, house 200yds on left*

Set in half an acre of lovely walled gardens, this Georgian house, built of mellow Bath stone, is within walking distance of the city centre. Many bedrooms have fine views over the city, and all are decorated in opulent style. Furnishings are elegant and facilities modern. The lounge is comfortable and relaxing, and breakfast is served in the smart dining room. Hospitality and service here are friendly and professional.

Rooms 11 en suite (2 fmly) (4 GF) S £65–£89; D £69–£160✶
Facilities FTV TVB tea/coffee Direct dial from bedrooms Cen ht Wi-fi available **Parking** 11 **Notes LB** ⊗ Closed 3 days Xmas

See advert on page 417

Premier Collection

★★★★★ GUEST ACCOMMODATION
The Villa Magdala

Henrietta Rd BA2 6LX

☎ 01225 466329 📠 01225 483207

e-mail: office@VillaMagdala.co.uk

web: www.VillaMagdala.co.uk

dir: *A4 onto A36 Bathwick St, 2nd right*

This stylish Victorian house is just a short walk from the city's attractions and offers a haven of peace and tranquillity. There are pleasant views from the attractively furnished and spacious bedrooms, all of which are well equipped. The charming lounge and dining room overlook one of Bath's delightful parks.

Rooms 17 en suite (4 fmly) D £90–£170 **Facilities** TVB tea/coffee Direct dial from bedrooms Cen ht Wi-fi available **Parking** 17 **Notes LB** ⊗ No children 5yrs

★★★★★ 🅰 GUEST HOUSE
Carfax

13–15 Great Pulteney St BA2 4BS

☎ 01225 462089 📠 01225 443257

e-mail: reservations@carfaxhotel.co.uk

web: www.carfaxhotel.co.uk

dir: *A36 onto Great Pulteney St*

Rooms 31 en suite (5 fmly) (4 GF) **Facilities** STV TVB tea/coffee Direct dial from bedrooms Lift Cen ht Dinner Last d 6.30pm Wi-fi available Playstations for hire **Conf** Max 30 Thtr 25 Class 25 Board 15 **Parking** 13 **Notes** ⊗ No coaches

★★★★ GUEST ACCOMMODATION
Brocks Guest House

32 Brock St BA1 2LN

☎ 01225 338374 📠 01225 338425

e-mail: brocks@brocksguesthouse.co.uk

web: www.brocksguesthouse.co.uk

dir: *Just off A4 between Circus & Royal Crescent*

A warm welcome is extended at this delightful Georgian property, located in the heart of the city just a few hundred yards from Royal Crescent. All rooms reflect the comfortable elegance of the Georgian era. A traditional breakfast is served in the charming dining room, which also offers a lounge area with comfortable seating.

Rooms 6 en suite (2 fmly) S £65–£70; D £79–£99✶ **Facilities** FTV TVB tea/coffee Cen ht **Parking** 2 **Notes** ⊗ Closed 24 Dec–1 Jan

★★★★ GUEST ACCOMMODATION
The Hollies

Hatfield Rd BA2 2BD

☎ 01225 313366

e-mail: davcartwright@lineone.net

dir: *A36 onto A367 Wells Rd & Wellsway, 0.7m right opp Devonshire Arms*

This delightful house stands in impressive gardens overlooking a magnificent church, and is within easy reach of the city centre. Individually decorated themed bedrooms are finished to provide excellent levels of comfort and facilities. Breakfast in the elegant dining room is an enjoyable start to the day.

Rooms 3 rms (2 en suite) (1 pri facs) S £60–£70; D £65–£75
Facilities TVB tea/coffee Cen ht Wi-fi available **Parking** 3 **Notes** ⊗ No children 16yrs Closed 15 Dec–20 Jan

★★★★ GUEST HOUSE
Oldfields

102 Wells Rd BA2 3AL

☎ 01225 317984 📠 01225 444471

e-mail: info@oldfields.co.uk

dir: *0.5m S of city centre. A36 onto A367*

This accommodation has been sensitively developed both to maintain some period features and to offer guests luxurious comfort. The attractive, light and airy bedrooms, some of which have four-poster beds and Jacuzzis, are well equipped with considerate extras. The

CONTINUED

lounge has an open fire during colder days. The elegant dining room, offers a choice of dishes for breakfast.

Rooms 16 en suite (4 fmly) (2 GF) S £49–£65; D £65–£150✲ **Facilities** STV TVB tea/coffee Direct dial from bedrooms Cen ht Wi-fi available **Parking** 12 **Notes** LB ⊗ No coaches Closed 24–26 Dec

★★★★ GUEST ACCOMMODATION

St Leonards

Warminster Rd BA2 6SQ

☎ 01225 465838 📄 01225 442800

e–mail: stay@stleonardsbath.co.uk

dir: *1m E of city centre. A4 onto A36 Warminster Rd, up hill 200yds on left*

Located in grounds on the eastern side of the city, this impressive Victorian home with its high ceilings has superb views over the town and surrounding countryside. The stylish bedrooms and bathrooms are spacious and very comfortable, and a full English breakfast is served in the attractive dining room.

Rooms 6 en suite (2 fmly) (2 GF) **Facilities** TVB tea/coffee Cen ht **Parking** 8 **Notes** No children 6yrs Closed Xmas

★★★★ GUEST ACCOMMODATION

The Town House

7 Bennett St BA1 2QJ

☎ 01225 422505 📄 01225 422505

e–mail: stay@thetownhousebath.co.uk

dir: *400yds N of city centre. Off A4 Roman Rd at lights onto Lansdown Hill, 2nd on left*

Bath's historical attractions and shops are on the doorstep when you stay here. The Town House is located alongside the Assembly Rooms and just a stone's throw away from the Royal Crescent. This stylish Georgian accommodation offers a good level of comfort. Bedrooms are finished with many thoughtful extras and the friendly hosts are attentive. At breakfast time the atmosphere is relaxed and memorable, with a good choice of freshly prepared dishes enjoyed around a communal table.

Rooms 3 en suite D £94–£120✲ **Facilities** TVB tea/coffee Cen ht Wi-fi available **Parking** 1 **Notes** ⊗ No children 14yrs Closed Jan

★★★★ GUEST ACCOMMODATION

Aquae Sulis

174/176 Newbridge Rd BA1 3LE

☎ 01225 420061 📄 01225 446077

e–mail: enquiries@aquaesulishotel.co.uk

web: www.aquaesulishotel.co.uk

dir: *On A4 1.8m W of city centre, on A4 (Upper Bristol Rd)*

Located within easy reach of the city centre, this attractive Edwardian house offers a genuine welcome. Bedrooms are of a good size and well equipped with many modern facilities such as internet access. There are two inviting lounges, one with a small but well-stocked bar. Breakfast is served in the comfortable dining room.

Rooms 13 rms (11 en suite) (2 pri facs) 1 annexe en suite (5 fmly) (3 GF) S £59–£89; D £65–£110✲ **Facilities** STV FTV TVB tea/coffee Direct dial from bedrooms Cen ht TVL Wi-fi available **Parking** 12 **Notes** LB ⊗ Closed 24–30 Dec

★★★★ GUEST ACCOMMODATION

Ashley Villa

26 Newbridge Rd BA1 3JZ

☎ 01225 421683 📄 01225 313604

e–mail: reservations@ashleyvilla.co.uk

web: www.ashleyvilla.co.uk

dir: *A4 Upper Bristol Rd W from Bath, fork left onto A4 Newbridge Rd, 200yds on right*

Located within walking distance of the city centre, Ashley Villa offers a range of bedrooms and bathrooms. Facilities include a lounge bar, a patio and an outdoor swimming pool. Breakfast is served in the bright attractive dining room.

Rooms 13 en suite (2 fmly) (4 GF) S £49–£69; D £59–£89✲ **Facilities** FTV TVB tea/coffee Direct dial from bedrooms Cen ht TVL Dinner Last d 9pm Wi-fi available ⚓ **Parking** 8 **Notes** LB ⊗ RS Xmas & New Year

★★★★ GUEST HOUSE

The Bailbrook Lodge

35/37 London Rd West BA1 7HZ

☎ 01225 859090 📄 01225 852299

e–mail: hotel@bailbrooklodge.co.uk

web: www.bailbrooklodge.co.uk

dir: *M4 junct 18, A46 S to A4 junct, left signed Batheaston, Lodge on left*

Set in extensive gardens on the east edge of the city, this imposing Georgian building provides smart accommodation. The well-equipped bedrooms include some with four-poster beds and period furniture, and service is professional and efficient. The inviting lounge has a small bar, and light snacks are available from noon until evening. Breakfast is served in the elegant dining room.

Rooms 15 rms (14 en suite) (1 pri facs) (5 fmly) (1 GF) S £59–£70; D £75–£160 **Facilities** STV TVB tea/coffee Licensed Cen ht Wi-fi available **Conf** Max 20 Thtr 20 Class 10 Board 12 Del from £110 **Parking** 15 **Notes** LB ⊗ Civ Wed 40

★★★★ GUEST ACCOMMODATION

The Bath House

40 Crescent Gardens BA1 2NB

☎ 0117 937 4495 📄 0117 937 4921

e–mail: info@thebathhouse.org

web: www.thebathhouse.org

dir: *100yds from Queen Sq on A431*

Now refurbished to high quality specifications, this accommodation is stylish and just a few minutes level walk from the city. Bedrooms are attractive, spacious, light and airy and equipped with modern accessories, including flat screen televisions and Wi-fi internet connection. Breakfast is room service only and a full height dining table provided in the bedroom ensures guests enjoy their meal experience. Limited parking space is available.

Rooms 4 en suite (1 GF) S £65–£95; D £79–£105✲ **Facilities** FTV TVB tea/coffee Cen ht Wi-fi available **Parking** 4 **Notes** LB ⊗ No children 8yrs

BATH CONTINUED

★★★★ BED & BREAKFAST
Cranleigh

159 Newbridge Hill BA1 3PX
☎ 01225 310197 📠 01225 423143
e–mail: cranleigh@btinternet.com
web: www.cranleighguesthouse.com

dir: *1.2m W of city centre on A431*

This pleasant Victorian house is in a quiet location near the city centre.
The well-equipped bedrooms, some on the ground floor, are
decorated in the period style and two rooms have four-poster beds.
Breakfast is served in the elegant dining room, and there is also an
attractive garden which includes a popular hot tub.

Rooms 9 en suite (2 fmly) (2 GF) S £55–£80; D £60–£115✳
Facilities FTV TVB tea/coffee Direct dial from bedrooms Cen ht Wi-fi
available Garden hot tub **Parking** 5 **Notes** ⊗ No children 5yrs Closed
25–26 Dec

★★★★ BED & BREAKFAST
Dolphin House

8 Northend, Batheaston BA1 7EN
☎ 01225 858915
e–mail: georgeandjane@hotmail.com

dir: *2m NE of Bath. Off Batheaston High St to Northend, 100yds
on right*

This detached Grade II listed Georgian house is convenient for Bath
and has a delightful terraced walled garden. Bedrooms, including a
suite with lounge, twin bedroom and large bathroom, feature attractive
period decor. Continental breakfasts are served in the bedrooms or on
the terrace.

Rooms 2 rms (1 en suite) (1 pri facs) (1 GF) S £45–£65; D £60–£80✳
Facilities TVB tea/coffee Cen ht Wi-fi available **Parking** 2 **Notes** ⊗
No children 12yrs Closed Xmas RS 24–27 Dec 🐾

★★★★ GUEST ACCOMMODATION
Eagle House

Church St, Bathford BA1 7RS
☎ 01225 859946 📠 01225 859430
e–mail: jonap@eagleho.demon.co.uk
web: www.eaglehouse.co.uk

dir: *Off A363 onto Church St*

Set in attractive gardens, this delightful Georgian house is pleasantly
located on the outskirts of the city. Bedrooms are individually styled,
and each has a thoughtful range of extra facilities. The impressive
lounge is adorned with attractive pictures, and the dining room has
views of the grounds and tennis court.

Eagle House

Rooms 6 en suite 2 annexe en suite (2 fmly) (2 GF) S £48–£88.50;
D £56–£112✳ **Facilities** TVB tea/coffee Direct dial from bedrooms
Cen ht 🌳 🐾 **Conf** Max 18 Thtr 18 Class 18 Board 14 **Parking** 10
Notes LB Closed 12 Dec–8 Jan

★★★★ GUEST ACCOMMODATION
Grosvenor Lodge

Grosvenor Place, London Rd BA1 6BA
☎ 01225 420504

Set back from the main road leading into and out of Bath, this pleasant
accommodation has undergone careful re-decoration and
refurbishment by the new owners. Bedrooms offer a range of shapes
and sizes and guests are also welcome to use the spacious lounge. A
carefully prepared breakfast is offered in the stylish dining room.

Rooms 3 rms (1 en suite) (2 pri facs) **Facilities** TVB tea/coffee Cen ht
TVL **Parking** 2 **Notes** No children 7yrs 🐾

★★★★ GUEST ACCOMMODATION
Grove Lodge

11 Lambridge BA1 6BJ
☎ 01225 310860 📠 01225 429 630
e–mail: stay@grovelodgebath.co.uk

dir: *0.6m NE of city centre. Off A4, 400yds W from junct A46*

This fine Georgian house lies within easy reach of the city centre and is
reached by a stone path through a neat garden surrounded by trees.
The spacious bedrooms have period character and all are well
equipped. There is an attractive breakfast room and parking is available
in nearby side streets. Guests may venture into the city for evening
meals or alternatively, a short stroll along the canalside leads to an inn,
which serves food.

CONTINUED

CONTINUED

Rooms 5 rms (4 en suite) (1 pri facs) (1 GF) S £49–£60; D £66–£82✶
Facilities TVB tea/coffee Cen ht Wi-fi available Notes LB ⊗ No children
6yrs Closed Xmas & New Year

★★★★ GUEST ACCOMMODATION
Highways House
143 Wells Rd BA2 3AL
☎ 01225 421238 📄 01225 481169
e–mail: stay@highwayshouse.co.uk
dir: A36 onto A367 Wells Rd, 300yds on left

This elegant Victorian house is just a 10-minute walk from the city
centre (or alternatively, there is a frequent bus). The bedrooms are
individually styled, well equipped and homely; one is located on the
ground floor. A spacious attractive lounge is available. Breakfast is
served in the dining room at separate tables. Parking is a bonus.

Rooms 5 en suite (2 fmly) (1 GF) S £50–£55; D £72–£77✶
Facilities TVB tea/coffee Cen ht Wi-fi available Parking 6 Notes ⊗
No children 8yrs

★★★★ GUEST ACCOMMODATION
The Kennard
11 Henrietta St BA2 6LL
☎ 01225 310472 📄 01225 460054
e–mail: reception@kennard.co.uk
web: www.kennard.co.uk
dir: A4 onto A36 Bathwick St, 2nd right onto Henrietta Rd &
Henrietta St

This attractive Georgian house dates from 1794 and is situated just off
famous Great Pulteney Street, making it convenient for the city centre.
The house is decorated and furnished to retain an atmosphere in

keeping with the elegance of the architecture. Bedrooms, some located
at ground floor level, vary in terms of style and space. Breakfast is
served in the lower garden dining room and includes an excellent cold
buffet as well as a selection of hot items.

Rooms 12 rms (10 en suite) (2 GF) S £58–£89; D £98–£140✶
Facilities STV TVB tea/coffee Direct dial from bedrooms Cen ht Wi-fi
available Notes ⊗ No children 8yrs Closed 2 wks Xmas

★★★★ GUEST ACCOMMODATION
Marlborough House
1 Marlborough Ln BA1 2NQ
☎ 01225 318175 📄 01225 466127
e–mail: mars@manque.dircon.co.uk
web: www.marlborough-house.net
dir: 450yds W of city centre, at A4 junct

Marlborough House is situated opposite Royal Victoria Park and close
to the Royal Crescent. Some original features remain and the rooms
are decorated with period furniture and pictures. The atmosphere is
relaxed, and service is attentive and friendly. The breakfast, served from
an open-plan kitchen, is vegetarian and organic.

Rooms 6 en suite (2 fmly) (1 GF) S £75–£95; D £85–£135✶
Facilities TVB tea/coffee Direct dial from bedrooms Cen ht Wi-fi available
Parking 3 Notes LB Closed 24–25 Dec

★★★★ GUEST ACCOMMODATION
Number 30
30 Crescent Gardens BA1 2NB
☎ 01225 337393 📄 01225 337393
e–mail: david.greenwood12@btinternet.com
web: www.numberthirty.com
dir: 0.5m from Queens Sq towards Bristol

This cared-for accommodation is conveniently located just a stroll from
the city centre. The hosts are friendly, attentive and more than happy
to provide useful local information. The freshly prepared breakfast,
featuring home-made preserves and some interesting specials, is
served in the light, pleasant dining room with an original fireplace.
Limited parking is available.

Rooms 3 rms (2 en suite) (1 pri facs) S £65–£90; D £95–£130
Facilities TVB tea/coffee Cen ht Wi-fi available Parking 3 Notes LB
No children 12yrs Closed 18 Dec–24 Jan

CONTINUED

BATH CONTINUED

★★★ GUEST ACCOMMODATION
Devonshire House

143 Wellsway BA2 4RZ
☎ 01225 312495
e–mail: enquiries@devonshire-house.uk.com
web: www.devonshire-house.uk.com

dir: *1m S of city centre. A36 onto A367 Wells Rd & Wellsway*

Located within walking distance of the city centre this charming house maintains its Victorian style. Secure parking is available and the friendly proprietors make every effort to ensure your stay is pleasant and memorable. The attractive bedrooms, some appointed to a high quality standard, have many considerate extras. There is a small lounge area and freshly cooked breakfasts are served in the pleasant dining room.

Rooms 4 en suite (1 fmly) (1 GF) S £42–£63; D £68–£78✱
Facilities TVB tea/coffee Cen ht Wi-fi available **Parking** 6 **Notes LB** ⊗

★★★ GUEST ACCOMMODATION
Brooks Guesthouse

1 & 1A Crescent Gardens, Upper Bristol Rd BA1 2NA
☎ 01225 425543 📠 01225 318147
e–mail: info@brooksguesthouse.com
web: www.brooksguesthouse.com

dir: *On A4, 350yds W of Queens Square, before Royal Victoria Park*

Conveniently located just a few minutes stroll from the centre of Bath, guests here will enjoy the relaxed atmosphere and welcoming hospitality. Bedrooms and bathrooms vary for size but are generally spacious and well decorated. Breakfast is served in the cosy downstairs dining room.

Rooms 21 en suite (5 fmly) (6 GF) S £50–£90; D £60–£130
Facilities STV FTV TVB tea/coffee Cen ht Wi-fi available **Notes LB** ⊗ Closed 25 Dec

★★★ GUEST ACCOMMODATION
Hermitage

Bath Rd SN13 8DT
☎ 01225 744187 📠 01225 743447
e–mail: hermitagebb@btconnect.com
(For full entry see Box (Wiltshire))

★★★ GUEST ACCOMMODATION
Lamp Post Villa

3 Crescent Gardens, Upper Bristol Rd BA1 2NA
☎ 01225 331221
e–mail: lamppostvilla@aol.com

dir: *350yds W of city centre on A4*

Close to the city's attractions, Lamp Post Villa offers comfortable accommodation with good facilities and private parking. There is a lounge and a lower ground-floor dining room, and the freshly cooked breakfasts provide a substantial start to the day.

Rooms 4 en suite (1 fmly) (1 GF) **Facilities** TVB tea/coffee Direct dial from bedrooms Cen ht TVL Wi-fi available **Parking** 4 **Notes** ⊗ No children 6yrs

★★★ GUEST ACCOMMODATION
The Parade Park and Lambrettas Bar

8, 9, 10 North Pde BA2 4AL
☎ 01225 463384 📠 01225 442322
e–mail: info@paradepark.co.uk
web: www.paradepark.co.uk

dir: *In city centre. Off A36 Pulteney Rd onto North Parade Rd & North Parade*

This attractive Georgian property was formerly the home of William Wordsworth. The restored rooms are brightly decorated, and well equipped with modern facilities. Traditional breakfasts are served in the impressive, panelled first-floor dining room. The modern, Lambrettas theme-bar is open to the public.

Rooms 38 rms (32 en suite) (8 fmly) (2 GF) S £40–£55; D £55–£90✱
Facilities TVB tea/coffee Cen ht **Notes LB** ⊗ Closed Xmas

★★★ GUEST ACCOMMODATION
Pulteney House

14 Pulteney Rd BA2 4HA
☎ 01225 460991 📠 01225 460991
e–mail: pulteney@tinyworld.co.uk
web: www.pulteneyhotel.co.uk

dir: *A4 onto A36, 200yds past lights on right hand side*

This large detached property, situated in a colourful garden is within walking distance of the city centre. Bedrooms vary in size including some annexe rooms, and are well equipped with useful facilities. Full

CONTINUED

English breakfasts are served in the dining room at individual tables. A guest lounge and car park are both welcome features.

Rooms 12 rms (11 en suite) (1 pri facs) 5 annexe en suite (6 fmly) (2 GF) S £45–£55; D £70–£120 **Facilities** TVB tea/coffee Cen ht TVL Wi-fi available **Parking** 18 **Notes** LB ⊗

★★★ GUEST HOUSE
Waltons

17–19 Crescent Gardens, Upper Bristol Rd BA1 2NA
☎ 01225 426528 📄 01225 420350
e–mail: rose@waltonsguesthouse.co.uk
web: www.bathguesthouse.com

dir: *On A4 350yds W of city centre*

There is a warm welcome at Waltons, situated within strolling distance of the centre of Bath. The cosy bedrooms come with useful extra facilities, and a traditional English breakfast is served at individual tables in the dining room.

Rooms 7 en suite S £50–£65; D £65–£85 **Facilities** FTV TVB tea/coffee Direct dial from bedrooms Cen ht **Notes** ⊗ ⊜

★★★ 🅰 GUEST ACCOMMODATION
Edgar Townhouse

64 Great Pulteney St BA2 4DN
☎ 01225 420619 📄 01225 466916
e–mail: edgar-hotel@btconnect.com
web: www.edgar-hotel.co.uk

dir: *From A46 on to A4 for 1m. At lights turn left, continue to junct, turn right*

Rooms 18 en suite (3 fmly) S £63–£93; D £78–£93✳ **Facilities** TVB tea/coffee Cen ht TVL Wi-fi available **Notes** LB Closed 24–26 Dec

Ⓤ
One Three Nine

139 Wells Rd BA2 3AL
☎ 01225 314769 📄 01225 443079
e–mail: info@139bath.co.uk

dir: *M4 junct 19 onto A46. A4 towards Bath, then A367 towards Wells and Shepton Mallett. On left 500mtrs up hill*

At the time of going to press the rating for this establishment had not been confirmed. Please check the AA website www.theAA.com for up-to-date information.

Rooms 10 en suite (2 fmly) (2 GF) S £49–£110; D £65–£165✳ **Facilities** FTV TVB tea/coffee Direct dial from bedrooms Cen ht Wi-fi available **Parking** 10 **Notes** ⊗ Closed 24–25 Dec

---

BECKINGTON   MAP 04 ST85

★★★ ⊜ GUEST ACCOMMODATION
Pickford House

23 Bath Rd BA11 6SJ
☎ 01373 830329 📄 01373 830329
e–mail: AmPritchar@aol.com
web: www.pickfordhouse.com

dir: *Off A36 (Little Chef rdbt) signed Beckington, follow road for 300yds to 30mph signs by village hall, turn right then sharp left*

This peacefully located Regency-style house is set in secluded walled gardens. The proprietors are welcoming and attentive, and many guests visit this pleasant house on a regular basis. Dinner is an enjoyable experience with a 'pot luck' menu (unless you require vegetarian or special dietary dishes) and, along with the impressive wine list, provides fine dining.

Rooms 2 rms 3 annexe en suite (2 fmly) (1 GF) **Facilities** TVB tea/coffee Cen ht Dinner Last d 9pm ⤹ **Parking** 15 **Notes** Closed Xmas ⊜

BRIDGWATER   MAP 04 ST23

★★★★ FARM HOUSE
Ash-Wembdon Farm *(ST281382)*

Hollow Ln, Wembdon TA5 2BD
☎ 01278 453097 📄 01278 445856 Mr & Mrs Rowe
e–mail: mary.rowe@btinternet.com
web: www.farmaccommodation.co.uk

dir: *M5, A38, A39 to Minehead, at rdbt 3rd exit Homeburg Way, at lights B3339, right onto Hollow Ln*

Near the Quantock Hills, this is a 17th-century farmhouse on a working beef and arable farm offering homely and comfortable accommodation. All rooms have en suite showers or private bathrooms, and English or Continental breakfasts are served in the guest dining room. Guests also have use of a lounge and landscaped garden.

Rooms 3 rms (2 en suite) (1 pri facs) S £32–£35; D £50–£56 **Facilities** TVB tea/coffee Cen ht Wi-fi available **Parking** 3 **Notes** ⊗ No children 10yrs 340 acres Arable/Beef Closed 22 Dec–3 Jan

ENGLAND

★★★★ GUEST ACCOMMODATION
Model Farm
Perry Green, Wembdon TA5 2BA
☎ 01278 433999
e–mail: info@modelfarm.com
web: www.modelfarm.com

dir: *2.5m NW of Bridgwater. Off junct A39 & B3339 to Perry Green, at T-junct follow sign No Through Road, farm 2nd drive on left*

This extensive Victorian house enjoys a peaceful rural setting and has glorious country views. Guests are assured of a warm welcome and friendly hospitality throughout their stay. Bedrooms are very spacious and include thoughtful touches with a good selection of extras. By arrangement, the proprietors join their guests around the large dining room table for a carefully prepared three-course dinner using fresh local ingredients. A suite of conference rooms is located in the original cider press barn.

Rooms 3 en suite (1 fmly) S fr £42.50; D £75✻ **Facilities** tea/coffee Cen ht TVL Dinner Last d noon **Conf** Max 24 Thtr 24 Board 16 **Parking** 6 **Notes** No children 3yrs

★★★ INN
The Boat & Anchor Inn
Huntworth TA7 0AQ
☎ 01278 662473 📄 01278 662542

dir: *M5 junct 24, 500yds NE to Huntworth, 0.5m N of village across canal bridge*

This popular canal-side inn offers easy access to the M5 and is a useful stopover en route for the West Country. Bedrooms vary in size and style and are situated above the busy bars, where an impressive selection is offered from the blackboard menus.

Rooms 11 en suite (3 fmly) S £55–£65; D £69.50–£85✻ **Facilities** TVB tea/coffee Cen ht Dinner Last d 9pm **Conf** Thtr 80 Class 50 Board 45 **Parking** 100 **Notes LB** ✖ RS Nov–Mar

---

BROMPTON REGIS MAP 03 SS93

★★★★ 🍴 FARM HOUSE
Holworthy Farm *(SS978308)*
TA22 9NY
☎ 01398 371244 📄 01398 371244 Mrs G Payne
e–mail: holworthyfarm@aol.com
web: www.holworthyfarm.co.uk

dir: *2m E of Brompton Regis. Off A396 on E side of Wimbleball Lake*

Set in the south-east corner of Exmoor, this working livestock farm has spectacular views over Wimbleball Lake. Bedrooms are traditionally furnished and well equipped. The dining room overlooking the garden is the attractive setting for breakfast. Dinner is available by arrangement.

Rooms 5 rms (3 en suite) (2 pri facs) (2 fmly) (1 GF) **Facilities** TVB tea/coffee Cen ht TVL Dinner Last d previous evening **Conf** Max 20 **Parking** 8 **Notes** ✖ 200 acres beef/sheep 🍴

★★★ GUEST HOUSE
Bruneton House
TA22 9NN
☎ 01398 371224
e–mail: brunetonhouse@hotmail.com

dir: *Off A396 onto Watchet Rd at Machine Cross, signs for Brompton Regis, establishment 3m at end of churchyard*

The warmest of welcomes will be received at this 17th-century family home in the Exmoor National Park. It provides a true taste of the joys of rural life, as one side of the house operates as the village shop. Bedrooms are spacious and comfortable, and a brightly decorated lounge is available. Wonderful views can be enjoyed from the cottage garden.

Rooms 3 rms (1 en suite) (2 pri facs) S £25–£30; D £50–£60 **Facilities** tea/coffee Cen ht TVL Dinner Last d 5pm **Parking** 4 **Notes** ✖ No coaches Closed Xmas & New Year RS Sep–Etr 🍴

BURNHAM-ON-SEA

MAP 04 ST34

★★★★ GUEST HOUSE
Magnolia House

26 Manor Rd TA8 2AS
☎ 01278 792460 📠 01278 795190
e-mail: enquiries@magnoliahouse.gb.com
web: www.magnoliahouse.gb.com

dir: *M5 junct 22, follow signs to Burnham-on-Sea, at 2nd rdbt, Magnolia House on right*

Within walking distance of the town centre and beach, this elegant Edwardian house has been totally refurbished to an impressive standard. Contemporary bedrooms offer comfort and quality with many extras such as Wi-fi and a large DVD film library. Bathrooms are also modern and stylish with invigorating showers. A family suite is also offered with separate, interconnecting bedrooms. Traditional full English breakfast is served in the attractive, air-conditioned breakfast room with vegetarian and continental options available.

Rooms 4 en suite (2 fmly) S £30–£40; D £55–£60✱ **Facilities** FTV TVB tea/coffee Cen ht Wi-fi available **Parking** 7 **Notes LB** ⊗ No coaches

---

CASTLE CARY

MAP 04 ST63

★★★★ FARM HOUSE
Clanville Manor *(ST618330)*

BA7 7PJ
☎ 01963 350124 & 07966 512732 📠 01963 350719
Mrs S Snook
e-mail: info@clanvillemanor.co.uk
web: www.clanvillemanor.co.uk

dir: *A371 onto B3153, 0.75m entrance to Clanville Manor via white gate & cattle grid under bridge*

Built in 1743, Clanville Manor is situated on a beef-rearing holding, and has been owned by the Snook family since 1898. A polished oak staircase leads up to the individually decorated bedrooms, which retain a great deal of their original charm. Hearty breakfasts are served in the elegant dining room, which looks out over open meadows. There is also a spacious and comfortable sitting room.

Rooms 4 en suite S £32.50–£40; D £65–£80 **Facilities** FTV TVB tea/coffee Cen ht TVL Wi-fi available ⚲ ⚘ **Parking** 6 **Notes LB** ⊗ No children 12yrs 165 acres beef Closed 21 Dec–2 Jan

---

★★★★ ⚑ ⊜ INN
The Pilgrims

Lovington BA7 7PT
☎ 01963 240600
e-mail: jools@thepilgrimsatlovington.co.uk
web: www.thepilgrimsatlovington.co.uk

dir: *On B3153, 1.5m E of lights on A37 at Lydford*

This popular accommodation describes itself as "The pub that thinks it's a restaurant", which is pretty accurate. With a real emphasis on fresh, local and carefully prepared produce, both dinner and breakfast are the focus of any stay here. In addition, the resident family proprietors provide a friendly and relaxed atmosphere. Comfortable and well equipped bedrooms are available in the adjacent converted cider barn.

Rooms 5 annexe en suite (5 GF) D £80–£110✱ **Facilities** TVB tea/coffee Cen ht Dinner Last d 9pm **Parking** 5 **Notes LB** No children 14yrs No coaches RS Sun eve-Tue

---

CATCOTT

MAP 04 ST33

★★★★ GUEST ACCOMMODATION
Honeysuckle

King William Rd TA7 9HU
☎ 01278 722890

dir: *Off A39 to Catcott, pass King William pub, house 200yds on right*

Situated in the village centre, this delightful modern house is a good base for visiting the many attractions in the area. Bedrooms are comfortable, and there is a spacious lounge and a charming garden. Breakfast is served around a communal table in the pleasant dining room.

Rooms 3 rms (1 en suite) S £22; D £54–£60✱ **Facilities** TVB tea/coffee Cen ht **Parking** 3 **Notes** ⊗ No children 7yrs Closed 20 Dec–3 Jan ⊜

CHARD

MAP 04 ST30

Premier Collection

★★★★★ ⊛ ⚑ GUEST ACCOMMODATION
Bellplot House & Thomas's Restaurant

High St TA20 1QB
☎ 01460 62600 📠 01460 62600
e-mail: info@bellplothouse.co.uk
web: www.bellplothouse.co.uk

dir: *In town centre, 500yds from Guildhall*

This grand Georgian property in the centre of town provides stylish accommodation suitable for business and leisure. There is ample parking, and the atmosphere is friendly and relaxed. Bedrooms are well equipped, and the elegant restaurant has an innovative menu. Wi-fi access is available.

Rooms 7 en suite (1 fmly) (2 GF) S £69.50; D £79.50✱ (room only) **Facilities** STV TVB tea/coffee Direct dial from bedrooms Cen ht Dinner Last d 9pm Wi-fi available Pool Table **Conf** Max 20 Thtr 20 Class 20 Board 20 **Parking** 12 **Notes** ⊗

CHARD CONTINUED

★★★ GUEST HOUSE
Watermead

83 High St TA20 1QT
☎ 01460 62834 📠 01460 67448
e–mail: trudy@watermeadguesthouse.co.uk
web: www.watermeadguesthouse.co.uk

dir: *On A30 in town centre*

Guests will feel at home at this family-run house, a smart establishment in a convenient location. Hearty breakfasts are served in the dining room overlooking the garden. Bedrooms are neat, and the spacious, self-contained suite is popular with families. Free Wi-fi access is available.

Rooms 9 rms (6 en suite) 1 annexe en suite (1 fmly) S £29–£50;
D £59–£62✶ **Facilities** TVB tea/coffee Cen ht TVL Wi-fi available
Parking 10 **Notes LB** No coaches

CHEDDAR   MAP 04 ST45

See also Draycott

Premier Collection

★★★★★ 🍴 FARM HOUSE
Batts Farm *(ST462507)*

Nyland BS27 3UD
☎ 01934 741469 Mr & Mrs J Pike
e–mail: clare@batts-farm.co.uk
web: www.batts-farm.co.uk

dir: *A371 from Cheddar towards Wells, 2m right towards Nyland, Batts Farm 1m on left*

Nestled in an idyllic location at the bottom of Nyland Hill, Batts Farm is a 200-year-old property full of character. Its peaceful location overlooks open farmland and the moors at the foot of the Mendips. The spacious bedrooms are decorated and furnished to a high standard and include especially comfortable beds. Guests are welcome to use the relaxing lounge and the summerhouse in the delightful garden. Breakfast includes home-made breads and local jams.

Rooms 3 en suite 1 annexe en suite S £55–£65; D £75–£90✶
Facilities TVB tea/coffee Cen ht TVL **Parking** available **Notes LB** ⊗
No children 12yrs

★★★★ GUEST ACCOMMODATION
Tor Farm

Nyland BS27 3UD
☎ 01934 743710 & 07766 026175 📠 01934 743710
e–mail: info@torfarm.co.uk
web: www.torfarm.co.uk

dir: *A371 from Cheddar towards Wells, after 2m turn right towards Nyland. Tor Farm 1.5m on right*

Tucked away in the Somerset countryside, this attractive, comfortable establishment has many welcome extras, including its own heated swimming pool. The smartly furnished bedrooms, including several on the ground floor, have wonderful views and some have either a private terrace or balcony. Guests can relax in the cosy lounge, or enjoy barbecues in the garden during summer months.

Rooms 8 en suite (2 fmly) (5 GF) **Facilities** TVB tea/coffee Cen ht TVL
Wi-fi available ⏃ **Conf** Class 15 **Parking** 12 **Notes** ⊗

★★★ 🅰 BED & BREAKFAST
Constantine

Lower New Rd BS27 3DY
☎ 01934 741339

dir: *0.5m W of town centre. A371 onto B3151 signed Wedmore, over old railway bridge, Constantine on right opp left turn*

Rooms 4 rms (1 en suite) (1 fmly) S £22–£30; D £45–£50✶
Facilities TVB tea/coffee Cen ht Dinner Last d 2pm **Parking** 5
Notes ⊗ Closed Dec 🖭

CHILTON POLDEN   MAP 04 ST34

★★★★ RESTAURANT WITH ROOMS
The Olive Mill

Bath Rd, Chilton Polden Ridge TA7 9AH
☎ 01278 722202 📠 01278 723327
e–mail: enquiries@theolivemill.co.uk
web: www.theolivemill.co.uk

dir: *M5 junct 23, A39 towards Glastonbury. Mill in 5m on left*

Just five miles from the M5, this popular establishment has a stylish bar and lounge leading down to an atmospheric restaurant specialising in fresh fish and Mediterranean influenced cuisine. In summer the large patio is a great place to enjoy a leisurely meal accompanied by superb views. The modern bedrooms have a separate entrance and all provide

CONTINUED

good levels of comfort with impressive bathrooms. Some rooms have balconies with stunning views across to the Mendip Hills.

Rooms 7 en suite (1 fmly) (1 GF) **Facilities** TVB tea/coffee Lift Cen ht Dinner Last d 9.30pm **Parking** 100 **Notes** ⊗ RS Oct–Apr

See advert on this page

CLUTTON · MAP 04 ST65

★★★★ INN
The Hunters Rest

King Ln, Clutton Hill BS39 5QL
☎ 01761 452303 📠 01761 453308
e–mail: paul@huntersrest.co.uk
web: www.huntersrest.co.uk

dir: Off A37 onto A368 towards Bath, 100yds right onto lane, left at T-junct, inn 0.25m on left

The Hunters Rest was originally built around 1750 as a hunting lodge for the Earl of Warwick. Set in delightful countryside, it is ideally located for Bath, Bristol and Wells. Bedrooms and bathrooms are furnished and equipped to excellent standards, and the ground floor combines the character of a real country inn with an excellent range of home-cooked meals.

Rooms 5 en suite (1 fmly) S £62.50–£79.50; D £87.50–£125✱ **Facilities** TVB tea/coffee Direct dial from bedrooms Cen ht Dinner Last d 9.45pm Wi-fi available **Conf** Max 40 Thtr 40 Class 25 Board 25 **Parking** 90 **Notes LB**

CREWKERNE · MAP 04 ST40

★★★★ BED & BREAKFAST
Greenways

Boozer Pit, Merriott TA16 5PW
☎ 01460 72830
e–mail: wardill.tim.martine@btinternet.com
web: www.martine-wardill.co.uk

dir: 2m N of Crewkerne. Off A356 into Merriott, at N end of village

Quietly located on the Somerset and Dorset borders, Greenways started life some 300 years ago as a cider house. The one bedroom with its large en suite bathroom is in a self-contained adjoining property with a private entrance. Breakfast is served in the pleasant conservatory where guests can also enjoy delicious home-cooked dinners by arrangement.

Rooms 1 en suite (1 GF) S £45; D £60✱ **Facilities** FTV TVB tea/coffee Cen ht Dinner Last d 3pm Wi-fi available Pool Table **Parking** 5 **Notes LB** ⊗ 🐾

★★★ GUEST ACCOMMODATION
Manor Farm

Wayford TA18 8QL
☎ 01460 78865 & 0776 7620031 📠 01460 78865
web: www.manorfarm.biz

dir: B3165 from Crewkerne to Lyme Regis, 3m in Clapton right onto Dunsham Ln, Manor Farm 0.5m up hill on right

Located off the beaten track, this fine Victorian country house has extensive views over Clapton towards the Axe Valley. The comfortably furnished bedrooms are well equipped, and front-facing rooms enjoy splendid views. Breakfast is served at separate tables in the dining room, and a spacious lounge is also provided.

Rooms 4 en suite 1 annexe en suite S £35–£40; D £65–£70✱ **Facilities** STV TV4B tea/coffee Cen ht TVL Fishing Riding **Parking** 14 **Notes** ⊗ 🐾

★★★ INN
The George
Market Square TA18 7LP
☎ 01460 73650 🖶 01460 72974
e–mail: georgecrewkerne@btconnect.com
web: www.thegeorgehotelcrewkerne.co.uk

dir: *In town centre on A30*

Situated in the heart of town, this welcoming inn has been providing rest and sustenance to travellers for over 400 years. The atmosphere is warm and inviting with the bar being the focal point for a natter and a satisfying pint. Comfortable bedrooms are traditionally styled and include four poster rooms. A choice of menus is available, served either in the bar or attractive restaurant.

Rooms 13 rms (8 en suite) (2 pri facs) (2 fmly) S £30–£100;
D £65–£150✳ **Facilities** FTV TVB tea/coffee Direct dial from bedrooms
Cen ht TVL Dinner Last d 9pm George Suite has a hydro-therapy spa bath
Conf Max 100 Thtr 100 Class 100 Board 50 **Notes LB**

★★★ INN
The Old Stagecoach Inn
Station Rd TA18 8AL
☎ 01460 72972 🖶 01460 77023
e–mail: info@stagecoach-inn.co.uk
web: www.stagecoach-inn.co.uk

dir: *1m from town centre next to station*

Well located for the railway station, and just a short walk from the centre of town, this relaxing inn provides informal and welcoming accommodation. Rooms are located around a rear courtyard, motel style. The proprietors are from Belgium, and offer a fine selection of beers and cuisine from their home country.

Rooms 13 annexe en suite (3 fmly) (13 GF) **Facilities** TVB tea/coffee
Direct dial from bedrooms Cen ht Dinner Last d 9.30pm **Conf** Max 25
Parking 25 **Notes** ⊗

Ⓤ
Manor Arms
Middle St, North Perrott TA18 7SG
☎ 01460 72901 🖶 01460 74055
e–mail: manorarmshotel@btconnect.com

dir: *In village on A3066*

At the time of going to press the rating for this establishment had not been confirmed. Please check the AA website www.theAA.com for up-to-date information.

Rooms 8 rms (6 en suite) (1 fmly) (3 GF) S £48–£60; D £60–£98✳
Facilities TVB tea/coffee Cen ht Dinner Last d 9pm **Conf** Max 18
Thtr 20 Class 15 Board 15 **Parking** 20 **Notes LB** ⊗ Closed 25–26 Dec

★★★ INN
Bull Terrier
BA5 3QJ
☎ 01749 343658
e–mail: barry.vidler@bullterrierpub.co.uk

dir: *On A371 by village cross*

Located in the centre of the village, this attractive country inn has a relaxed and friendly atmosphere. The public areas are particularly enjoyable, as the character of the inn has been retained with the flagstone floors and inglenook fireplace. Bedrooms are brightly decorated and well equipped. Freshly prepared lunches and dinners are available.

Rooms 2 en suite S £30–£35; D £55–£65✳ **Facilities** TVB tea/coffee
Cen ht Dinner Last d 9pm **Conf** Max 16 **Parking** 3 **Notes** ⊗
No children 10yrs RS Oct–Mar

★★★★ FARM HOUSE
Crapnell Farm *(ST597457)*
BA5 3HG
☎ 01749 342683 🖶 01749 342683 Mrs P J Keen
e–mail: pamkeen@yahoo.com

dir: *A371 from Shepton Mallet to Wells, after Croscombe right to Dinder, sharp right before village, Crapnell Farm 1.5m*

This charming farmhouse is thought to date from the 17th century. It provides attractive accommodation that includes a family bedroom. Breakfast is served in the dining room, which is equipped with period furniture, either at a communal or separate table. There is also a comfortable lounge, where log fires burn in the inglenook fireplace during cold weather. A very homely and comfortable establishment.

Rooms 3 en suite (1 fmly) **Facilities** TVB tea/coffee Cen ht TVL 3/4 size
snooker table, Splash pool **Parking** 8 **Notes** ⊗ Closed 18 Dec–3 Jan ⊛

DRAYCOTT   MAP 04 ST45

★★★★ GUEST ACCOMMODATION
Oakland House

Wells Rd BS27 3SU
☎ 01934 744195 📄 01934 744195
e–mail: enquiries@oakland-house.co.uk
web: www.oakland-house.co.uk

dir: *Off A371 at S end of village*

Situated a short distance from Cheddar, this friendly home provides comfortable and spacious accommodation. There are splendid views of the Somerset moors and Glastonbury Tor from the sun lounge and the well-appointed and attractive bedrooms. Dinner features fresh fruit and vegetables from the garden.

Rooms 3 en suite (1 fmly) S fr £40; D £65–£100 **Facilities** STV TVB tea/coffee Cen ht TVL Dinner Last d 24 hrs notice Pool Table **Parking** 6 **Notes** LB ⊗ 🐾

DULVERTON   MAP 03 SS92

See also Winsford

Premier Collection

★★★★★ 🏵 INN
Tarr Farm Inn

Tarr Steps, Exmoor National Park TA22 9PY
☎ 01643 851507 📄 01643 851111
e–mail: enquiries@tarrfarm.co.uk
web: www.tarrfarm.co.uk

dir: *4m NW of Dulverton. Off B3223 signed Tarr Steps, signs to Tarr Farm Inn*

Tarr Farm, dating from the 16th century, nestles on the lower slopes of Exmoor overlooking the famous old clapper bridge, Tarr Steps. The majority of rooms are in the bedroom block that provides very stylish and comfortable accommodation with an impressive selection of thoughtful touches. Tarr Farm Inn, with much character and traditional charm, draws the crowds for cream teas and delicious dinners which are prepared from good local produce.

Tarr Farm Inn

Rooms 9 en suite (4 GF) D fr £150✳ **Facilities** STV TVB tea/coffee Direct dial from bedrooms Cen ht Dinner Last d 9.30pm Wi-fi available Fishing Riding **Conf** Max 18 **Parking** 10 **Notes** LB No children 14yrs No coaches

★★★★ GUEST ACCOMMODATION
Threadneedle

EX16 9JH
☎ 01398 341598
e–mail: stay@threadneedlecottage.co.uk
web: www.threadneedlecottage.co.uk

dir: *On Devon/Somerset border just off B3227 between Oldways End & East Anstey*

Situated on the edge of Exmoor near Dulverton, Threadneedle is built in the style of a Devon longhouse. The spacious, well-appointed family home offers comfortable, en suite accommodation. Traditional West Country dishes are served, by arrangement, in the light airy dining room, which overlooks the garden and surrounding countryside.

Rooms 2 en suite (1 fmly) D £70–£80✳ **Facilities** FTV TVB tea/coffee Cen ht Dinner Last d 9am **Parking** 12 **Notes** LB 🐾

DUNSTER   MAP 03 SS94

★★★★ BED & BREAKFAST
Buttercross

36 Saint Georges St TA24 6RS
☎ 01643 821413
e–mail: info@buttercrossdunster.co.uk

dir: *Off A39 into Dunster, right after lights onto Saint Georges St, pass school and church, last white house on right*

Quietly situated on the edge of the village, this pleasant family home is just a short walk from Dunster Castle and the other interesting sights that the village has to offer. The spacious accommodation is smart, well equipped and has lovely views. A hearty cooked breakfast featuring local produce will certainly set guests up for the day.

Rooms 1 en suite (1 fmly) S £27.50–£30; D £55–£60✳ **Facilities** FTV TVB tea/coffee Cen ht **Parking** 2 **Notes** LB No children 5yrs Closed 21 Dec–4 Jan 🐾

CONTINUED

DUNSTER CONTINUED

★★★ 🏠 BED & BREAKFAST
Higher Orchard

30 Saint Georges St TA24 6RS

☎ 01643 821915

e–mail: lamacraft@higherorchard.fsnet.co.uk

web: www.higherorchard.fsnet.co.uk

dir: *In village. Off A396 Church St onto Saint Georges St*

Set in a fascinating historic village, this charming Victorian house has fine views over the church and castle. Guests can relax in the gardens surrounding the house or in the lounge. Breakfast is a selection of local produce, home-made marmalade, and eggs from the proprietor's own poultry.

Rooms 2 rms (1 en suite) (1 pri facs) S £35; D £60✳ **Facilities** TVB tea/coffee Cen ht **Parking** 2 **Notes** No children 10yrs Closed Xmas-New Year 🐾

EAST HARPTREE   MAP 04 ST55

Premier Collection

★★★★★ 🏠 🍴 GUEST ACCOMMODATION
Harptree Court

BS40 6AA

☎ 01761 221729

e–mail: location.harptree@tiscali.co.uk

dir: *From A368 take B3114 for Chewton Mendip. After 0.5m turn right into drive entrance, turn left at top of drive*

Harptree Court is a luxurious Georgian mansion set in 17 acres of grounds, peacefully located on the edge of the village. The resident proprietors are the third generation of owners from the same family, and ensure guests are very well looked after. Breakfast utilises fresh, local produce and dinner (available by prior arrangement) should not be missed.

Rooms 3 rms (2 en suite) (1 pri facs) S £65–£75; D £85–£110 **Facilities** TVB tea/coffee Cen ht TVL Dinner Last d 10am 🛏 🥄 **Conf** Max 20 Thtr 20 Class 20 Board 14 **Parking** 10 **Notes** ⊗ No children 12yrs Closed 23 Dec–Jan

FARMBOROUGH   MAP 04 ST66

★★★★ BED & BREAKFAST
School Cottages Bed & Breakfast

The Street, near Bath BA2 0AR

☎ 01761 471167

e–mail: tim@schoolcottages.co.uk

web: www.schoolcottages.co.uk

dir: *Off A39 in Farmborough onto The Street, 1st left opp village school*

This lovingly restored country house is conveniently located to the south-west of Bath in the pretty Somerset village of Farmborough. Contemporary, stylish bedrooms are equipped with Wi-fi, while excellent bathrooms may include a power shower or a spa bath. Homemade jams and freshly-laid eggs add to delicious breakfasts served in a charming conservatory overlooking the garden.

Rooms 3 en suite D fr £65✳ **Facilities** TVB tea/coffee Cen ht Wi-fi available **Parking** 3 **Notes** LB ⊗ 🐾

FITZHEAD   MAP 03 ST12

★★★★ INN
Fitzhead Inn

TA4 3JP

☎ 01823 400667

web: www.fitzheadinn.co.uk

dir: *Off A3065 Taunton to Wiveliscombe road just after Preston Bowyer*

Located in the village of Fitzhead and brimming with character, this delightful inn has a wealth of exposed beams and an inviting log fire.

CONTINUED

The charming bedrooms are in a converted barn and have modern facilities. Delicious lunches and dinners are served in the cosy bar.

Rooms 6 en suite (1 fmly) (3 GF) **Facilities** TVB tea/coffee Cen ht Dinner Last d 9.15pm **Notes** No coaches

---

FROME   MAP 04 ST74

Premier Collection

★★★★★ BED & BREAKFAST
Lullington House

Lullington BA11 2PG
☎ 01373 831406 📠 01373 831406
e–mail: info@lullingtonhouse.co.uk
web: www.lullingtonhouse.co.uk
dir: *2.5m N of Frome. Off A36 into Lullington*

Built in 1866 as a rectory, this quintessentially English stone country house stands in extensive grounds and gardens which convey an air of peace, quiet and tranquillity. The luxurious large bedrooms, some with four-poster beds, are decorated to high standards using beautiful fabrics, fine antique furniture and many extras such as Wi-fi, decanters of sherry, fresh flowers and well-stocked beverage trays. Breakfast is served in the impressive dining room with an excellent selection of dishes available.

Rooms 3 en suite S £70–£100; D £80–£120✱ **Facilities** FTV TVB tea/coffee Cen ht **Parking** 4 **Notes** ⊗ No children Closed Xmas & New Year 🐾

★★★★ INN
The Lamb Inn

1 Christchurch St East BA11 1QA
☎ 01373 472042
e–mail: info@thelambinnfrome.co.uk

Located at the top of the hill above the pleasant town of Frome, The Lamb Inn has undergone a major refurbishment programme. A selection of seven bedrooms and bathrooms of varying shapes and sizes is available, and all have been completed to a high standard of quality and comfort. The inn is owned by the Blindmans Brewery and as might be expected, an excellent selection of real ales is served in the modern bar. A range of dishes including homemade pies is also available.

Rooms 7 en suite (3 fmly) **Facilities** FTV TVB tea/coffee Direct dial from bedrooms Cen ht Dinner Last d 9pm Wi-fi available **Conf** Max 30 Class 30 Board 30 **Parking** 12 **Notes** ⊗ No coaches

★★★ INN
Fox & Hounds

Bulls Quarry Rd, Tytherington BA11 5BN
☎ 01373 473902
dir: *From Town Centre, up Bath Rd to A361, left at rdbt, turn right, on left*

This traditional inn is convenient for the countryside and within driving distance of Wells, Glastonbury and Longleat. Bedrooms are of individual size and style and are located at first floor level adjoining the bar/restaurant. Lunch and dinner are available, offering a good selection of freshly prepared dishes. The beer garden is the place to enjoy a long cool drink during the summer months.

Rooms 4 annexe en suite (1 fmly) **Facilities** TVB tea/coffee Dinner Last d 9pm **Parking** 25 **Notes** ⊗ Closed 25 Dec

★★★ FARM HOUSE
Brookover Farm *(ST775514)*

Orchardleigh BA11 2PH
☎ 01373 462806 Mr & Mrs Collingwood
e–mail: gcollingwood@btinternet.com
dir: *2m from Frome on A362, straight over x-rds and continue for 400yds, turn right, past farm buildings, 200yds on left*

This farmhouse has plenty of character and a homely, friendly environment. It is ideally placed for visiting the attractions of Somerset and Wiltshire and is within easy reach of Longleat. Bedrooms vary in size and are well equipped. A traditional cooked (or continental) breakfast is served in the cosy dining room where a log fire burns during colder months. For horse lovers, there is a riding school just next door.

Rooms 3 rms (2 en suite) (1 pri facs) (2 fmly) **Facilities** FTV TVB tea/coffee Cen ht Golf 18 **Notes** ⊗ 38 acres Arable/Horses

Ⓤ
The Blue Boar

15 Market Place BA11 1AN
☎ 01373 461530
dir: *Take A36 from Bath, follow signs for Frome town centre. Premises next to Woolworths*

At the time of going to press the rating for this establishment had not been confirmed. Please check the AA website www.theAA.com for up-to-date information.

Rooms 3 en suite (1 smoking) S £40–£50; D £50–£70✱ **Facilities** TVB tea/coffee Cen ht Pool Table **Parking** 4 **Notes** ⊗ No children 14yrs

FROME CONTINUED

The Place To Stay

Knoll Hill Farm, Trudoxhill BA11 5DP

☎ 01373 836266

web: www.theplacetostayuk.com

dir: *From Frome on A361 towards Shepton Mallet. Turn left for Trudoxhill, Knoll Hill Farm on left*

At the time of going to press the rating for this establishment had not been confirmed. Please check the AA website www.theAA.com for up-to-date information.

Rooms 5 annexe en suite (1 fmly) (5 GF) D £85–£125✱ **Facilities** TVB tea/coffee Cen ht Wi-fi available **Parking** 10 **Notes** ⊗ No children 12yrs ⊜

GLASTONBURY   MAP 04 ST53

See also Catcott & Somerton

★★★★ BED & BREAKFAST
Parsnips B&B

99 Bere Ln BA6 8BE

☎ 01458 835599

e–mail: parsnips.glastonbury@virgin.net

dir: *Opp Rural Life Museum at junct Bere Ln & Chilkwell St*

Located just a short walk from the town centre and near to the Tor, this accommodation is fresh, light and airy. Bedrooms are cosy, well equipped and attractively presented. There is a comfortable lounge for guest use and the hosts extend a warm, friendly welcome. Freshly prepared breakfast is served in the conservatory dining room. There is a pleasant garden with a seating area for relaxing during those warmer months.

Rooms 3 en suite S £45–£50; D £65–£70✱ **Facilities** TVB tea/coffee Cen ht **Parking** 3 **Notes** ⊗ ⊜

★★★★ BED & BREAKFAST
Wearyall Hill House

78 The Roman Way BA6 8AD

☎ 01458 835510

e–mail: enquiries@wearyallhillhouse.co.uk

dir: *0.5m SW of town centre. A39 rdbt towards Street, pass B&Q on right, left onto Roman Way*

Set on an elevated position on the edge of town, and close to places of interest, this delightful late Victorian residence affords sweeping views. Restored to its former glory by the present owners, the property is appropriately decorated and furnished with many extra facilities. The sumptuous breakfasts served in the attractive dining room are a highlight.

Rooms 3 en suite **Facilities** STV TVB tea/coffee Cen ht **Parking** 8 **Notes** ⊗ No children 10yrs ⊜

★★★ BED & BREAKFAST
Greenacres

Barrow Ln, North Wootton BA4 4HL

☎ 01749 890497

dir: *4m NE of Glastonbury. Off A39 at Browns garden centre, follow campsite signs. Or off A361 at Steanbow, follow campsite signs*

Quietly located within sight of Glastonbury Tor, this friendly home offers pleasant accommodation. The bright and comfortable bedrooms share adjacent bath and shower. A separate lounge is provided. Breakfast is served in the conservatory and there is a well-tended garden.

Rooms 2 rms D £55✱ **Facilities** TVB tea/coffee Cen ht TVL **Parking** 4 **Notes** ⊗ No children Closed end Sep–Mar ⊜

★★★ FARM HOUSE
Cradlebridge *(ST477385)*

BA16 9SD

☎ 01458 831827 Mrs J Tinney

dir: *A39 S from Glastonbury, after Morlands factory 2nd right signed Meare, Wedmore, Cradlebridge Farm signed 1m on left*

Cradlebridge is part of a 200-acre dairy farm with pleasant views over the Somerset Levels. The relaxing farmhouse offers spacious bedrooms, which have French doors that allow greater appreciation of the tranquil surroundings. A full English breakfast is served around a communal table in the dining room.

Rooms 2 en suite (2 fmly) (2 GF) S £35; D £60✱ **Facilities** TVB tea/coffee Cen ht **Parking** 6 **Notes** ⊗ No children 5yrs 200 acres dairy ⊜

★★★ GUEST HOUSE
No 1 Park Terrace

Street Rd BA6 9EA

☎ 01458 835845 📄 01458 833296

e–mail: info@no1parkterrace.co.uk

dir: *From High St, onto Magdalene St. At mini rdbt turn right, 100mtrs on right*

A spacious and charming Victorian guest house located within walking distance of the High Street and ruins, close to the centre of Glastonbury. The fully licensed restaurant provides a Spanish influenced menu. The proprietors are friendly and welcoming; bedrooms are bright and airy with singles available. Limited car parking.

Rooms 5 rms (2 en suite) (1 pri facs) S fr £35; D fr £70✱ **Facilities** TVB tea/coffee Licensed Cen ht Dinner Last d 9pm Wi-fi available **Conf** Max 20 **Parking** 5 **Notes** LB ⊗ No coaches

★★★ GUEST ACCOMMODATION
The Priestess House at Pilgrims B & B
12/13 Norbins Rd BA6 9JE
☎ 01458 834722
e–mail: pilgrimsbb@hotmail.com
web: www.pilgrimsbb.co.uk

dir: *In town centre. From St John's Church on High St onto Archers Way, left onto St Edmunds Rd, right onto Norbins Rd*

Just a short walk from the town centre, this comfortable accommodation has two rooms on the ground floor. Breakfast is served around one large table in the kitchen-dining room. There is also a lounge and a small garden to relax in during warm weather. Guests are invited to enjoy the homely environment.

Rooms 4 rms (3 en suite) (1 fmly) (2 GF) S £30–£40; D £55–£65✶
Facilities tea/coffee Cen ht TVL Wi-fi available **Notes** LB ⊗ ⊚

★★ BED & BREAKFAST
25 Leg of Mutton Road
BA6 8HH
☎ 01458 831886
e–mail: ammonmarie@yahoo.co.uk

dir: *At top of High St turn left onto Wells Rd. Take 2nd right, B&B is on the right*

Located in a quiet residential area, this homely accommodation with a single and twin bedded rooms is well situated for touring Somerset and Wiltshire. The atmosphere is relaxed and the host is friendly and welcoming, guests are invited to share the cosy lounge. A healthy cooked breakfast with homemade preserves and many organic ingredients is served in the kitchen/dining room around a communal table. On-street parking is always available.

Rooms 2 rms **Facilities** tea/coffee Cen ht **Notes** ⊗ No children 10yrs ⊚

HIGHBRIDGE   MAP 04 ST34

★★★★ GUEST ACCOMMODATION
Greenwood Lodge
76 Main Rd, West Huntspill TA9 3QU
☎ 01278 795886 📄 01278 795886
e–mail: info@greenwood-lodge.co.uk
web: www.greenwood-lodge.co.uk

dir: *On A38 in West Huntspill village, between Orchard Inn & Sundowner Hotel*

Set in two acres of land, this 18th-century former farmhouse and family home offers comfortable accommodation in a friendly environment. Breakfast, featuring home-made preserves, is served in the dining room and home-cooked dinners are available by arrangement. There is a lounge for relaxation and the family dog adds to the welcome.

Greenwood Lodge

Rooms 7 rms (6 en suite) (1 pri facs) (3 fmly) (1 GF) S £47.50; D £68✶
Facilities TVB tea/coffee Cen ht TVL Dinner Last d 6pm Wi-fi available Treatment room **Conf** Max 30 Thtr 30 Class 20 Board 12 Del from £77.50✶ **Parking** 8 **Notes** LB

ILCHESTER   MAP 04 ST52

★★★★ BED & BREAKFAST
Liongate House B&B
Liongate House, Northover BA22 8NG
☎ 01935 841741
e–mail: marlene@liongatehouse.com

dir: *0.5m from A303 junct signed to Ilchester, opposite Texaco garage*

These former stables have been developed to provide light and airy, contemporary-style accommodation. Bedrooms, one located at ground floor level, are individually designed, but each is comfortable and equipped with many considerate extras, including fresh flowers and fruit. Bathrooms are fresh and a pleasure to use. Breakfast is served in the lounge/dining room around a communal table.

Rooms 3 en suite (1 fmly) (1 GF) **Facilities** FTV TVB tea/coffee Cen ht TVL **Parking** 3 **Notes** Closed 23 Dec–21 Jan

ILMINSTER   MAP 04 ST31

Ⓤ
The New Inn
Dowlish Wake TA19 0NZ
☎ 01460 52413
e–mail: newinn-ilminster@tiscali.co.uk

dir: *A358 or A303, follow signs for Perry's Cider, well-signed in village*

At the time of going to press the rating for this establishment had not been confirmed. Please check the AA website www.theAA.com for up-to-date information.

Rooms 4 annexe en suite (4 GF) S £50–£70; D £60–£80 **Facilities** FTV TVB tea/coffee Cen ht Dinner Last d 8.30pm **Parking** 20 **Notes** LB

CONTINUED

ENGLAND

KEYNSHAM · MAP 04 ST66

★★★★ GUEST HOUSE
Grasmere Court
22–24 Bath Rd BS31 1SN
☎ 0117 986 2662 📠 0117 986 2762
e–mail: grasmerecourt@aol.com
web: www.grasmerecourthotel.co.uk

dir: *On B3116 just off A4*

This very friendly, family-run establishment is located between Bath and Bristol. Bedrooms vary in size and one has a four-poster bed. A comfortable lounge and a well-stocked bar are available, and good-value, freshly prepared food is served in the attractive dining room.

Rooms 16 en suite (2 fmly) (4 GF) **Facilities** STV TVB tea/coffee Direct dial from bedrooms Licensed Cen ht TVL Dinner Last d 7.45pm **Conf** Max 30 Thtr 30 Class 20 Board 20 **Parking** 18 **Notes** ⊗ No coaches

KILVE · MAP 03 ST14

★★★★ INN
Hood Arms Inn
TA5 1EA
☎ 01278 741210 📠 01278 741477
e–mail: enquiries@thehoodarms.com

dir: *12m W of Bridgwater on A39, halfway between Bridgwater & Minehead*

Located in the village of Kilve, this popular 17th-century inn offers well-equipped bedrooms with a good range of facilities. A selection of tasty dishes is available on the blackboard menus in the beamed bars.

Rooms 8 en suite 4 annexe en suite (4 fmly) (2 GF) S £49–£65; D £72–£85✳ **Facilities** TVB tea/coffee Direct dial from bedrooms Cen ht TVL Dinner Last d 9.15pm Wi-fi available **Conf** Max 20 Class 20 Board 16 Del from £70 ✳ **Parking** 12 **Notes** LB

LANGPORT · MAP 04 ST42

★★★ INN
The Old Pound Inn
Aller TA10 0RA
☎ 01458 250469
e–mail: oldpoundinn@btconnect.com
web: www.oldpoundinn.co.uk

dir: *On A372 in village centre*

Situated in the heart of a charming village, just two miles from Langport, this popular inn was once a cider house, and dates back to 1571. Its long tradition of hospitality continues with a convivial and welcoming atmosphere to both locals and visitors alike. Bedrooms are soundly appointed and include a four-poster room and connecting family room. Public areas include the traditional bar, together with a 'snug' and a la carte restaurant. There is also a skittle alley for those who fancy some competition with their pint.

Rooms 8 en suite (2 fmly) **Facilities** TVB tea/coffee Cen ht Dinner Last d 9pm Pool Table **Conf** Max 90 Thtr 90 Class 90 Board 90 **Parking** 15 **Notes** ⊗

LOWER VOBSTER · MAP 04 ST74

★★★★ ⊛ INN
The Vobster Inn
BA3 5RJ
☎ 01373 812920 📠 01373 812920
e–mail: rdavila@btinternet.com

dir: *From A361 follow signs for Whatley & Mells, then Vobster*

Peacefully located in four acres of Somerset countryside, this is the ideal village inn with a real sense of personal attention and a genuine welcome from the resident proprietors. Bedrooms and bathrooms provide high levels of quality and comfort. Dinner places an emphasis on high quality, simply prepared dishes with regular seasonal changes, and includes several dishes demonstrating the Spanish heritage of the chef proprietor.

Rooms 3 annexe en suite (1 fmly) (3 GF) S £55–£85; D £65–£95✳ **Facilities** FTV TVB tea/coffee Cen ht Dinner Last d 9.30pm Petanque **Conf** Max 40 Thtr 25 Class 32 Board 32 **Parking** 60 **Notes** LB ⊗

MARTOCK · MAP 04 ST41

★★★★ BED & BREAKFAST
Higher Farm
Bladon Hill, Kingsbury Episcopi TA12 6BJ
☎ 01935 823099
e–mail: boltonali@aol.com

dir: *2m NW of Martock. Off B3165 to Kingsbury Episcopi, left at Wyndham Arms, farm on right*

Located in the scenic village of Kingsbury Episcopi, Higher Farm provides comfortable accommodation with a relaxed and friendly atmosphere. Breakfast is served in the pleasant dining room, which opens onto the rear garden and patio. Two pubs serving evening meals are just a 5-minute walk in either direction.

CONTINUED

Higher Farm

Rooms 2 en suite (2 fmly) S £35; D £55–£70✳ **Facilities** TVB tea/coffee Cen ht **Parking** 6 **Notes** ⊗ ⊜

MINEHEAD MAP 03 SS94

See also Dunster

★★★★ GUEST HOUSE
Glendower House
30–32 Tregonwell Rd TA24 5DU
☎ 01643 707144 📠 01643 708719
e–mail: info@glendower-house.co.uk
web: www.glendower-house.co.uk

dir: *A39 into Minehead, last exit at mini-rdbt, 200yds right by school onto Ponsford Rd & Tregonwell Rd*

The family-run Glendower House is near the seafront, harbour and town centre. A friendly atmosphere prevails, and there are comfortable bedrooms and smart bathrooms. Public areas are spacious and guests can relax in the garden in the summer. Ample parking is a bonus.

Rooms 11 en suite (2 GF) S £35–£50; D £60–£80✳ **Facilities** TVB tea/coffee Cen ht **Parking** 14 **Notes** ⊗ No coaches Closed mid Dec–Feb

★★★★ GUEST ACCOMMODATION
Kenella House
7 Tregonwell Rd TA24 5DT
☎ 01643 703128 & 07710 889079 📠 01643 703128
e–mail: kenellahouse@fsmail.net
web: www.kenellahouse.co.uk

dir: *Off A39 onto Townsend Rd & right onto Ponsford Rd & Tregonwell Rd*

A warm welcome and relaxed atmosphere are found at Kenella House. Located close to the town centre, the guest house is also convenient for walkers (heated boot cupboard available) and visitors to the steam railway. The well-maintained bedrooms are very comfortable and have many extras. Home-cooked dinners, available by arrangement, and hearty breakfasts are served in the smart dining room.

Rooms 6 en suite (1 GF) D £60–£70✳ **Facilities** TVB tea/coffee Cen ht Dinner Last d am same day **Parking** 8 **Notes** LB ⊗ No children 14yrs Closed 23 Dec–2 Jan ⊜

NETHER STOWEY MAP 04 ST13

★★★★★ ⊜ GUEST ACCOMMODATION
Castle of Comfort Country House
TA5 1LE
☎ 01278 741264 📠 01278 741144
e–mail: reception@castle-of-comfort.co.uk
web: www.castle-of-comfort.co.uk

dir: *On A39 1.3m W of Nether Stowey on left*

Dating in part from the 16th century, this former inn is situated beside the A39 on the northern slopes of the Quantock Hills in an Area of Outstanding Natural Beauty. Bedrooms and bathrooms are well equipped, and the public rooms are smart and comfortable. The delightful gardens and a heated swimming pool are available to guests in the summer. An imaginative choice of dishes, using good local produce, is offered at dinner.

Rooms 5 en suite 1 annexe en suite (2 fmly) (1 GF) S £42–£92; D £104–£142✳ **Facilities** TVB tea/coffee Direct dial from bedrooms Cen ht Dinner Last d 8pm ⋏ Stabling with access to bridle paths **Conf** Max 20 Thtr 20 Class 20 Board 12 Del from £70 ✳ **Parking** 10 **Notes** LB Closed 24 Dec–2 Jan

---

NORTH CURRY MAP 04 ST32

★★★★ ⊜ BED & BREAKFAST
Helland House
Helland TA3 6DU
☎ 01823 490003
e–mail: gillvlasto@yahoo.co.uk

This elegant Georgian home has been newly refurbished to provide accommodation of style and quality. Peacefully located in an idyllic rural location, the house is close to the village of North Curry with its local amenities and popular pub. Bedrooms combine comfort and charm with excellent modern bathrooms, and a guest lounge is also available. Breakfast is a leisurely treat and can be served outside when the sun shines. Dinner also comes highly recommended and utilises local organic produce.

Rooms 2 en suite (2 fmly) S £40; D £75✳ **Facilities** FTV TVB tea/coffee Cen ht Dinner Last d noon Wi-fi available **Notes** ⊗ ⊜

ENGLAND

NORTH WOOTTON   MAP 04 ST54

★★★ GUEST ACCOMMODATION
Crossways

Stocks Ln BA4 4EU

☎ 01749 899000 📄 01749 890476

e–mail: enquiries@thecrossways.co.uk

dir: *Exit M5 junct 22 towards Shepton Mallet, 0.2m from Pilton*

Family run and tucked away in a quiet lane, yet with easy access to Wells, Glastonbury and other interesting areas of Wiltshire and Somerset. The rooms are spacious and there is a large bar-restaurant and a smaller dining room where breakfast is served. The extensive menu features many home-cooked dishes.

Rooms 21 en suite (4 fmly) **Facilities** TVB tea/coffee Cen ht Dinner Last d 9pm Pool Table **Conf** Max 40 Thtr 40 Class 40 Board 25 **Parking** available **Notes** ⊗ Closed 25 Dec RS 26 Dec–2 Jan Civ Wed 100

PORLOCK   MAP 03 SS84

★★★★ RESTAURANT WITH ROOMS
Andrews on the Weir

Porlock Weir TA24 8PB

☎ 01643 863300 📄 01643 863311

e–mail: info@andrewsontheweir.co.uk

web: www.andrewsontheweir.co.uk

dir: *Off A39 in Porlock signed Harbour, Porlock Weir 1.5m*

Enjoying a delightful elevated position overlooking Porlock Bay, Andrews on the Weir is furnished and decorated in country house style. Bedrooms are spacious and comfortable, and one room boasts a four-poster bed. The sitting room/bar is elegant and a log fire creates a cosy atmosphere.

Rooms 5 en suite S £75–£135; D £100–£180✳ **Facilities** TVB tea/coffee Cen ht Dinner Last d 2.30pm **Parking** 6 **Notes** LB No children 12yrs Closed Dec 22–Jan 2 & Mon–Tue

★★★★ BED & BREAKFAST
The Cottage

High St TA24 8PU

☎ 01643 862996 📄 01643 862996

e–mail: cottageporlock@aol.com

web: www.cottageporlock.co.uk

dir: *In village centre on A39*

One of the oldest local houses, The Cottage is located right in the heart of this ancient village, ideally placed to explore Exmoor and walk the South West coastal path. Bedrooms are well equipped and there is a comfortable lounge solely for guest use. Breakfast is served in the pleasant dining room at the front of the house.

Rooms 3 en suite (1 fmly) **Facilities** TVB tea/coffee Cen ht Dinner Last d 10am **Parking** 2 **Notes** ⊗ Closed Nov–Jan

RUDGE   MAP 04 ST85

★★★★ 🍺 INN
The Full Moon Inn

BA11 2QF

☎ 01373 830936

e–mail: info@thefullmoon.co.uk

dir: *A36 S from Bath 10m, turn left at Standerwick beside The Bell pub. 1m from Warminster*

Peacefully located in the quiet village of Rudge, this traditional inn offers a warm welcome and a proper country pub atmosphere. In the bar area, guests mix well with the locals to enjoy a selection of real ales and a log fire in the colder months. In addition to bar meals, a comfortable restaurant serving excellent home cooked dishes is also available. Bedrooms include some at the main inn and more in an adjacent annexe – all are comfortable and well equipped.

Rooms 5 en suite 11 annexe en suite (1 fmly) (2 GF) **Facilities** TVB tea/coffee Cen ht Dinner Last d 9pm 🔆 **Conf** Max 65 Thtr 30 Class 12 Board 18 **Parking** 25

SALTFORD

MAP 04 ST66

★★★★ BED & BREAKFAST

The White House

2 Beech Rd BS31 3BE

☎ 01225 872167

e–mail: white-house@blueyonder.co.uk

web: www.white-house.pwp.blueyonder.co.uk

dir: *50mtrs from A4 in centre of village by Saltford Motors*

Located just off the A4 to Bath, this modern, detached house has been appointed to a very high standard, and provides high quality bedrooms and bathrooms. Guests receive a friendly welcome ensuring a relaxed stay. A number of inns and restaurants are all within easy walking distance.

Rooms 4 en suite (2 fmly) S £50–£60; D £65✳ **Facilities** TVB tea/coffee Cen ht Wi-fi available Golf 18 **Parking** 5 **Notes** ⊗

SHEPTON MALLET

MAP 04 ST64

★★★★ GUEST ACCOMMODATION

Cannards Grave Farmhouse

Cannards Grave BA4 4LY

☎ 01749 347091 🗎 01749 347091

e–mail: sue@cannardsgravefarmhouse.co.uk

web: www.cannardsgravefarmhouse.co.uk

dir: *On A37 between Shepton Mallet & The Bath & West Showground, 100yds from Highwayman pub towards showground on left*

Conveniently located for the Bath and West showground, Longleat, Glastonbury and Wells, this 17th-century house provides thoughtfully equipped en suite bedrooms. There is also a well-furnished lounge. The proprietors offer warm hospitality. Breakfast is served in the conservatory dining room.

Rooms 5 en suite (2 fmly) (1 GF) S £40–£50; D £55–£65✳ **Facilities** FTV TVB tea/coffee Cen ht TVL Wi-fi available **Parking** 6 **Notes** ⊗

★★★★ ⊛ INN

Thatched Cottage

63–67 Charlton Rd BA4 5QF

☎ 01749 342058 🗎 01749 343265

e–mail: enquiries@thatchedcottage.info

web: www.thatchedcottage.info

dir: *0.6m E of town centre on A361*

This delightful Grade II listed, 17th-century hostelry has been renovated and upgraded while retaining its original character. The modern accommodation is well equipped with spacious bedrooms and the public areas are light, airy and very attractively appointed. The inn offers a good choice of carefully prepared dishes in the restaurant or lighter options in the bar.

Rooms 8 en suite S £75–£115; D £90–£135✳ **Facilities** STV TVB tea/coffee Direct dial from bedrooms Cen ht TVL Dinner Last d 9.30pm Wi-fi available **Conf** Max 45 Thtr 45 Class 35 Board 30 **Parking** 40 **Notes** LB

★★★★ ⊛ INN

The Three Horseshoes

Batcombe BA4 6HE

☎ 01749 850359 🗎 01749 850615

e–mail: shirley@thethreehorsesinn.co.uk

dir: *3m from Bruton signed on A359*

The Three Horseshoes is a traditional freehouse that dates back to the 17th century. The long, low bar with its cream-painted beams and inglenook fireplace is a great place for a pint or a delicious meal. In the garden is an ornamental fish pond and a patio for alfresco dining. Bedrooms are very comfortable with useful facilities and charming rustic décor.

Rooms 3 rms (2 en suite) (1 pri facs) (1 fmly) S £55–£75; D £75✳ **Facilities** TVB tea/coffee Cen ht Dinner Last d 9pm **Parking** 30 **Notes** No coaches RS Mon

★★★ BED & BREAKFAST

The Abbey Barn

Doulting BA4 4QD

☎ 01749 880321

e–mail: abbeybarn@btconnect.com

dir: *2m E of Shepton Mallet on A361 in the centre of Doulting*

Located in the pretty village of Doulting, the Abbey Barn retains many original features. The attractive public area is enhanced by memorabilia and a roaring log fire during the cooler months, which creates an inviting atmosphere. Bedrooms have period furniture and modern shower rooms. Fully licensed, guests may enjoy a drink or two.

Rooms 3 en suite (1 fmly) S £47–£70; D £70 **Facilities** TVB tea/coffee **Parking** 10 **Notes** LB ⊗ No children

SHEPTON MALLET CONTINUED

★★★ GUEST ACCOMMODATION
L'Abri B&B

Portman House, Pylle-on-the-Fosse BA4 6TA

☎ 01749 830150

e–mail: moonbase@sky.com

dir: *On A37, 2m S of Shepton Mallet*

Conveniently located near the Bath and West Showground, this establishment, which was formerly an inn, offers annexe bedrooms, each having their own front door leading to the back garden. Rooms are situated at ground floor level. Dinner is available by prior arrangement and features a selection of home-made dishes.

Rooms 3 en suite (3 GF) D £50✱ **Facilities** FTV TVB tea/coffee Cen ht Dinner Last d by arrangement **Parking** 10 **Notes** ⊗ No children 14yrs Closed 24–31 Dec

---

SOMERTON   MAP 04 ST42

★★★★ FARM HOUSE
Lower Farm *(ST527309)*

Kingweston TA11 6BA

☎ 01458 223237 📄 01458 223276 Mrs J Sedgman

e–mail: lowerfarm@btconnect.com

web: www.lowerfarm.net

dir: *3m NE of Somerton. On B3153 in Kingweston*

Set in the heart of Somerset, this Grade II listed stone farmhouse has been home to the same family for several generations. Furnished in cottage style, the cosy bedrooms combine period charm with modern comforts and have spectacular rural views. Guests are served a hearty breakfast in the Georgian dining room.

Rooms 2 en suite S £50–£60; D £65✱ **Facilities** FTV TVB tea/coffee Cen ht **Conf** Max 36 Thtr 36 Class 30 Board 20 **Parking** 8 **Notes** ⊗ 500 acres Arable Closed Xmas & New Year

★★★★ GUEST ACCOMMODATION
Somerton Court Country House

TA11 7AH

☎ 01458 274694 📄 01458 274694

e–mail: enquiries@somertoncourt.co.uk

web: www.somertoncourt.co.uk

dir: *Leave A303 onto A372 at Podimore rdbt. After 3m turn right onto B3151 to Somerton & follow B&B signs*

Dating back to the 17th century and set in extensive gardens and grounds, Somerton Court Country House is a tranquil haven away from the pressures of modern life. The comfortable bedrooms have lovely views, and breakfast is served in a delightful dining room that overlooks the gardens.

Rooms 6 en suite (2 fmly) S £40–£50; D £80✱ **Facilities** TVB tea/coffee Cen ht Riding **Conf** Max 150 Thtr 200 Class 150 **Parking** 30 **Notes** ⊗ Closed Xmas & New Year Civ Wed 150

★★★ ⚜ INN

The Devonshire Arms

Long Sutton TA10 9LP

☎ 01458 241271 📄 01458 241037

e–mail: mail@thedevonshirearms.com

web: www.thedevonshirearms.com

dir: *Off A303 onto A372 at Podimore rdbt. After 4m, left onto B3165, signed Martock and Long Sutton*

This inn provides stylish public rooms and accommodation. The bedrooms have contemporary furnishings and the spacious public areas are comfortable. A choice of ales, wines and spirits, and interesting cuisine complete the picture in the bar-restaurant.

Rooms 7 rms (6 en suite) (1 pri facs) 2 annexe en suite (1 fmly) (2 GF) S £70–£130; D £80–£130✱ **Facilities** FTV TVB tea/coffee Cen ht Dinner Last d 9.30pm Wi-fi available ⚓ **Parking** 6 **Notes LB**

SOUTH PETHERTON   MAP 04 ST41

★★★★ ⬭ BED & BREAKFAST

Old Harp House

Over Stratton TA13 5LB

☎ 01460 242301 📄 01460 242301

e–mail: anne.larpent@btinternet.com

web: www.oldharphouse.com

Peacefully located in an engaging Somerset village, just a short distance from the A303, this Grade II listed Somerset farmhouse dates back to the early 17th century. Many fascinating original features have been retained, such as a Tudor hamstone fireplace and winder staircase. Bedrooms are individually styled with luxurious touches, and breakfast and dinner (by prior arrangement) utilise local produce and are served in the elegant dining room.

Rooms 3 en suite S £60–£80; D £60–£80✱ **Facilities** FTV TVB tea/coffee Cen ht TVL Dinner Last d noon Wi-fi available Riding **Parking** 6 **Notes** ⊗ No children 12yrs ⓔ

STANTON DREW   MAP 04 ST56

★★★★ FARM HOUSE
Greenlands *(ST597636)*

BS39 4ES

☎ 01275 333487 📄 01275 331211 Mrs J Cleverley

dir: *A37 onto B3130, on right before Stanton Drew Garage*

Situated near the ancient village of Stanton Drew in the heart of the Chew Valley, Greenlands is convenient for Bristol Airport and Bath, Bristol and Wells. There are comfortable, well-equipped bedrooms and a downstairs lounge, and breakfast is the highlight of any stay here.

CONTINUED

Greenlands

Rooms 4 en suite S £25–£30; D £50✳ **Facilities** STV FTV TVB tea/coffee Cen ht TVL **Parking** 8 **Notes** No children 12yrs 3 acres Hobby Farming – Poultry 🐾

★★★★ BED & BREAKFAST
The Tithe Barn
Sandy Ln BS39 4EL
☎ 01275 331887
e–mail: stephen.jcroucher@btinternet.com
web: www.thetithebarnsomerset.co.uk

Peacefully located in the pleasant village of Stanton Drew, this property is full of character and charm and as the name suggests, has been tastefully converted from a previous existence as a barn. Bedrooms are comfortably decorated and furnished, and overlook the surrounding grounds. Carefully prepared breakfast includes a range of dishes utilising local produce and is served in the bright, spacious conservatory. Guests are also welcome to use the comfortable lounge with large fireplace.

Rooms 3 rms (2 en suite) (1 pri facs) S £50–£60; D £80–£90✳ **Facilities** TVB tea/coffee Cen ht TVL Dinner Last d 9.30pm 🏇 Stabling for own horses **Parking** 5 **Notes** ❊ 🐾

★★★★ BED & BREAKFAST
Valley Farm
Sandy Ln BS39 4EL
☎ 01275 332723 & 07799 768161 📠 01275 332723
e–mail: valleyfarm2000@tiscali.co.uk
dir: *Off B3130 into Stanton Drew, right onto Sandy Ln*

Located on a quiet country lane, Valley Farm offers relaxing and friendly accommodation. All bedrooms are comfortable and well

CONTINUED

equipped, and each room has pleasant views over the surrounding countryside. Breakfast is served around a communal table in the dining room, and although dinner is not available the village pub is just a stroll away.

Rooms 3 en suite (1 fmly) (1 GF) **Facilities** TVB tea/coffee Cen ht TVL **Parking** 6 **Notes** ❊ No children 8yrs Closed 24–26 Dec 🐾

STAPLE FITZPAINE   MAP 04 ST21

★★★★ 🍴 INN
Greyhound
TA3 5SP
☎ 01823 480227 📠 01823 481117
e–mail: thegreyhound-inn@btconnect.com
web: www.greyhoundinn.biz
dir: *M5 junct 25, A358 signed Yeovil. In 3m turn right, signed Staple Fitzpaine.*

Set in an Area of Outstanding Natural Beauty, this picturesque village inn has great atmosphere and character, complete with flagstone floors and open fires. An imaginative choice of freshly-prepared seasonal dishes using locally-sourced ingredients is featured on the ever-changing blackboard menu. The delightful bedrooms are spacious, comfortable, and well equipped with many extra facilities.

Rooms 4 en suite S £60; D £90 **Facilities** TVB tea/coffee Direct dial from bedrooms Cen ht Dinner Last d 9pm Wi-fi available Pool Table **Conf** Max 60 Thtr 60 Class 30 Board 20 **Parking** 40 **Notes** No children 10yrs

STOGUMBER   MAP 03 ST03

★★★★ 🅰 GUEST HOUSE
Wick House
Brook St TA4 3SZ
☎ 01984 656422
e–mail: sheila@wickhouse.co.uk
web: www.wickhouse.co.uk
dir: *Off A358 into village, left at the x-rds, Wick House 3rd on left*

Rooms 5 en suite (1 GF) S £30–£40; D £60–£68 **Facilities** TVB tea/coffee Licensed Cen ht TVL Dinner Last d 2pm Wi-fi available Stairlift **Parking** 6 **Notes** LB ⊗ No coaches

STREET   MAP 04 ST43

★★★★ INN
The Bear Inn
High St BA16 0EF
☎ 01458 442021
e–mail: bearinn.street@marstons.co.uk
This centrally located inn is just a stroll away from the Clarks Village Outlet Shopping. All the spacious bedrooms and bathrooms have been impressively refurbished to a high level and are located in the main building or annexe cottages. Part of Marston's Inns and Taverns, the popular bar restaurant is open all day.

Rooms 9 en suite 15 annexe en suite (12 fmly) (6 GF) S £79.95; D £79.95✳ **Facilities** FTV TVB tea/coffee Cen ht Dinner Wi-fi available **Conf** Max 30 **Parking** 50 **Notes** ⊗

★★★★ BED & BREAKFAST
The Birches
13 Housman Rd BA16 0SD
☎ 01458 442902
e–mail: askins@ukonline.co.uk
dir: *Off B3151 onto Portway at Cider Farm sign. 1st right onto Housman Rd*
The Birches is a modern house located in a quiet residential area, just ten minutes walk from Clarks Village Outlet Shopping. Bedrooms, one situated on the ground floor, are well equipped and have spacious private bathrooms. A freshly cooked breakfast, featuring home-made and garden produce is served in the pleasant dining room/lounge around a family table. A pub serving evening meals is just a stroll away.

Rooms 2 rms (2 pri facs) (1 fmly) (1 GF) S £35–£50; D £58–£60✳ **Facilities** TVB tea/coffee Cen ht **Parking** 2 **Notes** ⊗ 🐾

★★★ BED & BREAKFAST
Kasuli
71 Somerton Rd BA16 0DN
☎ 01458 442063
dir: *B3151 from Street rdbt for Somerton, house 400yds past Street Inn on left*
This family home is located close to Clarks Village Outlet Shopping and with easy access to local places of historical interest. Friendliness and a

CONTINUED

homely atmosphere are offered, and bedrooms are neatly presented. An enjoyable traditional breakfast is served in the dining room around the family dining table.

Rooms 2 rms S £24–£26; D £46–£50✳ **Facilities** TVB tea/coffee Cen ht **Parking** 2 **Notes** ⊗ No children 10yrs 🐾

TAUNTON   MAP 04 ST22

See also Staple Fitzpaine

Premier Collection

★★★★★ BED & BREAKFAST
Elm Villa
Private Rd, Staplegrove Rd TA2 6AJ
☎ 01823 336165
e–mail: ferguson@elmvilla10.freeserve.co.uk
dir: *M5 junct 25, take A358 Minehead Rd to Staplegrove Inn, left and left again into Private Rd*
This spacious and comfortable Victorian villa enjoys distant views of the Blackdown Hills, yet is within walking distance of town centre, theatre, station and County Cricket Ground. All bedrooms are en suite and have plenty of facilities. Ample parking is available.

Rooms 2 en suite S £40–£44; D £54–£58 **Facilities** TVB tea/coffee Cen ht **Parking** 2 **Notes** ⊗ No children 10yrs 🐾

★★★★ GUEST ACCOMMODATION
Cutsey House
Cutsey, Trull TA3 7NY
☎ 01823 421705 📠 01823 421294
e–mail: cutseyhouse@btconnect.com
dir: *M5 junct 26, into West Buckland, right at T-junct, 2nd left, next right*
A Victorian house set in over 20 acres of gardens and grounds with parts of the building dating back to the 15th century. The comfortable spacious bedrooms have glorious views of the countryside towards the Blackdown Hills. Dinner is available by arrangement and guests can enjoy their drinks in the library.

Rooms 3 en suite (1 smoking) S £35–£45; D £60–£70✳ **Facilities** TVB Cen ht TVL Dinner Last d 5pm Snooker **Conf** Max 12 **Parking** 11 **Notes** ⊗ Closed Xmas-Etr 🐾

★★★★ BED & BREAKFAST
4 Elm Grove B&B
4 Elm Grove TA1 1EG
☎ 01823 354653
e–mail: stirlings.taunton@tiscali.co.uk
Quietly located in a leafy residential area, just a short stroll from the centre of Taunton, this elegant establishment offers a warm and genuine welcome with every effort made to ensure a comfortable and relaxing stay. The tastefully appointed bedrooms offer a host of luxurious extras such as robes, fluffy towels and power showers. Breakfast consists of a substantial continental offering, served around the dining room table.

Rooms 2 en suite S £35–£45; D £50–£65✳ **Facilities** TVB tea/coffee Cen ht TVL Wi-fi available **Notes** ⊗ No children 12yrs 🐾

★ ★ ★ ★ 🍽 GUEST ACCOMMODATION
The Spinney
Curland TA3 5SE
☎ 01460 234362 & 234193 🖺 01460 234362
e–mail: enquiries@spinneybedandbreakfast.co.uk
web: www.spinneybedandbreakfast.co.uk

dir: *2m W off A358 Taunton-Ilminster road*
A warm welcome awaits at this delightful family home, set in well-tended gardens and magnificent views of the Blackdown, Quantock and Mendip Hills. The attractive bedrooms are equipped with modern comforts and include a ground floor room with level access. Using the best local produce, delicious dinners are available by arrangement and guests may bring their own wine.

Rooms 3 en suite (2 GF) S £48–£50; D £62–£65
Facilities FTV TVB tea/coffee Cen ht TVL Dinner Last d 4pm Wi-fi available **Parking** 6 **Notes** ⊗ No children

★ ★ ★ ★ GUEST HOUSE
Brookfield House
16 Wellington Rd TA1 4EQ
☎ 01823 272786 🖺 01823 272786
e–mail: info@brookfieldguesthouse.uk.com
web: www.brookfieldguesthouse.uk.com

dir: *From town centre signs to Musgrove Hospital, onto A38 Wellington Rd, on right opp turning to hospital*
This charming Grade II listed Georgian house is just a 5-minute level walk from the town centre. The family take great pride in caring for guests, and the brightly decorated bedrooms are well equipped. Breakfast, featuring local ingredients, is served in the attractive dining room. The property is non-smoking.

Rooms 7 en suite (1 fmly) S £50–£55; D £70–£85✳ **Facilities** TVB tea/coffee Cen ht Dinner Last d 8.30pm Wi-fi available **Parking** 8 **Notes** ⊗ No children 7yrs No coaches

★ ★ ★ ★ BED & BREAKFAST
Creechbarn
Vicarage Ln, Creech-St-Michael TA3 5PP
☎ 01823 443955
e–mail: mick@somersite.co.uk

dir: *M5 junct 25, A358 to Creech St Michael, follow canal boat signs to end Vicarage Ln. Through brick gateposts, turn right*
Located next to the canal and on a Sustrans cycle route, this traditional Somerset barn was lovingly converted by the current owners. Bedrooms are comfortable and there is a spacious sitting room with books, a television and table tennis. Breakfast is carefully prepared with free-range eggs and home-made bread.

▶**Rooms** 3 rms (1 en suite) S £33–£44; D £44–£55✳ **Facilities** TV1B tea/coffee Direct dial from bedrooms Cen ht TVL Wi-fi available **Parking** 6 **Notes** LB Closed 20 Dec–6 Jan 🍽

★ ★ ★ ★ FARM HOUSE
Lower Farm *(ST281241)*
Thornfalcon TA3 5NR
☎ 01823 443549 Mrs D Titman
e–mail: doreen@titman.eclipse.co.uk
web: www.somersite.co.uk

dir: *M5 junct 25, 2m SE on A358, left opp Nags Head pub, farm signed 1m on left*

This charming, thatched, 15th-century farmhouse is set in lovely gardens and is surrounded by open countryside. Hearty breakfasts, served in the farmhouse kitchen, feature home-produced eggs. Some bedrooms are located in the converted granary, some on the ground floor. There is a comfortable sitting room with a log fire.

Rooms 2 rms (1 en suite) (1 pri facs) 9 annexe rms (7 en suite) (2 annexe pri facs) (2 fmly) (7 GF) S fr £45; D fr £70✳ **Facilities** TV9B tea/coffee Cen ht TVL Wi-fi available **Parking** 10 **Notes** LB ⊗ No children 5yrs 10 acres beef cows poultry

★ ★ ★ ★ FARM HOUSE
Lower Manor Farm *(ST281240)*
Thornfalcon TA3 5NR
☎ 01823 443634 & 443222 Mrs M Cottey-Burt
e–mail: marion@lowermanorfarm.co.uk
web: www.lowermanorfarm.co.uk

dir: *M5 junct 25, A358 SE onto dual carriageway, 2nd sign left to Thornfalcon, left by war memorial, farm next right*
In a delightful rural setting, Lower Manor Farm provides a high standard of comfortable, well-furnished accommodation. All bedrooms are dual aspect, with views across the surrounding countryside. Tempting breakfasts, featuring home produce when available, are served at individual tables in a cosy dining room.

Rooms 3 rms (2 en suite) (1 pri facs) S £40–£45; D £60–£65 **Facilities** TVB tea/coffee Cen ht Wi-fi available **Parking** 10 **Notes** LB ⊗ No children 3 acres non-working 🍽

TAUNTON CONTINUED

★★★★ FARM HOUSE
Lower Marsh Farm *(ST224279)*
Kingston St Mary TA2 8AB
☎ 01823 451331 📠 01823 451331 Mr & Mrs J Gothard
e–mail: b&b@lowermarshfarm.co.uk

dir: M5 junct 25. Farm between Taunton & Kingston St Mary just past King's Hall School on right

Located at the foot of the Quantock Hills, this delightful family-run farm provides bright, comfortable bedrooms, complemented by numerous, thoughtful extra facilities. Evening meals are available by arrangement. Guests enjoy a hearty breakfast around one large table in the attractive dining room; a spacious lounge with log fire in winter is also available.

Rooms 3 en suite (1 fmly) **Facilities** TVB tea/coffee Cen ht TVL Dinner Last d noon **Parking** 6 **Notes** ⊗ 300 acres arable/sheep/horses 🐾

★★★★ 🍴 GUEST ACCOMMODATION
Meryan House
Bishop's Hull TA1 5EG
☎ 01823 337445 📠 01823 322355
e–mail: meryanhousehotel@btclick.com
web: www.meryanhouse.co.uk

dir: 1.5m W of town centre. Off A38 into Bishop's Hull

Located in its own grounds just over a mile from the town centre, this 17th-century property has delightful individually furnished rooms. The comfortable bedrooms feature antiques along with modern facilities. Interesting dishes are available at dinner, and there is also a cosy bar and a spacious lounge.

Rooms 12 en suite (2 fmly) (2 GF) **Facilities** STV TVB tea/coffee Direct dial from bedrooms Cen ht TVL Dinner Last d 7.30pm Wi-fi available **Conf** Max 25 Thtr 25 Class 25 Board 18 **Parking** 17 **Notes** ⊗ RS Sun

★★★ GUEST ACCOMMODATION
Blorenge House
57 Staple Grove Rd TA1 1DG
☎ 01823 283005 📠 01823 283005
e–mail: enquiries@blorengehouse.co.uk

dir: M5 junct 25, towards cricket ground & Morrisons on left, left at lights, right at 2nd lights, house 150yds on left

This fine Victorian property offers spacious accommodation within walking distance of the town centre. The bedrooms (some at ground floor level and some with four-poster beds) are individually furnished and vary in size. A lounge is available, and the garden with outdoor swimming pool is open to guests during daytime hours most days of the week. There is also ample parking.

Rooms 25 rms (20 en suite) (4 fmly) (3 GF) S £48–£70; D £70–£125✱ **Facilities** TVB tea/coffee Cen ht TVL Wi-fi available ⚲ **Conf** Max 20 **Parking** 25 **Notes LB**

★★★ INN
The Hatch Inn
Village Rd, Hatch Beauchamp TA3 6SG
☎ 01823 480245
e–mail: gemma@thehatchinn.co.uk
web: www.thehatchinn.co.uk

dir: M5 junct 25, 3m S off A358

With easy access to both the A303 and M5, this 18th-century, family-run coaching inn is very much the village local, complete with crackling logs fires and a convivial atmosphere. Bedrooms offer good levels of comfort with well appointed bathrooms. Public areas include a choice of bars serving local ales, and the menu features honest, home-cooked cuisine with a focus upon local produce.

Rooms 5 en suite (1 fmly) S £35; D £70–£80✱ **Facilities** TVB tea/coffee Cen ht Dinner Last d 9pm Wi-fi available Pool Table skittle alley **Notes** No coaches

★★★ FARM HOUSE
Higher Dipford *(ST216205)*
Trull TA3 7NU
☎ 01823 275770 & 257916 📠 01823 257916
Mrs M Fewings
e–mail: mafewings@tesco.net

dir: A38 S from town centre on Honiton Rd to Trull, right onto Dipford Rd, farm on left

This Grade II listed 17th-century longhouse is part of a working dairy farm. Steeped in character with elm beams and inglenook fireplaces, the house provides well-equipped and homely accommodation. Bedrooms are comfortable and individually decorated, and there is an honesty bar and lounge. Breakfasts and home-cooked dinners, featuring local produce, are served in the spacious dining room.

Rooms 3 en suite **Facilities** STV TVB tea/coffee Cen ht TVL Dinner Last d 8pm Pool Table **Parking** 6 **Notes** ⊗ 120 acres beef 🐾

TINTINHULL
MAP 04 ST41

★★★★ ☀ INN

Crown & Victoria

Farm St BA22 8PZ

☎ 01935 823341 📄 01935 825786

e–mail: info@thecrownandvictoria.co.uk

dir: *Off A303, signs for Tintinhull Gardens*

Appointed to a high standard, the light and airy accommodation has very well-equipped bedrooms. The staff ensure guests are cared for, and the contemporary bar and restaurant provide a good selection of carefully prepared dishes.

Rooms 5 en suite S £65; D £85✳ **Facilities** TVB tea/coffee Cen ht Dinner Last d 9pm Wi-fi available **Parking** 60 **Notes** No coaches

WATCHET
MAP 03 ST04

★★★★ BED & BREAKFAST

The Linhay B&B

Williton Rd TA23 0NU

☎ 01984 641252 & 07940 894009

e–mail: linhaybnb@aol.com

dir: *A39 towards Minehead, 2.5m after Williton*

Convenient for coastal and country attractions, Linhay offers spacious and friendly accommodation. Hospitality is a feature and guests are made to feel at home. The bedrooms are particularly well appointed and well equipped, and a hearty breakfast is served in the conservatory. There is an attractive garden with pool, a sauna and ample parking.

Rooms 3 en suite (3 GF) S £40–£60; D £60–£80✳ **Facilities** TVB tea/coffee Cen ht ⤴ Sauna **Parking** 3 **Notes** LB ⊗ Closed Xmas & New Year ⊛

★★★★ GUEST HOUSE

The Georgian House

28 Swain St TA23 0AD

☎ 01984 639279

e–mail: georgianhouse_watchet@virgin.net

dir: *A39 over railway bridge onto Watchet main street*

This elegant Georgian house is situated in the heart of this increasingly popular coastal resort within a short walk of the impressive new marina. The comfortable bedrooms combine quality and individuality. Breakfast (and dinner by arrangement) is served in the well-appointed dining room. Additional facilities include a lounge and the garden.

Rooms 3 en suite S fr £35; D £60–£90✳ **Facilities** TVB Cen ht Dinner Last d 9pm **Parking** 2 **Notes** LB ⊗ No coaches ⊛

WATERROW
MAP 03 ST02

★★★★ 🛏 INN

The Rock

TA4 2AX

☎ 01984 623293 📄 01984 623293

e–mail: matt@rockinn.co.uk

dir: *On B3227*

Set in the lush greenery of the Tone Valley, this 16th-century inn, as its name suggests, is built against the rock face. There is an abundance of character and the friendly atmosphere draws both locals and visitors. A range of freshly prepared, imaginative meals is available in the bar or restaurant, including Aberdeen Angus steaks from the owner's farm. The bedrooms are comfortable, light and airy.

Rooms 8 en suite (1 fmly) **Facilities** FTV TVB tea/coffee Direct dial from bedrooms Cen ht TVL Dinner Last d 10pm Pool Table **Parking** 25

WELLINGTON
MAP 03 ST12

★★★★ FARM HOUSE

Thorne Manor *(ST097210)*

Thorne St Margaret TA21 0EQ

☎ 01823 672264 Mrs P Hasell

e–mail: hasell@thornemanor.wanadoo.co.uk

web: www.thorne-manor.co.uk

dir: *3m W of Wellington. Off A38 to Thorne St Margaret*

There is a tangible sense of history at this engaging 16th-century manor house which stands in a small village near the Blackdown Hills. The centuries old front door opens to reveal accommodation of genuine character and good levels of comfort, with inglenook fireplaces in the dining room and the lounge. The spacious bedroom is well equipped and guests will be well cared for by the hosts. The well-tended garden provides space for relaxation, and breakfast features local produce.

Rooms 1 en suite S £40–£45; D £60–£65 **Facilities** tea/coffee TVL **Parking** 2 **Notes** ⊗ No children 175 acres Mixed Closed mid Dec–mid Jan ⊛

WELLS MAP 04 ST54

See also Croscombe

Double-Gate Farm

Premier Collection

★★★★★ 🛏 BED & BREAKFAST
Beaconsfield Farm

Easton BA5 1DU
☎ 01749 870308
e–mail: carol@beaconsfieldfarm.co.uk
web: www.beaconsfieldfarm.co.uk

dir: *2.5m from Wells on A371, on right just before village of Easton*

Set in pleasant, well-tended gardens on the west side of the Mendip Hills, Beaconsfield Farm is a convenient base for visiting this attractive area. The welcoming hosts are most friendly and attentive and many guests return on a regular basis. Bedrooms, which are very comfortable and equipped with many extra facilities, are delightfully decorated with co-ordinated colours and fabrics. A choice of well-cooked dishes featuring fresh local produce is offered at breakfast.

Rooms 3 en suite D £80–£85 **Facilities** FTV TVB tea/coffee Cen ht TVL Wi-fi available **Parking** 10 **Notes** ⊗ No children 8yrs Closed 22 Dec–3 Jan 🐾

★★★★★ 🄰 BED & BREAKFAST
Beryl

Hawkers Ln BA5 3JP
☎ 01749 678738 📠 01749 670508
e–mail: stay@beryl-wells.co.uk

dir: *Off B3139 Radstock Rd, signed The Horringtons, onto Hawkers Ln to end*

Rooms 9 rms (8 en suite) (1 pri facs) (2 fmly) **Facilities** TVB tea/coffee Direct dial from bedrooms Lift Cen ht TVL ⚞ 🛝 childrens play area **Parking** 20 **Notes** Closed 25–26 Dec

★★★★ FARM HOUSE
Double-Gate Farm *(ST484424)*

Godney BA5 1RX
☎ 01458 832217 📠 01458 835612 Mrs H Millard
e–mail: doublegatefarm@aol.com
web: www.doublegatefarm.com

dir: *A39 from Wells towards Glastonbury, at Polsham right signed Godney/Polsham, 2m to x-rds, continue to farmhouse on left after inn*

Expect a warm welcome not only from the owners, but also Jasper and Paddy, their friendly retrievers. Set on the banks of the River Sheppey on the Somerset Levels, this comfortable farmhouse is well-known for its attractive summer flower garden, as well as delicious breakfasts. Guests have use of a games room, and free internet access in the lounge.

Rooms 3 en suite 3 annexe en suite (1 fmly) (1 GF) S £50–£55; D £65–£70✳ **Facilities** FTV TVB tea/coffee Cen ht TVL Dinner Last d day before Fishing Snooker Table tennis **Parking** 13 **Notes** ⊗ 100 acres mixed Closed 21 Dec–4 Jan

★★★★ 🛏 GUEST ACCOMMODATION
Hollow Tree Farm

Launcherley BA5 1QJ
☎ 01749 673715 & 07704 506513 📠 01749 673715

dir: *A39 from Wells for Glastonbury, 1st left at Brownes Garden Centre, farm 0.75m on right*

Delightfully appointed rooms with bright, cheery colour schemes and comfortable furnishings are provided at this non-working farm. Spectacular views of Wells Cathedral and Glastonbury Tor and delightful flower-filled gardens add to the charm. The friendly hosts are most welcoming and attentive and home-baked bread, jams and marmalade are only a part of the delicious breakfast.

Rooms 3 rms (2 en suite) (1 pri facs) (1 fmly) (3 GF) S £30; D £46 **Facilities** TVB tea/coffee Cen ht TVL **Parking** 4 **Notes** ⊗ No children 12yrs Closed mid Dec–mid Jan 🐾

★★★★ BED & BREAKFAST
Riverside Grange

Tanyard Ln, North Wootton BA4 4AE
☎ 01749 890761
e–mail: riversidegrange@hotmail.com

dir: *2.5m SE of Wells in North Wootton*

A delightful restored tannery, built in 1853, the foundations of which actually sit in the River Redlake, which runs alongside the house. A warm welcome and attentive service is guaranteed from the friendly proprietor, who makes every effort to make guests feel at home. The house, furnished throughout with rosewood, is most comfortable. The bedrooms are stylishly co-ordinated and guests may relax in the attractive garden in summer or the cosy snug overlooking the orchard in winter.

Rooms 2 rms (1 en suite) (1 pri facs) S £55; D £65✳ **Facilities** TVB tea/-coffee Cen ht Wi-fi available **Parking** 6 **Notes** ⊗ No children 10yrs Closed Xmas & New Year 🐾

CONTINUED

ENGLAND

★★★★ GUEST ACCOMMODATION
Glengarth House

7 Glastonbury Rd BA5 1TW
☎ 01749 674792 📄 01749 674792
e-mail: glengarthhouse@tiscali.co.uk

dir: *On A39 S, on left past mini-rdbt*

This pleasant guest accommodation is located on the edge of Wells, just a short walk from the central attractions. A continental breakfast is provided in the light and airy dining room. The comfortable bedrooms are modern and brightly decorated, and guests will benefit from the limited off-road parking.

Rooms 5 en suite (1 fmly) **Facilities** TVB tea/coffee Cen ht Wi-fi available **Parking** 5 **Notes** ⊗ 🐾

★★★★ BED & BREAKFAST
Highfield

93 Portway BA5 2BR
☎ 01749 675330

dir: *Enter Wells & signs for A371 Cheddar, Highfield on Portway after last lights at top of hill*

Within walking distance of the city and cathedral, this delightful home maintains its Edwardian style and provides comfortable accommodation. A warm welcome is assured while bedrooms are well equipped. Breakfast is served at one large table in the smart dining room, which overlooks the pretty garden.

Rooms 3 en suite (1 fmly) **Facilities** TVB tea/coffee Cen ht **Parking** 7 **Notes** ⊗ No children 2yrs Closed 23 Dec–1 Jan 🐾

★★★★ BED & BREAKFAST
Highgate Cottage

Worth BA5 1LW
☎ 01749 674201 📄 01749 674201

dir: *B3139 into Worth, Pheasant pub on left, Highgate Cottage 200yds on right*

Located in the village of Worth to the west of Wells and set in two acres of land, access to this delightful stone cottage is over its own private bridge. The attractive bedrooms are comfortable and quiet. Full English breakfasts are served at individual tables in the lounge-dining room.

Rooms 2 en suite (1 fmly) S £35; D £55✳ **Facilities** TVB tea/coffee Cen ht Wi-fi available **Parking** 6 **Notes** LB Closed Dec–Jan 🐾

★★★★ BED & BREAKFAST
Infield House

36 Portway BA5 2BN
☎ 01749 670989 📄 01749 679093
e-mail: infield@talk21.com
web: www.infieldhouse.co.uk

dir: *500yds W of city centre on A371 Portway*

This charming Victorian house offers comfortable, spacious rooms of elegance and style. The friendly hosts are very welcoming and provide a relaxing home from home. Guests may bring their pets, by arrangement. Dinners, also by arrangement, are served in the pleasant dining room where good home cooking ensures an enjoyable and varied range of options.

Rooms 3 en suite D £58–£60✳ **Facilities** TVB tea/coffee Cen ht Dinner Last d 10.30am Wi-fi available **Parking** 3 **Notes** No children 12yrs

★★★★ GUEST ACCOMMODATION
Littlewell Farm

Coxley BA5 1QP
☎ 01749 677914
e-mail: enquiries@littlewellfarm.co.uk
web: www.littlewellfarm.co.uk

dir: *A39 from Wells towards Glastonbury, farm 1m on right opp sign for Coxley*

This charming house stands in spacious gardens at Coxley, on the outskirts of Wells. It provides well-equipped accommodation and has a smart, comfortable lounge. Breakfast, featuring local produce when possible, is served in the bright, modern dining room at separate tables.

Rooms 5 rms (4 en suite) (1 pri facs) (1 GF) S £35–£40; D £58–£60✳ **Facilities** TVB tea/coffee Cen ht TVL **Parking** 10 **Notes** ⊗ Closed 25 Dec 🐾

WELLS CONTINUED

★★★ BED & BREAKFAST
Amber House

Coxley BA5 1QZ

☎ 01749 679612

e–mail: amberhouse@wellscity27.freeserve.co.uk

dir: On A39 in village, 0.25m S past Pound Inn on right

Located just 1.5 miles south of the centre of Wells and ideally placed for touring the area's historic sites and countryside, this friendly family home offers a relaxed atmosphere. Bedrooms are well equipped; some look out over open countryside and farmland to the rear. A traditional English breakfast is served, at separate tables, in the cosy dining room, which guests are welcome to use at other times, if they so wish.

Rooms 2 en suite D £46–£52✶ **Facilities** TVB tea/coffee Cen ht
Parking 3 **Notes** ⊗ ⊚

★★★ GUEST ACCOMMODATION
Birdwood House

Birdwood, Bath Rd BA5 3EW

☎ 01749 679250

e–mail: info@birdwood-bandb.co.uk

web: www.birdwood-bandb.co.uk

dir: 1.5m NE of city centre. On B3139 between South & West Horrington

Set in extensive grounds and gardens just a short drive from the town centre, this imposing detached house dates from the 1850s. The bedrooms are comfortable and equipped with a number of extra facilities. Breakfast is served around a communal table in the pleasant dining room or conservatory, which is also available for guest use and enjoyment throughout the day.

Rooms 3 rms (2 en suite) (1 pri facs) (1 fmly) **Facilities** TVB tea/coffee
Cen ht TVL ⅃ **Parking** 12 **Notes** ⊗ ⊚

★★ BED & BREAKFAST
19 St Cuthbert Street

BA5 2AW

☎ 01749 673166

dir: At bottom of High St opp St Cuthbert's Church

Guests are assured of a friendly welcome at this charming terrace house, which is within walking distance of the cathedral and bus

CONTINUED

station. The accommodation is fresh, light and comfortable and the atmosphere homely. Bedrooms are well appointed and there is a comfortable lounge. Breakfast, featuring home-made marmalade, is served in the dining room around a family table.

Rooms 2 rms S £30–£35; D £50–£55✶ **Facilities** TVB tea/coffee Cen ht
TVL **Notes** No children 5yrs ⊚

WESTON-SUPER-MARE MAP 04 ST36

★★★★★ ▤ BED & BREAKFAST
Church House

27 Kewstoke Rd, Kewstoke BS22 9YD

☎ 01934 633185

e–mail: churchhouse@kewstoke.net

web: www.churchhousekewstoke.co.uk

dir: From M5 junct 21 follow signs for Kewstoke 2.5m, next to Kewstoke Church

In a peaceful location at the foot of Monk's Hill, this delightful property enjoys wonderful views over the Bristol Channel and across to Wales on clear days. Bedrooms are stylish and spacious, with lots of thoughtful extras and well-equipped en suites. Public areas include a pleasant conservatory and an elegant dining room where impressive breakfasts are served.

Rooms 5 en suite S £55–£60; D £75–£85 **Facilities** TVB tea/coffee
Cen ht Wi-fi available **Parking** 10 **Notes** LB

★★★★ GUEST ACCOMMODATION
The Beaches

36 Beach Rd BS23 1BG

☎ 01934 629529 📄 01934 629529

e–mail: info@beacheshotel.co.uk

dir: M5 junct 21 onto A370, follow signs for beach

This attractive Victorian property enjoys wonderful sea views from its front-facing bedrooms. Immaculately presented and family run with a relaxed atmosphere, the accommodation is bright and comfortable and parking is available at the rear.

Rooms 10 en suite (3 fmly) S £27.50–£30; D £50–£55✶ **Facilities** TVB
tea/coffee Cen ht TVL **Parking** 8 **Notes** LB ⊗ Closed 29 Oct–Mar

★★★★ BED & BREAKFAST
Camellia Lodge

76 Walliscote Rd BS23 1ED
☎ 01934 613534 📄 01934 613534
e–mail: dachefscamellia@aol.com

dir: 200yds from seafront

Guests return regularly for the warm welcome they receive at this immaculate Victorian family home, which is just off the seafront and within walking distance of the town centre. Bedrooms have a range of thoughtful touches, and carefully prepared breakfasts are served in the relaxing dining room. Home-cooked dinners are also available by prior arrangement.

Rooms 5 rms (4 en suite) (1 pri facs) (2 fmly) S £27.50–£35; D £55–£65✱ **Facilities** TVB tea/coffee Cen ht Dinner Last d 10.30am **Notes** ⊛

★★★★ GUEST HOUSE
Jamesfield Guest House

1A Ellenborough Park North BS23 1XH
☎ 01934 642898 📄 01934 624933
e–mail: jamesfield1@aol.com

Well-maintained property in an ideal location, a short walk from the seafront and only a few minutes stroll into town. Bedrooms are all comfortably furnished and well decorated, and include rooms on the ground floor. Guests are welcome to use the relaxing lounge, and the accommodation also benefits from its own car park.

Rooms 7 rms (6 en suite) (1 pri facs) (2 GF) S £25; D £50✱ **Facilities** TVB tea/coffee Cen ht TVL **Parking** 9 **Notes** ⊗ No coaches

★★★★ GUEST HOUSE
Oakover

25 Clevedon Rd BS23 1DA
☎ 01934 620125 📄 01934 620173
e–mail: info@oakover.co.uk
web: www.oakover.co.uk

dir: Off A370 Beach Rd near Sea Life Aquarium onto Clevedon Rd

Oakover is a substantial Victorian property situated a short level walk from the town centre and seafront. Bedrooms and bathrooms offer very good levels of quality and comfort. A varied breakfast menu is offered in the bright dining room. The friendly resident proprietor maintains an easy-going and welcoming establishment.

Rooms 6 en suite (2 GF) **Facilities** STV TVB tea/coffee Cen ht Wi-fi available **Parking** 7 **Notes** ⊗ No children 12yrs No coaches

★★★★ BED & BREAKFAST
The Owls Crest House

39 Kewstoke Rd, Kewstoke BS22 9YE
☎ 01934 417672
e–mail: theowlscrest1@btinternet.com

dir: M5 junct 21, follow A370 to Weston, take 1st left to Kewstoke

Located in the pleasant village of Kewstoke, guests will find an especially friendly welcome from the resident Irish hosts at this relaxed accommodation. Bedrooms and bathrooms offer good comfort and provide plenty of useful extras. Traditional home-cooked breakfasts are served in the relaxing dining room. Guests are welcome to use the comfortable lounge and a car park is also available.

Rooms 4 en suite (1 fmly) S £48–£50; D £58–£62✱ **Facilities** TVB tea/coffee Cen ht TVL Last d 7pm Wi-fi available **Parking** 5 **Notes** LB No children 5yrs Closed 28 Dec–2 Jan & annual holidays ⊛

★★★★ GUEST ACCOMMODATION
Rookery Manor

Edingworth Rd, Edingworth BS24 0JB
☎ 01934 750200 📄 01934 750014
e–mail: enquiries@rookery-manor.co.uk
web: www.rookery-manor.co.uk

dir: M5 junct 22, A370 towards Weston, 2m right to Rookery Manor

Situated in its own delightful gardens and grounds within easy reach of the M5 and all the resort attractions of Weston-Super-Mare, this 16th-century manor house is best known for its extensive wedding and conference facilities. Bedrooms, each with its own access to the garden, are modern and bright. A carte menu is offered in Truffles Restaurant.

Rooms 22 en suite (2 fmly) (10 GF) **Facilities** TVB tea/coffee Direct dial from bedrooms Cen ht TVL Dinner Last d 9pm Golf 9 ♨ Riding Snooker Pool Table ⚓ ♪ **Conf** Max 800 Thtr 800 Class 120 Board 120 **Parking** 460 **Notes** ⊗ Civ Wed 400

★★★★ GUEST ACCOMMODATION
Timbertop Aparthotel

8 Victoria Park BS23 2HZ
☎ 01934 631178 & 424348 📄 01934 414716
e–mail: stay@aparthoteltimbertop.com
web: www.aparthoteltimbertop.com

dir: Follow signs to pier, then 1st right after Winter Gardens, 1st left (Lower Church Rd). Left, then right to Timbertop

Located in a quiet, mainly residential area, Timbertop offers a varied range of bedrooms and bathrooms to suit the majority of requirements. All rooms are comfortably furnished and include a range of welcome extras. A relaxed and friendly welcome is provided at all times by the resident proprietor. A small bar and seating area are also available.

Rooms 8 en suite 5 annexe en suite (2 fmly) S £35–£50; D £70–£100✱ **Facilities** TVB tea/coffee Cen ht TVL Wi-fi available **Parking** 15 **Notes** LB ⊗

See advert on page 449

ENGLAND

★★★ GUEST HOUSE
Bella Vista

19 Upper Church Rd BS23 2DX
☎ 01934 631931 🖨 01934 620126
web: www.bellavistawsm.co.uk

dir: *A370 to town and seafront, right past Grand Pier. Right after 300yds onto Upper Church Rd & right at x-rds*

Situated close to the seafront and town centre, this delightful terrace property has an attractive patio with seating at the front. The bedrooms have televisions and hospitality trays and are well decorated throughout. There is a cosy dining room where full English breakfasts are served and a large comfortable lounge is also available.

Rooms 8 en suite (3 fmly) S £25–£45; D £45–£60✱ **Facilities** TVB tea/coffee Cen ht TVL **Notes LB** ⊗ No coaches Closed 12 Dec–2 Jan ⊜

★★★ GUEST HOUSE
Beverley

11 Whitecross Rd BS23 1EP
☎ 01934 622956 🖨 01934 622956
e–mail: beverley11@hushmail.com
web: www.beverleyguesthouse.co.uk

dir: *Off A370 Beach Rd onto Ellenborough Park Rd South & take 2nd right*

Expect a warm greeting on arrival at this Victorian house set in a quiet residential street close to the seafront, the railway station and the town centre. The individually-styled bedrooms are thoughtfully equipped and include a family suite. There is a small conservatory-lounge next to the dining room, where hearty breakfasts using local produce are served.

Rooms 5 en suite (3 fmly) (1 GF) S £37–£60; D £60–£65✱ **Facilities** TVB tea/coffee Cen ht Wi-fi available **Notes LB** ⊗ No coaches Closed Xmas

★★★ GUEST HOUSE
Edelweiss Guest House

24 Clevedon Rd BS23 1DG
☎ 01934 624705 🖨 01934 624705
e–mail: edelweissguesthouse@tiscali.co.uk

dir: *Turn onto Clevedon Rd off Beach Rd (Seafront) opposite Tropicana. Edelweiss 75yds on right*

Located in a residential area around a hundred yards from the seafront and beach, Edelweiss is a traditional and comfortable guest house run in a welcoming manner. Bedrooms vary in size but all are nicely decorated. Although dinner is not available, guests are welcome to select from a snack and beverage menu up until 10pm.

Rooms 5 rms (4 en suite) (1 pri facs) (3 fmly) (2 GF) S £25–£30; D £52–£64✱ **Facilities** FTV TVB tea/coffee Cen ht **Notes LB** ⊗ No coaches Closed Xmas wk

★★★ GUEST HOUSE
Goodrington

23 Charlton Rd BS23 4HB
☎ 01934 623229
e–mail: vera.bishop@talk21.com
web: www.goodrington.info

dir: *A370 Beach Rd S onto Uphill Rd, left onto Charlton Rd*

The owners make every effort to ensure that guests enjoy their stay at this charming Victorian house tucked away in a quiet residential area. The bedrooms are comfortably furnished, and there is an attractive lounge. Families are especially welcome and this is a good holiday base.

Rooms 3 rms (2 en suite) (1 pri facs) (1 fmly) (1 GF) S £30–£35; D £50–£60✱ **Facilities** FTV TVB tea/coffee Cen ht TVL Dinner Last d 24hr notice **Notes LB** ⊗ No coaches RS Oct–Mar ⊜

★★★ GUEST ACCOMMODATION
Linden Lodge Guest House

27 Clevedon Rd BS23 1DA
☎ 01934 645797
e–mail: info@lindenlodge.com

dir: *Follow signs to seafront. 0.5m S of grand pier turn onto Clevedon Road*

Just a short walk from the town centre and the seafront, Linden Lodge offers a traditional style of welcoming hospitality and guest care. Bedrooms offer a range of shapes and sizes and all are well decorated and equipped. A good selection is offered at breakfast and served in the pleasant conservatory.

Rooms 5 en suite (1 fmly) **Facilities** TVB tea/coffee Cen ht **Parking** 3 **Notes** ⊗

★★★ GUEST HOUSE
Milton Lodge

15 Milton Rd BS23 2SH
☎ 01934 623161 🖨 01934 623210
e–mail: info@milton-lodge.co.uk
web: www.milton-lodge.co.uk

dir: *M5 junct 21, towards Weston-Super-Mare, onto Locking Rd & Milton Rd*

Located within walking distance of the town centre and the seafront attractions, this comfortable guest house offers spacious, attractive and

CONTINUED

well-equipped bedrooms, including one on the ground floor. The atmosphere is relaxed and friendly and there is a lounge and attractive dining room. Off-road parking is also available.

Rooms 6 en suite (1 fmly) (1 GF) S £42–£48; D £60–£90✹
Facilities TVB tea/coffee Cen ht TVL Wi-fi available **Parking** 6
Notes LB ⊗ No children 12yrs No coaches

★★★ GUEST ACCOMMODATION
The Sunfold

39 Beach Rd BS23 1BG
☎ 01934 624700 📄 01934 624700
e–mail: enquiries@sunfold-hotel.co.uk
web: www.sunfold-hotel.co.uk

Located right on the seafront opposite the Tropicana building, this family-run accommodation offers a relaxed atmosphere and friendly welcome. Traditionally-furnished bedrooms include some with sea-facing views and a number of family rooms. Enjoyable home-cooked dinners are available in the downstairs dining room where a small bar is also open to guests.

Rooms 11 en suite (4 fmly) (2 GF) S £40–£50; D £55–£75✹
Facilities TVB tea/coffee Cen ht TVL Dinner Last d 7.30pm Wi-fi available **Parking** 5 **Notes LB** RS Xmas & New Year

★★★ GUEST HOUSE
Weston Bay Guest House

2–4 Clevedon Rd BS23 1DG
☎ 01934 628903 📄 01934 417661
e–mail: westonbayhotel@btinternet.com
web: www.westonbayhotel.co.uk

dir: Opp SeaQuarium on seafront

Located on the seafront, this family-run property has generally spacious, well-equipped bedrooms with modern en suites. The comfortable lounge and attractive breakfast room have sea views, and packed lunches are available on request. There is a small private car park.

Rooms 9 en suite (5 fmly) (1 GF) S £50–£55; D £65–£69✹
Facilities TVB tea/coffee Cen ht TVL **Parking** 11 **Notes LB** ⊗
No coaches Closed mid Nov–mid Mar

★★★ BED & BREAKFAST
Ynishir B&B

74 Uphill Way BS23 4TN
☎ 01934 412703 & 0771 495 0023
e–mail: simon.bilkus@homecall.co.uk

dir: A370 follow signs to hospital (Grange Rd), right at mini-rdbt, left onto Uphill Way

Set in pleasant countryside just a short distance from the sea, Ynishir has one bedroom with en suite facilities, and would be ideal accommodation for anyone who wants to walk the Mendip Way.

Rooms 1 en suite (1 fmly) (1 GF) (1 smoking) S £30; D £50–£60✹
Facilities FTV TVB tea/coffee Cen ht TVL **Parking** 1 **Notes** ⊜

★★ GUEST HOUSE
Corbiere

24 Upper Church Rd BS23 2DX
☎ 01934 629607 📄 01934 629607
e–mail: corbierehotel@aol.com

dir: M5 junct 21 take A370 to town/seafront. Turn right for pier along Knightstone Rd, approx 300yds turn right onto Upper Church Rd & right at x-rds

Located within walking distance of the city centre, this charming house maintains its Victorian style. Friendly proprietors make every effort to ensure a stay is pleasant and memorable. The attractive bedrooms have many considerate extras. There is a lounge, and freshly cooked breakfasts are served in the pleasant dining room.

Rooms 10 en suite (4 fmly) (2 GF) **Facilities** TVB tea/coffee Cen ht TVL Dinner Last d at breakfast **Notes** ⊗ No coaches ⊜

WHEDDON CROSS   MAP 03 SS93

★★★★ 🍴 🛏 FARM HOUSE
North Wheddon Farm *(SS923385)*
TA24 7EX
☎ 01643 841791 Mrs R Abraham
e–mail: rachael@go-exmoor.co.uk
web: www.go-exmoor.co.uk
dir: *500yds S of village x-rds on A396. Pass Moorland Hall on left, driveway next right*

North Wheddon Farm is a delightfully friendly and comfortable environment with great views. The tranquil grounds include a pleasant garden, and the memorable dinners and breakfasts feature local and the farm's own fresh produce. The bedrooms are thoughtfully equipped, and beds are most comfortable.

Rooms 3 rms (2 en suite) (1 pri facs) S £35–£37.50; D £70–£75
Facilities TVB tea/coffee Licensed Cen ht Dinner Last d 10am Wi-fi available Riding **Parking** 5 **Notes** LB 17 acres Mixed

★★★★ INN
The Rest and Be Thankful Inn
TA24 7DR
☎ 01643 841222 📄 01643 841813
e–mail: stay@restandbethankful.co.uk
dir: *M5 junct 25, A358 to Minehead, left onto B3224 at sign to Wheddon Cross*

The Rest and Be Thankful stands in the highest village on Exmoor, overlooking Dunkery Beacon. The comfortable bedrooms are extremely well equipped with extras such as mini-bars and trouser presses. The convivial bar, complete with crackling log fires is a popular meeting point for locals and visitors alike. A range of wholesome dishes is offered either in the bar or restaurant.

Rooms 8 en suite (1 fmly) S £36–£40; D £66–£75✳ **Facilities** TVB tea/coffee Direct dial from bedrooms Cen ht Dinner Last d 9pm Wi-fi available Pool Table Skittle alley **Conf** Max 50 Class 50 Board 50 **Parking** 10 **Notes** ⊗ Closed 25 Dec

WILLITON   MAP 03 ST04

★★★★ GUEST HOUSE
The White House
11 Long St TA4 4QW
☎ 01984 632306
e–mail: thewhitehouse@stefanroberts.orangehome.co.uk
dir: *A39 Bridgwater to Minehead, In Williton on right prior to Watchet turning*

A relaxed and easy-going atmosphere is the hallmark of this charming Georgian property. Bedrooms in the main building are more spacious than those in the courtyard, but all are well equipped with extra touches that make the White House a home-from-home.

Rooms 6 rms (5 en suite) (1 pri facs) 4 annexe en suite (3 fmly) (4 GF) S £37.50–£42.50; D £65–£75✳ **Facilities** TVB tea/coffee Licensed Cen ht Dinner Last d 2pm **Parking** 12 **Notes** LB No coaches

WINCANTON   MAP 04 ST72

★★★★ BED & BREAKFAST
Brookleigh
Holton BA9 8AE
☎ 01963 34685
e–mail: theclementss@hotmail.com
dir: *A371 from Wincanton towards Templecombe, at rdbt 1st exit onto A357, B&B signed*

Just a stone's throw from the A303, this well-kept family home is a good stopover or useful base for touring Somerset and Wiltshire, with easy access to Stourhead and Longleat. The clean, fresh bedrooms are attractively co-ordinated, and there is also a lounge. Breakfast, served in the conservatory dining room, features eggs from the neighbour's chickens.

Rooms 3 en suite S £25–£30; D £50 **Facilities** TVB tea/coffee Cen ht TVL **Parking** 6 **Notes** ⊗ 🖘

WINSFORD

MAP 03 SS93

★ ★ ★ ★ 🏵 GUEST HOUSE

Karslake House

Halse Ln TA24 7JE
☎ 01643 851242 📠 01643 851242
e–mail: enquiries@karslakehouse.co.uk
web: www.karslakehouse.co.uk
dir: *In village centre, past the pub and up the hill*

The 15th-century Karslake House stands in a peaceful Exmoor village. Its public rooms feature original beams and fireplaces, and an interesting menu of delicious meals is available in the dining room. Bedrooms are thoughtfully furnished and have a number of extra touches.

Rooms 6 rms (5 en suite) (1 pri facs) (1 GF) S £60–£80; D £85–£120✱ **Facilities** TVB tea/coffee Licensed Cen ht Dinner Last d 8.15pm Aromatherapist & Masseuse **Parking** 15 **Notes** No children 12yrs No coaches Closed Feb & Mar RS Nov–Jan

WITHYPOOL

MAP 03 SS83

Premier Collection

★ ★ ★ ★ ★ 🛏 BED & BREAKFAST

Kings Farm

TA24 7RE
☎ 01643 831381 📠 01643 831381
e–mail: info@kingsfarmexmoor.co.uk
dir: *Off B3223 to Withypool, over bridge & sharp left to farm*

Over two acres of landscaped gardens beside the river form the backdrop of this delightful farmhouse, set in an idyllic valley beside the Barle. It combines all the character and charm of its 19th-century origins with every modern comfort. From the carefully planned bedrooms to the sumptuously furnished sitting room, delicious home-cooked breakfasts and the warmest of welcomes, top quality is most definitely the hallmark of Kings Farm. Stabling and fishing available.

Rooms 2 rms (1 en suite) (1 pri facs) S £55; D £79–£89✱ **Facilities** STV TVB tea/coffee Cen ht Wi-fi available Fishing **Parking** 3 **Notes** No children 14yrs

★ ★ ★ ★ 🍽 INN

The Royal Oak Inn

TA24 7QP
☎ 01643 831506 📠 01643 831659
e–mail: enquiries@royaloakwithypool.co.uk
dir: *7m N of Dulverton, off B3223*

Set in the heart of the beautiful Exmoor landscape, this long established and popular inn has been providing rest and sustenance for weary travellers for many years. The atmosphere is warm and engaging with the bar always frequented by cheery locals with a story to tell! Bedrooms and bathrooms are stylish and very well appointed with added touches of luxury such as Egyptian cotton linen, bath robes and cosseting towels. Menus feature local produce and can be enjoyed either in the bars or in the elegant restaurant.

Rooms 8 rms (7 en suite) (1 pri facs) S £75; D £120✱ **Facilities** TVB tea/coffee Direct dial from bedrooms Cen ht Dinner Last d 9.30pm **Parking** 10 **Notes LB** No children 10yrs No coaches

WIVELISCOMBE

MAP 03 ST02

★ ★ ★ ★ INN

White Hart

West St TA4 2JP
☎ 01984 623344 📠 01984 624748
e–mail: reservations@whitehartwiveliscombe.co.uk
dir: *M5 junct 25 then A38 to Taunton. Follow signs for A358 to Minehead then B3227 to Wiveliscombe*

This establishment is the focal point of this delightful town situated near the foot of the Quantock Hills. Exmoor is on the doorstep and the coast is just a few miles' drive away. Bedrooms have been refurbished and offer contemporary accommodation with a good range of facilities. Innovative dishes are offered in the restaurant and the bar has good range of locally brewed beers.

Rooms 16 en suite (2 fmly) **Facilities** TVB tea/coffee

YEOVIL   MAP 04 ST51

See also Crewkerne

Premier Collection

★★★★★ ⚛⚛⚛ 🍷
RESTAURANT WITH ROOMS
Little Barwick House

Barwick Village BA22 9TD
☎ 01935 423902 📄 01935 420908
e–mail: littlebarwick@hotmail.com

dir: From Yeovil A37 towards Dorchester, left at 1st rdbt, 1st left, 0.25m on left

Situated in a quiet hamlet in 3.5 acres of gardens and grounds, this listed Georgian dower house is an ideal retreat for those seeking peaceful surroundings and good food. Just one of the highlights of a stay here is a meal in the restaurant, where good use is made of local ingredients. Each of the bedrooms has its own character, and a range of thoughtful extras such as fresh flowers, bottled water and magazines.

Rooms 6 en suite S £80–£126; D fr £138✳ **Facilities** TVB tea/coffee Direct dial from bedrooms Cen ht Dinner Last d 9pm **Parking** 30 **Notes LB** No children 5yrs RS Sun eve & Mon

★★★★ 🍽 INN
The Masons Arms

41 Lower Odcombe BA22 8TX
☎ 01935 862591 📄 01935 862591
e–mail: paula@masonsarmsodcombe.co.uk
web: www.masonsarmsodcombe.co.uk

dir: From A303 take A3088 to Yeovil, follow signs to Montacute after village, 3rd turning on right

Dating back to the 16th century, this charming inn claims to be the oldest building in this small country village on the outskirts of Yeovil. The spacious bedrooms are contemporary in style, with clean lines, high level of comfort and a wide range of considerate extras. The friendly hosts run their own micro-brewery, and their ales are available at the bar along with others. Public areas include the bar/restaurant, which offers a full menu of freshly prepared dishes, along with a choice of lighter snacks. There is a small caravan/touring park at the rear of the inn.

Rooms 5 en suite (5 GF) S £70; D £85✳ **Facilities** FTV TVB tea/coffee Direct dial from bedrooms Cen ht Dinner Last d 9.30pm Wi-fi available **Conf** Max 15 Class 15 Board 15 **Parking** 35 **Notes** No coaches

★★★★ ⚛ INN
The Helyar Arms

Moor Ln, East Coker BA22 9JR
☎ 01935 862332 📄 01935 864129
e–mail: info@helyar-arms.co.uk

dir: 3m S of Yeovil. Off A30 or A37 into East Coker

A charming 15th-century inn, serving real food in the heart of a pretty Somerset village. The traditional friendly bar with hand-drawn ales retains many original features while the bedrooms offer well equipped, attractive accommodation and modern facilities.

Rooms 6 en suite (3 fmly) **Facilities** TVB tea/coffee Direct dial from bedrooms Cen ht Dinner Last d 9.30pm Wi-fi available Skittle alley **Conf** Max 40 Thtr 40 Class 20 Board 30 **Parking** 40 **Notes** RS 25 Dec

★★★ INN
The Half Moon Inn

Main St, Mudford BA21 5TF
☎ 01935 850289 📄 01935 850842
e–mail: enquiries@thehalfmooninn.co.uk

dir: A303 at Sparkford onto A359 to Yeovil, 3.5m on left

Situated north of Yeovil, this delightful village inn dates from the 17th century. It has a wealth of character, enhanced by exposed beams and flagstone floors. The inn is very popular for its extensive range of wholesome food, and there is a choice of bar and dining area. Most of the spacious, well-equipped bedrooms are on the ground floor of a separate adjacent building.

Rooms 14 en suite (4 fmly) (9 GF) S £59.95; D £64.95(room only) **Facilities** STV TV13B tea/coffee Cen ht Dinner Last d 9.45pm Wi-fi available **Parking** 36 **Notes** ⊗ Closed 25–26 Dec

★★★ INN
The Halfway House Inn Country Lodge

Ilchester Rd BA22 8RE
☎ 01935 840350 📄 01935 849006
e–mail: paul@halfwayhouseinn.com
web: www.halfwayhouseinn.com

dir: A303 onto A37 Yeovil road at Ilchester, inn 2m on left

This roadside inn offers comfortable accommodation, which consists of bedrooms in the main house and other contemporary style rooms, each having its own front door, in the annexe. All rooms are bright and well equipped. Meals of generous portion are available in the cosy restaurant and bar, where friendly staff ensure a warm welcome.

Rooms 11 en suite 10 annexe en suite (6 fmly) (10 GF) **Facilities** STV TVB tea/coffee Cen ht TVL Dinner Last d 9pm Wi-fi available Fishing Pool Table **Conf** Max 120 Thtr 120 Class 50 Board 40 **Parking** 49

ENGLAND

STAFFORDSHIRE

ABBOTS BROMLEY
MAP 10 SK02

★★★★ FARM HOUSE
Marsh Farm *(SK069261)*
WS15 3EJ
☎ 01283 840323 Mrs M K Hollins
e–mail: marshfarm@meads1967.co.uk
web: www.marshfarmstaffs.co.uk

dir: *1m N of Abbots Bromley on B5013*

Guests are welcome to walk around the fields at this working farm and watch the activities. The farmhouse has been modernised and bedrooms are carefully furnished and equipped; three rooms are located in a sympathetic barn conversion. Comprehensive breakfasts are served in the spacious cottage-style dining room, which operates as a popular tea room during the summer.

Rooms 5 rms (3 en suite) (1 fmly) (1 GF) S £30–£35; D £60–£65✱
Facilities TVB tea/coffee Cen ht TVL **Parking** 6 **Notes** ⊗ 20 acres mixed Closed 25–27 Dec

ADBASTON
MAP 15 SJ72

★★★ 🅰 FARM HOUSE
Offley Grove Farm *(SJ760270)*
ST20 0QB
☎ 01785 280205 & 07745 170279 📠 01785 280205
Mrs M Hiscoe-James
e–mail: enquiries@offleygrovefarm.co.uk
web: www.offleygrovefarm.co.uk

dir: *3m from A519*

Rooms 2 en suite (1 fmly) S fr £34; D £54–£58✱ **Facilities** TVB tea/coffee Cen ht TVL Wi-fi available Fishing 🦢 **Conf** Max 24 Thtr 24 Class 24 Board 20 **Parking** 10 **Notes** ⊗ 45 acres Beef Closed 24–31 Dec Civ Wed 39 🍽

ALTON
MAP 10 SK04

★★★★ BED & BREAKFAST
Chained Oak Farm
Farley Ln ST10 4BZ
☎ 01538 702104
e–mail: cross@barn.fslife.co.uk
web: www.chainedoak.com

dir: *Between Alton & Farley, opp Alton Towers*

This modern detached house stands in delightful grounds including extensive woodlands and affords fine all-round views. It is very close to Alton Towers and offers spacious bedrooms, three of which are located in the renovated former stables. Families are especially welcome and warm hospitality is assured.

Rooms 1 en suite 3 annexe en suite (2 fmly) (4 GF) D £52✱
Facilities TVB tea/coffee Cen ht TVL **Parking** 10 **Notes** LB ⊗ 🍽 🍽

AUDLEY
MAP 15 SJ75

★★★★ FARM HOUSE
Domvilles Farm *(SJ776516)*
Barthomley Rd ST7 8HT
☎ 01782 720378 📠 01782 720883 Mrs E E Oulton
e–mail: eileen.oulton@virgin.net

dir: *M6 junct 16, B5078 towards Alsager, 0.5m left to Barthomley, left at White Lion, Domvilles 0.5m on left*

This 260-acre dairy farm is a short drive from major roads, and is delightfully presented throughout. Quality décor, antiques and memorabilia highlight the original features of the elegant Georgian property, and bedrooms feature fine Victorian four-poster, half-tester and brass beds. Imaginative food is served and a warm welcome is assured.

Rooms 5 en suite (1 fmly) (3 GF) S £35; D £60✱ **Facilities** TVB tea/coffee Cen ht TVL Dinner Last d 7pm Fishing **Conf** Max 40 Board 40 **Parking** 10 **Notes** LB ⊗ 260 acres Dairy/sheep

BREWOOD
MAP 10 SJ80

★★★★ BED & BREAKFAST
The Old Vicarage
Vicarage Rd ST19 9HA
☎ 01902 850210

dir: *From A449 to Brewood, right onto The Pavement, then right onto Vicarage Rd, on left*

Located close to the village centre, this elegant period house stands in pretty mature gardens and has been sympathetically renovated to provide modern facilities, while keeping lots of character. Bedrooms provide a wealth of thoughtful extras, and comprehensive breakfasts are taken at an antique oak table in the dining room, which overlooks the grounds.

Rooms 3 rms (2 en suite) (1 pri facs) S £38–£42; D £64–£69✱
Facilities TVB tea/coffee Cen ht Wi-fi available 🌳 **Parking** 5 **Notes** ⊗ Closed Xmas & New Year 🍽

BURTON UPON TRENT MAP 10 SK22

★★★★ GUEST ACCOMMODATION
The Delter

5 Derby Rd DE14 1RU
☎ 01283 535115 📄 01283 845261
e-mail: info@delterhotel.co.uk
web: www.thedelter.co.uk

dir: A511 rdbt onto A5121 Derby Rd, 50yds on left

This relaxing guest house is on the outskirts of Burton upon Trent, close to the famous Bass Museum. Bedrooms are thoughtfully equipped and carefully decorated, while the public areas consist of a pleasant breakfast room. Expect friendly and attentive service.

Rooms 7 en suite (2 fmly) (2 GF) S £40–£45; D £55–£65✱ **Facilities** FTV TVB tea/coffee Cen ht Wi-fi available **Parking** 8 **Notes** ⊗ Closed Xmas

★★★★ GUEST HOUSE
The Edgecote

179 Ashby Rd DE15 0LB
☎ 01283 568966
e-mail: susanmccabe@hotmail.co.uk

dir: 0.5m E of town centre on A511

Located in a residential area on the outskirts of town, this impressive Edwardian house provides a range of thoughtfully-equipped bedrooms, mostly en suite or with private facilities. A comprehensive breakfast is served in the oak-panelled dining room and there is a quiet lounge.

Rooms 11 rms (5 en suite) (2 pri facs) (1 fmly) **Facilities** TVB tea/coffee Cen ht **Parking** 6 **Notes** ⊗ No coaches

CHEDDLETON MAP 16 SJ95

Premier Collection

★★★★★ BED & BREAKFAST
Choir Cottage and Choir House

Ostlers Ln ST13 7HS
☎ 01538 360561 & 07719 617078
e-mail: enquiries@choircottage.co.uk

dir: Off A520 opp Red Lion onto Hollow Ln, pass church & left onto Ostlers Ln, cottage on right at top of hill

Original features complement this carefully decorated 17th-century stone cottage. The bedrooms have lots of thoughtful extras and feature four-poster beds, modern bathrooms and private entrances. Spacious lounge areas are available in an adjacent house, and the attractive dining room is the setting for breakfast.

Rooms 1 en suite 2 annexe en suite (1 fmly) (2 GF) S £55–£65; D £70–£75✱ **Facilities** TVB tea/coffee Direct dial from bedrooms Cen ht **Parking** 5 **Notes LB** ⊗ Closed Xmas ⊛

★★★★ GUEST HOUSE
Prospect House

334 Cheadle Rd ST13 7BW
☎ 01782 550639
e-mail: prospect@talk21.com
web: www.prospecthouseleek.co.uk

dir: 4m S of Leek on A520

Prospect House was built from local stone in 1838, and stands on the A520 between Cheddleton and Wetley Rocks. Bedrooms are in a converted coach house behind the house, and facilities include a traditionally-furnished dining room together with a cosy lounge, and a pleasant garden with a conservatory.

Rooms 5 en suite (1 fmly) (2 GF) S £25–£30; D £30–£50✱ **Facilities** FTV TVB tea/coffee Direct dial from bedrooms Cen ht TVL Dinner Last d 3pm Wi-fi available **Parking** 5 **Notes LB** ⊗ No coaches

CODSALL MAP 10 SJ80

★★★ GUEST ACCOMMODATION
Moors Farm

Chillington Ln WV8 1QF
☎ 01902 842330 📄 01902 847878
e-mail: enquiries@moorsfarm-hotel.co.uk
web: www.moorsfarmhotel.co.uk

dir: Between Codsall & Codsall Wood, onto Chillington Ln to T-junct & turn right

Located to the north of Codsall village and within easy reach of the M54, this farm provides friendly hospitality and thoughtfully equipped and comfortable accommodation. A self-catering apartment is also available. Wholesome breakfasts are served in the spacious dining room.

Rooms 6 rms (4 en suite) (1 fmly) S £35–£45; D £70✱ **Facilities** TVB tea/coffee Cen ht **Parking** 20 **Notes LB** ⊗ No children 4yrs

ECCLESHALL MAP 15 SJ82

★★★★ FARM HOUSE
Slindon House Farm (SJ826324)

Slindon ST21 6LX
☎ 01782 791237 Mrs H Bonsall
e-mail: helenbonsall@btconnect.com

dir: 2m N of Eccleshall on A519

This large, charming, Victorian farmhouse is fronted by a lovely garden and situated on a dairy, arable and sheep farm in the village of Slindon some 2.5 miles from Eccleshall. It has one twin and one double-bedded room, both of which are thoughtfully equipped. Breakfast is served at individual tables in the traditionally-furnished combined breakfast room and lounge.

Rooms 2 rms (1 en suite) (1 pri facs) S fr £35; D £50✱ **Facilities** TVB tea/coffee Cen ht TVL **Parking** 4 **Notes** ⊗ 175 acres arable dairy sheep beef Closed 23 Dec–3 Jan ⊛

EDINGALE　　　　MAP 10 SK21

★ ★ ★ BED & BREAKFAST
Oakwood Barn B&B
Oakwood Barn, Lullington Rd B79 9JA
☎ 01827 383916
e–mail: edingalequeenbee@yahoo.co.uk

dir: *From Lichfield take A38, right onto A513. Left towards Croxall, then right towards Edingdale, 900mtrs on Lullington Road, B&B on right*

Oakwood Barn dates back to the 16th century and is set in the wonderful Staffordshire countryside. The well equipped en suite bedrooms provide good comfort. Awake to the early morning dawn chorus of birds and enjoy a hearty breakfast with eggs supplied by the chickens in the garden.

Rooms 2 en suite (1 GF) D £65–£75✱ **Facilities** FTV TVB tea/coffee Cen ht Wi-fi available **Parking** 6 **Notes** ⊛ No children Closed Xmas & New Year ⊛

ELLASTONE　　　　MAP 10 SK14

★ ★ ★ ★ 🄰 BED & BREAKFAST
Cross Farm
Main Rd DE6 2GZ
☎ 01335 324668
e–mail: jane@cross-farm.co.uk
web: www.cross-farm.co.uk

dir: *On B5032 in village centre on corner of Dove St/Main Rd*

Rooms 2 en suite (2 fmly) S £27–£35; D £50–£55 **Facilities** TVB tea/coffee Cen ht **Parking** 6 **Notes LB** ⊛ ⊛

FROGHALL　　　　MAP 10 SK04

★ ★ ★ FARM HOUSE
Hermitage Working Farm (SK037497)
ST10 2HQ
☎ 01538 266515 📄 01538 266155 Mrs W Barlow
e–mail: wilma@hermitagefarm.co.uk
web: www.hermitagefarm.co.uk

dir: *A52 onto B5053 in Froghall, farm 0.5m on left at top of hill*

Parts of this charming sandstone house date from the 16th century. It is quietly located on an elevated position with panoramic views. There is traditionally-furnished accommodation in the main house as well as a converted barn that offers rooms suitable for families. Handy for visiting Alton Towers.

Rooms 3 en suite 6 annexe en suite (3 fmly) (3 GF) **Facilities** TVB tea/coffee Cen ht Riding Shooting **Parking** 12 **Notes** ⊛ 75 acres beef, sheep, poultry RS Nov–Mar

LICHFIELD　　　　MAP 10 SK10

★ ★ ★ ★ BED & BREAKFAST
Abbey House
Walsall Rd WS13 6RF
☎ 01543 301509 & 07977 183317
e–mail: jan@abbeyhousebnb.co.uk
web: www.abbeyhousebnb.co.uk

dir: *From Bowling Green Island in Lichfield, take A51 to Rugeley, 1st right house on left*

A few minutes walk from the historic centre and Lichfield Cathedral, this immaculately maintained house has been sympathetically renovated to provide high standards of comfort and facilities. Smart modern bathrooms complement thoughtfully furnished bedrooms, and comprehensive breakfasts are taken in an attractive dining room.

Rooms 3 en suite S £32; D £52–£54✱ **Facilities** FTV TVB tea/coffee Cen ht **Parking** 4 **Notes** ⊛ No children 14yrs Closed 24–26 Dec

---

★ ★ ★ ★ GUEST ACCOMMODATION
Coppers End
Walsall Rd, Muckley Corner WS14 0BG
☎ 01543 372910 📄 01543 360423
e–mail: info@coppersendguesthouse.co.uk
web: www.coppersendguesthouse.com

dir: *A5 onto A461 N for 100yds*

Formerly the police station, this family-run guest house provides well-appointed modern accommodation. Two bedrooms are on the ground floor, and most have smart en suites. There is a comfortable lounge, and breakfast is served in a modern conservatory overlooking the pretty rear gardens.

Rooms 6 rms (4 en suite) (2 GF) S £35–£42; D £52–£64✱ **Facilities** TVB tea/coffee Cen ht TVL Wi-fi available **Parking** 9 **Notes LB** ⊛ Closed Xmas & New Year

ENGLAND

LICHFIELD CONTINUED

★★★★ GUEST HOUSE
Netherstowe House

Netherstowe Ln WS13 6AY
☎ 01543 254270 📠 01543 254270
e–mail: reservations@netherstowehouse.com
web: www.netherstowehouse.com

dir: *A38 onto A5192, 0.3m on right, turn onto Netherstowe Ln.
Take 1st left & 1st right down private drive*

Located in a residential area a few minutes drive from city centre, this
elegant Georgian house provides a range of bedrooms, some of which
are quite spacious. Comprehensive breakfasts are taken in a cosy
dining room and a comfortable guest lounge is also available.

Rooms 12 en suite 8 annexe en suite (2 fmly) (5 GF) S £75–£95;
D £75–£95✱ **Facilities** FTV TVB tea/coffee Cen ht TVL Wi-fi available
Gymnasium 🏊 **Parking** 35 **Notes LB** ⊗

★★★ BED & BREAKFAST
Moat Cottage

29 Gaia Ln WS13 7LW
☎ 01543 419823 📠 01543 419823
e–mail: paynemoat@waitrose.com

dir: *From cathedral, Gaia Ln 1st on right after the Close*

This pretty, white-painted cottage, with mature gardens to the rear, is
located close to the city centre and cathedral. The beamed,
ground-floor twin bedroom has a spacious shower room. Memorable
breakfasts are served in the cosy hall-dining room, which also contains
comfortable lounge seating.

Rooms 1 en suite (1 GF) D £55✱ **Facilities** STV TVB tea/coffee Cen ht
Parking 3 **Notes** ⊗ No children ⊜

★★★ BED & BREAKFAST
The Hawthorns

30 Norwich Close WS13 7SJ
☎ 01543 250151
e–mail: bambrushton@hotmail.com

dir: *1m N of city centre. Off A5192 Eastern Ave nr Vauxhall
garage onto Norwich Close*

Located in a residential area on the outskirts of the city, this modern
house provides a homely bedroom with separate side entrance to the
property and a modern private shower room. Breakfast is taken in an
attractive kitchen/dining room overlooking a pretty rear garden.

Rooms 1 rms (1 pri facs) (1 GF) S £32; D £45✱ **Facilities** TVB tea/
coffee Cen ht Wi-fi available **Parking** 2 **Notes** ⊗ No children ⊜

★★ BED & BREAKFAST
8 The Close

8 The Close WS13 7LD
☎ 01543 418483 & 07812 202415
e–mail: gill@theclose.fsnet.co.uk
web: www.ldb.co.uk/accommodation.htm

dir: *In city centre opposite the Cathedral and next door to the
Cathedral bookshop. Off Beacon St into The Close (cathedral)*

Idyllic location opposite the 7th-century cathedral, this late Georgian
terrace house offers homely accommodation and a warm welcome is
assured. Breakfasts, which are taken at one table in the cosy hall dining
room, feature fine local or homemade produce. Free parking is
available within easy walking distance.

Rooms 3 rms (1 en suite) S £34–£44; D £54–£64✱ **Facilities** TVB tea/
coffee Cen ht Wi-fi available **Notes** ⊗ ⊜

LONGNOR   MAP 16 SK06

★★★★ ⊕ RESTAURANT WITH ROOMS
The Black Grouse

SK17 0NS
☎ 01298 83205 & 83194 📠 01298 83689
e–mail: food@theblackgrouse.co.uk

dir: *In village centre on B5053*

Located in the heart of the Peak District National Park this 18th-century
coaching inn offers stylish, fully equipped bedrooms each with a
modern en suite. Public areas include the oak-panelled bar (featuring
real ales) and separate dining room – both offering a tempting range
of bar meals and a frequently changing carte menu, using fresh, local
ingredients.

Rooms 8 en suite 3 annexe rms (3 fmly) (1 GF) S £60–£100;
D £100–£160✱ **Facilities** STV FTV TV8B tea/coffee Direct dial from
bedrooms Cen ht Dinner Last d 9.30pm Wi-fi available **Conf** Max 25
Board 25 **Parking** 100 **Notes LB** Civ Wed 50

OAKAMOOR

MAP 10 SK04

★★★★ GUEST HOUSE
The Beehive Guest House

Churnet View Rd ST10 3AE
☎ 01538 702420 📠 01538 702420
e-mail: thebeehiveoakamoor@btinternet.com
web: www.thebeehiveguesthouse.co.uk

dir: *Off B5417 in village N onto Eaves Ln, sharp left onto Churnet View Rd*

Standing in the centre of the village and overlooking the river, this spacious detached house offers thoughtfully equipped and comfortable bedrooms. There is also a comfortable lounge-dining room, where substantial breakfasts are served. This guest house is renowned for its hospitality.

Rooms 5 en suite (1 fmly) (1 GF) S £35–£54; D £54–£58 **Facilities** TVB tea/coffee Cen ht TVL Dinner Last d 6pm **Parking** 6 **Notes LB** ⊗ No children 5yrs No coaches

★★★★ FARM HOUSE
Crowtrees Farm (SK049459)

Eaves Ln ST10 3DY
☎ 01538 702260 Mrs D Bickle
e-mail: dianne@crowtreesfarm.co.uk
web: www.crowtreesfarm.co.uk

dir: *Off B5417 in village N onto Eaves Ln, 1m on left*

This impeccably maintained 200-year-old farmhouse is convenient for the Potteries, the Peak District and Alton Towers. Bedrooms are comfortable and well equipped. It is still a working farm with splendid views, and has a variety of pets. The friendly owners create a relaxing atmosphere.

Rooms 3 en suite 5 annexe en suite (2 fmly) **Facilities** TVB tea/coffee Cen ht **Parking** 6 **Notes** ⊗ 55 acres beef/sheep Closed 25–26 Dec

★★★★ GUEST HOUSE
The Laurels Guest House

Star Bank ST10 3BN
☎ 01538 702629 📠 01538 702796
e-mail: bbthelaurels@aol.com
web: www.thelaurels.co.uk

dir: *On B5147 from Cheadle, 250yds on right past Cricketers Arms public house in Oakamoor*

At the edge of Oakamoor village, offering comfortable bedrooms and a bar lounge and a spacious dining room, this friendly guest house is ideally located for families wishing to visit Alton Towers or touring rural Staffordshire and the Potteries.

The Laurels Guest House

Rooms 9 en suite (5 fmly) (1 GF) **Facilities** FTV TVB tea/coffee Licensed Cen ht TVL Dinner Last d 8.30pm Pool Table **Parking** 9 **Notes** ⊗ No coaches

★★★★ GUEST HOUSE
Tenement Farm

Three Lows, Ribden ST10 3BW
☎ 01538 702333 📠 01538 703603
e-mail: stanleese@aol.com
web: www.tenementfarm.co.uk

dir: *2m NE of Oakamoor. Off A52 onto B5417, 1st drive on left, signed*

Families are particularly welcome at this non-smoking former farmhouse, which has been renovated to provide high standards of comfort throughout. Popular with visitors to Alton Towers, bedrooms are equipped with homely extras. Public areas include a comfortable lounge with honesty bar, an attractive dining room and a children's play room.

Rooms 8 en suite (6 fmly) (2 GF) D £60–£70✱ **Facilities** TVB tea/coffee Licensed Cen ht TVL Dinner Last d 6.30pm **Parking** 12 **Notes LB** ⊗ No coaches Closed Nov–Feb

★★★ GUEST HOUSE
Admirals House

Mill Rd ST10 3AG
☎ 01538 702187
e-mail: admiralshouse@btinternet.com

dir: *A52 onto B5417. In Oakamoor village opposite picnic site*

Within the heart of the village a few minutes drive from Alton Towers, this half-timbered house is a popular community meeting point for a range of tasty bar meals and real ales. Homely bedrooms are equipped with thoughtful extras and family rooms are also available.

Rooms 6 en suite (4 fmly) (1 GF) S £25–£35; D £40–£50✱ **Facilities** TVB tea/coffee Licensed Cen ht Dinner Last d 8.30pm **Parking** 10 **Notes** ⊗ No coaches Closed 23 Dec–3 Jan RS Nov–Mar

CONTINUED

RUGELEY   MAP 10 SK01

Premier Collection

★★★★★ 🏠 GUEST HOUSE
Colton House
Colton WS15 3LL
☎ 01889 578580 📄 01889 578580
e–mail: mail@coltonhouse.com
web: www.coltonhouse.com

dir: *1.5m N of Rugeley. Off B5013 into Colton, 0.25m on right*

Set within the pretty village of Colton, this elegant early 18th-century house has been restored to retain original character and provide high standards of comfort and facilities. Bedrooms have a wealth of thoughtful extras, there is a spacious and comfortable lounge and a 1.5 acre garden.

Rooms 4 en suite S £50–£75; D £66–£96 **Facilities** FTV TVB tea/coffee Licensed Cen ht TVL Dinner Last d 1pm Wi-fi available **Conf** Max 15 Thtr 15 Class 15 Board 15 **Parking** 15 **Notes** ⊗ No children 12yrs No coaches

★★★★ 🏵 🏠 INN
The Plum Pudding
Rugeley Rd, Armitage WS15 4AZ
☎ 01543 490330 📄 01543 491229
e–mail: enquiries@plumpudding.co.uk
web: www.theplumpudding.co.uk

dir: *2.5m SE of Rugeley. On A513 at W end of Armitage*

Situated on the banks of the Trent and Mersey Canal, this property has been restored to offer comfortable, well-equipped accommodation.

CONTINUED

Meals are served in the brasserie where guests can relax beside the canal, enjoy a refreshing drink, and choose from a large selection of tempting, freshly prepared dishes.

Rooms 4 annexe en suite (1 fmly) (2 GF) S £55; D £55–£80 **Facilities** TVB tea/coffee Cen ht Dinner Last d 9.30pm Wi-fi available **Parking** 50 **Notes** ⊗ No children 2yrs No coaches Closed 25–26 Dec, 1 Jan

STAFFORD   MAP 10 SJ92

★★★★ FARM HOUSE
Haywood Park Farm *(SJ991207)*
Shugborough ST17 0XA
☎ 01889 882736 📄 01889 882736 Mr T Nichols
e–mail: haywood.parkfarm@btopenworld.com
web: www.haywoodparkfarm.co.uk

dir: *4m SE of Stafford off A513. Brown signs to Shugborough, on right 400yds past estate exit*

Part of the Shugborough Estate, this historic house commands panoramic views over the fruit, flower and sheep farm. Delightfully furnished bedrooms have a wealth of thoughtful extras, and breakfast is served in the attractive lounge-dining room and features home grown and local produce

Rooms 2 en suite D £70–£80✴ **Facilities** STV TVB tea/coffee Cen ht TVL Fishing Riding **Parking** 4 **Notes** LB ⊗ No children 14 yrs 120 acres sheep/horse livery/fruit farm 🅿

★★★ GUEST HOUSE
Leonards Croft
80 Lichfield Rd ST17 4LP
☎ 01785 223676 📄 01785 223676
e–mail: leonardscroft@hotmail.com

dir: *A34 from town centre signed Cannock, 0.5m on left*
Located south of the town centre, this well-proportioned late Victorian house has been carefully renovated to provide a range of practically furnished bedrooms, two of which are situated on the ground floor. A range of popular evening dishes is available in addition to comprehensive breakfasts, and a spacious lounge is also available. The gardens are extensive.

Rooms 9 en suite (3 fmly) (2 GF) **Facilities** TVB tea/coffee Licensed Cen ht TVL Dinner Last d 7pm **Parking** 12 **Notes** No coaches

★★★ BED & BREAKFAST
Old School
Newport Rd, Haughton ST18 9JH
☎ 01785 780358 🖷 01785 780358
e-mail: info@theoldsc.co.uk

dir: *A518 W from Stafford, 3m to Haughton, Old School next to church*

Located in the heart of Haughton village, this Grade II listed former Victorian school has been renovated to provide a range of modern bedrooms equipped with thoughtful extras. Breakfast is served at a family table in a cosy lounge-dining room.

Rooms 3 rms (3 GF) S £25; D £50 **Facilities** TVB tea/coffee Cen ht **Parking** 3 **Notes** ✆

★★ GUEST HOUSE
The Windsor
69 Lichfield Rd ST17 4LW
☎ 01785 258531 🖷 01785 246875
e-mail: info@abbeyhotelstafford.co.uk

dir: *0.6m SE of town centre on A34*

The Windsor is popular with contractors and overseas students. It has a range of practically equipped bedrooms, and a large car park. Breakfast is served in the dining room of the adjacent Abbey Hotel, which is under the same ownership.

Rooms 14 rms (3 en suite) S £28–£56; D £48–£70✳ **Facilities** FTV TVB tea/coffee Licensed Cen ht TVL Dinner Last d 8pm **Parking** 16 **Notes** ✆ No coaches Closed 21 Dec–6 Jan

Ⓤ
The Yew Tree Inn & Restaurant
Long Compton, Ranton ST18 9JT
☎ 01785 282278 🖷 01785 282278

dir: *M6 junct 14 towards Bridgeford, turn left to Woodseaves. At x-rds follow brown signs to inn, on left*

At the time of going to press the rating for this establishment had not been confirmed. Please check the AA website www.theAA.com for up-to-date information.

Rooms 3 en suite S fr £45; D fr £65✳ **Facilities** TVB tea/coffee Cen ht Dinner Last d 9pm **Parking** 60 **Notes** ✆

STONE
MAP 10 SJ93

★★★ BED & BREAKFAST
Field House
59 Stafford Rd ST15 0HE
☎ 01785 605712 🖷 01785 605712
e-mail: fieldhouse@ntlworld.com

dir: *A34 NW into town centre, right onto Stafford Rd, opp Walton Grange*

This family home stands in secluded, pretty gardens close to the town centre. The Georgian house has traditionally furnished bedrooms, some with family pieces. Guests breakfast together in the lounge-dining room, and hospitality is very welcoming.

Rooms 3 rms (1 en suite) (2 fmly) **Facilities** TVB tea/coffee Cen ht TVL Art tuition on request **Parking** 4 **Notes** ✆ ✆

Ⓤ
Langtrys
1–3 Oulton Rd ST15 8EB
☎ 01785 818724

At the time of going to press the rating for this establishment had not been confirmed. Please check the AA website www.theAA.com for up-to-date information.

Rooms 3 en suite **Facilities** TVB tea/coffee Cen ht **Parking** 33 **Notes** ✆ No children 16yrs

Ⓤ
Ye Olde Post Office
32 Church Ln, Oulton ST15 8UE
☎ 01785 813215 & 07867 813403
e-mail: jenny@yeoldepostoffice.co.uk

dir: *A520 to Leek, left before Trout Farm*

At the time of going to press the rating for this establishment had not been confirmed. Please check the AA website www.theAA.com for up-to-date information.

Rooms 2 rms S fr £30; D fr £45 **Facilities** TVB tea/coffee Cen ht **Parking** 3 **Notes** LB ✆

ENGLAND

STRETTON MAP 10 SJ81

★★ BED & BREAKFAST
Cottage Garden Roses
Woodlands House ST19 9LG
☎ 01785 840217 📠 01902 850193
e–mail: teresa@cottagegardenroses.com

dir: *M6 junct 12, A5 towards Telford, after 0.5m Gailey Island rdbt, after 2m follow brown tourist signs for cottage*

This charming former farmhouse dates from the mid 18th century. The delightful garden contains many Old English roses, and a range of organic skin care products made here are a feature of the bedroom. The traditionally furnished twin-bedded room with private bathroom has both elegance and atmosphere.

Rooms 1 en suite **Facilities** tea/coffee Cen ht TVL Dinner Last d day before **Parking** 6 **Notes** Closed Xmas & 2wks annual holiday

TAMWORTH MAP 10 SK20

Premier Collection

★★★★★ GUEST HOUSE
Oak Tree Farm
Hints Rd, Hopwas B78 3AA
☎ 01827 56807 📠 01827 56807
e–mail: oaktreefarm1@aol.com
web: www.oaktreefarmhotel.co.uk

dir: *2m NW of Tamworth. Off A51 in Hopwas*

A warm welcome is assured at this sympathetically restored farmhouse, located in peaceful rural surroundings yet only a short drive from the NEC. Spacious bedrooms are filled with homely extras. The elegant dining room, adorned with Oriental artefacts, is the setting for memorable breakfasts. A small conference room is available.

Rooms 2 en suite 5 annexe en suite (2 fmly) (2 GF) **Facilities** TVB tea/coffee Cen ht TVL Wi-fi available ⓕ Fishing Sauna **Conf** Max 15 Thtr 15 Class 9 Board 15 **Parking** 20 **Notes** No coaches

★★★★ INN
Globe Inn
Lower Gungate B79 7AW
☎ 01827 60455 📠 01827 63575
e–mail: info@theglobetamworth.com

Located in the centre of Tamworth, this popular inn provides well-equipped and pleasantly decorated accommodation. The public areas include a spacious lounge bar and a relaxed dining area where a varied selection of dishes is available. There is also a function room and adjacent parking.

Rooms 18 en suite (2 fmly) (18 smoking) S fr £50; D fr £50✷ **Facilities** STV TVB tea/coffee Cen ht Dinner Last d 9pm **Conf** Thtr 90 Class 90 Board 90 **Parking** 30 **Notes** ⊗ Closed 25 Dec

★★★★ GUEST HOUSE
Harlaston Post Office
Main Rd, Harlaston B79 9JU
☎ 01827 383324 & 383746 📠 01827 383746
e–mail: info@harlastonpostoffice.co.uk

dir: *4.5m N, off A513 into Harlaston village*

Part of the village stores and Post Office, this guest house stands opposite the ancient church. The individually-styled bedrooms provide a range of modern facilities in addition to thoughtful extras. Hearty cooked breakfasts can be enjoyed in the attractive dining room and a conservatory lounge overlooks the pretty garden.

Rooms 4 en suite (1 fmly) (1 GF) **Facilities** STV TVB tea/coffee Direct dial from bedrooms Lift Cen ht TVL **Parking** 5 **Notes** ⊗ No coaches ⊜

★★★★ Ⓐ GUEST ACCOMMODATION
Middleton House Farm
Tamworth Rd, Middleton B78 2BD
☎ 01827 873474 📠 01827 872246
e–mail: rob.jane@tinyonline.co.uk

dir: *4m S of Tamworth on A4091*

Rooms 6 en suite S fr £45; D £65–£85✷ **Facilities** FTV TVB tea/coffee Cen ht TVL Wi-fi available **Parking** 8 **Notes** ⊗ No children 12yrs Closed Xmas & New Year

UTTOXETER MAP 10 SK03

★★★★ BED & BREAKFAST
High View Cottage
Toothill Rd ST14 8JU
☎ 01889 568183
e–mail: info@highviewcottage.co.uk

dir: *1m S of town centre. Off B5017 Highwood Rd onto Toothill Rd*

Located on the edge of Uttoxeter and close to the racecourse, High View Cottage offers comfortable, well-equipped accommodation and a friendly atmosphere. Bedrooms are equipped with lots of thoughtful extras, and hearty breakfasts are served in the attractive Garden Room which overlooks the courtyard.

Rooms 5 en suite (2 fmly) (5 GF) S £25–£45; D £50–£65✷ **Facilities** FTV TVB tea/coffee Cen ht Wi-fi available Pool Table **Conf** Max 8 Board 8 **Parking** 10 **Notes** ⊗

★★★ GUEST HOUSE
Oldroyd Guest House & Motel
18–22 Bridge St ST14 8AP
☎ 01889 562763 📄 01889 568916
e–mail: enquiries@oldroyd-guesthouse.com

dir: *On A518 near racecourse*

This privately owned and personally run guest house is close to the town centre and eight miles from Alton Towers. Bedrooms have modern facilities, and some family and ground-floor rooms are available. Breakfast is served at separate tables in the bright and pleasant breakfast room.

Rooms 12 rms (10 en suite) 3 annexe en suite (7 fmly) (5 GF)
Facilities TVB tea/coffee Cen ht TVL **Parking** 20

WOODSEAVES   MAP 15 SJ72

★★★★ FARM HOUSE
Tunstall Hall Farm *(SJ771273)*
ST20 0NH
☎ 01785 280232 📄 01785 280232 Mrs Cooke
e–mail: isabel.cooke@btinternet.com

dir: *2m NW of Woodseaves. A41 onto A519, 1st left to Shebdon, continue for 3m and turn right towards Woodseaves, Bishops Offley 1m on right*

Located in a quiet hamlet, this impressive renovated farmhouse dates from the early 18th century and retains original exposed beams and open fires. The thoughtfully furnished bedrooms have smart modern shower rooms en suite, and breakfast is served in the attractive conservatory.

Rooms 2 en suite (1 fmly) S £25–£45; D £50–£60✳ **Facilities** TVB tea/coffee Cen ht TVL **Parking** 6 **Notes** ⊗ 280 acres Mixed dairy ⊜

SUFFOLK

ALDEBURGH   MAP 13 TM45

★★★★ GUEST HOUSE
The Toll House
50 Victoria Rd IP15 5EJ
☎ 01728 453239 & 454474
e–mail: tollhouse@fsmail.net
web: www.tollhouse.travelbugged.com

dir: *B1094 into town until rdbt, B&B on right*

Expect a warm welcome at this delightful red brick property situated just a short walk from the seafront and town centre. Bedrooms are tastefully furnished, have co-ordinated fabrics and many thoughtful touches. Breakfast is served at individual tables in the smart dining room, which overlooks the garden.

Rooms 7 en suite (3 GF) S £65–£70; D £70–£75✳ **Facilities** TVB tea/coffee Cen ht **Parking** 6 **Notes** ⊗ No coaches

★★★ INN
The Mill Inn
Market Cross Place IP15 5BJ
☎ 01728 452563 📄 01728 452563
e–mail: peeldennisp@aol.com

A traditional seafront inn in a bustling coastal town. Public areas include a lounge bar, a restaurant and a public bar frequented by local fishermen and the lifeboat crew. Bedrooms are simply decorated and well equipped; some rooms have lovely sea views.

Rooms 4 rms S £45–£50; D £65–£75✳ **Facilities** TVB tea/coffee Cen ht Dinner Last d 9pm **Notes** No children 8yrs

BARNINGHAM   MAP 13 TL97

★★★★ BED & BREAKFAST
College House Farm
Bardwell Rd IP31 1DF
☎ 01359 221512 📠 01359 221512
e–mail: jackie.brightwell@talk21.com

dir: *Off B1111 to village x-rds & onto Bardwell Rd*

A charming Grade II-listed Jacobean property, which stands in a peaceful location close to Bury St Edmunds. Its abundant original character is complemented by fine period furnishings. Bedrooms are generally quite spacious and thoughtfully equipped. Public rooms include an elegant dining room and a cosy lounge.

Rooms 4 rms (1 en suite) 2 annexe en suite (4 fmly) **Facilities** TVB tea/coffee Cen ht Dinner 🥄 **Conf** Max 10 **Parking** 8 **Notes** No children 5yrs ⊕

BEYTON   MAP 13 TL96

Premier Collection

★★★★★ 🏠 BED & BREAKFAST
Manorhouse
The Green IP30 9AF
☎ 01359 270960
e–mail: manorhouse@beyton.com
web: www.beyton.com

dir: *4m E of Bury St Edmunds. Beyton signed off A14 junct 46*

This charming 15th-century Suffolk longhouse is set in immaculate gardens in the heart of the village. The restored property retains many original features, such as exposed beams and roaring log fires. Bedrooms, two of which are in an adjacent barn conversion, are very spacious. Each is carefully furnished and filled with lots of thoughtful touches. Breakfast is served in the elegant dining room and there is a relaxing lounge.

Rooms 2 en suite 2 annexe en suite (2 GF) S £50–£60; D £66–£76 **Facilities** FTV TVB tea/coffee Cen ht Wi-fi available **Parking** 6 **Notes** ⊗ No children 12yrs Closed Xmas ⊕

BUNGAY   MAP 13 TM38

★★★★ FARM HOUSE
Earsham Park Farm *(TM304883)*
Old Railway Rd, Earsham NR35 2AQ
☎ 01986 892180 📠 01986 894796 Mrs B Watchorn
e–mail: aa@earsham-parkfarm.co.uk
web: www.earsham-parkfarm.co.uk

dir: *3m SW of Bungay on A143*

A superb detached Victorian property overlooking open countryside and forming part of a working farm. The property has been restored by the enthusiastic owners and retains many original features. Bedrooms and public areas are attractively furnished, and the excellent breakfasts feature home-made produce including sausages and bacon from the organically reared pigs.

Rooms 3 en suite S £46–£68; D £70–£92 **Facilities** FTV TVB tea/coffee Cen ht Wi-fi available **Conf** Max 16 Board 16 **Parking** 11 **Notes** 589 acres arable, pigs (outdoor)

BURY ST EDMUNDS   MAP 13 TL86

Premier Collection

★★★★★ ◉ GUEST ACCOMMODATION
Clarice House
Horringer Court, Horringer Rd IP29 5PH
☎ 01284 705550 📠 01284 716120
e–mail: bury@claricehouse.co.uk
web: www.claricehouse.co.uk

dir: *1m SW from town centre on A143 towards Horringer*

A large country property set amidst pretty landscaped grounds a short drive from the historic town centre. The spacious, well-equipped bedrooms have coordinated fabrics and many thoughtful touches. Public rooms have a wealth of charm and include a smart lounge bar, an intimate restaurant, a further lounge and a conservatory. The property also has superb leisure facilities.

Rooms 13 en suite S £55–£75; D £85–£100 **Facilities** STV FTV TVB tea/coffee Direct dial from bedrooms Lift Cen ht Dinner Last d 8.45pm ⊙ Sauna Solarium Gymnasium Spa & Beauty facilities **Conf** Max 50 Thtr 50 Class 50 Board 50 Del from £75 ✳ **Parking** 85 **Notes** LB ⊗ No children 5yrs Closed 24–26 Dec & 31 Dec–1 Jan

★★★★ INN
The Black Boy
69 Guildhall St IP33 1QD
☎ 01284 752723

dir: *Off A14 to town centre*

A popular inn situated in the centre of this historic town. The spacious bedrooms have co-ordinated fabrics, pine furniture and many thoughtful touches. Public areas feature a large open-plan bar with a good selection of ales and a range of bar snacks are also available.

Rooms 5 en suite **Facilities** tea/coffee Cen ht Dinner Last d 9pm **Parking** 6 **Notes** ⊗ No coaches

★★★★ BED & BREAKFAST
Brambles Lodge
Welham Ln, Risby IP28 6QS
☎ 01284 810701 📄 01284 810701

dir: *4m W of Bury. Off A14 junct 41 into Risby. Down South St, past Crown & Castle on left into Welham Ln. 2nd drive on right*

This establishment stands amid attractive landscaped gardens in the peaceful village of Risby. Breakfast is served at a large table in the smart conservatory that overlooking the garden with its duck pond. All the bedrooms are on the ground floor level, and have tea and coffee making facilities along with colour TV.

Rooms 2 en suite 1 annexe en suite (1 fmly) (3 GF) S £35–£40; D £60–£65 **Facilities** TV4B tea/coffee Cen ht **Parking** 5 **Notes** ⊗ No children ☺

★★★★ ➡ GUEST ACCOMMODATION
The Chantry
8 Sparhawk St IP33 1RY
☎ 01284 767427 📄 01284 760946
e–mail: chantryhotel1@aol.com

dir: *From cathedral S onto Crown St, left onto Sparhawk St*

Expect a warm welcome at this attractive Georgian property, just a short walk from the town centre. The individually decorated bedrooms are furnished with well-chosen pieces and have many thoughtful touches. Dinner and breakfast are served in the smart restaurant, and there is a cosy lounge-bar.

Rooms 12 en suite 3 annexe en suite (1 GF) S £69–£84; D £89–£99✳ **Facilities** TVB tea/coffee Direct dial from bedrooms Cen ht Dinner Last d 7pm Wi-fi available **Parking** 16 **Notes** LB

★★★★ BED & BREAKFAST
83 Whiting Street
83 Whiting St IP33 1NX
☎ 01284 704153
e–mail: gordon.wagstaff@btinternet.com

dir: *In town centre*

An attractive three-storey terrace property convenient for exploring this historic town. The spacious, individually decorated bedrooms are furnished with pine and equipped with modern facilities. Breakfast is served in the beamed dining room that features an open fireplace and a wall painting dating from 1530.

Rooms 4 en suite S £40; D fr £60✳ **Facilities** TV3B tea/coffee Cen ht **Notes** ⊗ ☺

★★★★ INN
The Fox & Hounds
Felsham Rd, Bradfield St George IP30 0AB
☎ 01284 386379
e–mail: bradfieldfox@aol.com

dir: *Off A134 Bury onto Sudbury Rd, at Sicklesmere turning to Little Welnetham & Bradfield St George*

Delightful inn set in a peaceful rural location surrounded by open countryside. The spacious bedrooms are in a converted barn to the rear of the inn; each one has pine furniture and a good range of useful extras. Public areas include a smart restaurant, a cosy bar and a small conservatory.

Rooms 2 annexe en suite (2 GF) **Facilities** TVB tea/coffee Cen ht Dinner Last d 9pm Petanque pitch **Parking** 30 **Notes** Closed 2–9 Jan

★★★★ ➡ INN
The Six Bells at Bardwell
The Green, Bardwell IP31 1AW
☎ 01359 250820 📄 01359 250820
e–mail: sixbellsbardwell@aol.com
web: www.sixbellsbardwell.co.uk

dir: *8m NE, off A143 on edge of viillage. Follow brown signs from A143*

This 16th-century inn lies in the peaceful village of Bardwell. The bedrooms are in a converted stable block next to the main building, and are furnished in a country style and thoughtfully equipped. Public rooms have original character and provide a choice of areas in which to relax.

Rooms 10 annexe en suite (1 fmly) (10 GF) S £52.50–£75; D £70–£95✳ **Facilities** FTV TVB tea/coffee Cen ht Dinner Last d 8.30pm **Parking** 50 **Notes** LB Closed 25 Dec–3 Jan

★★★★ INN
The Three Kings
Hengrave Rd, Fornham All Saints IP28 6LA
☎ 01284 766979
e–mail: thethreekings@keme.co.uk
web: www.the-three-kings.com

dir: *A14 junct 42, B1106 to Fornham, left onto B1101, establishment on left*

Attractive inn situated in the pleasant village of Fornham All Saints. The bedrooms are in a building adjacent to the main property; each one is smartly furnished and thoughtfully equipped. Public rooms feature a smart lounge bar, a conservatory, and a comfortable restaurant.

Rooms 9 annexe en suite (2 fmly) (6 GF) S £62–£80; D £80✳ **Facilities** TVB tea/coffee Direct dial from bedrooms Cen ht Dinner Last d 9pm Wi-fi available Pool Table **Conf** Max 45 Thtr 12 Class 24 Board 24 **Parking** 28 **Notes** ⊗

ENGLAND

★★★ GUEST ACCOMMODATION
The Abbey
35 Southgate St IP33 2AZ
☎ 01284 762020 ▤ 01284 724770
e–mail: 01284762020@tel-w.com

dir: *A14 junct 44, A1302 to town centre, onto Southgate St, premises 400yds*

The Abbey is well placed for visiting the historic town centre. The property is split between several historic buildings, the main core dating from the 15th century. The public rooms in the Tudor inn section feature a comfortable lounge and an informal dining area. Bedrooms vary in size and style, but all are comfortably furnished and well equipped.

Rooms 9 en suite 3 annexe en suite (1 fmly) (2 GF) S £68–£88; D £88–£98✳ **Facilities** TVB tea/coffee Cen ht **Parking** 12 **Notes** ⊗ No children 3yrs

★★★ INN
Dog & Partridge, The Old Brewers House
29 Crown St IP33 1QU
☎ 01284 764792
e–mail: 1065@greeneking.co.uk
web: www.oldenglish.co.uk

dir: *In town centre. Off A134 Parkway onto Westgate St & left onto Crown St*

Charming inn situated just a short walk from the town centre. Public rooms include a smart conservatory, a lounge bar, a small dining area and a smartly decked terrace to the rear of the property for alfresco dining. Bedrooms are pleasantly decorated, have co-ordinated fabrics, natural wood furniture and many thoughtful touches.

Rooms 9 en suite (2 fmly) (3 GF) **Facilities** STV TVB tea/coffee Direct dial from bedrooms Dinner Last d 9pm **Parking** 11 **Notes** ⊗

★★★ BED & BREAKFAST
5/6 Orchard Street
IP33 1EH
☎ 01284 750191 & 07946 590265
e–mail: mariellascarlett@hotmail.com

dir: *In town centre near St John's Church on one-way system*

Expect a warm welcome from the caring hosts at this terrace property situated just a short walk from the town centre. The pleasant bedrooms are comfortably appointed and have a good range of useful extras. Breakfast is served at a large communal table in the cosy dining room.

Rooms 3 rms S £24–£26; D £36–£38✳ **Facilities** TVB tea/coffee Cen ht **Notes** No children 6yrs Closed Aug ⊛

★★★ BED & BREAKFAST
Hamilton House
4 Nelson Rd IP33 3AG
☎ 01284 703022 & 07787 146553 ▤ 01284 703022
e–mail: hamiltonhouse@hotmail.co.uk

dir: *A14 junct 43, A134, left onto Risbygate St, 1st right*

A warm welcome awaits at this relaxing Edwardian villa, which is situated in a quiet side road just a short walk from the town centre. The bedrooms are brightly decorated with co-ordinated fabrics and have a good range of facilities. Breakfast is served at a large communal table in the dining room.

Rooms 4 rms (2 en suite) (1 fmly) S £25–£30; D £50–£55✳ **Facilities** TVB tea/coffee Cen ht Wi-fi available **Notes** ⊗ ⊛

★★★ ⬩ INN
Old Cannon Brewery
86 Cannon St IP33 1JR
☎ 01284 768769
e–mail: stay@oldcannonbrewery.co.uk

dir: *A14 junct 43, A134 towards town centre. At rdbt after Tesco left then sharp right onto Cadney Ln, left onto Cannon St, on left*

This delightful Victorian property was originally a beer house and brewery. The present owner has renovated the building and reopened the brewery, and the finished products can be sampled in the bar. The bar-dining area features a unique mirror-polished stainless-steel mash tun and boiler. Bedrooms are in an adjacent building; each one is pleasantly decorated and well equipped.

Rooms 5 en suite (1 GF) S £65; D £79✳ **Facilities** FTV TVB tea/coffee Cen ht Dinner Last d 9.15pm Wi-fi available Micro Brewery on premises, tours available **Parking** 6 **Notes** ⊗ No children 14yrs No coaches RS Xmas/New Year

★★★ BED & BREAKFAST
St Andrews Lodge
30 Saint Andrews St North IP33 1SZ
☎ 01284 756733
e–mail: standrewslodge@hotmail.com

dir: *A14 junct 43, A134 towards town centre, left onto Saint Andrews St North, Lodge on right*

This delightful property which is ideally situated close to the A14 and town centre. The well-equipped modern bedrooms are on the ground floor of a separate purpose-built building to the rear of the house. Breakfast is served at individual tables in the smart dining room, which overlooks the neat courtyard.

Rooms 3 annexe en suite (3 GF) S fr £45; D fr £60✳ **Facilities** FTV TVB tea/coffee Cen ht **Parking** 3

★★★ **A** GUEST HOUSE
Dunston Guest House
8 Springfield Rd IP33 3AN
☎ 01284 767981 📠 01284 764574
web: www.dunstonguesthouse.co.uk

dir: *A14 from Cambridge, 1st slip road onto A1302, in 1.5m after pedestrian crossing & Falcon pub left onto Springfield Rd*

Rooms 11 rms (7 en suite) (4 pri facs) 6 annexe rms (2 en suite) (5 fmly) (4 GF) S £30–£45; D £65–£75 **Facilities** TVB tea/coffee Cen ht TVL **Parking** 10 **Notes** ⊗ ☻

★★ GUEST ACCOMMODATION
Avery House
2 Newmarket Rd IP33 3SN
☎ 01284 755484

dir: *1m from Bury St Edmunds West, junct off A14 towards town centre*

Large detached, purpose-built property situated on the edge of town within easy walking distance of the shops. The property is popular with contractors and offers value for money accommodation. The practically equipped bedrooms are comfortable and a full English breakfast is provided in the cafeteria style dining room.

Rooms 6 en suite (1 fmly) (3 GF) S £35–£40; D £45–£50✱ **Facilities** TVB tea/coffee Cen ht **Parking** 7 **Notes** ⊗ ☻

U
The Olde Bull Inn
The Street, Barton Mills IP28 6AA
☎ 01638 711001 📠 01638 712003
e-mail: bookings@bullinn-bartonmills.com

At the time of going to press the rating for this establishment had not been confirmed. Please check the AA website www.theAA.com for up-to-date information.

Rooms 14 en suite S £60–£80; D £70–£90 (room only)

CAMPSEA ASH   MAP 13 TM35

★★★ **A** GUEST ACCOMMODATION
Dog and Duck
Station Rd IP13 0PT
☎ 01728 748439

dir: *Off A12 for Framlingham, onto B1078, 1.5m on left*

Rooms 5 annexe en suite (2 fmly) (4 GF) **Facilities** TVB tea/coffee Cen ht Dinner Last d 9pm **Parking** 20 **Notes** ⊗

CLARE   MAP 13 TL74

★★★★ GUEST ACCOMMODATION
Ship Stores
22 Callis St CO10 8PX
☎ 01787 277834 📠 01787 277183
e-mail: shipclare@aol.com

dir: *A1092 to Clare, onto B1063, past church 100yds on right*

A charming property situated in the heart of an historic market town. Bedrooms are split between the main house and a converted stable block; each room is furnished in a country style with bright, co-ordinated soft furnishings and many thoughtful touches. Public areas include a lounge with comfy sofas, and a contemporary breakfast room with a stripped pine floor.

Rooms 4 en suite 2 annexe en suite (1 fmly) (3 GF) S £45–£57; D £57–£62✱ **Facilities** TVB tea/coffee Cen ht Wi-fi available **Parking** 3 **Notes** LB ⊗

ELMSWELL   MAP 13 TL96

★★★★ GUEST HOUSE
Kiln Farm Guest House
Kiln Ln IP30 9QR
☎ 01359 240442
e-mail: davejankilnfarm@btinternet.com

dir: *Exit A14 junct 47 for A1088. Entrance to Kiln Ln off east bound slip road.*

A delightful Victorian farmhouse situated in a peaceful rural location amid three acres of landscaped grounds. The bedrooms are housed in converted farm buildings; each is smartly decorated and furnished in country style. Breakfast is served in the bar-dining room and there is a cosy lounge.

Rooms 2 en suite 6 annexe en suite (2 fmly) (6 GF) S £40–£50; D £80–£100✱ **Facilities** TVB tea/coffee Licensed Cen ht TVL Dinner Last d 6pm Wi-fi available **Parking** 20 **Notes** No coaches

465

EYE   MAP 13 TM17

★★★★ INN
The White Horse Inn
Stoke Ash IP23 7ET
☎ 01379 678222   📠 01379 678800
e-mail: mail@whitehorse-suffolk.co.uk
web: www.whitehorse-suffolk.co.uk
dir: *On A140 halfway between Ipswich & Norwich*

A 17th-century coaching inn situated in the village of Stoke Ash.
Bedrooms are located in an annexe adjacent to the main building;
each one is smartly decorated in pastel shades, tastefully furnished
with co-ordinated fabrics and thoughtfully equipped. An interesting
choice of dishes is served in the restaurant, which features exposed
beams and inglenook fireplaces.

Rooms 11 annexe en suite (1 fmly) (9 GF) S £49.50; D £49.90–£59.50✱
Facilities FTV TVB tea/coffee Direct dial from bedrooms Cen ht Dinner
Last d 9.30pm Wi-fi available **Conf** Max 50 Thtr 50 Class 50 **Parking** 60
Notes LB ⊗

FELIXSTOWE   MAP 13 TM33

★★★★ A GUEST HOUSE
Castle Lodge
Chevalier Rd IP11 7EY
☎ 01394 282149
dir: *A14 to town centre from Hamilton Rd, 3rd left & 1st right onto
Chevalier Rd*

Rooms 10 rms (9 en suite) (1 pri facs) (2 fmly) (1 GF) S £40–£50;
D £60–£70✱ **Facilities** TVB tea/coffee Licensed Cen ht Dinner Last d
4pm **Parking** 5 **Notes LB** No coaches Closed 24 Dec

FRAMLINGHAM   MAP 13 TM26

★★★★ FARM HOUSE
Woodlands Farm *(TM269709)*
Brundish IP13 8BP
☎ 01379 384444 Mrs J Graham
e-mail: jillatwoodlands@aol.com
dir: *4m N of Framlingham. Off A1120 onto B1116 N, 4th left,
0.5m left onto no-through road*

Quietly located north of the town, this charming house has a wealth of
character, including original exposed beams and inglenook fireplaces
CONTINUED

in the sitting room and the elegant dining room. The pleasant
bedrooms are carefully decorated and thoughtfully equipped.

Rooms 3 en suite S £30–£35; D £50–£60✱ **Facilities** tea/coffee Cen ht
TVL **Parking** 6 **Notes** ⊗ No children 10yrs 4 acres Small Holding Closed
24 Dec–2 Jan ⊜

★★★ GUEST ACCOMMODATION
Church Farm
Church Rd, Kettleburgh IP13 7LF
☎ 01728 723532
e-mail: jbater@suffolkonline.net
dir: *Off A12 to Wickham Market, signs to Easton Farm Park &
Kettleburgh 1.25m, house behind church*

A charming 300-year-old farmhouse situated close to the village church
amid superb grounds with a duck pond, mature shrubs and sweeping
lawns. The converted property retains exposed beams and open
fireplaces. Bedrooms are pleasantly decorated and equipped with
useful extras, and a ground-floor bedroom is available.

Rooms 3 rms (1 en suite) (1 GF) S £32–£34; D £64–£68 **Facilities** tea/
coffee Cen ht TVL Dinner Last d 7.30pm Fishing **Parking** 10 **Notes** ⊜

HADLEIGH   MAP 13 TM04

★★★★★ GUEST ACCOMMODATION
Edge Hall
2 High St IP7 5AP
☎ 01473 822458   📠 01473 822458
e-mail: r.rolfe@edgehall.co.uk
dir: *B1070 into Hadleigh. 1st property in High St on right*

This imposing 16th-century building is situated at the quiet end of High
Street and has been run by the same family for over 25 years. The
spacious bedrooms are individually decorated and carefully furnished
in period style – one room has a superb four-poster bed. Breakfast is
served in the elegant dining room and there is also a comfortable
lounge.

CONTINUED

Edge Hall

Valley Farm

Rooms 6 en suite 4 annexe en suite (2 fmly) (1 GF) S £57.50–£67.50;
D £85–£110✱ **Facilities** TVB tea/coffee Cen ht ✍ **Conf** Max 12
Parking 20 **Notes** LB 🐾

Rooms 2 en suite (1 fmly) S £60; D £54–£70✱ **Facilities** FTV TVB tea/
coffee Cen ht Wi-fi available 🐾 **Parking** 15 **Notes** LB ⊗ 🐾

HOLTON   MAP 13 TM47

Premier Collection

★★★★★ BED & BREAKFAST
Valley Farm
Bungay Rd IP19 8LY
☎ 01986 874521
e–mail: mail@valleyfarmholton.co.uk
web: www.valleyfarmholton.co.uk

dir: *A144 onto B1123 to Holton, left at fork in village, left at
school, 500yds on left*

Expect a warm welcome from the caring hosts at this charming red
brick farmhouse situated in a peaceful rural location a short drive from
Halesworth. The individually decorated bedrooms are tastefully
appointed with coordinated soft furnishings and many thoughtful
touches. Breakfast, which features locally sourced and home grown
produce, is served at a large communal table in the smartly appointed
dining room. The property has lovely landscaped grounds, a summer
house, and an indoor heated swimming pool.

IPSWICH   MAP 13 TM14

★★★ INN
The Shipwrights Arms
55–61 Wherestead Rd IP2 8JJ
☎ 01473 602261 📄 01473 604255

dir: *A14 onto A137 Ipswich Centre, at West Dock, turn left at Audi
garage, 50yds on right*

A smartly presented inn situated just a few minutes walk from the town
centre. Bedrooms are generally quite spacious; each one is smartly
decorated with co-ordinated soft furnishings and has many thoughtful
touches. Public rooms include a small bar area, two dining rooms and
a lovely conservatory.

Rooms 9 en suite (2 GF) S £55–£85; D £55–£85✱ **Facilities** TVB tea/
coffee Cen ht TVL Dinner Last d 9pm **Parking** 6 **Notes** ⊗ No coaches
RS Sun

LAVENHAM   MAP 13 TL94

Premier Collection

★★★★★ ◉◉ 🍷 RESTAURANT WITH ROOMS
Lavenham Great House 'Restaurant With Rooms'
Market Place CO10 9QZ
☎ 01787 247431 📄 01787 248007
e–mail: info@greathouse.co.uk
web: www.greathouse.co.uk

dir: *Off A1141 onto Market Ln, behind cross on Market Place*

The 18th-century front on Market Place conceals a 15th-century
timber-framed building that houses a restaurant with rooms. The Great
House has recently undergone major refurbishment, and remains a
pocket of France offering high-quality rural cuisine served by French
staff. The spacious bedrooms are individually decorated and
thoughtfully equipped with many useful extras; some rooms have a
separate lounge area.

Rooms 5 en suite (1 fmly) S £85–£180; D £85–£180✱ (room only)
Facilities FTV TVB tea/coffee Direct dial from bedrooms Cen ht Dinner
Last d 9.30pm Wi-fi available **Notes** LB Closed Jan RS Sun eve & Mon

CONTINUED

467

LAVENHAM CONTINUED

Premier Collection

★★★★★ BED & BREAKFAST

Lavenham Priory

Water St CO10 9RW

☎ 01787 247404 📄 01787 248472

e–mail: mail@lavenhampriory.co.uk

web: www.lavenhampriory.co.uk

dir: A1141 to Lavenham, turn by side of Swan onto Water St & right after 50yds onto private drive

A superb Grade I listed building, dating from the 15th century that once belonged to Benedictine monks and has been lovingly restored to maintain its original character. Individually decorated bedrooms are very spacious; each is beautifully furnished and thoughtfully equipped. Breakfast is served in the spectacular Merchants room or in the sheltered courtyard herb garden. Guests also have use of the Great Hall, with inglenook fireplace, and an adjoining lounge.

Rooms 6 en suite S £75–£85; D £100–£165✳ **Facilities** TVB tea/coffee Cen ht TVL Wi-fi available **Parking** 11 **Notes** No children 10yrs Closed 21 Dec–2 Jan

★★★★ BED & BREAKFAST

Wood Hall

Little Waldingfield CO10 0SY

☎ 01787 247362

e–mail: susan@woodhallbnb.fsnet.co.uk

web: www.thewoodhall.com

dir: A1141 onto B1115 into Little Waldingfield, Wood Hall 200yds on left past Swan pub

This is a delightful 15th-century property just a short drive from historic Lavenham. The spacious, individually decorated bedrooms are thoughtfully equipped. Breakfast is served in the elegant dining room, which features a superb inglenook fireplace with a wood-burning stove. Parking at rear.

Rooms 2 en suite S £50–£85; D £80–£85✳ **Facilities** TVB tea/coffee Cen ht Dinner Last d 48hrs before Wi-fi available 🐾 **Parking** 4 **Notes** ⊗ No children 10yrs Closed 21 Dec–2 Jan

★★★★ 🅰 BED & BREAKFAST

Brett Farm

The Common CO10 9PG

☎ 01787 248533

e–mail: brettfarmbandb@aol.com

web: www.brettfarm.com

dir: In Lavenham turn by Swan Hotel onto Water St, 4th left & 1st right over white bridge, farm on right

Rooms 3 rms (2 en suite) (3 GF) S £40–£65; D £65–£70✳ **Facilities** TVB tea/coffee Cen ht Wi-fi available Carriage rides Bike hire **Parking** 6 **Notes** ⊗ 🐾

◉ 🅤

The Angel

Market Place CO10 9QZ

☎ 01787 247388 📄 01787 248344

e–mail: angel@maypolehotels.com

web: www.maypolehotels.com

dir: From A14 take Bury E & Sudbury turn onto A143. After 4m take A1141 to Lavenham. Off High Street

At the time of going to press the rating for this establishment had not been confirmed. Please check the AA website www.theAA.com for up-to-date information.

Rooms 8 en suite (1 fmly) (1 GF) S £70; D £85✳ **Facilities** FTV TVB tea/coffee Direct dial from bedrooms Cen ht TVL Dinner Last d 9.15pm Wi-fi available **Parking** 5

LEISTON   MAP 13 TM46

★★★★ GUEST HOUSE

Field End

1 Kings Rd IP16 4DA

☎ 01728 833527 📄 01728 833527

e–mail: herbert@herbertwood.wanadoo.co.uk

web: www.fieldendbedandbreakfast.co.uk

dir: In town centre off B1122

This Edwardian house has been refurbished to a high standard and is impeccably maintained by the present owners. Bedrooms have coordinated soft furnishings and many thoughtful touches. Breakfast is served in an attractive dining room, which has a large sofa and a range of puzzles and games.

CONTINUED

Rooms 5 rms (2 en suite) (1 pri facs) (1 fmly) (1 GF) S fr £30;
D fr £60✳ **Facilities** TVB tea/coffee Cen ht TVL **Parking** 5 **Notes** ⊗
No children 6mths No coaches ⊛

LOWESTOFT   MAP 13 TM59

★★★★ GUEST ACCOMMODATION
Abbe Guest House

322 London Rd South NR33 0BG

☎ 01502 581083

e-mail: abbehouse@btconnect.com

dir: *On A12, 1.5m from the Pakefield Water Tower rdbt, 50yds past Rectory Rd*

Expect a warm welcome from the caring hosts at this charming property situated just a short walk from the seafront and town centre. Bedrooms are pleasantly decorated, have coordinated soft furnishings and benefit from many thoughtful touches. Breakfast is served in the smart dining room, and guests have the use of a cosy lounge bar with plush leather sofas.

Rooms 4 rms (3 en suite) (1 pri facs) (1 fmly) **Facilities** FTV TVB tea/coffee Cen ht TVL Dinner Last d 11am **Notes** ⊗ No children 5yrs Closed 21 Dec–6 Jan

★★★★ GUEST ACCOMMODATION
Somerton House

7 Kirkley Cliff NR33 0BY

☎ 01502 565665 📠 01502 501176

e-mail: pippin.somerton@btinternet.com

dir: *On the old A12, 100yds from Claremont Pier*

Somerton House is a Grade II Victorian terrace situated in a peaceful area of town overlooking the sea. Bedrooms are smartly furnished in a period style and have many thoughtful touches; some rooms have four poster or half-tester beds. Breakfast is served in the smart dining room and guests have the use of a cosy lounge.

Rooms 7 rms (5 en suite) (2 pri facs) (1 fmly) (1 GF) S £35–£36;
D £40–£41✳ **Facilities** STV FTV TVB tea/coffee Cen ht TVL Dinner Last d noon Wi-fi available **Notes LB** Closed 25–26 Dec

★★★ GUEST ACCOMMODATION
Katherine

49 Kirkley Cliff Rd NR33 0DF

☎ 01502 567858 📠 01502 581341

e-mail: beauthaicuisine@aol.com

web: www.beauthaikatherine.co.uk

dir: *On A12 seafront road next to Kensington Garden*

This large Victorian property lies opposite the beach in the quiet part of town. The spacious public rooms include a smart lounge bar with plush leather sofas and an intimate restaurant serving authentic Thai cuisine. The pleasant bedrooms have coordinated fabrics and many thoughtful touches.

Rooms 10 en suite (5 fmly) S £35–£50; D £55–£65✳ **Facilities** TVB tea/coffee Direct dial from bedrooms Cen ht Dinner Last d 10.30pm **Parking** 4 **Notes LB**

★★★ GUEST HOUSE
Coventry House

8 Kirkley Cliff NR33 0BY

☎ 01502 573865 📠 01502 573865

dir: *On A12 opp Claremont Pier, 0.25m S from Harbour Bridge*

An impressive Victorian terrace house situated on the seafront opposite the pier. The pleasant bedrooms are thoughtfully equipped and many rooms have lovely sea views. Breakfast is served in the carefully appointed dining room and there is a comfortable lounge.

Rooms 7 rms (5 en suite) (2 pri facs) (3 fmly) (1 GF) S £25–£35;
D £55–£60✳ **Facilities** TVB tea/coffee Cen ht TVL **Parking** 4 **Notes LB** No coaches Closed 24–27 Dec ⊛

★★★ GUEST HOUSE
Edingworth

395 London Rd South NR33 0BJ

☎ 01502 572051 📠 01502 572051

e-mail: enquiries@edingworth.co.uk

web: www.edingworth.co.uk

dir: *On A12 through Lowestoft towards Great Yarmouth*

A friendly, family-run guest house situated within easy walking distance of the town centre and seafront. The spacious bedrooms are pleasantly decorated and thoughtfully equipped. Breakfast is served in the smart dining room and there is a comfortable television lounge.

Rooms 6 rms (6 pri facs) (5 fmly) (1 GF) S £30–£32; D £52–£54
Facilities STV TVB tea/coffee Cen ht Dinner Last d noon **Parking** 3
Notes LB ⊗ No coaches Closed 24–26 Dec ⊛

ENGLAND

LOWESTOFT CONTINUED

★★★ GUEST HOUSE
Fairways

398 London Rd South NR33 0BQ
☎ 01502 572659
e–mail: amontali@netmatters.co.uk

dir: *S of town centre on A12, 1m from railway and bus station*

A friendly, family-run guest house located at the southern end of the town. Bedrooms come in a variety of sizes and styles; each room is pleasantly decorated and thoughtfully equipped. Breakfast is served in the smart dining room and there is also a cosy lounge.

Rooms 7 rms (4 en suite) (2 fmly) S fr £20✱ **Facilities** TVB tea/coffee Cen ht TVL

★★★ GUEST HOUSE
Highbury House

397 London Rd South NR33 0BJ
☎ 01502 589064 & 07760 227245
e–mail: highbury.house@hotmail.co.uk

dir: *On A12 follow signs to Lowestoft then London Rd S.*

A friendly, family-run guest house situated just a short walk from the town centre and seafront. Bedrooms are generally quite spacious; each one is pleasantly decorated and equipped with a good range of useful facilities. Breakfast and dinner are served at individual tables in the dining room.

Rooms 5 en suite S £28–£30; D £50–£52✱ **Facilities** FTV TVB tea/coffee Cen ht Dinner Last d noon **Notes** ⊗ No coaches ⊜

★★★ GUEST HOUSE
Kingsleigh

44 Marine Pde NR33 0QN
☎ 01502 572513
e–mail: levett@kingsleigh.wanadoo.co.uk

dir: *On A12 S from Lowestoft town centre, house on right, 0.25m from Harbour Bridge*

A warm welcome is to be expected on arrival at this well-maintained Victorian property, situated on the south side of town just a short walk from the shops. Bedrooms are attractively decorated in pastel shades and have coordinated soft furnishings and many thoughtful touches. Most rooms have superb sea views.

Rooms 5 rms (3 en suite) (1 fmly) **Facilities** FTV TVB tea/coffee Cen ht **Notes** No coaches ⊜

★★★ GUEST ACCOMMODATION
Seavilla

43 Kirkley Cliff Rd NR33 0DF
☎ 01502 574657 📠 01502 574657

dir: *A12 into town, right at South Beach, 300yds past Claremont Pier*

Expect a warm welcome at the Seavilla which is situated on the southern side of town overlooking the beach. The pleasant bedrooms are thoughtfully equipped and many have superb sea views. Breakfast is served at individual tables in the attractive dining room and guests have the use of a cosy lounge.

Rooms 9 rms (5 en suite) S £25–£40; D £50–£60 **Facilities** FTV TVB tea/coffee Cen ht TVL **Notes LB**

★★★ GUEST HOUSE
Wavecrest Guest House

31 Marine Pde NR33 0QN
☎ 01502 561268 📠 01502 561268
e–mail: wavecrestguesthouse@googlemail.com

dir: *On seafront just S of Lowestoft Bridge*

This Victorian terrace house is situated on the seafront, overlooking the award-winning beach and within easy walking distance of the town centre. The bedrooms are smartly decorated with coordinated soft furnishings and equipped with modern facilities. Public areas include an elegant dining room where breakfast is served at individual tables.

Rooms 5 rms (4 en suite) (1 pri facs) (1 fmly) S £25–£35; D £47–£60✱ **Facilities** TVB tea/coffee Cen ht Wi-fi available **Notes** ⊗ No coaches Closed 24–31 Dec

---

MENDHAM   **MAP 13 TM28**

★★★★ BED & BREAKFAST
Weston House Farm

IP20 0PB
☎ 01986 782206
e–mail: holden@farmline.com
web: www.westonhousefarm.co.uk

dir: *Off A143 or B1123 signed Mendham, signs from village centre*

Well maintained Grade II listed, 17th-century farmhouse set in an acre of pleasant gardens in the heart of the Waveny valley. The individually decorated bedrooms are generally quite spacious, thoughtfully furnished and well-equipped. Breakfast is served in the smart dining room which overlooks the garden.

Rooms 3 en suite (1 GF) S £34–£42; D £54–£65✱ **Facilities** TVB tea/coffee Cen ht TVL Wi-fi available **Parking** 6 **Notes** No children 10yrs Closed Dec–Feb ⊜

NAYLAND   MAP 13 TL93

★★★★ GUEST ACCOMMODATION

The Steam Mill House

1 Fen St CO6 4HT

☎ 01206 262818 📠 01206 262818

e-mail: brendaassing@tiscali.co.uk

web: www.thesteammillhouse.com

dir: *A134 onto B1087 into Nayland, bear right 0.5m. Fen St is 1st on left*

Dating back to 1811, the Steam Mill House is situated in the beautiful, tranquil village of Nayland. Rooms are comfortable and individually decorated. Breakfast is served in the dining room, offering homemade jams and locally produced bacon and sausages.

Rooms 3 en suite (2 fmly) (1 GF) S £50–£55; D £60–£65 **Facilities** TVB tea/coffee Cen ht Wi-fi available **Parking** 3 **Notes** ⊗ No children 4yrs Closed 22 Dec–3 Jan ●

★★★★★ ●● INN

White Hart Inn

High St CO6 4JF

☎ 01206 263382 📠 01206 263638

e-mail: nayhart@aol.com

dir: *Off A134 into village centre*

Relaxation and a warm welcome are guaranteed at this delightful 15th-century inn, in a charming village in the heart of Constable Country. The bedrooms are individually decorated and carefully furnished, while the elegant restaurant offers seasonal, local produce.

Rooms 6 en suite S £76–£109; D £96–£129✱ **Facilities** FTV TVB tea/coffee Direct dial from bedrooms Cen ht Dinner Last d 9pm Wi-fi available **Conf** Max 20 Thtr 20 Class 20 Board 20 **Parking** 8 **Notes** ⊗ Civ Wed 50

★★★★ BED & BREAKFAST

Hill House

Gravel Hill CO6 4JB

☎ 01206 262782

e-mail: heighamhillhouse@hotmail.com

dir: *In village centre. Off B1087 Birch St onto Gravel Hill. Premises 100yds up hill on right hand side.*

Set in secluded grounds in a peaceful village on the edge of Constable Country, this Grade II listed, 16th-century timber-framed building has a wealth of exposed beams, a flagstone hall and inglenooks. The attractive bedrooms are well equipped and overlook the pretty garden. Breakfast is served around a large communal table in the attractive, beamed dining room.

Rooms 2 en suite S £32–£38; D £64–£70 **Facilities** TVB tea/coffee Cen ht ⚐ **Parking** 4 **Notes** LB ⊗ No children 12yrs Closed 20 Dec–1 Jan ●

NEWMARKET   MAP 12 TL66

See also Kirtling (Cambridgeshire)

★★★★ BED & BREAKFAST

Birdcage Walk

2 Birdcage Walk CB8 0NE

☎ 01638 669456 📠 01638 669456

e-mail: patmerry@btinternet.com

dir: *Off A14 High St onto Birdcage Walk*

A warm welcome awaits at this delightful house located close to the racecourse and only a short walk to the town centre. Bedrooms and bathrooms are smartly appointed and thoughtfully equipped with a host of thoughtful extra touches. A hearty breakfast is served in the elegant dining room, overlooking the well-tended garden.

Rooms 2 en suite S £50; D £65–£70 **Facilities** TVB tea/coffee Cen ht Dinner Last d 7pm **Parking** 6 **Notes** ⊗ No children 12yrs Closed Xmas & New Year ●

★★★★ 🏠 BED & BREAKFAST

Bloodstock Barn

Mill Rd, Ashley CB8 9EE

☎ 01638 730263

e-mail: bruce@bloodstockbarn.com

dir: *From Newmarket take B1063, left at The Crown on to Mill Rd. 100yds on right*

Located amongst many notable stud farms within a conservation village three miles from the town centre, sympathetic renovation of this period property has resulted in high standards of comfort and facilities. Bedrooms provide many thoughtful extras and warm hospitality is complimented by memorable breakfasts, taken at a fine antique table in an elegant dining room, which also contains a lounge area.

Rooms 3 annexe en suite (3 GF) S £40–£80; D £70–£100✱ **Facilities** TVB tea/coffee Cen ht Wi-fi available **Parking** 6

ENGLAND

NEWMAKET *CONTINUED*

★★★★ BED & BREAKFAST
The Garden Lodge

11 Vicarage Ln, Woodditton CB8 9SG
☎ 01638 731116
e–mail: swedishgardenlodge@hotmail.com
web: www.gardenlodge.net

dir: *3m S of Newmarket in Woodditton village*

A warm welcome is assured in this home-from-home, not far from the famous racecourse. The accommodation, within quality chalets, is very well equipped and features a wealth of thoughtful extras. Freshly prepared home-cooked breakfasts are served in an elegant dining room in the main house.

Rooms 3 en suite (3 GF) S £30–£35; D £50–£60✱ **Facilities** TVB tea/coffee Cen ht Dinner Last d noon **Parking** 6 **Notes** ✉

SAXMUNDHAM   MAP 13 TM36

★★★★ BED & BREAKFAST
Sandpit Farm

Bruisyard IP17 2EB
☎ 01728 663445
e–mail: smarshall@aldevalleybreaks.co.uk
web: www.aldevalleybreaks.co.uk

dir: *4m W of Saxmundham. A1120 onto B1120, 1st left for Bruisyard, house 1.5m on left*

A delightful Grade II listed farmhouse set in 20 acres of grounds. Bedrooms have many thoughtful touches and lovely country views, and there are two cosy lounges to enjoy. Breakfast features quality local produce and freshly laid free-range eggs.

Rooms 2 en suite S £40–£60; D £65–£80✱ **Facilities** tea/coffee Cen ht TVL ☕ Riding ⚐ **Parking** 4 **Notes LB** Closed 24–26 Dec ✉

SOUTHWOLD   MAP 13 TM57

Premier Collection

★★★★★ ◉◉ ⌂ RESTAURANT WITH ROOMS
Sutherland House

56 High St IP18 6DN
☎ 01502 724544
e–mail: enquiries@sutherlandhouse.co.uk
web: www.sutherlandhouse.co.uk

dir: *A1095 into Southwold, on High St on left after Victoria St*

A delightful 16th-century house situated in the heart of the bustling town centre. The property has a wealth of original character that includes oak beams, exposed brickwork, open fireplaces and two superb ornate plasterwork ceilings. The stylish bedrooms are tastefully decorated, have co-ordinated fabrics and many thoughtful touches. Public rooms feature a large open-plan contemporary style restaurant with plush furniture.

Rooms 4 en suite (1 fmly) **Facilities** STV TVB tea/coffee Direct dial from bedrooms Cen ht Dinner Last d 9pm **Conf** Max 60 Thtr 80 Class 30 Board 30 **Parking** 2

★★★★ BED & BREAKFAST
Home at 21 North Parade

21 North Pde IP18 6LT
☎ 01502 722573
e–mail: pauline.archer@btconnect.com

dir: *A12 onto B1095. Mini rdbt, left onto Pier Avenue, right onto North Parade. Premises 100yds on right*

A lovely Victorian property situated on the promenade overlooking the sea. The stylish bedrooms have co-ordinated soft furnishings and many thoughtful touches, and some rooms have superb sea views. Breakfast, which includes fresh local produce, is served in the smart lounge/dining room at a large polished table.

Rooms 3 rms (2 en suite) (1 pri facs) S £60–£75; D £85–£95✱ **Facilities** FTV TVB tea/coffee Cen ht Golf 18 ☕ **Notes LB** No children 10yrs Closed Xmas & New Year ✉

★★★ GUEST ACCOMMODATION
The Hemsley's
28 Fieldstile Rd IP18 6LD
☎ 01502 723588
dir: *300yds N of town centre. Off A1095 Station Rd onto Fieldstile Rd towards seafront*

Expect a warm welcome at this small family-run bed and breakfast situated close to the centre of town. Bedrooms are pleasantly decorated with co-ordinated fabrics and have many thoughtful touches. Breakfast is served at a large communal table in the smart dining room.

Rooms 3 rms (1 fmly) (1 GF) **Facilities** TVB Cen ht **Notes** Closed Nov–Feb 🐾

Premier Collection
★★★★★ 🏠 GUEST ACCOMMODATION
Bays Farm
Forward Green IP14 5HU
☎ 01449 711286
e–mail: information@baysfarmsuffolk.co.uk
web: www.baysfarmsuffolk.co.uk
dir: *A14 junct 50, onto A1120. 1m after Stowupland, turn right at sharp left hand bend signed Broad Green. Bays Farm 1st house on right*

Tea and home-made cake are offered on arrival at this delightful 17th-century former farmhouse, situated amid four acres of mature grounds. The property has a wealth of character. Bedrooms are carefully decorated and have co-ordinated soft furnishings as well as many thoughtful touches. Breakfast, which includes locally sourced produce, is served around a large polished table in the stylish dining room.

Rooms 3 en suite S £60–£100; D £70–£110✳ **Facilities** TVB tea/coffee Cen ht **Parking** 3 **Notes** No children 12yrs

★★★★★ 🏠 GUEST ACCOMMODATION
Haughley House
Haughley IP14 3NS
☎ 01449 673398 📠 01449 673170
e–mail: bowden@kerne.co.uk
web: www.haughleyhouse.co.uk
dir: *Exit A14 junct 48 0.5m, fork right, 100yds on right*
Rooms 3 en suite S £60; D £90✳ **Facilities** tea/coffee Cen ht TVL Dinner 🍴 **Conf** Max 12 **Parking** 3 **Notes** ⊗

★★★★ 🏠 RESTAURANT WITH ROOMS
The Case Restaurant with Rooms
Further St, Assington CO10 5LD
☎ 01787 210483 📠 01787 211725
e–mail: restaurant@thecaserestaurantwithrooms.co.uk
dir: *Exit A12 at Colchester and take A134 to Sudbury. 7m from Colchester on left*
Rooms 7 en suite (2 fmly) **Facilities** FTV tea/coffee Cen ht Dinner Last d 9.30 Wi-fi available **Parking** 25 **Notes** ⊗

★★★★ BED & BREAKFAST
Folly House Bed & Breakfast
Folly Ln IP29 4TJ
☎ 01284 735207 & 07990 943060 📠 01284 735207
e–mail: lowerlinda@hotmail.com
dir: *Off B1066 onto Rectory Rd 1.5m, at T-junct turn right, Folly Ln on right*

This former alehouse dates back to the 1830s and is set amid landscaped grounds in peaceful countryside. The spacious bedroom has co-ordinated fabrics and many thoughtful touches. Public rooms include an elegant dining room, a conservatory-lounge and an indoor swimming pool.

Rooms 3 rms (1 en suite) (1 fmly) S £40–£65; D £50–£75✳ **Facilities** TVB tea/coffee Cen ht TVL Dinner Last d 9am 🐕 **Parking** 10 **Notes** ⊗ 🐾

ENGLAND

WINGFIELD   MAP 13 TM27

★★★★ BED & BREAKFAST
Gables Farm
Earsham St IP21 5RH
☎ 01379 586355
e–mail: enquiries@gablesfarm.co.uk
web: www.gablesfarm.co.uk
dir: *B1118 left to Wingfield Green, turn right after 1m, B&B 1.7m on right*

A warm welcome awaits at this delightful Grade II listed farmhouse, set amid two acres of moated gardens on the outskirts of the village. The spacious bedrooms are carefully furnished and thoughtfully equipped. Breakfast, which includes locally sourced produce, is served in the smart dining room at individual tables.

Rooms 3 en suite (1 fmly) **Facilities** TVB tea/coffee TVL **Parking** 5 **Notes** Closed 20–25 Dec ⊛

WOODBRIDGE

Ⓤ
Grove House
39 Grove Rd 1P12 4LG
☎ 01394 382202
e–mail: reception@grovehouse.hotel.ltd.uk
dir: *W of town centre on A12*

At the time of going to press the rating for this establishment had not been confirmed. Please check the AA website www.theAA.com for up-to-date information.

Rooms 10 en suite (1 fmly) (6 GF) S fr £50; D fr £65✱ **Facilities** TVB tea/coffee Cent ht Dinner Last d 9pm Wi-fi available **Conf** Max 20 Thtr 20 Class 20 Board 20 **Parking** 12 **Notes** LB ⊛

YAXLEY   MAP 13 TM17

Premier Collection

★★★★★ ⊛⊛ ⚗ RESTAURANT WITH ROOMS
The Auberge
Ipswich Rd IP23 8BZ
☎ 01379 783604 📋 01379 788486
e–mail: deestenhouse@fsmail.net
web: www.the-auberge.co.uk
dir: *On A140 between Norwich & Ipswich at B1117 x-rds Eye/Stadbloke*

A warm welcome awaits at this charming 15th-century property, which has been lovingly converted by the present owners into a smart restaurant with rooms. The public areas have a wealth of character, such as exposed brickwork and beams. The spacious bedrooms are tastefully appointed and have many thoughtful touches.

Rooms 4 en suite (2 GF) **Facilities** TVB tea/coffee Direct dial from bedrooms Cen ht Dinner Last d 9pm **Conf** Max 46 Thtr 30 Class 30 Board 20 **Parking** 40 **Notes** ⊛

SURREY

BETCHWORTH   MAP 06 TQ25

Ⓤ
The Red Lion
Old Rd, Buckland RH3 7DS
☎ 01737 843336 📋 01737 845242
e–mail: redlionsurrey@btconnect.com
dir: *Off A25 travelling from Reigate to Dorking turn left to Betchworth*

At the time of going to press the rating for this establishment had not been confirmed. Please check the AA website www.theAA.com for up-to-date information.

Rooms 6 annexe en suite (3 GF) D £55–£85 **Facilities** FTV TVB tea/coffee Dinner Last d 9pm Cricket pitch **Conf** Max 40 Thtr 40 Class 25 Board 25 **Parking** 40

See advert on opposite page

CAMBERLEY   MAP 06 SU86

Premier Collection

★★★★★ GUEST ACCOMMODATION
Maywood House
Maywood Dr GU15 1LH
☎ 01276 601730 📋 0845 0540909
e–mail: reservations@maywoodhouse.com

Maywood House provides comfortable accommodation in a secluded location but convenient for the M3. Amenities include extremely well equipped bedrooms and modern bathrooms with powerful showers. Delicious breakfasts are served in the airy dining room that overlooks beautiful gardens.

Rooms 5 en suite S £130–£150; D £145–£165✱ **Facilities** FTV TVB tea/coffee Direct dial from bedrooms Cen ht TVL Dinner Last d 24hrs in advance **Conf** Board 12 **Parking** 10 **Notes** ⊛ No children Closed 22 Dec–2 Jan

★★★★ GUEST ACCOMMODATION
Burwood House
15 London Rd GU15 3UQ
☎ 01276 685686 📋 01276 62220
e–mail: enquiries@burwoodhousehotel.co.uk
dir: *On A30 between Camberley and Bagshot*

Burwood House is a very stylish establishment with 19 individually designed bedrooms that offer all modern conveniences including Wi-fi. Every Monday to Thursday evening the kitchen offers a varied menu full of traditional favourites, as well as seasonal house specialties. Breakfast can be taken either buffet-style or as a fresh-cooked meal prepared upon request. Public areas include a lounge, bar and garden.

Rooms 19 en suite (3 fmly) (7 GF) **Facilities** tea/coffee Direct dial from bedrooms Cen ht TVL Dinner Last d 9pm Wi-fi available ⚘ ⚘ **Conf** Max 60 Thtr 50 Class 16 Board 20 **Parking** 22 **Notes** ⊛ Closed 22 Dec–4 Jan

CHARLWOOD   MAP 06 TQ24

*For accommodation details see under **Gatwick Airport (London), (Sussex, West)***

CHIDDINGFOLD   MAP 06 SU93

★★★★ INN
The Swan Inn

Petworth Rd GU8 4TY

☎ 01428 682073 📄 01428 683259

e–mail: the-swan-inn@btconnect.com

dir: *A3 onto A283 signposted Milford, past village green on left*

The 14th-century village inn offers home-cooked food, real ales, and a good choice of wines. There are terraced gardens and parking is available. The dining area has a friendly atmosphere.

Rooms 11 en suite (1 fmly) S £75–£145; D £75–£145✳ **Facilities** TVB tea/coffee Direct dial from bedrooms Dinner Last d 10pm Wi-fi available **Parking** 40 **Notes** No coaches

CHOBHAM   MAP 06 SU96

★★★★ GUEST ACCOMMODATION
Pembroke House

Valley End Rd GU24 8TB

☎ 01276 857654 📄 01276 858445

e–mail: pembroke_house@btinternet.com

dir: *A30 onto B383 signed Chobham, 3m right onto Valley End Rd, 1m on left*

Proprietor Julia Holland takes obvious pleasure in treating you as a friend at her beautifully appointed and spacious home. The elegantly proportioned public areas include an imposing entrance hall and dining room with views over the surrounding countryside. Bedrooms are restful and filled with thoughtful extras.

Rooms 4 rms (2 en suite) (2 pri facs) S £40–£70; D £100–£140✳ **Facilities** STV TVB tea/coffee Cen ht Wi-fi available 🍳 **Parking** 10 **Notes** No children 6yrs 🕸

CRANLEIGH   MAP 06 TQ03

[U]
Petersgate

Avenue Rd GU6 7LL

☎ 01483 273940

e–mail: agbrown@ukgateway.net

dir: *Take Horsham Rd at east end of Cranleigh (petrol station on right), 5th road on left into Avenue Rd, B&B on left, just after Grove Rd.*

At the time of going to press the rating for this establishment had not been confirmed. Please check the AA website www.theAA.com for up-to-date information.

Rooms 3 rms (1 pri facs) (1 fmly) S £25–£30; D £60–£70✳ **Facilities** tea/coffee Cen ht TVL **Parking** 2 **Notes** 🕸 No children 12yrs 🕸

FARNHAM — MAP 05 SU84

Premier Collection

★★★★★ BED & BREAKFAST

Bentley Mill

Bentley GU10 5JD

☎ 01420 23301 & 07768 842729 📠 01420 22538

e-mail: ann.bentleymill@supanet.com

web: www.bentleymill.com

dir: *Off A31 Farnham-Alton road, opp Bull Inn, turn left onto Gravel Hill Rd*

This delightful former corn mill, sitting beside the River Wey in beautifully tended gardens, has been expertly converted to provide two bedroom suites of the highest standard. Luxurious beds, antique furnishings and a host of thoughtful extra touches compliment the original features and maximise the immense character and charm of this Georgian property. Ann and David Hallett's hospitality knows no bounds: they do everything to ensure you enjoy their wonderful country home.

Rooms 2 rms (2 pri facs) 2 annexe en suite (3 fmly) (1 GF) S £80–£85; D £105–£130✲ **Facilities** STV TVB tea/coffee Cen ht Fishing ♨ **Parking** 6 **Notes** LB ⊗ No children 8yrs

★★★★ GUEST HOUSE

Dares Farm House

Farnham Rd, Ewshot GU10 5BB

☎ 01252 851631 📠 01252 852367

e-mail: daresfarm@tiscali.co.uk

dir: *3m NW of Farnham. M3 junct 5, A287 towards Farnham for 5m, up hill past Dares Ln, 1st left*

This attractive Grade II listed, 17th-century timber-framed cottage property is within easy reach of the M3 and A31. You can expect a warm welcome and a comfortable sleep in the cosy, individually decorated bedrooms. The hearty breakfast in the farmhouse kitchen sets you up for the day.

Rooms 4 en suite **Facilities** TVB tea/coffee Cen ht TVL **Parking** 5 **Notes** ⊗ No children 14yrs No coaches ⊜

★★★ BED & BREAKFAST

Sandiway

24 Shortheath Rd GU9 8SR

☎ 01252 710721

e-mail: john@shortheath.freeserve.co.uk

dir: *Onto A287 Hindhead, at lights at top of hill right onto Ridgway Rd, past green on left, Sandiway 300yds on right*

Guests are warmly welcomed at this delightful house, set in attractive gardens in a quiet residential area. Smart bedrooms have a thoughtful range of facilities and share a spacious, well-appointed bathroom. Guests have use of a comfortable lounge during the day and evening, which doubles as the dining room at breakfast.

Rooms 3 rms S £27.50–£30; D £45–£50✲ **Facilities** tea/coffee Cen ht TVL Wi-fi available **Parking** 3 **Notes** ⊗ Closed 21–31 Dec ⊜

★★★ INN

The Mulberry

Station Hill GU9 8AD

☎ 01252 726673

e-mail: info@exchangehotel.co.uk

Located close to the centre of town and the railway station, the Mulberry offers comfortable, well-equipped accommodation. A wide variety of meals are available in the Seafood and Steak restaurant, and there is a bar and a large beer garden.

Rooms 9 en suite **Facilities** TVB tea/coffee Cen ht TVL Dinner Last d 9.30pm Wi-fi available **Conf** Max 14 Thtr 14 Class 14 Board 14 **Parking** 14 **Notes** ⊗

GUILDFORD — MAP 06 SU94

★★★★ 🍴 GUEST ACCOMMODATION

Asperion Hillside

Perry Hill, Worplesdon GU3 3RF

☎ 01483 232051 📠 01483 237051

e-mail: info@thehillsidehotel.com

Located just a short drive away from central Guildford this accommodation is popular with both business and leisure travellers. Bedrooms are comfortable and well equipped with good facilities. Public areas include a spacious lounge bar where dinner is served, and a bright well-styled breakfast room. Gardens are well maintained and are enhanced by a guest terrace. Intimate meetings and events can also be catered for here.

Rooms 15 en suite (6 GF) S £65; D £80–£120✲ **Facilities** TVB tea/coffee Cen ht Dinner Last d 9pm Wi-fi available **Conf** Max 16 Thtr 16 Class 10 Board 16 **Parking** 15 **Notes** ⊗ Closed 21 Dec–7 Jan

★★★★ GUEST ACCOMMODATION

Asperion

73 Farnham Rd GU2 7PF

☎ 01483 579299 📠 01483 457977

e-mail: enquiries@asperion.co.uk

The stylish and luxurious Asperion provides contemporary rooms, a healthy organic breakfast, and caring service.

CONTINUED

Rooms 15 rms (14 en suite) (1 pri facs) (1 fmly) (9 GF) S £50–£65;
D £85–£120✶ **Facilities** STV TVB tea/coffee Direct dial from bedrooms
Cen ht TVL Dinner Last d 8.30pm Mon–Thu **Parking** 11 **Notes** ⊗
No children 12yrs Closed 21 Dec–5 Jan

★★★ GUEST ACCOMMODATION
Blanes Court Guest House
Albury Rd GU1 2BT
☎ 01483 573171 🗎 01483 532780
e–mail: reservations@blanes.demon.co.uk
web: www.blanes.demon.co.uk

dir: *0.7m E of town centre, off A246 Epsom Rd*

This large Edwardian house stands in a quiet residential area close to
the town centre and has ample private parking. Public areas include a
small seating area with a bar, and a conservatory overlooking the
attractive rear garden. Bedrooms vary in size, but each is individually
decorated and all offer a useful range of facilities.

Rooms 17 rms (16 en suite) (1 pri facs) (3 fmly) (6 GF) S £64–£86;
D £90–£95✶ **Facilities** FTV TVB tea/coffee Cen ht Wi-fi available
Parking 22 **Notes LB** ⊗ Closed 1wk Xmas

HASLEMERE   **MAP 06 SU93**

★★★ ⇔ INN
Wheatsheaf
Grayswood Rd, Grayswood GU27 2DE
☎ 01428 644440 🗎 01428 641285
e–mail: ken@thewheatsheafgrayswood.co.uk
web: www.wheatsheafgrayswood.co.uk

dir: *1m N of Haslemere on A286 in Grayswood*

Situated in a small village just outside Haslemere, this well-presented
inn has a friendly atmosphere. The smart conservatory restaurant is a
new addition, which complements the attractive dining area and
popular bar. Bedrooms are furnished to a good standard, all but one
on the ground floor.

Rooms 7 en suite (6 GF) S £55–£60; D £75–£80✶ **Facilities** TVB tea/
coffee Direct dial from bedrooms Cen ht Dinner Last d 9.45pm Wi-fi
available **Parking** 21 **Notes** No coaches

★★ FARM HOUSE
Ashleigh *(SU949313)*
Fisherstreet Farm GU28 9EJ
☎ 01428 707229 🗎 01428 707229 Mr & Mrs S Thomas
e–mail: gu284sx@yahoo.co.uk

dir: *3.5m E of Haslemere. B2131 onto A283 S*

Stephen and Madeleine Thomas make you feel like friends at their
charming farmhouse. A homely ambience is evident throughout the
spacious bedrooms, the cosy lounge and the elegant dining room.
Breakfast, served family style, uses farm produce whenever possible.

Rooms 3 rms (1 pri facs) (1 fmly) S £27.50–£35; D £55–£65✶
Facilities STV TVB tea/coffee Cen ht TVL Dinner Last d noon Wi-fi
available **Parking** 6 **Notes** ⊗ 450 acres Beef/Arable ⊜

HORLEY   **MAP 06 TQ24**

*For accommodation details see under Gatwick
Airport (London), (Sussex, West)*

SUSSEX, EAST

BATTLE   **MAP 06 TQ71**

★★★★ 🍴 FARM HOUSE
Fox Hole Farm *(TQ694166)*
Kane Hythe Rd TN33 9QU
☎ 01424 772053 Mr & Mrs P Collins
e–mail: foxholefarm@kanehythe.orangehome.co.uk

dir: *Off A271 onto B2096 farm 0.75m from junct on right*

A delightful 18th-century woodcutter's cottage set in forty acres of
grounds a short drive from historic Battle. The spacious bedrooms are
individually decorated and thoughtfully equipped. Breakfast includes
home-baked bread and is served in the charming dining room. The
cosy sitting room has exposed beams and an inglenook fireplace.

Rooms 3 en suite (1 GF) S £45–£49; D £62–£69✶ **Facilities** TVB tea/
coffee Cen ht **Parking** 6 **Notes** 40 acres ducks sheep chickens Closed Jan

BRIGHTON & HOVE   **MAP 06 TQ30**

★★★★ GUEST ACCOMMODATION
Brighton Pavilions
7 Charlotte St BN2 1AG
☎ 01273 621750 🗎 01273 622477
e–mail: sanchez-crespo@lineone.net
web: www.brightonpavilions.com

dir: *A23 to Brighton Pier, left onto A259 Marine Parade, Charlotte
St 15th left*

This well-run operation is in one of Brighton's Regency streets, a short
walk from the seafront and town centre. Bedrooms have style themes
such as Mikado or Pompeii, and are very smartly presented with many
thoughtful extras. The bright breakfast room is styled after a Titanic
garden restaurant.

Rooms 10 rms (7 en suite) (1 fmly) (1 GF) S £46–£65; D £92–£152✶
Facilities TVB tea/coffee Direct dial from bedrooms Cen ht **Notes LB**

BRIGHTON & HOVE CONTINUED

★★★★ GUEST ACCOMMODATION
Five
5 New Steine BN2 1PB
☎ 01273 686547 📄 01273 625613
e-mail: info@fivehotel.com

dir: *Along A259 heading E, 8th turning on left into the square*

An attractive townhouse in a traditional Georgian square just a stone's throw from the famous Brighton beaches, cafés and shops. Comfortable bedrooms and bathrooms are well equipped. A copious organic breakfast is served by cheerful hosts in the spacious, contemporary dining room.

Rooms 10 rms (8 en suite) (4 fmly) S £35–£75; D £70–£160✳ **Facilities** TVB tea/coffee Cen ht TVL Wi-fi available **Conf** Max 20 Board 20 **Notes** ⊗

★★★★ GUEST ACCOMMODATION
The Kelvin Guest House
9 Madeira Place, Kemptown BN2 1TN
☎ 01273 603735
e-mail: enquiries@thekelvin.co.uk

The Kelvin is a Regency townhouse elegantly refurbished in a modern contemporary style with beautifully furnished bedrooms equipped with flatscreen TVs, Freeview and Wi-fi. Breakfast is served in the bright, cheery dining room, and an attractive deck patio is available for guest use. Restaurants, shops and the beach are minutes away.

Rooms 10 rms (7 en suite) (3 pri facs) (1 fmly) (1 GF) **Facilities** FTV TVB tea/coffee Cen ht Wi-fi available **Notes** ⊗ No children 12yrs

★★★★ 🏢 GUEST ACCOMMODATION
Lansdowne Guest House
3 The Red House, 21 Lansdowne Rd BN3 1FE
☎ 07803 484775 📄 01273 773718
e-mail: lansdowneguesthouse@hotmail.co.uk

This modern and spacious suite is within a large 19th-century house originally built by Lord Caernarvon and retains much of the original charm. There are two large bedrooms, a private sitting room, an elegant lounge and a dining room where a substantial breakfast is served.

Rooms 2 rms (1 en suite) (1 pri facs) S £65–£75; D £75–£85✳ **Facilities** FTV TVB tea/coffee Cen ht TVL Dinner Last d 24hrs notice **Notes LB** ⊗ Closed 24–27 Dec ⊛

See advert on opposite page

★★★★ 🏢 🍴 GUEST ACCOMMODATION
New Steine
10 New Steine BN2 1PB
☎ 01273 695415 & 681546 📄 01273 622663
e-mail: reservation@newsteinehotel.com

dir: *A23 to Brighton Pier, left onto Marine Parade, New Steine on left after Wentworth St*

This guest house is close to the seafront off the Esplanade. The spacious bedrooms are well equipped and some have sea views. There is a cosy lounge, where a wide choice of English, vegetarian, vegan or continental breakfasts is served. There is street parking in front of the property.

Rooms 20 rms (16 en suite) (4 fmly) (2 GF) S £32–£49; D £49–£125✳ **Facilities** FTV TVB tea/coffee Direct dial from bedrooms Cen ht TVL Dinner Last d 9.30pm Wi-fi available **Conf** Max 55 Thtr 55 Class 50 Board 35 Del from £79 ✳ **Notes LB** No children 5yrs

★★★★ GUEST ACCOMMODATION
The Twenty One Guest House
21 Charlotte St, Marine Pde BN2 1AG
☎ 01273 686450
e-mail: enquiries@thetwentyone.co.uk
web: www.thetwentyone.co.uk

dir: *From Brighton Pier turn left on to Marine Parade, 16th turning on left*

This stylishly refurbished townhouse property is situated in Kemp Town within easy reach of clubs, bars and restaurants and just a short walk from the beach. Rooms are elegantly furnished and comfortable with an abundance of thoughtful extras provided. A smart dining room is the setting for a delicious freshly cooked breakfast.

Rooms 8 en suite (1 fmly) S £45–£58; D £85–£139✳ **Facilities** FTV TVB tea/coffee Cen ht Wi-fi available Sauna **Notes LB** ⊗

See advert on opposite page

★ ★ ★ ★ GUEST ACCOMMODATION
The White House

6 Bedford St BN2 1AN
☎ 01273 626266
e–mail: info@whitehousebrighton.com
web: www.whitehousebrighton.com

dir: *Arrive into Brighton A23 & follow signs to city centre. At rdbt opposite pier take 1st exit, continue through 2 sets of lights, turn left onto Bedford St*

The White House is a small Regency residence only 100 metres from the seafront, and a short walk from Brighton's centre. There are sea views from the south-facing rooms and a courtyard garden where guests may sit and relax. All rooms are smartly and stylishly decorated and guests can expect a relaxed atmosphere. Breakfast is served in the dining room, or al fresco. The extensive breakfast menu uses only best quality ingredients.

Rooms 10 rms (8 en suite) (2 GF) S £55; D £85–£200 **Facilities** TVB tea/coffee Cen ht Wi-fi available **Notes** ⊗ Closed Jan

★ ★ ★ ★ GUEST ACCOMMODATION
Alvia

36 Upper Rock Gardens BN2 1QF
☎ 01273 682939 📄 01273 626287
e–mail: enquiries@alviahotel.co.uk
web: www.alviahotel.co.uk

dir: *A23 to Brighton Pier, left onto Marine Parade, 500yds left at lights onto Lower Rock Gdns & Upper Rock Gdns*

This fine Victorian house is just a short walk from the seafront and town centre, and offers a choice of comfortable and well-equipped bedrooms. Full English and vegetarian breakfasts are offered, served in the bright dining room. Some parking is available, which should be booked in advance.

Rooms 10 rms (9 en suite) (1 fmly) S £30–£48; D £65–£180
Facilities TVB tea/coffee Cen ht Wi-fi available **Parking** 4 **Notes** LB ⊗

ENGLAND

BRIGHTON & HOVE CONTINUED

★★★★ GUEST ACCOMMODATION
Ambassador Brighton
22–23 New Steine, Marine Pde BN2 1PD
☎ 01273 676869 📠 01273 689988
e–mail: info@ambassadorbrighton.co.uk
web: www.ambassadorbrighton.co.uk

dir: *A23 to Brighton Pier, left onto A259, 9th left, onto Garden Sq, 1st left*

At the heart of bustling Kemp Town, overlooking the attractive garden square next to the seaside, this well-established property has a friendly and relaxing atmosphere. Bedrooms are well equipped and vary in size, with the largest having the best views. A small lounge with a separate bar is available.

Rooms 24 en suite (9 fmly) (3 GF) S £40–£75; D £65–£115✱ **Facilities** TVB tea/coffee Direct dial from bedrooms Cen ht **Conf** Max 20 Thtr 20 Board 14 Del from £75 ✱ **Notes LB**

★★★★ GUEST ACCOMMODATION
Aquarium Guest House
13 Madeira Place BN2 1TN
☎ 01273 605761
e–mail: info@aquarium-guesthouse.co.uk
web: www.aquarium-guesthouse.co.uk

dir: *A23 to Brighton Pier, left onto A259, 5th left*

Located close to Brighton Pier and the town centre, Aquarium Guest House offers comfortable accommodation and a friendly atmosphere. Bright and well appointed bedrooms, mainly en suite, are equipped with a number of thoughtful extras. An appetising breakfast is available in the bright basement dining room.

Rooms 7 rms (6 en suite) (1 pri facs) (1 GF) D £64–£100✱ **Facilities** FTV TVB tea/coffee Cen ht Wi-fi available **Notes LB** ⊗ No children 9yrs

★★★★ GUEST ACCOMMODATION
Bannings Guest House
14 Upper Rock Gardens, Kemptown BN2 1QE
☎ 01273 681403
e–mail: christopher.c.darnell@btinternet.com

dir: *Left onto A259 heading towards pier front, left at next lights, left to Tower Rock Garden and straight on to Upper Rock Gdns*

This attractive Victorian property is situated close to the seafront and just steps away from restaurants and shops. The comfortably furnished bedrooms are fresh and bright, and the cheerful dining room is the setting for a healthy breakfast. Parking tokens are available for a small charge.

Rooms 6 rms (5 en suite) (1 pri facs) (1 fmly) **Facilities** TVB tea/coffee Cen ht **Notes** ⊗

★★★★ 🏠 GUEST ACCOMMODATION
Brighton House
52 Regency Square BN1 2FF
☎ 01273 323282
e–mail: info@brighton-house.co.uk
web: www.brighton-house.co.uk

dir: *Opp West Pier*

Situated close to the seafront is the elegant, environmentally-friendly, Brighton House. Comfortably appointed bedrooms and bathrooms come in a variety of sizes and are located on four floors. An impressively abundant, organic continental breakfast is served in the spacious elegant dining room. Parking is in the nearby underground car park.

Rooms 16 en suite (2 fmly) S £40–£60; D £65–£125✱ **Facilities** TVB tea/coffee Cen ht **Notes** ⊗ No children 12yrs

★★★★ GUEST ACCOMMODATION
Colson House
17 Upper Rock Gardens BN2 1QE
☎ 01273 694922 📠 01273 694922
e–mail: info@colsonhouse.co.uk

dir: *From Brighton Pier, east on A259 then left at lights*

Just a short walk from Kemp Town this listed Regency property offers a warm friendly welcome and some comfortable accommodation. Bedrooms are named after movie icons and include DVD players with films by the artiste. Breakfast is served in a light and airy dining room.

Rooms 8 en suite (1 GF) **Facilities** TVB tea/coffee Cen ht Wi-fi available **Notes** ⊗ No children 12yrs

★★★★ GUEST ACCOMMODATION
Four Seasons Guest House
3 Upper Rock Gardens BN2 1QE
☎ 01273 673574
e–mail: info@fourseasonsbrighton.com
web: www.fourseasonsbrighton.com

dir: *At rdbt take first exit proceed along Marine Parade, at lights, turn left onto Lower Rock Gdns*

Caring hosts William and Thommy provide smart accommodation with a variety of stylish contemporary bedrooms, each with ample facilities including Wi-fi and hairdryers. A healthy breakfast is served in the sunny dining room. Beaches, restaurants and shops are within close walking distance

Rooms 7 rms (6 pri facs) (1 GF) S £39–£49; D £79–£120✱ **Facilities** FTV TVB tea/coffee Cen ht Wi-fi available **Notes LB** ⊗ No children 10yrs

★★★★ GUEST ACCOMMODATION
George IV

34 Regency Square BN1 2FJ
☎ 01273 321196 & 07940 808753
e-mail: georgeiv@stevesue.plus.com
web: www.georgeivbrighton.co.uk

dir: *Opp West Pier, at top of square*

Situated at the top of the prominent Regency square overlooking the gardens and sea, this restored property provides smartly furnished bedrooms with modern bathrooms and good facilities. There is a lift to all floors and a freshly prepared continental breakfast is served in your bedroom.

Rooms 8 en suite (1 fmly) S £45–£55; D £65–£130✱ (room only) **Facilities** TVB tea/coffee Lift Cen ht Wi-fi available **Notes** ⊗ Closed Jan

★★★★ GUEST ACCOMMODATION
Gullivers

12a New Steine, Marine Pde BN2 1PB
☎ 01273 681546 & 695415 📄 01273 622663
e-mail: reservation@gullivershotel.com
web: www.gullivershotel.com

dir: *A23 to Brighton Pier, left onto Marine Parade, premises 300yds on left*

Situated in an impressive Regency square close to the town and seafront, the New Steine has much to offer. Compact rooms use clever design and contemporary colours to ensure comfort, and some have quality shower rooms en suite. The lounge, decorated with fine art, and brasserie are super areas in which to relax and dine.

Rooms 12 rms (9 en suite) (1 GF) (4 smoking) S £29–£44.50; D £49–£125✱ **Facilities** FTV TVB tea/coffee Direct dial from bedrooms Cen ht TVL Dinner Last d 9.45pm Wi-fi available **Conf** Max 50 Thtr 50 Class 30 Board 30 Del from £89 ✱ **Notes LB** ⊗ No children 4yrs

★★★★ GUEST ACCOMMODATION
Marine View

24 New Steine BN2 1PD
☎ 01273 603870 📄 01273 357257
e-mail: info@mvbrighton.co.uk
web: www.mvbrighton.co.uk

dir: *From A23, left onto Marine Pde, left onto New Steine, 300mtrs*

Overlooking the elegant Steine Square with the sea just a glance away, this 18th-century property offers comfortable, well designed accommodation. Plenty of accessories are provided, including free Wi-fi. A hearty breakfast is available in the bright lounge/dining room.

Rooms 11 rms (8 en suite) (2 fmly) (2 GF) S £35–£60; D £60–£100 **Facilities** TVB tea/coffee Cen ht Wi-fi available **Notes LB** ⊗

★★★★ GUEST ACCOMMODATION
Nineteen

19 Broad St BN2 1TJ
☎ 01273 675529 📄 01273 675531
e-mail: info@hotelnineteen.co.uk
web: www.hotelnineteen.co.uk

dir: *A23 to Brighton Pier, left onto Marine Parade, Broad St 3rd on left*

This contemporary establishment lies close to the town centre, only minutes from Brighton Pier. Bedrooms are decorated with white walls, wooden floors and stylish artworks. The continental breakfast (served with champagne at the weekend) is superb, providing a fine start to the day.

Rooms 8 en suite (2 GF) S £56–£126; D £65–£180✱ **Facilities** FTV TVB Cen ht Wi-fi available Outdoor Hot Tub in 1 bedroom **Conf** Max 8 Board 8 **Notes** ⊗ No children 10yrs Closed 24–26 Dec

★★★★ 🍴 GUEST ACCOMMODATION
Paskins Town House

18/19 Charlotte St BN2 1AG
☎ 01273 601203 📄 01273 621973
e-mail: welcome@paskins.co.uk
web: www.paskins.co.uk

dir: *A23 to pier, turn left, Charlotte St 11th left*

This environmentally-friendly, family-run Victorian house is in a quiet street within walking distance of the seafront and town centre. Bedrooms are a comfortable mix of Victorian and art nouveau styles. The Art Deco breakfast room offers a variety of vegetarian and vegan dishes and traditional English breakfasts, featuring home-made vegetarian sausages and much organic produce.

Rooms 19 rms (16 en suite) (2 fmly) S £45–£60; D £90–£155✱ **Facilities** FTV TVB tea/coffee Direct dial from bedrooms Cen ht Wi-fi available **Notes LB**

★★★★ GUEST ACCOMMODATION
Snooze

25 St George Ter BN2 1JJ
☎ 01273 605797
e-mail: info@snoozebrighton.com

This splendid Victorian terraced property is close to the beach and the popular Kemptown bars and restaurants. Bedrooms have a distinctly 'retro' feel and are all comfortably presented. A choice of hearty breakfasts is served in the spacious dining room enhanced with large bay windows.

Rooms 10 rms (9 en suite) (1 pri facs) (2 GF) S £35–£40; D £60–£120✱ **Facilities** TVB tea/coffee Cen ht Wi-fi available **Notes** ⊗ No children 12yrs

ENGLAND

BRIGHTON & HOVE CONTINUED

★★★★ 🅐 GUEST ACCOMMODATION
Cavalaire House
34 Upper Rock Gardens BN2 1QF
☎ 01273 696899
e–mail: welcome@cavalaire.co.uk
web: www.cavalaire.co.uk

dir: *A23 to seafront, left onto A259, left at 1st lights onto Lower Rock Gdns & over next lights onto Upper Rock Gdns*

Rooms 10 en suite S £35–£95; D £60–£160✱ **Facilities** TVB tea/coffee Cen ht Wi-fi available **Parking** 3 **Notes** LB ⊗ No children 9yrs

★★★ GUEST ACCOMMODATION
Millards
23 Broad St BN2 1TJ
☎ 01273 694314 📠 01273 676826
e–mail: info@millards-hotel-brighton.com

dir: *A23 to Brighton Pier, left onto Marine Parade, left onto Manchester St, right onto Saint James St & 2nd right*

This refurbished establishment is near to the seafront and town centre. Bedrooms are stylishly comfortable and finished with considerate extras including Freeview TV and a safe. Breakfast is served in the modern dining area next to the reception.

Rooms 8 en suite (2 GF) **Facilities** TVB tea/coffee Direct dial from bedrooms Cen ht **Notes** ⊗

★★★ 🍴 GUEST ACCOMMODATION
Motel Schmotel
37 Russell Square BN1 2EF
☎ 01273 326129
e–mail: info@motelschmotel.co.uk

Charming family-run establishment situated on a quiet square just minutes away from beaches and shops. Bright en suite bedrooms include thoughtful amenities such as free Wi-fi and Freeview TV. A substantial breakfast menu uses fresh, local produce and is served in rooms.

Rooms 9 en suite (1 fmly) (2 GF) **Facilities** TVB tea/coffee Cen ht Wi-fi available **Parking** 2 **Notes** ⊗

★★★ GUEST ACCOMMODATION
Ainsley House Ltd
28 New Steine BN2 1PD
☎ 01273 605310 📠 01273 688604
e–mail: rooms@ainsleyhotel.com

Situated on the stylish Steine Square and with good views of the Pier, this popular property has a range of well equipped rooms; most are en suite and all are comfortably presented. Breakfast, served by the cheerful proprietor, is in the well positioned dining room with views over the square.

Rooms 12 rms (10 en suite) (3 fmly) **Facilities** TV11B tea/coffee Cen ht TVL

★★★ GUEST ACCOMMODATION
The Amblecliff
35 Upper Rock Gardens BN2 1QF
☎ 01273 681161 📠 01273 676945

dir: *A23 to Brighton, left at rdbt and turn right to Lower Rock Gdns. Straight up hill, on right*

Attractive Victorian property close to all the famous Brighton attractions and just a short walk from the beach. Bedrooms vary in size from stylish family rooms to singles, all are en suite and comfortably furnished, and some boast impressive bay windows. Limited off-road parking available by appointment

Rooms 14 rms (12 en suite) (4 fmly) (1 GF) **Facilities** TVB tea/coffee Cen ht Wi-fi available **Parking** 3

★★★ GUEST ACCOMMODATION
Avalon
7 Upper Rock Gardens BN2 1QE
☎ 01273 692344 📠 01273 692344
e–mail: info@avalonbrighton.co.uk

dir: *A23 to Brighton Pier, left onto Marine Parade, 300yds at lights left onto Lower Rock Gdns, over lights Avalon on left*

A warm welcome is assured at this guest house just a short walk from the seafront and The Lanes. Bedrooms, some redecorated, vary in size and style. Parking is restricted but vouchers are available for purchase from the proprietor.

Rooms 7 en suite (1 fmly) (1 GF) S £35–£39; D £65–£115✱ **Facilities** FTV TVB tea/coffee Cen ht

★★★ GUEST ACCOMMODATION
The Heathers
4 & 5 Lower Rock Gardens BN2 1PG
☎ 01273 626545 📠 01273 608350
e–mail: angelique@lincarhotels.co.uk
web: www.lincarhotels.co.uk

Close to the beaches, this friendly guest house has been refurbished in a modern style. Bedrooms are varied in size with some rooms equipped for families. Bathrooms have good showers. The breakfast room and lounge are fresh and comfortable.

Rooms 19 rms (18 en suite) (1 pri facs) (5 fmly) (5 GF) **Facilities** STV TVB tea/coffee Cen ht **Parking** 3

★★★ GUEST ACCOMMODATION
Marina West
26 Oriental Place BN1 2LL
☎ 01273 323087 📠 01273 206888
e–mail: info@marinawest.co.uk

dir: *A23 to Brighton Pier, right along seafront past West Pier, 3rd right onto Oriental Place*

Located just a stroll from the seafront or the town centre, this popular accommodation has undergone refurbishment to provide well-decorated bedrooms and a comfortable lounge. Rooms on the upper floors share a bathroom but others are en suite.

Rooms 11 rms (3 en suite) (1 fmly) (1 GF) **Facilities** STV TVB tea/coffee Direct dial from bedrooms Cen ht TVL **Conf** Thtr 22 Class 22 Board 22 **Notes** ⊗

★★★ GUEST ACCOMMODATION
The Oriental
9 Oriental Place BN1 2LJ
☎ 01273 205050 📠 01273 205050
e–mail: info@orientalbrighton.co.uk

dir: *A23 right onto A259 at seafront, right into Oriental Place, on right*

The Oriental is situated close to the sea front and enjoys easy access to all areas. The accommodation is comfortable and modern, and has a licensed bar. The owners offer friendly and welcoming service in a relaxed atmosphere.

Rooms 9 en suite (4 fmly) (1 GF) S £50–£65; D £80–£210✳ **Facilities** FTV TVB tea/coffee Cen ht Wi-fi available Massage & Aromatherapy **Conf** Max 10 Thtr 10 Class 10 Board 10 Del from £120 ✳

★★★ GUEST ACCOMMODATION
Regency Landsdowne Guest House
45 Landsdowne Place BN3 1HF
☎ 01273 321830 📠 01273 777067
e–mail: regencylansdowne@aol.com
web: www.regencylansdowne.co.uk

dir: *A23 to Brighton Pier, right onto A259, 1m right onto Lansdowne Place, house on left before Western Rd*

A warm welcome is guaranteed at this Regency house, located only minutes from the seafront. Comfortable bedrooms are functionally equipped with a good range of facilities. An extensive continental breakfast is served at a communal table overlooking attractive gardens. On-road parking a short walk away.

Rooms 7 rms (5 en suite) (1 pri facs) S £29–£55; D £44–£85✳ **Facilities** STV FTV TVB tea/coffee Lift Cen ht Wi-fi available **Notes** ⊗

★★★ GUEST ACCOMMODATION
Westbourne Guest House
46 Upper Rock Gardens BN2 1QF
☎ 01273 686920 📠 01273 686920
e–mail: welcome@westbournehotel.net

dir: *A23 to Brighton Pier, left onto Marine Parade, 100yds left at lights, premises on right*

Just a short walk from the seafront, this Victorian house is run by friendly owners. The attractive bedrooms are bright and well furnished, and some have flat screen TVs. Spacious dining area is complimented by a large bay window.

Rooms 11 rms (7 en suite) (1 fmly) (2 GF) S £35–£50; D £63–£100✳ **Facilities** FTV TVB tea/coffee TVL Wi-fi available **Parking** 1 **Notes** ⊗ Closed 23–30 Dec

★★★ 🅰 GUEST HOUSE
Sandpiper Guest House
11 Russell Square BN1 2EE
☎ 01273 328202 📠 01273 329974
e–mail: sandpiper@brighton.co.uk

dir: *After conference centre on King's Rd, right onto Cannon Place. Russell Sq at end of street*

Rooms 6 rms (1 fmly) **Facilities** TVB tea/coffee Cen ht **Notes** ⊗ No coaches

★★ INN
The Market Inn
1 Market St BN1 1HH
☎ 01273 329483 📠 01273 777227
e–mail: marketinn@reallondonpubs.com
web: www.reallondonpubs.com/market.html

dir: *In city centre, on pedestrian road 50yds from junct North St & East St*

This lively period inn is within walking distance of many local attractions. Bedrooms are attractively decorated and feature a range of extra facilities. Breakfast is served in the bedrooms, and popular bar food is served at lunchtimes in the bar, which retains its original character.

Rooms 2 en suite S £50; D £65–£75✳ **Facilities** FTV TVB tea/coffee Cen ht Dinner Last d 9pm Wi-fi available **Notes LB** No children No coaches

🆄
Brighton Marina House
8 Charlotte St BN2 1AG
☎ 01273 605349 📠 01273 679484
e–mail: rooms@jungs.co.uk

At the time of going to press the rating for this establishment had not been confirmed. Please check the AA website www.theAA.com for up-to-date information.

Rooms 9 rms (6 en suite) (3 pri facs) (3 fmly) S £29–£49; D £65–£99✳ **Facilities** FTV TVB tea/coffee Cen ht Wi-fi available **Notes LB** ⊗

ENGLAND

CROWBOROUGH   MAP 06 TQ53

★★★ INN
Plough & Horses

Walshes Rd TN6 3RE

☎ 01892 652614 📄 01892 652614

dir: *A26 onto B2100, under railway bridge, right onto Western Rd, over railway to Walshes Rd*

This pleasant inn has been welcoming guests for many years, and over the last two decades the present owners have made this a very attractive and popular place. The spacious bedrooms feature well-chosen pine furniture, and public rooms include a traditional bar, a restaurant, and a further lounge bar.

Rooms 15 en suite (3 fmly) **Facilities** TVB tea/coffee Cen ht TVL Dinner Last d 10pm **Parking** 40 **Notes** Closed 24–25 Dec

EASTBOURNE   MAP 06 TV69

★★★★★ BED & BREAKFAST
The Manse B & B

7 Dittons Rd BN21 1DW

☎ 01323 737851

e–mail: anne@themansebandb.co.uk

web: www.themansebandb.co.uk

dir: *A22 to town centre railway station, onto Old Orchard Rd, right onto Arlington Rd*

This delightful home is in a quiet residential area only a five minute walk from the town centre. Built as a Presbyterian manse at the turn of the 19th century, much of the original character has been retained. The beautifully decorated bedrooms are very comfortable and have a wide range of accessories such as flat screen TV and DVD. Breakfast is served in the elegant dining room, with its stripped wooden floors and pretty courtyard view.

Rooms 3 en suite S £45–£55; D £74–£84✱ **Facilities** FTV TVB tea/coffee Cen ht Wi-fi available **Parking** 2 **Notes** ⊗

★★★★★ BED & BREAKFAST
Ocklynge Manor

Mill Rd BN21 2PG

☎ 01323 734121 & 07979 627172

e–mail: ocklyngemanor@hotmail.com

web: www.ocklyngemanor.co.uk

dir: *From Eastbourne Hospital follow town centre/seafront sign, 1st right onto Kings Av, Ocklynge Manor at top of road*

This charming home has seen a variety of uses through the years, including as a commanderie for the Knights of St John in the 12th century. An air of peace and relaxation is evident in the delightful public rooms, well-tended gardens and the spacious, comfortable

bedrooms filled with thoughtful extras, including free Wi-fi. Hospitality is a plus and home-baked bread is just one of the delights on offer.

Ocklynge Manor

Rooms 3 rms (2 en suite) (1 pri facs) (1 fmly) S £45–£60; D £70–£80✱ **Facilities** FTV TVB tea/coffee Cen ht Wi-fi available **Parking** 3 **Notes** ⊗ No children 16yrs ⊚

★★★★★ GUEST ACCOMMODATION
The Berkeley

3 Lascelles Ter BN21 4BJ

☎ 01323 645055 📄 01323 400128

e–mail: info@theberkeley.net

dir: *Follow seafront from the pier and take 7th turning on right*

The Berkeley's central location is convenient for seafront, theatre and the town centre. Spacious bedrooms are smartly furnished. A stylish lounge is provided for guests to relax, and breakfast is served in the attractive dining room.

Rooms 13 en suite (4 fmly) (1 GF) S £39–£45; D £79–£89✱ **Facilities** STV TVB tea/coffee Cen ht Wi-fi available

★★★★★ BED & BREAKFAST
The Gables

21 Southfields Rd BN21 1BU

☎ 01323 644600

e–mail: info@gablesbandb.co.uk

dir: *A2270 into town centre, 2nd exit at rdbt by station, bear right into Southfields Rd*

The Gables is a splendid Edwardian property with lots of character, spacious accommodation and friendly hosts. A freshly-cooked breakfast is served in the elegant dining room. Free Wi-fi is available for guests. A short walk will take you to the station, town centre and pier. Some off-road parking is available.

Rooms 3 rms (2 en suite) (1 pri facs) D £68–£76✱ **Facilities** TVB tea/coffee Lift Cen ht TVL Wi-fi available **Parking** 2 **Notes** ⊗ ⊚

CONTINUED

★★★★ GUEST ACCOMMODATION
The Camelot Lodge

35 Lewes Rd BN21 2BU
☎ 01323 725207 📠 01323 722799
e–mail: info@camelotlodgehotel.com
web: www.camelotlodgehotel.com

dir: *A22 onto A2021, premises 0.5m after hospital on the lefthand side*

This delightful Edwardian property is within walking distance of the seafront and local amenities. The beautifully styled bedrooms feature a range of facilities including free Wi-fi access, and there is a spacious lounge-bar area. Meals are served in the conservatory dining room, and dinner is available by arrangement.

Rooms 8 en suite (3 fmly) (1 GF) S £29.95–£45; D £59.90–£80✳
Facilities FTV TVB tea/coffee Cen ht TVL Dinner Last d 7.30pm Wi-fi available **Parking** 11 **Notes LB** ⊗

★★★★ GUEST ACCOMMODATION
Arden House

17 Burlington Place BN21 4AR
☎ 01323 639639 📠 01323 417840
e–mail: info@theardenhotel.co.uk
web: www.theardenhotel.co.uk

dir: *Eastbourne seafront, head W, 5th turning after the pier*

This attractive Regency property sits just minutes away from the seafront and town centre. Bedrooms are comfortable and bright, many with new en suite bathrooms. Guests can enjoy a hearty breakfast at the beginning of the day then relax in the cosy lounge in the evening.

Rooms 11 rms (10 en suite) (1 pri facs) (1 fmly) S £30–£37; D £50–£60✳ **Facilities** TVB tea/coffee Cen ht TVL Wi-fi available **Parking** 5 **Notes LB**

★★★★ GUEST ACCOMMODATION
The Bay Lodge

61–62 Royal Pde BN22 7AQ
☎ 01323 732515 📠 01323 735009
e–mail: baylodgehotel@fsmail.net

dir: *From A22 follow signs to seafront. Bay Lodge is on right opposite Pavilion Tea Gardens*

This family-run guest house offers a warm welcome in comfortable surrounds opposite the Redoubt and Pavilion gardens. Bedrooms are bright and spacious, some with balconies. There is a sun lounge and a cosy bar overlooking the superb sea views.

Rooms 11 rms (10 en suite) (1 pri facs) (1 fmly) (2 GF) S £25–£28; D £50–£70✳ **Facilities** TVB tea/coffee Cen ht TVL Dinner Last d 10am Wi-fi available **Parking** 7 **Notes LB** ⊗

★★★★ GUEST ACCOMMODATION
Bella Vista

30 Redoubt Rd BN22 7DH
☎ 01323 724222
e–mail: enquiries@hotelbellavista.co.uk

dir: *500yds NE of town centre. Off A259 Seaside Rd*

Situated on the east side of town, just off the seafront, this is an attractive flint house with the bonus of a car park. Bedrooms are generally spacious, comfortable and neatly appointed with modern facilities including free Wi-fi. There is a large lounge and dining room where dinner and breakfast is served.

Rooms 12 en suite (1 fmly) (3 GF) **Facilities** TVB tea/coffee Cen ht TVL Dinner Last d 24hrs before **Parking** 10 **Notes** ⊗

★★★★ GUEST ACCOMMODATION
Far End

139 Royal Pde BN22 7LH
☎ 01323 725666
e–mail: ross.gowling@btconnect.com

dir: *0.5m NE of pier. A259 onto Channel View Rd & Royal Parade, next to Princess Park*

Located north-east of the town centre, next to the popular Princess Park and the Marina, this family-run guest house offers a warm and friendly welcome. Bedrooms vary in size but are well appointed, some having sea views. Breakfast and dinner are served in the bright ground-floor dining room.

Rooms 10 rms (6 en suite) **Facilities** TVB tea/coffee Cen ht Dinner Last d 2pm **Parking** 8 **Notes** No children 6yrs

EASTBOURNE CONTINUED

★★★★ GUEST ACCOMMODATION
The Gladwyn

16 Blackwater Rd BN21 4JD
☎ 01323 733142
e–mail: contact@thegladwyn.com
web: www.thegladwyn.com

dir: *250yds S of town centre. Off A259 South St onto Hardwick Rd & 1st right*

A warm welcome is guaranteed at this delightful guest house located opposite the famous tennis courts. Art work and interesting collectables feature throughout the property, including public areas and bedrooms. Freshly prepared breakfasts are served in the cosy dining room overlooking the attractive garden, which is available during the summer.

Rooms 10 en suite (1 fmly) (2 GF) S £40–£45; D £70–£80
Facilities TVB tea/coffee TVL Wi-fi available **Notes LB**

★★★★ GUEST ACCOMMODATION
Ivydene

5–6 Hampden Ter, Latimer Rd BN22 7BL
☎ 01323 720547 📄 01323 411247
e–mail: ivydenehotel@hotmail.co.uk
web: www.ivydenehotel-eastbourne.co.uk

dir: *From town centre/pier NE along seafront, towards Redoubt Fortress, onto St Aubyns Rd, 1st right onto Hampden Terrace*

This friendly family-run property is situated a short walk from the pier and seafront. Bedrooms are bright and cheerful with comfortable, stylish furnishings. Public areas include a spacious lounge/bar, sunny conservatory and attractive dining room.

Rooms 14 en suite (2 fmly) (1 GF) S £27–£35; D £54–£75
Facilities TVB tea/coffee Lift Cen ht Dinner Last d 2pm Wi-fi available
Notes LB ⊗ RS Oct–Etr

★★★★ GUEST ACCOMMODATION
The Mowbray

2 Lascelles Ter BN21 4BJ
☎ 01323 720012
e–mail: info@themowbray.com
dir: *Opp Devonshire Park Theatre*

This elegant townhouse is located opposite The Devonshire Theatre and a few minutes walk from the seafront. Bedrooms, that are accessible by a lift to all floors, vary in size, but all are attractively furnished and comfortable. There is a spacious well presented lounge, small modern bar and a stylish dining room. Breakfast is home-cooked, as are evening meals that are available by prior arrangement

Rooms 13 en suite (4 fmly) (1 GF) S £34–£45; D £68–£90✱
Facilities TVB tea/coffee Lift Cen ht Dinner Last d 6.30pm Wi-fi available **Conf** Max 20 Thtr 20 Class 10 Board 10 **Notes LB**

★★★★ GUEST ACCOMMODATION
The Sherwood

7 Lascelles Ter BN21 4BJ
☎ 01323 724002 📄 01323 400133
e–mail: info@thesherwood.net

dir: *Follow signs to seafront (Grand parade), next to the Eastbourne Centre*

Attractive Victorian property just a minute's walk from the seafront, offering well-appointed bedrooms with comfortable furnishings. The bright attractive dining room serves a fine selection of evening dishes and a robust breakfast.

Rooms 13 en suite (5 fmly) (1 GF) S £34–£39; D £68–£78✱
Facilities STV TVB tea/coffee Cen ht Dinner Last d 3pm Wi-fi available

★★★ GUEST ACCOMMODATION
Beach Haven

61 Pevensey Rd BN21 3HS
☎ 01323 726195
e–mail: enquiries@beach-haven.co.uk
web: www.beach-haven.co.uk

dir: *250yds E of town centre off A259*

The attractive terrace property is just a short walk from the seafront and attractions. Bedrooms are located on three floors, some offer en suite facilities and all have a thoughtful range of guest extras. There is also a comfortable dining room, a cosy lounge and a small private chapel.

Rooms 8 rms (3 en suite) (1 GF) S £30–£35; D £60–£70✱ **Facilities** TVB tea/coffee Cen ht Dinner Last d 10am **Notes LB** ⊗ No children 1yr

★★★ GUEST HOUSE
Beachy Rise

5 Beachy Head Rd BN20 7QN
☎ 01323 639171 📄 01323 645006
e–mail: susanne234@hotmail.co.uk

dir: *1m SW of town centre. Off B2103 Upper Dukes Rd*

This friendly family-run guest house has a quiet residential location close to Meads Village. Bedrooms are individually styled with coordinated soft furnishings and feature some useful extras. Breakfast is served in the light and airy dining room overlooking the garden, which guests are welcome to use.

Rooms 4 en suite (2 fmly) S £30–£45; D £50–£70✳ **Facilities** TVB tea/coffee Cen ht Wi-fi available **Notes** No coaches ☻

★★★ GUEST ACCOMMODATION
Rosedale

13 Bourne St BN21 3ES
☎ 01323 720215 📄 01323 727760
e–mail: rosedale13@btinternet.com
web: www.rosedale-eastbourne.co.uk

dir: *Off A259 corner of Bourne St and Ceylon Place*

This friendly establishment is well situated just a stone's throw from the pier and close to restaurants and shops. Bedrooms are bright and cheerful with comfortable furnishings and sparkling en suite bathrooms. A locally sourced English breakfast is served in the ground floor dining room and dinner is available by prior arrangement.

Rooms 6 rms (6 pri facs) (2 fmly) (3 smoking) **Facilities** TVB tea/coffee Cen ht Dinner Last d 24hrs

★★★ GUEST ACCOMMODATION
The Sheldon

9–11 Burlington Place BN21 4AS
☎ 01323 724120 📄 01323 430406
e–mail: sheldonhotel@tiscali.co.uk
web: www.thesheldonhotel.co.uk

dir: *500yds SE of pier off seafront Parade*

This impressive Victorian house is convenient for the town centre and only a short walk from the seafront. Bedrooms vary in size but are well equipped and cheerfully decorated. Traditional home-cooked food is served in the smart dining room.

The Sheldon

Rooms 28 en suite (5 fmly) (2 GF) **Facilities** TVB tea/coffee Direct dial from bedrooms Lift Cen ht TVL Dinner Last d 4pm Wi-fi available **Parking** 20 **Notes** ⊗

★★ GUEST ACCOMMODATION
Birling Gap

Seven Sisters Cliffs, Birling Gap, East Dean BN20 0AB
☎ 01323 423197 📄 01323 423030
e–mail: reception@birlinggaphotel.co.uk
web: www.birlinggaphotel.co.uk

dir: *4m W of Eastbourne. Off A259 at East Dean onto Gilberts Dr, Birling Gap 1.5m*

Friendly, family-run and situated in a superb cliff-top location. Bedrooms are suitably decorated and equipped, and many have lovely sea views. Public rooms include a spacious lounge bar and restaurant, which offers a wide range of popular dishes and a coffee shop.

Rooms 9 en suite (3 fmly) (9 GF) **Facilities** STV TVB tea/coffee Direct dial from bedrooms Cen ht Dinner Last d 9pm Pool Table **Conf** Max 150 Thtr 150 Class 100 Board 80 **Parking** 100

HALLAND   MAP 06 TQ41

Premier Collection

★★★★★ GUEST ACCOMMODATION
Tamberry Hall

Eastbourne Rd BN8 6PS
☎ 01825 880090 📄 01825 880090
e–mail: bedandbreakfast@tamberryhall.fsbusiness.co.uk
web: www.tamberryhall.co.uk

dir: *In Halland on A22, 200yds N of junct with B2192 at Black Lion Inn*

A warm welcome is assured at this attractive house sitting in three acres of wonderful landscaped gardens. Individually decorated bedrooms vary in size and are all equipped with a variety of thoughtful extras. An inglenook fireplace and exposed beams are a character of this establishment. Hearty breakfasts are served in a delightful dining room or on the terrace, weather permitting.

Rooms 3 en suite (1 fmly) S £65–£80; D £73–£85 **Facilities** TVB tea/coffee Cen ht TVL **Parking** 3 **Notes** LB ⊗ RS 24–27 Dec

CONTINUED

HASTINGS & ST LEONARDS   MAP 07 TQ80

Premier Collection

★★★★★ GUEST ACCOMMODATION
Stream House

Pett Level Rd, Fairlight TN35 4ED

☎ 01424 814916 & 0794 191 1379

e–mail: info@stream-house.co.uk

web: www.stream-house.co.uk

dir: *4m NE of Hastings. Off A259 on unclassified road between Fairlight & Cliff End*

Lovingly converted from three cottages, the house stands in three acres of tranquil grounds, just one mile from Winchelsea beach. The well-appointed bedrooms are beautifully decorated. Delicious breakfasts are served in the lounge-dining room with an original inglenook fireplace, and during warmer months you can enjoy the extensive garden with its rippling stream and Koi pond.

Rooms 3 rms (1 en suite) (2 pri facs) D £65–£85✱ **Facilities** TV2B tea/coffee Cen ht TVL Wi-fi available Table tennis **Parking** 4 **Notes** ⊗ No children 10yrs Closed Dec–Feb ☻

★★★★ GUEST ACCOMMODATION
Parkside House

59 Lower Park Rd TN34 2LD

☎ 01424 433096 🖩 01424 421431

e–mail: bkentparksidehse@aol.com

dir: *A2101 to town centre, right at rdbt, 1st right*

You can expect a friendly welcome at this attractive Victorian house overlooking Alexandra Park, just a 10-minute walk from the town

centre and seafront. The bedrooms are carefully furnished and have many thoughtful touches, and the cosy lounge has plush furniture. Breakfast is served at individual tables in the elegant dining room.

Rooms 5 rms (4 en suite) (1 fmly) D £65–£75 **Facilities** TVB tea/coffee Cen ht TVL Wi-fi available **Notes LB** ⊗

★★★★ GUEST ACCOMMODATION
Tower House 1066

26–28 Tower Rd West, St Leonards TN38 0RG

☎ 01424 427217

e–mail: reservations@towerhousehotel.com

dir: *1m NW of Hastings centre. Off A21 London Rd onto A2102 London Rd, 250yds right onto Tower Rd West*

An elegant double-fronted Victorian property situated on an elevated position in a peaceful residential area. Bedrooms are carefully furnished and beautifully presented. Ground-floor areas include a sumptuous lounge, an honesty bar, and a superb conservatory-dining room with access to immaculate gardens. Home-cooked dinners are available by arrangement. All special dietary requirements catered for.

Rooms 6 en suite 4 annexe en suite (3 fmly) (4 GF) **Facilities** TVB tea/coffee Cen ht TVL Dinner Last d noon Wi-fi available **Notes** ⊗

★★★★ GUEST ACCOMMODATION
White Cottage

Battery Hill, Fairlight TN35 4AP

☎ 01424 812528 🖩 01424 812285

e–mail: juneandjohn@whitecottagebb.fsnet.co.uk

dir: *3m E off A259 (Hastings-Rye), signed Fairlight*

This modern house is set among mature gardens on the outskirts of the peaceful village of Fairlight, between Hastings and Rye. White Cottage offers pleasantly decorated, thoughtfully furnished and well-equipped bedrooms. Breakfast is served in the bright and airy lounge-dining area which overlooks the beautiful garden.

Rooms 3 en suite (1 GF) D £65–£70✱ **Facilities** TVB tea/coffee Cen ht **Parking** 4 **Notes LB** ⊗ No children 12yrs Closed Dec ☻

★★★★ 🅰 GUEST HOUSE
Seaspray

54 Eversfield Place TN37 6DB

☎ 01424 436583

e–mail: jo@seaspraybb.co.uk

web: www.seaspraybb.co.uk

dir: *A21 to town centre & seafront, Seaspray 100yds W of pier*

Rooms 10 rms (8 en suite) (3 fmly) (1 GF) S £30–£45; D £60–£75 **Facilities** FTV TVB tea/coffee Cen ht Wi-fi available **Notes LB** ⊗ No coaches ☻

CONTINUED

★★★ GUEST ACCOMMODATION
Eagle House
Pevensey Rd TN38 0JZ
☎ 01424 430535 & 441273 📠 01424 437771
e–mail: info@eaglehousehotel.co.uk
dir: *Off seafront onto London Rd, premises next to St Leonards Shopping Centre*

Victorian property situated in a peaceful residential area within easy walking distance of the shops, college and seafront. Public areas are sumptuously decorated in a traditional style and the spacious 'retro' bedrooms are simply furnished. A hearty breakfast can be enjoyed in the dining room, which overlooks the gardens.

Rooms 20 en suite (2 fmly) **Facilities** TVB tea/coffee Direct dial from bedrooms Cen ht **Parking** 13 **Notes** ⊗

HERSTMONCEUX   MAP 06 TQ61

Premier Collection

★★★★★ GUEST ACCOMMODATION
Wartling Place
Wartling Place, Wartling BN27 1RY
☎ 01323 832590 📠 01323 831558
e–mail: accom@wartlingplace.prestel.co.uk
dir: *2.5m SE of Herstmonceux. Off A271 to Wartling, Wartling Place opp village church*
Located in a sleepy village, this beautiful Grade II listed country home is set in two acres of well-tended gardens. The individually decorated bedrooms, two featuring four-poster beds, are luxurious and have a host of thoughtful extras. Delicious breakfasts are served in the elegant dining room. For business travellers, there is free broadband access.

Rooms 4 en suite (1 fmly) **Facilities** TVB tea/coffee Cen ht Dinner Last d 24hrs in advance **Conf** Max 12 **Parking** 10 **Notes** ⊗

HOVE   MAP 06 TQ20

See Brighton & Hove

LEWES   MAP 06 TQ41

★★★★ GUEST ACCOMMODATION
Nightingales
The Avenue, Kingston BN7 3LL
☎ 01273 475673 📠 01273 475673
e–mail: jean.hudson@xln.co.uk
dir: *2m SW of Lewes. A23 onto A27 to Lewes, at Ashcombe rdbt exit for Kingston, under railway bridge, right at 30mph sign, house 2nd from end on right*

A warm welcome is assured at this delightful modern bungalow, set in beautifully kept gardens and grounds. The spacious bedrooms and bathrooms are well appointed and come with a wide range of thoughtful extras, including fresh fruit and sherry. Refreshment is served on arrival in either the lounge or conservatory, both of which overlook the garden.

Rooms 2 en suite (2 GF) S £45–£65; D £65–£75✳ **Facilities** TVB tea/coffee Cen ht TVL **Parking** 2 **Notes** ⊗ No children

★★★★ ⇔ INN
The Blacksmiths Arms
London Rd, Offham BN7 3QD
☎ 01273 472971
e–mail: blacksmithsarms@tiscali.co.uk
web: www.theblacksmithsarms-offham.co.uk
dir: *2m N of Lewes. On A275 in Offham*

Situated just outside Lewes, this is a great location for touring the South coast, offering high quality accommodation in comfortable bedrooms. Enjoyable meals are available in the cosy bar downstairs and this is where the hearty cooked breakfast is also served.

Rooms 4 en suite S £45–£55; D £60–£80✳ **Facilities** TVB tea/coffee Cen ht Dinner Last d 9pm Wi-fi available **Parking** 22 **Notes** ⊗ No children 5yrs No coaches

489

ENGLAND

NEWHAVEN

MAP 06 TQ40

★★★ 🅰 BED & BREAKFAST

Newhaven Lodge

12 Brighton Rd BN9 9NB

☎ 01273 513736

e-mail: info@newhavenlodge.co.uk

dir: *250yds W of town centre on A259*

Rooms 6 rms (3 en suite) (4 fmly) (2 GF) S £25–£35; D £50–£70✱
(room only) **Facilities** TVB tea/coffee Cen ht **Parking** 5 **Notes LB**

★★ INN

The Harbourside

Fort Rd BN9 9EL

☎ 01273 513340 📄 01273 512372

dir: *A259 into Newhaven, signs to Fort, left onto South Rd & Fort Rd*

This Victorian inn is, as the name suggests, conveniently situated for the ferry terminals and harbour attractions. Bedrooms are spacious and a hearty meal can be enjoyed in the attractive bar and dining area. There is also a useful car park to the rear.

Rooms 10 rms (3 en suite) (5 fmly) **Facilities** TVB tea/coffee Cen ht
Dinner Last d 8.50pm Pool Table **Conf** Max 50 **Parking** 25 **Notes** ⊗

RYE

MAP 07 TQ92

See also Hastings & St Leonards

Premier Collection

★★★★★ GUEST ACCOMMODATION

Jeake's House

Mermaid St TN31 7ET

☎ 01797 222828 📄 01797 222623

e-mail: stay@jeakeshouse.com

web: www.jeakeshouse.com

dir: *Approach from High St or The Strand*

Previously a 17th-century wool store and then a 19th-century Baptist school, this delightful house stands on a cobbled street in one of the most beautiful parts of this small, bustling town. The individually decorated bedrooms combine elegance and comfort with modern

CONTINUED

facilities. Breakfast is served at separate tables in the galleried dining room, and there is an oak-beamed lounge as well as a stylish book-lined bar with old pews.

Rooms 11 rms (10 en suite) (1 pri facs) (2 fmly) S £70–£79; D £90–£126
Facilities TVB tea/coffee Direct dial from bedrooms Cen ht **Parking** 21
Notes No children 8yrs

See advert on opposite page

Premier Collection

★★★★★ 📞 🛏 GUEST ACCOMMODATION

Manor Farm Oast

Windmill Ln TN36 4WL

☎ 01424 813787 📄 01424 813787

e-mail: manor.farm.oast@lineone.net

web: www.manorfarmoast.co.uk

dir: *4m SW of Rye. A259 W past Icklesham church, left at x-rds onto Windmill Ln, after sharp left bend left into orchards*

Charming 19th-century, environmentally friendly oast house peacefully located amid orchards in open countryside. Spacious bedrooms are individually styled and include numerous thoughtful extras including free Wi-fi. A choice of lounges is available, one heated by a roaring log fire during the winter, and locally sourced, home-produced dinners are a feature of any stay.

Rooms 3 rms (2 en suite) (1 pri facs) (1 fmly) S £54–£60; D £90–£94
Facilities TVB tea/coffee Cen ht Dinner Last d 7.30pm Wi-fi available
Conf Max 20 Thtr 20 Board 12 **Parking** 8 **Notes LB** ⊗ No children
11yrs Closed 23 Dec–15 Jan Civ Wed 70

Premier Collection

★★★★★ GUEST ACCOMMODATION

Olde Moat House

TN29 0AZ

☎ 01797 344700 📄 01797 343919

e-mail: oldemoathouse@hotmail.com

web: www.oldemoathouse.co.uk

(For full entry see Ivychurch (Kent))

Premier Collection

★★★★★ GUEST ACCOMMODATION

Willow Tree House

113 Winchelsea Rd TN31 7EL

☎ 01797 227820

e–mail: info@willow-tree-house.com

web: www.willow-tree-house.com

This grade II listed house alongside the A259 is just a short walk from the hub of Rye. It has been totally refurbished by the charming hosts. Bedrooms ooze quality and character and shower bathrooms are well equipped. Breakfast in the conservatory dining room is a great start to the day with well-sourced local products.

Rooms 6 en suite (1 fmly) S £70–£85; D £80–£120✳ **Facilities** FTV TVB tea/coffee Cen ht Wi-fi available **Parking** 8 **Notes** ⊗

Premier Collection

★★★★★ RESTAURANT WITH ROOMS

White Vine House

24 High St TN31 7JF

☎ 01797 224748

e–mail: info@whitevinehouse.co.uk

dir: *In the middle of Rye high street*

Situated in the heart of the ancient Cinque Port town of Rye, White Vine House's origins go back to the 13th century. The cellar is the oldest part, but the current building dates from 1560, and boasts an impressive Georgian frontage. The original timber framework is visible in many areas, and certainly adds to the house's feeling of history. The bedrooms have period furniture along with luxury bath or shower rooms. One bedroom has an antique four-poster which tops off the atmosphere for a special stay.

Rooms 7 en suite (1 fmly) S fr £75; D £125–£165✳ **Facilities** TVB tea/coffee Cen ht Dinner Last d 9.30pm Wi-fi available **Conf** Max 30 Thtr 30 Class 30 Board 30 **Notes LB** ⊗ Civ Wed 30

★★★★★ 🅰 GUEST ACCOMMODATION

Oaklands

Udimore Rd TN31 6AB

☎ 01797 229734 📄 01797 229734

e–mail: info@oaklands-rye.co.uk

web: www.oaklands-rye.co.uk

dir: *Take B2089 from Rye 1.3m, Oaklands drive on right*

Rooms 3 en suite D £80–£95 **Facilities** FTV TVB tea/coffee Cen ht 🤟 **Parking** 5 **Notes** ⊗

★★★★ 🛉 🖴 GUEST ACCOMMODATION

Strand House

Tanyards Ln, Winchelsea TN36 4JT

☎ 01797 226276 📄 01797 224806

e–mail: info@thestrandhouse.co.uk

web: www.thestrandhouse.co.uk

dir: *M20 junct 10 onto A2070 to Lydd. Follow A259 through Rye to Winchelsea, 2m past Rye*

This charming 15th-century house is just a few miles from Rye. Traditional character is maintained in comfortably appointed rooms and public areas. Local produce is a feature of the home-cooked evening meals and breakfasts. Marry Sullivan was a finalist for the AA Friendliest Landlady of the Year 2008 Award.

Rooms 10 rms (9 en suite) (1 pri facs) (3 fmly) (1 GF) S £50–£65; D £65–£120✳ **Facilities** FTV TVB tea/coffee Cen ht TVL Dinner Last d 7pm Wi-fi available **Parking** 12 **Notes** No children 12yrs RS wknds (high season) Civ Wed 30

RYE CONTINUED

★★★★ GUEST ACCOMMODATION
Little Saltcote

22 Military Rd TN31 7NY
☎ 01797 223210 📠 01797 224474
e–mail: info@littlesaltcote.co.uk
web: www.littlesaltcote.co.uk

dir: *0.5m N of town centre. Off A268 onto Military Rd signed Appledore, house 300yds on left*

This delightful family-run guest house stands in quiet surroundings within walking distance of Rye town centre. The bright and airy en suite bedrooms are equipped with modern facilities including Wi-fi, and you can enjoy afternoon tea in the garden conservatory. A hearty breakfast is served at individual tables in the dining room.

Rooms 4 en suite (2 fmly) (1 GF) S £40–£65; D £63–£80 **Facilities** TVB tea/coffee Cen ht Wi-fi available **Parking** 5 **Notes** LB

★★★★ GUEST ACCOMMODATION
The Windmill Guest House

Ferry Rd TN31 7DW
☎ 01797 224027
e–mail: info@ryewindmill.co.uk
web: www.ryewindmill.co.uk

This white smock windmill has been a Rye landmark since 1820 and was more recently a bakery. Bedrooms located in the purpose-built extension have good beds and en suite facilities that are generously proportioned. Breakfast taken in the old granary is a freshly-cooked affair from well-sourced local ingredients including local butchers' sausages and some good local fruit juices.

Rooms 8 en suite (4 GF) S £45–£55; D £60–£75✱ **Facilities** FTV TVB tea/coffee Cen ht TVL **Parking** 8 **Notes** No children 12yrs Closed 24–26 Dec

★★★ FARM HOUSE
Cliff Farm *(TQ933237)*

Military Rd, Iden Lock TN31 7QE
☎ 01797 280331 📠 01797 280331 Mrs P Sullivin
e–mail: info@cliff-farm.com

dir: *2m along Military Rd to Appledore, turn left at hanging milk churn*

Beautiful views and wonderful hospitality are what you'll find at this farmhouse situated in a peaceful rural location just a short drive from Rye and Hastings. Bedrooms are pleasantly decorated and comfortably furnished. Breakfast is served at individual tables in the dining room, and there is also a cosy sitting room with a wood-burning stove and television.

Rooms 3 rms (1 fmly) S £28; D £46–£48✱ **Facilities** tea/coffee Cen ht TVL **Parking** 6 **Notes** LB 6 acres smallholding Closed Nov–Feb 🅓

★★★ GUEST ACCOMMODATION
Tiffanys

51 Wincheslsea Rd TN31 7EL
☎ 01797 225693 📠 01797 225693
e–mail: terry.rosscoulson@btinternet.com

dir: *Situated on A259 Hastings, opposite Total Garage*

This friendly family-run establishment is ideally located next to the harbour and within easy walking distance of the town's famous antique stores. Comfortable bedrooms are bright and airy and a cosy dining room provides the setting for a hearty cooked breakfast.

Rooms 3 rms (1 en suite) (2 pri facs) (1 GF) **Facilities** FTV TVB tea/coffee Cen ht Dinner Last d 9pm **Notes** ⊗ 🅓

ST LEONARDS	MAP 07 TQ80

See Hastings & St Leonards

SEAFORD	MAP 06 TV49

★★★★ BED & BREAKFAST
Ab Fab Rooms

11 Station Rd, Bishopstone BN25 2RB
☎ 01323 895001 📠 0870 127 1624
e–mail: steve@abfabfood.co.uk

Just a short walk from Bishopstone station and sandy beaches, this is a perfect base for visiting local sights and attractions. Contemporary-styled bedrooms offer superior comfort and amenities. Breakfast, served in the garden conservatory, includes homemade jams and local Sussex produce. Steve Mitchell was a finalist for the AA Friendliest Landlady of the Year 2008.

Rooms 3 en suite S £50–£70; D £55–£75✱ **Facilities** STV TVB tea/coffee Cen ht Wi-fi available **Parking** 2 **Notes** ⊗ 🅓

★ ★ ★ GUEST ACCOMMODATION
The Avondale

Avondale Rd BN25 1RJ
☎ 01323 890008 📄 01323 490598
e–mail: avondalehotel@btconnect.com

dir: *In town centre, off A259 behind war memorial*

A warm welcome is offered by the caring owners at this friendly, family-run guest accommodation which is ideally placed for the Newhaven to Dieppe ferry service. The bedrooms are pleasantly furnished and thoughtfully equipped. Breakfast is served in the attractive dining room and guests also have the use of a cosy lounge.

Rooms 14 rms (8 en suite) (4 fmly) **Facilities** TVB tea/coffee Lift Cen ht TVL Wi-fi available **Conf** Max 15 Class 15 Board 15 **Notes** ⊗

★ ★ ★ GUEST ACCOMMODATION
Silverdale

21 Sutton Park Rd BN25 1RH
☎ 01323 491849 📄 01323 890854
e–mail: silverdale@mistral.co.uk
web: www.silverdale.mistral.co.uk

dir: *On A259 in the centre of Seaford, close to memorial*

A warm welcome is assured at this family-run establishment, which is well situated for the town centre and the seafront. The pleasant bedrooms have many useful extras, and breakfast and dinner are served in the dining room. The cosy well-stocked lounge bar specialises in English wines and malt whiskies.

Rooms 7 en suite (2 fmly) (1 GF) **Facilities** TVB tea/coffee Direct dial from bedrooms Cen ht Dinner Last d 2pm **Parking** 3

WADHURST   MAP 06 TQ63

★ ★ ★ ★ FARM HOUSE
Little Tidebrook Farm *(TQ621304)*

Riseden TN5 6NY
☎ 01892 782688 Mrs Sally Marley-Ward
e–mail: info@littletidebrook.co.uk
web: www.littletidebrook.co.uk

dir: *A267 from Tunbridge Wells to mark Cross, left onto B2100, 2m turn right at Best Beech Inn, left after 1m, farm on left after 0.25m*

This traditional farmhouse has cosy log fires in winter and wonderful garden dining in warm months. The imaginative décor combines with modern amenities such as Wi-fi to provide leisure and business travellers with the ideal setting. Close to Bewl Water and Royal Tunbridge Wells.

Rooms 4 rms (2 en suite) (1 pri facs) D £50–£80✳ **Facilities** TVB tea/coffee Cen ht TVL Wi-fi available **Parking** 8 **Notes** No children 12yrs 40 acres Horses 🐾

WILMINGTON   MAP 06 TQ50

★ ★ ★ ★ ◉◉ RESTAURANT WITH ROOMS
Crossways

Lewes Rd BN26 5SG
☎ 01323 482455 📄 01323 487811
e–mail: stay@crosswayshotel.co.uk
web: www.crosswayshotel.co.uk

dir: *On A27 between Lewes & Polegate, 2m E of Alfriston rdbt*

A well-established restaurant with a good local reputation is the focus of this attractive property. Bedrooms are also provided, and all are individually decorated with taste and style and superior rooms are available. Guest comfort is paramount so there are excellent facilities and the kind of hospitality that ensures guests return often.

Rooms 7 en suite S £72; D £115–£135 **Facilities** TVB tea/coffee Direct dial from bedrooms Cen ht Dinner Last d 8.30pm Wi-fi available **Parking** 30 **Notes LB** ⊗ No children 12yrs Closed 24 Dec–23 Jan

ENGLAND

SUSSEX, WEST

ALDINGBOURNE   MAP 06 SU90

★★★★ BED & BREAKFAST
Mill Cottage
Oving Rd PO20 3TP
☎ 01243 545188
e–mail: chris.standing@btconnect.com
web: www.theoldwatermeadows.com

dir: *From A27 take B2233. Take 3rd turning on right, Mill cottage 0.5m on left*

Set in an acre of gardens in the Sussex countryside, halfway between Arundel and Chichester, Mill Cottage was once an old labourers' living quarters associated with the neighbouring water mill. Bedrooms are homely, as is the dining room where breakfast is served overlooking the mill pond.

Rooms 2 en suite **Facilities** TVB tea/coffee Cen ht **Parking** 4 **Notes** ⊗ Closed Xmas & New Year 🐾

AMBERLEY   MAP 06 TQ01

★★★★ BED & BREAKFAST
Stream Cottage
The Square BN18 9SR
☎ 01798 831266 📠 01798 831266
e–mail: enquiries@streamcottage.co.uk
web: www.streamcottage.co.uk

dir: *Off B2139 into village centre*

Located on the edge of the South Downs and within easy reach of Arundel, Goodwood and Chichester, this picturesque thatched cottage has a wealth of beams and brick floors, and was reputedly built in 1587. The comfortable, well-equipped bedroom comes with a private sitting room. Breakfast is a wealth of imaginative ideas.

Rooms 1 rms (1 pri facs) (1 fmly) S £60; D £80✱ **Facilities** TVB tea/coffee Cen ht TVL **Parking** 1 **Notes LB** ⊗ Closed Xmas & New Year 🐾

★★★★ BED & BREAKFAST
Woody Banks Cottage
Crossgates BN18 9NR
☎ 01798 831295 & 07719 916703
e–mail: woodybanks@btinternet.com
web: www.woodybanks.co.uk

dir: *Off B2139 into village, right at Black Horse pub, Woody Banks 0.5m on left past Sportsman pub*

Located close to Arundel on an elevated position with stunning views over the Wildbrooks, this immaculately maintained house and gardens is very popular with walkers. It provides two comfortable, homely bedrooms filled with thoughtful extras. Imaginative breakfasts are served in the panoramic lounge-dining room.

Rooms 2 rms (1 pri facs) (1 fmly) D £60–£70 **Facilities** TVB tea/coffee Cen ht TVL **Parking** 3 **Notes LB** ⊗ No children 6yrs Closed 24–27 Dec 🐾

ANGMERING   MAP 06 TQ00

★★★★ GUEST ACCOMMODATION
Angmering Manor
High St BN16 4AG
☎ 01903 859849 📠 01903 783268
e–mail: angmeringmanor@thechapmansgroup.co.uk
web: www.angmeringmanorhotel.co.uk

dir: *Follow A27 towards Portsmouth, exit A280, follow signs for Angmering*

This former manor house in the heart of the village has been stylishly refurbished. It offers good food, a bar, an indoor pool, and good parking. Staff are friendly and helpful and rooms are very comfortable.

Rooms 8 en suite (3 fmly) **Facilities** FTV TVB tea/coffee Direct dial from bedrooms Cen ht Dinner Last d 9.30pm Wi-fi available ⓢ Sauna Gymnasium Beauty salon **Conf** Max 20 Class 20 **Parking** 25 **Notes** ⊗

ARUNDEL   MAP 06 TQ00

See also Amberley

★★★★ ⓢ RESTAURANT WITH ROOMS
The Townhouse
65 High St BN18 9AJ
☎ 01903 883847
web: www.thetownhouse.co.uk

dir: *Follow A27 to Arundel, onto High Street, establishment on left at top of hill*

This an elegant, Grade II-listed Regency building overlooking Arundel Castle, just a short walk from the shops and sights of Arundel. Bedrooms and public areas retain the unspoilt style of the building. The ceiling in the dining room is particularly spectacular, and comes all the way from 16th-century Florence. The owners can be justifiably proud of the enterprise they took on just a short years ago.

Rooms 4 en suite D £85–£120✱ **Facilities** FTV TVB tea/coffee Cen ht Dinner Last d 9.30pm Wi-fi available **Notes** ⊗ Closed 2wks Jan & 2wks Oct RS Sun–Mon

★★★ GUEST ACCOMMODATION
Arden

4 Queens Ln BN18 9JN

☎ 01903 882544

e-mail: terryandann@talktalkbusiness.net

dir: *From station, at rdbt take turning for town centre. Take next left onto Queens Ln*

This is a comfortable guest house situated a few minutes from Arundel village and station. The property has a selection of single, double and twin bedrooms, some of which are en suite. The dining room, where a traditional cooked breakfast is served, is situated in the well-lit basement. Off-street parking is available.

Rooms 8 rms (5 en suite) (2 GF) S £38–£45; D £56–£64✳ **Facilities** TVB tea/coffee **Parking** 5 **Notes** ⊗ No children 14yrs Closed 31 Dec 🐾

BOGNOR REGIS　　　　　　　　**MAP 06 SZ99**

★★★★ GUEST HOUSE
Old Priory

80 North Bersted St PO22 9AQ

☎ 01243 863580 📠 01243 826597

e-mail: old.priory@btinternet.com

web: www.old-priory.com

dir: *1.6m NW of Bognor. Off A259 Chichester Rd to North Bersted, Old Priory sign on left*

Located in the mainly residential area of North Bersted, this 400-year-old property retains many original features. Bedrooms which are all individual in style are homely and one has a four-poster waterbed and a double air bath. There is an outdoor pool and attractive grounds, perfect for the summer.

Rooms 2 en suite 3 annexe en suite (3 GF) S £40–£50; D £65–£100✳ **Facilities** STV TVB tea/coffee Cen ht ⤳ **Parking** 6 **Notes** ⊗ No coaches

★★★★ 🅰 GUEST HOUSE
Trevali Guest House

Belmont St PO21 1LE

☎ 01243 862203

e-mail: info@trevaliguesthouse.co.uk

dir: *Follow signs to seafront, then signs for Tourist Information*

Rooms 8 rms (5 en suite) (3 pri facs) (2 fmly) (2 GF) **Facilities** FTV TVB tea/coffee Cen ht **Notes** ⊗

★★★ GUEST HOUSE
Jubilee

5 Gloucester Rd PO21 1NU

☎ 01243 863016 & 07702 275967 📠 01243 868017

e-mail: jubileeguesthouse@tiscali.co.uk

web: www.jubileeguesthouse.com

dir: *A259 to seafront, house opp Day Entrance to Butlins Family Entertainment Resort*

This property is close to Butlins, the seafront and the town centre. The brightly decorated and well-equipped bedrooms vary in size. A generous and freshly cooked breakfast, including provision for vegetarians, is served in the attractive dining room.

Rooms 6 rms (2 en suite) (3 fmly) **Facilities** TVB tea/coffee Cen ht **Parking** 4 **Notes** ⊗ No coaches Closed Xmas, Jan & Feb

★★ GUEST ACCOMMODATION
Regis Lodge

3 Gloucester Rd PO21 1NU

☎ 01243 827110

e-mail: frank.regislodge@btinternet.com

web: www.regislodge.co.uk

dir: *A259 to Bognor, signs for Southcoast World, Regis Lodge opposite day visitors entrance to Southcoast World*

Located within easy walking distance of the seafront and attractions, this family-run guest house offers a high standard of hospitality. Bedrooms vary in size and are well presented and suitably equipped. The brightly decorated dining room has separate tables and a good choice is offered at breakfast.

Rooms 6 en suite (5 fmly) **Facilities** TVB tea/coffee Cen ht **Parking** 4 **Notes** ⊗

BOSHAM
MAP 05 SU80

★★★★ BED & BREAKFAST

Charters B&B

Bosham Ln PO18 8HG

☎ 01243 572644

e–mail: louise@chartersbandb.co.uk

dir: *A27 onto A259, 3m left at rdbt, right at T-junct, 100yds on right*

Charters B&B provides comfortable accommodation in a peaceful location close to Bosham Harbour and Goodwood race circuit. Bedrooms and bathrooms are spacious, stylish and modern with their own separate, self contained entrances. A continental breakfast is served in the comfort of guest bedrooms mid-week and a fully cooked freshly prepared hot breakfast is provided for guests on a Saturday and Sunday morning, served in the bright and airy conservatory.

Rooms 2 annexe en suite (1 GF) S £70–£100; D £80–£100✱ **Facilities** TVB tea/coffee Cen ht **Parking** 3 **Notes** ⊗ No children 10yrs Closed Xmas & New Year

★★★★ BED & BREAKFAST

White Barn

Crede Ln PO18 8NX

☎ 01243 573113   📠 01243 573113

e–mail: chrissie@whitebarn.biz

web: www.whitebarn.biz

dir: *A259 Bosham rdbt, turn S signed Bosham Quay, 0.5m to T-junct, left signed White Barn, 0.25m turn left signed White Barn, 50yds turn right*

This delightful single storey property is close to Bosham Harbour, Goodwood Race Circuit, Chichester and Portsmouth, and has cosy

CONTINUED

bedrooms with colour coordinated soft furnishings and many thoughtful extras. The open-plan dining room overlooks an attractive garden, where breakfast is served if the weather permits.

Rooms 2 en suite 1 annexe en suite (3 GF) S £60–£65; D £70–£95✱ **Facilities** STV FTV TVB tea/coffee Cen ht **Parking** 3 **Notes** ⊗ No children 12yrs

BURGESS HILL
MAP 06 TQ31

★★★★ BED & BREAKFAST

Abbey House

2 The Holt RH15 0RF

☎ 01444 233299

e–mail: info@abbey-house.biz

dir: *0.5m E of town centre. Off A2113 Folders Ln onto Kings Way, 3rd left onto The Holt*

This excellent accommodation is set within a comfortable family home, in a pleasant residential area: just a short walk from the town centre and railway station. The modern bedrooms are well equipped and include hair dryers, televisions, fridges and CD players. Welcoming touches include wine and fruit. A good breakfast is served around a large communal dining table.

Rooms 3 rms (2 en suite) (1 pri facs) (2 fmly) **Facilities** FTV TVB tea/coffee Direct dial from bedrooms Cen ht **Notes** ⊗ No children 10yrs Closed 24 Dec–2 Jan

★★★★ 🍴 GUEST ACCOMMODATION

The Homestead

Homestead Ln, Valebridge Rd RH15 0RQ

☎ 01444 246899 & 0800 064 0015 📠 0870 165 6035

e–mail: homestead@burgess-hill.co.uk

web: www.burgess-hill.co.uk

dir: *0.5m N of Burgess Hill. From Wivelsfield station onto Valebridge Rd, 0.5m turn right to end of Homestead Ln*

The Homestead has a country setting surrounded by 8 acres of garden and woodland just a short distance from the town centre. Bedrooms vary in size but all are well equipped and include generous extras. A great choice of breakfast includes vegetarian options. The attractive dining room overlooks the garden and there is a comfortable conservatory-lounge and good leisure facilities.

Rooms 3 en suite (2 GF) S £40; D £80 **Facilities** STV FTV TVB tea/coffee Direct dial from bedrooms Cen ht Wi-fi available 🎾 Gymnasium Hot tub **Parking** 50 **Notes** ⊗ No children 12yrs Closed 23 Dec–2 Jan

CHARLTON   MAP 06 SU81

★★★★ 🅰 GUEST HOUSE
Woodstock House
PO18 0HU

☎ 01243 811666 📄 01243 811666

e-mail: info@woodstockhousehotel.co.uk

web: www.woodstockhousehotel.co.uk

dir: *Off A286 at Singleton, 1m to Charlton, premises on left*

Rooms 11 en suite 2 annexe en suite (1 fmly) (2 GF) **Facilities** FTV TVB tea/coffee Direct dial from bedrooms Licensed Cen ht **Parking** 13 **Notes** No coaches

CHICHESTER   MAP 05 SU80

See also Bosham & Chilgrove

Premier Collection

★★★★★ 🏠 GUEST HOUSE
Rooks Hill
Lavant Rd, Lavant PO18 0BQ

☎ 01243 528400

e-mail: enquiries@rookshill.co.uk

Rooks Hill Guest House occupies a convenient and picturesque location near to Goodwood and the city of Chichester. The warm and friendly proprietors create a wonderful home-from-home atmosphere whether visiting for business or leisure. Accommodation offers superbly finished bedrooms, powerful thermostatic showers and additional thoughtful extras. A delicious breakfast served in the stylish dining room or on the patio overlooking the pretty gardens in warmer weather provides a substantial start to the day.

Rooms 6 en suite (2 GF) D £105–£125✱ **Facilities** FTV TVB tea/coffee Cen ht Wi-fi available **Parking** 6 **Notes LB** ⊗ No children 12yrs No coaches

Premier Collection

★★★★★★ 🍴🍴🍴 RESTAURANT WITH ROOMS
West Stoke House
Downs Rd, West Stoke PO18 9BN

☎ 01243 575226 📄 01243 574655

e-mail: info@weststokehouse.co.uk

dir: *3m NW of Chichester. Off B286 to West Stoke, next to St Andrew's Church*

This fine country house, part Georgian and part medieval, with over five acres of lawns and gardens, lies on the edge of the South Downs. The large uncluttered bedrooms have smart modern bathrooms and great country views. The restaurant provides very good cooking in a relaxed atmosphere. Public rooms have a light-filled elegance and are adorned with an eclectic mix of period furniture and contemporary art.

Rooms 8 rms (7 en suite) (1 pri facs) (1 fmly) S £95–£115; D £130–£215✱ **Facilities** TV6B tea/coffee Direct dial from bedrooms Cen ht Dinner Last d 9pm Wi-fi available ⚓ **Conf** Max 60 Thtr 60 Class 30 Board 20 **Parking** 20 **Notes LB** Closed 24–28 Dec Civ Wed 60

Premier Collection

★★★★★ 🍴 INN
The Royal Oak
Pook Ln PO18 0AX

☎ 01243 527434 📄 01243 775062

e-mail: info@royaloaklavant.co.uk

dir: *2m N of Chichester. Off A286 into East Lavant village centre*

Located close to the Goodwood estate and Rolls Royce HQ this delightful inn is full of character with beamed ceilings, timber floors and open fires in the public areas. Bedrooms are finished to a very high standard with comfortable beds and state of the art electronic equipment. Award winning meals are served in the popular restaurant.

Rooms 3 en suite 5 annexe en suite (1 fmly) **Facilities** STV TVB tea/coffee Direct dial from bedrooms Cen ht Dinner Last d 9.30pm Riding **Parking** 25 **Notes** No coaches

ENGLAND

CHICHESTER CONTINUED

★★★★ GUEST ACCOMMODATION
Abelands Barn

Bognor Rd, Merston PO20 1DY

☎ 01243 533826 & 783576 📄 01243 783576

e–mail: snooze@abelandsbarn.co.uk

dir: *2.5m E of city centre on A259*

Located between Chichester and Bognor Regis, this beautifully restored barn offers an elegant and tranquil retreat. Public areas include a characterful upstairs lounge and an open-plan dining room, while the bedrooms are located in the main house and annexe. A substantial breakfast en famille complete with country views rounds off the stay.

Rooms 4 rms (2 en suite) (2 pri facs) 1 annexe en suite (1 fmly) (2 GF) **Facilities** tea/coffee Cen ht TVL Dinner Last d 10pm Wi-fi available **Parking** 5 **Notes** ⊗

★★★★ BED & BREAKFAST
82 Fishbourne

82 Fishbourne Rd West PO19 3JL

☎ 07854 051013

e–mail: nik@nikwestacott.plus.com

web: www.82fishbourne.co.uk

dir: *A27 Chichester rdbt, towards Fishbourne and Bosham on A259. 0.5m on right diagonally opp Woolpack pub*

Warm and friendly hospitality abounds at 82 Fishbourne which is located only a short drive from the historic cathedral city of Chichester. Accommodation is spacious and well equipped for the business traveller or leisure guest. Breakfast provides a substantial start to the day and includes delicious fresh eggs from the free range hens which live in the back garden. Scheduled activities include 'Mushroom Hunts' and wine tastings throughout the year.

Rooms 3 en suite (1 fmly) (1 GF) S £45–£75; D £50–£100✶ **Facilities** FTV TVB tea/coffee Cen ht Dinner Last d 36hrs notice Wi-fi available **Parking** 3

★★★★ BED & BREAKFAST
Englewood B&B

East Ashling PO18 9AS

☎ 01243 575407

e–mail: sjenglewood@hotmail.co.uk

dir: *Bosham rdbt A259, N exit. At T-junct turn right, next left to B2178, left again, Englewood is on left*

Set well back from the main road, in an Area of Outstanding Natural Beauty, Englewood has a very pretty garden, and is surrounded by pleasant lanes and footpaths. The two bedrooms have lots of thoughtful facilities and extras including bottled water, boiled sweets and fruit squash.

Rooms 2 rms (1 en suite) (1 pri facs) (2 GF) S £35–£40; D £50–£64✶ **Facilities** TVB tea/coffee Cen ht **Parking** 2 **Notes** LB ⊗ No children ⊛

★★★★ BED & BREAKFAST
Gable End

Main Rd, Nutbourne PO18 8RT

☎ 01243 573356

e–mail: jill@po188rt.freeserve.co.uk

dir: *A259 W past Barleycorn pub on left, after 0.3m turn left & immediately right at Tamarind restaurant. 150yds on left*

You are guaranteed a genuinely warm welcome at Gable End which occupies a peaceful location close to Bosham and Emsworth Marina. Enjoy a delicious home cooked breakfast in attractive surroundings with views from the rear of the property overlooking the sea and pretty garden.

Rooms 1 rms (1 pri facs) D £70–£90✶ **Facilities** tea/coffee Cen ht Dinner **Parking** 8 **Notes** ⊗ No children 11yrs Closed 23 Dec–2 Jan ⊛

★★★★ INN
Horse and Groom

East Ashling PO18 9AX

☎ 01243 575339 📄 01243 575560

e–mail: info@thehorseandgroomchichester.co.uk

web: www.thehorseandgroomchichester.co.uk

dir: *On B2178 3m N of Chichester on road to Rowlands Castle*

The Horse and Groom is a unique 17th-century country pub and restaurant offering spacious and comfortable accommodation, and warm, friendly hospitality. Substantial freshly prepared breakfasts, lunches and dinners are available making good use of freshly caught fish and locally sourced ingredients.

Rooms 11 en suite (11 GF) S £45–£55; D £70–£80 **Facilities** TVB tea/coffee Cen ht Dinner Last d 9.15pm **Parking** 40 **Notes** RS Sun eve

★★★★ BED & BREAKFAST
Old Chapel Forge

Lower Bognor Rd, Lagness PO20 1LR
☎ 01243 264380
e–mail: info@oldchapelforge.co.uk

dir: *4m SE of Chichester. Off A27 Chichester bypass at Bognor rdbt signed Pagham/Runcton, onto B2166 Pagham Rd & Lower Bognor Rd, Old Chapel Forge on right*

Great local produce features in the hearty breakfasts at this comfortable, eco-friendly property, an idyllic 17th-century house and chapel set in mature gardens with panoramic views of the South Downs. Old Chapel Forge is a short drive from Chichester, Goodwood, Pagham Harbour Nature Reserve and the beach. Bedrooms, including suites in the chapel, are luxurious, and all have internet access.

Rooms 4 annexe en suite (2 fmly) (4 GF) S £35–£55; D £50–£110
Facilities TVB tea/coffee Cen ht Dinner Last d Breakfast Wi-fi available
Parking 6 **Notes LB**

★★★★ GUEST ACCOMMODATION
Old Orchard Guest House

8 Lyndhurst Rd PO19 7PF
☎ 01243 536547
e–mail: info@oldorchardguesthouse.co.uk

dir: *In city centre, behind Old Cattle Market, follow Market Av, Stirling Rd, Caledonian Rd onto Lyndhurst Rd*

Old Orchard Guest House occupies a convenient location only a few minutes walk from the centre of the historic city of Chichester. Hospitality is genuinely warm and friendly and smart, stylish accommodation is very comfortable. A fully cooked breakfast is available served at separate tables in the bright dining room.

Rooms 3 en suite S £40–£60; D £60–£80✳ **Facilities** FTV TVB tea/coffee Cen ht TVL **Parking** 2 **Notes** ⊗ No children 12yrs

★★★★ GUEST ACCOMMODATION
Trents

50 South St PO19 1DS
☎ 01243 773714
e–mail: enquiries@trentchichester.co.uk

dir: *Enter Chichester from M27 Stockbridge rdbt straight ahead onto South St. Trents on right*

Trents is a friendly brasserie situated in the heart of Chichester. The sun terrace is perfect for al fresco dining, weather permitting.

Contemporary bedrooms, which are all en suite, are very comfortable.

Rooms 5 en suite (1 fmly) S £60–£70; D £70–£99✳ (room only)
Facilities TVB tea/coffee Direct dial from bedrooms Cen ht Dinner Last d 9pm Wi-fi available **Notes** ⊗

★★★★ BED & BREAKFAST
Wilbury House

Main Rd, Fishbourne PO18 8AT
☎ 01243 572953 📠 01243 572953
e–mail: jackiepenfold@onetel.com

dir: *Off A27 Chichester bypass onto A259 W to Fishbourne and Bosham, 1m on left from Tesco rdbt*

This modern and well-appointed house is located on the edge of the village surrounded by countryside. Personally supervised by the charming owner, the atmosphere is friendly. Bedrooms are individually decorated, nicely furnished and include two ground-floor garden rooms. A generous English breakfast is served in the kitchen, overlooking the rear garden or in the dining room.

Rooms 1 rms (1 pri facs) 2 annexe en suite (2 GF) S £45–£60; D £75–£80 **Facilities** TVB tea/coffee Cen ht Wi-fi available **Parking** 7 **Notes** ⊗ No children 6yrs Closed mid Dec–mid Jan 🐾

★★★★ 🅰 BED & BREAKFAST
The Bruford's

66 The Street, Boxgrove PO18 0EE
☎ 01243 774085 & 775146 📠 01243 781235
e–mail: room4me@brufords.org
web: www.brufords.org

dir: *3m NE of Chichester. Off A27 into Boxgrove, signed on right*

Rooms 2 en suite 3 annexe en suite (4 GF) **Facilities** TVB tea/coffee Cen ht Snooker **Parking** 4 **Notes** ⊗ No children 12yrs

CONTINUED

CHICHESTER CONTINUED

★★★ GUEST ACCOMMODATION

Grandwood House

Watergate, West Marden PO18 9EG

☎ 07971 845153 & 023 9263 1436 📠 023 9263 1436

e–mail: info@grandwoodhouse.co.uk

web: www.grandwoodhouse.co.uk

Set in the South Downs and built in 1907, Grandwood House was originally a lodge belonging to Watergate House, which was accidentally burnt down by troops during WWII. Only a short walk away is the local pub in nearby Walderton which serves lunches and evening meals. All rooms are en suite and enjoy views of the garden, open farmland or both. Large security gates leading onto the driveway ensures secure parking at all times.

Rooms 4 annexe en suite (4 GF) **Facilities** FTV TVB tea/coffee Cen ht Wi-fi available **Parking** 8

★★★ INN

The Vestry

23 Southgate PO19 1ES

☎ 01243 773358 📠 01243 530633

e–mail: info@the-vestry.com

Just 15 minutes from the sea, at the heart of the city, the modern yet traditionally-styled Vestry offers en suite rooms with plenty of useful facilities. In the public areas, relax in one of many comfortable sofas, and enjoy a roaring log fire in the cooler months. The restaurant has a casual dining lunch menu along with weekly specials and bar snacks Sunday to Friday evenings.

Rooms 11 en suite (2 fmly) S £65–£85; D £75–£95✳ **Facilities** FTV TVB tea/coffee Direct dial from bedrooms Dinner Last d 7.45pm Wi-fi available **Notes** Closed 24–26 Dec & 31 Dec–1 Jan

---

CHILGROVE   MAP 05 SU81

★★★★ 🅰 BED & BREAKFAST

Chilgrove Farm

PO18 9HU

☎ 01243 519436 📠 01243 519438

e–mail: simonrenwick@aol.com

dir: A286 onto B2141 Chilgrove 3.5m, turn right onto Chilgrove Park Rd, 0.5m on right

Rooms 1 en suite 2 annexe en suite (2 fmly) (2 GF) S £50–£100; D £90–£120✳ **Facilities** FTV TVB tea/coffee Cen ht **Parking** 6 **Notes** LB ⊗

◉◉ 🆄

The Fish House (formerly White Horse)

PO18 9HX

☎ 01243 535219 & 519444 📠 01243 519499

e–mail: info@fishhouse.co.uk

dir: From Chichester take A286 N, turn left onto B2141 to village

At the time of going to press the rating for this establishment had not been confirmed. Please check the AA website www.theAA.com for up-to-date information.

Rooms 17 en suite (11 GF) S £90–£150; D £120–£220✳ **Facilities** STV FTV TVB tea/coffee Direct dial from bedrooms Cen ht Dinner Last d 9.45pm Wi-fi available Sauna **Conf** Max 20 Thtr 20 Class 20 Board 20 Del from £150 ✳ **Parking** 50 **Notes** LB Civ Wed 100

CRAWLEY   MAP 06 TQ23

For accommodation details see **Gatwick Airport** *(London)*

GATWICK AIRPORT   MAP 06 TQ24
(LONDON)

★★★★ GUEST ACCOMMODATION

Latchetts Cottage

Norwood Hill RH6 0ET

e–mail: davidjlees@tiscali.co.uk

web: www.latchettscottage.co.uk

dir: On A217, 2m S of Reigate turn right onto Ironsbottom, then 2nd right onto Collendean Ln, 0.9m straight over x-rds, 200yds on left

This picturesque cottage with its flower-filled garden boasts unspoilt country views. Charming bedrooms are comfortable with lots of thoughtful extras. A hearty breakfast is served in the cosy dining room. Gatwick Airport is within convenient reach and airport parking is available.

Rooms 3 rms S £30–£40; D £55–£60 **Facilities** FTV TVB tea/coffee Cen ht TVL Wi-fi available **Parking** 10 **Notes** ⊗ No children 5yrs Closed 25–26 Dec

★★★★ GUEST ACCOMMODATION
Acorn Lodge Gatwick
79 Massetts Rd RH6 7EB
☎ 01293 774550
e–mail: info@acornlodgegatwick.co.uk
web: www.acornlodgegatwick.co.uk

dir: *M23 junct 9, A23 into Horley, off A23 Brighton Rd*
This recently refurbished accommodation provides a 24-hour transfer service to the airport and has on-site parking. Bedrooms are comfortably furnished, come with a practical desk area and useful touches. Breakfast is a good start to your travels and is served in a comfortable dining room, where dinner is also available.

Rooms 13 en suite (4 fmly) (6 GF) **Facilities** TVB tea/coffee Cen ht TVL Dinner Last d 10pm **Parking** 20 **Notes** ⊛

★★★★ GUEST ACCOMMODATION
Corner House
72 Massetts Rd RH6 7ED
☎ 01293 784574 🖷 01293 784620
e–mail: info@thecornerhouse.co.uk
web: www.thecornerhouse.co.uk

dir: *M23 junct 9, to Gatwick,1st rdbt, 2nd exit (straight ahead) next rdbt 4th exit signed Redhill onto A23 towards Redhill, turn off 2nd right Massetts Rd, on left*
Well located for Gatwick Airport with a 24-hour courtesy transfer service, the Corner House provides a range of thoughtfully furnished bedrooms, some in a separate house. Ground-floor areas include an attractive dining room and a comfortable lounge bar.

Rooms 19 rms (13 en suite) 12 annexe en suite (6 fmly) (9 GF) S £41–£51; D £61–£71✱ **Facilities** FTV TVB tea/coffee Direct dial from bedrooms Cen ht TVL Dinner Last d 10pm Golf 18 Membership to local sports centre **Conf** Max 15 Class 15 Board 15 **Parking** 12

★★★★ GUEST ACCOMMODATION
Rosemead
19 Church Rd RH6 7EY
☎ 01293 784965 🖷 01293 430547
e–mail: info@rosemeadguesthouse.co.uk
web: www.rosemeadguesthouse.co.uk

dir: *M23 junct 9, A23 into Horley, off A23 Brighton Rd*
This large Edwardian guest house is ideally located for Gatwick Airport and is within walking distance of the town centre, with a wealth of local amenities. Bedrooms are individually furnished with coordinated décor, and secure parking is provided, along with airport transfers. Freshly cooked breakfast is served in the bright dining room.

Rooms 6 rms (5 en suite) (1 pri facs) (2 fmly) **Facilities** STV TVB tea/coffee Cen ht **Parking** 30

★★★★ GUEST HOUSE
Trumbles
Stan Hill RH6 0EP
☎ 01293 863418 🖷 01293 862925
e–mail: trumbles-gatwick@fsmail.net
web: www.trumbles.co.uk

dir: *0.5m N of Charlwood. From village centre onto Norwoodhill Rd, 1st left onto Stan Hill*
This attractive house, within easy reach of Gatwick, enjoys a quiet and secluded setting in this charming village. Bedrooms are spacious with a good range of facilities. The conservatory offers an ideal environment for guests to relax and enjoy either continental or full English breakfast. Parking is available, along with airport transfers.

Rooms 6 en suite (2 fmly) (1 GF) S £50–£60; D £65–£70✱ **Facilities** TVB tea/coffee Cen ht Wi-fi available **Parking** 20 **Notes** ⊛ No coaches Closed 24–26 Dec

★★★★ BED & BREAKFAST
Vulcan Lodge
27 Massetts Rd RH6 7DQ
☎ 01293 771522 🖷 01293 775376
e–mail: reservations@vulcan-lodge.com

dir: *M23 junct 9, A23 into Horley, off A23 Brighton Rd*

A particularly warm and friendly welcome is offered by the hosts of this charming period house, which sits back from the main road and is convenient for Gatwick Airport. Bedrooms are all newly decorated, well equipped and feature many thoughtful extras. A choice of breakfast is offered, including vegetarian, and is served in a delightful dining room.

Rooms 4 rms (3 en suite) (1 pri facs) (1 fmly) S £36–£40; D £50–£55✱ **Facilities** FTV TVB tea/coffee Cen ht TVL Wi-fi available **Parking** 13

GATWICK AIRPORT (LONDON) continued

★★★ GUEST HOUSE
Cumberland House

39 Brighton Rd RH6 7HH
☎ 01293 825800
e–mail: carmel@cumberlandhs.com
web: www.cumberlandhs.com

dir: *M23 junct 9, A23 into Horley, on A23 Brighton Rd at corner of Church Rd, left and left again into carpark*

This attractive and well-run guest house is convenient for Gatwick Airport. The comfortable bedrooms are carefully decorated and have a good range of facilities, and breakfast is served in the first-floor dining room. Ample off-road holiday parking.

Rooms 6 en suite (2 fmly) (1 GF) **Facilities** TVB tea/coffee Cen ht Wi-fi available Golf **Parking** 15 **Notes** ⊗

★★★ GUEST HOUSE
Gainsborough Lodge

39 Massetts Rd RH6 7DT
☎ 01293 783982 📠 01293 785365
e–mail: enquiries@gainsborough-lodge.co.uk

dir: *2m NE of airport off A23 Brighton Rd*

Close to Gatwick, this fine Edwardian house offers a courtesy service to and from the airport. The bright bedrooms are comfortably appointed, and a varied breakfast, including a vegetarian option, is served in the cheerful conservatory-dining room. There is also an attractive lounge and bar.

Rooms 16 rms (14 en suite) 14 annexe en suite (5 fmly) (12 GF) **Facilities** TVB tea/coffee Direct dial from bedrooms Cen ht TVL Free membership of local Gym **Parking** 30 **Notes** ⊗ No coaches

★★★ GUEST ACCOMMODATION
Gatwick White House

50–52 Church Rd RH6 7EX
☎ 01293 402777 & 784322 📠 01293 424135
e–mail: hotel@gwhh.com
web: www.gwhh.com

dir: *In Horley centre off A23 Brighton Rd*

Convenient for the airport and major routes, this establishment offers efficient and functional accommodation. There is a bar, restaurant with good curries as well as traditional dishes, good parking, and a 24-hour transfer service to Gatwick is available on request.

Rooms 27 en suite (2 fmly) (10 GF) S £40–£50; D fr £65 **Facilities** TVB tea/coffee Direct dial from bedrooms Cen ht TVL Dinner Last d 6pm Wi-fi available **Parking** 30 **Notes** ⊗

HAMBROOK	MAP 05 SU70

★★ 🅰 BED & BREAKFAST
Willow Brook Riding Centre

Hambrook Hill South PO18 8UJ
☎ 01243 572683
e–mail: willowbrookrc@btconnect.com
web: www.willowbrook-stables.co.uk

Rooms 3 rms (2 fmly) (1 GF) S £30; D £60✱ **Facilities** TVB tea/coffee Cen ht Wi-fi available Riding **Parking** 12 **Notes** LB

HENFIELD	MAP 06 TQ21

★★★★ 🏠 FARM HOUSE
Frylands *(TQ231197)*

Wineham BN5 9BP
☎ 01403 710214 📠 01403 711449 Mrs S Fowler
e–mail: b&b@frylands.co.uk

dir: *2m NE of Henfield. Off B2116 towards Wineham, 1.5m left onto Fryland Ln, Frylands 0.3m on left*

The friendly hosts offer comfortable accommodation at this delightful 16th-century timber-framed farmhouse, set in peaceful countryside. Day rooms and bedrooms are full of character and the well-appointed dining room is the setting for freshly cooked breakfasts. Ample off-road parking and free car storage for travellers using Gatwick Airport is available.

Rooms 3 rms (1 pri facs) (1 fmly) S £32.50–£37.50; D £55–£60 **Facilities** TVB tea/coffee Cen ht ↖ Fishing **Parking** 6 **Notes** 250 acres Mixed Closed 20 Dec–1 Jan ☻

HORSHAM   MAP 06 TQ13

★★★★ BED & BREAKFAST
Denham Cottage
1 Friday St, Warnham RH12 3QY
☎ 01403 243362
e-mail: info@denhamcottage.co.uk
dir: *From A24, into Warnham, past church on left, 2nd right, cottage is 2nd on left*

Denham Cottage is situated in the picturesque village of Warnham, near Horsham on the edge of the famous deer park. Very smart and spacious refurbished accommodation with a private lounge/study adjoining and lots of useful extras, whether staying on business or for pleasure.

Rooms 1 en suite S £30; D £60 **Facilities** TVB tea/coffee Cen ht TVL **Parking** 2 **Notes** ⊗ Closed Xmas ⊜

★★★★ ⊜ GUEST ACCOMMODATION
Random Hall
Stane St, Slinfold RH13 0QX
☎ 01403 790558 📄 01403 791046
e-mail: nigelrandomhall@btconnect.com
web: www.randomhall.co.uk

dir: *4m W of Horsham. On A29 W of Slinfold*
This 16th-century farmhouse combines character with good quality accommodation and service from the resident proprietors. The comfortable bedrooms are equipped with useful extras. Beams, flagstone floors and quality fabrics add style to the bar and public areas, and an enjoyable dinner is served Monday to Thursday.

Rooms 13 en suite (5 GF) S £75; D £110✻ **Facilities** STV TVB tea/coffee Direct dial from bedrooms Cen ht Dinner Last d 9pm Golf 18 **Conf** Max 16 Thtr 20 Class 16 Board 16 Del £130 ✻ **Parking** 50 **Notes** LB ⊗

LINDFIELD   MAP 06 TQ32

Premier Collection
★★★★★ GUEST ACCOMMODATION
The Pilstyes
106–108 High St RH16 2HS
☎ 01444 484101 📄 01444 484100
e-mail: carolpontifex@hotmail.com
web: www.sussex-bedandbreakfast.co.uk

dir: *On High Street (B2028) 8 houses down from church*
Pilstyes is a Grade II-listed village house built around 1575. The spacious bedrooms are beautifully furnished and provide all the comforts of home. A healthy breakfast is served in the charming country kitchen or, on sunny days, in the flower-filled cottage courtyard. Carol and Roy are caring hosts providing a warm welcome and ensuring a pleasant stay.

Rooms 2 en suite D £65–£90✻ **Facilities** FTV TVB tea/coffee Cen ht TVL Wi-fi available **Parking** 4 **Notes** ⊗ No children 5yrs

LITTLEHAMPTON   MAP 06 TQ00

★★★★ GUEST ACCOMMODATION
Leeside
Rope Walk BN17 5DE
☎ 01903 723666
e-mail: leeside1@tiscali.co.uk

dir: *Off A259. Onto Ferry Road 1m, turn right*
This bright, newly remodelled bungalow is close to local sailing clubs, the River Arun and the beach. Visitors will enjoy a warm welcome, comfortable modern bedrooms; including free Wi-fi and flat screened TVs, and a hearty breakfast to start the day.

Rooms 4 rms (3 en suite) (1 pri facs) (3 GF) S £35; D £60 **Facilities** FTV TVB tea/coffee Cen ht TVL Wi-fi available **Parking** 4 **Notes** ⊗ No children 14yrs Closed Xmas

★★★★ 🏠 BED & BREAKFAST
Racing Greens
70 South Ter BN17 5LQ
☎ 01903 732972 📄 01903 719389
e-mail: racinggreens@aol.com
web: www.littlehampton-racing-greens.co.uk

dir: *A259 onto B2187 for Littlehampton seafront, brown signs to seafront, B&B faces the Greens and sea near Harbour Park Entertainment Centre*
This Victorian seafront home offers bright, spacious, comfortable accommodation. Bedroom amenities include Wi-fi and Freeview TV. Breakfast, featuring local and organic produce and a variety of breads, is served around a large table in the airy dining room overlooking the Greens.

Rooms 2 rms (1 en suite) (1 pri facs) S £40–£85; D £60–£85✻ **Facilities** FTV TVB tea/coffee Cen ht Wi-fi available **Notes** LB ⊗ No children

MIDHURST
MAP 06 SU82

See also Rogate

Premier Collection

★★★★★ 🏠 GUEST ACCOMMODATION
Park House

Bepton GU29 0JB
☎ 01730 819000 📠 01730 819099
e–mail: reservations@parkhousehotel.com
web: www.parkhousehotel.com

dir: *3m SW of Midhurst off A286*

This delightful, family-run guest house stands in landscaped gardens in the peaceful village of Bepton. The attractive, spacious bedrooms are thoughtfully equipped, and there is an elegant drawing room and an honesty bar. Breakfast and dinner are served in the dining room.

Rooms 12 en suite 3 annexe en suite (2 fmly) (1 GF) **Facilities** STV TV14B tea/coffee Direct dial from bedrooms Cen ht Dinner Last d 8.45pm ⤩ ☺ ⤷ ♪ **Conf** Max 50 Thtr 50 Class 50 Board 25 **Parking** 30 **Notes** Civ Wed 54

Premier Collection

★★★★★ BED & BREAKFAST
Rivermead House

Hollist Ln GU29 9RS
☎ 01730 810907 & 07885 699479
e–mail: mail@bridgetadler.com
web: www.bridgetadler.com

dir: *1m NW of Midhurst. Off A286 towards Woolbeding*

Rivermead House is situated in a semi-rural area on the outskirts of Midhurst, in a quiet location, offering friendly and relaxed accommodation. The bedroom is on the front of the house and enjoys wonderful south-facing views over the garden and farmland with distant views of the South Downs. It is spacious and comfortable, and breakfast is served in the farmhouse style kitchen.

Rooms 1 en suite (1 fmly) **Facilities** TVB tea/coffee Cen ht Dinner Last d 6pm Golf **Parking** 2 **Notes** ⊗ Closed 24–26 Dec ⊛

★★★★ GUEST ACCOMMODATION
Amberfold

Amberfold, Heyshott GU29 0DA
☎ 01730 812385 📠 01730 813559
e–mail: erlingamberfold@aol.com
web: www.amberfold.co.uk

dir: *Off A286 signed Graffham/Heyshott, after 1.5m pass pond, Amberfold on left*

A delightful 17th-century, Grade II listed cottage, set in mature and attractive gardens in peacefully idyllic countryside. The accommodation is provided in two very different self-contained units, a cottage annexe and a modern open-plan lodge. Each bedroom is tastefully appointed with many thoughtful extras.

Rooms 2 annexe en suite (2 GF) **Facilities** FTV TVB tea/coffee Cen ht **Parking** 2 **Notes** ⊗ No children 14yrs Closed 16 Dec–8 Feb ⊛

★★★★ GUEST ACCOMMODATION
Cowdray Park Golf Club

GU29 0BB
☎ 01730 813599 📠 01730 815900
e–mail: enquiries@cowdraygolf.co.uk

dir: *1m E on A272*

This renovated lodge provides contemporary bedrooms, with some rooms overlooking the internationally famous polo grounds. The immaculate golf course itself provides a challenge to members and visitors. Refreshments and meals are taken in the new clubhouse with modern facilities.

Rooms 7 en suite (5 GF) S £60–£80; D £80–£120✶ **Facilities** STV TVB tea/coffee Cen ht TVL Dinner Last d 8pm Golf 18 ♪ **Conf** Max 60 Thtr 60 Class 60 Board 20 **Parking** 10 **Notes** LB ⊗ No children 10yrs

---

★★★★ BED & BREAKFAST
Holly Tree Lodge

Easebourne St GU29 0BE
☎ 01730 813729 & 07746 523094 📠 01730 813729
e–mail: eabhamilton@yahoo.co.uk

dir: *1.5m NE of town centre. Off A272 at Easebourne church onto Easebourne St, premises on left after 600mtrs*

A warm welcome is guaranteed at this family home, set in lovely gardens, just one mile from the centre of Midhurst. The large, bright en suite bedroom can accommodate a family, and a cosy double room

CONTINUED

is available. Breakfast is served in the sunny dining room or conservatory overlooking pretty gardens.

Rooms 2 rms (1 en suite) (2 GF) D £50–£90✳ **Facilities** TVB tea/coffee Cen ht **Parking** 5 **Notes** ✖ ⊕

★★★★ FARM HOUSE
Loves Farm *(SU912235)*

Easebourne St GU29 0BG
☎ 01730 813212 & 07789 228400 Mr J Renwick
e–mail: renwick@lovesl.fsnet.co.uk

dir: *2m NE of town centre. Off A272 at Easebourne church onto Easebourne St, signs for Loves Farm*

This 17th-century farmhouse is set on a 300-acre farm with wonderful views of the South Downs from the windows. The two comfortable rooms have their own entrance and both benefit from king size beds and en suite or private shower rooms. A great location for access to Midhurst, Cowdray Park and Goodwood.

Rooms 3 rms (2 en suite) (1 pri facs) (2 fmly) (1 GF) S £40–£50; D £65–£80✳ **Facilities** TVB tea/coffee Cen ht **Parking** 3 **Notes** ✖ 300 acres Arable/Sheep/Horses ⊕

PULBOROUGH   MAP 06 TQ01

★★★★ BED & BREAKFAST
Orchard Mead

Toat Ln RH20 1BZ
☎ 01798 872640
e–mail: siggy.rutherford@ukonline.co.uk

dir: *Off A29 1m N of Pulborough onto Blackgate Ln, left onto Pickhurst Ln & right onto Toat Ln, Orchard Mead at end*

A long winding road leads you this delightful detached home. Set in a peaceful rural location and only a short drive from the local train station. Bedrooms are comfortably furnished with thoughtful touches. A delicious light supper or full dinner can be provided on request.

Rooms 2 en suite (2 GF) **Facilities** TVB tea/coffee Cen ht TVL Dinner Last d 10am **Parking** 2 **Notes** ✖ No children 12yrs Closed Xmas & Etr ⊕

★★★ BED & BREAKFAST
Arun House

Bury RH20 1NT
☎ 01798 831736
e–mail: arunway@hotmail.com
web: www.arunhousesussex.co.uk

dir: *5m S of Pulborough. On A29, signed near Carringdales & Turners garages*

Located on the A29 and convenient for Arundel, Amberley Castle and the South Downs Way, this friendly family home is popular with ramblers and cyclists and offers comfortable accommodation. Guests may sit on the terrace and enjoy the views across the garden, with its pond, ducks and free-range chickens. The adjoining café is most welcoming.

Rooms 3 rms (1 fmly) S £30; D £50✳ **Facilities** TVB tea/coffee Cen ht **Parking** 6 **Notes** ✖ ⊕

★★★ BED & BREAKFAST
Harkaway

8 Houghton Ln, Bury RH20 1PD
☎ 01798 831843
e–mail: carol@harkaway.org.uk
web: www.harkaway.org.uk

dir: *5m S of Pulborough. Off A29 into Bury, at x-rds onto Houghton Ln, on left past Coombe Crescent*

Located north of Arundel in the pretty village of Bury, this property was once the home of John Galsworthy, author of *The Forsyte Saga*. The homely bedrooms include one on the ground floor and all areas of the house are non-smoking. Breakfast is served in the attractive communal dining room overlooking the well-maintained garden.

Rooms 4 rms (1 en suite) (1 GF) **Facilities** Cen ht TVL Wi-fi available **Parking** 2 **Notes** ✖ No children 6yrs ⊕

ROGATE   MAP 05 SU82

Premier Collection
★★★★★ BED & BREAKFAST
Mizzards

GU31 5HS
☎ 01730 821656 📠 01730 821655
e–mail: francis@mizzards.co.uk

dir: *0.6m S from Rogate x-rds, over river & signed 300yds on right*

This charming 16th-century house stands near the River Rother in two acres of resplendent landscaped gardens with a lake and the proprietor's own sculptures. Relax in either the conservatory or the split-level drawing room, and the airy, well-appointed bedrooms look over the grounds. There is an entrance hall dining room, and a swimming pool is available in summer.

Rooms 3 en suite S £55–£60; D £80–£88 **Facilities** TVB tea/coffee Cen ht ⤳ ⤴ **Parking** 12 **Notes** ✖ No children 9yrs Closed Xmas ⊕

RUSTINGTON

MAP 06 TQ00

★★★★ GUEST ACCOMMODATION

Kenmore

Claigmar Rd BN16 2NL

☎ 01903 784634 🖹 01903 784634

e–mail: thekenmore@hotmail.co.uk

dir: *A259 follow signs for Rustington, turn for Claigmar Rd by war memorial. Kenmore on right as Claigmar Rd bends*

A warm welcome is assured at this Edwardian house, located close to the sea and convenient for touring West Sussex. Spacious bedrooms, all individually decorated, are provided with many useful extras. There is a comfortable lounge in which to relax and a bright dining room where a good choice of breakfast is served.

Rooms 7 rms (6 en suite) (2 fmly) (2 GF) S £28–£35✱ **Facilities** TVB tea/coffee Cen ht **Parking** 7

SELSEY

MAP 05 SZ89

★★★★ GUEST ACCOMMODATION

St Andrews Lodge

Chichester Rd PO20 0LX

☎ 01243 606899 🖹 01243 607826

e–mail: info@standrewslodge.co.uk

web: www.standrewslodge.co.uk

dir: *B2145 into Selsey, on right just before the church*

This friendly lodge is just half a mile from the seafront. The refurbished bedrooms are bright and spacious, and have a range of useful extras. Five ground-floor rooms, one with easier access, overlook the large south-facing garden, which is perfect for a drink on a summer evening.

Rooms 5 en suite 5 annexe en suite (3 fmly) (5 GF) S £36–£50; D £62.50–£85 **Facilities** TVB tea/coffee Direct dial from bedrooms Cen ht TVL **Conf** Max 15 **Parking** 14 **Notes LB** Closed 21 Dec–11 Jan

★★★★ 🅰 BED & BREAKFAST

Greenacre

5 Manor Farm Court PO20 0LY

☎ 01243 602912

e–mail: greenacre@zoom.co.uk

dir: *B2145 to Selsey, over a small rdbt, next left (Manor Farm Court), bear left & Greenacre on left*

Rooms 4 rms (3 en suite) (1 fmly) (1 GF) **Facilities** STV TVB tea/coffee Cen ht TVL **Parking** 7

SIDLESHAM

MAP 05 SZ89

Premier Collection

★★★★★ 🏵 RESTAURANT WITH ROOMS

The Crab & Lobster

Mill Ln PO20 7NB

☎ 01243 641233

e–mail: enquiries@crab-lobster.co.uk

dir: *A27 onto B2145 Selsey. Take 1st left after garage at Sidlesham onto Rookery Ln. Follow road to Crab and Lobster*

Hidden away on the South Coast near Pagham Harbour and only a short drive from Chichester is where you will find the stylish Crab & Lobster. Bedrooms are superbly appointed and bathrooms are a feature with luxury toiletries and powerful 'raindrop' showers. Enjoy lunch or dinner in the smart restaurant where the menu offers a range of locally caught fresh fish amongst other regionally sourced seasonal produce.

Rooms 4 en suite **Facilities** FTV TVB tea/coffee Cen ht Dinner Last d 9.30pm **Parking** 12 **Notes** 🚫

★★★★ GUEST ACCOMMODATION

Landseer House

Cow Ln PO20 7LN

☎ 01243 641525 🖹 01243 641525

e–mail: enq@landseerhouse.co.uk

web: www.landseerhouse.co.uk

dir: *A27 Chichester bypass, take B2145 towards Selsey. After Hunston & Sidlesham, pass garage 0.5m, turn right signed Highleigh. Turn onto Keynor Ln, then 2nd left onto Cow Ln, House 0.5m last on right*

Landseer House offers tranquillity and benefits from its peaceful location close to Pagham Harbour yet only a ten minute drive from the centre of the historic Cathedral City of Chichester. The hands-on proprietors provide genuinely warm and friendly hospitality. Bedrooms and bathrooms are furnished to an excellent standard offering comfort. Breakfast which is freshly cooked to order provides a substantial start to the day.

CONTINUED

Landseer House

Rooms 4 rms (3 en suite) (1 pri facs) S £75–£120; D £80–£150✱
Facilities FTV TVB tea/coffee Cen ht TVL Wi-fi available **Parking** 14
Notes No children 12yrs

SOUTH HARTING   MAP 05 SU71

★★★★ GUEST ACCOMMODATION
Torberry Cottage

Hurst GU31 5RG
☎ 01730 826883 📠 01730 826883
e–mail: torberry.cottage@virgin.net
dir: *1m W of South Harting on B2146*

Located in a rural setting north of the South Downs, this pleasantly
furnished house offers well-equipped bedrooms and fine hospitality.
Breakfasts, using fresh produce and served around a large table, are a
feature. The house stands in very pleasant gardens.

Rooms 2 en suite S fr £40; D £65✱ **Facilities** TVB tea/coffee Cen ht
Parking 4 **Notes** ⊗ No children 10yrs Closed Xmas RS wknds 🖳

WORTHING   MAP 06 TQ10

★★★★ GUEST ACCOMMODATION
The Beacons

18 Shelley Rd BN11 1TU
☎ 01903 230948
e–mail: thebeacons@btconnect.com
dir: *0.5m W of town centre. Off A259 Richmond Rd onto Crescent
Rd & 3rd left*

This splendid Edwardian property is ideally situated close to the
shopping centre, marine garden and pier. Bedrooms are bright,
spacious and attractively furnished with many thoughtful amenities,
including free Wi-fi. Guests can enjoy the comfortable lounge with
honesty bar and breakfast is served in the sunny dining room.

Rooms 8 en suite (1 fmly) (3 GF) S £40–£45; D £70–£80✱
Facilities tea/coffee Cen ht Wi-fi available **Parking** 8

★★★★ GUEST ACCOMMODATION
The Burlington

Marine Pde BN11 3QL
☎ 01903 211222 📠 01903 209561
e–mail: info@theburlingtonworthing.co.uk
web: www.theburlingtonworthing.co.uk
dir: *On seafront 0.5m W of Worthing Pier, Wordsworth Rd junct*

Imposing seafront building offers a modern contemporary look that
appeals to a mainly youthful clientele. The light spacious bar and
terrace extends to a night club open at the weekends. Bedrooms are
spacious and thoughtfully furnished with some modern touches.
Friendly staff.

Rooms 26 en suite (6 fmly) S £65; D £85 **Facilities** FTV TVB tea/coffee
Direct dial from bedrooms Cen ht Dinner Last d 8.45pm Wi-fi available
Conf Max 100 Thtr 50 Class 35 Board 40 Del from £90 ✱ **Notes** ⊗

★★★★ GUEST ACCOMMODATION
The Conifers

43 Parkfield Rd BN13 1EP
☎ 01903 265066 & 07947 321096
e–mail: conifers@hews.org.uk
dir: *A24 or A27 onto A2031 at Offington rdbt, over lights,
Parkfield Rd 5th right*

This charming home with its award-winning garden is located in a
quiet residential area within easy reach of the town centre. Bedrooms
are bright and comfortable with plenty of thoughtful extras. A hearty
English breakfast is served by friendly host Barbara in a traditionally
furnished, oak-panelled dining room.

Rooms 2 rms (1 pri facs) (1 fmly) S £37.50–£40; D £65–£80✱
Facilities TVB tea/coffee Cen ht **Parking** 2 **Notes** ⊗ No children 12yrs
Closed Xmas 🖳

★★★★ INN
John Henry's Inn
The Forge, Nepcote Ln, Findon Village BN14 0SE
☎ 01903 877277 & 07850 661230 📠 01903 877178
e–mail: enquiries@john-henrys.com

dir: Off A24 rdbt into Findon village, over x-rds at bottom of hill, 300yds on left

Located in a quiet village, this delightful converted cottage provides accommodation which varies in size, and offers comfortable beds and good facilities. A sports room is on-site. Dinner and breakfast are served in the bar brassiere just opposite. Parking available.

Rooms 5 en suite (3 fmly) (2 GF) S £65; D£85 **Facilities** TVB tea/coffee Cen ht Dinner Last d 9pm Pool Table **Parking** 12 **Notes** ⊗ No coaches

★★★★ GUEST ACCOMMODATION
Moorings
4 Selden Rd BN11 2LL
☎ 01903 208882 📠 01903 236878
e–mail: themooringsworthing@hotmail.co.uk

dir: 0.5m E of pier off A259 towards Brighton

This well-presented Victorian house is located in a quiet residential street just a short walk from the seafront and town centre. Bedrooms are attractively coordinated with plenty of extras such as Wi-fi and Freeview TV. Breakfast is served in a smart dining room and there is a small lounge with books and games.

Rooms 6 en suite (1 fmly) **Facilities** FTV TVB tea/coffee Direct dial from bedrooms Cen ht Wi-fi available **Notes** ⊗

★★★★ GUEST ACCOMMODATION
Olinda Guest House
199 Brighton Rd BN11 2EX
☎ 01903 206114
e–mail: info@olindaguesthouse.co.uk
web: www.olindaguesthouse.co.uk

dir: 1m E of pier on Brighton Rd along Worthing sea front

Guests are assured a warm welcome at this establishment which is located on the seafront just a walk away from the town centre. The bedrooms are cosy and comfortable and breakfast is taken in the attractively appointed dining room overlooking the seafront.

Rooms 6 rms (3 en suite) S £25–£35; D £50–£70 **Facilities** TVB tea/coffee Cen ht Wi-fi available **Notes** ⊗ No children 12yrs

★★★★ GUEST ACCOMMODATION
The Park House
4 St Georges Rd BN11 2DS
☎ 01903 207939 📠 01902 207939
e–mail: theparkhouse@aol.com

This stylish Victorian property is located in a quiet side street a short walk from the seafront and town centre. A friendly welcome from affable hosts is matched by an elegant oriental-style dining room where breakfast is served. Bedrooms are well equipped and comfortable.

Rooms 7 en suite (2 fmly) **Facilities** TVB tea/coffee Cen ht **Parking** 4

★★★★ GUEST ACCOMMODATION
Tudor Guest House
5 Windsor Rd BN11 2LU
☎ 01903 210265
e–mail: info@tudor-worthing.co.uk

dir: Off A259 seafront road

The Tudor Guest House is a friendly and attractive establishment situated just off the seafront on the east side of town. Bedrooms are generally spacious and neatly appointed with modern facilities. Fresh organic produce is served in the bright breakfast room.

Rooms 8 en suite (2 GF) **Facilities** TVB tea/coffee Cen ht **Parking** 5 **Notes** ⊗ No children 8yrs Closed 24 Dec–3 Jan

★★★ GUEST ACCOMMODATION
Avalon
8 Windsor Rd BN11 2LX
☎ 01903 233808 📠 01903 215201
e–mail: avalon.worthing@ntlworld.com

dir: 0.75m E from town centre off A259 seafront road

This family-run guest house provides a warm welcome and is only a stroll from the beach. Bedrooms vary in size but all are well appointed, suiting a variety of travellers. Hearty breakfasts are served in the bright and cheerful ground-floor dining room.

Rooms 7 rms (2 en suite) (1 fmly) (1 GF) S fr £25; D fr £50✳ **Facilities** TVB tea/coffee Cen ht Wi-fi available **Parking** 3 **Notes** ⊗ No children 5yrs

TYNE & WEAR

GATESHEAD   **MAP 21 NZ26**

GUEST ACCOMMODATON OF THE YEAR FOR ENGLAND
Premier Collection

★ ★ ★ ★ ★ GUEST HOUSE

The Stables Lodge

South Farm, Lamesley NE11 0ET

☎ 0191 492 1756 📠 0191 410 6192

e-mail: janet@thestableslodge.co.uk

dir: *From A1, take Team Valley/Retail World slip road and turn off towards Lamesley/Kibblesworth*

The Stables Lodge is in a semi-rural setting not far from Newcastle and Gateshead, with the Metro Centre and Angel of the North only minutes away. The Stables was thoughtfully converted presenting a "Hunting Lodge" theme. Features include luxurious surroundings and excellent guest care. The red room has a sauna and steam room, while the garden room has an outside seating area.

Rooms 3 en suite (1 fmly) (1 GF) **Facilities** STV TVB tea/coffee Cen ht TVL Sauna **Parking** 6 **Notes** ⊗ No coaches

★ ★ ★ INN

The Angel View Inn

Low Eighton NE9 7UB

☎ 0191 410 3219 📠 0191 492 4350

e-mail: reception@angelviewinn.co.uk

dir: *Follow brown tourist signs to Angel of the North. At rdbt, take 4th exit B1295, 1st left to Angel View Inn*

The inn was originally built as a farmhouse and stables, it has been extended and is modern in style. Offering thoughtfully equipped accommodation, with uninterrupted views of the famous Angel of the North. Perfectly located for access to the north or south bound A1. An extensive menu is available either in the lounge bar or in the restaurant.

Rooms 19 en suite 8 annexe en suite (1 fmly) (6 GF) S £52–£62; D £70–£80✱ **Facilities** TVB tea/coffee Direct dial from bedrooms Cen ht TVL Dinner Last d 9.30pm **Conf** Max 120 Thtr 100 Class 45 Board 45 **Parking** 100 **Notes** ⊗ Closed 25 Dec

SOUTH SHIELDS   **MAP 21 NZ36**

★ ★ ★ ★ GUEST HOUSE

Forest Guest House

117 Ocean Rd NE33 2JL

☎ 0191 454 8160 📠 0191 454 8160

e-mail: enquiries@forestguesthouse.com

dir: *Take A194 into South Shields to Ocean Rd*

Close to parks, beaches and the town centre, this cosy and tastefully decorated house offers a variety of room sizes, all well equipped and many benefiting from en suite bath or shower rooms. Breakfast is served in the smart open-plan kitchen/dining room.

Rooms 4 en suite (2 fmly) S £26–£30; D £50–£55✱ **Facilities** STV FTV TVB tea/coffee Cen ht Wi-fi available **Notes** LB ⊗ No children 6yrs No coaches

★ ★ ★ ★ GUEST HOUSE

Ocean Breeze

11 Urfa Ter NE33 2ES

☎ 0191 456 7442

e-mail: info@oceanbreezeguesthouse.co.uk

dir: *A183 towards town centre, onto Lawe Rd, 3rd left*

Situated within a short walk of the seafront and town centre, this smartly appointed terrace house offers modern, fully-equipped bedrooms, most with en suite shower rooms. Guests are given a genuine warm welcome and hearty breakfasts, made using fresh local ingredients are served in the pleasant dining room.

Rooms 6 rms (3 en suite) (1 fmly) **Facilities** FTV TVB tea/coffee Cen ht Wi-fi available **Notes** ⊗ No children 5yrs No coaches Closed 16 Dec–6 Jan

SUNDERLAND   **MAP 19 NZ35**

★ ★ ★ GUEST HOUSE

Mowbray

6 Mowbray Rd SR2 8HU

☎ 0191 510 9611

dir: *0.5m S of city centre off A1018 Ryhope Rd*

This substantial and long established family house stands in a leafy residential area south of the centre. Bedrooms are mainly well-proportioned, furnished in pine, and have modern bathrooms en suite. There is a spacious lounge-dining room.

Rooms 8 en suite (2 fmly) **Facilities** TVB tea/coffee Cen ht TVL **Parking** 6 **Notes** ⊗ No coaches ⊛

Sandsides Guest House

Whitley Bay, Tyne & Wear
Tel: 0191 253 0399
Email: sandsides@btinternet.com

This family-run bed & breakfast is ideal for families and couples looking for a peaceful, relaxing place to stay whilst enjoying all that the North East of England has to offer. Whitley Bay and the surrounding area has something for everyone from award-winning beaches to attractions and shops.

Rooms are cosy and traditionally furnished, most are ensuite.

High standards guaranteed.

ENGLAND

ENGLAND

SUNNISIDE   MAP 19 NZ25

Premier Collection

★★★★★ GUEST ACCOMMODATION
Hedley Hall Country House
Hedley Ln NE16 5EH
☎ 01207 231835
e-mail: hedleyhall@aol.com
web: www.hedleyhall.com

dir: *From A1 follow signs for Lanseley, at mini rdbt turn right 2m, left at Birkheads Garden/Nursery sign. Straight over x-rds, turn left to Hedley Hall Country House*

Located within easy reach of Beamish, Hedley Hall Country House was once a working farm that was part of the Queen Mother's estate. A warm welcome and quality accommodation is guaranteed. The stylish modern bedrooms, one with a superking-sized bed, are very thoughtfully equipped. Delightful day rooms include a spacious lounge with deep sofas. Breakfasts are served in the conservatory or the elegant dining room.

Rooms 3 en suite (1 fmly) S £50–£55; D £75–£80✱ **Facilities** TVB tea/coffee Cen ht TVL Dinner Last d noon Wi-fi available **Parking** 6 **Notes LB** ⊗ Closed 22 Dec–2 Jan

WHITLEY BAY   MAP 21 NZ37

★★★★ GUEST HOUSE
Lindsay Guest House
50 Victoria Av NE26 2BA
☎ 0191 252 7341 🗏 0191 252 7505
e-mail: info@lindsayguesthouse.co.uk

dir: *Off Promenade by tennis courts and bowling green*

The Lindsay forms part of a terrace close to the seafront. Behind the unassuming façade is a stylish and immaculately maintained guest house, with contemporary, eye-catching furniture in the lounge and dining room. Modern bathrooms complement smart bedrooms.

Rooms 4 en suite (4 fmly) S £39–£45; D £65–£75✱ **Facilities** STV TVB tea/coffee Cen ht TVL **Parking** 3 **Notes** No coaches

★★★★ 🅰 GUEST ACCOMMODATION
Marlborough
20–21 East Pde, Central Promenade NE26 1AP
☎ 0191 251 3628 🗏 0191 252 5033
e-mail: reception@marlborough-hotel.com
dir: *In town centre. Off A193 onto Promenade*

Rooms 16 rms (15 en suite) (4 fmly) (2 GF) **Facilities** FTV TVB tea/coffee Direct dial from bedrooms TVL Wi-fi available **Parking** 7 **Notes** ⊗ Closed Xmas & New Year

★★★ GUEST ACCOMMODATION
Sandsides Guest House
122 Park Av NE26 1AY
☎ 0191 253 0399 & 07947 447695
e-mail: sandsides@btinternet.com

dir: *A19 Tyne Tunnel exit A1058. At rdbt follow A192 Whitley Bay, next rdbt turn left. Located in one-way system*

Situated opposite the park and close to the beach and town centre. The tastefully decorated house offers a variety of room sizes, two have en suite shower rooms and the others have shared facilities. Breakfast is served in the dining room offering freshly cooked breakfasts.

Rooms 5 rms (2 en suite) (2 fmly) S £18–£22; D £40–£60✱ **Facilities** tea/coffee **Parking** 1 **Notes LB** ⊗ ⊜

See advert on page 509

WARWICKSHIRE

ALCESTER   MAP 10 SP05

★★★ INN
The Green Dragon
The Green, Sambourne B96 6NU
☎ 01527 892465 & 07759 288890 🗏 01527 893255
e-mail: greendragon@sambourne.com
dir: *3m NW of Alcester. Off A435 to Sambourne village*

Located on the village green in pretty Sambourne, the early 18th-century inn is a focal point of the community and hosts meetings of vintage car enthusiasts. The cosy, traditionally furnished areas are the setting for imaginative food and a good range of real ales. The chalet style bedrooms are next to the colourful beer garden.

Rooms 6 en suite (6 GF) **Facilities** TVB tea/coffee Direct dial from bedrooms Cen ht Dinner Last d 9pm Wi-fi available **Parking** 30 **Notes** ⊗

ATHERSTONE   MAP 10 SP39

Premier Collection

★★★★★ ⊛ RESTAURANT WITH ROOMS
Chapel House

Friar's Gate CV9 1EY

☎ 01827 718949 📄 01827 717702

e-mail: info@chapelhousehotel.co.uk

web: www.chapelhousehotel.co.uk

dir: *A5 to town centre, right onto Church St. Right onto Sheepy Rd & left onto Friar's Gate*

Sitting next to the church this 18th-century town house offers excellent hospitality and service while the cooking, using much local produce, is very notable. Bedrooms are well equipped and lounges are extensive; there is also a delightful walled garden for guests to use.

Rooms 12 en suite **Facilities** TVB tea/coffee Direct dial from bedrooms Cen ht Dinner Last d 9pm Wi-fi available **Notes** ⊗ Closed Etr wk, Aug BH wk & Xmas wk

BAGINTON   MAP 11 SP37

★★★★ INN
Old Mill

Mill Hill CV8 3AH

☎ 024 7630 2241 📄 024 7630 7070

e-mail: oldmillinn@thespiritgroup.com

dir: *In village centre (0.25m from junct A45 & A46)*

Enjoying a peaceful riverside location, yet within easy reach of the motorway networks, the Old Mill has been furnished to a high standard. Public areas include the popular Chef & Brewer bar and restaurant, with a pleasant patio for summer evenings. Spacious bedrooms are smartly appointed and well equipped.

Rooms 27 en suite (6 fmly) **Facilities** TVB tea/coffee Direct dial from bedrooms Dinner Last d 9.30pm **Conf** Max 18 Thtr 30 Class 16 Board 20 **Parking** 200 **Notes** ⊗

★★★ INN
The Oak

Coventry Rd CV8 3AU

☎ 024 7651 8855 📄 024 7651 8866

e-mail: thebagintonoak@aol.com

web: http://theoak.greatpubs.net

Located close to major road links and Coventry Airport, this popular inn provides a wide range of food throughout themed open plan public areas. Families are especially welcome. Modern well equipped bedrooms are situated within a separate accommodation building.

The Oak

Rooms 13 annexe en suite (1 fmly) (6 GF) S £40–£60; D £40–£60 **Facilities** FTV TVB tea/coffee Cen ht Dinner Last d 9pm Wi-fi available Free use of local gym **Conf** Max 40 Thtr 40 Class 40 Board 25 **Parking** 110

BARNACLE   MAP 11 SP38

★★★★ GUEST ACCOMMODATION
Park Farm House

Spring Rd CV7 9LG

☎ 024 7661 2628 📄 024 7661 6010

dir: *M6 junct 2 onto B4065 to Shilton. Left at lights, left again over M69, right into Barnacle*

Excellent accommodation and hospitality in a peaceful location is provided at this delightful farmhouse which dates from 1655. The spacious bedrooms are well equipped and there is a cosy lounge. Good breakfasts are provided around a large table and dinner is available by arrangement.

Rooms 3 en suite **Facilities** TVB tea/coffee Cen ht Dinner Last d 12hrs notice **Conf** Max 8 Board 8 **Parking** 6 **Notes** ⊗ No children 12yrs ⊛

COLESHILL   MAP 10 SP28

★★★ BED & BREAKFAST
The Old Vicarage

Shawbury Ln, Shustoke B46 2LA

☎ 01675 481331 📄 01675 481331

e-mail: jbhawk@doctors.org.uk

dir: *A446 onto B4114 for Coleshill, B4114 Coleshill-Nuneaton road for Shustoke, 0.5m after village right at sharp left bend (Griffin Inn) & sharp left towards church*

Standing opposite the magnificent church of St Cuthbert, at the edge of Shustoke, this impressive guest house is set in pretty mature gardens. The house is stylishly decorated and furnished throughout, and retains many original features. Bedrooms are filled with a wealth of thoughtful extras and superb breakfasts are served in an elegant dining room or attractive patio during the warmer months.

Rooms 3 rms (2 en suite) (1 pri facs) **Facilities** TVB tea/coffee Cen ht **Parking** 6 **Notes** ⊗ Closed Xmas

CONTINUED

COLESHILL CONTINUED

★★★ GUEST HOUSE
Ye Olde Station
Church Rd, Shustoke B46 2AX
☎ 01675 481736 🖹 01675 481736
e-mail: patr@freeuk.com
web: www.yeoldestationguesthouse.co.uk

dir: *2.5m NE, on B4114 300yds past Griffin pub*

This converted Victorian railway station has been modernised to provide a range of practically furnished bedrooms with efficient bathrooms. Ground-floor areas include a lounge-dining room and a games room with pool table.

Rooms 9 en suite (1 fmly) S £45; D £65✳ **Facilities** TVB tea/coffee Cen ht TVL Pool Table **Parking** 16

ETTINGTON   MAP 10 SP24

Premier Collection

★★★★★ 🍴 BED & BREAKFAST
Fulready Manor
Fulready CV37 7PE
☎ 01789 740152 🖹 01789 740247
e-mail: stay@fulreadymanor.co.uk
web: www.fulreadymanor.co.uk

dir: *2.5m SE of Ettington. 0.5m S off A422 at Pillerton Priors*

Located in 120 acres of arable farmland, this impressive, new Cotswold-stone house provides very high levels of comfort. The spacious ground-floor areas are furnished with quality and flair, and feature fine furniture and art. The individually themed bedrooms have a wealth of thoughtful extras, and memorable breakfasts are served in the elegant dining room overlooking immaculate gardens.

Rooms 3 en suite D £120–£140 **Facilities** Cen ht Wi-fi available **Parking** 6 **Notes** ⊗ No children 15yrs 🐾

★★★ 🅰 INN
The Houndshill
Banbury Rd CV37 7NS
☎ 01789 740267 🖹 01789 740075

dir: *4m S of Stratford-upon-Avon. 1m N of Ettington village on A422*

Rooms 8 en suite (2 fmly) **Facilities** TVB tea/coffee Direct dial from bedrooms Cen ht Dinner Last d 9.30 pm **Conf** Thtr 30 Board 18 **Parking** 50 **Notes** Closed 25–28 Dec

See advert on opposite page

GREAT WOLFORD   MAP 10 SP23

Premier Collection

★★★★★ BED & BREAKFAST
The Old Coach House
CV36 5NQ
☎ 01608 674152
e-mail: theoldcoachhouse@thewolfords.net
web: www.theoldcoachhouseatthewolfords.co.uk
dir: *Off A44/A3400 to village centre*

Located in a historic Cotswold village next to a fine country inn, this former coach house has been restored to provide high levels of comfort and facilities. Bedrooms are equipped with a wealth of thoughtful extras, and quality decor and furnishings enhance the intrinsic charm of the property.

Rooms 2 en suite S £50; D £80 **Facilities** TVB tea/coffee Cen ht TVL **Conf** Max 6 Board 6 **Parking** 2 **Notes** LB ⊗ No children 10yrs

★★★★ 🍴 INN
The Fox & Hounds Inn
CV36 5NQ
☎ 01608 674220
e-mail: enquiries@thefoxandhoundsinn.com
dir: *Off A3400, 1.5m to Great Wolford*

Very much a focal point of the local community, this 16th-century inn retains many original features, which are enhanced by rustic furniture and memorabilia. The thoughtfully furnished bedrooms are in converted outbuildings, and a warm welcome is assured.

Rooms 3 annexe en suite S £50; D £80 **Facilities** TVB tea/coffee Cen ht Dinner Last d 9pm Wi-fi available **Parking** 12 **Notes** RS Sun & Mon

ENGLAND

★★★★★ 🅐 GUEST HOUSE
Loweridge Guest House
Hawkesworth Dr CV8 2GP
☎ 01926 859522
e-mail: info@loweridgeguesthouse.co.uk
dir: *A429 (Coventry to Kenilworth), left at Tainters Hill and left onto Hawkesworth Dr*
Rooms 4 en suite (3 fmly) (3 GF) S £70–£80; D £90–£95✱
Facilities TVB tea/coffee Cen ht TVL Dinner Last d 6pm **Parking** 7
Notes No coaches

★★★★ GUEST HOUSE
Stoneleigh Park Lodge
Stoneleigh Park CV8 2LZ
☎ 024 7669 0123 📄 024 7669 0789
e-mail: info@stoneleighparklodge.com
web: www.stoneleighparklodge.com
dir: *2m E of Kenilworth in National Agricultural Centre*
Stoneleigh Park Lodge lies within the National Agricultural Centre grounds and provides modern, well-equipped accommodation. Meals, using local produce, are served in the Park View Restaurant overlooking the showground. Various conference and meeting facilities are available.
Rooms 58 en suite (4 fmly) (26 GF) S £70–£100; D £80–£115✱
Facilities FTV TVB tea/coffee Direct dial from bedrooms Licensed Cen ht TVL Dinner Last d 9.30pm Wi-fi available Fishing **Conf** Max 10 **Parking** 60 **Notes** No coaches Closed Xmas

★★★★ GUEST ACCOMMODATION
Victoria Lodge
180 Warwick Rd CV8 1HU
☎ 01926 512020 📄 01926 858703
e-mail: info@victorialodgehotel.co.uk
dir: *250yds SE of town centre on A452 opp St John's Church*

Situated on the fringe of the historic town, Victoria Lodge is a family run establishment. All of the highly appointed rooms are en suite and are thoughtfully furnished with homely extras. There is a car park and a Victorian walled garden for guests use. Victoria Lodge is situated within walking distance of Kenilworth Castle and the towns many acclaimed restaurants.
Rooms 10 en suite (1 fmly) (2 GF) S £49–£62; D £72–£80
Facilities TVB tea/coffee Direct dial from bedrooms Cen ht Wi-fi available **Parking** 9 **Notes** ⊗ Closed 24 Dec–1 Jan

★★★ GUEST ACCOMMODATION
Hollyhurst
47 Priory Rd CV8 1LL
☎ 01926 853882 📄 01926 853882
e-mail: admin@hollyhurstguesthouse.co.uk
dir: *On A452 in town centre*
Located on a mainly residential avenue within easy walking distance of the castle and town centre, this constantly improving establishment offers a range of bedrooms, some of which have the benefit of modern shower rooms. Ground-floor areas include a comfortable lounge in addition to an attractive dining room.
Rooms 7 rms (3 en suite) (1 pri facs) (1 fmly) S £32–£36; D £52–£55
Facilities TVB tea/coffee Cen ht TVL **Parking** 7 **Notes** ⊗ Closed Xmas & New Year 🅑

THE
HOUNDSHILL

The Houndshill is a family-run Inn, ideally situated for visitors to the Heart of England whether for business or pleasure. Stratford-upon-Avon, home of Shakespeare and the world-famous Shakespeare Theatre, is just four miles away, the Cotswold villages in some of England's most beautiful countryside, close by, and Oxford, Coventry and Birmingham are all within easy reach.

We are a fully licensed free house; the bar serves a full range of traditional beers. Our standard Menu is supplemented by the Specials Board and Vegetarian meals.

Above all our aim is to provide a personal service and to ensure your stay is a happy one.

All rooms have their own bathroom and tea/coffee making facilities. We look forward to welcoming you. The informal and friendly atmosphere will make your stay that much more enjoyable!	Banbury Road, Ettington, Stratford-upon-Avon Warwickshire CV37 7NS Tel: 01789 740267 Fax: 01789 740075

CONTINUED

KENILWORTH CONTINUED

★★ BED & BREAKFAST
Howden House

170 Warwick Rd CV8 1HS
☎ 01926 850310

dir: *From the A46 take the Lemington exit to the A452 follow sign to Kenilworth*

You will find a warm welcome at Howden House which is nestled at the end of the main high street, convenient for the town centre. Rooms are homely and comfortable. Howden House is convenient for the National Exhibition Centre and motorway networks.

Rooms 3 rms (1 fmly) (1 GF) D £50–£65✳ **Facilities** TVB tea/coffee Cen ht TVL Golf 36 ⚲ **Parking** 1 **Notes** ⊗ Closed Xmas & New Year ⊜

LEAMINGTON SPA (ROYAL)   MAP 10 SP36

★★★★ GUEST ACCOMMODATION
The Adams

22 Avenue Rd CV31 3PQ
☎ 01926 450742 ▤ 01926 313110
e–mail: bookings@adams-hotel.co.uk

dir: *500yds W of town centre. Off A452 Adelaide Rd onto Avenue Rd*

Just a short walk from town centre, this elegant 1827 Regency house offers a relaxing setting and quality accommodation. Public areas include a lounge bar with leather armchairs, and a pretty garden. The attractive bedrooms are very well appointed, and have modem points and bathrobes.

Rooms 10 en suite (2 GF) S £68.50; D £85–£90✳ **Facilities** TVB tea/coffee Direct dial from bedrooms Cen ht Wi-fi available **Parking** 14 **Notes** ⊗ No children 12yrs Closed 23 Dec–2 Jan

★★★★ GUEST ACCOMMODATION
Bubbenhall House

Paget's Ln CV8 3BJ
☎ 024 7630 2409 & 07746 282541 ▤ 024 7630 2409
e–mail: wharrison@bubbenhallhouse.freeserve.co.uk

dir: *5m NE of Leamington. Off A445 at Bubbenhall S onto Paget's Ln, 1m on single-track lane (over 4 speed humps)*

Located between Leamington Spa and Coventry in extensive mature grounds with an abundance of wildlife, this impressive late Edwardian house was once the home of Alexander Issigonis, designer of the Mini. It contains many interesting features including a Jacobean-style staircase. Thoughtful extras are provided in the bedrooms, and public areas include an elegant dining room and choice of sumptuous lounges.

Rooms 5 en suite (1 GF) S £50; D £70–£75✳ **Facilities** FTV TVB tea/coffee Cen ht TVL Wi-fi available ⚲ ⚲ **Parking** 12 **Notes LB** ⊜

LIGHTHORNE   MAP 10 SP35

★★★★ BED & BREAKFAST
Redlands Farm

Banbury Rd CV35 0AH
☎ 01926 651241
e–mail: redlandsfarm@btinternet.com

dir: *Off B4100, 5m S of Warwick*

Redlands Farm offers a tranquil location, conveniently located just six miles from Warwick, Leamington Spa and Stratford Upon Avon. Bedrooms offer a comfortable stay, and breakfast guarantees fresh eggs provided by the chickens in the garden.

Rooms 3 en suite (1 fmly) S £35; D £65✳ **Facilities** TVB tea/coffee Cen ht TVL ⤳ **Parking** 7 **Notes** ⊗ No children 7yrs Closed Xmas & New Year Civ Wed

LONG COMPTON   MAP 10 SP23

★★★★ INN
The Red Lion
Main St CV36 5JJ
☎ 01608 684221   🖷 01608 684968
e–mail: info@redlion-longcompton.co.uk
dir: *5m S of Shipston on Stour on A3400*

Located in the pretty rural village of Long Compton, this mid–18th-century posting house retains many original features, highlighted by rustic furniture in the public areas. A good range of ales is offered, and interesting menus make good use of quality local produce. Newly refurbished bedrooms are well appointed, and furnished with a good range of facilities.

Rooms 5 en suite (1 fmly) S £45–£55; D £75–£110✳ **Facilities** TVB tea/coffee Cen ht Dinner Last d 9pm Wi-fi available **Parking** 60 **Notes** No coaches

★★★★ BED & BREAKFAST
Tallet Barn B & B
Yerdley Farm CV36 5LH
☎ 01608 684248   🖷 01608 684248
e–mail: talletbarn@tiscali.co.uk
dir: *Off A3400 in village onto Vicarage Ln opp Post Office/stores*
A converted barn and grain store in the heart of this unspoiled Cotswold village provide comfortable bedrooms with thoughtful extras. Comprehensive breakfasts are served in the elegant beamed dining room in the main house, which also has a comfortable lounge.

Rooms 2 annexe en suite (1 fmly) (1 GF) S £40–£45; D £60–£65 **Facilities** TVB tea/coffee Cen ht **Parking** 3 **Notes** ⊛ No children 6yrs ⊛

SHIPSTON ON STOUR   MAP 10 SP24

★★★★ 🏠 BED & BREAKFAST
Holly End Bed & Breakfast
London Rd CV36 4EP
☎ 01608 664064
e–mail: hollyend.hunt@btinternet.com
web: www.holly-end.co.uk
dir: *0.5m S of Shipston on Stour on A3400*
Located between Oxford and Stratford-upon-Avon and a short walk from town centre, this immaculate detached house offers bedrooms with lots of thoughtful extras. Comprehensive breakfasts use the best of local produce.

Rooms 3 rms (2 en suite) (1 pri facs) (1 fmly) S £50–£60; D £75–£100 **Facilities** FTV TVB tea/coffee Cen ht Wi-fi available **Parking** 6 **Notes LB** ⊛ No children 9yrs ⊛

★★★★ 🅰 GUEST ACCOMMODATION
Folly Farm Cottage
Ilmington CV36 4LJ
☎ 01608 682425
e–mail: bruceandpam@follyfarm.co.uk
dir: *A3400 S of Stratford-upon-Avon, turn right signed Wimpstone/Ilmington*

Rooms 3 en suite S £55; D £68–£84✳ **Facilities** TVB tea/coffee Cen ht Dinner Last d 4pm **Parking** 8 **Notes LB** ⊛ No children 18yrs

STRATFORD-UPON-AVON   MAP 10 SP25

Premier Collection

★★★★★ GUEST HOUSE
Cherry Trees
Swans Nest Ln CV37 7LS
☎ 01789 292989
e–mail: gotocherrytrees@aol.com
web: www.cherrytrees-stratford.co.uk
dir: *250yds SE of town centre over bridge. Off A422, next to Butterfly Farm*
Comfortably located close to the theatre and the centre of town, Cherry Trees offers spacious, luxurious, well-equipped rooms. Guests have a separate entrance and hearty breakfasts are served in the attractive upstairs dining room.

Rooms 3 en suite (3 GF) S £55–£65; D £80–£110✳ **Facilities** FTV TVB tea/coffee Cen ht Wi-fi available **Parking** 11 **Notes LB** ⊛ No children 10yrs No coaches

STRATFORD-UPON-AVON *CONTINUED*

★★★★ GUEST HOUSE
Ambleside
41 Grove Rd CV37 6PB
☎ 01789 297239 📄 01789 295670
e–mail: ruth@amblesideguesthouse.com
dir: *On A4390 opp Firs Park*

This attractive, spotlessly clean and friendly house is situated close to the market square and town centre. The bedrooms are carefully decorated, well appointed and some have smart modern shower rooms. Breakfast is served in the light airy dining room overlooking the pretty front garden. There is a free private car park at the rear of the house.

Rooms 6 rms (5 en suite) (4 fmly) (1 GF) S £28–£32; D £60–£80
Facilities TVB tea/coffee Cen ht Wi-fi available Golf **Parking** 7
Notes ⊗ No children 5yrs

★★★★ BED & BREAKFAST
Cross o'th' Hill Farm
Broadway Rd CV37 8HP
☎ 01789 204738
e–mail: decimanoble@hotmail.com
web: www.crossothhillfarm.com

dir: *0.5m S of Stratford. A3400 S from Stratford for Shipston, 0.75m onto B4632, farm signed 0.25m on right, farmhouse 200yds*

This large farmhouse, dating from 1860, stands among pasture and a small orchard a short walk from the centre of Stratford. Original architectural details have been lovingly preserved, and relaxed, understated elegance marks the bedrooms and public areas.

CONTINUED

Rooms 3 rms (2 en suite) (1 pri facs) S fr £60; D fr £80✳ **Facilities** TVB tea/coffee Cen ht TVL Wi-fi available 🐾 **Parking** 22 **Notes** ⊗ No children 5yrs Closed 25 Dec–Feb 🖭

★★★★ FARM HOUSE
Clopton Orchard Farm *(SP165455)*
Lower Clopton, Upper Quinton CV37 8LH
☎ 01386 438669 & 07765 414636 📄 01386 438669
Mrs A Coldicott
e–mail: mail@clopton-orchard.fsnet.co.uk

dir: *6m S of Stratford on B4632. S through Lower Clopton, on right opposite farm shop*

A warm welcome is assured at this attractive modern farmhouse located between Broadway and Stratford-upon-Avon. The spacious bedrooms come with practical and thoughtful extras, and comprehensive breakfasts are served around a family table in the cosy pine-furnished first-floor dining room.

Rooms 2 en suite (1 fmly) S £40–£50; D fr £65 **Facilities** TVB tea/coffee Cen ht **Parking** 5 **Notes** LB ⊗ 300 acres arable sheep pigs geese 🖭

★★★★ GUEST ACCOMMODATION
Emsley Guest House
4 Arden St CV37 6PA
☎ 01789 299557 📄 01789 299557
e–mail: val@theemsley.co.uk
web: www.theemsley.co.uk

dir: *A46 onto A3400 into Stratford, right at lights onto A4390 Arden St*

Emsley Guest House is just a short walk from Stratford centre and the railway station, and is a good base for visiting the many local attractions. Bedrooms are carefully decorated and well equipped. Substantial breakfasts, including vegetarian options, are served in the attractive dining room. There is also a comfortable lounge, and parking nearby is arranged by the owners.

Rooms 5 en suite (3 fmly) D £70–£80 **Facilities** TVB tea/coffee Cen ht TVL **Parking** 20 **Notes** ⊗ Closed 24 Dec–1 Jan

★★★★ INN
The Fox & Goose Inn
Armscote CV37 8DD
☎ 01608 682293 📄 01608 682293
e–mail: mail@foxandgoose.co.uk
web: www.foxandgoose.co.uk

dir: *S of Stratford-upon-Avon. Off A3400 near church in Newbold on Stour signed Armscote 1m, bear right in village*

A conversion of two cottages and a blacksmith's forge, this inn retains many original features that are enhanced by the quality furnishings and decor. The Cluedo-themed bedrooms are designed with individual flair, and imaginative and hearty food is served in the candlelit dining room.

Rooms 3 en suite **Facilities** TVB tea/coffee Cen ht Dinner Last d 9.30pm
Conf Max 20 Thtr 20 Class 20 Board 20 Del from £55 ✳ **Parking** 20
Notes ⊗ No coaches

★★★★ FARM HOUSE
Monk's Barn (SP206516)
Shipston Rd CV37 8NA
☎ 01789 293714 Mrs R M Meadows
e–mail: ritameadows@btconnect.com
dir: *2m S of Stratford on A3400, on right after bungalows on left*

With stunning views of the surrounding countryside, a warm welcome
is assured at this impressive renovated house. Bedrooms, some of
which are located in former outbuildings, are filled with a wealth of
thoughtful extras. Memorable breakfasts are served in the spacious and
cosy lounge-dining room.

Rooms 4 rms (3 en suite) 3 annexe en suite (4 GF) S £26–£28.50;
D £52–£57 **Facilities** TVB tea/coffee Cen ht TVL **Parking** 7 **Notes** ⊗
75 acres mixed Closed 25–26 Dec

★★★★ GUEST ACCOMMODATION
Moonraker House
40 Alcester Rd CV37 9DB
☎ 01789 268774 📠 01789 268774
e–mail: moonrakerhouse@btinternet.com
dir: *200yds from railway station on A422 Alcester Rd*
Just a short walk from the railway station and the central attractions,
this establishment provides a range of stylish bedrooms. The sitting
area during the day is the setting for the freshly cooked breakfasts. The
attractive exterior is enhanced by a magnificent floral display during the
warmer months.

Rooms 7 en suite (1 fmly) (2 GF) S £40–£47; D £65–£85✳
Facilities FTV TVB tea/coffee Cen ht Wi-fi available **Parking** 7
Notes LB ⊗ No children 6yrs

★★★★ GUEST ACCOMMODATION
Twelfth Night
13 Evesham Place CV37 6HT
☎ 01789 414595
e–mail: twelfthnight@fsmail.net
web: www.twelfthnight.co.uk
dir: *In town centre off A4390 Grove Rd*

This delightful Victorian villa is within easy walking distance of the town
centre. Quality décor and furnishings enhance the charming original
features, and the elegant dining room is the setting for imaginative
English breakfasts.

Rooms 7 rms (6 en suite) (1 pri facs) S £40–£50; D £55–£85
Facilities TVB tea/coffee Cen ht **Parking** 6 **Notes** ⊗ Closed 11–25 Feb

★★★★ GUEST HOUSE
Victoria Spa Lodge
Bishopton Ln, Bishopton CV37 9QY
☎ 01789 267985 📠 01789 204728
e–mail: ptozer@victoriaspalodge.demon.co.uk
web: www.stratford-upon-avon.co.uk/victoriaspa.htm
dir: *A3400 1.5m N to junct A46, 1st left onto Bishopton Ln, 1st
house on right*

Located within immaculate mature gardens beside the canal on the
outskirts of town, this impressive Victorian house retains many original
features enhanced by the furnishings and décor. Bedrooms are filled
with thoughtful extras and the spacious dining room, furnished with
quality antiques and ornaments, also contains a cosy lounge area.

Rooms 7 en suite (3 fmly) S £50–£55; D £65–£70✳ **Facilities** TVB tea/
coffee Cen ht Wi-fi available **Parking** 12 **Notes** ⊗ No coaches Closed
Xmas & New Year

STRATFORD-UPON-AVON continued

★★★ GUEST HOUSE
Arden Way Guest House
22 Shipston Rd CV37 7LP
☎ 01789 205646 📠 01789 205646
e-mail: info@ardenwayguesthouse.co.uk
web: www.ardenwayguesthouse.co.uk

dir: *On A3400 S of River Avon, 100mtrs on left*

A warm welcome is assured at this constantly improving no-smoking house, located within easy walking distance of the Butterfly Farm and cricket ground. The homely bedrooms are filled with lots of thoughtful extras and an attractive dining room, overlooking the pretty rear garden, is the setting for comprehensive breakfasts.

Rooms 6 rms (5 en suite) (1 pri facs) (2 fmly) (2 GF) S £28–£55; D £56–£68✱ **Facilities** FTV TVB tea/coffee Cen ht **Parking** 6 **Notes** ⊗ No coaches

★★★ BED & BREAKFAST
Clomendy
10 Broad Walk CV37 6HS
☎ 01789 266957
e-mail: clomendy@amserve.com
web: www.clomendy.co.uk

dir: *In town centre, turn left off B439 at Evesham Place*

Located on a peaceful avenue within easy walking distance of central attractions, this immaculately maintained house offers homely, thoughtfully equipped bedrooms with modern bathrooms. Breakfast is served at a family table in the elegant dining room, which opens to the pretty rear patio garden.

Rooms 2 rms (1 en suite) (1 pri facs) S £45; D £50–£60 **Facilities** TVB tea/coffee Cen ht **Parking** 1 **Notes LB** ⊗ No children 5yrs ⊛

★★★ GUEST ACCOMMODATION
Forget-me-Not
18 Evesham Place CV37 6HT
☎ 01789 204907 📠 01789 204907
e-mail: kate@forgetmenotguesthouse.co.uk

dir: *W side of town centre on A4390 ring road, near Chestnut Walk junct*

This guest house benefits from lots of care and attention applied by its enthusiastic owners. Bedrooms of varying sizes offer comfortable beds and modern shower rooms. Breakfast is offered in a pretty, bright ground-floor dining room.

Rooms 5 en suite (1 fmly) S £30–£60; D £45–£80 **Facilities** TVB tea/coffee Cen ht **Parking** 2 **Notes LB** ⊗

★★★ GUEST ACCOMMODATION
Stretton House
38 Grove Rd CV37 6PB
☎ 01789 268647 📠 01789 268647
e-mail: shortpbshort@aol.com
web: www.strettonhouse.co.uk

dir: *On A439 in town centre road behind police station*

This attractive Edwardian terrace house is within easy walking distance of the railway station and Shakespeare's birthplace. Bedrooms are carefully decorated, well equipped, and many have modern shower rooms en suite. The pretty front garden is a very welcoming feature.

Rooms 6 rms (5 en suite) (1 pri facs) (3 fmly) (1 GF) S £30–£35; D £65–£70 **Facilities** TVB tea/coffee Cen ht Wi-fi available **Parking** 7

★★★ GUEST ACCOMMODATION
Travellers Rest
146 Alcester Rd CV37 9DR
☎ 01789 266589
e-mail: enquiries@travellersrest.biz
web: www.travellersrest.biz

dir: *0.5m W of town centre on A422, past railway station*

Located on the Alcester Road with easy access to town centre, this attractive semi-detached house provides cosy bedrooms, each with a modern shower room, and filled with thoughtful extras. Breakfast is taken in an attractive front-facing dining room and a warm welcome is assured.

Rooms 3 en suite (1 fmly) **Facilities** TVB tea/coffee Cen ht **Parking** 5 **Notes** Closed 24–26 Dec ⊛

★★★ 🛏 FARM HOUSE
Whitchurch Farm *(SP222485)*
Whitchurch CV37 8PD
☎ 01789 450359 📠 01789 450359 Mrs E James
e-mail: jweeah@aol.com

dir: *A3400 S from Stratford-upon-Avon. After 4m, turn right for Wimpstone, then left at telephone box, 0.5m through village*

Dating back in parts to the 17th century, this characteristic farmhouse enjoys a peaceful rural setting and yet is only a short drive away from the attractions of Stratford-Upon-Avon. The spacious bedrooms offer country views while Mrs James' award-winning cuisine utilises locally sourced produce wherever possible.

CONTINUED

Rooms 3 en suite (2 fmly) S £30–£40; D £70–£75✶ **Facilities** FTV TVB tea/coffee Cen ht TVL Dinner Last d Breakfast Wi-fi available **Parking** 5 **Notes** ⊗ 400 acres sheep/arable/beef Closed Dec–Jan

★★★ 🅰 GUEST HOUSE
Salamander
40 Grove Rd CV37 6PB
☎ 01789 205728 📄 01789 205728
e–mail: p.delin@btinternet.com
web: www.salamanderguesthouse.co.uk

dir: *250yds W of town centre on A439 ring road, opp Firs Garden*

Rooms 7 rms (6 en suite) (1 pri facs) (5 fmly) (1 GF) **Facilities** TVB tea/coffee Cen ht Dinner Last d 2wks prior Wi-fi available **Parking** 12

★★ BED & BREAKFAST
Barbette Guest House
165 Evesham Rd CV37 9BP
☎ 01789 297822
e–mail: barbette@sitgetan.demon.co.uk

dir: *B439 S, 0.5m from town centre*

Expect a friendly welcome at Barbette Guest House, a compact but comfortable establishment close to the main road with ample car parking and a landscaped rear garden. Bedrooms are comfortable and well-equipped and guests have use of a TV lounge.

Rooms 4 rms (1 en suite) **Facilities** FTV TVB tea/coffee Cen ht TVL **Parking** 5 **Notes** ⊗ 📧

See also Lighthorne

★★★★ GUEST HOUSE
Croft
Haseley Knob CV35 7NL
☎ 01926 484447 📄 01926 484447
e–mail: david@croftguesthouse.co.uk
web: www.croftguesthouse.co.uk

dir: *4.5m NW of Warwick. Off A4177 into Haseley Knob, follow B&B signs*

Friendly proprietors provide homely accommodation at this modern detached house, set in peaceful countryside and convenient for Warwick and the NEC, Birmingham. The conservatory dining room overlooks large well-kept gardens. Fresh eggs from home-reared chickens are used for memorable English breakfasts.

Rooms 7 rms (5 en suite) (2 pri facs) 2 annexe rms (1 en suite) (1 annexe pri facs) (2 fmly) (4 GF) S £40–£45; D £60–£65✶ **Facilities** TVB tea/coffee Cen ht TVL Wi-fi available **Parking** 9 **Notes** No coaches Closed Xmas wk

★★★★ INN
The Mary Arden Inn
The Green CV37 9XJ
☎ 01789 267030 📄 01789 204875
e–mail: info@mary-arden.co.uk
web: www.mary-arden.co.uk

Dating back to the 1700s and described as a 'traditional inn with rooms', the Mary Arden sits directly opposite Mary Arden's house in the centre of the picturesque village of Wilmcote, three miles from Stratford-upon-Avon. Public areas offer a flexible and comfortable range of day rooms, while the accommodation is well appointed and thoughtfully equipped.

Rooms 11 en suite (1 fmly) **Facilities** TVB tea/coffee Direct dial from bedrooms Cen ht TVL Dinner Last d 9pm **Conf** Max 12 Thtr 20 Board 12 **Parking** 20

WEST MIDLANDS

BIRMINGHAM   MAP 10 SP08

Premier Collection

★★★★★ GUEST ACCOMMODATION
Westbourne Lodge

25–31 Fountain Rd, Edgbaston B17 8NJ
☎ 0121 429 1003 🖹 0121 429 7436
e–mail: info@westbournelodge.co.uk
web: www.westbournelodge.co.uk

dir: *100yds from A456*

Located on a quiet residential avenue close to the Hagley Rd, this well-maintained property provides a range of non-smoking, thoughtfully furnished bedrooms, some of which are on the ground floor. Breakfast, and dinner by arrangement, are served in an attractive dining room overlooking a pretty patio garden. A comfortable sitting room and lounge bar are also available.

Rooms 24 en suite (7 fmly) (3 GF) S £49.50–£59.50; D £69.50–£89.50✳
Facilities FTV TVB tea/coffee Direct dial from bedrooms Cen ht TVL Dinner Last d 8pm Wi-fi available **Parking** 12 **Notes** Closed 24 Dec–1 Jan

★★★★ GUEST HOUSE
Black Firs

113 Coleshill Rd, Marston Green B37 7HT
☎ 0121 779 2727 🖹 0121 779 2727
e–mail: julie@b-firs.co.uk
web: www.b-firs.co.uk

dir: *M42 junct 6, A45 W, onto B4438, signs for Marston Green*

This elegant house is set in immaculate gardens in a mainly residential area close to the NEC. Thoughtfully equipped bedrooms with Wi-fi access are complemented by smart shower rooms. Memorable breakfasts are served in an attractive dining room and a lounge is also available.

Rooms 6 en suite **Facilities** TVB tea/coffee Cen ht TVL **Conf** Max 14 **Parking** 6 **Notes** ⊗ No coaches 📵

★★★★ GUEST HOUSE
Olton Cottage

School Ln, Old Yardley Village, Yardley B33 8PD
☎ 0121 783 9249 🖹 0121 789 6545
e–mail: olton.cottage@virgin.net

dir: *3.5m E of city centre. Off A45 onto A4040 to Yardley, 1m right onto Vicarage Rd, right onto Church Rd, left onto School Ln*

A warm welcome is assured at this carefully renovated Victorian house, located in a peaceful residential area close to the city centre. The cosy bedrooms contain a wealth of thoughtful extras and ground-floor areas include a cottage-style dining room and comfortable lounge overlooking the pretty enclosed garden.

Rooms 6 rms (2 en suite) (1 fmly) **Facilities** TVB tea/coffee Cen ht TVL **Parking** 2 **Notes** ⊗ 📵

★★★ GUEST ACCOMMODATION
Tri-Star

Coventry Rd, Elmdon B26 3QR
☎ 0121 782 1010 & 782 6131 🖹 0121 782 6131

dir: *On A45*

Located a short drive from the airport, the international station and the NEC, this owner-managed property provides a range of thoughtfully furnished bedrooms with modern bathrooms. The open-plan ground-floor area includes a bright, attractive dining room, a comfortable lounge bar and a separate conference room.

Rooms 15 en suite (3 fmly) (6 GF) **Facilities** TVB tea/coffee Cen ht TVL Dinner Last d 8pm Pool Table Games room **Conf** Max 20 Thtr 20 Class 10 Board 20 **Parking** 25 **Notes** ⊗

★★★ GUEST ACCOMMODATION
Central

1637 Coventry Rd, South Yardley B26 1DD
☎ 0121 706 7757 🖹 0121 706 7757
e–mail: stay@centralguesthouse.com
web: www.centralguesthouse.com

dir: *3.5m SE of city centre. M42 junct 6, A45 W, past McDonalds & shops, on left*

Located between the airport and city centre, this comfortable house is made a real home from home by the friendly and attentive proprietors. Bedrooms are equipped with plenty of thoughtful extras. Breakfast is served in an attractive dining room and you can relax in the attractive garden.

Rooms 5 en suite (1 fmly) **Facilities** TVB tea/coffee Cen ht TVL **Parking** 4

★★ GUEST HOUSE
Awentsbury

21 Serpentine Rd, Selly Park B29 7HU
☎ 0121 472 1258 🖹 0121 472 1258
e–mail: ian@awentsbury.com

dir: *A38 2m SW from city centre, left onto Bournbrook Rd, left & 1st right*

This large Victorian house is in a quiet residential area within easy walking distance of the university and local restaurants. Bedrooms are simply furnished and many have showers en suite. Breakfast is served in the lounge-dining room, which overlooks the garden.

Rooms 16 rms (7 en suite) (1 fmly) (4 GF) S £36–£52; D £56–£64✳
Facilities TV15B tea/coffee Direct dial from bedrooms Cen ht **Parking** 12

★★ GUEST ACCOMMODATION
Rollason Wood
130 Wood End Rd, Erdington B24 8BJ

☎ 0121 373 1230 📄 0121 382 2578

e-mail: rollwood@globalnet.co.uk

dir: *M6 junct 6, A5127 to Erdington, right onto A4040, 0.25m on left*

Well situated for routes and the city centre, this owner-managed establishment is popular with contractors. The choice of three different bedroom styles suits most budgets, and rates include full English breakfasts. Ground-floor areas include a popular bar, cosy television lounge and a dining room.

Rooms 35 rms (11 en suite) (5 fmly) **Facilities** TVB tea/coffee Cen ht TVL Dinner Last d 8.30pm Pool Table **Parking** 35

BIRMINGHAM   MAP 10 SP08

(NATIONAL EXHIBITION CENTRE)

See Hampton-in-Arden & Solihull

COVENTRY   MAP 10 SP37

★★★★ GUEST HOUSE
Acacia
11 Park Rd, Cheyles More CV1 2LE

☎ 024 7663 3622 📄 024 7663 3622

e-mail: acaciaguesthouse@hotmail.com

dir: *Off city ring road junct 6 to railway station & left*

Located within easy walking distance of the train station and city centre, the Acacia provides a range of carefully furnished bedrooms, many of which are on the ground floor. A cosy lounge bar is available.

CONTINUED

Rooms 14 rms (13 en suite) (1 pri facs) (6 fmly) (6 GF) **Facilities** TVB tea/coffee Cen ht TVL Dinner Last d 8.30pm **Parking** 12 **Notes** ⊗ Closed Xmas 🐾

★★★ GUEST ACCOMMODATION
Croft on the Green
23 Stoke Green, off Binley Rd CV3 1FP

☎ 024 7645 7846 📄 024 7645 7846

e-mail: croftonthegreen@aol.com

web: www.croftonthegreen.co.uk

dir: *1m E of city centre off A428 Binley Rd*

An impressive Victorian villa located within a conservation area close to the city centre. A range of practically furnished bedrooms is provided and ground floor areas include a spacious attractive dining room overlooking the pretty garden, and a comfortable lounge bar.

Rooms 12 rms (9 en suite) (2 fmly) S £28-£39; D £45-£48✱ **Facilities** TVB tea/coffee Cen ht TVL Wi-fi available **Parking** 12 **Notes** ⊗

★★★ 🅰 GUEST HOUSE
Ashdowns
12 Regent St CV1 3EP

☎ 024 7622 9280

dir: *A429 to city centre, over rdbt before ring road, 1st left onto Grosvenor Rd, right onto Westminster Rd, right onto Regent St*

Rooms 8 rms (7 en suite) (3 fmly) (1 GF) S £30-£35; D £50-£55 **Facilities** TVB tea/coffee Cen ht TVL **Parking** 8 **Notes** LB ⊗ No children 13yrs Closed 22 Dec-1 Jan 🐾

DORRIDGE   MAP 10 SP17

★★★★ ◉◉ RESTAURANT WITH ROOMS
The Forest
25 Station Rd B93 8JA

☎ 01564 772120 📄 01564 732680

e-mail: info@forest-hotel.com

web: www.forest-hotel.com

dir: *In town centre near station*

The well-established and very individual establishment is well placed for routes to Birmingham, Stratford-upon-Avon and Warwick. Rooms are very well equipped with modern facilities, and imaginative food is served in the bars and intimate restaurant. A warm welcome is assured.

Rooms 12 en suite S £95-£120; D £110-£130✱ **Facilities** TVB tea/coffee Direct dial from bedrooms Cen ht Dinner Last d 10pm Wi-fi available **Conf** BC Max 100 Thtr 100 Class 60 Board 40 **Parking** 50 **Notes** ⊗ RS Sun eve Civ Wed 120

HAMPTON-IN-ARDEN MAP 10 SP28

★★★★ GUEST HOUSE
The Cottage Guest House
Kenilworth Rd B92 0LW
☎ 01675 442323 🗏 01675 443323
e–mail: cottage.roger88@virgin.net
web: www.cottageguesthouse.net

dir: *2m SE of Hampton on A452*

A fine collection of antique memorabilia adorns the public areas of this delightful cottage, which is convenient for visiting the NEC, Birmingham, or exploring the area. Many guests return for the friendly and relaxing atmosphere and the attentive service. Freshly cooked traditional breakfasts, served in the cottage dining room, provide a good start to the day.

Rooms 9 en suite (2 GF) S £35–£50; D £50–£70✶ **Facilities** TVB tea/coffee Cen ht TVL **Parking** 14 **Notes** Closed Xmas ◎

SOLIHULL MAP 10 SP17

★★★ BED & BREAKFAST
The Gate House
Barston Ln, Barston B92 0JN
☎ 01675 443274
e–mail: enquiries@gatehousesolihull.co.uk
web: www.gatehousesolihull.co.uk

dir: *4m E of Solihull. Off B4101 or B4102 to Barston, on W side of village*

This elegant Victorian building stands in landscaped grounds with secure parking, and is within easy driving distance of the NEC, Birmingham. The resident proprietor is most welcoming and provides spacious comfortable accommodation. Breakfast is served in an elegant dining room overlooking the pretty gardens.

Rooms 4 rms (2 en suite) S £30–£50; D £65–£80 **Facilities** TVB tea/coffee Cen ht Wi-fi available **Parking** 20 **Notes** ⊗ No children 5yrs ◎

SUTTON COLDFIELD MAP 10 SP19

★★★★ 🚿 BED & BREAKFAST
Windrush
337 Birmingham Rd, Wylde Green B72 1DL
☎ 0121 384 7534
e–mail: windrush59@hotmail.com

dir: *M6 junct 6, on A5127 to Sutton Coldfield, pass shopping centre on left. 75yds then house just before Hawthorn's Surgery on right*

A warm welcome is assured at this elegant Victorian house, located between the city centre and Sutton Coldfield. Bedrooms are filled with a wealth of thoughtful extras and the bathroom contains a modern shower. Memorable breakfasts are served in an elegant dining room.

Rooms 2 rms (1 en suite) S £35–£38; D £50–£60✶ **Facilities** FTV TVB tea/coffee Cen ht **Parking** 5 **Notes** ⊗ No children 16yrs Closed 19 Dec–3 Jan ◎

WIGHT, ISLE OF

ARRETON MAP 05 SZ58

★★★★ BED & BREAKFAST
Blandings
Horringford PO30 3AP
☎ 01983 865720 & 865331 🗏 01983 862099
e–mail: robin.oulton@horringford.com
web: www.horringford.com/bedandbreakfast.htm

dir: *S through Arreton (B3056), pass Stickworth Hall on your right, 300yds on left farm entrance signed Horringford Gdns. Take U turn to left, drive to end of poplar trees, turn right. Blandings on left*

This recently-built detached home stands in the grounds of Horringford Gardens. The bedroom has private access and has a decking area for warm summer evenings. Breakfast is a highlight with local island produce gracing the table.

Rooms 1 en suite (1 GF) D £60✶ **Facilities** FTV TVB tea/coffee Cen ht **Parking** 3 **Notes** LB ◎

BEMBRIDGE MAP 05 SZ68

★★★★ INN
Crab & Lobster Inn
32 Forelands Field Rd PO35 5TR
☎ 01983 872244
e–mail: crab.lobster@bluebottle.com

A traditional beamed inn enjoying a coastal location overlooking Bembridge Ledge with panoramic sea views. Bedrooms and bathrooms are traditionally fitted, comfortable and spacious, offering a good range of accessories. Locally-caught crab and lobster is the specialty during lunch and dinner at this popular dining destination.

Rooms 5 en suite (1 fmly) S £47.50–£70; D £80–£100✶ **Facilities** TVB tea/coffee Cen ht Dinner Last d 9pm **Parking** 20 **Notes** ⊗ No coaches RS 24–26 Dec

See advert on opposite page

★★★★ BED & BREAKFAST
Sheepstor Cottage
West Green, St Helens PO33 1XA
☎ 01983 873132

dir: *A3055 onto B3330 to the Green, left onto Field Ln, 3rd house on right*

A friendly welcome awaits you from the proprietor and her family of cats at this cosy cottage-style guest house. The attractive bedrooms are en suite, and freshly prepared breakfasts are served in the pleasant dining room, which looks over the surrounding countryside.

Rooms 2 en suite (1 fmly) S £30; D £60✶ **Facilities** TVB tea/coffee Cen ht **Notes** ⊗ ◎

BONCHURCH   MAP 05 SZ57

Premier Collection

★★★★★ GUEST HOUSE
Winterbourne Country House
Bonchurch Village Rd PO38 1RQ

☎ 01983 852535 📄 01983 857529

e–mail: info@winterbournehouse.co.uk

dir: *1m E of Ventnor. Off A3055 into Bonchurch village*

During his stay in 1849, Charles Dickens described Winterbourne as 'the prettiest place I ever saw in my life, at home or abroad'. Today, the comfortable bedrooms are all well equipped and differ in size, and include luxurious rooms with sea views. There are two lounges and a secluded terrace.

Rooms 7 rms (6 en suite) (1 pri facs) S £65–£150; D £110–£190✳ **Facilities** TVB tea/coffee Direct dial from bedrooms Licensed Cen ht TVL ⤳ **Parking** 8 **Notes** No children 10yrs No coaches Closed Xmas

---

BRIGHSTONE   MAP 05 SZ48

★★★ BED & BREAKFAST
"Teapots"
9 St Mary's Court, Main Rd PO30 4AH

☎ 01983 740998

dir: *Village centre on B3399. Entrance opposite Mace shop*

A warm welcome awaits at this modern, detached house, situated in the centre of this picturesque village. It provides thoughtfully equipped bedrooms and a pleasant breakfast room, where all share one table. There is also a very attractive garden.

Rooms 3 rms (1 pri facs) (1 fmly) **Facilities** TVB tea/coffee Cen ht TVL **Parking** 2 **Notes** ⊗ Closed Xmas & New Year ⊜

CHALE   MAP 05 SZ47

★★★★ 🛏 BED & BREAKFAST
The Old House
Gotten Manor, Gotten Ln PO38 2HQ

☎ 01983 551368 & 07746 453398

e–mail: aa@gottenmanor.co.uk

web: www.gottenmanor.co.uk

dir: *1m N of Chale. Turn right off B3399 onto Gotten Ln (opp chapel), house at end*

Located in countryside close to the coast, this 17th-century house has 18th- and 19th-century additions. Restoration has created comfortable, rustic bedrooms with antique bathtubs. Comprehensive breakfasts using the finest ingredients are served in the cosy dining room, and there is a spacious lounge with an open fire.

Rooms 2 en suite D £80–£95 **Facilities** STV FTV TVB tea/coffee Cen ht Wi-fi available ⤳ **Parking** 4 **Notes** LB ⊗ No children 12yrs ⊜

COWES   MAP 05 SZ49

★★★ BED & BREAKFAST
Medina Post Office
5–7 York St PO31 7BS

☎ 01983 292665 📄 01983 292665

e–mail: info@medinapost.co.uk

web: www.medinapost.co.uk

dir: *Off A3020 Mill Hill Rd in West Cowes, 200yds from floating bridge*

A warm welcome is to be expected at this charming terrace property, which is situated close to the town centre and ferry terminal. Bedrooms are pleasantly decorated with coordinated fabrics and have a good range of facilities. Breakfast is served at separate tables in the sunny conservatory.

Rooms 2 rms (1 en suite) (1 pri facs) D £50–£75✳ **Facilities** TVB tea/coffee Cen ht TVL Wi-fi available **Notes** Closed Nov–Feb

---

COWES CONTINUED

★★★ GUEST ACCOMMODATION
Windward House

69 Mill Hill Rd PO31 7EQ

☎ 01983 280940 & 07771 573580 📠 01983 280940

e–mail: sueogston1@tiscali.co.uk

dir: *A320 Cowes-Newport, halfway up Mill Hill Rd on right from floating bridge from E Cowes (Red Funnel Ferries)*

A friendly atmosphere prevails at this comfortable Victorian house, located close to the centre of Cowes. Bedrooms are bright and neat, and downstairs there is a spacious lounge equipped with satellite television, video and music systems. Breakfast is served in a separate dining room around a shared table.

Rooms 6 rms (3 en suite) (2 fmly) (1 GF) S £25–£40; D £50–£70✱ **Facilities** TVB tea/coffee Cen ht TVL ᕃ **Parking** 4 **Notes** 🌐

FRESHWATER   MAP 05 SZ38

★★★★ GUEST ACCOMMODATION
Seagulls Rest

Colwell Chine Rd PO40 9NP

☎ 01983 754037 & 754929

e–mail: selena.flint@btinternet.com

web: www.seagullsrest.com

dir: *A3054 W from Yarmouth, 2.5m at Colwell Bay Inn right for beach, 300yds on left*

Situated just a stroll from the beach, this smart modern detached house has bright and spacious bedrooms, and there is a comfortable lounge. Breakfast and evening meals (by arrangement) are served in the cheery dining room.

Rooms 4 en suite (2 fmly) (1 GF) S £28–£40; D £56–£60 **Facilities** TVB tea/coffee Cen ht Dinner Last d 10am **Parking** 9 **Notes LB** 🚫 🌐

★★★★ GUEST ACCOMMODATION
Buttercup House

Camp Rd PO40 9HL

☎ 01983 752772

e–mail: enquiries@buttercuphouse.co.uk

Situated on the quieter, western side of the island, this attractive stone house dates back in part to 1836. The atmosphere is relaxed and welcoming. Bedrooms are comfy and spacious and have a number of extra facilities. Breakfast is served around the dining room table, providing a tasty and satisfying start to the day, perhaps before setting off to explore on foot or bicycle.

Rooms 3 en suite (1 fmly) S £35–£40; D £60–£80 **Facilities** FTV TVB tea/coffee Cen ht **Parking** 3 **Notes** 🚫 No children 8yrs 🌐

GODSHILL   MAP 05 SZ58

Premier Collection

★★★★★ BED & BREAKFAST
Godshill Park Farm House

Shanklin Rd PO38 3JF

☎ 01983 840781

e–mail: info@godshillparkfarm.uk.com

web: www.godshillparkfarm.uk.com

dir: *From ferry teminal towards Newport, onto A3020 & signs to Sandown, at Blackwater Corner right to Godshill, farm on right after Griffin pub*

This delightful 200-year-old stone farmhouse is set in 270 acres of organic farmland with lakes and woodlands. Bedrooms, one with a four-poster bed and the other overlooking the millpond, are comfortably furnished with many extra facilities. Delicious full English breakfasts are served at one large table in the oak panelled Great Hall.

Rooms 2 en suite (1 fmly) S fr £50; D £90–£99✱ **Facilities** TVB Direct dial from bedrooms Cen ht Fishing **Parking** 4 **Notes** 🚫 No children 8yrs

Premier Collection

★★★★★ 🛏 BED & BREAKFAST
Koala Cottage

Church Hollow PO38 3DR

☎ 01983 842031

e–mail: info@koalacottage.co.uk

web: www.koalacottage.co.uk

Nestled in the quaint village of Godshill is the hidden gem which is Koala Cottage. Bedrooms and bathrooms are furnished to a luxury standard and equipped with endless thoughtful accessories. Leisure facilities include a hot tub and sauna; beauty treatments are available in the comfort of guest bedrooms by prior arrangement. Enjoy a delicious freshly cooked breakfast each morning.

Rooms 4 en suite (1 fmly) (3 GF) **Facilities** STV FTV TVB tea/coffee Cen ht Wi-fi available Sauna Spa **Parking** 5 **Notes** 🚫 No children 18yrs

★★★★ BED & BREAKFAST
'Arndale'
High St PO38 3HH
☎ 01983 842003
e–mail: arndalebandb@aol.com
dir: *On A3020 High St*
Arndale is situated in the pretty village of Godshill. Expect a warm welcome from the resident dogs, Bayley and Arrow. The private lounge-dining room is where dinner is served by arrangement. Guests have access to the patio and garden.

Rooms 2 rms (2 pri facs) (2 fmly) (1 GF) **Facilities** TVB Cen ht TVL Dinner Last d 7pm Riding **Parking** 4 **Notes** ⊗ No children 14yrs ⊛

NEWPORT   MAP 05 SZ58

★★★★ GUEST ACCOMMODATION
Braunstone House
33 Lugley St PO30 5ET
☎ 01983 822994 📄 01983 526300
e–mail: lugleys@uwclub.net

Occupying a central location in Newport, this Georgian house has lots of charm. Bedrooms retain elegant proportions and ambience and are well provided with extras. The popular brasserie restaurant has a modern aspect and well-prepared and appealing cuisine.

Rooms 5 rms (4 en suite) (1 pri facs) **Facilities** TVB tea/coffee Cen ht Dinner Last d 9.30pm Wi-fi available **Notes** ⊗

★★★ GUEST ACCOMMODATION
Castle Lodge
54 Castle Rd PO30 1DP
☎ 01983 527862 & 07789 228203 📄 01983 559030
e–mail: castlelodge@hotmail.co.uk
dir: *0.5m SW of town centre. On B3323 towards Carisbrooke Castle*
This well-presented establishment is located in a quiet residential area within close walking distance of the famous Carisbrooke Castle. A comfortable stay is assured with attractive and restful bedrooms together with a bright and airy dining room where a substantial breakfast can be enjoyed.

Rooms 3 rms (2 en suite) (1 pri facs) 5 annexe rms (4 en suite) (1 annexe pri facs) (1 fmly) (5 GF) S £25–£30; D £50–£60✱ **Facilities** TVB tea/coffee Cen ht **Parking** 8 **Notes** ⊗

NITON   MAP 05 SZ57

AA FUNKIEST B&B OF THE YEAR
Premier Collection

★★★★★ GUEST ACCOMMODATION
Enchanted Manor
Sandrock Rd PO38 2NG
☎ 01983 730215
e–mail: info@enchantedmanor.co.uk
web: www.enchantedmanor.co.uk
This delightful property, set in charming grounds, enjoys an enviable location within walking distance of the sea. An enchanted theme prevails throughout the beautifully appointed suites and spacious public areas that are all furnished and decorated to a very high standard. A host of extra touches are provided such as DVD players, well-stocked mini-fridges and welcome baskets. Guests are ensured of friendly, attentive personalised service and an excellent breakfast.

Rooms 7 en suite (2 GF) **Facilities** STV FTV TVB tea/coffee Cen ht Wi-fi available ⌁ Snooker Pool Table Spa/hot tub Massage beauty treatment room **Conf** Max 30 Board 30 **Parking** 15 **Notes** No children Civ Wed 50

RYDE   MAP 05 SZ59

★★★★ BED & BREAKFAST
Grange Farm B&B
Grange Farm, Staplers Rd, Wootton PO33 4RW
☎ 01983 882147
e–mail: grange@wightfarmholiday.co.uk
dir: *4m W of Ryde next to Butterfly World, Wootton Common*
The homely, family-run property is in a quiet rural setting between Newport and Ryde. The comfortable bedrooms and bathrooms are equipped with a large range of extra facilities, and there is also a cosy lounge. Substantial English breakfasts are served house-party style around one large table.

Rooms 2 en suite **Facilities** TVB tea/coffee Cen ht TVL **Parking** 6 **Notes** ⊗ No children 4yrs

★★★★ BED & BREAKFAST
1 The Lawn
Spencer Rd PO33 2NU
☎ 01983 568742
e–mail: n@cross3524.freeserve.co.uk
dir: *A3054, left into West St. Left at T-junct, 100yds on left*
Attractive Victorian house in quiet area, convenient for town centre as well as hovercraft and Catamaran terminals. Off-road parking is available.

Rooms 2 rms (2 pri facs) **Facilities** TV1B tea/coffee Cen ht **Parking** 2 **Notes** ⊗ No children 5yrs ⊛

SANDOWN — MAP 05 SZ58

★★★★ GUEST HOUSE
Montague House

109 Station Av PO36 8HD
☎ 01983 404295
e–mail: enquiries@montaguehousehotel.fsnet.co.uk

dir: *A3055 from Ryde to Sandown, onto Station Av following signs for beach*

This large, detached, late Victorian house is just a short walk from the town centre and seafront. The friendly hosts have recently renovated the property extensively to provide good quality, well-equipped modern accommodation. Separate tables are provided in the very attractive dining room and you can relax in the pleasant conservatory.

Rooms 11 rms (9 en suite) (2 fmly) (3 GF) S £25–£30; D £50–£60✱
Facilities TVB tea/coffee Cen ht TVL **Notes LB** ⊗ No children 5yrs No coaches ⊛

★★★★ GUEST HOUSE
Carisbrooke House

11 Beachfield Rd PO36 8NA
☎ 01983 402257 ▤ 01983 402257
e–mail: wmch583@aol.com

dir: *2 minutes from Sandown town, beach and leisure centre, opposite Ferncliff Gardens*

Expect a friendly welcome at this family run guest-house situated opposite Ferncliff Gardens and within walking distance of the town centre and seafront. A full English breakfast is served in the dining room overlooking the sun terrace. Enjoy a drink in the bar/lounge. Dinner by arrangement

Rooms 11 rms (9 en suite) (2 pri facs) (3 fmly) (3 GF) S £27–£30; D £54–£70✱ **Facilities** TVB tea/coffee Licensed Cen ht TVL Dinner Last d breakfast same day Wi-fi available **Parking** 3 **Notes LB**

★★★★ GUEST ACCOMMODATION
The Lawns

72 Broadway PO36 9AA
☎ 01983 402549
e–mail: lawnshotel@aol.com
web: www.lawnshotelisleofwight.co.uk

dir: *On A3055 N of town centre*

The Lawns stands in grounds just a short walk from the beach, public transport and town centre. There is a comfortable lounge and bar, and evening meals (by arrangement) and breakfast are served in the bright dining room. Service is friendly and attentive, and the bedrooms are comfortably equipped.

The Lawns

Rooms 13 en suite (5 fmly) (2 GF) S £29–£36; D £58–£88✱
Facilities FTV TVB tea/coffee Direct dial from bedrooms Cen ht TVL Dinner Last d noon **Parking** 15 **Notes LB** ⊗

★★★ GUEST HOUSE
Chester Lodge

7 Beachfield Rd PO36 8NA
☎ 01983 402773

dir: *On B3395 S from seafront/High St*

This family-run property is within walking distance of the seafront and shops. The neat bedrooms include some on the ground floor with easier access, and there is a comfortable bar and lounge. Breakfast is served in the bright dining room.

Rooms 13 en suite (3 fmly) (4 GF) **Facilities** TVB tea/coffee Licensed TVL Dinner Last d tbc **Parking** 14 **Notes** ⊗

★★★ A GUEST HOUSE
The Montpelier

Pier St PO36 8JR
☎ 01983 403964 ▤ 07092 212734
e–mail: info@themontpelier.co.uk
web: www.themontpelier.co.uk

dir: *A3055 onto Melville St, over junct onto Pier St*

Rooms 8 en suite (2 fmly) S £23–£29; D £46–£58✱ **Facilities** TVB tea/coffee Cen ht **Notes LB** ⊗ No coaches

SHANKLIN — MAP 05 SZ58

Premier Collection

★★★★★ GUEST ACCOMMODATION
Foxhills

30 Victoria Av PO37 6LS
☎ 01983 862329 ▤ 01983 866666
e–mail: info@foxhillsofshanklin.co.uk
web: www.foxhillsofshanklin.co.uk

dir: *A3020 from Shanklin centre towards Newport, Foxhills 450yds on left*

An idyllic getaway for the weary business traveller and leisure guest alike, Foxhills offers something a little bit special. Individually styled

CONTINUED
CONTINUED

rooms offer high levels of comfort and many thoughtful extras, and any stay here isn't complete without using the spa or having a treatment in the beauty salon.

Foxhills

Rooms 8 en suite (1 GF) S £44–£108; D £88–£118 **Facilities** TVB tea/coffee Direct dial from bedrooms Cen ht Wi-fi available Solarium Health & beauty treatments & whirlpool spa **Conf** Max 25 Class 20 Board 12 **Parking** 13 **Notes LB** ⊗ No children 14yrs Closed 3–31 Jan

★★★★ GUEST ACCOMMODATION
Aqua

17 The Esplanade PO37 6BN
☎ 01983 863024 📄 01983 864841
e–mail: aa@aquahotel.co.uk
web: www.aquahotel.co.uk

dir: *Off A3055 North Rd onto Hope Rd & seafront Esplanade*

This friendly, family-run establishment has been in the same hands since 1980. The bright and airy public areas include a spacious lounge bar, where live entertainment is available on most evenings, and the attractive Boaters Restaurant, which serves a selection of freshly-made dishes. Many of the well-equipped bedrooms have sea views and some have a balcony.

Rooms 22 en suite (4 fmly) **Facilities** TVB tea/coffee Cen ht Dinner Last d 4pm **Notes** ⊗ Closed 21 Dec–Jan

★★★★ GUEST ACCOMMODATION
The Avenue

6 Avenue Rd PO37 7BG
☎ 01983 862746
e–mail: info@avenuehotelshanklin.co.uk

dir: *A3055 from Sandown, through Lake, right onto Avenue Rd before x-rds lights*

This friendly, family-run guest house is in a quiet location just a 5-minute walk from the town centre and beaches. The well-equipped bedrooms are generally spacious, and there is a bar-lounge, a conservatory and a comfortable breakfast room. An attractive terraced courtyard lies to the rear.

Rooms 10 en suite (2 fmly) (2 GF) S £29–£39; D £58–£66✳ **Facilities** TVB tea/coffee Cen ht Wi-fi available **Parking** 6 **Notes LB** ⊗ Closed Nov–Feb

★★★★ GUEST ACCOMMODATION
Belmont

8 Queens Rd PO37 6AN
☎ 01983 867875 & 862864
e–mail: enquiries@belmont-iow.co.uk
web: www.belmont-iow.co.uk

dir: *From Sandown (on A3055), half left at Fiveways lights signed Ventnor. Belmont 400mtrs on right, opp St Saviour's church*

This Victorian residence stands in well-tended grounds a short walk from the picturesque old village and Shanklin Chine. Bedrooms are comfortable and some have distant sea views. There is also a spacious and well-proportioned lounge, a cosy bar and an elegant breakfast room overlooking the swimming pool.

Rooms 13 en suite (4 fmly) (2 GF) S £31–£61; D £54–£84✳ **Facilities** TVB tea/coffee Direct dial from bedrooms Cen ht ⋩ Pool heated late May–early Sep **Parking** 9 **Notes LB** ⊗ No children 5yrs Closed Nov–Feb

★★★★ GUEST ACCOMMODATION
Courtlands

15 Paddock Rd PO37 6PA
☎ 01983 862167 📄 01983 863308
e–mail: enquiries@courtlandshotel.co.uk
web: www.courtlandshotel.co.uk

dir: *In town centre. Off A3020 Victoria Av onto Highfield Rd, 1st left*

Located just a short walk from the High Street and the old village, this welcoming establishment offers comfortable accommodation, a spacious bar area and a comfortable lounge. Breakfast is served in the dining room and dinner is available by arrangement.

Rooms 19 rms (18 en suite) (4 fmly) (6 GF) S £33–£37; D £66–£74✳ **Facilities** TVB tea/coffee Cen ht TVL ⋩ Pool Table **Parking** 12 **Notes LB** ⊗ Closed Oct–Mar

SHANKLIN CONTINUED

★★★★ GUEST HOUSE
Glendene Guest House

7 Carter Av PO37 7LQ

☎ 01983 862924

e–mail: jpierceglendene@aol.com

dir: *A3020 into Shanklin, left onto St John's Rd & Brook Rd to Carter Av x-rds*

Located in the heart of Shanklin and within walking distance of the sandy beach, Glendene offers comfortable accommodation within a friendly environment. Breakfast is served in the attractive dining room and a delicious home-cooked dinner is available by arrangement.

Rooms 7 rms (4 en suite) (2 pri facs) (2 fmly) S £24–£30; D £48–£60 **Facilities** TVB tea/coffee TVL Dinner Last d breakfast Wi-fi available **Parking** 6 **Notes LB** ⊗ No coaches

★★★★ GUEST ACCOMMODATION
The Grange

9 Eastcliff Rd PO37 6AA

☎ 01983 867644 🖷 01983 865537

e–mail: jenni@thegrangebythesea.com

web: www.thegrangebythesea.com

dir: *Off A3055 High St*

This delightful house specialises in holistic breaks and enjoys a tranquil yet convenient setting in manicured grounds close to the seafront and village centre. Extensive refurbishment has resulted in beautifully presented bedrooms and spacious public areas. Dinner and breakfast are taken en famille (outside in fine weather).

Rooms 17 rms (16 en suite) (1 pri facs) (1 fmly) (6 GF) S £69–£77; D £88–£104✳ **Facilities** TVB tea/coffee Cen ht TVL Dinner Wi-fi available Sauna **Parking** 8 **Notes LB** ⊗ Civ Wed 100

★★★★ 🕸 GUEST ACCOMMODATION
Hayes Barton

7 Highfield Rd PO37 6PP

☎ 01983 867747 🖷 01983 862104

e–mail: williams.2000@virgin.net

web: www.hayesbarton.co.uk

dir: *A3055 onto A3020 Victoria Av, 3rd left*

Hayes Barton has the relaxed atmosphere of a family home and provides well-equipped bedrooms and a range of comfortable public areas. Dinner is available from a short selection of home-cooked dishes and there is a cosy bar lounge. The old village, beach and promenade are all within walking distance.

Rooms 9 en suite (4 fmly) (2 GF) D £52–£68✳ **Facilities** TVB tea/coffee Cen ht TVL Dinner Last d noon **Parking** 8 **Notes LB** Closed Nov–Mar

★★★★ 🍴 GUEST ACCOMMODATION
Keats Cottage Restaurant & Guest Accommodation

76 High St PO37 6NJ

☎ 01983 865518 🖷 01983 863837

e–mail: jillrowe9@btinternet.com

dir: *From Newport take A3020 to Shanklin, at lights turn right, located on the left*

Keats Cottage is convenient for shops, pubs, restaurants, the theatre, and Shanklin's blue flag beach. It's also an ideal base for walking holidays. The rear part of the building encompasses the historic Eglantine Cottage, which is where the legendary Mrs Williams played host to John Keats, the romantic poet; George Morland, the artist; and Thomas Morton, the dramatist. The consumptive Keats particularly appreciated Mrs Williams' care and attention, and the bedrooms are named after these illustrious visitors. Please note that this is an authentic historic building with stairs to all rooms and is not suitable for some disabled people or persons who have difficulty negotiating stairs.

Rooms 4 en suite **Facilities** TVB tea/coffee Cen ht Dinner Last d 9.30pm **Notes** No children 14yrs

★★★★ GUEST HOUSE
The Richmond

23 Palmerston Rd PO37 6AS
☎ 01983 862874
e–mail: info@richmondhotel-shanklin.co.uk

dir: *Off Shanklin High St at Conservative Club*

This friendly guest house is a stroll from the town centre and beach. The carefully furnished bedrooms have a good range of facilities, and the public rooms include a cosy lounge bar and an attractive dining room.

Rooms 9 en suite (3 fmly) S £26–£28; D £52–£56✱ **Facilities** TVB tea/coffee Licensed Cen ht TVL Dinner Last d 1pm **Parking** 5 **Notes LB** ⊗ No coaches

★★★★ GUEST ACCOMMODATION
Rowborough

32 Arthurs Hill PO37 6EX
☎ 01983 866072 & 863070 ▤ 01983 867703
e–mail: mister.paulwood@virgin.net
web: www.rowborough-hotel.com

dir: *Between Sandown and Shanklin*

Located on the main road into town, this charming, family-run establishment provides comfortable bedrooms with many extra facilities. The non-smoking conservatory overlooks the garden, along with a lounge and a bar. Dinner is available by arrangement.

Rooms 9 en suite (5 fmly) (1 GF) S £28–£32; D £56–£64✱ **Facilities** TVB tea/coffee Cen ht TVL Dinner Last d 4pm Wi-fi available DVD players in all rooms **Parking** 5 **Notes LB**

★★★★ GUEST ACCOMMODATION
St Brelades

15 Hope Rd PO37 6EA
☎ 01983 862967
e–mail: info@st-brelades-hotel.co.uk
web: www.st-brelades-hotel.co.uk

dir: *A3055 into Shanklin, left onto Hope Rd signed Esplanade*

A warm welcome is assured at this delightful family-run establishment, located within easy walking distance of the beach and town centre. The cosy bedrooms are brightly decorated and equipped with many useful extras. There is also a lounge and bar, and tasty evening meals are available by arrangement.

Rooms 15 en suite (4 fmly) (4 GF) S £30–£40; D £56–£66✱ **Facilities** TVB tea/coffee Cen ht TVL Dinner Last d by prior notice Wi-fi available **Parking** 10 **Notes LB** ⊗ RS Nov–Feb

★★★★ GUEST ACCOMMODATION
St Georges House

2 St Georges Rd PO37 6BA
☎ 01983 863691 ▤ 01983 861597
e–mail: stgeorgesiow@isleofwight.com
web: www.stgeorgesiow.com

dir: *Heading S from Fiveways turn 2nd right off A3055, next right*

A warm welcome is assured at this family-run property located in a quiet area between the town centre and cliff top. Bedrooms which vary in size provide comfort and are well appointed. Guests have use of the lounge and bar, and dinners are available by appointment during the winter months.

Rooms 9 en suite (1 fmly) (1 GF) S £27–£37; D £54–£74 **Facilities** FTV TVB tea/coffee Cen ht TVL Dinner Last d late am Wi-fi available **Parking** 7 **Notes LB** Closed mid Dec–mid Jan

★★★ GUEST ACCOMMODATION
The Bedford Lodge

4 Chine Av PO37 6AQ
☎ 01983 862416 ▤ 01983 868704
e–mail: mail@bedfordlodge.co.uk

dir: *A3055 onto Chine Av, opp Tower Cottage Gardens*

A particularly warm welcome is guaranteed here at this delightful property. The Bedford Lodge benefits from an unspoilt and quiet location with pretty gardens and is extremely close to Old Shanklin and Shanklin beach. Bedrooms are well equipped and comfortable. A delicious breakfast is served at individual dining tables in the attractive dining room; in addition a bar and lounge is available for guests' use.

Rooms 14 en suite (4 fmly) (3 GF) **Facilities** TVB Cen ht TVL **Parking** 8 **Notes** ⊗ No children 5yrs

★★★ GUEST HOUSE
The Braemar

1 Grange Rd PO37 6NN
☎ 01983 863172 ▤ 01983 863172
e–mail: djsherfield@aol.com

Tucked away in Shanklins Old Village, expect a warm welcome at this family-run, licensed guest house. Bedrooms are comfortable and vary in size. Breakfast is served in the bright dining room overlooking the gardens. Home-cooked evening meals by arrangement.

Rooms 11 en suite (1 fmly) (3 GF) **Facilities** TVB tea/coffee Licensed Cen ht TVL Dinner Last d 4pm Pool Table **Parking** 10 **Notes** No coaches

SHORWELL

MAP 05 SZ48

★★ BED & BREAKFAST
Malt House Cottage

Walkers Ln PO30 3JZ
☎ 01983 740870 & 07877 048499
e–mail: maltcottage@yahoo.co.uk

dir: *B3323 from Newport 5m. Opposite pub car park*

Enjoying a location close to the castle and historic old town, this atmospheric building was previously the High School. Public rooms have been converted from the original classrooms and retain many interesting features. Bedrooms are more modern in style and comfortably equipped.

Rooms 3 rms (1 en suite) (2 pri facs) (1 fmly) D £50–£60(room only) **Facilities** TVB tea/coffee Cen ht TVL **Parking** 4 **Notes** LB ⊗ ⊜

TOTLAND BAY

MAP 05 SZ38

★★★★ BED & BREAKFAST
The Golf House

Alum Bay New Rd PO39 0JA
☎ 01983 753293
e–mail: sue@thegolfhouse.info

dir: *Totland B3322, at War Memorial rdbt take 2nd exit onto Church Hill 1m, entrance on right*

The Golf House is a detached house in its own grounds situated at the western tip of the Isle of Wight. It is surrounded by National Trust land in an Area of Outstanding Natural Beauty and enjoys amazing views from every window. Local produce is used wherever possible and a number of eating establishments are within a short driving distance. A games room is available, and transport to and from Yarmouth can be arranged.

Rooms 3 rms (1 en suite) (2 pri facs) D £32.50–£39.50✱ **Facilities** STV FTV TVB tea/coffee Cen ht TVL Wi-fi available Snooker **Parking** 3 **Notes** LB ⊗

★★★★ BED & BREAKFAST
The Hoo

Colwell Rd PO39 0AB
☎ 01983 753592 🖺 01983 753592
e–mail: jerjohnston@btinternet.com

dir: *From Yarmouth ferry right onto A3054, 2.25m enter Colwell Common, The Hoo is on corner of Colwell Rd & Warden Rd*

Located close to the port and beaches, this friendly family home provides a peaceful setting. The house has many Japanese features and guests are asked to wear slippers. The spacious bedrooms are well equipped and comfortably furnished. English breakfast is most enjoyable and is served overlooking the attractive gardens.

Rooms 3 rms (1 en suite) (2 fmly) S £25–£48; D £40–£77 **Facilities** FTV TVB tea/coffee Cen ht **Parking** 1 **Notes** No children 5yrs Closed 2 Jan–3 Mar

---

★★★ GUEST ACCOMMODATION
The Hermitage

Cliff Rd PO39 0EW
☎ 01983 752518
e–mail: blake_david@btconnect.com
web: www.thehermitagebnb.co.uk

dir: *Church Hill B3322, right onto Eden Rd, left onto Cliff Rd, 0.5m on right*

The Hermitage is an extremely pet and people friendly establishment which occupies a stunning and unspoilt location near to the cliff top in Totland Bay. Extensive gardens are well maintained and off road car parking is a bonus. Accommodation is comfortable and you are assured of a genuinely warm welcome and friendly service at this traditionally styled establishment. A range of delicious items at breakfast provide a substantial start to the day.

Rooms 4 rms (3 en suite) (1 pri facs) (1 fmly) S £30–£40; D £50–£70✱ **Facilities** TVB tea/coffee TVL Dinner Last d at breakfast **Parking** 6 **Notes** LB

VENTNOR

MAP 05 SZ57

Premier Collection

★★★★★ ⚘⚘ RESTAURANT WITH ROOMS
Hambrough

Hambrough Rd PO38 1SQ
☎ 01983 856333 🖺 01983 857260
e–mail: info@thehambrough.com

A former Victorian villa set on the hillside above Ventnor and with memorable views out to sea. It has a modern, stylish interior with well-equipped and comfortable bedrooms. The team's passion for food is clearly evident in the superb cuisine served in the minimalist themed restaurant.

Rooms 7 en suite D £130–£220 **Facilities** TVB tea/coffee Direct dial from bedrooms Cen ht Dinner Wi-fi available **Conf** Thtr 30 Class 20 Board 14 Del from £235 **Notes** LB No children 8yrs

---

Premier Collection

★★★★★ ⚘ 🛏 GUEST ACCOMMODATION
The Leconfield

85 Leeson Rd, Upper Bonchurch PO38 1PU
☎ 01983 852196 🖺 01983 856525
e–mail: enquiries@leconfieldhotel.com
web: www.leconfieldhotel.com

dir: *On A3055, 3m from Old Shanklin village*

This country house is situated on an elevated position with panoramic seaviews above the historic village of Bonchurch. Luxury finished bedrooms and suites are spacious and individually styled, finished with many thoughtful extras to enhance comfort. Public rooms include two lounges and a conservatory in addition to the Sea Scape restaurant, named after the views, where freshly prepared breakfast and imaginative dinner menus are served. Additional facilities include the outdoor pool, terrace area and ample off-road parking.

CONTINUED

Rooms 7 en suite 5 annexe en suite (3 GF) S £48–£57; D £92–£194✳
Facilities TVB tea/coffee Cen ht Dinner Last d 8pm Wi-fi available ⏀
Parking 14 **Notes LB** ⊗ No children 16yrs

See advert on this page

Premier Collection

★★★★★ GUEST HOUSE
Horseshoe Bay House

Shore Rd PO38 1RN
☎ 01983 856800
e-mail: howard@horseshoebayhouse.com

dir: *0.5m E of Ventnor. Off A3055 to Bonchurch, house opp pond*

Set at the very edge of the beach in the pretty village of Bonchurch, this super place offers spacious accommodation in a memorable location. Hospitality is friendly and the proprietors here are attentive hosts. Bedrooms are smartly styled in tranquil colours and comfortably appointed; most rooms enjoy the spectacular views. Breakfast offers a good range of choice and provides an excellent start to the day.

Rooms 6 rms (5 en suite) (1 pri facs) (1 fmly) (1 GF) S £40–£55;
D £80–£95✳ **Facilities** TVB tea/coffee Licensed Cen ht TVL Wi-fi available **Parking** 6 **Notes LB** ⊗ No children 8yrs No coaches

Premier Collection

★★★★★ GUEST HOUSE
Winterbourne Country House

Bonchurch Village Rd PO38 1RQ
☎ 01983 852535 📄 01983 857529
e-mail: info@winterbournehouse.co.uk

(For full entry see Bonchurch)

★★★★ GUEST ACCOMMODATION
The Lake

Shore Rd, Bonchurch PO38 1RF
☎ 01983 852613
e-mail: enquiries@lakehotel.co.uk

dir: *0.5m E of Ventnor. Off A3055 to Bonchurch, opp village pond*

A warm welcome is assured at this friendly, family-run property set in two acres of well-tended gardens close to the sea. Bedrooms are equipped with modern facilities and the elegant public rooms offer a high standard of comfort. A choice of menus is offered at dinner and breakfast.

Rooms 11 en suite 9 annexe en suite (7 fmly) (4 GF) S £44;
D £72–£88✳ **Facilities** TVB tea/coffee Cen ht TVL Dinner Last d 6.30pm **Parking** 20 **Notes LB** No children 3yrs RS Nov–Feb

★★★★ GUEST HOUSE
Burwynns

9 Steephill Rd PO38 1UF
☎ 01983 854172 📄 01983 854172

dir: *A3055 from Ventnor towards St Lawrence, house 0.25m on the right beyond Ventnor Park*

Burwynns Guest House, located 0.5 miles from the centre of Ventnor, provides comfortable accommodation within a homely and friendly environment. Breakfast is served in the pleasantly appointed dining room, which overlooks the rear garden and swimming pool.

Rooms 4 rms (3 en suite) (1 pri facs) (1 fmly) S £32–£34; D £54–£58
Facilities TVB tea/coffee Cen ht TVL ⏀ **Parking** 4 **Notes LB** ⊗ No children 10yrs No coaches ⊜

VENTNOR CONTINUED

★★★★ GUEST ACCOMMODATION
The Hillside
Mitchell Av PO38 1DR
☎ 01983 852271 ▤ 01983 852271
e-mail: aa@hillside-hotel.co.uk
web: www.hillsideventnor.co.uk

dir: *Exit A3055 onto B3327, premises 600yds on right behind tennis courts*

Hospitality is an important factor at this friendly establishment. Built as an inn during the 18th century, it enjoys some beautiful views of the sea and back onto St Boniface Downs. Bedrooms are individually furnished and are all en suite. Guests can relax in the cosy bar, elegant lounge and plant-filled conservatory. Breakfast is served at an unhurried pace in the bright dining room.

Rooms 12 en suite (1 fmly) (1 GF) S £40–£43; D £80–£86
Facilities TVB tea/coffee Cen ht ⬚ **Parking** 12 **Notes LB** No children 5yrs Closed Xmas

★★★★ GUEST ACCOMMODATION
St. Augustine Villa
Esplanade PO38 1TA
☎ 01983 852285 ▤ 01983 856630
e-mail: info@harbourviewhotel.co.uk
web: www.harbourviewhotel.co.uk

dir: *Opp harbour*

Located on an elevated position with spectacular sea views, this delightful Victorian property next to the Winter Gardens provides well-equipped and comfortable bedrooms. Public areas include a conservatory dining room, lounge, cosy bar, small garden and patio area, all with sea views.

Rooms 9 en suite **Facilities** STV FTV TVB tea/coffee Direct dial from bedrooms Cen ht TVL Wi-fi available **Parking** 8 **Notes** ⊗ No children 21yrs Closed 5 Jan–1 Feb

★★★★ GUEST ACCOMMODATION
St Maur
Castle Rd PO38 1LG
☎ 01983 852570 & 853645 ▤ 01983 852306
e-mail: sales@stmaur.co.uk

dir: *Exit A3055 at the end of Park Ave onto Castle Rd, premises 150yds on the left*

A warm welcome awaits guests at this Victorian villa, which is pleasantly and quietly located in an elevated position overlooking the bay. The well-equipped bedrooms are traditionally decorated while public areas include a spacious lounge and cosy residents' bar. The gardens here are a delight.

Rooms 9 en suite (2 fmly) **Facilities** STV TVB tea/coffee Cen ht Dinner Last d 7pm **Parking** 9 **Notes** ⊗ No children 5yrs Closed Dec

★★★ GUEST ACCOMMODATION
Cornerways
39 Madeira Rd PO38 1QS
☎ 01983 852323 ▤ 01983 852323
e-mail: cornerwayshotel@aol.com

dir: *Off Trinity Rd (south coast road) near Trinity Church onto Madeira Rd, house on left*

This guest house is quietly located between Bonchurch and the town centre, yet is only a stroll from the beach, shops and many places of interest. Bedrooms are comfortable and well equipped and there is a lounge and cosy bar. Full English breakfasts are served at individual tables.

Rooms 9 en suite (1 fmly) (1 GF) S £27–£34; D £54–£68✳
Facilities TVB tea/coffee Cen ht TVL **Parking** 4 **Notes LB** ⊗ No children 5yrs ⊜

★★★ GUEST HOUSE
Llynfi

23 Spring Hill PO38 1PF
☎ 01983 852202 🖹 01983 852202
e-mail: info@llynfihotel.co.uk
dir: *A3055 from Shanklin, right before sharp S-bend onto St Boniface Rd, left onto Spring Hill*

You are assured of a warm welcome at this family-run property, located just a short way up the hill from the main street. Bedrooms are bright and comfortably appointed, and the extensive public areas include a conservatory with an adjoining terrace, and a cosy bar and a dining room. Dinner is available by arrangement.

Rooms 9 rms (8 en suite) (1 pri facs) (5 fmly) S £27–£30; D £54–£60✱ **Facilities** TVB tea/coffee Licensed Dinner Last d 4pm **Parking** 7 **Notes** LB ⊗

YARMOUTH   MAP 05 SZ38

★★★ INN
Bugle Coaching Inn

The Square PO41 0NS
☎ 01983 760272 🖹 01983 760883
e-mail: buglecoachinginn@btconnect.com
web: www.buglecoachinginn.co.uk
dir: *220yds from Yarmouth Wightlink Ferry Terminal, in town square*

Taking pride of place in the market square, this listed 17th-century building is close to the ferry and has ample car parking. Spacious, well-furnished bedrooms are available. A selection of bars and lounges offer contemporary style and comfort. A varied range of delicious home-cooked meals is offered including daily specials.

Rooms 7 en suite (1 fmly) **Facilities** TVB tea/coffee Direct dial from bedrooms Dinner Last d 9.30pm **Parking** 8

WILTSHIRE

ALDBOURNE   MAP 05 SU27

★★★★ INN
Crown at Aldbourne

The Square SN8 2DU
☎ 01672 540214 🖹 01672 540214
e-mail: info@crownataldbourne.co.uk
web: www.crownataldbourne.co.uk
dir: *M4 junct 15 head N on A419, signed to Aldbourne*

The Crown has been recently refurbished to return it to its traditional village inn roots. The cosy bar offers a range of real ales while the comfortable dining room provides plenty of character in which to enjoy the excellent selection of home-cooked dishes. Friendly hospitality and relaxed and welcoming service are delivered throughout any stay. Bedrooms and bathrooms vary slightly in size but are all well decorated and comfortably furnished.

Rooms 4 en suite S fr £49.95; D fr £69.95✱ **Facilities** TVB tea/coffee Cen ht Dinner Last d 9.30pm **Conf** Max 30 Thtr 20 Class 12 Board 10 **Notes** LB

AMESBURY MAP 05 SU14

★★★★ GUEST ACCOMMODATION
Mandalay
15 Stonehenge Rd SP4 7BA
☎ 01980 623733 📠 01980 626642
e-mail: nick.ramplin@btinternet.com
dir: *500yds W of town centre, off High St onto Church St &*
Stonehenge Rd

Quietly located on the edge of the town, yet within easy reach of
Stonehenge and the cathedral, this delightful property provides
individually decorated rooms. Freshly cooked breakfasts are served in
the pleasant breakfast room, which overlooks the landscaped gardens.

Rooms 5 en suite (2 fmly) S £40–£55; D £55–£75 **Facilities** TVB tea/
coffee Cen ht TVL **Parking** 5 **Notes** ⊗

★★★★ GUEST ACCOMMODATION
Park House Motel
SP4 0EG
☎ 01980 629256 📠 01980 629256
dir: *5m E of Amesbury. Junct A303 & A338*

This family-run establishment offers a warm welcome and is extremely
convenient for the A303. Bedrooms are practically equipped with
modern facilities and come in a variety of sizes. There is a large dining
room where dinner is served during the week, and a cosy bar in which
to relax.

Rooms 30 rms (27 en suite) (1 pri facs) (9 fmly) (25 GF) S £56–£62;
D £70 **Facilities** STV TVB tea/coffee Cen ht TVL Dinner Last d 8.30pm
Wi-fi available **Parking** 40

See advert on page 533

★★★ BED & BREAKFAST
Catkin Lodge
93 Countess Rd SP4 7AT
☎ 01980 624810 & 622139 📠 01980 622139
e-mail: info@catkinlodge.fsnet.co.uk
web: www.catkinlodge.fsnet.co.uk
dir: *A303 at Amesbury onto A345 Marlborough road, 400yds on*
left

Popular for business and leisure, Catkin Lodge is close to Stonehenge
and offers off-road parking. The three bedrooms, including two on the
ground floor, offer good levels of comfort and can accommodate
children if required. The artwork of the talented proprietor is displayed
around the property, adding further interest.

Rooms 3 en suite (1 fmly) (2 GF) S £35–£50; D £60–£75✳
Facilities FTV TVB tea/coffee Cen ht **Parking** 7 **Notes** ⊗ No children
7yrs ✉

BOX MAP 04 ST86

★★★★★ 🛏 BED & BREAKFAST
Foggam Barn Bed and Breakfast
Box Hill SN13 8ES
☎ 01225 744888 📠 01225 744888
e-mail: denise@foggambarn.com
web: www.foggambarn.com

Foggam Barn is a delightful, detached house with pleasant gardens
and excellent views over the surrounding countryside. Chippenham or
Bath are just a short drive away. The two bedrooms are very
comfortably furnished and decorated, and guests are welcome to use
the relaxing lounge. Breakfast, made with high quality local and
homemade produce, is served in the spacious conservatory.

Rooms 2 rms (1 en suite) (1 pri facs) (4 fmly) D £75–£95✳
Facilities STV TVB tea/coffee Cen ht TVL Wi-fi available **Parking** 8
Notes ⊗ No children ✉

★★★★★ BED & BREAKFAST
Spinney Cross
Lower Kingsdown Rd, Kingsdown SN13 8BA
☎ 01225 742019 & 461518
e-mail: dotcom@spinneycross.co.uk
dir: *Bath A4 toward Chippenham, A353 from Bathford to*
Bradford on Avon. Under railway bridge, left at Crown PH to
Kingsdown, left at Swan PH, bear right at bottom of hill, Spinney
Cross 500yds on left

A warm welcome is assured at this delightful home located in the quiet
village of Kingsdown. The views are a pleasure to behold. Bedrooms
are spacious and attractively styled, and all have their own private
access to the patio and garden. A varied range of tasty options is
available at breakfast.

Rooms 3 rms (2 en suite) (1 fmly) (3 GF) S £60–£85; D £60–£85✳
Facilities TVB tea/coffee Cen ht Wi-fi available **Parking** 6 **Notes LB** ⊗

★★★★ BED & BREAKFAST
White Smocks
Ashley SN13 8AJ
☎ 01225 742154 📄 01225 742212
e–mail: whitesmocksashley@hotmail.com
dir: *A4 1m W of Box turn opp The Northy, at T-junct White Smocks right of thatched cottage*

Quietly located in the pleasant village of Ashley, and just a short drive from Bath with its many attractions, White Smocks offers a relaxing escape where guests are encouraged to enjoy the pleasant garden in the summer, real fires in the winter and the jacuzzi all year round. The two bedrooms and bathrooms are immaculately presented and comfortably furnished. Guests are also welcome to use the lounge.

Rooms 2 en suite (1 fmly) S £45–£55; D £65–£70✷ **Facilities** TVB tea/coffee Cen ht TVL Dinner **Parking** 3 **Notes LB** ⊗

★★★ GUEST ACCOMMODATION
Hermitage
Bath Rd SN13 8DT
☎ 01225 744187 📄 01225 743447
e–mail: hermitagebb@btconnect.com
dir: *On A4 at W end of village*

This 16th-century house is located in a pleasant village five miles from Bath. The spacious bedrooms are comfortably furnished, with two rooms in a small adjacent cottage. Breakfast is served in the dining room. There is also a lounge area, and delightful gardens with a heated swimming pool.

Rooms 3 en suite 2 annexe en suite (1 fmly) (1 GF) S £35–£45; D £55–£65✷ **Facilities** TVB tea/coffee Cen ht ₹ **Parking** 6 **Notes** ⊗ Closed 22 Dec–6 Jan 🍴

[U]
Lorne House
London Rd SN13 8NA
☎ 01225 742597
e–mail: info@lornehousebox.co.uk
web: www.lornehousebox.co.uk
dir: *On A4 in village, E of High St*

At the time of going to press the rating for this establishment had not been confirmed. Please check the AA website www.theAA.com for up-to-date information.

Rooms 4 en suite (2 fmly) S £40–£50; D £70–£80✷ **Facilities** FTV TVB tea/coffee Cen ht TVL Wi-fi available ⅃ **Parking** 6 **Notes** ⊗ Closed Xmas & New Year

BRADFORD-ON-AVON MAP 04 ST86

Premier Collection

★★★★★ 🛏 BED & BREAKFAST
Bradford Old Windmill

4 Masons Ln BA15 1QN
☎ 01225 866842 📄 01225 866648
e–mail: aa@bradfordoldwindmill.co.uk

dir: *300yds N of town centre off A363. Driveway on E side of Masons Ln, no sign or number*

This unique property has been restored to retain many original features. Bedrooms are individually decorated, and include a number of interesting options such as a round room, a waterbed or a suite with minstrels' gallery. An extensive breakfast menu, featuring local and organic products whenever possible, offers a range of alternatives from devilled mushrooms or passion fruit pancakes to the more traditional choices. A comfortable lounge is also available.

Rooms 3 en suite (1 fmly) S £79–£99; D £79–£109 **Facilities** TVB tea/coffee Cen ht Dinner Last d previous day **Parking** 3 **Notes** ⊗ No children 6yrs Closed Dec–Jan RS Tue, Fri & Sun (Mar–Oct)

★★★★ ◉◉ INN
The Tollgate Inn

Ham Green, Holt BA14 6PX
☎ 01225 782326 📄 01225 782805
e–mail: alison@tollgateholt.co.uk
web: www.tollgateholt.co.uk

dir: *2m E on B3107, at W end of Holt village*

The Tollgate Inn combines the comforts of a traditional inn with excellent quality food served in delightful surroundings. It stands near the village green at Holt, and is only a short drive from Bath. Bedrooms, varying in size, are well decorated and thoughtfully equipped with welcome extras.

Rooms 4 en suite S £50–£100; D £80–£100✱ **Facilities** TVB tea/coffee Direct dial from bedrooms Cen ht Dinner Last d 9.30pm Wi-fi available **Conf** Max 30 Thtr 36 Board 30 Del from £100 ✱ **Parking** 40 **Notes** ⊗ No children 16yrs No coaches

★★★★ BED & BREAKFAST
Home Farm

Farleigh Rd, Wingfield BA14 9LG
☎ 01225 764492 📄 01225 764492
e–mail: info@homefarm-guesthouse.co.uk

dir: *2m S in Wingfield village on A366*

This delightful former farmhouse offers comfortable, well-equipped accommodation. Guests are assured of a warm welcome, and are free to use the charming gardens, which have wonderful views over farmland. A full English breakfast is served at individual tables.

Rooms 3 en suite (1 fmly) (1 GF) **Facilities** TVB tea/coffee Cen ht TVL **Parking** 30 **Notes** ⊗

★★★★ BED & BREAKFAST
Midway Cottage

Farleigh Wick BA15 2PU
☎ 01225 863932
e–mail: midwaycottage@btinternet.com
web: www.midwaycottage.co.uk

dir: *2m NW of Bradford on A363, next to Fox & Hounds pub*

A warm welcome is assured at this delightful Victorian cottage, located near Bradford-on-Avon and Bath. The comfortable bedrooms are equipped with a variety of thoughtful extras, and there is a pleasant garden. Breakfast is served around a communal table in the lounge-dining room.

Rooms 3 en suite (1 GF) **Facilities** TVB tea/coffee Cen ht TVL **Parking** 3 **Notes** ⊗ No children 5yrs Closed Xmas–5 Jan

★★★★ BED & BREAKFAST
Serendipity

19f Bradford Rd, Winsley BA15 2HW
☎ 01225 722380
e–mail: vanda.shepherd@tesco.net

dir: *A36 onto B3108, 1.5m right into Winsley, establishment on right on main road*

Set in a quiet residential area, Serendipity is convenient for visiting nearby Bath. The proprietors are friendly and welcoming, and bedrooms are brightly decorated and equipped with a range of extras. Two are on the ground floor. Guests can watch badgers and local wildlife in the gardens during the evening. Breakfast is served in the conservatory overlooking the garden.

Rooms 3 en suite (1 fmly) (2 GF) S £40–£62; D £49–£64 **Facilities** FTV TVB tea/coffee Cen ht Wi-fi available 🐾 **Parking** 5 **Notes** LB ⊗ 🐾

★★ 🅰 BED & BREAKFAST
Conifers
4 King Alfred Way, Winsley BA15 2NG
☎ 01225 722482

dir: *A363 onto B3108 2m, 2nd left onto Dane Rise, 2nd right*

Rooms 2 rms S £25–£30; D £45–£50✶ **Facilities** TV1B tea/coffee
Cen ht TVL **Parking** 4 **Notes** ⊛

CHIPPENHAM   MAP 04 ST97

★★★ BED & BREAKFAST
Diana Lodge Bed & Breakfast
Grathie Cottage, 72 Marshfield Rd SN15 1JR
☎ 01249 650306
e–mail: apple@onetel.net

dir: *500yds NW of town centre on A420, into West End Club car park*

A cheerful welcome awaits guests at this late 19th-century cottage, within walking distance of the town centre and the railway station. Comfortable bedrooms are well decorated and adjacent car parking is available.

Rooms 4 rms (2 en suite) (4 fmly) (1 GF) **Facilities** TVB tea/coffee
Cen ht TVL **Parking** available **Notes** ⊗

CORSHAM   MAP 04 ST87

★★★★ BED & BREAKFAST
Thurlestone Lodge
13 Prospect SN13 9AD
☎ 01249 713397 & 07815 731131
e–mail: v_ogilvie_robb@hotmail.com
web: www.thurlestone.webeden.co.uk

dir: *0.25m from Corsham Centre on B3353. 150yds on right after Great Western pub halfway between turnings to Lypiatt Rd & Dicketts Rd*

This charming Victorian house is delightfully located in the attractive town of Corsham, convenient for the countryside and attractions of the Cotswolds and Bath areas. Bedrooms are comfortable, spacious and well appointed. Breakfast is served in the spacious dining room and provides a hearty start to the day.

Rooms 2 en suite (1 fmly) S £48–£58; D £60–£70✶ **Facilities** TVB tea/coffee Cen ht Wi-fi available **Parking** 5 **Notes** ⊗ Closed Xmas & New Year RS 22 Dec–2 Jan ⊛

★★★★ FARM HOUSE
Pickwick Lodge Farm *(ST857708)*
Guyers Ln SN13 0PS
☎ 01249 712207 📄 01249 701904 Mrs G Stafford
e–mail: b&b@pickwickfarm.co.uk
web: www.pickwickfarm.co.uk

dir: *Off A4, Bath side of Corsham, onto Guyers Ln, farmhouse at end on right*

This Grade II listed, 17th-century farmhouse is peacefully located on a 300-acre beef and arable farm, within easy reach of Bath. The spacious bedrooms are well-equipped with modern facilities and many thoughtful extras. A hearty breakfast using the best local produce is served at a communal table in the dining room.

Rooms 3 rms (2 en suite) (1 pri facs) D £65–£70✶ **Facilities** FTV TVB tea/coffee Cen ht TVL Wi-fi available Fishing **Parking** 6 **Notes** LB ⊗ No children 12yrs 300 acres arable beef ⊛

CRICKLADE   MAP 05 SU09

★★★ BED & BREAKFAST
Upper Chelworth Farm
Upper Chelworth SN6 6HD
☎ 01793 750440

dir: *1.5m W of Cricklade. Off B4040 x-rds for Chelworth Upper Green*

Close to the M4 and Swindon, Upper Chelworth Farm offers a genuinely friendly welcome in addition to comfortable bedrooms of varying sizes. There is a spacious lounge with a wood-burning stove, games room with a pool table, and a lovely garden. Breakfast is served in the dining room.

Rooms 7 rms (6 en suite) (1 fmly) **Facilities** TV6B tea/coffee Cen ht TVL Pool Table **Parking** 10 **Notes** No children 5yrs Closed mid Dec–mid Jan ⊛

DEVIZES
MAP 04 SU06

★★★★★ 🛏 BED & BREAKFAST

Blounts Court Farm

Coxhill Ln, Potterne SN10 5PH

☎ 01380 727180

e–mail: carys@blountscourtfarm.co.uk

dir: *A360 to Potterne, turn onto Coxhill Ln opp George & Dragon, at fork turn left and follow drive to farmhouse*

A warm welcome is assured at this delightful arable farm, overlooking the village cricket field. The barn and cider press have been converted to provide three attractive bedrooms on the ground floor, one of which has a four-poster bed. The elegant decor is in keeping with the exposed beams and character of the house. Breakfast, which features home-made and local produce, is served in the farmhouse dining room.

Rooms 3 en suite (3 GF) S £36–£42; D £58–£70✳ **Facilities** TVB tea/coffee Cen ht TVL Wi-fi available **Parking** 20 **Notes** ✖ No children 8yrs

★★★★ 🅰 BED & BREAKFAST

Glebe House

Chittoe SN15 2EL

☎ 01380 850864 📠 01380 850189

e–mail: gscrope@aol.com

web: www.glebehouse-chittoe.co.uk

dir: *Off A342 to Chittoe & Spye Park, over x-rds, 2nd house on left*

Rooms 3 rms (1 GF) **Facilities** tea/coffee Cen ht TVL Dinner Last d 9pm Fishing Riding **Parking** 4 **Notes** ✖ No children 8yrs Closed Xmas & New Year 📧

★★★ GUEST ACCOMMODATION

Littleton Lodge

Littleton Panell (A360), West Lavington SN10 4ES

☎ 01380 813131 📠 01380 816969

e–mail: stay@littletonlodge.co.uk

web: www.littletonlodge.co.uk

dir: *On A360 in Littleton Panell*

Convenient for Stonehenge and for touring the many attractions of this pleasant area, Littleton Lodge offers spacious and comfortable accommodation and a relaxed friendly atmosphere. Breakfast is served in the stylish dining room and freshly cooked dishes provide a pleasant start to the day.

Rooms 3 en suite **Facilities** TVB tea/coffee Cen ht Golf **Parking** 4 **Notes** ✖

DINTON
MAP 04 SU03

★★★★ 🅰 FARM HOUSE

Marshwood Farm B&B *(SU005327)*

SP3 5ET

☎ 01722 716334 Mrs F J Lockyer

e–mail: marshwood1@btconnect.com

dir: *A30 onto B3089 into Dinton, turn right to Wylye, B&B 0.5m on left*

Rooms 2 en suite (1 fmly) S £40–£65; D £55–£65 **Facilities** TVB tea/coffee Cen ht 🛎 **Parking** 4 **Notes** LB ✖ 580 acres Arable/sheep

FIRSDOWN
MAP 05 SU23

★★★★ BED & BREAKFAST

Junipers

3 Juniper Rd SP5 1SS

☎ 01980 862330

e–mail: junipersbedandbreakfast@btinternet.com

web: www.junipersbedandbreakfast.co.uk

dir: *5m from Salisbury on A30, A343 to London follow Junipers brown signs into Firsdown*

Located in a quiet residential area, just five miles from the city, this homely accommodation is located at ground floor level. Bedrooms are well equipped with thoughtful extras. The hosts, who have craft skills, are happy to show guests their interesting items constructed in medieval style. Breakfast, featuring local produce, is served in the cosy dining room/lounge.

Rooms 3 en suite (3 GF) D £60–£65 **Facilities** TVB tea/coffee Cen ht **Parking** 6 **Notes** LB ✖ No children

FONTHILL BISHOP
MAP 04 ST93

★★★ GUEST HOUSE

The River Barn

SP3 5SF

☎ 01747 820232

dir: *Off A303 to Tisbury/Fonthill Bishop. 1m to junct then right onto B3089, 100yds on left*

Surrounded by lawns stretching down the river, The River Barn is the central hub of the village of Fonthill Bishop. Parts of the barn are 600

CONTINUED

years old and it has operated as a business for the last 100 years. The annexe bedrooms are spacious and well appointed. The café-bar offers sumptuous cakes and cream teas, light lunches and evening meals.

Rooms 4 annexe en suite (1 fmly) (3 GF) S £40–£50; D £60–£65✳ **Facilities** TVB tea/coffee Licensed Cen ht Dinner Last d day before **Parking** 20 **Notes LB** No coaches

GRITTLETON　　　　　　　MAP 04 ST88

★★ BED & BREAKFAST
Staddlestones
SN14 6AW

☎ 01249 782458 🖹 01249 782458

e–mail: staddlestonesbb@btinternet.com

dir: *500yds E of village x-rds*

The large modern bungalow lies at the east end of the small village, and is convenient for the M4. The local pub is just a stroll away and ample parking is available.

Rooms 3 rms (3 GF) S £35–£70; D £50–£80✳ **Facilities** TVB tea/coffee Cen ht TVL **Parking** 5 **Notes** ⊛

HIGHWORTH　　　　　　　MAP 05 SU29

Premier Collection
★★★★★ ⊛⊛ 🛎 RESTAURANT WITH ROOMS
Jesmonds of Highworth
Jesmond House SN6 7HJ

☎ 01793 762364 🖹 01793 861201

e–mail: info@jesmondsofhighworth.com

web: www.jesmondsofhighworth.com

dir: *A419 onto B4019 to Highworth, left at lights, establishment on left*

Jesmonds offers high quality bedrooms and bathrooms in addition to a contemporary restaurant providing memorable cuisine. The young team of staff here offer an effortless mix of professional service delivered in a relaxed and welcoming manner. In addition to a comfortable bar and separate lounge, guests are encouraged to enjoy the pleasant Zen-inspired rear garden with water feature. Head Chef William Guthrie and his team utilise high quality produce with a skilful combination of textures and flavours.

Rooms 10 en suite (2 fmly) **Facilities** FTV TVB tea/coffee Direct dial from bedrooms Cen ht Dinner Last d 9.15pm Wi-fi available **Conf** Class 18 Board 24 **Parking** 20 **Notes** ⊛ RS Mon

★★★★ GUEST HOUSE
Highlands of Highworth
1 Swindon Rd SN6 7DE

☎ 01793 765131

e–mail: highlandsofhighworth@yahoo.co.uk

dir: *A361 from Swindon, after Shell garage, last house on left before rdbt*

Conveniently located on the edge of Highworth, this detached accommodation offers a range of very well decorated and equipped bedrooms including one on the ground floor. Extras such as free Wi-fi in rooms are welcome features. Ample car parking is provided, and a good selection of pubs and restaurants are within easy walking distance.

Rooms 4 en suite (1 GF) S £30; D £55–£60✳ **Facilities** FTV TVB tea/coffee Cen ht TVL Wi-fi available **Parking** 6 **Notes LB** ⊛ No children 12yrs No coaches

HINDON　　　　　　　MAP 04 ST93

★★★★ INN
The Lamb Inn
SP3 6DP

☎ 01747 820573 🖹 01747 820605

e–mail: manager@lambathindon.co.uk

dir: *Off B3089 in village centre*

The 17th-century coaching inn is in a pretty village within easy reach of Salisbury and Bath. It has been refurbished in an eclectic style, and some of the well-equipped bedrooms have four-poster beds. Enjoyable, freshly prepared dishes are available at lunch and dinner in the restaurant or bar, where log fires provide a welcoming atmosphere on colder days.

Rooms 14 en suite (1 fmly) S £70; D £99–£135✳ **Facilities** STV TVB tea/coffee Direct dial from bedrooms Cen ht Dinner Last d 9.30pm **Conf** Max 40 Thtr 40 Class 16 Board 24 Del from £100 ✳ **Parking** 16 **Notes LB**

LACOCK   MAP 04 ST96

★★★★ ⬭ 🍴 GUEST ACCOMMODATION
At the Sign of the Angel
6 Church St SN15 2LB
☎ 01249 730230 📠 01249 730527
e–mail: angel@lacock.co.uk
web: www.lacock.co.uk
dir: *Off A350 into Lacock, follow Local Traffic Sign*

Visitors will be impressed by the character of this 15th-century former wool merchant's house, set in the National Trust village of Lacock. Bedrooms come in a range of sizes and styles including the atmospheric rooms in the main house and others in an adjacent new building. Excellent dinners and breakfasts are served in the beamed dining rooms, and there is also a first-floor lounge and a pleasant rear garden.

Rooms 6 en suite 5 annexe en suite (1 fmly) (4 GF) S £72–£85; D £132–£155✶ **Facilities** FTV TVB tea/coffee Direct dial from bedrooms Cen ht Dinner Last d 9pm **Conf** Max 14 Board 14 **Parking** 7 **Notes** Closed 23–30 Dec RS Mon (ex BHs) Civ Wed 25

★★★★ 🅰 GUEST ACCOMMODATION
The Old Rectory
Cantax Hill SN15 2JZ
☎ 01249 730335 📠 01249 730166
e–mail: sexton@oldrectorylacock.co.uk
web: www.oldrectorylacock.co.uk
dir: *A350 S from Chippenham , left at lights into Lacock, The Old Rectory 1st on right*

Rooms 6 rms (4 en suite) (2 pri facs) (2 fmly) (1 GF) S £40–£70; D £70–£80✶ **Facilities** TVB tea/coffee Cen ht TVL Wi-fi available ⬭ **Conf** Max 20 Board 14 **Parking** 8 **Notes** LB No children 10yrs Closed 24–26 Dec

LANDFORD   MAP 05 SU21

★★★★ GUEST ACCOMMODATION
New Forest Lodge
Southampton Rd SP5 2ED
☎ 01794 390999 📠 01794 390066
e–mail: info@newforestlodge.co.uk
A well established, purpose built property on the A36 Salisbury to Southampton road with good parking. Rooms are bright and spacious with extremely comfortable beds, and bathrooms are modern and well equipped.

Rooms 14 en suite (6 fmly) (6 GF) **Facilities** TVB tea/coffee Direct dial from bedrooms Cen ht TVL Dinner Last d 11pm Wi-fi available **Parking** 35

LOWER CHICKSGROVE   MAP 04 ST92

★★★★ ❀ INN
Compasses Inn
SP3 6NB
☎ 01722 714318 📠 01722 714318
e–mail: thecompasses@aol.com
web: www.thecompassesinn.com

dir: *Off A30 signed Lower Chicksgrove, 1st left onto Lagpond Ln, single-track lane to village*

This charming 17th-century inn, within easy reach of Bath, Salisbury, Glastonbury and the Dorset coast, offers comfortable accommodation in a peaceful setting. Carefully prepared dinners are enjoyed in the warm atmosphere of the bar-restaurant, while breakfast is served in a separate dining room.

Rooms 5 en suite (1 fmly) S £65–£90; D £85–£90 **Facilities** FTV TVB tea/coffee Cen ht Dinner Last d 9.30pm **Conf** Max 14 **Parking** 40 **Notes** LB Closed 25–26 Dec

MALMESBURY   MAP 04 ST98

★★★★ 🅰 FARM HOUSE
Lovett Farm *(ST975850)*
Little Somerford SN15 5BP
☎ 01666 823268 & 07808 858612 📠 01666 823268
Mrs S Barnes
e–mail: sue@lovettfarm.co.uk
web: www.lovettfarm.co.uk
dir: *3m from Malmesbury on B4042 opp 2nd turning to the Somerfords*

Rooms 2 en suite S £30–£50; D £60–£70✶ **Facilities** TVB tea/coffee Cen ht **Parking** 4 **Notes** ⊗ No children 12yrs 75 acres Beef

MERE	MAP 04 ST83

★★★★ GUEST ACCOMMODATION
Chetcombe House
Chetcombe Rd BA12 6AZ
☎ 01747 860219 📄 01747 860111
e–mail: mary.butchers@lineone.net
dir: *Off A303*

Chetcombe House has wonderful views across an acre of well-tended gardens towards Gillingham and the Blackmore Vale. The house, built in 1937, provides elegance and charm, and is pleasantly spacious, comfortable and fresh. The bedrooms are well equipped and are provided with many extra facilities. Breakfast is served in the attractive dining room, which overlooks the rear garden.

Rooms 5 en suite (1 fmly) S £45; D £60✶ **Facilities** TVB tea/coffee Cen ht Wi-fi available **Parking** 10 **Notes** ⊗ Closed Xmas & New Year ⊜

★★★ INN
The George Inn
The Square BA12 6DR
☎ 01747 860427
e–mail: una.white@btconnect.com
web: www.thegeorgeinnmere.co.uk

dir: *A303 junct signed Mere. Centre of town, opposite clock tower*
In the heart of Mere, just off the A303, The George Inn is a traditional country pub with rooms, complete with many original features, including stone walls, flag floors and a huge open fireplace. Dining is in the bar, richly decorated restaurant or alfresco during the summer. Choose from traditional home made offerings such as delicious soups, pie of the day or locally reared lamb and beef dishes.

Rooms 7 en suite (3 fmly) S fr £45; D fr £65✶ **Facilities** TVB tea/coffee Cen ht Dinner Last d 8.30pm **Conf** Max 40 **Notes** ⊗

NETTLETON	MAP 04 ST87

★★★★ ⊜ BED & BREAKFAST
Fosse Farmhouse Chambre d'Hote
Nettleton Shrub SN14 7NJ
☎ 01249 782286 📄 01249 783066
e–mail: caroncooper@compuserve.com
web: www.fossefarmhouse.com

dir: *1.5m N from Castle Combe on B4039, left at Gib, 1m on right*
Set in quiet Wiltshire countryside close to Castle Combe, this guest house has well-equipped bedrooms decorated in keeping with its 18th-century origins. Excellent dinners are served in the farmhouse, and cream teas can be enjoyed in the old stables or the delightful garden.

Rooms 3 en suite (1 fmly) S £65–£70; D £90–£140✶ **Facilities** TVB tea/coffee Cen ht Dinner Last d 8.30pm Golf 18 **Conf** Max 15 Thtr 10 Class 10 Board 10 Del from £110 ✶ **Parking** 12 **Notes LB**

PURTON	MAP 05 SU08

Premier Collection
★★★★★ ⌂ GUEST ACCOMMODATION
The Old Farmhouse
Bagbury Ln, Restrop SN5 4LX
☎ 01793 770130
e–mail: stay@theoldfarmhouse.net
web: www.theoldfarmhouse.net

dir: *M4 junct 16, signs for Purton, right at 1st x-rds, Bagbury Ln 1st left*

The Old Farmhouse's tranquil countryside location is convenient for the motorway and close to Swindon centre. Each bedroom is individually styled, comfortably furnished and includes a host of facilities and thoughtful extras. The proprietors are most friendly and attentive, and an impressive continental breakfast is served in each room. Guests will enjoy the private, nine-hole golf course and a recently completed spa with hot tub and treatments.

Rooms 6 annexe en suite (4 GF) D £85–£180✶ **Facilities** TVB tea/coffee Direct dial from bedrooms Cen ht Golf 9 Sauna ♨ Hot tub, Beauty & treatments **Parking** 20 **Notes LB** ⊗ No children

ENGLAND

REDLYNCH   MAP 05 SU22

★★★ BED & BREAKFAST

Rookseat B&B

Grove Ln SP5 2NR

☎ 01725 512522

e-mail: deanransome@btinternet.com

Expect a friendly welcome at this family-run bed and breakfast situated in the quiet New Forest village of Redlynch, perfect for visiting Salisbury and Bournemouth. Comfortable bedrooms all have en suite shower rooms. A delicious breakfast with plenty of choice is served in the dining room.

Rooms 3 en suite **Facilities** TVB tea/coffee Cen ht **Parking** 3 **Notes** ⊗ No children 12yrs

ROWDE   MAP 04 ST96

★★★★ ⊛⊛ RESTAURANT WITH ROOMS

The George & Dragon

High St SN10 2PN

☎ 01380 723053

e-mail: thegandd@tiscali.co.uk

dir: 1.5m from Devizes on A350 towards Chippenham

The George & Dragon dates back to the 14th century when it was a meeting house. Exposed beams, wooden floors, antique rugs and open fires create a warm atmosphere in the bar and restaurant. Bedrooms and bathrooms are very well decorated and equipped with some welcome extras. Dining in the bar or restaurant should not be missed, as local produce and fresh fish deliveries from Cornwall are offered from the daily-changing blackboard menu.

Rooms 3 rms (2 en suite) (1 pri facs) (1 fmly) D fr £75✶ **Facilities** TVB tea/coffee Cen ht Dinner Last d 10pm **Parking** 15 **Notes** ⊗

SALISBURY   MAP 05 SU12

See also Amesbury & Stoford

★★★★ GUEST ACCOMMODATION

St Anns House

32–34 Saint Ann St SP1 2DP

☎ 01722 335657

e-mail: info@stannshouse.co.uk

web: www.stannshouse.co.uk

dir: From Brown St turn left onto Saint Ann St

St Ann's House is a newly refurbished former public house close to the Cathedral and city centre. Lovingly restored with many original features and modern creature comforts such as flat screen televisions, this is a high quality operation with a friendly host.

Rooms 8 en suite S £65–£75; D £90–£120 **Facilities** FTV TVB tea/coffee Cen ht TVL Wi-fi available **Conf** Max 30 Thtr 18 Class 18 Board 18 **Notes** ⊗ No children 9yrs Closed 23 Dec–2 Jan

★★★★ BED & BREAKFAST

Salisbury Old Mill House

Warminster Rd, South Newton SP2 0QD

☎ 01722 742458

e-mail: salisburymill@yahoo.com

dir: 4m NW of Salisbury on A36 in South Newton

This restored watermill exudes character, and the mill machinery is still on view. Friendly and welcoming, the property offers comfortable, well-appointed bedrooms, a lounge with wood-burning stove, and a dining area where delicious dinners are available by arrangement. The garden features the original millpond.

Rooms 4 en suite (1 fmly) S £30–£45; D £55–£85✶ **Facilities** TVB tea/coffee Cen ht Dinner Last d 24hr prior **Parking** 10 **Notes** ⊗ Closed 25 Dec & 1 Jan ⊛

★★★★ GUEST HOUSE

Websters

11 Hartington Rd SP2 7LG

☎ 01722 339779

e-mail: enquiries@websters-bed-breakfast.com

dir: From city centre onto A360 Devizes Rd, 1st turning on left

A warm welcome is assured at this delightful property, located in a quiet cul-de-sac close to the city centre. The charming, well-presented bedrooms are equipped with numerous extras including broadband. There is one ground-floor room with easier access.

Rooms 5 en suite (1 GF) S £40–£45; D £55–£60✶ **Facilities** TVB tea/coffee Cen ht TVL Wi-fi available **Parking** 5 **Notes LB** ⊗ No children 12yrs No coaches Closed 31 Dec & 1 Jan RS Xmas & New Year

★★★★ BED & BREAKFAST

Avonlea House

231 Castle Rd SP1 3RY

☎ 01722 338351

e-mail: guests@avonleahouse.co.uk

web: www.avonleahouse.co.uk

dir: 1.5m N of city centre. On A345 near Old Sarum

The Avonlea has very comfortable and well equipped bedrooms. Breakfast is offered with a choice of fresh local items. The property is located close to Old Sarum and within walking distance of Salisbury city centre for the Cathedral and riverside walks. There are leisure facilities close by in the shape of a swimming pool and gym, and there is easy access to Stonehenge, the New Forest and the South coast.

Rooms 3 en suite D £58.50–£65✶ **Facilities** TVB tea/coffee Cen ht Wi-fi available **Parking** 3 **Notes** ⊗ No children 12yrs Closed Xmas & New Year

★★★★ GUEST ACCOMMODATION
Cathedral View

83 Exeter St SP1 2SE

☎ 01722 502254

e–mail: wenda.rampton@btopenworld.com

dir: *200yds E of cathedral. Off A338 ring road onto Exeter St, signs for Old George Mall*

The friendly home has views of the cathedral, which is just a two minute walk away, and provides attractive refurbished bedrooms with numerous thoughtful extras. Breakfast is a good selection served around one large table in the dining room.

Rooms 4 en suite (1 fmly) D £75 **Facilities** FTV TVB tea/coffee Cen ht Wi-fi available **Notes** ⊗ No children 10yrs ☜

★★★★ GUEST ACCOMMODATION
Cricket Field House

Skew Bridge, Wilton Rd SP2 9NS

☎ 01722 322595 📄 01722 322595

e–mail: cricketfieldcottage@btinternet.com

web: www.cricketfieldhouse.co.uk

dir: *A36 W of Salisbury, towards Wilton and Warminster*

The 19th-century gamekeeper's cottage stands in award-winning gardens overlooking the South Wiltshire Cricket Ground. Within walking distance of the city centre and railway station, Cricket Field House provides a high level of accommodation, hospitality and customer care.

Rooms 7 en suite 10 annexe en suite (1 fmly) (10 GF) S £50–£75; D £65–£95✱ **Facilities** FTV TVB tea/coffee Cen ht Wi-fi available **Conf** Thtr 20 Class 14 Board 16 **Parking** 25 **Notes** ⊗ No children 14yrs RS 24–26 Dec

★★★★ GUEST HOUSE
The Edwardian Lodge

59 Castle Rd SP1 3RH

☎ 01722 413329 📄 01722 503105

e–mail: enquiries@edwardianlodge.co.uk

web: www.edwardianlodge.co.uk

dir: *0.5m N of city centre on A345. Turn onto Victoria Rd to car park*

Located close to the city centre, this fine Edwardian home is convenient for the many nearby places of interest. It has spacious, comfortably

CONTINUED

furnished and well-equipped bedrooms, some located on the ground floor. Breakfast is served in the conservatory.

Rooms 8 en suite (1 fmly) (3 GF) S £42–£50; D £60–£70✱ **Facilities** TVB tea/coffee Cen ht Wi-fi available **Parking** 7 **Notes** ⊗ Closed 20–28 Dec

★★★★ FARM HOUSE
Newton Farmhouse *(SU230223)*

Southampton Rd SP5 2QL

☎ 01794 884416 Mr & Mrs Guild

e–mail: lizzie@newtonfarmhouse.com

web: www.newtonfarmhouse.com

(For full entry see Whiteparish)

★★★★ GUEST ACCOMMODATION
The Old House

161 Wilton Rd SP2 7JQ

☎ 01722 333433 📄 01722 335551

dir: *1m W of city centre on A36*

Located close to the city centre, this non-smoking property dates from the 17th century. Bedrooms have modern facilities and one room has a four-poster bed. There is a spacious lounge, cosy cellar bar, and large gardens to enjoy – weather permitting.

Rooms 7 en suite (1 fmly) S £38–£60; D £60–£65✱ **Facilities** TVB tea/coffee Cen ht TVL **Parking** 10 **Notes LB** ⊗ No children 7yrs

★★★★ GUEST ACCOMMODATION
2 Park Lane

2 Park Ln SP1 3NP

☎ 01722 321001

web: www.2parklane.co.uk

A stylish period property that has been completely renovated within walking distance of the city centre and its attractions. Light, airy rooms, comfortable beds and good off-road parking are available.

Rooms 6 en suite D £70–£85 **Facilities** FTV TVB tea/coffee Cen ht Wi-fi available **Parking** 6 **Notes** ⊗ No children 6yrs

★★★★ 🅰 BED & BREAKFAST
Wyndham Park Lodge

51 Wyndham Rd SP1 3AB

☎ 01722 416517 📄 01722 328851

e–mail: enquiries@wyndhamparklodge.co.uk

dir: *Off A36 S onto Castle St towards city centre, 2nd left*

Rooms 3 en suite 1 annexe en suite (1 fmly) (1 GF) S £40–£45; D £55–£60✱ **Facilities** FTV TVB tea/coffee Cen ht Wi-fi available **Parking** 3 **Notes** ⊗ Closed Xmas & New Year

SALISBURY CONTINUED

★★★ GUEST ACCOMMODATION
City Lodge

33 Milford St SP1 2AP

☎ 01722 326600 📠 01722 338686

e–mail: info@citylodge.biz

Citylodge offers excellent value lodge style accommodation in a converted 15th-century Merchant House in the centre of Salisbury. Newly refurbished, with a wealth of original beams and features, the lodge also boasts free Wi-fi, flat screen digital TVs, and en suite bathrooms in all bedrooms. No meals are served, but friendly helpful staff are on hand to assist with dining recommendations.

Rooms 23 en suite (5 fmly) (5 GF) **Facilities** FTV TVB tea/coffee Cen ht Wi-fi available **Notes** ⊗

★★★ GUEST ACCOMMODATION
Byways Guest House

31 Fowlers Rd SP1 2QP

☎ 01722 328364 📠 01722 322146

e–mail: info@bywayshouse.co.uk

web: www.bywayshouse.co.uk

dir: *500yds E of city centre. A30 onto A36 signed Southampton, follow Youth Hostel signs to hostel, Fowlers Rd opp*

Located in a quiet street with off-road parking, Byways is within walking distance of the town centre. Several bedrooms have been decorated in a Victorian style and another two have four-poster beds. All rooms offer good levels of comfort, with one adapted for easier access.

Rooms 23 rms (19 en suite) (6 fmly) (13 GF) S £39–£60; D £55–£80✳
Facilities TVB tea/coffee Cen ht Wi-fi available **Conf** Max 8 **Parking** 15
Notes Closed Xmas & New Year

★★★ INN
Kings Head Inn

1 Bridge St SP1 2ND

☎ 01722 438400 📠 01722 326743

e–mail: salisburylodge@jdwetherspoon.co.uk

dir: *Off A30 Salisbury ring road, follow signs to train station, 300mtrs on right*

Centrally located, with some rooms overlooking the high street, this lodge offers a lively atmosphere with its popular Lloyds No.1 bar and extensive menus. The well-equipped bedrooms have a number of welcome extras. Some outdoor seating is available in the summer.

Rooms 32 en suite (3 fmly) (14 GF) **Facilities** TVB tea/coffee Direct dial from bedrooms Lift Cen ht Wi-fi available **Notes** ⊗

★★★ BED & BREAKFAST
Melbury House

46 Stonehenge Rd, Durrington SP4 8BP

☎ 01980 653151

e–mail: jwcw@freenet.co.uk

dir: *From A303 Countess Rd rdbt, take A345. At rdbt turn right signed Durrington 5yds, turn left onto Stonehenge Rd*

Melbury House is a traditional small bed and breakfast with warm, friendly hosts. Rooms are fresh and comfortable and it has a great location, handy for Stonehenge and Salisbury. Breakfast is at a family table and is freshly cooked to order – a good start to the day.

Rooms 2 rms (1 en suite) (1 pri facs) (2 fmly) (2 GF) **Facilities** TVB tea/coffee Cen ht **Parking** 4 **Notes** ⊗ No children 🐾

★★★ BED & BREAKFAST
Sarum Heights
289 Castle Rd SP1 3SB

☎ 01722 421596 & 07931 582357

e–mail: sarumheights@ntlworld.com

Sarum Heights is a large family home on the outskirts of the city with good off-road parking. Rooms are smart, clean and well appointed with quality beds and linen. Freshly-cooked breakfasts are served at a family table in the kitchen.

Rooms 3 rms (2 en suite) (1 pri facs) S £35–£45; D £55–£65
Facilities TVB tea/coffee Cen ht Wi-fi available **Parking** 3 **Notes LB** ⊗ ⊜

STAPLEFORD   MAP 05 SU03

★★★ BED & BREAKFAST
Oak Bluffs
4 Church Furlong SP3 4QE

☎ 01722 790663 & 07796 893502 📄 01722 790663

dir: *In village centre off B3083*

A warm and friendly welcome awaits you at this immaculately presented bungalow situated in a delightful village, complete with ancient church and many thatched properties. Well located for visiting Stonehenge, the well appointed bedroom has its own separate entrance, with lots of thoughtful extras provided. A couple of pubs are within walking distance.

Rooms 1 en suite (1 GF) S £35–£40; D £55–£60✷ **Facilities** TVB tea/coffee Cen ht **Parking** 1 **Notes** ⊗ ⊜

STOFORD   MAP 05 SU03

★★★ INN
The Swan Inn
Warminster Rd SP2 0PR

☎ 01722 790236

e–mail: info@theswanatstoford.co.uk

web: www.theswanatstoford.co.uk

dir: *On A36 in village centre*

This centrally located, family-run inn is ideal for touring the area. Good-sized bedrooms are available, and the newly refurbished bar and restaurant serve an excellent choice of meals with an emphasis on locally sourced produce. Other facilities include Wi-fi, private fishing on the river and a skittle alley.

Rooms 9 en suite (2 fmly) S fr £55; D fr £65✷ **Facilities** TVB tea/coffee Cen ht Dinner Last d 9.15pm Wi-fi available Fishing Pool Table Skittle alley **Conf** Thtr 40 Class 30 Board 20 **Parking** 70 **Notes** ⊗

STOURTON   MAP 04 ST73

★★★★ ⊜ INN
Spread Eagle Inn
Church Lawn BA12 6QE

☎ 01747 840587 📄 01747 840954

e–mail: enquiries@spreadeagleinn.com

web: www.spreadeagleinn.com

dir: *0.5m W off B3092 at entrance to Stourhead Gardens*

Set in the beautiful grounds of Stourhead House with its Palladian temples, lakes and vistas, the Spread Eagle is an impressive red brick building with a good reputation for simple, honest, locally-sourced food. In the bedrooms, National Trust antiques sit side by side with modern comforts. The large Georgian windows, low ceilings and uneven floors give the feel of a comfortable country house.

Rooms 5 en suite S £80; D £110✷ **Facilities** TVB tea/coffee Direct dial from bedrooms Cen ht Dinner Last d 9pm Wi-fi available **Conf** Max 30 Thtr 30 Board 20 **Notes LB** ⊗

SWINDON   MAP 05 SU18

Premier Collection
★★★★★ 🏛 GUEST ACCOMMODATION
The Old Farmhouse
Bagbury Ln, Restrop SN5 4LX

☎ 01793 770130

e–mail: stay@theoldfarmhouse.net

web: www.theoldfarmhouse.net

(For full entry see Purton)

SWINDON CONTINUED

★★★★ GUEST ACCOMMODATION
Ardecca

Fieldrise Farm, Kingsdown Ln, Blunsdon SN25 5DL
☎ 01793 721238 & 07791 120826
e-mail: chris-graham.ardecca@fsmail.net
web: www.ardecca-bedandbreakfast.co.uk

dir: Off A419 for Blunsdon & Swindon, onto B4019. Right at Cold Harbour pub, 1st on left

Ardecca is quietly located in sixteen acres of pastureland with easy access to Swindon and the Cotswolds. All rooms are on the ground floor and are well furnished and equipped. An especially friendly welcome is provided and freshly-cooked home-made dinners are available by arrangement. Arts and crafts workshops are available on site.

Rooms 4 rms (4 pri facs) (1 fmly) (4 GF) S £40; D £60✱ **Facilities** TVB tea/coffee Cen ht Dinner Last d prior notice needed Wi-fi available Art & Crafts workshops **Conf** Class 16 **Parking** 5 **Notes** ⊗ No children 6yrs ⊜

★★★★ GUEST HOUSE
The Old Post Office Guest House

Thornhill Rd, South Marston SN3 4RY
☎ 01793 823114 📄 01793 823441
e-mail: theoldpostofficeguesthouse@yahoo.co.uk
web: www.theoldpostofficeguesthouse.co.uk

dir: A420 onto Thornhill Rd at Gablecross rdbt 0.75m on left before Old Vicarage Lane

Sympathetically extended, this attractive property is about two miles from Swindon. Guests are welcomed by the enthusiastic owner, a professional opera singer with a wonderful sense of humour. The comfortable bedrooms vary in size, and all are equipped with numerous facilities. An extensive choice is offered at breakfast, freshly cooked using the best of local produce.

Rooms 5 en suite (1 fmly) **Facilities** FTV TVB tea/coffee Cen ht Wi-fi available **Parking** 6 **Notes** ⊗ No coaches

See advert on opposite page

★★★★ GUEST ACCOMMODATION
Portquin

Broadbush, Broad Blunsdon SN26 7DH
☎ 01793 721261
e-mail: portquin@msn.com

dir: A419 onto B4019 at Blunsdon signed Highworth, continue 0.5m

This friendly guest house near Swindon provides a warm welcome and views of the Lambourn Downs. The rooms vary in shape and size, with six in the main house and three in an adjacent annexe. Full English breakfasts are served at two large tables in the kitchen-dining area.

Rooms 6 en suite 3 annexe en suite (2 fmly) (4 GF) S £40–£45; D £50–£70 **Facilities** TVB tea/coffee Cen ht Wi-fi available **Conf** Max 20 Thtr 20 Class 20 Board 20 Del from £40 **Parking** 12

★★★★ INN
Tawny Owl

Queen Elizabeth Dr, Taw Hill SN25 1WP
☎ 01793 706770 📄 01793 706785
e-mail: tawnyowl@arkells.com

dir: 2.5m NW of town centre, signed from A419

Expect a genuinely friendly welcome from the staff at this modern inn on the north-west outskirts of Swindon. It has comfortable, well-equipped bedrooms and bathrooms. A varied selection of enjoyable home-cooked meals is on offer at dinner, and a range of Arkells ales and wines. A private function room is available.

Rooms 5 en suite (1 fmly) **Facilities** TVB tea/coffee Direct dial from bedrooms Cen ht TVL Dinner Last d 9pm Stairlift **Conf** Max 55 Thtr 55 Class 55 Board 55 **Parking** 75 **Notes** ⊗ RS Xmas/New Year Civ Wed 50

★★★ INN
Crown Inn

Ermin St SN3 4NL
☎ 01793 827530 📄 01793 831683
e-mail: thecrownstratton@arkells.com

dir: A419 onto B4006 Stratton St Margaret, left onto Ermin St

This popular inn, dating back to 1868, is situated in Stratton St Margaret near to Swindon centre and the M4. Public areas are furnished in traditional style with crackling log fires that add to the character of the place. Bedrooms are located within the main building and in a newer adjacent block.

CONTINUED

Crown Inn

Rooms 21 en suite (7 GF) **Facilities** STV TVB tea/coffee Direct dial from bedrooms Cen ht Dinner Last d 9.15pm Wi-fi available **Parking** 60 **Notes** No coaches

★★★ GUEST HOUSE
Fairview Guest House
52 Swindon Rd, Wootton Bassett SN4 8EU
☎ 01793 852283 📄 01793 848076
e–mail: fairview@woottonb.wanadoo.co.uk
web: http://fairviewguesthouse.mysite.orange.co.uk

dir: *On A3102 to Wootton Bassett, 1.25m from M4 junct 16 & 5m from Swindon centre*

Family-run property with easy access to the M4 and the town of Swindon. Bedrooms are between the main house and the bungalow annexe, and breakfast is served in an open-plan dining/sitting room with an open fire on cooler mornings.

Rooms 8 rms (3 en suite) 4 annexe rms (3 en suite) (1 annexe pri facs) (2 fmly) (4 GF) S £30–£38; D £48–£50✶ **Facilities** TVB tea/coffee Cen ht TVL Wi-fi available **Parking** 14 **Notes** LB ⊗ No coaches

★★★ GUEST ACCOMMODATION
Fir Tree Lodge
17 Highworth Rd, Stratton St Margaret SN3 4QL
☎ 01793 822372 📄 01793 822372
e–mail: info@firtreelodge.com

dir: *1.5m NE of town centre. A419 onto B4006 signed Stratton/ Town Centre, premises 200yds opp Rat Trap pub*

Fir Tree Lodge is a modern guest house offering a range of comfortable bedrooms including rooms on the ground floor. The resident proprietors provide a relaxed and friendly welcome. The guest house benefits from a large secure car park.

Rooms 12 en suite 2 annexe rms (2 annexe pri facs) (1 fmly) (5 GF) (2 smoking) S £35–£40; D £55–£60✶ **Facilities** FTV TVB tea/coffee Cen ht **Parking** 13

★★★ INN
Heart in Hand
43 High St, Blunsdon SN26 7AG
☎ 01793 721314 📄 01793 727026
e–mail: leppardsteve@aol.com
dir: *Off A419 at High St, 200yds on right*

Located in the village centre, this family-run inn offers a relaxed and friendly welcome together with a wide selection of home-cooked food. Bedrooms are spacious, well equipped and offer a number of useful extras. A pleasant patio and rear garden with seating is also available.

Rooms 4 en suite (1 fmly) **Facilities** TVB tea/coffee Cen ht Dinner Last d 9pm **Parking** 17 **Notes** ⊗

★★★ BED & BREAKFAST
Internos B & B
3 Turnpike Rd, Blunsdon SN26 7EA
☎ 01793 721496 📄 01793 721496
web: www.internos-bedandbreakfast.co.uk
dir: *4m N of Swindon. Alongside A419 access from Cold Harbour End*

Situated just off the A419 towards Cirencester, this establishment offers comfortable accommodation and a relaxed and friendly atmosphere. The gardens open onto a field, which is a haven for wildlife. Guests enjoy a freshly-cooked breakfast served in the dining room, and a cosy lounge is also available.

Rooms 3 rms (1 fmly) S £25–£27; D £45✶ **Facilities** FTV TVB tea/ coffee Cen ht TVL Wi-fi available **Parking** 6 **Notes** ⊗ 🐾

The Old Post Office Guest House
Thornhill Road, South Marston, Swindon SN3 4RY

This attractive property is about two miles from Swindon and makes an excellent base for touring the West Country. Guests are welcomed by the enthusiastic owners. The house has been in the Sansum family for four generations and Jackie Sansum is a professional opera singer with a wonderful sense of humour. The comfortable and prettily decorated en suite bedrooms – including one family room – vary in size, and all come with numerous facilities. An extensive, sumptuous choice is offered at breakfast. All dishes are freshly cooked using the best of local produce.

Tel: 01793 823114
Email: theoldpostofficeguesthouse@yahoo.co.uk
Website: theoldpostofficeguesthouse.co.uk

SWINDON CONTINUED

★★ INN
Saracens Head
High St, Highworth SN6 7AG
☎ 01793 762284 🖥 01793 767869
e-mail: arkells@arkells.com

dir: *5m NE of Swindon*

The Saracens Head stands on the main street of this pleasant market town, close to Swindon. It offers plenty of character, including a popular bar dating from 1828. A fine selection of real ales and home-cooked food are highlights. Bedrooms, which vary in size, are generally compact. A rear car park and a patio area are available.

Rooms 13 en suite (2 fmly) **Facilities** TVB tea/coffee Direct dial from bedrooms Cen ht Dinner Wi-fi available **Conf** Max 10 Thtr 10 Class 10 Board 10 **Parking** 30

TROWBRIDGE   MAP 04 ST85

★★★★ BED & BREAKFAST
Eastbrook Cottage
Hoopers Pool, Southwick BA14 9NG
☎ 01225 764403
e-mail: enquiries@eastbrookcottage.co.uk
web: www.eastbrookcottage.co.uk

dir: *2m SW of Trowbridge. Off A361 between Rode & Southwick*

This cottage, situated just off the main Frome road, offers fresh, smart accommodation. Although the bedrooms are not the most spacious, they are finished to a high level of quality and equipped with many thoughtful extras. To add to this, the host offers genuine hospitality and friendliness. Guests may not want to move from the wood-burning stove in the snug lounge. Breakfast, featuring local produce wherever possible, is enjoyed around a large oak table.

Rooms 3 rms (2 en suite) (1 pri facs) S £35–£45; D £60–£70✳ **Facilities** TVB tea/coffee Cen ht Wi-fi available **Parking** 5 **Notes** ⊗ No children 10yrs ⊜

★★★ 🅰 BED & BREAKFAST
Paxcroft Cottage
62B Paxcroft Cottages, Devizes Rd, Hilperton BA14 6JB
☎ 01225 765838
e-mail: paxcroftcottages@hotmail.com
web: www.paxcroftcottages.pwp.blueyonder.co.uk

dir: *2m NE of Trowbridge. On A361 near Paxcroft Farm, 0.5m from the Paxcroft Mead Estate*

Rooms 3 en suite (1 fmly) S £30–£35; D £50–£55✳ **Facilities** FTV TVB tea/coffee Cen ht TVL **Parking** 6 **Notes LB** ⊗ ⊜

★★ BED & BREAKFAST
Bridge House Bed & Breakfast
Canal Bridge, Semington BA14 6JT
☎ 01225 703281 & 706101 🖥 01225 790888
e-mail: jeanpayneDHPS@aol.com

dir: *3m NE of Trowbridge. Off A361 into Semington, over bridge, house on right*

The front garden of this charming house leads directly to the canal, which offers a wonderful opportunity for cyclists, dedicated ramblers and strollers, who may choose to travel to heritage towns such as Bradford-on-Avon. Bedrooms are pretty and well equipped. Breakfast, featuring home-made preserves, is served around a farmhouse table in the pleasant dining room, adjacent to the kitchen.

Rooms 4 rms S £27–£30; D £50–£54✳ **Facilities** TVB tea/coffee **Parking** 6 **Notes** ⊗ Closed 20 Dec–3 Jan ⊜

WARMINSTER   MAP 04 ST84

★★★★ BED & BREAKFAST
Deverill End
Sutton Veny BA12 7BY
☎ 01985 840356

dir: *2.5m SE of Warminster. Off A36 at Heytesbury rdbt to Sutton Veny, over x-rds, 200yds on left*

This farmside B&B is located midway between Bath and Salisbury and within easy reach of Stonehenge, Longleat and Stourhead, guests are made to feel at home and invited to share the spectacular southern views and pretty garden. Bedrooms are comfortable, well equipped and all on the ground floor. Breakfast features home-grown produce (when in season) and own free range eggs.

Rooms 3 en suite (3 GF) S £50–£65; D £65 **Facilities** TVB tea/coffee Cen ht **Parking** 4 **Notes** ⊗ No children 10yrs Closed Xmas & Jan ⊜

★★★★ INN
The George Inn
Longbridge Deverill BA12 7DG
☎ 01985 840396 🖥 01985 841333
web: www.thegeorgeinnlongbridgedeverill.co.uk

dir: *3m S on the A350*

The George Inn combines a friendly village pub atmosphere with modern well-equipped bedrooms, one of which has a four-poster bed. In addition to the pleasant bar/restaurant, there is a cosy first floor lounge and a pleasant river garden in which to enjoy a cool summer drink. There is an extensive menu available, featuring home-cooked dishes.

Rooms 11 en suite (5 fmly) S fr £65; D fr £85✳ **Facilities** TVB tea/coffee Direct dial from bedrooms Cen ht Dinner Last d 9.30pm **Conf** Max 120 Thtr 50 Class 50 Board 30 **Notes** ⊗ RS Xmas

★★★★ BED & BREAKFAST
The Granary Bed & Breakfast
Manor Farm, Upton Scudamore BA12 0AG
☎ 01985 214835 🖹 01985 214835

dir: *2m NW of Warminster. Off A350 into Upton Scudamore*

The Granary is located in the peaceful village of Upton Scudamore and has delightful country views. It offers ground-floor bedrooms, each with a private terrace, stylishly decorated with coordinated fabrics and comfortable furnishings. The many thoughtful extras include a fridge, and breakfast is served in your room.

Rooms 2 annexe en suite (2 GF) S fr £50; D £65✱ **Facilities** FTV TVB tea/coffee Cen ht Wi-fi available **Parking** 3 **Notes LB** ⊗ No children 8yrs Closed 20 Dec–3 Jan ⊛

★★★★ GUEST ACCOMMODATION
White Lodge
22 Westbury Rd BA12 0AW
☎ 01985 212378 🖹 01985 212378
e–mail: carol@lioncountry.co.uk

dir: *0.5m N of town centre. Off High St onto Portway signed Westbury, White Lodge 0.75m on left*

Situated on the outskirts of Warminster, this attractive house, with art deco features, is well placed for touring Wiltshire and Somerset. Individually styled bedrooms, which overlook well-tended grounds, are comfortable and well-appointed.

Rooms 3 rms (1 en suite) (2 pri facs) (1 fmly) S fr £50; D fr £68 **Facilities** TVB tea/coffee Cen ht **Parking** 8 **Notes** ⊗ No children 5yrs Closed Xmas RS Jan–Feb ⊛

★★★ ⊜ INN
The Dove Inn
Corton BA12 0SZ
☎ 01985 850109 🖹 01985 851041
e–mail: info@thedove.co.uk

dir: *5m SE of Warminster. Off A36 to Corton village*

This relaxing inn stands in the heart of a peaceful village. There are carefully furnished courtyard rooms and a conservatory, and in cooler months a roaring log fire accompanies the imaginative bar menu. Home-cooked dishes and a selection of real ales are highlights of any stay here.

Rooms 5 annexe en suite (1 fmly) (4 GF) **Facilities** TVB tea/coffee Cen ht Dinner Last d 9pm **Parking** 24

★★★★ BED & BREAKFAST
Brayford
Newton Ln SP5 2QQ
☎ 01794 884216
e–mail: reservations@brayford.org.uk

dir: *Off A36 at Newton x-rds onto Newton Ln towards Whiteparish, Brayford 150yds on right*

A genuine welcome awaits guests at this comfortable family home. Peacefully located with views over neighbouring farmland, the house is just a short drive off the A36. Suitable for business and leisure travellers, bedrooms are well equipped with many thoughtful extras. Guests are invited to relax in the lounge dining room, where a tasty breakfast is served.

Rooms 3 rms (2 pri facs) (1 fmly) (2 GF) S £35–£45; D £60–£65 **Facilities** FTV TVB tea/coffee Cen ht TVL Gymnasium **Parking** 2 **Notes** ⊗ Closed Xmas & New Year ⊛

★★★★ FARM HOUSE
Newton Farmhouse *(SU230223)*
Southampton Rd SP5 2QL
☎ 01794 884416 Mr & Mrs Guild
e–mail: lizzie@newtonfarmhouse.com
web: www.newtonfarmhouse.com

dir: *7m SE of Salisbury on A36, 1m S of A27 junct*

Dating back to the 16th century, this delightful farmhouse was gifted to Lord Nelson's family as part of the Trafalgar estate. The house has been thoughtfully restored and bedrooms, most with four-poster beds, have been adorned with personal touches. Delicious breakfasts are available in the relaxing conservatory. The pleasant gardens include an outdoor swimming pool.

Rooms 6 en suite 3 annexe en suite (2 fmly) (5 GF) S £55–£90; D £70–£110✱ **Facilities** TVB tea/coffee Cen ht TVL Wi-fi available 🌂 🐴 **Parking** 9 **Notes LB** ⊗ 2 acres Non-working

ENGLAND

WHITLEY   MAP 04 ST86

◉◉ [U]

The Pear Tree Inn
Top Ln SN12 8QX
☎ 01225 709131 📠 01225 702276
e–mail: peartreeinn@maypolehotels.com

At the time of going to press the rating for this establishment had not been confirmed. Please check the AA website www.theAA.com for up-to-date information.

Rooms 4 en suite 4 annexe en suite (2 fmly) (4 GF) S fr £75; D fr £110✱
Facilities FTV TVB tea/coffee Cen ht Dinner Last d 9.30pm **Parking** 45
Notes ⊗

WORCESTERSHIRE

ABBERLEY   MAP 10 SO76

★★★★ BED & BREAKFAST

Orleton Court B & B
WR6 6SU
☎ 01584 881248 📠 01584 881159
e–mail: pmspilsbury@aol.com

dir: *4m W of Abberley. A443 onto B4203 through Stanford Bridge, 1st right, 1m right into Orleton Court*

This Georgian farmhouse situated by the River Teme is part of a working hop farm. There are two comfortable en suite bedrooms. Hearty breakfasts are served in the parlour and a comfortable lounge is available. Coarse fishing, golf and shooting are available by arrangement.

Rooms 3 rms (2 en suite) (2 fmly) **Facilities** TV2B tea/coffee Cen ht
TVL Fishing **Parking** 20 **Notes** ⊗ ⊜

★★★ INN

The Manor Arms at Abberley
Netherton Ln WR6 6BN
☎ 01299 896507 📠 01299 896723
e–mail: info@themanorarms.co.uk
web: www.themanorarms.co.uk

dir: *Off the A443 at Abberley, leave A443 at Abberley, follow brown signs to Manor Arms*

The Manor Arms has been part of the village for over 300 years, and was originally owned by the Lord of the Manor. While a number of changes have been made to the interior of the inn over a period of years, it still retains much of its original status and interest. Bedrooms are individually furnished, and all offer en suite facility. The traditional lounge bar offers cask marque ales and a good choice of meals from bar snacks to an a la carte menu.

Rooms 10 en suite (1 fmly) (3 GF) S £45–£55; D £60–£70✱
Facilities TVB tea/coffee Direct dial from bedrooms Cen ht Dinner Last
d 9pm **Conf** Max 20 Del from £75 ✱ **Parking** 20 **Notes** LB

ALVECHURCH   MAP 10 SP07

★★★★ BED & BREAKFAST

Woodlands Bed and Breakfast
Coopers Hill B48 7BX
☎ 0121 445 6774 📠 0121 505 1801
e–mail: john.impey@gmail.com
web: www.woodlands-bed-and-breakfast.com

dir: *From Red Lion, Alvechurch, enter Tanyard Ln over canal, under railway. Woodlands 2nd on left*

Woodlands is set is 18 acres of delightful countryside with extensive gardens, a heated swimming pool (in season) and croquet lawn. A warm welcome is offered by John and Amanda your hosts. Bedrooms are spacious and comfortable, and a substantial breakfast is served in the elegant dining room. Situated within 10 miles of the centre of Birmingham and a short drive from Stratford and Warwick.

Rooms 3 en suite 1 annexe en suite (2 fmly) (1 GF) S fr £42; D fr £75✱
Facilities FTV TVB tea/coffee Cen ht Dinner Last d 9pm Wi-fi available
↖ Fishing Gymnasium ♨ Table Tennis **Parking** 10 **Notes** Closed Xmas/
Etr wks

ENGLAND

★★★ 🅰 FARM HOUSE
Alcott Farm *(SP056739)*
Icknield St, Weatheroak B48 7EH
☎ 01564 824051 🖹 01564 829799 Mrs J Poole
e–mail: alcottfarm@btinternet.com
web: www.alcottfarm.co.uk

dir: *2m NE of Alvechurch. M42 junct 3, A435 for Birmingham, left signed Weatheroak, left at x-rds down steep hill, left past pub, farm 0.5m on right up long driveway*

Rooms 4 en suite (1 GF) S £40; D £60 **Facilities** TVB tea/coffee Cen ht TVL Fishing **Parking** 20 **Notes** ⊗ No children 10yrs 66 acres Horses 🐾

ASTWOOD BANK   MAP 10 SP06

☆☆☆ BED & BREAKFAST
Corner Cottage
1194 Evesham Rd B96 6AA
☎ 01527 459122
e–mail: marilyn_alan1194@hotmail.co.uk

dir: *A441 through Astwood Bank, at T-lights*

Conveniently located just 12 miles from Stratford upon Avon, Marilyn and Alan offer a superb warm welcome into their Victorian home set in the pristine village of Astwood Bank. Rooms are compact but offer a comfortable stay. The walled garden can be enjoyed by all.

Rooms 3 rms (2 en suite) (1 pri facs) (3 fmly) D £45–£55✳
Facilities TVB tea/coffee Cen ht TVL **Parking** 3 **Notes LB** ⊗ 🐾

★★ BED & BREAKFAST
Orchard Farm
96 The Ridgeway B96 6LX
☎ 01527 892441

dir: *On the A441, approx 4m from Redditch, opposite The Why Not Inn*

Ideally located for the Cotswolds and Stratford-upon-Avon, this period house provides comfortable bedrooms equipped with a wealth of thoughtful extras which share a modern efficient bathroom. Comprehensive breakfasts are taken in a cosy dining room and a warm welcome is assured. No commercial vehicles or trailers please.

Rooms 2 rms S fr £30; D fr £60✳ **Facilities** TVB tea/coffee Cen ht TVL **Parking** 3 **Notes** 🐾

BECKFORD   MAP 10 SO93

★★★★ INN
The Beckford
Cheltenham Rd GL20 7AN
☎ 01386 881532 🖹 01386 882021
e–mail: norman@thebeckford.com

dir: *Off A46 nr junct Station Rd to Beckford*

Looking more like a country mansion than a typical inn, this is a superb Cotswold stone building with 18th-century origins. Comfortable accommodation is provided in the eight bedrooms and a good range of choices for dinner and breakfast is offered. The Beckford is a splendid venue for parties, weddings or conferences. The Garden Restaurant is well-appointed with 84 covers. A snug is available with a wall-mounted widescreen television, where you can watch your favourite sports or other programmes. There is ample parking surrounding this established property with disabled access.

Rooms 10 rms (8 en suite) (2 pri facs) S £50–£60; D £70–£100✳
Facilities TVB tea/coffee Direct dial from bedrooms Cen ht TVL Dinner Last d 9.40pm **Conf** Max 100 Thtr 100 Board 100 **Parking** 70 **Notes LB** ⊗ Civ Wed 60

551

ENGLAND

BEWDLEY   MAP 10 SO77

Premier Collection

★★★★★ 🛏 BED & BREAKFAST
Number Thirty
30 Gardners Meadow DY12 2DG
☎ 01299 402404 📠 01299 402404
e–mail: info@numberthirty.net

dir: *Off Load St/Bewdley bridge onto Severnside South, 2nd right*
A warm welcome is assured at this smart modern house, a short stroll
from the River Severn and Georgian town centre. Bedrooms are
luxuriously furnished and have lots of thoughtful extras.
Comprehensive breakfasts are taken in an attractive dining room
overlooking immaculate gardens and cricket ground and guests can
enjoy the game from a raised sun deck. A sumptuous guest lounge is
also available.

Rooms 4 rms (3 en suite) (1 pri facs) **Facilities** TVB tea/coffee Cen ht
TVL **Parking** 6 **Notes** ❸ No children 10yrs ⊛

★★★★ INN
The Mug House Inn
12 Severnside North DY12 2EE
☎ 01299 402543
e–mail: drew@mughousebewdley.co.uk
web: www.mughousebewdley.co.uk

dir: *In town centre on riverfront*

Located on the opposite side of the River Severn to Bewdley Rowing
Club, this 18th-century inn has been renovated to combine high
standards of comfort and facilities with the original features. Bedrooms
are thoughtfully furnished, there is a separate breakfast room, and
imaginative dinners are served in the restaurant.

Rooms 4 en suite 3 annexe en suite (2 fmly) (1 GF) S £60–£95;
D £75–£120✳ **Facilities** TVB tea/coffee Cen ht Dinner Last d 9pm Wi-fi
available **Notes** ❸ No coaches

★★★★ ⊜ INN
Royal Forester Country Inn
Callow Hill DY14 9XW
☎ 01299 266286
e–mail: contact@royalforesterinn.co.uk
www.royalforesterinn.co.uk
Located opposite The Wyre Forest on the town's outskirts, this inn
dates back to 1411 and has been sympathetically restored to provide
high standards of comfort. Stylish modern bedrooms are
complimented by smart bathrooms and equipped with many
thoughtful extras. Décor styles throughout the public areas highlight
the many retained period features and the restaurant serves
imaginative food featuring locally sourced produce.

Rooms 7 en suite (2 fmly) S £55–£75; D £79–£99✳ **Facilities** STV FTV
TVB tea/coffee Cen ht Dinner Last d 9.30pm Wi-fi available **Parking** 40
Notes LB No coaches

★★★ BED & BREAKFAST
Bank House
14 Lower Park DY12 2DP
☎ 01299 402652
e–mail: fleur.nightingale@virgin.net
web: www.bewdley-accommodation.co.uk

dir: *In town centre. From junct High St & Lax Ln, Bank House
after junct on left*
Once a private bank, this Victorian house retains many original features
and offers comfortable accommodation. The cosy dining room is the
setting for tasty English breakfasts served at one family table. Owner
Mrs Nightingale has a comprehensive knowledge of the town and its
history.

Rooms 4 rms (1 fmly) S £30–£32; D £54–£56✳ **Facilities** TVB tea/
coffee Cen ht **Parking** 2 **Notes** ❸ Closed 24–26 Dec RS 27–31 Dec ⊛

★★★ BED & BREAKFAST
Pewterers' House
Pewterers' Alley DY12 1AE
☎ 01299 401956
e–mail: pewterershouse@tiscali.co.uk
web: www.pewterershouse.co.uk

dir: *250yds NE of town centre. On B4190 E of bridge, opp Black
Boy Hotel*
A short walk from the River Severn and historic centre, this deceptively
spacious period cottage has been sympathetically renovated to provide
high standards of comfort and facilities. Bedrooms are equipped with a
wealth of thoughtful extras and efficient modern shower rooms.
Comprehensive breakfasts feature local produce and a warm welcome
is assured.

Rooms 3 rms (2 en suite) **Facilities** TVB tea/coffee Cen ht **Parking** 2
Notes ⊛

★★★ INN
Woodcolliers Arms

76 Welch Gate DY12 2AU
☎ 01299 400589 📄 01299 400589
e–mail: roger@woodcolliers.co.uk
web: www.woodcolliers.co.uk

dir: *Exit A456, follow road behind church and turn left into Welch Gate (B4190)*

Dating from before 1780, the Woodcolliers is a family-run establishment located in the renowned Georgian town of Bewdley. A traditional inn offering an interesting menu with both traditional British pub food and a speciality Russian menu. Accommodation is comfortable and rooms are well equipped.

Rooms 4 rms (3 en suite) (1 pri facs) S £25–£40; D £55–£90✳
Facilities TVB tea/coffee Cen ht Dinner Last d 9pm Sauna **Parking** 2
Notes LB No coaches

BROADWAY   MAP 10 SP03

Premier Collection

★★★★★ 🏛 BED & BREAKFAST
Mill Hay House

Snowshill Rd WR12 7JS
☎ 01386 852498 📄 01386 858038
e–mail: millhayhouse@aol.com
web: www.millhay.co.uk

dir: *0.7m S of Broadway towards Snowshill, house on right*

Set in three acres of immaculate grounds beside a medieval watermill, this impressive early 18th-century stone house has many original features complemented by quality décor, period furniture and works of art. The spacious bedrooms are filled with thoughtful extras and one has a balcony. Imaginative breakfasts are served in the elegant dining room and there is a spacious drawing room.

Rooms 3 en suite **Facilities** FTV TVB tea/coffee Direct dial from bedrooms Cen ht TVL Wi-fi available **Parking** 15 **Notes** ⊗ No children 12yrs

Premier Collection

★★★★★ ◉◉ RESTAURANT WITH ROOMS
Russell's

20 High St WR12 7DT
☎ 01386 853555 📄 01386 853555
e–mail: info@russellsofbroadway.com

dir: *Opposite village green*

Situated in the centre of a picturesque Cotswold village this restaurant with rooms is a great base for exploring local attractions. Bedrooms, each with their own character, boast superb quality, air conditioning and a wide range of extras for guests. Cuisine is a real draw with freshly-prepared local produce used with skill.

Rooms 4 en suite 3 annexe en suite (4 fmly) **Facilities** STV TV3B tea/coffee Direct dial from bedrooms Cen ht Dinner Last d 9.30pm
Conf Max 12 Board 12 **Parking** 16

★★★★ FARM HOUSE
Bowers Hill Farm *(SP086420)*

Bowers Hill, Willersey WR11 7HG
☎ 01386 834585 & 07966 171861
📄 01386 830234 Mr & Mrs M Bent
e–mail: sarah@bowershillfarm.com
web: www.bowershillfarm.com

dir: *3m NW of Broadway. A44 onto B4632 to Willersey, at mini rdbt signs to Badsey/industrial estate, farm 2m on right by postbox*

An impressive Victorian house set in immaculate gardens on a diverse farm, where point-to-point horses are also bred. The house has been renovated to provide very comfortable bedrooms with modern bathrooms. Breakfast is served in the elegant dining room or the magnificent conservatory, and a lounge with open fire is also available.

Rooms 3 en suite (1 fmly) S £40–£50; D £65–£75 **Facilities** TVB tea/coffee Cen ht TVL Wi-fi available **Conf** Max 8 Class 8 Board 8 **Parking** 5 **Notes LB** ⊗ 40 acres horse breeding, grassland

★★★★ GUEST ACCOMMODATION
Leasow House

Laverton Meadows WR12 7NA
☎ 01386 584526 📄 01386 584596
e–mail: leasow@hotmail.com
web: www.leasow.co.uk

(For full entry see Laverton (Gloucestershire))

★★★★ GUEST ACCOMMODATION
Cowley House

Church St WR12 7AE
☎ 01386 858148
e–mail: cowleyhouse.broadway@tiscali.co.uk

dir: *Follow signs for Broadway village, Church St adjacent to village green, 3rd on left*

A warm welcome is assured at this 18th-century Cotswold-stone house, just a stroll from the village green. Fine period furniture enhances the interiors, and the elegant hall has a polished flagstone floor. Tastefully equipped bedrooms include thoughtful extras, smart modern shower rooms and comprehensive breakfasts feature local produce.

Rooms 6 rms (5 en suite) (1 pri facs) (1 fmly) (2 GF) S £45–£50; D £58–£85✳ **Facilities** TVB tea/coffee Cen ht Wi-fi available **Parking** 6 **Notes LB**

ENGLAND

BROADWAY CONTINUED

★★★★ INN
Horse & Hound
54 High St WR12 7DT
☎ 01386 852287 📠 01386 853784
e-mail: k2mtk@aol.com

dir: *Off A46 to Evesham*

The Horse and Hound is at the heart of this beautiful Cotswold village. A warm welcome is guaranteed whether dining in the inviting pub or staying overnight in the attractive and well-appointed bedrooms. Breakfast and dinner are features not to be missed, and both use carefully prepared local produce.

Rooms 5 en suite (1 fmly) D £80✱ **Facilities** TVB tea/coffee Cen ht Dinner Last d 9pm **Parking** 15 **Notes** RS Winter

★★★★ FARM HOUSE
Mount Pleasant Farm (SP056392)
Childswickham WR12 7HZ
☎ 01386 853424 📠 01386 853424 Mrs H Perry
e-mail: helen@mount-pleasant.fslife.co.uk

dir: *Onto B4632 for Winchcombe, 50yds right to Childswickham (3m). Farm 1.5m W on left*

Located in immaculate, mature grounds in a pretty hamlet, this impressive Victorian house provides spacious, traditionally furnished bedrooms with smart modern bathrooms. Comprehensive breakfasts are served in an elegant dining room, and a comfortable lounge is available.

Rooms 3 en suite (1 fmly) **Facilities** TVB tea/coffee Cen ht **Parking** 10 **Notes** ⊗ No children 5yrs 950 acres Arable

★★★★ 🏆 GUEST ACCOMMODATION
Whiteacres Guest House
Station Rd WR12 7DE
☎ 01386 852320
e-mail: whiteacres@btinternet.com
web: www.broadwaybandb.com

dir: *500yds NW from E end of High St*

Located a few minutes walk from the historic village centre, this elegant Edwardian house has been lovingly renovated to provide high standards of comfort and facilities. Bedrooms are equipped with a wealth of thoughtful extras, and memorable breakfasts are taken in an attractive dining room. A comfortable guest lounge is also available and a warm welcome is assured.

Rooms 5 en suite S £55–£65; D £65–£80✱ **Facilities** TVB tea/coffee Cen ht TVL Wi-fi available **Parking** 5 **Notes LB** No children 5yrs

---

BROMSGROVE   MAP 10 SO97

★★★ FARM HOUSE
Lower Bentley (SO962679)
Lower Bentley B60 4JB
☎ 01527 821286 Mr & Mrs A Gibbs
e-mail: anthony@lowerbentleyfarm.force9.co.uk
web: www.lowerbentleyfarm.co.uk

dir: *B4091 S past Navigation pub, left signed Woodgate, 1st right onto Woodgate Rd, 3rd left onto Lower Bentley Ln*

Located a short drive from major roads, this impressive red brick Victorian house is full of original features and is stylishly decorated and furnished throughout. Bedrooms are filled with lots of thoughtful extras and a comfortable lounge is provided in addition to an elegant dining room, the setting for memorable breakfasts.

Rooms 2 en suite S £35–£37; D £55✱ **Facilities** TVB tea/coffee Cen ht **Parking** 5 **Notes** ⊗ 346 acres dairy ☎

FLYFORD FLAVELL   MAP 10 SO95

★★★★ 🍽 INN
The Boot Inn
Radford Rd WR7 4BS
☎ 01386 462658 📠 01386 462547
e-mail: enquiries@thebootinn.com
web: www.thebootinn.com

dir: *In village centre, signed from A422*

An inn has occupied this site since the 13th century, though the Boot itself dates from the Georgian period. Modernisation has retained its historic charm, while the bedrooms, furnished in antique pine, are equipped with practical extras and have modern bathrooms. A range of ales, wines and imaginative food is offered in the cosy public areas, which include an attractive conservatory and patio.

Rooms 5 annexe en suite (2 GF) S £50–£60; D £60–£90 **Facilities** TVB tea/coffee Cen ht Dinner Last d 9.45pm Wi-fi available Golf 27 Pool Table **Parking** 30 **Notes LB**

ENGLAND

KEMPSEY   MAP 10 SO84

★★★ INN
Walter de Cantelupe Inn
Main Rd (A38) WR5 3NA
☎ 01905 820572
e–mail: walter.depub@fsbdial.co.uk
web: www.walterdecantelupeinn.com

dir: *On A38 in village centre*

This inn provides cosy bedrooms with smart bathrooms, and is convenient for the M5 and Worcester. The intimate, open-plan public areas are the setting for a range of real ales, and imaginative food featuring local produce and a fine selection of British cheeses.

Rooms 3 rms (2 en suite) (1 pri facs) **Facilities** TVB tea/coffee Cen ht Dinner Last d 9pm (Fri/Sat 10pm) Wi-fi available **Parking** 24 **Notes** No coaches

KIDDERMINSTER   MAP 10 SO87

★★★★ GUEST HOUSE
Bewdley Hill House
8 Bewdley Hill DY11 6BS
☎ 01562 60473 📠 0871 236 1608
e–mail: info@bewdleyhillhouse.co.uk
web: www.bewdleyhillhouse.co.uk

dir: *A456 W from town centre, on left before fuel station*

Located on the edge of Kidderminster, Bewdley Hill offers comfortable accommodation in a friendly family atmosphere and makes a good business or leisure base for the surrounding areas. Rooms are freshly decorated and well equipped and breakfast is served in an attractive dining room.

Rooms 6 en suite (2 fmly) (1 GF) S £35; D £60 **Facilities** TVB tea/coffee Cen ht Wi-fi available **Parking** 6 **Notes** ⊗ No coaches No children 3yrs Closed 22 Dec–5 Jan

★★★ GUEST ACCOMMODATION
Victoria House
15 Comberton Rd DY10 1UA
☎ 01562 67240
e–mail: victoriakidderminster@yahoo.co.uk

dir: *0.5m from town centre on A448, 200yds from Kidderminster station*

Located a short walk from the Severn Valley Railway, this impressive Victorian house has been renovated to provide homely bedrooms, filled with thoughtful extras and some with modern compact shower rooms. Breakfast is served in a spacious, attractive dining room and private car parking is also available.

Rooms 7 rms (5 en suite) (1 fmly) S £29–£34; D £49 **Facilities** TVB tea/coffee Cen ht **Parking** 5 **Notes** ⊗ No children 5yrs

MALVERN   MAP 10 SO74

★★★★ BED & BREAKFAST
The Dell House
Green Ln, Malvern Wells WR14 4HU
☎ 01684 564448 📠 01684 893974
e–mail: burrage@dellhouse.co.uk
web: www.dellhouse.co.uk

dir: *2m S of Great Malvern on A449. Turn left off A449 onto Green Ln. House at top of road on right*

This impressive, well-proportioned Victorian house retains many unique features, several of which were introduced by the resident scholar and vicar during its period as a rectory. Spacious bedrooms are filled with thoughtful extras and a comprehensive breakfast is served in an elegant dining room with superb views of the surrounding countryside and mature grounds in which the house sits.

Rooms 3 en suite **Facilities** TVB tea/coffee Cen ht TVL Wi-fi available **Parking** 6 **Notes** ⊗ No children 10yrs 🐾

ENGLAND

★★★★ GUEST ACCOMMODATION
Bredon House

34 Worcester Rd WR14 4AA
☎ 01684 566990 📠 01684 577530
e–mail: enquiries@bredonhouse.co.uk
web: www.bredonhouse.co.uk

dir: *200yds N of Great Malvern centre on A449, large fir tree in front car park*

Superbly located on the east side of the Malvern Hills, with stunning views of the Vale of Evesham and the Severn valley, this elegant Regency house retains many original features. Bedrooms, some with stunning rear views, offer both thoughtful and practical extras, and a comfortable lounge is also available.

Rooms 10 en suite (2 fmly) (1 GF) **Facilities** TVB tea/coffee Direct dial from bedrooms Cen ht TVL Wi-fi available **Parking** 7

★★★★ BED & BREAKFAST
Woodpeckers

66 Peachfield Rd, Malvern Wells WR14 4AL
☎ 01684 562827 📠 01684 562827
e–mail: woodpeckers@cmail.co.uk
web: www.wood-pecker.co.uk

dir: *1m S of town centre. Off B4208 onto Peachfield Rd, left onto private road before railway bridge*

Set in an unspoiled wooded hollow close to the Three Counties Showground, this attractive bungalow provides homely accommodation with quality modern bathrooms. Breakfast is served in the cosy dining room, which has a glass wall overlooking the pretty, mature garden. The interior is enhanced by the proprietor's fine original art and sculpture.

Rooms 2 en suite (2 GF) S £35–£45; D £60–£70✳ **Facilities** TVB tea/coffee Cen ht Wi-fi available **Parking** 2 **Notes** LB ⊗ No children 12yrs ⊜

★★★ GUEST ACCOMMODATION
The Pembridge

114 Graham Rd WR14 2HX
☎ 01684 574813 📠 01684 566885

dir: *A449 onto Church St, 1st left*

Located on a leafy residential road close to the town centre, this large Victorian house retains many original features, including a superb staircase. Bedrooms, which include a ground-floor room, are well equipped. Other areas include a comfortable sitting room with a small bar and an elegant dining room.

Rooms 8 en suite (1 fmly) (1 GF) S £48–£60; D £58–£68✳
Facilities TVB tea/coffee Direct dial from bedrooms Cen ht TVL
Conf Max 8 **Parking** 10 **Notes** LB ⊗ No children 7yrs RS 25–26 Dec

★★★ BED & BREAKFAST
Portocks End House

Little Clevelode WR13 6PE
☎ 01684 310276
e–mail: mpa-cameron@countyside-inter.net

dir: *On B4424, 4m N of Upton-On-Severn, opposite Riverside Caravan Park*

Peacefully located but convenient for the Showground and major road links, this period house retains many original features, and traditional furnishing and décor styles highlight the intrinsic charm. Bedrooms are equipped with lots of thoughtful extras and breakfasts are taken in a cosy dining room, overlooking the pretty garden.

Rooms 2 rms (2 pri facs) (1 fmly) S £26; D £48✳ **Facilities** tea/coffee
Parking 4 **Notes** Closed Dec–Feb ⊜

★★★ GUEST ACCOMMODATION
Sidney House

40 Worcester Rd WR14 4AA
☎ 01684 574994 📠 01684 574994
e–mail: info@sidneyhouse.co.uk
web: www.sidneyhouse.co.uk

dir: *On A449, 200yds N from town centre*

This impressive Grade II Georgian house is close to the central attractions and has stunning views. Bedrooms are filled with thoughtful extras, and some have small shower rooms en suite. The spacious dining room overlooks the Cotswold escarpment and a comfortable lounge is also available.

Rooms 8 rms (6 en suite) (1 fmly) S £25–£55; D £59–£75✳
Facilities TVB tea/coffee Cen ht TVL **Parking** 9 **Notes** Closed 24 Dec–3 Jan

★★★ INN
Wyche Inn

74 Wyche Rd WR14 4EQ

☎ 01684 575396 📄 01684 575396

e–mail: reservations@thewycheinn.co.uk

dir: *1.5m S of Malvern. On B4218 towards Malvern and Colwall. Off A449 (Worcester to Ross/Ledbury) road*

Located in an elevated position on the outskirts, with stunning views over the surrounding countryside, this inn is popular with both locals and visiting walkers. Thoughtfully furnished bedrooms provide good levels of comfort and a good range of ale and food is offered, with some value 'specials' nights.

Rooms 4 en suite **Facilities** TVB tea/coffee Cen ht Dinner Last d 8.30pm Pool Table **Parking** 4 **Notes** No coaches

★★ GUEST ACCOMMODATION
Four Hedges

The Rhydd, Hanley Castle WR8 0AD

☎ 01684 310405

e–mail: fredgies@aol.com

dir: *4m E of Malvern at junct of B4211 & B4424*

Situated in a rural location, this detached house stands in mature grounds with wild birds in abundance. The bedrooms are equipped with thoughtful extras. Tasty English breakfasts, using free-range eggs, are served in a cosy dining room at a table made from a 300-year-old elm tree.

Rooms 4 rms (2 en suite) S fr £20; D fr £40 **Facilities** TV1B tea/coffee Cen ht TVL Fishing ⬥ **Parking** 5 **Notes** Closed Xmas ⊜

MARTLEY   MAP 10 SO76

★★★★ INN
Admiral Rodney Inn

Berrow Green WR6 6PL

☎ 01886 821375

e–mail: rodney@admiral.fslife.co.uk

dir: *A44 onto B4197 at Knightwick, 2m on left*

Located in the pretty village of Berrow Green, this 16th-century inn has been renovated to provide high standards of comfort and facilities. New hosts Karen and Desmond offer a warm welcome to all their customers, and provide spacious, carefully furnished bedrooms,

CONTINUED

complemented by luxurious modern bathrooms. Ground-floor areas include quality bars with log fires and a unique tiered and beamed restaurant, where imaginative dishes are served. There are also outside seating areas to front and rear, and excellent parking facilities.

Rooms 3 en suite D £55–£65✱ **Facilities** TVB tea/coffee Direct dial from bedrooms Cen ht Wi-fi available Pool Table **Parking** 40

WORCESTER   MAP 10 SO85

★★★★ INN
Bants

Worcester Rd WR7 4NN

☎ 01905 381282 📄 01905 381173

e–mail: info@bants.co.uk

web: www.bants.co.uk

dir: *5m E of Worcester. On A422 at Upton Snodsbury*

A family-run 16th-century pub with a modern atmosphere. Bedrooms are carefully decorated and well equipped, with some rooms separate from the inn. A wide range of freshly-cooked meals is available in the free-house bar or served in the large conservatory.

Rooms 3 en suite 5 annexe en suite (3 GF) S £75–£125; D £85–£150✱ **Facilities** FTV TVB tea/coffee Cen ht Dinner Last d 9pm Wi-fi available **Conf** Max 50 **Parking** 40 **Notes** LB ⊗ No children 12yrs No coaches

★★★★ BED & BREAKFAST
Burgage House

4 College Precincts WR1 2LG

☎ 01905 25396 📄 01905 25396

e–mail: louise.newsholme@googlemail.com

dir: *M5 junct 7, A44 into city centre, after 7th set of lights left onto Edgar St, College Precinct is pedestrian only on right*

Located next to the cathedral and the historic centre, this impressive Georgian house has original features, including a fine stone staircase, enhanced by the décor and furnishings. Bedrooms, including the ground-floor Cromwell Room, are spacious and homely. An elegant dining room is the setting for comprehensive English breakfasts.

Rooms 4 en suite (1 fmly) (1 GF) S £32–£36; D £60–£65✱ **Facilities** TVB tea/coffee Cen ht **Notes** ⊗ Closed 23–30 Dec ⊜

★★★★ GUEST ACCOMMODATION
Oaklands B&B

Claines WR3 7RS

☎ 01905 458871 📄 01905 759362

e–mail: barbara.gadd@zoom.co.uk

A warm welcome is guaranteed at this converted stable, which is well located in a peaceful setting just a short drive from major routes. The property stands in abundant mature gardens, and the well-appointed bedrooms are mostly spacious. There is also a snooker room and parking is available.

Rooms 4 en suite (2 fmly) **Facilities** TVB tea/coffee Cen ht Snooker **Parking** 6 **Notes** Closed Xmas & New Year ⊜

WORCESTER CONTINUED

★★★★ GUEST HOUSE
Wyatt

40 Barbourne Rd WR1 1HU
☎ 01905 26311 📄 01905 26311
e–mail: wyatt.guest@virgin.net

dir: *On A38 0.5m N from city centre*

Located within easy walking distance of shops, restaurants and central attractions, this constantly improving Victorian house provides a range of thoughtfully furnished bedrooms. Breakfast is served in an attractive dining room, a warm welcome is assured and the attractive frontage is a regular winner in the Worcester Britain in Bloom competition.

Rooms 8 rms (7 en suite) (3 fmly) (1 GF) S £32–£37; D £50–£52
Facilities STV TVB tea/coffee Cen ht Wi-fi available **Notes** No coaches

★★ GUEST HOUSE
Croft Guest House

Bransford WR6 5JD
☎ 01886 832227
e–mail: accom@brianporter.orangehome.co.uk
web: www.croftguesthouse.com

dir: *4m SW of Worcester. On A4103 Leigh exit at Bransford rdbt, driveway on left after 30yds*

This cottage-style property, dating in parts from the 16th century, is convenient for the city centre and the Malverns. Freshly-cooked breakfasts feature home-made sausages. Bedrooms are homely and the pretty gardens have a water feature. Dogs are welcome with a current vaccination certificate.

Rooms 4 rms (3 en suite) (1 fmly) S £28–£39; D £48–£64✳
Facilities FTV TVB tea/coffee Licensed Cen ht TVL Dinner Last d 10am
Parking 5 **Notes LB** No coaches

YORKSHIRE, EAST RIDING OF

BEVERLEY
MAP 17 TA03

See also Leven

Premier Collection

★★★★★ GUEST ACCOMMODATION
Burton Mount Country House

Malton Rd, Cherry Burton HU17 7RA
☎ 01964 550541 📄 01964 551955
e–mail: pg@burtonmount.co.uk
web: www.burtonmount.co.uk

dir: *3m NW of Beverley. B1248 for Malton, 2m right at x-rds, house on left*

A charming country house three miles from Beverley, set in delightful gardens and offering luxurious accommodation. Bedrooms are well equipped and have thoughtful extra touches. The spacious drawing room has a blazing fire in the cooler months, and an excellent, Aga-cooked Yorkshire breakfast is served in the morning room. Pauline Greenwood is renowned locally for her customer care, culinary skills and warm hospitality.

Burton Mount Country House

Rooms 3 en suite **Facilities** STV TVB tea/coffee Cen ht TVL Dinner Last d 4.30pm 🍷 ♨ **Conf** Max 30 Thtr 30 Class 20 Board 20 **Parking** 20 **Notes** ⊗ No children 12yrs

BRIDLINGTON
MAP 17 TA16

Premier Collection

★★★★★ GUEST ACCOMMODATION
Marton Grange

Flamborough Rd, Marton cum Sewerby YO15 1DU
☎ 01262 602034 📄 01262 602034
e–mail: martongrange@talk21.com
web: www.marton-grange.co.uk

dir: *2m NE of Bridlington. On B1255, 600yds W of Links golf club*

There is a welcoming atmosphere at this country guest house and the bedrooms are all of high quality, with a range of extra facilities; ground-floor rooms are available. There are attractive lounges with views over the immaculate gardens while substantial breakfasts are served in the delightful dining room.

Rooms 11 en suite (3 GF) S £45–£52; D £70–£84✳ **Facilities** TVB tea/coffee Lift Cen ht **Parking** 11 **Notes** No children 12yrs Closed Dec–Feb

CONTINUED

★★★★ GUEST ACCOMMODATION
Burlington Quays
20 Meadowfield Rd YO15 3LD
☎ 01262 676052
e–mail: burlingtonquays@axis-connect.com

dir: A165 into Bridlington, take 1st right past golf course onto Kingston Rd. Bear left to seafront, turn 3rd left

In a peaceful street close to the seafront, this spacious house features modern, well appointed bedrooms, all in suite bath or shower rooms. Guests also have use of a comfortable lounge and a cosy, fully licensed bar. Tasty breakfasts are served in the pleasant dining room at individual tables.

Rooms 5 en suite (4 fmly) S £36–£38; D £52–£56✶ **Facilities** TVB tea/coffee Cen ht TVL **Parking** 2 **Notes** ⊗ ⊜

★★★★ BED & BREAKFAST
Longleigh
12 Swanland Av YO15 2HH
☎ 01262 676234 & 07980 310777
e–mail: geraldineross@hotmail.co.uk

dir: Flamborough Rd, N past Holy Trinity Church

In a quiet location ten minutes walk from the town centre or beach, Longleigh offers comfortable, tastefully appointed accommodation in a friendly atmosphere. Rooms are well equipped and breakfast is served in the attractive dining room.

Rooms 3 en suite S fr £28; D £50–£56 **Facilities** TVB tea/coffee Cen ht TVL **Notes** ⊗ ⊜

★★★★ GUEST ACCOMMODATION
The Mount
2 Roundhay Rd YO15 3JY
☎ 01262 672306
e–mail: mounthotel01@btconnect.com

dir: M62 junct 37 onto A164, pass golf course, right onto Shaftesbury Av, Roundham Rd 3rd on left, The Mount on right

This spacious Victorian house offers friendly and attentive service. Bedrooms are attractively presented and well furnished. Home-cooked five-course meals are available with prior arrangement and are served in the bright dining room. Guests are also welcome to use the comfortable lounge that leads through to a fully licensed bar.

Rooms 8 rms (6 en suite) (2 pri facs) (2 fmly) S £30; D £60✶ **Facilities** TVB tea/coffee Cen ht TVL Dinner Last d 1pm Wi-fi available **Notes LB** ⊗

★★★★ GUEST ACCOMMODATION
The Royal Bridlington
1 Shaftesbury Rd YO15 3NP
☎ 01262 672433 ▤ 01262 672118
e–mail: info@royalhotelbrid.co.uk

dir: A615 N to Bridlington (Kingsgate), right onto Shaftesbury Rd

Located just off the promenade, this immaculate property has a range of thoughtfully furnished bedrooms with smart modern bathrooms.

CONTINUED

Spacious public areas include a large dining room, conservatory-sitting room, and a cosy television lounge. Freshly-cooked dinners are a feature and a warm welcome is assured.

Rooms 15 rms (14 en suite) (1 pri facs) 2 annexe en suite (7 fmly) (3 GF) S £36–£42; D £62–£74✶ **Facilities** FTV TVB tea/coffee Cen ht TVL Dinner Last d 6pm Wi-fi available **Conf** Max 85 Thtr 85 Class 20 Board 40 Del from £70 ✶ **Parking** 7 **Notes LB** ⊗

★★★★ GUEST ACCOMMODATION
The Ryburn
31 Flamborough Rd YO15 2JH
☎ 01262 674098 ▤ 01262 674098

dir: From harbour take B1255 towards Flamborough. Ryburn 300mtrs on left after leisure centre

This attractive Tudor-style accommodation stands in a prominent position just a short walk from the town centre. A variety of rooms are available: some suitable for families, one is on the ground floor, and one has private balcony. Public areas include a dining room and an attractive lounge. This is a non-smoking establishment.

Rooms 7 en suite (2 fmly) (1 GF) S £35–£37.50; D £66–£70 **Facilities** TVB tea/coffee Cen ht TVL **Parking** 6 **Notes** ⊗ No children 5yrs Closed 6–27 Nov

★★★ GUEST HOUSE
Westward-Ho Guest House
8 West St YO15 3DX
☎ 01262 670110
e–mail: westward.ho@homecall.co.uk

dir: 250yds S of town centre. Off A1038 at harbour onto South Cliff Rd, right onto Windsor Crescent & West St

Situated in a side road, close to the harbour and Spa centre, this family-owned guest house offers good hospitality. Contemporary bedrooms (including family rooms) are attractively presented and feature smart en suites or private shower room. Hearty breakfasts are served in the open plan guest lounge and dining room which also has a small bar.

Rooms 5 rms (4 en suite) (1 pri facs) (1 fmly) **Facilities** FTV TVB tea/coffee Cen ht TVL **Notes** ⊗ No coaches ⊜

★★★ GUEST HOUSE
Aidansdale
92 Trinity Rd YO15 2HF
☎ 01262 676723

This friendly family run house is located on a street next to North Beach and is only five minutes from the town centre. The attractive bedrooms are comfortable and well equipped, with good quality en suite shower rooms. Tasty breakfasts are served in the pleasant dining room and service is very attentive.

Rooms 7 rms (6 en suite) (4 fmly) D £46–£54✶ **Facilities** tea/coffee Cen ht TVL **Notes LB** ⊜

BRIDLINGTON CONTINUED

★★★ GUEST ACCOMMODATION
The Langdon

13–16 Pembroke Ter YO15 3BX

☎ 01262 400124 🖷 01262 605377

e–mail: cruxon@fsmail.net

dir: *250yds SW of town centre. Off seafront South Marine*

Located on the seafront, the Langdon has a cosy bar and lounge where regular evening entertainment is held, and the reception rooms extend to a small garden porch. Home-cooked meals are served in the cheerful dining room or the stylish new restaurant.

Rooms 30 en suite (7 fmly) S £25–£35; D £50–£70✳ **Facilities** STV TVB tea/coffee Lift Cen ht TVL Dinner Last d noon Pool Table **Conf** Max 50 Board 50 Del from £50 ✳ **Notes LB** ⊗

★★★ GUEST ACCOMMODATION
The Ransdale

30 Flamborough Rd YO15 2JQ

☎ 01262 674334

Close to all main attractions this establishment offers comfortable bedrooms and friendly service. Guests have use of a small, modern lounge. Evening meals and tasty breakfasts are served in the spacious dining room which also has a bar area. Limited off-street parking is also available.

Rooms 16 en suite (4 fmly) (4 GF) S £40–£60; D £60✳ **Facilities** TVB tea/coffee Cen ht TVL Dinner Last d 9pm Wi-fi available **Parking** 10 **Notes LB** ⊗

★★★ GUEST ACCOMMODATION
Richmond Guest House

9 The Crescent YO15 2NX

☎ 01262 674366 & 07773 100387

dir: *In town centre. Off B1254 Promenade onto Cliff St towards harbour, left onto The Crescent*

Located a short walk from the seafront and the central attractions, this Victorian terrace property looks out across a garden to the sea. There is a range of homely bedrooms and comprehensive breakfasts are served in an attractive dining room.

Rooms 9 rms (7 en suite) (2 pri facs) (2 fmly) (1 GF) S £15–£25; D £40–£70✳ **Facilities** TVB tea/coffee Stairlift **Parking** 2 **Notes LB** ⊗ Closed Xmas & New Year ⊕

★★★ GUEST HOUSE
Sandra's Guest House

6 Summerfield Rd, South Marine Dr YO15 3LF

☎ 01262 677791

e–mail: sandra@axis-connect.com

dir: *250yds SW of town centre. Off seafront South Marine Dr*

Close to the south beach and the Spa Theatre, this friendly guest house offers very homely and comfortable accommodation with good home cooking. There is a comfortable lounge and the dining room has a bar.

Rooms 8 rms (7 en suite) (1 pri facs) (1 GF) S £25–£30; D £45–£50✳ **Facilities** TVB tea/coffee Licensed Cen ht Dinner Last d 4pm **Notes LB** ⊗ No children 12yrs No coaches RS Xmas (3 day package) ⊕

★★★ GUEST HOUSE
Shearwater

22 Vernon Rd YO15 2HE

☎ 01262 679883

e–mail: shearwaterhotel@amserve.com

dir: *In town centre. Off B1254 Promenade onto Trinity Rd & Vernon Rd*

A friendly welcome awaits you at this well-furnished house in a residential area near the seafront. Bedrooms are very comfortably furnished and equipped. There is a cosy lounge, and quality home-cooked meals are provided in the modern dining room.

Rooms 7 en suite (3 fmly) (1 GF) S £30; D £50✳ **Facilities** TVB tea/ coffee Cen ht Dinner Last d 4.30pm **Notes LB** ⊕

★★★ GUEST ACCOMMODATION
The Tennyson

19 Tennyson Av YO15 2EU

☎ 01262 604382 & 07729 149729

e–mail: dianew2@live.co.uk

web: www.thetennysonhotel.co.uk

dir: *500yds NE of town centre. B1254 Promenade from town centre towards Flamborough, Tennyson Av on left*

Situated in a quiet side road close to the town centre and attractions, this friendly guest house offers attentive service, comfortable bedrooms and a cosy bar.

Rooms 7 rms (6 en suite) (1 pri facs) (1 fmly) S £26–£35; D £52–£60✳ **Facilities** TVB tea/coffee Cen ht TVL Dinner Last d 10am **Notes LB**

★★★ GUEST HOUSE
Three Gables

37 Windsor Crescent YO15 3HZ

☎ 01262 673826 & 07732 336246

e–mail: threegables@fsmail.net

A spacious Victorian house with lots of character and period features. Bedrooms are comfortable and all guests are given a warm welcome and offered a choice of home cooked meals. There is a large dining room and a guest lounge.

Rooms 10 en suite S £30; D £52✳ **Facilities** TVB tea/coffee Cen ht TVL Dinner Last d 3pm **Parking** 10 **Notes** No children 10yrs Closed 24–26 Dec ⊕

CONTINUED

★★★ 🅰 GUEST HOUSE
Ivanhoe Guesthouse
63 Cardigan Rd YO15 3JS
☎ 01262 675983
e-mail: bookings@ivanhoeguesthouse.co.uk
dir: *500yds SW of town centre. Off A1038 Hilderthorpe Rd onto Cardigan Rd*

Rooms 8 en suite (4 fmly) **Facilities** TVB tea/coffee Licensed Cen ht TVL Dinner Last d noon Wi-fi available **Parking** 9 **Notes** ⊗ No coaches

★★ GUEST HOUSE
The Chimes Guest House
9 Wellington Rd YO15 2BA
☎ 01262 401659
e-mail: sandsbb@aol.com

dir: *A165 into town centre, Quay Rd, 3rd left after level crossing at Christchurch*

Town centre location close to beach and shops, yet in a quiet side road, this family home provides family accommodation and well-equipped cosy bedrooms. A fresh breakfast is carefully prepared to order, and friendliness is both sincere and helpful.

Rooms 8 rms (1 en suite) (2 fmly) **Facilities** FTV TVB tea/coffee Cen ht TVL Dinner Last d Lunchtime **Parking** 3

HUGGATE   MAP 19 SE85

★★★ ⌂ INN
The Wolds Inn
Driffield Rd YO42 1YH
☎ 01377 288217
e-mail: huggate@woldsinn.freeserve.co.uk
dir: *Huggate signed off A166 & brown signs to Wold Inn*

At the end of the highest village in the Yorkshire Wolds, midway between York and the coast, this ancient inn is a rural haven beside the Wolds Way walk. Substantial meals are served in the dining room and a good range of well-kept beers is available in the bar. Bedrooms, varying in size, are well equipped and comfortable.

Rooms 3 en suite S fr £40; D fr £50(room only) **Facilities** FTV TVB tea/coffee Cen ht Dinner Last d 9pm Pool Table **Parking** 50 **Notes** ⊗

LEVEN   MAP 17 TA14

★★★ INN
The New Inn
44 South St HU17 5NZ
☎ 01964 542223 📄 01964 545828
dir: *Off A1035, in village centre*

This central red-brick inn was built in the early 19th century. The modern bedrooms are brightly decorated and all rooms have showers en suite. There is an attractive breakfast room and a friendly atmosphere in the bars where traditional ales are served. The property has ample parking.

Rooms 10 en suite (1 fmly) **Facilities** TVB tea/coffee Cen ht TVL Dinner Last d 9pm Golf 18 Pool Table **Parking** 55

MARKET WEIGHTON   MAP 17 SE84

★★★ GUEST ACCOMMODATION
Robeanne House
Driffield Ln, Shiptonthorpe YO43 3PW
☎ 01430 873312 📄 01430 879142
e-mail: enquiries@robeannehouse.co.uk
web: www.robeannehouse.co.uk
dir: *1.5m NW on A614*

Set back off the A614 in a quiet location, this delightful modern family home was built as a farmhouse. York, the coast, and the Yorkshire Moors and Dales are within easy driving distance. All bedrooms have country views and include a large family room. A charming wooden chalet is available in the garden.

Rooms 2 en suite 5 annexe en suite (2 fmly) (2 GF) S £30–£45; D fr £60✳ **Facilities** TVB tea/coffee Cen ht TVL Dinner Last d 24hrs prior **Parking** 10 **Notes LB**

SOUTH CAVE   MAP 17 SE93

★★★★ 🍴 ⇔ GUEST ACCOMMODATION
Rudstone Walk
HU15 2AH
☎ 01430 422230 📄 01430 424552
e-mail: office@rudstone-walk.co.uk
web: www.rudstone-walk.co.uk
dir: *M62 junct 38, onto B1230, over A1034, Rudstone Walk 200yds on left*

Set among 80 acres of green fields and lawns, on the edge of the Yorkshire Wolds, this converted 17th-century farm is ideal as a relaxing retreat for both tourists and conferences, and is just one mile from the M62 and a short drive from the town of Beverley. Bedrooms form a garden courtyard around the farmhouse, which is where all meals are served. Self-catering accommodation is also available.

Rooms 14 en suite (2 fmly) (10 GF) **Facilities** TVB tea/coffee Direct dial from bedrooms Cen ht Dinner Last d 7pm **Conf** Max 120 Thtr 50 Class 30 Board 26 **Parking** 50 **Notes** RS 24–28 Dec & 31 Dec–2 Jan Civ Wed 50

YORKSHIRE, NORTH

ALDBROUGH ST JOHN   MAP 19 NZ21

★★★ GUEST ACCOMMODATION
Lucy Cross Farm
DL11 7AD
☎ 01325 374319 & 07931 545985
e–mail: sally@lucycross.co.uk
web: www.lucycross.co.uk

dir: *A1 junct 56 onto B6275 at Barton, white house 3m from Barton rdbt on left towards Piercebridge*

Located close to major road links, a relaxed atmosphere and friendly welcome is assured. Traditionally furnished bedrooms are very comfortably equipped; one is on the ground floor. A lounge is available and hearty breakfasts are served in the pleasant dining room.

Rooms 5 rms (3 en suite) (2 pri facs) (1 fmly) (1 GF) S £30–£40; D £56–£65 **Facilities** FTV TVB tea/coffee Cen ht TVL Dinner Last d 8pm Wi-fi available Fishing Riding **Conf** Max 12 Board 12 **Parking** 10 **Notes** LB

AMPLEFORTH   MAP 19 SE57

Premier Collection

★★★★★ 🏠 ➡ GUEST ACCOMMODATION
Shallowdale House
West End YO62 4DY
☎ 01439 788325 📠 01439 788885
e–mail: stay@shallowdalehouse.co.uk
web: www.shallowdalehouse.co.uk

dir: *Off A170 at W end of village, on turning to Hambleton*

An outstanding example of an architect-designed 1960s house, Shallowdale lies in two acres of hillside gardens. There are stunning views from every room, and the elegant public rooms include a choice of lounges. Spacious bedrooms blend traditional and 1960s style with many home comforts. Expect excellent service and genuine hospitality from Anton and Phillip. The very imaginative, freshly cooked dinners are not to be missed.

CONTINUED

Shallowdale House

Rooms 3 rms (2 en suite) (1 pri facs) S £75–£85; D £95–£115 **Facilities** TVB tea/coffee Cen ht Dinner Last d 48hrs Wi-fi available **Parking** 3 **Notes** ⊗ No children 12yrs Closed Xmas & New Year

---

APPLETREEWICK   MAP 19 SE06

Premier Collection

★★★★★ 🏠 BED & BREAKFAST
Knowles Lodge
BD23 6DQ
☎ 01756 720228 📠 01756 720381
e–mail: pam@knowleslodge.com
web: www.knowleslodge.com

dir: *From Bolton Abbey B6160 3.5m, turn right after Barden Tower 1m, entrance on left*

Located in the heart of Wharfedale and surrounded by 17 acres of meadow and woodland, this delightful Canadian-style ranch has been lovingly restored. The house is attractively furnished, with well appointed bedrooms, and whether guests are there to walk, cycle, fish, or simply relax and enjoy the scenery, they are sure to be given a warm welcome. Delicious breakfasts featuring home-made dishes are served around a large gate-leg table.

Rooms 3 en suite (2 GF) S £55; D £90 **Facilities** STV TV1B tea/coffee Cen ht TVL Wi-fi available Fishing 🎣 Boule Pit **Parking** 6 **Notes** No children 8yrs Civ Wed 75

ASKRIGG   MAP 18 SD99

★★★★ BED & BREAKFAST
Whitfield
Helm DL8 3JF
☎ 01969 650565 📠 01969 650565
e–mail: bookings@askrigg-cottages.co.uk
web: www.askrigg-cottages.co.uk

dir: *Off A684 at Bainbridge signed Askrigg, right at T-junct, 150yds to No Through Rd sign, left up hill 0.5m*

Set high in the fells, this smart accommodation is in a carefully converted barn, built of Yorkshire limestone. Both bedrooms are homely, and have stunning views of the Wensleydale countryside. Hearty breakfasts are served around a communal table in the inviting lounge-dining room.

Rooms 2 en suite S £45; D fr £58 **Facilities** TVB tea/coffee Cen ht TVL **Parking** 1 **Notes** LB Closed 23 Dec–2 Jan 🐾

AYSGARTH — MAP 19 SE08

★★★★ 🛏 GUEST ACCOMMODATION
Stow House

DL8 3SR
☎ 01969 663635
e–mail: info@stowhouse.co.uk
web: www.stowhouse.co.uk

dir: *0.6m E of Aysgarth on A684*

Set back from the road, in its own grounds, this former Victorian vicarage is delightfully furnished and decorated throughout. Bedrooms, most offering panoramic views over the Dales, are bright and homely. The smart dining room is the venue for hearty, carefully prepared breakfasts. Creative dinners are a highlight of any stay.

Rooms 9 en suite (1 GF) S £48–£53; D £76–£96✱ **Facilities** TVB tea/coffee Cen ht Dinner Last d 2pm 🛎 🛜 **Parking** 10 **Notes LB** Closed 24–26 Dec

BEDALE — MAP 19 SE28

Premier Collection

★★★★★ 🏠 FARM HOUSE
Mill Close Farm *(SE232922)*

Patrick Brompton DL8 1JY
☎ 01677 450257 📠 01748 813612 Mrs P Knox
e–mail: pat@millclose.co.uk
web: www.millclose.co.uk

dir: *3m NW of Bedale. A684 to Patrick Brompton & brown tourist signs to farm*

A real home from home atmosphere prevails at this working farm. Bedrooms are furnished with quality and style; one has a four-poster and two have spa baths, but all rooms feature homely extras including fridges. Well-prepared breakfasts are one of the highlights of a stay and feature home-made produce cooked in the Aga of the farm kitchen.

Rooms 3 en suite S £55–£65; D £80–£90✱ **Facilities** TVB tea/coffee Cen ht **Parking** 6 **Notes LB** ⊗ No children 10yrs 240 acres Mixed Closed Dec–Feb

★★★★ GUEST HOUSE
Elmfield House

Arrathorne DL8 1NE
☎ 01677 450558 📠 01677 450557
e–mail: stay@elmfieldhouse.co.uk
web: www.elmfieldhouse.co.uk

dir: *4m NW of Bedale. A684 from Bedale for Leyburn, right after Patrick Brompton towards Richmond, B&B 1.5m on right*

Originally a gamekeeper's cottage, and now carefully extended, Elmfield House has uninterrupted views of the surrounding countryside. The comfortable bedrooms are generally spacious and very well equipped. The attractive public rooms are also well proportioned and offer a cosy lounge area, as well as a conservatory-lounge and games area. Dinners are available by prior arrangement.

Rooms 4 en suite 3 annexe en suite (2 fmly) (2 GF) S £55–£60; D £76–£88 **Facilities** TVB tea/coffee Licensed Cen ht Dinner Last d at booking Wi-fi available Fishing **Parking** 7 **Notes LB** ⊗ No coaches

★★★★ INN
Castle Arms

Snape DL8 2TB
☎ 01677 470270 📠 01677 470837
e–mail: castlearms@aol.com

dir: *2m S of Bedale. Off B6268 into Snape*

Nestled in the quiet village of Snape, this former coaching inn is full of character. Bedrooms are in a converted barn, and each room is very comfortable and carefully furnished. The restaurant and public bar offer a good selection of fine ales, along with an interesting selection of freshly-prepared dishes.

Rooms 9 annexe en suite (8 GF) S £55–£58; D £75–£85✱ **Facilities** TVB tea/coffee Cen ht Dinner Last d 8.30pm **Parking** 15 **Notes LB** No coaches

BISHOP MONKTON MAP 19 SE36

★★★★ INN
Lamb & Flag Inn
Boroughbridge Rd HG3 3QN
☎ 01765 677322
e–mail: carol@lambandflagbarn.co.uk

dir: *A61 turn E onto Moor Rd crossing Knaresbrough Rd*

A delightful country inn set in the countryside yet close to Harrogate, York and Leeds. The inn provides a warm welcome and freshly prepared local food. The three comfortably furnished and equipped bedrooms are a conversion from a barn and are annexed next to the pub.

Rooms 3 annexe en suite (1 fmly) (3 GF) S fr £50; D fr £60✳
Facilities FTV TVB tea/coffee Cen ht Dinner Last d 8.45pm Pool Table
Parking 20 **Notes** ⊗

BOLTON ABBEY MAP 19 SE05

★★★★ GUEST ACCOMMODATION
Howgill Lodge
Barden BD23 6DJ
☎ 01756 720655
e–mail: info@howgill-lodge.co.uk

dir: *B6160 from Bolton Abbey signed Burnsall, 3m right at Barden Tower signed Appletreewick, Howgill Lodge 1.25m on right at phone box*

Having an idyllic position high above the valley, this converted stone granary provides a quality get-away-from-it-all experience. The uniquely styled bedrooms provide a host of thoughtful touches and are designed to feature original stonewalls, flagstone floors and timber beams. All of the rooms boast spectacular, memorable views. Breakfasts make excellent use of fresh local ingredients.

Rooms 4 en suite (4 GF) S £45; D £70✳ **Facilities** TVB tea/coffee Cen ht **Parking** 6 **Notes** ⊗ Closed 24–26 Dec

BURNSALL MAP 19 SE06

★★★★ RESTAURANT WITH ROOMS
Devonshire Fell
BD23 6BT
☎ 01756 729000 ▤ 01756 729009
e–mail: manager@devonshirefell.co.uk

dir: *On B6160, 6m from Bolton Abbey rdbt A59 junct*

Located on the edge of the attractive village of Burnsall, Devonshire Fell offers comfortable, well equipped accommodation in a relaxing atmosphere. There is an extensive menu featuring local produce, and meals can be taken either in the bar area or the more formal restaurant. A function room with views over the valley is also available.

Rooms 12 en suite D £130–£265✳ **Facilities** STV FTV TVB tea/coffee Direct dial from bedrooms Cen ht Dinner Last d 7.30pm Wi-fi available Fishing **Conf** Max 50 Thtr 50 Class 30 Board 24 Del from £135 ✳ **Parking** 30 **Notes LB** Civ Wed 90

CARPERBY MAP 19 SE08

★★★ Ⓐ INN
The Wheatsheaf
DL8 4DF
☎ 01969 663216 ▤ 01969 663019
e–mail: wheatsheaf@paulmit.globalnet.co.uk

dir: *Off A684 signed Aysgarth Falls to village centre*

Rooms 8 en suite 5 annexe en suite (1 fmly) (1 GF) S £35; D £68–£85✳ **Facilities** TVB tea/coffee Cen ht Dinner Last d 9pm Wi-fi available Fishing **Conf** Max 20 Board 20 **Parking** 40 **Notes LB** RS Mon

CATTERICK MAP 19 SE29

★★★ GUEST ACCOMMODATION
Rose Cottage
26 High St DL10 7LJ
☎ 01748 811164

dir: *Off A1 in village centre, opp newsagents*

Convenient for exploring the Dales and Moors, this well-maintained guest house lies in the middle of Catterick. Bedrooms are nicely presented and comfortable. The cosy public rooms include a cottage-style dining room adorned with Mrs Archer's paintings, and a lounge. Dinner is available by arrangement during the summer.

Rooms 4 rms (2 en suite) (1 fmly) (4 smoking) S £29–£35; D £46–£52 **Facilities** TVB tea/coffee Cen ht Dinner Last d 9.30am **Parking** 4 **Notes** Closed 24–26 Dec ⊜

CLAPHAM MAP 18 SD76

★★★ GUEST HOUSE
Brookhouse Guest House
Station Rd LA2 8ER
☎ 015242 51580
e–mail: admin@brookhouseclapham.co.uk
web: www.brookhouse-clapham.co.uk

dir: *Off A65 into village*

Located in the pretty conservation village of Clapham beside the river, this well-maintained and friendly guest house provides thoughtfully furnished bedrooms and a popular ground floor café, serving a selection of meals and snacks through the day.

Rooms 3 rms (1 fmly) S £28; D £50–£60✳ **Facilities** FTV TVB tea/coffee Cen ht Dinner Last d 9pm Golf 18 ⊵ **Notes LB** ⊗ No coaches ⊜

ENGLAND

CLOUGHTON
MAP 19 TA09

★★★★ INN
Blacksmiths Arms
High St YO13 0AE
☎ 01723 870244
e–mail: enquiries@blacksmithsarmsinn.co.uk
dir: *On A171 in village centre*

Located six miles north of Scarborough, this inn features smartly furnished bedrooms. Four are in converted stone buildings that have private entrances. A good range of dishes is served in the bar and dining room, which have the ambience of a country inn, including open fires and traditional furniture.

Rooms 6 en suite 4 annexe en suite (1 fmly) (4 GF) S £40–£70; D £70–£72✶ **Facilities** FTV TVB tea/coffee Cen ht Dinner Last d 9.30pm **Parking** 35 **Notes LB** ⊗ No coaches RS 25–27 Dec

★★★★ GUEST ACCOMMODATION
Rockhaven
Newlands Rd YO13 0AR
☎ 01723 871971
e–mail: bbclevelandway@talktalk.net
dir: *6m N of Scarborough on A171. At junct of Staintondale Rd & Hood Ln*

A delightful Victorian detached house with views across open countryside and out to sea. Superbly furnished with comfortable beds and a spacious guest lounge, Rockhaven offers freshly-cooked breakfasts, and is set in ideal countryside for walking, cycling or touring.

Rooms 3 en suite **Facilities** TVB tea/coffee Cen ht Dinner Last d noon **Parking** 6 **Notes** ⊗ Closed Dec–Jan RS Feb–Mar, Oct–Nov ⊛

CRAYKE
MAP 19 SE57

★★★★ Ⓐ RESTAURANT WITH ROOMS
The Durham Ox
Westway YO61 4TE
☎ 01347 821506 🖹 01347 823326
e–mail: enquiries@thedurhamox.com
dir: *A19 to Easingwold. Through market place to Crayke, 1st left up hill*

Rooms 4 annexe en suite (2 fmly) (2 GF) S £60–£80; D £80–£120✶ **Facilities** TVB tea/coffee Dinner Last d 9.30pm Wi-fi available Shooting, fishing, riding by arrangement **Conf** Max 18 Thtr 18 Board 18 **Parking** 35 **Notes LB** RS 25 Dec

FILEY
MAP 17 TA18

★★★★ GUEST HOUSE
Gables
2A Rutland St YO14 9JB
☎ 01723 514750
e–mail: thegablesfiley@aol.com
dir: *Off A165 signs for town centre, right onto West Av, 2nd left onto Rutland St, the Gables opp church on corner*

Located in a quiet residential area, just a stroll from the centre and promenade, this smart Edwardian house extends a warm welcome. Bedrooms are brightly decorated and well equipped and some are suitable for families. Breakfasts are substantial and a varied evening menu is available.

Rooms 5 en suite (2 fmly) D £60–£76✶ **Facilities** TVB tea/coffee Cen ht Dinner Last d noon Wi-fi available Golf 18 ⛳ **Parking** 2 **Notes LB** No coaches

FLIXTON
MAP 17 TA07

★★★★ GUEST ACCOMMODATION
Orchard Lodge
North St YO11 3UA
☎ 01723 890202 🖹 01723 890202
e–mail: c.pummell@btinternet.com
web: www.orchard-lodge.com
dir: *Off A1039 in village centre*

Located six miles south of Scarborough, just off the main road, this establishment offers spacious and comfortable bedrooms. It is a good base for touring the coast, the North York Moors or the Wolds. Hearty breakfasts feature home-made preserves.

Rooms 6 en suite S £45–£50; D £70–£80✶ **Facilities** TVB tea/coffee Cen ht **Parking** 8 **Notes LB** ⊗ No children 3yrs Closed Jan–Feb

ENGLAND

GIGGLESWICK
MAP 18 SD86

★★★★ 🅰 INN
Harts Head Inn
Belle Hill BD24 0BA
☎ 01729 822086 📠 01729 824992
e–mail: info@hartsheadinn.co.uk
web: www.hartsheadinn.co.uk
dir: *On B6480, 1m from A65*

Rooms 7 en suite 3 annexe en suite (1 fmly) S fr £37.50; D £79✱
Facilities STV TVB tea/coffee Cen ht Dinner Last d 9pm Wi-fi available
Snooker Pool Table **Conf** Max 30 Class 30 Board 20 **Parking** 25
Notes LB

GILLING EAST
MAP 19 SE67

★★★★ 🍽 RESTAURANT WITH ROOMS
The Fairfax
Main St YO62 4JH
☎ 01439 788212
e–mail: mail@thefairfax.co.uk

dir: *From A170 turn right onto B1257, right again onto B1363 to Gilling East*

This 17th-century coaching inn has been refurbished and now offers a spacious contemporary restaurant with a bar area available for guests to enjoy a pre-dinner drink. The focus is on food with a wide choice of meals available, featuring locally sourced ingredients. A range of stylish bedrooms are available including high quality suites in the courtyard building.

Rooms 12 en suite (2 fmly) (2 GF) **Facilities** FTV TVB tea/coffee Cen ht
Dinner Last d 10pm Wi-fi available Golf 9 **Parking** 14 **Notes** RS Tue
(Winter)

GOLDSBOROUGH
MAP 19 SE35

Premier Collection

★★★★★ GUEST ACCOMMODATION
Goldsborough Hall
Church St HG5 8NR
☎ 01423 867321 📠 0870 285 1327
e–mail: accommodation@goldsboroughhall.com

dir: *A1(M) junct 47, take A59 to Knaresborough. Take 2nd left onto Station Rd, at T-junct left onto Church St*

It's not everyday that you get the chance to stay in the former residence of a Royal Princess, in this case HRH Princess Mary. Hospitality at Goldsborough Hall is second to none. Six luxury rooms have been refurbished to the highest standards, and the bathrooms offer a real "wow" factor. Bedrooms feature hand-made mahogany 8ft four-poster beds, Chesterfields and 50-inch televisions.

Rooms 6 en suite (2 fmly) D £150–£395✱ **Facilities** FTV TV3B tea/
coffee Direct dial from bedrooms Lift Cen ht TVL Wi-fi available Outdoor
Hot Tub **Conf** Max 150 Thtr 150 Class 50 Board 30 **Parking** 50
Notes LB Civ Wed 110

GRASSINGTON	MAP 19 SE06

Premier Collection

★★★★★ 🍸 🍷 GUEST ACCOMMODATION
Ashfield House

Summers Fold BD23 5AE
☎ 01756 752584 📠 07092 376562
e–mail: info@ashfieldhouse.co.uk
web: www.ashfieldhouse.co.uk

dir: *B6265 to village centre Main St, left onto Summers Fold*

Guests are greeted like old friends at this beautifully maintained 17th-century house, peacefully tucked away a few yards from the village square. The smart lounges offer a high level of comfort and an honesty bar. The freshly prepared three-course dinner (by arrangement) is a highlight of any stay. The attractive bedrooms are well furnished and thoughtfully equipped.

Rooms 8 rms (7 en suite) (1 pri facs) S £65.25–£85.25; D £91–£129✳ **Facilities** TVB tea/coffee Cen ht Dinner Last d 24hrs in advance Wi-fi available **Conf** Max 8 Board 8 Del from £160 ✳ **Parking** 8 **Notes LB** ⊗ No children 5yrs RS Nov–Mar

★★★★ 🏵 🍸 INN
Gamekeeper's Inn

Long Ashes Park, Threshfield BD23 5PN
☎ 01756 752434 📠 01756 752876
e–mail: info@gamekeeperinn.co.uk
web: www.gamekeeperinn.co.uk

dir: *From Skipton take the B6265 towards Grassington and Threshfield, then take B6160 towards Kettlewell, inn signed from road*

Situated within Long Ashes Park, this friendly inn offers thoughtfully equipped and comfortably furnished bedrooms. The restaurant offers an interesting selection of freshly-prepared dishes. Guests also have free use of the Long Ashes leisure centre.

Rooms 5 en suite (1 fmly) S £55–£65; D £75–£85✳ **Facilities** TVB tea/coffee Cen ht Dinner Last d 8.30pm Wi-fi available ⊗ Sauna Solarium Gymnasium **Conf** Max 10 Thtr 12 Class 10 Board 10 **Parking** 20 **Notes LB** No coaches

GREAT AYTON	MAP 19 NZ51

★★★ INN
Royal Oak

123 High St TS9 6BW
☎ 01642 722361 & 723270 📠 01642 724047
e–mail: info@royaloak-hotel.co.uk

dir: *Off the A173, on High Street*

This 18th-century former coaching inn is very popular with locals and visitors to the village. Bedrooms are all comfortably equipped. The restaurant and public bar retain many original features and offer a good selection of fine ales; an extensive range of food is available all day and is served in the bar or the dining room.

Rooms 5 en suite S £35–£45; D £70✳ **Facilities** TVB tea/coffee Direct dial from bedrooms Cen ht Dinner Last d 9.30pm **Conf** Max 30 Thtr 30 Class 30 Board 30 **Notes** No coaches

GUISBOROUGH	MAP 19 NZ61

★★★★ GUEST ACCOMMODATION
The Kings Head at Newton

The Green TS9 6QR
☎ 01642 722318 📠 01642 724750
e–mail: info@kingsheadhotel.co.uk
web: www.kingsheadhotel.co.uk

dir: *A171 towards Guisborough, at rdbt onto A173 to Newton under Roseberry, under Roseberry Topping landmark*

Converted from a row of traditional cottages, the friendly, family-owned Kings Head offers modern accommodation with original features. The stylish modern bedrooms are thoughtfully equipped, and the adjacent restaurant offers a choice of wines, beers and a very good range of dishes.

Rooms 8 en suite (1 fmly) (2 GF) S £59.50–£85; D £75–£110✳ **Facilities** FTV TVB tea/coffee Direct dial from bedrooms Cen ht TVL Dinner Last d 9.30pm Wi-fi available Mountain biking **Parking** 100 **Notes** ⊗ Closed 25–26 Dec & 1 Jan

ENGLAND

★★★★ ⑱ RESTAURANT WITH ROOMS

Pinchinthorpe Hall

Pinchinthorpe TS14 8HG

☎ 01287 630200 📠 01287 632000

e–mail: sales@nybrewery.co.uk

dir: *2m SW of Guisborough on A173*

An elegant 17th-century country manor house that has stylish bedrooms, each very individually and tastefully decorated, and completed with many thoughtful extras. The Brewhouse Bistro serves interesting dishes using home-grown and local produce, along with attentive service.

Rooms 6 en suite S fr £85; D fr £130✱ (room only) **Facilities** TVB tea/ coffee Direct dial from bedrooms Cen ht Dinner Last d 9.30pm **Conf** Max 50 Thtr 50 Class 20 Board 24 **Parking** 110 **Notes LB** ⊗ Civ Wed 80

HACKNESS   MAP 19 SE99

★★★★ GUEST ACCOMMODATION

Troutsdale Lodge

Troutsdale YO13 0BS

☎ 01723 882209

e–mail: clive@troutsdalelodge.fsnet.co.uk

web: www.troutsdalelodge.com

dir: *Off A170 at Snainton signed Troutsdale*

Commanding magnificent views across a peaceful valley and the forest beyond, this Edwardian house showcases many original features combined with modern art. Bedrooms offer good all-round comforts and guests receive fine hospitality from the resident owners.

Rooms 4 en suite (1 fmly) (4 GF) **Facilities** TVB tea/coffee Cen ht TVL Dinner Last d 8pm 🐾 **Parking** 8 **Notes** ⊛

HARROGATE   MAP 19 SE35

★★★★★ Ⓐ GUEST ACCOMMODATION

Cold Cotes

Cold Cotes Rd, Felliscliffe HG3 2LW

☎ 01423 770937

e–mail: info@coldcotes.com

web: www.coldcotes.com

dir: *W of Harrogate. Off A59 after Black Bull, 3rd entrance on right*

Rooms 3 en suite 2 annexe en suite (2 GF) D £80–£95✱ **Facilities** FTV TVB tea/coffee Cen ht Dinner Last d 8pm Wi-fi available **Conf** Max 50 Thtr 30 Class 24 Board 14 **Parking** 20 **Notes** ⊗ No children 12yrs Closed 2–16 Jan

★★★★ GUEST HOUSE

Alexa House & Stable Cottages

26 Ripon Rd HG1 2JJ

☎ 01423 501988 📠 01423 504086

e–mail: enquires@alexa-house.co.uk

web: www.alexa-house.co.uk

dir: *On A61, 0.25m from junct A59*

This popular establishment has stylish, well-equipped bedrooms split between the main house and cottage rooms. All rooms come with homely extras. The opulent day rooms include an elegant lounge with honesty bar, and a bright dining room. The hands-on proprietors ensure high levels of customer care.

Rooms 9 en suite 4 annexe en suite (2 fmly) (4 GF) S £55–£65; D £85–£95✱ **Facilities** TVB tea/coffee Licensed Cen ht Wi-fi available **Conf** Max 10 Class 10 **Parking** 10 **Notes** No coaches Closed 23–26 Dec

★★★★ GUEST ACCOMMODATION

April House

3 Studley Rd HG1 5JU

☎ 01423 561879

e–mail: info@aprilhouse.com

dir: *Off A59/A61 onto Kings Rd signed Harrogate International Centre. Opposite Holiday Inn turn onto Alexandra Rd. Establishment at top of road*

Located in a quiet residential area just a short walk from the conference centre, this impeccable Victorian house retains many

CONTINUED

original features. The comfortable bedrooms come with an array of homely touches, and breakfast is served in an attractive dining room.

Rooms 5 rms (4 en suite) (1 pri facs) (1 fmly) S £40–£45; D £70–£80✳
Facilities TVB tea/coffee Wi-fi available **Notes** LB ⊗

★★★★ GUEST ACCOMMODATION
Ashwood House
7 Spring Grove HG1 2HS
☎ 01423 560081 🖹 01423 527928
e–mail: ashwoodhouse@aol.com
web: www.ashwoodhouse.co.uk
dir: *A61 Ripon Rd onto Springfield Av, 3rd left*

This delightfully decorated and furnished Edwardian house is situated in a quiet area of town. The spacious bedrooms are individually styled and thoughtfully equipped, and one has a four-poster bed. There is a cosy lounge and an elegant dining room where full English breakfasts are served.

Rooms 5 en suite (1 fmly) **Facilities** TVB tea/coffee Cen ht TVL
Parking 3 **Notes** ⊗ No children 7yrs Closed Xmas & New Year

★★★★ GUEST ACCOMMODATION
The Camberley
52–54 Kings Rd HG1 5JR
☎ 01423 561618 🖹 01423 536360
e–mail: camberleyhotelharrogate@yahoo.co.uk
dir: *Opposite Harrogate International Centre*
Located directly opposite the convention centre and with the benefit of private car parking, this constantly improving owner-managed guest house provides comfortable accommodation and a warm welcome is assured. A spacious guest lounge is available in addition to a period themed basement dining room, the setting for comprehensive breakfasts utilising local produce.

Rooms 11 rms (9 en suite) (2 pri facs) (2 fmly) (1 GF) S £30–£45;
D £60–£75✳ **Facilities** TVB tea/coffee Cen ht **Parking** 10 **Notes** LB ⊗
Closed 24–25 Dec

★★★★ GUEST ACCOMMODATION
The Dales
101 Valley Dr HG2 0JP
☎ 01423 507248
e–mail: reservations@dales-hotel.co.uk
dir: *A61 N into Harrogate, left before Bettys on Parliament St, to rdbt & 2nd exit, left onto Valley Dr*
Set in a peaceful residential area overlooking Valley Gardens, the cosy property has well-equipped bedrooms with either en suite or private facilities. Relax in the stylish lounge; an honesty bar is also available. Quality breakfasts are served in the dining room, and service is friendly and attentive.

Rooms 8 rms (6 en suite) (2 pri facs) S £40; D £70–£75 **Facilities** FTV
TVB tea/coffee Cen ht TVL Wi-fi available **Notes** LB ⊗

★★★★ GUEST ACCOMMODATION
Fountains B & B
27 Kings Rd HG1 5JY
☎ 01423 530483 🖹 01423 705312
e–mail: dave@fountains.fsworld.co.uk
dir: *500yds N of town centre. Off A59 Skipton Rd onto Kings Rd, 0.75m on right on corner of Coppice Dr*
This delightful guest house offers very comfortable accommodation close to the conference centre. Carefully decorated throughout, the bedrooms have co-ordinated soft fabrics, and some have period furniture. The elegant lounge is available for guests use. Substantial breakfasts are served in the breakfast room.

Rooms 10 en suite (2 fmly) (2 GF) S £40–£57; D £68 **Facilities** FTV
TVB tea/coffee Cen ht Wi-fi available **Parking** 8 **Notes** No children 6yrs
Closed 24 Dec–2 Jan

★★★★ GUEST ACCOMMODATION
The Grafton
1–3 Franklin Mount HG1 5EJ
☎ 01423 508491 🖹 01423 523168
e–mail: enquiries@graftonhotel.co.uk
web: www.graftonhotel.co.uk
dir: *Follow signs to International Centre, onto Kings Rd with Centre on left, Franklin Mount 450yds on right*
The delightful family-run Grafton is in a quiet location just a short walk from the conference centre and town. Bedrooms are well appointed and comfortably furnished, and there are lounges with a small cosy bar. Breakfast is served in the light and spacious dining room, which overlooks the garden.

Rooms 17 en suite (3 fmly) S £45–£65; D £80–£95 **Facilities** FTV TVB
tea/coffee Direct dial from bedrooms Cen ht TVL Wi-fi available
Parking 3 **Notes** LB ⊗ Closed 15–28 Dec

HARROGATE CONTINUED

★★★★ GUEST ACCOMMODATION
Ruskin

1 Swan Rd HG1 2SS
☎ 01423 502045 📄 01423 506131
e–mail: ruskin.hotel@virgin.net

dir: *Off A61 Ripon road, left opp The Majestic Hotel*

The mid 19th-century house stands in secluded tree-studded gardens, only a 5-minute walk from the town centre. It retains many original features and has a relaxing lounge. Breakfasts are served in the elegant dining room, and the thoughtfully equipped bedrooms range from compact to spacious, all furnished in stylish Victorian pine.

Rooms 7 en suite (2 fmly) (1 GF) **Facilities** TVB tea/coffee Direct dial from bedrooms Cen ht **Parking** 7

★★★★ GUEST HOUSE
Shannon Court

65 Dragon Av HG1 5DS
☎ 01423 509858 📄 01423 530606
e–mail: info@shannoncourtguesthouse.co.uk
web: www.shannoncourtguesthouse.co.uk

dir: *Located on corner of Dragon Avenue and Mornington Crescent, parallel to A59 Skipton Rd*

Situated within easy walking distance of the town centre, this friendly guest house offers individually decorated, pleasantly furnished and thoughtfully equipped bedrooms. There is a comfortable dining room where hearty breakfasts are served at individual tables and also a cosy lounge area for guests to relax in.

Rooms 8 en suite (2 fmly) S £50–£80; D £75–£80 **Facilities** TVB tea/coffee Cen ht Wi-fi available **Parking** 2 **Notes LB** ⊗ No coaches

★★★★ GUEST ACCOMMODATION
Shelbourne

78 Kings Rd HG1 5JX
☎ 01423 504390 📄 01423 504390
e–mail: sue@shelbournehouse.co.uk
web: www.shelbournehouse.co.uk

dir: *Signs to International Centre, over lights by Moat House Hotel, premises on right*

Situated opposite the conference centre and near to the town centre, this elegant Victorian house extends a warm welcome to all guests. Bedrooms are tastefully decorated and well equipped. There is a guest's lounge and an attractive breakfast room where hearty breakfasts are served at the individual tables.

Rooms 8 en suite (2 fmly) S £40–£45; D £70–£80✳ **Facilities** TVB tea/coffee Cen ht TVL **Conf** Board 16 **Parking** 1 **Notes LB** ⊗

★★★★ GUEST ACCOMMODATION
Wynnstay House

60 Franklin Rd HG1 5EE
☎ 01423 560476
e–mail: wynnstayhouse@tiscali.co.uk
web: www.wynnstayhouse.com

dir: *Off A61 in town centre onto Kings Rd, right onto Strawberry Dale, 2nd left*

Located in a residential area a short distance from the conference centre, shops and attractions, this friendly, family-run guest house is ideal for business or leisure. There is a passion for ruined castles at Wynnstay House: the attractive, well-equipped bedrooms are each named after a spectacular fortress.

Rooms 6 en suite S £47.50–£80; D £60–£80✳ **Facilities** TVB tea/coffee Cen ht Wi-fi available **Notes LB** ⊗ No children 14yrs

★★★ GUEST ACCOMMODATION
Pigeon Olde Farm Lodge

Bilton Hall Dr HG1 4DW
☎ 01423 868853
e–mail: maureen@tatemd.fsnet.co.uk

dir: *2.5m NE of Harrogate. Off A59 Forest Ln Head opp golf club onto Bilton Hall Dr*

A warm welcome awaits you at this delightful guest house converted from farm buildings and barns. It has a peaceful location opposite Harrogate Golf Club, and Knaresborough and Harrogate town centres are within easy reach. The smart bedrooms are attractively furnished and well equipped.

Rooms 2 en suite 4 annexe en suite (6 GF) D £64✳ **Facilities** TVB tea/coffee Cen ht **Parking** 10 **Notes** ⊗ ⊜

★★★ GUEST ACCOMMODATION
Harrogate Brasserie with Rooms

28–30 Cheltenham Pde HG1 1DB
☎ 01423 505041 📄 01423 722300
e–mail: info@harrogatebrasserie.co.uk
web: www.harrogatebrasserie.co.uk

dir: *On A61 town centre behind theatre*

This town centre establishment is distinctly continental in style. The brasserie covers three cosy dining areas richly decorated and adorned with artefacts. Live jazz is featured on Wednesday, Friday and Sunday nights. The individual bedrooms feature period collectibles; many rooms have DVD players and all have lots to read.

Rooms 17 en suite (3 fmly) **Facilities** TVB tea/coffee Direct dial from bedrooms Dinner **Parking** 12 **Notes** ch fac Closed 26 Dec–2 Jan

See advert on opposite page

HAWES
MAP 18 SD88

★★★★ GUEST ACCOMMODATION

Steppe Haugh
Town Head DL8 3RH

☎ 01969 667645

e–mail: info@steppehaugh.co.uk

dir: *On A684, W side of Hawes, next to fuel station*

Over 350 years old, the stone house retains much original charm and offers a very welcoming atmosphere. The thoughtfully furnished bedrooms are cosy, and the spacious lounge has a welcoming log fire in the cooler seasons. Private parking is available.

Rooms 5 en suite S £36–£38; D £64–£66 **Facilities** TVB tea/coffee Cen ht TVL **Parking** 5 **Notes** No children 7yrs Closed Dec–Jan ⊛

HAWNBY
MAP 19 SE58

★★★★ GUEST ACCOMMODATION

Laskill Grange
YO62 5NB

☎ 01439 798268

e–mail: laskillgrange@tiscali.co.uk

web: www.laskillgrange.co.uk

dir: *6m N of Helmsley on B1257*

Country lovers will enjoy this charming 19th-century farmhouse. Guests can take a walk in the surrounding countryside, fish the River Seph which runs through the grounds, or visit nearby Rievaulx Abbey. Comfortable bedrooms are in the main house and are well furnished and supplied with many thoughtful extras.

Rooms 3 annexe rms (2 en suite) (1 annexe pri facs) (3 GF) S £35–£40; D £70–£80✻ **Facilities** FTV TVB tea/coffee Cen ht TVL Fishing Riding **Conf** Max 20 **Parking** 20 **Notes LB** Closed 25 Dec

---

HELLIFIELD
MAP 18 SD85

★★★★★ GUEST ACCOMMODATION

Ribblecote Manor
Swinden BD23 4LS

☎ 01729 850446 🖷 01729 850446

e–mail: harrison.ribblecote@virgin.net

dir: *2m S of Hellifield. Off A682 to Swinden*

This impressive stone house stands on pretty landscaped grounds. The carefully furnished bedrooms are equipped with thoughtful extras and one has a spa bath. Additional facilities include an indoor swimming pool and a games room with a full-size snooker table. Breakfasts, using quality local produce, are served in an attractive dining room, and a spacious lounge is available.

Rooms 3 en suite (1 fmly) **Facilities** TVB tea/coffee Cen ht TVL Dinner Last d 24hrs ⊗ Snooker **Parking** 4 **Notes** ⊗ No children 2yrs ⊛

HELMSLEY
MAP 19 SE68

See also Hawnby

★★★★★ 🍴 🚲 GUEST ACCOMMODATION

Shallowdale House
West End YO62 4DY

☎ 01439 788325 🖷 01439 788885

e–mail: stay@shallowdalehouse.co.uk

web: www.shallowdalehouse.co.uk

(For full entry see Ampleforth)

★★★★ GUEST ACCOMMODATION

Plumpton Court
High St, Nawton YO62 7TT

☎ 01439 771223

e–mail: mail@plumptoncourt.com

web: www.plumptoncourt.com

dir: *2.5m E of Helmsley. Off A170 in Nawton, signed*

Located in the village of Nawton, in the foothills of the North Yorkshire Moors, this characteristic 17th-century, stone-built house offers a warm welcome. The cosy lounge bar has an open fire. Bedrooms are comfortable, modern and well equipped, one with a four-poster bed.

Rooms 7 en suite (1 GF) S £40; D £59–£63✻ **Facilities** FTV TVB tea/coffee Cen ht **Parking** 8 **Notes** ⊗ No children 12yrs Closed Dec–Jan

HELMSLEY CONTINUED

★★★★ A GUEST HOUSE
The Carlton Lodge

Bondgate YO62 5EY
☎ 01439 770557 📄 01439 772378
e–mail: enquiries@carlton-lodge.com
web: www.carlton-lodge.com

dir: *400yds E of Market Sq on A170*

Rooms 8 rms (7 en suite) (1 pri facs) (2 GF) S £45–£55; D £75–£90✳
Facilities FTV TVB tea/coffee Direct dial from bedrooms Licensed Cen ht
Last d 8pm Wi-fi available **Parking** 10 **Notes** LB No coaches

★★★★ A INN
The Crown Inn

21 Market Place YO62 5BJ
☎ 01439 770297
e–mail: info@tchh.co.uk
web: www.tchh.co.uk

dir: *A19 onto A170 at the top of market square*

Rooms 12 en suite 7 annexe en suite (2 fmly) (6 GF) S £50–£80;
D £80–£160✳ **Facilities** TVB tea/coffee Cen ht TVL Dinner **Parking** 30
Notes LB

HUBY   MAP 19 SE56

★★★ GUEST ACCOMMODATION
The New Inn Motel

Main St YO61 1HQ
☎ 01347 810219 📄 01347 810219
e–mail: enquiries@newinnmotel.freeserve.co.uk
web: www.newinnmotel.co.uk

dir: *Off A19 E into village centre, motel on left*

Located behind the New Inn, this modern motel-style accommodation
has a quiet location in the village of Huby, nine miles north of York.
Comfortable bedrooms are spacious and neatly furnished, and
breakfast is served in the cosy dining room. The reception area hosts
an array of tourist information and the resident owners provide a
friendly and helpful service.

Rooms 8 en suite (3 fmly) (8 GF) S £35–£50; D £60–£70✳
Facilities TVB tea/coffee Cen ht **Parking** 8 **Notes** LB Closed mid
Nov–mid Dec & part Feb

HUNTON   MAP 19 SE19

★★★ ➡ INN
The Countryman's Inn

Bedale DL8 1PY
☎ 01677 450554
e–mail: tony@countrymansinn.co.uk

dir: *Located between Bedale and Leyburn 2m N of A684*

Set in the heart of this quiet village, the inn is popular with visitors and
locals and serves good home-made food. The resident owner and staff
provide warm hospitality, and the bedrooms are smartly furnished and
comfortably equipped.

Rooms 3 en suite **Facilities** FTV TVB tea/coffee Cen ht TVL Dinner Last
d 8.45pm Wi-fi available **Parking** 11 **Notes** RS Mon–Tue

INGLETON   MAP 18 SD67

★★★★ BED & BREAKFAST
Gale Green Cottage

Westhouse LA6 3NJ
☎ 015242 41245 & 077867 82088
e–mail: jill@galegreen.com

dir: *2m NW of Ingleton. S of A65 at Masongill x-rds*

Peacefully located in a rural hamlet, this 300-year-old house has been
lovingly renovated to provide modern facilities without compromising
original charm and character. Thoughtfully furnished bedrooms feature
smart modern en suite shower rooms and a guest lounge is also
available.

Rooms 3 en suite (1 fmly) S £29; D £58 **Facilities** FTV TVB tea/coffee
Cen ht TVL **Parking** 6 **Notes** ➡

★★★★ GUEST ACCOMMODATION
Inglenook

20 Main St LA6 3HJ
☎ 01524 241270
e–mail: inglenook20@hotmail.com
web: www.inglenookguesthouse.com

dir: *Off A65 New Rd onto Main St*

Close to the River Greta with lovely views of Ingleborough peak, this
comfortable Victorian house extends a warm welcome. Bedrooms are
freshly decorated and have a host of comforts. A lounge is also
available.

Rooms 4 rms (3 en suite) (1 pri facs) 1 annexe en suite (1 GF) ⊛
D £50–£56 **Facilities** FTV TVB tea/coffee Cen ht TVL **Notes** LB ⊗
No children 5yrs Closed Xmas

KIRKBYMOORSIDE   MAP 19 SE68

★★★★ ⊠ FARM HOUSE
Brickfields Farm *(SE704852)*

Kirby Mills YO62 6NS
☎ 01751 433074 Mrs J Trousdale
e–mail: janet@brickfieldsfarm.co.uk
web: www.brickfieldsfarm.co.uk

dir: *A170 E from Kirkbymoorside, 0.5m right into Kirby Mills (signed), farm 1st right*

Rooms 2 en suite 4 annexe en suite (6 GF) S £50–£60; D £76–£90✱
Facilities FTV TVB tea/coffee Cen ht Wi-fi available Golf **Parking** 8
Notes LB ⊗ No children 15 acres non-working ⊜

KNARESBOROUGH   MAP 19 SE35

Premier Collection

★★★★★ ⋒ ⇔ GUEST HOUSE
Gallon House

47 Kirkgate HG5 8BZ
☎ 01423 862102
e–mail: gallon-house@ntlworld.com
web: www.gallon-house.co.uk

dir: *Adjacent to railway station*

This delightful building has spectacular views over the River Nidd, and offers very stylish accommodation and a homely atmosphere. The bedrooms are all individual with many homely extras. Rick's culinary delights are not to be missed. Dinner (by arrangement) and breakfast, feature quality local and home-made produce. Sue and Rick Hodgson were finalists for the AA Friendliest Landlady of the Year 2008 Award.

Rooms 3 en suite S £60–£85; D £90–£120✱ **Facilities** FTV TVB tea/coffee Licensed Cen ht Dinner Last d 24hrs notice Wi-fi available
Notes LB No coaches ⊜

See advert on this page

Premier Collection

★★★★★ ⊛⊛ RESTAURANT WITH ROOMS
General Tarleton Inn

Boroughbridge Rd, Ferrensby HG5 0PZ
☎ 01423 340284 ▤ 01423 340288
e–mail: gti@generaltarleton.co.uk

dir: *A1(M) junct 48 at Boroughbridge, take A6055 to Knaresborough. 4m on right*

Food is a real feature here with skilfully prepared meals served in the restaurant, traditional bar and modern conservatory. Accommodation is provided in brightly decorated and airy rooms, and the bathrooms are thoughtfully equipped. Enjoying a country location, yet close to the A1(M), the inn remains popular with both business and leisure guests.

Rooms 14 en suite (7 GF) S fr £107; D fr £129✱ **Facilities** TVB tea/coffee Direct dial from bedrooms Cen ht Dinner Last d 9.15pm Wi-fi available **Conf** Max 40 Thtr 40 Class 35 Board 20 Del £165 ✱
Parking 40 **Notes LB** ⊗

★★★★ ⋒ GUEST ACCOMMODATION
Newton House

5–7 York Place HG5 0AD
☎ 01423 863539 ▤ 01423 869748
e–mail: newtonhouse@btinternet.com
web: www.newtonhouseyorkshire.com

dir: *On A59 in Knaresborough, 500yds from town centre*

The delightful 18th-century former coaching inn is only a short walk from the river, castle and market square. The property is entered by an archway into a courtyard. The attractive, very well-equipped bedrooms include some four-posters and also king-size doubles. There is a comfortable lounge, and memorable breakfasts are served in the attractive dining room.

Rooms 9 rms (8 en suite) (1 pri facs) 2 annexe en suite (3 fmly) (3 GF) S £50–£85; D £75–£100✱ **Facilities** FTV TVB tea/coffee Direct dial from bedrooms Cen ht TVL Wi-fi available **Parking** 10 **Notes LB** Closed 1wk Xmas

LEYBURN MAP 19 SE19

★★★★★ BED & BREAKFAST

Thorney Hall

Spennithorne DL8 5PW

☎ 01969 622120 & 07836 269453

e–mail: nesbit1954@btinternet.com

This beautiful, lovingly restored country house offers period features, open fireplaces and elegant furnishings. Bedrooms are well appointed and each has either a modern en suite or private bathroom. Guests receive a warm welcome and have use of an attractive lounge. Well-cooked evening meals and hearty breakfasts are served at a traditional table in the grand dining room. Jan Scott-Collier was a finalist for the AA Friendliest Landlady of the Year 2008 Award.

Rooms 3 rms (2 en suite) (1 pri facs) S £75; D £90✱ **Facilities** TVB tea/coffee Cen ht Dinner Last d 4pm Golf 🏌 🏄 **Parking** 10 **Notes** No children 12yrs 🐾

LONG PRESTON MAP 18 SD85

Ⓤ

Boars Head

9 Main St BD23 4ND

☎ 01729 840217 📠 01729 840217

e–mail: darrenjmonks@hotmail.co.uk

web: www.yorkshirenet.co.uk/stayat/theboarshead/

dir: *On A65 between Skipton and Settle*

At the time of going to press the rating for this establishment had not been confirmed. Please check the AA website www.theAA.com for up-to-date information.

Rooms 5 en suite (2 fmly) S £37.50; D £50✱ **Facilities** TVB tea/coffee Cen ht Dinner Last d 9pm Wi-fi available Pool Table **Parking** 25 **Notes** 🐾 ch fac

---

LOW ROW MAP 18 SD99

★★★★ INN

The Punch Bowl Inn

DL11 6PF

☎ 01748 886233 📠 01748 886945

e–mail: info@pbinn.co.uk

dir: *From Scotch Corner take A6108 to Richmond then B6270 to Low Row*

This friendly inn has recently been refurbished in a contemporary style. Real ales and freshly-cooked meals are served in either the spacious bar or dining room. The modern bedrooms are simply furnished and stylish, with well-equipped bathrooms. Guests also have use of a lounge, which like all rooms has stunning views of the Dales.

Rooms 9 en suite 2 annexe en suite (1 GF) D £72.50–£110✱ **Facilities** TVB tea/coffee Direct dial from bedrooms Cen ht TVL Dinner Last d 9pm Fishing Riding **Parking** 20 **Notes** LB 🐾 Closed 25 Dec

---

MALHAM MAP 18 SD96

★★★★ 🏠 🍽 GUEST HOUSE

River House

BD23 4DA

☎ 01729 830315

e–mail: info@riverhousehotel.co.uk

web: www.riverhousehotel.co.uk

dir: *Off A65, N to Malham*

A warm welcome awaits you at this attractive house, which dates from 1664. The bedrooms are bright and comfortable, with one on the ground floor. Public areas include a cosy lounge and a large, well-appointed dining room. Breakfasts and evening meals offer choice and quality above expectation and are well worthy of the Breakfast and Dinner Awards held.

Rooms 8 en suite (1 GF) S £45–£60; D £60–£100 **Facilities** TVB tea/coffee Licensed Cen ht Dinner Last d 8pm Wi-fi available **Parking** 5 **Notes** LB No children 9yrs No coaches

---

★★★ GUEST HOUSE

Beck Hall

Cove Rd BD23 4DJ

☎ 01729 830332

e–mail: alice@beckhallmalham.com

web: www.beckhallmalham.com

dir: *A65 to Gargrave, turn right to Malham. 100yds on right after mini rdbt*

A small stone bridge over Malham Beck leads to this delightful property. Dating from 1710, the house has true character, with bedrooms carefully furnished with four-poster beds. Delicious afternoon teas are available in the colourful garden in warmer months, while roaring log fires welcome you in the winter.

Rooms 10 rms (9 en suite) (1 pri facs) 7 annexe en suite (4 fmly) (4 GF) S £25–£60; D £54–£80✱ **Facilities** STV TV15B tea/coffee Licensed Cen ht Dinner Last d 6pm Wi-fi available Fishing Riding **Conf** Max 35 Thtr 30 Class 30 Board 30 Del from £29 ✱ **Parking** 40 **Notes** LB

MASHAM	MAP 19 SE28

★★★★ 🏠 🍽 GUEST HOUSE
Bank Villa
HG4 4DB
☎ 01765 689605
e–mail: bankvilla@btopenworld.com
web: www.bankvilla.com
dir: *Enter on A6108 from Ripon, property on right*

An elegant Georgian house set in a pretty walled garden. Individually decorated bedrooms feature stripped pine, period furniture and crisp white linen. Imaginative home-cooked meals are served in the attractive dining room. Character public rooms include a choice of lounges, or relax in the garden in summer.

Rooms 6 rms (4 en suite) (2 pri facs) (2 fmly) S £50–£65; D £55–£95✻
Facilities tea/coffee Licensed Cen ht TVL Dinner Last d breakfast
Parking 6 **Notes LB** ⊗ No children 5yrs No coaches

MIDDLESBROUGH	MAP 19 NZ41

★★★★ GUEST ACCOMMODATION
The Grey House
79 Cambridge Rd, Linthorpe TS5 5NL
☎ 01642 817485 🖷 01642 817485
e–mail: denistaylor–100@btinternet.com
web: www.greyhousehotel.co.uk
dir: *A19 N onto A1130 & A1032 Acklam Rd, right at lights*
This Edwardian mansion stands in mature gardens in a quiet residential area, and is lovingly maintained to provide a relaxing retreat. The master bedrooms are well sized, and the upper rooms, though smaller, also offer good comfort. Downstairs there is an attractive lounge and the breakfast room.

Rooms 9 en suite (1 fmly) S £48; D £65✻ **Facilities** FTV TVB tea/coffee Direct dial from bedrooms Cen ht TVL Wi-fi available **Parking** 10 **Notes LB**

MUKER	MAP 18 SD99

★★★★ FARM HOUSE
Oxnop Hall *(SD931973)*
Low Oxnop, Gunnerside DL11 6JJ
☎ 01748 886253 🖷 01748 886253 Mrs A Porter
dir: *Off B6270 between Muker and Gunnerside*

Set in beautiful Swaledale scenery, this smartly presented 17th-century farmhouse has been furnished with thought and care. The attractive bedrooms are well equipped and some boast original exposed beams and mullion windows. Hearty farmhouse breakfasts are served, using local and home-made produce where possible. A cosy lounge is also available.

Rooms 4 en suite 1 annexe en suite (1 GF) S £33–£42; D £64–£74✻
Facilities FTV TVB tea/coffee Cen ht **Parking** 10 **Notes** ⊗ No children 10yrs 1300 acres beef sheep hill farming Closed Dec–15 Feb RS 22 Mar 🍽

NORTHALLERTON	MAP 19 SE39

★★★★ GUEST HOUSE
Windsor Guest House
56 South Pde DL7 8SL
☎ 01609 774100 🖷 01609 774100
e–mail: windsorguesthouse@yahoo.co.uk
dir: *On A684 at S end of High St*
This Victorian terrace house is convenient for the town centre. The well maintained accommodation consists of bright, cheerful, and thoughtfully equipped bedrooms with en suite bathrooms. The attractive dining room looks out to the back garden and is a pleasant venue for tasty breakfasts served by the friendly proprietors.

Rooms 6 rms (5 en suite) (1 pri facs) S £35; D £55✻ **Facilities** FTV TVB tea/coffee Cen ht TVL Wi-fi available **Parking** 1 **Notes** ⊗ No coaches

OLDSTEAD MAP 19 SE57

◉ U

The Black Swan at Oldstead

YO61 4BL

☎ 01347 868387 & 868634

e–mail: enquiries@blackswanoldstead.co.uk

dir: *Leave A19 3m S Thirsk for Coxwold, left in Coxwold, left at Byland Abbey for Oldstead*

At the time of going to press the rating for this establishment had not been confirmed. Please check the AA website www.theAA.com for up-to-date information.

Rooms 4 annexe en suite (4 GF) S £50–£100; D £95–£130✱
Facilities FTV TVB tea/coffee Cen ht Dinner Last d 9pm Wi-fi available
Parking 4 **Notes LB** ⊗

OSMOTHERLEY MAP 19 SE49

★★★ INN

Queen Catherine

7 West End DL6 3AG

☎ 01609 883209

e–mail: info@queencatherinehotel.co.uk

dir: *Off A19 into village centre*

This traditional inn nestles in the heart of a picturesque village. Bedrooms are compact yet comfortably equipped and decorated. The cosy bar offers imaginative menus and the hearty breakfasts make good use of fresh local produce.

Rooms 5 en suite S £32.50; D £65✱ **Facilities** TVB tea/coffee Cen ht TVL Dinner Last d 8.45pm

PATELEY BRIDGE MAP 19 SE16

★★★★ GUEST ACCOMMODATION

Foxfield Bed and Breakfast

Ripon Rd HG3 5NJ

☎ 01423 711685 📠 01423 715804

e–mail: foxfieldeaxis-connect.com

web: www.foxfieldbnb.co.uk

A warm welcome awaits you at Foxfield, which is in a quiet residential area on the southern fringe of Pateley Bridge. The immaculate house provides comfortable bedrooms with homely extras; the front bedrooms and dining room boast panoramic views across the Dales.

Rooms 3 en suite (1 fmly) **Facilities** TVB tea/coffee Cen ht Wi-fi available **Parking** 4 **Notes** ⊗ Closed Xmas & New Year ⊜

★★★ GUEST ACCOMMODATION

Roslyn House

9 King St HG3 5AT

☎ 01423 711374 📠 01423 715995

e–mail: roslynhousepb@aol.com

web: www.roslynhouse.co.uk

dir: *B6165 into Pateley Bridge, end of High St turn right at newsagents, house 200yds on left*

You are assured of a very warm welcome at this well-maintained guest house in the village centre. Bedrooms are sensibly furnished and offer many homely touches. A very comfortable lounge is available and hearty breakfasts set you up for the day. Roslyn House caters well for cyclists and walkers on the famous Nidderdale Way.

Rooms 6 en suite (6 fmly) S £40–£49; D £59–£64✱ **Facilities** TVB tea/coffee Cen ht TVL Wi-fi available **Conf** Max 8 Board 8 **Parking** 4 **Notes LB** ⊗ No children 12yrs ⊜

PICKERING MAP 19 SE78

Premier Collection

★★★★★ ⬥ GUEST ACCOMMODATION

17 Burgate

17 Burgate YO18 7AU

☎ 01751 473463

e–mail: info@17burgate.co.uk

dir: *From A170 follow sign to Castle passing 17 Burgate on right*

An elegant market town house close to the centre and the castle, offering comfortable individually designed bedrooms with all modern facilities including free broadband. Public areas include a comfortable lounge bar, and breakfast includes a wide choice of local, healthy foods.

Rooms 5 en suite S £70–£75; D £85–£115 **Facilities** FTV TVB tea/coffee Direct dial from bedrooms Cen ht Wi-fi available **Parking** 7 **Notes LB** ⊗ No children 10yrs

RAVENSCAR MAP 19 NZ90

★★★★ 🅰 GUEST ACCOMMODATION

Smugglers Rock Country House

YO13 0ER

☎ 01723 870044

e–mail: info@smugglersrock.co.uk

dir: *0.5m S of Ravenscar. Off A171 towards Ravenscar, opp stone windmill*

Rooms 8 en suite (3 fmly) S £36–£40; D £62–£70✱ **Facilities** TVB tea/coffee Cen ht TVL **Parking** 12 **Notes LB** ⊗ No children 5yrs Closed Nov–Mar RS end Mar–early Oct

REETH
MAP 19 SE09

★★★★ ➲ INN
Charles Bathurst Inn
Arkengarthdale DL11 6EN
☎ 01748 884567 📄 01748 884599
e–mail: info@cbinn.co.uk

dir: *B6270 to Reeth, at Buck Hotel turn N to Langthwaite, pass church on right, inn 0.5m on right*

The CB Inn, as it is known, is surrounded by magnificent scenery high in the Dales. Food is the focus of the pub, where a choice of rustic eating areas makes for atmospheric dining. The well-equipped bedrooms blend contemporary and traditional styles and cosy lounge areas are available. A well-equipped function suite is also available.

Rooms 19 en suite (2 fmly) (5 GF) D £72.50–£115✱ **Facilities** TVB tea/coffee Direct dial from bedrooms Cen ht Dinner Last d 9pm Wi-fi available Fishing Riding Pool Table **Conf** Max 100 Thtr 100 Class 30 Board 30 Del from £89.80 ✱ **Parking** 35 **Notes** LB ⊗ Closed 25 Dec

RICCALL
MAP 16 SE63

★★★★ GUEST ACCOMMODATION
The Park View
20 Main St YO19 6PX
☎ 01757 248458 📄 01757 249211
e–mail: mail@parkviewriccall.co.uk
web: www.parkviewriccall.co.uk

dir: *A19 from Selby, left for Riccall by water tower, 100yds on right*

The well-furnished and comfortable Park View stands in grounds and offers well-equipped bedrooms. There is a cosy lounge plus a small bar, while breakfasts are served in the dining room. Dinner is available midweek.

Rooms 7 en suite (1 fmly) S £49–£51; D £71–£74✱ **Facilities** TVB tea/coffee Cen ht TVL Dinner Last d at booking Mon–Thu Wi-fi available **Parking** 10

★★★★ 🄰 GUEST ACCOMMODATION
Dairymans of Riccall
14 Kelfield Rd YO19 6PG
☎ 01757 248532 📄 0871 251 3863
e–mail: bookings@dairymansriccall.co.uk

dir: *Off A19 into village, off Main St onto Silver St & Kelfield Rd*

Rooms 4 en suite (1 fmly) S £30; D £60✱ **Facilities** FTV TVB tea/coffee Cen ht TVL Wi-fi available **Notes** ⊗

★★★★ 🄰 BED & BREAKFAST
White Rose Villa
33 York Rd YO19 6QG
☎ 01757 248115
e–mail: whiterosevilla@btinternet.com
web: www.whiterosevilla-info.com

dir: *From A19, signed Riccall, 50mtrs on right*

Rooms 3 en suite (2 fmly) S £30–£35; D £56✱ **Facilities** TVB tea/coffee **Parking** 4 **Notes** LB ⊗ Closed 24–26 & 31 Dec ⊚

RICHMOND
MAP 19 NZ10

See also Reeth

★★★★ FARM HOUSE
Whashton Springs Farm *(NZ149046)*
DL11 7JS
☎ 01748 822884 📄 01748 826285 Mrs J M Turnbull
e–mail: whashtonsprings@btconnect.com

dir: *In Richmond N at lights towards Ravensworth, 3m down steep hill, farm at bottom on left*

A friendly welcome awaits you at this farmhouse accommodation, situated in the heart of the countryside yet convenient for major routes. Bedrooms are split between the courtyard rooms and the main farmhouse. Hearty breakfasts are served in the spacious dining room overlooking the gardens. A stylish lounge is also available.

Rooms 3 en suite 5 annexe en suite (2 fmly) (5 GF) **Facilities** TVB tea/coffee Cen ht **Conf** Max 16 Board 16 **Parking** 10 **Notes** ⊗ No children 5yrs 600 acres arable beef mixed sheep Closed late Dec–Jan ⊚

★★★ 🄰 GUEST HOUSE
Pottergate
4 Pottergate DL10 4AB
☎ 01748 823826

dir: *A1608 to Richmond, over 1st rdbt & lights, 50yds on left*

Rooms 6 rms (1 en suite) (2 pri facs) (1 fmly) S £25–£45; D £55–£65 **Facilities** TV1B tea/coffee Cen ht **Parking** 2 **Notes** ⊗ No children 3yrs No coaches ⊚

RICHMOND CONTINUED

★★ GUEST HOUSE
The Moat House
9 Castle Hill DL10 4QP
☎ 01748 823285
e–mail: themoathousehotel@hotmail.com

Located close to Richmond Castle and the Market Place this friendly guest house offers bedrooms divided between the main house and adjacent cottage, with a few en suite rooms available. Breakfast and other home cooked meals are served throughout the day in the café on the ground floor, and a small bar with pool table is available on the first floor.

Rooms 13 rms (13 pri facs) 1 annexe en suite (4 fmly) (3 GF)
Facilities FTV TVB tea/coffee Licensed Cen ht TVL Dinner Last d 9.30pm Pool Table **Notes** Civ Wed

---

RIPON
MAP 19 SE37

Premier Collection

★★★★★ 🏠 FARM HOUSE
Mallard Grange *(SE270704)*
Aldfield HG4 3BE
☎ 01765 620242 📠 01765 620242 Mrs M Johnson
e–mail: maggie@mallardgrange.co.uk
web: www.mallardgrange.co.uk
dir: *B6265 W fom Ripon, Mallard Grange 2.5m on right*

Located near Fountains Abbey a genuine welcome is always guaranteed here. The original features of this early 16th-century, Grade II-listed farmhouse are highlighted by quality furnishings and décor. Bedrooms, two of which are in a converted smithy, are filled with a wealth of thoughtful extras, and comprehensive breakfasts feature home-reared and local produce.

Rooms 2 en suite 2 annexe en suite (2 GF) D £75–£105 **Facilities** TVB tea/coffee Cen ht Wi-fi available **Parking** 6 **Notes LB** ⊗ No children 12yrs 500 acres Mixed, beef, sheep, arable Closed Xmas & New Year

★★★★★ 🅰 GUEST ACCOMMODATION
The Old Coach House
2 Stable Cottages, North Stainley HG4 3HT
☎ 01765 634900 📠 01765 635352
e–mail: enquiries@oldcoachhouse.info
web: www.oldcoachhouse.info

dir: *From Ripon take A6108 to Masham. Once in North Stainley, on left opposite Staveley Arms*

Rooms 8 en suite (4 GF) **Facilities** FTV TVB tea/coffee Direct dial from bedrooms Cen ht **Parking** 8 **Notes** ⊗ No children 14yrs Closed Jan

See advert on opposite page

★★★★ 🏠 FARM HOUSE
Bay Tree Farm *(SE263685)*
Aldfield HG4 3BE
☎ 01765 620394 📠 01765 620394 Mrs V Leeming
e–mail: val@btfarm.entadsl.com
web: www.baytreefarm.co.uk
dir: *4m W of Ripon. S off B6265*

A warm welcome awaits you at this farmhouse set in the countryside close to Fountains Abbey and Studley Park. Bedrooms are suitably equipped, there is a cosy lounge with a log-burning stove, and breakfast is traditional home-cooked fare. Dinner is available for groups of eight or more by arrangement. Val Leeming was a finalist for the AA Friendliest Landlady of the Year 2008.

Rooms 4 en suite 2 annexe en suite (1 fmly) (3 GF) S £45–£60; D £80–£95✷ **Facilities** TVB tea/coffee Cen ht Dinner Last d 10am **Parking** 10 **Notes** 400 acres beef arable

★★★★ FARM HOUSE
St George's Court (SE237697)
Old Home Farm, Grantley HG4 3PJ
☎ 01765 620618 Mrs Hitchen
e-mail: stgeorgescourt@bronco.co.uk
web: www.stgeorges-court.co.uk
dir: B6265 W from Ripon, right signed Grantley & Winksley, up hill 1m past Risplith sign & next right

This renovated farmhouse is a great location to get away from it all, in the delightful countryside close to Fountains Abbey. Attractive, well-equipped ground-floor bedrooms are located around a central courtyard. Imaginative breakfasts are served in the conservatory-dining room, which has splendid views of the surrounding countryside.

Rooms 5 en suite (1 fmly) (5 GF) S £45–£55; D £65–£75✱
Facilities TVB tea/coffee Cen ht Fishing **Conf** Max 12 **Parking** 12
Notes LB 20 acres beef /sheep/pigs

ROBIN HOOD'S BAY   MAP 19 NZ90

★★★ INN
The Flask Inn
Fylingdales YO22 4QH
☎ 01947 880305
e-mail: admin@theflaskinn.com
dir: On A171, 7m S from Whitby

The Flask, originally a 16th-century hostel, is now a comfortable inn offering a good range of real ales and food. Thoughtfully equipped bedrooms are furnished in attractive pine and have modern shower rooms en suite. The spacious bar has a friendly atmosphere.

Rooms 6 en suite (2 fmly) **Facilities** TVB tea/coffee Cen ht Dinner Last d 9pm Pool Table **Conf** Max 40 **Parking** 20

The Old Coach House
2 Stable Cottages, North Stanley, Ripon HG4 3HT

The Old Coach House is an accommodation jewel and one of Yorkshire's best kept secrets. The 18th century coaching house stands proud in the grounds of North Stanley Hall in the picturesque village of North Stanley, just north of Ripon.

This 5 star luxury guesthouse is nestled between The Yorkshire Dales and North Yorkshire Moors National Park and is a great location to explore these beautiful areas of outstanding natural beauty as well as The Yorkshire Wolds, Nidderdale, Harrogate and York.

The area is steeped in history with the historic city of Ripon nearby as well as countryside walks, attractions, plentiful restaurants and country pubs.

All eight rooms are en-suite and designed with modern living in mind. Each room offers a range of contemporary high quality fittings and facilities including tea/coffee, safe, telephone, hair dryer, flat screen TV, alarm clock and refrigerator.

With Oak beams in some of the guest rooms this high quality bed and breakfast really gives that feeling of staying in a rustic, character property.

Tel: 01765 634900   **Fax:** 01765 635352   **Website:** www.oldcoachhouse.info   **Email:** enquiries@oldcoachhouse.info

ROBIN HOOD'S BAY continued

★★★ 🍽 RESTAURANT WITH ROOMS
Bramblewick

2 King St YO22 4SH

☎ 01947 880960 & 880339 📄 01947 880960

e–mail: bramblewick@btinternet.com

dir: *A171 onto B1447 to rdbt, straight over & down steep hill into 'Old Village', establishment at bottom on left*

Only yards from the lifeboat slipway and the beach, this building dates from the 17th century. Modern en suite bedrooms have great atmosphere with low beams, and below is a popular daytime café that changes to offer intimate candlelight dinner in the evenings. Parking is at Bank Top, a five minute walk from the old village. Cars can stop briefly in the old village, to drop off or pick up passengers.

Rooms 3 en suite D £65–£70 **Facilities** TVB tea/coffee Cen ht Dinner Last d 8.30pm **Notes LB** ⊗ Closed 24–26 Dec

---

ROSEDALE ABBEY   MAP 19 SE79

★★★★ GUEST ACCOMMODATION
Sevenford House

YO18 8SE

☎ 01751 417283

e–mail: sevenford@aol.com

web: www.sevenford.com

dir: *Off A170 at sign for Rosedale Abbey, in village turn sharp left at Coach & House Restaurant & right at White Horse*

Set in the heart of the national park, this elegant Victorian house stands in a peaceful garden within walking distance of the village. The well-proportioned bedrooms are comfortable, well equipped and have stunning panoramic views. There is also an inviting lounge and a spacious breakfast room with grand piano.

Rooms 3 en suite (1 fmly) S fr £40; D fr £60 **Facilities** TVB tea/coffee Cen ht Wi-fi available **Parking** 6 **Notes LB** ⊗ 🐾

SCARBOROUGH   MAP 17 TA08

★★★★★ 🍴 BED & BREAKFAST
Holly Croft

28 Station Rd, Scalby YO13 0QA

☎ 01723 375376 & 07759 429706

e–mail: christine.goodall@tesco.net

web: www.holly-croft.co.uk

dir: *A171 at Scalby x-rds, turn right at tennis courts, 500yds on right*

A beautifully appointed detached Victorian house in a quiet residential area in the village of Scalby. All rooms including the spacious bedrooms are furnished with family antiques and thoughtful accessories are provided. Guests can relax in the lounge and there is also a billiard room and large garden.

Rooms 2 rms (1 en suite) (1 pri facs) S £45–£50; D £70–£75✱
Facilities tea/coffee Cen ht TVL Dinner Last d 10am Wi-fi available
Parking 2 **Notes LB** ⊗ No children 5yrs Closed Xmas & New Year 🐾

★★★★ GUEST ACCOMMODATION
Columbus

124 Columbus Ravine YO12 7QZ

☎ 01723 374634 & 07930 545964

e–mail: hotel.columbus@lineone.net

dir: *On A165 towards North Bay, near Peasholm Park*

Yorkshire hospitality at its best is offered here, and Bonnie Purchon is a welcoming hostess. The establishment is well located for the beach and attractions. Bedrooms are compact, well equipped and homely. A very comfortable lounge is provided. In the dining room a good breakfast is served, as are evening meals during the main season.

Rooms 10 en suite (2 fmly) S £34–£40; D £68–£78✱ **Facilities** TVB tea/coffee Cen ht Dinner Last d am **Parking** 8 **Notes LB** ⊗ No children 3yrs

★★★★ GUEST ACCOMMODATION
The Danielle

9 Esplanade Rd, South Cliff YO11 2AS

☎ 01723 366206

e–mail: hoteldanielle@yahoo.co.uk

dir: *S of town centre. Off A165 Filey Rd onto Victoria Av, left onto Esplanade, left onto Esplanade Rd*

A warm welcome is assured at this elegant Victorian house situated a short walk from the Spa Cliff Lift. Bedrooms are equipped with thoughtful extras, and day rooms include an attractive dining room and a lounge.

Rooms 9 rms (7 en suite) (3 fmly) S £26–£28; D £56–£68✱
Facilities TVB tea/coffee Cen ht TVL **Notes LB** ⊗ No children 2yrs Closed Dec–mid Feb

ENGLAND

★★★★ GUEST ACCOMMODATION
The Hillcrest

2 Peasholm Av YO12 7NE

☎ 01723 361981

e-mail: enquiries@hillcresthotel.co.uk

dir: *A165 to North Bay/leisure parks, onto Peasholm Dr & Peasholm Crescent*

Hillcrest is in a residential area close to Peasholm Park, within walking distance of the cricket ground and the North Bay attractions, and its individually furnished bedrooms contain many extras. There is a spacious guest lounge with video library and an attractive breakfast room.

Rooms 7 en suite (1 fmly) S £25–£35; D £50–£60✳ **Facilities** FTV TVB tea/coffee Cen ht TVL Dinner Last d 10am **Parking** 3 **Notes LB** ⊗ Closed 22–29 Dec

★★★★ GUEST ACCOMMODATION
Olivers

34 West St YO11 2QP

☎ 01723 368717

e-mail: olivershotel@scarborough.co.uk

dir: *Take A64 to B1427 (Margarets Rd). Right onto A165 (Filey Rd). Take 2nd left onto Granville Rd*

Well-equipped, spacious bedrooms are a feature of this Victorian gentleman's residence, and one bedroom was originally the nursery. Close to the cliff lift down to the spa, beaches and gardens, and centrally located on the South Cliff.

Rooms 6 en suite (2 fmly) (1 GF) **Facilities** TVB tea/coffee Cen ht Dinner Last d breakfast **Notes** ⊗ Closed 20–28 Dec

★★★★ GUEST ACCOMMODATION
Paragon

123 Queens Pde YO12 7HU

☎ 01723 372676 🖻 01723 372676

e-mail: enquiries@paragon-hotel.fsnet.co.uk

web: www.paragonhotel.com

dir: *On A64, follow signs for North Bay. Establishment on clifftop*

This welcoming Victorian terrace house has been carefully renovated to provide stylish, thoughtfully equipped, non-smoking accommodation. Hearty English breakfasts are served in the attractive dining room and there is also a lounge bar with a fabulous sea view.

Rooms 14 en suite (1 fmly) **Facilities** TVB tea/coffee Direct dial from bedrooms Cen ht Dinner Last d 1pm **Parking** 6 **Notes** No children 3yrs Closed 20 Nov–24 Jan

★★★★ GUEST ACCOMMODATION
The Ramleh

135 Queens Pde YO12 7HY

☎ 01723 365745

e-mail: info@theramleh.co.uk

dir: *A64/A165 to North Bay & Alexandra Bowling Centre. At Bowling Centre, follow Queens Parade*

Overlooking North Bay, this welcoming terrace house has a friendly atmosphere. The modern bedrooms are bright and comfortable, and tasty breakfasts are served in the spacious dining room, which also has a well-stocked bar and a stunning view.

Rooms 9 rms (8 en suite) (1 pri facs) (3 fmly) S £25–£35; D £50–£60✳ **Facilities** TVB tea/coffee Cen ht TVL Dinner Last d 10am **Parking** 6 **Notes LB** ⊗ Closed 24–29 Dec

★★★★ GUEST ACCOMMODATION
The Whiteley

99/101 Queens Pde YO12 7HY

☎ 01723 373514 🖻 01723 373007

e-mail: whiteleyhotel@bigfoot.com

dir: *A64/A165 to North Bay & Peasholm Park, right onto Peasholm Rd, 1st left*

The Whiteley is an immaculately run, sea-facing home from home. Bedrooms, if compact, are carefully decorated and have many thoughtful extras. There's a small garden at the rear, a choice of lounges, and a bar. The establishment has some superb views, and the owners provide personal attention and a substantial breakfast.

Rooms 10 en suite (3 fmly) (1 GF) S £30.50–£32; D £49–£60 **Facilities** TVB tea/coffee Cen ht TVL **Parking** 8 **Notes LB** ⊗ No children 3yrs Closed 30 Nov–Jan

SCARBOROUGH CONTINUED

★★★★ GUEST ACCOMMODATION
The Windmill Bed & Breakfast
Mill St, Off Victoria Rd YO11 1SZ
☎ 01723 372735 📄 01723 377190
e-mail: info@windmill-hotel.co.uk
web: www.windmill-hotel.co.uk

dir: *A64 into Scarborough, pass Sainsbury's, left onto Victoria Rd, 3rd left onto Mill St*

Situated in the centre of town but having its own car park, this unique establishment has modern bedrooms situated around a courtyard next to a windmill dating from 1784. The base of the mill includes a spacious breakfast room and a toy museum which is only viewable by guests.

Rooms 11 en suite (3 fmly) (6 GF) D £64–£110 **Facilities** TVB tea/coffee Cen ht **Parking** 7 **Notes** ⊗

★★★★ 🅰 GUEST ACCOMMODATION
The Wharncliffe
26 Blenheim Ter YO12 7HD
☎ 01723 374635
e-mail: info@thewharncliffescarborough.co.uk

dir: *Follow signs to Castle, left onto Blenheim St, left onto Blenheim Ter*

Rooms 12 en suite D £58–£68 **Facilities** FTV TVB tea/coffee Cen ht TVL Wi-fi available **Notes LB** ⊗ No children 18yrs

★★★ GUEST ACCOMMODATION
Chessington
The Crescent YO11 2PP
☎ 01723 365207 📄 01723 375206
e-mail: info@thechessington.co.uk
web: www.thechessington.co.uk

dir: *A64 to town centre lights, right, left at next lights & right at next lights, Chessington on left*

This Grade II listed building occupies a fine position overlooking the Crescent and is close to the town centre. The bedrooms are well equipped, and the spacious dining room is the setting for comprehensive breakfasts. A sitting room and lounge bar are available.

Rooms 10 en suite (2 fmly) **Facilities** TVB tea/coffee Cen ht TVL **Conf** Max 10 **Notes** ⊗ Closed Dec & Jan

★★★ ⚓ GUEST ACCOMMODATION
The Croft
87 Queens Pde YO12 7HT
☎ 01723 373904
e-mail: information@crofthotel.co.uk
web: www.crofthotel.co.uk

dir: *Follow tourist signs for North Bay seafront, along front towards castle headland, right turn up cliff, right at top, premises on left*

A flexible approach to your needs is a key feature of this friendly establishment. It overlooks the bay, so you can enjoy the spectacular view from the comfortable lounge or from the patio in fine weather. Meals are served in the very pleasant well-appointed dining room.

Rooms 6 rms (5 en suite) (1 pri facs) (4 fmly) S £24–£27.50; D £48–£55✱ **Facilities** TVB tea/coffee Cen ht TVL **Parking** 4 **Notes LB** ⊗ Closed Dec–Feb

★★★ GUEST ACCOMMODATION
The Moorings
3 Burniston Rd YO12 6PG
☎ 01723 373786
e-mail: post@scarboroughmoorings.co.uk

dir: *From N Bay, the Moorings is on the main A165 opposite Kinderland*

Located in a quiet area close to the North Bay, this large detached house offers a friendly welcome, spacious dining room and private parking. There are a variety of bedroom styles including family rooms, a wheelchair accessible annexe room and several with separate lounges.

Rooms 11 en suite 1 annexe en suite (2 fmly) (1 GF) S £32–£35; D £64–£80✱ **Facilities** FTV TVB tea/coffee Cen ht TVL Wi-fi available **Parking** 12 **Notes LB** ⊗ Closed 2wks Xmas

★★★ FARM HOUSE
Plane Tree Cottage Farm *(SE999984)*
Staintondale YO13 0EY
☎ 01723 870796 Mrs M A Edmondson

dir: *A171 N from Scarborough. At Cloughton onto Staintondale road, farm 2m N of Cloughton*

The Edmondson family are welcoming hosts, and the animals on the farm include unusual breeds of sheep and hens. This is an interesting

CONTINUED

and pleasant venue, either for its tranquil, secluded setting, or as a base for walking. There is good home cooking, comfortable bedrooms, and a cosy lounge and dining room.

Rooms 3 rms (2 en suite) (1 GF) D £56 **Facilities** tea/coffee Cen ht TVL Dinner Last d 10am **Parking** 3 **Notes** ⊗ No children 60 acres sheep hens, highland cattle Closed Oct–Mar ⊜

★★★ GUEST HOUSE
Argo
134 North Marine Rd YO12 7HZ
☎ 01723 375745

This friendly house is a haven for cricket fans, with some of the comfortable bedrooms overlooking the championship ground. Day rooms include a well appointed lounge and a dining room where tasty cooked breakfasts are served at individual tables.

Rooms 8 rms (5 en suite) (2 fmly) S £19–£20; D £44–£46✳ **Facilities** TVB tea/coffee Cen ht TVL **Notes** ⊗ No children 5yrs No coaches ⊜

★★★ GUEST ACCOMMODATION
Jalna House
168 North Marine Rd YO12 7HZ
☎ 01723 360668 📠 01723 360668

dir: A165 to Peasholm Park, onto Peasholm Rd & North Marine Rd, near cricket ground

A well-furnished guest house close to Peasholm Park and within walking distance of the North Beach attractions, cricket field and the town centre. Compact bedrooms are comfortable, there is a cosy lounge and a dining room serving tasty home-cooked meals.

Rooms 10 rms (6 en suite) (6 fmly) (2 GF) **Facilities** TVB tea/coffee Cen ht TVL Dinner Last d noon **Notes** Closed 21 Dec–7 Jan ⊜

★★★ GUEST ACCOMMODATION
North End Farm Country Guesthouse
88 Main St, Seamer YO12 4RF
☎ 01723 862965
e–mail: northendfarm@tiscali.co.uk

dir: A64 N onto B1261 through Seamer, farmhouse next to rdbt

Located in Seamer, a village inland from Scarborough, this 18th-century farmhouse contains comfortable, well-equipped en suite bedrooms. Breakfast is served at individual tables in the smart dining room, and the cosy lounge has a large-screen television.

Rooms 3 en suite S £30–£35; D £50–£60✳ **Facilities** TVB tea/coffee Cen ht TVL **Parking** 6 **Notes** ⊜

★★★ GUEST ACCOMMODATION
Parmelia
17 West St YO11 2QN
☎ 01723 361914
e–mail: parmelia.hotel@btconnect.com
web: www.parmeliahotel.co.uk

dir: Off A64 at The Mere onto Queen Margarets Rd, left at next rdbt (A165) onto Ramshill Rd, right for Esplanade Gdns Rd

Only a short walk from the Esplanade on the south cliff, this large guest house provides modern coordinated bedrooms. Cheerful hospitality makes you feel at home, and there is an attractive lounge where you can relax.

Rooms 15 rms (12 en suite) (1 pri facs) (4 fmly) (2 GF) **Facilities** TVB tea/coffee Cen ht TVL **Notes** ⊗ No children 4yrs Closed Dec–Feb ⊜

★★★ GUEST ACCOMMODATION
Peasholm Park
21–23 Victoria Park YO12 7TS
☎ 01723 500954
e–mail: peasholmparkhotel@btconnect.com
web: www.peasholmpark.co.uk

dir: Opp entrance to Peasholm Park

A warm welcome awaits you at this family-run guest house, which is within easy walking distance of the beach or the town centre. Bedrooms are comfortable, and feature homely extras. Evening meals are available by arrangement.

Rooms 12 en suite (3 fmly) S £28–£38; D £56–£72 **Facilities** TVB tea/coffee Cen ht TVL Dinner Last d noon **Parking** 2 **Notes** LB ⊗ No children 4yrs RS 22 Dec–2 Jan

SCARBOROUGH *CONTINUED*

★★★ GUEST ACCOMMODATION
Scarborough Fayre

143–147 Queens Pde YO12 7HU
☎ 01723 361677
e–mail: info@scarboroughfayrehotel.com

dir: *Off N Marine Road, near cricket ground*

Overlooking the North Bay, a warm welcome is assured at
Scarborough Fayre, and guests have use of a comfortable lounge, fully
licensed bar and spacious restaurant. Bedrooms are well equipped,
most benefiting from compact en suites and some with stunning sea
views.

Rooms 24 rms (23 en suite) (1 pri facs) (4 fmly) (1 GF) S £30–£45;
D £60–£90 **Facilities** TVB tea/coffee Cen ht TVL Dinner Last d noon
Wi-fi available **Parking** 23 **Notes** LB ⊗

★★ GUEST ACCOMMODATION
Falcon

5–7 Falconers Square YO11 2EJ
☎ 01723 500701
e–mail: info@skikero.co.uk

dir: *From A1/M1, take A64 to Scarborough. After B&Q, right at
next rdbt, at T-junct turn left*

Tucked away in a town centre square this family run property is
convenient for all attractions. Bedrooms are simply furnished in a
contemporary style and vary in size with some en suite rooms
available. Meals are served in the attached Portofino Italian restaurant
by friendly, professional staff (closed on Monday evenings).

Rooms 15 rms (9 en suite) (1 pri facs) (3 fmly) S £20–£30; D £44–£80✻
Facilities FTV TVB tea/coffee Cen ht Last d 10pm **Notes** LB

★★ GUEST ACCOMMODATION
The Grosvenor

51 Grosvenor Rd YO11 2LZ
☎ 01723 363801 📄 01723 363801
e–mail: grosvenorhotelscarborough@msn.com
web: www.grosvenor-scarborough.co.uk

dir: *Follow signs for South Bay along Valley Rd, Grosvenor Rd on
right*

You can expect good hospitality from all the family at the Grosvenor,
situated a short walk from the town and the seafront. This friendly

CONTINUED

guest house offers comfortable accommodation and a spacious
lounge.

Rooms 14 en suite (3 fmly) (3 GF) S £25–£35; D £50–£70✻
Facilities TVB tea/coffee Cen ht TVL **Notes** LB ⊗ Closed 10 Dec–10 Jan

★★ GUEST ACCOMMODATION
Warwick House

70 Westborough YO11 1TS
☎ 01723 374343 📄 01723 374343
e–mail: warwick@onetel.net

dir: *On outskirts of town centre, just before railway station on left*

Close to the Stephen Joseph Theatre, station and shops, this friendly
guest house has comfortable rooms, a smart bright lounge and a
pleasant basement dining room. Private parking is available.

Rooms 6 rms (2 en suite) (4 fmly) S £17–£20; D £34–£40✻ (room only)
Facilities TVB tea/coffee Cen ht TVL Wi-fi available **Parking** 5
Notes LB ⊛

SCOTCH CORNER   MAP 19 NZ20

★★★ 🅰 INN
The Vintage

DL10 6NP
☎ 01748 824424 & 822961 📄 01748 826272
e–mail: thevintagescotchcorner@btinternet.com
web: www.thevintagehotel.co.uk

dir: *A1 at Scotch Corner onto A66 towards Penrith, premises
200yds on left*

Rooms 8 rms (5 en suite) S £25–£39.50; D £39.50–£49.50✻ (room only)
Facilities TVB tea/coffee Direct dial from bedrooms Cen ht TVL Dinner
Last d 9pm **Conf** Max 48 Thtr 40 Class 24 Board 20 **Parking** 40
Notes LB ⊗ Closed Xmas & New Year

SETTLE   MAP 18 SD86

See also Clapham, Hellifield & Long Preston

★★★★ GUEST ACCOMMODATION
Whitefriars Country Guesthouse

Church St BD24 9JD
☎ 01729 823753
e–mail: info@whitefriars-settle.co.uk

dir: *Off A65 through Settle market place, premises signed 50yds
on left*

This friendly, family-run house stands in peaceful gardens just a stroll
from the town centre and railway station. Bedrooms, some quite
spacious, are attractively furnished in a traditional style and thoughtfully
equipped. A hearty breakfast is served in the traditional, beamed
dining room, and a cosy lounge is available.

Rooms 10 rms (6 en suite) (1 pri facs) (1 fmly) S £33–£35; D £50–£64
Facilities TVB tea/coffee Cen ht TVL **Parking** 10 **Notes** ⊗ Closed
25 Dec ⊛

SKIPTON MAP 18 SD95

★★★★ GUEST ACCOMMODATION
Clay Hall
Broughton Rd BD23 3AA
☎ 01756 794391

dir: *On A6069, 1m from Skipton towards Broughton*
A warm welcome is assured here on the outskirts of the town next to the Leeds and Liverpool canal. The house has been restored to provide carefully furnished bedrooms with smart modern shower rooms en suite, and a wealth of thoughtful extras. Comprehensive breakfasts are served in an attractive dining room.

Rooms 2 en suite S £40–£45; D £50–£55✱ **Facilities** TVB tea/coffee Cen ht **Parking** 4 **Notes** ⊗ No children 12yrs ⊜

★★★★ 🛏 GUEST HOUSE
Westfield House
50 Keighley Rd BD23 2NB
☎ 01756 790849

dir: *500yds S of town centre on A6131, S of canal bridge*
Just a stroll from the town centre, this friendly, non-smoking guest house provides smart accommodation. Bedrooms are well presented and most have large beds and many accessories including bathrobes. A hearty breakfast is served in the cosy dining room, and permission to use nearby parking is a bonus. Hospitality here is warm and nothing is too much trouble for the owners.

Rooms 4 en suite D £52–£58✱ **Facilities** TVB tea/coffee Cen ht **Notes** ⊗ No children No coaches ⊜

★★★ GUEST ACCOMMODATION
Rockwood House
14 Main St, Embsay BD23 6RE
☎ 01756 799755 & 07976 314980 📠 01756 799755
e–mail: rwh@ezeedsl.co.uk
web: www.stayinyorkshire.co.uk

dir: *2m NE of Skipton. Off A59 into Embsay village centre*
This Victorian terrace house has a peaceful location in the village of Embsay. Bedrooms are thoughtfully furnished, individually styled and reassuringly comfortable. The traditionally styled dining room sets the venue for hearty breakfasts. Hospitality is a feature here with a genuine and friendly welcome.

Rooms 3 en suite (1 fmly) (1 GF) S £30–£50; D £55–£70✱ **Facilities** TVB tea/coffee Direct dial from bedrooms Cen ht TVL **Parking** 3 **Notes LB** ⊗

SUTTON-ON-THE-FOREST MAP 19 SE56

★★★★★ ⊛ INN
The Blackwell Ox Inn
Huby Rd YO61 1DT
☎ 01347 810328 & 690758 📠 01904 691529
e–mail: enquiries@blackwelloxinns
web: www.blackwelloxinn.co.uk

dir: *Off A1237, onto B1363 to Sutton-on-the-Forest. Left at T-junct, 50yds on right*
Standing in the lovely village, this refurbished inn and restaurant offers very good bedrooms and pleasing public rooms. Cooking is well worth seeking out and staff are very keen and friendly.

Rooms 5 en suite S £65–£110; D £95–£110✱ **Facilities** TVB tea/coffee Direct dial from bedrooms Lift Cen ht TVL Dinner Last d 9.30pm **Parking** 18 **Notes** ⊗ No coaches

★★★★ FARM HOUSE
Goose Farm *(SE593629)*
Eastmoor YO61 1ET
☎ 01347 810577 📠 01347 810577 Mr G Rowson
e–mail: stay@goosefarm.fsnet.co.uk
web: www.goosefarm.co.uk

dir: *York outer ring road A1237 onto B1363 N. Take 2nd right, 1st Farm on left*
Situated on a quiet countryside road, this 19th-century farmhouse is convenient for the many attractions of York. Guests are sure of a friendly welcome, comfortable bedrooms and hearty breakfasts.

Rooms 3 en suite S £29–£38; D £64–£68✱ **Facilities** TVB tea/coffee Cen ht **Parking** 4 **Notes** ⊗ 25 acres Beef

TADCASTER MAP 16 SE44

★★★ BED & BREAKFAST
The Old Presbytery Guest House
London Rd, Saxton LS24 9PU
☎ 01937 557708 & 557392 📠 01937 557392
e–mail: guest@presbytery.plus.com
web: www.presbyteryguesthouse.co.uk

dir: *4m S of Tadcaster on A162. 100yds N of Barkston Ash on E side of road*
Dating from the 18th century, this former dower house has been modernised to provide comfortable accommodation with original features. The hall lounge features a wood-burning stove, and extensive breakfasts are served at an old oak dining table in a cosy breakfast room.

Rooms 4 rms (3 en suite) (1 pri facs) (1 fmly) S £37–£45; D £70✱ **Facilities** TVB tea/coffee Cen ht TVL Wi-fi available Golf 18 **Conf** Max 8 Board 8 **Parking** 6 **Notes** ⊗

THIRSK   MAP 19 SE48

Premier Collection

★★★★★ 🏠 🍽 GUEST ACCOMMODATION

Spital Hill

York Rd YO7 3AE

☎ 01845 522273 📠 01845 524970

e–mail: spitalhill@spitalhill.entadsl.com

web: www.spitalhill.co.uk

dir: 1.5m SE of town, set back 200yds from A19, driveway marked by 2 white posts

Set in gardens, this substantial Victorian country house is delightfully furnished. The spacious bedrooms are thoughtfully equipped with many extras, one even has a piano, but no televisions or kettles; the proprietor prefers to offer tea as a service. Delicious meals feature local and home-grown produce and are served house-party style around one table in the interesting dining room.

Rooms 3 rms (2 en suite) (1 pri facs) 2 annexe en suite (1 GF) S £58–£63; D £88–£103 **Facilities** Direct dial from bedrooms Cen ht TVL Dinner Last d 2pm 🐾 **Parking** 6 **Notes LB** ⊗ No children 12yrs

THORNTON WATLASS   MAP 19 SE28

Premier Collection

★★★★★ GUEST ACCOMMODATION

Thornton Watlass Hall

HG4 4AS

☎ 01677 422803 📠 01677 424160

e–mail: enquiries@thorntonwatlasshall.co.uk

dir: Off B6268, at N end of village

Thornton Watlass Hall dates from the 11th century and has been occupied by the same family for just under 1000 years. The Hall has featured in TV dramas over the years such as All Creatures Great and Small and it has also been the home to 'Lord Ashfordly', as Ashfordly Hall in Heartbeat. The Hall is finely furnished in period style and is unspoilt but still offers all the modern amenities. David and Liz Smith-Dodsworth offer a very friendly welcome and breakfasts are served in the grand dining room offering local produce. Relax in the palatial drawing room with its large open fireplace and honesty bar.

Rooms 6 en suite (1 fmly) S £75; D £120–£130 **Facilities** TVB tea/coffee Direct dial from bedrooms Cen ht TVL Wi-fi available Snooker 🐾 **Parking** 50 **Notes** Closed 24 Dec–1 Jan RS 2 Jan–Apr

★★★ INN

Buck Inn

HG4 4AH

☎ 01677 422461 📠 01677 422447

e–mail: innwatlass1@btconnect.com

dir: From A1 at Leeming Bar take A684 towards Bedale, B6268 towards Masham 2m, turn right at x-rds to Thornton Watlass

This traditional country inn is situated on the edge of the village green overlooking the cricket pitch. Cricket prints and old photographs are found throughout and an open fire in the bar adds to the warm and intimate atmosphere. Wholesome lunches and dinners, from an extensive menu, are served in the bar or dining room. Bedrooms are brightly decorated and well equipped.

Rooms 7 rms (5 en suite) (1 fmly) (1 GF) S £55–£60; D £75–£85✳ **Facilities** TVB tea/coffee Cen ht TVL Dinner Last d 9.15pm Wi-fi available Fishing Pool Table Quoits **Conf** Max 50 Thtr 50 Class 45 Board 30 Del from £65 ✳ **Parking** 10 **Notes LB** RS 24–25 Dec

WESTOW   MAP 19 SE76

★★★★ FARM HOUSE

Woodhouse Farm (SE749637)

YO60 7LL

☎ 01653 618378 & 07904 293422 📠 01653 618378

Mrs S Wardle

e–mail: stay@wood-house-farm.co.uk

web: www.wood-house-farm.co.uk

dir: Off A64 to Kirkham Priory & Westow. Right at T-junct, farm drive 0.5m out of village on right

The owners of this house are a young farming family who open their home and offer caring hospitality. Home-made bread, preserves and farm produce turn breakfast into a feast, and the views from the house across open fields are splendid.

Rooms 3 en suite (1 fmly) S £40–£45; D £60–£70 **Facilities** TVB tea/coffee Cen ht TVL Wi-fi available Fishing **Parking** 12 **Notes LB** ⊗ 500 acres arable, beef, sheep Closed Xmas, New Year & Mar–mid Apr 🐾

★★★ FARM HOUSE
Clifton Farm *(SE776463)*
YO60 7LS
☎ 01653 658557 & 07776 112530 📄 01653 658557
Ms L Laughton
e–mail: lynn@cliftonfarm.co.uk
web: www.cliftonfarm.co.uk

dir: *2m SE of Westow. Off A64 signed Harton then Howsham, pass Howsham towards Leavening, over x-rds & Clifton Farm 1m on right*

Situated in countryside on the edge of Leavening village, this comfortable, well-furnished farmhouse offers outstanding hospitality and service. Bedrooms are well equipped, breakfasts are hearty, and a lounge is available.

Rooms 3 rms (2 en suite) (1 pri facs) (1 fmly) S £30–£45; D £60–£70✱ **Facilities** TVB tea/coffee Cen ht TVL Wi-fi available **Parking** 6 **Notes LB** No children 5yrs 120 acres Mixed

---

WHITBY   MAP 19 NZ81

See also Robin Hood's Bay

★★★★★ 🅰 GUEST HOUSE
The Haven
4 East Crescent YO21 3HD
☎ 01947 603842 📄 0870 094 1103
e–mail: info@thehavenwhitby.co.uk
web: www.thehavenwhitby.co.uk

dir: *A171 onto A174 in Whitby. At rdbt left onto Chubb Hill, next rdbt 4th exit onto St Hilda's Ter, left onto Cliff St, left onto East Crescent*

Rooms 8 en suite S £33; D £60–£67✱ **Facilities** TVB tea/coffee Cen ht TVL Wi-fi available **Notes** ⊗ No children 15yrs No coaches ✆

★★★★ ⊚ 🍴 RESTAURANT WITH ROOMS
Estbek House
East Row, Sandsend YO21 3SU
☎ 01947 893424 📄 01947 893625
e–mail: info@estbekhouse.co.uk

dir: *On Cleveland Way, within Sandsend, next to East Beck*

A speciality seafood restaurant on the first floor is the focus of this listed building in a small coastal village north west of Whitby. Below is

CONTINUED

a small bar and breakfast room, while up above are four individually presented bedrooms offering luxury and comfort.

Estbek House

Rooms 4 rms (3 en suite) (1 pri facs) **Facilities** TVB tea/coffee Cen ht Dinner Last d 9pm Wi-fi available **Conf** Board 20 **Parking** 6 **Notes** ⊗ No children 14yrs

---

★★★★★ 🍷 🚬 GUEST ACCOMMODATION
Netherby House
90 Coach Rd, Sleights YO22 5EQ
☎ 01947 810211 📄 01947 810211
e–mail: info@netherby-house.co.uk
web: www.netherby-house.co.uk

dir: *In village of Sleights, off A169 Whitby-Pickering road*

This fine Victorian house has been lovingly refurbished and now offers thoughtfully furnished, individually styled bedrooms together with delightful day rooms. There is a fine conservatory and the grounds are extensive, with exceptional views from the summerhouse at the bottom of the garden. Imaginative dinners feature produce from the extensive kitchen garden.

Rooms 6 en suite 5 annexe en suite (1 fmly) (5 GF) S £36–£44.50; D £72–£89✱ **Facilities** TVB tea/coffee Cen ht Dinner Last d 7.30–9pm ↪ **Parking** 17 **Notes LB** ⊗ No children 2yrs Closed 25–26 Dec

★★★★ GUEST HOUSE
Chiltern Guest House
13 Normanby Ter, West Cliff YO21 3ES
☎ 01947 604981
e-mail: Jjchiltern@aol.com

dir: *Whalebones next to Harbour, sea on right. Royal Hotel on left, 200yds. Royal Gardens turn left, 2nd road on left 6th house on right*

The Victorian terrace house offers a warm welcome and comfortable accommodation within walking distance of the town centre and seafront. Public areas include a smartly decorated lounge and a bright, attractive dining room. Bedrooms are thoughtfully equipped and many have modern en suites.

Rooms 8 rms (7 en suite) (3 fmly) S £25–£35; D £56–£62✶
Facilities TVB tea/coffee Cen ht TVL Wi-fi available Golf 18 **Notes LB**
⊛

★★★★ GUEST ACCOMMODATION
Corra Lynn
28 Crescent Av YO21 3EW
☎ 01947 602214 📄 01947 602214

dir: *Corner A174 & Crescent Av*

Occupying a prominent corner position, this property mixes traditional values with a trendy and artistic style. Bedrooms are thoughtfully equipped, individually furnished and have bright colour schemes, but it is the delightful dining room with corner bar and a wall adorned with clocks that takes the eye.

Rooms 5 en suite (1 fmly) S £28–£30; D £56–£60✶ **Facilities** STV TVB tea/coffee Direct dial from bedrooms Cen ht **Parking** 5 **Notes** ⊗ Closed 21 Dec–5 Jan ⊛

See advert on opposite page

★★★★ GUEST ACCOMMODATION
Kimberley House
7 Havelock Place YO21 3ER
☎ 01947 604125
e-mail: enquiries@kimberleyhouse.com
web: www.kimberleyhouse.com

dir: *Follow signs to West Cliff, A174 onto Crescent Av, right onto Hudson St, next junct*

This 19th-century house was built for a local seafaring family. It stands in a quiet residential area within walking distance of the West Cliff promenades and the historic town centre. Bedrooms are well equipped and comfortable, and a wide choice of breakfasts is available.

Rooms 8 rms (7 en suite) (1 pri facs) (1 GF) S £30; D fr £62✶
Facilities TVB tea/coffee Cen ht **Notes LB** ⊗ No children 12yrs Closed Dec–Jan ⊛

★★★★ GUEST HOUSE
Rosslyn Guest House
11 Abbey Ter YO21 3HQ
☎ 01947 604086
e-mail: rosslynhouse@googlemail.com

Located close to the sea front this friendly house offers well furnished bedrooms, high standards of cleanliness and friendly service. A wide choice is offered for breakfast, which is served in the beautifully appointed dining room. A small kitchen area is also available for guest use.

Rooms 5 en suite (2 fmly) S £29–£39; D £50–£58 **Facilities** TVB tea/coffee Cen ht Wi-fi available **Parking** 3 **Notes LB** ⊗ No coaches

★★★★ GUEST HOUSE
The Waverley
17 Crescent Av YO21 3ED
☎ 01947 604389 📄 08700 063 3129
e-mail: stephen@whitbywaverley.com

dir: *A174 towards Saltburn, turn right, 250mtrs on right at bend*

This terraced house was originally built as a guesthouse in 1898 and is located on the West Cliff. Bedrooms vary in size, but all are comfortable and well equipped. Day rooms include a smartly appointed dining room and first floor lounge. All guests are assured a warm welcome and a hearty breakfast.

Rooms 6 rms (5 en suite) (1 pri facs) (1 fmly) **Facilities** TVB tea/coffee Cen ht TVL **Parking** 3 **Notes** ⊗ No children 2yrs No coaches Closed Nov–Jan

★★★★ GUEST ACCOMMODATION
Whitehaven
29 Crescent Av YO21 3EW
☎ 01947 601569
e-mail: simon@whitehavenguesthouse.co.uk
web: www.whitehavenguesthouse.co.uk

dir: *Signs to West Cliff, A174 onto Crescent Av*

Occupying a corner position close to the sports complex and indoor swimming pool, this house provides colourful bedrooms in contrasting styles. All rooms have mini-fridges and most have DVD facilities. Vegetarian options are available at breakfast served in the attractive dining room.

Rooms 4 rms (3 en suite) (1 pri facs) D £60–£70 **Facilities** FTV TVB tea/coffee Cen ht **Notes LB** ⊗ Closed 18–27 Dec ⊛

★★★★ A GUEST ACCOMMODATION
The Leeway
1 Havelock Place YO21 3ER
☎ 01947 602604
e-mail: enquiries@theleeway.co.uk
web: www.theleeway.co.uk

Rooms 6 rms (5 en suite) (1 pri facs) (1 GF) S £30–£35; D £64–£80
Facilities TVB tea/coffee Cen ht Wi-fi available **Notes LB** ⊗ No children 10yrs Closed 24–26 Dec

ENGLAND

★★★ GUEST ACCOMMODATION
Arundel House
Bagdale YO21 1QJ
☎ 01947 603645 📠 08709 157628
e-mail: arundel_house@hotmail.com

dir: *A171 town centre, onto Arundel Pl at bottom of hill*

In a prime location within walking distance of all the attractions, Arundel House's bedrooms are simply furnished and offer good value for money. Expect a helping of true Yorkshire hospitality, and look out for the unique collection of walking canes on show in the house.

Rooms 12 en suite (2 fmly) (2 GF) **Facilities** TVB tea/coffee Cen ht Wi-fi available **Parking** 6

★★★ GUEST HOUSE
The Sandbeck
1 & 2 Crescent Ter, West Cliff YO21 3EL
☎ 01947 604012 & 603349
e-mail: dysonsandbeck@tesco.net

dir: *On West Cliff opp theatre booking office*

Commanding a prominent corner position on the seafront, Sandbeck is being progressively upgraded. Bedrooms are generally well proportioned and front rooms have fine sea views. Public rooms comprise a bar, quiet lounge, and a spacious dining room offering various breakfast options.

Rooms 23 en suite (4 fmly) S £39; D £62–£92✱ **Facilities** TVB tea/coffee Licensed Lift Cen ht **Notes** ⊗ No children 5yrs No coaches Closed Dec

★★★ ⊛ RESTAURANT WITH ROOMS
The White Horse & Griffin
Church St YO22 4BH
☎ 01947 825026 & 604857 📠 01947 604857
e-mail: info@whitehorseandgriffin.co.uk
web: www.whitehorseandgriffin.co.uk

dir: *From town centre E across Bridge St bridge, 2nd left, 50mtrs on right next to Whitby bookshop*

This historic inn, now a restaurant with rooms, is as quaint as the cobbled side street in which it lies. Cooking is good with the emphasis on fresh fish. The bedrooms, some reached by steep staircases, retain a rustic charm but are well equipped and include CD players.

Rooms 10 en suite 10 annexe rms (3 en suite) (7 annexe pri facs) (1 fmly) S £50–£130; D £65–£220✱ **Facilities** TV14B tea/coffee Cen ht Dinner Last d 9pm Wi-fi available **Conf** Max 30 Thtr 30 Class 12 Board 15 **Parking** 1 **Notes LB** ⊗

Ⓤ
Sandpiper Guest House
4 Belle Vue Ter YO21 3EY
☎ 01947 600246
e-mail: enquiries@sandpiperhouse.wanadoo.co.uk

dir: *A169, 2nd left at rdbt signed Whitby, follow signs to West Cliffe on N Prom, 4th right, take Esplanade straight onto Belle Vue Terrace. B&B on left*

At the time of going to press the rating for this establishment had not been confirmed. Please check the AA website www.theAA.com for up-to-date information.

Rooms 7 en suite (1 fmly) (1 GF) S £31.50–£40; D £63–£80✱ **Facilities** TVB tea/coffee Cen ht Wi-fi available **Parking** 3 **Notes LB** ⊗ No children 4yrs ⊜

CONTINUED

ENGLAND

YORK   MAP 16 SE65

See also Sutton-on-the-Forest

★★★★ 🔒 GUEST HOUSE
Burswood Guest House
68 Tadcaster Rd, Dringhouses YO24 1LR
☎ 01904 702582 📠 01904 708377
e–mail: burswood.guesthouse@virgin.net

dir: *Tadcaster Rd A1036 opposite racecourse, from the A64 on S side of the city*

Guests are sure of a warm welcome at this modern dormer bungalow. Bedrooms are richly furnished and very well equipped. Freshly cooked breakfasts are served in the conservatory/breakfast room which overlooks the well-tended garden. Good car parking is available at the front of the house and Burswood is easily accessible for the city centre and the racecourse.

Rooms 5 en suite (1 fmly) (3 GF) **Facilities** FTV TVB tea/coffee Cen ht **Parking** 6 **Notes** ⊗ No coaches

★★★★ GUEST ACCOMMODATION
The Hazelwood
24–25 Portland St YO31 7EH
☎ 01904 626548 📠 01904 628032
e–mail: reservations@thehazelwoodyork.com
web: www.thehazelwoodyork.com

dir: *400yds N of York Minster, off inner ring road Gillygate*

A renovation of two elegant Victorian houses in a residential side street near the Minster. Bedrooms are equipped with thoughtful extras, and comprehensive breakfasts are served in an attractive dining room. There is a cosy garden-level lounge and a private car park.

Rooms 13 en suite (2 fmly) (2 GF) S £50–£105; D £80–£122✱ **Facilities** TVB tea/coffee Cen ht Wi-fi available **Parking** 8 **Notes LB** ⊗ No children 8yrs

★★★★ GUEST ACCOMMODATION
Ascot House
80 East Pde YO31 7YH
☎ 01904 426826 📠 01904 431077
e–mail: admin@ascothouseyork.com
web: www.ascothouseyork.com

dir: *0.5m NE of city centre. Off A1036 Heworth Green onto Mill Ln, 2nd left*

June and Keith Wood provide friendly service at the 1869 Ascot House, a 15-minute walk from the town centre. Bedrooms are thoughtfully equipped, many with four-poster or canopy beds and other period furniture. Reception rooms include a cosy lounge that also retains its original features.

Rooms 13 rms (12 en suite) (1 pri facs) (3 fmly) (2 GF) S £55–£70; D £70–£80 **Facilities** TVB tea/coffee Cen ht TVL Wi-fi available Sauna **Parking** 14 **Notes LB** Closed 21–28 Dec

★★★★ GUEST HOUSE
Ashley Guest House
76 Scott St YO23 1NS
☎ 01904 647520
e–mail: taylor.philip.j@googlemail.com

dir: *Pass racecourse, turn right at 2nd set of lights onto Scarcroft Rd. Scott St is 2nd last street on right*

A Victorian end terrace that has been given a very modern treatment with stylish interiors and distinctive character. Attractively furnished bedrooms and caring hospitality are hallmarks of this well located city centre guest house.

Rooms 5 rms (4 en suite) (1 pri facs) S £35–£68; D £50–£96✱ **Facilities** TVB tea/coffee Cen ht Wi-fi available **Notes** ⊗ No children 10yrs

★★★★ GUEST ACCOMMODATION
City Guest House

68 Monkgate YO31 7PF
☎ 01904 622483
e-mail: info@cityguesthouse.co.uk
dir: *NE of city centre on B1036*

Just a stroll from the historic Monk Bar, this guest house is well located for business, shopping and sightseeing. Carefully furnished bedrooms boast stylish interior design and come equipped with a host of thoughtful touches. The smart dining room is the venue for a good breakfast.

Rooms 7 en suite (1 fmly) (1 GF) **Facilities** TVB tea/coffee Cen ht **Parking** 6 **Notes** ⊗ No children 8yrs Closed 20 Dec–1 Feb

★★★★ GUEST ACCOMMODATION
The Heathers

54 Shipton Rd, Clifton-Without YO30 5RQ
☎ 01904 640989 📄 01904 640989
e-mail: reservations@heathers-guest-house.co.uk
web: www.heathers-guest-house.co.uk
dir: *N of York on A19, halfway between A1237 ring road & York city centre*

Recent remodelling and refurbishment at this house has resulted in a most comfortable and welcoming establishment. Heather and Graham Fisher have designed each room, individually using quality fabrics and decor to provide a feeling of luxury in the bedrooms. The light and airy breakfast room looks out on to a well tended garden area.

The Heathers

Rooms 6 rms (4 en suite) (2 pri facs) (2 fmly) D £56–£120 **Facilities** TVB tea/coffee Cen ht TVL Wi-fi available **Parking** 9 **Notes** ⊗ No children 10yrs Closed Xmas

★★★★ GUEST ACCOMMODATION
Holly Lodge

204–206 Fulford Rd YO10 4DD
☎ 01904 646005
e-mail: geoff@thehollylodge.co.uk
web: www.thehollylodge.co.uk
dir: *On A19 south side, 1.5m on left from A64/A19 junct, or follow A19 Selby signs from city centre to Fulford Rd*

Located just a short walk from the historic centre, this pleasant Georgian property has coordinated, well-equipped bedrooms. The spacious lounge houses a grand piano, and hearty breakfasts are served in the cosy dining room. You may also enjoy the delightful walled garden.

Rooms 5 en suite (1 fmly) (1 GF) S £58–£88; D £78–£88 **Facilities** TVB tea/coffee Cen ht **Parking** 6 **Notes** ⊗ No children 7yrs Closed 24–27 Dec

★★★★ Ⓐ GUEST HOUSE
Curzon Lodge and Stable Cottages

23 Tadcaster Rd, Dringhouses YO24 1QG
☎ 01904 703157 📄 01904 703157
e-mail: admin@curzonlodge.com
dir: *1m SW of city walls and 1.5m NE of A64 (York West exit) on A1036 between Holiday Inn & Marriott Hotel*

Rooms 5 en suite 5 annexe en suite (1 fmly) (4 GF) **Facilities** TVB tea/coffee Cen ht Wi-fi available **Parking** 16 **Notes** ⊗ No children 10yrs No coaches Closed 24 Dec–1 Jan

CONTINUED

YORK CONTINUED

★★★★ A GUEST HOUSE
Midway House

145 Fulford Rd YO10 4HG

☎ 01904 659272

e–mail: info@midwayhouseyork.co.uk

dir: *A64 to York, 3rd exit A19 to York city centre, over 2nd lights & house 50yds on right*

Rooms 12 rms (10 en suite) (3 fmly) (1 GF) S £40–£65; D £60–£85✳
Facilities TVB tea/coffee Cen ht TVL Wi-fi available **Parking** 14
Notes LB ⊗ No children 6yrs No coaches Closed 23 Dec–1 Feb

★★★ GUEST ACCOMMODATION
Church View B & B

87 The Village, Stockton on the Forest YO32 9UP

☎ 01904 400403 & 07752 273371 📄 01904 400325

e–mail: manners@87churchview.fsnet.co.uk

web: www.churchviewyork.co.uk

dir: *4.5m NE of York. Off A64 to Stockton on the Forest, Church View opp church*

Set in the centre of the village, this 200-year-old house offers three very well-equipped bedrooms, one on the ground floor and two reached by a spiral staircase. CD and video players are provided. There is a very cosy lounge and dining room and hospitality is very good as is the service provided. Dinner is available by arrangement.

Rooms 3 en suite (3 fmly) (1 GF) **Facilities** TVB tea/coffee Cen ht TVL
Dinner Last d 10am Golf 18 **Parking** 3 **Notes** ⊗ Closed 20 Dec–1 Jan

★★★ GUEST HOUSE
Cumbria House

2 Vyner St, Haxby Rd YO31 8HS

☎ 01904 636817

e–mail: candj@cumbriahouse.freeserve.co.uk

web: www.cumbriahouse.com

dir: *A1237 onto B1363 S towards city centre, pass hospital, left at lights, 400yds on left*

Expect a warm welcome at this family-run guest house, which is ten minutes walk from the Minster. The attractive bedrooms are well furnished and equipped with many useful extras. Freshly-cooked breakfasts are served in the smart dining room at individual tables.

Rooms 6 rms (2 en suite) (2 fmly) S £28–£30; D £56–£60✳
Facilities TVB tea/coffee Cen ht **Parking** 5 **Notes** LB ⊗ No coaches
Closed 24–28 Dec

★★★ GUEST HOUSE
Greenside

124 Clifton YO30 6BQ

☎ 01904 623631 📄 01904 623631

e–mail: greenside@surfree.co.uk

web: www.greensideguesthouse.co.uk

dir: *A19 N towards city centre, over lights for Greenside, on left opp Clifton Green*

Overlooking Clifton Green, this detached house is just within walking distance of the city centre. Accommodation consists of simply furnished bedrooms and there is a cosy lounge and a dining room, where dinners by arrangement and traditional breakfasts are served. It is a family home, and other families are welcome.

Rooms 6 rms (3 en suite) (2 fmly) (3 GF) S fr £28; D fr £48✳
Facilities TVB tea/coffee Cen ht TVL Wi-fi available **Parking** 6
Notes LB No coaches Closed Xmas & New Year ☺

★★★ GUEST ACCOMMODATION
St Georges

6 St Georges Place, Tadcaster Rd YO24 1DR

☎ 01904 625056 📄 01904 625009

e–mail: sixstgeorg@aol.com

web: www.stgeorgesyork.com

dir: *A64 onto A1036 N to city centre, as racecourse ends, St Georges Place on left*

Located near the racecourse, this family-run establishment is within walking distance of the city. The attractive bedrooms are equipped with modern facilities, and some rooms have four-poster beds and others can accommodate families. A cosy lounge is available and hearty breakfasts are served in the delightful dining room.

Rooms 10 en suite (5 fmly) (1 GF) S £30–£50; D £58–£65✳
Facilities TVB tea/coffee Cen ht Wi-fi available **Parking** 7 **Notes** LB
Closed 20 Dec–2 Jan

★★★ Ⓐ GUEST HOUSE
The St Denys

St Denys Rd YO1 9QD
☎ 01904 622207 📠 01904 624800
e–mail: info@stdenyshotel.co.uk
web: www.stdenyshotel.co.uk

dir: *A1079 to inner ring road, through Walmgate Bar, 500yds left, premises opp St Deny's Church*

Rooms 13 en suite (4 fmly) (3 GF) S £50–£79; D £59–£99✳
Facilities TVB tea/coffee Direct dial from bedrooms Licensed Cen ht TVL Wi-fi available **Parking** 7 **Notes LB** ⊗ No coaches

Ⓤ
Astley House

123 Clifton YO30 6BL
☎ 01904 634745 📠 01904 634745
e–mail: astleyhouse@btinternet.com

At the time of going to press the rating for this establishment had not been confirmed. Please check the AA website www.theAA.com for up-to-date information.

Rooms 12 en suite 1 annexe en suite (3 fmly) (1 GF) S £25–£35; D £55–£85 **Facilities** TVB tea/coffee Direct dial from bedrooms Cen ht Dinner Last d 24hrs notice Wi-fi available **Parking** 8 **Notes LB** ⊗

Ⓤ
Caesars Haxby

169 York Rd, Haxby YO32 3HB
☎ 01904 758864

At the time of going to press the rating for this establishment had not been confirmed. Please check the AA website www.theAA.com for up-to-date information.

Rooms 7 en suite S £35–£47.50; D £60–£85✳ **Facilities** Cen ht Dinner **Conf** Thtr 30 Class 15 Board 20 Del from £120 ✳ **Parking** 36 **Notes LB**

YORKSHIRE, SOUTH

DONCASTER   MAP 16 SE50

★★★★ GUEST ACCOMMODATION
Canda Lodge

Hampole Balk Ln, Skellow DN6 8LF
☎ 01302 724028 📠 01302 727999

dir: *NW of Doncaster. Off A1 onto B1220 into Skellow*

Well located for the A1, this stone house has well-tended gardens and spacious parking. Garden bedrooms are attractively decorated, well-equipped and delightfully furnished. The public areas consist of a pleasant breakfast room with individual tables and a small lounge area. Service is friendly and caring.

Rooms 2 rms 4 annexe en suite (1 fmly) (6 GF) S £36–£38; D £48–£50✳ **Facilities** TVB tea/coffee Direct dial from bedrooms Cen ht TVL **Parking** 20 **Notes** ⊗ No children 13yrs

HOOTON PAGNELL   MAP 16 SE40

★★★ 🏠 FARM HOUSE
Rock Farm *(SE484081)*

DN5 7BT
☎ 01977 642200 & 07785 916186 📠 01977 642200
Ms Harrison
e–mail: info@rockfarm.info
web: www.rockfarm.info

dir: *A1(M) junct 38, follow Wakefield signs. In 1m turn left, next left & left again. Farm 1st on right*

A few minutes from the A1, and located in the heart of this Domesday village beside 'The Hostel' and the ancient butter cross, this working farmhouse offers well-equipped spacious beamed bedrooms and warm hospitality in a Grade II listed building with excellent fresh breakfasts.

Rooms 3 rms (1 en suite) (1 fmly) S £28–£37; D £50–£60 **Facilities** TVB tea/coffee Cen ht TVL **Parking** 15 **Notes** ⊗ 200 acres Horses/arable/beef ⊗

ROTHERHAM   MAP 16 SK49

★★★★ GUEST ACCOMMODATION
The Stonecroft

138 Main St, Bramley S66 2SF
☎ 01709 540922 📠 01709 540922
e–mail: stonecrofthotel@btconnect.com
web: www.stonecrofthotel.com

dir: *3m E of Rotherham. Off A631 into Bramley village centre*

These converted stone cottages in the centre of Bramley provide a good base for visiting Rotherham or Sheffield. Some bedrooms are around a landscaped courtyard with private parking, and there is a lounge with a bar. Imaginative home-cooked meals are available.

Rooms 3 en suite 4 annexe en suite (1 fmly) (4 GF) S £56–£63; D £72–£78✳ **Facilities** FTV TVB tea/coffee Cen ht TVL Dinner Last d 8pm Wi-fi available **Parking** 7 **Notes LB** ⊗ Closed 25–26 Dec

ENGLAND

SHEFFIELD   MAP 16 SK38

★★★★ ☕ GUEST HOUSE
Quarry House

Rivelin Glen Quarry, Rivelin Valley Rd S6 5SE

☎ 0114 234 0382 📠 0114 234 0382

e–mail: penelopeslack@aol.com

web: www.quarryhouse.org.uk

dir: *2.5m W of Sheffield. Off A6101 Rivelin Valley Rd at sharp bend, uphill to car park, signed*

A warm welcome is given at this delightful former quarry master's house in the picturesque Rivelin valley. Well-appointed bedrooms include many thoughtful extras. The tasty evening meals and comprehensive breakfasts have a strong organic influence, and there is a cosy lounge and a smart dining room.

Rooms 3 rms (2 en suite) (1 pri facs) (1 fmly) (1 GF) S fr £40; D fr £80✻ (room only) **Facilities** TVB tea/coffee Cen ht TVL Dinner Last d 6pm Wi-fi available **Parking** 8 **Notes** No coaches ☻

★★★★ GUEST ACCOMMODATION
Westbourne House Guest Accommodation

25 Westbourne Rd, Broomhill S10 2QQ

☎ 0114 266 0109 📠 0114 266 7778

e–mail: guests@westbournehousehotel.com

web: www.westbournehousehotel.com

dir: *A61 onto B6069 Glossop Rd, past university, after Hallamshire Hospital over lights, next left*

A Victorian residence situated in beautiful gardens close to the university and hospitals. There is an attractive licensed restaurant where carefully prepared imaginative meals are served by arrangement. The modern bedrooms are individually furnished and decorated, and extremely well equipped. A comfortable lounge overlooks the terrace and garden.

Rooms 8 rms (7 en suite) (2 fmly) S £55–£79; D £85–£97✻ **Facilities** FTV TVB tea/coffee Cen ht Wi-fi available **Conf** Max 15 Thtr 15 Class 15 Board 15 **Parking** 6 **Notes** ⊗ Closed Xmas

★★★★ GUEST ACCOMMODATION
Padley Farm B & B

Dungworth Green S6 6HE

☎ 0114 285 1427 📠 0114 285 1427

e–mail: aandlmbestall@btinternet.com

web: www.padleyfarm.co.uk

dir: *M1 junct 33 follow ring road (A61 Barnsley), turn left onto B6077 signed Bradfield*

The barn conversion offers high quality en suite rooms with spectacular views of open countryside. An allergy free environment and warm hospitality ensure a pleasant stay.

Padley Farm B&B

Rooms 7 en suite (4 fmly) (2 GF) S £30–£37; D £54–£60✻ **Facilities** FTV TVB tea/coffee Cen ht Snooker **Conf** Max 15 Class 15 **Parking** 8 **Notes** LB ⊗

WORTLEY   MAP 16 SK39

★★★ GUEST ACCOMMODATION
Wortley Hall

Worltey Village S35 7DB

☎ 0114 288 2100 📠 0114 283 0695

e–mail: info@wortleyhall.org.uk

web: www.wortleyhall.org.uk

dir: *Exit M1 junct 35a, straight over 2nd rdbt signed A616/ Manchester. In 3m turn left to Wortley*

Standing in 26 acres of parkland, this listed country house has been in the custody of the Trades Union Movement for the last 50 years and displays much of their history. Bedrooms are mixed in size and quality, but all are comfortable and there are spacious day rooms reminiscent of the hall's original grandeur.

Rooms 49 en suite (7 fmly) (4 GF) S fr £40; D fr £80✻ **Facilities** TVB tea/coffee Direct dial from bedrooms Lift Cen ht TVL Dinner Wi-fi available **Conf** Thtr 150 Class 70 Board 30 Del from £105 ✻ **Parking** 60 **Notes** ⊗ Civ Wed 100

YORKSHIRE, WEST

HALIFAX   MAP 19 SE02

★★★★ ◉ INN
Shibden Mill

Shibden Mill Fold, Shibden HX3 7UL

☎ 01422 365840 📠 01422 362971

e–mail: shibdenmillinn@zoom.co.uk

web: www.shibdenmillinn.com

dir: *3m NE of Halifax off A58*

Nestling in a fold of Shibden Dale, this 17th-century inn features exposed beams and open fires. Guests can dine well in the two lounge-style bars, the restaurant, or outside in summer. The stylish bedrooms come in a variety of sizes, and all are thoughtfully equipped and have access to a free video library. Service is friendly and obliging.

CONTINUED   *CONTINUED*

Shibden Mill

Rooms 11 en suite (1 GF) **Facilities** FTV TVB tea/coffee Direct dial from bedrooms Cen ht Dinner Last d 9.30pm Wi-fi available **Conf** Max 50 Thtr 50 Class 21 Board 24 **Parking** 100

HAWORTH
MAP 19 SE03

★★★ ◉ RESTAURANT WITH ROOMS

Weavers Restaurant with Rooms

13/17 West Ln BD22 8DU

☎ 01535 643822 📠 01535 644832

e-mail: weaversinnhaworth@aol.com

dir: *In village centre. Pass Brontë Weaving Shed on right, 100yds left to Parsonage car park*

Centrally located on the cobbled main street, this family-owned restaurant with rooms provides well-equipped, stylish and comfortable accommodation. Each of the three rooms is en suite and has many thoughtful extras. The kitchen serves both modern and traditional dishes with flair and creativity.

Rooms 3 en suite S £59–£69; D £89–£99✱ **Facilities** FTV TVB tea/coffee Direct dial from bedrooms Cen ht Dinner Last d 9pm **Notes** ✪ RS Mon & Sun

---

HEBDEN BRIDGE
MAP 19 SD92

★★★★ RESTAURANT WITH ROOMS

The Dusty Miller & Coiners Restaurant

Burnley Rd, Mytholmroyd HX7 5LH

☎ 01422 885959

e-mail: thedustymiller@hotmail.co.uk

web: www.dustymiller.co.uk

Situated in the Calder Valley, this Grade II-listed building offers a relaxing bar, with comfortable seating and a contemporary restaurant. Accommodation consists of five fully equipped bedrooms; ample car parking is provided.

Rooms 5 en suite (1 fmly) S £49; D £65✱ **Facilities** TVB tea/coffee Cen ht Dinner Last d 9pm Wi-fi available **Parking** 25 **Notes LB** ✪

HOLMFIRTH
MAP 16 SE10

★★★★ 🅐 GUEST ACCOMMODATION

Uppergate Farm

Hepworth HD9 1TG

☎ 01484 681369 📠 01484 687343

e-mail: info@uppergatefarm.co.uk

dir: *0.5m off A616*

Rooms 2 en suite (1 fmly) S £50; D £70–£75 **Facilities** TVB tea/coffee Cen ht TVL Wi-fi available 🕙 Sauna **Parking** 6 **Notes LB** ✪

HUDDERSFIELD
MAP 16 SE11

★★★★ ◉◉ RESTAURANT WITH ROOMS

Weavers Shed Restaurant with Rooms

86–88 Knowl Rd, Golcar HD7 4AN

☎ 01484 654284 📠 01484 650980

e-mail: info@weaversshed.co.uk

web: www.weaversshed.co.uk

dir: *3m W of Huddersfield. A62 onto B6111 to Milnsbridge & Scar Ln to Golcar, right onto Knowl Rd, signed Colne Valley Museum*

This converted house has spacious bedrooms named after local textile mills; all are extremely well equipped. An inviting bar-lounge leads into the well known restaurant where fresh produce, much from the establishment's own gardens, forms the basis of excellent meals.

Rooms 5 en suite (2 GF) S fr £80; D fr £100✱ **Facilities** TVB tea/coffee Direct dial from bedrooms Cen ht Dinner Last d 9pm **Conf** Max 16 Board 16 **Parking** 20 **Notes LB** ✪ Closed Xmas/New Year

---

★★★★ GUEST ACCOMMODATION

The Huddersfield Central Lodge

11/15 Beast Market HD1 1QF

☎ 01484 515551 📠 01484 432349

e-mail: enquiries@centrallodge.com

web: www.centrallodge.com

dir: *In town centre off Lord St, signs for Beast Market from ring road*

This friendly, family-run operation offers smart spacious bedrooms with modern en suites. Some rooms are in the main building, while new rooms, many with kitchenettes, are situated across a courtyard. Public rooms include a bar and a conservatory, and there are arrangements for local restaurants to charge meals to guests' accounts. Secure complimentary parking.

Rooms 9 en suite 13 annexe en suite (2 fmly) (6 smoking) S £47–£50; D £57–£67✱ **Facilities** STV TVB tea/coffee Direct dial from bedrooms Cen ht TVL Wi-fi available **Parking** 50

HUDDERSFIELD CONTINUED

★★★★ INN
The Woodman Inn
Thunderbridge Ln HD8 0PX
☎ 01484 605778 📄 01484 604110
e–mail: thewoodman@connectfree.co.uk
web: www.woodman-inn.co.uk
(For full entry see Kirkburton)

★★★ GUEST HOUSE
Griffin Lodge Guest House
273 Manchester Rd HD4 5AG
☎ 01484 431042 📄 01484 431043
e–mail: info@griffinlodge.co.uk
web: www.griffinlodge.co.uk
Located on the outskirts of Huddefield and close to the villages of
Holmfirth and Marsden, Griffin Lodge is family run and offers
comfortable well appointed accommodation. Hearty breakfasts are
served in the small dining room and there is secure parking to the rear.
Rooms 6 en suite (4 fmly) (6 GF) S fr £35; D fr £45✱ (room only)
Facilities FTV TVB tea/coffee Cen ht Wi-fi available **Parking** 10

KIRKBURTON   MAP 16 SE11

★★★★ INN
The Woodman Inn
Thunderbridge Ln HD8 0PX
☎ 01484 605778 📄 01484 604110
e–mail: thewoodman@connectfree.co.uk
web: www.woodman-inn.co.uk
dir: *1m SW of Kirkburton. Off A629 in Thunder Bridge*
The Woodman offers traditional innkeeping and is extremely popular
with locals. The air-conditioned restaurant holds an extensive range of
wines, while the popular bar offers a wide selection of ales and lagers.
Bedrooms are comfortable and comprehensively furnished, making
this an ideal base for walking, visiting the National Mining Museum, or
simply escaping to the country.
Rooms 12 en suite (3 GF) **Facilities** TVB tea/coffee Direct dial from
bedrooms Cen ht Dinner Last d 9pm Pool Table **Conf** Max 60 Thtr 50
Class 60 Board 30 **Parking** 50 **Notes** ⊗

MARSDEN   MAP 16 SE01

★★★★ ⚛ RESTAURANT WITH ROOMS
The Olive Branch Restaurant with Rooms
Manchester Rd HD7 6LU
☎ 01484 844487
e–mail: mail@olivebranch.uk.com
web: www.olivebranch.uk.com
dir: *1m NE of Marsden on A62*
The Olive Branch was a roadside inn, which has now developed into a
popular restaurant with three comfortable bedrooms. The menu
features the best of seasonal produce cooked with flair and
enthusiasm. The surrounding countryside has many historic attractions
and pleasant walking.
Rooms 3 en suite S £55; D £70✱ (room only) **Facilities** TVB tea/coffee
Direct dial from bedrooms Cen ht Dinner Last d 9.30pm **Parking** 25
Notes ⊗ Closed 2–17 Jan

OSSETT   MAP 16 SE22

★★★★ GUEST ACCOMMODATION
Heath House
Chancery Rd WF5 9RZ
☎ 01924 260654 📄 01924 263131
e–mail: jo.holland@amserve.net
web: www.heath-house.co.uk
dir: *M1 junct 40, A638 towards Dewsbury, at end dual
carriageway exit rdbt 2nd left, house 20yds on right*
The spacious Victorian family home stands in 4 acres of tranquil
gardens a short distance from the M1. It has elegant en suite
bedrooms, and the courteous and friendly owners provide healthy,
freshly-cooked breakfasts.
Rooms 2 en suite 2 annexe en suite (1 fmly) (2 GF) **Facilities** TVB tea/
coffee Cen ht Fishing small farm, sheep, hens, rabbits & ferrets
Parking 16

PONTEFRACT   MAP 16 SE42

★★★★ GUEST ACCOMMODATION
Wentvale
Great North Rd, Knottingley WF11 8PF
☎ 01977 676714
e–mail: wentvale1@btconnect.com
dir: *1.5m NE of Pontefract. Off A1 S for A645, sharp right*
Original features at this welcoming Victorian house include the
stained-glass front door and a panelled hall. Double-glazing in the
attractive, well-equipped bedrooms provides effective sound insulation.
There is an elegant lounge and a charming dining room where hearty
breakfasts are served.
Rooms 8 en suite 3 annexe en suite (4 GF) S £39; D £58✱
Facilities TVB tea/coffee Cen ht TVL **Parking** 15 **Notes** ⊗ No children
12yrs Closed Xmas & New Year

WAKEFIELD   MAP 16 SE32

★★★★ 🅰 GUEST ACCOMMODATION
Midgley Lodge Motel and Golf Course

Barr Ln, Midgley WF4 4JJ
☎ 01924 830069 📄 01924 830087
e–mail: midgleylodgemotel@tiscali.co.uk

dir: *6 miles SW of Wakefield. M1 junct 38, A637 Huddersfield road to Midgley*

Rooms 25 en suite (10 fmly) (13 GF) S fr £39.95; D fr £48(room only) Facilities STV TVB tea/coffee Direct dial from bedrooms Cen ht TVL Golf 9 Parking 90 Notes ⊗ Closed 25 Dec–2 Jan

★★★ GUEST HOUSE
Stanley View Guest House

226–230 Stanley Rd WF1 4AE
☎ 01924 376803 📄 01924 369123
e–mail: enquiries@stanleyviewguesthouse.co.uk

dir: *M62 junct 30, follow Aberford Rd 3m. Signed on left*

Part of an attractive terrace, this well established guest house is just half a mile from the city centre and has private parking at the rear. The well equipped bedrooms are brightly decorated, and there is a licensed bar and comfortable lounge. Hearty home cooked meals are served in the attractive dining room.

Rooms 17 rms (13 en suite) (6 fmly) (7 GF) S £25–£34; D £40–£45✶ Facilities STV TVB tea/coffee Direct dial from bedrooms Licensed Cen ht TVL Dinner Last d 8.30pm Parking 10 Notes No coaches

CHANNEL ISLANDS
GUERNSEY

FOREST   MAP 24

★★★★ GUEST HOUSE
Maison Bel Air Guest House

La Chene GY8 0AL
☎ 01481 238503 📄 01481 239403
e–mail: juliette@maisonbelair.com

The Maison Bel Air is set in peaceful landscaped gardens just a short drive from the airport and well-placed for touring the island. The attractive bedrooms are pleasantly decorated and thoughtfully

CONTINUED

equipped. Breakfast is served at individual tables in the smart dining room and there is also a cosy lounge.

Rooms 6 en suite (1 fmly) S £30–£44; D £50–£68✶ Facilities TVB tea/coffee Cen ht Parking 8 Notes LB ⊗ No children 3yrs No coaches

JERSEY

ST AUBIN   MAP 24

Premier Collection

★★★★★ 🏠 GUEST ACCOMMODATION
The Panorama

La Rue du Crocquet JE3 8BZ
☎ 01534 742429 📄 01534 745940
e–mail: info@panoramajersey.com
web: www.panoramajersey.com

dir: *In village centre*

Having spectacular views across St Aubin's Bay, the Panorama is a long-established favourite with visitors. The welcome is genuine and many of the well-equipped bedrooms have wonderful views, with most bathrooms upgraded recently. Public areas also look seaward and have attractive antique fireplaces. Breakfast is excellent and served in two dining areas.

Rooms 14 en suite (3 GF) S £40–£65; D £80–£130 Facilities STV TVB tea/coffee Cen ht Wi-fi available Notes ⊗ No children 18yrs Closed mid Oct–mid Apr

★★★ GUEST ACCOMMODATION
Peterborough House

La Rue du Croquet JE3 8BZ
☎ 01534 741568 📄 01534 746787
e–mail: fernando@localdial.com

dir: *A13 to St Aubin, left at La Haule Slip, 1st left. Left fork, half way down on left*

Situated on the old St Aubin high street, this well-presented guest house dates from 1690. The bedrooms are comfortably appointed and the sea-facing rooms are always in high demand. One of the two lounge areas has a bar, or you can enjoy the view with a drink on the outdoor terrace. Breakfast has a choice of traditional and continental options.

Rooms 14 rms (12 en suite) (1 fmly) (2 GF) S £29–£39; D £48–£68✶ Facilities TVB tea/coffee Cen ht TVL Notes LB ⊗ No children 12yrs Closed Nov–Feb

ENGLAND

ST HELIER   MAP 24

★★★★ GUEST ACCOMMODATION
Bay View Guest House
12 Havre des Pas JE2 4UQ
☎ 01534 720950 & 07797 720100 📧 01532 720950
e–mail: bayview.guesthouse@jerseymail.co.uk

dir: *Through tunnel, right at rdbt, down Green St & left, 100yds on left*

The Bay View is located across the road from the Havre des Pas Lido and beach, and just a ten minute walk from the centre of St Helier. Bedrooms are well equipped, and extra facilities include a bar and a television lounge with free Wi-fi internet access. There is a small garden terrace to the front of the establishment.

Rooms 13 rms (11 pri facs) (3 fmly) S £28–£46; D £56–£92✳
Facilities TVB tea/coffee Cen ht TVL Wi-fi available **Notes LB** ⊗

MAN, ISLE OF

DOUGLAS   MAP 24 SC37

★★★★ BED & BREAKFAST
Dreem Ard
Ballanard Rd IM2 5PR
☎ 01624 621491 📧 01624 621491

dir: *From St Ninian's Church along Ballanard Rd for 1m, over Johnny Watterson Ln x-rds, past farm on left, Dreem Ard on left*

Dreem Ard is a relaxing sanctuary, with superb views over the glens just to the north of Douglas. Bedrooms are spacious and well equipped, and the caring hosts are genuinely hospitable and attentive. Breakfast and dinner are served around a large table, where good food and good company go hand-in-hand.

Rooms 3 en suite (1 fmly) (2 GF) S £40–£60; D £59–£79✳
Facilities STV TVB tea/coffee Cen ht Dinner Last d breakfast **Parking** 6
Notes LB ⊗ No children 8yrs ☻

★★★ A GUEST HOUSE
All Seasons
11 Clifton Ter, Broadway IM2 3HX
☎ 0871 855 0603 📧 0871 855 0603
e–mail: hansonsales@pilogene.co.uk

dir: *Off Central Promenade at Villa Marina, premises in 1st row of hotels on left*

Rooms 6 rms (4 en suite) (2 pri facs) (6 fmly) S £27–£55; D £54–£98
Facilities TVB tea/coffee Licensed Cen ht TVL Dinner Last d 5pm Wi-fi available ☼ **Notes LB** ⊗ No children 12yrs No coaches

PORT ST MARY   MAP 24 SC26

Premier Collection

★★★★★ 🍴 GUEST HOUSE
Aaron House
The Promenade IM9 5DE
☎ 01624 835702
web: www.aaronhouse.co.uk

dir: *Signs for South & Port St Mary, left at Post Office, house in centre of Promenade overlooking harbour*

Aaron House is truly individual. From the parlour down to the detail of the cast-iron baths, the house has been restored to its Victorian origins. The family work hard to offer the best quality, whether its providing luxury and comfort in the bedrooms, or even to offering home-made cakes on arrival.

Rooms 4 rms (2 en suite) (2 pri facs) **Facilities** tea/coffee Cen ht TVL
Notes ⊗ No children 14yrs No coaches Closed 21 Dec–3 Jan ☻

ST JOHN'S   MAP 24 SC28

★★★★ 🍴 INN
Glen Helen Inn
Glen Helen IM4 3NP
☎ 01624 801294 📧 01624 803294
e–mail: info@glenheleninn.com
web: www.glenheleninn.com

This charming inn is in a glorious location in the heart of the Island and close to some lovely country walks. Bedrooms are all very well planned and have a contemporary appearance. The stylish bar is ideal for pre dinner drinks and the inn has a popular restaurant, which serves a wide range of dishes.

Rooms 14 en suite (3 fmly) **Facilities** TVB tea/coffee Cen ht Dinner Last d 9.30pm **Conf** Max 80 Thtr 80 Class 24 Board 40 **Parking** 70

Scotland

Glen Coe, Highlands

CITY OF ABERDEEN

ABERDEEN   MAP 23 NJ90

★★★★ GUEST HOUSE
The Jays Guest House
422 King St AB24 3BR
☎ 01224 638295 📄 01224 638360
e–mail: alice@jaysguesthouse.co.uk
web: www.jaysguesthouse.co.uk
dir: *A90 from S onto Main St & Union St & A92 to King St N*
Guests are warmly welcomed to this attractive granite house on the
north side of the city. Maintained in first-class order throughout, it
offers attractive bedrooms, smartly furnished to appeal to business
guests and tourists. Freshly prepared breakfasts are enjoyed in the
carefully appointed dining room.
Rooms 10 rms (8 en suite) (2 pri facs) (1 GF) S £45–£60; D £90–£110✶
Facilities STV TVB tea/coffee Cen ht Wi-fi available **Parking** 9 **Notes** ⊗
No children 12yrs No coaches Closed mid Dec–mid Jan

★★★ GUEST HOUSE
Arkaig
43 Powis Ter AB25 3PP
☎ 01224 638872 📄 01224 622189
e–mail: info@arkaig.co.uk
dir: *On A96 at junct with Bedford Rd*
A friendly welcome and relaxed atmosphere is assured at this
well-presented guest house, situated on the north side of the city close
to the university and city centre. Bedrooms vary in size, are attractively
decorated and are all thoughtfully equipped to appeal to business and
leisure guests. There is a cosy sun lounge with magazines, and an
attractive breakfast room where delicious freshly cooked breakfasts are
served. Parking is also available.
Rooms 8 rms (6 en suite) (1 fmly) (5 GF) **Facilities** TVB tea/coffee
Direct dial from bedrooms Cen ht TVL **Parking** 10

PETERCULTER   MAP 23 NJ80

★★★ 🅰 GUEST HOUSE
Furain
92 North Deeside Rd AB14 0QN
☎ 01224 732189 📄 01224 739070
e–mail: furain@btinternet.com
dir: *7m W of city centre on A93*
Rooms 8 en suite (2 fmly) (3 GF) S £42–£48; D £54–£64✶
Facilities TVB tea/coffee Cen ht **Parking** 7 **Notes** No coaches Closed
Xmas & New Year

ABERDEENSHIRE

BALLATER   MAP 23 NO39

★★★★ ◉◉ RESTAURANT WITH ROOMS
The Green Inn
9 Victoria Rd AB35 5QQ
☎ 013397 55701
e–mail: info@green-inn.com
web: www.green-inn.com
dir: *In centre of village*
A former temperance hotel, the Green Inn enjoys a central location in
the pretty village of Ballater. Bedrooms are all of a high standard and
attractively presented. The restaurant has a strong reputation for its fine
cuisine, which can be enjoyed in the stylish conservatory restaurant.
Breakfast is equally enjoyable and not to be missed. Genuine
hospitality from the enthusiastic proprietors is a real feature of any stay.
Rooms 3 en suite S £50–£60; D £70–£90✶ **Facilities** TVB tea/coffee
Cen ht TVL Dinner Last d 9pm Wi-fi available **Notes** Closed 1st 2 wks
Nov, last 2 wks Jan

BRAEMAR   MAP 23 NO19

★★★★ GUEST HOUSE
Callater Lodge Guest House
9 Glenshee Rd AB35 5YQ
☎ 013397 41275
e–mail: info@hotel-braemar.co.uk
web: www.callaterlodge.co.uk
dir: *Next to A93, 300yds S of Braemar centre*
Located in the picturesque village of Braemar, a very well presented
property under the new ownership of the Shores. Bedrooms are
comfortable with many thoughtful extras provided as standard. Public
areas are welcoming with a home away from home feel. Breakfast is
served on individual tables with local quality ingredients used. The
gardens are a feature and are pleasing to the eye.
Rooms 6 en suite (1 fmly) S £35–£40; D £66–£72✶ **Facilities** TVB tea/
coffee Licensed Cen ht **Parking** 6 **Notes** ⊗ No coaches Closed Xmas

FRASERBURGH   MAP 23 NJ96

★★★★★ 🅰 BED & BREAKFAST
Lonmay Old Manse
Lonmay AB43 8UJ
☎ 01346 532227 📄 01346 532227
e–mail: info@lonmay.co.uk
web: www.lonmay.co.uk
dir: *From A90 onto B9033 St Combs, 1.5m left for Cairness
House. Turn right in 500yds*
Rooms 3 en suite S £50; D £64–£70✶ **Facilities** TVB Cen ht Dinner
Last d 24hr notice 🍴 **Parking** 6 **Notes** ⊗

SCOTLAND

INVERURIE
MAP 23 NJ72

[U]
Kintore Arms
83 High St AB51 3QJ
☎ 01467 621367 ▤ 01467 625620
e–mail: manager.kintore@ohiml.com
web: www.oxfordhotelsandinns.com
dir: *From A96 at rdbt turn signed Inverurie, onto main High St, on left*

At the time of going to press the rating for this establishment had not been confirmed. Please check the AA website www.theAA.com for up-to-date information.

Rooms 19 en suite (1 fmly) S £65; D £75✱ **Facilities** FTV TVB tea/coffee Cen ht TVL Dinner Last d 9pm Wi-fi available **Conf** Max 150 Thtr 150 Class 75 Board 75 **Parking** 30 **Notes** Civ Wed 150

MINTLAW
MAP 23 NJ94

[U]
Country Park Inn
Station Rd AB42 5EB
☎ 01771 622622
e–mail: manager.countrypark@ohiml.com
At the time of going to press the rating for this establishment had not been confirmed. Please check the AA website www.theAA.com for up-to-date information.

Rooms 3 rms (2 en suite) (1 pri facs) S fr £35; D fr £50✱ **Facilities** STV TVB Cen ht Dinner **Conf** Max 100 Thtr 80 Class 60 Board 60 Del from £85 ✱ **Notes** ⊗

OLDMELDRUM
MAP 23 NJ82

★★★★ [A] BED & BREAKFAST
Cromlet Hill
South Rd AB51 0AB
☎ 01651 872315 ▤ 01651 872164
e–mail: johnpage@cromlethill.co.uk
dir: *In town centre*

Rooms 3 en suite (1 fmly) S £40–£50; D £56–£70✱ **Facilities** TVB tea/coffee Cen ht TVL **Parking** 4 **Notes** ⊗ ⊛

STONEHAVEN
MAP 23 NO88

★★★★ GUEST ACCOMMODATION
Woodside Of Glasslaw
AB39 3XQ
☎ 01569 763799 ▤ 01569 763799
e–mail: aileenpaton@hotmail.com
dir: *A90 N, 1st sign for Stonehaven, at end bend turn right, next left*

Set amid farmland and gardens, yet close to major roads, this guest house is popular with business and leisure guests. The comfortable bedrooms are spacious and attractively decorated, and hearty breakfasts are served at individual tables lounge-dining room.

Rooms 6 en suite (1 fmly) (4 GF) S fr £35; D fr £55✱ **Facilities** TVB tea/coffee Cen ht TVL Wi-fi available **Parking** 6 **Notes** Closed Xmas

ANGUS

INVERKEILOR
MAP 23 NO64

★★★★ ⊛⊛ RESTAURANT WITH ROOMS
Gordon's
Main St DD11 5RN
☎ 01241 830364 ▤ 01241 830364
e–mail: gordonsrest@aol.com
dir: *Off A92, follow signs for Inverkeilor*

It's worth a detour off the main road to this family-run restaurant with rooms set in the centre of the village. It has earned AA Rosettes for its dinners, though the excellent breakfasts are equally memorable. A huge fire dominates the restaurant on cooler evenings and there is a small lounge with limited seating. The attractive bedrooms are tastefully decorated and thoughtfully equipped, the larger two being furnished in pine.

Rooms 3 rms (2 en suite) (1 pri facs) S £60–£75; D £90–£100✱ **Facilities** TVB Cen ht Dinner Last d 9pm **Parking** 6 **Notes** ⊗ No children 12yrs Closed 2 wks Jan

MONIFIETH
MAP 21 NO43

[U]
Panmure
Tay St DD5 4AX
☎ 01382 532911 ▤ 01382 535859
e–mail: generalmanager.panmure@ohiml.com
At the time of going to press the rating for this establishment had not been confirmed. Please check the AA website www.theAA.com for up-to-date information.

Rooms 13 en suite (3 fmly) S £50–£70; D £70–£90✱ **Facilities** TVB tea/coffee Lift Cen ht TVL Dinner Last d 10pm Wi-fi available Golf 18 **Conf** Max 150 Thtr 150 Class 80 Board 50 Del from £39.95 ✱ **Parking** 50 **Notes** LB Civ Wed 100

SCOTLAND

MONTROSE
MAP 23 NO75

★★★ GUEST HOUSE
Oaklands
10 Rossie Island Rd DD10 9NN
☎ 01674 672018 📄 01674 672018
e–mail: oaklands1@btopenworld.com

dir: *On A92 at S end of town*

A genuine welcome and attentive service are assured at this smart detached house situated on the south side of the town. Bedrooms come in a variety of sizes and are neatly presented. There is a lounge on the ground floor next to the attractive dining room, where hearty breakfasts are served. Motorcycle guided tours can be arranged with tourists travelling with their own motorbikes.

Rooms 7 en suite (1 fmly) (1 GF) S £30–£35; D £50–£65✳
Facilities FTV TVB tea/coffee Cen ht TVL Wi-fi available **Parking** 8
Notes ⊗ No coaches

ARGYLL & BUTE

APPIN
MAP 20 NM94

Premier Collection

★★★★★ 🍴 GUEST HOUSE
Bealach Country House
Duror PA38 4BW
☎ 01631 740298
e–mail: info@bealach-house.co.uk
web: www.bealach-house.co.uk

dir: *Off A828, 2m S of Duror. 1.5m into the Glen*

Set one and a half miles off the main Oban to Fort William road, surrounded by nothing but rolling hills, the meandering drive up the track to the property is well worth the journey. Bedrooms and bathrooms are very comfortable and cater well for the needs of the modern guest. Public areas are a home away from home. Dinner is available, and the breakfast is very impressive.

Rooms 3 en suite S £40–£65; D £80–£100 **Facilities** tea/coffee Cen ht TVL Dinner Last d 6pm Wi-fi available **Parking** 6 **Notes** ⊗ No children 14yrs No coaches Closed Dec & Jan

---

ARROCHAR
MAP 20 NN20

★★★★ BED & BREAKFAST
Burnbrae
Shore Rd G83 7AG
☎ 01301 702988 📄 01301 702988
e–mail: janice.mathieson1@btopenworld.com
web: www.scotland2000.com/burnbrae

dir: *A82 at Tarbet onto A83 2m. A814 for 1m, house before The Village Inn*

Overlooking the majestic Loch Long, perched on a small knoll with a bubbling burn running alongside the property. High standards of hospitality and customer care are evident from your hosts. Bedrooms are well appointed and equipped, catering for the needs of the modern traveller. A very good breakfast includes award winning homemade preserves and gives the guest a wonderful start to their day regardless of the planned activities. Burnbrae has a mooring on the loch if required.

Rooms 2 en suite S £60–£75; D £70–£80 **Facilities** TVB tea/coffee Cen ht **Parking** 3 **Notes** No children 10yrs ⊛

CAMPBELTOWN
MAP 20 NR72

★★★ 🅰 GUEST HOUSE
Westbank Guest House
Dell Rd PA28 6JG
☎ 01586 553660 📄 01586 553660

dir: *A83 to Campbeltown turn right at T-junct follow signs for Southend, B842, through S-bend, Heritage centre on left, 1st right Dell Rd*

Rooms 7 rms (6 en suite) (1 pri facs) (3 fmly) **Facilities** TVB tea/coffee Cen ht TVL **Notes** No coaches

---

CARDROSS
MAP 20 NS37

Premier Collection

★★★★★ GUEST ACCOMMODATION
Kirkton House
Darleith Rd G82 5EZ
☎ 01389 841951 📄 01389 841868
e–mail: aa@kirktonhouse.co.uk
web: www.kirktonhouse.co.uk

dir: *0.5m N of village. Turn N off A814 onto Darleith Rd at W end of village. Kirkton House 0.5m on right*

Dating from the 18th century, this converted farmstead around an attractive courtyard has stunning views over the Clyde estuary from its elevated location. The individually styled bedrooms are well equipped and generally spacious, with two on the ground floor. Stone walls and large fireplaces feature in public areas, and home-cooked meals using fresh produce are served in the delightful dining room.

Rooms 6 en suite (4 fmly) (2 GF) S £40–£45; D £50–£70 **Facilities** FTV TVB tea/coffee Direct dial from bedrooms Cen ht TVL Wi-fi available Riding **Parking** 12 **Notes LB** Closed Dec–Jan

CONTINUED

CARRADALE   MAP 20 NR83

★★★★ ⊛ GUEST ACCOMMODATION
Dunvalanree
Port Righ Bay PA28 6SE
☎ 01583 431226 📠 01583 431339
e–mail: stay@dunvalanree.com
web: www.dunvalanree.com
dir: *From centre of Carradale, turn right at x-rds and continue to end of road*

Set in some stunning scenery on the Mull of Kintyre, Dunvalanree is a small non-smoking accommodation that has been welcoming guests for over 70 years. The restaurant menu, which has earned itself an AA Rosette, uses local sea food and farm produce. Standing in delightful gardens on the edge of Port Righ Bay, Dunvalanree enjoys splendid views over Kilbrannan Sound, to the Isle of Arran.

Rooms 5 en suite (1 GF) S £75–£90; D £130–£150(incl. dinner) **Facilities** TVB tea/coffee Cen ht Dinner Last d 7.30pm Wi-fi available Golf 9 Fishing ⚓ **Parking** 8 **Notes LB** ⊛

CONNEL   MAP 20 NM93

★★★★ 🍴 GUEST HOUSE
Ards House
PA37 1PT
☎ 01631 710255 📠 01631 710857
e–mail: info@ardshouse.com
web: www.ardshouse.com

dir: *On A85, 4m N of Oban*

This delightful Victorian villa on the approaches to Loch Etive has stunning views over the Firth of Lorne and the Morven Hills beyond. The stylish bedrooms come with added touches such as home-made shortbread and mineral water. There is an inviting drawing room complete with piano, games and books, plus a fire on cooler evenings. The attractive dining room is the setting for delicious breakfasts.

Rooms 4 en suite S £50–£65; D £76–£90✱ **Facilities** FTV TVB tea/coffee Cen ht TVL **Parking** 12 **Notes LB** ⊛ No children 10yrs No coaches Closed mid Dec–mid Jan

★★★★ GUEST HOUSE
Ronebhal Guest House
PA37 1PJ
☎ 01631 710310 📠 01631 710310
e–mail: ronebhal@btinternet.com

dir: *A85 W from village centre, 4th house after turning for Fort William*

The Strachan family extends a friendly welcome to their lovely detached home, which has stunning views of Loch Etive. The bedrooms are well equipped and comfortably furnished in modern styles. There is a sitting room, and an attractive dining room where hearty traditional breakfasts are served at individual tables. Gardens are pleasing on the eye.

Rooms 5 rms (4 en suite) (1 pri facs) (1 fmly) (1 GF) S £25–£50; D £50–£80 **Facilities** FTV TVB tea/coffee Cen ht TVL **Parking** 6 **Notes LB** ⊛ No children 7yrs No coaches Closed Nov–Feb

HELENSBURGH   MAP 20 NS28

See also Cardross

Premier Collection

★★★★★ GUEST ACCOMMODATION
Lethamhill
West Dhuhill Dr G84 9AW
☎ 01436 676016 & 07907 977652 📠 01436 676016
e–mail: Lethamhill@talk21.com
web: www.lethamhill.co.uk

dir: *1m N of pier/town centre. Off A818 onto West Dhuhill Dr. Cross Upper Colcough St, then 3rd entrance on right*

From the red phone box in the garden to the old typewriters and slot machines inside, this fine house is an Aladdin's cave of unusual collectibles and memorabilia. The house itself offers spacious and comfortable bedrooms with superb bathrooms. The home-cooked breakfasts and delicious baking earn much praise.

Rooms 3 en suite S £55–£70; D £80–£120 **Facilities** TVB tea/coffee Cen ht TVL Wi-fi available **Parking** 6 **Notes LB** ⊛

SCOTLAND

LOCHGILPHEAD   MAP 20 NR88

★★★★ 🅰 BED & BREAKFAST

Corbiere

Achnabreac PA31 8SG

☎ 01546 602764

e–mail: joan.sinclair4@btinternet.com

dir: *A83 to Lochgilphead, right onto A816. 1st right after the Achnebreac Cemetery.*

Rooms 2 rms (1 en suite) (1 pri facs) (2 fmly) D £50–£55✻
Facilities TVB tea/coffee Cen ht TVL **Parking** 5 **Notes** ⊗ No children 10yrs 🐾

OBAN   MAP 20 NM82

Premier Collection

★★★★★ GUEST HOUSE

Blarcreen House

Ardchattan, Connel PA37 1RG

☎ 01631 750272 📄 01631 750132

e–mail: info@blarcreenhouse.com

web: www.blarcreenhouse.com

dir: *9.5m NE of Oban. N over Connel Bridge, 1st right for 7m, pass church and Ardchattan Priory Gardens, Blarcreen House 2m*

Built in 1886 this elegant Victorian farmhouse stands on the shores of Loch Etive and has lovely views of the surrounding mountains. Bedrooms are beautifully furnished and very well equipped. There is a comfortable drawing room with deep sofas, a plentiful supply of books and videos, and a log-burning fire. Delicious home-cooked fare featuring the very best of local produce is served in the dining room. Hospitality is strong and the atmosphere relaxed in this charming house.

Rooms 3 en suite S £69.50–£75; D £79–£110✻ **Facilities** STV TVB tea/coffee Licensed Cen ht TVL Dinner Last d 24hrs prior Wi-fi available **Parking** 5 **Notes LB** ⊗ No children 16yrs No coaches

★★★★ 🍴 GUEST HOUSE

Glenburnie House

The Esplanade PA34 5AQ

☎ 01631 562089 📄 01631 562089

e–mail: graeme.strachan@btinternet.com

dir: *On Oban seafront. Follow signs for Ganavan*

This impressive seafront Victorian house has been lovingly restored to a high standard. Bedrooms (including a four-poster room and a mini-suite) are beautifully decorated and very well equipped. There is a cosy ground-floor lounge and an elegant dining room, where hearty traditional breakfasts are served at individual tables.

Rooms 12 en suite (2 GF) S £45–£50; D £75–£100 **Facilities** FTV TVB tea/coffee Cen ht Wi-fi available **Parking** 12 **Notes LB** ⊗ No children 12yrs No coaches Closed Nov–Mar

★★★★ GUEST HOUSE

Alltavona House

Corran Esplanade PA34 5AQ

☎ 01631 565067 & 07771 708301 📄 01631 565067

e–mail: carol@alltavona.co.uk

dir: *From Oban centre along seafront past cathedral, 5th house from the end of Esplanade*

Alltavona is an elegant Victorian villa with a delightful location on the Corran Esplanade with stunning views over Oban Bay to the islands of Lismore and Kererra. The attractive bedrooms are individually styled and feature quality furnishings. Delicious breakfasts featuring the best of local produce are served in the charming dining room.

Rooms 6 en suite (3 fmly) **Facilities** TVB tea/coffee Cen ht **Parking** 6 **Notes** ⊗ No children 12yrs No coaches Closed 12–30 Dec

★★★★ GUEST HOUSE

Braeside

Kilmore PA34 4QR

☎ 01631 770243 📄 01631 770343

e–mail: braeside.guesthouse@virgin.net

web: www.braesideguesthouse.net

dir: *On A816 5m from Oban*

The family-run bungalow stands in gardens overlooking the spectacular Loch Feochan. Bedrooms, all en suite, are bright and airy, well equipped and have easy access. The lounge-dining room has a loch view, a bar with a range of single malts and wines, and offers a varied choice of tasty home-cooked evening meals and breakfasts.

Rooms 5 en suite (1 fmly) (5 GF) S £30–£60; D £54–£60✻
Facilities TVB tea/coffee Licensed Cen ht Dinner Last d noon Wi-fi available **Parking** 6 **Notes LB** ⊗ No children 8yrs No coaches

★★★★ GUEST HOUSE
Corriemar House
Corran Esplanade PA34 5AQ
☎ 01631 562476 📠 01631 564339
e−mail: info@corriemarhouse.co.uk
web: www.corriemarhouse.co.uk

dir: *A85 to Oban. Down hill in right lane & follow sign for Gamavan at mini rdbt onto Esplanade*

Billy and Sandra Russell have created a stylish haven of tranquillity at this detached Victorian house close to the town centre. Bedrooms are furnished with panache, range from massive to cosy, and even include a suite. Those to the front of the house have stunning views across Oban Bay to the Isle of Mull. Expect a substantial breakfast and friendly attentive service.

Rooms 9 en suite 4 annexe en suite (3 fmly) (1 GF) **Facilities** TVB tea/coffee Cen ht **Parking** 9 **Notes** ⊗

★★★★ GUEST HOUSE
Greencourt
Benvoullin Rd PA34 5EF
☎ 01631 563987
e−mail: relax@greencourt-oban.co.uk

dir: *At Oban, left at Kings Knoll Hotel, over x-rds & follow Dalriach Rd. Pass leisure centre and bowling green on left then turn left. Left again and sharp left onto lane, Greencourt 2nd house on left*

This welcoming family home stands on an elevated location overlooking the bowling green and leisure centre. The delightful detached house has attractive, comfortable bedrooms of varying sizes, and all are well equipped. Freshly prepared breakfasts are served in the bright airy dining room, which has lovely views.

Rooms 6 rms (5 en suite) (1 pri facs) (6 GF) S £30−£37; D £60−£74✳ **Facilities** TVB tea/coffee Cen ht **Parking** 6 **Notes LB** ⊗ No coaches Closed Dec−Jan

★★ GUEST ACCOMMODATION
Lancaster
Corran Esplanade PA34 5AD
☎ 01631 562587 📠 01631 562587
e−mail: john@lancasteroban.com

dir: *On seafront next to Columba's Cathedral*

There are lovely views over the bay towards the Isle of Mull from this welcoming, family-run establishment on the Esplanade. Public areas include a choice of lounges and bars.

Rooms 27 rms (24 en suite) (3 fmly) (27 smoking) S £35−£40; D £74−£82✳ **Facilities** TVB tea/coffee Cen ht TVL 🦜 Sauna Pool Table Jacuzzi, steam room **Conf** Max 30 Thtr 30 Class 20 Board 12 **Parking** 20 **Notes LB**

TARBERT LOCH FYNE
MAP 20 NR86

Ⓤ
The Victoria
Barmore Rd PA29 6TW
☎ 01880 820236 📠 01880 820638
At the time of going to press the rating for this establishment had not been confirmed. Please check the AA website www.theAA.com for up-to-date information.

Rooms 5 en suite S fr £45; D fr £70✳ **Facilities** TVB tea/coffee Cen ht Wi-fi available **Notes** ⊗

CLACKMANNANSHIRE

TILLICOULTRY
MAP 21 NS99

★★★★ BED & BREAKFAST
Westbourne House
10 Dollar Rd FK13 6PA
☎ 01259 750314
e−mail: info@westbournehouse.co.uk

dir: *A91 to St Andrews. Establishment on left just past mini rdbt*

This former mill-owner's home, set in wooded gardens on the edge of the village, is adorned with memorabilia gathered by the owners during their travels abroad. They offer a friendly welcome and an excellent choice is offered at breakfast.

Rooms 3 rms (2 en suite) (1 pri facs) (1 fmly) (1 GF) S £35−£40; D £58−£60✳ **Facilities** TVB tea/coffee Cen ht TVL 🦮 **Parking** 3 **Notes** Closed Xmas-New Year

DUMFRIES & GALLOWAY

ANNAN
MAP 21 NY16

★★ 🅰 GUEST HOUSE
Rowanbank Guest House
20 St Johns Rd DG12 6AW
☎ 01461 204200
e−mail: rowanbankguests@btconnect.com

dir: *Off A75 at Annan. S for Bank St at lights. Property 200yds on left.*

Rooms 10 en suite (3 fmly) (5 GF) S £33; D £60−£77✳ **Facilities** FTV TVB tea/coffee Cen ht TVL Wi-fi available **Parking** 4 **Notes** No coaches ⊕

CASTLE DOUGLAS MAP 21 NX76

★★★★ 🛏 🍴 GUEST HOUSE

Craigadam

Craigadam DG7 3HU

☎ 01556 650233 & 650100 📄 01556 650233

e–mail: inquiry@craigadam.com

web: www.craigadam.com

dir: *From Castle Douglas E on A75 to Crocketford. In Crocketford turn left on A712 for 2m. House on hill*

Set on a farm, this elegant country house offers gracious living in a relaxed environment. The large bedrooms, most set around a courtyard, are strikingly individual in style. Public areas include a billiard room with comprehensive honesty bar, and the panelled dining room features a magnificent 15-seater table, the setting for Celia Pickup's delightful meals.

Rooms 10 en suite (2 fmly) (7 GF) **Facilities** TVB tea/coffee Licensed Cen ht Dinner Last d 8am Fishing Snooker ⚓ **Conf** Max 22 **Parking** 12 **Notes** No coaches Closed Xmas & New Year Civ Wed 150

DUMFRIES MAP 21 NX97

★★★★ BED & BREAKFAST

Wallamhill House

Kirkton DG1 1SL

☎ 01387 248249

e–mail: wallamhill@aol.com

dir: *3m N of Dumfries. Off A701 signed Kirkton, 1.5m on right*

Wallamhill House is set in well-tended gardens, in a delightful rural area three miles from Dumfries. Bedrooms are spacious and extremely well equipped. There is a peaceful drawing room, and a mini health club with sauna, steam shower and gym equipment.

Rooms 3 en suite (1 fmly) S £35–£40; D £60 **Facilities** FTV TVB tea/coffee Cen ht TVL Sauna Gymnasium ⚓ Steam room **Parking** 6 **Notes** LB ⊗

★★★★ GUEST HOUSE

Rivendell

105 Edinburgh Rd DG1 1JX

☎ 01387 252251 📄 01387 263084

e–mail: info@rivendellbnb.co.uk

web: www.rivendellbnb.co.uk

dir: *On A701 Edinburgh Rd, 400yds S of A75 junct*

Situated just north of the town and close to the bypass, this lovely 1920s house, standing in extensive landscaped gardens, has been restored to reflect the period style of the property. Bedrooms are thoughtfully equipped, many are spacious and all offer modern facilities. Traditional breakfasts are served in the elegant dining room.

Rooms 5 en suite (2 fmly) S £30–£45; D £52–£58 **Facilities** TVB tea/coffee Cen ht Wi-fi available **Parking** 12 **Notes** LB ⊗ No coaches

★★★★ GUEST ACCOMMODATION

Southpark House

Quarry Rd, Locharbriggs DG1 1QG

☎ 01387 711188 & 0800 970 1588 📄 01387 711155

e–mail: info@southparkhouse.co.uk

web: www.southparkhouse.co.uk

dir: *3.5m NE of Dumfries. Off A701 in Locharbriggs onto Quarry Rd, last house on left*

Having a peaceful location with stunning views, this well-maintained property offers comfortable, attractive and well-equipped bedrooms. The peaceful lounge has a log fire on colder evenings, and fax and e-mail facilities are available. Friendly proprietor Ewan Maxwell personally oversees the hearty Scottish breakfasts served in the recently-built conservatory breakfast room.

Rooms 4 en suite (1 fmly) S £30–£50; D £50–£75 **Facilities** STV FTV TVB tea/coffee Cen ht TVL Wi-fi available 2 acres of garden **Parking** 13 **Notes** LB ⊗

GRETNA　　　　　MAP 21 NY36
(WITH GRETNA GREEN)

★★★ GUEST ACCOMMODATION
Barrasgate
Millhill DG16 5HU
☎ 01461 337577 & 07711 661938 📠 01461 337577
e–mail: info@barrasgate.co.uk
web: www.barrasgate.co.uk

dir: *A74(M) junct 24. 1m E take 2nd left signed Gretna Green
establishment on left*

This detached house lies in attractive gardens in a rural setting near the Blacksmith Centre and motorway links. Bedrooms are equipped with thoughtful extras and have fine country views. Hearty breakfasts, featuring local produce, are taken in an attractive dining room, overlooking the gardens.

Rooms 4 en suite (1 fmly) (1 GF) **Facilities** TV3B tea/coffee Cen ht TVL **Parking** 8 **Notes** ☺

★★★ GUEST ACCOMMODATION
Surrone House
Annan Rd DG16 5DL
☎ 01461 338341 📠 01461 338341
e–mail: enquiries@surronehouse.co.uk
web: www.surronehouse.co.uk

dir: *In town centre on B721*

You are assured of a warm welcome at this well-maintained guest house set in attractive gardens well back from the road. Bedrooms are sensibly furnished and including a delightful honeymoon suite. Dinner, drinks and light refreshments are available.

Rooms 7 rms (6 en suite) (1 pri facs) (3 fmly) (2 GF) S £45–£50; D £60–£65✳ **Facilities** FTV TVB tea/coffee Cen ht TVL Dinner Last d 8pm Wi-fi available **Parking** 10 **Notes** ☺

★★★ 🅐 BED & BREAKFAST
Kirkcroft Guest House
Glasgow Rd DG16 5DU
☎ 01461 337403 📠 01461 337403
e–mail: info@kirkcroft.co.uk

dir: *On B7076 next to railway station, at bottom of drive to Gretna Hall*

Rooms 3 en suite S £40; D £54✳ **Facilities** FTV TVB tea/coffee Cen ht **Parking** 5 **Notes** LB ☺

KIRKCUDBRIGHT　　　　　MAP 20 NX65

★★★★ BED & BREAKFAST
Baytree House
110 High St DG6 4JQ
☎ 01557 330824
e–mail: ruary@baytreekirkcudbright.co.uk

dir: *Off main street onto Saint Cuthbert's St & Castle St*

Baytree House is a beautifully restored Georgian house close to the town centre. The attractive bedrooms are thoughtfully equipped and furnished in keeping with style of the house, and the bright airy ground-floor dining room with a cosy lounge area overlooks the secluded garden.

Rooms 3 en suite (1 GF) S £40–£64; D £60–£64✳ **Facilities** TVB tea/coffee Cen ht TVL Wi-fi available **Notes** LB No children 12yrs ☺

MOFFAT　　　　　MAP 21 NT00

Premier Collection
★★★★★ ◉◉ GUEST ACCOMMODATION
Well View
Ballplay Rd DG10 9JU
☎ 01683 220184
e–mail: johnwellview@aol.com

dir: *Leave Moffat on A708 towards Selkirk 0.5m, turn left onto Ballplay Rd, 300mtrs on right*

Well View is a well-established building set on an elevated position with outstanding views. The house is tastefully and traditionally decorated and furnished with many personal touches. Service and attention to detail are key features at Well View as is the fine food that is personally cooked by the proprietors.

Rooms 3 en suite S £65–£75; D £90–£110✳ **Facilities** TVB tea/coffee Cen ht Dinner Last d 7.30pm **Parking** 4 **Notes** LB

SCOTLAND

MOFFAT CONTINUED

★★★★ 🍴 GUEST HOUSE
Bridge House
Well Rd DG10 9JT
☎ 01683 220558 📠 01683 220558
e–mail: info@bridgehousemoffat.co.uk
dir: *Off A708 The Holm onto Burnside & Well Rd, house 0.5m on left*

A fine Victorian property, Bridge House lies in attractive gardens in a quiet residential area on the fringe of the town. The atmosphere is very friendly and relaxed. The chef-proprietor provides interesting dinners (by arrangement) featuring local produce. The cosy guest lounge is the ideal venue for pre-dinner drinks.

Rooms 7 en suite (1 fmly) S £45–£50; D £65–£95✳ **Facilities** TVB tea/coffee Licensed Cen ht Dinner Last d 7pm **Parking** 7 **Notes** LB ⊗ No children 2yrs No coaches Closed 23 Dec–13 Feb

★★★★ ⚙ GUEST HOUSE
Hartfell House & The Limetree Restaurant
Hartfell Crescent DG10 9AL
☎ 01683 220153
e–mail: enquiries@hartfellhouse.co.uk
dir: *Off High St at war memorial onto Well St & Old Well Rd, Hartfell Crescent on right*

Built in 1850, this impressive Victorian house is in a peaceful terrace high above the town, having lovely views of the surrounding countryside. Beautifully maintained, its bedrooms offer high quality and comfort. The attractive dining room is transformed in the evening

CONTINUED

into the Lime Tree restaurant (previously in the town centre) offering Chef Matt Seddon's culinary delights.

Rooms 7 en suite (2 fmly) (1 GF) S £40; D £70 **Facilities** TVB tea/coffee Licensed Cen ht Dinner Last d 8.30pm Wi-fi available **Parking** 6 **Notes** LB ⊗ No coaches Closed Xmas

★★★★ GUEST ACCOMMODATION
Limetree House
Eastgate DG10 9AE
☎ 01683 220001
e–mail: info@limetreehouse.co.uk
web: www.limetreehouse.co.uk
dir: *Off High St onto Well St, left onto Eastgate, house 100yds*

A warm welcome is assured at this well-maintained guest house, quietly situated behind the main high street. Recognisable by its colourful flower baskets in season, it provides an inviting lounge and bright cheerful breakfast room. Bedrooms are smartly furnished and include a large family room.

Rooms 6 en suite (1 fmly) (1 GF) S fr £42.50; D £65–£75✳ **Facilities** FTV TVB tea/coffee Cen ht Dinner Last d 5pm **Parking** 3 **Notes** LB No children 5yrs RS Xmas & New Year

★★★ INN
The Balmoral
High St DG10 9DL
☎ 01683 220288 📠 01683 220451
web: www.thebalmoralhotel-moffat.co.uk
dir: *0.5m from A/M74 junct 15, halfway up High St on right*

The Balmoral is situated in the centre of Moffat with free parking in the town square, a friendly welcome is guaranteed. Fully licensed with bar meals available all day until 9.30pm. Bedrooms are very comfortably equipped with thoughtful extras. A former spa town and an ideal tourist location within easy reach of the major tourist attractions.

Rooms 16 en suite (2 fmly) S £32.50; D £53✳ **Facilities** TVB tea/coffee Dinner **Notes** ⊗

★★ GUEST ACCOMMODATION
Barnhill Springs Country Guest House
DG10 9QS
☎ 01683 220580
dir: *A74(M) junct 15, A701 towards Moffat, Barnhill Rd 50yds on right*

This former farmhouse has a quiet rural location south of the town and within easy reach of the M74. Bedrooms are well proportioned; one having a bathroom en suite. There is a comfortable lounge and separate dining room.

Rooms 5 rms (1 en suite) (2 pri facs) (1 fmly) (1 GF) S £30; D £60 **Facilities** tea/coffee Cen ht TVL Dinner Last d 9am **Parking** 10 **Notes** 🍴

THORNHILL   MAP 21 NX89

Premier Collection

★★★★★ GUEST ACCOMMODATION
Gillbank House

8 East Morton St DG3 5LZ
☎ 01848 330597 📄 01848 331713
e–mail: hanne@gillbank.co.uk
web: www.gillbank.co.uk

dir: *In town centre off A76*

Gillbank House was originally built for a wealthy Edinburgh merchant. Convenient for the many outdoor pursuits in this area, such as fishing and golfing, this delightful house offers comfortable and spacious bedrooms and smart shower rooms en suite. Breakfast is served at individual tables in the bright, airy dining room, which is next to the comfortable lounge.

Rooms 6 en suite (2 GF) S £45; D £65 **Facilities** TVB tea/coffee Cen ht **Parking** 8 **Notes** ⊗ No children 8yrs

EAST AYRSHIRE

SORN   MAP 20 NS52

★★★★ ֍֍ RESTAURANT WITH ROOMS
The Sorn Inn

35 Main St KA5 6HU
☎ 01290 551305 📄 01290 553470
e–mail: craig@sorninn.com

dir: *A70 from S or A76 from N onto B743 to Sorn*

Centrally situated in this rural village, which is convenient for many of Ayrshire's attractions, this renovated inn is now a fine dining restaurant with a cosy lounge area. There is also a popular chop house with a pub-like environment. The freshly decorated bedrooms have comfortable beds and good facilities.

Rooms 4 en suite (1 fmly) S £40–£45; D £70–£95✳ **Facilities** TVB tea/coffee Direct dial from bedrooms Cen ht Dinner Last d 9pm Wi-fi available Fishing **Parking** 9 **Notes** Closed 2wks Jan RS Mon

EAST LOTHIAN

GIFFORD   MAP 21 NT56

[U]
Tweeddale Arms

High St EH41 4QU
☎ 01620 810240 📄 01620 810488
e–mail: managertweeddalearms@ohiml.com

dir: *Take A1 to Haddington, signed to Gifford*

At the time of going to press the rating for this establishment had not been confirmed. Please check the AA website www.theAA.com for up-to-date information.

Rooms 13 en suite (2 fmly) S fr £45; D £75–£90✳ **Facilities** TVB tea/coffee Cen ht Dinner Last d 8.30pm Wi-fi available **Conf** Max 50 Class 50 Board 30 **Notes** Civ Wed 50

HADDINGTON   MAP 21 NT57

★★★★ 🅐 BED & BREAKFAST
Eaglescairnie Mains

By Gifford EH41 4HN
☎ 01620 810491 📄 01620 810491
e–mail: williams.eagles@btinternet.com

dir: *3.5m S of Haddington. B6368 from Haddington signed Humbie & Bolton. Through Bolton, at top of hill fork left signed Eaglescairnie & Gifford, 0.5m on left*

Rooms 3 en suite S £40–£50; D £65–£75✳ **Facilities** tea/coffee TVL Wi-fi available ⚲ **Parking** 10 **Notes** Closed Xmas

CITY OF EDINBURGH

EDINBURGH   MAP 21 NT27

See also East Calder (West Lothian)

Premier Collection

★★★★★ 🏠 GUEST ACCOMMODATION
Elmview

15 Glengyle Ter EH3 9LN
☎ 0131 228 1973
e–mail: nici@elmview.co.uk
web: www.elmview.co.uk

dir: *0.5m S of city centre. Off A702 Leven St onto ValleyField St, one-way to Glengyle Ter*

Elmview offers stylish accommodation on the lower ground level of a fine Victorian terrace house. The bedrooms and smart bathrooms are comfortable and extremely well equipped, with thoughtful extras such as safes, and fridges with fresh milk and water. Breakfasts are excellent and are served at a large, elegantly appointed table in the charming dining room.

Rooms 3 en suite (3 GF) S £75–£100; D £95–£120✳ **Facilities** FTV TVB tea/coffee Direct dial from bedrooms Cen ht Wi-fi available **Notes** ⊗ No children 15yrs Closed Dec–Feb

CONTINUED

SCOTLAND

EDINBURGH CONTINUED

Premier Collection

★★★★★ GUEST ACCOMMODATION

Kew House

1 Kew Ter, Murrayfield EH12 5JE
☎ 0131 313 0700 🖷 0131 313 0747
e-mail: info@kewhouse.com
web: www.kewhouse.com

dir: *1m W of city centre A8*

Forming part of a listed Victorian terrace, Kew House lies within walking distance of the city centre, and is convenient for Murrayfield rugby stadium and tourist attractions. Meticulously maintained throughout, it offers attractive bedrooms in a variety of sizes, all thoughtfully equipped to suit business and leisure guests. There is a comfortable lounge offering a supper and snack menu. Internet access is also available.

Rooms 6 en suite (1 fmly) (2 GF) S £84–£90; D £105–£180✶
Facilities FTV TVB tea/coffee Direct dial from bedrooms Cen ht Last d 8pm Wi-fi available **Parking** 6

Premier Collection

★★★★★ ❀ 🍴 RESTAURANT WITH ROOMS

The Witchery by the Castle

352 Castlehill, The Royal Mile EH1 2NF
☎ 0131 225 5613 🖷 0131 220 4392
e-mail: mail@thewitchery.com
web: www.thewitchery.com

dir: *Top of Royal Mile at gates of Edinburgh Castle*

Originally built in 1595, the Witchery by the Castle is situated in a historic building at the gates of Edinburgh Castle. The two luxurious and theatrically decorated suites, known as the Inner Sanctum and the Old Rectory are located above the restaurant and are reached via a winding stone staircase. Filled with antiques, opulently draped beds, large roll-top baths and a plethora of memorabilia, this ancient and exciting establishment is often described as one of the country's most romantic destinations.

Rooms 2 en suite 5 annexe en suite (1 GF) **Facilities** STV FTV TVB tea/coffee Direct dial from bedrooms Cen ht Dinner Last d 11.30pm
Notes ⊗ No children 12yrs Closed 25–26 Dec Civ Wed 60

★★★★ GUEST HOUSE

Aonach Mor Guest House

14 Kilmaurs Ter EH16 5DR
☎ 0131 667 8694
e-mail: info@aonachmor.com
web: www.aonachmor.com

dir: *A7 to Cameron Toll rdbt, follow city centre signs, Dalkeith Rd 5th on right*

Situated in a residential area within easy reach of the city centre and major tourist attractions, Aonach Mor offers stylish well-equipped accommodation, especially the four poster feature room which even boasts its own steam room. The comfortable combined lounge dining room has recently been refurbished and now boast a working open fire place. Internet access is available in this location too.

Rooms 7 rms (5 en suite) (2 fmly) S £35–£55; D £60–£120✶
Facilities FTV TVB tea/coffee Cen ht Wi-fi available Steam room
Notes ⊗ No children 3yrs

★★★★ GUEST HOUSE

Bonnington Guest House

202 Ferry Rd EH6 4NW
☎ 0131 554 7610 🖷 0131 554 7610
e-mail: booking@thebonningtonguesthouse.com
web: www.thebonningtonguesthouse.com

dir: *On A902, near corner of Ferry Rd and Newhaven Rd*

This delightful Georgian house offers individually furnished bedrooms on two floors, that retain many of their original features. Family rooms are also available. A substantial freshly prepared breakfast is served in the newly refurbished dining room. Off-street parking is an added bonus.

Rooms 7 rms (5 en suite) (2 pri facs) (4 fmly) (1 GF) **Facilities** FTV TVB tea/coffee Cen ht Wi-fi available **Parking** 9 **Notes** ⊗ No coaches

★ ★ ★ ★ ☰ GUEST HOUSE
Southside

8 Newington Rd EH9 1QS

☎ 0131 668 4422 🖹 0131 667 7771

e–mail: info@southsideguesthouse.co.uk

web: www.southsideguesthouse.co.uk

dir: *E end of Princes St onto North Bridge to Royal Mile, continue S 0.5m, house on right*

Situated within easy reach of the city centre and convenient for the major attractions, Southside is an elegant sandstone house. Bedrooms are individually styled, comfortable and thoughtfully equipped. Traditional, freshly cooked Scottish breakfasts are served at individual tables in the smart ground-floor dining room.

Rooms 8 en suite (2 fmly) (1 GF) S £55–£80; D £70–£160✻
Facilities TVB tea/coffee Direct dial from bedrooms Licensed Cen ht Wi-fi available **Notes LB** ⊗ No children 10yrs No coaches

★ ★ ★ ★ GUEST ACCOMMODATION
Allison House

17 Mayfield Gardens EH9 2AX

☎ 0131 667 8049 🖹 0131 667 5001

e–mail: info@allisonhousehotel.com

web: www.allisonhousehotel.com

Part of a Victorian terrace, Allison House offers modern comforts in a splendid building. It's convenient for the city centre, theatres, tourist attractions and is on the main bus route. The attractive bedrooms are generally spacious and very well equipped. Breakfast is served at individual tables in the ground-floor dining room. Off-road parking is available.

Rooms 11 rms (10 en suite) (1 pri facs) (1 fmly) (2 GF) (2 smoking) S £47.50–£65; D £60–£120 **Facilities** TVB tea/coffee Direct dial from bedrooms Cen ht Wi-fi available **Parking** 6 **Notes LB** ⊗

★ ★ ★ ★ GUEST HOUSE
Ashlyn Guest House

42 Inverleith Row EH3 5PY

☎ 0131 552 2954

e–mail: peter@pkelsey.wanadoo.co.uk

web: www.ashlyn-edinburgh.co.uk

dir: *Adjacent to Edinburgh Botanic Gardens, follow signs for North Edinburgh & Botanics thereafter*

The Ashlyn Guest House is a warm and friendly Georgian home, ideally located to take advantage of Edinburgh's attractions. The city centre is within walking distance and the Royal Botanical Gardens are minutes away. Bedrooms are all individually decorated and furnished to a high standard. A generous and hearty breakfast gives a great start to the day.

Ashlyn Guest House

Rooms 8 rms (4 en suite) (2 pri facs) (1 fmly) (1 GF) S £30–£40; D £60–£90✻ **Facilities** TVB tea/coffee Cen ht TVL **Notes** ⊗ No children 7yrs No coaches Closed 23–28 Dec

★ ★ ★ ★ GUEST HOUSE
Ellesmere House

11 Glengyle Ter EH3 9LN

☎ 0131 229 4823

e–mail: ruth@edinburghbandb.co.uk

web: www.edinburghbandb.co.uk

dir: *S of city centre off A702*

This delightful terrace house overlooks Bruntsfield Links and is convenient for the city centre. Currently benefitting from investment from the new proprietors, the attractive bedrooms vary in size and have many thoughtful touches. Breakfast, featuring the best of local produce, is enjoyed in the elegant dining room.

Rooms 4 en suite **Facilities** FTV TVB tea/coffee Cen ht TVL Wi-fi available **Notes** ⊗ No coaches 🖃

CONTINUED

EDINBURGH CONTINUED

★★★★ GUEST ACCOMMODATION
Fraoch House
66 Pilrig St EH6 5AS
☎ 0131 554 1353
e–mail: info@fraochhouse.com
dir: *1m from Princes St*

Situated within walking distance of the city centre and convenient for many attractions, Fraoch House, which dates from the 1900s, has been carefully refurbished to offer well-equipped and thoughtfully furnished bedrooms. Delicious, freshly cooked breakfasts are served in the charming dining room on the ground floor.

Rooms 6 rms (4 en suite) (2 pri facs) (1 fmly) **Facilities** TVB tea/coffee Cen ht Free use of DVDs and CDs, and internet access **Notes** ⊗

★★★★ BED & BREAKFAST
The Hedges
19 Hillside Crescent EH7 5EB
☎ 0131 478 9555
e–mail: thehedgesguesthouse@hotmail.co.uk
Well situated on the approach into Edinburgh. Newly refurbished property with very good result achieved. Bedrooms differ in size but all are of a good quality. The well cooked breakfast in served in the garden room on individual tables. Many thoughtful extras are provided as standard.

Rooms 3 en suite (3 GF) D £80–£130 **Facilities** TVB tea/coffee Cen ht Wi-fi available **Notes LB** ⊗

★★★★ GUEST HOUSE
Heriott Park
256 Ferry Rd, Goldenacre EH5 3AN
☎ 0131 552 3456
e–mail: reservations@heriottpark.co.uk
web: www.heriottpark.co.uk
dir: *1.5m N of city centre on A902*

A conversion of two adjoining properties, which retain many original features. The guest house is on the north side of the city and has lovely panoramic views of the Edinburgh skyline including Edinburgh Castle and Arthur's Seat. The attractive bedrooms are well equipped and have excellent bathrooms en suite.

Rooms 15 rms (14 en suite) (1 pri facs) (7 fmly) (1 GF) S £35–£80; D £60–£100 **Facilities** FTV TVB tea/coffee Cen ht Wi-fi available **Notes** ⊗

★★★★ GUEST HOUSE
International Guest House
37 Mayfield Gardens EH9 2BX
☎ 0131 667 2511 🖨 0131 667 1112
e–mail: intergh1@yahoo.co.uk
web: www.accomodation-edinburgh.com
dir: *On A701 1.5m S of Princes St*

Guests are assured of a warm and friendly welcome at this attractive Victorian terraced house situated to the south of the city centre. The smartly presented bedrooms are thoughtfully decorated, comfortably furnished and well equipped. Hearty Scottish breakfasts are served at individual tables in the traditionally styled dining room, which boasts a beautiful ornate ceiling.

Rooms 9 en suite (3 fmly) (1 GF) S £35–£75; D £60–£130✳ **Facilities** STV TVB tea/coffee Direct dial from bedrooms Cen ht Wi-fi available **Parking** 3 **Notes LB** ⊗

See advert on opposite page

SCOTLAND

★★★★ GUEST HOUSE

Sherwood

42 Minto St EH9 2BR

☎ 0131 667 1200 📄 0131 667 2344

e–mail: enquiries@sherwood-edinburgh.com

web: www.sherwood-edinburgh.com

dir: *On A701 S of the city centre*

Lying on the south side of the city, this guest house is immaculately maintained and attractively presented throughout. Bedrooms vary in size, the smaller ones being thoughtfully appointed to make the best use of space. All include iron/board and several come with a fridge and microwave. Continental breakfast is served in the elegant dining room.

Rooms 6 rms (5 en suite) (1 pri facs) (2 fmly) (1 GF) **Facilities** FTV TVB tea/coffee Cen ht **Parking** 3 **Notes** ⊗ Closed 20–29 Dec

★★★★ GUEST ACCOMMODATION

23 Mayfield

23 Mayfield Gardens EH9 2BX

☎ 0131 667 5806 📄 0131 667 6833

e–mail: info@23mayfield.co.uk

web: www.23mayfield.co.uk

dir: *A720 bypass S, follow city centre signs. Left at Craigmillar Park, 0.5m on right*

Well located on route into Edinburgh with the added benefit of off-road car parking. Spacious accommodation with many of the original features of this period house being retained. Breakfast is a real delight with the very best local produce used to give the guest a great start to their day. Many thoughtful extras are provided in accord with the needs of the modern traveller.

Rooms 9 en suite (2 fmly) (2 GF) S £45–£80; D £65–£125✱ **Facilities** FTV TVB tea/coffee Cen ht Wi-fi available **Parking** 10 **Notes LB** No children 5yrs

★★★★ 🅰 GUEST HOUSE

The Ben Doran

11 Mayfield Gardens EH9 2AX

☎ 0131 667 8488 📄 0131 667 0076

e–mail: info@ben-doran.com

dir: *1.5m SE of city centre on A701*

Rooms 11 rms (7 en suite) S £54–£125; D £65–£203✱ **Facilities** FTV TVB tea/coffee Direct dial from bedrooms Cen ht Dinner Last d 8.30pm Wi-fi available **Parking** 8 **Notes LB** ⊗ No children 12yrs No coaches Closed 24 & 25 Dec

★★★★ 🅰 GUEST HOUSE

Gildun

9 Spence St EH16 5AG

☎ 0131 667 1368 📄 0131 668 4989

e–mail: gildun.edin@btinternet.com

dir: *A720 city bypass to Sheriffhall rdbt onto A7 for 4m to Cameron Toll rdbt go under railway bridge follow A7 sign onto Dalkeith Rd, Spence St is 4th on left opp church*

Rooms 8 rms (6 en suite) (5 fmly) (2 GF) S £30–£50; D £60–£120 **Facilities** FTV TVB tea/coffee Cen ht Wi-fi available **Parking** 4 **Notes LB** No coaches

★★★ GUEST HOUSE

Abbotsford

36 Pilrig St EH6 5AL

☎ 0131 554 2706 📄 0131 555 4550

e–mail: info@abbotsfordguesthouse.co.uk

web: www.abbotsfordguesthouse.co.uk

Situated just off Leith Walk and within easy walking distance of the city centre, this charming and friendly guest house offers individually decorated, pleasantly furnished and thoughtfully equipped bedrooms. There is an elegant ground-floor dining room where hearty breakfasts are served at individual tables.

Rooms 8 rms (5 en suite) S £30–£50; D £60–£130✱ **Facilities** STV TVB tea/coffee Cen ht **Notes** ⊗

EDINBURGH CONTINUED

★★★ GUEST HOUSE
Arden Guest House
126 Old Dalkeith Rd EH16 4SD
☎ 0131 664 3985 📠 0131 621 0866
e–mail: ardenedinburgh@aol.com

dir: *2m SE of city centre nr Craigmillar Castle. On A7 200yds W of hospital*

Colourful flowering baskets adorn the front of this welcoming, personally-run guest house situated on the south side of the city, convenient for leisure and business travellers. The modern bedrooms offer good overall freedom of space. Traditional Scottish breakfasts are served at individual tables in the conservatory-dining room. Off-road car parking is a bonus.

Rooms 11 en suite (3 fmly) (6 GF) S £35–£90; D £50–£110✱
Facilities STV TVB tea/coffee Cen ht Wi-fi available Golf **Parking** 12
Notes LB

★★★ GUEST HOUSE
Corstorphine Lodge
186–188 St Johns Rd, Corstorphine EH12 8SG
☎ 0131 539 4237 & 476 7116 📠 0131 539 4945
e–mail: corsthouse@aol.com
web: www.corstorphinehotels.co.uk

dir: *From M8 take city bypass N towards city centre for 1m along A8. Located on left*

Occupying two large detached Victorian villas, Corstorphine is convenient for the airport and the city centre. Bedrooms, which vary in size, are carefully decorated and well equipped. There is a spacious conservatory-dining room where traditional, continental or vegetarian breakfasts can be enjoyed at individual tables. Ample off-road parking is available.

Rooms 12 en suite 5 annexe en suite (8 fmly) (5 GF) S £39–£69; D £49–£139 **Facilities** STV FTV TVB tea/coffee Cen ht TVL Wi-fi available **Parking** 14 **Notes LB** ⊗

★★★ GUEST HOUSE
Ecosse International
15 McDonald Rd EH7 4LX
☎ 0131 556 4967 📠 0131 556 7394
e–mail: erlinda@ecosseguesthouse.fsnet.co.uk

dir: *Off A900 NE of city centre*

Situated just off Leith Walk to the north, and within easy walking distance of the city centre, this well-maintained guest house offers comfortable and cheerful accommodation. The cosy lounge area and the adjacent dining room, where hearty breakfasts are served at individual tables, are situated on the lower-ground floor.

Rooms 5 en suite (3 fmly) **Facilities** TVB tea/coffee Cen ht TVL **Notes** ⊗ No coaches

★★★ GUEST HOUSE
Elder York
38 Elder St EH1 3DX
☎ 0131 556 1926 📠 0131 624 7140
e–mail: reception@elderyork.co.uk
web: www.elderyork.co.uk

dir: *From Princes St onto Queen St, then York Place*

Occupying the third and fourth floors of a terrace building, this guest house offers comfortable accommodation and is well situated for Princes Street and the city's attractions. Refurbishment has resulted in smartly appointed bedrooms. A freshly prepared breakfast is served in the spacious dining room.

Rooms 13 rms (8 en suite) (1 fmly) S £30–£80; D £50–£120✱
Facilities FTV TVB tea/coffee Cen ht **Notes LB** ⊗

★★★ GUEST HOUSE
Galloway
22 Dean Park Crescent EH4 1PH
☎ 0131 332 3672 📠 0131 332 3672
e–mail: galloway_theclarks@hotmail.com

dir: *0.5m NW of castle & Princes St. Off A90 onto Comely Bank Av & Dean Park*

Located in a peaceful residential area, conveniently situated for both the shops and bistros north of the city centre, this guest house provides smart, thoughtfully equipped bedrooms. Breakfasts featuring a comprehensive selection of starters and hot dishes are served in the ground floor dining room.

Rooms 10 rms (6 en suite) (1 pri facs) (6 fmly) (1 GF) **Facilities** TVB tea/coffee Cen ht

★★★ GUEST HOUSE
Garfield Guest House
264 Ferry Rd EH5 3AN
☎ 0131 552 2369
e–mail: enquiries@garfieldguesthouse.co.uk

Friendly hospitality and good value, no-frills accommodation offering modern comfortable bedrooms. Well situated within easy striking distance of the centre of Edinburgh and well serviced by a regular bus service.

Rooms 7 rms (6 en suite) (1 pri facs) (1 GF) **Facilities** TVB tea/coffee Cen ht

★★★ GUEST HOUSE
Kariba Guest House
10 Granville Ter EH10 4PQ
☎ 0131 229 3773 📠 0131 229 4968
e–mail: karibaguesthouse@hotmail.com
web: www.karibaguesthouse.co.uk

Recognised by its colourful flower displays in summer, this guest house lies to the south-west of the city centre. The pine-furnished bedrooms include some with spacious accommodation for families, and there is a bright and attractive breakfast room.

Rooms 9 rms (8 en suite) (1 pri facs) (3 fmly) **Facilities** TVB tea/coffee Cen ht TVL **Parking** 7 **Notes** No coaches

★★★ GUEST HOUSE
The Lairg

11 Coates Gardens EH12 5LG

☎ 0131 337 1050 📠 0131 346 2167

e–mail: lairgmarie@aol.com

dir: *From A8 under rail bridge, stately home 150yds on left, Coates Gardens next 2nd left*

Situated in a residential area close to the Haymarket at the west end of the city, The Lairg is well located for the train station, Murrayfield, the city centre and tourist attractions. It offers attractive, generally spacious, well-equipped accommodation in a friendly relaxed environment. Breakfasts featuring the best of local produce are served at individual tables in the elegant ground-floor dining room.

Rooms 9 en suite (2 fmly) (1 GF) **Facilities** TVB tea/coffee Direct dial from bedrooms Cen ht **Notes** ⊗ No coaches

★★★ GUEST HOUSE
Relax Guest House

11 Eyre Place EH3 5ES

☎ 0131 556 1433 📠 0131 466 8281

e–mail: info@relaxguesthouse.co.uk

web: www.relaxguesthouse.co.uk

dir: *Off B901 N of city centre*

Relax Guest House offers comfortable well-equipped accommodation within walking distance of the city centre and major attractions. Bedrooms are bright and airy, and are en suite. Delicious traditional breakfasts are served at individual tables in the spacious lounge-dining room. A stair lift goes up to the first floor.

Rooms 10 en suite (3 fmly) **Facilities** STV FTV TVB tea/coffee Direct dial from bedrooms Licensed Lift Cen ht TVL Dinner Last d 5pm **Conf** Max 20 **Parking** 1 **Notes** ⊗

★★★ GUEST HOUSE
Six Mary's Place

6 Mary's Place, Raeburn Place, Stockbridge EH4 1JH

☎ 0131 332 8965 📠 0131 624 7060

e–mail: info@sixmarysplace.co.uk

web: www.sixmarysplace.co.uk

dir: *From Waverley station W onto Princes St, right onto Fredrick St & Howe St, left onto Circus Place, house 0.5m on left before rugby grounds*

A relaxed and friendly atmosphere is assured at this Georgian terrace property, located in a popular suburb. In contrast to the original facade, the public areas and bedrooms are bright and contemporary. There is an inviting lounge with internet access, and a conservatory dining room where tasty vegetarian breakfasts can be enjoyed overlooking the pretty, enclosed garden.

Rooms 8 rms (7 en suite) (1 pri facs) (1 fmly) (1 GF) S £40–£55; D £60–£98✱ **Facilities** TVB tea/coffee Direct dial from bedrooms Cen ht TVL Wi-fi available **Conf** Thtr 12 Board 8 **Notes** ⊗ ch fac No coaches Closed 24–27 Dec

★★★ Ⓐ BED & BREAKFAST
Ardbrae House

85 Drum Brae South, Corstorphine EH12 8TD

☎ 0131 467 5787

e–mail: info@ardbrae.com

dir: *From W enter Edinburgh on A8. At PC World/Drum Brae rdbt turn left and proceed up hill, on left, next to speed camera*

Rooms 3 en suite (3 GF) S £35–£60; D £50–£90✱ **Facilities** FTV TVB tea/coffee Cen ht Wi-fi available **Parking** 5 **Notes** LB ⊗ Closed 24–28 Dec

★★★ Ⓐ GUEST HOUSE
Charleston House

38 Minto St EH9 2BS

☎ 0131 667 6589 & 07904 022205 📠 0131 668 3800

e–mail: joan_wightman@hotmail.com

web: www.charleston-house.co.uk

dir: *1.5m SE of city centre on A701 at corner Duncan St*

Rooms 5 rms (2 en suite) (2 fmly) (1 GF) S £25–£65; D £50–£85✱ **Facilities** FTV TVB tea/coffee Cen ht TVL Wi-fi available **Notes** LB Closed 24–27 Dec

SCOTLAND

EDINBURGH CONTINUED

★★★ Ⓐ GUEST HOUSE
Classic House

50 Mayfield Rd EH9 2NH

☎ 0131 667 5847 📄 0131 662 1016

e–mail: info@classicguesthouse.co.uk

web: www.classichouse.demon.co.uk

dir: *Join bypass follow signs for A701 city centre. At Liberton Brae, keep left, 0.5m on left*

Rooms 7 rms (6 en suite) (1 pri facs) (2 fmly) S £30–£50; D £50–£80✳
Facilities TVB Cen ht TVL **Notes LB** ⊗ No coaches

★★★ Ⓐ GUEST HOUSE
Ravensdown Guest House

248 Ferry Rd EH5 3AN

☎ 0131 552 5438

e–mail: david@ravensdownhouse.com

web: www.ravensdownhouse.com

Rooms 7 rms (6 en suite) (1 pri facs) (5 fmly) (1 GF) S £45–£65;
D £70–£110 **Facilities** FTV TVB tea/coffee Cen ht Wi-fi available
Parking 2 **Notes** ⊗

★★★ Ⓐ GUEST HOUSE
The St Valery

36 Coates Gardens, Haymarket EH12 5LE

☎ 0131 337 1893 📄 0131 346 8529

e–mail: info@stvalery.co.uk

web: www.stvalery.com

dir: *A8 towards city centre, pass Donaldson school on left, two streets before Haymarket station on left*

Rooms 11 en suite (3 fmly) (1 GF) S £42–£56; D £56–£108✳
Facilities STV FTV TVB tea/coffee Direct dial from bedrooms Cen ht
TVL Dinner Wi-fi available

★★ GUEST HOUSE
Averon City Centre Guest House

44 Gilmore Place EH3 9NQ

☎ 0131 229 9932

e–mail: info@averon.co.uk

web: www.averon.co.uk

dir: *From W end of Princes St onto A702, right at Kings Theatre*
Situated within walking distance of the west end of the city and close to the Kings Theatre, this guest house offers comfortable good value accommodation, with a secure car park to the rear.

Rooms 10 rms (6 en suite) (3 fmly) S £26–£48; D £52–£96
Facilities TVB tea/coffee Cen ht **Parking** 19 **Notes** ⊗

See advert on this page

★★ GUEST ACCOMMODATION
The Osbourne

51–59 York Place EH1 3JD

☎ 0131 556 5577 📄 0131 556 1012

e–mail: reservations@osbournehotel.com

web: www.osbournehotel.com

The friendly Osbourne offers budget accommodation ideally located at the east end of the city centre, close to the bus station and Harvey Nichols. The bedrooms vary in size but all offer good overall ease of use, the property also benefits from a lounge on the ground floor. Traditional breakfasts are served at individual tables in the spacious dining room.

Rooms 57 rms (54 en suite) (10 fmly) S £35–£65; D £50–£80✳
Facilities TVB tea/coffee Direct dial from bedrooms Lift Cen ht TVL Wi-fi available **Notes** ⊗

FIFE

ANSTRUTHER
MAP 21 NO50

★★★★ 🍴 GUEST HOUSE
The Spindrift
Pittenweem Rd KY10 3DT
☎ 01333 310573 📠 01333 310573
e–mail: info@thespindrift.co.uk
web: www.thespindrift.co.uk
dir: *Entering town from W on A917, 1st building on left*

This immaculate Victorian villa stands on the western edge of the village. The attractive bedrooms offer a wide range of extra touches; the Captain's Room, a replica of a wood-panelled cabin, is a particular feature. The inviting lounge has an honesty bar, while imaginative breakfasts, and enjoyable home-cooked meals by arrangement, are served in the cheerful dining room.

Rooms 8 rms (7 en suite) (1 pri facs) (2 fmly) S £40–£48; D £60–£76
Facilities FTV TVB tea/coffee Direct dial from bedrooms Licensed Cen ht
TVL Dinner Last d noon Wi-fi available **Parking** 12 **Notes** LB
No children 10yrs No coaches Closed Xmas-late Jan

★★★★ RESTAURANT WITH ROOMS
The Waterfront
18–20 Shore St KY10 3EA
☎ 01333 312200 📠 01333 312288
e–mail: chris@anstruther-waterfront.co.uk
dir: *Off A917 opposite marina*

Situated overlooking the harbour, the Waterfront offers spacious, stylish, contemporary accommodation with bedrooms located in lovingly restored buildings situated in a courtyard behind the restaurant. There is a comfortable lounge with a smartly fitted kitchen and dining room, and laundry facilities are available in the granary. Dinner and breakfast are served in the attractive restaurant that offers a comprehensive menu featuring the best of local produce.

Rooms 8 annexe en suite (3 fmly) (1 GF) S £20–£38; D £40–£75✳
Facilities STV TVB tea/coffee Cen ht TVL Dinner Last d 10pm
Notes LB ⊗

INVERKEITHING
MAP 21 NT18

★★★★ BED & BREAKFAST
The Roods
16 Bannerman Av KY11 1NG
☎ 01383 415049 📠 01383 415049
e–mail: isobelmarley@hotmail.com
web: www.the-roods.co.uk
dir: *N of town centre off B981 Church St-Chapel Pl*

This charming house stands in secluded, well-tended gardens close to the station. Bedrooms are individually styled and have new state-of-the-art bathrooms. There is an inviting lounge, and breakfast is served at individual tables in an attractive conservatory.

Rooms 2 en suite (2 GF) **Facilities** TVB tea/coffee Direct dial from
bedrooms Cen ht TVL Dinner Last d 9am **Parking** 4 **Notes** ⊗ ⊜

LEUCHARS
MAP 21 NO42

★★★★ GUEST HOUSE
Hillpark House
96 Main St KY16 0HF
☎ 01334 839280 📠 01334 839051
e–mail: enquiries@hillparkhouse.com
web: www.hillparkhouse.com
dir: *Leaving Leuchars for St Michaels, house last on right*

Lying peacefully on the edge of the village, Hillpark House is an impressive Edwardian home offering comfortable, well-appointed and equipped bedrooms. There is an inviting lounge, a conservatory and a peaceful dining room.

Rooms 5 rms (3 en suite) (1 pri facs) (1 fmly) S fr £38; D fr £70✳
Facilities TVB tea/coffee Cen ht TVL Wi-fi available Golf **Parking** 6
Notes ⊗ No coaches

CONTINUED

SCOTLAND

★★★★ GUEST HOUSE
Dunclutha Guest House
16 Victoria Rd KY8 4EX
☎ 01333 425515 📠 01333 422311
e–mail: pam.leven@blueyonder.co.uk
web: www.dunclutha.myby.co.uk

dir: *A915, B933 Glenlyon Rd into Leven, rdbt left onto Commercial Rd & Victoria Rd, Dunclutha opp church on right*

Set in a quiet street close to the town centre, Dunclutha is an inviting Victorian property that was formerly the rectory for the nearby Episcopalian church. Lovingly restored and refurbished to its original splendour it offers comfortable, well-equipped accommodation. A splendid lounge adjoins the dining room where hearty breakfasts are served at individual tables.

Rooms 4 rms (3 en suite) (1 pri facs) (2 fmly) S £35–£45; D £60–£70✳ **Facilities** TVB tea/coffee Cen ht TVL Piano **Parking** 3 **Notes** ⊗ No coaches RS 2 wks Jan

★★★★ 🅐 BED & BREAKFAST
Sandilands
20 Leven Rd, Lundin Links KY8 6AH
☎ 01333 329881 📠 01333 329881
e–mail: info@sandilandsfife.co.uk

dir: *2m NE of Leven. On A915 in village centre*

Rooms 3 en suite D £50–£60✳ **Facilities** FTV TVB tea/coffee Cen ht Wi-fi available **Parking** 3 **Notes** ⊗ No children 5yrs Closed Dec–Feb

★★★★ RESTAURANT WITH ROOMS
Town House
1 High St KY7 6DQ
☎ 01592 758459 📠 01592 755039
e–mail: townhousehotel@aol.com
web: www.townhousehotel-fife.co.uk

dir: *In town centre opposite railway station*

Well situated on the edge of town and close to the railway station, this friendly establishment offers well presented bedrooms with pleasant colour schemes, modern furnishings, and a good range of facilities and extras. The attractive bar-restaurant is popular with locals and serves a choice of good-value dishes.

Rooms 3 en suite (1 fmly) S £45; D £70–£80✳ **Facilities** FTV TVB tea/coffee Cen ht Dinner Last d 9pm Wi-fi available **Notes** ⊗ Closed 25–26 Dec & 1–2 Jan

★★★ INN
The Abbey Inn
East Port KY14 6EZ
☎ 01337 840761 📠 01337 840761
e–mail: wo6whiskers04@aol.com
web: www.theabbeyinn.com

dir: *On A913 High St*

Located at the east end of the village, the Abbey Inn offers accommodation and situated on the first floor. Bedrooms are bright and well appointed with many thoughtful extras provided as standard. There is a popular public lounge bar where meals can be provided for residents by prior arrangement.

Rooms 3 en suite S fr £30; D fr £60✳ **Facilities** TVB tea/coffee Cen ht Dinner Last d 9pm Pool Table **Notes** LB No coaches

Premier Collection

★★★★★ ◉◉ RESTAURANT WITH ROOMS
The Peat Inn
KY15 5LH
☎ 01334 840206 📠 01334 840530
e–mail: stay@thepeatinn.co.uk

dir: *At junct of B940 & B941, 5m SW of St Andrews*

This 300-year-old former coaching inn enjoys a rural location yet is close to St Andrews. The spacious accommodation is very well appointed and all rooms have lounge areas. The inn is steeped in history and is a real haven for food lovers. The three dining areas create a romantic setting. Expect open fires and a relaxed ambiance.

Rooms 8 annexe en suite (2 fmly) (8 GF) S £95–£125; D £145–£175✳ **Facilities** FTV TVB tea/coffee Direct dial from bedrooms Cen ht Dinner Last d 9pm **Parking** 24 **Notes** LB Closed 25–26 Dec & 1–3 Jan RS Sun–Mon

ST ANDREWS

MAP 21 NO51

Premier Collection

★★★★★ ≘ GUEST ACCOMMODATION
The Paddock

Sunnyside, Strathkinness KY16 9XP
☎ 01334 850888 📄 01334 850870
e-mail: thepaddock@btinternet.com
web: www.thepadd.co.uk

dir: *3m W from St Andrews off B939. The Paddock signed from village centre*

Situated in a peaceful village overlooking rolling countryside, this friendly, family-run guest house offers stylish and very well-equipped bedrooms. Superb fish tanks, one freshwater, the other salt, line the entrance hall and contain beautiful and unusual fish. The lounge-dining room in the conservatory is a lovely setting for the delicious breakfasts.

Rooms 4 en suite (1 fmly) (2 GF) **Facilities** TVB tea/coffee Cen ht Wi-fi available **Parking** 8 **Notes** ⊗ Closed 1–27 Dec

★★★★ ≘ GUEST HOUSE
Glenderran

9 Murray Park KY16 9AW
☎ 01334 477951 📄 01334 477908
e-mail: info@glenderran.com
web: www.glenderran.com

dir: *In town centre. Off North St onto Murray Place & Murray Park*

This smart terrace house has a super location just minutes from the town centre, seafront, West Sands beach and the Old Course. Aviation-theme pictures and memorabilia decorate the public rooms. Well-equipped bedrooms come in a variety of sizes, and carefully prepared breakfasts are enjoyed in the ground-floor dining room.

Rooms 5 rms (4 en suite) (1 pri facs) S £35–£45; D £70–£100 **Facilities** FTV TVB tea/coffee Cen ht TVL Wi-fi available **Notes LB** ⊗ No children 12yrs No coaches

★★★★ GUEST HOUSE
Annandale Guest House

23 Murray Park KY16 9AW
☎ 01334 475310 📄 01334 475310
e-mail: info@annandale-standrews.com

dir: *A91 to St Andrews. Onto one-way system, right again, 1st guest house on left*

Forming part of a Victorian row, this welcoming guest house is convenient for the seafront and central amenities. The comfortable bedrooms are bright, modern and well equipped. Hearty breakfasts are served in the lounge-dining room. Internet access is available.

Rooms 6 en suite (2 fmly) **Facilities** TVB tea/coffee Cen ht **Notes** ⊗ No children 5yrs No coaches Closed 17 Dec–10 Jan

★★★★ INN
Barns

5 Main St, Kingsbarns KY16 8TA
☎ 01334 460820 📄 01334 460821
e-mail: info@barnsatkingsbarns.com

Located in the East Neuk of Fife this small inn offers modern and wonderfully comfortably equipped bedrooms and bathrooms that surpass expectations with the many extras that are provided as standard. The snug bar and lounge are enhanced with golfing objet d'art and art work from the surrounding golf courses and local towns. Outdoor seating in the courtyard offers al fresco dining if the mood should take you. Good quality comfort food is served in the dining room.

Rooms 4 en suite (2 fmly) (2 GF) S £50–£120; D £90–£160✶ **Facilities** STV TVB tea/coffee Direct dial from bedrooms Cen ht TVL Dinner Last d 9.45pm Golf 18 **Parking** 25 **Notes LB**

★★★★ GUEST HOUSE
Craigmore

3 Murray Park KY16 9AW
☎ 01334 472142 📄 01334 477963
e-mail: info@standrewscraigmore.com
web: www.standrewscraigmore.com

dir: *In town centre. Off North St onto Murray Place & Murray Park*

Lying between the town centre and the seafront, this immaculately maintained guest house forms part of a Victorian row. Close to the Old Course, it is adorned with lots of amusing golfing touches. The stylish bedrooms are attractively decorated and well equipped. Breakfast is served at individual tables in the elegant lounge-dining room.

Rooms 7 en suite (4 fmly) (1 GF) S £60–£74; D £70–£92✶ **Facilities** FTV TVB tea/coffee Cen ht TVL Wi-fi available **Notes LB** ⊗ No coaches

ST ANDREWS CONTINUED

★★★★ ⑳⑳ INN
The Inn at Lathones
Largoward KY9 1JE
☎ 01334 840494 📠 01334 840694
e–mail: lathones@theinn.co.uk
web: www.theinn.co.uk

dir: *5m S of St Andrews on A915, 0.5m before village of Largoward on left just after hidden dip*

This lovely country inn, parts of which are 400 years old, is full of character and individuality. The friendly staff help to create a relaxed atmosphere. Smart contemporary bedrooms are in two separate wings. The colourful, cosy restaurant is the main focus, the menu offering modern interpretations of Scottish and European dishes.

Rooms 13 annexe en suite (1 fmly) (11 GF) **Facilities** STV TVB tea/coffee Direct dial from bedrooms Cen ht TVL Dinner Last d 9.30pm Wi-fi available **Conf** BC Max 40 Thtr 40 Class 10 Board 20 **Parking** 35 **Notes** Closed 26 Dec & 3–16 Jan RS 24 Dec Civ Wed 45

★★★★ GUEST HOUSE
Lorimer House
19 Murray Park KY16 9AW
☎ 01334 476599 📠 01334 476599
e–mail: info@lorimerhouse.com
web: www.lorimerhouse.com

dir: *A91 to St Andrews, left onto Golf Place, right onto The Scores, right onto Murray Park*

A warm and friendly welcome is assured at this delightful Victorian terrace house, situated within easy reach of the famous Old Course, the seafront and town centre. Bedrooms are attractive, comfortably furnished and well equipped. Freshly prepared Scottish breakfasts are served in the stylish dining room, which also has a lounge area and offers free broadband internet access.

Rooms 5 en suite (1 GF) D £60–£98✳ **Facilities** STV FTV TVB tea/coffee Cen ht TVL Wi-fi available **Notes** ⊗ No children 12yrs No coaches

★★★★ GUEST HOUSE
Nethan House
17 Murray Park KY16 9AW
☎ 01334 472104 📠 01334 850870
e–mail: enquiries@nethan-standrews.com

dir: *A91 towards St Andrews, over 2nd rdbt onto North St, Murray Park on left before cinema*

This large Victorian terrace house is set in the heart of St Andrews; a short walk from the main tourist attractions and the famous St Andrews golf course. The house has been totally refurbished, and the bright bedrooms are stylish and well appointed. The freshly cooked breakfast is a highlight and is served in the attractive dining room.

Rooms 7 en suite (1 fmly) (1 GF) **Facilities** FTV TVB tea/coffee Cen ht TVL Wi-fi available **Notes** ⊗ No coaches Closed 24–26 Dec

★★★★ FARM HOUSE
Spinkstown Farmhouse *(NO541144)*
KY16 8PN
☎ 01334 473475 📠 01334 473475 Mrs A E Duncan
e–mail: anne@spinkstown.com

dir: *2m E on A917 to Crail, 3rd farmhouse on right*

This immaculately maintained modern farmhouse is surrounded by gently rolling countryside. Bedrooms are stylish, spacious and well-equipped. The comfortable lounge, complete with baby grand piano, overlooks the well-tended rear garden. Breakfast is served around a communal table in the dining room.

Rooms 3 en suite S fr £35; D fr £60✳ **Facilities** TVB tea/coffee Cen ht TVL **Parking** 3 **Notes** ⊗ 250 acres arable/cattle/sheep

CITY OF GLASGOW

GLASGOW   MAP 20 NS56

★★★★ GUEST ACCOMMODATION
The Kelvingrove
944 Sauchiehall St G3 7TH
☎ 0141 339 5011 📠 0141 339 6566
e–mail: info@kelvingrovehotel.com
web: www.kelvingrove-hotel.co.uk

dir: *M8 junct 18, 0.5m along road signed Kelvingrove Museum, on left*

This friendly, well-maintained establishment is in a terrace just west of the city centre, and is easily spotted in summer with its colourful floral displays. Bedrooms, including several rooms suitable for families, are well equipped and have smart, fully tiled en suite bathrooms. There is a bright breakfast room, and the reception lounge is open 24 hours.

Rooms 22 en suite (5 fmly) (3 GF) **Facilities** TVB tea/coffee Direct dial from bedrooms Cen ht

★★★ GUEST HOUSE
Botanic Guest House

1 Alfred Ter, Great Western Rd G12 8RF

☎ 0141 337 7007 📠 0141 337 7070

e–mail: info@botanichotel.co.uk

dir: *15 mins by car from Glasgow airport and 10 mins from city centre train station.*

The Botanic is located just off the Great Western Road alongside other guest accommodation and residential properties only 2 miles from the heart of the city centre. Comfortable bedrooms and well-presented bathrooms provide good value for money. A generous breakfast makes a good start to the day.

Rooms 16 rms (13 en suite) (5 fmly) (3 GF) S £20–£50; D £40–£70✳
Facilities TVB tea/coffee Direct dial from bedrooms **Notes LB** No coaches

★★★ GUEST HOUSE
Clifton Guest House

26–27 Buckingham Ter, Great Western Rd G12 8ED

☎ 0141 334 8080 📠 0141 337 3468

e–mail: kalam@cliftonhotelglasgow.co.uk

dir: *1.25m NW of city centre off A82 Inverquhomery Rd*

Located north-west of the city centre, the Clifton forms part of an elegant terrace and is ideal for business and leisure. The attractive bedrooms are spacious, and there is an elegant lounge. Hearty breakfasts are served at individual tables in the dining room.

Rooms 23 rms (17 en suite) (6 fmly) (3 GF) S £39–£75; D £59–£95✳
Facilities STV TVB tea/coffee Direct dial from bedrooms Cen ht TVL
Parking 8 **Notes** ⊛

★★★ GUEST HOUSE
Kelvin

15 Buckingham Ter, Great Western Rd, Hillhead G12 8EB

☎ 0141 339 7143 📠 0141 339 5215

e–mail: enquiries@kelvinhotel.com

web: www.kelvinhotel.com

dir: *M8 junct 17, A82 Kelvinside/Dumbarton, 1m on right before Botanic Gardens*

Two substantial Victorian terrace houses on the west side of the city have been combined to create this friendly establishment close to the Botanical Gardens. The attractive bedrooms are comfortably proportioned and well equipped. The dining room on the first floor is the setting for hearty traditional breakfasts served at individual tables.

Rooms 21 rms (9 en suite) (4 fmly) (2 GF) (14 smoking) S £28–£45; D £48–£62✳ **Facilities** FTV TVB tea/coffee Cen ht **Parking** 5

★★★ GUEST ACCOMMODATION
Lomond

6 Buckingham Ter, Great Western Rd, Hillhead G12 8EB

☎ 0141 339 2339 📠 0141 339 0477

e–mail: info@lomondhotel.co.uk

web: www.lomondhotel.co.uk

dir: *M8 junct 17, A82 Dumbarton, 1m on right before Botanic Gardens*

Situated in the west end of the city in a tree-lined Victorian terrace, the Lomond offers well maintained, good value accommodation in a friendly environment. Bedrooms are brightly appointed and suitably equipped for leisure guests. Hearty breakfasts are served at individual tables in the bright ground-floor dining room.

Rooms 17 rms (6 en suite) (5 fmly) (3 GF) S £20–£50; D £40–£70✳
Facilities TVB tea/coffee Direct dial from bedrooms Cen ht **Notes LB**

★★ 🅰 BED & BREAKFAST
Craigielea House B&B

35 Westercraigs G31 2HY

☎ 0141 554 3446

e–mail: craigieleahouse@yahoo.co.uk

dir: *1m E of city centre. M8 junct 15, onto A8, left onto Duke St, pass Tennents Brewery & left into road after lights into Craigpark. 3rd on left, then right into Westercraigs*

Rooms 3 rms (1 GF) S fr £25; D £40–£44✳ **Facilities** TVB tea/coffee
Cen ht **Parking** 3 **Notes** ⊛ No children 3yrs 🔄

GLASGOW CONTINUED

★ GUEST HOUSE
Georgian House
29 Buckingham Ter, Great Western Rd,
Kelvinside G12 8ED
☎ 0141 339 0008 & 07973 971563
e–mail: thegeorgianhouse@yahoo.com
web: www.thegeorgianhousehotel.com

dir: *M8 junct 17 towards Dumbarton, right into Queen Margaret Dr, through 4 sets of lights & right into Buckingham Ter*

The friendly guest house offers good value accommodation at the west end of the city in a peaceful tree-lined Victorian terrace near the Botanic Gardens. Bedrooms vary in size and are furnished in modern style. Only a continental style breakfast is served which is in the first-floor lounge-dining room.

Rooms 11 rms (9 en suite) (1 pri facs) (4 fmly) (3 GF) **Facilities** TVB tea/coffee Cen ht TVL Wi-fi available **Conf** Max 20 **Parking** 7 **Notes** ⊗

HIGHLAND

ARDELVE
MAP 22 NG82

★★★ GUEST HOUSE
Caberfeidh House
IV40 8DY
☎ 01599 555293
e–mail: info@caberfeidh.plus.com
web: www.caberfeidh.plus.com

dir: *A87 over Dornie Bridge into Ardelve, 1st left, 100yds on right*

Set in a peaceful location overlooking Lochs Alsh and Duich, Caberfeidh House offers good value, comfortable accommodation in relaxed and friendly surroundings. Bedrooms are traditionally furnished and thoughtfully equipped, and there is a cosy lounge with a wide selection of books, games and magazines. Hearty breakfasts are served at individual tables in the dining room.

Caberfeidh House

Rooms 5 rms (4 en suite) (1 pri facs) (3 fmly) S £26–£28; D £52–£56✱ **Facilities** TVB tea/coffee Cen ht TVL **Parking** 4 **Notes** ⊗ No coaches Closed 25–26 Dec

★★★ GUEST HOUSE
Eilean a Cheo
Dornie IV40 8DY
☎ 01599 555485
e–mail: stay@scothighland.com
web: www.scothighland.com

dir: *A87 N of Dornie Bridge, turn for Ardelve 110yds on right*

Set in a quiet location overlooking Loch Duich and the famous Eilean Donan castle, this well maintained house offers well-equipped bedrooms, some of which benefit from the view. Breakfast is freshly prepared and served in the tidy breakfast room, with a natural fire burning on cooler mornings.

Rooms 5 en suite (3 GF) S £36–£70; D £40–£70 **Facilities** TVB tea/coffee Cen ht Dinner Last d 24hrs before Wi-fi available **Parking** 6 **Notes** ⊗ No coaches

AVIEMORE
MAP 23 NH81

Premier Collection

★★★★★ GUEST HOUSE
The Old Minister's House
Rothiemurchus PH22 1QH
☎ 01479 812181 ▤ 0871 661 9324
e–mail: kate@theoldministershouse.co.uk
web: www.theoldministershouse.co.uk

dir: *B970 from Aviemore signed Glenmore & Coylumbridge, establishment 0.75m at Inverdruie*

Built originally as a manse in 1906, the Old Minister's House stands in well-tended grounds close to Aviemore. The house is beautifully furnished and immaculately maintained. Bedrooms are spacious, attractively decorated and thoughtfully equipped. There is an inviting lounge and a dining room where hearty breakfasts are served.

CONTINUED

CONTINUED

The Old Minister's House

Rooms 4 en suite (1 fmly) S £45–£60; D £76–£84✳ **Facilities** TVB tea/coffee Cen ht Wi-fi available **Parking** 4 **Notes** ⊛ No children 12yrs No coaches

★★★★ BED & BREAKFAST
Dell Druie Guest House
Inverdruie, Rothiemurchus PH22 1QH
☎ 01479 810934
e–mail: general@delldruieguesthouse.com
web: www.delldruieguesthouse.com

dir: *0.75m S of Aviemore. Off B9152 onto B970 to Coylumbridge and Cairngorm Mountain, sharp left after Rothiemurchus Vistor Centre, last house in cul-de-sac*

Dell Druie offers stylish and comfortable accommodation and is situated in the Cairngorms National Park. The River Druie runs past the house, and guests often relax in the landscaped garden, an ideal point for watching wildlife. All bedrooms have recently been refurbished to a very high standard and include DVD players, Sky TV, luxurious bathrobes and free Wi-fi internet connection. Breakfast is served in the Garden Room and there is an extensive choice on the menu, including a Highland breakfast, Scottish smoked salmon and a range of seasonal fruits. Margaret Capsomidis was a finalist for the AA Friendliest Landlady of the Year Award 2008.

Rooms 3 rms (2 en suite) (1 pri facs) (1 GF) S £70–£90; D £80–£110 **Facilities** STV TVB tea/coffee Cen ht TVL Wi-fi available Golf 18 Fishing **Parking** 6 **Notes** ⊛ No children 14yrs

★★★★ GUEST HOUSE
Ravenscraig
Grampian Rd PH22 1RP
☎ 01479 810278 📄 01479 810210
e–mail: info@aviemoreonline.com
web: www.aviemoreonline.com

dir: *N end of main street, 250yds N of police station*

This friendly, family-run guest house is on the north side of the village, a short walk from local amenities. Bedrooms vary between the traditionally styled rooms in the main house and modern spacious rooms in a brand new chalet-style annexe. There is a relaxing lounge and separate dining room, where freshly prepared breakfasts are served at individual tables.

Rooms 6 en suite 6 annexe en suite (6 fmly) (6 GF) **Facilities** TVB tea/coffee Cen ht TVL Wi-fi available **Parking** 15 **Notes** ⊛

BOAT OF GARTEN · MAP 23 NH91

★★★ GUEST HOUSE
Heathbank House
Drumuillie Rd PH24 3BD
☎ 01479 831234
e–mail: enquiries@heathbankhouse.co.uk

dir: *100yds from Strathspey steam railway station*

Heathbank House is set in the heart of the beautiful Cairngorms National Park. Built in 1897 it still retains many of its original Victorian features, but also benefits from plenty of modern amenities. Two of the six en suite bedrooms have four posters, and guests have the use of two lounges. All meals are home-cooked, using fresh local produce wherever possible, and are served in the Charles Rennie Mackintosh-inspired dining room. Dinner must be booked in advance.

Rooms 6 en suite (1 GF) **Facilities** TVB tea/coffee Licensed Cen ht TVL Dinner Last d 11am **Parking** 8 **Notes** ⊛ No children 12yrs No coaches

---

BONAR BRIDGE · MAP 23 NH69

★★★ GUEST ACCOMMODATION
Kyle House
Dornoch Rd IV24 3EB
☎ 01863 766360 📄 01863 766360
e–mail: kylehouse360@msn.com

dir: *On A949 N from village centre*

A spacious house with splendid views of the Kyle of Sutherland and the hills beyond. Bedrooms are comfortably furnished in traditional style and equipped with all the expected facilities. There is a lounge and hearty breakfasts are enjoyed in the dining room.

Rooms 5 rms (3 en suite) (2 fmly) S £26; D £52✳ **Facilities** TVB tea/coffee Cen ht TVL **Parking** 5 **Notes** ⊛ No children 5yrs Closed Dec–Jan RS Oct & Apr 🏴

BRORA MAP 23 NC90

★★★★★ BED & BREAKFAST
Glenaveron
Golf Rd KW9 6QS
☎ 01408 621601
e–mail: alistair@glenaveron.co.uk
web: www.glenaveron.co.uk

dir: *A9 NE into Brora, right onto Golf Rd, 2nd house on right*

Glenaveron stands in attractive landscaped gardens a short distance from the beach and golf course. There are two lovely well proportioned bedrooms upstairs, and a ground-floor twin bedroom for easier access. The lounge is great for relaxation, and excellent breakfasts are served house-party style in the elegant dining room.

Rooms 3 en suite (1 GF) S £45–£55; D £66–£70✱ **Facilities** FTV TVB tea/coffee Cen ht Wi-fi available **Parking** 6 **Notes** ⊗ Closed 8–23 Oct, Xmas & New Year

---

CARRBRIDGE MAP 23 NH92

★★★★ ◭ GUEST HOUSE
Craigellachie Guest House
Main St PH23 3AS
☎ 01479 841641 📄 01479 841415
e–mail: info@craigellachiehouse.co.uk
web: www.craigellachiehouse.co.uk

dir: *A95 N from Aviemore, after 4m left to Carrbridge*

Rooms 5 rms (3 en suite) (2 pri facs) (2 fmly) S £26–£28; D £52–£56 **Facilities** tea/coffee Cen ht TVL **Parking** 7 **Notes** LB ⊗ No children 4yrs No coaches

★★★ BED & BREAKFAST
Pines Country House
Duthil PH23 3ND
☎ 01479 841220 📄 01479 841220
e–mail: lynn@thepines-duthil.co.uk

dir: *2m E of Carrbridge in Duthil on A938*

A warm welcome is assured at this comfortable home in the Cairngorms National Park. The bright bedrooms are traditionally

CONTINUED

furnished and offer good amenities. Enjoyable home-cooked fare is served around a communal table. Relax in the conservatory-lounge and watch squirrels feed in the nearby wood.

Rooms 4 en suite (1 fmly) (1 GF) S £35–£40; D £50–£55 **Facilities** STV TVB tea/coffee Cen ht Dinner Last d 4pm **Parking** 5 **Notes** LB

★★★ ◭ INN
The Cairn
Main Rd PH23 3AS
☎ 01479 841212 📄 01479 841362
e–mail: info@cairnhotel.co.uk
web: www.cairnhotel.co.uk

dir: *In village centre*

Rooms 7 rms (5 en suite) (2 fmly) S £26–£38; D £52–£56✱ **Facilities** STV TVB tea/coffee Dinner Last d 8.30pm Wi-fi available Pool Table **Parking** 20 **Notes** Closed 25 Dec

---

DORNOCH MAP 23 NH78

★★★★★ ◉◉ RESTAURANT WITH ROOMS
2 Quail Restaurant and Rooms
Castle St IV25 3SN
☎ 01862 811811
e–mail: theaa@2quail.com

dir: *On main street, 200yds from cathedral*

The saying "small is beautiful" aptly applies to this restaurant with rooms. Though set in the main street, the careful reproduction of its Victorian past transports you back in time. Cosy public rooms are ideal for conversation, but there are masses of books for those just wishing to relax. The stylish, individual bedrooms match the character of the house but are thoughtfully equipped to include DVD players. Food is the main feature however, with excellent breakfasts and set four course dinners.

Rooms 3 en suite (1 fmly) S £75–£120; D £85–£120 **Facilities** TVB tea/coffee Direct dial from bedrooms Cen ht Dinner Last d 10pm Wi-fi available **Notes** LB ⊗ No children 8yrs Closed Xmas & 2 wks Feb/Mar RS Nov–Mar

DRUMNADROCHIT MAP 23 NH53

★★★★ BED & BREAKFAST
Ferness Cottage
Lewiston IV63 6UW
☎ 01456 450564
e–mail: info@lochnessaccommodation.co.uk
web: www.lochnessaccommodation.co.uk

dir: *A82, from Inverness turn right after Esso service station, from Fort William left before Esso service station, 100mtrs telephone box on left. 100mtrs on right*

This rose-covered cottage dating from the 1840s has a peaceful location within easy walking distance of the village centre. The two charming bedrooms are well equipped, with many thoughtful extra touches. Traditional breakfasts in the cosy lounge-dining room feature the best of local produce. Guests can use the grassed riverbank with a seated area beside the River Coiltie, where fishing is available.

Rooms 2 en suite S £50–£65; D £50–£65 **Facilities** TVB tea/coffee Cen ht Fishing **Parking** 2 **Notes** LB ⊗ No children 10yrs

★★★★ BED & BREAKFAST
Glen Rowan
West Lewiston IV63 6UW
☎ 01456 450235
e–mail: info@glenrowan.co.uk

dir: *From Inverness A82 to Drumnadrochit & Lewiston, right after Esso station, Glen Rowan 600yds on left*

Set in a peaceful village, this friendly family home offers attractive, smartly furnished and well-equipped accommodation. Neat gardens surround the house and rooms at the rear overlook the River Coiltie. There is a choice of comfortable lounges, and a smart dining room where delicious home-cooked fare is served at individual tables. Bicycle storage and drying facilities are available.

Rooms 3 en suite (2 fmly) (3 GF) S £32–£60; D £42–£60✳
Facilities TVB tea/coffee Cen ht Dinner Last d 6pm Wi-fi available Fishing **Parking** 5 **Notes** LB ⊗

FORT WILLIAM MAP 22 NN17

See also Spean Bridge

Premier Collection

★★★★★ GUEST ACCOMMODATION
The Grange
Grange Rd PH33 6JF
☎ 01397 705516
e–mail: info@thegrange-scotland.co.uk
web: www.thegrange-scotland.co.uk

dir: *A82 S from Fort William, 300yds from rdbt left onto Ashburn Ln, at top on left*

This lovely Victorian villa stands in immaculate gardens on an elevated position with beautiful views of Loch Linnhe. Attractive decor and pretty fabrics have been used to good effect in the charming bedrooms, two of which have loch views. There is ample provision of books and fresh flowers in the carefully furnished lounge, and the elegant dining room is a lovely setting for hearty breakfasts.

Rooms 4 en suite **Facilities** TVB tea/coffee Cen ht Wi-fi available
Parking 4 **Notes** ⊗ No children 13yrs Closed Nov–Mar

Premier Collection

★★★★★ ▤ GUEST ACCOMMODATION
Ashburn House
8 Achintore Rd PH33 6RQ
☎ 01397 706000 📠 01397 702024
e–mail: christine@no–1.fsworld.co.uk
web: www.scotland2000.com/ashburn

dir: *500yds S of town centre on A82*

Having spectacular views of Loch Linnhe and the Ardgour Hills, this elegant Victorian villa is within easy walking distance of the town centre. It has been lovingly restored to its former glory and offers spacious, individually decorated and well-equipped bedrooms. There is a sunny conservatory lounge and an attractive dining room, which is an appropriate setting for the delicious breakfasts.

Rooms 7 en suite (2 GF) S £40–£50; D £80–£100✳ **Facilities** TVB tea/ coffee Cen ht Wi-fi available **Parking** 8 **Notes** LB ⊗ No children 12yrs Closed Xmas

SCOTLAND

FORT WILLIAM CONTINUED

★★★★ GUEST HOUSE
Distillery House
Nevis Bridge, North Rd PH33 6LR
☎ 01397 700103
e–mail: disthouse@aol.com

dir: *A82 from Fort William towards Inverness, on left after Glen Nevis rdbt*

Situated in the grounds of the former Glenlochy Distillery, this friendly guest house was once the distillery manager's home. Bedrooms are attractively decorated, comfortably furnished and very well equipped. There is a relaxing lounge, which features a superb range of games, and a bright airy dining room where traditional Scottish breakfasts are served at individual tables.

Rooms 10 en suite (1 fmly) (1 GF) S £30–£50; D £60–£104✳
Facilities TVB tea/coffee Licensed Cen ht **Parking** 21 **Notes LB** ⊗ No coaches

★★★★ GUEST HOUSE
Lochan Cottage
Lochyside PH33 7NX
☎ 01397 702695
e–mail: lochanco@btopenworld.com
web: www.fortwilliam-guesthouse.co.uk

dir: *A82 N from Fort William signed Inverness, left onto A830, left onto B8006 by Farm Foods to Lochyside*

A friendly welcome is extended at this charming house, situated in an acre of beautiful well-tended gardens with stunning panoramic views over Ben Nevis and Aonach Mor. Bedrooms are comfortable, attractive and well equipped. There is a spacious lounge and a charming conservatory-style dining room where delicious breakfasts are served.

Rooms 6 en suite (6 GF) S £24–£66; D £48–£66✳ **Facilities** TVB tea/coffee Cen ht **Parking** 10 **Notes LB** ⊗ No children 16yrs No coaches Closed Nov–Jan

★★★★ GUEST HOUSE
Mansefield Guest House
Corpach PH33 7LT
☎ 01397 772262 & 0845 6449432
e–mail: mansefield@btinternet.com
web: www.fortwilliamaccommodation.com

dir: *2m N of Fort William A82 onto A830, house 2m on A830 in Corpach*

Peacefully set in its own well-tended garden this friendly, family-run guest house provides comfortable, attractively decorated and well-equipped accommodation. There is a cosy lounge, where a roaring coal fire burns on cold evenings, and an attractive dining room where delicious, home-cooked evening meals and breakfasts are served at individual tables.

Rooms 6 en suite (1 fmly) (1 GF) S £25–£35; D £50–£80✳
Facilities TVB tea/coffee Cen ht TVL Dinner Last d noon Wi-fi available **Parking** 7 **Notes LB** ⊗ No children 12yrs No coaches

★★★ GUEST ACCOMMODATION
Glenlochy
Nevis Bridge PH33 6LP
☎ 01397 702909
e–mail: glenlochy1@aol.com
web: www.glenlochy.co.uk

dir: *A82 from Inverness, guest house on left after 2nd lights*

The well-tended garden of this friendly, family-run guest house marks the end of the famous West Highland Way. Bedrooms are pleasantly decorated and well equipped. There is a comfortable first-floor lounge and a bright, airy ground-floor dining room, where hearty breakfasts are served at individual tables.

Rooms 10 en suite 1 annexe en suite (2 fmly) (7 GF) S £25–£70; D £50–£76✳ **Facilities** TVB tea/coffee Cen ht TVL **Parking** 13 **Notes LB** ⊗

★★★ BED & BREAKFAST
Stobhan B & B
Fassifern Rd PH33 6BD
☎ 01397 702790 📠 01397 702790
e-mail: boggi@supanet.com

dir: *In town centre. A82 onto Victoria Rd beside St Mary's Church, right onto Fassifern Rd*

Stobhan B & B occupies an elevated location overlooking Loch Linnhe and offers comfortable, good-value accommodation. Bedrooms, one of which is on the ground floor, are traditionally furnished and have en suite facilities. Breakfast is served in the ground-floor dining room, which is adjacent to the lounge.

Rooms 4 en suite (1 GF) **Facilities** TVB tea/coffee Cen ht

★★★ 🅰 GUEST HOUSE
Berkeley House
Belford Rd PH33 6BT
☎ 01397 701185
e-mail: berkeleyhouse67@hotmail.com

dir: *On A82 at N end of town adjacent to St Mary's Church*

Rooms 7 en suite (1 fmly) (1 GF) **Facilities** TVB tea/coffee Cen ht TVL **Parking** 7 **Notes** ⊗ No coaches Closed 23–27 Dec

★★★ 🅰 GUEST HOUSE
Lochview
Heathercroft, Argyll Rd PH33 6RE
☎ 01397 703149
e-mail: info@lochview.co.uk

dir: *Off A82 rdbt at S end of town centre onto Lundavra Rd, left onto Argyll Ter, 1st right onto Heathercroft to top*

Rooms 6 en suite S £38–£45; D £60–£70 **Facilities** TVB tea/coffee Cen ht Wi-fi available **Parking** 6 **Notes** ⊗ No coaches Closed Oct–Apr

---

FOYERS MAP 23 NH42

★★★★ ◎◎ RESTAURANT WITH ROOMS
Craigdarroch House
IV2 6XU
☎ 01456 486400 📠 01456 486444
e-mail: info@hotel-loch-ness.co.uk

dir: *Take B862 from either end of loch, then B852 signed Foyers*

Opened in 1994 Craigdarroch commands an elevated position high above Loch Ness on the south side of the Loch. Bedrooms vary in style and size but all are comfortable and well equipped with front facing having wonderful Loch views. Dinner is not to be missed and breakfasts also impressed.

Rooms 10 en suite S £70–£120; D £100–£180✳ (room only) **Facilities** FTV TVB tea/coffee Direct dial from bedrooms Cen ht Dinner Last d 8pm Wi-fi available **Parking** 24 **Notes** No children 12yrs Civ Wed 30

★★★ GUEST HOUSE
Foyers Bay Country House
Lochness IV2 6YB
☎ 01456 486624 📠 01456 486337
e-mail: enquiries@foyersbay.co.uk

dir: *Off B852 into Lower Foyers*

This delightful Victorian villa is situated on sloping grounds and surrounded by pines and abundant colourful rhododendrons and stunning views of Loch Ness. The attractive, well-equipped bedrooms vary in size, and front facing first-floor bedrooms overlook the loch. There is a comfortable lounge next to the plant-filled conservatory-café, where evening meals and traditional breakfasts are served.

Rooms 6 en suite (1 GF) S £55–£65; D £80–£90 **Facilities** TVB tea/coffee Licensed Cen ht Dinner Last d 8pm Wi-fi available **Conf** Max 20 Thtr 20 Class 20 Board 20 **Parking** 6 **Notes** LB ⊗ No children 16yrs No coaches

---

GAIRLOCH MAP 22 NG87

★★★ 🛏 INN
The Old Inn
Flowerdale Glen IV21 2BD
☎ 01445 712006 📠 01445 712445
e-mail: info@theoldinn.net
web: www.theoldinn.co.uk

dir: *A832 into Gairloch, establishment on right opp Gairloch harbour*

Situated close to the harbour, this well-established and lively inn has an idyllic location overlooking the burn and the old bridge. A good range of meals, many featuring seafood, are served in the bars and dining areas, and outside at picnic tables on finer days. Live music is a feature several evenings a week. Bedrooms are well equipped and attractively decorated.

Rooms 14 en suite (3 fmly) (2 GF) **Facilities** STV TVB tea/coffee Direct dial from bedrooms Cen ht Dinner Last d 9.30pm Wi-fi available Pool Table **Conf** Max 20 Thtr 35 Class 15 Board 20 **Parking** 40 **Notes** No coaches Civ Wed 40

GLENCOE MAP 22 NN15

★★★★ GUEST HOUSE
Lyn-Leven
West Laroch PH49 4JP
☎ 01855 811392 📠 01855 811600
e-mail: macleodcilla@aol.com
web: www.lynleven.co.uk
(For full entry see South Ballachulish)

GLENCOE CONTINUED

★★★★ GUEST ACCOMMODATION
Scorrybreac
PH49 4HT
☎ 01855 811354
e–mail: info@scorrybreac.co.uk
web: www.scorrybreac.co.uk
dir: *Off A82 just outside village, 500yds from the River Coe bridge*

Having a stunning location above the village and overlooking the loch, this charming family-run guest house offers guests a warm welcome. Bedrooms are attractive, well equipped and comfortably furnished. There is a cosy lounge with plenty of books, board games and maps, and a bright airy dining room where delicious breakfasts are served at individual tables.

Rooms 6 en suite (6 GF) S £36–£44; D £48–£58✹ **Facilities** TVB tea/coffee Cen ht **Parking** 8 **Notes LB** ⊗ Closed 25 Dec

★★★ GUEST ACCOMMODATION
Fern Villa
Loanfern PH49 4JE
☎ 01855 811393 📠 01855 811727
e–mail: ghfernvilla@aol.com
web: www.fernvilla.org.uk
(For full entry see South Ballachulish)

GOLSPIE   **MAP 23 NC80**

★★★★ GUEST ACCOMMODATION
Granite Villa Guest House
Fountain Rd KW10 6TH
☎ 01408 633146
e–mail: info@granite-villa.co.uk
dir: *Left from A9 (Nbound) onto Fountain Rd, immediately before pedestrian crossing lights*

Originally built in 1892 for a wealthy local merchant, this traditional Victorian house has been sympathetically restored in recent years. Bedrooms are comfortable and all come with a range of thoughtful extras. Guests can relax in the large lounge, with its views over the landscaped garden where complimentary tea and coffee is often served. A warm welcome is assured in this charming period house.

Rooms 5 en suite (1 fmly) (1 GF) (2 smoking) S £40; D £60✹ **Facilities** FTV TVB tea/coffee Cen ht Wi-fi available **Parking** 6 **Notes** ⊛

GRANTOWN-ON-SPEY   **MAP 23 NJ02**

Premier Collection

★★★★★ GUEST HOUSE
An Cala
Woodlands Ter PH26 3JU
☎ 01479 873293 📠 01479 873610
e–mail: ancala@globalnet.co.uk
web: www.ancala.info
dir: *From Aviemore on the A95 bear left on the B9102 at the rdbt outside Grantown. After 400yds, 1st left & An Cala opp*

An Cala is an impressive Victorian house set in attractive gardens within easy walking distance of the town centre. Bedrooms are individually furnished with period pieces, attractively decorated and thoughtfully equipped. There is a comfortable lounge complete with log-burning stove and an elegant dining room where first class breakfasts (and dinners by arrangement) are served.

Rooms 4 en suite (1 fmly) S £55–£65; D £68–£80 **Facilities** FTV TVB tea/coffee Cen ht TVL Dinner Last d 24hrs notice Wi-fi available **Parking** 6 **Notes LB** ⊗ No children 3yrs No coaches Closed Xmas

SCOTLAND

★★★★ GUEST ACCOMMODATION
Holmhill House
Woodside Av PH26 3JR
☎ 01479 873977
e-mail: enquiries@holmhillhouse.co.uk
web: www.holmhillhouse.co.uk

dir: *S of town centre off A939 Spey Av*

Built in 1895, and situated in a large well-tended garden within walking distance of the town centre, Holmhill House combines Victorian character with modern comforts. The attractive bedrooms are well equipped, and are en suite. There is a games room suitable for all ages, and a ramp and lift is available for easier access plus a specially equipped bathroom. Children are also well catered for with games, toys, crayons and videos available.

Rooms 4 en suite (2 fmly) D £65–£70✶ **Facilities** TVB tea/coffee Lift Cen ht Wi-fi available **Parking** 8 **Notes** ⊗ Closed Nov–Mar

★★★★ 🅰 GUEST HOUSE
Dunallan House
Woodside Ave PH26 3JN
☎ 01479 872140
e-mail: enquiries@dunallan.com

dir: *From Granton Square lights, opposite Co-op, follow Forest Rd, right into Woodside Ave*

Rooms 7 rms (6 en suite) (1 pri facs) (1 fmly) (1 GF) S £40–£48; D £60–£76✶ **Facilities** TVB tea/coffee Cen ht TVL Wi-fi available **Parking** 8 **Notes** ⊗ No coaches

★★★★ 🅰 GUEST HOUSE
Rossmor Guest House
Woodlands Ter PH26 3JU
☎ 01479 872201
e-mail: rossmorgrantown@yahoo.com
web: www.rossmor.co.uk

dir: *500yds SW of village centre on B9102*

Rooms 6 en suite D £60–£70✶ **Facilities** TVB tea/coffee Cen ht Wi-fi available **Parking** 6 **Notes** ⊗ No children 8yrs No coaches

★★★ 🅰 GUEST HOUSE
Willowbank Guest House
High St PH26 3EN
☎ 01479 872089
e-mail: info@wbgh.co.uk
web: www.wbgh.co.uk

dir: *200yds SW of village centre on B9102*

Rooms 9 rms (6 en suite) (1 pri facs) (2 fmly) (2 GF) S £30–£45; D £52–£59✶ **Facilities** TVB tea/coffee Licensed Cen ht Dinner Last d 1pm Wi-fi available **Parking** 8 **Notes** No coaches

INVERGARRY
MAP 22 NH30

★★★ 🅰 GUEST HOUSE
Forest Lodge Guest House
South Laggan PH34 4EA
☎ 01809 501219 & 07790 907477
e-mail: info@flgh.co.uk
web: www.flgh.co.uk

dir: *2.5m S of Invergarry. Off A82 in South Laggan*

Rooms 7 rms (6 en suite) (1 pri facs) (3 fmly) (3 GF) S £34–£38; D £52–£56✶ **Facilities** TV1B tea/coffee Licensed Cen ht TVL Dinner Last d 24hrs Wi-fi available **Parking** 10 **Notes LB** No coaches Closed 20 Dec–7 Jan

INVERNESS
MAP 23 NH64

Premier Collection

★★★★★ 🖺 GUEST ACCOMMODATION
Daviot Lodge
Daviot Mains IV2 5ER
☎ 01463 772215 📄 01463 772099
e-mail: margaret.hutcheson@btopenworld.com
web: www.daviotlodge.co.uk

dir: *Off A9 5m S of Inverness onto B851 signed Croy. 1m on left*

Standing in 80 acres of peaceful pasture land, this impressive establishment offers attractive, well-appointed and equipped bedrooms. The master bedroom is furnished with a four-poster bed. There is a tranquil lounge with deep sofas and a real fire, and a peaceful dining room where hearty breakfasts featuring the best of local produce are served. Full disabled access for wheelchairs.

Rooms 7 en suite (1 GF) **Facilities** TVB tea/coffee Direct dial from bedrooms Cen ht TVL Wi-fi available **Parking** 10 **Notes** No children 5yrs

INVERNESS CONTINUED

Premier Collection

★★★★★ 🛏 GUEST HOUSE

Trafford Bank

96 Fairfield Rd IV3 5LL

☎ 01463 241414

e–mail: enquiries@invernesshotelaccommodation.co.uk

dir: Off A82 at Kenneth St, Fairfield Rd 2nd left, 600yds on right

This impressive Victorian house lies in a residential area close to the canal. Lorraine Freel has utilised her interior design skills to blend the best in contemporary styles with the house's period character and the results are simply stunning. Delightful public areas offer a choice of lounges, while breakfast is taken in a beautiful conservatory featuring eye-catching wrought-iron chairs. Bedrooms are all unique and boast TV/DVD/CD, sherry, silent mini fridge and much more.

Rooms 5 en suite (2 fmly) S £60–£85; D £80–£120 **Facilities** STV FTV TVB tea/coffee Cen ht TVL Wi-fi available **Parking** 8 **Notes** LB ⊗

See advert on opposite page

Premier Collection

★★★★★ GUEST HOUSE

Ballifeary Guest House

10 Ballifeary Rd IV3 5PJ

☎ 01463 235572 📠 01463 717583

e–mail: william.gilbert@btconnect.com

web: www.ballifearyguesthouse.co.uk

dir: Off A82, 0.5m from town centre, turn left onto Bishops Rd & sharp right onto Ballifeary Rd

This charming detached house has a peaceful residential location within easy walking distance of the town centre and Eden Court Theatre. The attractive bedrooms are carefully appointed and well equipped. There is an elegant ground-floor drawing room and a comfortable dining room, where delicious breakfasts, featuring the best of local produce, are served at individual tables.

Ballifeary Guest House

Rooms 6 en suite (1 GF) S £35–£70; D £70–£78 **Facilities** TVB tea/coffee Cen ht Wi-fi available **Parking** 6 **Notes** LB ⊗ No children 15yrs No coaches Closed 24–28 Dec

★★★★ GUEST ACCOMMODATION

Moyness House

6 Bruce Gardens IV3 5EN

☎ 01463 233836 📠 01463 233836

e–mail: stay@moyness.co.uk

web: www.moyness.co.uk

dir: Off A82 Fort William road, almost opp Highland Regional Council headquarters

Situated in a quiet residential area just a short distance from the city centre, this elegant Victorian villa dates from 1880 and offers beautifully decorated, comfortable bedrooms and well-appointed bathrooms. There is an attractive sitting room and an inviting dining room, where traditional Scottish breakfasts are served. Guests are welcome to use the secluded and well-maintained back garden.

Rooms 6 en suite (1 fmly) (2 GF) **Facilities** TV7B tea/coffee Cen ht Wi-fi available **Parking** 10

CONTINUED

★★★★ GUEST ACCOMMODATION
Westbourne
50 Huntly St IV3 5HS
☎ 01463 220700 📠 01463 220700
e-mail: richard@westbourne.org.uk

dir: *A9 onto A82 at football stadium over 4 rdbts, 1st left onto Wells St & Huntly St*

The immaculately maintained Westbourne looks across the River Ness to the city centre. This friendly, family-run house has bright modern bedrooms of varying size, all attractively furnished in pine and very well equipped. The ground-floor bedroom has been specially furnished for easier access. A relaxing lounge with internet access, books, games and puzzles is available.

Rooms 9 en suite (2 fmly) **Facilities** TVB tea/coffee Cen ht Wi-fi available **Parking** 6 **Notes** Closed Xmas & New Year

★★★★ 🏠 GUEST HOUSE
The Alexander
16 Ness Bank IV2 4SF
☎ 01463 231151 📠 01463 232220
e-mail: info@thealexander.net
web: www.thealexander.net

dir: *On E bank of river, opposite the cathedral*

Built in 1830 this impressive house has been extensively renovated by the current owners and many of the original Georgian features have been retained. Bedrooms are simply furnished and beds have luxurious mattresses dressed in fine Egyptian cotton. Public rooms include a charming lounge with views over the River Ness and the house is a short walk from the city centre.

Rooms 7 en suite 3 annexe en suite (1 GF) S £40–£55; D £70–£90✳ **Facilities** TVB tea/coffee Cen ht Wi-fi available **Parking** 8 **Notes** ⊗ No coaches

★★★★ BED & BREAKFAST
The Ghillies Lodge
16 Island Bank Rd IV2 4QS
☎ 01463 232137 📠 01463 713744
e-mail: info@ghillieslodge.com

dir: *1m SW from town centre on B862, pink house facing the river*

Situated on the banks of the River Ness not far from the city centre, Ghillies Lodge offers comfortable accommodation in a relaxed, peaceful environment. The attractive bedrooms, one of which is on the ground floor, are all en suite, and are individually styled and well equipped. There is a comfortable lounge-dining room, and a conservatory that overlooks the river.

Rooms 3 en suite (1 GF) **Facilities** STV TVB tea/coffee Cen ht TVL Wi-fi available **Parking** 4

INVERNESS CONTINUED

★★★★ GUEST HOUSE
Lyndon Guest House

50 Telford St IV3 5LE

☎ 01463 232551 📄 01463 225827

e–mail: lyndonguesthouse@btopenworld.com

web: www.lyndon-guest-house.co.uk

dir: *From A9 onto A82 over Friars Bridge, right at rdbt onto Telford street, on right hand side*

A warm Highland welcome awaits at this family-run accommodation close to the centre of Inverness. All rooms are en suite and are equipped with plenty of useful facilities including full internet access. Gaelic Spoken.

Rooms 6 en suite (4 fmly) (2 GF) S £25–£38; D £50–£65 **Facilities** STV TVB tea/coffee Cen ht TVL Wi-fi available **Parking** 6 **Notes** ⊗ Closed 20 Dec–5 Jan

★★★★ Ⓐ GUEST HOUSE
Avalon Guest House

79 Glenurquhart Rd IV3 5PB

☎ 01463 239075 📄 01463 709827

e–mail: avalon@inverness-loch-ness.co.uk

web: www.inverness-loch-ness.co.uk

Rooms 6 rms (5 en suite) (1 pri facs) (2 fmly) (4 GF) S £45–£65; D £50–£70✳ **Facilities** FTV TVB tea/coffee Cen ht TVL Wi-fi available **Parking** 12 **Notes LB** No coaches

★★★ GUEST ACCOMMODATION
St Ann's House

37 Harrowden Rd IV3 5QN

☎ 01463 236157 📄 01463 236157

e–mail: stannshous@aol.com

dir: *Off rdbt junct A82 & A862 on W side of bridge*

Located only a ten-minute walk from the city centre, this family-run guest house offers a warm welcome. The attractive bedrooms are well equipped, and refreshments can be enjoyed in the inviting lounge. Tasty breakfasts are served at individual tables in the bright airy dining room, which overlooks the delightful rear garden.

Rooms 6 rms (5 en suite) (1 pri facs) (1 fmly) (1 GF) S £28; D £58✳ **Facilities** TVB tea/coffee Cen ht TVL **Parking** 4 **Notes** ⊗ ⊜

★★★ GUEST HOUSE
Acorn House

2A Bruce Gardens IV3 5EN

☎ 01463 717021 & 240000 📄 01463 714236

e–mail: enquiries@acorn-house.freeserve.co.uk

web: www.acorn-house.freeserve.co.uk

dir: *From town centre onto A82, on W side of river, right onto Bruce Gardens*

This is an attractive detached house that is just a 5-minute walk from the town centre. Bedrooms are smartly presented and well equipped. Breakfast and dinner are served at individual tables in the spacious dining room and can be followed by coffee served in the comfortable lounge.

Rooms 6 en suite (3 fmly) S £49.95; D £70–£75✳ **Facilities** STV TVB tea/coffee Cen ht TVL Sauna Hot Tub **Parking** 7 **Notes LB**

★★★ INN
Crown Court

25 Southside Rd IV2 3RG

☎ 01463 234816 📄 01463 714900

e–mail: manager.crowncourt@ohiml.com

dir: *From S take Rainmore junct off A9, follow hospital signs, right into Anfield Rd, 800mtrs on right*

On a quiet side street and a short walk from the city centre the Crown Court has a range of well equipped bedrooms. Evening meals are served in the popular Bistro and freshly prepared breakfasts can be enjoyed in the quaint dining room. Ample secure car parking is also available at the inn.

Rooms 9 en suite (1 fmly) (1 GF) **Facilities** FTV tea/coffee Direct dial from bedrooms **Conf** Thtr 180 Class 60 Board 60 **Parking** 28 **Notes** No coaches

★★★ GUEST ACCOMMODATION
Fraser House
49 Huntly St IV3 5HS
☎ 01463 716488 📠 01463 716488
e–mail: fraserlea@btopenworld.com
web: www.fraserhouse.co.uk
dir: *A82 W over bridge, left onto Huntly St, house 100yds*

Situated on the west bank of the River Ness, Fraser House has a commanding position overlooking the city, and is within easy walking distance of the central amenities. Bedrooms, all en suite, vary in size and are comfortably furnished and well equipped. The ground-floor dining room is the setting for freshly cooked Scottish breakfasts.

Rooms 5 en suite (2 fmly) S £30–£35; D £50–£60 **Facilities** TVB tea/coffee Cen ht **Notes** ◉

★★★ GUEST ACCOMMODATION
Sunnyholm
12 Mayfield Rd IV2 4AE
☎ 01463 231336 📠 01463 715788
e–mail: sunnyholm@aol.com
web: www.invernessguesthouse.com
dir: *500yds SE of town centre. Off B861 Culduthel Rd onto Mayfield Rd*

Situated in a peaceful residential area within easy walking distance of the city centre, Sunnyholm offers comfortably proportioned and well-equipped bedrooms. A spacious conservatory-lounge overlooks the rear garden, and there is a another lounge next to the bright, airy dining room.

Rooms 4 en suite (4 GF) S £35–£39; D £50–£58✳ **Facilities** TVB tea/coffee Cen ht **Parking** 6 **Notes** ⊗ No children 3yrs ◉

KINGUSSIE   MAP 23 NH70

★★★★★ ◉◉◉ RESTAURANT WITH ROOMS
The Cross at Kingussie
Tweed Mill Brae, Ardbroilach Rd PH21 1LB
☎ 01540 661166 📠 01540 661080
e–mail: relax@thecross.co.uk
dir: *From lights in Kingussie centre along Ardbroilach Rd, 300yds left onto Tweed Mill Brae*

Situated in the valley above the town of Kingussie, this former tweed mill sits next to a river, with wild flower gardens and a sunny terrace. Hospitality and food are clearly highlights of any stay at this special restaurant with rooms. Locally sourced produce is carefully prepared with passion and skill. Bedrooms are spacious and airy, while fluffy towels and hand-made toiletries provide extra luxury.

Rooms 8 en suite (1 fmly) S £125–£180; D £170–£280✳ (incl. dinner) **Facilities** TVB Direct dial from bedrooms Cen ht Dinner Last d 8.30pm Wi-fi available Petanque **Conf** Max 20 Thtr 20 Class 20 Board 20 **Parking** 12 **Notes LB** ⊗ No children 8yrs Closed Xmas & Jan (ex New Year) RS Sun & Mon

LYBSTER   MAP 23 ND23

🅄
Portland Arms
Main St KW3 6BS
☎ 01593 721721 📠 01593 721722
e–mail: manager.portlandarms@ohiml.com
web: www.portlandarms.co.uk
dir: *On main A99, 4m N of Thruso junct*

At the time of going to press the rating for this establishment had not been confirmed. Please check the AA website www.theAA.com for up-to-date information.

Rooms 22 en suite (4 fmly) (4 GF) S £50–£70; D £70–£86✳ **Facilities** FTV TVB tea/coffee Direct dial from bedrooms Cen ht Dinner Last d 8.45pm Wi-fi available **Conf** Max 150 Thtr 150 Class 150 Board 50 Del from £80 ✳ **Parking** 22 **Notes LB** Civ Wed 100

NAIRN   MAP 23 NH85

★★★★ BED & BREAKFAST
North End
18 Waverley Rd IV12 4RQ
☎ 01667 456338
e–mail: reservations@northendnairn.co.uk
dir: *On corner of A96 (Academy St) and Waverley Rd*

Built in 1895, North End is a delightful Victorian villa that has been sympathetically restored in recent years. The spacious bedrooms are comfortable and well equipped. The cosy lounge has a wood-burning stove and the original features of the house are complimented by contemporary furnishings. The house is within easy walking distance of Nairn and is a twenty minute drive from Inverness.

Rooms 3 rms (2 en suite) (1 pri facs) S £24–£27; D £48–£54✳ **Facilities** TVB tea/coffee Cen ht TVL **Parking** 4 **Notes LB** ⊗ ◉

SCOTLAND

NEWTONMORE   MAP 23 NN79

Premier Collection

★★★★★ 🏛 GUEST HOUSE

Ard-Na-Coille

Kingussie Rd PH20 1AY

☎ 01540 673214 📄 01540 673214

e–mail: jacquie@ard-na-coille.co.uk

dir: *Exit A9 at Newtonmore, opp Highland Folk Museum*

This large period house has been totally refurbished by its current owners and it is set in its own landscaped grounds. The house overlooks the open fields and enjoys a stunning location. Bedrooms are of a very high standard, spacious and with a host of thoughtful extras. The public areas include a large lounge with its open fires and delicious breakfasts are served in the light filled dining room.

Rooms 3 en suite S £75–£85; D £85–£95✳ **Facilities** STV FTV TVB tea/coffee Direct dial from bedrooms Licensed Cen ht TVL Wi-fi available Golf 18 Snooker **Parking** 10 **Notes LB** ⊗ No children

★★★★ GUEST HOUSE

Crubenbeg House

Falls of Truim PH20 1BE

☎ 01540 673300

e–mail: enquiries@crubenbeghouse.com

web: www.crubenbeghouse.com

dir: *4m S of Newtonmore. Off A9 for Crubenmore, over railway bridge & right, signed*

Set in peaceful rural location, Crubenbeg House has stunning country views and is well located for touring the Highlands. The attractive bedrooms are individually styled and well equipped, while the ground-floor bedroom provides easier access. You can enjoy a dram in front of the fire in the inviting lounge, while breakfast features the best of local produce in the adjacent dining room.

Rooms 4 rms (3 en suite) (1 pri facs) (1 GF) S £30–£36; D £50–£80 **Facilities** STV TVB tea/coffee Licensed Cen ht Dinner Last d 4pm Wi-fi available **Parking** 10 **Notes LB** No children No coaches

SHIEL BRIDGE   MAP 22 NG91

★★★★ ⚜ RESTAURANT WITH ROOMS

Grants at Craigellachie

Craigellachie, Ratagan IV40 8HP

☎ 01599 511331

e–mail: info@housebytheloch.co.uk

dir: *From A87 turn to Glenelg, 1st right to Ratagn, opp Youth Hostel sign*

Nestled on the tranquil shores of Loch Duin and overlooked by the Five Sisters Mountains, Grants really does enjoy a stunning location. The restaurant has a well deserved reputation for its fine dining and the recently upgraded bedrooms are stylish and have all the creature comforts. Guests are guaranteed a warm welcome at this charming house.

Rooms 2 en suite 2 annexe en suite (3 GF) D £149–£189✳ (incl. dinner) **Facilities** STV TVB tea/coffee Cen ht Dinner Last d 8.30pm **Parking** 8 **Notes LB** No children 12yrs Closed 2wks mid Nov & mid Jan–mid Feb RS Oct–Apr

SOUTH BALLACHULISH   MAP 22 NN05

★★★★ 🏛 ⚘ GUEST HOUSE

Craiglinnhe House

Lettermore PH49 4JD

☎ 01855 811270

e–mail: info@craiglinnhe.co.uk

web: www.craiglinnhe.co.uk

dir: *From village A82 onto A828, Craiglinnhe 1.5m on left*

Built during the reign of Queen Victoria, Craiglinnhe House enjoys an elevated position with stunning views across Loch Linnhe to the village of Onich, and up to the Ballachulish Bridge and the Pap of Glencoe. The attractive bedrooms vary in size, are stylishly furnished, and are well equipped. There is a ground-floor lounge and a charming dining room where delicious breakfasts, and evening meals by arrangement, are served at individual tables.

Rooms 5 en suite S £42–£60; D £56–£80✳ **Facilities** TVB tea/coffee Licensed Cen ht Dinner Last d 10am **Parking** 5 **Notes LB** ⊗ No children 13yrs No coaches Closed 24–26 Dec

★★★★ GUEST HOUSE
Lyn-Leven
West Laroch PH49 4JP
☎ 01855 811392 🖹 01855 811600
e–mail: macleodcilla@aol.com
web: www.lynleven.co.uk
dir: *Off A82 signed on left West Laroch*

Genuine Highland hospitality and high standards are part of the appeal of this comfortable guest house. The attractive bedrooms vary in size, are well equipped, and offer many thoughtful extra touches. There is a spacious lounge and a smart dining room where delicious home-cooked evening meals and breakfasts are served at individual tables.

Rooms 8 en suite 4 annexe en suite (3 fmly) (12 GF) **Facilities** TVB tea/coffee Cen ht TVL Dinner Last d 7pm **Parking** 12 **Notes** Closed Xmas

★★★ GUEST ACCOMMODATION
Fern Villa
Loanfern PH49 4JE
☎ 01855 811393 🖹 01855 811727
e–mail: ghfernvilla@aol.com
web: www.fernvilla.org.uk
dir: *Off A82 into village, off Albert Rd onto Loanfern*

A warm welcome is assured at this elegant Victorian house. The bedrooms are well equipped and maintained, with those at the front of the house providing breathtaking views of the stunning scenery. There is a comfortable lounge with a selection of board games.

Rooms 5 en suite (1 GF) S £20–£37; D £40–£54✳ **Facilities** TVB tea/coffee Cen ht TVL **Parking** 5 **Notes** LB ✪

SPEAN BRIDGE   **MAP 22 NN28**

★★★★ 🛏 GUEST HOUSE
Corriechoille Lodge
PH34 4EY
☎ 01397 712002
web: www.corriechoille.com
dir: *Off A82 signed Corriechoille, continue 2.25m, left at road fork (10mph sign). At end of tarmac, turn right up hill & left*

This fine country house stands above the River Spean. There are magnificent views of the Nevis range and surrounding mountains from the comfortable first-floor lounge and some of the spacious, well-appointed bedrooms. Friendly and attentive service is provided, as are traditional breakfasts and delicious evening meals by arrangement.

Rooms 4 en suite (2 fmly) (1 GF) S £40–£46; D £72–£60✳
Facilities TVB tea/coffee Licensed Cen ht Dinner Last d previous day Wi-fi available **Parking** 7 **Notes** ✪ No children 7yrs No coaches Closed Nov–Mar RS Mon–Tue

★★★★ ◉◉ RESTAURANT WITH ROOMS
The Smiddy House
Roy Bridge Rd PH34 4EU
☎ 01397 712335 🖹 01397 712043
e–mail: enquiry@smiddyhouse.co.uk
web: www.smiddyhouse.co.uk
dir: *In village centre, A82 onto A86*

Set within the 'Great Glen', which stretches from Fort William to Inverness, this was once the village smithy, and is now a friendly establishment. The attractive bedrooms, which are named after Scottish places, are comfortably furnished and well equipped. A relaxing garden room is available for guest use. Delicious evening meals are served in Russell's restaurant.

Rooms 4 en suite (1 fmly) S £60–£75; D £60–£80✳ **Facilities** TVB tea/coffee Dinner Last d 9.30pm **Parking** 15

SCOTLAND

SPEAN BRIDGE continued

★★★★ Ⓐ GUEST HOUSE
Distant Hills Guest House

Roy Bridge Rd PH34 4EU

☎ 01397 712452

e–mail: enquiry@distanthills.com

dir: *A82 onto A86 at Spean Bridge, 0.5m on right*

Rooms 7 en suite (7 GF) S £40–£80; D £65–£90✳ **Facilities** TVB tea/coffee Cen ht TVL Dinner Last d 24hrs Wi-fi available **Parking** 10 **Notes** ⊗

★★★ FARM HOUSE
Achnabobane *(NN195811)*

PH34 4EX

☎ 01397 712919 Mr and Mrs N Ockenden

e–mail: enquiries@achnabobane.co.uk

web: www.achnabobane.co.uk

dir: *2m S of Spean Bridge on A82*

With breathtaking views of Ben Nevis, Aonach Mhor and the Grey Corries, the farmhouse offers comfortable, good-value accommodation in a friendly family environment. Bedrooms are traditional in style and well equipped. Breakfast and evening meals are served in the conservatory-dining room. Pets welcome.

Rooms 4 rms (1 en suite) (1 fmly) (1 GF) S £28; D £56✳ **Facilities** TVB tea/coffee Cen ht TVL Dinner Last d 1pm Wi-fi available **Parking** 5 **Notes** Closed Xmas

---

STRATHPEFFER   MAP 23 NH45

★★★ GUEST HOUSE
Inver Lodge

IV14 9DL

☎ 01997 421392

e–mail: derbyshire@inverlg.fsnet.co.uk

dir: *A834 through Strathpeffer centre, turn beside Spa Pavilion signed Bowling Green, Inver Lodge on right*

You are assured of a warm welcome at this Victorian lodge, secluded in its own tree-studded gardens yet within easy walking distance of the town centre. Bedrooms are comfortable and well equipped, and the cosy lounge is ideal for relaxation. Breakfasts and (by arrangement) evening meals are also served here at a communal table.

Rooms 2 rms (1 fmly) S £30–£35; D £50 **Facilities** TVB tea/coffee Cen ht Dinner Last d 4pm **Parking** 2 **Notes LB** ⊗ No coaches Closed Xmas & New Year ◉

STRATHY POINT   MAP 23 NC86

★★★★ BED & BREAKFAST
Catalina

Aultivullin KW14 7RY

☎ 01641 541395 📠 0871 900 2537

e–mail: catalina.bandb@virgin.net

dir: *A836 at Strathy onto Strathy Point Rd, 1.5m then left & 1m to end*

Having a tranquil setting close to the sea, this former croft house provides a getaway location for those seeking relaxation. The self-contained bedroom is in a wing that includes a dining room and a cosy lounge. Cuisine is home-cooked and meal times are flexible.

Rooms 1 en suite (1 GF) S £35; D £52 **Facilities** TVB tea/coffee Cen ht TVL Dinner Last d 7.15pm **Parking** 2 **Notes** ⊗ No children ◉

TOMATIN   MAP 23 NH82

★★★ GUEST HOUSE
Glenan Lodge

IV13 7YT

☎ 01808 511217

e–mail: enquiries@glenanlodge.co.uk

web: www.glenanlodge.co.uk

dir: *Off A9 to Tomatin, signed to Lodge*

Peacefully located on the edge of the village, this relaxed and homely guest house offers a warm welcome. The comfortable bedrooms are traditionally furnished and suitably equipped. An inviting lounge is available, and delicious home-cooked evening meals and breakfasts are served in the dining room. A two mile stretch of the River Findhorn is available for fly-fishing, and golfers, walkers and bird watchers are also well provided for locally.

Rooms 7 en suite (2 fmly) S £27; D £54✳ **Facilities** TVB tea/coffee Licensed Cen ht TVL Dinner Last d 6pm Wi-fi available Fishing **Parking** 7 **Notes LB** ⊗ No children 5yrs no coaches

---

TORRIDON   MAP 22 NG95

Ⓤ
The Torridon Inn

IV22 2EY

☎ 01445 791242 📠 01445 712253

e–mail: inn@thetorridon.com

At the time of going to press the rating for this establishment had not been confirmed. Please check the AA website www.theAA.com for up-to-date information.

Rooms 12 en suite (3 fmly) (5 GF) D £74–£80✳ **Facilities** STV TVB tea/coffee Cen ht Dinner Last d 8.45pm Wi-fi available Fishing Pool Table ⤴ **Conf** Max 35 Thtr 35 Board 16 Del £120✳ **Parking** 12 **Notes LB** Closed Nov–Feb Civ Wed 40

ULLAPOOL   MAP 22 NH19

★★★★ A GUEST HOUSE
Dromnan Guest House
Garve Rd IV26 2SX
☎ 01854 612333 📠 01854 613364
e-mail: info@dromnan.com
web: www.dromnan.com
dir: *A835 S into town, left at 30mph sign*

Rooms 7 en suite (2 fmly) S £50–£60; D £60–£70✶ **Facilities** FTV TVB tea/coffee Cen ht TVL Wi-fi available free entry to Lochbroom Leisure Centre **Parking** 7 **Notes** ⊗ No coaches

WICK   MAP 23 ND35

★★★★ BED & BREAKFAST
The Clachan
13 Randolph Place, South Rd KW1 5NJ
☎ 01955 605384
e-mail: enquiry@theclachan.co.uk
dir: *Off A99 0.5m S of town centre*

A warm welcome is assured at this immaculate detached home, by the main road on the south edge of the town. The bright, airy bedrooms (all on the ground floor) though compact, are attractively furnished to make good use of available space. Breakfast offers an extensive choice and is served at individual tables in the cosy dining room.

Rooms 3 en suite (3 GF) S £38–£40; D £48–£50✶ **Facilities** FTV TVB tea/coffee Cen ht Wi-fi available **Parking** 3 **Notes** ⊗ No children 12yrs Closed Xmas & New Year ⊛

MIDLOTHIAN

PENICUIK   MAP 21 NT25

U
Craigiebield House
50 Bog Rd EH26 9BZ
☎ 01968 672557
e-mail: reservations.craigiebield@ohiml.com

At the time of going to press the rating for this establishment had not been confirmed. Please check the AA website www.theAA.com for up-to-date information.

Rooms 17 en suite (4 fmly) S £65–£85; D £75–£120✶ **Facilities** FTV TVB tea/coffee Direct dial from bedrooms Cen ht Dinner Last d 9pm Wi-fi available **Conf** Max 200 Thtr 200 Class 100 Board 50 Del from £99✶ **Parking** 40 **Notes** ⊗ Civ Wed 150

See advert on this page

ROSLIN   MAP 21 NT26

★★★ INN
The Original Roslin Inn
4 Main St EH25 9LE
☎ 0131 440 2384 📠 0131 440 2514
e-mail: enquiries@theoriginalhotel.co.uk
dir: *Off city bypass at Straiton for A703, inn is close to Roslin Chapel*

Whether you find yourself on the Da Vinci Code trail or in the area on business, this property is within easy distance of the famous Roslin Chapel which is well worth the visit. A delightful village inn offers well-equipped bedrooms with upgraded en suites. Four of the rooms have four-poster beds. The Grail Restaurant, the lounge and conservatory offer a comprehensive selection of dining options.

Rooms 6 en suite (2 fmly) S £65–£75; D £85–£100✶ **Facilities** STV TVB tea/coffee Cen ht Dinner Last d 9.30pm **Conf** Max 100 Thtr 130 Class 80 Board 60 **Parking** 8 **Notes LB** Civ Wed 180

MORAY

CULLEN
MAP 23 NJ56

★★★ 🅰 GUEST HOUSE
Norwood Guest House

11 Seafield Place AB56 4TE
☎ 01542 840314
e–mail: info@norwoodguesthouse.com

dir: *From A98, turn onto Seafield Place from Main St, Cullen*

Rooms 6 rms (3 en suite) (3 pri facs) (1 GF) **Facilities** TVB tea/coffee
Licensed Cen ht Dinner Last d 9am **Parking** 4 **Notes** ⊗ No coaches

KEITH
MAP 23 NJ45

★★★ FARM HOUSE
The Haughs Farm Guest House
(NJ416515)

AB55 6QN
☎ 01542 882238 📠 01542 882238 Mrs J Jackson
e–mail: jiwjackson@aol.com
web: www.haughsfarmbedandbreakfast.net

dir: *0.5m NW of Keith off A96, signed Inverness*

Expect a friendly welcome at this comfortable farmhouse on the
outskirts of town. The spacious bedrooms are inviting and have a
comprehensive range of accessories. Public areas include a relaxing
lounge, and meals are served in the sun room overlooking the garden.

Rooms 3 en suite (1 fmly) (3 GF) (3 smoking) S £35–£37; D £48–£52✳
Facilities TVB tea/coffee Cen ht TVL Wi-fi available **Parking** 11
Notes ⊗ 165 acres beef mixed sheep Closed Oct/Etr ⊜

★★★ GUEST ACCOMMODATION
The Royal

Church Rd AB55 5BR
☎ 01542 886978 📠 01542 889919
e–mail: royalhotelkeith@ohiml.com

dir: *On A96*

Located in the heart of Keith within good stricking distance for both
Aberdeen and Inverness. Bedrooms are of a good size and well
presented. Guests have a choice of two bars and dinner can be taken
in one of two locations. Breakfast is served on invidual tables in the
first floor restaurant.

Rooms 10 en suite (1 fmly) S £30–£45; D £55–£80✳ **Facilities** TVB tea/
coffee Cen ht Dinner Last d 8.30pm Wi-fi available Pool Table
Conf Max 150 Thtr 150 Class 100 Board 90 **Parking** 6

NORTH AYRSHIRE

ARDROSSAN
MAP 20 NS24

🆄
Lauriston

15 South Crescent Rd KA22 8EA
☎ 01294 463771 📠 01294 470345
e–mail: manager.lauriston@ohiml.com

dir: *A78 onto A738 in town*

At the time of going to press the rating for this establishment had not
been confirmed. Please check the AA website www.theAA.com for
up-to-date information.

Rooms 5 en suite (1 fmly) S £30–£55; D £30–£55✳ (room only)
Facilities FTV TVB tea/coffee Cen ht Dinner Last d 9pm **Conf** Max 200
Thtr 200 Class 150 Board 35 **Parking** 31 **Notes** ⊗ Civ Wed

LARGS
MAP 20 NS25

★★★★ GUEST HOUSE
Whin Park

16 Douglas St KA30 8PS
☎ 01475 673437
e–mail: enquiries@whinpark.co.uk
web: www.whinpark.co.uk

dir: *N of Largs off A78 signed Brisbane Glen*

Situated just a stroll from the seafront, this comfortable bungalow takes
its name from the gorse bushes that grow in profusion on the
surrounding hillsides. Bedrooms are attractively decorated and well
equipped. There is an elegant lounge and a lovely dining room.
Resident proprietors provide excellent levels of customer care.

Rooms 4 en suite (1 fmly) S £36–£38; D £64–£68✳ **Facilities** TVB tea/
coffee **Parking** 4 **Notes** ⊗ No coaches Closed Feb

★★★★ 🛏 BED & BREAKFAST
South Whittlieburn Farm

Brisbane Glen KA30 8SN
☎ 01475 675881 📠 01475 675080
e–mail: largsbandb@southwhittlieburnfarm.freeserve.co.uk

dir: *2m NE of Largs off A78 signed Brisbane Glen, after Vikingar
centre*

This comfortable and welcoming farmhouse is on a working sheep
farm surrounded by gently rolling countryside. The attractive bedrooms
are well equipped with all having DVD and video players. There is a
spacious ground-floor lounge and a bright airy dining room where
delicious breakfasts are served.

Rooms 3 en suite (1 fmly) S £35–£40; D £58–£65✳ **Facilities** STV TVB
tea/coffee Cen ht TVL Golf 18 **Parking** 10 **Notes LB** ⊗ RS Xmas ⊜

SALTCOATS

MAP 20 NS24

Premier Collection

★★★★★ 🏠 GUEST ACCOMMODATION

Lochwood Farm Log Cabin

KA21 6NG

☎ 01294 552529

e–mail: info@lochwoodfarm.co.uk

dir: *1m off Saltcoats-Dalry road (B714)*

The log cabin is a recent addition to the Steading operation. Set in 200 acres of glorious rolling countryside, this immaculately maintained dairy and arable farm offers warm hospitality with delicious food. The cabin boasts its own lounge and attractive bedroom with many extras as standard. Across in the converted traditional stone byre there is a further choice of lounges and a spacious dining room where hearty farmhouse breakfasts are served at a large communal table. The cabin also boasts an outdoor Jacuzzi hot tub to relax in. Lochwood Farm Log Cabin was the AA's Family-Friendly B&B of the Year for 2007.

Rooms 1 en suite (1 GF) D £95–£105✳ **Facilities** FTV TVB tea/coffee Cen ht TVL Wi-fi available Jacuzzi Hot tub **Parking** 10 **Notes LB** ⊗

NORTH LANARKSHIRE

AIRDRIE

MAP 21 NS76

★★★ GUEST HOUSE

Shawlee Cottage

108 Lauchope St, Chapelhall ML6 8SW

☎ 01236 753774 📠 01236 749300

e–mail: shawleecottage@blueyonder.co.uk

web: www.csaitken.fsbusiness.co.uk/index.htm

dir: *M8 junct 6, A73 to Chapelhall, left onto B799, Shawlee 600yds on right*

Shawlee Cottage is close to motorway and rail networks, and within easy reach of Edinburgh and Glasgow. This delightful cottage dates from the 19th century and has comfortable, well-equipped bedrooms with wide doors and a ramp at the entrance. Scottish breakfasts (and dinner by arrangement) are served in the attractive dining room.

Rooms 5 en suite (5 GF) S £30–£40; D £50–£60 **Facilities** TVB tea/coffee Direct dial from bedrooms Cen ht Wi-fi available **Parking** 6 **Notes** ⊗ No coaches

COATBRIDGE

MAP 20 NS76

★★★ GUEST HOUSE

Auchenlea

153 Langmuir Rd, Bargeddie G69 7RT

☎ 0141 771 6870 & 07775 791381 📠 0141 771 6870

e–mail: helenbarr06@btinternet.com

dir: *N off A8 onto A752 for 0.4m*

Backing onto farmland, yet only a short distance from the motorway, this detached house is well placed for Glasgow and Edinburgh. Satisfying, well-cooked breakfasts are served at a communal table in

CONTINUED

the bright dining room, and there is an attractive conservatory and adjoining lounge. The bedrooms, all on the ground floor, are modern in style with one designed for easier access.

Rooms 6 en suite (1 fmly) (6 GF) S £30–£35; D £60–£70✳ **Facilities** TVB tea/coffee Cen ht TVL **Parking** 10 **Notes** ⊗ ⊜

KILSYTH

MAP 20 NS77

Ⓤ

The Coachman

4 Parkfoot St G65 0SP

☎ 01236 821649 📠 01326 823850

web: www.oxfordhotelsand inns.com

At the time of going to press the rating for this establishment had not been confirmed. Please check the AA website www.theAA.com for up-to-date information.

Rooms 11 en suite (1 fmly) S £35–£45; D £60–£70✳ **Facilities** TVB tea/coffee Direct dial from bedrooms **Parking** 20 **Notes** Closed 1 Jan RS Xmas

PERTH & KINROSS

ALYTH

MAP 23 NO24

Premier Collection

★★★★★ 🏠 ⊜ GUEST ACCOMMODATION

Tigh Na Leigh Guesthouse

22–24 Airlie St PH11 8AJ

☎ 01828 632372 📠 01828 632279

e–mail: bandcblack@yahoo.co.uk

web: www.tighnaleigh.co.uk

dir: *In town centre on B952*

Situated in the heart of this country town, Tigh Na Leigh is Gaelic for "The house of the Doctor or Physician". Its location and somewhat sombre façade are in stunning contrast to what lies inside. The house has been completely restored to blend its Victorian architecture with contemporary interior design. Bedrooms include a superb suite and state-of-the-art bathrooms. Public rooms offer three entirely different lounges, while delicious meals are served in the conservatory/dining room overlooking a spectacular landscaped garden.

Rooms 5 en suite (1 GF) S £40; D £80–£110✳ **Facilities** FTV TVB tea/coffee Cen ht TVL Dinner Last d 8pm Wi-fi available **Parking** 5 **Notes** No children 12yrs Closed Dec–Feb

BLAIRGOWRIE   MAP 21 NO14

★★★★ BED & BREAKFAST
Gilmore House

Perth Rd PH10 6EJ
☎ 01250 872791 📄 01250 872791
e–mail: jill@gilmorehouse.co.uk

dir: *On A93 S*

This Victorian villa stands in a well-tended garden on the south side of town. Sympathetically restored to enhance its period features it offers individual bedrooms tastefully furnished in antique pine, and thoughtfully equipped to include modern amenities such as Freeview TV. There are two inviting lounges, one of which has lovely views over the gardens. Hearty traditional breakfasts are served in the attractive dining room.

Rooms 3 en suite D £50–£60 **Facilities** FTV TVB tea/coffee Cen ht TVL Wi-fi available **Parking** 3 **Notes** Closed Xmas

COUPAR ANGUS   MAP 21 NO23

★★★ GUEST HOUSE
Enverdale House

6 Pleasure Rd PH13 9JB
☎ 01828 627606 📄 01828 627239

Enverdale House is located on a quiet road and is a short walk from the centre of the small market town of Couper Angus. This family run guesthouse has attractively presented bedrooms, and public rooms include a spacious lounge bar along with spacious conference facilities. An extensive breakfast menu is provided and evening meals are served in the stylish restaurant.

Rooms 5 en suite (1 fmly) **Facilities** FTV TVB tea/coffee Licensed Cen ht Dinner Last d 9pm Wi-fi available **Notes** ⊗ Civ Wed 200

CRIEFF   MAP 21 NN82

★★★★ BED & BREAKFAST
Merlindale

Perth Rd PH7 3EQ
☎ 01764 655205 📄 01764 655205
e–mail: merlin.dale@virgin.net
web: www.merlindale.co.uk

dir: *On A85 350yds from E end of High St*

Situated in a quiet residential area within walking distance of the town centre, this delightful detached house stands in well-tended grounds and offers a warm welcome. The pretty bedrooms are comfortably furnished and well equipped. There is a spacious lounge, an impressive library, and an elegant dining room where delicious evening meals and traditional breakfasts are served.

Rooms 3 en suite (1 fmly) **Facilities** STV TVB tea/coffee Cen ht TVL Dinner Last d 24hrs notice Wi-fi available **Parking** 3 **Notes** ⊗ Closed 9 Dec–10 Feb 🌐

GLENDEVON   MAP 21 NN90

★★★★ ⊛ INN
An Lochan Tormaukin

FK14 7JY
☎ 0845 371 1414
e–mail: info@anlochan.co.uk

A delightful country inn dating back to the 17th century, located in a secluded idyllic setting not far from the famous Gleneagles Championship golf courses. This well-presented property is currently enjoying a rolling programme of refurbishment. Open log fires and bare stone walls add to the character of this property where the small team are friendly and welcoming. Food is a strong aspect of this inn with the best made of locally sourced foods.

Rooms 13 en suite **Facilities** Direct dial from bedrooms Cen ht Dinner Last d 9pm Wi-fi available **Parking** 50

GLENSHEE (SPITTAL OF),   MAP 21 NO17

★★★★ BED & BREAKFAST
Dalhenzean Lodge

PH10 7QD
☎ 01250 885217 📄 0871 733 5419
e–mail: mikepurdie@onetel.com

dir: *On A93 2m S of Spittal of Glenshee*

Dalhenzean Lodge was built in 1715, and is situated in the shadow of Meall Uaine, overlooking Shee Water. Some seven miles from the ski slopes at The Cairnwell, it is well located for fishing, hill walking and climbing, with the Cateran Trail nearby. Bedrooms are beautifully decorated and have many thoughtful extras. Hearty breakfasts featuring the best of local produce are served in the ground-floor dining room.

Rooms 2 rms (1 en suite) (1 pri facs) D £50–£55✱ **Facilities** STV FTV TVB tea/coffee Cen ht **Parking** 2 **Notes** LB 🌐

PERTH   MAP 21 NO12

★★★★ GUEST ACCOMMODATION
Cherrybank Guesthouse

217–219 Glasgow Rd PH2 0NB
☎ 01738 451982 📄 01738 561336
e–mail: m.r.cherrybank@blueyonder.co.uk

dir: *1m SW of town centre on A93*

Convenient for the town and major roads, Cherrybank has been extended and carefully refurbished to offer well equipped and beautifully presented bedrooms, one of which is on the ground floor. The delightful lounge is ideal for relaxation, while delicious breakfasts are served at individual tables in the bright airy dining room.

CONTINUED

Cherrybank Guesthouse

Rooms 5 rms (4 en suite) (1 pri facs) (2 fmly) (1 GF) **Facilities** TVB tea/coffee Cen ht Wi-fi available **Parking** 4 **Notes** ⊗

★★★★ BED & BREAKFAST
Westview

49 Dunkeld Rd PH1 5RP
☎ 01738 627787 📠 01738 447790
e–mail: angiewestview@aol.com

dir: *On A912, 0.5m NW from town centre opp Royal Bank of Scotland*

Expect a warm welcome from enthusiastic owner Angie Livingstone. She is a fan of Victoriana, and her house captures that period, one feature being the teddies on the stairs. Best use is made of available space in the bedrooms, which are full of character. Public areas include an inviting lounge and a dining room.

Rooms 5 rms (3 en suite) (1 fmly) (1 GF) **Facilities** STV TVB tea/coffee Cen ht TVL Dinner Last d 12.30pm **Parking** 4 **Notes** ⊛

★★★ GUEST HOUSE
Clunie

12 Pitcullen Crescent PH2 7HT
☎ 01738 623625 📠 01738 623238
e–mail: ann@clunieguesthouse.co.uk

dir: *On A94 on E side of river*

Lying on the north east side of town, this family-run guest house offers a friendly welcome. The comfortable bedrooms, which vary in size, are attractively decorated and well equipped. Breakfast is served at individual tables in the elegant ground-floor dining room.

Rooms 7 en suite (1 fmly) S £30–£40; D £50–£70✱ **Facilities** TVB tea/coffee Cen ht **Parking** 8 **Notes LB** No coaches

Premier Collection

★★★★★ 🍴 BED & BREAKFAST
Easter Dunfallandy House

Logierait Rd PH16 5NA
☎ 01796 474128
e–mail: sue@dunfallandy.co.uk
web: www.dunfallandy.co.uk

dir: *1m S of Pitlochry. Off A924 Perth Rd in town onto Bridge Rd, fork left, house 1m on right*

A splendid country house, Dunfallandy lies peacefully in an elevated position on the western side of the Tummel Valley. Immaculately maintained, it retains many original features including fine woodwork. The lounge is very relaxing, and the dining room, with its magnificent wood-panelled ceiling, is the setting for breakfast served to one large table. Bedrooms are well proportioned and thoughtfully equipped.

Rooms 3 en suite (1 GF) S £47.50–£62.50; D £75–£85✱ **Facilities** STV TVB tea/coffee Cen ht TVL Wi-fi available **Parking** 10 **Notes LB** ⊗ Closed Xmas

★★★★ GUEST HOUSE
Craigroyston House

2 Lower Oakfield PH16 5HQ
☎ 01796 472053 📠 01796 472053
e–mail: reservations@craigroyston.co.uk
web: www.craigroyston.co.uk

dir: *In town centre near information centre car park*

The Maxwell family delight in welcoming you to their home, an impressive detached Victorian villa set in a colourful garden. The bedrooms have pretty colour schemes and are comfortably furnished in period style. There is an inviting sitting room, complete with deep sofas for those wishing to relax and enjoy the tranquillity. Scottish breakfasts are served at individual tables in the attractive dining room.

Rooms 8 en suite (1 fmly) (1 GF) D £60–£76 **Facilities** TVB tea/coffee Cen ht **Parking** 9 **Notes LB** ⊗ No coaches ⊛

SCOTLAND

SCOTLAND

PITLOCHRY CONTINUED

★★★★ 🏠 GUEST HOUSE
Beinn Bhracaigh
High Oakfield PH16 5HT
☎ 01796 470355
e–mail: info@beinnbhracaigh.com

dir: *From S, take 2nd right after railway arch, then 2nd left into Higher Oakfield*

Beinn Bhracaigh enjoys a prominent position overlooking the charming town of Pitlochry. A great deal of refurbishment has taken place at the house under its new owners, including the upgraded bedrooms which are most impressive. Public areas are very well presented and guests have a choice of lounges. Breakfast is served at individual tables in the bright, spacious dining room with its views over the gardens and the town below.

Rooms 10 en suite (1 fmly) (4 GF) S £40–£65; D £55–£95 **Facilities** TVB tea/coffee Licensed Cen ht Wi-fi available **Conf** Max 10 Thtr 10 Class 10 Board 10 **Parking** 12 **Notes** LB ⊗ No children 5yrs No coaches

★★★★ GUEST HOUSE
Torrdarach House
Golf Course Rd PH16 5AU
☎ 01796 472136 📄 01796 472136
e–mail: torrdarach@msn.com

dir: *In town centre. Off A924 Atholl Rd onto Larchwood Rd to top of hill, left, red house on right*

From its elevated location overlooking the Tummel Valley, this impressive, detached Victorian villa stands in a delightful secluded garden, home to a family of red squirrels. The attractive bedrooms are comfortably furnished and well equipped. Delicious, freshly cooked breakfasts are served at individual tables in the ground-floor dining room.

Rooms 7 rms (6 en suite) (1 pri facs) (1 GF) **Facilities** TVB tea/coffee Licensed Cen ht **Parking** 7 **Notes** ⊗ No coaches

★★★★ GUEST HOUSE
Wellwood House
13 West Moulin Rd PH16 5EA
☎ 01796 474288 📄 01796 474299
e–mail: wellwoodhouse@aol.com
web: www.wellwoodhouse.com

dir: *In town centre opp town hall*

Set in lovely grounds on an elevated position overlooking the town, Wellwood House has stunning views of the Vale of Atholl and the surrounding countryside. The comfortably proportioned bedrooms are attractively decorated and well equipped. The elegant lounge has an honesty bar and a fire on cooler evenings, and the spacious dining room is the setting for hearty breakfasts served at individual tables.

Rooms 10 en suite (8 en suite) (2 pri facs) (1 fmly) (1 GF) S £40–£55; D £55–£80✱ **Facilities** FTV TVB tea/coffee Licensed Cen ht TVL Wi-fi available **Parking** 20 **Notes** ⊗ No coaches Closed 22–29 Dec

PAISLEY   MAP 20 NS46

★★★★ 🅰 GUEST HOUSE
Ashtree House
9 Orr Square PA1 2DL
☎ 0141 848 6411 📄 0141 848 6659
e–mail: booking@ashtreehousehotel.com

dir: *M8 junct 27 or 29, follow signs for town centre/museum. After 1.5m turn onto New St, left onto High St, right onto Orr Sq*

Rooms 12 en suite (2 GF) S £50–£60; D £75–£90✱ **Facilities** FTV TVB tea/coffee Direct dial from bedrooms Cen ht TVL Dinner Last d 5pm Wi-fi available **Conf** Max 35 Thtr 35 Class 35 Board 15 Del from £70 ✱ **Parking** 15 **Notes** LB ⊗ No coaches

BROUGHTON   MAP 21 NT13

★★★ 🏠 🍽 GUEST ACCOMMODATION
The Glenholm Centre
ML12 6JF
☎ 01899 830408
e–mail: info@glenholm.co.uk

dir: *1m S of Broughton. Off A701 to Glenholm*

Surrounded by peaceful farmland, this former schoolhouse has a distinct African theme. The home-cooked meals and baking have received much praise and are served in the spacious lounge-dining room. The bright airy bedrooms are thoughtfully equipped, and the service is friendly and attentive. Computer courses are available.

Rooms 3 en suite 1 annexe en suite (1 fmly) (2 GF) S £33–£43; D £54–£66✱ **Facilities** TVB tea/coffee Cen ht TVL Dinner Last d 10am Wi-fi available ⅃ **Conf** Max 24 Thtr 24 Class 24 Board 24 Del from £57 ✱ **Parking** 14 **Notes** LB Closed 20 Dec–1 Feb

CRAILING   MAP 21 NT62

★★★★ 🏠 🍽 GUEST HOUSE
Crailing Old School Guest House
TD8 6TL
☎ 01835 850382
e–mail: jean.player@virgin.net
web: www.crailingoldschool.co.uk

dir: *A698 onto B6400 signed Nisbet, Crailing Old School also signed*

This delightful rural retreat, built in 1887 as the village school, has been imaginatively renovated to combine Victorian features with modern comforts. The spacious bedrooms are beautifully maintained and decorated, and filled with homely extras. The lodge annexe suite located 10 yards from the house offers easier ground-floor access. The best of local produce produces tasty breakfasts, served in the stylish lounge-dining room (evening meals by arrangement).

CONTINUED

Crailing Old School Guest House

Rooms 3 rms (1 en suite) 1 annexe en suite (1 GF) S £37.50–£45;
D £60–£70 **Facilities** TVB tea/coffee Cen ht TVL Dinner Last d 7.30pm
Wi-fi available **Parking** 7 **Notes** No children 9yrs No coaches Closed
24 Dec–2 Jan, 1 wk Feb & 2wks Autumn

EDDLESTON   MAP 21 NT24

★★★★ ◉◉◉ RESTAURANT WITH ROOMS
The Horseshoe Inn
EH45 8QP
☎ 01721 730225 📠 01721 730268
e–mail: reservations@horseshoeinn.co.uk
web: www.horseshoeinn.co.uk

dir: *A703, 5m N of Peebles*

The Horseshoe Inn is five miles north of Peebles and only 18 miles
south of Edinburgh. Originally a blacksmith's shop, it was significantly
refurbished by Vivienne Steele and her partner, Chef Director Patrick
Bardoulet. It is now a restaurant with rooms which has a very good
reputation for fine dining, and a delightful atmosphere. There are eight
bedrooms and ample customer parking to the rear.

CONTINUED

Rooms 8 en suite (1 fmly) (6 GF) S fr £70; D fr £100✱ **Facilities** TVB
tea/coffee Direct dial from bedrooms Cen ht Dinner Last d 9pm (9.30pm
Fri–Sat) Wi-fi available **Parking** 20 **Notes LB** Closed 25 Dec & Mon

---

GALASHIELS   MAP 21 NT43

★★ FARM HOUSE
Over Langshaw *(NT524400)*
Langshaw TD1 2PE
☎ 01896 860244 📠 01896 860668 Mrs S Bergius
e–mail: overlangshaw@btconnect.com

dir: *3m N of Galashiels. A7 N from Galashiels, 1m right signed
Langshaw, right at T-junct into Langshaw, left signed Earlston,
Over Langshaw 1m, signed*

There are fine panoramic views from this organic hillside farm. It offers
two comfortable and spacious bedrooms. Hearty breakfasts are
provided at individual tables in the lounge and a friendly welcome is
guaranteed.

Rooms 2 en suite (1 fmly) (1 GF) S £35–£40; D £64–£72 **Facilities** tea/
coffee Cen ht TVL **Parking** 4 **Notes** 500 acres dairy/sheep/organic ◉

HAWICK   MAP 21 NT51

★★★ ⒶRESTAURANT WITH ROOMS
Mosspaul
Teviothead TD9 0LP
☎ 01450 850245 📠 01450 850631
e–mail: mosspaulinn@aol.com

dir: *Immediately adjacent to A7. 10m N of Langholm*

Rooms 5 en suite (1 fmly) (1 GF) S £37.50; D £59.50–£79.50✱
Facilities TVB tea/coffee Cen ht TVL Dinner Last d 8.30pm Sauna
Conf Max 30 Thtr 30 Class 20 Board 18 **Parking** 30 **Notes LB** Closed
1–24 Jan

JEDBURGH   MAP 21 NT62

★★★★ GUEST ACCOMMODATION
Allerton House
Oxnam Rd TD8 6QQ
☎ 01835 869633 📠 01835 869885
e–mail: info@allertonhouse.co.uk

dir: *Off A68 bypass onto Oxnam Rd at Laidlaw Memorial
Swimming pool, 200mtrs on right*

Set in gardens within a quiet residential area a short walk from the
town centre, this fine Georgian house has been refurbished in a bright
contemporary style. Smart bedrooms include DVD players, mini-bars
and internet access. An attractive lounge-dining room provides daily
papers and enjoyable breakfasts. Service is truly friendly.

Rooms 6 en suite (1 fmly) (2 GF) S £37.50–£42.50; D £75–£85✱
Facilities STV TVB tea/coffee Cen ht Dinner Last d 9pm Wi-fi available
Complimentary use of local swimming pool **Conf** Max 20 **Parking** 7
Notes ⊗

SCOTLAND

JEDBURGH CONTINUED

★★ GUEST HOUSE
Ferniehirst Mill Lodge

TD8 6PQ
☎ 01835 863279
e–mail: ferniehirstmill@aol.com
web: www.ferniehirstmill.co.uk

dir: *2.5m S on A68, onto private track to end*

Reached by a narrow farm track and a rustic wooden bridge, this chalet-style house has a secluded setting by the River Jed. Bedrooms are small and functional but there is a comfortable lounge in which to relax. Home-cooked dinners are available by arrangement, and hearty breakfasts are served in the cosy dining room.

Rooms 7 en suite (1 GF) S £22–£27; D £44–£54 **Facilities** tea/coffee Direct dial from bedrooms Licensed Cen ht TVL Dinner Last d 5pm Fishing Riding **Parking** 10 **Notes** No coaches

---

LAUDER   MAP 21 NT54

★★★★ 🏚 🍴 INN
The Black Bull

Market Place TD2 6SR
☎ 01578 722208 📄 01578 722419
e–mail: enquiries@blackbull-lauder.com
web: www.blackbull-lauder.com

dir: *On A68 in village centre*

This 18th-century coaching inn has been completely transformed. The lovely bedrooms are furnished in the period character and thoughtfully equipped with modern amenities. All with wooden floors, the cosy bar and four dining areas are charming, the main dining room being a former chapel. A tremendous range of food makes this a destination gastro-pub.

Rooms 8 en suite (2 fmly) **Facilities** TVB tea/coffee Direct dial from bedrooms Cen ht Dinner Last d 9pm **Conf** Max 40 **Parking** 8 **Notes** Closed 1st 3 wks of Feb Civ Wed 40

MELROSE   MAP 21 NT53

GUEST ACCOMMODATON OF THE YEAR FOR SCOTLAND
Premier Collection

★★★★★ 🏚 GUEST HOUSE
Fauhope House

Gattonside TD6 9LU
☎ 01896 823184 📄 01896 823184
e–mail: fauhope@bordernet.co.uk

dir: *0.7m N of Melrose over River Tweed. N off B6360 at Gattonside 30mph sign (E) up long driveway*

It's hard to imagine a more complete experience than a stay at Fauhope, set high on a hillside on the north-east edge of the village. Hospitality is first class, breakfasts are excellent, and the delightful country house has a splendid interior. Bedrooms are

CONTINUED

---

luxurious, each individual and superbly equipped. Public areas are elegantly decorated and furnished, and enhanced by beautiful floral arrangements; the dining room is particularly stunning.

Fauhope House

Rooms 3 en suite S fr £60; D £80–£100✱ **Facilities** TVB tea/coffee Cen ht Dinner Last d 7.30pm 🐎 Riding **Parking** 10 **Notes LB** ⊗ No coaches

---

SWINTON   MAP 21 NT84

★★★★ ◉◉ RESTAURANT WITH ROOMS
Wheatsheaf at Swinton

TD11 3JJ
☎ 01890 860257 📄 01890 860688
e–mail: reception@wheatsheaf-swinton.co.uk

dir: *In village centre on A6112*

Overlooking the village green, this restaurant with rooms has built its reputation on excellent food. Bedrooms are stylishly furnished, all with smart en suite facilities, the largest ones featuring a bath and separate shower cubicle. Recently added executive bedrooms are of a very high standard.

Rooms 10 en suite (2 fmly) (1 GF) S £71–£99; D £108–£144✱ **Facilities** FTV TVB tea/coffee Direct dial from bedrooms Cen ht Dinner Last d 9pm Wi-fi available **Conf** Max 18 Thtr 18 Class 18 Board 12 **Parking** 7 **Notes LB** ⊗ Closed 25–27 Dec, 31 Jan Civ Wed 50

SOUTH AYRSHIRE

AYR   MAP 20 NS32

See also Dunure

Premier Collection

★★★★★ GUEST HOUSE
The Crescent

26 Bellevue Crescent KA7 2DR
☎ 01292 287329
e–mail: carrie@26crescent.freeserve.co.uk
web: www.26crescent.freeserve.co.uk

dir: *Leave A79 onto rdbt, 3rd exit onto King St. Left onto Bellevue Crescent*

Located in a quiet residential area of Ayr, close to the seafront, town centre and race course. This guest house offers a traditional warm

CONTINUED

welcome with well appointed and comfortable bedrooms. Bathrooms are of a high standard, as is the hearty breakfast served on individual tables in the charming dining room.

The Crescent

Rooms 4 en suite S £45–£55; D £60–£65✳ **Facilities** FTV TVB tea/coffee Cen ht Wi-fi available **Notes LB** ☒ No coaches

★★★★ GUEST HOUSE
Daviot House

12 Queens Ter KA7 1DU

☎ 01292 269678

e–mail: daviothouse@hotmail.com

web: www.daviothouse.com

dir: *Off A719 onto Wellington Sq & Bath Place, turn right*

This well-maintained Victorian house stands in a peaceful location close to the beach and town centre. Bedrooms are modern in style and well equipped. Hearty breakfasts are served in the dining room. A member of Golf South Ayrshire Hoteliers golf booking service for local municipal courses.

Rooms 5 rms (4 en suite) (1 pri facs) (1 fmly) S £35–£45; D £50–£60✳ **Facilities** FTV TVB tea/coffee Cen ht **Notes** ☒ No children No coaches

★★★★ BED & BREAKFAST
Greenan Lodge

39 Dunure, Doonfoot KA7 4HR

☎ 01292 443939

e–mail: helen@greenanlodge.com

dir: *2m S of town centre on A719 coastal road*

Guests are made to feel truly welcome at this modern bungalow in a quiet residential area, convenient for the coast and attractions around Ayr. The bright, well-furnished bedrooms offer numerous extras and there is a spacious lounge. Expect a generous Scottish breakfast.

Rooms 3 en suite (3 GF) **Facilities** TVB tea/coffee Cen ht TVL **Parking** 10 **Notes** No children 7yrs ☺

DUNURE   **MAP 20 NS21**

★★★★ FARM HOUSE
Dunduff *(NS265160)*

Dunure KA7 4LH

☎ 01292 500225 🖷 01292 500222 Mrs A Gemmell

e–mail: gemmelldunduff@aol.com

dir: *On A719 400yds past village school*

Parts of this working farm date from the 15th and 17th centuries. It stands on an elevated position with stunning views across the Firth of the Clyde towards Arran and the Mull of Kintyre. Bedrooms are comfortable and well-equipped, with a comfortable lounge enhancing the home away from home feel. Expect genuine Scottish hospitality, and breakfast specialities including locally smoked kippers.

Rooms 3 rms (2 en suite) (1 pri facs) (2 fmly) **Facilities** TVB tea/coffee Cen ht TVL Fishing **Parking** 10 **Notes** ☒ 600 acres beef sheep Closed Nov–Feb

MAYBOLE

MAP 20 NS20

Premier Collection

★★★★★ 🏠 🍴 GUEST ACCOMMODATION

Ladyburn

KA19 7SG

☎ 01655 740585 📠 01655 740580

e–mail: jh@ladyburn.co.uk

dir: *A77 (Glasgow/Stranraer) at Maybole turn to B7023 to Crosshill and right at War Memorial. In 2m turn left for approx 1m on right*

This charming country house is the home of the Hepburn family, who take great pride in the warmth of their welcome. Sitting in open countryside with attractive gardens, it's a great place to come to relax. Classically styled bedrooms, two with four-poster beds, offer every comfort and are complemented by the library and the drawing room. Dinner comprises a carefully cooked three course set menu, and is served in a gracious candlelit setting.

Rooms 5 en suite **Facilities** tea/coffee Direct dial from bedrooms 🐾 **Parking** 12 **Notes** ⊗

SOUTH LANARKSHIRE

STRATHAVEN

MAP 20 NS74

★★★ 🏵 RESTAURANT WITH ROOMS

Rissons at Springvale

18 Lethame Rd ML10 6AD

☎ 01357 521131 & 520234 📠 01357 521131

e–mail: rissons@msn.com

dir: *A71 into Strathaven, W of town centre off Townhead St*

You are assured of a warm welcome at this charming establishment close to the town centre. The bedrooms and bathrooms are stylish and well-equipped. Food, though, is the main feature, and a range of interesting, well-prepared dishes is served in Rissons Restaurant.

Rooms 11 en suite (1 fmly) (2 GF) S £40–£55; D £70✳ **Facilities** TVB tea/coffee Cen ht Dinner Last d 9.30pm Wi-fi available **Parking** 10 **Notes** ⊗ Closed 1st wk Jan

STIRLING

BALMAHA

MAP 20 NS49

★★★ INN

Oak Tree Inn

G63 0JQ

☎ 01360 870357 📠 01360 870350

e–mail: info@oak-tree-inn.co.uk

dir: *A811 onto B837 to Balmaha village*

Standing in the shade of a magnificent 500-year-old oak tree on the quiet eastern shore of Loch Lomond, this friendly family-run inn is a great base for exploring the surrounding countryside. The attractive

CONTINUED

bedrooms have been refurbished to a high standard and are individually styled and well equipped. The rustic bar is complete with beams, a roaring log fire and local memorabilia, while the dining room serves delicious home-cooked fare.

Oak Tree Inn

Rooms 8 en suite (1 fmly) S £75; D £75✳ **Facilities** TVB tea/coffee Cen ht Dinner Last d 8.45pm **Parking** 6 **Notes** ⊗ No coaches Closed 25 Dec, 1 Jan

CALLANDER

MAP 20 NN60

★★★★ 🏠 GUEST ACCOMMODATION

Arden House

Bracklinn Rd FK17 8EQ

☎ 01877 330235

e–mail: ardenhouse@onetel.com

dir: *Off A84 Main St onto Bracklinn Rd, house 200yds on left*

This impressive Victorian villa lies in beautiful mature grounds in a peaceful area of the town. It featured in the 1960s hit television series *Dr Finlay's Casebook* and is a friendly, welcoming house. The comfortable bedrooms are thoughtfully furnished and equipped. There is a stylish lounge in addition to the attractive breakfast room where delicious breakfasts are served at individual tables. Ian and William were runners up for the AA Friendliest Landlady of the Year Award 2008.

Rooms 6 en suite (2 GF) S fr £37.50; D £70–£80✳ **Facilities** TVB tea/coffee Cen ht Wi-fi available 🛗 **Parking** 10 **Notes** ⊗ No children 14yrs Closed Nov–Mar

★★★★ GUEST HOUSE

Lubnaig House

Leny Feus FK17 8AS

☎ 01877 330376

e–mail: info@lubnaighouse.co.uk

web: www.lubnaighouse.co.uk

dir: *From centre A84 W, right onto Leny Feus, located after Poppies Hotel*

Lubnaig House is set in a delightful tree-lined secluded garden just a 5-minute walk from the town centre. The house, built in 1864, has been modernised to provide comfortable well-appointed bedrooms. There are two cosy lounges, and an impressive dining room where hearty traditional breakfasts are served at individual tables.

Rooms 6 en suite 2 annexe en suite S £45–£55; D £72–£78✳
Facilities TVB tea/coffee Cen ht Wi-fi available **Parking** 10 **Notes LB** ⊗
No children 7yrs No coaches Closed Nov–Apr

★★★★ GUEST HOUSE

Annfield Guest House

18 North Church St FK17 8EG

☎ 01877 330204 🖻 01877 330674

e–mail: reservations@annfieldguesthouse.co.uk

dir: *Off A84 Main St onto North Church St, at top on right*

Situated within easy reach of the town centre, this welcoming guest house offers comfortable, good-value accommodation. The spacious bedrooms are attractively decorated and well equipped. An elegant first-floor lounge is ideal for relaxation, and hearty breakfasts are served at individual tables in the pretty dining room. Self-catering accommodation is also available.

Rooms 7 rms (4 en suite) (1 pri facs) (1 fmly) S £30–£40; D £55–£65
Facilities TVB tea/coffee Cen ht Wi-fi available **Parking** 7 **Notes LB** ⊗
No children 6yrs No coaches Closed Xmas & New Year ⊛

★★★★ ⊛ RESTAURANT WITH ROOMS

Callander Meadows

24 Main St FK17 8BB

☎ 01877 330181

e–mail: mail@callandermeadows.co.uk

web: www.callandermeadows.co.uk

dir: *M9 junct 10 onto A84 to Callander, on main street just past A81 junct*

Located on the high street in Callender, this family-run business offers comfortable accommodation and a restaurant that has quickly become

very popular with the locals. Private parking is available to the rear, and out of the three bedrooms, two have been refurbished to a very high standard.

Callander Meadows

Rooms 3 en suite D £60–£70✳ **Facilities** TVB tea/coffee Cen ht Dinner
Parking 4 **Notes** ⊗ RS Winter

CRIANLARICH MAP 20 NN32

★★★★ GUEST HOUSE

The Lodge House

FK20 8RU

☎ 01838 300276

e–mail: admin@lodgehouse.co.uk

dir: *From Crianlarich village follow A82 N, Lodge House 1m on right*

The Lodge House benefits from a peaceful location with picture postcard views of the surrounding countryside including Ben More. Bedrooms are comfortable and well equipped, with Wi-fi facilities available. Dinner is available by prior arrangement. A range of therapies are also available by appointment including aromatherapy and reflexology.

Rooms 3 en suite 1 annexe en suite (1 fmly) (1 GF) S £30–£45;
D £60–£75 **Facilities** TVB tea/coffee Licensed TVL Dinner Last d 11am
Wi-fi available **Parking** 5 **Notes** ⊗ No coaches

CONTINUED

LOCHEARNHEAD MAP 20 NN52

★★★★ GUEST HOUSE
Mansewood Country House
FK19 8NS
☎ 01567 830213
e–mail: stay@mansewoodcountryhouse.co.uk
dir: A84 N to Lochearnhead, 1st building on left

Mansewood Country House is a spacious former manse that dates back to the 18th century and lies in a well-tended garden to the south of the village. Bedrooms are well appointed and equipped and offer high standards of comfort. Refreshments can be enjoyed in the cosy bar or the elegant lounge, and meals prepared with flair are served in the attractive restaurant. There is also a log cabin where pets are allowed.

Rooms 6 en suite (1 GF) S £40; D £60✱ **Facilities** TVB tea/coffee Licensed Cen ht TVL Dinner Last d 7.15pm Wi-fi available **Parking** 6 **Notes LB** ⊛ No coaches RS Nov–Mar

★★★★ BED & BREAKFAST
Tigh Na Crich
FK19 8PR
☎ 01567 830235
e–mail: johntippett2@aol.com
web: www.tighnacrich.co.uk
dir: On junct of A84 & A85, next to village shop

Located in the heart of the small village of Lochearnhead and surrounded by mountains on three sides and Loch Earn on the fourth. Very well presented accommodation with many thoughtful extras provided. The generous breakfast is served in the comfortable dining room on individual tables looking out to the front of the property.

Rooms 3 en suite D £52–£55✱ **Facilities** TVB tea/coffee Cen ht **Parking** 3 **Notes** ⊛

STIRLING MAP 21 NS79

★★★★ GUEST HOUSE
Linden Guest House
22 Linden Av FK7 7PQ
☎ 01786 448850 & 07974 116573 ▤ 01786 448850
e–mail: fay@lindenguesthouse.co.uk
web: www.lindenguesthouse.co.uk
dir: 0.5m SE of city centre off A9

Situated within walking distance of the town centre, this friendly guest house offers attractive and very well-equipped bedrooms, including a large family room that sleeps five comfortably. There is a bright dining room where delicious breakfasts are served at individual tables with quality Wedgwood crockery.

Rooms 4 en suite (2 fmly) (1 GF) S £50–£60; D £60–£70✱ **Facilities** STV TVB tea/coffee Cen ht Wi-fi available **Parking** 2 **Notes LB** No coaches

STRATHYRE MAP 20 NN51

Premier Collection

★★★★★ ⊛⊛ RESTAURANT WITH ROOMS
Creagan House
FK18 8ND
☎ 01877 384638 ▤ 01877 384319
e–mail: eatandstay@creaganhouse.co.uk
web: www.creaganhouse.co.uk
dir: 0.25m N of Strathyre on A84

Originally a farmhouse dating from the 17th century, Creagan House has operated as a restaurant with rooms for many years. The baronial-style dining room provides a wonderful setting for sympathetic cooking. Warm hospitality and attentive service are the highlights of any stay.

Rooms 5 en suite (1 fmly) (1 GF) S £70–£85; D £120–£130 **Facilities** FTV TVB tea/coffee Cen ht Dinner Last d 8.30pm **Conf** Max 35 Thtr 35 Class 12 Board 35 **Parking** 26 **Notes LB** Closed 21 Jan–5 Mar & 1–19 Nov RS Wed & Thu

WEST DUNBARTONSHIRE

BALLOCH   MAP 20 NS38

★★★ BED & BREAKFAST
Sunnyside
35 Main St G83 9JX
☎ 01389 750282 & 07717 397548
e–mail: enquiries@sunnysidebb.co.uk
dir: *From A82 take A811 then A813 for 1m, over mini-rdbt 150mtrs on left*

Set in its own grounds well back from the road by Loch Lomond, Sunnyside is an attractive, traditional detached house, parts of which date back to the 1830s. Bedrooms are attractively decorated and provide comfortable modern accommodation. The dining room is located on the ground floor, and is an appropriate setting for hearty Scottish breakfasts.

Rooms 6 en suite (2 fmly) (1 GF) S £25–£40; D £40–£60✱
Facilities TVB tea/coffee Cen ht **Parking** 8

DUMBARTON   MAP 20 NS37

*See **Cardross (Argyll & Bute)***

WEST LOTHIAN

BLACKBURN   MAP 21 NS96

★★★ GUEST ACCOMMODATION
Cruachan B & B
78 East Main St EH47 7QS
☎ 01506 655221 ▤ 01506 652395
e–mail: enquiries@cruachan.co.uk
web: www.cruachan.co.uk
dir: *On A705 in Blackburn, 1m from M8 junct 4*

Ideally located for both the leisure and business traveller to central Scotland, with Edinburgh's city centre only some 30 minutes away by train from nearby Bathgate and Glasgow only 35 minutes away by car. Cruachan is the comfortable, friendly home of the Harkins family. Bedrooms are bright, attractive and very well equipped. Breakfast, featuring the best of local produce is served at individual tables in the ground-floor dining room.

Rooms 4 rms (3 en suite) (1 pri facs) (1 fmly) S £40–£60; D £60–£70
Facilities FTV TVB tea/coffee Cen ht Wi-fi available **Parking** 5 **Notes** ✪

EAST CALDER   MAP 21 NT06

Premier Collection

★★★★★ GUEST HOUSE
Ashcroft Farmhouse
EH53 0ET
☎ 01506 881810 ▤ 01506 884327
e–mail: scottashcroft7@aol.com
web: www.ashcroftfarmhouse.com
dir: *On B7015, off A71, 0.5m E of East Calder, near to Almondell Country Park*

With over 40 years' experience in caring for guests, Derek and Elizabeth Scott ensure a stay at Ashcroft will be memorable. Their modern home sits in lovely award-winning landscaped gardens and provides attractive and well-equipped ground-floor bedrooms. The comfortable lounge includes a video and DVD library. Breakfast, featuring home-made sausages and the best of local produce, is served at individual tables in the stylish dining room. Free Wi-fi is now available, and a Park & Ride facility is nearby.

Rooms 6 en suite (2 fmly) (6 GF) D £70–£80✱ **Facilities** TVB tea/coffee Cen ht TVL Wi-fi available **Parking** 8 **Notes** ✪ No children 12yrs No coaches

See advert on page 653

SCOTLAND

SCOTLAND

EAST CALDER CONTINUED

★★★★ BED & BREAKFAST
Whitecroft

7 Raw Holdings EH53 0ET
☎ 01506 882494 📄 01506 882598
e-mail: lornascot@aol.com
dir: *A71 onto B7015, establishment on right*

A relaxed and friendly atmosphere prevails at this charming modern guest house. The bedrooms, all of which are on the ground floor, are attractively colour coordinated, well-equipped and contain many thoughtful extra touches. Breakfast is served at individual tables in the smart dining room.

Rooms 3 en suite S £40–£50; D £60–£70✱ **Facilities** TVB tea/coffee Cen ht Wi-fi available **Parking** 5 **Notes** ⊗ No children 12yrs

---

LINLITHGOW   MAP 21 NS97

Premier Collection

★★★★★ 🍴 GUEST ACCOMMODATION
Arden Country House

Belsyde EH49 6QE
☎ 01506 670172 📄 01506 670172
e-mail: info@ardencountryhouse.com
dir: *1.3m SW of Linlithgow. A706 over Union Canal, entrance 200yds on left at Lodge Cottage*

Situated in the picturesque grounds of the Belsyde Country Estate and close to the Royal Burgh of Linlithgow, Arden Country House offers immaculate, stylishly furnished and spacious bedrooms. There is a cosy ground-floor lounge and a charming dining room where delicious breakfasts feature the best of local produce. Beth Cruickshank was a finalist for the AA Friendliest Landlady of the Year 2008 Award.

Rooms 3 en suite (1 GF) S £48–£80; D £76–£100 **Facilities** TVB tea/coffee Cen ht Wi-fi available **Parking** 4 **Notes LB** ⊗ No children 12yrs Closed 25–26 Dec

★★★★ GUEST ACCOMMODATION
Belsyde House

Lanark Rd EH49 6QE
☎ 01506 842098 📄 01506 842098
e-mail: hay@belsydehouse.co.uk
web: www.belsydehouse.co.uk
dir: *1.5m SW on A706, 1st left over Union Canal*

Reached by a tree-lined driveway, this welcoming farmhouse is peacefully situated in attractive grounds close to the Union Canal. There are well-proportioned double, twin and family rooms, and a cosy single. All are nicely furnished and well equipped. Breakfast, including a vegetarian menu, is served at good-sized tables in the dining room, next to the lounge.

Rooms 3 rms (1 en suite) (1 fmly) **Facilities** TVB tea/coffee Cen ht TVL Wi-fi available **Parking** 10 **Notes** ⊗ Closed Xmas

★★★★ GUEST HOUSE
Bomains Farm

Bo'Ness EH49 7RQ
☎ 01506 822188 & 822861 📄 01506 824433
e-mail: bunty.kirk@onetel.net
web: www.bomains.co.uk
dir: *A706 1.5m N towards Bo Ness, left at golf course x-rds, 1st farm on right*

From its elevated location this friendly farmhouse has stunning views of the Firth of Forth. The bedrooms which vary in size are beautifully decorated, well equipped and enhanced by quality fabrics, with many thoughtful extra touches. Delicious home-cooked fare featuring the best of local produce is served a stylish lounge-dining room.

CONTINUED

Edinburgh and Glasgow this friendly family home offers spotless, comfortable and stylish accommodation in a relaxed environment. Bedrooms are attractive and well equipped with two situated on the ground floor. Hearty breakfasts are served in the smart dining room.

Rooms 3 en suite (2 GF) **Facilities** TVB tea/coffee Cen ht Wi-fi available **Parking** 6 **Notes** ✷ 🅿

Bomains Farm

Rooms 5 rms (4 en suite) (1 pri facs) S £35–£40; D £50–£70
Facilities STV TVB tea/coffee Cen ht TVL Dinner Last d 5.30pm Golf 18
Parking 12 **Notes** No coaches

★★★★ BED & BREAKFAST
Whitecroft
7 Raw Holdings EH53 0ET
☎ 01506 882494 📄 01506 882598
e–mail: lornascot@aol.com
(For full entry see East Calder)

LIVINGSTON   MAP 21 NT06

★★★★ BED & BREAKFAST
Redcraig
Redcraig, Midcalder EH53 0JT
☎ 01506 884249 📄 01506 884249
e–mail: jcampbelljack@aol.com
web: www.redcraigbedandbreakfast.co.uk
dir: *Off A71, take road for Morton between Lizzie Brice rdbt (Livingston) and Kirknewton T-lights*

Enjoying a peaceful location within easy reach of central Scotland's major motorway and rail network, and situated half way between

CONTINUED

SCOTTISH ISLANDS
ARRAN, ISLE OF

BRODICK   MAP 20 NS03

★★★★ GUEST HOUSE
Allandale
KA27 8BJ
☎ 01770 302278
e–mail: info@allandalehouse.co.uk
dir: *500yds S of Brodick Pier, off A841 towards Lamlash, up hill 2nd left at Corriegills sign*

Under enthusiastic ownership, this comfortable guest house is set in delightful gardens in beautiful countryside. Guests can relax in the lounge with its attractive garden views. Bedrooms vary in size and have pleasing colour schemes and mixed modern furnishings along with thoughtful amenities. In a peaceful location, Allandale is convenient for the CalMac Ferry and Brodick centre.

Rooms 4 rms (3 en suite) (1 pri facs) 2 annexe en suite (3 fmly) (2 GF) S £45; D £68–£74✷ **Facilities** FTV TVB tea/coffee Cen ht **Parking** 6 **Notes LB** ✷ No coaches Closed Nov–Feb

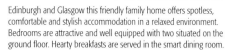

BRODICK CONTINUED

★★★★ GUEST HOUSE
Dunvegan House

Dunvegan Shore Rd KA27 8AJ

☎ 01770 302811 📄 01770 302811

e–mail: dunveganhouse1@hotmail.com

dir: *Turn right from ferry terminal, 500yds along Shore Rd*

Dunvegan is a delightful detached home overlooking the bay towards Brodick Castle with Goat Fell beyond. The comfortable lounge and attractive dining room, as well as the pine-furnished bedrooms, enjoy the views. A daily-changing dinner menu and an interesting wine list encourage guests to dine in.

Rooms 9 en suite (1 fmly) (3 GF) S £50; D £80✱ **Facilities** TVB tea/coffee Licensed Cen ht Dinner Last d 4pm **Parking** 10 **Notes** ⊗ No coaches Closed Xmas & New Year 🐾

HARRIS, ISLE OF

SCARISTA   **MAP 22 NG09**

★★★★ ⊛⊛ RESTAURANT WITH ROOMS
Scarista House

HS3 3HX

☎ 01859 550238 📄 01859 550277

e–mail: timandpatricia@scaristahouse.com

dir: *On A859, 15m S of Tarbert*

A former manse, Scarista House is now a haven for food lovers who seek to explore the magnificent island of Harris. The house enjoys breathtaking views of the Atlantic and is just a short stroll from miles of golden sandy beaches. The house is run in a relaxed country-house manner by the friendly hosts. Expect wellies in the hall and masses of books and CDs in one of two lounges. Bedrooms are cosy, and delicious set dinners and memorable breakfasts are provided.

Rooms 3 en suite 2 annexe en suite (2 GF) S £125–£150; D £175–£199 **Facilities** tea/coffee Direct dial from bedrooms Cen ht Dinner Last d 8pm **Parking** 12 **Notes LB** Closed Xmas, Jan & Feb Civ Wed 40

ISLAY, ISLE OF

BOWMORE   **MAP 20 NR35**

Premier Collection

★★★★★ ⊛⊛ RESTAURANT WITH ROOMS
The Harbour Inn and Restaurant

PA43 7JR

☎ 01496 810330 📄 01496 810990

e–mail: info@harbour.inn.com

dir: *Next to harbour*

No trip to Islay would be complete without experiencing a night or two at the Harbour Inn. The humble whitewashed exterior conceals a sophisticated, quality environment that draws discerning travellers from all over the world. Spacious bedrooms are appointed to a high standard and the conservatory-lounge has stunning views over Loch

Indaal to the peaks of Jura. The cosy bar is popular with locals, while the smart dining room showcases some of the finest seafood in British waters. Welcome peat fires burn in cooler months.

Rooms 7 en suite (1 GF) **Facilities** TVB tea/coffee Direct dial from bedrooms Dinner Last d 9pm Complimentary use of local leisure centre **Notes** ⊗ No children 10yrs

SHETLAND

LERWICK   **MAP 24 HU44**

★★★★ GUEST HOUSE
Glen Orchy House

20 Knab Rd ZE1 0AX

☎ 01595 692031 📄 01595 692031

e–mail: glenorchy.house@virgin.net

dir: *Next to coastguard station*

This welcoming and well-presented house lies above the town with views over the Knab, and is within easy walking distance of the town centre. Bedrooms are modern in design and there is a choice of lounges with books and board games, one with an honesty bar. Substantial breakfasts are served, and the restaurant offers a delicious Thai menu.

Rooms 24 en suite (4 fmly) (4 GF) **Facilities** STV FTV TVB tea/coffee Licensed Cen ht TVL Dinner Last d 9pm Wi-fi available **Parking** 10 **Notes** No coaches

SKYE, ISLE OF

DUNVEGAN   **MAP 22 NG24**

Ⓤ
Roskhill House

Roskhill IV55 8ZD

☎ 01470 521317

e–mail: stay@roskhillhouse.co.uk

web: www.roskhillhouse.co.uk

dir: *3m S of Dunvegan off A836 Dunvegan*

At the time of going to press the rating for this establishment had not been confirmed. Please check the AA website www.theAA.com for up-to-date information.

Rooms 5 en suite (2 GF) S £50; D £60–£74✱ **Facilities** tea/coffee Cen ht TVL Dinner Last d 9.30am Wi-fi available **Parking** 6 **Notes** No children 7yrs Closed Nov–mid Mar

CONTINUED

EDINBANE MAP 22 NG35

★ ★ ★ ★ 🏠 GUEST ACCOMMODATION

Shorefield House

Edinbane IV51 9PW

☎ 01470 582444 📄 01470 582414

e–mail: shorefieldhouse@aol.com

dir: *12m from Portree & 8m from Dunvegan, off A850 into Edinbane, 1st on right*

Shorefield stands in the village of Edinbane and looks out to Loch Greshornish. Bedrooms range from single to family, while a ground-floor room has easier access. All rooms are thoughtfully equipped and have CD players. Breakfast is an impressive choice and there is also a child-friendly garden.

Rooms 4 en suite (1 fmly) (3 GF) D £74–£90 **Facilities** TV2B tea/coffee Cen ht TVL **Parking** 10 **Notes** ⊗ Closed Oct–Etr

---

PORTREE MAP 22 NG44

★ ★ ★ ★ BED & BREAKFAST

'Medina'

Coolin Hills Gardens IV51 9NB

☎ 01478 612821

e–mail: medinaskye@yahoo.co.uk

web: www.medinaskye.co.uk

dir: *From Portree centre, A855 to Staffin, at large sign for Cullin Hills Hotel turn right, then at second large sign turn hard left up hill*

A delightful bungalow quietly located in a small residential development in the former walled gardens of the Cuillin Hills Hotel. The two ground floor bedrooms are spacious, comfortable and well equipped, and guests also have the use of an elegant and comfortable lounge, where breakfast is served around a communal table.

Rooms 2 en suite (2 GF) D £64–£72✱ **Facilities** TVB tea/coffee Cen ht TVL **Parking** 2 **Notes** ⊗ No children 14yrs Closed Nov–Feb ⊛

STRUAN MAP 22 NG33

Premier Collection

★ ★ ★ ★ ★ ★ ◉◉◉ 🏠
RESTAURANT WITH ROOMS

Ullinish Country Lodge

IV56 8FD

☎ 01470 572214 📄 01470 572341

e–mail: ullinish@theisleofskye.co.uk

dir: *N on A863*

Set in some of Scotland's most dramatic landscape, with views of the Black Cuillin and MacLeod's Tables, Ullinish Country Lodge has lochs on three sides. Samuel Johnson and James Boswell stayed here in 1773 and were impressed with the hospitality even then! Hosts Brian and Pam hope to extend the same welcome to their guests today. As you would expect, all bedrooms have amazing views, and come with half-tester beds. The restaurant's offerings are very impressive.

Rooms 6 en suite S £90–£120; D £120–£160✱ **Facilities** TVB tea/coffee Cen ht Dinner Last d 8.30pm **Parking** 8 **Notes LB** ⊗ No children 16yrs Closed Jan & 1 wk Nov

---

UIG MAP 22 NG36

🅄

Woodbine House

IV51 9XP

☎ 01470 542243 📄 01470 542243

e–mail: contact@skyeactivities.co.uk

dir: *From Portree into Uig Bay, pass Ferry Inn & right onto A855 Staffin Rd, house 300yds on right*

At the time of going to press the rating for this establishment had not been confirmed. Please check the AA website www.theAA.com for up-to-date information.

Rooms 4 en suite (1 fmly) S £25–£59; D £50–£59✱ **Facilities** TVB tea/coffee Cen ht Dinner Last d 3pm Wi-fi available Archery, Mountain bike/sea kayak hire & boat trips **Parking** 4 **Notes LB**

Wales
Snowdonia National Park

ANGLESEY, ISLE OF

BEAUMARIS   MAP 14 SH67

Premier Collection

★★★★★ ◉◉ INN
Ye Olde Bulls Head Inn

Castle St LL58 8AP
☎ 01248 810329 🖷 01248 811294
e–mail: info@bullsheadinn.co.uk

Charles Dickens and Samuel Johnson were regular visitors to this inn
which features exposed beams and antique weaponry. Richly
decorated bedrooms are well equipped and there is a spacious lounge.
Meetings and small functions are catered for and food continues to
attract praise in both The Loft restaurant and the less formal brasserie.
New for 2008 is a sympathetic renovation of an adjacent period
property to provide additional quality accommodation in contemporary
style.

Rooms 12 en suite 1 annexe en suite (2 GF) **Facilities** TVB tea/coffee
Direct dial from bedrooms Wi-fi available **Conf** Max 16 Board 16
Parking 10 **Notes** ⊗

CEMAES BAY   MAP 14 SH39

★★★★ BED & BREAKFAST
Hafod Country House

LL67 0DS
☎ 01407 711645
e–mail: hbr1946@aol.com

dir: 0.5m S of Cemaes. Off A5025 Cemaes rdbt signed
Llanfechell, Hafod 500yds on left

Guests are assured of a warm welcome at this large and spacious
Edwardian house, which stands in extensive gardens and is quietly
located on the outskirts of the village. It provides well equipped
accommodation, as well as a comfortable lounge and a pleasant
breakfast room, where separate tables are provided.

Rooms 3 en suite S £35–£40; D £60–£65✱ **Facilities** TVB tea/coffee
Cen ht **Parking** 3 **Notes** ⊗ No children 7yrs Closed Oct–Mar

HOLYHEAD   MAP 14 SH28

★★ GUEST HOUSE
Wavecrest

93 Newry St LL65 1HU
☎ 01407 763637 🖷 01407 764862
e–mail: cwavecrest@aol.com
web: www.holyheadhotels.com

dir: Left at end A55, 600yds turn by railings, premises 100yds up
hill on right

Well located for the Irish ferry terminals and within easy walking
distance of the town centre, the Wavecrest is proving to be a popular
overnight stop-off. Pretty bedrooms are equipped with satellite
television and other modern facilities. There is a comfortable lounge
and evening meals may be booked in advance.   *CONTINUED*

Rooms 4 rms (2 en suite) (3 fmly) **Facilities** STV TVB tea/coffee Cen ht
TVL Dinner Last d 3pm **Parking** 1 **Notes** No coaches Closed 24–31 Dec
⊗

LLANERCHYMEDD   MAP 14 SH48

★★★★ FARM HOUSE
Tre-Wyn (SH454851)

Maenaddwyn LL71 8AE
☎ 01248 470875 Mrs N Bown
e–mail: nia@trewyn.fsnet.co.uk

dir: A5025 to Benllech Bay, B5108 to Brynteg x-rds, take
Llannerchymedd road 3m to Maenaddwyn. Right after 6 houses,
0.5m to farm

An extremely friendly welcome is extended at this spacious farmhouse.
Rooms are well equipped and attractively furnished. The dining room
and the relaxing lounge with its log fire have wonderful views across
the gardens and countryside to Bodafon Mountain.

Rooms 3 en suite (1 fmly) **Facilities** TVB tea/coffee Cen ht TVL
Parking 5 **Notes** ⊗ 240 acres arable beef sheep

LLANGEFNI   MAP 14 SH47

★★★★ INN
Bull

Bulkley Square LL77 7LR
☎ 01248 722119 🖷 01248 750488
e–mail: bull@welsh-historic-inns.com
web: www.welsh-historic-inns.com

dir: 5 mins from A55 junct 6

This town centre hostelry was built in 1817, and provides well-
equipped, tastefully furnished accommodation both in the main
building and the annexe, including a room with a four-poster bed and
a family room. Public areas offer a choice of bars, a spacious and
traditional restaurant together with a comfortable, relaxing lounge.

Rooms 15 en suite 7 annexe en suite (2 fmly) (7 GF) **Facilities** STV TVB
tea/coffee Direct dial from bedrooms Cen ht TVL Dinner Last d 9pm
Conf Max 60 Thtr 60 Class 40 Board 40 **Parking** 15 **Notes** ⊗
No coaches

MENAI BRIDGE   MAP 14 SH57

Premier Collection

★★★★★ 🗟 FARM HOUSE
Wern Farm (SH550740)

Pentraeth Rd LL59 5RR
☎ 01248 712421 🖷 01248 715421 Mr & Mrs P Brayshaw
e–mail: wernfarmanglesey@onetel.com
web: www.angleseyfarms.com/wern.htm

dir: A55 junct 8 over Britannia Bridge onto A5025, over rdbt &
pass large garage, farm on right

A warm welcome is assured at this immaculate farm house, located in
superb grounds, which include an ornamental pond and all-weather
CONTINUED

WALES

tennis court. Spacious bedrooms are furnished with style and a wealth of thoughtful extras enhance guest comfort. Memorable breakfasts are served in the attractive conservatory-dining room, and a sumptuous lounge and games room, featuring an antique three-quarter size billiard table, are also benefits of this home from home.

Rooms 3 rms (2 en suite) (2 fmly) D £75–£80✳ **Facilities** FTV TVB tea/coffee Cen ht TVL ⌕ Snooker ⥁ **Parking** 10 **Notes** ⊗ No children 12yrs 150 acres mixed Closed Nov–Feb

---

VALLEY   MAP 14 SH27

★★★ Ⓐ INN
Valley
London Rd LL65 3DU

☎ 01407 740203 & 740299 🖶 01407 740686

e–mail: valley-hotel@tinyworld.com

web: www.valley-hotel-anglesey.co.uk

dir: Leave A55 at exit 3 and follow signs to Valley, situated at lights in Valley on A5

Rooms 19 en suite (6 fmly) **Facilities** FTV TVB tea/coffee Cen ht Dinner Last d 9.15pm **Conf** Max 120 Thtr 100 Class 70 Board 50 **Parking** 100

BRIDGEND

BRIDGEND   MAP 09 SS97

★★★★ Ⓐ BED & BREAKFAST
Ewenny Woods Bed and Breakfast
The Trip, Ewenny CF35 5BZ

☎ 01656 766421

e–mail: info@ewennywoods.co.uk

dir: B4265 to Ewenny, over river and turn left towards Corntown. 500mtrs on right

Rooms 3 en suite S £40–£50; D £50–£70 **Facilities** TVB tea/coffee Cen ht Wi-fi available Bowls & Badminton **Parking** 7 **Notes** LB ⊗

★★★ Ⓐ GUEST HOUSE
Hunters Gate
Maudlam CF33 4PL

☎ 01656 740735

e–mail: janehampton@maudlam.fsnet.co.uk

dir: 6m W of Bridgend. M4 junct 37, A4229 for Porthcawl, right at 1st rdbt onto B4283 through North Cornelly, left at x-rds to Maudlam, left after Angel Inn to village

Rooms 3 rms (2 en suite) (1 pri facs) S fr £30; D fr £50 **Facilities** TVB tea/coffee Cen ht TVL Dinner Last d 5pm **Parking** 6 **Notes** No children 9yrs No coaches ⊛

CAERPHILLY

CAERPHILLY   MAP 09 ST18

★★★ GUEST HOUSE
The Cottage
Mountain View, Pwllypant CF83 3HW

☎ 029 2086 9160 🖶 029 2086 9160

e–mail: cottageguesthouse@tiscali.co.uk

dir: 1m N of town centre. On rdbt junct A468 & A469

Enthusiastic proprietor Carole Beacham welcomes you to her 300-year-old home, which occupies a convenient roadside location near to the town centre. Bedrooms are well and thoughtfully appointed, and there is a spacious and comfortable lounge. Breakfast is served in the attractive dining room.

Rooms 3 en suite **Facilities** TVB tea/coffee Cen ht TVL **Parking** 8 **Notes** ⊗ No coaches ⊛

CARDIFF

CARDIFF   MAP 09 ST17

★★★★ GUEST HOUSE
Annedd Lon
157 Cathedral Rd, Pontcanna CF11 9PL

☎ 029 2022 3349

web: www.anneddlon.co.uk

dir: From Cardiff Castle, W across the river Taff. 1st right is Cathedral Rd. On left just after 4th side street

Just a leisurely stroll from Sophia Gardens and the Millennium Stadium, this impressive Victorian house is ideally located. The house retains many original features and is attractively furnished. Elegant public areas include a comfortable lounge as well as a cosy dining room.

Rooms 6 rms (5 en suite) (2 fmly) S £40–£45; D £55–£70 **Facilities** FTV TVB tea/coffee Cen ht **Parking** 6 **Notes** ⊗ No coaches Closed 24–29 Dec

WALES

CARDIFF CONTINUED

★★★★ GUEST ACCOMMODATION
The Big Sleep Cardiff
Bute Ter CF10 2FE
☎ 029 2063 6363 ▤ 029 2063 6364
e–mail: bookings.cardiff@thebigsleephotel.com

dir: *Opp Cardiff International Arena*
Part of the Cardiff skyline, this city-centre establishment offers
well-equipped bedrooms ranging from standard to penthouse, with
spectacular views over the city towards the bay. There is a bar on the
ground floor and secure parking. Choose between a continental
breakfast or Breakfast to Go, an alternative for travellers making an
early start.

Rooms 81 en suite (8 fmly) D £45–£120 **Facilities** FTV TVB tea/coffee
Direct dial from bedrooms Lift Cen ht Wi-fi available **Conf** Max 60
Thtr 60 Class 20 Board 20 **Parking** 20 **Notes LB** Closed 24 & 25 Dec

★★★★ GUEST HOUSE
Marlborough
98 Newport Rd CF24 1DG
☎ 029 2049 2385 ▤ 029 2046 5982
web: www.marlboroughguesthouse.co.uk

This friendly, family-run guest house is just a short walk from the city
centre. Bedrooms are mostly spacious and all are well furnished and
equipped. Bathrooms are particularly well fitted. Hearty breakfasts are
served in the pleasant breakfast room.

Rooms 8 rms (6 en suite) (2 fmly) **Facilities** STV TVB tea/coffee Cen ht
TVL **Parking** 8 **Notes** ⊗

★★★★ ⊛ RESTAURANT WITH ROOMS
The Old Post Office
Greenwood Ln, St Fagans CF5 6EL
☎ 029 2056 5400 ▤ 029 2056 3400
e–mail: info@theoldpostofficerestaurant.co.uk

dir: *4m W of city centre. M4 junct 33 onto A4232, onto A48 for
Cardiff & 1st left for St Fagans*
Located just five miles from Cardiff in the historic village of St Fagans,
this establishment offers contemporary style based on New England
design. Bedrooms, like the dining room, feature striking white walls
with spotlights emphasising the fresh, clean design. Delicious meals
include a carefully prepared selection of local produce.

CONTINUED

Rooms 6 en suite (2 fmly) (6 GF) S £90–£130; D £100–£150✳ (incl.
dinner) **Facilities** FTV TVB tea/coffee Cen ht Dinner Last d 9.30pm
Wi-fi available **Parking** 20 **Notes LB** ⊗ Closed mid-end Jan

★★★★ 🅰 BED & BREAKFAST
Number 62
62 Cathedral Rd CF11 9LL
☎ 029 2041 2765 ▤ 029 2064 1199
e–mail: stay@number62.com
web: www.number62.com

dir: *W of castle, over River Taff, take 1st right, 0.5m on right*
Rooms 3 en suite S £60–£110; D £70–£130✳ **Facilities** FTV TVB tea/
coffee Cen ht Wi-fi available **Conf** Max 10 Board 10 **Notes LB** ⊗
No children 8yrs

★★★ GUEST HOUSE
Tanglewood
4 Tygwyn Rd, Penylan CF23 5JE
☎ 029 2047 3447 & 07971 546812 ▤ 0870 706 1808
e–mail: reservations@tanglewoodguesthouse.com
web: www.tanglewoodguesthouse.com

dir: *Towards Cardiff E & Docks. 3rd exit at rdbt. Next rdbt 1st exit.
Left at lights. Right just past next lights. Establishment 120yds on
right*
An elegant, well-kept Edwardian house, Tanglewood is in a quiet
residential district and has attractive gardens. The pleasant bedrooms
are thoughtfully equipped and there is a comfortable lounge
overlooking the gardens.

Rooms 4 rms (1 en suite) **Facilities** TVB tea/coffee Cen ht TVL
Parking 8 **Notes** ⊗ No coaches Closed 15 Dec–10 Jan ⊜

CARMARTHENSHIRE

AMMANFORD   **MAP 08 SN61**

★★ 🅰 BED & BREAKFAST
Bryncoch Farm
Llandyfan SA18 2TY
☎ 01269 850480 ▤ 01236 850480
e–mail: robrich@bryncochfarm.co.uk

dir: *M4 junct 29, A483 to Ammanford, onto A474, 0.75m left
signed Trap, farm 3m*
Rooms 3 en suite (1 fmly) S £25; D £40✳ **Facilities** FTV TVB tea/
coffee Cen ht TVL **Parking** 10

WALES

CARMARTHEN
MAP 08 SN42

See also Cwmduad

★★★★ 🖳 GUEST ACCOMMODATION
Capel Dewi Uchaf Country House
Capel Dewi SA32 8AY
☎ 01267 290799 📄 01267 290003
e–mail: uchaffarm@aol.com
dir: On B4300 between Capel Dewi & junct B4310

Located in 35 acres of grounds with stunning views and private fishing in the River Towy, this Grade II listed, 16th-century house retains many magnificent features and has a wealth of character. Generous Welsh breakfasts are a feature here.

Rooms 3 en suite **Facilities** TVB tea/coffee Cen ht TVL Dinner Last d 10am Fishing Riding **Conf** Max 8 Board 8 **Parking** 10 **Notes** ❷ Closed Xmas

★★★★ GUEST ACCOMMODATION
Sarnau Mansion
Llysonnen Rd SA33 5DZ
☎ 01267 211404 📄 01267 211404
e–mail: fernihough@so1405.force9.co.uk
web: www.sarnaumansion.co.uk
dir: 5m W of Carmarthen. Off A40 onto B4298 & Bancyfelin road, Sarnau on right

Located west of Carmarthen in sixteen acres of grounds and gardens, including a tennis court, this large Grade II listed, late-Georgian house retains much original character and is stylishly decorated. There is a lounge with a log fire, an elegant dining room, and spacious bedrooms with stunning rural views.

Rooms 3 en suite S £45; D £65–£70✱ **Facilities** TVB tea/coffee Cen ht TVL Dinner Last d 24hrs 🍵 **Parking** 10 **Notes** ❷ No children 5yrs

★★★★ BED & BREAKFAST
Shakeshafts
Lower Penddaulwyn, Capel Dewi SA32 8AY
☎ 01267 290627
e–mail: elaine@shakeshafts.com
web: www.shakeshafts.com
dir: On B4300 3m E of Carmarthen

Peacefully located in the beautiful Towy Valley with three acres of grounds to the rear, Shakeshafts offers a friendly and relaxing style of accommodation. The modern bedrooms and bathrooms are newly furnished and comfortable. Guests are welcome to enjoy the surrounding gardens, or on colder days they may prefer the latest addition of a conservatory.

Rooms 3 en suite (1 GF) S £35–£45; D £54–£60 **Facilities** TVB tea/coffee Cen ht ⌁ **Parking** 10 **Notes** LB ❷ No children 8yrs ❸

CWMDUAD
MAP 08 SN33

★★★ GUEST HOUSE
Neuadd-Wen
SA33 6XJ
☎ 01267 281438 📄 01267 281438
e–mail: goodbourn@neuaddwen.plus.com
dir: On A484, 9m N of Carmarthen, towards Cardigan

Excellent customer care is assured at this combined Post Office and house situated in pretty gardens in an unspoiled village. Bedrooms are filled with thoughtful extras and there is a choice of lounges. One bedroom is in a carefully renovated Victorian toll cottage across the road. There is an attractive dining room that serves imaginative dinners using fresh local produce.

Rooms 9 rms (6 en suite) 1 annexe en suite (2 fmly) (2 GF) S £22–£26; D £44–£52 **Facilities** TV9B tea/coffee Direct dial from bedrooms Licensed Cen ht TVL Dinner Last d 5pm **Parking** 12 **Notes** LB No coaches

FELIN GWM UCHAF
MAP 08 SN52

★★★★ 🖳 FARM HOUSE
Allt Y Golau Farmhouse *(SN510261)*
Allt Y Golau Uchaf SA32 7BB
☎ 01267 290455 📄 01267 290743 Dr C Rouse
e–mail: alltygolau@btinternet.com
web: www.alltygolau.com
dir: A40 onto B4310, N for 2m. 1st on left after Felin gwm Uchaf

This delightful Georgian stonewalled farmhouse has been furnished and decorated to a high standard by the present owners. Allt y Golau Uchaf enjoys panoramic views over the Tywi Valley and beyond to the Black Mountains. Take a relaxing walk through two acres of mature garden. Accommodation is comfortable and there are many thoughtful extras provided in the bedrooms, as well as a separate lounge. Breakfast is provided in the cosy dining room around a communal table. Jacquie Rouse was a finalist for the AA Friendliest Landlady of the Year Award 2008.

Rooms 3 rms (2 en suite) (1 pri facs) (2 GF) S £45; D £65 **Facilities** tea/coffee Cen ht TVL **Parking** 3 **Notes** ❷ 2 acres Small Holding Closed 20 Dec–2 Jan ❸

LAUGHARNE MAP 08 SN31

★★★★ BED & BREAKFAST
Keepers Cottage Bed and Breakfast
SA33 4QN
☎ 01994 427404
e-mail: info@keepers-cottage.com
web: www.keepers-cottage.com
dir: *On A4066, St Clears to Laugharne road, opp blue village sign*
A warm welcome awaits at this delightful cottage-style property and its
hosts, Marj and Rose. Bedrooms including a ground floor room offer
comfort with many extras provided. There is a lounge facility with
stunning views which extend to The Gower Peninsular. The welcoming
dining room is set with separate tables and is the venue for a hearty
breakfast. The Dylan Thomas Boat House and Laugharne Castle, are
both just a short walk away. Cyclists, walkers and fishermen will find
this a particularly useful establishment as there is a lock-up unit with a
washing and drying facility.
Rooms 3 en suite (1 GF) **Facilities** FTV TVB tea/coffee Cen ht TVL
Parking 6 **Notes** ⊗ No children 10yrs

LLANDEILO MAP 08 SN62

★★★★ Ⓐ BED & BREAKFAST
Blaen-Y-Garn
Manordeilo SA19 7BG
☎ 01550 777707
e-mail: blaenygarn@btinternet com
dir: *On A40 between Llandeilo & Llandovery*
Rooms 2 rms (1 en suite) (1 pri facs) (1 GF) S £35; D £50–£55✶
Facilities TVB tea/coffee Cen ht Wi-fi available **Parking** 5 **Notes** ⊗

LLANDYBIE MAP 08 SN61

★★★ BED & BREAKFAST
Glynhir Mansion
Glynhir Rd SA18 2TD
☎ 01269 850438 📄 01269 851275
e-mail: enquiries@theglynhirestate.com
web: www.theglynhirestate.com
dir: *1m N of Ammanford on A483*
Nestling at the foot of the Black Mountains in an Area of Outstanding
Natural Beauty, Glynhir Mansion dates from the end of the 17th
century. The dining room and lounge have open fires and attractive
period furnishings. The 200 acres of grounds include some lovely
walks alongside the River Loughor, where a 30 foot waterfall is a
spectacle not to be missed.
Rooms 4 en suite (1 fmly) S £40; D £70✶ **Facilities** Cen ht TVL Dinner
Last d 10.30am Golf 18 Pool Table Table tennis **Conf** Max 40 Thtr 40
Class 40 Board 30 Del from £80 ✶ **Parking** 12 **Notes** LB ⊗ Closed
mid Dec–mid Jan RS mid Jan–Mar Civ Wed 45

LLANELLI MAP 08 SN50

★★ GUEST ACCOMMODATION
Coastal Park Guest House
86 Queen Victoria Rd SA15 2TH
☎ 01554 755357 📄 01554 755357
e-mail: office@awelymor.fsnet.co.uk
dir: *500yds SW of town centre. A484 onto B4304, left at rdbt onto
Queen Victoria Rd*
This friendly and relaxed guest house is situated close to the town
centre and offers bright accommodation, including some family rooms.
Public areas include a smart lounge and cosy bar with a separate
dining room, and there is an enclosed rear car park.
Rooms 11 rms (7 en suite) (3 fmly) (1 GF) S £32.50–£37; D £50–£55✶
Facilities TVB tea/coffee Cen ht TVL Dinner Last d 5pm **Parking** 10
Notes LB

PENCADER MAP 08 SN43

★★★★ 🍽 BED & BREAKFAST
Hollyville Cottage B&B
Hollyville, Maesycrugiau SA39 9DL
☎ 01559 395301
e-mail: bizzylizzy_hollyville@btinternet.com
dir: *From Camarthen A485 16m. Left past builder merchants,
right at x-rd/s. B&B on left in 1.5m*
This restored Victorian Welsh stone cottage is located in the peaceful
Teifi Valley in the small village of Maesycrugiau. The pretty cottage
bedrooms are decorated in period style and provide many extras for
guests comfort. There are two en suite bedrooms in the converted
coach house adjoining which can also be let as self-catering. The
welcoming dining room furnishes a communal table where guests can
enjoy a country feast, using fresh ingredients, using their own hens'
eggs, homemade preserves and honey from Elizabeth's bees. The
peaceful garden may be enjoyed by guests on sunnier days.
Rooms 1 rms (1 pri facs) 2 annexe en suite (1 fmly) S £35–£40;
D £60–£80 **Facilities** TV2B tea/coffee Cen ht TVL Dinner Last d day
before Wi-fi available **Parking** 3 **Notes** LB ⊗

ST CLEARS MAP 08 SN21

Premier Collection

★★★★★ 🍽 BED & BREAKFAST
Coedllys Country House
Llangynin SA33 4JY
☎ 01994 231455 📄 01994 231441
e-mail: keith@harber.fsworld.co.uk
web: www.coedllyscountryhouse.co.uk
Set in a peaceful valley with rolling countryside, Coedllys is the
beautiful home of Mr and Mrs Harber, who are adept at making visitors
feel like honoured guests. Bedrooms are lavishly furnished, and the
thoughtful and useful extras make a stay more memorable. There is a
cosy well-furnished lounge, and an extensive menu choice at breakfast
is served in the pleasant dining room. For the energetic there is the
CONTINUED

WALES

fitness suite, or relax in the small indoor pool or sauna which are available for guest use.

Coedllys Country House

Rooms 3 en suite S £52.50–£62.50; D £80–£95✱ **Facilities** FTV TVB tea/coffee Cen ht Dinner Last d 24hrs prior Wi-fi available 🌀 Sauna Gymnasium **Parking** 6 **Notes LB** No children 10yrs Closed Xmas

CEREDIGION

ABERAERON **MAP 08 SN46**

Premier Collection

★ ★ ★ ★ ★ 🏵️🏵️ 🍴

RESTAURANT WITH ROOMS

Ty Mawr Mansion

Cilcennin SA48 8DB

☎ 01570 470033

e-mail: info@tymawrmansion.co.uk

web: www.tymawrmansion.co.uk

dir: *on A482 (Lampeter to Aberaeron road) 4m from Aberaeron*

Surrounded by rolling countryside in its own naturally beautiful gardens, this fine country mansion house is a haven of perfect peace and tranquillity. Careful renovation has seen it restored to its former glory and, combined with lush fabrics, top quality beds and sumptuous furnishings, the accommodation is spacious, superbly equipped and very comfortable. Award-winning chefs create mouth-watering dishes from local and seasonal produce, and Martin and Cath McAlpine offer the sort of welcome which makes every visit here a memorable one. Ty Mawr was AA Guest Accommodation of the Year for Wales 2007–2008.

Rooms 8 en suite 1 annexe en suite (1 fmly) (2 GF) S £85–£120; D £120–£280✱ **Facilities** FTV TVB tea/coffee Direct dial from bedrooms Cen ht Dinner Last d 9pm Wi-fi available Fishing Snooker Pool Table outdoor hot tub **Conf** Max 25 Thtr 25 Class 25 Board 16 **Parking** 20 **Notes LB** ⊗ No children 12yrs Closed 25 Dec–8 Jan

Premier Collection

★ ★ ★ ★ ★ 🏵️ INN

The Harbourmaster

Pen Cei SA46 0BA

☎ 01545 570755

e-mail: info@harbour-master.com

web: www.harbour-master.com

dir: *In town centre beside tourist office and harbour*

Located right on the harbour, this Grade II listed building was previously the harbourmaster's house. The bedrooms are delightfully furnished and have excellent showers, and the proprietors and staff are very friendly and professional. Dinner and breakfast are a real treat too, a varied range of carefully prepared dishes using much local produce.

Rooms 13 rms (10 en suite) (3 pri facs) S £55–£60; D £90–£200✱ **Facilities** FTV TVB tea/coffee Direct dial from bedrooms Lift Cen ht Dinner Last d 9pm Wi-fi available **Parking** 7 **Notes LB** ⊗ No children 5yrs No coaches Closed 25 Dec RS Mon lunch

★ ★ ★ ★ GUEST HOUSE

Arosfa Harbourside Guesthouse

SA46 0BU

☎ 01545 570120

e-mail: arosfabandb@btinternet.com

dir: *A487 in town centre onto Market St towards sea, 150yds to Arosfa, car park*

A warm welcome is assured at this renovated Georgian house, located by the historic harbour. Bedrooms are filled with thoughtful extras and have modern bathrooms. Other areas include a cosy lounge, stairways enhanced by quality art and memorabilia, and a bright, attractive dining room, the setting for imaginative Welsh breakfasts.

Rooms 3 en suite 1 annexe en suite (1 fmly) (1 GF) S £35–£60; D £60–£100 **Facilities** FTV TVB tea/coffee Cen ht Wi-fi available **Notes LB** ⊗ No coaches 📧

WALES

CONTINUED

ABERYSTWYTH MAP 08 SN58

Premier Collection

★★★★★ BED & BREAKFAST

Awel-Deg

Capel Bangor SY23 3LR

☎ 01970 880681

e-mail: awel-deg@tiscali.co.uk

web: www.awel-deg.co.uk

dir: *5m E of Aberystwyth. On A44 in Capel Bangor*

Located five miles from the historic university town, this attractive bungalow, set in pretty gardens, provides high standards of hospitality, comfort and facilities. Immaculately maintained throughout, spacious bedrooms are equipped with a wealth of thoughtful extras and smart, modern en suite shower rooms. Comprehensive breakfasts are served at one table in the elegant dining room and a choice of lounges is available.

Rooms 2 en suite (2 GF) S £40; D £58 **Facilities** FTV TVB tea/coffee Cen ht TVL **Parking** 8 **Notes LB** ✖ No children 11yrs Closed 20–30 Dec ✆

★★★★ GUEST HOUSE

Bodalwyn

Queen's Av SY23 2EG

☎ 01970 612578 📠 01970 639261

e-mail: enquiries@bodalwyn.co.uk

web: www.bodalwyn.co.uk

dir: *500yds N of town centre. Off A487 Northgate St onto North Rd to end*

Located a short walk from the promenade, this imposing Edwardian house, built for a college professor, has been totally refurbished to

CONTINUED

provide high standards of comfort and good facilities. Smart modern bathrooms complement the spacious bedrooms, which are equipped with a wealth of thoughtful extras. Family rooms are available. Comprehensive Welsh breakfasts are served in the elegant conservatory-dining room.

Rooms 8 en suite (2 fmly) S £35–£47.50; D £55–£65✸ **Facilities** TVB tea/coffee Cen ht Wi-fi available **Notes** ✖ No coaches Closed 24 Dec–1 Jan ✆

★★★★ GUEST HOUSE

Glyn-Garth

South Rd SY23 1JS

☎ 01970 615050 📠 01970 636835

e-mail: glyngarth@aol.com

web: www.glyngarthgh.cjb.net

dir: *In town centre. Off A487 onto South Rd*

Privately owned and personally run by the same family for over 50 years, this immaculately maintained guest house provides a range of thoughtfully furnished bedrooms with smart modern bathrooms. Breakfast is served in the attractive dining room and a lounge is also available.

Rooms 10 rms (6 en suite) (2 fmly) (1 GF) S £28–£60; D £56–£70✸ **Facilities** STV TVB tea/coffee Cen ht TVL **Parking** 2 **Notes** ✖ No coaches Closed 2 wks Xmas & New Year ✆

★★★★ GUEST HOUSE

Llety Ceiro Country House

Peggy Ln, Bow St, Llandre SY24 5AB

☎ 01970 821900 📠 01970 820966

e-mail: marinehotel1@btconnect.com

dir: *4m NE of Aberystwyth. Off A487 onto B4353 for 300yds*

Located north of Aberystwyth, this house is immaculately maintained throughout. Bedrooms are equipped with a range of thoughtful extras in addition to smart modern bathrooms. A spacious conservatory lounge is available in addition to an attractive dining room, and bicycle hire is also available.

Rooms 11 en suite (2 fmly) (3 GF) (1 smoking) S £35–£75; D £50–£95 **Facilities** TVB tea/coffee Direct dial from bedrooms Licensed Cen ht TVL Dinner Last d 8pm Free use of facilities at sister hotel **Conf** Max 55 Thtr 60 Class 40 Board 40 **Parking** 21 **Notes LB** Civ Wed 65

★★★★ GUEST HOUSE

Yr Hafod

1 South Marine Ter SY23 1JX

☎ 01970 617579 📠 01970 636835

e-mail: johnyrhafod@aol.com

dir: *On south promenade between harbour & castle*

An immaculately maintained, end of terrace Victorian house in a commanding location overlooking the South Bay. The spacious bedrooms are comfortable and some have smart modern shower rooms. Breakfast is served in the attractive front-facing dining room.

Rooms 7 rms (2 en suite) S £28–£29; D £56–£74✸ **Facilities** TVB tea/coffee Cen ht TVL Wi-fi available **Parking** 1 **Notes** ✖ No coaches Closed Xmas & New Year ✆

WALES

★★★ BED & BREAKFAST
Y Gelli

Dolau, Lovesgrove SY23 3HP
☎ 01970 617834
e–mail: pat.twigg@virgin.net
dir: *Off A44 2.75m E of town centre*

Located in spacious grounds on the town's outskirts, this modern detached house contains a range of practically furnished bedrooms and three further rooms are available in an adjacent Victorian property. Comprehensive breakfasts are served in the attractive dining room and a lounge is also available.

Rooms 6 rms (2 en suite) 3 annexe rms (1 en suite) (3 fmly) (1 GF)
Facilities TVB tea/coffee Cen ht TVL Dinner Last d early morning Snooker Pool Table Table tennis, Stabling can be provided **Conf** Thtr 30 Class 30 Board 20 **Parking** 20 **Notes** ⊗ ⊜

LAMPETER   MAP 08 SN54

★★★★ BED & BREAKFAST
Haulfan

6 Station Ter SA48 7HH
☎ 01570 422718
e–mail: haulfanguesthouse@lampeter.freeserve.co.uk
dir: *From S, A485 through town centre, right by fountain, next right*

Very popular for visitors to the nearby university, this Victorian house provides modern furnished and equipped bedrooms. There is a homely, comfortable lounge and generous breakfasts are served in the cosy dining room, where separate tables are provided. A warm welcome is assured from proprietors, who have an excellent knowledge of the area.

Rooms 3 rms (2 en suite) (1 fmly) (1 GF) S £25–£35; D £50–£55✷
Facilities TVB tea/coffee Cen ht TVL **Parking** 1 **Notes LB** ⊗ Closed 20 Dec–mid Jan ⊜

★★★★ 🅐 GUEST HOUSE
Rhyd Y Groes

SA48 8QN
☎ 01570 470188 🖹 01570 470188
e–mail: enquiries@rhyd-y-groes.com

Rooms 3 rms (1 en suite) (1 pri facs) (1 fmly) (1 GF) S £29; D £58–£78✷ **Facilities** TVB tea/coffee Cen ht TVL Dinner Last d 2pm ⟲ Riding Hot tub **Conf** Max 20 **Parking** 12 **Notes LB** ⊗ No coaches

---

CONWY

ABERGELE   MAP 14 SH97

Premier Collection

★★★★★ ⊛ RESTAURANT WITH ROOMS
The Kinmel Arms

The Village, St George LL22 9BP
☎ 01745 832207 🖹 01745 822044
e–mail: info@thekinmelarms.co.uk
dir: *From A55 junct 24a to St George. E on A55, junct 25. 1st left to Rhuddlan, then 1st right into St George. Take 2nd right*

This converted 17th-century coaching inn stands close to the church in the village of St George in the beautiful Elwy Valley. The popular, restaurant specialises in produce from Wales and North West England, and the friendly and helpful staff ensures an enjoyable stay. The accommodation consists of four attractive, well-equipped suites, and substantial continental breakfasts are served in the rooms.

Rooms 4 en suite (2 GF) **Facilities** STV TVB tea/coffee Cen ht Dinner Last d 9.30pm **Parking** 8 **Notes** ⊗ No children 16yrs Closed 25 Dec & 1 Jan RS Sun & Mon

---

BETWS-Y-COED   MAP 14 SH75

Premier Collection

★★★★★ ⊜ GUEST ACCOMMODATION
Penmachno Hall

LL24 0PU
☎ 01690 760410 🖹 01690 760410
e–mail: stay@penmachnohall.co.uk
web: www.penmachnohall.co.uk
dir: *4m S of Betws-y-Coed. A5 onto B4406 to Penmachno, over bridge, right at Eagles pub signed Ty Mawr*

Set in over two acres of mature grounds including a mountain stream and woodland, this impressive Victorian rectory has been lovingly restored to provide high standards of comfort and facilities. Stylish décor and quality furnishings highlight the many original features throughout the ground-floor areas, and the bedrooms have a wealth of thoughtful extras.

Rooms 3 en suite S £75–£90; D £75–£90 **Facilities** TVB tea/coffee Cen ht Dinner Last d 24hrs before Wi-fi available **Parking** 3 **Notes LB** ⊗ Closed Xmas & New Year RS Sun–Mon

WALES

BETWS-Y-COED CONTINUED

GUEST ACCOMMODATON OF THE YEAR FOR WALES
Premier Collection

★★★★★ ◉◉◉ GUEST HOUSE

Tan-y-Foel Country House

Capel Garmon LL26 0RE

☎ 01690 710507 🖹 01690 710681

e–mail: enquiries@tyfhotel.co.uk

web: www.tyfhotel.co.uk

dir: *1.5m E of Betws-y-Coed. Off A5 onto A470 N, 2m right for Capel Garmon, establishment signed 1.5m on left*

Situated high above the Conwy valley and set in six acres of woodland with attractive gardens and country walks leading from the grounds, this delightful 17th-century country house has superb views in all directions. The bedrooms are individually decorated and include four-poster king, canopied and king-size beds along with modern facilities. There is a stylish sitting room and restaurant where fires burn in winter, and fresh local produce features on the small but interesting menu.

Rooms 3 en suite 2 annexe en suite (1 GF) S £110–£155; D £149–£200✷ **Facilities** TVB tea/coffee Direct dial from bedrooms Licensed Cen ht Dinner Last d 7.30pm **Parking** 14 **Notes LB** ⊗ No children 12yrs No coaches Closed Dec RS Jan

★★★★ GUEST HOUSE

Afon View Guest House

Holyhead Rd LL24 0AN

☎ 01690 710726 🖹 01690 710726

e–mail: welcome@afon-view.co.uk

web: www.afon-view.co.uk

dir: *On A5 150yds E of HSBC bank*

A warm welcome is assured at this elegant Victorian house, located between Waterloo Bridge and village centre. Bedrooms are equipped with lots of thoughtful extras and day rooms include an attractive dining room and comfortable guest lounge. Afternoon teas are served during the summer months.

Rooms 7 en suite (1 fmly) S £40–£45; D £60–£85✷ **Facilities** TVB tea/coffee Cen ht Wi-fi available **Parking** 7 **Notes LB** ⊗ No children 4yrs

★★★★ GUEST HOUSE

Bryn Bella Guest House

Lon Muriau, Llanrwst Rd LL24 0HD

☎ 01690 710627

e–mail: welcome@bryn-bella.co.uk

web: www.bryn-bella.co.uk

dir: *A5 onto A470, 0.5m right onto driveway signed Bryn Bella*

Located on an elevated position on the town's outskirts and having stunning views of the surrounding countryside, this elegant Victorian house provides a range of thoughtfully equipped bedrooms with smart modern bathrooms. A fine collection of memorabilia adorns the public areas, which include an attractive dining room and a comfortable lounge. A warm welcome is assured and guest services include a daily weather forecast.

Rooms 5 en suite (1 GF) D £55–£70✷ **Facilities** TVB tea/coffee Cen ht TVL Wi-fi available **Parking** 7 **Notes LB** ⊗ No coaches

★★★★ GUEST ACCOMMODATION

The Courthouse (Henllys)

Old Church Rd LL24 0AL

☎ 01690 710534

e–mail: welcome@guesthouse-snowdonia.co.uk

web: www.guesthouse-snowdonia.co.uk

dir: *Off A5 in village centre onto Old Church Rd towards golf club*

Superbly located in immaculate gardens beside the river, the Victorian former police station and magistrates' court have been renovated to provide accommodation of immense charm; one bedroom is a former cell, and memorable breakfasts are served in the original courtroom. A warm welcome is assured.

Rooms 4 en suite (1 fmly) D £60–£90✷ **Facilities** TVB tea/coffee Cen ht Wi-fi available **Parking** 4 **Notes LB** ⊗ No children 4yrs Closed Jan

WALES

★★★★ FARM HOUSE
Cwmanog Isaf Farm *(SH799546)*
Fairy Glen LL24 0SL
☎ 01690 710225 & 07808 421634 Mrs H M Hughes
e–mail: heather.hughes3@tesco.net

dir: *1m S of Betws-y-Coed off A470 by Fairy Glen Hotel, 500yds on farm lane*

Peacefully located on 30 acres of undulating land, which also contains the renowned Fairy Glen, this 200-year-old house on a working livestock farm has been restored to provide comfortable, thoughtfully furnished bedrooms. Breakfast and dinners use home-reared or organic produce, and the raised position of the property provides stunning views of the surrounding countryside.

Rooms 3 rms (2 en suite) (1 pri facs) (1 GF) D £56–£60✱ **Facilities** STV TVB tea/coffee Cen ht Dinner Last d 10am **Parking** 4 **Notes** ⊗ No children 15yrs 30 acres Mixed Closed 15 Dec–7 Feb ⊛

★★★★ GUEST HOUSE
Park Hill
Llanrwst Rd LL24 0HD
☎ 01690 710540 🖷 01690 710540
e–mail: welcome@park-hill.co.uk
web: www.park-hill.co.uk

dir: *0.5m N of Betws-y-Coed on A470 Llanrwst road*

This friendly guest house benefits from a peaceful location overlooking the village. Comfortable bedrooms come in a wide range of sizes and are well equipped, one with a four-poster bed. There is a choice of lounges, a heated swimming pool, sauna and whirlpool bath for guests' use.

Rooms 9 en suite S £55–£84; D £60–£84 **Facilities** TVB tea/coffee Licensed Cen ht TVL Dinner Last d 4pm ⌧ Sauna **Parking** 11 **Notes** LB ⊗ No children 8yrs No coaches

★★★★ Ⓐ BED & BREAKFAST
Bridge View Bed & Breakfast
Old Church Rd LL24 0AL
☎ 01690 710127
e–mail: welcome@betwsguesthouse.co.uk
web: www.betwsguesthouse.co.uk
Rooms 3 en suite S £74; D £74–£84✱ **Facilities** TVB

★★★★ Ⓐ GUEST HOUSE
The Ferns Guest House
Holyhead Rd LL24 0AN
☎ 01690 710587
e–mail: ferns@betws-y-coed.co.uk
web: www.ferns-guesthouse.co.uk

dir: *On A5 near Waterloo Bridge*

Rooms 7 en suite (2 fmly) S £38–£40; D £56–£65✱ **Facilities** TVB tea/coffee Cen ht TVL Wi-fi available **Parking** 7 **Notes** ⊗ No children 5yrs No coaches

★★★ INN
Ty Gwyn Inn
LL24 0SG
☎ 01690 710383 🖷 01690 710383
e–mail: mratcl1050@aol.com

dir: *Junct of A5 & A470, by Waterloo Bridge*

Situated on the edge of the village, close to the Waterloo Bridge, this historic coaching inn retains many original features. Quality furnishing styles and memorabilia throughout enhance its intrinsic charm. Bedrooms, some of which feature antique beds, are equipped with thoughtful extras and imaginative food is provided within the cosy bars or restaurant.

Rooms 13 rms (10 en suite) (2 fmly) (1 GF) S £40–£65; D £72–£120✱ **Facilities** TVB tea/coffee Cen ht TVL Dinner Last d 9pm Wi-fi available **Parking** 14 **Notes** LB Closed Mon–Wed in Jan

See advert on this page

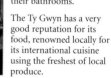

BETWS-Y-COED CONTINUED

★★★ INN
The White Horse Inn

Capel Garmon LL26 0RW

☎ 01690 710271 📄 01690 710721

dir: *A470 Llanwrst to Betws road, left at Snowdonia and Capel Garmon sign*

This 16th-century inn has a wealth of character, enhanced by original exposed timbers, stone walls and log fires. The bars feature an impressive collection of pottery and china. A good selection of home-cooked food is available, served in either the bars or in the cottage-style restaurant. The bedrooms are compact and thoughtfully furnished with modern facilities.

Rooms 5 en suite S £40–£45; D £60–£66✱ **Facilities** TVB tea/coffee Cen ht Dinner Last d 9pm Pool Table **Parking** 20 **Notes LB** No children Closed 25 Dec

---

BYLCHAU   MAP 14 SH96

Premier Collection

★★★★★ 🛏 🍽 FARM HOUSE
Hafod Elwy Hall *(SH938562)*

LL16 5SP

☎ 01690 770345 📄 01690 770266 Mrs W Charles-Warner

e–mail: enquiries@hafodelwyhall.co.uk

web: www.hafodelwyhall.co.uk

dir: *A5 onto A543, 5.5m right onto track signed Hafod Elwy Hall*

A warm welcome awaits you at this charming house, which originates from the 14th century. The peaceful property overlooks the surrounding countryside and is located on a 60-acre sheep and pig-rearing holding. Rooms are well equipped and have many thoughtful extras.

Rooms 3 rms (2 en suite) (1 pri facs) (1 GF) S £40–£70; D £60–£100 **Facilities** STV TV1B tea/coffee Cen ht TVL Dinner Last d 2pm Fishing **Parking** 4 **Notes LB** No children 16yrs 60 acres Mixed small holding

---

COLWYN BAY   MAP 14 SH87

★★★★ GUEST HOUSE
Whitehall

51 Cayley Promenade, Rhos-on-Sea LL28 4EP

☎ 01492 547296

e–mail: mossd.cymru@virgin.net

dir: *A55 onto B5115 Brompton Av, right at rdbt onto Whitehall Rd to seafront*

Overlooking Rhos-on-Sea promenade, this popular, family-run establishment is convenient for shopping and local amenities. Attractively appointed bedrooms include family rooms and a room on ground floor level. All benefit from an excellent range of facilities such as video and CD players, as well as air-conditioning. Facilities include a bar and a foyer lounge. Home-cooked dinners are available.

Rooms 12 en suite (4 fmly) S £32; D £64–£76✱ **Facilities** FTV TVB tea/coffee Direct dial from bedrooms Licensed Cen ht TVL Dinner Last d 4.30pm Wi-fi available **Parking** 5 **Notes LB**

★★★ GUEST HOUSE
The Northwood

47 Rhos Rd, Rhos-on-Sea LL28 4RS

☎ 01492 549931

e–mail: welcome@thenorthwood.co.uk

web: www.thenorthwood.co.uk

dir: *A55 onto B5115 Brompton Av, over rdbt, 2nd right*

A short walk from the seafront and shops, the Northwood has a warm and friendly atmosphere and welcomes back many regular guests. Bedrooms are furnished in modern style and freshly prepared meals can be enjoyed in the spacious dining room/bar while light refreshments are offered in the lounge.

Rooms 11 rms (10 en suite) (1 pri facs) (3 fmly) (2 GF) S £25–£35; D £50–£70 **Facilities** TVB tea/coffee Licensed Cen ht TVL Dinner Last d 7pm Wi-fi available **Conf** Max 20 Class 20 Board 20 **Parking** 12 **Notes LB** No coaches

See advert on opposite page

CONWY

MAP 14 SH77

★★★★★ 🛏 GUEST ACCOMMODATION

The Old Rectory Country House

Llanrwst Rd, Llansanffraid Glan Conwy LL28 5LF

☎ 01492 580611

e–mail: info@oldrectorycountryhouse.co.uk
web: www.oldrectorycountryhouse.co.uk

dir: 0.5m S from A470/A55 junct on left, by 30mph sign

This very welcoming accommodation has fine views over the Conwy estuary and towards Snowdonia. The elegant day rooms are luxurious and afternoon tea is available in the lounge. Bedrooms share the delightful views and are thoughtfully furnished, while the genuine hospitality creates a real home from home.

Rooms 4 en suite 2 annexe en suite **Facilities** TVB tea/coffee Direct dial from bedrooms Cen ht **Parking** 10 **Notes** No children 5yrs Closed 14 Dec–15 Jan

★★★★★ ◉ GUEST ACCOMMODATION

Sychnant Pass Country House

Sychnant Pass Rd LL32 8BJ

☎ 01492 585486 📠 01492 585486

e–mail: info@sychnantpasscountryhouse.co.uk
web: www.sychnantpasscountryhouse.co.uk

dir: 1.75m W of Conwy. Off A547 Bangor Rd in town onto Mount Pleasant & Sychnant Pass Rd, 1.75m on right near top of hill

Fine views are to be had from this Edwardian house set in landscaped grounds. Bedrooms, including suites and four poster rooms, are individually furnished and equipped with a range of thoughtful extras. Lounges, warmed by open fires in the chillier months, are comfortable and inviting, and imaginative dinners and suppers are served in the attractive dining room.

Rooms 12 en suite (3 fmly) (2 GF) S £75–£160; D £95–£180✳ **Facilities** TVB tea/coffee Cen ht Dinner Last d 8.30pm Wi-fi available ⓢ Sauna Solarium Gymnasium **Parking** 30 **Notes** LB Closed 24–26 Dec & Jan Civ Wed 100

★★★★ GUEST ACCOMMODATION

Gwern Borter Country Manor

Barkers Ln LL32 8YL

☎ 01492 650360 📠 01492 650360

e–mail: mail@snowdoniaholidays.co.uk

dir: From Conwy B5106 for 2.25m, right towards Rowen for 0.5m then right, left as road forks, Gwern Borter 0.5m on left

This delightful mansion has walls covered in climbing plants and is set in several acres of lawns and gardens. Children are very welcome and there is a rustic play area, games room and many farmyard pets. Bedrooms are furnished with antiques and modern facilities, and one room has an Edwardian four-poster bed. There is an elegant lounge and Victorian-style dining room, where freshly cooked breakfasts are served. Self-catering cottages are also available.

Rooms 4 rms (3 en suite) (1 pri facs) (1 fmly) S £45–£60; D £80–£90✳ **Facilities** STV FTV TVB tea/coffee Cen ht TVL Wi-fi available Riding Sauna Gymnasium Pool Table **Parking** 4 **Notes** LB ⊗ No children 4yrs

WALES

CONWY CONTINUED

★★★ GUEST HOUSE
Glan Heulog
Llanrwst Rd, Woodlands LL32 8LT
☎ 01492 593845
e–mail: glanheulog@no1guesthouse.freeserve.co.uk
web: www.walesbandb.co.uk

dir: *From Conwy Castle take B5106, house 0.25m on left*

This late 19th-century house lies in an elevated location, with fine views over the town and castle from many rooms. Bedrooms are decorated with pretty wallpapers, are well equipped and one has a four-poster bed. A pleasant breakfast room and conservatory are provided and hospitality from the proprietors is very friendly.

Rooms 7 rms (6 en suite) (1 pri facs) (1 fmly) S £35–£40; D £54–£64 Facilities TVB tea/coffee Cen ht TVL Parking 8 Notes No coaches

---

GWYTHERIN   MAP 14 SH86

★★★★ INN
The Lion Inn Gwytherin
LL22 8UU
☎ 01745 860123 📠 01745 860556
e–mail: info@thelioninn.net
web: www.thelioninn.net

dir: *Take A548 onto B5384*

Located in an award winning village within an area of outstanding natural beauty, this local stone built inn has been sympathetically renovated to provide high standards of comfort and facilities. Bedrooms are equipped with both practical and thoughtful extras and a wide range of food and ales are available within the bar or restaurant.

Rooms 5 en suite 1 annexe en suite (1 fmly) S fr £49; D fr £79✱ Facilities tea/coffee Direct dial from bedrooms Cen ht Dinner Last d 8.45pm Conf Max 25 Thtr 20 Class 20 Board 15 Del from £90 ✱ Parking 8 Notes ⊗ No coaches

---

LLANDUDNO   MAP 14 SH78

★★★★ GUEST HOUSE
Abbey Lodge
14 Abbey Rd LL30 2EA
☎ 01492 878042 📠 01492 878042
e–mail: enquiries@abbeylodgeuk.com

dir: *A546 to N end of town, onto Clement Av, right onto Abbey Rd*

This impressive Victorian villa is on a leafy avenue within easy walking distance of the promenade. It has been lovingly restored, and stylish décor and furniture add to its charm. Bedrooms come with a wealth of thoughtful extras, and there is a choice of sumptuous lounges and an elegant dining room.

Abbey Lodge

Rooms 4 en suite S £40; D £75 Facilities FTV TVB tea/coffee Cen ht Wi-fi available Parking 4 Notes ⊗ No children 12yrs No coaches Closed Dec–1 Feb ⊛

★★★★ GUEST HOUSE
Brigstock House
1 St David's Place LL30 2UG
☎ 01492 876416
e–mail: mmemory@btinternet.com

dir: *A470 into Llandudno, left onto The Parade promenade, left onto Lloyd St, left onto St David's Rd & left onto St David's Place*

This impressive Edwardian property is in a quiet residential cul-de-sac within easy walking distance of the seafront and central shopping area. The attractive bedrooms are very well equipped, and a comfortable lounge is available. Substantial breakfasts and dinners (by arrangement) are served in the elegant dining room.

Rooms 9 rms (8 en suite) (1 pri facs) S £29; D £58–£66✱ Facilities TVB tea/coffee Licensed Cen ht TVL Dinner Last d 10am Wi-fi available Parking 6 Notes ⊗ No children 12yrs No coaches Closed Xmas

★★★★ GUEST HOUSE
Bryn Derwen
34 Abbey Rd LL30 2EE
☎ 01492 876804 📠 01492 876804
e–mail: brynderwen@fsmail.net
web: www.bryn-derwen.co.uk

dir: *A470 into Llandudno, left at The Parade promenade to cenotaph, left, over rdbt, 4th right onto York Rd, Bryn Derwen at top*

A warm welcome is assured at this impressive Victorian house, which retains original tiled floors and some fine stained-glass windows.

CONTINUED

CONTINUED

Quality décor and furnishings highlight the historic charm of the property, which is apparent in the sumptuous lounges and attractive dining room, the setting for imaginative dinners and breakfasts. Bedrooms are equipped with a wealth of thoughtful extras, and the establishment also has a fully-equipped beauty salon.

Rooms 9 en suite (1 fmly) S £46–£50; D £76–£96✳ **Facilities** FTV TVB tea/coffee Licensed Cen ht TVL Dinner Last d 4pm Wi-fi available Solarium Beauty Salon **Parking** 9 **Notes LB** ⊗ No children 12yrs No coaches Closed Dec–Feb

★★★★ GUEST HOUSE
Britannia Guest House
Promenade, 15 Craig-y-Don Pde LL30 1BG
☎ 01492 877185

dir: *On seafront close to Llandudno Conference Centre*

This friendly guesthouse is conveniently located on the promenade and offers comfortably furnished and thoughtfully equipped bedrooms. A lot of refurbishment has recently been carried out and benefitted all areas. The pleasant breakfast room overlooks the pretty front garden and sea front.

Rooms 10 rms (9 en suite) (1 pri facs) (3 fmly) (2 GF) S £35–£50; D £50–£74✳ **Facilities** TVB tea/coffee Cen ht Dinner Last d noon **Notes LB** ⊗ No coaches Closed Dec–Jan

★★★★ GUEST ACCOMMODATION
Bryn-y-Mor
25 North Pde LL30 2LP
☎ 01492 876790 🖹 01492 874990
e–mail: info@bryn-y-mor.net
web: www.bryn-y-mor.net

dir: *A55 take Llandudno junct, head for Promenade turn left, by pier on left*

Located at the foot of the Great Orme and close to the town centre and its main attractions, the family run Bryn-y-Mor offers comfortable well – equipped rooms, many with sea views. There is an attractive lounge looking over the bay to the little Orme. There is also a small bar and an outside patio which also overlooks the bay.

Rooms 12 en suite S £50–£62; D £64–£88✳ **Facilities** TVB tea/coffee Cen ht **Notes** ⊗ No children 16yrs Closed 15 Nov–9 Feb

★★★★ GUEST ACCOMMODATION
Can-Y-Bae
10 Mostyn Crescent, Central Promenade LL30 1AR
☎ 01492 874188 🖹 01492 868376
e–mail: canybae@btconnect.com

dir: *A55 junct 10 onto A470, signed Llandudno/promenade. Can-Y-Bae located on sea front promenade between Venue Cymru Theatre & Band Stand*

A warm welcome is assured at this tastefully renovated house, centrally located on the Promenade. Bedrooms are equipped with both practical and homely extras and upper floors are serviced by a modern lift. Day rooms include a panoramic lounge, cosy bar and attractive basement dining room.

Can-Y-Bae

Rooms 16 en suite (1 fmly) (2 GF) S £35–£45; D £70–£80 **Facilities** TVB tea/coffee Direct dial from bedrooms Lift Cen ht Dinner Last d 6pm Wi-fi available **Notes LB**

★★★★ GUEST HOUSE
The Cliffbury
34 St David's Rd LL30 2UH
☎ 01492 877224
e–mail: info@thecliffbury.co.uk

Located on a leafy avenue within easy walking distance of the town centre, this elegant Edwardian house has been sympathetically refurbished to provide high standards of comfort. Bedrooms, furnished in minimalist style, provide a range of practical and thoughtful extras and smart modern bath/shower rooms are an additional benefit. Breakfast is taken in an attractive dining room and a warm welcome is assured.

Rooms 7 en suite **Facilities** FTV TVB tea/coffee Cen ht Dinner Wi-fi available **Parking** 3 **Notes** ⊗ No children 11yrs No coaches

★★★★ GUEST HOUSE
Glenavon Guest House
27 St Mary's Rd LL30 2UB
☎ 01492 877687 🖹 0870 706 2247
e–mail: postmaster@glenavon.plus.com

dir: *From A470 signed Llandudno, turn left at lights onto Trinity Avenue, St Mary's Rd is the 3rd on right Glenavon is on the right*

Supporters of Liverpool Football Club are especially welcome here and they can admire the extensive range of memorabilia throughout the comfortable day rooms. Bedrooms are equipped with thoughtful extras and Welsh breakfasts provide a good start to the day.

Rooms 7 en suite (1 fmly) S £35–£45; D £60–£75✳ **Facilities** FTV TVB tea/coffee Cen ht TVL Dinner Last d 10am Wi-fi available **Parking** 4 **Notes LB** ⊗ No coaches

CONTINUED

WALES

LLANDUDNO CONTINUED

★★★★ GUEST HOUSE
The Hilary Guesthouse
32 St David's Rd LL30 2UL
☎ 01492 875623
e–mail: thehilary@fsmail.net
web: www.thehilaryguesthouse-llandudno.co.uk

dir: *A470 to town centre, take the first left after train station, then the 4th right*

A warm and friendly welcome awaits at this very pleasant guesthouse. It is located in a quiet residential area, yet within easy reach of the town centre and other amenities. It provides soundly maintained accommodation which is equally suitable for holidaymakers and commercial visitors.

Rooms 8 en suite S £37–£55; D £60–£75✱ **Facilities** FTV TVB tea/coffee Cen ht Wi-fi available **Parking** 6 **Notes LB** ⊗ No children

★★★★ GUEST ACCOMMODATION
Lynton House
80 Church Walks LL30 2HD
☎ 01492 875057 & 875009 📠 01492 875057
e–mail: info@lyntonhousellandudno.co.uk

dir: *A546 The Parade towards pier, right at T-junct by cenotaph, left at rdbt after pier, premises on right*

A warm welcome is assured at this constantly improving family run establishment, located close to promenade, pier and town centre. Bedrooms are equipped with lots of thoughtful extras and breakfast is taken in an attractive dining room overlooking the pretty front patio garden. A spacious comfortable lounge includes a well stocked honesty bar.

Rooms 14 en suite (3 fmly) (1 GF) **Facilities** FTV TVB tea/coffee Direct dial from bedrooms Cen ht TVL Wi-fi available **Parking** 4 **Notes** ⊗ Closed 17–30 Dec

★★★★ GUEST ACCOMMODATION
St Hilary Guest House
The Promenade, 16 Craig-Y-Don Pde LL30 1BG
☎ 01492 875551 📠 01492 877538
e–mail: info@sthilaryguesthouse.co.uk
web: www.sthilaryguesthouse.co.uk

dir: *0.5m E of town centre. On B5115 seafront road near North Wales Theatre*

This very soundly maintained guest house is at the eastern end of the promenade and some of the attractive modern bedrooms have sea views. Family rooms are available, and other facilities include a cosy lounge and a pleasant breakfast room with separate tables. Unrestricted parking is normally available nearby.

Rooms 10 rms (9 en suite) (1 pri facs) (3 fmly) (2 GF) S £32–£50; D £48–£76✱ **Facilities** FTV TVB tea/coffee Cen ht Wi-fi available **Notes LB** ⊗ Closed end Nov–early Feb

★★★★ GUEST ACCOMMODATION
The Stratford House Guest Accommodation
8 Craig-y-Don Pde, Promenade LL30 1BG
☎ 01492 877962
e–mail: stratfordhtl@aol.com
web: www.stratfordguesthouse.com

dir: *A55 onto A470 to Llandudno, at rdbt 4th exit signed Craig-y-Don, right at Promenade*

Located at the Craig-y-Don end of Promenade, this constantly improving establishment provides a range of thoughtfully furnished bedrooms with smart modern en suite bath or shower rooms. Comprehensive breakfasts are taken in an attractive dining room with stunning sea views.

Rooms 10 en suite (3 fmly) (2 GF) S £36–£40; D £48–£60✱ **Facilities** TVB tea/coffee Cen ht **Notes LB** ⊗

★★★★ 🅰 GUEST HOUSE
Ashdale Guest House
3 St Davids Rd LL30 2UL
☎ 01492 877089 📠 01492 877089
e–mail: srule@btconnect.com

dir: *A470 towards town centre, continue through rdbts and keep left. After station at lights turn left, 4th right*

Rooms 8 rms (7 en suite) (1 pri facs) (1 fmly) S £25–£36; D £50–£72✱ **Facilities** TVB tea/coffee Cen ht TVL Dinner Last d 10am **Parking** 3 **Notes** ⊗ No coaches

★★★ GUEST ACCOMMODATION
"All Seasons"
7–8 Hill Ter LL30 2LS
☎ 01492 876277 📠 01492 876277
e–mail: all.seasons@virgin.net

Family-run and friendly, 'All Seasons' stands on the Great Orme overlooking Llandudno Bay and close to the centre of town. Rooms are comfortable and well equipped and many have sea views. Meals are served in the attractive restaurant and there is a selection of lounges and an outside patio overlooking the bay.

Rooms 24 en suite (4 fmly) (2 GF) **Facilities** TVB tea/coffee TVL Dinner Last d 5pm **Parking** 5 **Notes** ⊗ Closed Jan

★★★ GUEST ACCOMMODATION
The Kestrel
25 Deganwy Av LL30 2YB
☎ 01492 875108
e–mail: kestrelllandudno@msn.com
web: www.kestrelllandudno.co.uk

dir: *A55 onto A546 for 4m, right onto Gloddaeth Av, Deganwy Av 4th on right*

A warm welcome is assured at this Victorian terrace house close to the main shopping centre and leisure facilities. Bedrooms feature some

CONTINUED

family accommodation and ground-floor areas include an attractive dining room with adjacent lounge bar.

Rooms 9 en suite (1 fmly) (3 smoking) S £26; D £50–£60✲
Facilities TVB tea/coffee Cen ht TVL Dinner Last d before lunch Golf 18
Parking 4 **Notes LB** No children 3yrs ☻

★★★ GUEST ACCOMMODATION
Minion
21–23 Carmen Sylva Rd, Craig-y-Don LL30 1EQ
☎ 01492 877740

dir: *A55 junct 19 onto A470 to Llandudno. At 4th rdbt take Craig-y-Don turn-off. 2nd right after park*

Situated in a quiet residential area a few minutes walk from the eastern promenade, the Minion has been owned by the same family for over 60 years and continues to extend a warm welcome. Bedrooms are smart and comfortable, and two are on the ground floor. There is a cosy bar and a colourful garden.

Rooms 10 en suite (1 fmly) (2 GF) S £22.50–£25; D £45–£50✲
Facilities FTV TVB tea/coffee TVL Dinner Last d 4pm **Parking** 8
Notes No children 2yrs Closed Nov–Mar ☻

RHOS-ON-SEA   **MAP 14 SH88**

See also Colwyn Bay

Premier Collection

★★★★★ ☷ GUEST ACCOMMODATION
Plas Rhos
Cayley Promenade LL28 4EP
☎ 01492 543698 🖶 01492 540088
e–mail: info@plasrhos.co.uk

dir: *A55 junct 20 onto B5115 for Rhos-on-Sea, right at rdbt onto Whitehall Rd to promenade*

Stunning sea views are a feature of this renovated Victorian house, which provides high standards of comfort and hospitality. Cosy bedrooms are filled with a wealth of thoughtful extras, and public areas include a choice of sumptuous lounges featuring smart décor, quality soft furnishings and memorabilia. Breakfast is served in the attractive dining room, overlooking the pretty patio garden.

Rooms 8 en suite S £45–£65; D £70–£98 **Facilities** FTV TVB tea/coffee
Cen ht TVL Wi-fi available **Parking** 4 **Notes LB** ✖ No children 12yrs
Closed 21 Dec–Jan

TREFRIW   **MAP 14 SH76**

★★★★ GUEST ACCOMMODATION
Hafod Country House
LL27 0RQ
☎ 01492 640029 🖶 01492 641351
e–mail: stay@hafod-house.co.uk

dir: *On B5106 entering Trefriw from S, house on right*

This former farmhouse is personally run and friendly with a wealth of charm and character. The tasteful bedrooms feature period furnishings and thoughtful extras such as fresh fruit. There is a comfortable sitting room and a cosy bar. The fixed-price menu is imaginative and makes good use of fresh, local produce while the breakfast menu offers a wide choice.

Rooms 6 en suite **Facilities** TVB tea/coffee Direct dial from bedrooms
Cen ht Dinner Last d 9pm **Parking** 14 **Notes** No children 11yrs Closed
Jan RS Feb–Mar

DENBIGHSHIRE

CORWEN   **MAP 15 SJ04**

Premier Collection

★★★★★ ☷ GUEST HOUSE
Bron-y-Graig
LL21 0DR
☎ 01490 413007 🖶 01490 413007
e–mail: info@north-wales-hotel.co.uk
web: www.north-wales-hotel.co.uk

dir: *On A5 on E edge of Corwen*

A short walk from the town centre, this impressive Victorian house retains many original features including fireplaces, stained glass and a tiled floor in the entrance hall. Bedrooms, complemented by luxurious bathrooms, are thoughtfully furnished, and two are in a renovated coach house. Ground-floor areas include a traditionally furnished dining room and a comfortable lounge. A warm welcome, attentive service and imaginative food is assured.

Rooms 8 en suite 2 annexe en suite (3 fmly) S £39–£49; D £59
Facilities STV TVB tea/coffee Direct dial from bedrooms Licensed Cen ht
Dinner Last d 9.30pm **Conf** Max 20 Class 20 Board 15 **Parking** 15
Notes LB

WALES

WALES

CORWEN CONTINUED

★★★★ GUEST ACCOMMODATION

Plas Derwen Country House

London Rd LL21 0DR

☎ 01490 412742

e–mail: bandb@plasderwen.supanet.com

dir: *On A5 0.5m E of Corwen*

Set in four acres of fields and mature gardens in an elevated position with superb views of the River Dee, this elegant late 18th-century house has been restored to provide high levels of comfort and facilities. Quality furnishings and décor highlight the many original features and a warm welcome is assured.

Rooms 3 rms (2 en suite) (1 pri facs) (2 fmly) **Facilities** TVB tea/coffee Cen ht TVL Wi-fi available **Parking** 6 **Notes** ⊗ Closed Dec–Jan ◉

★★★★ BED & BREAKFAST

Powys Country House

Holyhead Rd, Bonwm LL21 9EG

☎ 01490 412367 🗐 01490 412367

e–mail: info@powyscountryhouse.co.uk

dir: *On A5 1m E from Corwen, on left*

Located two miles south of Corwen in extensive gardens, which include a tennis court, this recently refurbished period property provides good standards of comfort and facilities. Bedrooms are equipped with lots of homely extras and day rooms include a cosy lounge and spacious dining room, the setting for comprehensive breakfasts.

Rooms 5 en suite (2 fmly) S £40–£50; D £60–£70✹ **Facilities** STV FTV TVB tea/coffee Cen ht TVL ♨ Full size chess set **Parking** 12 **Notes LB** ⊗ No children 3yrs Closed end Nov–end Mar

★★★★ 🄰 BED & BREAKFAST

The Cottage Bed & Breakfast

Carrog LL21 9AP

☎ 01490 430644

e–mail: enquiries@thecottagecarrog.co.uk

dir: *W along A5 from Llangollen for 7m. Turn right, signed Carrog. Down hill past the Steam Railway Station and over River Dee. Turn left, up the hill, through village for 0.25m, The Cottage on left*

Rooms 2 en suite S £35–£50; D £55–£66✹ **Facilities** TVB tea/coffee Cen ht Wi-fi available Fishing **Parking** 2 **Notes LB** ⊗ No children 5yrs Closed Nov–Etr

DENBIGH   MAP 15 SJ06

See also Bylchau (Conwy)

★★★ GUEST HOUSE

Cayo

74 Vale St LL16 3BW

☎ 01745 812686

e–mail: stay@cayo.co.uk

dir: *Off A525 into town, at lights turn up hill, supermarket on right. Guest house up hill on left*

A warm welcome is assured at this Victorian house, which is situated on the main street, just a short walk from the town centre. Bedrooms are comfortably and thoughtfully furnished with lots of homely extras. Good home cooking is provided in a Victorian-themed dining room, and a cosy basement lounge is also available.

Rooms 4 en suite S £27; D £54✹ **Facilities** TVB tea/coffee Cen ht TVL Wi-fi available **Notes** No coaches Closed Xmas-New Year

LLANDRILLO   MAP 15 SJ03

Premier Collection

★★★★★ ◉◉ 🍴 RESTAURANT WITH ROOMS

Tyddyn Llan

LL21 0ST

☎ 01490 440264 🗐 01490 440414

e–mail: tyddynllan@compuserve.com

web: www.tyddynllan.co.uk

dir: *Take B4401 from Corwen to Llandrillo. Tyddyn Llan on right leaving village*

An elegant Georgian house set in its own grounds in a peaceful and relaxing location. Bedrooms vary in size but all are comfortably furnished and include some welcome extras. The restaurant and lounges are quite delightful and offer pleasant views over the surrounding gardens. Emphasis is on local produce, carefully prepared by the chef/proprietor and his team.

Rooms 13 en suite (1 GF) S £100–£130; D £200–£340✹ (incl. dinner) **Facilities** FTV TVB tea/coffee Direct dial from bedrooms Cen ht Dinner Last d 9.30pm ♨ **Conf** Max 30 Thtr 30 Class 10 Board 20 Del from £160✹ **Parking** 20 **Notes LB** Closed 2 wks Jan RS Nov–Mar Civ Wed 40

LLANDYRNOG
MAP 15 SJ16

Premier Collection

★★★★★ GUEST ACCOMMODATION
Pentre Mawr Country House

LL16 4LA

☎ 01824 790732 📄 01492 585486

e-mail: info@pentremawrcountryhouse.co.uk

dir: *From Denbigh follow signs to Bodfari/Llandyrnog. Left at rdbt to Bodfari, after 50yds turn left onto country lane, follow road and Pentre Mawr on left*

Expect a warm welcome from Graham and Bre at this superb family country house set in nearly 200 acres of meadows, park and woodland. The property has been in Graham's family for over four hundred years. Bedrooms are individually decorated, very spacious and each is thoughtfully equipped. Breakfast is served in either the morning room or, on warmer mornings, on the Georgian terrace. Dinner is served in the formal dining room. There is a salt water swimming pool in the walled garden.

Rooms 5 en suite S £75–£100; D £90–£120✳ **Facilities** TVB tea/coffee Cen ht Dinner Last d 7pm Wi-fi available ↘ ♨ Fishing ↩ **Conf** Max 10 **Parking** 8 **Notes LB** No children 13yrs Closed Nov–Feb ☺

LLANGOLLEN
MAP 15 SJ24

See also Corwen

★★★★ GUEST HOUSE
Oakmere

Regent St LL20 8HS

☎ 01978 861126

e-mail: oakmeregh@aol.com

web: www.oakmere.llangollen.co.uk

dir: *A5 from lights in Llangollen towards Oswestry, 300yds on right*

A well-proportioned Victorian house standing on pretty grounds. Furnishings and decor highlight the many retained original features and bedrooms are spacious and comfortable. Ground-floor areas include a large dining room with a Gothic-style conservatory and a lounge.

Oakmere

Rooms 6 rms (4 en suite) (2 pri facs) (1 fmly) S £50–£60; D £65✳ **Facilities** TVB tea/coffee Cen ht Wi-fi available **Parking** 10 **Notes** ⊗ No children 10yrs No coaches ☺

★★★★ BED & BREAKFAST
Tyn Celyn Farmhouse

Tyndwr LL20 8AR

☎ 01978 861117 📄 01978 861771

e-mail: j.m.bather-tyncelyn@talk21.com

web: www.smoothhound.co.uk/hotels/tyncelyn.html

dir: *A5 to Llangollen, pass golf club on right, next left signed Youth Hostel, 0.5m sharp left onto Tyndwr Rd, past activity centre on left. Tyn Celyn 0.5m on left*

This 300-year-old timber-framed farmhouse has stunning views over the Vale of Llangollen. Bedrooms, one of which is located on the ground floor, provide a range of thoughtful extras in addition to fine period furniture. Breakfast is served at a magnificent carved table in a spacious sitting-dining room.

Rooms 3 en suite (1 fmly) (1 GF) D fr £60 **Facilities** TVB tea/coffee Cen ht TVL **Parking** 5 **Notes LB** ⊗ ☺

CONTINUED

WALES

LLANGOLLEN CONTINUED

★★★★ BED & BREAKFAST
Whitegate

Grange Rd LL20 8AP
☎ 01978 860960 📠 01978 861699
e–mail: veda@whitegate-llangollen.co.uk

dir: *No car access on Grange Rd. Up Hill St (behind Grapes Hotel on A5) & past Plas Newydd on left. Whitegate on right after short narrow road*

This impressive Edwardian family house is a short walk from the town centre, and stands in pretty gardens. The comfortable, traditionally furnished bedrooms have thoughtful extras in addition to modern showers en suite; two rooms have fine views over the Vale of Llangollen. There is a comfortable lounge-dining room and at breakfast the emphasis is on fresh local produce.

Rooms 3 en suite S £40; D £60✳ **Facilities** tea/coffee Cen ht TVL
Parking 8 **Notes** LB ✖ 🐾

RHYL　　　　　　　　　　MAP 14 SJ08

★★★★ ◉◉ 🍴 RESTAURANT WITH ROOMS
Barratt's at Ty'n Rhyl

Ty'n Rhyl, 167 Vale Rd LL18 2PH
☎ 01745 344138 & 0773 095 4994 📠 01745 344138
e–mail: ebarratt5@aol.com

dir: *A55 onto A525 to Rhyl, pass Sainsburys & B&Q, garden centre on left, Barratt's 400yds on right*

This delightful 16th-century house lies in a secluded location surrounded by attractive gardens. The quality of food reflects the skill of the owner-chef. Public areas are smartly furnished and include a panelled lounge and separate bar with attractive conservatory. Bedrooms are comfortable and equipped with lots of thoughtful extras.

Rooms 3 en suite **Facilities** TVB tea/coffee Cen ht TVL Dinner Last d 9pm Wi-fi available ⚓ **Parking** 20 **Notes** ✖

RUTHIN　　　　　　　　　　MAP 15 SJ15

★★★★ GUEST ACCOMMODATION
Eyarth Station

Llanfair Dyffryn Clwyd LL15 2EE
☎ 01824 703643 📠 01824 707464
e–mail: stay@eyarthstation.com

dir: *1m S of Ruthin. Off A525 onto lane, 600yds to Eyarth Station*
Until 1964 and the Beeching cuts, this was a sleepy country station. A comfortable lounge and outdoor swimming pool occupy the space once taken up by the railway and platforms. Bedrooms are carefully decorated and full of thoughtful extras. Family rooms are available, and two rooms are in the former stationmaster's house adjoining the main building.

Rooms 4 en suite 2 annexe en suite (2 fmly) (4 GF) S £50; D £72✳
Facilities TV1B tea/coffee Cen ht TVL Dinner Last d 7pm ⚓ **Parking** 6
Notes LB Closed 2 wks Jan

★★★★ 🏠 ➾ BED & BREAKFAST
Firgrove Country House B & B

Firgrove, Llanfwrog LL15 2LL
☎ 01824 702677 📠 01824 702677
e–mail: meadway@firgrovecountryhouse.co.uk
web: www.firgrovecountryhouse.co.uk

dir: *0.5m SW of Ruthin. A494 onto B5105, 0.25m past Llanfwrog church on right*

Standing in immaculate mature gardens in a peaceful rural location, this well-proportioned house retains many original features, highlighted by the quality décor and furnishings. Bedrooms are equipped with a wealth of thoughtful extras and memorable breakfasts, using home-made or local produce, are served in the elegant dining room.

Rooms 2 en suite 1 annexe en suite (1 GF) D £70–£100✳ **Facilities** FTV TVB tea/coffee Cen ht Dinner Last d 24hrs Wi-fi available **Parking** 4
Notes ✖ No children Closed Nov–Feb

★★★★ ◉◉ RESTAURANT WITH ROOMS

The Wynnstay Arms

Well St LL15 1AN

☎ 01824 703147

e–mail: resevations@wynnstayarms.com

web: www.wynnstayarms.com

dir: *In town centre*

This former town centre period inn has been sympathetically renovated to provide good quality accommodation and a smart café-bar. Imaginative food is served in Fusions Brasserie, where a contemporary decor style highlights the many retained period features.

Rooms 7 en suite (1 fmly) S £45–£65; D £70–£110✱ **Facilities** FTV TVB tea/coffee Cen ht Dinner Last d 9.30pm Wi-fi available **Conf** Max 30 Thtr 30 Class 20 Board 16 **Parking** 14 **Notes** LB

★★★★ FARM HOUSE

Tyddyn Chambers *(SJ102543)*

Pwllglas LL15 2LS

☎ 01824 750683 Mrs E Williams

e–mail: williams@tyddynchambers.fsnet.co.uk

web: www.tyddynchambers.co.uk

dir: *3m S of Ruthin. W off A494 after the Fox & Hounds pub in Pwllglas, signed*

This charming little farmhouse has been extended to provide carefully appointed, modern accommodation, which includes a family room. The pleasant, traditionally furnished breakfast room has separate tables and a lounge is also available. The house stands in an elevated position with panoramic views.

Rooms 3 en suite (1 fmly) S £30–£35; D £50–£60 **Facilities** TVB tea/coffee Cen ht TVL **Parking** 3 **Notes** LB ⊗ 180 acres Beef, sheep Closed Xmas & New Year ⊜

★★★ BED & BREAKFAST

Plas Efenechtyd Cottage Bed & Breakfast

Efenechtyd LL15 2LP

☎ 01824 704008

e–mail: info@plas-efenechtyd-cottage.co.uk

dir: *From Ruthin follow A494 and take B5105 1.2m. Turn left into narrow lane*

Located two miles from town centre in the ancient hamlet of Efenechtyd, overlooking the Vale of Clwyd, this 200 year old cottage stands on one acre of mature gardens, a magnet for local wildlife. Furnishing and décor styles highlight the many retained period features and a warm welcome is assured.

Rooms 3 en suite S £35; D £55✱ **Facilities** FTV TVB tea/coffee Cen ht Wi-fi available **Parking** 3 **Notes** LB ⊗ ⊜

ST ASAPH   MAP 15 SJ07

Premier Collection

★★★★★ GUEST HOUSE

Tan-Yr-Onnen Guest House

Waen LL17 0DU

☎ 01745 583821 🖷 01745 583821

e–mail: tanyronnenvisit@aol.com

web: www.northwalesbreaks.co.uk

dir: *W on A55 junct 28, turn left in 300yds*

A warm welcome is assured at this extensively modernised house which is quietly located in six acres of grounds and gardens, yet conveniently close to the A55. It opened in Easter 2006 and provides very high quality, modern, well-equipped accommodation, including a suite and ground floor rooms. There is a spacious lounge, and hearty breakfasts are served in the adjacent dining room.

Rooms 6 en suite (1 fmly) (4 GF) S £50–£80; D £70–£100✱ **Facilities** FTV TVB tea/coffee Cen ht Wi-fi available **Parking** 8 **Notes** No coaches

★★★★ FARM HOUSE

Bach-Y-Graig *(SJ075713)*

Tremeirchion LL17 0UH

☎ 01745 730627 🖷 01745 730627 Mrs A Roberts

e–mail: anwen@bachygraig.co.uk

dir: *3m SE of St Asaph. Off A525 at Trefnant onto A541 to x-rds with white railings, left down hill, over bridge & then right*

Dating from the 16th century, this listed building was the first brick-built house in Wales and retains many original features including a wealth of exposed beams and inglenook fireplaces. Bedrooms are furnished with fine period pieces and quality soft fabrics. Ground floor areas include a quiet lounge and a combined sitting and dining room, featuring a superb Jacobean oak table.

Rooms 3 rms (2 en suite) (1 pri facs) (1 fmly) S £40–£55; D £70–£85 **Facilities** FTV TVB tea/coffee Cen ht TVL Wi-fi available Fishing Woodland trail **Parking** 3 **Notes** LB ⊗ 200 acres dairy Closed Xmas & New Year ⊜

WALES

FLINTSHIRE

HOLYWELL
MAP 15 SJ17

★★★ Ⓐ FARM HOUSE
Greenhill Farm *(SJ186776)*

CH8 7QF

☎ 01352 713270 Mrs M Jones

e–mail: mary@greenhillfarm.fsnet.co.uk

web: www.greenhillfarm.co.uk

dir: *From Holywell signs to St Winfred's Well, left opp Royal Oak pub to end of lane*

Rooms 4 rms (2 en suite) (2 pri facs) (2 fmly) S fr £30; D fr £60
Facilities TVB tea/coffee Cen ht TVL Wi-fi available Childrens play area
Parking 6 **Notes LB** ⊗ 120 acres dairy mixed RS Dec–Jan

NANNERCH
MAP 15 SJ16

★★★★ GUEST ACCOMMODATION
The Old Mill Guest Accommodation

Melin-Y-Wern, Denbigh Rd CH7 5RH

☎ 01352 741542

e–mail: mail@old-mill.co.uk

web: www.old-mill.co.uk

dir: *A541 NW from Mold, 7m enter Melin-Y-Wern, Old Mill on right*

This converted stone stable block was once part of a Victorian watermill complex. The site also includes a restaurant and wine bar. The non-smoking guest accommodation offers modern, well-equipped bedrooms with private bathrooms, suitable for leisure and business.

Rooms 6 en suite (2 GF) S £45–£57; D £60–£78✶ **Facilities** FTV TVB tea/coffee Direct dial from bedrooms Cen ht Wi-fi available **Parking** 12 **Notes LB** ⊗ Closed 1–30 Nov

GWYNEDD

ABERDYFI
MAP 14 SN69

★★★★ GUEST ACCOMMODATION
Penmaendyfi Country House

Cwrt, Pennal SY20 9LD

☎ 01654 791246 🖹 01654 791616

e–mail: shana@penmaendyfi.co.uk

dir: *4m W of Machynlleth on A493*

Delightfully located within sweeping grounds, Penmaendyfi offers a wealth of history in addition to stunning views over the Dyfi estuary to the mountains beyond. Bedrooms and bathrooms are particularly spacious and include one on the ground floor. Guests are welcome to use the comfortable lounge with honesty bar and the large outdoor swimming pool.

Rooms 6 en suite (2 fmly) (1 GF) S £50–£65; D £80–£90✶ **Facilities** TVB tea/coffee Direct dial from bedrooms Cen ht ↖ ⌁ **Parking** 10 **Notes** ⊗ Closed Dec–Jan

ABERSOCH
MAP 14 SH32

★★★★ GUEST HOUSE
Llysfor Guest House

LL53 7AL

☎ 01758 712248 🖹 01758 712248

e–mail: emma@llysforguesthouse.co.uk

web: www.llysforguesthouse.com

dir: *Take A499, at bottom of hill on right*

This large Victorian house stands opposite the harbour and is within a short walk of the beach and the town centre. It provides good quality,

CONTINUED

modern accommodation, which is complemented by a pleasant lounge and an attractive breakfast room.

Rooms 6 rms (4 en suite) (2 pri facs) S £45–£50; D £70–£80✳
Facilities TVB tea/coffee Cen ht **Parking** 8 **Notes** ⊗ No coaches Closed Dec–Feb ⊛

BALA   MAP 14 SH93

★★★★ GUEST HOUSE
Erw Feurig
Cefnddwysarn LL23 7LL
☎ 01678 530262 & 07786 168399 ▤ 01678 530262
e–mail: erwfeurig@yahoo.com
web: www.erwfeurig.com

dir: 3m NE of Bala off A494. 2nd left after telephone box, B&B signed

A warm welcome is assured at this delightful and peaceful farm cottage situated on a hillside with panoramic views of the Berwyn Mountains. The individually styled bedrooms have a range of additional extras, and a cosy lounge and a cheerful ground-floor breakfast room are available.

Rooms 4 rms (2 en suite) (2 pri facs) (1 GF) S £30; D £55✳
Facilities TVB tea/coffee Cen ht TVL Fishing **Parking** 6 **Notes LB** ⊗
No children No coaches Closed Nov–Feb ⊛

★★★★ FARM HOUSE
Pen-Y-Bryn Farmhouse *(SH967394)*
Sarnau LL23 7LH
☎ 01678 530389 ▤ 01678 530389 Mrs E Jones
e–mail: jonespenbryn@lineone.net
web: www.bala-wales.com/penbryn/

dir: 3m NE of Bala off A494. Pass Cefnddwysarn, 2nd left, B&B signed

A genuine welcome is assured at this stone Victorian house, located on an elevated position overlooking Sarnau and the surrounding mountains. Bedrooms are thoughtfully furnished and have modern en suite facilities. Hearty breakfasts are served in the attractive conservatory with stunning views.

Rooms 3 en suite (1 GF) S £30–£32; D £52 **Facilities** tea/coffee Cen ht TVL Bird watching, walking, cycling **Parking** 8 **Notes LB** ⊗ 70 acres mixed Closed 25–26 Dec ⊛

★★★★ INN
The White Lion Royal
High St LL23 7AE
☎ 01678 520314 ▤ 01678 521669
e–mail: lion@welsh-historic-inns.com

dir: From the north or south take the A494, White Lion located in town centre.

Located a few minutes walk from Llyn Tegid, this historic coaching inn has been sympathetically renovated to provide high standards of comfort and facilities. Thoughtfully furnished bedrooms benefit from smart efficient en suite bathrooms, and public areas retain original charm and character.

Rooms 26 en suite (4 fmly) S £60–£80; D £65–£110✳ **Facilities** STV TVB tea/coffee Direct dial from bedrooms Cen ht TVL Dinner Last d 9pm **Conf** Max 60 Thtr 60 Class 40 Board 40 Del from £70 ✳
Parking 20 **Notes LB** ⊗

★★★ INN
Gwesty'r Plas Coch Cyf
High St LL23 7AB
☎ 01678 520309 ▤ 01678 521135
e–mail: plascoch@tiscali.co.uk

A focal point in a bustling town, this 18th-century former coaching inn is popular with locals and resident guests alike. The public areas are very attractive and bedrooms are spacious.

Rooms 10 en suite (4 fmly) S £35–£45; D £55–£69✳ **Facilities** TVB tea/coffee Direct dial from bedrooms Cen ht TVL Dinner Last d 9pm Golf 10 Pool Table **Conf** Max 35 Thtr 35 **Parking** 15

BARMOUTH   MAP 14 SH61

See also Dyffryn Ardudwy

★★★★ GUEST HOUSE
Richmond House
High St LL42 1DW
☎ 01341 281366 & 07976 833069
e–mail: info@barmouthbedandbreakfast.co.uk
web: www.barmouthbedandbreakfast.co.uk

dir: In town centre. Car park at rear on Jubilee Rd

A warm welcome awaits you at this lovely Victorian house, which has been modernised to provide good quality and thoughtfully equipped accommodation. Two of the bedrooms have sea views, as do the lounge and dining room, where there are separate tables. There is also a pleasant garden.

Rooms 3 en suite (1 fmly) S £55; D fr £65✳ **Facilities** TVB tea/coffee Cen ht Wi-fi available **Parking** 5 **Notes LB** ⊗ No coaches

WALES

BARMOUTH CONTINUED

★★★★ 🍽 GUEST ACCOMMODATION
Llwyndu Farmhouse
Llanaber LL42 1RR
☎ 01341 280144
e–mail: Intouch@llwyndu-farmhouse.co.uk
web: www.llwyndu-farmhouse.co.uk

dir: *A496 towards Harlech where street lights end, on outskirts of Barmouth, take next right*

This converted 16th-century farmhouse retains many original features including inglenook fireplaces, exposed beams and timbers. There is a cosy lounge and meals are enjoyed at individual tables in the character dining room. Bedrooms are modern and well equipped, and some have four-poster beds. Four rooms are in nearby buildings.

Rooms 3 en suite 4 annexe en suite (2 fmly) D £80–£94✱
Facilities TVB tea/coffee Cen ht TVL Dinner Last d 6pm **Parking** 10
Notes LB Closed 25–26 Dec RS Sun

★★★★ 🏠 🍽 GUEST ACCOMMODATION
Morwendon House
Llanaber LL42 1RR
☎ 01341 280566 📠 07092 197785
e–mail: info@morwendon-house.co.uk

dir: *A496 at Llanaber N of Barmouth. On Seaward side 250yds past Llanaber Church*

With its impressive position overlooking Cardigan Bay, Morwendon House is an ideal base for exploring the surrounding area and its many attractions. The bedrooms offer well-equipped accommodation, with many rooms having sea views. Dinner is available by arrangement and

CONTINUED

meals are taken in the attractive dining room overlooking the bay. There is also a comfortable lounge, again with views over the bay.

Rooms 5 en suite 1 annexe en suite (1 fmly) (1 GF) **Facilities** TVB tea/coffee Cen ht TVL Dinner Last d 7pm **Parking** 7 **Notes** ⊗ No children 5yrs

★★★★ INN
Tal-y-Don Inn
High St LL42 1DL
☎ 01341 280508 📠 01341 280885
e–mail: david@tal-y-don.co.uk
web: www.tal-y-don.co.uk

dir: *A496 one-way system, right onto Beach Rd, right at end*

This very friendly and popular town centre hostelry provides attractive, good-quality accommodation. Public areas include lounge and public bar areas and a beer garden. A good range of freshly prepared food is available, served in either the pleasant restaurant or in the bar.

Rooms 5 en suite **Facilities** TVB tea/coffee Direct dial from bedrooms Cen ht Dinner Last d 8.45pm **Notes** ⊗ No coaches

---

BEDDGELERT   MAP 14 SH54

★★★★ 🍽 GUEST ACCOMMODATION
Sygun Fawr Country House
LL55 4NE
☎ 01766 890258 📠 01766 890258
e–mail: sygunfawr@aol.com
web: www.sygunfawr.co.uk

dir: *A498 N, turn right over river at brown sign onto lane*

Sygun Fawr is set in a spectacular location within the Snowdonia National Park. The surrounding countryside and immaculate gardens are a mass of colour in the spring. Bedrooms are neat and pretty and many have superb views. Stone walls and exposed timbers abound, and a cosy bar and several comfortable sitting rooms are provided.

Rooms 11 en suite (1 GF) S £59; D £78–£105✱ **Facilities** tea/coffee Cen ht TVL Dinner Last d 8pm **Conf** Thtr 10 Board 10 **Parking** 20 **Notes LB** Closed Jan

WALES

WALES

★★★★ INN
Tanronnen Inn

LL55 4YB

☎ 01766 890347 📄 01766 890606

This delightful inn offers comfortable, well equipped and attractively appointed accommodation, including a family room. There is also a selection of pleasant and relaxing public areas. The wide range of bar food is popular with tourists, and more formal meals are served in the restaurant.

Rooms 7 en suite (3 fmly) **Facilities** TVB tea/coffee Direct dial from bedrooms Dinner **Parking** 15 **Notes** ⊗

BETWS GARMON   MAP 14 SH55

★★★★ 🛏 BED & BREAKFAST
Betws Inn

LL54 7YY

☎ 01286 650324

e–mail: stay@betws-inn.co.uk

dir: *On A4085 Caernarfon to Beddgelert, opp Bryn Gloch Caravan Park*

Set in the western foothills of the Snowdonia, this 17th-century former inn has been restored to create an establishment of immense charm. A warm welcome and caring service are assured. Bedrooms have a wealth of homely extras, and imaginative dinners feature local produce. Breakfast includes home-made bread and preserves.

Rooms 3 en suite S £50–£60; D £70–£80✱ **Facilities** tea/coffee Cen ht TVL Dinner Last d 2pm **Parking** 3 **Notes** ⊗

CAERNARFON   MAP 14 SH46

See also Clynnog Fawr & Penygroes

★★★★ FARM HOUSE
Pengwern *(SH459587)*

Saron LL54 5UH

☎ 01286 831500 📄 01286 830741 Mr & Mrs G Rowlands

e–mail: janepengwern@aol.com

web: www.pengwern.net

dir: *A487 S from Caernarfon, pass supermarket on right, right after bridge, 2m to Saron, over x-rds, 1st driveway on right*

A beautifully maintained farmhouse surrounded by 130 acres of farmland running down to Foryd Bay, which is noted for its birdlife. Spacious bedrooms are equipped with modern, efficient bathrooms in addition to a wealth of thoughtful extras. Imaginative breakfasts are served in an elegant dining room and a lounge is also available.

Pengwern

Rooms 3 en suite S £45; D £70–£90 **Facilities** TVB tea/coffee Cen ht Dinner Last d noon **Parking** 3 **Notes** LB ⊗ 130 acres beef sheep Closed Oct–Apr

★★★★ GUEST HOUSE
Caer Menai

15 Church St LL55 1SW

☎ 01286 672612

e–mail: info@caermenai.co.uk

web: www.caermenai.co.uk

dir: *Follow signs to the Castle & Old Town Walls, Caer Menai is 250yds from the castle within the walled town*

This friendly guest house, originally the late 19th-century county school, is within the walled town, close to the castle. The medieval town wall forms the boundary of the back garden. There is an attractive breakfast room and a lounge, and the cheerful bedrooms are equipped with modern facilities.

Rooms 7 en suite (2 fmly) S £40–£60; D £60–£65✱ **Facilities** FTV TVB tea/coffee Cen ht TVL Wi-fi available **Notes** LB ⊗ No coaches 🐾

★★★★ 🅰 GUEST ACCOMMODATION
Bron Menai Guest House

North Rd LL55 1BA

☎ 01286 675589 📄 01286 673689

e–mail: enquiries@bronmenai.co.uk

dir: *A487 into Caernarfon, at large rdbt signed to town centre. 25yds on left opposite Church*

Rooms 8 en suite (1 GF) S £35–£55; D £60–£75✱ **Facilities** FTV TVB tea/coffee Cen ht TVL Dinner Last d 10am Wi-fi available **Parking** 8 **Notes** LB ⊗ No children 10yrs

★★★★ 🅰 GUEST ACCOMMODATION
Plas Dinas Country House

Bontnewydd LL54 7YF

☎ 01286 830214

e–mail: info@plasdinas.co.uk

web: www.plasdinas.co.uk

dir: *On A487 from Caernarfon, set back 0.5m down private drive*

Rooms 10 en suite (1 GF) S £79–£159; D £89–£169✱ **Facilities** FTV TVB tea/coffee Direct dial from bedrooms Cen ht TVL Dinner Last d 8pm Wi-fi available **Conf** Max 20 Thtr 20 Class 20 Board 16 **Parking** 50 **Notes** LB Civ Wed 60

CONTINUED

CLYNNOG-FAWR   MAP 14 SH44

★★★★ GUEST HOUSE

Bryn Eisteddfod Country House

Clynnog Fawr LL54 5DA

☎ 01286 660431

e–mail: info@bryneisteddfod.com

dir: *Off A499 at village*

This Victorian house, near the Lleyn Peninsula and Snowdonia, offers comfortable accommodation and is especially popular with golfers. The traditionally furnished bedrooms are well equipped. There is a comfortable lounge and a large attractive conservatory bar-dining room, where evening meals can be served.

Rooms 7 rms (6 en suite) (1 pri facs) (2 fmly) S £52.50; D £70✶ **Facilities** TVB tea/coffee Licensed Cen ht Dinner Last d 8.45pm **Conf** Max 40 **Parking** 25 **Notes** ⊗ No coaches

---

CRICCIETH   MAP 14 SH43

★★★★ GUEST ACCOMMODATION

The Abereistedd

West Pde LL52 0EN

☎ 01766 522710 📠 01766 523526

e–mail: info@abereistedd.co.uk

web: www.abereistedd.co.uk

dir: *A487 through Criccieth towards Pwllheli, left 400yds after fuel station following signs for beach, on left at seafront*

An extremely warm welcome is assured at this Victorian property with uninterrupted mountain and coastal views. The attractive bedrooms

are very well equipped with thoughtful extras, the ground-floor lounge has a bar extension, and the bright dining room overlooks the seafront.

Rooms 12 en suite (2 fmly) S £35; D £58–£70✶ **Facilities** TVB tea/coffee Direct dial from bedrooms Cen ht Dinner Last d 2pm **Parking** 9 **Notes LB** ⊗ Closed Nov–Mar

★★★★ GUEST ACCOMMODATION

Bron Rhiw

Caernarfon Rd LL52 0AP

☎ 01766 522257

e–mail: clairecriccieth@yahoo.co.uk

web: www.bronrhiwhotel.co.uk

dir: *Off High St onto B4411*

A warm welcome and high standards of comfort and facilities are assured at this constantly improving Victorian property, just a short walk from the seafront. Bedrooms are equipped with lots of thoughtful extras and ground-floor areas include a sumptuous lounge, a cosy bar, and an elegant dining room, the setting for imaginative breakfasts.

Rooms 9 en suite (2 fmly) S £46–£70; D £70–£74 **Facilities** TVB tea/coffee Cen ht **Parking** 3 **Notes LB** ⊗ No children 5yrs Closed Nov–Feb

★★★★ GUEST HOUSE

Cefn Uchaf Farm Guest House

Garndolbenmaen LL51 9PJ

☎ 01766 530239

e–mail: enquiries@cefnuchaf.co.uk

dir: *5m N of Porthmadog. Left off A487 after Dolbenmaen. 4m N Criccieth right off B4411 Rhoslan*

The large, pleasant farmhouse stands in a remote location amid stunning scenery. Some of the thoughtfully furnished modern bedrooms are ideal for families, and a spacious lounge is available. Meals are served in the bright dining room.

Rooms 8 rms (7 en suite) (1 pri facs) (3 fmly) S £40–£45; D £54–£60✶ **Facilities** TVB tea/coffee Cen ht TVL Dinner Last d noon **Parking** 12

CONTINUED

★★★★ GUEST HOUSE
Min y Gaer
Porthmadog Rd LL52 0HP
☎ 01766 522151 📠 01766 523540
e–mail: info@minygaer.co.uk
dir: On A497 200yds E of junct with B4411

The friendly, family-run Min y Gaer has superb views from many of the rooms. The smart, modern bedrooms are furnished in pine, and the welcoming proprietors also provide a bar and a traditionally furnished lounge.

Rooms 10 en suite (2 fmly) S £30–£33; D £60–£70 Facilities TVB tea/coffee Licensed Cen ht TVL Wi-fi available ♨ Parking 12 Notes No coaches Closed 17 Dec–14 Mar

---

DOLGELLAU   MAP 14 SH71

Premier Collection

★★★★★ FARM HOUSE
Tyddynmawr Farmhouse (SH704159)
Cader Rd, Islawrdref LL40 1TL
☎ 01341 422331 Mrs Evans

dir: From town centre left at top of square, left at garage onto Cader Rd for 3m, 1st farm on left after Gwernan Lake

A warm welcome is assured at this 18th-century farmhouse which lies at the foot of Cader Idris amidst breathtaking scenery. Bedrooms are spacious, with Welsh Oak furniture; the upper one has a balcony and the ground-floor room has a patio area. Bathrooms are large and luxurious. Superb breakfasts are a feast of home-made items; bread, preserves, muesli or smoked fish – the choice is excellent. Self-catering cottages are also available.

CONTINUED

Rooms 3 en suite (1 GF) S £58; D £68 Facilities TVB tea/coffee Cen ht TVL Fishing Parking 8 Notes ⊗ No children 800 acres beef sheep Closed Jan ⊚

★★★★ ☞ BED & BREAKFAST
Coed Cae
Taicynhaeaf LL40 2TU
☎ 01341 430628 & 07909 996983
e–mail: info@coedcae.co.uk
dir: 3m NW of Dolgellau. N off A496 opp toll bridge

A warm welcome awaits at this charming old house, which is set in its own extensive wooded grounds, overlooking spectacular views of the Mawddach Estuary. The thoughtfully equipped accommodation includes a bedroom on ground floor level. All share one table in the spacious combined dining room and lounge, where guests can enjoy skilfully prepared, imaginative food.

Rooms 3 rms (2 en suite) (1 pri facs) (1 fmly) (1 GF) S £45–£55; D £60–£85✳ Facilities TVB tea/coffee Cen ht Dinner Last d 4pm Conf Max 8 Board 8 Del from £40 ✳ Parking 8 Notes LB ⊗

★★★★ GUEST HOUSE
Dolgun Uchaf Guesthouse
Dolgun Uchaf LL40 2AB
☎ 01341 422269
e–mail: dolgunuchaf@aol.com
web: www.guesthousessnowdonia.com

dir: Off A470 at Little Chef just S of Dolgellau, Dolgun Uchaf 1st property on right

Located in a peaceful area with stunning views of the surrounding countryside, this 500-year-old late medieval hall house retains many original features, including exposed beams and open fireplaces. Bedrooms are equipped with thoughtful extras and a lounge is also available.

Rooms 3 en suite 1 annexe en suite (1 GF) Facilities TVB tea/coffee Cen ht TVL Dinner Last d 24hrs prior Parking 6 Notes No children 5yrs

WALES

WALES

DOLGELLAU CONTINUED

★★★ GUEST HOUSE

Ivy House

Finsbury Square LL40 1RF

☎ 01341 422535 📠 01341 422689

e-mail: marg.bamford@btconnect.com

dir: *In town centre. From top of main square, house on left after bend*

Friendly hospitality is offered at this house, situated in the centre of Dolgellau at the foot of Cader Idris. Bedrooms are brightly decorated and thoughtfully equipped. Ground floor rooms include a comfortable lounge and a spacious dining room where dinner is available by arrangement.

Rooms 6 rms (4 en suite) (1 fmly) S £37–£45; D £55–£65✱
Facilities TVB tea/coffee Cen ht TVL Dinner Last d 4pm **Notes** ⊗
No coaches Closed 24–26 Dec

DYFFRYN ARDUDWY   MAP 14 SH52

★★★★ INN

Cadwgan Inn

LL44 2HA

☎ 01341 247240

e-mail: cadwgan.hotel@virgin.net

dir: *In Dyffryn Ardudwy onto Station Rd, over railway crossing*

This very pleasant, privately-owned pub stands in grounds close to Dyffryn Ardudwy station, between Barmouth and Harlech. The beach is a short walk away. The good quality, well-equipped modern accommodation includes family rooms and a room with a four-poster

bed. Public areas include a family room with games, a meeting room and a beer garden

Rooms 6 en suite (3 fmly) **Facilities** TVB tea/coffee Cen ht TVL Dinner
Last d 9.30pm Sauna Gymnasium Pool Table **Notes** ⊗ No coaches Civ
Wed 60

★★★★ GUEST HOUSE

The Old Farmhouse

Tyddyn Du LL44 2DW

☎ 01341 242711 📠 01341 242711

e-mail: metcalfe.oldfarmhouse@virgin.net

dir: *Signed on A496 between Harlech & Barmouth, 0.5m from road*

Located in well-maintained grounds including a swimming pool and hot tub, this renovated former farmhouse provides a range of thoughtfully furnished bedrooms, two of which are in a separate garden cottage. The comfortable sitting-dining room has stunning views of the surrounding coastline.

Rooms 3 en suite 2 annexe en suite (2 fmly) (5 GF) **Facilities** STV TVB
tea/coffee Cen ht TVL ⚒ **Parking** 10 **Notes** ⊗ No children 5yrs
No coaches Closed 24–31 Dec ☺

FFESTINIOG   MAP 14 SH74

★★★★ BED & BREAKFAST

Ty Clwb

The Square LL41 4LS

☎ 01766 762658 📠 01766 762658

e-mail: tyclwb@talk21.com

web: www.tyclwb.co.uk

dir: *On B4391 in of Ffestiniog, opp church*

Located opposite the historic church, this elegant house has been carefully modernised and is immaculately maintained throughout. Bedrooms are thoughtfully furnished and in addition to an attractive dining room, a spacious lounge with sun patio provides stunning views of the surrounding mountain range.

Rooms 3 en suite D £50–£60 **Facilities** tea/coffee Cen ht TVL

★★★ GUEST ACCOMMODATION

Morannedd

Blaenau Rd LL41 4LG

☎ 01766 762734

e-mail: morannedd@talk21.com

dir: *At edge of village on A470 towards Blaenau Ffestiniog*

This guest house is set in the Snowdonia National Park and is well located for touring north Wales. A friendly welcome is offered and the atmosphere is relaxed and informal. Bedrooms are smart and modern and a cosy lounge is available. Hearty home cooking is a definite draw.

Rooms 4 en suite **Facilities** TVB tea/coffee Cen ht **Notes** Closed Xmas
☺

CONTINUED

HARLECH   MAP 14 SH53

★★★★ GUEST HOUSE
Gwrach Ynys Country

Talsarnau LL47 6TS

☎ 01766 780742 📄 01766 781199

e-mail: deborah@gwrachynys.co.uk

web: www.gwrachynys.co.uk

dir: *2m N of Harlech on A496*

This delightful Edwardian house nestles in idyllic lawns and gardens with dramatic views of the surrounding mountains. Bedrooms are thoughtfully equipped with modern facilities. Two comfortably furnished lounges promote a home from home feel and hospitality is welcoming. Hearty meals can be enjoyed at separate tables in the dining room.

Rooms 7 rms (6 en suite) (1 pri facs) (3 fmly) S £28–£30; D £56–£70✱ **Facilities** TVB tea/coffee Cen ht TVL **Parking** 10 **Notes LB** ⊗ Closed mid Nov–mid Jan ⊜

LLANBEDR   MAP 14 SH52

★★★★ GUEST HOUSE
Bryn Artro Country House

LL45 2LE

☎ 01341 241619 & 07775 585729

e-mail: julie@llanbedr-brynartro.com

dir: *On A496 3m S of Harlech, opp Maes Artro Centre*

Located in mature grounds with a water garden, this Victorian house, faced in local slate, has original tiled floors and stained-glass windows. Bedrooms are thoughtfully equipped with homely extras, and home-cooked dinners as well as comprehensive Welsh breakfasts are provided in a spacious dining room that overlooks the pretty rear gardens.

Rooms 7 en suite (4 fmly) **Facilities** TVB tea/coffee Licensed Cen ht TVL Dinner Last d 8pm Bike hire **Conf** Max 16 **Parking** 20 **Notes** ⊗

★★★★ INN
Victoria

LL45 2LD

☎ 01341 241213 📄 01341 241644

e-mail: junevicinn@aol.com

dir: *In village centre*

This former coaching inn lies beside the River Artro in a very pretty village. Many original features remain, including the Settle bar with its flagstone floor, black polished fireplace and unusual circular wooden settle. The menu is extensive and is supplemented by blackboard specials. Bedrooms are spacious and thoughtfully furnished.

Victoria

Rooms 5 en suite **Facilities** TVB tea/coffee Cen ht Dinner Last d 9pm **Conf** Max 30 **Parking** 75 **Notes** ⊗

LLANDDEINIOLEN   MAP 14 SH56

★★★★★ 🅰 GUEST ACCOMMODATION
Ty'n-Rhos Country House & Restaurant

Seion LL55 3AE

☎ 01248 670489 📄 01248 671772

e-mail: enquiries@tynrhos.co.uk

web: www.tynrhos.co.uk

dir: *A55 junct 11 onto A5 for 50yds turn right at mini-rdbt onto A4244. After 4m, take 2nd exit at rdbt, signed in 0.5m*

Rooms 11 en suite 3 annexe en suite (2 fmly) (2 GF) S fr £75; D £80–£130✱ **Facilities** FTV TVB tea/coffee Wi-fi available Fishing 🎣 **Conf** Max 50 Thtr 50 Class 40 Board 40 Del from £120 ✱ **Parking** 50 **Notes** No children 6yrs Civ Wed 30

MALLWYD   MAP 14 SH81

★★★★ INN
Brigand's Inn

SY20 9HJ

☎ 01650 511999 📄 01650 531208

e-mail: info@brigandsinn.co.uk

dir: *In village at junct A458 & A470*

This 15th-century inn has extensive shooting and fishing rights, and has been renovated to provide high standards of comfort and facilities. Quality furnishing and décor highlight the many original features, and comfortable bedrooms have luxurious bathrooms with power showers.

Rooms 10 en suite (1 fmly) **Facilities** TVB tea/coffee Direct dial from bedrooms Cen ht Dinner Last d 9pm Fishing **Conf** Max 120 Thtr 100 Class 90 Board 100 **Parking** 150 **Notes** ⊗ Civ Wed 120

CONTINUED

PENYGROES
MAP 14 SH45

★★ FARM HOUSE
Llwyndu Mawr *(SH475536)*
Carmel Rd LL54 6PU
☎ 01286 880419 📠 01286 880845 Mrs N R Williams

dir: From village onto B4418, 500yds left for Carmel, 500yds up hill after cemetery, 1st left

This hillside farmhouse dates from the 19th century and is quietly located on the outskirts of the village. Home from home hospitality is provided and you are welcome to take part in the life of this working sheep farm, where there is also a boarding kennel.

Rooms 4 rms (2 en suite) (1 fmly) (1 GF) S £22–£25; D £44–£50✳
Facilities TVB tea/coffee Cen ht TVL Dinner Last d 4pm **Parking** 7
Notes LB 98 acres sheep, ducks, geese, chickens Closed 20 Dec–6 Jan ⊛

PORTHMADOG
MAP 14 SH53

★★★★ GUEST ACCOMMODATION
Tudor Lodge
Tan-Yr-Onnen, Penamser Rd LL49 9NY
☎ 01766 515530
e–mail: info@tudor-lodge.co.uk
web: www.tudor-lodge.co.uk

dir: At main Porthmadog rdbt turn onto Criccieth Rd, 40mtrs on left

This large guest house is conveniently located within a short walk of the town centre. It has recently been considerably renovated to provide good quality modern accommodation, including family rooms. Separate tables are provided in the breakfast room, where a substantial self-service continental breakfast buffet is provided. There is also a pleasant garden for guests to use.

Rooms 13 en suite (4 fmly) (6 GF) S £39; D £64–£84 **Facilities** STV TVB tea/coffee Cen ht Wi-fi available **Parking** 11 **Notes** LB ⊛

TYWYN
MAP 14 SH50

★★★★ FARM HOUSE
Eisteddfa *(SH651055)*
Eisteddfa, Abergynolwyn LL36 9UP
☎ 01654 782385 📠 01654 782228 Mrs G Pugh

dir: 5m NE of Tywyn on B4405 nr Dolgoch Falls

Eisteddfa is a modern stone bungalow situated less than a mile from Abergynolwyn, in a spot ideal for walking or for visiting the local historic railway. Rooms are well equipped and stunning views are a feature from the attractive dining room.

Rooms 3 rms (2 en suite) (3 GF) **Facilities** STV TVB tea/coffee Cen ht TVL **Notes** 1200 acres mixed Closed Dec–Feb ⊛

MERTHYR TYDFIL

MERTHYR TYDFIL
MAP 09 SO00

★★★★ GUEST HOUSE
Penrhadw Farm
Pontsticill CF48 2TU
☎ 01685 723481 & 722461 📠 01685 722461
e–mail: info@penrhadwfarm.co.uk
web: www.penrhadwfarm.co.uk

dir: 5m N of Merthyr Tydfil, map on website

Expect a warm welcome at this former Victorian farmhouse in the glorious Brecon Beacons National Park. The house has been totally refurbished to provide quality modern accommodation. The well-equipped, spacious bedrooms include two large suites in cottages adjacent to the main building. There is also a comfortable lounge. Separate tables are provided in the cosy breakfast room.

Rooms 5 en suite (2 fmly) (1 GF) S £46–£60; D £65–£100✳
Facilities STV TVB tea/coffee Cen ht TVL Dinner Last d by arrangement Wi-fi available **Conf** Max 10 Thtr 10 Class 10 **Parking** 22 **Notes** LB ⊛

★★★★ GUEST HOUSE
Llwyn Onn
Cwmtaf CF48 2HT
☎ 01685 384384 📠 01685 359310
e–mail: reception@llwynonn.co.uk

dir: Off A470 2m N of Cefn Coed, overlooking Llwyn-on Reservoir

Fronted by a large pleasant garden, this delightful house overlooks Llwyn-on Reservoir. Recently added to this property are a further seven new bedrooms which are spacious, comfortable and carefully appointed. The cosy lounge opens onto the terrace and garden, as does the bright breakfast room.

Rooms 11 en suite (3 GF) S £40–£60; D £70–£100✳ **Facilities** STV TVB tea/coffee Cen ht TVL **Conf** Max 10 Class 10 Board 10 **Parking** 9 **Notes** LB ⊛ No coaches RS 2 wks Xmas

MONMOUTHSHIRE

ABERGAVENNY MAP 09 SO21

★★★★ A GUEST HOUSE

Black Lion Guest House

43 Hereford Rd NP7 5PY

☎ 01873 851920 01873 857885

e-mail: blacklionaber@aol.com

Rooms 5 rms (2 en suite) (3 pri facs) (1 fmly) S £30–£40; D £60–£80 **Facilities** STV FTV TVB tea/coffee Cen ht Dinner Last d 8.30pm **Parking** 3 **Notes** No coaches

★★★★ A FARM HOUSE

Penyclawdd *(SO291173)*

Llanvihangel Crucorney NP7 7LB

☎ 01873 890591 Mrs A Davies

e-mail: info@penyclawdd.co.uk

web: www.penyclawdd.co.uk

dir: *5m N of Abergavenny. Off A465 to Hereford, turn 2nd left after rdbt on outskirts. After 0.75m, on right, signed*

Rooms 2 en suite (1 fmly) S £30; D £60* **Facilities** TVB tea/coffee Cen ht TVL **Parking** 5 **Notes** 160 acres Cattle & Sheep

★★★ FARM HOUSE

Hardwick Farm *(SO306115)*

NP7 9BT

☎ 01873 853513 & 07773 775179

01873 854238 Mrs A Price

e-mail: carol.hardwickfarm@virgin.net

dir: *1m from Abergavenny, off A4042, farm sign on right*

Quietly located in the Usk valley with wonderful views, this large family-run farmhouse provides warm hospitality. The spacious bedrooms are comfortably furnished, well equipped, and include one suitable for a family. Farmhouse breakfasts are served at separate tables, in the traditionally furnished dining room.

Rooms 2 en suite (1 fmly) **Facilities** TVB tea/coffee Cen ht **Parking** 2 **Notes** 230 acres dairy mixed Closed Xmas

★★★ A GUEST ACCOMMODATION

Pentre Court Country House

Llanwenarth Citra NP7 7EW

☎ 01873 853545 01873 851354

e-mail: judith@pentrecourt.com

web: www.pentrecourt.com

dir: *On A40 opp Lamb and Flag Inn*

Rooms 3 en suite (1 fmly) **Facilities** TVB tea/coffee Cen ht TVL Dinner Last d Day before **Parking** 6 **Notes** Closed 23 Dec–1 Jan

See advert on this page

LLANDOGO MAP 04 SO50

★★★★ INN

The Sloop Inn

NP25 4TW

☎ 01594 530291

e-mail: thesloopinn@btconnect.co.uk

dir: *On A466 in village centre*

This welcoming inn is centrally located close to the River Wye in a valley of outstanding natural beauty. The inn offers a selection of traditional food, as well as friendly hospitality. The dining room has delightful views over the valley, and the spacious bedrooms and recently refurbished bathrooms are equipped for business and leisure guests.

Rooms 4 en suite (1 fmly) S £30–£35; D £50–£55 **Facilities** TVB tea/coffee Cen ht Dinner Last d 9pm Pool Table **Parking** 50 **Notes** LB RS Mon–Fri

Pentre Court Guest House

Pentre Court is a small Georgian country house beautifully located half a mile outside Abergavenny in South Wales. Pentre Court is surrounded by beautiful gardens and some of the most picturesque landscape to be found in the UK.

The house is beautifully set just inside the Brecon Beacons National Park in 4 acres of well-wooded gardens and paddock through which runs the stream Nantiago.

In the garden is a heated swimming pool with diving board, changing room and sun terrace.

Adjacent to the house are footpaths to the River Usk and Sugar Loaf Mountain.

Accommodation includes en-suite bedrooms, central heating, a dining room and drawing room with open fire and colour TV.

Meals include a typical British or Continental breakfast.

Evening meals can be provided by prior arrangement and packed lunches and special dietary needs can be accommodated.

Brecon Road, Abergavenny, Monmouthshire NP7 7EW
Tel: 01873 853545
Website: www.pentrecourt.com
Email: judith@pentrecourt.com

LLANTRISANT   MAP 09 ST39

★★★ 🅰 INN
Greyhound Inn
NP15 1LE

☎ 01291 673447 & 672505 📠 01291 673255

e–mail: enquiry@greyhound-inn.com

web: www.greyhound-inn.com

dir: *M4 junct 24, A449, 1st exit for Usk, 2.5m from town square, follow Llantrisant signs*

Rooms 10 en suite (2 fmly) (5 GF) S £60; D £80✱ **Facilities** TVB tea/coffee Direct dial from bedrooms Wi-fi available **Notes** ⊗ No coaches Closed 25–26 Dec RS Sun eve

---

MONMOUTH   MAP 10 SO51

★★★★ BED & BREAKFAST
Penylan Farm
The Hendre NP25 5NL

☎ 01600 716435 📠 01600 719391

e–mail: penylanfarm@gmail.com

dir: *5m NW of Monmouth. B4233 through Rockfield towards Hendre. 0.5m before Hendre turn right towards Newcastle. After 1.5m turn left, farm 0.5 m on right.*

This converted barn was originally part of the Hendre Estate, once owned by the Rolls family. The bedrooms are housed in a former granary, and are equipped with many thoughtful extras. There is also a self-catering accommodation which is suitable for short term letting. Breakfasts focus on local produce, and a lounge is available.

Rooms 5 rms (3 en suite) (1 fmly) (2 GF) S £38–£45; D £55–£70✱ **Facilities** TVB tea/coffee Cen ht Dinner Last d 24hrs prior Wi-fi available ⚓ **Parking** 5 **Notes** LB ⊗ Closed Xmas & New Year

---

★★★ GUEST HOUSE
Church Farm
Mitchel Troy NP25 4HZ

☎ 01600 712176

e–mail: info@churchfarmguesthouse.eclipse.co.uk

dir: *From A40 S, left onto B4293 for Trelleck before tunnel, 150yds turn left and follow signs to Mitchel Troy. Guest House on main road, on left 200yds beyond campsite*

Located in the village of Mitchel Troy, this 16th-century former farmhouse retains many original features including exposed beams and open fireplaces. There is a range of bedrooms and a spacious lounge, and breakfast is served in the traditionally furnished dining room. Dinner is available by prior arrangement.

Rooms 9 rms (7 en suite) (2 pri facs) (3 fmly) S £29–£31; D £58–£62 **Facilities** TV2B tea/coffee Cen ht TVL Dinner Last d noon **Parking** 12 **Notes** LB No coaches Closed Xmas ⊛

ROCKFIELD   MAP 09 SO41

★★★★ ⊛⊛ RESTAURANT WITH ROOMS
The Stonemill & Steppes Farm Cottages
NP25 5SW

☎ 01600 775424 📠 01600 715257

e–mail: michelle@thestonemill.co.uk

dir: *A48 to Monmouth, B4233 to Rockfield. 2.6m from Monmouth town centre*

Located in Rockfield, a small hamlet just west of Monmouth, close to the Forest of Dean and Wye Valley, this operation offers accommodation comprising of six very well-appointed cottages. The comfortable rooms (for self-catering or on a B&B basis) are architect designed, and lovingly restored with many of the original features remaining. This is also handy for golfers, with a choice of courses within the locality. In a separate, converted 16th-century barn is the Stonemill Restaurant with oak beams, vaulted ceilings and an old cider press. Breakfast is served in the cottages on request.

Rooms 6 en suite (6 fmly) (6 GF) **Facilities** TVB tea/coffee Cen ht TVL Dinner Last d 9.30pm Free golf **Parking** 53 **Notes** ⊗ RS Sun eve & Mon

WALES

Premier Collection

★ ★ ★ ★ ★ ◉◉ RESTAURANT WITH ROOMS

The Bell at Skenfrith

NP7 8UH

☎ 01600 750235 📄 01600 750525

e–mail: enquiries@skenfrith.co.uk

web: www.skenfrith.co.uk

dir: *On B4521 in Skenfrith, opposite castle*

The Bell is a beautifully restored, 17th-century former coaching inn which still retains much of its original charm and character. It is peacefully situated on the banks of the Monnow, a tributary of the River Wye. Natural materials have been used to create a relaxing atmosphere, while the bedrooms, which include full suites and rooms with four-poster beds, are stylish, luxurious and equipped with DVD players.

Rooms 11 en suite S £75–£120; D £110–£220✶ **Facilities** TVB tea/coffee Direct dial from bedrooms Cen ht Dinner Last d 9.30pm Wi-fi available **Conf** Max 20 Thtr 20 Board 16 Del £185 ✶ **Parking** 36 **Notes** No children 8yrs Closed last wk Jan–1st wk Feb RS Oct–Mar

---

TINTERN PARVA

★ ★ ★ ★ 🍴 GUEST HOUSE

Parva Farmhouse Riverside Guest House & Restaurant

Monmouth Rd NP16 6SQ

☎ 01291 689411 📄 01291 689941

e–mail: parvahoteltintern@fsmail.net

dir: *On A466 at N edge of Tintern. Next to St Michael's Church on the riverside*

This relaxed and friendly family-run guest house is situated on a sweep of the River Wye with far reaching views of the valley. Originally a farmhouse dating from the 17th century, many original features have been retained, providing character and comfort in an informal atmosphere. The Inglenook Restaurant has a cosy atmosphere where quality ingredients are prepared for dinner and breakfast. The individually designed bedrooms are tastefully decorated and enjoy pleasant views; one has a four-poster.

Rooms 8 en suite S £45–£60; D £65–£80✶ **Facilities** TVB tea/coffee Licensed Cen ht Dinner Last d Same day **Parking** 8 **Notes** No children 12yrs No coaches

Premier Collection

★ ★ ★ ★ ★ ◉◉ RESTAURANT WITH ROOMS

The Crown at Whitebrook

NP25 4TX

☎ 01600 860254 📄 01600 860607

e–mail: info@crownatwhitebrook.co.uk

dir: *4m from Monmouth on B4293, left at sign to Whitebrook, 2m on unmarked road, Crown on right*

In a secluded spot in the wooded valley of the River Wye this former drover's cottage dates back to the 17th century. Refurbished and individually decorated bedrooms boast a contemporary feel with smart modern facilities. The restaurant and lounge combine many original features with a bright fresh look. Memorable cuisine features locally sourced ingredients skilfully prepared.

Rooms 8 en suite S £80–£100; D £115–£140✶ **Facilities** FTV TVB tea/ coffee Direct dial from bedrooms Cen ht Dinner Last d 9.15pm Fishing Shooting **Conf** Max 12 Thtr 12 Board 12 **Parking** 20 **Notes** LB ⊗ No children 12yrs Closed 24 Dec–7 Jan RS Sun–Tue

See advert on this page

The Crown at Whitebrook
near Monmouthshire NP25 4TX

The Crown at Whitebrook is set in 3 acres of gardens surrounded by forest views in the heart of the breathtakingly beautiful Wye Valley. Eight luxurious bedrooms have been furnished to the highest standard with attention to detail throughout. Individual themes and character define each room. All boast modern en-suite bathrooms with under-floor heating, high-speed Internet access and flat screen televisions. The restaurant has a warm, relaxed ambience and a superb Modern British fine dining menu draws from the best of local ingredients.

Tel: 01600 860254   Fax: 01600 860607
Email: info@crownatwhitebrook.co.uk
Website: www.crownatwhitebrook.co.uk

WALES

WALES

NEATH PORT TALBOT

NEATH
MAP 09 SS79

★★★★ GUEST HOUSE
Cwmbach Cottages Guest House
Cwmbach Rd, Cadoxton SA10 8AH
☎ 01639 639825
e–mail: l.morgan5@btinternet.com
web: www.cwmbachcottages.co.uk
dir: *1.5m NE of Neath. A465 onto A474 & A4230 towards Aberdulais, left opp Cadoxton church, guest house signed*

A terrace of former miners' cottages has been restored to provide a range of thoughtfully furnished bedrooms, with one on the ground floor for easier access. Spacious public areas include a comfortable lounge and a pleasant breakfast room with separate tables. A superb decked patio overlooks a wooded hillside rich with wildlife.

Rooms 5 en suite (1 fmly) (1 GF) S £34–£42; D £52–£62✶
Facilities TVB tea/coffee Cen ht TVL Wi-fi available Golf 18 **Parking** 9
Notes LB ⊗ ⊜

NEWPORT

CAERLEON
MAP 09 ST39

★★★★★ ⊜ BED & BREAKFAST
Radford House
Broadway NP18 1AY
☎ 01633 430101
e–mail: radfordhouse@btconnect.com
web: www.radfordhouse.co.uk
dir: *In town centre opp museum & church*

Located in the heart of the historic town of Caerleon, refurbished Radford House more than meets its brochure description of providing rooms of distinction for the discerning traveller. The spacious bedrooms and bathrooms have been beautifully designed and sumptuously furnished, and include fresh flowers, bottles of water, an extensive selection of teas, chocolates, fresh fruit, and flat-screen televisions. A comfortable drawing room, impressive staircase and smart breakfast room add to the air of luxury and relaxation.

Rooms 3 en suite S £55–£65; D £75–£85✶ **Facilities** FTV TVB tea/
coffee Cen ht Wi-fi available **Notes** ⊗ No children 12yrs

NEWPORT
MAP 09 ST38

★★★★ GUEST HOUSE
Hazel Court Guest House
Langstone Court Rd, Llanwern NP18 2DS
☎ 01633 411033 📄 01633 411033
e–mail: noelle.williams@hazel-court.co.uk
dir: *Exit M4 junct 24 and take A48 Docks and Civic Centre. Take 1st turning left into Llanwern Village, 1st left 0.5m*

A warm welcome awaits all guests from the friendly proprietor at this well-presented property, set in rolling countryside in an acre of its own grounds. Hazel Court is not far from Newport and within easy reach of the M4. Bedrooms are comfortable and include thoughtful extras including Wi-fi. A hearty breakfast is served around the communal table in the bright dining room. Off-road parking is provided.

Rooms 6 rms (5 en suite) (1 pri facs) (1 fmly) (2 GF) S £38; D £50✶
Facilities TVB tea/coffee Cen ht Wi-fi available **Parking** 8 **Notes** ⊗
No coaches

★★★★ GUEST HOUSE
Labuan Guest House
464 Chepstow Rd NP19 8JF
☎ 01633 664533 📠 01633 664533
e–mail: patricia.bees@ntlworld.com
dir: *M4 junct 24, 1.5m on B4237*

Expect a warm welcome from owners Pat and John at this delightful guest house which is set on the main road into Newport. Accommodation is comfortable and includes a ground floor twin room. All rooms are of a good size and bathrooms feature a wide range of extras. The hearty breakfast is taken in the welcoming dining room at separate tables, where a good choice from the menu is available. Off street parking available.

Rooms 5 rms (3 en suite) (2 pri facs) (1 GF) S £38–£45; D £68–£75✳
Facilities TVB tea/coffee Cen ht TVL Dinner Last d 5pm Wi-fi available
Parking 6 **Notes LB** No children 🐾

★★★ GUEST HOUSE
Kepe Lodge
46A Caerau Rd NP20 4HH
☎ 01633 262351 📠 01633 262351
e–mail: kepelodge@hotmail.com

dir: *500yds W of town centre. M4 junct 27, town centre signs, 2nd lights left, premises on right*

This attractive guest house in a quiet residential area is set back from the road in pleasant gardens. Guests can expect attentive service and comfortable homely bedrooms. Breakfast is served at individual tables in the well-appointed dining room. A comfortable lounge is also available.

Rooms 8 rms (3 en suite) S £30–£49; D £60✳ **Facilities** FTV TVB tea/coffee Cen ht **Parking** 12 **Notes** 🐾 No children 10yrs No coaches 🐾

★★★ INN
The Rising Sun
1 Cefn Rd, Rogerstone NP10 9AQ
☎ 01633 895126 📠 01633 891020
dir: *M4 junct 27, B4591 signed Highcross, establishment 0.5m on left*

Located a short drive from the M4 in the community of Rogerstone, this Edwardian inn provides high levels of comfort and facilities. Bedrooms are equipped with quality furnishings and lots of thoughtful extras. Spacious public rooms include a magnificent split-level conservatory, and the grounds feature a children's play area.

Rooms 6 rms (5 en suite) (1 pri facs) (1 fmly) (6 smoking) S £45–£55; D £65–£75✳ **Facilities** FTV TVB tea/coffee Cen ht Dinner Last d 9.30pm Pool Table Childrens play area **Parking** 100 **Notes** 🚫 RS Mon–Thu 3.30–5.30pm, Sun 3.30–7pm

---

REDWICK   MAP 09 ST48

★★★★ GUEST HOUSE
Brickhouse Country Guest House
North Row NP26 3DX
☎ 01633 880230 📠 01633 882441
e–mail: brickhouse@compuserve.com

dir: *M4 junct 23A, follow steelworks road for 1.5m. Left after sign for Redwick, Brickhouse 1.5m on left*

This impressive country house is in a peaceful location with attractive, well-tended gardens. The friendly hosts are most attentive and provide a relaxing atmosphere. Bedrooms are spacious and traditionally furnished, while the public areas include a choice of lounges. Dinners featuring home-grown produce are sometimes available by prior arrangement.

Rooms 7 rms (5 en suite) (1 fmly) **Facilities** TVB Licensed Cen ht TVL Dinner Last d noon **Parking** 7 **Notes** 🚫 No children 10yrs No coaches

WALES

ST BRIDES WENTLOOGE   MAP 09 ST28

Premier Collection

★★★★★ ◉ INN
The Inn at the Elm Tree
NP10 8SQ
☎ 01633 680225 📠 01633 681035
e–mail: inn@the-elm-tree.co.uk
dir: *4m SW of Newport. On B4239 in St Brides village*
This stylish barn conversion on the tranquil Wentlooge Levels offers individually decorated bedrooms that combine the traditional and the contemporary:- hand-made brass beds, beamed ceilings and sumptuous fabrics blend with minimalist bathrooms (some with Jacuzzi), ISDN lines and business services. The restaurant offers an extensive choice including seafood and game in season, with the emphasis on quality ingredients.

Rooms 10 en suite (1 fmly) (2 GF) S £80–£90; D £90–£110✳
Facilities TVB tea/coffee Direct dial from bedrooms Cen ht Dinner Last d 9.30pm **Conf** Max 20 Board 20 Del £150 ✳ **Parking** 30 **Notes LB** Civ Wed 60

PEMBROKESHIRE

FISHGUARD   MAP 08 SM93

★★★★ FARM HOUSE
Erw-Lon *(SN028325)*
Pontfaen SA65 9TS
☎ 01348 881297 Mrs L McAllister
e–mail: lilwenmcallister@btinternet.com
dir: *5.5m SE of Fishguard on B4313*

Located in the Pembrokeshire Coast National Park, with stunning views of the Gwaun Valley, this attractive farmhouse has been converted to provide modern well-equipped bedrooms with a wealth of homely extras. The McAllisters give the warmest of welcomes, and their memorable dinners feature the finest local produce.

Rooms 3 rms (2 en suite) (1 pri facs) S £35–£40; D £60–£66
Facilities TVB tea/coffee Cen ht TVL Dinner Last d 24hrs in advance
Parking 5 **Notes LB** ⊗ No children 10yrs 128 acres beef sheep Closed Dec–Mar ◉

HAVERFORDWEST   MAP 08 SM91

See also Narberth

★★★★ GUEST HOUSE
College Guest House
93 Hill St, St Thomas Green SA61 1QL
☎ 01437 763710 📠 01437 763710
e–mail: colinlarby@aol.com
dir: *In town centre, along High St, pass church, keep in left hand lane. Take 1st exit by Stonemason Arms pub, follow signs for St Thomas Green. 300mtrs on left by no entry sign*

Located in a mainly residential area within easy walking distance of the attractions, this impressive Georgian house has been upgraded to offer good levels of comfort and facilities. There is range of practically equipped bedrooms, along with public areas that include a spacious lounge (with internet access) and an attractive pine-furnished dining room, the setting for comprehensive breakfasts.

Rooms 8 en suite (4 fmly) S £45–£50; D £65–£70✳ **Facilities** TVB tea/coffee Cen ht TVL Wi-fi available **Parking** 2

★★★★ FARM HOUSE
Lower Haythog Farm *(SM996214)*
Spittal SA62 5QL
☎ 01437 731279 📠 01437 731279 Mrs N M Thomas
e–mail: nesta@lowerhaythogfarm.co.uk
web: www.lowerhaythogfarm.co.uk
dir: *5m N on B4329 to railway bridge, farmhouse entrance on right*
Located in 250 acres of unspoiled countryside, this 14th-century farmhouse with adjacent cottage provides high standards of comfort and good facilities. Bedrooms, including a two-bedroom family suite, are modern and well equipped. The elegant oak-beamed dining room is the setting for imaginative home-cooked dinners. Welcoming real fires burn during cold weather in the comfortable lounge, and a second conservatory-lounge overlooks the large, attractive garden.

Rooms 6 en suite (2 fmly) (1 GF) **Facilities** TVB tea/coffee Cen ht TVL Dinner Fishing **Parking** 5 **Notes** 250 acres dairy ◉

★★★★ GUEST HOUSE
Manian Lodge
Begelly SA68 0XE
☎ 01834 813273 📄 01834 811591
e–mail: information@manianlodge.com

dir: *A447 N onto A478, 0.5m on right in Begelly*

Manian Lodge is convenient for Tenby and the South Pembrokeshire Heritage Coast, and also the Pembroke Dock ferry terminal. The owners provide well-equipped modern bedrooms, including some on the ground floor. There is a comfortable lounge bar, a lounge, and a very attractive restaurant where a good choice of meals is offered. Self-catering accommodation is also available.

Rooms 6 en suite (1 GF) S £40–£49.50; D £60–£70✱ **Facilities** TVB tea/coffee Licensed Cen ht Dinner Last d 9pm Wi-fi available **Conf** Max 40 Thtr 40 Class 10 Board 18 **Parking** 19 **Notes LB** ⊛

★★★ FARM HOUSE
Highland Grange Farm *(SN077154)*
Robeston Wathen SA67 8EP
☎ 01834 860952 📄 01834 860952 Mrs N Jones
e–mail: info@highlandgrange.co.uk
web: www.highlandgrange.co.uk

dir: *2m NW of Narberth on A40 Robeston Wathen, near Bush Inn*

A warm welcome can be expected along with comfortable accommodation at this farmhouse property, where all the spacious bedrooms are on the ground floor. The property is set on the main A40 road in the small village of Robeston Wathen, between Whitland and Haverfordwest. The dining room has separate tables where a good hearty breakfast is provided. There is also a spacious and comfortable lounge where a real fire is lit in cold weather.

Rooms 3 rms (2 en suite) (1 fmly) (3 GF) **Facilities** TVB tea/coffee Licensed Cen ht TVL Dinner Last d 5pm **Parking** 6 **Notes** ⊛ 50 acres Mixed, sheep ⊜

★★★★ INN
Trewern Arms
SA42 0NB
☎ 01239 820395 📄 01239 820173
e–mail: trewern.arms@virgin.net

dir: *Off A48. Midway between Cardigan & Fishguard*

Set in a peaceful and picturesque village, this charming 16th-century inn is well positioned to offer a relaxing stay. There are many original features to be seen in the two character bars and attractive restaurant, and the spacious bedrooms are appointed to a high standard and include some family rooms.

Rooms 10 en suite (4 fmly) **Facilities** TVB Fishing Riding **Parking** 100

NEWPORT

★★★ A INN
Salutation Inn
Filindre Farchog SA41 3UY
☎ 01239 820564 📄 01239 820355
e–mail: johndenley@aol.com
web: www.salutationcountryhotel.co.uk

dir: *On A487 between Cardigan & Fishguard. 3m N of Newport*

Rooms 8 en suite (2 fmly) (8 GF) S £50; D £70✱ **Facilities** TVB tea/coffee Direct dial from bedrooms Cen ht Dinner Last d 9.30pm Wi-fi available Pool Table **Conf** Max 25 Thtr 25 Class 12 Board 12 **Parking** 60 **Notes LB**

WALES

WALES

ST DAVID'S

MAP 08 SM72

See also Solva

★★★★ 🏠 🍽 GUEST HOUSE

Ramsey House

Lower Moor SA62 6RP

☎ 01437 720321

e–mail: info@ramseyhouse.co.uk

web: www.ramseyhouse.co.uk

dir: *From Cross Sq in St Davids towards Porthclais, house 0.25m on left*

This pleasant guest house is under the new ownership of Suzanne and Shaun Ellison, who offer the ideal combination of professional hotel management and the warmth of a family-run guest house. The property is quietly located on the outskirts of St David's surrounded by unspoilt countryside. It provides modern, well-equipped bedrooms with a good range of welcome extras. Carefully prepared dinners by award-winning chef Shaun feature quality local Welsh produce, and breakfast provides a choice of homemade items including breads and preserves.

Rooms 6 rms (5 en suite) (1 pri facs) (3 GF) S £50–£80; D £80✱ **Facilities** TVB tea/coffee Licensed Cen ht Dinner Wi-fi available **Parking** 10 **Notes LB** No coaches ☺

★★★★ BED & BREAKFAST

The Waterings

Anchor Dr, High St SA62 6QH

☎ 01437 720876 📠 01437 720876

e–mail: waterings@supanet.com

web: www.waterings.co.uk

dir: *On A487 on E edge of St David's*

Situated a short walk from the centre of St David's, the Waterings offers spacious bedrooms that are accessed from a courtyard garden. Most rooms have their own separate seating area. Breakfast, from a good selection of local produce, is served in a smart dining room in the main house.

Rooms 5 annexe en suite (4 fmly) (5 GF) S £50–£80; D £75–£80✱ **Facilities** FTV TVB tea/coffee Cen ht 🌳 **Conf** Max 15 Board 15 **Parking** 20 **Notes** ⊗ No children 5yrs ☺

★★★★ GUEST HOUSE
Y-Gorlan

77 Nun St SA62 6NU
☎ 01437 720837 & 07974 108029
e-mail: mikebohlen@aol.com

dir: *In centre of St David's*

This personally-run guest house is just a stroll from the city's attractions. The well-maintained accommodation includes a family room and a room with a four-poster bed. The comfortable first-floor lounge has excellent views towards the coast across the surrounding countryside. A hearty breakfast is offered with a good choice of items available.

Rooms 5 en suite (1 fmly) S £35–£38; D £68–£74✳ **Facilities** STV TVB tea/coffee Cen ht TVL **Parking** 3 **Notes** ⊗ No children 5yrs No coaches

---

SAUNDERSFOOT   MAP 08 SN10

★★★★ GUEST HOUSE
Vine Cottage

The Ridgeway SA69 9LA
☎ 01834 814422
e-mail: enquiries@vinecottageguesthouse.co.uk
web: www.vinecottageguesthouse.co.uk

dir: *A477 S onto A478, left onto B4316, after railway bridge right signed Saundersfoot, cottage 100yds beyond 30mph sign*

A warm welcome awaits guests at this pleasant former farmhouse, conveniently located on the outskirts of Saundersfoot, yet within easy walking distance of this delightful village. A feature is the extensive mature gardens which display some rare and exotic plants, also a summer house at the rear of the garden where guests can sit and relax in the warmer evenings. Bedrooms, which include a ground-floor room, are modern and well equipped, and some are suitable for families. There is a comfortable, airy lounge. Dinner (available on request), and breakfast are served in the cosy dining room.

Rooms 5 en suite (2 fmly) (1 GF) S £35–£70; D £56–£70✳ **Facilities** TVB tea/coffee Cen ht Dinner Last d 10am **Parking** 10 **Notes LB** No children 6yrs No coaches 🐾

SOLVA   MAP 08 SM82

★★★★★ 🛏 FARM HOUSE
Lochmeyler Farm Guest House
(SM855275)

Llandeloy SA62 6LL
☎ 01348 837724 📠 01348 837622 Mrs M Jones
e-mail: stay@lochmeyler.co.uk
web: www.lochmeyler.co.uk

dir: *From Haverfordwest A487 St David's Rd to Penycwm, right to Llandeloy*

Located on a 220-acre dairy farm in an Area of Outstanding Natural Beauty, Lochmeyler provides high levels of comfort and excellent facilities. The spacious bedrooms, some in converted outbuildings, are equipped with a wealth of thoughtful extras and four have private sitting rooms. Comprehensive breakfasts are served in the dining room as well as dinner on request, and a sumptuous lounge is also available.

Rooms 12 en suite (6 GF) S £30–£50; D £60–£70 **Facilities** TVB tea/coffee Direct dial from bedrooms Licensed Cen ht Dinner Last d 2pm **Parking** 12 **Notes LB** No children 14yrs 220 acres dairy

WALES

TENBY   MAP 08 SN10

★★★★ 🍴 GUEST ACCOMMODATION

Panorama

The Esplanade SA70 7DU

☎ 01834 844976 🖨 01834 844976

e–mail: mail@tenby-hotel.co.uk

web: www.tenby-hotel.co.uk

dir: *A478 follow South Beach & Town Centre signs. Sharp left under railway arches, up Greenhill Rd, onto South Pde then Esplanade*

This charming property is part of a Victorian terrace, overlooking the South Beach and Caldy Island in Tenby. All the bedrooms are well equipped and comfortable. Facilities include a cosy seating area and a large elegant dining room with sea views. Breakfast offers a good selection prepared from fresh and local ingredients.

Rooms 8 en suite (1 fmly) **Facilities** TVB tea/coffee **Notes** ⊗ No children 5yrs

★★★★ GUEST ACCOMMODATION

Rosendale

Lydstep SA70 7SQ

☎ 01834 870040

e–mail: rosendalewales@yahoo.com

web: www.rosendalepembrokeshire.co.uk

dir: *3m SW of Tenby. A4139 W towards Pembroke, Rosendale on the right after Lydstep village*

A warm welcome awaits all guests at this family-run guest accommodation, ideally located on the outskirts of the pretty village of Lydstep, not far from the seaside town of Tenby. Rosendale provides modern, well-equipped bedrooms, some with coast or country views.

CONTINUED

Three rooms are on the ground floor of a separate building to the rear of the main house. The attractive dining room is the setting for breakfast, and there is also a large, comfortable lounge.

Rooms 6 en suite (3 GF) **Facilities** TVB tea/coffee Cen ht **Parking** 6 **Notes** No children 16yrs Closed Dec–Jan

★★★★ GUEST ACCOMMODATION

Esplanade

The Esplanade SA70 7DU

☎ 01834 842760 & 843333 🖨 01834 845633

e–mail: esplanade.tenby@virgin.net

web: www.esplanadetenby.co.uk

dir: *Signs to South Beach, premises on seafront next to town walls*

Located beside the historic town walls of Tenby and with stunning views over the sea to Caldey Island, the Esplanade provides a range of standard and luxury bedrooms, some ideal for families. Breakfast is offered in the elegant front-facing dining room, which contains a comfortable lounge-bar area.

Rooms 14 en suite (3 fmly) (1 GF) S £50–£85; D £70–£130 **Facilities** TVB tea/coffee Direct dial from bedrooms Cen ht Wi-fi available **Notes LB** Closed 23–27 Dec

★★★ GUEST ACCOMMODATION

Giltar Grove Country House

Penally SA70 7RY

☎ 01834 871568

e–mail: giltarbnb@aol.com

dir: *2m SW of Tenby. Off A4139, 2nd right after railway bridge*

Just a short walk from the spectacular Pembrokeshire Coastal Path, this impressive Victorian farmhouse retains many original features. The

CONTINUED

non-smoking bedrooms include rooms with four-poster beds and rooms on the ground floor. All are filled with homely extras. There is a cosy sitting room, an elegant dining room, and spacious conservatory that is used for breakfast.

Rooms 6 rms (5 en suite) (1 pri facs) (2 GF) S £30–£35; D £60–£70 **Facilities** TVB tea/coffee Cen ht **Parking** 10 **Notes** ⊗ No children 10yrs Closed Dec–Feb ◉

POWYS

BRECON   MAP 09 SO02

See also Sennybridge

Premier Collection

★★★★★ BED & BREAKFAST
Canal Bank

Ty Gardd LD3 7HG
☎ 01874 623464 & 625844
e–mail: enquiries@accommodation-breconbeacons.co.uk
web: www.accommodation-breconbeacons.co.uk

dir: *B4601 signed Brecon, left over bridge before fuel station, turn right & continue to end of road*

Expect a warm welcome at this delightful property, which was developed from a row of five 18th-century cottages. It provides very high quality, comfortable and well-equipped accommodation, and stands alongside the canal in a semi-rural area on the outskirts of Brecon, yet within walking distance of the town centre. Facilities here include a comfortable lounge, a very attractive breakfast room and a lovely garden.

Rooms 3 en suite S £50–£85; D £65–£85✹ **Facilities** TVB tea/coffee Cen ht Wi-fi available **Parking** 5 **Notes** ⊗ No children ◉

Premier Collection

★★★★★ GUEST ACCOMMODATION
The Coach House

Orchard St LD3 8AN
☎ 01874 620043 ▤ 01874 622454
e–mail: info@coachhousebrecon.com

dir: *From town centre W over bridge onto B4601, Coach House 200yds on right*

A warm welcome awaits you at this former coach house, now transformed into modern contemporary accommodation. The friendly and enthusiastic proprietors ensure your stay is something to remember. The bedrooms are well equipped and extremely comfortable. A selection of imaginative Welsh home-cooked breakfast items are served in the relaxing spacious dining room. The Coach House is within easy walking distance of Brecon and also benefits from a lovely garden.

Rooms 7 en suite S £50–£75; D £65–£98 **Facilities** STV TVB tea/coffee Direct dial from bedrooms Cen ht Dinner Last d 8pm Wi-fi available Resident holistic therapist, massage & reflexology **Conf** Max 24 Thtr 24 Board 16 Del from £100 **Parking** 7 **Notes** ⊗ No children 16yrs

★★★★ ◉◉ INN
The Felin Fach Griffin

Felin Fach LD3 0UB
☎ 01874 620111 ▤ 01874 620120
e–mail: enquiries@eatdrinksleep.ltd.uk
web: www.eatdrinksleep.ltd.uk

dir: *4m NE of Brecon on A470*

This delightful inn stands in an extensive garden at the northern end of Felin Fach village. The public areas have a wealth of rustic charm and provide the setting for the excellent food. Service and hospitality are commendable. The bedrooms are carefully appointed and have modern equipment and facilities.

Rooms 7 en suite (1 fmly) **Facilities** tea/coffee Direct dial from bedrooms Cen ht Dinner Last d 9.30pm ⌣ **Conf** Max 15 Board 15 **Parking** 61 **Notes** No coaches Closed 25–26 Dec RS Mon (ex BH's)

WALES

BRECON *CONTINUED*

★★★★ FARM HOUSE
Llanddetty Hall Farm *(SO124205)*
Talybont-on-Usk LD3 7YR
☎ 01874 676415 📠 01874 676415 Mrs H E Atkins
dir: *SE of Brecon. Off B4558*

This impressive Grade II listed 17th-century farmhouse in the beautiful Usk valley is full of character, and the friendly proprietors ensure a comfortable stay. Bedrooms are very pleasant and feature traditional furnishings, exposed timbers and polished floorboards. Welcoming log fires are lit during cold weather in the comfortable lounge, and guests dine around one table in the dining room.

Rooms 3 rms (2 en suite) (1 pri facs) 1 annexe en suite (1 GF) S £35; D £58–£60✳ **Facilities** TV1B tea/coffee Cen ht TVL **Parking** 6 **Notes** ⊗ No children 12yrs 48 acres sheep Closed 16 Dec–14 Jan RS Feb–Apr 🐾

★★★★ 🌸🌸 RESTAURANT WITH ROOMS
Peterstone Court
Llanhamlach LD3 7YB
☎ 01874 665387
e–mail: info@peterstone-court.com
dir: *3m from Brecon on A40 towards Abergavenny*

This establishment affords stunning views as it stands on the edge of the Brecon Beacons and overlooks the River Usk. The style is friendly and informal, without any unnecessary fuss. No two bedrooms are alike, but all share comparable levels of comfort, quality and elegance. Public areas reflect similar standards, eclectically styled with a blend of contemporary and traditional. Quality produce is cooked with care in a range of enjoyable dishes.

Rooms 8 en suite 4 annexe en suite (2 fmly) S £85–£190; D £110–£220✳ **Facilities** TVB tea/coffee Direct dial from bedrooms Cen ht Dinner Last d 9.30pm Wi-fi available ⚓ Sauna Gymnasium Pool open mid Apr–1 Oct **Conf** Max 100 Thtr 100 Class 100 Board 60 Del £140 ✳ **Parking** 60 **Notes LB** Civ Wed

★★★★ 🌸 INN
The Usk Inn
Station Rd, Talybont-on-Usk LD3 7JE
☎ 01874 676251 📠 01874 676392
e–mail: stay@uskinn.co.uk
dir: *Off A40 6m E of Brecon*

This delightful inn is personally run in a friendly manner by the new owners who have renovated the property to a high standard. The thoughtfully equipped and well-appointed bedrooms include a family room and one room with a four-poster bed. Public areas have a wealth of charm and the inn has a well-deserved reputation for its food.

Rooms 11 en suite (1 fmly) S £50–£80; D £80–£120✳ **Facilities** TVB tea/coffee Direct dial from bedrooms Cen ht TVL Dinner Last d 9.30pm **Conf** Max 40 Thtr 60 Class 40 Board 20 **Parking** 30 **Notes LB** ⊗ Closed 25–27 Dec

★★★ GUEST HOUSE
The Beacons Guest House
16 Bridge St LD3 8AH
☎ 01874 623339 📠 01874 623339
e–mail: guesthouse@thebreconbeacons.co.uk
dir: *On B4601 opp Christ College*

Located west of the historic town centre over the bridge, this 17th-century former farmhouse by the river has been renovated to provide a range of homely bedrooms, some in converted barns and outbuildings. There is a guests' lounge and a cosy bar. This is a non-smoking establishment.

Rooms 11 rms (9 en suite) 3 annexe en suite (4 fmly) (3 GF) S £35–£52.50; D £44–£78✳ **Facilities** TVB tea/coffee Licensed Cen ht TVL Wi-fi available **Parking** 20 **Notes LB** ⊗

WALES

★★★ GUEST ACCOMMODATION
Borderers
47 The Watton LD3 7EG
☎ 01874 623559
e–mail: info@borderers.com
web: www.borderers.com

dir: *200yds SE of town centre on B4601, opp church*
This guest house was originally a 17th-century drovers' inn. The courtyard, now a car park, is surrounded by many of the bedrooms, and pretty hanging baskets are seen everywhere. The non-smoking bedrooms are attractively decorated with rich floral fabrics. A room suitable for easier access is available.

Rooms 4 rms (3 en suite) (1 pri facs) 5 annexe en suite (2 fmly) (4 GF) S £40–£60; D £60–£70 **Facilities** TVB tea/coffee Cen ht **Parking** 6

★★★ INN
Brecon Castle
Castle Square LD3 9DB
☎ 01874 624611 📠 01874 623737
e–mail: hotel@breconcastle.co.uk
Under new ownership, this former coaching inn occupies an elevated position overlooking the River Usk. This view is shared by the restaurant and some of the spacious comfortable bedrooms, while the remaining public areas are designed with a contemporary, roomy and relaxed feel and log burning fires for colder days. Function and meeting rooms are available and incorporate one of the castle walls, parking is ample to the front of the property. All meals are freshly prepared and taken in the separate dining and breakfast rooms.

Rooms 30 en suite (3 fmly) (3 GF) **Facilities** STV FTV TVB tea/coffee Direct dial from bedrooms Wi-fi available **Conf** Max 100 Thtr 100 Board 50 **Parking** 30 **Notes** No coaches Civ Wed 200

★★★ INN
The Old Ford Inn
Llanhamlach LD3 7YB
☎ 01874 665391 & 665220

dir: *3m SE from Brecon on A40*
Parts of this former drovers' inn date from the Middle Ages. The non-smoking bedrooms, which include family rooms, have modern facilities and most look out towards the Brecon Beacons. Public areas have a wealth of character and include a choice of bars and a cottage-style dining room.

Rooms 5 rms (5 pri facs) (1 fmly) **Facilities** TVB tea/coffee Cen ht Dinner Last d 8.45pm **Parking** 20 **Notes** ⊗

★★★ 🅰 BED & BREAKFAST
Wye Knot Stop
Llyswen LD3 0UR
☎ 01874 754247
e–mail: info@wyeknotstop.co.uk

dir: *On main A470, N of Brecon, at junct of A470 & A479*
Rooms 1 en suite 1 annexe en suite (2 fmly) (1 GF) S £35; D £60✱ **Facilities** TVB tea/coffee Cen ht Dinner Last d 7pm Wi-fi available **Parking** 7 **Notes LB** Closed Jan

---
BUILTH WELLS   **MAP 09 SO05**

Premier Collection
★★★★★ ◉◉ RESTAURANT WITH ROOMS
The Drawing Room
Cwmbach, Newbridge-on-Wye LD2 3RT
☎ 01982 552493
e–mail: post@the-drawing-room.co.uk

dir: *3m NW of Builth on A470*
This delightful Georgian country house has been extensively and tastefully renovated by the present owners, to provide three comfortable and very well equipped bedrooms, all with luxurious en suite facilities. Public rooms include two comfortable lounges with welcoming log fires, a room for private dining and a very elegant and intimate dining room, which provides the ideal setting for the cooking skills of Colin Dawson.

Rooms 3 en suite D £230–£260✱ (incl. dinner) **Facilities** TVB Cen ht Dinner Last d 9pm **Parking** 14 **Notes** ⊗ No children 12yrs

---
CAERSWS   **MAP 15 SO09**

Premier Collection
★★★★★ ◉◉ RESTAURANT WITH ROOMS
The Talkhouse
Pontdolgoch SY17 5JE
☎ 01686 688919 📠 01686 689134
e–mail: info@talkhouse.co.uk

dir: *1.5m NW of Caersws on A470*
A highlight of this delightful 19th-century inn is the food, home-made dishes making good use of local produce. Bedrooms offer luxury in every area and the cosy lounge, filled with sofas, is the place to while away some time with a glass of wine or a pot of tea. The bar features a large fireplace.

Rooms 3 en suite **Facilities** TVB Cen ht Dinner Last d 8.45pm **Parking** 50 **Notes** ⊗ No children 14yrs Closed 1st 2 wks Jan RS Sun eve & Mon

WALES

CRICKHOWELL
MAP 09 SO21

Premier Collection

★★★★★ BED & BREAKFAST
Glangrwyney Court

NP8 1ES
☎ 01873 811288 📠 01873 810317
e-mail: info@glancourt.co.uk
web: www.glancourt.co.uk

dir: *2m SE of Crickhowell on A40 (near county boundary)*

Located in extensive mature grounds, this impressive Georgian house has been renovated to provide high standards of comfort and facilities. The spacious bedrooms are equipped with a range of homely extras, and bathrooms include a Jacuzzi or steam shower. The interior has been decorated with style. There are also comfortable bedrooms in an annexe with two having their own lounge and kitchen area. Comprehensive breakfasts are taken in the elegant dining room and a luxurious lounge is also provided.

Rooms 6 rms (5 en suite) (1 pri facs) 4 annexe en suite (1 fmly) (1 GF) **Facilities** STV TVB tea/coffee Cen ht TVL Dinner Last d 72 hrs notice Wi-fi available ➘ ➚ Boules **Parking** 12 **Notes** Civ Wed 23

See advert on opposite page

CRIGGION
MAP 15 SJ21

★★★★ FARM HOUSE
Brimford House *(SJ310150)*

SY5 9AU
☎ 01938 570235 Mrs Dawson
e-mail: info@brimford.co.uk

dir: *Off B4393 after Crew Green turn left for Criggion Brimford 1st on left after pub*

This elegant Georgian house stands in lovely open countryside and is a good base for touring central Wales and the Marches. Bedrooms are spacious, and thoughtful extras enhance guest comfort. A cheery log fire burns in the lounge during colder weather and the hospitality is equally warm, providing a relaxing atmosphere throughout.

Rooms 3 en suite S £45–£60; D £55–£70✱ **Facilities** TVB tea/coffee Cen ht TVL Fishing **Parking** 4 **Notes** LB 250 acres Arable, beef, sheep ☻

★★★ 🅰 FARM HOUSE
Lane Farm *(SJ305161)*

SY5 9BG
☎ 01743 884288 📠 01743 885126 Mrs L Burrowes
e-mail: lane.farm@ukgateway.net

dir: *Situated on B4393 between Crew Green and Llandrinio*

Rooms 4 en suite (2 GF) S £30–£35; D £50–£54 **Facilities** TVB tea/coffee Cen ht Fishing **Parking** 8 **Notes** LB ⊗ 380 acres Organic beef/sheep Closed 23–27 Dec ☻

DYLIFE
MAP 14 SN89

★★ INN
Star

SY19 7BW
☎ 01650 521345

dir: *1.5m off B4518 between Llanidloes & Machynlleth*

This friendly historic inn is a popular watering hole amid beautiful countryside. It's a good base for active walking, cycling, birdwatching, or just relaxing. The menu offers a wide choice and the comfortable bedrooms are practically furnished.

Rooms 6 rms (2 en suite) (1 fmly) S £25–£38; D £42–£44✱ **Facilities** FTV TV2B tea/coffee Cen ht TVL Dinner Last d 10pm Pool Table **Parking** 30 **Notes** LB RS Winter

ERWOOD
MAP 09 SO04

★★★★ 🍽 BED & BREAKFAST
Hafod-y-Garreg

LD2 3TQ
☎ 01982 560400
e-mail: john-annie@hafod-y.wanadoo.co.uk
web: www.hafodygarreg.co.uk

dir: *1m S of Erwood. Off A470 at Trericket Mill, sharp right, up track past cream farmhouse towards pine forest, through gate*

This remote Grade II listed farmhouse dates in part from 1401 and is the oldest surviving traditional house in Wales. It has tremendous character and has been furnished and decorated to befit its age, while the bedrooms have modern facilities. There is an impressive dining room and a lounge with an open fireplace. Warm hospitality from John and Annie McKay is a major strength here.

Rooms 2 en suite (1 fmly) D £65 **Facilities** STV TVB tea/coffee Cen ht Dinner Last d Day before Wi-fi available **Parking** 6 **Notes** LB Closed Xmas ☻

See also Erwood

★★★★ ◉ INN
Old Black Lion Inn
26 Lion St HR3 5AD
☎ 01497 820841 📠 01497 822960
e–mail: info@oldblacklion.co.uk

This fine old coaching inn, with a history stretching back several centuries, has a wealth of charm and character. It was occupied by Oliver Cromwell during the siege of Hay Castle. Privately owned and personally run, it provides cosy and well-equipped bedrooms, some located in an adjacent building. A wide range of well-prepared food is provided, and the service is relaxed and friendly.

Rooms 6 rms (5 en suite) (1 pri facs) 4 annexe en suite (2 GF)
Facilities STV TVB tea/coffee Direct dial from bedrooms Cen ht Dinner Last d 9.30pm **Parking** 12 **Notes** ⊗ No children 8yrs Closed 24–26 Dec

★★★ INN
Baskerville Arms
Clyro HR3 5RZ
☎ 01497 820670 📠 0870 705 8427
e–mail: info@baskervillearms.co.uk
dir: *From Hereford follow A438 into Clyro, signed*
Situated near Hay-on-Wye in the peaceful village of Clyro, this former Georgian coaching inn is personally run by its friendly and enthusiastic owners. Bedrooms offer a range of styles while public areas include a bar with a village inn atmosphere, a separate restaurant and a comfortable residents' lounge. There is also a large function room, plus a meeting room.

Rooms 13 en suite (1 fmly) S £45–£55; D £65–£85 **Facilities** TVB tea/coffee Cen ht TVL Dinner Last d 8.30pm Wi-fi available Pool Table **Conf** Thtr 80 Class 60 Board 60 Del from £115 ✳ **Parking** 12 **Notes** LB Civ Wed 120

★★★★★ 🏠 🍴 GUEST ACCOMMODATION
Guidfa House
Crossgates LD1 6RF
☎ 01597 851241 📠 01597 851875
e–mail: guidfa@globalnet.co.uk
web: www.guidfa-house.co.uk
dir: *3m N of Llandrindod Wells, at junct of A483 & A44*

Expect a relaxed and pampered stay at this elegant Georgian house just outside the town. Comfort is the keynote here, whether in the attractive and well-equipped bedrooms or in the homely lounge, where a real fire burns in cold weather. Food is also a strength, due to the proprietor's skilful touch in the kitchen.

Rooms 5 en suite 1 annexe en suite (1 GF) S fr £55; D £70–£95✳
Facilities TVB tea/coffee Cen ht Dinner Last d previous day Wi-fi available **Parking** 10 **Notes** LB ⊗ No children 10yrs

WALES

LLANDRINDOD WELLS CONTINUED

★★★★ FARM HOUSE
Holly *(SO045593)*

Holly Farm, Howey LD1 5PP

☎ 01597 822402 🖺 01597 822402 Mrs R Jones

dir: *2m S on A483 near Howey*

This working farm dates from Tudor times. Bedrooms are homely and full of character, and the comfortable lounge has a log fire in cooler months. Traditional home cooking using local produce can be sampled in the dining room.

Rooms 3 en suite (1 fmly) S £32–£35; D £52–£60✶ **Facilities** TVB tea/coffee Cen ht TVL Dinner Last d 5pm **Parking** 4 **Notes LB** ⊗ 70 acres beef sheep

---

LLANGEDWYN   **MAP 15 SJ12**

★★★★ GUEST HOUSE
Plas Uchaf

SY10 9LD

☎ 01691 780588 🖺 0845 280 2188

e–mail: maureenwise@hotmail.com
web: www.welsh-bed-breakfast.co.uk

dir: *Mile End services Oswestry 483/Welshpool, 2m White Lion right, 4.5m Llangedwyn, 150yds after school on right*

A very warm welcome awaits at this large and impressive late 17th-century mansion that stands in extensive grounds, and is situated on a hillside in the picturesque Tanat Valley. It provides traditionally furnished, spacious bedrooms including a two bedroom suite, and a choice of comfortable sitting rooms. All share one huge table in the dining room, where home-cooked dinners are available. The house is understandably becoming popular as a venue for weddings.

Rooms 7 rms (4 en suite) (3 pri facs) (2 fmly) **Facilities** TV5B tea/coffee Licensed Cen ht Dinner Last d 2pm 🎣 Fishing Pool Table 🌙 ⚓ **Conf** Max 15 **Parking** 30 **Notes** ⊗ Civ Wed 40 ⊛

LLANGURIG   **MAP 09 SN97**

★★★★ GUEST HOUSE
The Old Vicarage

SY18 6RN

☎ 01686 440280 🖺 01686 440280

e–mail: info@theoldvicaragellangurig.co.uk

dir: *A470 onto A44, signed*

Located on pretty mature grounds, which feature a magnificent holly tree, this elegant Victorian house provides a range of thoughtfully furnished bedrooms, some with fine period items. Breakfast is served in a spacious dining room and a comfortable guest lounge is also available. Afternoon teas are served in the garden during the warmer months.

Rooms 4 en suite (1 fmly) S £30–£40; D £48–£54✶ **Facilities** TVB tea/coffee Licensed Cen ht TVL Dinner Last d 5pm Wi-fi available **Parking** 6 **Notes LB** ⊗ No coaches ⊛

LLANIDLOES   **MAP 09 SN98**

★★★ INN
Mount

China St SY18 6AB

☎ 01686 412247 🖺 01686 412247

e–mail: mountllani@aol.com

dir: *In town centre*

This establishment is believed to occupy part of the site of a motte and bailey castle and started life as a coaching inn. The traditional bars are full of character, with exposed beams and timbers as well as cobbled flooring and log fires. Bedrooms, which include some in a new separate building, are carefully furnished and equipped with practical and thoughtful extras. CONTINUED

Rooms 3 en suite 6 annexe en suite (3 fmly) (3 GF) S £39; D £59✱
Facilities TVB tea/coffee Cen ht TVL Dinner Last d 9pm Pool Table
Conf Max 20 Class 20 Board 12 Parking 12

LLANWRTYD WELLS   MAP 09 SN84

★★★★ ◉◉◉ RESTAURANT WITH ROOMS
Carlton Riverside

Irfon Crescent LD5 4SP
☎ 01591 610248
e–mail: info@carltonrestaurant.co.uk

dir: *In town centre next to bridge*

Guests become part of the family at this character property, set beside
the river in Wales's smallest town. Carlton Riverside offers
award-winning cuisine for which Mary Ann Gilchrist relies on the very
best of local ingredients. The set menu is complemented by a
well-chosen wine list and dinner is served in the delightfully stylish
restaurant which offers a memorable blend of traditional comfort,
modern design and river views. Four comfortable bedrooms have
tasteful combinations of antique and contemporary furniture, along
with welcome personal touches.

Rooms 4 en suite S £40–£50; D £65–£100✱ Facilities TVB tea/coffee
Cen ht Dinner Last d 8.30pm Notes LB Closed Dec

★★★★ ◉◉ RESTAURANT WITH ROOMS
Lasswade Country House

Station Rd LD5 4RW
☎ 01591 610515 🖹 01591 610611
e–mail: info@lasswadehotel.co.uk

dir: *Off A483 into Irfon Terrace, right into Station Rd, 350yds on
right*

This friendly establishment on the edge of the town has impressive
views over the countryside. Bedrooms are comfortably furnished and
well equipped, while the public areas consist of a tastefully decorated
lounge, an elegant restaurant with a bar, and an airy conservatory
which looks out on to the neighbouring hills. The kitchen utilises fresh,
local produce to provide an enjoyable dining experience.

Rooms 8 en suite Facilities TVB Notes Civ Wed

LLANYMYNECH   MAP 15 SJ22

★★★★ INN
The Bradford Arms

Llanymynech SY22 6EJ
☎ 01691 830582 🖹 01691 839009
e–mail: cateloo@tesco.net

(For full entry see Oswestry (Shropshire))

★★★ BED & BREAKFAST
Ty-Coch Bungalow

Four Crosses SY22 6QZ
☎ 01691 830361
e–mail: bill_lee@talk21.com

dir: *1m S of Llanymynech on A483*

Built in 1984, this large bungalow provides friendly hospitality, modern
accommodation and a comfortable lounge. Guests share one large
breakfast table in the kitchen-dining room.

Rooms 2 en suite (2 GF) S £35; D £56 Facilities TVB tea/coffee Cen ht
TVL Dinner Last d 24hrs notice Parking 6 Notes LB ⊗ ⊜

MACHYNLLETH   MAP 14 SH70

★★★★ 🅰 BED & BREAKFAST
Dolgelynen Farm B & B

Dolgelynen SY20 9JR
☎ 01654 702026 🖹 01654 702026
e–mail: elinordyfi@tiscali.co.uk
web: www.dolgelynenfarmhouse.co.uk

dir: *1.5m NW of Machynlleth. A487 onto A493, 1st left onto Farm
Ln, follow river 1m to farm*

Rooms 3 rms (2 en suite) (1 pri facs) S £30; D £50–£60✱ Facilities TVB
tea/coffee Cen ht Parking 4 Notes ⊗ No children 12yrs Closed Nov–Etr
⊜

★★★ GUEST HOUSE
Maenllwyd

Newtown Rd SY20 8EY
☎ 01654 702928 🖹 01654 702928
e–mail: maenllwyd@btinternet.com
web: www.maenllwyd.co.uk

dir: *On A489 opp hospital*

Maenllwyd is a Victorian house set on the outskirts of this historic
town, a short walk from local amenities. A warm welcome has been
offered to guests here for many years and the hospitality is very
enjoyable. Bedrooms are attractively decorated with modern facilities
provided. There is a comfortable lounge and a separate dining room.

Rooms 8 en suite (1 fmly) S £45; D £60–£65✱ Facilities TVB tea/coffee
Cen ht TVL Parking 11 Notes No coaches Closed 25-26 Dec

WALES

NEWTOWN   MAP 15 SO19

★★★★★ A GUEST HOUSE
The Old Vicarage
Dolfor SY16 4BN
☎ 01686 629051
e–mail: tim@theoldvicaragedolfor.co.uk

dir: *3.5m from Newtown on A483 signed Llandrindod Wells*

Rooms 3 en suite S fr £65; D fr £100✳ Facilities FTV TVB Licensed
Cen ht Dinner Last d 9pm Wi-fi available Parking 8 Notes ⊗
No children 12yrs No coaches 🐾

★★★ GUEST ACCOMMODATION
Yesterdays
Severn Sq SY16 2AG
☎ 01686 622644
e–mail: info@yesterdayshotel.com
web: www.yesterdayshotel.com

dir: *Off junct High St & Broad St onto Severn St to Severn Sq*

Dating from the 17th century, this attractive guest house has spacious
rooms equipped with many thoughtful extras. The friendly hosts
provide a genuine welcome and attentive service in the centre of this
fine market town, which lies on the Severn Way long-distance path.

Rooms 5 en suite 1 annexe en suite (2 fmly) (2 GF) S £35–£40;
D £60–£65 Facilities TVB tea/coffee Cen ht Wi-fi available Notes ⊗

SENNYBRIDGE   MAP 09 SN92

★★★ GUEST ACCOMMODATION
Maeswalter
Heol Senni LD3 8SU
☎ 01874 636629
e–mail: joy@maeswalter.fsnet.co.uk
web: www.maeswalter.co.uk

dir: *A470 onto A4215, 2.5m left for Heol Senni, 1.5m on right
over cattle grid*

Set in a peaceful country location with splendid views of the Senni
Valley, this 17th-century farmhouse offers a friendly and relaxing place
to stay. The accommodation is well maintained and includes a suite on
the ground floor of an adjacent building. A lounge-dining room is
provided, and freshly cooked farmhouse breakfasts are a pleasure.

CONTINUED

Rooms 4 rms (3 en suite) (1 pri facs) (1 fmly) (2 GF) S £35–£40;
D £54–£68✳ Facilities STV TVB tea/coffee Cen ht TVL Dinner Last d
noon Parking 12 Notes LB ⊗ No children 5yrs

WELSHPOOL   MAP 15 SJ20

See also Criggion

Premier Collection

★★★★★ BED & BREAKFAST
Moors Farm B&B
Oswestry Rd SY21 9JR
☎ 01938 553395 & 07957 882967
e–mail: moorsfarm@tiscali.co.uk
web: www.moors-farm.com

dir: *1.5m NE of Welshpool off A483*

A very warm welcome awaits you at this impressive house, parts of
which date from the early 18th century. It has a wealth of character,
including exposed beams and log-burning fires, and has been carefully
renovated to provide very good quality spacious accommodation.

Rooms 5 en suite (2 fmly) Facilities TVB tea/coffee Cen ht TVL
Notes ⊗

★★★ 🏠 FARM HOUSE
Heath Cottage (SJ239023)
Kingswood, Forden SY21 8LX
☎ 01938 580453 📠 01938 580453 Mr & Mrs M C Payne
e–mail: heathcottagewales@tiscali.co.uk

dir: *4m S of Welshpool. Off A490 behind Forden Old Post Office,
opp Parrys Garage*

Furnishings and décor highlight the original features of this early
18th-century farmhouse. Bedrooms have stunning country views, and
a choice of lounges, one with a log fire, is available. Memorable
breakfasts feature free-range eggs and home-made preserves.

Rooms 3 en suite (1 fmly) S £27.50; D £55 Facilities tea/coffee Cen ht
TVL Parking 4 Notes ⊗ 6 acres Poultry/sheep Closed Oct–Etr 🐾

RHONDDA CYNON TAFF

PONTYPRIDD   MAP 09 ST08

★★★ BED & BREAKFAST
Tyn-Y-Wern Country House
Ynysybwl CF37 3LY
☎ 01443 790551 📠 01443 790551
e–mail: tynywern2002@yahoo.com

dir: *B4273 from Pontypridd, war memorial on left. 1st right turn
after row of modern terrace houses on right*

This large Victorian house, once a mine manager's residence, is in a
quiet location three miles from Pontypridd, and its elevated position
provides good views. It has been extensively restored and provides

CONTINUED

modern yet traditionally furnished accommodation, plus an attractive dining room and a lounge. There is an extensive garden with self-catering cottages, a games room and a laundry room.

Rooms 3 rms (1 en suite) **Facilities** TVB tea/coffee Cen ht Wi-fi available Pool Table **Parking** 10 **Notes** Closed 20 Dec–6 Jan ⊛

SWANSEA

LLANGENNITH   MAP 08 SS49

★★★★ INN
Kings Head

Town House SA3 1HX

☎ 01792 386212 📄 01792 386477

e–mail: info@kingsheadgower.co.uk

The Kings Head is made up from three 17th-century buildings set behind a splendid rough stone wall, and stands opposite Llangennith Church in this coastal village on the Gower peninsula. In a separate building are the seven well equipped and comfortable bedrooms. This is an ideal base for exploring the Gower peninsula, whether for walking, cycling or surfing. Evening meals and breakfasts can be taken in the pub.

Rooms 7 en suite (3 fmly) (4 GF) D £70–£90✱ **Facilities** FTV TVB tea/coffee Cen ht Dinner Last d 9pm Pool Table **Parking** 10 **Notes** LB

MUMBLES   MAP 08 SS68

Premier Collection

★★★★★ GUEST ACCOMMODATION
Little Langland

2 Rotherslade Rd, Langland SA3 4QN

☎ 01792 369696

e–mail: enquiries@littlelangland.co.uk

dir: Off A4067 in Mumbles onto Newton Rd, 4th left onto Langland Rd, 2nd left onto Rotherslade Rd

Little Langland has recently had a total refurbishment which proprietors Christine and Roger Johnson take great pride in. Little Langland is only five miles from Swansea City Centre and within easy access of the stunning Gower Peninsula with its many coves and bays. The bedrooms are stylish, comfortable and include free broadband. There is a brand new cafe bar, ideal for a relaxing drink, and there is also a

bar menu of freshly prepared snacks available along with a variety of coffees and wines. Breakfast is served in the comfortable dining area.

Rooms 6 en suite S £65–£70; D £85–£100✱ **Facilities** FTV TVB tea/coffee Direct dial from bedrooms Cen ht **Parking** 6 **Notes** ⊗ No children 8yrs

★★★★ A GUEST HOUSE
Alexandra House

366 Mumbles Rd SA3 5TN

☎ 01792 406406 📄 01792 405605

dir: M4 junct 42 onto A483 onto A4067 to Mumbles 500yds after West Cross Inn

Rooms 6 en suite (1 fmly) (1 GF) **Facilities** TVB tea/coffee Cen ht **Parking** 6 **Notes** ⊗ No children 5yrs No coaches Closed 23 Dec–2 Jan ⊛

PARKMILL (NEAR SWANSEA)   MAP 08 SS58

★★★★ FARM HOUSE
Parc-le-Breos House (SS529896)

SA3 2HA

☎ 01792 371636 📄 01792 371287 Mrs O Edwards

dir: On A4118, right 300yds after Shepherds shop, next left, signed

This imposing early 19th-century house is at the end of a forest drive and set in 70 acres of delightful grounds. Many charming original features have been retained in the public rooms, which include a lounge and a games room. The bedrooms have comfortable furnishings, and many are suitable for families.

Rooms 10 en suite (7 fmly) (1 GF) **Facilities** TVB tea/coffee Licensed Cen ht TVL Dinner Last d 3pm Riding Pool Table **Conf** Max 30 Thtr 30 **Parking** 12 **Notes** ⊗ 65 acres arable horses pigs chickens Closed 25–26 Dec

CONTINUED

WALES

WALES

REYNOLDSTON
MAP 08 SS48

Premier Collection

★★★★★ ◎◎ RESTAURANT WITH ROOMS

Fairyhill

SA3 1BS

☎ 01792 390139 🖩 01792 391358

e–mail: postbox@fairyhill.net

dir: *M4 junct 47 onto A483, at next rdbt turn right onto A484. At Gowerton take B4295 10m*

Peace and tranquillity are never far away at this charming Georgian mansion set in the heart of the beautiful Gower peninsula. Bedrooms are furnished with care and are filled with many thoughtful extras. There is also a range of comfortable seating areas with crackling log fires to choose from, and a smart restaurant offering menus based on local produce, complemented by an excellent wine list.

Rooms 8 en suite S £145–£250; D £165–£275✳ **Facilities** FTV TVB Direct dial from bedrooms Cen ht TVL Dinner Last d 9pm Wi-fi available 🌱 Holistic treatments **Conf** Max 32 Thtr 32 Board 16 **Parking** 50 **Notes** LB ❸ No children 8yrs Closed 1–24 Jan RS Nov–Mar

SWANSEA
MAP 09 SS69

★★★★ GUEST HOUSE

Crescent Guest House

132 Eaton Crescent, Uplands SA1 4QR

☎ 01792 466814 🖩 01792 466814

e–mail: crescentguesthouse@hotmail.co.uk

web: www.crescentguesthouse.co.uk

dir: *0.5m W of town centre. Off A4118, 1st left after St James's Church*

This friendly guest house is on a leafy avenue close to the restaurants, bars and shops of Swansea's Uplands area. The Edwardian house has been refurbished to provide well-equipped bedrooms with modern en suites, internet connections and flat-screen televisions. Family rooms are also available. Breakfast is served in a cosy dining room, and the spacious lounge has impressive views of Swansea Bay.

Rooms 6 en suite (1 fmly) S £36–£45; D £56–£70✳ **Facilities** FTV TVB tea/coffee Cen ht TVL Wi-fi available **Parking** 6 **Notes** ❸ No coaches

★★★ GUEST HOUSE

Hurst Dene

10 Sketty Rd, Uplands SA2 0LJ

☎ 01792 280920 🖩 01792 280920

e–mail: hurstdenehotel@yahoo.co.uk

dir: *1m W of city centre. A4118 through Uplands shopping area onto Sketty Rd, Hurst Dene on right*

This friendly guest house has a private car park and provides soundly maintained bedrooms with modern furnishings and equipment. Facilities include an attractive breakfast room with separate tables and there is a small comfortable lounge.

Rooms 10 rms (8 en suite) (3 fmly) (1 GF) S £35–£40; D £60–£65✳ **Facilities** TVB tea/coffee Cen ht TVL **Parking** 7 **Notes** ❸ Closed 22 Dec–1 Jan

See advert on opposite page

★★★ GUEST ACCOMMODATION

The White House

4 Nyanza Ter SA1 4QQ

☎ 01792 473856 🖩 01792 455300

e–mail: reception@thewhitehousehotel.co.uk

dir: *On A4118, 1m W of city centre*

Part of a short early Victorian terrace within fashionable Uplands, this house retains many original features. It has been restored to provide thoughtfully furnished and equipped quality accommodation. Bedrooms are filled with many extras, and the memorable Welsh breakfasts include cockles and laverbread.

Rooms 9 en suite (4 fmly) S £42; D £72 **Facilities** STV FTV TVB tea/coffee Direct dial from bedrooms Cen ht TVL Dinner Last d 8.15pm **Conf** Max 16 Thtr 16 Class 16 Board 10 Del £95 ✳ **Parking** 8 **Notes** LB

TORFAEN

PONTHIR
MAP 09 ST39

★★★★ BED & BREAKFAST

The Annex

Stokes Farm, Stokes Dr NP18 1PG

☎ 01633 422383 🖩 01633 422383

e–mail: jasponthir@hotmail.co.uk

web: www.stokes-farm.co.uk

dir: *On B4236 from Caerleon towards Cwmbran. Turn right immediately before Ponthir House Public House*

Not your typical bed and breakfast, here guests have exclusive use of a large, high quality annex building. This includes a luxurious bed, spacious lounge with large flat screen TV, and a separate kitchen area where guests are invited to prepare their own continental breakfast from the substantial range of cold meats, cheeses and fresh fruit provided. The friendly proprietor is always on hand and in the morning delivers fresh bread and croissants to the door.

Rooms 1 en suite (1 fmly) (1 GF) D fr £75 **Facilities** TVB Cen ht TVL **Parking** 4 **Notes** LB ❸

PONTYPOOL MAP 09 SO20

★★★★ FARM HOUSE
Ty-Cooke Farm (SO310052)
Mamhilad NP4 8QZ
☎ 01873 880382 📠 01873 880382 Mrs M Price
e–mail: tycookefarm@hotmail.com
dir: Off A4042 to Mamhilad, in 2m 1st farm on left past Horseshoe Inn
This working farm is quietly located in an attractive setting with lovely views. It is thought to date from 1700 and has a wealth of character. Breakfasts are served at one table near a magnificent ornate marble fireplace. There is also a small lounge on the ground floor of the barn accommodation.
Rooms 6 en suite (1 fmly) (1 GF) S fr £45; D fr £65✱ **Facilities** TV3B tea/coffee Cen ht TVL **Parking** 6 **Notes** ✖ 135 acres beef sheep

HANMER MAP 15 SJ43

★★★★ INN
The Hanmer Arms
SY13 3DE
☎ 01948 830532 📠 0148 830740
e–mail: info@hanmerarms.co.uk
web: www.hanmerarms.co.uk
dir: On A539, just off A525 Whitchurch/Wrexham road
Located in the centre of the village and also home to the local crown green bowling club, this former farm has been sympathetically renovated to provide a good range of facilities. Well equipped bedrooms are situated in the former stables or barns, and rustic furniture styles highlight the many period features within public areas, which also feature an attractive first floor function room.
Rooms 12 annexe en suite (2 fmly) (5 GF) S £49.50–£59.50; D £79.50–£89.50✱ **Facilities** FTV TVB tea/coffee Cen ht Dinner Last d 9pm **Conf** Max 140 Thtr 140 Class 100 Board 60 Del from £89.50 ✱ **Parking** 50 **Notes LB** Civ Wed 60

LLANARMON DYFFRYN CEIRIOG MAP 15 SJ13

★★★★ ⊕ 🍴 INN
The Hand at Llanarmon
LL20 7LD
☎ 01691 600666 📠 01691 600262
e–mail: reception@thehandhotel.co.uk
dir: Turn off A5 at Chirk onto B4500 signed Ceiriog Valley, continue for 11m
This small, pleasant, privately owned and run accommodation is located in the village centre and has a wealth of charm and character. Apart from warm and friendly hospitality, it provides a variety of bedroom styles, including rooms on ground floor level and two in a

separate building. A large wood-carved hand extends a welcome at front entrance and a good choice of competently prepared food is provided.

The Hand at Llanarmon

Rooms 13 en suite (4 GF) S £40–£70; D £80–£110✱ **Facilities** TVB tea/coffee Direct dial from bedrooms Cen ht Dinner Last d 8.45pm Wi-Fi available **Parking** 19 **Notes LB** RS 24–26 Dec Civ Wed 60

CONTINUED

WALES

Ireland
Rosmuck, Galway

NORTHERN IRELAND
CO ANTRIM

BUSHMILLS

MAP 01 C6

Premier Collection

★★★★★ GUEST ACCOMMODATION
Whitepark House

150 Whitepark Rd, Ballintoy BT54 6NH
☎ 028 2073 1482
e–mail: bob@whiteparkhouse.com

dir: *On A2 at Whitepark Bay, 6m E of Bushmills*

Whitepark House nestles above a sandy beach and has super views of the ocean and Scotland's Western Isles. The house features bijouterie gathered from Far Eastern travels, while the traditional bedrooms are homely. Breakfasts are served around a central table in the open-plan hallway, and hospitality is warm and memorable.

Rooms 3 en suite S £75; D £100 **Facilities** tea/coffee Cen ht Wi-fi available **Parking** 6 **Notes** ⊗ No children 10yrs

---

CUSHENDUN

MAP 01 D6

★★★★ FARM HOUSE
The Villa Farm House *(D 250341)*

185 Torr Rd BT44 0PU
☎ 028 2176 1252 📄 028 2176 1252 Mrs Scally
e–mail: maggie.scally@hotmail.co.uk

dir: *From Cushendun on B92 right onto Torr Rd, 0.5m right at T-junct, farmhouse 3rd left, black & white sign at end of road. 400mtrs through farm*

This delightful Tudor-style two-storey farmhouse sits in well-kept gardens and provides stunning views of the Bay of Cushendun and the village, which houses the smallest pub in Ireland. The well-equipped bedrooms are traditionally styled and some are suitable for families. Friendly service and freshly cooked meals are assured.

Rooms 4 en suite (2 fmly) S £35; D fr £60 **Facilities** TVB tea/coffee Cen ht TVL Stairlift **Parking** 25 **Notes** LB ⊗ 40 acres sheep Closed Nov–Jan ⊛

LARNE

MAP 01 D5

★★★★ GUEST ACCOMMODATION
Derrin House

2 Princes Gardens BT40 1RQ
☎ 028 2827 3269 📄 028 2827 3269
e–mail: info@derrinhouse.co.uk

dir: *Off A8 Harbour Highway onto A2 coast route, 1st left after lights at Main St*

Just a short walk from the town centre, and a short drive from the harbour, this comfortable Victorian house offers a very friendly welcome. The bedrooms are gradually being refurbished to offer smartly presented modern facilities. Public areas are light and inviting, hearty breakfasts are offered in the stylish dining room.

Rooms 7 rms (6 en suite) (1 pri facs) (2 fmly) (2 GF) S £35–£38; D £55–£60 **Facilities** TVB tea/coffee Cen ht TVL Wi-fi available **Parking** 6 **Notes** LB

★★★★ GUEST HOUSE
Manor

23 Older Fleet Rd, Harbour Highway BT40 1AS
☎ 028 2827 3305 📄 028 2826 0505
e–mail: welcome@themanorguesthouse.com
web: www.themanorguesthouse.com

dir: *Near Larne ferry terminal & harbour train station*

This grand Victorian house continues to prove popular with travellers thanks to its convenient location next to the ferry terminal. There is an elegant sitting room and a separate cosy breakfast room. The well-equipped bedrooms vary in size and are furnished in modern or period style. Hospitality is especially good and ensures a real home from home experience.

Rooms 8 en suite (2 fmly) S £30–£35; D £55–£60 **Facilities** TVB tea/coffee Cen ht Wi-fi available **Parking** 6 **Notes** LB ⊗ Closed 25–26 Dec

---

PORTRUSH

MAP 01 C6

★★★ GUEST ACCOMMODATION
Beulah Guest House

16 Causeway St BT56 8AB
☎ 028 7082 2413
e–mail: stay@beulahguesthouse.com

dir: *Approach Portrush, signs for Bushmills/East Strand car park, onto Causeway St, house 300yds on left*

Situated just a stroll from the East Strand and the town's attractions, this guest house offers a friendly welcome. Bright and attractive throughout, the comfortable bedrooms are well equipped. There is also a first-floor lounge and secure parking behind the house.

Rooms 9 en suite (3 fmly) S £30–£35; D £60–£70✱ **Facilities** TVB tea/coffee Cen ht TVL **Parking** 10 **Notes** LB ⊗ Closed 25–26 Dec

BELFAST

BELFAST MAP 01 D5

★★★★ GUEST ACCOMMODATION
Tara Lodge
36 Cromwell Rd BT7 1JW
☎ 028 9059 0900 ▤ 028 9059 0901
e–mail: info@taralodge.com
web: www.taralodge.com

dir: *M1 onto A55, left onto A1, right onto Fitzwilliam St, left onto University Rd, proceed to Botanic*

Friendly staff and comfortable bedrooms make this new establishment popular for tourism and business. The stylish dining room is the scene for memorable breakfasts, while secure off-road parking is a bonus so close to the city centre.

Rooms 19 en suite 9 annexe en suite (3 GF) S £70–£80; D £85–£95✱ **Facilities** STV FTV TVB tea/coffee Direct dial from bedrooms Lift Cen ht TVL Wi-fi available **Parking** 19 **Notes LB** ✪ Closed 24–28 Dec

CO DOWN

BANGOR MAP 01 D5

Premier Collection

★★★★★ BED & BREAKFAST
Hebron House
68 Princetown Rd BT20 3TD
☎ 028 9146 3126 ▤ 028 9146 3126
e–mail: reception@hebron-house.com
web: www.hebron-house.com

dir: *A20 onto B20 for 3m, 1st rdbt onto Princetown Rd*

Hebron House stands in a peaceful elevated location within easy walking distance of the town amenities. Bedrooms are luxuriously furnished and have many thoughtful extras. The elegant lounge is richly styled and very comfortable. Breakfast offers home-made and local produce around a communal table in the smart dining room.

Hebron House

Rooms 3 en suite (1 GF) S £50–£80; D £75–£80 **Facilities** TVB tea/coffee Cen ht TVL Wi-fi available **Parking** 2 **Notes** ✪ Closed 22 Dec–1 Jan

★★★★ GUEST HOUSE
Shelleven House
61 Princetown Rd BT20 3TA
☎ 028 9127 1777 ▤ 028 9127 1777
e–mail: shellevenhouse@aol.com
web: www.shellevenhouse.com

dir: *A2 from Belfast, left at rail station rdbt. Onto Dufferin Av, proceed to rdbt, over to Princetown Rd*

Shelleven is a large Victorian Townhouse situated in a quiet conservation area and close to the marina, the promenade and a short walk from the town centre. Bedrooms are all spacious and very comfortable, with rooms at the front of the house having wonderful sea views. There is an extensive choice available at breakfast, which is served in the elegant dining room.

Rooms 10 en suite (2 fmly) (1 GF) S £36–£60; D £70–£85✱ **Facilities** STV TVB tea/coffee Direct dial from bedrooms Licensed Cen ht TVL **Parking** 10 **Notes LB** ✪ No coaches

IRELAND

CONTINUED

BANGOR CONTINUED

★★★ GUEST ACCOMMODATION
Tara Guest House

49/51 Princetown Rd BT20 3TA

☎ 028 9145 8820 ▤ 028 9146 8924

e–mail: taraguesthouse@lineone.net

dir: *A2 to Bangor, down Main St, left onto Queens Parade to mini-rdbt (Gray Hill) right onto Princetown Rd*

Located just a short walk from the town centre this traditionally styled house provides spacious, well-equipped bedrooms, many for which are suitable for families. Some bedrooms also boast sea views while spa baths are provided in others. There is a comfortable lounge and bright dining room.

Rooms 13 en suite (4 fmly) S fr £35; D fr £60 **Facilities** TVB tea/coffee Direct dial from bedrooms Cen ht TVL Wi-fi available **Parking** 8 **Notes** Closed 25–30 Dec

See advert on this page

COMBER   MAP 01 D5

★★★★ GUEST HOUSE
The Old Schoolhouse Inn

Castle Espie BT23 6EA

☎ 028 9754 1182 ▤ 028 9754 2583

e–mail: info@theoldschoolhouseinn.com

dir: *A22 to Comber, right at end of road. 0.5m past Castle Espie*

This privately owned and personally run establishment originated as a school built in 1929. The school itself is now a charming restaurant, while the modern bedrooms are spacious and well equipped.

Rooms 12 en suite (12 GF) **Facilities** STV TVB tea/coffee Direct dial from bedrooms Licensed Cen ht TVL Dinner Last d 9.30pm Golf 9 **Conf** Max 60 Thtr 60 Class 30 Board 30 **Parking** 100

HOLYWOOD   MAP 01 D5

Premier Collection

★★★★★ ⊜ GUEST HOUSE
Rayanne House

60 Desmesne Rd BT18 9EX

☎ 028 9042 5859 ▤ 028 9042 5859

e–mail: rayannehouse@hotmail.com

web: www.rayannehouse.com

dir: *Exit A2 at Holywood, left onto Jacksons Rd, pass golf club, 200yds on right*

This elegant period house, set in its own grounds, is full of charm and enjoys a commanding position overlooking Belfast Lough and the Antrim Hills beyond. Bedrooms are all of a high standard and a host of thoughtful extras is provided. The house is a short drive from Belfast City centre and the City Airport. Breakfasts are not to be missed and evening meals are served in the spacious dining room.

Rooms 10 en suite (2 fmly) (1 GF) **Facilities** FTV TVB tea/coffee Direct dial from bedrooms Licensed Cen ht Dinner Last d 9pm Wi-fi available Golf 18 **Conf** Max 17 Thtr 17 Class 17 Board 17 **Parking** 15 **Notes** ⊗ No coaches RS 25–26 Dec

---

NEWTOWNARDS   MAP 01 D5

★★★★ GUEST HOUSE
Ballynester House

1a Cardy Rd, Greyabbey BT22 2LS

☎ 028 4278 8386 ▤ 028 4278 8986

e–mail: rc.davison@virgin.net

dir: *A20 S from Newtownards to Greyabbey, or A20 N from Portaferry to Greyabbey, signed at Greyabbey rdbt*

Located in the rolling hills above Strangford Lough, this stylish, modern house provides a tranquil haven and a warm welcome. Smart day rooms make the most of the super views; hearty breakfasts are served in the bright dining room. Richly furnished bedrooms include a host of thoughtful extras.

Rooms 3 en suite (1 fmly) (3 GF) **Facilities** TVB tea/coffee Cen ht Wi-fi available Professional Genealogy consultation for guests **Parking** 10 **Notes** ⊗ No children 7yrs No coaches

IRELAND

CONTINUED

CO FERMANAGH

ENNISKILLEN   MAP 01 C5

★★★★ GUEST HOUSE
Arch House Tullyhona Farm Guest House
Marble Arch Rd, Florencecourt BT92 1DE
☎ 028 6634 8452
e–mail: tullyguest60@hotmail.com
web: www.archhouse.com

dir: *A4 from Enniskillen towards Sligo, 2.5m onto A32, right at NT sign for Florence Court*

This delightful house nestles in a tranquil country setting very close to the Marble Arch Caves and Florence Court. The refurbished bedrooms are stylish, and Tullyhona's restaurant is open for all-day breakfasts, as well as a range of traditional evening meals.

Rooms 4 en suite (4 fmly) S £38–£45; D £52–£54 **Facilities** TVB Direct dial from bedrooms Cen ht TVL Dinner Last d 6.30pm Riding Farm tours Trampoline Table tennis Badminton **Conf** Max 70 Thtr 70 Class 50 **Parking** 8 **Notes LB**

★★★★ GUEST HOUSE
Willowbank House
60 Bellvue Rd BT74 4JH
☎ 028 6632 8582 📠 028 6632 8582
e–mail: joan@willowbankhouse.com
web: www.willowbankhouse.com

dir: *A4 from Enniskillen towards Belfast, 0.25m right after Killy Helvin Hotel signed Upper Lough Erne & Willowbank House, 2m on left*

This peacefully situated house commands an elevated position in attractive grounds just a short drive from the town. Bedrooms, all on the ground floor, vary in size and some are suitable for families. There is a comfortable lounge and substantial breakfasts are served in the conservatory dining room, overlooking the lake.

Rooms 5 en suite (2 fmly) (5 GF) S £40–£45; D £55–£60✱ **Facilities** FTV TVB tea/coffee Cen ht TVL Wi-fi available **Parking** 6 **Notes LB** ✪ No coaches Closed Xmas RS New Year

★★★ INN
Aghnacarra House
Carrybridge, Lisbellaw BT94 5HX
☎ 028 6638 7077
e–mail: normaensor@talk21.com
web: www.guesthouseireland.com

dir: *From Belfast A4 left to Lisbellaw-Carrybridge*

Surrounded by spacious grounds, gardens and countryside on the shores of Lough Erne, this delightful modern extended house is a haven of peace and quiet. It is understandably very popular with anglers, who may fish from the grounds. Bedrooms are well maintained, and day rooms include an elegant lounge, bright dining room and a spacious bar and games room

Rooms 7 en suite (3 fmly) (5 GF) S £35; D £60 **Facilities** TV2B tea/coffee Cen ht TVL Dinner Last d 24hrs notice Pool Table **Parking** 8 **Notes LB** ✪

CO LONDONDERRY

CASTLEDAWSON   MAP 01 C5

Premier Collection

★★★★★ ◉ INN
The Inn at Castle Dawson
47 Main St BT45 8AA
☎ 028 7946 9777 📠 028 7946 9888
e–mail: info@theinnatcastledawson.co.uk
web: www.theinnatcastledawson.co.uk

dir: *Off Castledawson rdbt on A6*

Built on the original site of the 200-hundred year old Castledawson House, the inn has twelve bedrooms, a small conference facility and an 80-seat restaurant. The bedrooms at the inn are spacious and coupled with metropolitan furnishings. Bedrooms at the rear offer views over the fast-flowing river and the countryside beyond. Fine dining can be enjoyed in the restaurant with a more casual menu served in the bar.

Rooms 12 en suite (6 GF) S £59; D £79✱ **Facilities** FTV TVB tea/coffee Direct dial from bedrooms Cen ht TVL Dinner Last d 9pm Golf 18 Fishing Riding **Conf** Max 20 Thtr 20 Class 20 Board 20 **Parking** 15 **Notes LB** ✪

IRELAND

COLERAINE

MAP 01 C6

Premier Collection

★★★★★ FARM HOUSE

Greenhill House (C 849210)

24 Greenhill Rd, Aghadowey BT51 4EU

☎ 028 7086 8241 📄 028 7086 8365 Mrs E Hegarty

e–mail: greenhill.house@btinternet.com

web: www.greenhill-house.co.uk

dir: *A29 from Coleraine south for 7m, left onto B66 Greenhill Rd for 300yds. House on right, AA sign at front gate*

Located in the tranquil Bann Valley, overlooking the Antrim Hills, this delightful Georgian house nestles in well-tended gardens with views to open rolling countryside. Public rooms are traditionally styled and include a comfortable lounge and an elegant dining room. The pleasant bedrooms vary in size and style and have a host of thoughtful extras.

Rooms 6 en suite (2 fmly) S £40; D £60 **Facilities** TVB tea/coffee Direct dial from bedrooms Cen ht TVL Wi-fi available **Parking** 10 **Notes** ⊗ 150 acres beef Closed Nov–Feb RS Mar–Oct

★★★★ GUEST HOUSE

Bellevue Country House

43 Greenhill Rd, Aghadowey BT51 4EU

☎ 028 7086 8797 📄 028 7086 8780

e–mail: info@bellevuecountryhouse.co.uk

dir: *On B66 just off A29, 7m S of Coleraine*

This fine country house, dating from 1840, stands in peaceful grounds. A variety of bedrooms are offered, including a family room and ground-floor accommodation, and there is also a comfortable drawing room. Generous breakfasts are freshly prepared and served around one large table.

Rooms 3 en suite (1 fmly) (1 GF) **Facilities** TVB tea/coffee Cen ht TVL Fishing **Parking** 9 **Notes** ⊗ No coaches Closed Nov –4 Jan 🐾

★★★★ FARM HOUSE

Heathfield (NW012782)

31 Drumcroone Rd, Killykergan BT51 4EB

☎ 028 2955 8245 📄 028 2955 8245 Ms H Torrens

e–mail: relax@heathfieldfarm.com

web: www.heathfieldfarm.com

dir: *8m S of Coleraine. On A29 nr Killykergan, 2m N of Garvagh*

Heathfield is a delightful traditional farmhouse that is an integral part of a working farm. The house enjoys a rural setting and is a short drive from the towns of Garvagh and Coleraine making it an ideal base from which to explore the North Antrim Coast. Bedrooms are comfortable and all enjoy views of the surrounding countryside. Guests can enjoy a hearty breakfast in the dining room or relax in the lounge after a day's sightseeing.

Rooms 3 en suite S £35–£40; D £60✳ **Facilities** TVB tea/coffee Cen ht TVL **Parking** 10 **Notes** ⊗ No children 10yrs Closed Xmas

LIMAVADY

MAP 01 C6

★★★★ GUEST HOUSE

Ballycarton House

239 Seacoast Rd BT49 0HZ

☎ 028 7775 0216 📄 028 7775 0231

e–mail: stay@ballycartonhouse.com

dir: *On the A2 coast road midway between Limavady and Castlerock*

Set in the beautiful Roe Valley, Ballycarton is overlooked by Benevenagh Mountain, and is close to Magilligan Point, which has one of the longest beaches in Northern Ireland. Wi-fi is available, along with a games room, a hot tub and sauna cabin, and an honesty bar.

Rooms 5 en suite **Facilities** TVB tea/coffee Direct dial from bedrooms Cen ht TVL Wi-fi available Sauna Pool Table Jacuzzi/Hot Tub **Parking** 8 **Notes** ⊗ No children 5yrs No coaches Closed 25–26 Dec

LONDONDERRY

MAP 01 C5

★★★ GUEST HOUSE

Clarence House

15 Northland Rd BT48 7HY

☎ 028 7126 5342 & 07786 801954 📄 028 7126 5377

e–mail: clarencehouse@zoom.co.uk

web: www.guesthouseireland.biz

dir: *From Belfast A6 next to University opp fire station & Radio Foyle*

This long-established, family-run guest house provides charming, well-equipped bedrooms. Traditionally styled day rooms include a spacious lounge and a smartly presented dining room where wholesome and generous meals are served.

Rooms 9 en suite (2 fmly) S £35–£45; D £75–£100 **Facilities** FTV TVB tea/coffee Direct dial from bedrooms Licensed Cen ht TVL Dinner Last d 1pm

IRELAND

[U]
Serendipity House
26 Marlborough St BT48 9AY

☎ 028 7126 4229 🖶 028 9095 0709

e–mail: m300pcl@hotmail.co.uk

At the time of going to press the rating for this establishment had not been confirmed. Please check the AA website www.theAA.com for up-to-date information.

Rooms 5 rms (4 en suite) (1 pri facs) (2 fmly) S £35–£45; D £50✱
Facilities TVB tea/coffee Cen ht TVL Dinner Last d 6pm Wi-fi available
Notes LB

CO TYRONE

DUNGANNON   MAP 01 C5

Premier Collection

★★★★★ 🍴 🛏 GUEST HOUSE
Grange Lodge
7 Grange Rd BT71 7EJ

☎ 028 8778 4212 🖶 028 8778 4313

e–mail: stay@grangelodgecountryhouse.com

web: www.grangelodgecountryhouse.com

dir: M1 junct 15, A29 towards Armagh, 1m Grange Lodge signed, 1st right & 1st white-walled entrance on right

Grange Lodge dates from 1698 and nestles in 20 acres of well-tended grounds. It continues to set high standards in hospitality and food, and excellent meals are served in the bright and airy extension. Home-baked afternoon teas can be enjoyed in the sumptuous drawing room.

Rooms 5 en suite S £60–£69; D £85–£89 **Facilities** STV FTV TVB tea/coffee Direct dial from bedrooms Cen ht TVL Dinner Last d 1pm previous day Wi-fi available 🍴 **Conf** Max 25 **Parking** 12 **Notes** ⊗ No children 12yrs No coaches Closed 21 Dec–9 Jan

★★★★ BED & BREAKFAST
Millbrook Bed & Breakfast
46 Moy Rd BT71 7DT

☎ 028 8772 3715

e–mail: info@millbrookonline.co.uk

dir: On A29 1m S of Dungannon, 0.25m N of M1 junct 15

This well-presented bungalow is situated just outside the town of Dungannon and close to main routes. Comfortable ground-floor bedrooms and a stylish lounge are complemented by a substantial, freshly prepared breakfast. The owners' natural hospitality is memorable.

Rooms 3 en suite (3 GF) S £40; D £60✱ **Facilities** TVB tea/coffee Cen ht TVL **Parking** 4 **Notes** ⊗ 🖼

REPUBLIC OF IRELAND
CO CARLOW

CARLOW   MAP 01 C3

★★★★ GUEST HOUSE
Barrowville Town House
Kilkenny Rd

☎ 059 914 3324

e–mail: barrowvilletownhouse@eircom.net

dir: N9 Kilkenny Rd near Institute of Technology

The Smyths are the friendly owners of this carefully maintained 18th-century town house. Many of the very comfortable bedrooms are spacious, and the public rooms are elegant and relaxing. The conservatory, with its fruiting vine, is where Barrowville's legendary breakfasts are served, overlooking well tended gardens. Ample car parking.

Rooms 7 en suite (3 fmly) S €55–€75; D €90–€130✱ **Facilities** STV TVB tea/coffee Direct dial from bedrooms Cen ht TVL Wi-fi available **Parking** 11 **Notes** ⊗ No children 10yrs Closed 24–26 Dec

RATHVILLY   MAP 01 D3

★★★★ FARM HOUSE
Baile Ricead (S 845836)
☎ 059 916 1120 Mrs M Corrigan

e–mail: minacorrigan@eircom.net

dir: 5km from Rathvilly. N9 S, left at Castle Inn, left next junct, 2nd right before Graney Bridge, left after water pump, house on bend

This delightful farmhouse has comfortable bedrooms furnished to a good standard. There is a lounge, and conservatory-dining room that looks out across the delightful gardens to the Wicklow Mountains. Guests can use the barbecue in the garden.

Rooms 4 rms (2 en suite) (1 fmly) **Facilities** TVB tea/coffee Cen ht TVL **Parking** 6 **Notes** 66 acres mixed Closed Nov–16 Mar

IRELAND

CO CAVAN

BALLYCONNELL   MAP 01 C4

★★★★ BED & BREAKFAST
Prospect Bay Lakeside Accommodation

Brackley Lake

☎ 049 952 3930 ▤ 049 952 3930

e–mail: info@prospectbay.ie

dir: *N87 through Ballyconnell and Bawnboy to Brackley Lake. 1st left after Lakeside car park*

Prospect Bay promises you eco-friendly comfort, hospitality and home baking. The accommodation is on a 30-acre site overlooking Brackley Lake, where boats are available for fishing. Bedrooms and guest sitting/dining room are all smartly appointed and lead on to the lovely garden patio. Convenient for Slieve Russell Hotel and golf course.

Rooms 4 en suite (2 fmly) (2 GF) S €50–€60; D €80–€90✳ **Facilities** TVB tea/coffee Cen ht TVL Wi-fi available Fishing Clay pigeon shooting, hovercrafting, mud buggies **Parking** 5 **Notes LB** Closed 20 Dec–6 Jan

CO CLARE

BALLYVAUGHAN   MAP 01 B3

Premier Collection

★★★★★ GUEST HOUSE
Rusheen Lodge

☎ 065 707 7092 ▤ 065 707 7152

e–mail: rusheen@iol.ie

dir: *On N67 1km from Ballyvaughan*

A charming house situated in the valley of The Burren, an area famous for its Arctic and Alpine plants. The McCann family were founders of the famous Aillwee Cave nearby and have a wealth of local folklore. The bedrooms are spacious and very attractively decorated, some with extra seating areas. Patio gardens lead from the cosy dining room.

Rooms 9 en suite (3 fmly) (3 GF) **Facilities** STV TVB tea/coffee Direct dial from bedrooms Cen ht TVL Wi-fi available **Parking** 12 **Notes** ⊗ Closed mid Nov–mid Feb

BUNRATTY   MAP 01 B3

★★★★ BED & BREAKFAST
Park House

Low Rd

☎ 061 369902 ▤ 061 369903

e–mail: parkhouse@eircom.net

dir: *From N18 take Bunratty exit, turn left at castle, pass Folk Park. Park House 4th house on left*

A purpose-built guest house with spacious bedrooms within walking distance of the castle. There is a lounge and a lovely garden.

Rooms 6 en suite (3 fmly) (2 GF) S €55; D €78✳ **Facilities** STV TVB tea/coffee Cen ht Dinner Wi-fi available **Parking** 6 **Notes** ⊗ Closed 25–26 Dec

CORROFIN   MAP 01 B3

★★★ FARM HOUSE
Fergus View *(R 265919)*

Kilnaboy

☎ 065 683 7606 ▤ 065 683 7192 Mrs M Kelleher

e–mail: deckell@indigo.ie

dir: *3.2km N of Corofin towards Kilfenora, past ruins of Kilnaboy Church on left on R476*

This fourth-generation family home is well located for touring the famous Burren area. A varied breakfast menu including home baking is on offer.

Rooms 6 rms (5 en suite) (1 fmly) S €53; D €76✳ **Facilities** Cen ht TVL Wi-fi available **Parking** 8 **Notes** ⊗ Closed 26 Oct–mid Mar 🐾

DOOLIN   MAP 01 B3

Premier Collection

★★★★★ 🔔 GUEST HOUSE
Ballyvara House

Ballyvara

☎ 065 707 4467 ▤ 065 707 4868

e–mail: info@ballyvarahouse.ie

dir: *Left at Fitzpatrick's Bar, up hill on left*

Once a 19th-century farm cottage, Ballyvara House has been transformed into a stylish guest house. Public areas and the spacious bedrooms are furnished to a high standard. The house is set in 8 hectares of unspoiled countryside close to Doolin, which is famous for traditional music, pubs and ferrys to the Aran Islands.

Rooms 11 en suite (2 fmly) (5 GF) S €70–€120; D €100–€180✳ **Facilities** STV TVB tea/coffee Direct dial from bedrooms Licensed Cen ht TVL Wi-fi available 🎱 Pool Table Childrens outdoor play area, Library **Parking** 10 **Notes LB** ⊗ Closed Oct–Apr

★★★ 🍽 GUEST HOUSE
Cullinan's Restaurant & Guesthouse

☎ 065 707 4183 ▤ 065 707 4239

e–mail: cullinans@eircom.net

dir: *In town centre at x-rds between McGanns Pub & O'Connors Pub*

This charming guest house and restaurant is situated in the village of Doolin. Bedrooms are attractive decorated and comfortable. Chef patron James features locally caught fresh fish on his dinner menu, along with steaks, lamb and vegetarian dishes and there is a popular Early Bird menu. Other facilities include a lounge, a patio, and gardens that run down to the River Aille.

Rooms 8 en suite (3 fmly) (3 GF) S €50–€80; D €70–€100✳ **Facilities** TV3B tea/coffee Direct dial from bedrooms Cen ht TVL Dinner Last d 9pm Wi-fi available **Parking** 15 **Notes** ⊗ No coaches Closed Jan–Feb

IRELAND

KILRUSH MAP 01 B3

★★★★ BED & BREAKFAST
Hillcrest View

Doonbeg Rd
☎ 065 905 1986 📠 065 905 1900
e–mail: ethnahynes@eircom.net

dir: *Off N67 Kilkee road, on Doonbeg road*

Within walking distance of the town centre and a short drive from the Killimer ferry, Hillcrest View has spacious and well-appointed bedrooms. There is a sitting-dining room with a breakfast conservatory, while patio seats look over the pretty garden.

Rooms 6 en suite (2 fmly) **Facilities** STV TVB tea/coffee Cen ht TVL **Parking** 7 **Notes** ⊗

★★★ BED & BREAKFAST
Cois Na Sionna

Ferry Junction, Killimer
☎ 065 905 3073 & 087 237 7285 📠 065 905 3073
e–mail: coisnasionna@eircom.net

dir: *On N67 at entrance to Killimer-Tarbert car ferry*

This modern house is close to the Killimer/Tarbert car ferry. Bedrooms offer good space and are bright and well appointed. There is a comfortable lounge and a traditional cooked breakfast is served in the dining room. A good base for visiting Clare and Kerry.

Rooms 4 en suite (3 fmly) **Facilities** TVB tea/coffee Cen ht TVL **Parking** 6

LAHINCH MAP 01 B3

Premier Collection

★★★★★ 🛏 🍴 GUEST HOUSE
Moy House

☎ 065 708 2800 📠 065 708 2500
e–mail: moyhouse@eircom.net
web: www.moyhouse.com

dir: *1km from Lahinch on Miltown Malbay Rd, signed from Lahinch*

This 18th-century house overlooks Lahinch's world-famous surfing beach and championship golf links. Individually designed bedrooms are decorated with luxurious fabrics and fine antique furniture. The elegant drawing room has an open turf fire and breathtaking views. The carefully prepared dinner menu has an emphasis on excellent seafood, and breakfast is noteworthy too.

Rooms 9 en suite (2 fmly) (4 GF) S €145–€175; D €185–€360✳ **Facilities** STV FTV TVB Direct dial from bedrooms Licensed Cen ht Dinner Last d 8.30pm Wi-fi available **Conf** Max 16 Board 16 **Parking** 30 **Notes** LB ⊗ Closed Jan–13 Feb

★★★ BED & BREAKFAST
Castleview Lodge

Ennistymon Rd
☎ 065 708 1648
e–mail: castleview_lodge@eircom.net

dir: *On N67 (Ennis-Shannon road)*

Castleview Lodge is located on the N67 within walking distance of Lahinch overlooking the Golf course at the north of the town and close to the beach and Cliffs of Moher. Bedrooms are well appointed and attractively decorated. There is ample off street car parking available.

Rooms 5 en suite S €45; D €70 **Facilities** STV FTV TVB tea/coffee Cen ht TVL **Parking** 5 **Notes** LB ⊗ 🍴

SCARRIFF MAP 01 B3

★★★★ BED & BREAKFAST
Clareville House

Tuamgraney
☎ 061 922925 & 087 686 7548 📠 061 922925
e–mail: clarevillehouse@ireland.com
web: www.clarevillehouse.net

dir: *On R352 in village adjacent to Scarriff*

Situated in the centre of the pretty lakeside village of Tuamgraney this purpose-built bed and breakfast is attractively decorated. The spacious bedrooms are furnished to a high standard and the cosy guest sitting room and dining room are also well furnished. Ample off-road parking is available.

Rooms 4 en suite (4 fmly) S €45–€50; D €70–€78 **Facilities** TVB tea/coffee Cen ht TVL Golf 18 Riding **Parking** 8 **Notes** ⊗ Closed 20–27 Dec

SPANISH POINT MAP 01 B3

Premier Collection

★★★★★ 🏅 GUEST HOUSE
Admiralty Lodge

☎ 065 708 5007 📠 065 708 5030
e–mail: info@admiralty.ie

This delightful country house is located on the coast road at Spanish Point and close to Doonbeg Golf links. It has been lovingly refurbished to a high standard by Aoife and Pat O'Malley. The stylish bedrooms are furnished with comfort in mind and relaxing lounges feature open fires and a cosy cocktail bar. French contemporary cuisine is served in the Piano restaurant. The gardens include a patio and heli pad.

Rooms 11 en suite (1 GF) (1 smoking) S €130–€150; D €150–€180 **Facilities** STV TVB Direct dial from bedrooms Licensed Cen ht Dinner Last d 9.30pm Golf Pool Table Library **Parking** 30 **Notes** LB Closed Jan–Feb

IRELAND

SPANISH POINT CONTINUED

Ⓤ
Red Cliff Lodge

☎ 065 708 5756 📄 065 708 5775
e–mail: info@redcliff.ie

dir: *R474 Ennis to Miltown Malbay, S on N67 for 1.5km*

At the time of going to press the rating for this establishment had not been confirmed. Please check the AA website www.theAA.com for up-to-date information.

Rooms 6 annexe en suite (6 GF) S €100–€150; D €150–€200
Facilities STV TVB tea/coffee Direct dial from bedrooms Cen ht TVL
Conf Max 12 Board 12 **Parking** 10 **Notes** LB ⊗ No children Closed Dec–1 Mar

CO CORK

BANDON   MAP 01 B2

★★★★ BED & BREAKFAST
Glebe Country House

Ballinadee

☎ 021 477 8294 📄 021 477 8456
e–mail: glebehse@indigo.ie

dir: *Off N71 at Innishannon Bridge signed Ballinadee, 8km along river bank, left after village sign*

This lovely guest house stands in well-kept gardens, and is run with great attention to detail. Antique furnishings predominate throughout this comfortable house, which has a lounge and an elegant dining room. An interesting breakfast menu offers unusual options, and a country-house style dinner is available by arrangement.

Rooms 4 en suite (2 fmly) S €60–€70; D €90–€110✱ **Facilities** tea/coffee Direct dial from bedrooms Cen ht TVL Dinner Last d noon Wi-fi available **Parking** 10 **Notes** LB Closed 21 Dec–3 Jan

BLARNEY   MAP 01 B2

Premier Collection

★★★★★ 🍴 🍽 GUEST HOUSE
Ashlee Lodge

Tower

☎ 021 4385346 📄 021 4385726
e–mail: info@ashleelodge.com

dir: *4km from Blarney on R617*

Ashley Lodge is a purpose-built guest house, situated in the village of Tower, close to Blarney and local pubs and restaurants. Bedrooms are decorated with comfort and elegance in mind, some with whirlpool baths, and one room has easier access. The extensive breakfast menu is memorable for Ann's home baking. You can unwind in the sauna or the outdoor hot tub. Transfers to the nearest airport and railway station can be arranged, and tee times can be booked at many of the nearby golf courses.

Rooms 10 en suite (2 fmly) (6 GF) S €75–€200; D €100–€250✱
Facilities STV FTV TVB tea/coffee Direct dial from bedrooms Licensed
CONTINUED

Cen ht TVL Dinner Last d 8.30pm Wi-fi available Sauna Hot tub **Parking** 12 **Notes** LB

★★★★ BED & BREAKFAST
Killarney House

Station Rd

☎ 021 4381841 📄 021 4381841
e–mail: info@killarneyhouseblarney.com

dir: *From N20 onto R617, right after Blarney fuel station turn right, 1km on Station Rd on right*

A no-smoking house with four ground-floor bedrooms in a new extension, and two on the first floor. Caroline Morgan is a charming, attentive hostess whose comfortable house is very well appointed. There is a television lounge, drying facilities for wet gear, and off-road parking. Golf available nearby.

Rooms 6 en suite (2 fmly) (4 GF) S €47–€55; D €66–€76
Facilities TVB tea/coffee Cen ht **Parking** 8 **Notes** LB ⊗ 🐾

★★★★ BED & BREAKFAST
White House

Shean Lower

☎ 021 4385338
e–mail: info@thewhitehouseblarney.com
web: www.thewhitehouseblarney.com

dir: *On R617 Cork-Blarney road*

Situated on an elevated position near to the town, with views of Blarney Castle, this carefully maintained bungalow lies in grounds. Bedrooms, with modern facilities, are well appointed and have comfortable armchairs. There is a television lounge and a breakfast room. A private car park is also available.

Rooms 6 en suite (1 fmly) (6 GF) S €50–€55; D €70–€77
Facilities STV TVB tea/coffee Cen ht Wi-fi available **Parking** 7 **Notes** ⊗ Closed 20 Dec–1 Jan 🐾

CLONAKILTY   MAP 01 B2

Premier Collection

★★★★★ 🍴 FARM HOUSE
An Garran Coir (W 332358)

Rathbarry, Rosscarbery Coast Route

☎ 023 48236 📄 023 48236 Mr & Mrs M Calnan
e–mail: angarrancoir@eircom.net
web: www.angarrancoir.com

dir: *Signed at Maxol station in Clonakilty. 6.5km W of town off N71, 1.5km on right*

Situated on the coast road to Rosscarbery from Clonakilty, close to sandy beaches and the village, this comfortable farmhouse has lovely views. Bedrooms are attractively decorated to a high standard with well fitted bathrooms. Joe Callinan's cooking is a special treat, evening meals are available on request with produce from the garden and fresh eggs from the farm. A tennis court and lovely garden are available to guests.

CONTINUED

Rooms 5 en suite (2 fmly) **Facilities** TVB tea/coffee Cen ht Dinner Last d 3pm ☕ Local leisure club available – rates negotiated **Parking** 5 **Notes** ⊗

★★★★ FARM HOUSE
Duvane House *(W 349405)*
Ballyduvane
☎ 023 33129 📠 023 33129 Mrs N McCarthy
e–mail: duvanefarm@eircom.net
dir: 2km SW from Clonakilty on N71

This Georgian farmhouse is on the N71 Skibbereen road. Bedrooms are comfortable and include four-poster and brass beds. There is a lovely sitting room and dining room, and a wide choice is available at breakfast (dinner is available by arrangement). Local amenities include Blue Flag beaches, riding and golf.

Rooms 4 en suite (1 fmly) **Facilities** TVB tea/coffee Cen ht TVL Dinner Last d 4pm Fishing Pool Table ⚓ **Parking** 20 **Notes** ⊗ 100 acres beef, dairy, mixed, sheep Closed Nov–Mar

★★★★ FARM HOUSE
Springfield House *(W 330342)*
Kilkern, Rathbarry, Castlefreke
☎ 023 40622 📠 023 40622 Mr & Mrs J Callanan
e–mail: jandmcallanan@eircom.net
dir: N71 from Clonakilty for Skibbereen, 0.5km left after Pike Bar & signed for 5km

A Georgian-style farmhouse in a picturesque rural setting. Maureen and John Callanan are genuine and welcoming hosts, and their comfortable home has well-appointed bedrooms and lovely gardens. You are welcome to watch the cows being milked. Home cooking is a speciality, and dinner is available by arrangement.

Rooms 4 rms (3 en suite) (2 fmly) **Facilities** TV3B Cen ht TVL Dinner Last d 3pm **Parking** 8 **Notes** ⊗ 130 acres dairy/beef Closed 20–27 Dec ☺

★★ FARM HOUSE
Desert House *(W 390411)*
Coast Rd
☎ 023 33331 📠 023 33048 Mrs D Jennings
e–mail: deserthouse@eircom.net
dir: 1km E of Clonakilty. Signed on N71 at 1st rdbt, house 500 mtrs on left

This comfortable Georgian farmhouse overlooks Clonakilty Bay and is within walking distance of the town. The estuary is of great interest to bird watching enthusiasts. It is a good base for touring west Cork and Kerry.

Rooms 5 rms (4 en suite) **Facilities** TVB tea/coffee Cen ht **Parking** 10 **Notes** 100 acres dairy mixed

---

CORK   **MAP 01 B2**

Premier Collection

★★★★★ 🏠 GUEST HOUSE
Lancaster Lodge
Lancaster Quay, Western Rd
☎ 021 4251125 📠 021 4251126
e–mail: info@lancasterlodge.com
dir: By Jurys Hotel

Situated just five minutes from the city centre, this modern guest house overlooks the River Lee. Public rooms include a spacious lounge and contemporary style restaurant. Bedrooms are spacious and feature an excellent range of facilities. Two ground-floor rooms have easier access. A wide choice is offered for breakfast.

Rooms 39 en suite (3 GF) **Facilities** STV TVB tea/coffee Direct dial from bedrooms Lift Cen ht TVL **Parking** 40 **Notes** ⊗ Closed 22–26 Dec

★★★★ GUEST HOUSE
Crawford House
Western Rd
☎ 021 4279000 📠 021 4279927
e–mail: info@crawfordguesthouse.com
dir: 0.8km from city on N22 Cork-Killarney road, opp University College

Two adjoining Victorian houses form this friendly guest house, close to the university and city centre. Refurbished in a contemporary style, the bedrooms have refreshing natural colour schemes. The attractive dining room and conservatory overlook a colourful patio. An interesting breakfast menu is available and there is ample secure parking.

Rooms 12 en suite (2 fmly) (1 GF) **Facilities** STV TVB tea/coffee Direct dial from bedrooms Cen ht Wi-fi available **Parking** 12 **Notes** ⊗ Closed 22 Dec–15 Jan

CORK CONTINUED

★★★★ GUEST HOUSE
Garnish House

1 Aldergrove, Western Rd
☎ 021 4275111 📄 021 4273872
e–mail: garnish@iol.ie

dir: *Opp Cork University College*

A stay in Garnish House is memorable for its carefully appointed rooms, with an optional Jacuzzi en suite, and the extensive breakfast menu. Only a 5-minute walk to the city centre, and convenient for the ferry and airport, the guest house has 24-hour reception for reservations, departures and late arrivals.

Rooms 13 en suite (4 fmly) (1 GF) **Facilities** STV TVB tea/coffee Direct dial from bedrooms Cen ht TVL **Parking** 10 **Notes** ⊗ No children No coaches

★★★★ GUEST HOUSE
Killarney

Western Rd
☎ 021 4270290 📄 021 4271010
e–mail: killarneyhouse@iol.ie

dir: *On N22 Cork-Killarney opp University College*

Mrs O'Leary is the welcoming owner of this well-equipped guest house, which stands near Cork University on the N22. The bedrooms all have televisions, telephones and tea and coffee facilities. A comfortable lounge is available, and there is car parking to the rear of the house.

Rooms 19 en suite (3 fmly) **Facilities** STV TVB tea/coffee Direct dial from bedrooms Cen ht TVL Wi-fi available **Parking** 15 **Notes** ⊗ Closed 24–26 Dec

★★★ GUEST HOUSE
Rose Lodge

Mardyke Walk, off Western Rd
☎ 021 4272958 📄 021 4274087
e–mail: info@roselodge.net

dir: *N22 from city centre, pass Jurys Hotel on left, right at University College gates, right again, Lodge on right*

This family-run guest house is close to UCC and just a 10-minute walk from the city centre. The en suite bedrooms are well appointed, and

there is a comfortable sitting room and an attractive breakfast room. Limited off-road parking is available.

Rooms 16 en suite (4 fmly) **Facilities** STV TVB tea/coffee Direct dial from bedrooms Cen ht TVL **Parking** 8 **Notes** ⊗

FERMOY	MAP 01 B2

Premier Collection

★★★★★ GUEST ACCOMMODATION
Ballyvolane House

Castlelyons
☎ 025 36349 📄 025 36781
e–mail: info@ballyvolanehouse.ie

dir: *N8 onto R628 & signed*

An Italianate country house, originally built in 1728, which has a magnificent setting in parkland and well-known gardens (open to the public in May). The Greens are exceptionally friendly hosts. Public areas are spacious, and bedrooms are comfortable. Dinner is served around a fine table. There are three lakes, one stocked with brown trout.

Rooms 6 en suite **Facilities** FTV TVB tea/coffee Cen ht Dinner Last d noon Wi-fi available Fishing ⚓ Trout lakes, bicycles, badminton **Conf** Max 50 Thtr 14 Class 45 Board 14 **Parking** 25 **Notes** ⊗ Closed 23–31 Dec

★★★★ BED & BREAKFAST
Abbeyville House

Abercomby Place
☎ 025 32767 📄 025 32767
e–mail: info@abbeyvillehouse.com

dir: *N8 Cork to Dublin Road, across road from town park. Located in town centre across from park*

This delightful 19th-century town house is situated on the crossroads of Munster, on the Rosslare to Killarney and Cork to Dublin routes. The smart bedrooms, drawing room and dining room are furnished to a high standard. Guests have complementary use of the facilities in the Health and Fitness Club in the town park near by.

Rooms 6 en suite (2 fmly) (1 GF) S €50–€80; D €110–€180✳ **Facilities** TVB tea/coffee Cen ht TVL Wi-fi available Free use of Carrig Court Health & Fitness Club **Parking** 12 **Notes** Closed 30 Oct–1 Apr

CONTINUED

IRELAND

GOLEEN — MAP 01 A1

★★★★ 🍽 BED & BREAKFAST
Heron's Cove
The Harbour
☎ 028 35225 📠 028 35422
e-mail: suehill@eircom.net
web: www.heronscove.com
dir: By harbour in Goleen

There are charming views of the harbour, fast-flowing steam and inland hills from Heron's Cove, at Ireland's most south-westerly point, near Mizen Head. The restaurant and wine bar is run by chef-patron Sue Hill, where the freshest fish and local produce feature. Bedrooms are comfortable, some with balconies overlooking the harbour.

Rooms 5 en suite (2 fmly) S €60–€100; D €70–€110 **Facilities** STV TVB tea/coffee Direct dial from bedrooms Cen ht Dinner Last d 9.30pm **Parking** 10 **Notes** ⊗ Closed Xmas & New Year

See advert on this page

KINSALE — MAP 01 B2

Premier Collection
★★★★★ GUEST HOUSE
Friar's Lodge
5 Friars St
☎ 086 289 5075 & 021 4777384 📠 021 4774363
e-mail: mtierney@indigo.ie
dir: In town centre next to parish church

This new, purpose built property near the Friary, has been developed with every comfort in mind. Bedrooms are particularly spacious. Located on a quiet street within minutes walk of the town centre, with secure parking to the rear. A very good choice is offered from the breakfast menu.

Rooms 18 en suite (2 fmly) (4 GF) (2 smoking) S €60–€80; D €90–€150✳ **Facilities** STV TVB tea/coffee Direct dial from bedrooms Lift Cen ht Wi-fi available **Parking** 20 **Notes** Closed Xmas 🍽

Premier Collection
★★★★★ GUEST HOUSE
Old Bank House
11 Pearse St
☎ 021 4774075 📠 021 4774296
e-mail: info@oldbankhousekinsale.com
dir: On main road into Kinsale from Cork Airport (R600). House on right at start of Kinsale, next to Post Office

The Fitzgerald family has restored this delightful Georgian house to its former elegance. The en suite bedrooms, with period furniture and attractive decor, combine charm with modern comforts. Sailing, deep-sea fishing and horse riding can be arranged. Dinner is available at the sister Blue Haven Hotel.

Rooms 17 en suite (3 fmly) **Facilities** STV TVB Direct dial from bedrooms Lift Cen ht Wi-fi available **Notes** ⊗ Closed 23–28 Dec

IRELAND

KINSALE CONTINUED

Premier Collection

★★★★★ GUEST HOUSE
Perryville House

☎ 021 4772731 📄 021 4772298

e–mail: sales@perryville.iol.ie

This elegant Georgian house in the centre of the town offers spacious, well-equipped accommodation. The comfortable drawing rooms are carefully decorated and the buffet breakfast is a highlight of the Perryville experience. A non-smoking property.

Rooms 26 en suite **Facilities** Direct dial from bedrooms **Parking** 10 **Notes** ⊗ No children 12yrs No coaches Closed Nov–Apr

★★★★ BED & BREAKFAST
Rivermount House

Knocknabinny, Barrells Cross

☎ 021 4778033 📄 021 4778225

e–mail: rivermnt@iol.ie

dir: *3km from Kinsale. R600 W towards Old Head of Kinsale, right at Barrels Cross*

There are spectacular views over the Bandon River from this charming modern family home which is close to the Old Head Golf links and Kinsale town off the R600. The smartly decorated bedrooms are furnished to a high standard with many thoughtful extras. Guests can relax in the contemporary conservatory lounge and sitting room where an interesting snack menu is available, Claire's breakfast and packed lunches are a speciality

Rooms 6 en suite (3 fmly) (2 GF) **Facilities** TVB tea/coffee Direct dial from bedrooms Cen ht TVL Wi-fi available **Parking** 10 **Notes** ⊗ Closed Dec– Jan

★★★★ BED & BREAKFAST
Chart House Luxury Accommodation

6 Denis Quay

☎ 021 4774568 📄 021 4777907

e–mail: charthouse@eircom.net

dir: *Off Pier Rd between Actons & Trident hotels onto Denis Quay, last house on right*

This 1790 Georgian house was once a sea captain's residence. It has been lovingly restored and the comfortable bedrooms are furnished with period pieces, while two have Jacuzzis. There is a cosy lobby lounge and a dining room where Mary O'Connor serves delicious breakfasts, including home-made breads. Afternoon tea and coffee are served on arrival. Being in a gourmet capital, dinner reservations can be arranged and golfing and touring trips organised.

Rooms 3 en suite D €110–€170✳ **Facilities** STV TVB Direct dial from bedrooms Cen ht **Notes** ⊗ No children Closed Xmas

★★★★ 🛏 GUEST HOUSE
Harbour Lodge

Scilly

☎ 021 4772376 📄 021 4772675

e–mail: relax@harbourlodge.com

web: www.harbourlodge.com

dir: *Enter Kinsale on R600. Take 1st left to Scilly. At Spaniard Bar turn right, follow road towards coast*

This well-appointed house has superb views of Kinsale Harbour and marina. Bedrooms are smartly decorated and enhanced with quality bedding and many thoughtful extras, including some with balconies. Dinner is a particular treat, menu includes local fish, and reservations are necessary. The Tiernan family are very hospitable hosts and will help to arrange fishing trips, or golf at one of the many golf courses near by.

Rooms 9 en suite (9 fmly) (4 GF) **Facilities** STV TVB Direct dial from bedrooms Licensed Cen ht TVL Dinner Last d noon **Conf** Max 15 Thtr 15 **Parking** 9 **Notes** ⊗

★★★★ BED & BREAKFAST
Old Presbytery

43 Cork St

☎ 021 4772027 📄 021 4772166

e–mail: info@oldpres.com

dir: *From Cork Rd to end of Pearse St, turn left, 1st right & 1st right again, establishment on right opp parish church*

This charming house, situated on a quiet street in the centre of the town, offers an elegant lounge and a delightful breakfast room. Bedrooms are traditional, with pine furnishings, brass beds and interesting memorabilia. One bedroom has external access via a staircase and is very peaceful. Sailing and sea fishing are available and there are plenty of excellent restaurants nearby. Booking is advised.

Rooms 6 en suite (1 fmly) (1 GF) **Facilities** STV FTV TVB tea/coffee Direct dial from bedrooms Cen ht TVL Wi-fi available **Parking** 6 **Notes** ⊗ Closed Dec–1 Mar

IRELAND

★★★★ BED & BREAKFAST
Waterlands
Cork Rd
☎ 021 477 2318 & 087 276 7917 ▤ 021 477 4873
e–mail: info@collinsbb.com
web: www.collinsbb.com

dir: *R600 to Kinsale, off at Welcome to Kinsale sign, Waterlands signed, turn right*

This house, located on an elevated position, provides luxury accommodation. A south-facing conservatory breakfast room overlooks the picturesque gardens and offers an extensive breakfast menu. The comfortable, well-decorated en suite bedrooms have electric blankets, hairdryers and clock radios.

Rooms 4 en suite (2 fmly) S €50–€60; D €70–€90✱ **Facilities** TVB tea/coffee Cen ht TVL **Parking** 10 **Notes** ⊗ Closed Dec–Feb

★★★★ ⊛ RESTAURANT WITH ROOMS
The White House
Pearse St, The Glen
☎ 021 4772125 ▤ 021 4772045
e–mail: whitehse@indigo.ie

dir: *In town centre*

Centrally located among the narrow, twisting streets of the charming town of Kinsale, this restaurant with rooms dates from 1850, and is a welcoming hostelry with modern, smart, and comfortable bedrooms. The bar and bistro is open for lunch and dinner, menu is varied with local fish and beef a speciality. The courtyard is perfect for the summer and there is traditional music in the bar most nights.

Rooms 10 en suite (2 fmly) **Facilities** STV TVB tea/coffee Direct dial from bedrooms Cen ht Dinner Last d 10pm Wi-fi available **Notes** ⊗ Closed 24–25 Dec

★★★★ BED & BREAKFAST
Woodlands House B&B
Cappagh
☎ 021 4772633 ▤ 021 4772649
e–mail: info@woodlandskinsale.com

dir: *R605 NW from Kinsale, pass St Multose's Church, 0.5km on left*

Situated on a height overlooking the town, about a 10-minute walk away on the Bandon road, this new house offers great comfort and the personal attention of Brian and Valerie Hosford. Rooms are individually decorated, some with views towards the harbour. Breakfast is a particular pleasure, featuring home-made breads and preserves. Free Wi-fi is also available.

Rooms 6 en suite (1 fmly) (2 GF) S €55–€80; D €80–€100 **Facilities** TVB tea/coffee Direct dial from bedrooms Cen ht TVL Wi-fi available **Parking** 8 **Notes** ⊗ Closed 16 Nov–Feb

★★★★ BED & BREAKFAST
Greenfield House B&B
Navigation Rd
☎ 022 50231 & 08723 63535
e–mail: greenfieldhouse@hotmail.com

dir: *N20 at Mallow rdbt onto N72 Killarney road, last house 300mtrs on left*

A purpose-built house, designed and furnished to the highest standards. Large, airy rooms look out over open country and all are luxuriously appointed with quality en suite facilities. Situated within walking distance of the town centre, station and Cork Racecourse. Parking facilities.

Rooms 6 en suite (3 fmly) (3 GF) **Facilities** STV TVB tea/coffee Cen ht TVL **Parking** 10 **Notes** ⊗

★★★★ BED & BREAKFAST
Oaklands House
Springwood, Killarney Rd
☎ 022 21127 ▤ 022 21127
e–mail: oaklands@eircom.net

dir: *Off N72 Killarney road at railway bridge, signed*

Situated in a quiet residential area on the edge of town, Winifred O'Donovan's home is inviting and attractively decorated throughout. The atmosphere is particularly tranquil, with a dining room overlooking the lovely gardens where guests can enjoy Winifred's cooking. The dining room has recently been extended to provide a conservatory where breakfast is served.

Rooms 4 en suite (1 fmly) **Facilities** STV TVB tea/coffee Cen ht TVL **Parking** 6 **Notes** ⊗ Closed Nov–Mar

Premier Collection

★★★★★ ⇔ GUEST HOUSE
Ballymaloe House
☎ 021 4652531 ▤ 021 4652021
e–mail: res@ballymaloe.ie

dir: *On L35 from Midleton, 3km beyond Cloyne on Ballycotton road*

This charming country house is on a 162-hectare farm, part of the Geraldine estate. Bedrooms range from one within the old castle walls, to some in the main house and yet more in the courtyard buildings. All are well appointed to high standards. Much of the food on offer in the restaurant is produced on the farm. There is a craft shop on the estate.

Rooms 23 en suite 11 annexe en suite (2 fmly) (4 GF) S €150–€195; D €220–€320✱ **Facilities** Direct dial from bedrooms Licensed Cen ht TVL Dinner Last d 9pm Wi-fi available ↘ Golf 9 ⚘ ⚓ ⚑ Children's sand pit/slide **Conf** Max 25 Thtr 25 Class 25 Board 25 Del from €120 ✱ **Parking** 30 **Notes** LB ⊗ Closed 23–26 Dec Civ Wed

IRELAND

SKIBBEREEN

MAP 01 B2

★★★ BED & BREAKFAST
Ilenroy House

10 North St

☎ 028 22751 & 22193 📄 028 23228

e–mail: ilenroyhouse@oceanfree.net

dir: *90mtrs from main street on N71 Clonakilty road*

Conveniently situated in the centre of Skibbereen, this well maintained house has comfortable bedrooms that are equipped to a high standard. This is an excellent base from which to tour South West Cork and the Islands.

Rooms 5 en suite (2 smoking) S €40–€50; D €75–€80 **Facilities** STV TVB tea/coffee Direct dial from bedrooms Cen ht **Notes** ⊗

YOUGHAL

MAP 01 C2

Premier Collection

★★★★★ 🍴 GUEST HOUSE
Ahernes

163 North Main St

☎ 024 92424 📄 024 93633

e–mail: ahernes@eircom.net

In the same family since 1923, Ahernes offers a warm welcome, with turf fires and a traditional atmosphere. Spacious bedrooms are furnished to the highest standard and include antiques and modern facilities. There is a restaurant, well known for its daily-changing menu of the freshest seafood specialities, in addition to a cosy drawing room.

Rooms 12 en suite (2 fmly) (3 GF) (3 smoking) S €125–€135; D €170–€210✳ **Facilities** TVB tea/coffee Direct dial from bedrooms Licensed Cen ht Dinner Last d 9.30pm Wi-fi available **Conf** Max 20 Thtr 20 Class 20 Board 12 **Parking** 20 **Notes** LB Closed 23–29 Dec

CO DONEGAL

BALLYSHANNON

MAP 01 B5

★★★★ GUEST HOUSE
Dún Na Sí

Bundoran Rd

☎ 071 985 2322

e–mail: dun-na-si@oceanfree.net

dir: *0.4km from Ballyshannon on R267*

A smart purpose-built guest house set back from the road and within walking distance of the town. The spacious bedrooms are comfortable and well equipped, and one of the two ground-floor rooms is suitable for the less mobile.

Rooms 7 en suite (2 fmly) (2 GF) S €45–€50; D €76–€90✳ **Facilities** STV TVB tea/coffee Direct dial from bedrooms Cen ht Wi-fi available **Parking** 15 **Notes** ⊗

★★★★ 🍴 RESTAURANT WITH ROOMS
Heron's Cove

Creevy, Rossnowlagh Rd

☎ 071 9822070 📄 071 9822075

e–mail: info@heronscove.ie

dir: *From N side of Ballyshannon at rdbt take R231 towards Rossnowlagh 2m. Just after Creevy National School on left*

Situated between Ballyshannon and Creevy Pier and close to the sandy beach at Rossnowlagh, the O'Toole family have refurbished Heron's Cove to a high standard. Bedrooms are comfortable, and there is a cosy lounge bar and charming restaurant where menus feature steaks and fresh fish from local suppliers.

Rooms 10 en suite (1 fmly) S fr €60; D fr €110✳ **Facilities** FTV TVB tea/coffee Direct dial from bedrooms Cen ht Dinner Last d 9pm **Parking** 60 **Notes** LB ⊗ Closed 24–28 Dec & Jan RS Oct–Mar

---

CARRIGANS

MAP 01 C5

★★★★ BED & BREAKFAST
Mount Royd Country Home

☎ 074 914 0163 📄 074 914 0400

e–mail: jmartin@mountroyd.com

dir: *Off N13/N14 onto R236. A40 from Northern Ireland*

Set in lovely mature gardens in the pretty village and a short distance from Derry, the Mount Royd is an attractive creeper-clad house. The River Foyle runs along the back boundary. The friendly Martins have brought hospitality to new heights – nothing is too much trouble for them. Breakfast is a feast of choices. Bedrooms are very comfortable, with lots of personal touches.

Rooms 4 en suite (1 fmly) (1 GF) S fr €40; D fr €70✳ **Facilities** TVB tea/coffee Cen ht TVL **Parking** 7 **Notes** LB ⊗ No children 12yrs Closed Jan RS Nov–Feb 🐾

IRELAND

DONEGAL

MAP 01 B5

★★★★ BED & BREAKFAST
The Arches Country House

Lough Eske

☎ 074 972 2029 ▤ 074 972 2029

e–mail: archescountryhse@eircom.net

dir: *5km from Donegal. Signed off N15, 300mtrs from garage*

Located on an elevated site overlooking Lough Eske, this fine house is set amid beautifully manicured lawns. Each of the bedrooms shares the spectacular view, as do the breakfast room and comfortable lounge. A warm welcome is assured from the McGinty family.

Rooms 6 en suite (3 fmly) (2 GF) S €50–€55; D €70–€75✳
Facilities TVB tea/coffee Cen ht TVL **Parking** 10 **Notes** ❂

★★★★ BED & BREAKFAST
Ardeevin

Lough Eske, Barnesmore

☎ 074 972 1790 ▤ 074 972 1790

e–mail: seanmcginty@eircom.net

dir: *N15 Derry road from Donegal for 5km, left at junct after garage for Ardeevin & Lough Eske & signs for Ardeevin*

This homely house has a lovely location high above Lough Eske and with superb views of lake and mountain. Well-appointed bedrooms have en suite facilities.

Rooms 6 en suite (2 fmly) (2 GF) S €50; D €70✳ **Facilities** STV FTV TVB tea/coffee Cen ht TVL **Parking** 10 **Notes** ❂ No children 9yrs Closed Dec–mid Mar ▣

★★★★ ➨ GUEST HOUSE
Ard Na Breatha

Drumrooske Middle

☎ 074 972 2288 & 086 842 1330 ▤ 074 974 0720

e–mail: info@ardnabreatha.com

web: www.ardnabreatha.com

dir: *From town centre onto Killybegs road, 2nd right, sharp right at Vivo shop*

This family-run guest house is just a short drive from the town centre. Bedrooms are all well-appointed and very comfortable, with plans for an additional lounge under way. Evening meals are served in the popular restaurant at weekends and during high season, but can be arranged for residents at other times.

Rooms 6 en suite (1 fmly) (3 GF) **Facilities** TVB tea/coffee Direct dial from bedrooms Licensed Cen ht TVL Dinner Last d 9.30pm
Conf Thtr 30 Class 40 Board 20 Del from €99 **Parking** 16 **Notes** LB Closed Dec–Jan RS Wknds

DUNKINEELY   MAP 01 B5

★★★★ ◉ RESTAURANT WITH ROOMS
Castle Murray House and Restaurant

St Johns Point

☎ 074 9737022 📄 074 9737330

e–mail: info@castlemurray.com

dir: *From Donegal take N56 towards Killybegs. Left to Dunkineely*

Situated on the coast road of St. John's Point, this charming family-run house and restaurant overlooks McSwynes Bay and the castle. The bedrooms are individually decorated with guest comfort very much in mind as is the cosy bar and sun lounge. There is a strong French influence in the cooking; locally landed fish, and prime lamb and beef are on the menus.

Rooms 10 en suite (2 fmly) S €70–€90; D €130–€150✱ **Facilities** FTV TVB tea/coffee Direct dial from bedrooms Cen ht Dinner Last d 9.30pm Wi-fi available **Parking** 40 **Notes LB** Closed mid Jan–mid Feb Civ Wed

See advert on page 725

LAGHEY   MAP 01 B5

Premier Collection

★★★★★ ◉ GUEST HOUSE
Coxtown Manor

☎ 074 9734575 & 9734574 📄 074 9734576

e–mail: coxtownmanor@oddpost.com

dir: *Off N15 between Ballyshannon & Donegal Town. On old Laghey-Ballintra Rd*

Coxtown Manor, which dates back to the 17th century, is situated close to Donegal town. Its Belgian owner, Chef Eduard Dewael cooks dinner

CONTINUED

nightly, using mainly organic local produce. Breakfast is also a treat. Bedrooms are in both the main house and the Coach House and are comfortably furnished and individually decorated. There is a cosy bar and delightful drawing room and dining room, all with welcoming open turf fires.

Rooms 9 en suite (4 fmly) (2 GF) **Facilities** STV TVB Direct dial from bedrooms Licensed Dinner Last d 9pm **Parking** 18 **Notes** ⊗ No coaches Closed Nov–12 Feb RS 12 Feb– Etr

LETTERKENNY   MAP 01 C5

★★★★ GUEST HOUSE
Ballyraine

Ramelton Rd

☎ 074 912 4460 & 912 0851 📄 074 912 0851

e–mail: ballyraineguesthouse@eircom.net

dir: *N13 onto R245*

This purpose-built guest house, 5 kilometres from the town centre, is well located for touring the Fanad and Inishowen Peninsula. Bedrooms are spacious and pleasantly decorated, some are suitable for families. There is a comfortable lounge and an attractive breakfast room.

Rooms 8 en suite (1 fmly) (2 GF) **Facilities** STV TVB tea/coffee Direct dial from bedrooms Cen ht TVL **Parking** 12 **Notes** ⊗

★★★ BED & BREAKFAST
Larkfield B&B

Drumnahoe

☎ 074 912 1478 & 086 0621263

e–mail: philomena21478@hotmail.com

dir: *1st left past Clanree Hotel. Signed N14 towards Letterkenny*

This house offers quiet and comfortable accommodation on the outskirts of Letterkenny. Mrs McDaid is a welcoming host and can advise on places to visit and restaurants for enjoyable evening meals. A good base for touring the Giant's Causeway and Glenveagh National Park.

Rooms 3 rms (2 en suite) (1 fmly) (3 GF) S €30–€45; D €64–€68✱ **Facilities** TVB tea/coffee Cen ht TVL **Parking** 4 **Notes LB** ⊗ Closed 21 Dec–2 Jan RS 3 Jan

DUBLIN

DUBLIN   MAP 01 D4

See also Howth (Co Dublin)

Premier Collection

★★★★★ GUEST HOUSE

Aberdeen Lodge

53 Park Av, Ballsbridge

☎ 01 2838155 📄 01 2837877

e–mail: info@aberdeen-lodge.com

web: www.aberdeen-lodge.com

dir: *From city centre onto Merrion road towards Sydney Parade Dart station, 1st left onto Park Av*

This particularly fine early Edwardian house stands on one of Dublin's most prestigious roads near to the Embassy suburb and DART or bus to accesses the city centre. Bedrooms are very well equipped, some with four-poster beds, and there is a relaxing comfortable lounge and the breakfast room has lovely views of the colourful garden.

Rooms 16 en suite (8 fmly) S €99–€129; D €119–€159 **Facilities** STV TVB tea/coffee Direct dial from bedrooms Licensed Cen ht Wi-fi available **Conf** Max 60 Thtr 60 Class 40 Board 40 Del from €140 **Parking** 16 **Notes** LB ⊗

Premier Collection

★★★★★ GUEST ACCOMMODATION

Blakes Townhouse

50 Merrion Rd, Ballsbridge

☎ 01 6688324 📄 01 6684280

e–mail: info@blakestownhouse.com

dir: *Merrion Rd S to Ballsbridge, Blakes opp RDS Convention Centre*

This luxurious house has been refurbished to a very high standard. Some of the spacious, air-conditioned bedrooms have four-poster beds, others have balconies overlooking the gardens, plus all the expected facilities. Parking available.

Rooms 13 en suite (1 fmly) (2 smoking) S €99–€139; D €119–€169 **Facilities** STV TVB tea/coffee Direct dial from bedrooms Cen ht Wi-fi available **Conf** Max 60 Thtr 60 Class 40 Board 40 Del from €140 **Parking** 6 **Notes** LB ⊗

Premier Collection

★★★★★ GUEST HOUSE

Butlers Town House

44 Lansdowne Rd, Ballsbridge

☎ 01 6674022 📄 01 6673960

e–mail: reservations@butlers-hotel.com

This fine Victorian house, in the heart of Dublin's Embassy belt, has been restored and retains the charm of a gracious family home. Bedrooms are air-conditioned and individually furnished and decorated. The public areas are particularly relaxing and there is a charming and comfortable drawing room and conservatory style breakfast room. Limited off-street parking is available.

Rooms 20 en suite **Facilities** STV TVB Direct dial from bedrooms Licensed **Parking** 14 **Notes** ⊗ No coaches Closed 22 Dec–8 Jan

DUBLIN CONTINUED

Premier Collection

★★★★★ GUEST HOUSE

Glenogra

64 Merrion Rd, Ballsbridge
☎ 01 6683661 📠 01 6683698
e–mail: info@glenogra.com
web: www.glenogra.com

dir: *Opp Royal Dublin Showgrounds & Four Seasons Hotel*

This fine brick house is situated in the pleasant suburb of Ballsbridge opposite the RDS and close to the city centre. Bedrooms are comfortably appointed with many thoughtful extras. There is an elegant drawing room and dining room with a rear garden where there is limited parking.

Rooms 13 en suite (1 fmly) S €85–€120; D €119–€199✱
Facilities STV TVB tea/coffee Direct dial from bedrooms Cen ht TVL
Wi-fi available **Parking** 10 **Notes LB** ⊗ No coaches Closed 21 Dec–5 Jan

Premier Collection

★★★★★ GUEST HOUSE

Harrington Hall

69–70 Harcourt St
☎ 01 4753497 📠 01 4754544
e–mail: harringtonhall@eircom.net
web: www.harringtonhall.com

dir: *St Stephens Green via O'Connell St, in Earlsfort Ter pass National Concert Hall & right onto Hatch St, right onto Harcourt St*

This restored Georgian house is on a one-way street, leading to St Stephen's Green in the centre of the city. The bedrooms and bathrooms are very comfortable and include two junior suites with galleried bedroom areas, and a full suite. A lovely plasterwork ceiling adorns the relaxing drawing room. Elevator, porter service and limited parking available.

Rooms 28 en suite (3 fmly) (3 GF) **Facilities** STV TVB tea/coffee Direct
dial from bedrooms Lift Cen ht **Conf** Max 20 Thtr 20 Class 6 Board 12
Parking 8 **Notes** ⊗

See advert on opposite page

Premier Collection

★★★★★ GUEST HOUSE

Merrion Hall

54–56 Merrion Rd, Ballsbridge
☎ 01 6681426 📠 01 6684280
e–mail: merrionhall@iol.ie

dir: *From city centre towards Dun Laoghaire Port, Ballsbridge 1.6km on main route, premises between British & US embassies*

This elegant house in Ballsbridge is convenient to the RDS and Lansdowne Road Stadium. Reception rooms are spacious, and the breakfast room overlooks the garden. The air-conditioned bedrooms are well appointed, and some rooms have balconies. Limited off-street parking is available.

Rooms 28 en suite (4 fmly) (4 GF) (2 smoking) S €99–€129;
D €119–€159 **Facilities** STV TVB tea/coffee Direct dial from bedrooms
Licensed Lift Cen ht Wi-fi available **Conf** Max 60 Thtr 60 Class 40
Board 40 Del from €140 **Parking** 10 **Notes LB** ⊗

Premier Collection

★★★★★ GUEST HOUSE

Pembroke Town House

90 Pembroke Rd, Ballsbridge
☎ 01 6600277 📠 01 6600291
e–mail: info@pembroketownhouse.ie

dir: *After Trinity College onto Nassan St & Northumberland Rd, onto lane to right of service station before lights, house 200mtrs on left*

Close to the city centre, three Georgian houses have been converted to make a comfortable guest house. The marble-tiled foyer, inviting lounge, and the friendly and attentive staff all combine to provide a welcoming atmosphere. The well-appointed bedrooms vary in style and some have a mezzanine sitting area. Secure parking is available behind the house.

Rooms 48 en suite (4 fmly) (10 GF) **Facilities** TVB tea/coffee Direct dial
from bedrooms Licensed Lift Cen ht TVL **Conf** Max 10 Board 10
Parking 20 **Notes** ⊗ Closed 22 Dec–2 Jan

★★★★ GUEST HOUSE

Charleville Lodge

268/272 North Circular Rd, Phibsborough
☎ 01 8386633 📠 01 8385854
e–mail: info@charlevillelodge.ie
web: www.charlevillelodge.ie

dir: *N from O'Connell St to Phibsborough, left fork at St Peter's Church, house 250mtrs on left*

Situated close to the city centre near Phoenix Park, this elegant terrace of Victorian houses has been restored to a high standard. The two interconnecting lounges are welcoming and the smart dining room offers a choice of breakfasts. Bedrooms are very comfortable with pleasant décor, and there is a secure car park.

Rooms 30 en suite (2 fmly) (4 GF) S €55–€150; D €70–€300✱
Facilities STV FTV TVB Direct dial from bedrooms Cen ht TVL
Conf Max 20 Thtr 20 Class 20 Board 20 **Parking** 18 **Notes LB** ⊗
Closed 21–26 Dec

★★★★ GUEST HOUSE
Eliza Lodge
23/24 Wellington Quay, Temple Bar
☎ 01 6718044 📄 01 6718362
e–mail: info@dublinlodge.com

Very smart accommodation in a completely refurbished building situated at the foot of the Millennium Bridge. Inviting, comfortable bedrooms are well equipped, and there is a lounge with a hospitality centre, and a fully licensed restaurant.

Rooms 18 en suite (2 fmly) **Facilities** STV TVB tea/coffee Direct dial from bedrooms Lift Cen ht TVL **Notes** ⊗ Closed 23 Dec–2 Jan

★★★★ GUEST ACCOMMODATION
Glenshandan Lodge
Dublin Rd, Swords
☎ 01 8408838 📄 01 8408838
e–mail: glenshandan@eircom.net

dir: *Beside Statoil on airport side of Swords Main St*

Family and dog-friendly house, with hospitable owners and good facilities including e-mail access. Bedrooms are comfortable and one room has easier access. Secure parking available. Close to pubs, restaurants, golf, airport and the Kennel Club.

Rooms 9 en suite (5 fmly) (5 GF) S €35–€65; D €80–€90 **Facilities** TVB tea/coffee Cen ht TVL Wi-fi available **Conf** Max 20 Del from €55 **Parking** 10 **Notes LB** Closed Xmas/New Year

★★★ BED & BREAKFAST
Aran House
5 Home Farm Rd, Drumcondra
☎ 01 8367395
e–mail: aranhouse@eircom.net

dir: *From city centre towards airport/Drumcondra road. Past St Patrick's College and Cat & Cage pub. 1st left after Skylon Hotel*

This comfortable, red-brick terrace house is just off the main airport road close to pubs and on a bus route to the city centre. The attractive dining room is an appropriate setting for delicious breakfasts and there is a cosy guest sitting room.

Rooms 4 en suite (2 fmly) S fr €60; D fr €90✻ **Facilities** TVB Cen ht TVL **Notes** Closed Nov–Feb 🐾

★★★ GUEST HOUSE
Ardagh House
1 Highfield Rd, Rathgar
☎ 01 4977068 📄 01 4973991
e–mail: enquiries@ardagh-house.ie

dir: *S of city centre through Rathmines*

Ardagh House has been refurbished and upgraded by Mary and Willie Doyle, and some of the comfortable, airy en suite rooms look over the attractive rear garden.

Rooms 19 en suite (4 fmly) (1 GF) S €70–€95; D €90–€150 **Facilities** FTV TVB tea/coffee Direct dial from bedrooms Cen ht TVL Wi-fi available **Parking** 20 **Notes** ⊗ Closed 22 Dec–3 Jan

★★★ GUEST HOUSE
Clifden
32 Gardiner Place
☎ 01 8746364 📄 01 8746122
e–mail: bnb@indigo.ie

dir: *From N end of O'Connell St, around Parnell Sq & exit at church onto Gardiner Row, over lights, house 4th on right*

This city centre house is just a short walk from O'Connell Street, and close to amenities. Facilities include a comfortable sitting room, cheerfully appointed breakfast room and a car park at the rear of the house.

Rooms 14 en suite (4 fmly) **Facilities** STV TVB tea/coffee Direct dial from bedrooms Cen ht TVL **Parking** 12 **Notes** ⊗ No coaches

Harrington Hall
70 Harcourt Street, Dublin 2

Harrington Hall has been awarded 5 stars from the AA and is a member of the prestigious Manor House Hotel group. It is a tranquil retreat in the heart of the city centre, close to the shopping mecca of Grafton Street. It is renowned for the personalised attention extended to all its guests. On site car park available.

Tel: +353 1 4753497   **Fax:** +353 1 4781557
Website: www.harringtonhall.com
Email: harringtonhall@eircom.net

DUBLIN CONTINUED

★★★ BED & BREAKFAST
Pairc na Bhfuiseog

55 Lorcan Crescent, Santry
☎ 01 8421318 📠 01 8421318
e-mail: rpjd@eircom.net

dir: *N1 Dublin Airport, Swords Rd to Santry, over flyover, sharp left at rdbt, to top of road. Right onto Lorcan Crescent*

An extended, modern semi-detached house, very nicely appointed throughout, with excellent en suite facilities. Convenient for Dublin Airport, ferries and city centre. The owners Ronald and Colette Downey provide a homely atmosphere and lots of local information.

Rooms 4 rms (3 en suite) (1 fmly) (1 GF) S €45–€47.50✳
Facilities STV TVB Cen ht **Parking** 4 **Notes** ⊗ No children 18yrs Closed 21 Dec–1 Jan

★★★ GUEST HOUSE
St Aiden's

32 Brighton Rd, Rathgar
☎ 01 4902011 & 4906178 📠 01 6864946
e-mail: staidens@eircom.net

dir: *M50 junct 11, towards city centre, premises 3rd left after lights in Terenure*

A fine Victorian house situated in a residential tree-lined road just 15 minutes from the city centre. The well-proportioned reception rooms are comfortable and relaxing, and a hospitality trolley is available. Bedrooms vary from spacious family rooms to snug singles, and all have modern comforts.

Rooms 8 en suite (2 fmly) S €55–€75; D €89–€110✳ **Facilities** STV TVB tea/coffee Direct dial from bedrooms Licensed Cen ht TVL Wi-fi available **Notes LB** ⊗

★★ GUEST HOUSE
Antrim Arms

27 Upper Drumcondra Rd
☎ 01 8375356 📠 01 8378769
e-mail: info@antrimarmsguesthouse.com

dir: *N1 to Dublin city, at the end of N1, after 1.6km onto Drumcondra Rd, house next to Skylon Hotel*

This fine, detached house is a 10-minute drive from Dublin Airport, the ferry port and the city centre. The attractive bedrooms, which vary in size, include some large family rooms and one room adapted for easier access. There is also a comfortable lounge and a dining room.

Rooms 24 en suite (3 fmly) (3 GF) **Facilities** TVB tea/coffee Cen ht TVL **Parking** 17 **Notes** ⊗ No children 16yrs Closed 22 Dec–3 Jan

CO DUBLIN

HOWTH — MAP 01 D4

★★★★ BED & BREAKFAST
Inisradharc

Balkill Rd
☎ 01 8322306
e-mail: harbour_view@msn.com

dir: *Off R105 past Howth Yacht Club onto Abbey St, bear right of church (in middle of road), house 0.6km up hill on right*

Set in a charming fishing village of Howth with lovely views of the harbour and Dublin Bay. The breakfast room also has fine views and there is a spacious television lounge. Well-kept gardens surround the property. Convenient for Dublin airport, ferry port and 20 minutes by DART to the city centre.

Rooms 3 en suite (1 fmly) (3 GF) D €80–€90✳ **Facilities** TVB tea/coffee Cen ht TVL **Parking** 3 **Notes** ⊗ No children 4yrs Closed 12 Dec–8 Jan

LUSK — MAP 01 D4

★★★ BED & BREAKFAST
Brookfield Lodge

Blakescross
☎ 01 8430043 📠 01 8430177
e-mail: trishb@indigo.ie

dir: *M1, R132 Donabate/Skerries for 3km, pass Esso station, at junct R132-N1 & R129*

Set in extensive gardens, this modern bungalow offers first-class hospitality and spacious, well-appointed rooms. Breakfasts are served in a conservatory-style dining room and there is also a comfortable lounge.

Rooms 3 en suite (2 fmly) **Facilities** STV TVB tea/coffee Cen ht TVL **Parking** 10 **Notes** ⊗ Closed 24–26 Dec

RUSH — MAP 01 D4

★★★★ BED & BREAKFAST
Sandyhills Bed & Breakfast

Sandyhills
☎ 01 8437148 & 086 242 3660 📠 01 8437148
e-mail: mary@sandyhills.ie

dir: *Exit M1 onto N1, turn right to Lusk on R127. 3rd exit on rdbt in Lusk to Rush. Right towards church carpark, right to Corrs Lane & then 2nd right*

Set just a stroll from the sea and the village of Rush, within easy reach of Dublin Airport, Sandyhills has spacious bedrooms, well equipped with thoughtful extra facilities. Breakfast is a special treat featuring local produce along with Mary Buckley's preserves, freshly baked cakes and breads. There is a cosy sitting room and a lovely garden with secure car parking.

Rooms 5 en suite (2 fmly) S fr €65; D €110✳ **Facilities** FTV TVB Direct dial from bedrooms Cen ht Wi-fi available **Parking** 20 **Notes LB** ⊗ No children 12yrs

SKERRIES　　　　　　　　　MAP 01 D4

★★★★ ⊕ RESTAURANT WITH ROOMS
Redbank House & Restaurant

5–7 Church St

☎ 01 8491005 📠 01 8491598

e–mail: sales@redbank.ie

dir: *N1 north past airport & bypass Swords. 3m N at end of dual carriageway at Esso station right towards Rush, Lusk & Skerries*

Adjacent to the well-known restaurant of the same name, this comfortable double fronted period town house has two reception rooms, en suite bedrooms and a secluded garden. The restaurant is the setting for quality local produce used with an emphasis on fresh fish in imaginative cooking, served by friendly and attentive staff. Convenient for Dublin airport and the ferry port.

Rooms 18 en suite (2 fmly) (7 GF) S €65–€75; D €90–€120✳ **Facilities** STV FTV TVB tea/coffee Direct dial from bedrooms Cen ht TVL Dinner Last d 9.45pm Wi-fi available **Conf** Max 25 Thtr 35 Class 25 Board 25 **Notes LB** Closed 24–28 Dec Civ Wed 55

CO GALWAY

CARNA (CARNA)　　　　　MAP 01 A4

★★★★ BED & BREAKFAST
Hillside House B&B

Kylesalia, Kilkieran

☎ 095 33420 📠 095 33420

e–mail: hillsidehouse@oceanfree.net

dir: *Off N59 at Maam Cross or Recess onto R340 or follow coast road from Galway R336*

At the foot of Mordan Mountain, this house is a good touring base. Bedrooms are comfortable, there are lovely gardens and secure parking. Snack service available. Near fishing and beach.

Rooms 4 en suite (4 fmly) **Facilities** STV TVB tea/coffee Cen ht TVL **Parking** 8 **Notes** ⊗ Closed Oct–Apr RS Apr–Oct

CLIFDEN　　　　　　　　　MAP 01 A4

★★★★ GUEST HOUSE
Buttermilk Lodge

Westport Rd

☎ 095 21951 📠 095 21953

e–mail: buttermilklodge@eircom.net

web: www.buttermilklodge.com

dir: *N59 from Galway. Right at Esso station onto Westport Rd, Lodge 400mtrs from junct on left. From Westport, Lodge on right after 50km road sign*

Expect carefully decorated and appointed bedrooms, four with luxury bath en suite and the remainder with shower en suite, along with many personal touches at this large house on the edge of town. Cathriona and Patrick O'Toole are welcoming hosts who offer fresh baking, tea and coffee on arrival.

Buttermilk Lodge

Rooms 11 en suite (2 fmly) (4 GF) S €50–€75; D €80–€100 **Facilities** STV FTV TVB Direct dial from bedrooms Cen ht Wi-fi available **Parking** 14 **Notes LB** ⊗ No children 5yrs Closed 1–27 Dec, 3 Jan–1 Mar

★★★★ FARM HOUSE
Ardmore House *(L 589523)*

Sky Rd

☎ 095 21221 📠 095 21100 Mr & Mrs J Mullen

e–mail: info@ardmore-house.com

web: www.ardmore-house.com

dir: *5km W of Clifden. From Clifden signs for Sky Rd, pass bank onto the Abbey Glen Castle, house signed*

Ardmore is set among the wild scenery of Connemara between hills and the sea on the Sky Road. Bedrooms are attractively decorated and the house is very comfortable throughout. A pathway leads from the house to the coast. A good hearty breakfast is provided featuring Kathy's home baking.

Rooms 6 en suite (3 fmly) (6 GF) D €70–€80 **Facilities** STV TVB tea/coffee Cen ht Wi-fi available **Parking** 8 **Notes LB** ⊗ 25 acres non-working Closed Oct–Mar 🐾

★★★★ FARM HOUSE
Faul House *(L 650475)*

Ballyconneely Rd

☎ 095 21239 📠 095 21998 Mrs K Conneely

e–mail: info@ireland.com

dir: *1.5km from town right at Connemara Pottery & signed Rockglen Hotel*

A fine modern farmhouse stands on a quiet and secluded road overlooking Clifden Bay. It is smart and comfortable with large bedrooms, all well furnished and with good views. Kathleen offers a hearty breakfast with home baking. There are Connemara ponies available for trekking.

Rooms 6 en suite (3 fmly) (3 GF) **Facilities** TVB tea/coffee Cen ht TVL Wi-fi available **Parking** 10 **Notes** ⊗ Closed Nov –17 Mar 🐾

IRELAND

CONTINUED

★★★★ BED & BREAKFAST
Mallmore House

Ballyconneely Rd
☎ 095 21460
e–mail: info@mallmore.com

dir: *1.5km from Clifden towards Ballyconneely and take 1st right*

A charming Georgian-style house built in the 17th century set in fourteen hectares of woodland overlooking Clifden Bay, close to the Rock Glen Hotel. Alan and Kathy Hardman have restored the house with parquet flooring and some favourite antiques, while turf fires provide warmth and atmosphere.

Rooms 6 en suite (2 fmly) (6 GF) D €80 **Facilities** TVB tea/coffee Cen ht Wi-fi available **Parking** 15 **Notes** ⊗ Closed Nov–1 Mar ⊜

★★★ GUEST HOUSE
Ben View House

Bridge St
☎ 095 21256 📠 095 21226
e–mail: benviewhouse@ireland.com

dir: *Enter town on N59, opp Esso fuel station*

This town-centre house offers good quality accommodation at a moderate cost, and is a good touring base.

Rooms 10 rms (9 en suite) (3 fmly) **Facilities** TV9B tea/coffee Cen ht TVL **Notes** ⊗

CRAUGHWELL   MAP 01 B3

Premier Collection

★★★★★ ⊜ GUEST HOUSE
St Clerans Manor House

☎ 091 846555 📠 091 846752
e–mail: info@stclerans.com

dir: *Athenry exit off N6 rdbt at Loughrea, left after 6km, signs for St Clerans*

A delightful 18th-century Georgian manor house set in 45 acres. Bedrooms and public areas have been lovingly restored to a high standard of luxury and comfort. Local produce and Oriental influences feature nightly on the dinner menu. Coarse fishing and croquet are available in the grounds. A helicopter pad and personalised chauffeur driven tours are available.

Rooms 12 en suite (2 fmly) (2 GF) **Facilities** STV FTV TVB Direct dial from bedrooms Cen ht TVL Dinner Last d 9pm Wi-fi available Fishing 🎣 **Conf** Max 20 Thtr 30 Class 15 Board 14 **Parking** 15 **Notes** ⊗ No coaches Closed 24–29 Dec Civ Wed 40

GALWAY   MAP 01 B3

★★★★ BED & BREAKFAST
Achill Lodge

5 Cashelmara, Upper Salthill
☎ 091 584709
e–mail: info@achill-lodge.com
web: www.achill-lodge.com

dir: *R336 from Galway City, continue through Salthill, passing the golf club*

Achill Lodge is a newly-constructed, purpose-built bed and breakfast located in the exclusive seaside resort of Salthill, just five minutes' drive from Galway. Bedrooms are carefully decorated and well equipped, with extra large en suite bathrooms. Some have lovely views over Galway Bay, as does the cosy guest sitting room and breakfast room. There is private off-road parking available.

Rooms 4 en suite (2 fmly) S €45–€80; D €70–€120✳ **Facilities** STV FTV TVB tea/coffee Cen ht TVL Wi-fi available **Parking** 8 **Notes** LB ⊗ Closed Nov–Feb

★★★★ BED & BREAKFAST
Almara House

2 Merlin Gate, Merlin Park, Dublin Rd
☎ 091 755345 & 086 2451220 📠 091 771585
e–mail: matthewkiernan@eircom.net

dir: *From Martin rdbt follow signs for Merlin Park. 0.2km Almara House is located on left*

Located in the eastern outskirts of Galway city, this attractive guest house offers well-appointed bedrooms with lots of thoughtful extras and Wi-fi access. Breakfast features Marie Kiernan's home baking. Almara House is well located for the Institute of Technology and off-road parking is available.

Rooms 5 en suite (2 fmly) (1 GF) S €40–€65; D €80–€110 **Facilities** STV FTV TVB tea/coffee Cen ht TVL Wi-fi available **Parking** 8 **Notes** LB ⊗ No children 4yrs Closed 20–30 Dec

★★★★ GUEST HOUSE
Marian Lodge
Knocknacarra Rd, Salthill Upper
☎ 091 521678 📠 091 528103
e-mail: celine@iol.ie

dir: *From Galway to Salthill on R336, through Salthill, 1st right after Spinnaker Hotel onto Knocknacarra Rd*

This large modern house is only 50 metres from the seafront. The fully equipped bedrooms have orthopedic beds and en suite facilities. There is also a lounge and separate breakfast room available.

Rooms 6 en suite (4 fmly) **Facilities** STV TVB tea/coffee Direct dial from bedrooms Cen ht TVL **Parking** 10 **Notes** ⊗ No children 3yrs Closed 23–28 Dec

★★★ BED & BREAKFAST
Four Seasons
23 College Rd
☎ 091 564078 📠 091 569765
e-mail: 4season@gofree.indigo.ie

dir: *From E or S exit motorway signed Galway City East then city centre, 5th house on right after sports ground/greyhound track*

This comfortable house adjacent to the city centre is the family home of Eddie and Helen Fitzgerald who will immediately make you feel at home and help you with itineraries and sight-seeing, and will recommend restaurants for evening meals.

Rooms 5 en suite 2 annexe en suite (3 fmly) **Facilities** STV TVB tea/coffee Cen ht TVL **Parking** 7 **Notes** ⊗

★★★ BED & BREAKFAST
Lakeland & Midsummer Lakehouse
Lakeland Angling Centre, Portacarron Bay
☎ 091 552121 📠 091 552146
e-mail: mayfly@eircom.net

dir: *Off N59 20 mins from Galway take 2nd right after Oughterard Golf Club sign. From Maam Cross through Oughterard, pass Gateway Hotel next left, house on lake shore*

Situated on the shores of the lough, this comfortable house offers a spacious television lounge, and a fine dining room with views across the water. Fishing and boat trips can be arranged, and dinner is available.

Rooms 9 rms (8 en suite) (3 fmly) **Facilities** tea/coffee Cen ht TVL Fishing **Parking** 20 **Notes** ⊗ Closed 10 Dec–16 Jan

ROUNDSTONE   MAP 01 A4

★★★★ BED & BREAKFAST
Ivy Rock House
Letterdyfe
☎ 095 35872 📠 095 35959
e-mail: ivyrockhouse@eircom.net

Overlooking Bertraghboy Bay this house has been decorated to a high standard and provides comfortable accommodation. Public rooms include two adjoining reception rooms and a first-floor sitting room with spectacular views. Bedrooms are well appointed. There are good restaurants nearby.

Rooms 6 en suite (4 fmly) (3 GF) **Facilities** TV4B Cen ht TVL Last d 3pm Riding locally **Parking** 10 **Notes** ⊗ Closed Oct–Mar

SALTHILL   MAP 01 B3

★★★★ BED & BREAKFAST
Rose Villa
10 Cashelmara, Knocknacarra Cross
☎ 091 584200 📠 091 584200
e-mail: kevin.ohare@ireland.com

dir: *1km from Salthill Promenade in upper Salthill on R336. On right after Golf Club before T-junct*

Rose Villa enjoys lovely views over the bay especially when the sun is going down. Bedrooms are comfortable and well appointed. There is a relaxing guest lounge and Marie and Kevin O'Hara serve a good breakfast. Off-street car parking is available.

Rooms 4 en suite (3 fmly) S €50–€70; D €100–€120✱ **Facilities** STV FTV TVB tea/coffee Cen ht TVL Wi-fi available **Parking** 7 **Notes** ⊗ Closed 30 Nov–7 Feb

SPIDDAL (AN SPIDÉAL)   MAP 01 B3

★★★★ BED & BREAKFAST
Ardmor Country House
Greenhill
☎ 091 553145 📠 091 553596
e-mail: ardmorcountryhouse@yahoo.com

dir: *On R336 coast road from Galway, 1km W of Spiddal*

There are superb views of Galway Bay and the Aran Islands from this beautifully appointed luxury home. Bedrooms are spacious and there are relaxing lounges, a well-stocked library and delightful gardens.

Rooms 7 en suite (4 fmly) S €45–€55; D €70–€74✱ **Facilities** TVB tea/coffee Cen ht TVL Wi-fi available **Parking** 20 **Notes** ⊗ Closed Dec–Feb RS Mar–Nov 🐾

IRELAND

SPIDDAL (AN SPIDÉAL) CONTINUED

★★★★ BED & BREAKFAST
Tuar Beag

Tuar Beag
☎ 091 553422
e-mail: tuarbeagbandb@eircom.net

dir: *On R336 coast road on W edge of Spiddal*

Tuar Beag is a prominent house, much extended from the 19th-century cottage where four generations of the proprietor's family grew up. The original stone walls and fireplace have been retained and the house now offers excellent accommodation overlooking Galway Bay and the Aran Islands. Breakfast is a notable feature.

Rooms 6 en suite (6 fmly) **Facilities** TVB tea/coffee Cen ht TVL **Parking** 20 **Notes** ⊗ No children 2yrs Closed 16 Nov–1 Mar ⊛

CO KERRY

BALLYBUNION   MAP 01 A3

Premier Collection

★★★★★ GUEST HOUSE
Cashen Course House

Golf Links Rd
☎ 068 27351 📠 068 28934
e-mail: golfstay@eircom.net
web: www.cashenguesthouse.com

dir: *200mtrs from Ballybunion Golf Club*

Overlooking the Cashen links, this spacious, purpose-built house offers comfortable well-appointed bedrooms. A warm welcome is assured from the O'Brien family who are on hand to advise and assist with tee bookings. A baby grand piano is a feature of the inviting lounge. Drying facilities are available.

Rooms 9 en suite (3 fmly) (3 GF) S €80–€120; D €120–€160✳ **Facilities** STV TVB tea/coffee Direct dial from bedrooms Cen ht TVL Wi-fi available Golf 18 2 golf courses opposite **Parking** 12 **Notes LB** ⊗ Closed Nov–Apr

CAHERDANIEL   MAP 01 A2
(CATHAIR DÓNALL)

★★★★ BED & BREAKFAST
Derrynane Bay House

☎ 066 9475404 & 08723 43974 📠 066 9475436
e-mail: dbhouse@eircom.net

dir: *1km on Waterville side of Caherdaniel village on N70 overlooking Derrynane Bay*

Situated on an elevated position with views over Derrynane Bay, this house is meticulously maintained. Carefully furnished throughout, there is a comfortable sitting and dining room, along with attractive bedrooms. The owner is very welcoming and offers a good breakfast menu. Walking, water sports, good beaches, fishing and golf are all nearby.

CONTINUED

Rooms 6 rms (5 en suite) (1 pri facs) (2 fmly) (4 GF) S €50–€60; D €80 **Facilities** STV FTV TVB tea/coffee Direct dial from bedrooms Cen ht TVL Dinner Last d noon **Parking** 10 **Notes** ⊗ Closed Nov–Dec RS 6 Jan–20 Mar

CASTLEGREGORY   MAP 01 A2

Premier Collection

★★★★★ BED & BREAKFAST
Shores Country House

Conor Pass Rd, Cappatigue
☎ 066 713 9196 & 713 9195 📠 066 713 9196
e-mail: theshores@eircom.net

dir: *N86/R560 through Stradbally village, continue 1.6km, house on left*

This charming house has panoramic views from its elevated position. Bedrooms and public rooms are all individually decorated to a very high standard. An interesting home-cooked dinner is available Monday to Friday, and features local and seasonal produce.

Rooms 6 en suite (1 fmly) (2 GF) S €40–€100; D €80–€100 **Facilities** STV TVB tea/coffee Direct dial from bedrooms Cen ht TVL Dinner Last d 5pm Library **Parking** 8 **Notes LB** ⊗ Closed mid Nov–mid Feb

★★★★ BED & BREAKFAST
Sea-Mount House

Cappatigue, Conor Pass Rd
☎ 066 7139229 📠 066 7139229
e-mail: seamount@unison.ie
web: www.seamounthouse.com

dir: *On Conor Pass road, 2.4km W of Stradbally, overlooking Brandon Bay*

Located on the Conor Pass road between Tralee and Dingle, this friendly house has great views of Brandon Bay. It is a good base for exploring the Dingle Peninsula. The cosy sitting areas and bedrooms make the most of the views, a great way to enjoy home baking and welcome tea on arrival.

Rooms 3 en suite (1 fmly) (2 GF) S €47–€50; D €70–€80✳ **Facilities** TVB tea/coffee Cen ht TVL **Parking** 5 **Notes LB** ⊗ Closed Nov–May ⊛

★★★ BED & BREAKFAST
Griffin's Palm Beach Country House

Goulane, Conor Pass Rd
☎ 066 7139147 📠 066 7139073
e-mail: griffinspalmbeach@eircom.net

dir: *1.5km from Stradbally village*

This farmhouse is a good base for exploring the Dingle Peninsula and unspoiled beaches. The comfortable bedrooms have fine views over Brandon Bay, and the delightful garden can be enjoyed from the dining room and sitting room. Mrs Griffin offers a warm welcome and her home baking is a feature on the breakfast menu.

Rooms 8 rms (6 en suite) (2 pri facs) (3 fmly) (1 GF) S €48–€51; D €90–€100✳ **Facilities** tea/coffee Cen ht TVL ♨ **Parking** 10 **Notes LB** Closed Nov–Feb

IRELAND

CASTLEMAINE — MAP 01 A2

★★★ FARM HOUSE
Murphys Farmhouse (R8801005)
Boolteens
☎ 066 976 7337 📄 066 976 7839 Mrs M Murphy
e-mail: info@murphysfarmhouse.com
dir: *From Castlemaine onto R561 Dingle road, signed*
The elevated position of this long established house offers marvellous views of Dingle Bay. Bedrooms are very comfortable, and a choice of two lounges is available for guests. Expect a warm welcome from Mrs Mary Murphy, whose family also own a traditional pub nearby, where dinner is served.

Rooms 14 en suite (5 fmly) (6 GF) **Facilities** TVB tea/coffee Cen ht TVL Dinner Last d 1pm **Parking** 16 **Notes** ⊗ 30 acres Dairy

CLOGHANE (AN CLOCHÁN) — MAP 01 A2

★★ ⇔ GUEST HOUSE
O'Connors Guesthouse
☎ 066 713 8113 📄 066 713 8270
e-mail: oconnorsguesthouse@eircom.net
dir: *In village centre*
Situated in a lovely village close to Castlegregory, the long-established, family-run house has a traditional bar and restaurant, and some of the bedrooms look over the bay and mountains.

Rooms 9 en suite (6 fmly) (2 GF) S €50-€65; D €80-€100 **Facilities** tea/coffee Direct dial from bedrooms Licensed Cen ht TVL Dinner Last d 8.30pm Wi-fi available **Parking** 20 **Notes** LB ⊗ Closed Nov-Feb

DINGLE (AN DAINGEAN) — MAP 01 A2

Premier Collection
★★★★★ GUEST ACCOMMODATION
Emlagh House
☎ 066 9152345 📄 066 9152369
e-mail: info@emlaghhouse.com
web: www.emlaghhouse.com
dir: *Pass fuel station at E entrance to town, turn left & house ahead*
Impressive Georgian-style house on the outskirts of Dingle where attention to detail and luxury combine to make a stay memorable. The stylish drawing room and dining room overlook the harbour. Bedrooms and bathrooms are individually decorated to a high standard with antique furniture, and ground floor rooms have private patios. Breakfasts are very special here and make good use of fresh local produce.

Rooms 10 en suite (1 fmly) (4 GF) S €125-€165; D €180-€290 **Facilities** STV TVB Direct dial from bedrooms Lift Cen ht Wi-fi available **Parking** 20 **Notes** LB ⊗ No children 8yrs Closed 5 Nov-10 Mar

Premier Collection
★★★★★ 🛏 GUEST HOUSE
Milltown House
☎ 066 9151372 📄 066 9151095
e-mail: info@milltownhousedingle.com
dir: *1.5km W of Dingle on Slea Head road. Cross Milltown Bridge & left*
Situated on a sea channel to the west of Dingle town, the house has been elegantly refurbished and has a warm inviting atmosphere, the Kerry family making guests feel really welcome. Bedrooms have attractive décor and are well appointed. There is also a cosy sitting room leading to a conservatory breakfast room.

Rooms 10 en suite (1 fmly) (3 GF) S €85-€145; D €130-€170 **Facilities** STV TVB tea/coffee Direct dial from bedrooms Cen ht **Parking** 10 **Notes** ⊗ No children 5yrs No coaches Closed 29 Oct-27 Apr

Premier Collection
★★★★★ GUEST HOUSE
Castlewood House
The Wood
☎ 066 915 2788 📄 066 915 2110
e-mail: castlewoodhouse@eircom.net
dir: *R559 from Dingle, 0.5km from Aquarium*
Located at the western edge of the town, Castlewood House has been recently built to a high specification. Each of the individually designed bedrooms is very comfortable and well equipped. There is lift access to the upper floor and a spa bath in each en suite. Both the sitting room and breakfast rooms make the most of the beautiful views.

Rooms 12 en suite (3 fmly) (4 GF) **Facilities** STV TVB tea/coffee Direct dial from bedrooms Lift Cen ht **Parking** 15 **Notes** ⊗ Closed 4-27 Dec, 4 Jan-4 Feb

Premier Collection
★★★★★ ⇔ GUEST HOUSE
Gormans Clifftop House & Restaurant
Glaise Bheag, Ballydavid
☎ 066 9155162 📄 066 9155003
e-mail: info@gormans-clifftophouse.com
dir: *From Dingle harbour to rdbt W of town, over rdbt signed An Fheothanach to coast, keep left at junct*
This traditional house is in a superb location overlooking Smerwick Harbour and the vastness of the Atlantic beyond. The Gorman family offer marvellous hospitality and the food is excellent. Lounges and restaurant enjoy stunning views. The comfortable bedrooms are most inviting, and one is adapted for the less mobile.

Rooms 9 en suite (2 fmly) (5 GF) **Facilities** TVB tea/coffee Direct dial from bedrooms Licensed Cen ht Dinner Last d 8.30pm Wi-fi available **Parking** 15 **Notes** ⊗ Closed 24-26 Dec RS Nov-Feb

IRELAND

735

DINGLE (AN DAINGEAN) CONTINUED

Premier Collection

★★★★★ GUEST HOUSE

Heatons

The Wood

☎ 066 9152288 📄 066 9152324

e-mail: heatons@iol.ie

dir: 0.6km beyond marina

A family-run guest house located on the waterfront and near the town. Most bedrooms have views of Dingle Bay and are very comfortable and well appointed. Guests can also enjoy the views and relax in the spacious foyer lounge. The breakfast room is brightly decorated and offers an impressive carte.

Rooms 16 en suite (2 fmly) (5 GF) **Facilities** STV TVB tea/coffee Direct dial from bedrooms Cen ht **Parking** 16 **Notes** ⊗ No children 8yrs Closed 5 Jan–1 Feb

★★★★ GUEST HOUSE

Alpine

Mail Rd

☎ 066 9151250 📄 066 9151966

e-mail: alpinedingle@eircom.net

dir: On right on N86 at entrance to town

On the edge of Dingle, this large, attractive three-storey guest house is run by the O'Shea family, who maintain excellent standards. The elegantly furnished bedrooms have large, spacious bathrooms. There is a private car park, and the guest house is just two minutes walk from the town centre.

Rooms 10 en suite (3 fmly) **Facilities** STV TVB tea/coffee Direct dial from bedrooms Cen ht TVL **Parking** 15 **Notes** ⊗

★★★ FARM HOUSE

Hurleys (Q 392080)

An Dooneen, Kilcooley

☎ 066 9155112 Ms Mary Hurley

e-mail: andooneen@eircom.net

dir: 11km W of Dingle town on Ballydavid-Muirioch road

Hurley's Farm is tucked away behind the church in Kilcooley, 1.5 kilometres from the beach and sheltered by Mount Brandon, a popular

place for hill walkers. Accommodation includes a cosy TV room, dining room and comfortable en suite bedrooms, graced by some special pieces of high quality furniture. The whole area is rich in early historic and prehistoric relics: ogham stones, ring forts and the famous dry-stone masonry 'beehive' huts.

Rooms 4 en suite (2 GF) S €45–€55; D €80–€86 **Facilities** Cen ht TVL **Parking** 6 **Notes LB** ⊗ Closed Nov–Mar ⊜

KENMARE   MAP 01 B2

From the 3rd of November 2008, phone numbers in this location will have 66 added to the start of their existing number. The dialling code remains the same.

★★★★ GUEST HOUSE

Davitts

Henry St

☎ 064 42741 📄 064 42757

e-mail: info@davitts-kenmare.com

dir: On N22 (Cork-Killarney rd) at Kenmare junct (R569). In town centre

This town-centre guest house has been decorated to a high standard. The spacious, well-appointed bedrooms are decorated in a contemporary style, and there is a cosy sitting room on the first floor. Davitt's Restaurant is at street level, a popular venue to meet friends and locals and enjoy the varied menu.

Rooms 11 en suite (1 fmly) S €50–€70; D €80–€100✳ **Facilities** STV TVB Direct dial from bedrooms Licensed Cen ht TVL Dinner Last d 9.45pm **Parking** 4 **Notes** ⊗ Closed 1–14 Nov & 24–26 Dec

★★★★ BED & BREAKFAST

Harbour View

Castletownbere Rd, Dauros

☎ 064 41755 📄 064 42611

e-mail: maureenmccarthy@eircom.net

dir: From Kenmare towards Glengurriffe, onto Castletownbere Haven road 571, 1st right after bridge, Harbour View 6.5km on left on seashore

This charming house is situated on the seashore, with lovely views of Kenmare Bay and the mountains beyond. Maureen McCarthy is a cheerful, caring hostess with infectious enthusiasm, and her attention to detail is evident throughout the comfortable bedrooms. The breakfast menu includes fresh and smoked seafood and the home baking is excellent.

CONTINUED

CONTINUED

IRELAND

Rooms 4 en suite (3 fmly) (4 GF) S €70–€90; D €90 **Facilities** STV TVB tea/coffee Cen ht TVL **Parking** 6 **Notes** ⊗ No children 6yrs Closed Nov–Feb ⊜

★★★★ GUEST HOUSE
Sea Shore Farm Guest House
Tubrid
☎ 064 41270 & 41675 📠 064 41270
e–mail: seashore@eircom.net

dir: *1.6km from Kenmare on N70 Ring of Kerry road. Signed at junct N70 & N71*

Overlooking Kenmare Bay on the Ring of Kerry road, this modern farm guest house is close to town and has spacious bedrooms. Ground-floor rooms open onto the patio and have easier access. Guests are welcome to enjoy the farm walks through the fields to the shore, and salmon and trout fishing on a private stretch of the Roughty River. There is a comfortable sitting room and dining room and a delightful garden.

Rooms 6 en suite (2 fmly) (2 GF) **Facilities** FTV TVB tea/coffee Direct dial from bedrooms Cen ht Wi-fi available **Parking** 10 **Notes** ⊗ Closed 15 Nov–Feb

★★★★ GUEST HOUSE
Virginia's Guesthouse
36 Henry St
☎ 064 41021 & 086 3720625
e–mail: virginias@eircom.net
web: www.virginias-kenmare.com

dir: *In town centre*

Virginia's is a well-presented house near the town green. Sharing an entrance with Mulcahy's Restaurant, the bedrooms are on the upper floors and are very comfortable. Breakfast features home-baked breads and there is a very comfortable guest sitting room.

Rooms 8 en suite (1 fmly) S €60–€85; D €70–€120 **Facilities** STV TVB Direct dial from bedrooms Cen ht **Notes LB** ⊗ No children 12yrs Closed 20–25 Dec

★★★ BED & BREAKFAST
Annagry House
Sneem Rd
☎ 064 41283
e–mail: info@annagryhouse.com

dir: *500mtrs from town centre, turn left onto N70 towards Sneem on the Ring of Kerry. 400mtrs on right*

Annagry House is situated on the Ring of Kerry road (N70) only minutes from Kenmare town. Bedrooms/bathrooms are spacious and ideally furnished for families and two rooms are on ground floor. The relaxing guest sitting room has books and maps of the area. The extensive breakfast menu includes Fionnuala's home baking, and Danny will advise on tours and activities available.

Rooms 6 en suite (3 fmly) (2 GF) D €76–€84 **Facilities** FTV TVB tea/coffee Cen ht TVL Wi-fi available **Parking** 11 **Notes** ⊗ Closed 26 Oct–Apr ⊜

KILGARVAN
MAP 01 B2

From the 3rd of November 2008, phone numbers in this location will have 66 added to the start of their existing number. The dialling code remains the same.

★★★★ BED & BREAKFAST
Birchwood
Church Ground
☎ 064 85473 📠 064 85570
e–mail: birchwood1@eircom.net

dir: *500mtrs E of Kilgarvan on R569*

Birchwood stands in extensive gardens facing a natural forest and backed by the Mangerton Mountains, an area ideal for hill-walking and touring. The MacDonnells are caring hosts in this tranquil location, and offer comfortable and attractively decorated bedrooms. Dinner is available, and the nearby Rivers Roughty and Slaheny provide good salmon and trout fishing.

Rooms 5 en suite (3 fmly) S €40–€45; D €60✶ **Facilities** FTV TVB tea/coffee Cen ht TVL Dinner Last d 6.30pm Fishing **Parking** 6 **Notes** ⊗ ⊜

KILLARNEY
MAP 01 B2

From the 3rd of November 2008, phone numbers in this location will have 66 added to the start of their existing number. The dialling code remains the same.

Premier Collection
★★★★★ GUEST HOUSE
Earls Court House
Woodlawn Junction, Muckross Rd
☎ 064 34009 📠 064 34366
e–mail: info@killarney-earlscourt.ie

dir: *Left at lights on Muckross Rd, Earls Court House 100mtrs on left*

Earls Court House is a charming guest house situated within walking distance of the town centre and National Park. Bedrooms are spacious and individually furnished with luxury and guest comfort in mind, some with four poster beds, Jacuzzi baths and balconies. The relaxing lounges have open fires and guests can enjoy the sun patio and garden. There is ample off-street parking available.

Rooms 30 en suite (3 fmly) (8 GF) **Facilities** STV TVB tea/coffee Direct dial from bedrooms Lift Cen ht TVL Wi-fi available **Parking** 30 **Notes** ⊗ Closed 13 Nov–11 Feb RS 6 Nov–Feb (group bookings 8+)

IRELAND

KILLARNEY *CONTINUED*

Premier Collection

★★★★★ 🏠 GUEST HOUSE
Kathleens Country House
Tralee Rd
☎ 064 32810 📄 064 32340
e–mail: info@kathleens.net

dir: *1.6km N of town centre on N22*

The modern, purpose-built guest house stands in lovely gardens amid scenic countryside. The family-run, luxury accommodation is a good touring centre. Bedrooms are furnished with antique pine and have excellent bathrooms, while the five sitting rooms all have different views. Breakfast is served in the elegant dining room overlooking the gardens.

Rooms 17 en suite (2 fmly) (2 GF) **Facilities** STV TVB tea/coffee Direct dial from bedrooms Cen ht Wi-fi available 🥢 **Parking** 20 **Notes** ⊗ No children 3yrs Closed mid Oct–mid Mar

Premier Collection

★★★★★ 🏠 GUEST HOUSE
Fairview
College St
☎ 064 34164 📄 064 71777
e–mail: info@fairviewkillarney.com

dir: *In town centre off College St*

This guest house is situated in the town centre and close to the railway station. Great attention to detail has been taken in the furnishing and design to ensure guest comfort in bedrooms. There is a lift to all floors and a penthouse suite enjoys views to the mountains. Dinner is served nightly in the Fifth Season Restaurant.

Rooms 29 en suite (1 GF) (2 smoking) **Facilities** STV TVB tea/coffee Direct dial from bedrooms Licensed Lift Cen ht TVL Dinner Last d 10pm Wi-fi available Jacuzzi suites available **Parking** 11

Premier Collection

★★★★★ 🛏 GUEST HOUSE
Foleys Town House
22/23 High St
☎ 064 31217 📄 064 34683
e–mail: info@foleystownhouse.com

dir: *In town centre*

Charming, individually-designed bedrooms are a feature of this well-established house, which has good parking facilities and a comfortable lounge. Family owned and run by Carol Hartnett who is also the chef in the adjoining restaurant that specialises in seafood.

Foleys Town House

Rooms 28 en suite S €75–€90; D €150–€160 **Facilities** STV TVB tea/coffee Direct dial from bedrooms Licensed Lift Cen ht TVL Dinner Last d 10.30pm Wi-fi available **Parking** 60 **Notes** LB ⊗ Closed 6 Nov–16 Mar

Premier Collection

★★★★★ GUEST HOUSE
Old Weir Lodge
Muckross Rd
☎ 064 35593 📄 064 35583
e–mail: oldweirlodge@eircom.net
web: www.oldweirlodge.com

dir: *On N71 Muckross Rd, 500mtrs from Killarney*

Welcoming, purpose-built Tudor-style lodge, set in attractive gardens. Maureen loves to cook and home-baking is a feature of the breakfasts; evening meals are also available by arrangement. Dermot will help with leisure activities such as boat trips on the Killarney Lakes or golf and fishing. The comfortable bedrooms are equipped to a high standard and there is a delightful sitting room overlooking the gardens. There is also a drying room and ample off-road parking.

Rooms 30 en suite (7 fmly) (6 GF) S €65–€95; D €90–€140 **Facilities** STV TVB tea/coffee Direct dial from bedrooms Licensed Lift Cen ht TVL Dinner Last d 8pm **Parking** 30 **Notes** ⊗ Closed 23–26 Dec

CONTINUED

IRELAND

★★★★ BED & BREAKFAST
Applecroft House

Woodlawn Rd

☎ 064 32782

e–mail: applecroft@eircom.net

dir: *N71 from Killarney on Muckross road for 500mtrs, left at 2nd set lights onto Woodlawn Rd for 500mtrs, sign on left*

Applecroft is a delightful home of the Brosnan family tucked away in a residential area, with beautiful landscaped gardens. Bedrooms are spacious and there is great attention to detail in the decoration. Guests can relax in the lounge or on the patio. Breakfast is served in the lovely dining room overlooking the garden.

Rooms 5 en suite (2 fmly) S €50–€60; D €70–€80 **Facilities** STV TVB Cen ht TVL **Parking** 5 **Notes** LB ⊗ Closed Dec–Feb RS 10 Feb–1 Dec

★★★★ GUEST HOUSE
Ashville

Rock Rd

☎ 064 36405 📠 064 36778

e–mail: info@ashvillekillarney.com

dir: *In town centre. Off N end of High St onto Rock Rd*

This inviting house is just a stroll from the town centre and near the N22 Tralee road. Bedrooms are comfortably furnished and there is a pleasant relaxing sitting room and dining room. There is a private car park and tours can be arranged.

Rooms 12 en suite (4 fmly) (4 GF) S €55–€120; D €74–€120 **Facilities** STV FTV TV10B tea/coffee Direct dial from bedrooms Cen ht TVL Wi-fi available **Parking** 13 **Notes** LB ⊗ Closed Nov–1 Mar

★★★★ GUEST HOUSE
Crystal Springs

Ballycasheen

☎ 064 33272 & 35518 📠 064 35518

e–mail: crystalsprings@eircom.net

web: www.crystalspringsbb.com

dir: *From Killarney town turn right off Cork Rd at 1st lights & Texaco. Left onto Rookery Rd, to end & Crystal Springs is across road at T-junct*

This luxurious house is on the outskirts of the town and the garden runs down to the River Flesk. It overlooks a historic mill and is close to

CONTINUED

the mountains, lakes, golf courses and Killarney National Park. Bedrooms are attractively decorated and well equipped and there is a charming lounge and dining room where delicious breakfasts are served.

Rooms 7 en suite (3 fmly) (3 GF) **Facilities** STV TVB tea/coffee Direct dial from bedrooms Cen ht TVL Dinner Last d 3pm Fishing **Parking** 14

★★★★ BED & BREAKFAST
Killarney Villa

Mallow Rd

☎ 064 31878 📠 064 31878

e–mail: killarneyvilla@ie-post.com

web: www.killarneyvilla.com

dir: *N22 E from Killarney, over 1st rdbt, continue after 2nd rdbt on N22 & N72 for 2km, left signed Mallow, Villa 300mtrs on right*

This luxurious country home has a rooftop conservatory where complimentary beverages are available. It is situated on the outskirts of the town within easy reach of the beautiful Killarney lakes and mountains. Bedrooms are very comfortable and well equipped, and there is a lovely dining room where a variety of dishes are available at breakfast.

Rooms 6 en suite S €45–€55; D €78–€94✳ **Facilities** STV TVB tea/coffee Cen ht TVL **Parking** 20 **Notes** LB ⊗ Closed Nov–Etr ⊛

★★★★ GUEST HOUSE
Kingfisher Lodge

Lewis Rd

☎ 064 37131 📠 064 39871

e–mail: kingfisherguesthouse@eircom.net

dir: *Dublin link straight through 1st rdbt. Right at next rdbt towards town centre, Lodge on left*

This welcoming, family-run modern guest house, situated within walking distance of the town centre, has comfortable well-appointed bedrooms. A delicious breakfast is served in the attractively decorated dining room and there is also a relaxing lounge. A drying room is available for fishing and wet gear. Golf, walking and fishing trips can be arranged.

Rooms 10 en suite (1 fmly) (2 GF) **Facilities** TVB tea/coffee Direct dial from bedrooms Cen ht TVL Wi-fi available Walking, fishing, horseriding, golf can be booked **Parking** 11 **Notes** No coaches Closed 15 Dec–13 Feb

★★★★ BED & BREAKFAST
Redwood

Tralee Rd

☎ 064 34754 & 087 299 8924 📠 064 34754

e–mail: redwd@indigo.ie

dir: *N22 N from Killarney, Redwood 3.2km from Cleeny rdbt on left*

Set in landscaped grounds 4 kilometres from the town centre, this is a very comfortable house. Bedrooms are well furnished, and the lounge and dining rooms are very spacious with picture windows framing the garden. A good choice is offered at breakfast.

Rooms 6 en suite (3 fmly) (2 GF) S fr €50; D €72–€90 **Facilities** STV TVB tea/coffee Cen ht Wi-fi available **Parking** 6 **Notes** LB ⊗

IRELAND

KILLARNEY *CONTINUED*

★★★★ BED & BREAKFAST
Shraheen House
Ballycasheen, Off Cork Rd (N22)
☎ 064 31286
e-mail: info@shraheenhouse.com

dir: *On Ballycasheen-Woodlawn road, 1.6km off N71 at lights by Dromhall Hotel. Off N22 at Whitebridge Caravan Park Sign*

The large modern house stands in extensive grounds on a quiet road. The bedrooms are all well equipped and have attractive soft furnishings. The quiet gardens and the pleasant sun lounge are very relaxing. Within easy reach of three golf courses or local fishing.

Rooms 6 en suite (2 fmly) (3 GF) S €55–€65; D €70–€77 **Facilities** STV TVB tea/coffee Cen ht TVL Wi-fi available **Parking** 8 **Notes** ⊗ No children 4yrs Closed Dec–Jan ⊛

KILLORGLIN   MAP 01 A2

Premier Collection

★★★★★ ⊛ GUEST HOUSE
Carrig House Country House & Restaurant
Caragh Lake
☎ 066 9769100 ▤ 066 9769166
e-mail: info@carrighouse.com

A warm and friendly atmosphere combines with a range of relaxing lounges to make a visit to Carrig House a truly memorable event. The house is in excellent condition, nestled among well-kept gardens by the shore of the lake. The spacious bedrooms are all individually decorated and many have superb views of the lake, as does the dining room, where delicious evening meals are available. The hospitality shown by hosts Mary and Frank and their team is outstanding.

Rooms 16 en suite **Facilities** Direct dial from bedrooms Licensed Cen ht TVL Dinner Last d 9.15pm Fishing ⤚ **Parking** 20 **Notes** No children 8yrs No coaches Closed Oct–Feb

★★★★ GUEST HOUSE
Grove Lodge
Killarney Rd
☎ 066 9761157 & 08720 73238 ▤ 066 9762330
e-mail: info@grovelodge.com

dir: *800mtrs from Killorglin Bridge on N72 Killarney road*

A lovely riverside house extended and developed to a high standard, with all the rooms en suite and fully equipped. Mrs Foley is an enthusiastic host who likes to please her guests and for those who just want to relax there is a patio seating area in the garden by the river.

Rooms 10 en suite (4 fmly) (4 GF) **Facilities** STV TVB tea/coffee Direct dial from bedrooms Cen ht Fishing **Parking** 15 **Notes** ⊗ Closed 22–30 Dec

★★★ FARM HOUSE
Dromin Farmhouse *(V 806902)*
Milltown Post Office
☎ 066 9761867 Mrs M Foley
e-mail: drominfarmhouse@yahoo.com

dir: *3km from Killorglin and Milltown. Off N70 1km from Killorglin at sign after factory, continue 2km*

Set on a sheep and cattle farm with fantastic mountain views, this elevated bungalow is near to local beaches, golf, fishing and horse riding. A television lounge is available and babysitting can be arranged. The interesting High Tea menu includes local seafood. Reservations are appreciated.

Rooms 4 en suite (2 fmly) (4 GF) **Facilities** TVB tea/coffee Cen ht TVL Dinner Last d noon **Parking** 10 **Notes** ⊗ 42 acres dairy sheep Closed Nov–16 Mar

★★★ FARM HOUSE
Hillview Farmhouse *(V 800908)*
☎ 066 9767117 ▤ 066 9767910 Ms D Stephens
e-mail: dstephens@eircom.net

dir: *On N70 between Killorgin and Milltown*

This working dairy and sheep farmhouse is a good base for touring Dingle and the Ring of Kerry. There are comfortable bedrooms, a cosy lounge, and a dining room where Dorothea Stephens' home baking is a speciality.

Rooms 4 en suite (3 fmly) (2 GF) **Facilities** Cen ht TVL **Parking** 8 **Notes** ⊗ 100 acres Mixed Closed Nov–Feb

★★★ BED & BREAKFAST
O'Regan's Country Home & Gardens
Bansha
☎ 066 9761200 ▤ 066 9761200
e-mail: jeromeoregan@eircom.net

dir: *1.6km from Killorglin on N70, turn right, beside Killorglin golf club*

This dormer bungalow is set in colourful-award-winning gardens just off the N70, adjacent to Killorglin Golf Club. The bedrooms are comfortable, there is an inviting breakfast room, and the lounge overlooks the beautiful garden.

Rooms 4 en suite (1 fmly) **Facilities** TVB tea/coffee Cen ht TVL Last d noon **Parking** 8 **Notes** ⊗ Closed Nov–Feb ⊛

IRELAND

TRALEE   MAP 01 A2

★★★★ BED & BREAKFAST
Brianville
Clogherbrien, Fenit Rd
☎ 066 7126645 📄 066 7126645
e–mail: michsmit@gofree.indigo.ie
web: www.brianville-tralee.com
dir: *R558 Tralee-Fenit road, 2km from Tralee*

This welcoming large yellow bungalow, situated on the road to Fenit on the outskirts of Tralee, is within easy reach of beaches, golf and the Aqua Dome. Bedrooms vary in size and are attractively furnished with hand-crafted pine. Breakfast is served in the bright sitting/dining room overlooking the well-tended garden.

Rooms 5 en suite (1 fmly) **Facilities** STV TVB tea/coffee Cen ht TVL **Parking** 10 **Notes** ⊗ @

★★★ GUEST HOUSE
Tralee Townhouse
1–2 High St
☎ 066 7181111 📄 066 7181112
e–mail: traleetownhouse@eircom.net
dir: *In town*

Located in the town centre, close to pubs, restaurants and Splash World, this friendly guest house offers well-equipped bedrooms with a lift to all floors. Guests can relax in the comfortable lounge and Eleanor Collins serves a variety of breakfast dishes and home baked breads.

Rooms 19 en suite (2 fmly) (9 smoking) **Facilities** STV FTV TVB tea/coffee Direct dial from bedrooms Lift Cen ht TVL Wi-fi available **Notes** ⊗ Closed 24–28 Dec

CO KILDARE

ATHY   MAP 01 C3

Premier Collection

★★★★★ BED & BREAKFAST
Coursetown Country House
Stradbally Rd
☎ 059 8631101 📄 059 8632740
e–mail: coursetown@hotmail.com
dir: *3km from Athy. N78 at Athy onto R428*

This charming Victorian country house stands on a 100-hectare tillage farm and bird sanctuary. It has been extensively refurbished, and all bedrooms are furnished to the highest standards. Convalescent or disabled guests are especially welcome, and Iris and Jim Fox are happy to share their knowledge of the Irish countryside and its wildlife.

Rooms 5 en suite (1 GF) **Facilities** TVB tea/coffee Direct dial from bedrooms Cen ht TVL **Parking** 22 **Notes** No children 12yrs Closed 15 Nov–15 Mar

CO KILKENNY

KILKENNY   MAP 01 C3

★★★★ GUEST HOUSE
Butler House
Patrick St
☎ 056 7765707 & 7722828 📄 056 7765626
e–mail: res@butler.ie
web: www.butler.ie
dir: *In centre near Kilkenny Castle*

Once the dower house of Kilkenny Castle, this fine Georgian building fronts onto the main street with secluded gardens at the rear, through which you stroll to have full breakfast in Kilkenny Design Centre. A continental breakfast is served in bedrooms, which feature contemporary décor. There is a comfortable foyer lounge and conference-banqueting suites.

Rooms 13 en suite (4 fmly) S €80–€155; D €120–€250✳ **Facilities** STV TVB tea/coffee Direct dial from bedrooms Cen ht Dinner Last d 10pm Wi-fi available **Conf** Max 120 Thtr 120 Class 40 Board 40 **Parking** 24 **Notes** LB ⊗ No coaches Closed 24–29 Dec Civ Wed 70

IRELAND

KILKENNY CONTINUED

★★★★ GUEST HOUSE
Rosquil House
Castlecomer Rd
☎ 056 7721419 📠 056 7750398
e–mail: info@rosquilhouse.com

dir: *From N77, 1km from rail & bus staions, near Newpark Hotel*
Newly built and furnished with great attention to detail and guest comfort in mind, Rosquil House is situated just a few minutes from the centre of Kilkenny. Bedrooms make good use of space with quality furnishings, as do the guest sitting room and breakfast room. Breakfast is a real treat with a choice of hot dishes complimented by Rhoda Nolan's home baking. Ample off-street parking available.

Rooms 7 en suite (1 fmly) (3 GF) **Facilities** STV TVB tea/coffee Direct dial from bedrooms Licensed Cen ht **Parking** 10 **Notes** ⊗ Closed 23–29 Dec

CO LAOIS

PORTLAOISE   MAP 01 C3

★★★ BED & BREAKFAST
O'Sullivan
8 Kelly Ville Park
☎ 0502 22774 📠 0502 80863

dir: *In town centre opp County Hall car park*
This family-run semi-detached house on the edge of the town offers a homely atmosphere. The en suite bedrooms are comfortable and secure parking is available.

Rooms 5 en suite (1 fmly) (2 GF) S €70; D €96✳ **Facilities** STV TVB Cen ht TVL **Parking** 8 **Notes LB** ⊗ Closed 21 Dec–1 Jan

CO LIMERICK

ADARE   MAP 01 B3

★★★★ BED & BREAKFAST
Berkeley Lodge
Station Rd
☎ 061 396857 📠 061 396857
e–mail: berlodge@iol.ie

dir: *In village centre*
Situated just off the main street of this pretty village, Berkeley Lodge offers comfortable, well equipped and carefully decorated accommodation. The lounge leads on to an attractive conservatory-style breakfast room, which offers an extensive menu.

Rooms 6 en suite (2 fmly) (1 GF) **Facilities** TVB tea/coffee Cen ht TVL **Parking** 6 **Notes** ⊗

★★★★ BED & BREAKFAST
Carrigane House
Rienroe
☎ 061 396778
e–mail: carrigane.house@oceanfree.net

dir: *Off N21 rdbt 0.4km NE of Adare onto Croom road, 2nd house on right*
Guests can be assured of a warm welcome at this purpose-built house situated close to the pretty village of Adare. There is a lovely colourful garden and a relaxing lounge, while breakfast is a particular treat. Bedrooms are attractively decorated, and one is on the ground floor. Ample parking is available.

Rooms 6 en suite (3 fmly) (1 GF) **Facilities** TVB tea/coffee Cen ht TVL **Parking** 10 **Notes** ⊗ Closed 15 Dec–10 Jan 🍴

GLIN   MAP 01 B3

Premier Collection

★★★★★ 🍴 GUEST ACCOMMODATION
Glin Castle
☎ 068 34173 & 34112 📠 068 34364
e–mail: knight@iol.ie
web: www.glincastle.com

dir: *Up Glin village Main St & 1st right*

Glin Castle was built in the 18th century and stands in a 202-hectare estate with formal gardens overlooking the Shannon estuary. The Knight of Glin has a famous collection of Irish prints and antiques, which furnish the elaborate reception rooms and sumptuous bedrooms. Family portraits hang in the dining room, and the dinner menu includes fruit and vegetables from the walled garden and quality local produce.

Rooms 15 en suite S €310–€495; D €310–€495✳ **Facilities** STV FTV TVB Direct dial from bedrooms Cen ht TVL Dinner Last d 9.30pm 🍴 **Conf** Max 20 Thtr 20 Class 20 Board 20 **Parking** 20 **Notes LB** No children 10yrs Closed 30 Nov–1 Mar

KILMALLOCK — MAP 01 B2

Premier Collection

★★★★★ FARM HOUSE
Flemingstown House *(R 629255)*
☎ 063 98093 📄 063 98546 Mrs I Sheedy-King
e–mail: info@flemingstown.com

dir: *On R512 Kilmallock-Fermoy route*
A lovely 18th-century farmhouse, which has been modernised to provide stylish facilities throughout. Public rooms include a comfortably furnished sitting room with antiques. At breakfast, Imelda's home baking and local produce are on offer in the delightful dining room overlooking the garden. Dinner is available by arrangement. The area is excellent for walkers, horse riders, hunting, anglers and golfers.

Rooms 5 en suite (2 fmly) S €65–€70; D €120✱ **Facilities** TVB tea/coffee Cen ht Dinner Last d noon Riding **Parking** 20 **Notes** No children 8yrs 120 acres Beef Closed Nov–Feb

LIMERICK — MAP 01 B3

★★★ GUEST HOUSE
Clifton House
Ennis Rd
☎ 061 451166 📄 061 451224
e–mail: cliftonhouse@eircom.net

dir: *On N18 towards Shannon Airport, opp Woodfield House Hotel*
Providing well-equipped, attractive and very comfortable bedrooms has been the aim of the refurbishment of Michael and Mary Powell's guest house. Complimentary tea and coffee are available in the spacious, relaxing lounge.

Rooms 16 en suite S €55; D €80–€90✱ **Facilities** STV TVB Direct dial from bedrooms Cen ht TVL **Parking** 22 **Notes** ⊗ Closed 21 Dec–2 Jan

CO LONGFORD

LONGFORD — MAP 01 C4

★★★★ BED & BREAKFAST
Longford Country House
Ennybegs
☎ 043 23320 📄 043 23516
e–mail: info@longfordcountryhouse.com
web: www.longfordcountryhouse.com

dir: *3rd exit off 2nd rdbt on N4 Longford bypass, 5km, left at x-rds after Old Forge pub, 2nd house on right*
A hospitable, Tudor-style house. The parlour has a wrought-iron spiral stairway to the library loft, as well as a cosy sitting room with turf fire and a dining room where dinner is served by arrangement. Other facilities include a games room and pitch and putt. Self-catering cottages are also available.

Rooms 6 rms (5 en suite) (2 fmly) **Facilities** FTV TVB tea/coffee Cen ht TVL Dinner Last d noon Pitch & putt course Games room Aromatherapy **Parking** 20 **Notes** ⊗ RS Nov–Mar (open by arrangement only)

CO LOUTH

CARLINGFORD — MAP 01 D4

Premier Collection

★★★★★ GUEST HOUSE
Beaufort House
Ghan Rd
☎ 042 9373879 📄 042 9373878
e–mail: michaelcaine@beauforthouse.net
web: www.beauforthouse.net

dir: *On shore of Carlingford Lough, S of East Pier of harbour*
Situated in a pretty village on Carlingford Lough, this charming guest house has spacious, well-equipped bedrooms and comfortable public rooms. An interesting breakfast menu includes fresh fish as well as traditional fare and home baking. Dinner is available for large parties by arrangement.

Rooms 5 en suite (2 fmly) (1 GF) **Facilities** TVB tea/coffee Direct dial from bedrooms Cen ht TVL Dinner Last d 8pm ⌁ Yacht charter and sailing school **Conf** Max 20 Board 20 **Parking** 20 **Notes** ⊗ No coaches

DUNDALK — MAP 01 D4

★★★★ GUEST ACCOMMODATION
Rosemount
Dublin Rd
☎ 042 9335878 📄 042 9335878
e–mail: maisieb7@eircom.net

dir: *On N1 2km S of Dundalk*
This handsome bungalow stands in beautiful gardens on the southern outskirts of the town close to Dundalk IT College. The nicely furnished bedrooms are attractively decorated and have many thoughtful extras. There is also a comfortable lounge and ample parking.

Rooms 6 annexe en suite (4 fmly) (6 GF) S €50; D €70✱ **Facilities** TVB tea/coffee Cen ht TVL **Parking** 8 **Notes** LB ⊛

CO MAYO

ACHILL ISLAND — MAP 01 A4

★★★★ GUEST HOUSE
Gray's
Dugort
☎ 098 43244 & 43315

dir: *11km NW of Achill Sound. Off R319 to Doogort*
This welcoming guest house is in Doogort, on the northern shore of Achill Island, at the foot of the Slievemore mountains. There is a smart conservatory and various lounges, the cosy bedrooms are well appointed, and dinner is served nightly by arrangement in the cheerful dining room. A self-contained villa, ideal for families, is also available.

Rooms 5 en suite 10 annexe en suite (4 fmly) (2 GF) S €55–€61; D €110 **Facilities** TVB tea/coffee Licensed Cen ht TVL Dinner Last d 6pm Pool Table ⌁ **Parking** 30 **Notes** Closed Oct–Feb ⊛

ACHILL ISLAND CONTINUED

★★★ GUEST ACCOMMODATION
Lavelle's Seaside House

Dooega

☎ 098 45116 & 01 2828142

e-mail: celialavelle@eircom.net

web: www.lavellesseasidehouse.com

dir: *R319 NW from Achill Sound, 4km turn left to Dooega*

Friendliness and good food are offered at this comfortable guest house close to the beach. Facilities include a lounge, breakfast room, and a traditional pub where seafood is available during the high season. The more-spacious bedrooms are in the new wing.

Rooms 14 en suite (5 fmly) **Facilities** tea/coffee Cen ht TVL Dinner Last d 4.30pm **Parking** 20 **Notes** ⊗ Closed 2 Nov–mid Mar RS Dinner served Jul/Aug only

---

CASTLEBAR   MAP 01 B4

★★★ GUEST ACCOMMODATION
Lough Lannagh Lodge

Old Westport Rd

☎ 094 902 7111 📄 094 902 7295

e-mail: llv@eircom.net

web: www.loughlannagh.ie

dir: *N5 around Castlebar. 3rd rdbt, 2nd exit. Next left, past playground 1st building on right*

Lough Lannagh is in a delightful wooded area within walking distance of Castlebar. There is a conference centre, fitness centre, tennis, table tennis, laundry and drying facilities, a private kitchen, and many activities for children. Bedrooms are well appointed and breakfast is served in the café. Dinner is available by appointment for groups.

Rooms 24 en suite (24 fmly) (12 GF) S €60; D €94 **Facilities** FTV TVB Direct dial from bedrooms Cen ht TVL Dinner Wi-fi available ॐ Sauna Gymnasium Steam room, table tennis, child activities Jul–Aug **Conf** Max 100 Thtr 100 Class 54 Board 34 **Parking** 24 **Notes LB** ⊗ Closed 9 Dec–11 Jan

---

WESTPORT   MAP 01 B4

★★★★ BED & BREAKFAST
Carrabaun House

Carrabaun, Leenane Rd

☎ 098 26196 📄 098 28466

e-mail: carrabaun@anu.ie

dir: *On N59 S. Leave Westport town, 1.6km pass Maxol station on left, house 200mtrs*

This elevated house has stunning views of Croagh Patrick and Clew Bay, situated on the outskirts of Westport town. The Gavin family are friendly hosts and serve a hearty breakfast. Bedrooms are attractively furnished and there is a comfortable guest sitting room and dining room. There is private parking, and lovely gardens surround the house.

Rooms 6 en suite (6 fmly) (1 GF) **Facilities** TVB tea/coffee Cen ht TVL **Parking** 12 **Notes** ⊗ Closed 16–31 Dec

★★★ FARM HOUSE
Bertra House *(L 903823)*

Thornhill, Murrisk

☎ 098 64833 📄 098 64833 Mrs M Gill

e-mail: bertrahse@eircom.net

dir: *W of Wesport off R335 near Croagh Patrick on L1833*

This attractive bungalow overlooks the Blue Flag Bertra beach. Four bedrooms are en suite and the fifth has its own bathroom. Breakfast is generous and Mrs Gill offers tea and home-baked cakes on arrival in the cosy lounge.

CONTINUED

CONTINUED

IRELAND

Rooms 5 rms (4 en suite) (3 fmly) (5 GF) S €51; D €76✳
Facilities FTV TVB tea/coffee Cen ht TVL **Parking** 7 **Notes** LB ⊗
40 acres beef Closed 15 Nov –15 Mar

CO MEATH

NAVAN
MAP 01 C4

★★★★ GUEST ACCOMMODATION
Killyon
Dublin Rd
☎ 046 907 1224 📠 046 907 2766
e–mail: info@killyonguesthouse.ie

dir: *On N3, River Boyne side, opp Ardboyne Hotel*
This luxurious house has fine views over the River Boyne from its
balcony. Comfortable, well-appointed bedrooms and an inviting
attractive lounge make this a popular place to stay. Owner Mrs Fogarty
offers a wide range of home cooking.

Rooms 6 en suite (1 fmly) (1 GF) S €45–€60; D €70–€80✳
Facilities STV TVB Direct dial from bedrooms Cen ht TVL Wi-fi available
Fishing **Parking** 10 **Notes** ⊗ Closed 23–25 Dec

★★★ BED & BREAKFAST
The Yellow House
Springfield Glen, Dublin Rd
☎ 046 9073338
e–mail: info@theyellowhouse.ie

dir: *N3 from Dublin, left at 2nd lights on approach to Navan*
Located on the southern approach to the town, this friendly house is
popular with return guests. It offers well-appointed rooms and a
comfortable lounge reserved for residents. A number of choices are
available at breakfast, and off-road parking is provided in mature
gardens.

Rooms 4 rms (3 en suite) (1 pri facs) (2 fmly) **Facilities** FTV TVB tea/
coffee Cen ht TVL Wi-fi available **Parking** 12 **Notes** ⊗

TRIM
MAP 01 C4

★★★ GUEST HOUSE
Brogans
High St
☎ 046 943 1237 📠 046 943 7648
e–mail: info@brogans.ie
web: www.brogans.ie

dir: *Leave M50 junct 6 at rdbt 1st exit to Blanchardstown, N3 rdbt
2nd exit, turn 1st left, & left again onto R154. Continue to High St*
Brogans is situated in the designated heritage town of Trim. It was built
nearly two centuries ago using much of the original stone from Trim
Castle. The bedrooms in the main house have been refurbished with
new rooms in the court yard, they are all very comfortable and
furnished to a high standard. There is a cosy traditional bar, and dinner
is available nightly in the smart Beacon Restaurant and bar. This guest
house is convenient to New Grange, The Hill of Tara and many
championship golf courses

CONTINUED

Rooms 18 en suite (3 fmly) (4 GF) **Facilities** STV TVB tea/coffee Direct
dial from bedrooms Licensed Cen ht TVL Dinner Last d 9.30pm
Conf Max 35 Thtr 35 Class 35 Board 35 **Notes** ⊗ Closed Good Fri &
25 Dec

CO ROSCOMMON

ROSCOMMON
MAP 01 B4

★★★ RESTAURANT WITH ROOMS
Gleesons Townhouse & Restaurant
Market Square
☎ 090 6626954 📠 090 6627425
e–mail: info@gleesonstownhouse.com

dir: *in town centre next to tourist office*
This 19th-century cut-limestone town house has been very tastefully
restored. The bedrooms and suites are decorated and furnished to a
high standard. Dinner is served nightly in the Manse Restaurant and
there is an extensive lunch and afternoon tea menu in the café or in
the beautifully landscaped front courtyard. Conference facilities and
secure car parking are available.

Rooms 19 rms (17 en suite) (2 pri facs) (1 fmly) **Facilities** STV FTV TVB
tea/coffee Direct dial from bedrooms Lift Cen ht TVL Dinner Last d
8.45pm Wi-fi available **Conf** Thtr 80 Class 40 Board 30 **Parking** 25
Notes Closed 25–26 Dec

CO SLIGO

ACLARE
MAP 01 B4

★★★ BED & BREAKFAST
Haggart Lodge
Lislea
☎ 071 9181954
e–mail: mleheny@eircom.net

Maeve Leheny welcomes guests to her comfortable home overlooking
the Ox Mountains in west Sligo, near the Mayo border. Traditional
country-cooked dinners are available if booked before midday, and
home baking is a feature of breakfast. This is a pet friendly property,
where resident dogs Tyke and Tyra will vacate their kennels if required.
There are stables available nearby.

Rooms 4 rms (3 en suite) S €45–€51 **Facilities** TVB Cen ht TVL
Dinner Last d 1pm Wi-fi available **Parking** 12 **Notes** LB

BALLINTOGHER MAP 01 B5

★★★★ GUEST HOUSE
Kingsfort Country House
☎ 071 911 5111
e-mail: bernard@kingsfortcountryhouse.com
dir: *From Collooney onto Ballygawley (8km), follow signs*
This charming guest house is situated in the village of Ballintogher south of Sligo town. Built in 1790 as a court house, it has been magnificently restored and decorated in an understated rustic style providing all modern comforts. Two of the bedrooms are in the main house, and six, including one adapted for the less able, are in the courtyard building. There is a sitting room and TV lounge for guests, and dinner is available by prior arrangement.
Rooms 2 en suite 6 annexe en suite (1 fmly) (3 GF) S €95–€105; D €170–€210✱ **Facilities** Direct dial from bedrooms Cen ht TVL Dinner **Parking** 10 **Notes** Closed Nov–Mar

BALLYMOTE MAP 01 B4

★★★★ BED & BREAKFAST
Church View
Main St, Gurteen
☎ 071 9182935
e-mail: info@thechurchview.com
dir: *From Ballymote at x-rds head towards Gurteen, on left beside church*
Located in the centre of Gurteen village, a half hour's drive from Knock airport, this architect designed townhouse is home to Jacci Conlon and her family. Bedrooms are spacious and individually decorated. A wide selection of breakfast options is available, served in the smart dining room.
Rooms 5 en suite (2 fmly) (1 GF) S €40–€46; D €70–€72✱ **Facilities** STV TVB tea/coffee Cen ht TVL Wi-fi available **Parking** 5 **Notes** ⊗

BALLYSADARE MAP 01 B5

★★★ BED & BREAKFAST
Seashore House
Lisduff
☎ 071 916 7827 📠 071 916 7827
e-mail: seashore@oceanfree.net
dir: *N4 onto N59 W at Ballisadore, 4km Seashore signed, 0.6km right to house*
An attractive dormer bungalow in a quiet seashore location. A comfortable lounge with open turf fire and sunny conservatory dining room looking out over attractive landscaped gardens to sea and mountain scenery. Bedrooms are attractively appointed and comfortable, and there is also a tennis court and bicycle storage.
Rooms 5 rms (4 en suite) (2 fmly) (3 GF) S €50–€55; D €76–€80✱ **Facilities** STV TVB Cen ht TVL ⌁ Solarium **Parking** 6 **Notes** LB ⊗ No children

DRUMCLIFFE MAP 01 B5

★★★ BED & BREAKFAST
Willsborough House B&B
Cullaghbeg
☎ 071 9173526
e-mail: willsboroughhouse@eircom.net
dir: *7km on N15 from Sligo, after restaurant on left, take 2nd on right*
This attractive house is tucked under Ben Bulben just off the N15 between Drumcliffe and Sligo town and within walking distance of Davis's pub and restaurant. The bedrooms are well appointed and suitable for families. Fiona and Anthony produce a fine breakfast with local produce and home baking a feature. Cycle routes, bike hire and horse riding near by.
Rooms 3 en suite (2 fmly) S €40; D €66✱ **Facilities** TVB tea/coffee Cen ht Bicycle hire, Dog boarding kennels **Parking** 4 **Notes** ⊗ 🐾

INISHCRONE MAP 01 B5

Premier Collection

★★★★★ BED & BREAKFAST
Seasons Lodge
Bartragh
☎ 096 37122
e-mail: dermot@seasonslodge.ie
web: www.seasonslodge.ie
dir: *Beside Enniscrone Golf Club*
This modern guest house is next to Enniscrone Golf Course and close to the famous seaweed baths and a lovely beach. The spacious bedrooms are fitted to a high standard, are all on the ground floor and have access to the garden. There is a relaxing sitting and dining room where breakfast is served. Proprietor Dermot O'Regan is happy to arrange golf or tours.
Rooms 4 en suite (2 fmly) (4 GF) **Facilities** STV TVB Direct dial from bedrooms Cen ht TVL **Parking** 10 **Notes** ⊗ No children 8yrs Closed Dec–Jan

SLIGO MAP 01 B5

★★★ BED & BREAKFAST
Aisling
Cairns Hill
☎ 071 916 0704 📠 071 916 0704
e-mail: aislingsligo@eircom.net
dir: *N4 to Sligo, right at 1st lights, S from Sligo past Esso fuel station, left at lights*
This delightful home of Des and Nan Faul has a beautiful garden and is conveniently situated on the southern end of the town and close to Sligo race course. Bedrooms are comfortably furnished and there is a cosy sitting and dining room for guests to relax and enjoy mountain views.
Rooms 5 rms (3 en suite) (2 fmly) (5 GF) **Facilities** STV TVB Cen ht TVL **Parking** 6 **Notes** ⊗ No children 6yrs Closed 24–28 Dec

TOBERCURRY   MAP 01 B4

★★★ BED & BREAKFAST
Cruckawn House
Ballymote/Boyle Rd
☎ 071 918 5188 📄 071 918 5188
e–mail: cruckawn@esatclear.ie

dir: *300mtrs off N17 on R294, on right, overlooking golf course*
Overlooking the golf course, just a short walk from the town centre,
Cruckawn House offers friendly hospitality. The dining room adjoins
the comfortable sun lounge, and there is also a television lounge.
Salmon and coarse fishing, horse riding and mountain climbing are all
available nearby and the area is renowned for traditional Irish music.

Rooms 5 en suite (2 fmly) **Facilities** TVB Cen ht TVL Dinner Last d
6pm Golf 9 Gymnasium Pool Table ⅃ Game & coarse fishing, bike hire
Parking 8 **Notes** ⊗ Closed Nov–Feb

CO TIPPERARY

BALLYKISTEEN   MAP 01 B3

★★★★ BED & BREAKFAST
Ballykisteen Lodge B&B
☎ 062 33403 📄 062 33711
e–mail: ballykisteenlodge@oceanfree.net
web: www.ballykisteenlodgebandb.net

dir: *3km from Tipperary on N24 opp Tipperary Racecourse*
This well-presented guesthouse is situated across from the Tipperary
racecourse and beside the Ballykisteen Golf Centre. There are attractive
bedrooms and a sitting room. Breakfast features home baking and a
variety of freshly cooked dishes, and is served in the cosy dining room
that looks over a delightful garden.

Rooms 4 en suite (3 fmly) **Facilities** TVB tea/coffee Cen ht TVL
Parking 10 **Notes** ⊗

CASHEL   MAP 01 C3

★★★★ BED & BREAKFAST
Ard Ri House
Dualla Rd
☎ 062 63143 📄 062 63037
e–mail: donalcreed@eircom.net

dir: *Turn 1st right after Information Office onto R688, turn left
after church onto R691, 1km on right*
A warm welcome awaits you at this non-smoking house, only a short
distance from the town on the Kilkenny Road. All of the bedrooms are
comfortably furnished with thoughtful extras, and are on the ground
floor. The breakfast served by Eileen features locally sourced
ingredients from a varied menu. Facilities are available for children.

Rooms 4 en suite (1 fmly) (4 GF) D €66–€76 **Facilities** TVB tea/coffee
Cen ht TVL Wi-fi available **Parking** 8 **Notes** Closed Nov–Feb

★★★★ GUEST HOUSE
Aulber House
Golden Rd
☎ 062 63713 & 087 6314720 📄 062 63715
e–mail: beralley@eircom.net
web: www.aulberhouse.com

dir: *From Cashel on N74. Last house on left*
A newly-built guest house, set in landscaped gardens just a 5-minute
walk from the Rock of Cashel and town centre. Spacious bedrooms are
thoughtfully furnished and equipped, and include one fitted for the
less mobile. Relax by the open fire in the sitting room, or enjoy views
of the surrounding countryside and the Rock from the first-floor
lounge.

Rooms 12 en suite (2 fmly) (3 GF) S €50–€80; D €80–€120✱
Facilities TVB tea/coffee Direct dial from bedrooms Cen ht TVL Wi-fi
available **Parking** 20 **Notes** ⊗ Closed 23 Dec–23 Jan

★★★★ BED & BREAKFAST
Thornbrook House
Dualla Rd
☎ 062 62388 📄 062 61480
e–mail: thornbrookhouse@eircom.net
web: www.thornbrookhouse.com

dir: *1st right after tourist office onto Friar St, left after church onto
R691, house 1km on right*
Visitors to Thornbrook will relish the combined skills of the Kennedys.
Mary runs this attractively appointed bungalow with great attention to
detail, while the superbly landscaped gardens are the handiwork of
Willie Kennedy. Comfortable lounge and bedrooms, ample parking.

Rooms 5 rms (3 en suite) (1 fmly) (5 GF) S €50–€60; D €70–€80
Facilities TVB tea/coffee Cen ht Wi-fi available **Parking** 8 **Notes** ⊗
No children 4yrs Closed Nov–Mar

★★★ BED & BREAKFAST
Ashmore House
John St
☎ 062 61286 📄 062 62789
e–mail: info@ashmorehouse.ie

dir: *Off N8 in town centre onto John St, house 100mtrs on right*
Ashmore House is set in a pretty walled garden in the town centre with
an enclosed car park. Guests have use of a large sitting and dining
room, and bedrooms come in a variety of sizes from big family rooms
to a more compact double.

Rooms 5 en suite (2 fmly) S €55–€70; D €70–€90✱ **Facilities** STV
TVB tea/coffee Cen ht TVL Dinner Last d 24hrs notice **Parking** 10
Notes ⊗

IRELAND

747

NENAGH — MAP 01 B3

★★★★ BED & BREAKFAST
Ashley Park House
☎ 067 38223 & 38013 📄 067 38013
e–mail: margaret@ashleypark.com
web: www.ashleypark.com
dir: *6.5km N of Nenagh. Off N52 across lake, signed on left & left under arch*

The attractive, colonial style farmhouse was built in 1770. Set in gardens that run down to Lake Ourna, it has spacious bedrooms with quality antique furnishings. Breakfast is served in the dining room overlooking the lake, and dinner is available by arrangement. There is a delightful walled garden, and a boat for the fishing on the lake is available.

Rooms 5 en suite (3 fmly) **Facilities** TVB tea/coffee Cen ht TVL Dinner Last d 9pm Wi-fi available Golf 18 Fishing Rowing boat on lake **Conf** Max 30 Board 30 **Parking** 30 **Notes** 🐾

THURLES — MAP 01 C3

★★★★★ 🍽 GUEST HOUSE
Inch House Country House & Restaurant
☎ 0504 51348 & 51261 📄 0504 51754
e–mail: mairin@inchhouse.ie
dir: *6.5km NE of Thurles on R498*

This lovely Georgian house was built in 1720 and the Egan family has restored the property. The elegant drawing room ceiling is particularly outstanding among the grand public rooms, and the spacious bedrooms are delightfully appointed. Reservations are essential in the fine restaurant, where an imaginative choice of freshly prepared dishes using local produce is on offer.

Rooms 5 en suite (1 fmly) S fr €75; D fr €130✳ **Facilities** TVB tea/coffee Direct dial from bedrooms Licensed Cen ht TVL Dinner Last d 9.30pm Wi-fi available **Parking** 40 **Notes** 🐾 No children Closed Xmas & Etr RS Sun & Mon

---

★★★★★ BED & BREAKFAST
The Castle
Twomileborris
☎ 0504 44324 📄 0504 44352
e–mail: b&b@thecastletmb.com
dir: *7km E of Thurles. On N75 200mtrs W of Twomileborris at Castle*

Pierce and Joan are very welcoming hosts. Their fascinating house, sheltered by a 16th-century tower house, has been in the Duggan family for 200 years. Bedrooms are comfortable and spacious, there is a relaxing lounge, and the dining room overlooks the delightful garden. Golf, fishing, hill walking, and traditional pubs and restaurants are all nearby. Dinner is available by arrangement.

Rooms 4 en suite (3 fmly) S €50–€70; D €80–€120✳ **Facilities** STV FTV TVB tea/coffee Cen ht TVL Dinner Last d 11am Wi-fi available 🐾 Fishing Pool Table ⚲ **Conf** Max 40 Board 20 **Parking** 30 **Notes** LB 🐾

TIPPERARY — MAP 01 C3

★★★ GUEST HOUSE
Ach-na-Sheen House
Clonmel Rd
☎ 062 51298 📄 062 80467
e–mail: gernoonan@eircom.net
dir: *In town centre*

This large, modern bungalow is set in a lovely garden and only five minutes walk from the main street of Tipperary town on the N24 road. Public areas include a guest sitting room and dining room and bedrooms are well appointed. There is good off-street parking.

Rooms 8 en suite (5 fmly) (6 GF) S €60; D €90✳ **Facilities** STV TVB tea/coffee Cen ht **Parking** 13 **Notes** 🐾 Closed 11 Dec–8 Jan

IRELAND

★★★ BED & BREAKFAST
Aisling
Glen of Aherlow
☎ 087 2278230 📠 062 82955
e–mail: ladygreg@oceanfree.net

dir: *In town, take R664 at T-lights at Main St*

Aisling is situated 3kms from Tipperary town on the R664 Glen of Aherlow road and close to the train station and Tipperary Golf club. Bedrooms are well furnished and attractively decorated. There is a comfortable guest sitting room and a delightful garden with patio seating. Marian and Bob will arrange day trips and have maps and good information on the locality.

Rooms 5 rms (4 en suite) (1 pri facs) (2 fmly) (5 GF) (2 smoking) S €35–€45; D €80 **Facilities** FTV TVB tea/coffee Cen ht TVL Dinner Last d 3pm Wi-fi available **Parking** 4 **Notes** LB

CO WATERFORD

From the 3rd of November 2008, phone numbers in this location will have 61 added to the start of their existing number. The dialling code remains the same.

BALLYMACARBRY   MAP 01 C2

Premier Collection

★★★★★ 🍽 FARM HOUSE
Glasha Farmhouse *(S1104106)*
Glasha
☎ 052 36108 📠 052 36108 Mr & Mrs P O'Gorman
e–mail: glasha@eircom.net

dir: *Signed off R671 between Clommel & Dungarvan*

Excellent accommodation and a warm welcome are assured at this comfortable country house. Two of the bedrooms are on the ground floor and all rooms are individually styled with smart furnishings and lots of personal touches. Home-cooking is a speciality and trout fishing is available on the river which runs through the grounds.

Rooms 8 en suite (5 fmly) (2 GF) **Facilities** TVB tea/coffee Cen ht TVL Dinner Last d 5.30pm Fishing **Parking** 10 **Notes** ⊛ 150 acres dairy Closed 20–27 Dec

Premier Collection

★★★★★ GUEST HOUSE
Hanoras Cottage
Nire Valley
☎ 052 36134 & 36442 📠 052 36540
e–mail: hanorascottage@eircom.net

dir: *From Clonmel or Dungarvan R67 to Ballymacarbry, at Melodys Bar turn into Nire Valley, establishment by bridge beside church*

Located in the beautiful Nire Valley, Hanoras Cottage offers spacious bedrooms with Jacuzzis. Lounge areas are very comfortable and the award-winning restaurant serves fresh local produce. Mrs Wall's breakfasts are a real feast and deserve to be savoured at leisure.

CONTINUED

Rooms 10 en suite S €100; D €190–€250 **Facilities** TVB tea/coffee Direct dial from bedrooms Licensed Cen ht TVL Dinner Last d 9pm **Parking** 15 **Notes** LB ⊛ No children No coaches Closed Xmas wk RS Sun

See advert on this page

DUNGARVAN   MAP 01 C2

Premier Collection

★★★★★ FARM HOUSE
Castle Country House *(S 192016)*
Millstreet, Cappagh
☎ 058 68049 Mrs J Nugent
e–mail: castlefm@iol.ie

dir: *15km off the N25 between Dungarvan and Cappoquin. House is signed on the N72 & the R671. From the N72, take R671 for 3.5m; turn right at Millstreet.*

This delightful house is in the west wing of a 15th-century castle. Guests are spoiled by host Joan Nugent who loves to cook and hunt out antiques for her visitors to enjoy. She is helped by her husband Emmett who enjoys showing off his high-tech dairy farm and is a fount of local knowledge. Bedrooms are spacious and enjoy lovely views. There is a river walk and a beautiful garden to relax in.

Rooms 5 en suite (1 fmly) S €65; D €105✳ **Facilities** FTV TVB tea/coffee Cen ht Dinner Last d 5pm Fishing Farm tour **Parking** 11 **Notes** LB 170 acres dairy & beef Closed Dec–Feb

---

Hanoras Cottage

Hanoras Cottage Country House & Restaurant is renowned for luxurious accommodation and food but most of all the hallmark of this little gem in the Comeragh Mountains is the hospitality that exudes from the Wall family and their staff, little wonder Hanoras is a national award winner of both guesthouse and breakfast of the year. Husband and wife chefs Eoin & Judith Wall are huge supporters of local produce and are delighted to cater for any special diets. Bedrooms are extremely comfortable with large bathrooms, super king-size beds and Jacuzzi, most have double tubs for that special occasion try Room 5. Enjoy the sheer bliss of an adult only house! Mid-week and weekend special offers.

IRELAND

DUNGARVAN CONTINUED

Premier Collection

★★★★★ 🏠 FARM HOUSE
Sliabh gCua Farmhouse *(S 191057)*
Touraneena, Ballinamult
☎ 058 47120 Mrs B Cullinan
e-mail: breedacullinan@sliabhgcua.com
web: www.sliabhgcua.com

dir: *From Dungarvan take R672 towards Clonmel, continue for 1km to village of Touraneena*

This creeper-clad farmhouse, set in landscaped grounds, is a sign of the warm welcome offered by the Cullinan family. Rooms are comfortably appointed, each with two views of the gardens. Breakfast is a particular delight, with bread baked each morning and a great selection of fruits.

Rooms 4 en suite (1 fmly) S €50; D €90✳ **Facilities** tea/coffee Cen ht TVL Children's Playground **Parking** 6 **Notes LB** ✪ 170 acres beef Closed Nov–Mar 🖨

★★★★ BED & BREAKFAST
Kilcannon House
Cappagh
☎ 058 68418
e-mail: kilcannonhouse@eircom.net

dir: *10km from Dungarvan, right after Cappagh post office*

A lovely old farm house with views of the Knockmealdown Mountains it is situated just off the main Rosslare/Killarney Road (N72) at Cappagh between Dungarvan and Lismore. Bedrooms are spacious and comfortable, the ground floor one has its own front door. Guests can relax by the fire in the sitting room or the delightful garden or watch the range of hens that supply eggs for the breakfast. Gertie Ormond's dinner or barbecue is a speciality and available by prior arrangement.

Rooms 2 en suite 1 annexe en suite (1 GF) S €55–€60; D €90–€100✳ **Facilities** TVB tea/coffee Cen ht TVL Dinner Last d noon Riding **Conf** Max 6 **Parking** 30 **Notes LB** No children 🖨

DUNMORE EAST · MAP 01 C2

★★★★ GUEST HOUSE
The Beach Guest House
Lower Village
☎ 051 383316 📠 051 383319
e-mail: beachouse@eircom.net

dir: *R684 from Waterford into Dunmore East, 1st left in village to sea wall, house on left*

This purpose-built guest house is family run and centrally placed facing the beach in this picturesque village. No two bedrooms are alike but all share high standards of comfort and quality with a wealth of thoughtful extras. Expect a delicious breakfast served in the conservatory-style dining room, and relax in the lounge or on the patio.

Rooms 7 en suite (1 fmly) (1 GF) S €50–€60; D €80–€100 **Facilities** TVB tea/coffee Direct dial from bedrooms Cen ht Wi-fi available **Parking** 11 **Notes LB** ✪ No children 6yrs No coaches Closed Nov–Feb

TRAMORE · MAP 01 C2

★★★★ BED & BREAKFAST
Glenorney
Newtown
☎ 051 381056 📠 051 381103
e-mail: glenoney@iol.ie

dir: *On R675 opp Tramore Golf Club*

A beautifully spacious and luxurious home with spectacular views of Tramore Bay, located opposite a championship golf course. Great attention has been paid to detail and there is an extensive breakfast menu. Bedrooms are carefully decorated and the lounge is comfortably furnished. There is also a sun room, patio and garden.

Rooms 6 en suite (2 fmly) (3 GF) **Facilities** TVB tea/coffee Direct dial from bedrooms Cen ht TVL **Parking** 6 **Notes** ✪ Closed Xmas

★★★★ BED & BREAKFAST
Cliff House
Cliff Rd
☎ 051 381497 & 391296 📠 051 381497
e-mail: hilary@cliffhouse.ie

dir: *Off R675, left at Ritz thatched pub*

This comfortable and spacious home of the O'Sullivan family is situated overlooking Tramore Bay and has beautiful gardens and a conservatory lounge where guests can relax while enjoying the breathtaking views. All bedrooms are decorated to a high standard, there are rooms with balconies and some rooms are suitable for families. The extensive breakfast menu offers many delicious choices.

Rooms 6 en suite (3 fmly) (3 GF) **Facilities** STV TVB tea/coffee Cen ht TVL **Parking** 10 **Notes** ✪ No children 6yrs Closed 20 Dec–Jan

★★★★ BED & BREAKFAST
Cloneen

Love Ln
☎ 051 381264 ▤ 051 381264
e-mail: cloneen@iol.ie

dir: *N25 onto R675 to Tramore, Majestic Hotel on right, continue up hill until road bears left, take 1st left*

This pleasant family home is situated on a quite residential area off the Coast road and within walking distance of the seaside town of Tramore. Bedrooms are stylishly furnished with guest comfort in mind, some with their own patio overlooking the garden. Three rooms are on the ground floor and there are two rooms suitable for families. Guests have use of a conservatory style sitting and separate dining room.

Rooms 5 en suite (2 fmly) S €50–€55; D €70–€80✳ **Facilities** STV TVB tea/coffee Cen ht TVL Wi-fi available **Parking** 8

WATERFORD   **MAP 01 C2**

Premier Collection
★★★★★ GUEST ACCOMMODATION
Foxmount Country House

Passage East Rd, Dunmore Rd
☎ 051 874308 ▤ 051 854906
e-mail: info@foxmountcountryhouse.com

dir: *From Waterford onto Dunmore East road, 2.5km fork left towards Passage East for 0.8km, right at next T-junct*

This charming 17th-century country house is set on a dairy farm amid beautiful lawns and colourful gardens. Carefully modernised, it offers bedrooms furnished with well-chosen antique furniture. Guests can relax in the drawing room by the fire or sit in the garden and enjoy the bird song. Margaret Kent's home baking is a special treat as is the breakfast featuring local products.

Rooms 4 en suite (1 fmly) **Facilities** Cen ht TVL 🐾 **Parking** 6 **Notes** ⊗ Closed early Nov–early Mar 🐾

Premier Collection
★★★★★ GUEST ACCOMMODATION
Sion Hill House & Gardens

Sion Hill, Ferrybank
☎ 051 851558 ▤ 051 851678
e-mail: sionhill@eircom.net

dir: *Near city centre on N25 to Rosslare*

Situated close to the city, this 18th-century residence has extensive peaceful gardens, which include a walled garden, a meadow and woodlands. Flanked by two pavilions, the house has been refurbished to provide two fine reception rooms and comfortable en suite bedrooms. The friendly owners like to mix with their guests, as the visitors' book shows.

Rooms 4 en suite (4 fmly) **Facilities** STV TVB tea/coffee Cen ht TVL **Parking** 16 **Notes** ⊗ Closed mid Dec–early Jan

★★★★ GUEST HOUSE
Diamond Hill Country House

Diamond Hill, Slieverue
☎ 051 832855 ▤ 051 832254
e-mail: info@stayatdiamondhill.com

dir: *2km from Waterford off N25 to Rosslare*

Extensive refurbishment has been carried out to a very high standard at this friendly house. These include spacious new bedrooms, comfortable lounges and a private car park. Diamond Hill is a welcoming home with lovely gardens and a sun terrace.

Rooms 17 en suite (6 fmly) (9 GF) S €40–€50; D €70–€90✳ **Facilities** STV TVB tea/coffee Direct dial from bedrooms Cen ht TVL Dinner Last d 8pm Wi-fi available **Parking** 20 **Notes** Closed 22–27 Dec

★★★ BED & BREAKFAST
Belmont House

Belmont Rd, Rosslare Rd, Ferrybank
☎ 051 832174 ▤ 051 832174
e-mail: belmonthouse@eircom.net

dir: *2km from Waterford on N25 to Rosslare road*

The dormer bungalow is convenient for the Waterford Glass Factory, golf clubs and the city centre. There are tea and coffee facilities in the sitting room and the dining room looks out across the garden to the countryside beyond. Bedrooms are comfortably furnished.

Rooms 6 rms (4 en suite) S €50–€55; D €60–€70✳ **Facilities** Cen ht TVL **Parking** 6 **Notes** ⊗ No children 7yrs Closed Nov–Apr 🐾

IRELAND

CO WESTMEATH

ATHLONE
MAP 01 C4

★★★★ BED & BREAKFAST
Shelmalier House

Cartontroy, Retreat Rd
☎ 090 647 2245 & 647 2145 📄 090 647 3190
e–mail: shelmalier@eircom.net

dir: *2km E of town centre*

Shelmalier is a modern house in a residential area, set in well-kept gardens. The décor is very attractive, and bedrooms offer good quality furnishings and facilities. There is a comfortable lounge and a breakfast room.

Rooms 7 en suite (2 fmly) (1 GF) **Facilities** STV TVB tea/coffee Direct dial from bedrooms Cen ht TVL Sauna Hot tub **Parking** 10 **Notes** ⊗ Closed 20 Dec–Jan

★★★★ ⊛ RESTAURANT WITH ROOMS
Wineport Lodge

Glasson
☎ 090 6439010 📄 090 6485471
e–mail: lodge@wineport.ie
web: www.wineport.ie

dir: *From N6 (Dublin/Galway road) take N55 north (Longford/Cavan exit) at Athlone. Left at Dog & Duck pub. Lodge 1m on left*

Set in a wonderful location right on the shores of the inner lakes of Lough Rea on the Shannon and three miles north of Athlone. Guests can arrive by road or water, dine on the deck or in the attractive dining room. Cuisine is modern with innovative use of the best of local produce. Most of the luxurious bedrooms and suites have balconies – the perfect setting for breakfast. There is a Canadian hot tub on the roof terrace.

Rooms 29 en suite (3 fmly) (15 GF) **Facilities** STV FTV TVB tea/coffee Direct dial from bedrooms Lift Dinner Wi-fi available Fishing Boat Hire Exercise Studio **Parking** 100 **Notes** ⊗

HORSELEAP
MAP 01 C4

★★★★ FARM HOUSE
Woodlands Farm House (N 286426)

Streamstown
☎ 044 26414 Mrs M Maxwell

dir: *N6 N onto R391 at Horseleap, farm signed 4km*

This very comfortable and charming farmhouse has a delightful setting on a 48-hectare farm. The spacious sitting and dining rooms are very relaxing, and there is a hospitality kitchen where tea and coffee are available at all times.

Rooms 5 rms (4 en suite) (1 pri facs) (2 fmly) (2 GF) **Facilities** Cen ht TVL Last d 5pm **Parking** available **Notes** 120 acres mixed ⊛

CO WEXFORD

BALLYHACK
MAP 01 C2

★★★★ BED & BREAKFAST
Marsh Mere Lodge

☎ 051 389186
e–mail: stay@marshmerelodge.com

dir: *R733 to Ballyhack*

This charming house, a short walk from the Ballyhack ferry, embodies relaxation and comfort. Each bedroom has an individual character and afternoon tea is served on the sunny veranda overlooking King's Bay and Waterford harbour.

Rooms 4 en suite (2 GF) S €60–€70; D €100–€110 **Facilities** Cen ht TVL **Parking** 5 **Notes LB** ⊗

CAMPILE
MAP 01 C2

Premier Collection

★★★★★ GUEST ACCOMMODATION
Kilmokea Country Manor & Gardens

Great Island
☎ 051 388109 📄 051 388776
e–mail: kilmokea@eircom.net

dir: *R733 from New Ross to Campile, right before village for Great Island & Kilmokea Gardens*

An 18th-century stone rectory, recently restored. Located in wooded gardens (open to the public), where peacocks wander and trout fishing is available on the lake. Comfortable bedrooms and public rooms are richly furnished, and a country-house style dinner is served nightly (booking essential). Take breakfast in the conservatory and tea overlooking the beautiful gardens.

Rooms 4 en suite 2 annexe en suite (1 fmly) (2 GF) S €75–€180; D €180–€300✳ **Facilities** STV TV2B tea/coffee Direct dial from bedrooms Cen ht TVL Dinner Last d 8.30pm Wi-fi available ⊗ ♨ Fishing Riding Sauna Gymnasium ⤴ **Conf** Max 75 Thtr 40 Class 30 Board 25 **Parking** 23 **Notes LB** RS Nov–end Jan

ENNISCORTHY

MAP 01 D3

★★★★ GUEST HOUSE
Lemongrove House
Blackstoops
☎ 05392 36115 📄 05392 36115
e-mail: lemongrovehouse@iolfree.ie
dir: *1km N of Enniscorthy at rdbt on N11*

A large house set on an elevated site surrounded by gardens. Lemongrove House offers en suite bedrooms which are all individually decorated in warm, cheerful colour schemes, and there is a comfortable sitting room and breakfast room. Plenty of parking.

Rooms 9 en suite (3 fmly) (5 GF) **Facilities** STV TVB tea/coffee Direct dial from bedrooms Cen ht TVL **Parking** 12 **Notes** ⊗ Closed 20–31 Dec

GOREY

MAP 01 D3

Premier Collection

★★★★★ BED & BREAKFAST
Woodlands Country House
Killinierin
☎ 0402 37125 📄 0402 37133
e-mail: info@woodlandscountryhouse.com
dir: *N11 junct 22, Arklow – Gorey bypass, sign for Gorey. Immediately after rdbt, sign for Woodlands on right*
The 1836 country house stands in extensive mature gardens with a courtyard of stone buildings. The O'Sullivan family offer warm hospitality (and home-made scones on arrival). Three rooms have balconies.

Rooms 6 en suite (3 fmly) S €70; D €110–€130✳ **Facilities** STV FTV TVB tea/coffee Cen ht TVL ♨ Pool Table **Parking** 10 **Notes** LB ⊗ Closed Oct–Mar

★★★★ BED & BREAKFAST
Hillside House
Tubberduff
☎ 053 9421726 📄 053 9422567
e-mail: hillsidehouse@eircom.net
web: www.hillsidehouse.net
dir: *N11 junct 22, take Gorey/Ballymoney Rd, & follow signs for Hillside House*

A pristine house with pretty garden set in a lovely rural location commanding panoramic views of mountains and the sea, only 3 kilometres from Ballymoney beach. Ann Sutherland is a good cook, providing guests with a variety of home baking. The reception rooms are spacious, bedrooms are very comfortable and attractively decorated.

Rooms 6 en suite (4 fmly) (4 GF) S €50–€60; D €80–€90 **Facilities** STV TVB tea/coffee Cen ht TVL Wi-fi available **Parking** 6 **Notes** LB ⊗ Closed 20–28 Dec

NEW ROSS
MAP 01 C3

★★★ BED & BREAKFAST
Woodlands House
Carrigbyrne

☎ 051 428287 📄 051 428287

e-mail: woodwex@eircom.net

dir: On N25 New Ross-Wexford route, 0.4km from Cedar Lodge Hotel towards New Ross

Commanding panoramic views, this is a recently refurbished bungalow with pretty gardens. It is only a 30-minute drive to Rosslare Harbour. Snacks are available, and dinner by arrangement. Bedrooms vary in size, though all are very comfortable. There is a guest sitting room.

Rooms 4 en suite (4 GF) **Facilities** TVB tea/coffee Cen ht Dinner Last d 10am **Parking** 6 **Notes** ⊗ No children 5yrs

ROSSLARE HARBOUR
MAP 01 D2

Premier Collection

★★★★★ 🍽 GUEST HOUSE
Churchtown House

☎ 053 913 2555 📄 053 913 2577

e-mail: info@churchtownhouse.com

dir: N25 onto R736 at Tagoat, turn between Cushens pub & church, house 0.8km on left

This charming house stands in mature grounds between Rosslare Strand and the Harbour port. Individually decorated bedrooms match the comfortable and relaxing lounge areas where hosts Patricia and Austin Cody are very welcoming. Dinner is served at 8 pm by arrangement, following sherry in the lounge.

Rooms 12 en suite (1 fmly) (5 GF) S €85–€110; D €130–€180 **Facilities** FTV TVB Direct dial from bedrooms Cen ht TVL Dinner Last d noon Wi-fi available 🌙 **Parking** 14 **Notes** LB ⊗ No coaches Closed Nov–Feb

★★★ BED & BREAKFAST
The Light House
Main Rd

☎ 053 913 3214 📄 053 913 3214

A contemporary bungalow set in grounds, The Light House is convenient for ferry users or for the beach and golf club. There is a

CONTINUED

television lounge and breakfast room in addition to the bedrooms, all of which have excellent en suite shower rooms.

Rooms 4 en suite (4 GF) S €40✱ **Facilities** TVB tea/coffee Cen ht TVL **Parking** 6 **Notes** ⊗ No children 18yrs Closed Nov–Feb 🎮

WEXFORD
MAP 01 D3

GUEST ACCOMMODATON OF THE YEAR FOR IRELAND
★★★★ FARM HOUSE
Killiane Castle *(T 058168)*
Drinagh

☎ 053 9158885 📄 053 9158885 Mr & Mrs J Mernagh

e-mail: killianecastle@yahoo.com

dir: Off N25 between Wexford and Rosslare

This 17th-century house is part of a 13th-century Norman castle where the Mernagh family run a charming house on a dairy farm close to Wexford town. The comfortable reception rooms and bedrooms are beautifully furnished. Breakfast is a real treat and includes farm produce and Kathleen's baking and preserves. There is a hard tennis court, croquet lawn, a golf driving range and walks that wander through the farm.

Rooms 8 en suite (2 fmly) S €75; D €100 **Facilities** TVB Cen ht TVL Wi-fi available 🎾 🏑 ⚡ Driving range **Parking** 8 **Notes** ⊗ 230 acres dairy Closed Dec–Feb

★★★★ BED & BREAKFAST
Maple Lodge
Castlebridge

☎ 053 9159195 & 9159062

e-mail: sreenan@eircom.net

dir: 5km N of Wexford. On R741 N on outskirts of Castlebridge, pink house on left

This imposing house, set in extensive mature gardens, is in a peaceful location close to Curracloe Beach. Eamonn and Margaret Sreenan offer warm hospitality in their comfortable home. There is a varied breakfast menu offered and secure parking in the grounds.

Rooms 4 en suite (2 fmly) **Facilities** STV TVB Cen ht TVL **Parking** 5 **Notes** ⊗ No children 10yrs Closed mid Nov–mid Mar

★★★★ 🍴 RESTAURANT WITH ROOMS
Newbay Country House & Restaurant
Newbay, Carrick

☎ 053 42779 📄 053 46318

e-mail: newbay@newbayhouse.com

dir: A11 from Wexford Bridge and turn right towards N25. Turn left before Quality Hotel and next right

Built in the 1820s, but only offering accommodation for some ten years, Newbay offers a choice of two dining areas, the casual Cellar Bistro on the lower floor, or the more formal restaurant in the original house. Unsurprisingly, seafood is a passion here. The freshest catch only has to travel a few hundred yards. The very comfortable

CONTINUED

IRELAND

bedrooms are situated in both the house and a wing. Some have four-posters and all have lovely views.

Rooms 11 en suite (1 fmly) (6 smoking) S €39–€85; D €78–€130 **Facilities** TVB tea/coffee Cen ht TVL Dinner Last d 9pm Wi-fi available **Notes** LB ⊗

★★★★ BED & BREAKFAST
Rathaspeck Manor
Rathaspeck
☎ 053 9141672 & 086 836 5764
e–mail: mickcuddihy@eircom.net

dir: *Signed on N25, near Johnstone Castle*

Standing in grounds that feature an 18-hole par-3 golf course, this Georgian country house is 0.8 kilometres from Johnstone Castle. The comfortable, spacious bedrooms are en suite and the public rooms are appointed with period furnishings.

Rooms 5 en suite S €70; D €140✱ **Facilities** TVB tea/coffee Cen ht TVL Golf 18 ⌂ **Parking** 8 **Notes** ⊗ No children 10yrs Closed 8 Nov–Jun ⊜

See advert on this page

★★★★ GUEST ACCOMMODATION
Slaney Manor
Ferrycarrig
☎ 053 91 20051 📠 053 91 20510
e–mail: slaneymanor@eircom.net

dir: *On N25, 0.8km W of N11 junct*

This attractive manor house stands in 24 hectares of woodland overlooking the River Slaney. Restored by the owners, the house retains many fine features. The elegant, high-ceilinged drawing room and dining room have views of the river, and four-poster beds feature in all bedrooms. The rooms in the converted coach house can be reserved on a room only basis for those travelling on the Rosslare ferry.

Rooms 9 en suite (2 fmly) (4 GF) S €70–€95; D €90–€190✱ **Facilities** TVB tea/coffee Direct dial from bedrooms Lift Cen ht TVL Dinner Last d noon **Parking** 30 **Notes** LB ⊗ Closed Xmas Civ Wed 60

CO WICKLOW

ARKLOW   MAP 01 D3

★★★ BED & BREAKFAST
Koliba Country Home
Beech Rd, Avoca
☎ 0402 32737 📠 0402 32737
e–mail: koliba@eircom.net

dir: *N11 onto R772 into Arklow, right at Rover garage, house 3km on right*

Situated halfway between Avoca and Arklow, this recently renovated house has panoramic views of the Vale of Avoca. Each cosy room is individually decorated. Rose and Brendan are very hospitable hosts and ensure a warm welcome.

Rooms 4 en suite (4 fmly) (4 GF) **Facilities** TVB tea/coffee Cen ht TVL **Parking** 8 **Notes** ⊗ Closed Nov–Mar

ASHFORD   MAP 01 D3

★★★★ ⌂ ⇔ GUEST HOUSE
Ballyknocken House & Cookery School
☎ 0404 44627 📠 0404 44696
e–mail: cfulvio@ballyknocken.com
web: www.ballyknocken.com

dir: *N11 S into Ashford, right after petrol station, house 5km on right*

This charming Victorian farmhouse stands in the foothills of the Wicklow Mountains. Catherine Fulvio is an enthusiastic hostess and reservations are necessary for dinner, which includes imaginative, freshly prepared dishes using produce from the garden and farm. The smart bedrooms are comfortable, and the farm buildings have been converted into a cookery school.

Rooms 7 en suite (1 fmly) S €69–€99; D €118–€134✱ **Facilities** TVB tea/coffee Direct dial from bedrooms Licensed Cen ht Dinner Last d day before ⌂ Cookery school **Conf** Max 80 Thtr 80 Class 50 Board 30 **Parking** 8 **Notes** LB ⊗ No coaches Closed Dec–Jan

IRELAND

AVOCA
MAP 01 D3

★★★★ BED & BREAKFAST
Cherrybrook Country Home
☎ 0402 35179 & 08761 05027 🖹 0402 35765
e–mail: cherrybandb@eircom.net

dir: *N11 S to Arklow, follow signs for Vale of Avola*

Set in the village made famous by the television series *Ballykissangel*, Cherrybrook has fine gardens with a barbeque area. It is a well-presented house with a lounge and conservatory dining room. Bedrooms are attractively decorated.

Rooms 5 en suite (2 fmly) (3 GF) **Facilities** TVB tea/coffee Cen ht TVL Wi-fi available **Parking** 5 **Notes** ⊗ No children 13yrs

★★★★ BED & BREAKFAST
Sheepwalk House & Cottages
Beech Rd
☎ 0402 35189 🖹 0402 35789
e–mail: sheepwalk@eircom.net
web: www.sheepwalk.com

dir: *2m from Avoca. Off N11 at Arklow junct take slip road towards Arklow. 1st right at Rover Garage (Beech Rd), Sheepwalk 2m on left*

An 18th-century Georgian house with lovely views across Arklow Bay. The cosy bedrooms are equipped with every thoughtful extra, and guests can breakfast in the informal sun lounge with sea views.

Rooms 6 en suite S €50; D €90 **Facilities** TVB tea/coffee Cen ht **Parking** 12 **Notes** ⊗ Closed Nov–14 Mar

DUNLAVIN
MAP 01 C3

Premier Collection

★★★★★ 🛎 GUEST HOUSE
Rathsallagh House
☎ 045 403112 🖹 045 403343
e–mail: info@rathsallagh.com

dir: *10.5km after end of M9 left signed Dunlavin, house signed 5km*

Surrounded by its own 18-hole championship golf course this delightful house was converted from Queen Ann stables in 1798 and now has the new addition of spacious and luxurious bedrooms with conference and leisure facilities. Food is country-house cooking at its best, and there is a cosy bar and comfortable drawing room to relax in. Close to Curragh and Punchestown racecourses.

Rooms 29 en suite (11 GF) S €195; D €270–€320✳ **Facilities** FTV TVB tea/coffee Direct dial from bedrooms Licensed Cen ht TVL Dinner Last d 9pm Wi-fi available Golf 18 ♨ Snooker Sauna 🏊 🏌 Golf academy with driving range **Conf** Max 160 Thtr 150 Class 75 Board 40 Del from €305 ✳ **Parking** 150 **Notes LB** No children 12yrs Closed 3 Jan–13 Feb Civ Wed

★★★★ FARM HOUSE
Tynte House (N 870015)
☎ 045 401561 🖹 045 401586 Mr & Mrs J Lawler
e–mail: info@tyntehouse.com
web: www.tyntehouse.com

dir: *N81 at Hollywood Cross, right at Dunlavin, follow finger signs for Tynte House, past market house in town centre*

The 19th-century farmhouse stands in the square of this quiet country village. The friendly hosts have carried out a lot of restoration resulting in comfortable bedrooms and a relaxing guest sitting room. Breakfast is a highlight of a visit to this house, which features Caroline's home baking.

Rooms 7 en suite (2 fmly) S €44–€54; D €70–€90 **Facilities** TVB tea/coffee Direct dial from bedrooms Cen ht TVL Wi-fi available Golf 18 ♨ Pool Table Playground Games room **Parking** 16 **Notes LB** 300 acres Beef & Tillage Closed 16 Dec–9 Jan

WICKLOW
MAP 01 D3

★★★★ FARM HOUSE
Kilpatrick House (T2257808)
Redcross
☎ 0404 47137 & 087 6358325
🖹 0404 47866 Mr Howard Kingston
e–mail: info@kilpatrickhouse.com

dir: *13km S, 3.2km off N11, signed from Jack Whites pub*

This elegant 18th-century Georgian residence is set on a beef and tillage farm just off the N11 north of Arklow. Bedrooms are carefully furnished and thoughtfully equipped. Dinner is available on request and the extensive breakfast menu includes Shirley's home baking and country produce. Close to Brittas Bay, there is a choice of golf courses and horse riding.

Rooms 4 rms (3 en suite) (1 pri facs) (2 fmly) S €55–€65; D €80–€96✳ **Facilities** TVB tea/coffee Cen ht TVL ♨ Fishing **Parking** 20 **Notes** ⊗ 150 acres Beef Closed Oct–Apr

County Maps

England

1 Bedfordshire
2 Berkshire
3 Bristol
4 Buckinghamshire
5 Cambridgeshire
6 Greater Manchester
7 Herefordshire
8 Hertfordshire
9 Leicestershire
10 Northamptonshire
11 Nottinghamshire
12 Rutland
13 Staffordshire
14 Warwickshire
15 West Midlands
16 Worcestershire

Scotland

17 City of Glasgow
18 Clackmannanshire
19 East Ayrshire
20 East Dunbartonshire
21 East Renfrewshire
22 Perth & Kinross
23 Renfrewshire
24 South Lanarkshire
25 West Dunbartonshire

Wales

26 Blaenau Gwent
27 Bridgend
28 Caerphilly
29 Denbighshire
30 Flintshire
31 Merthyr Tydfil
32 Monmouthshire
33 Neath Port Talbot
34 Newport
35 Rhondda Cynon Taff
36 Torfaen
37 Vale of Glamorgan
38 Wrexham

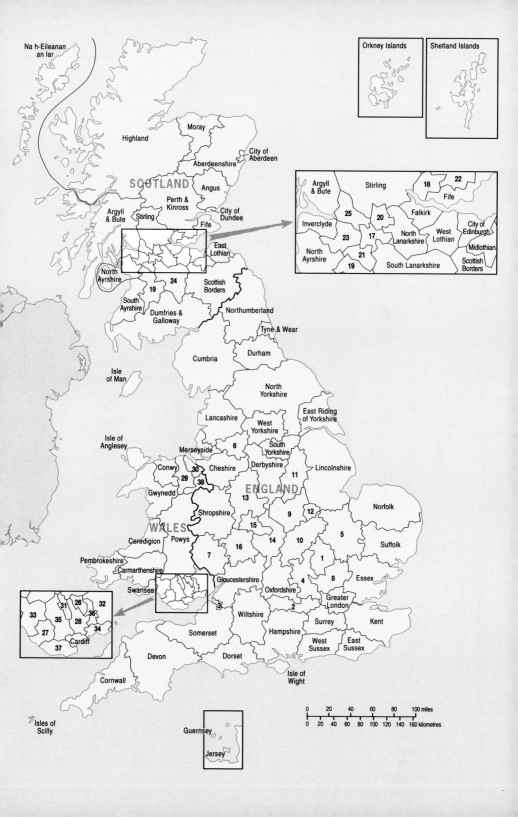

Na h-Eileanan an Iar

Orkney Islands

Shetland Islands

Highland

Moray

City of Aberdeen

SCOTLAND

Aberdeenshire

Angus

Perth & Kinross

City of Dundee

Argyll & Bute

Stirling

Fife

East Lothian

North Ayrshire

19   24

South Ayrshire

Dumfries & Galloway

Scottish Borders

Northumberland

Argyll & Bute

Stirling

18   22

Inverclyde

25   20

Fife

Falkirk

23   17

North Lanarkshire

West Lothian

City of Edinburgh

North Ayrshire

21

19

South Lanarkshire

Midlothian

Scottish Borders

Tyne & Wear

Cumbria

Durham

Isle of Man

North Yorkshire

Lancashire

West Yorkshire

East Riding of Yorkshire

Isle of Anglesey

Merseyside

6

South Yorkshire

Derbyshire

Lincolnshire

Conwy

30

Cheshire

11

Gwynedd

29   38

ENGLAND

Norfolk

13

WALES

Shropshire

9   12

Ceredigion

Powys

15

14   10

5

Suffolk

Pembrokeshire

7

16

4   8

Essex

Carmarthenshire

1

Swansea

Gloucestershire

Oxfordshire

2

Greater London

3

33   31   26   32

35   28   36

27   34

Cardiff

37

Wiltshire

Somerset

Hampshire

Surrey

West Sussex

East Sussex

Kent

Devon

Dorset

Isle of Wight

Cornwall

Isles of Scilly

Guernsey

Jersey

0   20   40   60   80   100 miles

0   20   40   60   80   100   120   140   160 kilometres

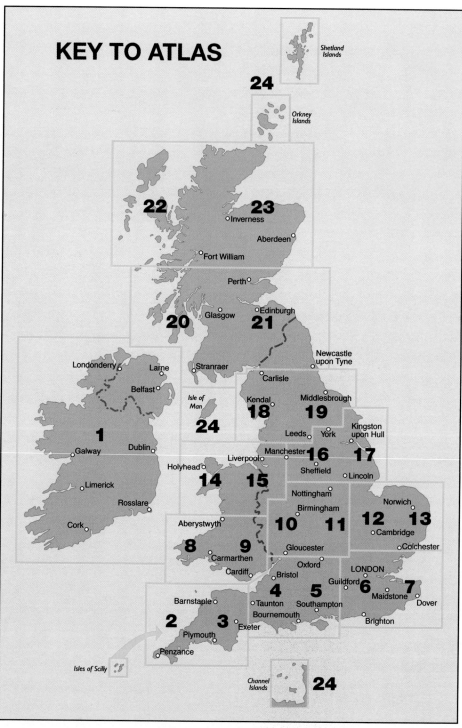

KEY TO ATLAS

Shetland Islands

24

Orkney Islands

22   **23**
○Inverness

Aberdeen○

○Fort William

Perth○

Glasgow○   ○Edinburgh
20   **21**

Londonderry○   Larne○   ○Stranraer   Newcastle upon Tyne○

Belfast○   Carlisle○

Isle of Man   Kendal○   Middlesbrough○

24   **18**   **19**

Leeds○   York○   Kingston upon Hull○

1   Liverpool○   Manchester○   **16**   **17**

Galway○   Dublin○   Sheffield○   ○Lincoln

Holyhead○   **14**   **15**   Nottingham○

Limerick○   Birmingham○   Norwich○

Rosslare○   Aberystwyth○   **10**   **11**   **12**   **13**

Cork○   ○Cambridge

8   **9**   Gloucester○   ○Colchester

Carmarthen○   Oxford○   LONDON

Cardiff○   ○Bristol   Guildford○   **6**   **7**

Barnstaple○   **4**   **5**   Maidstone○   Dover○

2   **3**   ○Taunton   Southampton○

Plymouth   Bournemouth○   Brighton○

Penzance○

Isles of Scilly

Channel Islands   **24**

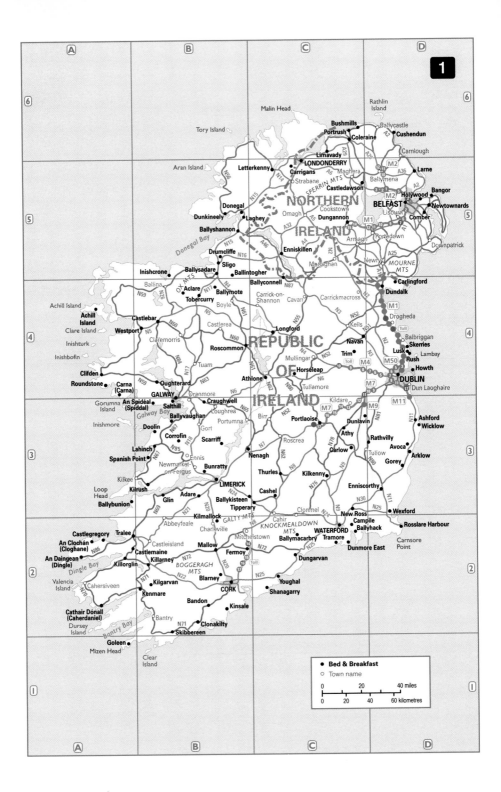

1

Malin Head

Tory Island

Rathlin Island

Bushmills
Ballycastle
Portrush
Cushendun
Coleraine
A2
Carnlough

Limavady
LONDONDERRY
M2
Larne
Aran Island
Letterkenny
Carrigans
Maghera
A36
Strabane
Ballymena
A2
Bangor

Castledawson
M2
Holywood
Newtownards
SPERRIN MTS
NORTHERN
BELFAST
Lisburn
Comber
Donegal
Omagh
Cookstown
M1
Dunkineely
Laghey
Dungannon
IRELAND
Ballyshannon
A32
Armagh
Portadown
Downpatrick

Donegal Bay
Drumcliffe
Enniskillen
Newry
A25
Inishcrone
Ballysadare
Sligo
Ballintogher
MOURNE MTS
Ballina
Ballyconnell
Carlingford
Aclare
Ballymote
Carrick-on-Shannon
Cavan
Carrickmacross
Dundalk
Tobercurry
Boyle
M1
Achill Island
Drogheda
Achill Island
Castlebar
Castlerea
Longford
Kells
Toll
Balbriggan
Westport
Roscommon
Navan
Skerries
Clare Island
Claremorris
Lusk
Lambay
Inishturk
Tuam
Trim
Rush
Inishbofin
Athlone
Mullingar
Toll
Howth
REPUBLIC
Horseleap
M4
M50
Clifden
Oughterard
Tullamore
DUBLIN
Roundstone
Carna
(Carna)
GALWAY
Dranmore
OF
M7
Dun Laoghaire
Gorumna Island
An Spidéal
(Spiddal)
Salthill
Craughwell
Kildare
M11
Ballyvaughan
Loughrea
IRELAND
M7
M9
Inishmore
Doolin
Gort
Portumna
Birr
Portlaoise
Ashford
Corrofin
Scarriff
Roscrea
Dunlavin
Wicklow
Lahinch
Ennis
Nenagh
Athy
Rathvilly
Spanish Point
Newmarket-on-Fergus
Bunratty
Thurles
Carlow
Avoca
Kilkee
Kilrush
Adare
LIMERICK
Cashel
Kilkenny
Gorey
Arklow
Loop Head
Glin
Tipperary
Enniscorthy
Ballybunion
Kilmallock
Ballykisteen
Clonmel
New Ross
Wexford
Castlegregory
Tralee
Abbeyfeale
GALTY MTS
Cahir
Campile
An Clochán
(Cloghane)
Castleisland
Mallow
Mitchelstown
KNOCKMEALDOWN MTS
WATERFORD
Ballyhack
Rosslare Harbour
An Daingean
(Dingle)
Castlemaine
Fermoy
Ballymacarbry
Tramore
Carnsore Point
Dingle Bay
Killorglin
Killarney
BOGGERAGH MTS
Toll
Dungarvan
Dunmore East
Valencia Island
Kilgarvan
Blarney
Youghal
Cahersiveen
Kenmare
CORK
Shanagarry
Cathair Dónall
(Caherdaniel)
Bandon
Kinsale
Dursey Island
Bantry
Clonakilty
Bantry Bay
Skibbereen
Goleen
Mizen Head
Clear Island

● Bed & Breakfast
○ Town name

0   20   40 miles

0   20   40   60 kilometres

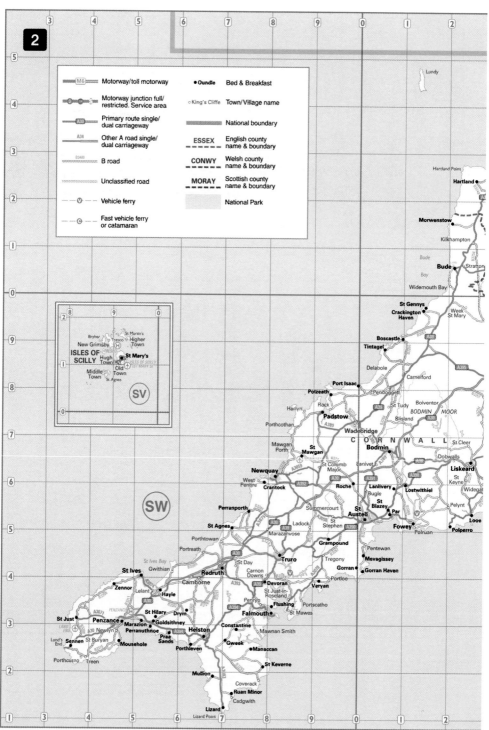

2

Legend

M6	Motorway/toll motorway
	Motorway junction full/restricted. Service area
A41	Primary route single/dual carriageway
A34	Other A road single/dual carriageway
B3400	B road
	Unclassified road
—V—	Vehicle ferry
—C—	Fast vehicle ferry or catamaran
● Oundle	Bed & Breakfast
○ King's Cliffe	Town/Village name
	National boundary
ESSEX	English county name & boundary
CONWY	Welsh county name & boundary
MORAY	Scottish county name & boundary
	National Park

ISLES OF SCILLY

Bryher · New Grimsby · Tresco · St Martin's · Higher Town · St Mary's · Hugh Town · Old Town · Middle Town · St Agnes · ISLES OF SCILLY (St Mary's)

SV

SW

Lundy

Hartland Point

Hartland ●

Morwenstow ●

Kilkhampton

Bude Bay · Bude ● · Stratton

Widemouth Bay

St Gennys ● · Week St Mary

Crackington Haven ●

Boscastle ●

Tintagel ●

Delabole · Camelford

Port Isaac ● · Pendoggett

Portzeath · Rock · St Tudy · Bolventor · BODMIN MOOR

Harlyn · Padstow ● · Blisland

Porthcothan · Wadebridge · Lanivet · Bodmin · CORNWALL · St Cleer

Mawgan Porth · St Mawgan · St Columb Major · Dobwalls

Newquay · Liskeard ●

West Pentire · Crantock · Roche · Lanlivery · St Keyne · Widega

Bugle · St Blazey · Lostwithiel ●

Perranporth · Summercourt · St Austell · Par · Pelynt

Ladock · St Stephen · Fowey · Looe ●

St Agnes ● · Marazanvose · Polruan · Polperro

Porthtowan · Grampound · Pentewan

Portreath · Tregony · Mevagissey ●

St Ives Bay · Gwithian · St Day · Truro · Gorran ● · Gorran Haven

St Ives ● · Carnon Downs · Portloe

Zennor · Redruth · Camborne · Devoran · Veryan

Lelant · Hayle · St Just-in-Roseland

St Just ● · Drym · Penryn · Flushing · Portscatho

Penzance · St Hilary · Goldsithney · Falmouth ● · St Mawes

Marazion · Helston · Constantine

Newlyn · Perranuthnoe · Mawnan Smith

Land's End · Sennen · St Buryan · Praa Sands · Porthleven · Gweek · Manaccan

Mousehole · St Keverne

Porthcurno · Treen · Mullion ●

Coverack

Ruan Minor · Cadgwith

Lizard · Lizard Point

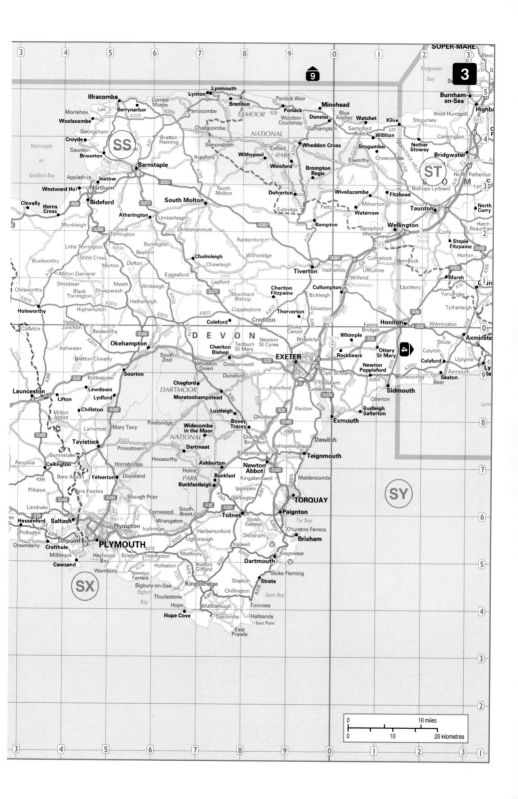

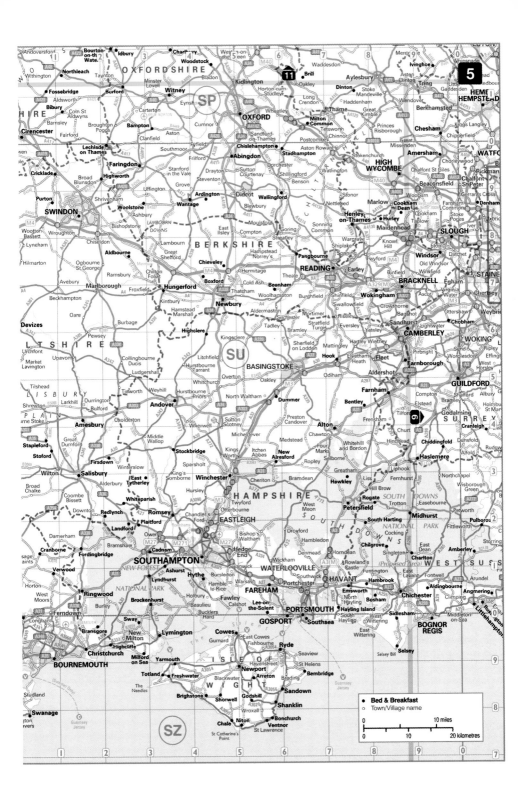

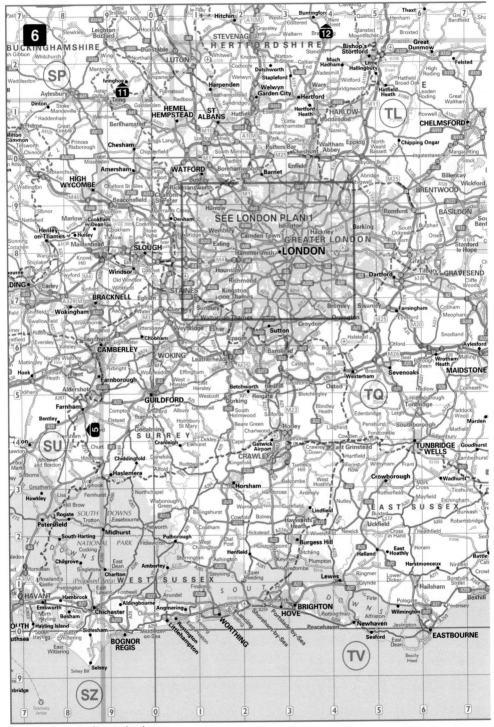

For continuation pages refer to numbered arrows

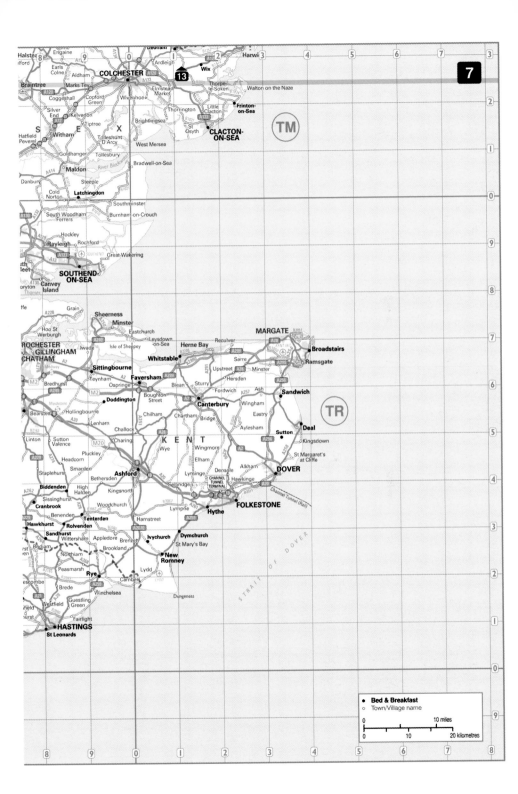

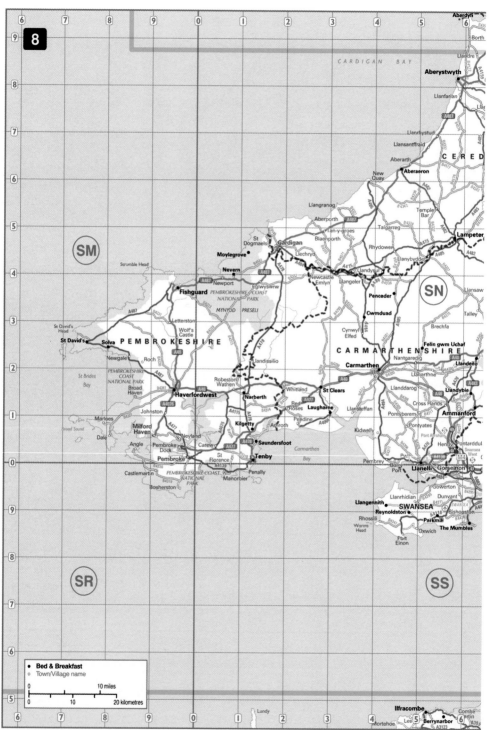

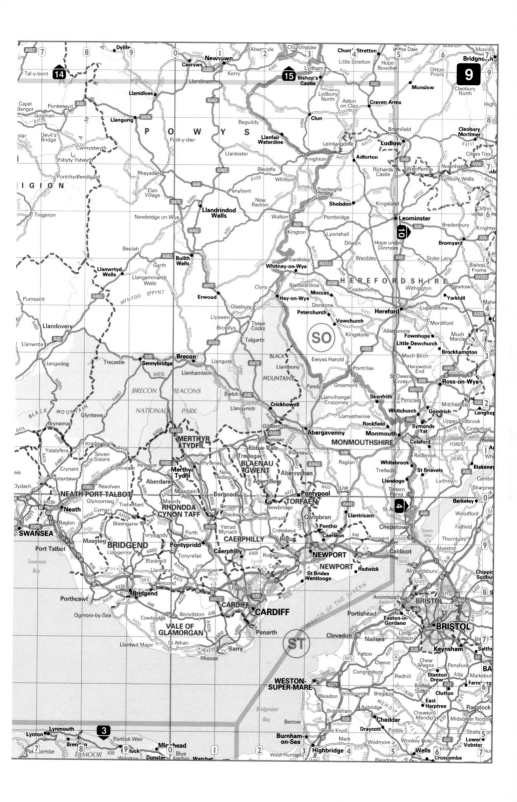

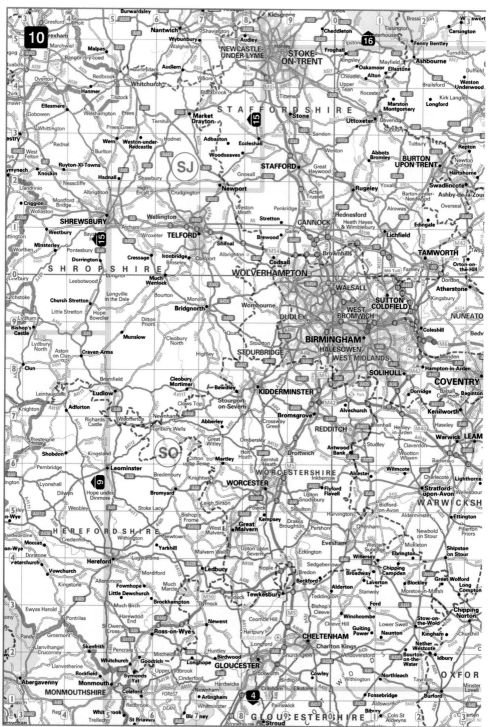

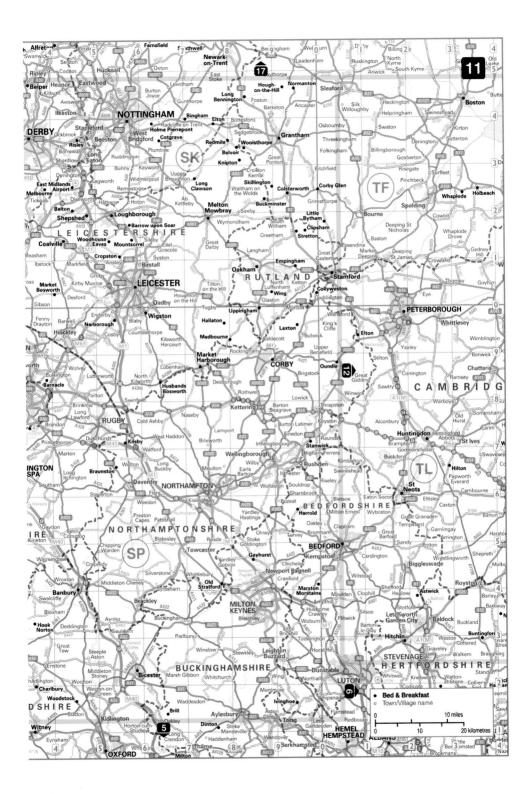

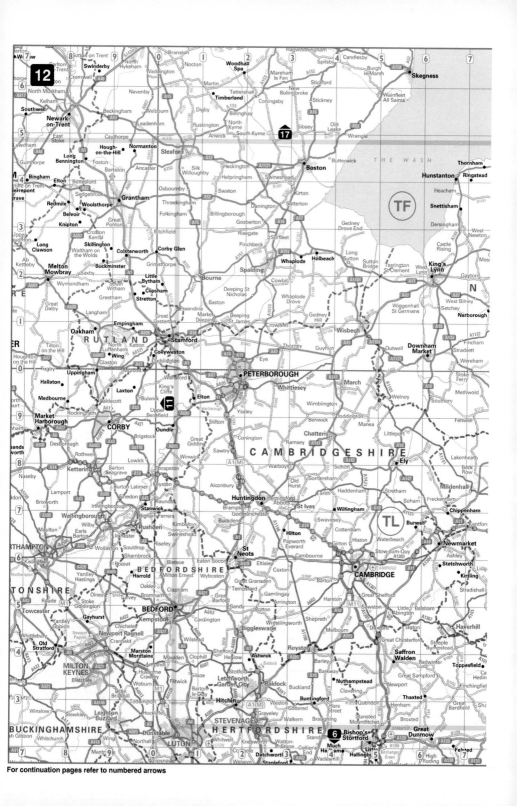

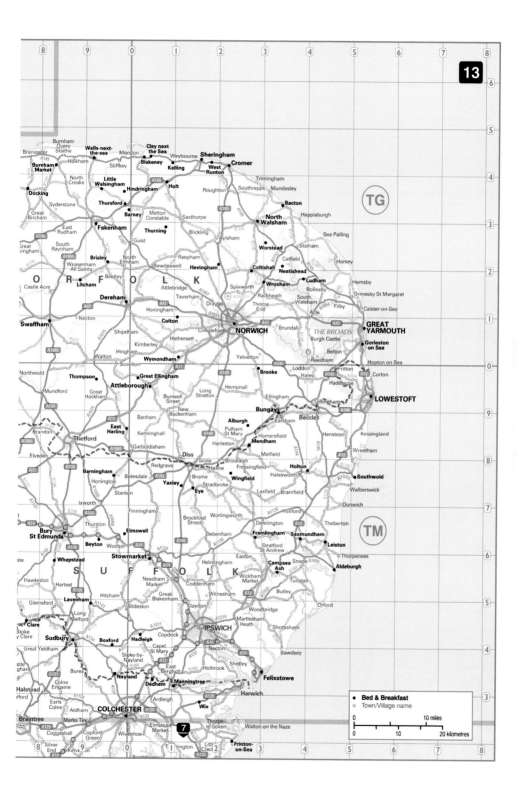

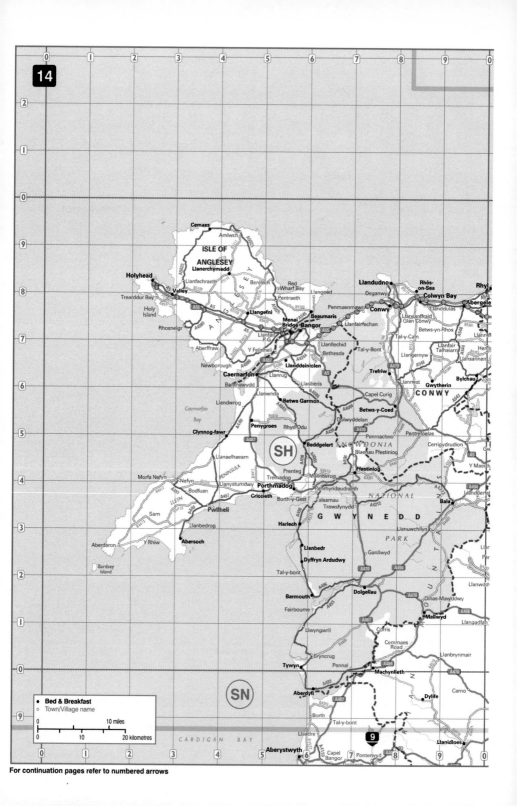

ISLE OF
ANGLESEY

CONWY

SNOWDONIA

NATIONAL

GWYNEDD

PARK

CARDIGAN BAY

SH

SN

Bed & Breakfast
○ Town/Village name

0   10 miles

0   10   20 kilometres

9

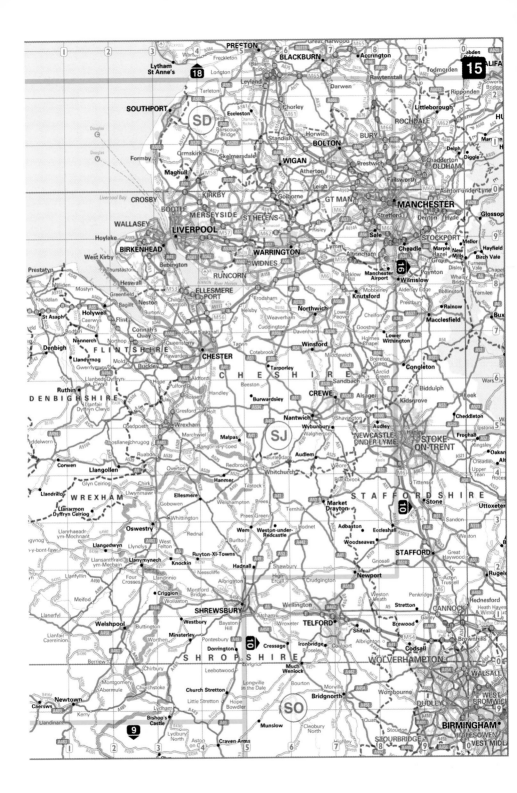

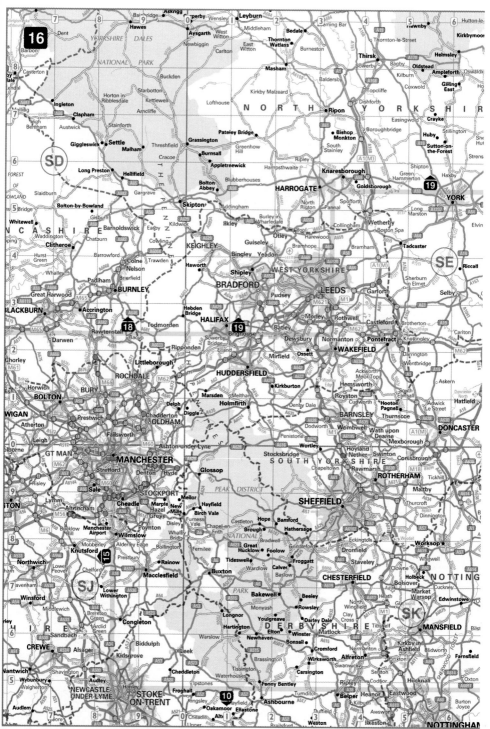

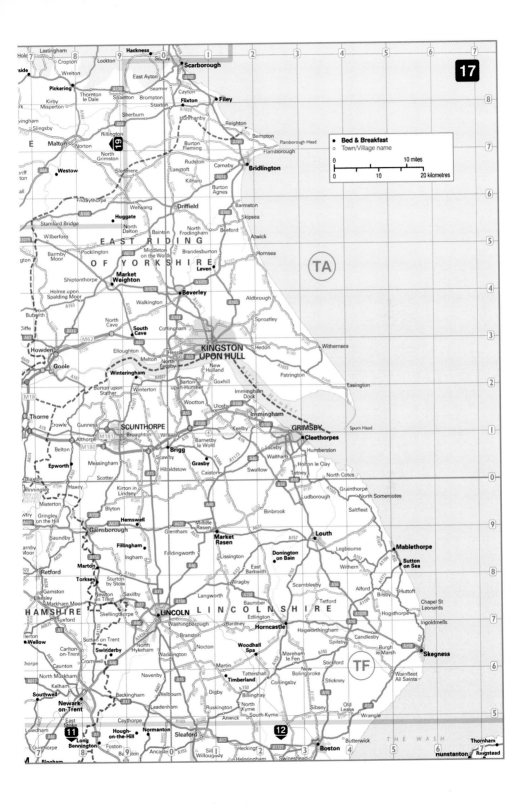

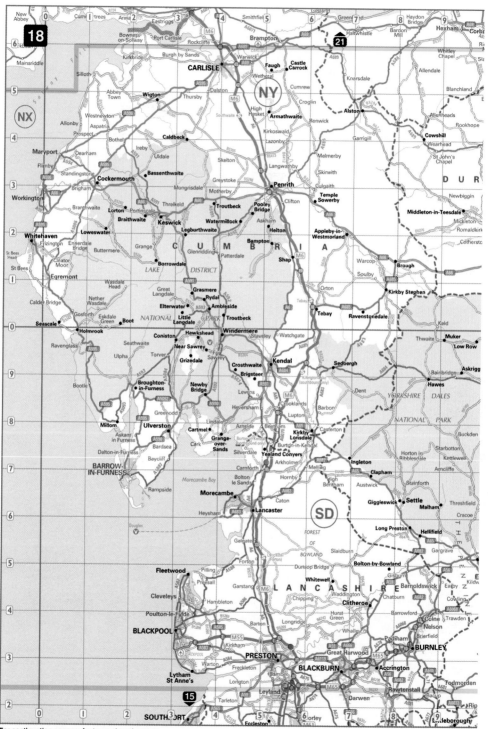

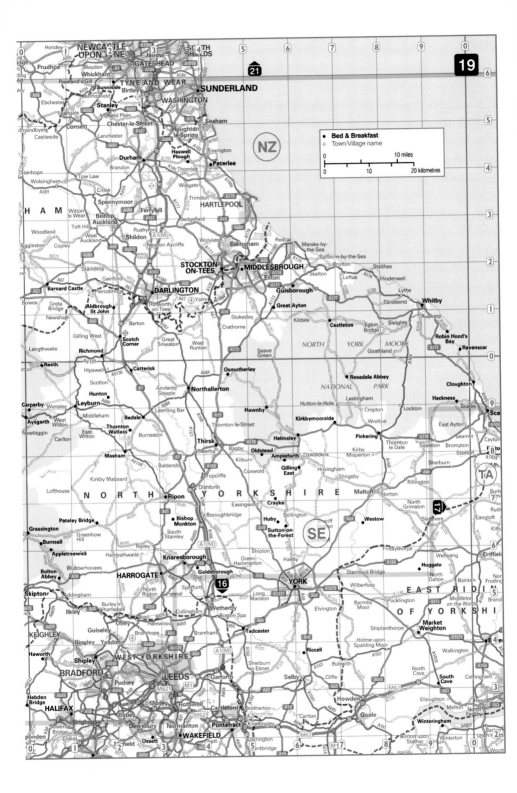

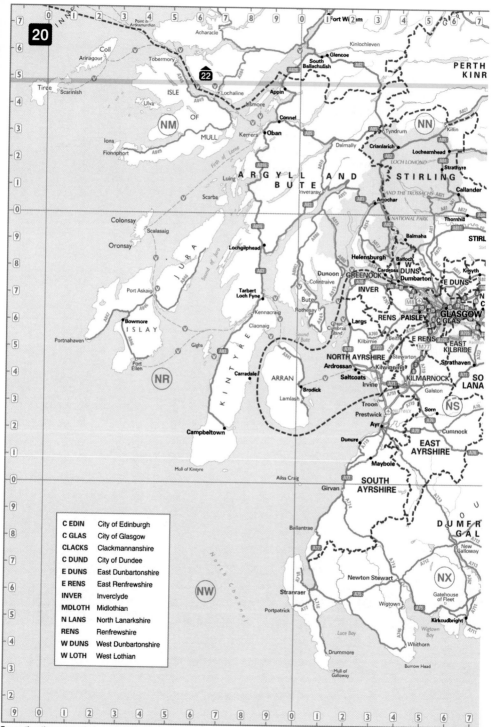

C EDIN	City of Edinburgh
C GLAS	City of Glasgow
CLACKS	Clackmannanshire
C DUND	City of Dundee
E DUNS	East Dunbartonshire
E RENS	East Renfrewshire
INVER	Inverclyde
MDLOTH	Midlothian
N LANS	North Lanarkshire
RENS	Renfrewshire
W DUNS	West Dunbartonshire
W LOTH	West Lothian

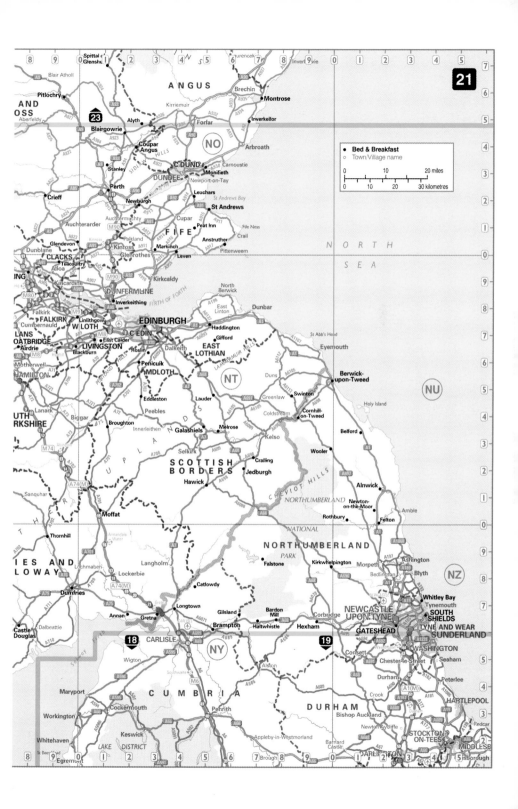

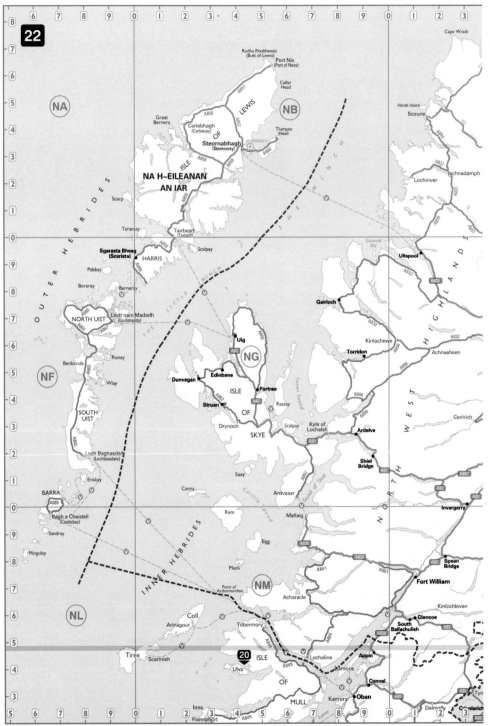

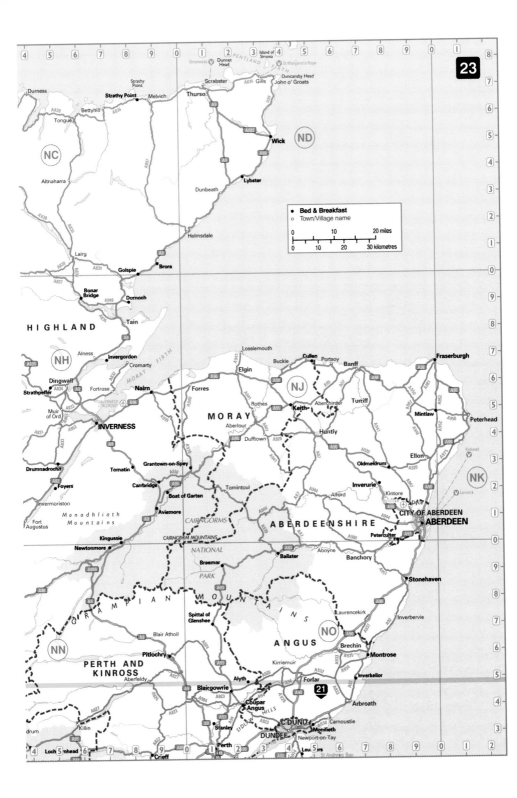

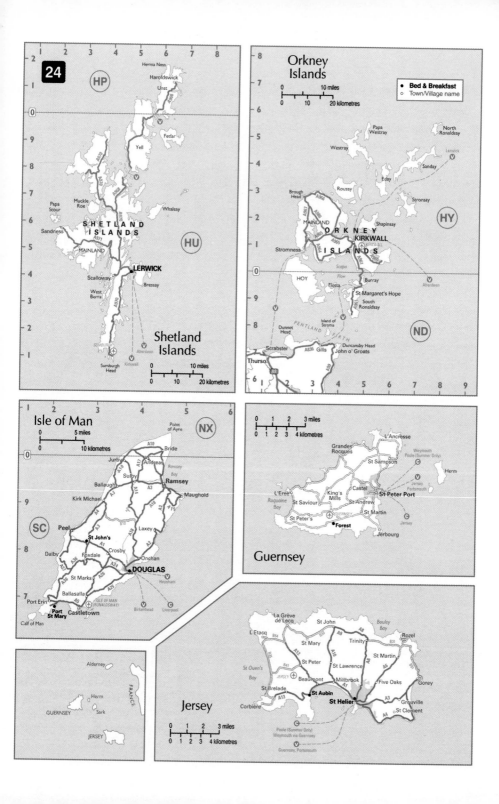

Central London

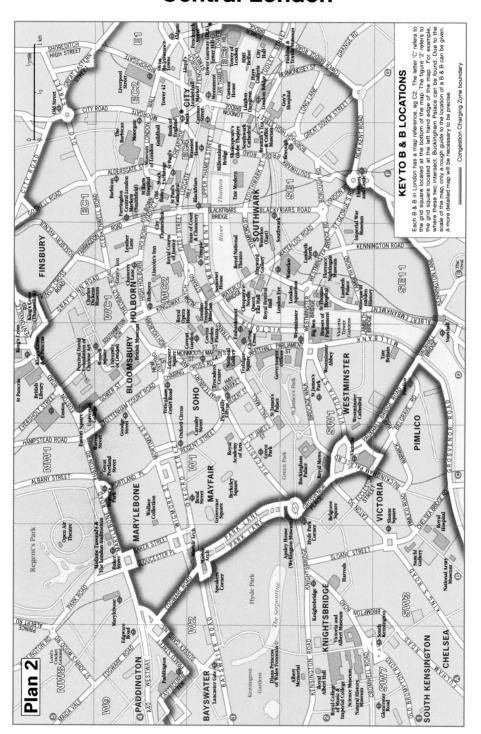

KEY TO B & B LOCATIONS

Each B & B in London has a map reference, eg C2. The letter 'C' refers to the grid square located at the bottom of the map. The figure '2' refers to the grid square located at the left hand edge of the map. For example, where these two intersect, Buckingham Palace can be found. Due to the scale of the map, only a rough guide to the location of a B & B can be given. A more detailed map will be necessary to be precise.

—— Congestion Charging Zone boundary

Plan 2

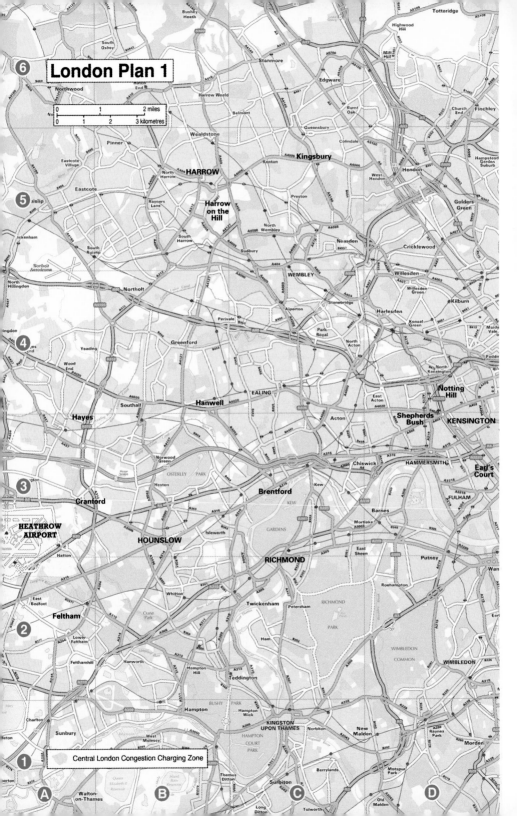

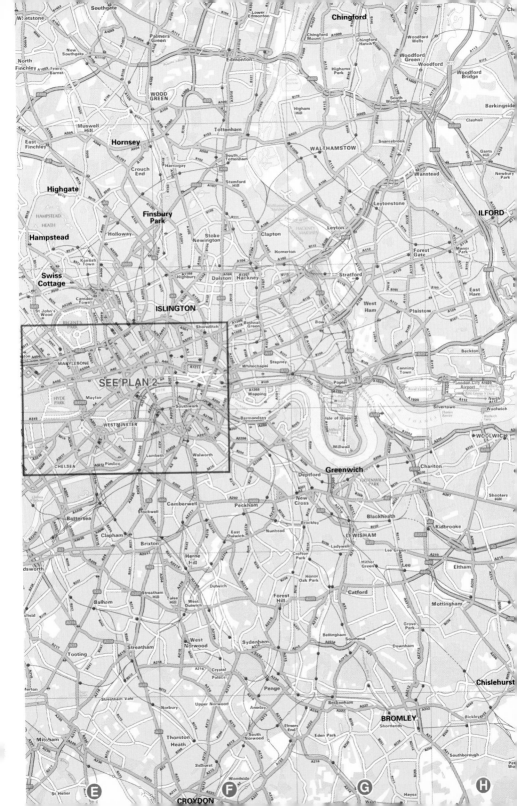

Index of locations

Index

Index

Index

Index

The Automobile Association would like to thank the following photographers, companies and picture libraries for their assistance in the preparation of this book.

Abbreviations for the picture credits are as follows: (t) top; (b) bottom; (l) left; (r) right; (AA) AA World Travel Library.

1 Royalty Free Photodisc; 3t Photodisc; 3bl San Domenico House; 3br Tan-y-Foel Country House; 4l © David Cook/www.blueshiftstudios.co.uk/Alamy; 4r AA/N Hicks; 5 Photodisc; 6 © David Cook/www.blueshiftstudios.co.uk/Alamy; 7t Photodisc; 7b Stockbyte Royalty Free; 9t Photodisc; 9b Tan-y-Foel Country House; 10t © David Cook/www.blueshiftstudios.co.uk/Alamy; 10b Royalty Free Photodisc; 11t Photodisc; 12t AA/C Jones; 12bl The Stables Lodge; 12br Fauhope House; 13t Royalty Free Photodisc; 13bl Tan-Y-Foel Country House; 13br Killiane Castle; 14t © David Cook/www.blueshiftstudios.co.uk/Alamy; 14c S Smyth; 15t Photodisc; 15b The Enchanted Manor; 16 AA/C Jones; 17 Royalty Free Photodisc; 18 AA/C Jones; 19 Royalty Free Photodisc; 20 AA/C Jones; 21t Royalty Free Photodisc; 21b AA/T Mackie; 599 AA/D Tarn; England AA/M Moody; Scotland AA/J Henderson; Wales AA/N Jenkins; Ireland AA/S Day

Every effort has been made to trace the copyright holders, and we apologise in advance for any accidental errors. We would be happy to apply the corrections in the following edition of this publication.

Please send this form to:
Editor, The B&B Guide,
Lifestyle Guides,
The Automobile Association,
Fanum House, FH13
Basingstoke RG21 4EA

Readers' Report Form

e-mail: lifestyleguides@theAA.com

Use this form to recommend any guest house, farmhouse or inn where you have stayed that is not already in the guide.

If you have any comments about your stay at an establishment listed in the Guide, please let us know, as feedback from readers helps to keep our Guide accurate and up to date. If you have a complaint during your stay, we recommend that you discuss the matter with the establishment.

Please note that the AA does not undertake to arbitrate between you and the establishment, to obtain compensation, or to engage in protracted correspondence.

Date:

Your name (block capitals)

Your address (block capitals)

....

....

....

....

e-mail address:

Name of hotel:

Comments (Please include the name & address of the establishment) ....

....

....

....

....

....

....

....

(please attach a separate sheet if necessary)

Please tick here if you DO NOT wish to receive details of AA offers or products ☐

PTO

The B&B Guide 2009

Have you bought this Guide before?   Yes   No

What other accommodation, restaurant, pub or food guides have you bought recently?

....

....

....

Why did you buy this Guide? (circle all that apply)

holiday   short break   business travel   special occasion

overnight stop   conference

other ....

How often do you stay in B&Bs? (circle one choice)

more than once a month   once a month   once in 2-3 months

once in six months   once a year   less than once a year

Please answer these questions to help us make improvements to the guide:

Which of these factors are most important when choosing a B&B?

price   location   awards/ratings   service

décor/surroundings   previous experience recommendation

other (please state) ....

Do you read the editorial features in the guide?   Yes   No

Do you use the location atlas?   Yes   No

What elements of the guide do you find the most useful when choosing somewhere to stay?

description   photo   advertisement   star rating

Can you suggest any improvements to the guide?

....

....

....

....

Thank you for returning this form

Please send this form to:
Editor, The B&B Guide,
Lifestyle Guides,
The Automobile Association,
Fanum House, FH13
Basingstoke RG21 4EA

Readers' Report Form

e-mail: lifestyleguides@theAA.com

Use this form to recommend any guest house, farmhouse or inn where you have stayed that is not already in the guide.

If you have any comments about your stay at an establishment listed in the Guide, please let us know, as feedback from readers helps to keep our Guide accurate and up to date. If you have a complaint during your stay, we recommend that you discuss the matter with the establishment.

Please note that the AA does not undertake to arbitrate between you and the establishment, to obtain compensation, or to engage in protracted correspondence.

Date:

Your name (block capitals)

Your address (block capitals)

....

....

....

....

e-mail address:

Name of hotel:

Comments (Please include the name & address of the establishment) ....

....

....

....

....

....

....

....

(please attach a separate sheet if necessary)

Please tick here if you DO NOT wish to receive details of AA offers or products ☐

PTO

The B&B Guide 2009

Have you bought this Guide before?   Yes   No

What other accommodation, restaurant, pub or food guides have you bought recently?

.... - -

.... - -

.... - -

Why did you buy this Guide? (circle all that apply)

holiday   short break   business travel   special occasion

overnight stop   conference

other .... - -

How often do you stay in B&Bs? (circle one choice)

more than once a month   once a month   once in 2-3 months

once in six months   once a year   less than once a year

Please answer these questions to help us make improvements to the guide:

Which of these factors are most important when choosing a B&B?

price   location   awards/ratings   service

décor/surroundings   previous experience   recommendation

other (please state) .... - -

Do you read the editorial features in the guide?   Yes   No

Do you use the location atlas?   Yes   No

What elements of the guide do you find the most useful when choosing somewhere to stay?

description   photo   advertisement   star rating

Can you suggest any improvements to the guide?

.... - -

.... - -

.... - -

.... - -

Thank you for returning this form